1987

Musical Applications of Microprocessors

Musical Applications of Microprocessors

SECOND EDITION

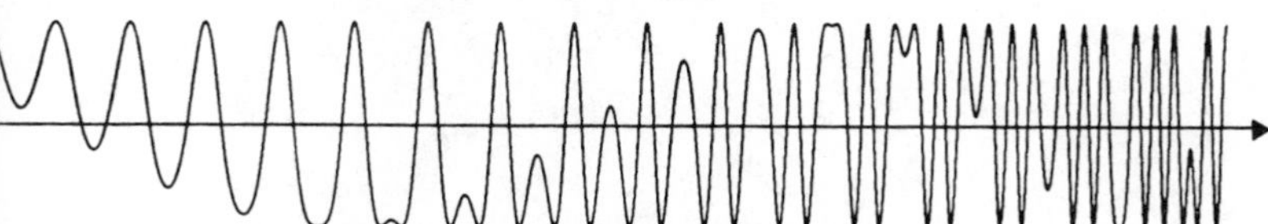

Hal Chamberlin

HAYDEN BOOKS

A Division of Howard W. Sams & Company

4300 West 62nd Street

Indianapolis, Indiana 46268 USA

SECOND EDITION
SECOND PRINTING—1987

International Standard Book Number: 0-8104-5768-7
Library of Congress Catalog Card Number: 85-24842

Acquisitions Editor: *Therese A. Zak*
Editors: *Ronnie Groff and Lori Williams*
Illustrator: *John McAusland*
Cover Design: *Jim Bernard*

Printed in the United States of America

Preface

The period encompassing the mid-1970s until now has seen an explosive growth in the application of digital logic, especially programmed logic and microcomputers. The key to this growth is the fantastic reduction in the cost of logic and memory and the development of the microprocessor. In particular, microprocessors and microcomputer systems built around them make it possible, practical, and even advisable to perform many functions using computer techniques that would have been done with conventional logic or analog circuits a very few years ago.

Although many computer music techniques were developed over a decade earlier, their widespread use in the broader area of electronic music has not yet materialized. Now, however, the increasing power of microprocessors and their fantastic low cost make such widespread use inevitable.

Many of these existing techniques cannot or should not be used directly, however. Although a microprocessor bears considerable resemblance to the large-scale machines on which these techniques were developed, there are important differences. Additionally, there are numerous new techniques that lend themselves well to microprocessor implementation but that are completely impractical using a large-scale mainframe or even minicomputer.

In the pages to follow, the application of all important electronic and computer music performance techniques to microprocessors will be covered. In addition, some new, not generally known, techniques that are only practical with microprocessors will be discussed. Finally, some of the extremely powerful big computer signal-processing techniques will be presented in nonmathematical language and applied to the more powerful 16-bit microprocessors that are becoming commonplace.

The text is divided into four major sections. Chapters 1 to 5 cover important background material, the understanding of which is necessary for full appreciation of the sections to follow. Chapters on analog music synthesis principles, digital music synthesis principles, and microprocessors should serve to acquaint the general reader with these areas as well as fill in the background of the specialized reader.

Chapters 6 to 11 cover the application of microprocessors to controlling conventional analog sound-synthesizing equipment. The first two chapters cover typical analog modules and interfacing techniques to microprocessors. The remaining four chapters are devoted to the control function itself, particularly the manner in which the human user interacts with the microprocessor–synthesizer combination.

Chapters 12 to 18 concentrate on purely digital synthesis techniques. These techniques have the greatest inherent generality and accuracy, but widespread use has so far been inhibited by high cost and operation outside of real time. Chapter 12 discusses the conversion of high-fidelity audio signals to and from the digital domain. Chapters 13 to 15 discuss digital signal generation and processing. The next three chapters describe the use and implementation of these digital techniques into practical equipment and systems.

Section IV covers actual applications of all of these techniques. Chapter 19 describes professional-quality usage of analog and digital technology in research installations and in several representative products. Chapter 20 examines the design of consumer-oriented and very low-cost music-synthesizing products. In so doing, it also provides a good summary of the strengths and weaknesses of the myriad synthesis techniques described in earlier chapters. Chapter 21 concludes by speculating on future developments in musical applications of microprocessors at all levels from novelties to serious musical research.

Throughout the discussions, the use of mathematics is minimized, and where present, is limited to elementary algebra and trigonometry. Instead, numerous charts, graphs, and sometimes computer programs in BASIC are used to illustrate important concepts. This does not mean that the more difficult concepts are skipped. For example, the fast Fourier transform and its workings are described and supported with a tested program listing in BASIC. Digital filters are also covered extensively.

The reader is not expected to merely study and marvel at the techniques described. Rather, he is urged to go out and try them, apply them, and enjoy the results. For this purpose, many actual programs and circuit diagrams are included. While not every topic is reduced to practice, enough information is supplied or pointed out in reference material to enable the industrious reader to experiment with and refine the technique.

HAL CHAMBERLIN

Contents

SECTION III: Digital Synthesis and Sound Modification 365

SECTION I

Background

Music is unique among the arts. Virtually everyone enjoys and appreciates it to some extent. It is certainly the richest of the fine arts, with the typical middle-class household spending hundreds of dollars annually on music hardware such as radios, phonographs, and hi-fi sound systems and software like records, tapes, and concert tickets. It is also unique in that it encompasses a very broad range of disciplines ranging from mathematics to physics to computer programming.

In the area of music synthesis by computer, it is necessary that the practitioner be somewhat familiar with these and other fields in order to master the medium. While detailed treatment of all necessary background material is impossible in five short chapters, that which is covered should serve to enlighten the reader in those areas outside of his or her primary interest.

1

Music Synthesis Principles

Creating and listening to music is one of man's oldest and most popular pastimes. Although natural sounds from both inanimate and animate sources may have some of the essential characteristics of music, only man can create and control sounds that simultaneously possess all of the characteristics of music.

Early peoples used many naturally occurring objects to create music. Sticks beaten together, stones pounded together, and logs being struck were certainly used for early rhythmic sounds. Later discovery of conch shell and ram's horn trumpets added pitched sounds to the available repertoire.

However, as the quest for new and different sounds continued, natural objects were modified specifically for the purpose of producing a wider range of sounds. Logs were hollowed and slotted for differently pitched sounds. Natural horns were modified in length or pierced with holes for the same purpose. At this point and for all of history to follow, music became completely artificial and was played on wholly artificial instruments.

Over the years, a great multitude of different instruments was invented and refined. Stringed instruments culminating in the piano and violin evolved from the earliest one-string harps. Wind instruments such as the trumpet and pipe organ developed from simple horns or reed pipes. Percussion instruments such as the timpani or vibraphone evolved from log drums.

Historically, musical instrument makers have been quick to adopt newly available technology. Perhaps since music is of such universal interest and is usually regarded as a pastime, it would be natural that technologists would want to utilize their expertise in an enjoyable manner. The experimental approach to utilizing new technology in music is quite reasonable, since the consequences of failure are nothing more than a heightened desire to succeed the next time. In addition, failure is not that well defined. Although the results may not have been expected, if they are different there are always some who would praise them. This would not be true in many other applications of technology such as bridge building or vehicle design.

It is not surprising, then, that musical instrument manufacturers have rapidly adopted this century's electronic and more recent computer technology. Modern electronic technology allows the design of compact instruments with a wider range of sounds and more precise player control of the sounds than had been previously available. Also of significance is the fact that these new instruments are often much easier to play. Perhaps the ultimate in playing ease is a programmable instrument such as a digital computer. Since time need no longer be a factor, very intricate, fast-moving music may be played as easily as it can be written down.

Often traditionalists, who may have spent many years perfecting the skills necessary to play traditional instruments, are loudly opposed to the utilization of this new technology because to them music so produced is artificial and mechanical. Nevertheless, there is no essential difference between the use of piston valve technology in trumpet design and computer programming technology in organ design. It is still the responsibility of the composer and performer to produce desirable musical results.

At this point it would be wise to develop a working definition of music. Most physics texts define a musical sound as one that possesses a degree of regularity, while noise as a sound does not possess such regularity. Clearly, this alone is not sufficient, since a snare drum beat would be classified as noise and fluorescent light buzz as music by this definition.

The arrangement, in time, of component sounds is as important as the sounds themselves. Furthermore, this arrangement must be orderly to be musical. However, excessive orderliness leads to boredom.

So far nothing has been said about the emotional aspect of music composition and performance. True, some of the world's best music has a strong emotional appeal but that alone is not sufficient. A mortal cry of anguish appeals emotionally to all who hear it but is certainly not music. A well-executed display of sound can be just as interesting to the ear as a fireworks display is to the eye.

In summary, then, good music must be composed of sounds that have regular vibrations but with enough variation to be continuously interesting. Likewise, the arrangement of sounds must be orderly but with enough variety to maintain interest. Music may either express an emotional point or merely be a spectacular display of sound. Above all, good music must hold the attention of the listener.

Goals of Music Synthesis

Certainly, all who study electronic music techniques in general and particularly the readers of this book must have some goal in mind. The vast majority of young music students today are still educated solely on the traditional musical instruments such as piano, organ, or any of a multitude of band and orchestra instruments. Most often this involvement is not completely spontaneous but rather is encouraged by parents and teachers, often as the result of a musical aptitude test. Children who get into music on their own are more apt to choose the guitar, drums, or vocal music perhaps because of the publicity that is continuously heaped upon players of those instruments or because of the ready market for combo dance music.

Electronic and computer music has an attraction to both beginning and thoroughly seasoned musicians. Its newness and unique capabilities are strong attractive qualities. Young musicians are attracted because the potential exists for creating sounds and music never before contemplated, let alone heard. Experienced musicians see the opportunity to express themselves in new ways unfettered by the constraints of conventional instruments or the classical rules of composition for them.

Wider Variety of Sounds

Probably the most obvious and commonly sought goal of electronic music practitioners is broadening the repertoire of sounds available for music composition. Any given traditional instrument is definitely limited in the pitch, loudness, and timbre range of sounds that it can produce. Orchestral composers have often been quite clever in combining the sounds of ordinary instruments to produce a composite sound that does not resemble the components at all. Indeed, it may be theoretically possible to produce any desired sound in this manner. However, the proper combination is not at all obvious and experimentation to discover it is not always practical due to the cost and time constraints of an orchestra.

Undoubtedly the first purely electronic sound available was the simple sine wave. Acoustically, a sine wave can be likened to pure refined sugar; good in small amounts but sickeningly sweet if overdone. The oscillators that produced the sine waves were usually continuously variable over a large frequency range making wide interval glissando (a continuous change in pitch from one note to the next) a reality.

Modern electronic music techniques are capable of an infinite variety of musical timbres. Whereas in the past a differently shaped or proportioned instrument was required to explore different timbres, the same can now be accomplished by knob twiddling or keying numbers on a computer terminal keyboard. Furthermore, timbre need not be unchanging. It is entirely possible for a note to begin sounding like a saxophone and end sounding like a flute with a smooth transition in between.

Because of the human hearing mechanism, a short, rapid sequence of sounds may have an entirely different effect than the same sequence presented more slowly. Electronic and computer techniques allow such sequences to be accurately specified, played, and easily modified. Changing the component sounds, the sequence, and the rate of presentation opens up a new infinity of sounds available for the composition of music.

Sheer dynamic range is a significant new musical tool. A single tone may start from the depths of inaudibility and creep upwards in pitch to the heights of inaudibility. Any sound may be made as loud or as soft as desired. Thunderous, gut-shaking bass chords are available as is the most subtle solo melody.

Certainly a musician working with electronics is not limited by the sounds available for composition.

Performance by the Composer

Another goal sought by many electronic musicians is, to be blunt, omnipotence. It is now possible for a single person to compose, perform, and criticize a piece of music of any degree of complexity desired. No longer is it necessary to write the music down part by part and find an orchestra to play it, and then correctly only after considerable practice. Instead, the composer can play the piece sequentially by part and have the parts combined in a recording studio. Or, with the aid of a computer, proper notation of the music is itself sufficient to precisely direct the performance.

Interpretation of conventional scores has always been a problem. Many important variables are left unspecified. Filling in these gaps is left to the conductor (who may indeed be the composer himself) and the individual players. In cases in which some aspect of the music is unconventional, the fact that the performers are musicians too with their own ideas may make execution according to the composer's wishes very difficult. With the use of electronics, the composer himself can be in complete control of the performance. Passages can be repeated and experimented with in search of perfection subject only to the patience of the composer. Nobody other than the composer himself needs to hear or judge the work until it is in final form.

Because of the vast repertoire of new sounds available, it is less likely that the desired sounds and their combinations can be chosen using only prior knowledge and imagination. Just as the classical composer worked with a piano to experiment with melodies and rhythms, the contemporary composer needs to experiment. Electronics allows such experimentation with immediate, or nearly so, feedback of results. Additionally, the costs are such that experimentation is usually practical as well as possible.

The majority of money spent on musical instruments in this country is by individuals who are not in any sense professional musicians. To these people, playing an instrument is a very enjoyable, creative pastime. The increasing popularity of organs over pianos and other instruments in the home is probably due to the greater versatility of the organ. Electronic organ manufacturers have been very quick to adopt new technology that increases the capabilities of their instruments and makes them easier to learn and use. In the not too distant future, programmable electronic instruments will allow anyone with clear ideas and time to try their hand at composing and performing truly serious music strictly for fun.

Certainly, a musician working with electronics is not limited by anyone else in what can be achieved.

Increased Precision

Another often desired goal that can only be fulfilled through the use of electronics is increased precision in the control of sounds. Additionally, aspects of sound that in the past have been left to chance or were predefined can now be precisely controlled. In fact, when a computer is involved, all of the parameters of sound must be specified somehow, even if the actual desire is to ignore some of them.

In many ways the human ear is very sensitive to and critical of imperfections in musical sounds. Small amounts of certain types of distortion can be very unpleasant. Relatively small shifts in pitch can break up an otherwise beautiful chord into a not so beautiful one. Many hours are spent in practice sessions getting the relative volume balance between instruments correct and repeatable.

Timing is another variable that must be controlled, since the ear is extremely sensitive to relative timing among musical events. Its capacity for following and analyzing rapid sound sequences exceeds the capabilities of conventionally played instruments. However, electronic instruments, particularly those involving computers, have control over time to any degree of accuracy desired.

In one technique of electronic tone production, for example, the user has complete control over the fundamental building blocks of timbre, the harmonic partials. Any timbre (within a broad class of timbres) may be created by combining the harmonics in different proportions. Timbres may be experimented with, saved for exact recall, and later utilized or refined further. The ability to document and accurately recreate timbres and sounds is as important as the ability to create them.

Extreme precision in all aspects of music performance is novel but not necessarily good. Many will argue that such precision leads to mechanical sounding music. Indeed, certain kinds of uncertainty or subtle variation are necessary to maintain listener interest. However, if one starts with a precise product, then the needed imperfections may be added in the precise quantity desired.

Certainly, a musician working with electronics is not limited by inaccuracies in the control of sounds.

Increased Complexity

Complexity is one of the hallmarks of contemporary music. It is used to increase the impact of the piece, display virtuosity both of the performer and the composer, and to create a rich "sound landscape" upon which the primary theme stands.

Complexity in this case means the quantity of musical events per unit of time. Thus, it may actually be either greater speed or more parts playing simultaneously or both. A modern recording studio can make a small ensemble sound like a vast collection of musicians through the use of overdubbing and reverberation techniques. The same studio can facilitate the rapid playing of music either by actually speeding up the tape or by relieving concern over the errors made during rapid playing.

The use of computers allows great but well-controlled complexity to be built up because the music can be programmed. The programming process is nothing more than notation of the music according to a rigid set of rules. In many computer-based music systems using purely digital synthesis techniques, there is no practical limit to the speed of playing or to the number of instruments or sounds that may be simultaneously present. The only penalty for adding additional parts is a longer waiting period during one phase of the music production.

Complexity in sound may also be quite subtle. Many natural sounds are really quite complex when described in terms of the fundamental parameters of sound. One interest area of many researchers is precise analysis of natural sounds, some of which are not normally easily repeatable. With information gleaned from the analysis, new sounds may be synthesized that resemble the original in controlled ways or emphasize one or more of its characteristics.

Certainly, a musician working with electronics is not limited by the degree of sound complexity possible.

Increased Spontaneity

Finally, a minority of people are looking for more randomness or spontaneity in the performance of music through the use of electronics. The wider range and greater ease of control of electronic instruments makes manual improvisation easier and more interesting.

Computers may generate and use random sequences to control some or all of the parameters of a sound. Certain mathematical processes, when used to control sound, lead to interesting, unpredictable results. Natural phenomena may also be captured electronically and used to control sound. One example is the use of brain waves as a control source for one or more oscillators. An entire record album has been created using fluctuations in the earth's magnetic field as a control source.

Certainly, a musician working with electronics is limited only by his own imagination.

The Fundamental Parameters of Sound

All music, whether it is conventional or electronic in origin, is an ordered collection of sounds. Accordingly, a working knowledge of the physics of sound is necessary to understand and intelligently experiment with the degree of control of sound offered by the use of computers in electronic music.

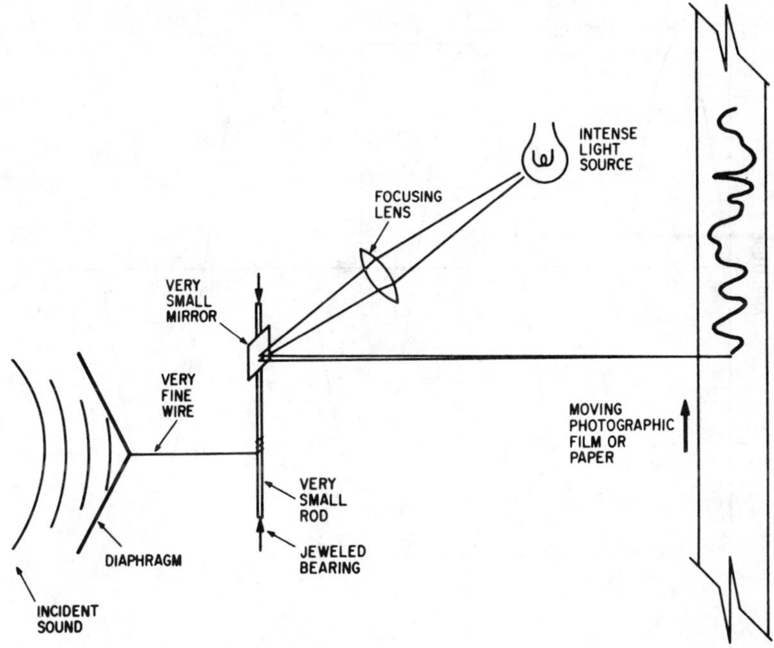

Fig. 1–1. Mechanical sound-waveform-tracing apparatus

Steady, unchanging sounds fall into two classes, pitched and unpitched. The two classes are not completely disjointed, however, since there are some sounds that possess characteristics of both groups. As will be shown later, all steady sounds can be described by a number of parameters that are also steady. In all cases, these parameters are scalar quantities, that is, a simple number with corresponding physical units. Changing sounds (all sounds change to some degree—otherwise they would have no beginning or end) are similar to steady sounds except that the parameters that describe them change with time.

One way to visualize a sound is to show its waveform or the manner in which air pressure changes with time. Before the discovery of electronics, mechanical instruments similar to the one shown schematically in Fig. 1–1 were used. Movement of the air caused by sound vibrations would be picked up by a diaphragm and cause a tiny mirror to rotate in synchronism with the vibration. A light beam reflected from the mirror onto moving photographic film would make a visibile waveform trace. The distance from the mirror to the film acted as a long but massless lever arm to effectively amplify the vibrations.

Of course, sound waveforms may now be photographed on the display screen of an oscilloscope. In order to do this, the sound is first directed into a

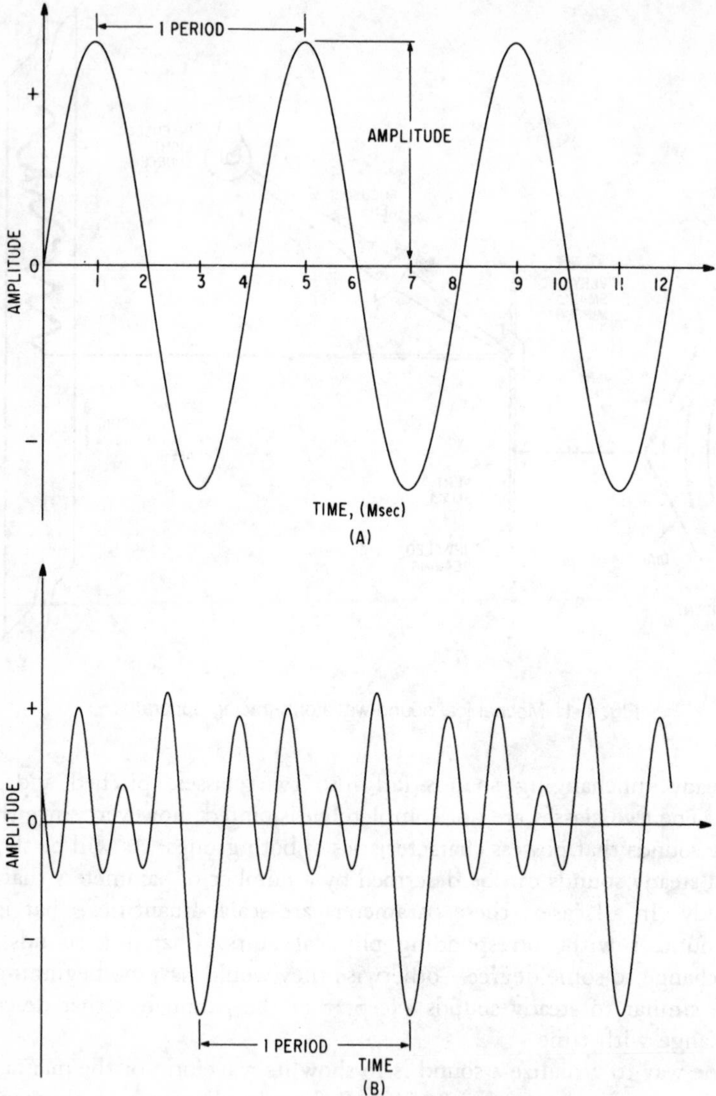

Fig. 1–2. Some typical waveforms of steady sounds

microphone that converts the air vibrations into equivalent electrical voltage vibrations. Electronic sounds, of course, already exist in electrical form. In either case, the electrical voltage variations control the vertical position of the oscilloscope beam while it is also sweeping from left to right at a constant rate. Thus, the plot on the screen shows equivalent air pressure on the vertical or Y axis and the passage of time on the horizontal or X axis. In the case of silence, a horizontal *baseline* is all that would be seen. This does not represent zero air pressure but instead represents zero *variation* from current atmospheric pressure. Since only relatively rapid variations in pressure can be heard, the baseline is usually taken as a zero reference and the positive and negative variation around zero is the quantity of interest.

Even using an oscilloscope presents some problems. One of these is that the screen is not very wide so only very short segments of the waveform may be conveniently displayed. The best way to visualize a waveform is to have a computer record it and display it on a graphic display or plot it on paper. From now on when the term "sound" or "vibration" is used, it is assumed to exist as an electrical signal. Listening to the sound is simply a matter of feeding the signal to a high-fidelity amplifier and quality speaker system.

Typical Sound Waveforms

Figure 1–2 shows some typical waveforms of steady sounds. The horizontal axis represents the passage of time and is marked off in milliseconds. The vertical axis represents air pressure but is marked off in volts due to the fact that the picture is actually of an electrical signal. The progression from left to right is from the simplest possible pitched sound (sine wave) through more complex pitched sounds to semipitched sounds and finally to the most fundamental unpitched sound (white noise).

The waveforms in Figs. 1–2A and B are from unquestionably pitched sounds. Their distinguishing feature is that the waveform repeats itself

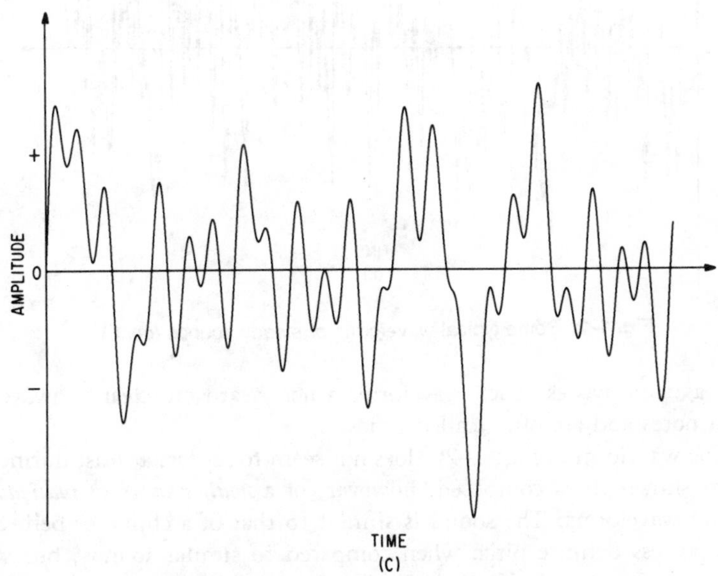

Fig. 1–2. Some typical waveforms of steady sounds (*cont.*)

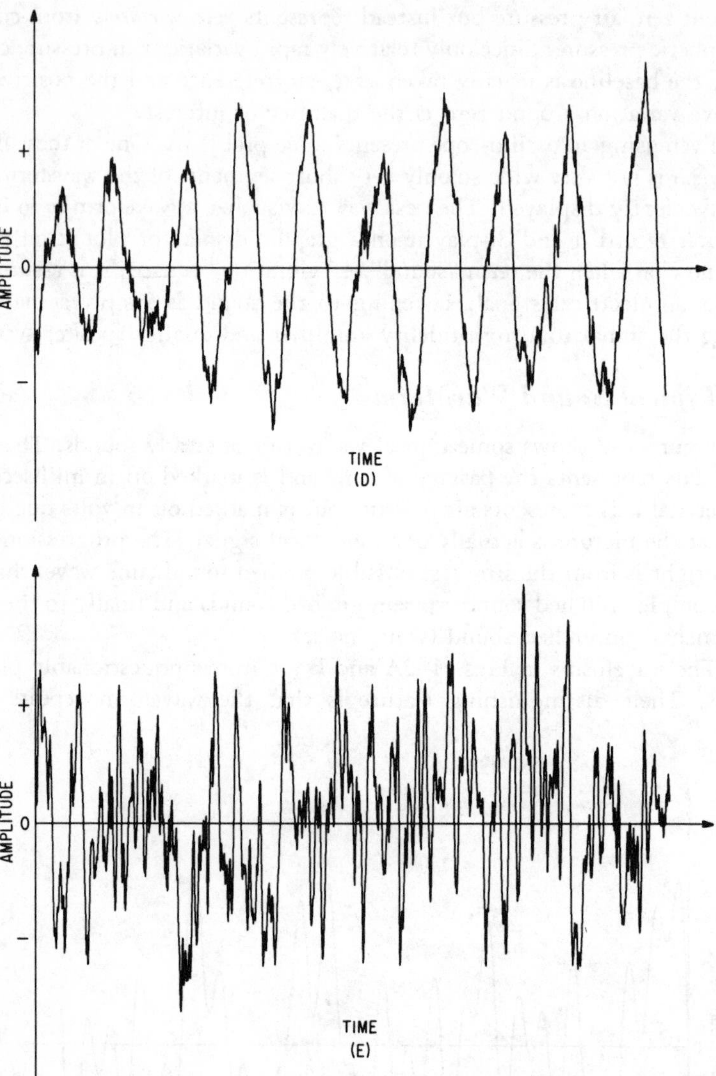

Fig. 1–2. Some typical waveforms of steady sounds (*cont.*)

exactly as time passes. Such waveforms when heard are clear, unwavering musical notes and are often called tones.

The waveform in Fig. 1–2C does not seem to repeat, at least during the segment shown. It is composed, however, of a *small number* of *individually* repeating waveforms. The sound is similar to that of a chime or bell. Such sounds possess definite pitch when compared to similar sounds, but when they are presented in isolation it is often impossible to say what the pitch really is in musical terms.

The waveforms in Figs. 1–2D and E do not repeat either, but each is composed of a very large (essentially infinite) number of repeating components. Waveform E, however, is composed of an equal mix of these components, whereas D contains a greater proportion of some components than others. The sound of waveform E is that of rushing air, whereas D is similar to whistling wind. Accordingly, E is purely unpitched and D is semipitched.

All of these waveforms can be described by means of *parameters*. Given these parameters and a synthesizer or computer, one could reproduce the essential characteristics of each of these waveforms and an infinity of others between the extremes. This does not mean that the same exact shape would be reproduced in all cases (although that too is possible if enough parameters are defined), but it does mean that those characteristics that are audible would be reproduced. Not all parameters are of equal importance in accurately describing the sound, as will be shown later.

The sine wave can be completely described with only two parameters. One of these is related to the time required for a single repetition of the waveshape and the other is related to the height of the waveform.

The Frequency Parameter

In Fig. 1-2A, the sine waveform repeats every 4 msec (thousandths of a second); thus, its *period* is 4 msec. Usually the reciprocal of the period is used and is called the *frequency*, which is measured in cycles per second according to the number of times the waveshape repeats in 1 sec. Recently, the composite unit cycles per second has been replaced by hertz as the unit of frequency. Thus, hertz or its abbreviation, Hz, will be used hereafter. Large values of frequency, usually called *high* frequencies, are measured in kilohertz (kHz) and megahertz (MHz), which are thousands and millions of hertz, respectively.

For the pure sine wave shown, the human ear is generally regarded as being capable of hearing frequencies between 20 Hz and 20 kHz. The 20-kHz upper frequency limit is usually a bit optimistic, however, with 15 kHz to 18 kHz being more common for young people. Advancing age pushes the upper limit lower yet. The lower limit of 20 Hz is somewhat arbitrary, since such low frequencies, if they are loud enough, make their presence known by rustling clothing, shaking floors, and rattling windows.

The frequency parameter of the sine wave is strongly related to the perceived pitch of the tone when heard. Whereas frequency is a physical parameter of the sound waveform, pitch is a subjective parameter that exists only in the mind of the listener. Without question, when frequency is increased, the perceived pitch also increases provided that the frequencies involved are in the audible range. The relationship between pitch and frequency is not linear, however. For example, an increase of 100 Hz from 100 Hz to 200 Hz results in a large pitch change upward, but a similar 100 Hz increase from 5 kHz to 5.1 kHz is a nearly imperceptible increase.

Listening tests have shown that the relation between frequency and pitch is an approximately *exponential* one. Thus, the increase from 100 Hz to 200 Hz represents a doubling in frequency so an equivalent pitch increase starting from 5 kHz would require doubling again to 10 kHz.

Musical Pitch

Musical pitch has its own system of measurement. Unlike frequency, the units are relative rather than absolute. The most fundamental unit is the *octave*. If tone B is one octave higher than tone A, then its frequency is exactly twice as high and the sensation of pitch would be twice as high. (In tests with musically inexperienced laymen, tone B would typically be judged to be less than twice as high in pitch as tone A, but such a tendency is usually eliminated by musical training.) Other units are the *half-step*, which is 1/12 of an octave or a frequency ratio of 1.05946, and the *cent*, which is 1/100 of a half-step or a ratio of about 1.00059, which is roughly 0.06%. A half-step is also the difference in pitch between two directly adjacent keys on a conventionally tuned piano. For moderately loud sounds around 1 kHz, the smallest change in frequency that can be perceived is around 5 cents.

Since these pitch units are purely relative, a basis point is needed if an absolute pitch scale is to be defined. One such basis point is the international pitch standard, which defines the note, A above middle-C, as being 440.0 Hz. The corresponding frequencies of all other musical notes can be obtained by applying the proper ratios to the 440-Hz standard.

Table 1–1 gives the frequencies of some musical notes. Note that two systems of tuning are represented, although there are others. The most popular tuning system is *equal temperment*, which is based solely on the frequency ratio of the half-step being the twelfth root of 2.0 or approximately 1.05946. The term equal temperment means that all half-steps are exactly the same size. The other system represented is the *just* system of tuning, which is based on rational fraction ratios with small numbers for numerator and denominator. The table shows these ratios in both fractional form and decimal form for comparison with the equally tempered scale frequencies. Note that the octave ratio is exact in both scales, but there are small differences in all of the other ratios.

Of the two scales, the just-tuned one is more musically accurate and pleasing to the ear particularly when chords are played. Musical accuracy here means accuracy of the important musical intervals such as the fifth, which is ideally a ratio of 3:2, and the third, which should be 5:4. Its disadvantage is that not all half-steps are the same size; thus, transposition from one key to another is not easily achieved. For example, the just scale shown is for the key of A major, meaning that the basis frequency chosen for application of the rational fraction ratios was 440 Hz. If another just scale was constructed using a C as a basis, most of the note frequencies would be slightly altered. As a result, the note D, for example, would have slightly different frequencies depending on the key of the music, which often changes in the course of a composition. This is a clearly impractical situation for all fixed-tuned instruments such as organs, pianos, guitars, etc. With equally tempered tuning, there is no problem in going from one key to another. For most musical applications, this advantage outweighs the sacrifice made in musical accuracy.

The equal-temperment system is also used almost exclusively in electronic music because it simplifies the electronic circuitry considerably. With a computer or microprocessor involved, however, it becomes feasible, although not necessarily simple, to handle just tuning and thus gain an extra measure of precision.

Table 1-1. Two Musical Tuning Systems

Equal temperment			*A Major just*			
Note	*Ratio*	*Frequency*	*Note*		*Ratio*	*Frequency*
A0	0.0625	27.500	A0	1/16	0.0625	27.500
A1	0.1250	55.000	A1	1/8	0.1250	55.000
A2	0.2500	110.000	A2	1/4	0.2500	110.000
A3	0.5000	220.000	A3	1/2	0.5000	220.000
A#3	0.5297	233.068				
B3	0.5612	246.928	B3	9/16	0.5625	247.500
C4	0.5946	261.624				
C#4	0.6300	277.200	C#4	5/8	0.6250	275.000
D4	0.6674	293.656	D4	4/6	0.6667	293.333
D#4	0.7071	311.124				
E4	0.7492	329.648	E4	3/4	0.7500	330.000
F4	0.7937	349.228				
F#4	0.8410	370.040	F#4	5/6	0.8333	366.667
G4	0.8910	392.040				
G#4	0.9439	415.316	G#4	15/16	0.9375	412.500
A4	1.0000	440.000	A4	1	1.0000	440.000
A#4	1.0594	466.136				
B4	1.1224	493.856	B4	9/8	1.1250	495.000
C5	1.1892	523.248				
C#5	1.2600	554.400	C#5	5/4	1.2500	550.000
D5	1.3348	587.312	D5	4/3	1.3333	586.667
D#5	1.4142	622.248				
E5	1.4984	659.296	E5	3/2	1.5000	660.000
F5	1.5874	698.456				
F#5	1.6820	740.080	F#5	5/3	1.6667	733.333
G5	1.7820	784.080				
G#5	1.8878	830.632	G#5	15/8	1.8750	825.000
A5	2.0000	880.000	A5	2	2.0000	880.000
A6	4.0000	1760.00	A6	4	4.0000	1760.00
A7	8.0000	3520.00	A7	8	8.0000	3250.00

The Amplitude Parameter

The other parameter that describes a sine wave is the *amplitude*. The amplitude parameter is related to the height of the wave in a plot such as in Fig. 1–2A. In the air, amplitude would actually relate to the degree of change in air pressure, whereas in an electronic circuit it would relate to the voltage or current in the circuit.

The most obvious way to specify the amplitude of a sine wave is to find the minimum voltage and the maximum voltage in the course of one cycle and express the amplitude as the difference between the extremes. This is termed the *peak-to-peak* amplitude. Another method is to specify the *average* amplitude, which is the long time average difference between the instantaneous waveform voltage and the baseline. A typical voltmeter would respond to this average rather than the actual peaks of the waveform. A third method relates the amount of heat produced in a resistor connected to the source of the sine wave voltage to the amount of heat produced when the same resistor is connected to a source of constant dc voltage. The dc voltage required to produce the same amount of heat is called the *effective* voltage of the sine wave or its *root-mean-square* value which is abbreviated rms. Of the amplitude specification methods, the rms technique most accurately correlates with what the ear hears, whereas the peak-to-peak method most accurately predicts the possibility of unwanted distortion in electronic recording and synthesis equipment.

The most common unit for amplitude specification when a waveform is being examined is simply the volt. In rare cases, a current waveform may be of interest so the amplitude would be specified in milliamperes or amperes. When a signal is being delivered to a speaker, however, the amplitude is usually expressed as power in watts. The power in a signal can be calculated in several ways. The simplest is to multiply the instantaneous voltage by the instantaneous current and average the product over one repetition of the waveform. Another method is to square the rms voltage of the waveform and divide the result by the speaker impedance, which is accurate only if the speaker impedance is purely resistive.

The human ear is capable of responding to a very wide range of sound amplitudes. The amount of sound power at 2,000 Hz that can be listened to without undue discomfort is about a trillion (10^{12}) times greater than the power in a barely audible sound. For convenience in working with such a wide range of power, the bel scale (named after Alexander Graham Bell) of sound intensity was developed. Like musical pitch units the bel scale is relative. The bel unit refers to a ratio of 10 between the power of two sounds. Thus, sound B contains 1.0 bel more power than sound A if it is 10 times as powerful. Conversely, sound A would be 1 bel less powerful or -1.0 bel with respect to sound B. Expressed using the bel scale, the range of hearing would be 12 bels.

In actual audio work, the unit decibel, which is a tenth of a bel, is more commonly used. It is abbreviated dB and represents a power ratio of about 1.259 to 1. Three decibels (which is 1.259^3) represents almost exactly a ratio of 2.0 and 6 dB is a ratio of 4:1. Note that these are *power* ratios. Since power increases as the square of voltage (assuming constant load resistance), a 10:1 ratio of voltage is equivalent to 100:1 ratio of power or 20 dB. Consequently, 6 dB represents only a doubling of voltage amplitude. Expressed as a voltage ratio, the 120-dB range of human hearing represents a million-to-one voltage range.

Since the decibel scale is relative, a basis point is needed if an absolute decibel scale is to be defined. For sound in air, the 0-dB reference is taken as 10^{-16} W/cm^2, a very small amount of power indeed. For electrical signals, the reference point is 0.001 W into a 600-ohm impedance or about 0.775 V. For the maximum amplitude of 120 dB, the figures would be 0.1 mW/cm^2 in air and a million kilowatts of electrical power, more than most generating plants put out. Clearly, the standardized electrical basis point has nothing to do with sound amplitude.

It should be apparent by now that there is a strong relationship between the amplitude of a sine wave and the loudness of the sound it represents. Also, as expected from the trillion-to-one audible amplitude range, the relationship is highly nonlinear. However, when amplitude is expressed in decibels, the relation is reasonably linear. The amplitude of a sound must be increased an average of 8.3 dB to be perceived as a doubling of loudness. For moderately loud sounds, 1 dB is about the smallest change in amplitude that is noticeable. The basis point of 10^{-16} W/cm^2 for sound in air is about the softest sine wave at 2 kHz that can be heard by a person with good hearing. The basis for the electrical 0-dB point is purely arbitrary.

Frequency and Amplitude Interaction

The frequency and amplitude parameters of a sine wave are completely independent. Thus, one may be varied over a wide range without affecting the value of the other whatsoever. This may not always be strictly true in a practical circuit for generating sine waves, but the amount of interaction in good-quality equipment is very small.

When this sound is heard by the human ear, however, there is significant interaction between loudness and pitch. The most dramatic interaction is the effect on the apparent loudness of a constant amplitude sine wave tone caused by changing its frequency.

Figure 1–3 shows the extent of this interaction. The curves show the amplitude change necessary to preserve constant loudness as frequency is varied. Note that there is relatively little interaction at large amplitudes, but, as the amplitude decreases, the lower-frequency sounds decrease in loudness much faster than higher-frequency sounds. For example, at an

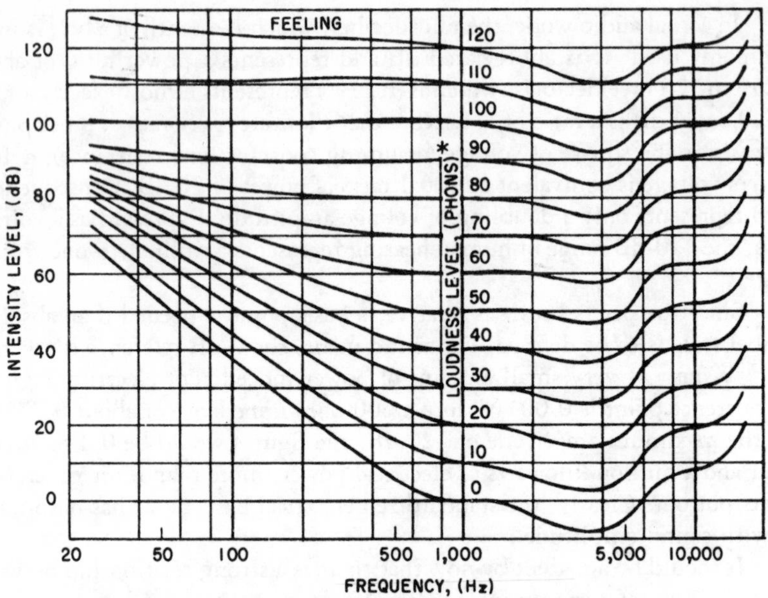

Fig. 1–3. Loudness as a function of amplitude and frequency

amplitude level of 60 dB (relative to 10^{-16} W/cm^2 in air) frequencies below 35 Hz would be too soft to be noticed. As frequency increases, loudness increases also up to about 800 Hz where it levels off to the comfortably loud level of normal conversation. As frequency approaches the upper limit of hearing, the apparent loudness again decreases.

The effect on pitch caused by an amplitude change is much smaller. Again the effect is greatest at the extremes of the frequency range. In particular, the pitch of a low-frequency (100 Hz) sine wave tone decreases as the amplitude increases. The pitch shift effect is small enough to be ignored, however, with more complex waveshapes.

The Mathematical Sine Shape

Before moving on to more complex waveshapes and other parameters, we need to look more closely at the sine shape itself. Why is it the simplest possible waveform and why is it so important? The name *sine* wave comes from the sine trigonometric function. For right triangles, the sine of one of the other angles is the ratio of the length of the side opposite the angle to the length of the hypotenuse.

Figure 1–4A shows how this trigonometric ratio can be converted into a sine wave shape. Assume that the crank, which represents the hypotenuse, is one unit in length and that it is being turned counterclockwise at a

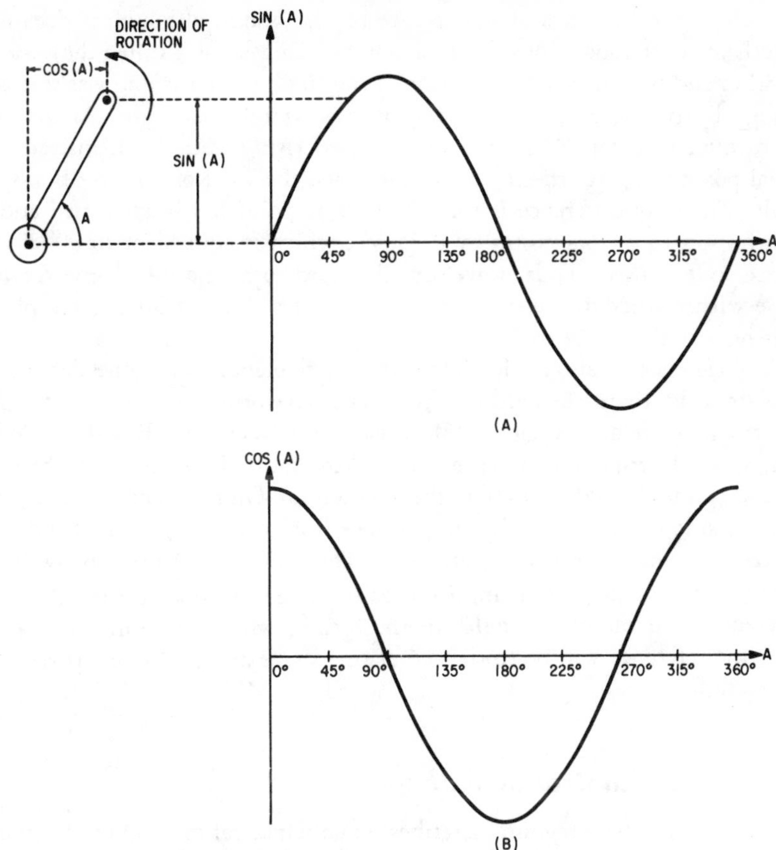

Fig. 1–4. Mathematical sine wave generator

constant speed. The angle, A, between the crank arm and the centerline of the crank axis is the angle of interest. As the crank turns and time passes, the angle gets progressively larger. The distance from the center of the handle to the horizontal centerline of the crank axis, which represents the side opposite the angle, is the sine of this progressively increasing angle.

Also shown is a graph of the sine as a function of the angle. If the crank is being turned one revolution per second, then the frequency of the sine wave on the graph is 1.0 Hz, and the horizontal axis units may be changed from degrees to time. If the speed of turning is increased, then the frequency of the sine wave would also be increased. Sometimes the term "instantaneous angular velocity" is used when the frequency varies. If rapid variations are encountered, simply counting the number of complete sine wave cycles in 1 second may not be precise enough. In such cases, angular velocity refers, conceptually, to the *speed* of crank turning, which can be measured very quickly.

One other factor is of importance on the graph, although it does not directly affect the sound of a single sine wave. This factor is called the *phase* of the wave and is related to the position of the crank when turning was started. In Fig. 1–4A, the initial crank position was straight out right. At time 0, the turning was started and the wave started rising initially. If instead the initial position was at the top of the arc, then the wave of Fig. 1–4B would result. The only difference is that the 0 time point has been shifted ahead with respect to the waveform by 0.25 sec, which is equivalent to 90° if the degree scale is used. Thus, waveform B is said to have a 90° degree *leading* phase with respect to waveform A and waveform A has a 90° *lagging* phase with respect to waveform B.

Since phase is also a relative quantity, a reference point is needed for an absolute scale. By mathematical convention, waveform B has a 0 phase angle. As a result, waveform A has a −90° phase angle. Waveform B is also called a *cosine* wave. In trigonometry, the cosine is the ratio of the length of the side *adjacent* the angle to the length of the hypotenuse. On the crank diagram, the adjacent side is represented by the distance from the center of the handle to the *vertical* centerline of the crank axis. The plot of a cosine wave will be exactly the same shape and amplitude as the sine wave done earlier; the only difference is in the phase angle. In the future, when the term *sine wave* is used, the reference will be to the actual sine shape and not to any particular phase angle.

The Mechanical Sine Shape

Although the foregoing describes a mathematical method of plotting a sine wave as accurately as desired, it does not explain why it is such an important waveshape. For the answer to that question consider the mechanical setup shown in Fig. 1–5. Here we have a weight hanging from a spring firmly attached to the ceiling. If the weight is pulled down somewhat and released, it will bounce up and down with a smooth motion that gradually diminishes. If the spring is of highly tempered steel and the experiment is performed in a vacuum, the vibration amplitude of the weight will decrease so slowly that for short observation times the amplitude will appear constant. The point is that the motion of the weight, if plotted as a function of time, is an essentially perfect sine wave. Any imperfections in the sine shape are due to defects in the spring and the fact that gravity is less at the top of the weight motion than at the bottom. The mathematical reason that two such different devices should have identical motion characteristics is beyond the scope of this discussion, however.

The frequency of vibration of the spring-mass system may be altered by either changing the amount of weight or the stiffness of the spring or both. With a stiff spring and light weight (or even the weight of the spring itself), the frequency can become high enough to be heard. Note that, as the

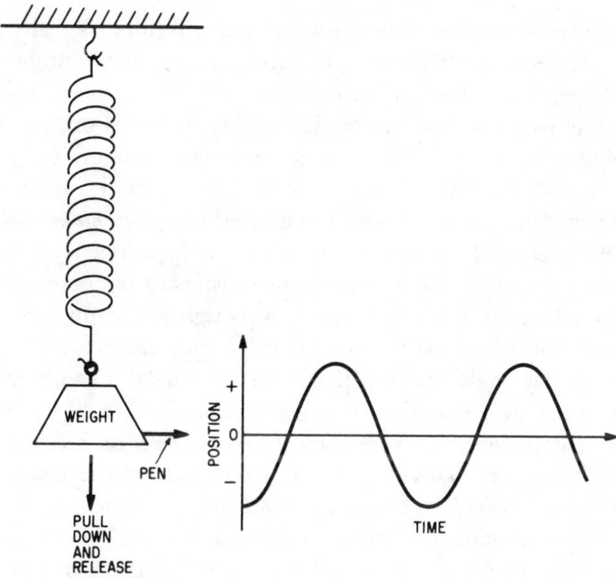

Fig. 1–5. Mechanical sine wave generator

amplitude of the vibrations gradually diminishes, the frequency remains the same. The rate of amplitude decay is dependent mainly on the amount of friction present. If the spring is held by a person rather than the ceiling, the vibrational energy lost to friction may be replenished by careful, synchronized movement of the spring.

The importance of the sine wave is obvious if one realizes that all natural sounds come from mechanical vibration. The vibrating members in all cases are actually tiny spring-mass systems. Pieces of metal, logs, and even the air itself have a degree of springiness and mass. Striking these objects or exciting them by other means creates the characteristic sine wave vibration of either the entire object or portions of it. In most cases, more than one spring-mass equivalent is vibrating simultaneously, so the resulting sound is actually a combination of sine waves of different frequencies and rates of decay.

Complex Waveforms

At this point, we are now prepared to discuss the most interesting parameter of all in repeating waveforms, namely the shape of the wave itself. The shape of a waveform influences its *timbre* or tone quality. Obviously, there is an infinite number of possible waveshapes (and only a few less timbres). The only restriction is that a waveshape must be a single-valued function, which essentially means that the horizontal progression from left to right can never reverse.

As mentioned earlier, any natural sound waveform is really a combination of sine waves originating from vibrating spring-mass systems. However, in the 17th century, a French mathematician by the name of Joseph Fourier proved mathematically that any waveform, regardless of origin, is actually a mixture of sine waves of different frequencies, amplitudes, and phases. Furthermore, he showed that if the waveform repeats steadily, then the frequencies of the component sine waves are restricted to being *integer multiples* of the repetition frequency of the waveform. Thus, if the frequency of repetition is 100 Hz, then the component sine waves must have frequencies of 100 Hz, 200 Hz, 300 Hz, etc., up to infinity, although any components above 20 kHz will not contribute to the sound, since they are inaudible. Of course, some of them may have zero amplitude, but in general it can be assumed that all of them exist in the audible frequency range.

These component sine waves are called *overtones* or *harmonics,* with the latter term preferred. The component having the same frequency as the overall waveshape is termed the *fundamental* frequency, which is also the first harmonic. The component having a frequency twice the fundamental is termed the first overtone or second harmonic. The third harmonic has a frequency three times the fundamental and so forth. Since the frequencies of the component waves are fixed, each one can be characterized by giving its amplitude and its phase angle either as an absolute quantity or with respect to the fundamental.

Figure 1–6 shows how harmonic sine waves can be combined together to produce a waveshape that is about as far as one can get from a curvy wave. Combining two waveforms really means adding them point by point as shown to get the combined result. A squared-off waveform such as this actually has an infinite number of harmonics with nonzero amplitudes. A practical synthesis of the waveform from harmonic components has to stop somewhere, of course, and leave all of the higher-frequency harmonics with a zero amplitude.

As can be seen, each additional harmonic gives a closer approximation to the desired rectangular-shaped wave. With the first 32 harmonics represented, the approximation is getting quite close with steeply rising sides and reasonably flat top; however, there is still a significant amount of overshoot and ringing. These imperfections are mainly due to using the set of harmonic amplitudes designed for an infinite series and stopping the series abruptly at the 32nd harmonic. A modification of the amplitudes taking into account the fact that no harmonics above 32 are allowed produces a visibly superior rendition of the desired shape.

The significance of Fourier's theorem can be realized by noting that all of the acoustically important aspects of the shape of a waveform can be specified with a comparatively small number of parameters. For example, a 1,000-Hz waveshape, no matter how complicated, can be specified by 20 amplitudes and 20 phase angles corresponding to the 20 audible harmonics.

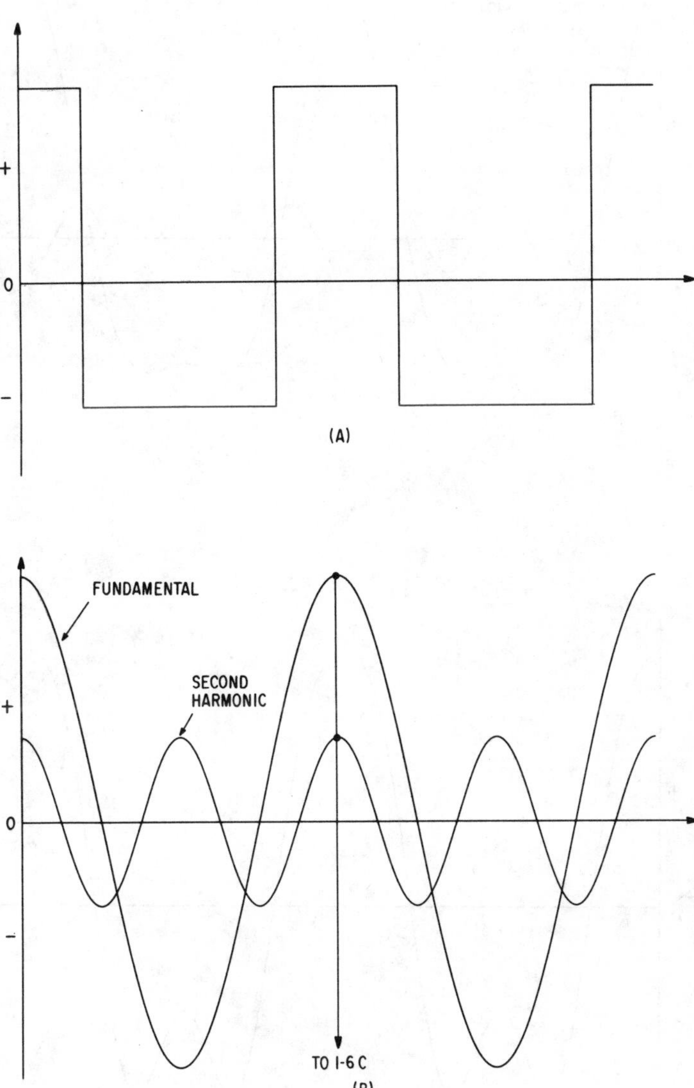

Fig. 1–6. Synthesis of a rectangle wave from sine waves. (A) Desired rectangular wave. (B) Fundamental and second harmonics separately.

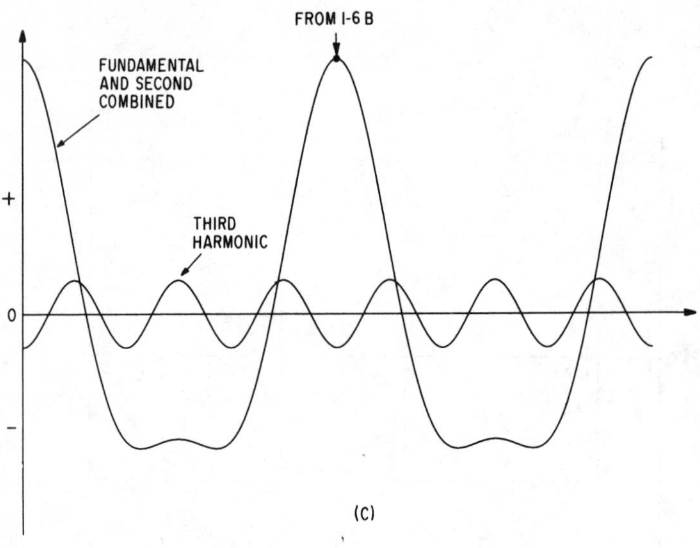

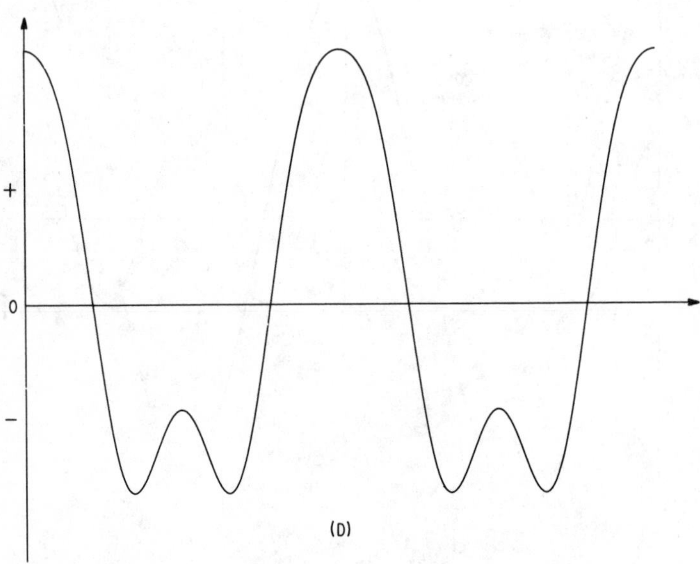

Fig. 1–6. Synthesis of a rectangle wave from sine waves (*cont.*). (C) Fundamental and second harmonics combined and separate third harmonic. (D) Fundamental, second, and third harmonics combined.

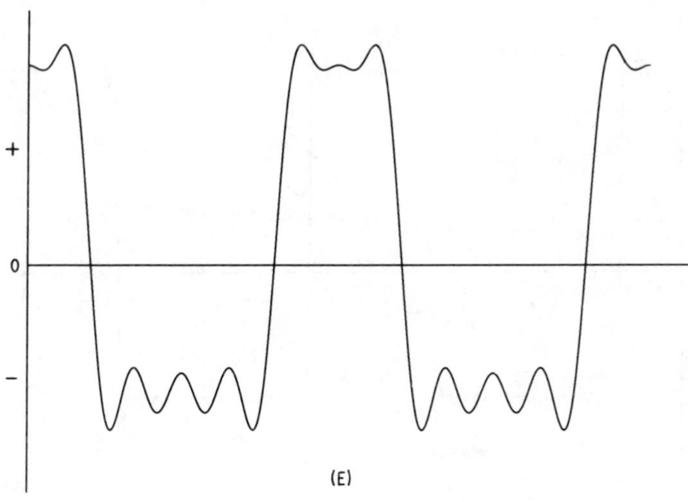

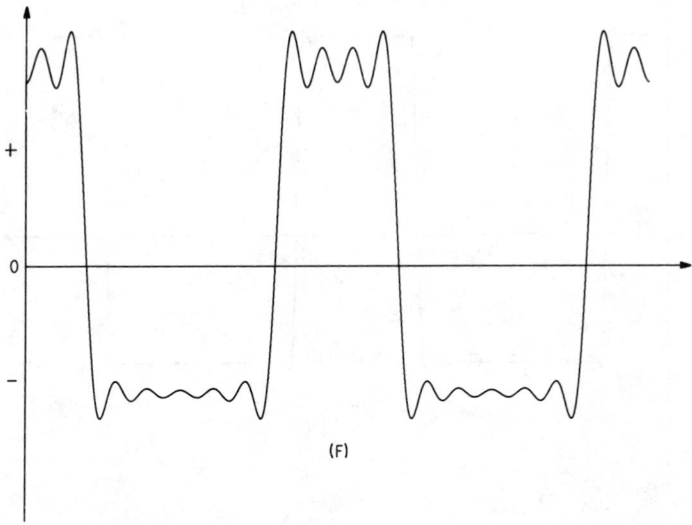

Fig. 1–6. Synthesis of a rectangle wave from sine waves (*cont*,). (E) Fundamental through sixth harmonics combined. (F) Fundamental through 10th harmonics combined.

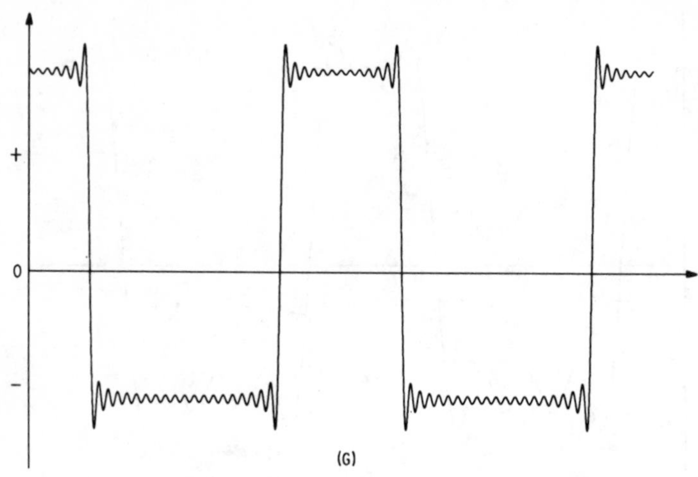

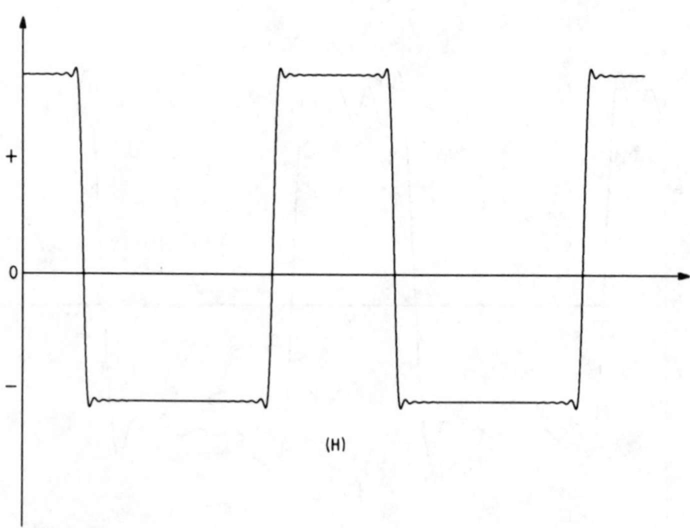

Fig. 1–6. Synthesis of a rectangle wave from sine waves (*cont.*). (G) Fundamental through 32nd harmonics combined. (H) Fundamental through 32nd harmonics combined with adjustment for a finite number of harmonics.

Human Ear Interpretation of Waveshape

Up to this point, the emphasis has been on the actual shape of a wave. However, the human ear does not work by tracing the waveform and reporting the various twists, turns, and undulations to the brain. Instead, the sound vibrations are crudely analyzed into sine wave components and the amplitudes of the components are sent to the brain for recognition. The phases of the harmonics with respect to the fundamental are of little importance in tones of moderate frequency and amplitude. As a result, phase can usually be ignored when synthesizing sound waveforms. For example, the tones of Fig. 1–7 would all sound alike provided the frequency was above a couple of hundred hertz and the amplitude was not excessively large. The amplitudes of the harmonics in Fig. 1–7A, B, and C are all the same, but in B the fundamental has been shifted 180° with respect to the other harmonics, and in C the phases of all of the components have been randomly redistributed.

Obviously, the waveshape is not really a very good indicator of the timbre of the resulting sound. Since the harmonic amplitudes are a good indicator of timbre, a different kind of graph called a *spectrum* plot is useful. Such a graph is shown in Fig. 1–8, which is the spectrum of the rectangular wave used earlier. The horizontal axis is now frequency and the vertical axis is amplitude, usually either the peak (half of peak-to-peak) value or the rms value. Each harmonic is represented by a vertical line whose height depends on its amplitude.

When evaluating timbre, particularly lower-frequency tones with a lot of harmonics, the human ear is not usually supersensitive about the exact amplitude of a particular harmonic. In most cases, the trend in amplitudes of

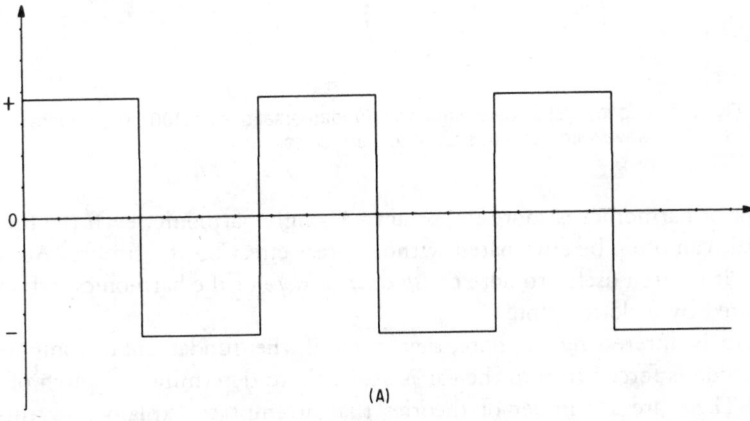

Fig. 1–7. (A) Normal square wave.

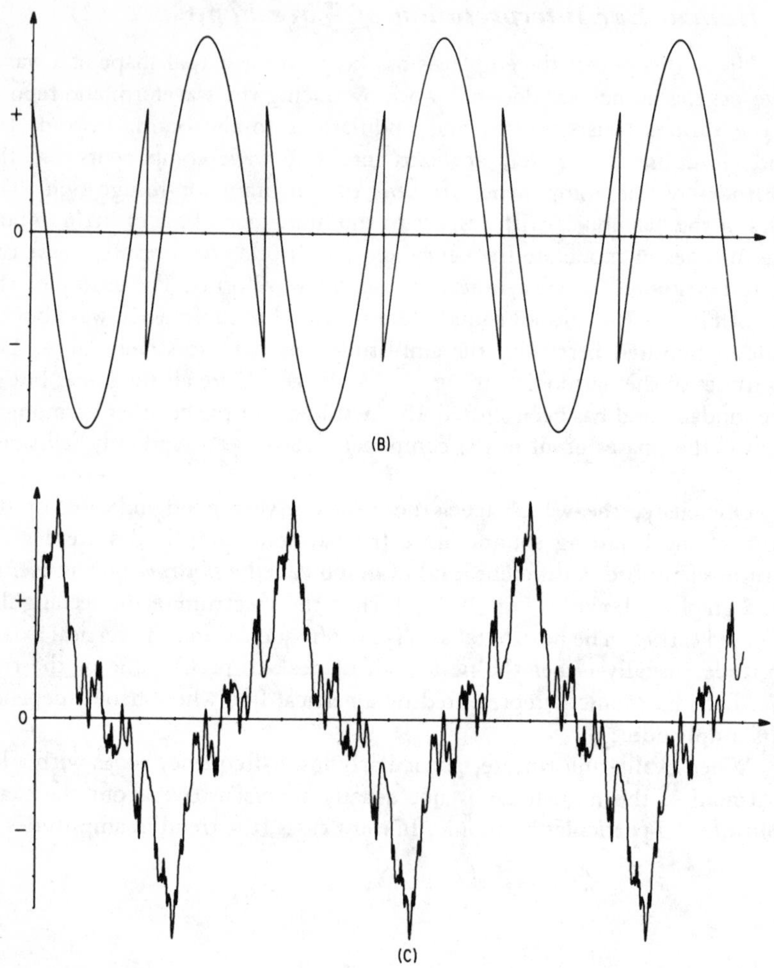

Fig. 1–7. (*Cont.*). (B) Square wave with fundamental shifted 180°. (C) Square wave with random shift of all harmonics.

groups of harmonics is more important. A single harmonic, even the fundamental, can often be eliminated without great effect on the timbre. Accordingly, it is often useful to note the *spectral envelope* of the harmonics, which is indicated by a dotted line.

It is interesting to note that even if the fundamental component amplitude is forced to zero the ear is still able to determine the pitch of the tone. There are a number of theories that attempt to explain how this is accomplished. One maintains that the ear is somehow capable of picking out the repetition rate of the waveform, which is not destroyed by removing the fundamental. Another suggests that all of the remaining component frequencies are ascertained, and the missing fundamental frequency is "computed" from them.

Nonrepeating Waveforms

With the basics of definitely pitched sounds with repeating waveforms in hand, let's examine more closely the last three waveforms in Fig. 1–2. As mentioned earlier, waveform C does not repeat but does have a pitch *sense* in relation to other similar sounds. Its spectrum is shown in Fig. 1–8B. Note that the sine wave component frequencies are *not* integral multiples of some fundamental frequency. This is the main reason that the waveform does not repeat and that it does not have an absolute pitch. However, since a small number of component frequencies relatively far from each other are involved, the sound is pleasing to hear, and the waveform trace is not unduly complex.

Actually, the statement about the waveform never repeating needs to be qualified a bit. If all of the frequencies are rational numbers it *will* repeat eventually. If one of the frequencies is irrational, such as π kHz, however, the waveshape will indeed never repeat. At the moment, the presence or

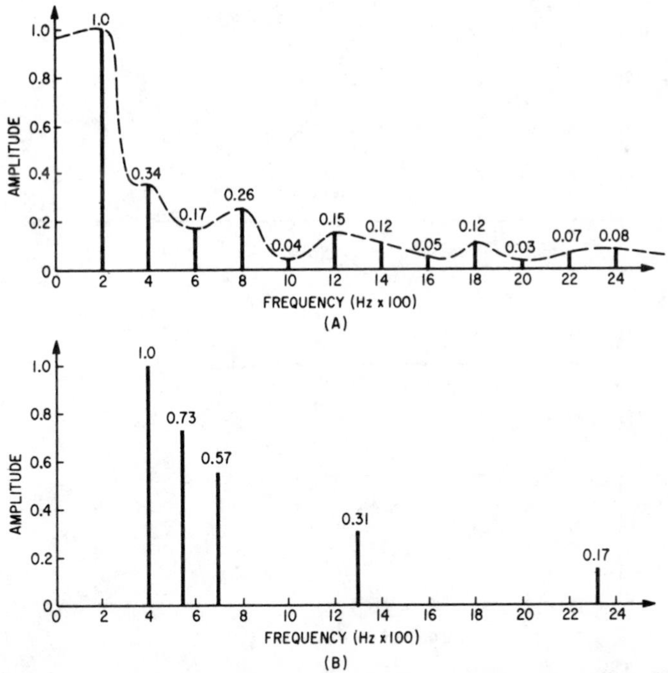

Fig. 1–8. Spectrum plot. (A) Rectangle wave of Fig. 1–7. (B) Waveform of Fig. 1–2C.

absence of a repeating wave pattern is rather academic, but it will be important later.

Unpitched sounds and most semipitched sounds are like the waveforms of Fig. 1–2D and E—real messes that look more like an infant's scribbling. Time waveforms of such sounds give almost no clues about how they will sound. A spectrum plot, however, will reveal quite a bit. The first obvious feature is that there is a very large number of lines representing component sine waves. With such a large number, the spectral envelope takes on added significance. In fact, most sounds of this type literally have an infinite number of component frequencies so the envelope is all that can be really plotted.

The spectrum in Fig. 1–8D is special. It is nothing more than a straight line! Such a sound is called *white noise* because it has an even mixture of all audible frequencies. This is analogous to white light, which is an even mixture of all visible light frequencies. Any departure from a straight spectral plot can be called coloring the sound, analogous to coloring light by making one group of frequencies stronger than others.

Pure white noise sounds like rushing air or distant surf. If the lower

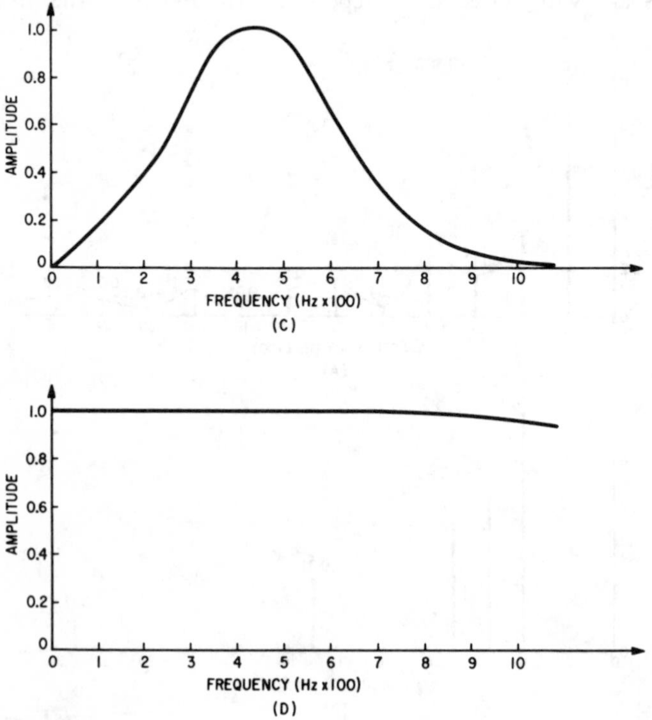

Fig. 1–8. Spectrum plot (*cont.*). (C) Waveform of Fig. 1–2D. (D) Waveform of Fig. 1–2E.

frequencies are emphasized (or the higher ones eliminated) the sound becomes a roar, or in an extreme case, a rumble. If the high frequencies predominate, a hiss is produced.

The middle frequencies can also be emphasized as in Fig. 1–8C. If a wide range of middle frequencies is emphasized, the sound is only altered slightly. However, if a sufficiently narrow range is strengthened, a vague sense of pitch is produced. The apparent frequency of such a sound is normally near the center of the group of emphasized frequencies. The narrower the range of frequencies that are emphasized, the more definite the pitch sensation. If the range is very narrow, such as a few hertz, a clearly pitched but wavering tone is heard. If the waveform of such a tone is examined over only a few cycles, it may even appear to be a pure, repeating, sine wave! Multiple groups of emphasized frequencies are also possible with a clearly different audible effect. In fact, any spectrum envelope shape is possible.

Parameter Variation

In review, then, all steady sounds can be described by three fundamental parameters: frequency if the waveform repeats, overall amplitude, and relative harmonic amplitudes or spectrum shape. The audible equivalents of these parameters are pitch, loudness, and timbre, respectively, with perhaps a limited degree of interaction among them.

What about unsteady sounds? All real sounds are unsteady to some extent with many useful musical sounds being particularly so. Basically a changing sound is a steady sound whose parameters change with time. Such action is frequently referred to as *dynamic* variation of sound parameters. Thus, changing sounds can be described by noting how the parameters vary with time.

Some terms that are often used in discussing parameter variation behavior are *steady state* and *transition*. If a parameter is changing only part of the time, then those times when it is not changing are called steady states. Usually a steady state is not an absolute cessation of change but instead a period of relatively little change. The transitions are those periods when movement from one steady state to another takes place. An infinite variety of transition shapes are possible from a direct, linear change from one steady state to another to a variety of different curves. Often it is the speed and form of the transitions that have the greatest influence on the overall audible impact of a sound.

Frequency Variation

Dynamic variation of frequency is perhaps the most fundamental. A simple one-voice melody is really a series of relatively long steady states with essentially instantaneous transitions between them. If the frequency transitions become fairly long, the audible effect is that of a glide from note to note.

Often with conventional instruments, a small but deliberate wavering of frequency is added to the extended steady states. This wavering is called *vibrato.* If the frequency parameter is plotted as a function of time on a graph, then the vibrato shows up as a small amplitude waveform with the baseline being the current steady state. This situation is termed *frequency modulation* because one waveform, the vibrato, is modulating the frequency of another waveform, the sound. We now have a whole new infinity of possible vibrato frequencies, amplitudes, and shapes. Vibrato waveforms for conventional instruments are usually around 6 Hz with an amplitude of 1% or so and a roughly sine waveshape.

Gross alterations in the typical vibrato waveform can also have a gross effect on the resulting sound. If the modulating wave amplitude is greatly increased to several percent or even tens of percent, the result can be a very boingy or spacey sound. If the modulating frequency is increased to tens or hundreds of hertz, the sound being modulated can be completely altered. Clangorous sounds resembling long steel pipes being struck or breaking glass are easily synthesized simply by having one waveform frequency modulate another. This phenomenon will be studied in greater depth later.

Amplitude Variation

Changes in amplitude are also fundamental. Again taking a one-voice melody as an example, it is the amplitude changes that separate one note from another, particularly when two consecutive notes are of the same frequency. Such an amplitude change delineating a note or other sound is frequently called an amplitude *envelope* or just envelope. The shape and duration of the amplitude envelope of a note has a profound effect on the overall perceived timbre of the note, often as important as the spectrum itself.

Figure 1–9 shows a generalized amplitude envelope. Since they are so important, the various transitions and steady states have been given names. The initial steady state is, of course, zero or silence. The intermediate steady state is called the *sustain,* which forms the body of many notes. The transition

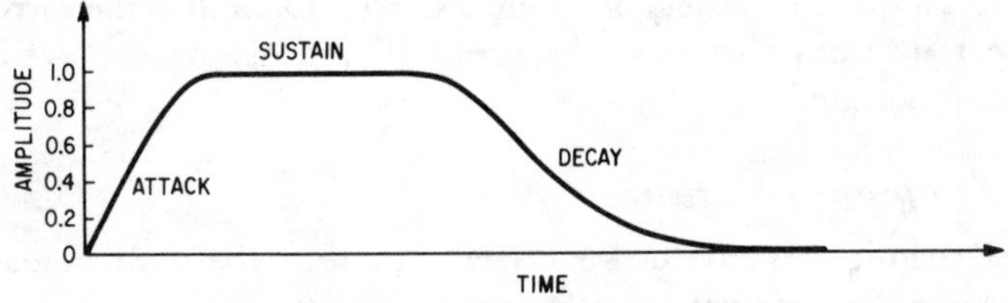

Fig. 1–9. Typical amplitude envelope shape.

from zero to the sustain is called the *attack*. The duration of the attack is of primary importance, although its shape may also be important, particularly if the attack is long. The transition from the sustain back to zero is the *decay*. Again, time is the major variable. Some notes, such as a piano note, have no real sustain and start to decay immediately after the attack. They may, however, have two different rates of decay, a slow initial one, which could be considered the sustain, even though it is decaying, and a faster final one. Other envelope shapes are, of course, possible and quite useful in electronic music.

As with frequency variation, an amplitude envelope may have a small wavering superimposed on the otherwise steady-state portions. Such amplitude wavering is called *tremolo* and, if small in amplitude, sounds much like vibrato to the untrained ear. Actually, the physical manipulation required to waver the tone of conventional instruments seldom results in pure vibrato or tremolo; usually both are present to some degree. Large-amplitude tremolo gives rise to an unmistakable throbbing sound. Generalized amplitude modulation of one waveform by another is also possible, and in many cases the effects are similar to frequency modulation. This will also be examined more closely later.

Spectrum Variation

Finally, dynamic changes in the spectrum of a tone are the most interesting and the most difficult to synthesize in general. The primary difference between spectrum variation and frequency or amplitude variation is that a spectrum shape is multidimensional and the other two parameters are single-dimensional. Because of this multidimensional nature, standard electronic synthesis techniques for dynamic spectrum changes generally utilize schemes that attempt to cover a wide range of timbres by varying only one or two parameters of a simplified spectrum shape.

One obvious way to control and vary the spectrum is to individually control the amplitudes of the individual harmonics making up the tone. This is a completely general technique applicable to any definitely pitched tone. The problem with actually accomplishing this is twofold. The first is the myriad of parameters to control—dozens of harmonic amplitudes for moderately pitched tones. Involving a computer or microprocessor is the only reasonable approach to such a control task. The other problem is deciding *how* the harmonic amplitudes *should* vary to obtain the desired effect, if indeed even that is known. There are methods such as analyzing natural sounds, evaluating mathematical formulas, or choosing amplitude contours at random and subjectively evaluating the results that work well in many instances. In any case, a computer would probably be involved in generating the data also.

As mentioned previously, common synthesis techniques aim at reducing the dimensionality of the spectral variation problem. Consider for a moment a spectral envelope like the one that was shown in Fig. 1–8C. Disregarding the exact shape of the bell-shaped curve, it should be obvious that three parameters can adequately describe the spectrum. First, there is the width and height of the peak on the curve, and finally the frequency at which the peak is highest. In a typical application, the width and height of the curve are related. Also, since only the *relative* height of one portion of the curve with respect to another is important, the absolute height parameter is usually eliminated. This leaves just the width and center frequency as variables. Note that for definitely pitched, periodic sound waveforms the spectrum curve being considered is really the *envelope* of the individual harmonic amplitudes.

It turns out that manipulation of these two variables is sufficient to create very interesting dynamic spectrum changes. In fact, if the width variable is set to a reasonable constant value such as ⅓ octave at the 6-dB down (with respect to the peak) points, then varying just the center frequency is almost as interesting. This in fact is the principle behind the "wah-wah" sound effect for guitars that became popular years ago.

Other methods for changing or distorting the spectrum under the influence of a small number of parameters exist and will be covered in more detail later.

Simultaneous Sounds

The preceding should serve as a brief introduction to the fundamental parameters of a single, isolated sound. Most interesting music, however, contains numerous simultaneous sounds. One common use for simultaneous sounds is chords and harmony. Another application is rhythm accompaniment. Sometimes quantities of sound are used simply as a kind of acoustical background for a simpler but more prominent foreground. The physics and fundamental parameters of each component sound remain unaltered, however. The real frontier in synthesis, after adequate control of the basic parameters of sound is accomplished, is applying this degree of control to numerous sounds, all simultaneously, and all under the direction of a single composer/performer. Extensive use of microprocessors in synthesis will be the final stride toward reaching this goal.

History of Electronic Sound Synthesis

Sound and music synthesis by electronic means has a long and interesting history. Although only the most significant milestones can be briefly described here, the effort is certainly worthwhile, since the ongoing evolution of synthesis techniques and equipment is far from complete. Without exception, significant developments in sound synthesis closely followed significant developments in electronic and computer technology. Often, however, there have been gaps of many years, even decades, between when it became possible to apply a technique and when it became practical to do so.

The Teleharmonium

One of the earliest serious musical instruments that produced sound by purely electrical means was conceived and built by Thaddius Cahill in 1903. The device was called the Teleharmonium, and the name fairly accurately described the principles involved. As with many synthesis developments, the profit motive was the major driving force. Cahill's basic concept was to generate music signals electrically and transmit them to subscriber's homes over telephone lines for a fee. The signals would be reproduced by loudspeakers for "the continuous entertainment of all present." The "harmonium" part of the name derives from the use of harmonically related sine waves for the synthesis of various timbres.

At the performer's end, the device resembled a conventional pipe organ console with two piano-like keyboards and numerous stops for controlling the timbre. Tone signals, however, were generated at kilowatt levels by specially constructed multipole, multiarmature electric generators located in the basement. Each generator had eight outputs representing a particular note pitch at octave intervals for the 8-octave range. Such generators were reasonably straightforward to build but were large, heavy, and expensive. Although 12 were planned to cover all of the notes in an octave, only 8 were actually built. The high power levels produced were needed to serve the large number of subscribers expected and overcome transmission losses.

In addition to the generators, special multiwinding "mixing transformers" were used to combine several tones together. A limited amount of harmonic mixing was utilized to vary the timbre. This was possible without additional windings on the generators, since the first six harmonics of any note on the equally tempered musical scale are also on the scale with very little error. The amplitude levels of the tones were controlled by means of inductors with movable cores to vary the inductance. In addition to the tonnage of iron, miles of wire were used to connect keyboard contacts to the other equipment. Overall, the machinery that was built weighed over 200 tons and required 30 railroad flatcars to move.

Generally, the device worked well and was adequately accurate and stable. One problem that was eventually overcome was key click. Since the tones were being continuously generated and merely switched on and off with contacts, the attack of a note was instantaneous. If a key contact closed at a time when the signal being switched was near a peak, a sharp rising transient would be generated in the output line. The solution to the problem was additional filter transformers to suppress the transients.

The other problems were mostly economic. Since the planned 12 generators were not available, some of the notes were missing, resulting in a restricted set of key signatures that could be played. Another difficulty was that the pressure of delivering continuous music to the subscribers already signed up severely limited the amount of machine time available for practice and further refinement.

Listeners' reactions to Teleharmonium music were interesting. The initial reaction was quite favorable and understandably so. No one had ever heard pure, perfectly tuned sine waves before and the sparkling clear unwavering quality of the sound was quite a novelty. Over long periods of time, however, the novelty was replaced by subtle irritation as the overly sweet nature of pure sine waves became apparent. The limited harmonic mixing technique that was later developed did little to remedy the situation, since six harmonics are too few for the lower-pitched tones and even fewer were provided for the higher-pitched ones due to generator limitations. A related problem was the extremely poor loudspeakers available at the time. Bass response was totally absent and the many sharp resonances of the metal horns would frequently emphasize particular notes or harmonics many times over their nominal amplitude.

For Cahill, the project was a financial disaster, its fate eventually sealed by radio broadcasting. The basic concepts live on, however, in the Hammond electronic organs. The "tone wheels" used in these instruments are electric generators that perform exactly as Cahill's except that the power output is only a few *micro*watts rather than many *kilo*watts. The needed amplification is supplied by electronic amplifiers. Mixing, click suppression, and harmonic amplitude control are performed by resistive networks requiring only additional amplifier gain to overcome their losses. The eighth harmonic, which is also on the equal-tempered scale, was added, skipping the seventh altogether. Still, the Hammond organ has a distinctive sound not found in any other type of electronic organ. Even if the reader has never heard one live, he has probably heard a record of one—over a background music system!

Soundtrack Art

Somewhat later, around 1930 after sound was added to motion pictures, some work was done with drawing sound waveforms directly onto film. Theoretically, this technique is infinitely powerful, since any conceivable sound within the frequency range of the film equipment could be drawn. The difficulty was in figuring out exactly what to draw and how to draw it accurately enough to get the desired result.

The magnitude of the problem can be appreciated by considering how a single, clear tone might be drawn. The clearness of a tone depends to a great degree on how accurately the waveform cycles repeat. Gradual variations from cycle to cycle are desirable, but imperfections in a single cycle add roughness to the tone. For even the simplest of tones, the waveform would have to be carefully drafted. More complex or simultaneous tones would be even more difficult. In spite of these problems, at least one interesting but short and simple piece was created in this way.

Like the Teleharmonium, the concept of drawing waveforms directly is now fairly common. Computers and sophisticated programs, however, do the tedious waveform calculation and combination tasks.

The Tape Recorder

Without question, the most significant development in electronics for music synthesis as well as music recording was the tape recorder. The Germans first developed the wire recorder during World War II, and it was subsequently refined to utilize iron-oxide-coated paper tape. Plastic film bases were later developed, and now magnetic tape is the highest fidelity analog sound recording technique in common use.

When on tape, sound becomes a physical object that can be cut, stretched, rearranged, molded, and easily re-recorded. A new breed of abstract composers did just that and the result, called "musique concrète," sounded like nothing that had ever been heard before. In fact, before the popularization of synthesizer music, the public's conception of electronic music was of this form, which they usually characterized as a seemingly random collection of outrageous sounds.

The name musique concrète stems from the fact that most, if not all, of the sounds used were *natural* in origin, i.e., concrete. Popular source material included water drips, sneezes, and squeaky door hinges. Typical manipulations included gross speeding or slowing of the recorded sound, dicing the tape and rearranging parts of the sound often with segments in reverse, overdubbing to create simultaneous copies of the sound, and other tricks. Occasionally, a small amount of electronic equipment was used to filter and modify the sound in various ways. Regardless of the actual source material, the distortions were so severe that the final result was completely unrecognizable.

Although usage of this sound material need not result in abstract compositions, it usually did. The primary difficulty was in achieving accurate enough control of the distortion processes to produce more conventional pitch and rhythmic sequences. Unfortunately, musique concrète did very little to popularize electronic music techniques, although it undoubtedly gratified a small circle of composers and listeners.

RCA Mark II Synthesizer

Over the years, many special-purpose electronic musical instruments were developed and used. One example is the theremin (1920), which was an electronic tone source whose frequency and amplitude could be independently controlled by hand-waving near two metal plates. Others include a host of keyboard instruments such as the Novachord (1938) and the Melochord (1949). In the early 1950s, however, work began on a general purpose instrument, the first electronic sound synthesizer.

The RCA Mark II Electronic Music Synthesizer could produce two tones at once in which all of the important parameters could be controlled. The control mechanism was a roll of punched paper tape, much like a player-piano roll. Thus, it was a *programmed* machine and as such allowed composers ample opportunity to carefully consider variations of sound parameters. The program tape itself consisted of 36 channels, which were divided into groups. Each group used a binary code to control the associated parameter. A typewriter-like keyboard was used to punch and edit the tapes.

Complex music could be built up from the basic two tones by use of a disk cutting lathe and disk player, which were mechanically synchronized to the program tape drive. Previously recorded material could be played from one disk, combined with new material from the synthesizer, and re-recorded onto another disk.

The RCA synthesizer filled a room, primarily because all of the electronic circuitry used vacuum tubes. Financing of the project was justified because of the potential for low-cost musical accompaniment of radio and television programming and the possibility of producing hit records. Extensive use of the machine emphasized the concept that programmed control was going to be necessary to adequately manipulate all of the variables that electronic technology had given the means to control.

Direct Computer Synthesis

The ultimate in programmed control was first developed in the middle 1960s and has undergone constant refinement ever since. Large digital computers not only controlled the generation and arrangement of sounds, they generated the sounds themselves! This was called *direct* computer synthesis of sound because there is essentially no intermediate device necessary to synthesize the sound. The only specialized electronic equipment beyond standard computer gear was a digital-to-analog converter (DAC), a comparatively simple device. Simply put, a DAC can accept a string of numbers from a computer and plot waveforms from them as an audio signal suitable for driving loudspeakers or recording.

Such a system is ultimately flexible. Absolutely any sound within a restricted frequency range (and that range can easily be greater than the range of hearing) can be synthesized and controlled to the Nth degree. Any source of sound, be it natural, electronic, or imaginary, can be described by a mathematical model and a suitable computer program can be used to exercise the model and produce strings of numbers representing the resulting waveform. Sounds may be as simple or as complex as desired, and natural sounds may be imitated with accuracy limited only by the completeness of the corresponding mathematical model.

No limit exists as to the number of simultaneous sounds that may be generated either. Often in such a system, a discrete sound source may be just a set of numbers describing the parameters of the sound. Usually this would take only a few words of computer storage out of the tens or hundreds of thousands typically available.

Obviously, such an all-powerful technique must have some limitation or else it would have completely superseded all other techniques. That limitation is time. Although large computers perform calculations at tremendous rates of speed, so many must be performed that several minutes of computer time are necessary to compute only a few seconds of music waveforms. The more complex the sound, the longer the calculations. The net result was that considerable time elapsed between the specification of sound and its actual production. Considerable usually meant at least half a day due to typical management practices in large computer centers.

Obviously, then, composing for the direct computer synthesis medium demanded considerable knowledge of the relation between mathematical models, sound parameters, and the ultimate sensation of the listener. It also required that the composer have a clear idea of what was to be accomplished. Without such foreknowledge and careful planning, the delays incurred by excessive experimentation would be unacceptable and the cost of computer time prohibitive. Nevertheless, many of the greatest electronic musical works were realized using this technique.

Voltage-Controlled Synthesizers

Perhaps the complete antithesis of direct computer synthesis started to emerge in the middle 1960s largely as the result of development of silicon transistors and other semiconductor devices. The concept was *modular* music synthesizing systems utilizing voltage-control concepts as a common organizational thread throughout the system. Each module in the system had a distinct function and usually these functions corresponded one for one with the fundamental parameters of sound. The modules could be easily connected together in an infinite variety of configurations that could be changed in seconds by rerouting patch cords or pins on patch boards. The whole assemblage could be played by a keyboard or a number of other manual-input devices.

In general, a voltage-controlled synthesizer module consists of a black box with inputs and outputs that are electrical signals. Signals are conceptually divided into audio signals that represent sound and control voltages that represent parameters. An amplifier module, for example, would have an audio signal input, a control input, and an audio signal output. Varying the dc voltage at the control input would change the gain of the amplifier. Thus, it could be considered that the amplifier module altered the amplitude parameter of the sound passing through in accordance to the voltage at the control input. A filter module likewise altered the timbre of a sound passing through according to a combination of one or two control inputs. Although oscillator modules had no signal inputs, control inputs altered the frequency of the output waveform and sometimes the waveform itself.

The real power of the voltage-control concept lies in the realization that the only difference between a *signal* voltage and a *control* voltage is in the typical rates of change. Properly designed modules could process control voltages as easily as signals and could also be cascaded for multiple operations on the same or different parameters.

Unlike direct computer synthesis, experimentation was encouraged due to the personal interaction and ease of use of the synthesizer. In addition, familiarity with the audible effect of different modules could be obtained in only a few hours of experimentation. Improvisation was also practical and widely practiced.

One limitation of voltage-controlled synthesizers until recently, however, was that they were essentially monophonic, i.e., one note at a time. The problem lies not in the voltage control technique but in the human interface devices such as keyboards and ultimately in the ability of the performer to handle all of the variables. This limitation has classically been overcome by the use of overdubbing to combine one musical line at a time with a multitrack tape recorder.

Perhaps the most significant event in the popular history of electronic music occurred when a recording created with voltage-controlled equipment by Walter Carlos called "Switched On Bach" was released in 1969. For the first time, the general public was exposed to electronic music that was "real music" with melody, rhythm, and harmony. This shattered the old myth that electronic music was always abstract and disorienting and created quite a bit of interest among performers, listeners, and advertising agencies.

Microprocessors

Today the microprocessor is the hottest technical development of the decade. The basic power of a computer that once cost thousands of dollars is now available for only tens of dollars. Electronic music technology has and certainly will continue to benefit from microprocessors. Ultimately, techniques with the generality of direct computer synthesis and the ease of interaction of voltage-controlled synthesis will become commonplace.

Microprocessors are ideally suited to automating and rendering programmable the standard voltage-controlled music synthesizer. The synthesizer's strong points such as ease of use and experimentation can be retained in the development stages of a composition, but the advantages of programmed operation can be realized when the final result is generated. A microprocessor can easily remember, catalog, and reproduce the numerous interconnection patterns and control sequences typically used. It can also generate its own control sequences based on mathematical models, inputs from other sources, or random chance. This entire application area of microprocessors is of great interest currently and is, of course, the subject of Section II of this book.

The faster and more sophisticated microprocessors are becoming powerful enough for direct synthesis techniques to be applied with performance approaching that of large machines of only a few years ago and price tags in the reach of the serious experimenter. Furthermore, costs of the faster but simpler microprocessors are such that a multiprocessor system, with a microprocessor for each sound to be synthesized simultaneously, is in the realm of practicality. What was once an oscillator circuit with separate waveforming circuits may become instead a microprocessor with suitably simplified direct synthesis programming. These are the application areas that are the subject of Section III.

2

Sound Modification Methods

All the different methods for generating the sound material necessary for electronic music can be roughly categorized into two groups: those that generate entirely new sounds via some kind of synthesis process and those that merely modify existing sounds. This dichotomy is not very rigid, however, since many synthesis methods depend heavily on modification of otherwise simple synthetic sounds for their results, and many modification methods so severely distort the original sound that the result could easily be considered to be synthetic. Nevertheless, the fundamental component techniques making up a methodology can be easily segregated into synthesis and modification processes.

Modification techniques are usually considered to be the older of the two. Before the appearance of musique concrète, pure synthesis was more common, but the fundamental goal of most of these early efforts was to build a solo instrument that would fit into an orchestra. The goal of musique concrète, on the other hand, was to replace the orchestra and produce works of the magnitude of a symphony entirely by electronic means.

Modification methods attack sound from every conceivable direction. Any of the simple sound parameters such as frequency, amplitude, or spectrum may be directly altered. Time sequencing of the envelopes of these parameters may be altered in numerous ways. Parameter envelopes characteristic of one sound may be extracted and applied to another. Even simple judicious selection of short portions of sounds can give a completely different effect.

Sound on Tape

As mentioned previously, sound on magnetic tape is a physical object that may be freely manipulated. The only tools required are a reel-to-reel tape recorder (two recorders are desirable), a good pair of nonmagnetic scissors, a splicing block with splicing tape, and imagination. A grease pencil is also necessary for marking the exact location of sound events on the tape.

A so-called "full-track" tape recorder is very helpful when extensively editing tape. Such machines record on the full width of the tape; thus, it may not be turned over for additional recording time. Although such machines are hard to come by in the consumer new equipment market, they are fairly common as professional equipment. Stereophonic effects are typically added as a separate step later after the basic composition has been completed. Also the higher tape speeds available are typically used. Besides better recording fidelity, the many pieces of tape to be manipulated will be larger and easier to handle.

Rearrangement

The most fundamental splicing modification is rearrangement of a previously recorded sequence of sounds. Since a fair amount of experimentation is usually required, the sequence is typically copied several times before cutting commences. One interesting introductory experiment is to record a scale from a musical instrument and rearrange it to form a melody. Timing is fairly easy to control since time = distance along the tape. Even 50 msec is 3/4 of an inch at 15 inches/sec.

More interesting results are obtained if parts of the envelopes of notes are removed or attacks and decays are interchanged. In particular, using just the attack portion of many musical instrument notes can create some very interesting results that usually will not resemble the source instrument at all.

A related procedure that works well with full-track recorders is to make an extended diagonal splice rather than the typical short diagonal or straight splice. The result will be that one sound will seem to dissolve into another. If a piece of tape is spliced in slightly crooked, the high frequencies will be lost on playback and the result is as if a curtain had been pulled over the sound source. The angle of the crooked piece determines the extent of high-frequency loss with greater angles producing greater losses.

With full-track equipment, a piece of tape may also be spliced in backward. At first that might not seem like a very powerful technique, but it is. For example, ordinary English speech becomes a very strange, gutteral sounding foreign language nearly impossible to repeat accurately. A very interesting experiment is to record a sentence and learn to repeat its backward sound. Then the sentence is spoken backward, recorded, and played backward again. The resulting accent is unbelievable!

A piano recording played backward sounds like an organ with the ends of notes "snuffed out" by a breath of air. This is one demonstration of the importance of the amplitude envelope in determining the overall timbre of a sound. A simple piano piece performed backward and then played backward so the music is forward is another interesting experiment.

Even ignoring envelopes, which is the case with relatively steady sounds, the character of many sounds is completely changed by playing them backward. If a recording of a contralto or bass singer is played backward, the cutting quality of the voice disappears and the result sounds more like a well-tuned belch. Although the exact explanation for this will be detailed later, it is one case in which the phase relationship among harmonics in a tone makes a big difference in timbre.

All kinds of percussive sounds are completely altered by backward playing. In most cases, if the percussive sound is pitched at all, the sense of pitch is heightened by being played backward. This is probably due to the fact that for a short period following a sharp attack transient the ear is recovering and is less able to perceive pitch.

Another possibility is splicing the same sound back to back to eliminate the sudden cutoff that occurs when percussive sounds are played backward. Using the attack portion for both the attack and decay, using the decay portion for both, or even using the attack from one sound and dissolving into the decay portion of another are all possibilities.

Speed Transposition

Another trick that nearly everyone who owns a reel-to-reel tape recorder has tried at least once is playing the tape at a different speed than it was recorded. A speed doubling changes speech into familiar monkey chatter, while a speed halving produces drawn out groans. More useful effects are created if, when producing the source material, the undesirable speedup or slowdown effects of the processing are compensated for. Such an example is the production of the once popular "chipmunk" records in which the original vocals were sung much more slowly than usual in order to have a reasonable tempo after the speed doubling.

More severe speed changes usually distort a sound beyond recognition. Male speech when slowed by a factor of 16 or more comes out sounding like rhythmic beating on a constantly changing drum. Other common, complex sounds take on a new dimension when slowed substantially. The fine structure that usually emerges is reminiscent of examining a pond water droplet through a microscope.

Although standard tape speeds are usually powers of two times the base speed of 15 inches/sec, many professional recorders can be easily run at intermediate speeds. These machines usually have synchronous motors whose speed is precisely determined by the power line *frequency* rather than voltage. If the motor circuit is separated from the rest of the electronics and connected to a power amplifier driven by a variable-frequency oscillator, the tape speed may be continuously varied over a fairly broad range. The newest professional recorders use a dc servo motor system whose speed is proportional to a reference voltage, which is normally tightly regulated. Disconnecting the reference and connecting a variable voltage source can give a very wide speed range.

With precisely variable speed, it is possible to record a *single* sound or note and convert it into all of the notes of the scale. A Christmas song "sung" with a single dog bark is one recent application of this technique. Great thunderous concluding chords from a symphony may be captured and likewise processed or even smoothly slid from one pitch to another. If the rotating mass in the recorder is relatively small, it may even be able to follow relatively complex frequency envelopes and play different pitches on command.

Many musical instruments have different *registers* or pitch ranges and produce substantially different timbres in the various registers. A particularly prominent example is the clarinet, which possesses a characteristic hollow woody sound in the lower register and a somewhat squawky sound in the upper register. With tape speed transposition, the connection between pitch register and actual pitch may be broken, resulting in a wider range of timbres than those produced by ordinary instruments.

Special equipment has been constructed that allows speech to be played faster or slower than it was recorded without any pitch change. The initial units used rotating tape heads that would essentially break the sound into short segments approximately 30 msec long. When in the speedup mode, a portion of each segment would be thrown away and the remainder stretched out to fill the space. The amount thrown away and the resulting degree of stretch was just enough to cancel the upward pitch tendency. Slowdown was accomplished in a similar manner except that a fraction of the segment would be repeated after the entire segment was played. Although useful for altering speech rates for talking books or stenographers, undesirable beating effects with music waveforms limited the use of such equipment. Improved designs using digital logic and memories instead of rotating tape heads allow variable segment size and much better results with musical tones.

Tape Reverberation

Reverberation may also be added to sound entirely through the use of tape equipment. Actually, echo would be a better term because the effect is really a series of distinct echos. Most of the better quality recorders have separate record and playback heads mounted side-by-side from 0.75 to 2 inches apart. Typically, the tape first passes the recording head and then passes the playback head, resulting in a delay between the original sound and the signal developed by the playback head. The magnitude of the delay depends on the exact tape speed and head spacing but is typically between 100 and 500 msec, well within the range of distinct echo perception.

A single echo is produced if the delayed playback signal is mixed with the original signal and recorded on another machine. Multiple echos, however, can be produced using *feedback* techniques and only one recorder. The trick is to mix the original signal and the delayed signal but feed the result back to the record head of the *same* machine. In operation, there is initially no playback signal so the original source merely passes through the mixer and is recorded. A split second later, this signal is picked up by the playback head, mixed with the continuation of the original, and recorded again. Two split seconds later, it is passed around the loop again and so on. If each re-recording of the echo is weaker than the previous one, the echos eventually die out like normal echos. However, if the re-recording is at the same or greater amplitude, the echos continue unabated or build up until distortion is produced.

Of course, the signal is degraded a little every time it is played and re-recorded. If the feedback factor is just a little beyond unity (re-recorded just a trifle louder than the original), the middle frequencies will continue to build up while the low and high extremes will slowly die out. If the original signal is an isolated sound shorter than the delay time, the result is an interesting change in timbre each time the sound repeats. If the process is allowed to continue long enough, the sound will eventually degrade into a howl with a periodic amplitude envelope. The user may also change the echo re-record volume in response to what he hears and improvise. Many sounds in the category of "the saucer lands" have been produced in exactly this way.

Tape echo in conjunction with other tape-editing tricks can also lead to interesting results. For example, if a recorded sound is played backward, is re-recorded with echo added, and the new recording is again played backward, the echos wind up *preceding* the sounds, a very strange effect. "Preverb" would be an apt name for such a process. Different effective echo times with fixed head spacing may be accomplished by a speed transposition prior to the addition of reverberation followed by an inverse transposition.

Tape-echo techniques are so powerful that specialized machines have been built exclusively for that purpose. Multiple playback heads with irregular spacing was one attempt to provide enough multiple, random echos so that the result resembled concert hall reverberation rather than Grand Canyon reverberation. Another refinement was easily movable playback heads to vary the echo rate. A particularly interesting effect is produced if the head is moved *while* the recording is made. The echos would then be of a different pitch than the original sound!

Multitrack Recorders

Finally, tape equipment can be, and usually is, used to combine sounds together for the final result. Unfortunately, direct recording of one sound on top of another on the same tape track cannot be done very well. The high-frequency bias signal necessary for high-fidelity tape recording tends to erase previously recorded sounds. Two recorders or a single multitrack recorder, however, can be used to combine sounds onto one track.

In a typical multitrack setup, the separate sounds to be combined are each recorded on a separate track of the same tape. When played, the signal from each track has its own separate gain control so that the relative contribution of each track to the resulting whole can be controlled. A final *mixdown* run is done in which the multiple sounds are combined and recorded onto the two- or four-track (for stereo or quad) master tape, which represents the final result. Commercial multitrack machines typically have 8, 16, or even 24 separate tracks. Most modern recording studios depend heavily on multitrack tape for most of their serious work.

Obviously, such a setup would allow a single performer to play all the parts of a piece one at a time and then combine them. Synchronization with previously recorded material is accomplished by temporarily using the section of the recording head that is scanning a previously recorded track for playback (at reduced fidelity) to the performer. Most complex music performed on voltage-controlled synthesizers is played in separate parts and combined with a multitrack tape machine.

By now it should be apparent that tape manipulation methods are very powerful sound modification techniques. One drawback, however, is that often a considerable amount of work is necessary, such as careful re-recording, accurate cutting, and keeping track of scores of little pieces of tape. Thus, experimentation is hampered somewhat by the possibility of wasted effort. Application of computer technology, even microcomputers, is now tremendously streamlining the process and even adding some new tricks.

Electronic Sound Modification

Over the years, quite a few "black boxes" and techniques have been developed for directly modifying sound. Generally, these devices consist entirely of electronic circuits. Rarely, however, a mechanical system does the bulk of the work and transducers are used for getting audio signals in and out. Such cases are frequently the subject of intensive research to find cost-effective electronic substitutes for the mechanical elements.

The uses for sound modifiers are varied but can be divided into two rough groups. Obviously, such devices are of great utility in the electronic music studio for adding complexity to basic electronic sounds that by themselves may be lifeless. The other application is as instrumental sound modifiers for rock bands and small combos. The devices for use by this group are usually named by the apparent effect produced. Thus, we have "fuzz boxes," "wah-wah pedals," and "infinity sustains." Fortunately, the physical effects of most of these can be easily explained in terms of the fundamental parameters of sound.

Nonlinear Amplifiers

Modification of the spectrum of a sound is perhaps the most dramatic. Spectrum modification devices range from simple distortion boxes to sophisticated variable filter banks. In all cases, the basic aim of a spectrum modification device is to change the relative amplitudes of the component harmonics of the sound. Although the overall amplitude of the waveform might also be altered by the process, it can easily be corrected later if undesirable.

The simplest spectrum modification device is a nonlinear amplifier circuit of some sort. Nonlinear in this sense simply means that the instantaneous output voltage is not a constant times the input voltage. Such nonlinearity is best described by means of a transfer function graph such as in Fig. 2–1. Voltage values corresponding to the input signal waveshape are plotted along the Y axis and the resulting output signal waveshape is plotted along the X axis. Assuming that the overall gain of the amplifier is unity, a perfectly linear response would be represented by a straight line to infinity as shown.

Any real amplifier, however, has an overload point beyond which the output voltage cannot deviate even though the input voltage does. Figure 2–2A shows the transfer function of a real amplifier. Assuming for the moment that a sine wave somewhat greater than the overload point is the input signal, it is apparent that the peaks of the waveform have been clipped off. In fact, circuits designed specifically for such waveform distortions are

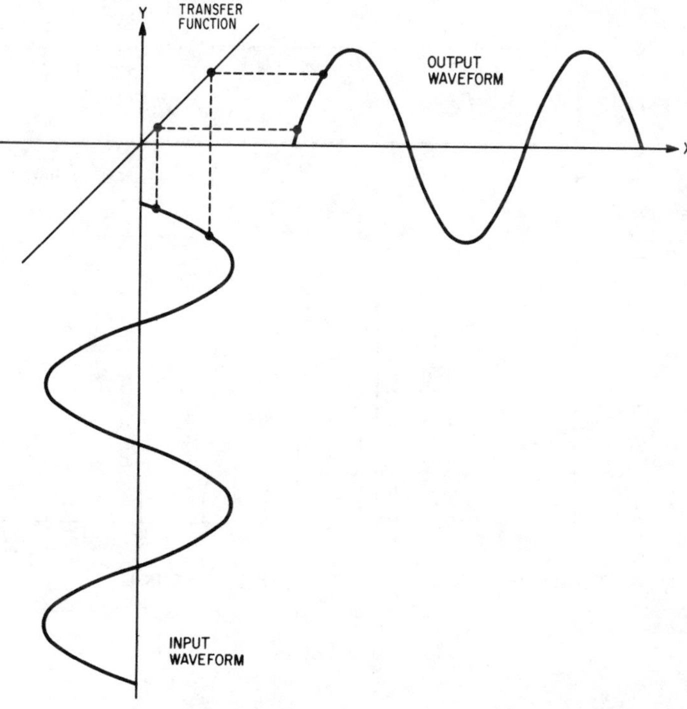

Fig. 2–1. Linear transfer function

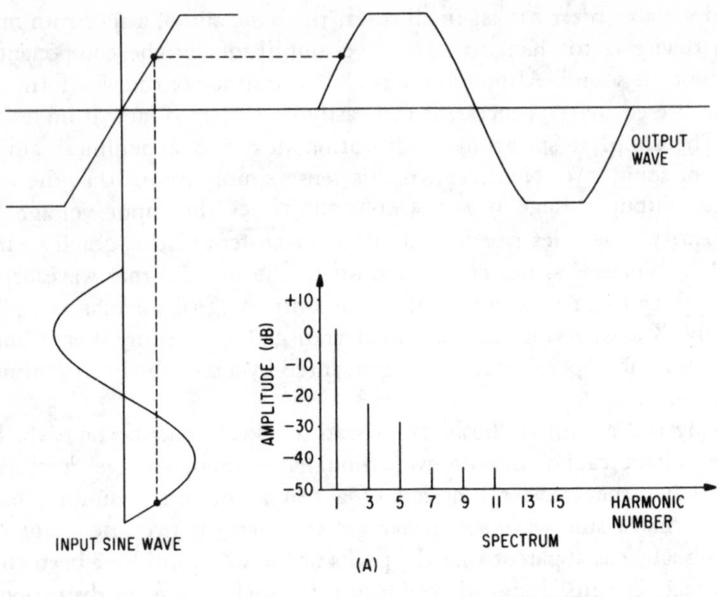

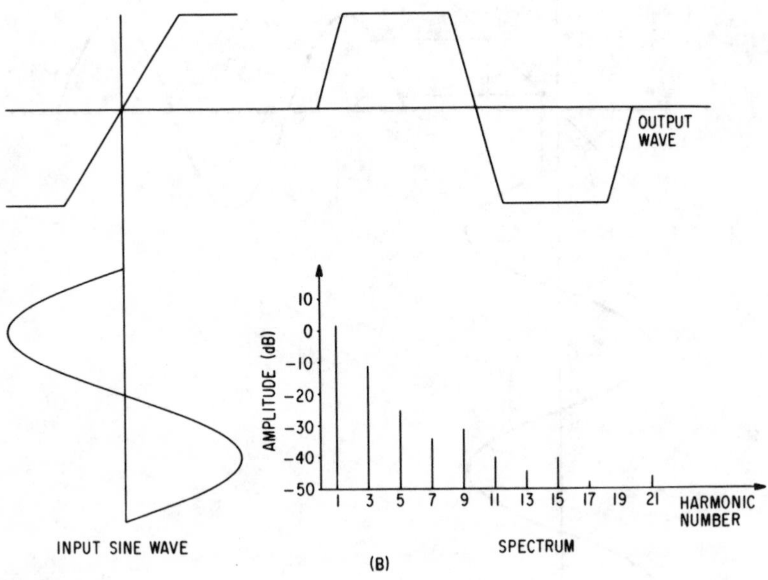

Fig. 2–2. Nonlinear waveshaping. (A) Slight clipping. (B) More severe clipping.

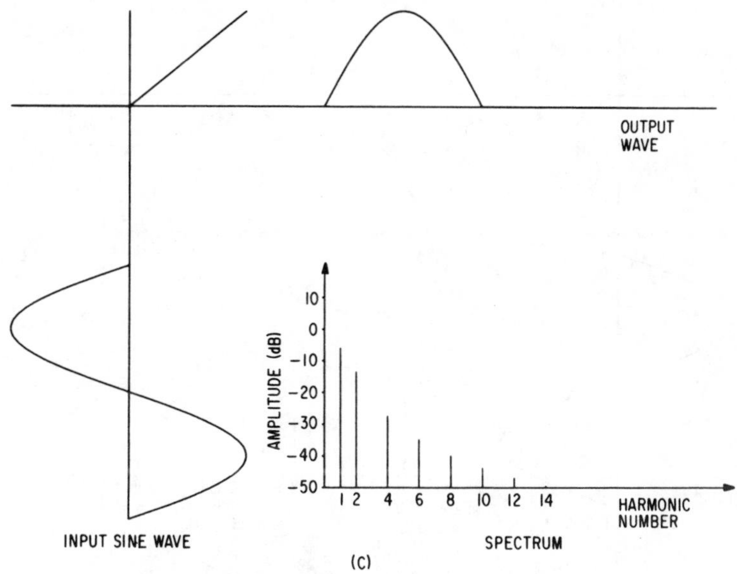

Fig. 2–2. Nonlinear waveshaping (*cont.*). (C) Half-wave rectification.

called clippers. The accompanying spectral plot shows that the distorted waveform now has some harmonics added that were not originally present although their amplitude is low. Increasing the input amplitude further results in more severe clipping and a greater proportion of high-frequency harmonics as shown in Fig. 2–2B. Thus, by varying the *amplitude* of the input, one may vary the *spectrum* of the output by using a clipper. In practice, however, clipping circuits usually allow adjustment of the clipping point of the transfer function, which produces the same effect. Thus, the clipping point becomes a *parameter* of the clipper that, when varied, changes the spectrum parameters of the output signal.

The preceding is called a *symmetrical* clipper because the positive and negative portions of the waveform are affected similarly. Thus, the harmonics added are of odd order only. A nonsymmetrical clipper of one type is shown in Fig. 2–2C. There is no output for negative input voltages, and for positive inputs, the output follows the input. The output spectrum now has both even and odd order harmonics that were not originally present. Changing the clipping point of this circuit, which is shown in Fig. 2–2D, increases the *proportion* of high-frequency harmonics, although the overall output amplitude has decreased.

The action of the circuit in Fig. 2–2E is somewhat interesting. None of the original input frequency component appears at the output and only even order harmonics are generated. The ear hears this result as a pitch doubling, since the resulting harmonic series is really an even and odd series for a

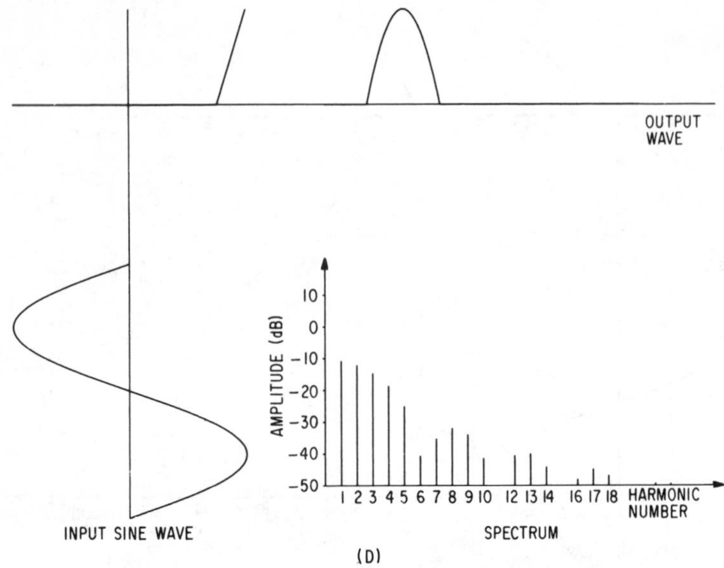

Fig. 2–2. Nonlinear waveshaping (*cont.*). (D) Half-wave rectification with offset.

fundamental at twice the frequency. Figure 2–2F shows the result of varying two possible parameters of the transfer curve; a center clipping threshold and the slope (gain) for positive input signals.

Actually, pure sine waves are seldom used as the source signal such as when a musical instrument's sound is being modified. Depending on the exact waveform, a given nonlinearity may increase some harmonics, reduce others, and leave some generally unchanged. Instrumental waveforms are not constant either. Frequently, slight changes in input waveform (from slight harmonic phase changes, for example) may result in large changes in output spectrum. One interesting waveform that is not affected by any kind of nonlinear device is the square wave. Although the amplitude may be changed, the square waveshape is never altered.

Of course, there are literally thousands of possible nonlinear curves, each with a set of parameters that may be changed to vary the output signal spectrum. There are important drawbacks to their use, however. One drawback is that the relationship between a parameter or parameters describing a certain class of transfer curves and the actual spectrum in terms of harmonics is not always simple. For example, increasing a clipper parameter may at first give increased high harmonic content, but further increases of the same parameter might actually reduce the high harmonics or shift the emphasis to middle harmonics. The situation gets much more complicated if a complex waveform is used for the input.

Another important drawback is that nonlinear devices generally give desirable results only with *single* tone inputs. If two simultaneous tones of

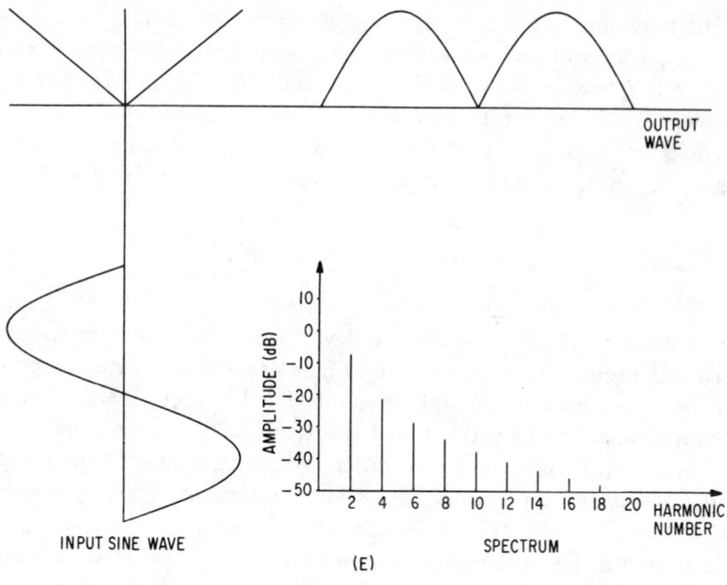

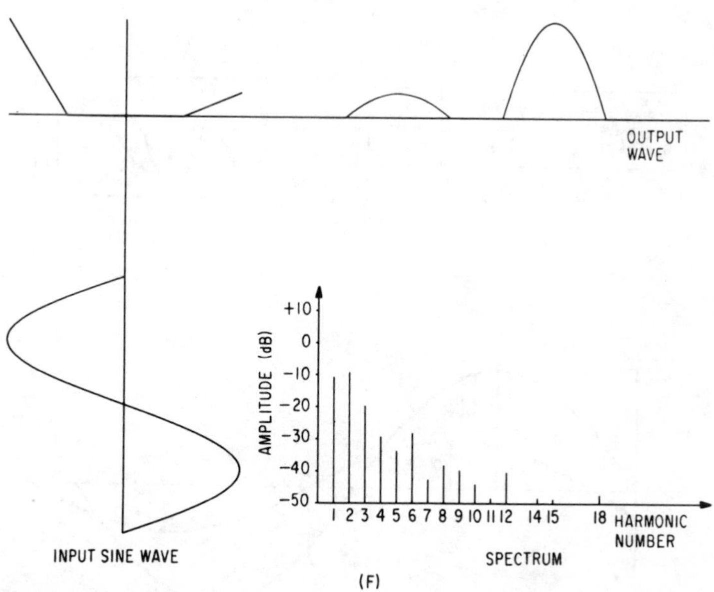

Fig. 2–2. Nonlinear waveshaping (*cont.*). (E) Full-wave rectification. (F) Nonsymmetrical rectification with offset.

different frequency are fed in, the output spectrum contains not only harmonic frequencies of each tone, but every possible combination of sum and difference frequencies between the tones and their harmonics. For musical instrument use, the resulting sound is close to garbage unless the input frequencies are simply related such as a 3:2 ratio. For more abstract goals, however, anything is potentially useful even if it is not predictable.

Filters

While nonlinear circuits are relatively simple spectrum modifiers, their action is indirect. A different class of device called *filters* acts directly on the spectrum changing the amplitude and phase of each sine wave component of the input signal by a predictable amount. Furthermore, their *action* on the spectrum is unaffected by the actual spectrum of the input signal.

Filters can be completely specified by giving a plot of their *amplitude* response and *phase* response as a function of frequency. Nearly always, the amplitude response is termed, incorrectly, the frequency response but the former term will be used exclusively in this book. The test setup shown in Fig. 2–3 can be used to make such plots. Here we have a variable-frequency sine wave signal generator, a calibrated oscilloscope with dual-trace capability, and the filter under test. The *gain* of the filter at a particular frequency may be determined by measuring the amplitude of the signal at the filter

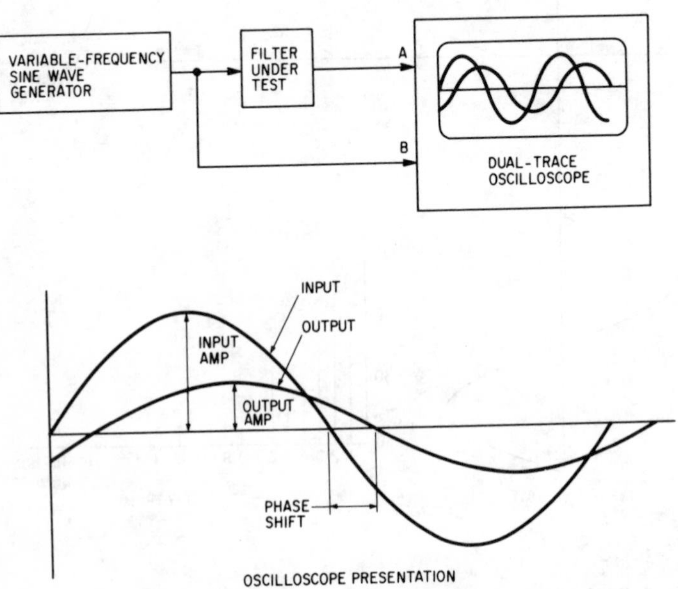

Fig. 2–3. Experimental setup for characterizing a filter

output and dividing it by the input amplitude, which usually remains constant. The *phase shift* at a particular frequency may be determined by comparing the two waveforms on the oscilloscope face. Note that phase shifts greater than 180° leading or lagging cannot be uniquely determined at an arbitrary frequency with this setup. However, a point of zero phase shift can usually be found and the trend away from zero followed.

The amplitude response then is plotted simply by varying the input frequency over the audible range and plotting the gain factor. Customarily, the frequency axis is logarithmic in order to accurately represent a wide range of frequencies, and the amplitude axis is scaled in decibels, which effectively makes it a log scale also. The phase response may be plotted similarly,

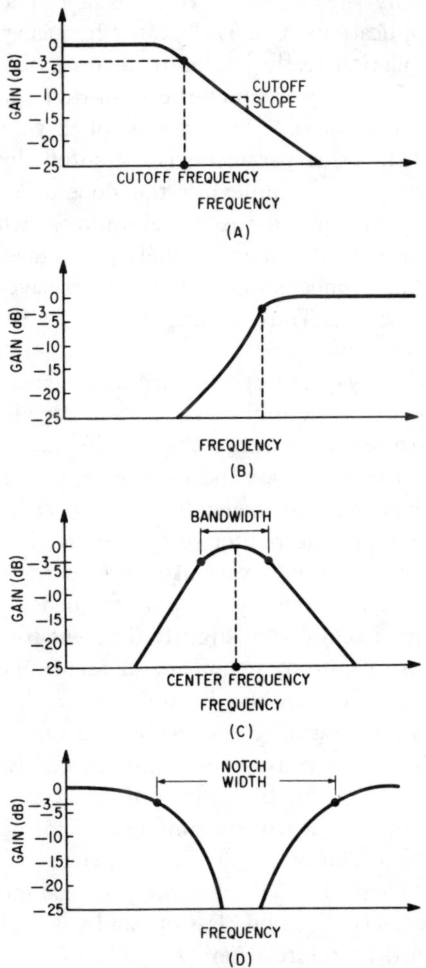

Fig. 2-4. Basic filter amplitude response curve shapes. (A) Low-pass. (B) High-pass. (C) Bandpass. (D) Band-reject.

although the phase axis is usually linear. Actually, for simple filter circuitry, the shape of the phase response is rigidly tied to the shape of the amplitude response. For use as a sound modifier, the phase response of a filter is usually ignored.

Theoretically, the shape of an amplitude response curve may be anything desired. However, like the principle that any waveshape may be built from sine shapes, amplitude response curves may be built from a small class of basic shapes. Figure 2–4 shows some of these..

Shape A is called a *low-pass* response because the lower frequencies are passed without *attenuation* (reduction in amplitude), while the higher frequencies are reduced considerably. Although several parameters may be necessary to fully specify such a shape, two are of primary importance in sound modification applications. One is the *cutoff* frequency or the frequency above which the attenuation really begins to increase. By convention, the cutoff frequency is the frequency at which the amplitude response is 3 dB less (one-half the power output or 0.7071 times as much voltage) than it is at very low frequencies. The other parameter is the cutoff slope. In a practical filter of minimal or moderate complexity, the slope of amplitude decrease beyond the cutoff frequency approaches an asymptote, which is a straight line. Cutoff slope is usually stated in decibels per octave, particularly for musical purposes. Actually, most simple filter circuits have cutoff slopes that are multiples of 6 dB/octave. Thus, a simple low-pass filter might have a slope of 6, 12, 18, etc., dB/octave.

Shape B is called a *high-pass* response for the same reason A was termed low-pass. The parameters of the high-pass response are also similar.

Shape C is called a *bandpass* response. This is because in the general case a small band of frequencies are passed and the others, both higher and lower, are rejected. Two parameters are generally used to characterize bandpass responses, although four are required for completeness. The frequency corresponding to the top of the peak is variously termed the center frequency, natural frequency, resonant frequency, or pole frequency. The natural and resonant frequencies are actually very slightly different from the true center frequency, but for musical purposes they are all identical.

The width of the curve can also be specified in different ways. One common method calls for measuring the frequencies of the two 3-dB down points, subtracting them, and calling the result the bandwidth in hertz. In music, it is more useful to specify bandwidth in octaves, thus the term "1/3 octave bandpass filter" is frequently encountered. A formula for the octave bandwidth in terms of the lower cutoff, FL, upper cutoff, FU, and center frequency, FC is $BW = \log_2 [1 + (FU-FL)/FC]$. A final method, which only applies to a certain but very common class of bandpass filters, is the quality factor or Q. Q is defined by the relation: $Q = FC/(FU - FL)$. The significance of Q will be studied in greater detail later.

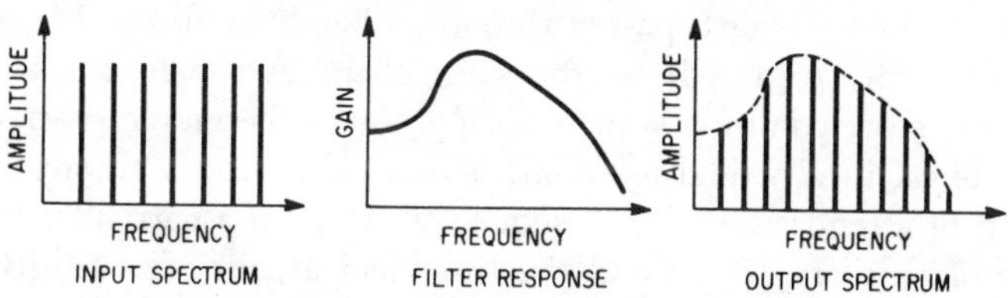

Fig. 2–5. Effect of filtering on the spectrum

The other two parameters are the two ultimate slopes of the sides of the bell-shaped curve. As before, they are usually multiples of 6 dB per octave. The slope just beyond the 3-dB points is usually steeper than the ultimate slope far from the center frequency and becomes more so for higher *Q*s (narrower bandwidths).

The final basic filter shape is called a *band-reject* (or notch) response and is shown in Fig. 2–4D. The center frequency is, of course, the frequency of greatest attenuation. Specification of the width parameter is not really standardized because the exact shape of the notch varies considerably with the filter circuit. However, one common specification is, again, the difference between the 3-dB down points. Often, a rough attempt at specifying the shape is made by specifying both the 3-dB and the 60-dB notch widths.

The effect of a filter on the spectrum of a sound can be easily determined graphically as in Fig. 2–5. As a simple case, consider a sound with all

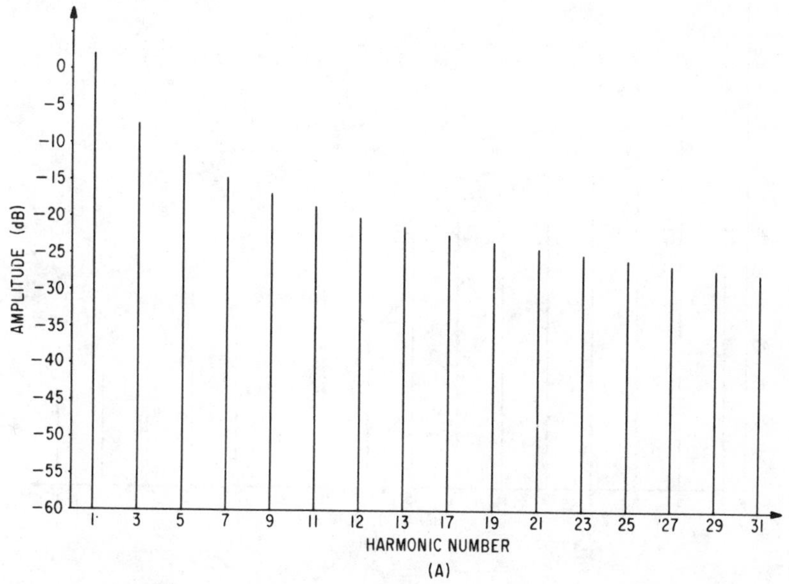

Fig. 2–6. Effect of filters on a square wave. (A) Original square wave.

harmonics of equal strength passed through a bandpass filter. The envelope of the output spectrum will be the same shape as the filter's amplitude response. For more common signals with a nonflat harmonic spectrum, the amplitude of each individual harmonic is modified directly according to the filter's gain or attenuation at that frequency. Thus, if a particular harmonic had an amplitude of −8 dB and the filter had a gain of −12 dB at that harmonic's frequency, then the same harmonic would have an amplitude of

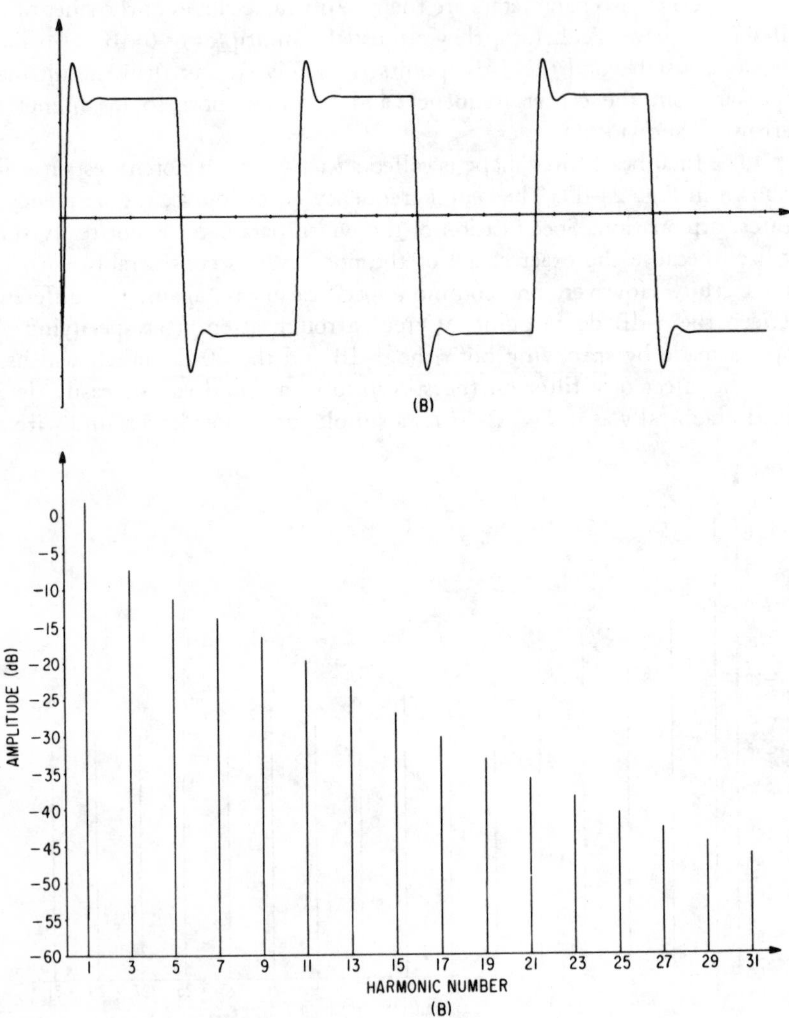

Fig. 2–6. Effect of filters on a square wave (*cont.*). (B) Low-pass filter.

−20 dB at the filter's output. For nonrepeating waveforms, the amplitude of each frequency component is similarly altered.

Although nonlinear circuits cannot alter the shape of a square wave, a filter can. Figure 2–6 shows both the waveshape and spectral effect of filter circuits on a 200-Hz square wave. Note that in the case of the bandpass filter, a rapidly decaying sine wave is generated on each edge of the square wave. The frequency of this sine wave is the actual natural frequency, which for practical purposes is the same as the filter's center frequency. The rate of

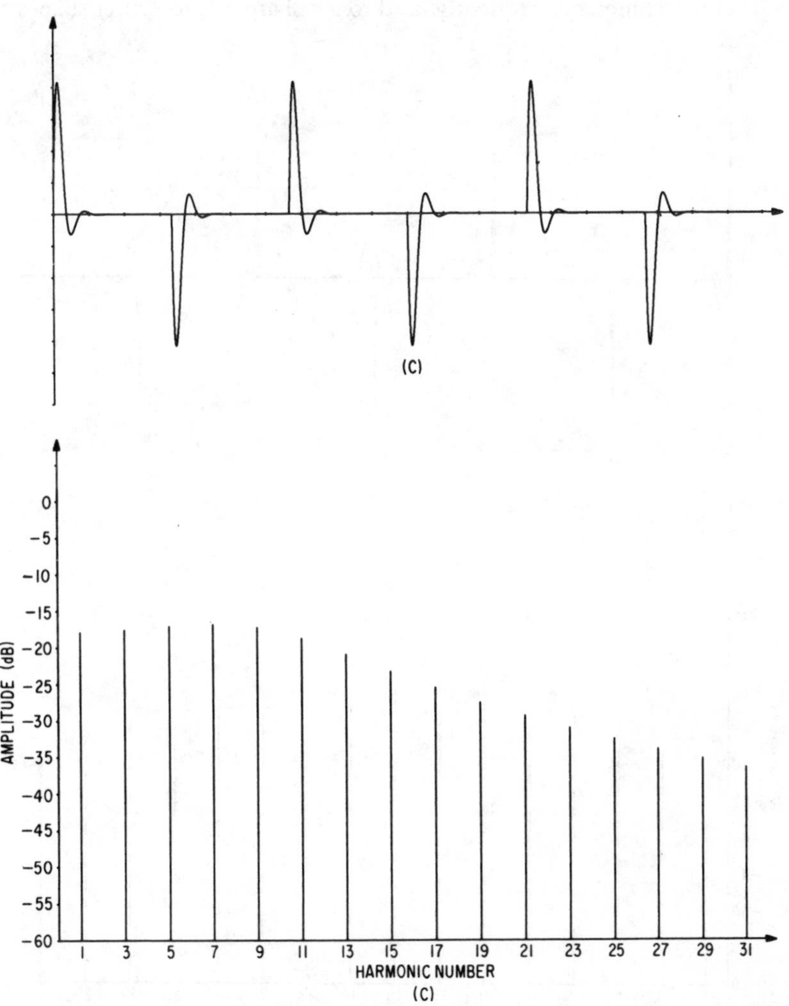

Fig. 2–6. Effect of filters on a square wave (*cont.*). (C) Bandpass filter.

decay is related to the filter's bandwidth or Q with narrower bandwidths (higher Q) resulting in a slower decay.

As mentioned previously, more complex filter amplitude response shapes may be obtained by combining basic shapes. The most predictable method for combining two shapes is to *cascade* two filter sections by feeding the filtered output from one filter into the input of another. The resulting response shape is just the point-by-point sum of the individual response shapes, provided that they were plotted in decibels. Values from a linear gain scale would have to be *multiplied* together for the result.

This technique is frequently used to get sharper cutoff filter shapes than

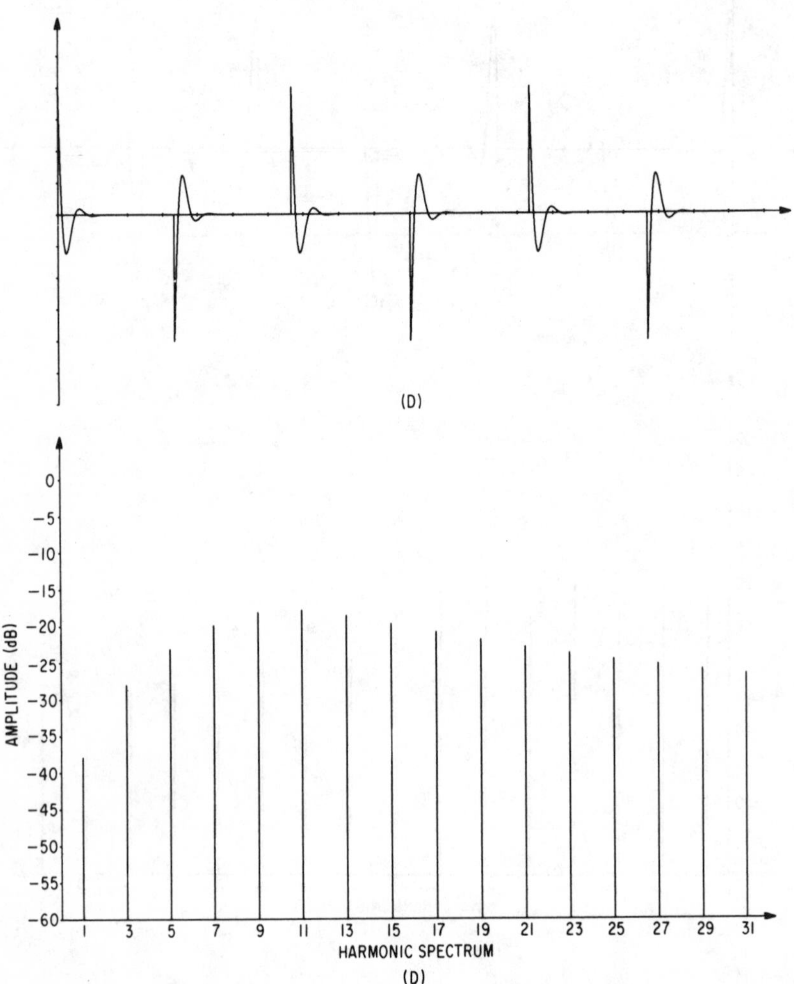

Fig. 2–6. Effect of filters on a square wave (*cont.*). (D) High-pass filter.

simple circuits provide. Figure 2–7, for example, shows how two rather sloppy low-pass shapes that can be obtained from simple circuits combine together to give a much improved low-pass shape.

Fixed filters (those with constant parameter values) are commonly used as equalizers in music systems. An equalizer is a filter that is intended to compensate for nonuniform amplitude response elsewhere in a high-fidelity sound system. For sound modification use, however, a fixed filter can be used to change the overall tonal quality of the sound. A low-pass filter, for example, gives a muffled effect, while a high-pass filter tends to give a thin or tinny effect. Bandpass filters, depending on the center frequency, may have

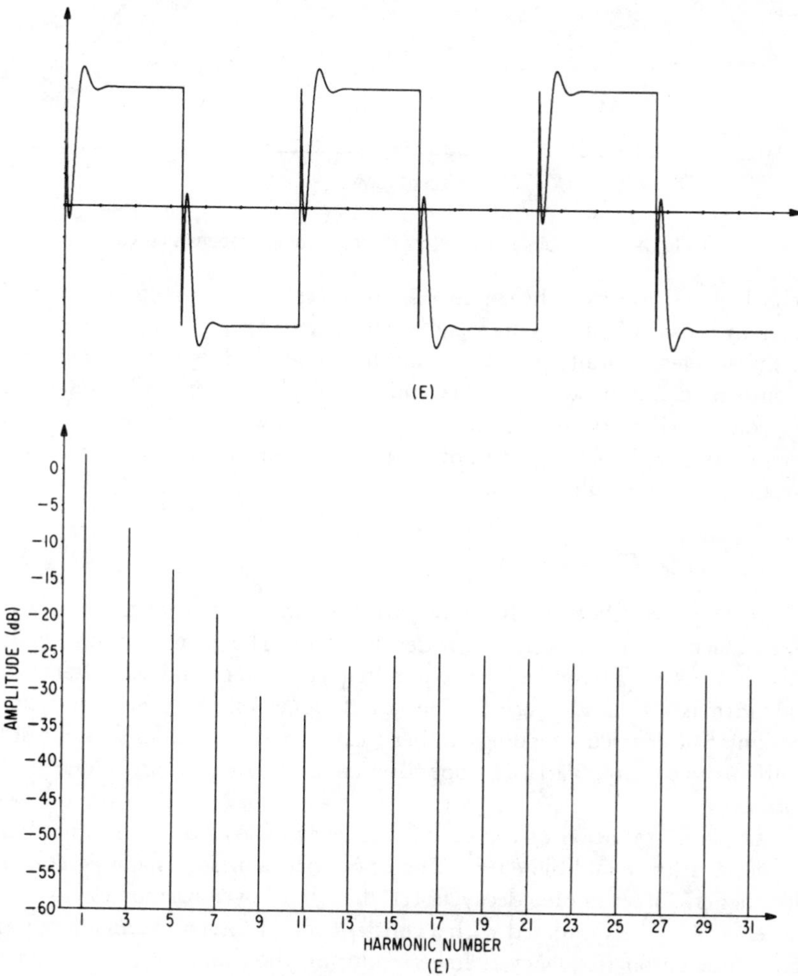

Fig. 2–6. Effect of filters on a square wave (*cont.*). (E) Band-reject filter.

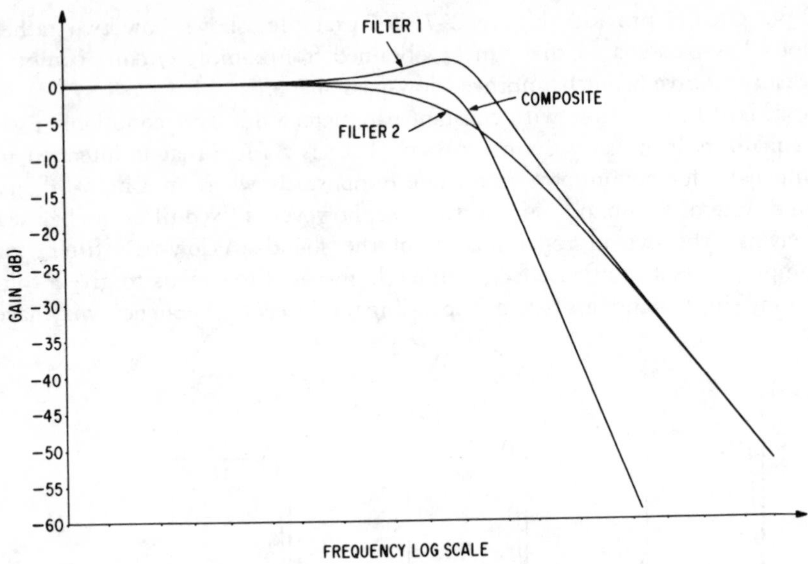

Fig. 2–7. Combining two filters to get a better response curve

a "conch shell" effect on the sound. Often the essential character of the tone of certain musical instruments may be simulated with a simple fixed filter and simple electronically generated waveforms. A double-humped bandpass response with humps at 1,200 Hz and 2,700 Hz, for example, resembles the resonance characteristics of an English horn. Sawtooth waveforms played through such a filter setup resemble the sound of an English horn. Such resonant peaks are called *formants*.

Variable Filters

Inexpensive filters with easily variable parameters that cover a wide range are actually a relatively recent development. The parameter most easily varied is the cutoff frequency or center frequency. For bandpass filters, the bandwidth is also easily varied. The cutoff slope, on the other hand, is a function of filter circuit topology rather than component values so as a result is difficult to control. Variable-slope filter circuits, however, are under investigation.

Dynamic variation of the cutoff frequency of low- or high-pass filters provides a definite audible effect. The upper harmonics of many percussion instruments, for example, decay faster than the lower harmonics do. The same effect may be simulated with a constant sound spectrum and a low-pass filter whose cutoff frequency is lowered during the course of the note. The opposite effect may be created by using a high-pass filter to increase high harmonic content as a note progresses.

The most dramatic variable filter effect, however, is produced by sweeping the center frequency of a bandpass filter. For moderate bandwidths (around 1/4 to 1/2 octave), the effect is similar to that of an opening and closing hat mute used with a trumpet or trombone. Such variable bandpass filters are popularly called "wah-wah" boxes due to their distinctive sound.

If the bandwidth is made smaller yet, only one harmonic will be emphasized by the narrow peak, and the others will be greatly attenuated. Varying the center frequency in this case gives the effect of a distinct scale of sine wave notes as each harmonic is approached and passed by. White noise passed through a variable narrow-band filter is given a definite although airy pitch that is easily controlled.

Several tunable bandpass filters may also be used to provide a number of independently movable formants. In fact, the voiced portions of human speech (vowels and dipthongs) may be simulated with a harmonically rich tone and two to four variable bandpass filters depending on the degree of naturalness desired. Each possible steady vowel corresponds to a particular steady-state combination of formant frequencies, while each dipthong corresponds to a particular pattern of formant frequency transitions. Of course, a good speech synthesizer requires more than this, although the formant generator and control means for producing accurate formant frequency variation constitute the majority of the circuitry.

Variable notch filters produce a somewhat more subtle effect. Using white noise as an input, a frequency sweeping notch filter will create a sound

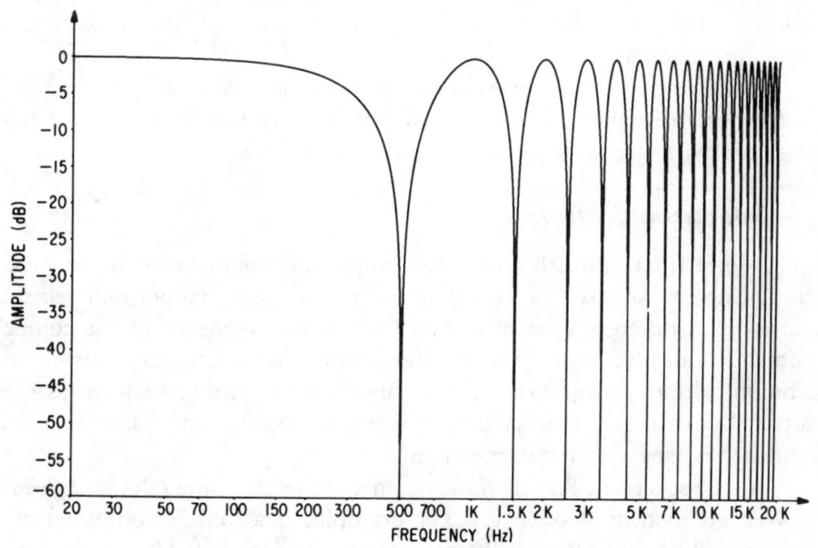

Fig. 2–8. Comb filter response shape

similar to a passing jet plane. A device for reproducing such an effect exactly is called a *comb* filter because its amplitude response curve, shown in Fig. 2–8, resembles a comb. Note that the comb filter response is like a bunch of notch filters with the notch frequencies regularly spaced a given number of hertz apart. Tuning of a notch filter amounts to increasing or decreasing the spacing between the notches, thus forcing the higher-frequency notches to move out faster than the lower-frequency ones.

As might be expected, an actual implementation of a comb filter is considerably simpler than a multitude of gang-tunable notch filters. The physical effect observed at an airport may be explained by noting that a passing jet is essentially a point source of white noise and that airports have smooth concrete runway surfaces. Thus, one ray of sound travels directly to the ear and another ray (there can only be one) bounces from the pavement before reaching the ear. These two paths differ slightly in length and the difference changes as the angle of the plane changes. Due to this difference in path lengths, some sound frequencies are reinforced when the two rays meet at the ear and others are cancelled. The same effect may be created by splitting an audio signal into two paths, inserting a short variable delay into one of the paths, and then recombining the two signals.

The initial implementation of this effect for processing arbitrary sound signals involved two identical tape recorders playing identical recordings of the sound to be processed. If the tapes were far out of synchronization, a distinct echo was heard. Closer synchronization produced the comb filter effect. Adjustments in the effective delay between the two signals were accomplished with light finger pressure on the tape reel flanges to slightly slow one of the recorders; the effect that was produced became known as "flanging" a sound.

Until recently, it was very difficult and expensive to construct a high-fidelity variable delay. However, now it is a fairly simple and inexpensive procedure with digital logic or analog delay line ICs.

Spectrum Shifters

While filters directly affect the amplitudes of the various frequency components of sounds, the actual frequency of these components remains unaltered. A different class of device changes the frequency of the components but, ideally, leaves the relative amplitudes alone. Of course, one technique already mentioned has the capability of shifting frequencies proportionally, that is, multiplying every frequency by the same value, and that technique is tape speed transposition.

A true spectrum shifter, however, maintains the same relative *difference* between component frequencies. For example, if a tone is composed of a fundamental of 200 Hz with harmonics at 400 Hz, 600 Hz, etc., then a spectrum shift of 31.4 Hz would result in frequency components of 231.4 Hz, 431.4 Hz, 631.4 Hz, and so forth. Note that these frequencies are no

longer harmonically related. Sounds that normally have harmonic spectra undergo a complete change in some aspects of their timbre when shifted a few tens of hertz, while other aspects are relatively unaffected. In particular, they tend to take on a sort of "watery" texture. Quality spectrum shifters that have good low-frequency response and work properly even with small amounts of shift are still relatively complex and expensive.

A related but much simpler device is the balanced modulator, which is also known as a ring modulator. The device has two signal inputs that are identical and an output. In operation, an instantaneous output voltage equal to the *product* of the two input voltages with all algebraic sign conventions observed is generated. Figure 2–9 shows the output waveform with two different frequency sine waves as inputs. Note that the output spectrum contains neither of the input frequencies but does contain a sum frequency of 1,200 Hz and a difference frequency of 800 Hz.

In order to more fully understand the physical effect, consider an experiment in which one of the inputs is connected to a complex waveform with a lot of frequency components and the other input is connected to a variable-frequency sine wave oscillator. With the oscillator set to zero frequency, the output is the same as the other input. As the oscillator frequency increases, a spectral plot of the output, as in Fig. 2–10, would show each frequency component splitting into two components, which then move away from each other. Thus, one copy of the input spectrum shifts down in

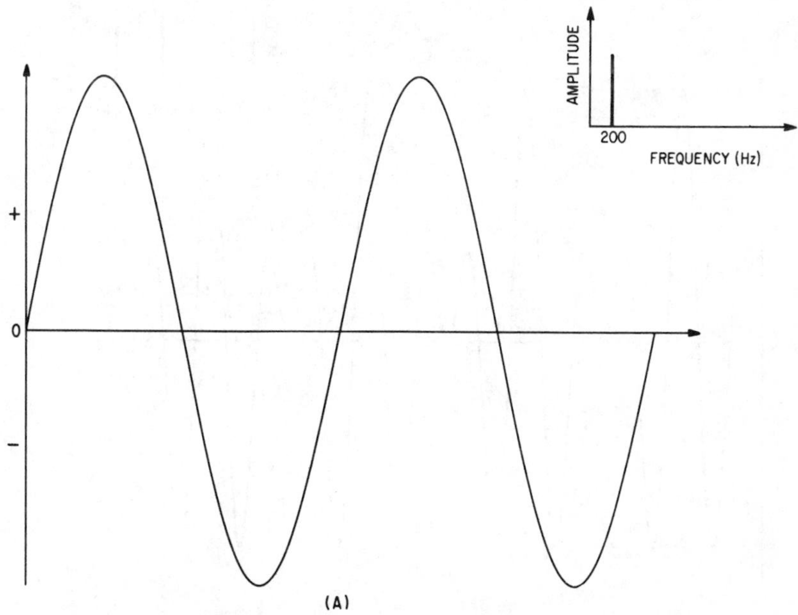

Fig. 2–9. Action of the balanced modulator. (A) Input to A.

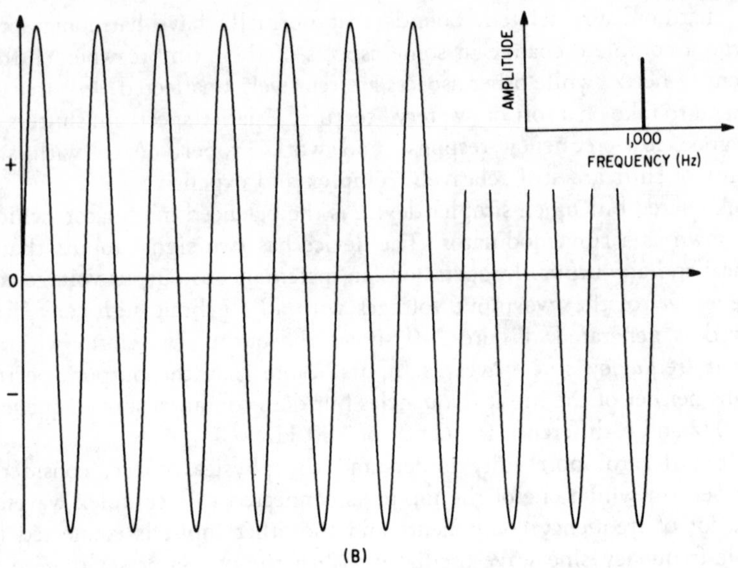

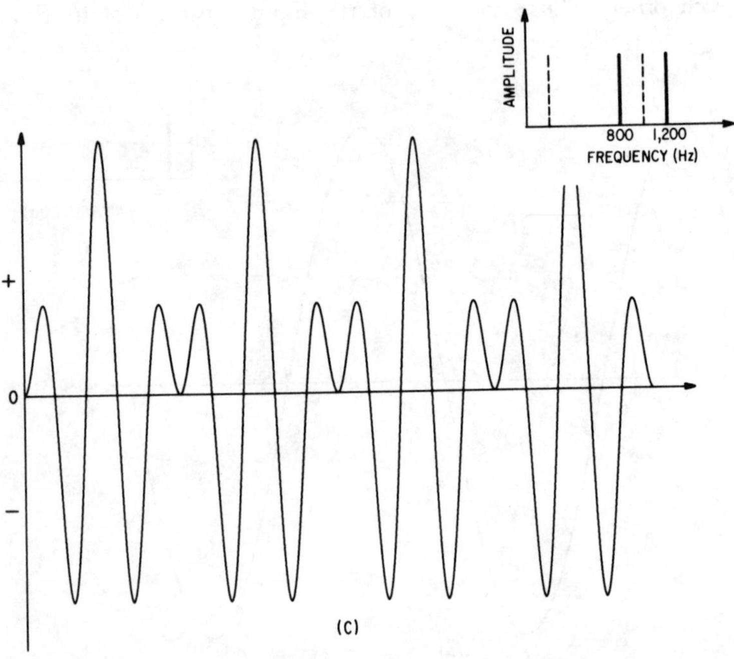

Fig. 2–9. Action of the balanced modulator (*cont.*). (B) Input to B. (C) Output.

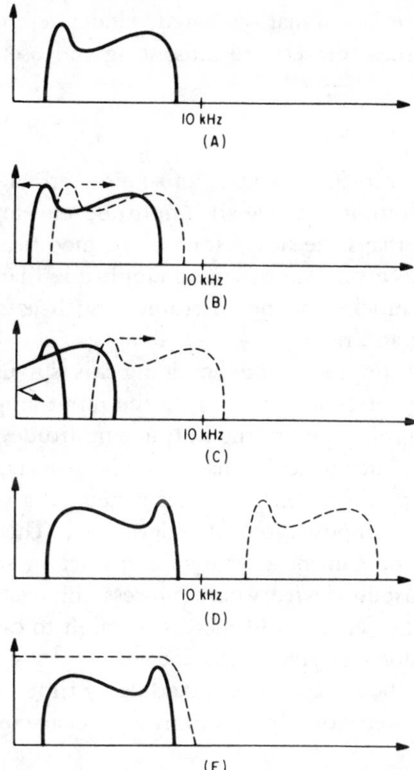

Fig. 2–10. Operation of a spectrum inverter. (A) Input spectrum. (B) Low frequency to balanced modulator. (C) Higher frequency to balanced modulator. (D) 10 kHz to balanced modulator. (E) Final inverted spectrum.

frequency, while the other copy shifts up. The envelope of the copies *individually* remains unaltered. Actually, a true spectrum shifter manages to suppress one of the copies.

If the oscillator frequency is made high enough, frequency components in the downward moving copy will eventually cross zero. As they do, they are reflected back upward with reversed phase, since a physically negative frequency is impossible. With a continuing increase in oscillator frequency, a point will eventually be reached in which the entire downward moving copy has been reflected and the upward moving copy ceases to overlap it. If a low-pass filter is now inserted in the output, only the reflected copy remains. The interesting point about the spectrum now is that it has been *inverted* with originally low-frequency components becoming high and vice versa.

Generally, balanced modulators and spectrum inverters severely distort sounds into an unrecognizable and usually unpleasant grating. In fact, spectrum inverters were once popular as speech scramblers, since a reinversion would restore the original signal unaltered. Under certain conditions, however, the effects of these devices are interesting and useful.

Envelope Modifiers

Although spectrum modification of sounds can have a profound effect on their timbre, altering the overall amplitude envelope can also have a significant effect. Perhaps the simplest envelope modification is flattening of the decay in order to give a steady sound amplitude that eventually cuts off suddenly. Thus, a plucked string instrument such as a guitar comes out sounding more like an organ.

The oldest and simplest method of doing this is to use a clipping circuit with a low clipping threshold. As long as the input amplitude was significantly above the clipping point, the output amplitude remained relatively constant. Of course, such a device also severely distorts the spectrum.

Later, envelope follower circuits that generated a voltage proportional to the amplitude of an input signal were developed. This voltage could then be used to control the gain of a separate amplifier in any desired manner. Thus, the guitar sustain device would process the evelope follower signal such that the amplifier gain would increase enough to cancel the decrease in input signal amplitude and give a constant output. By suitable processing of the envelope signal, the attack, sustain, and decay times of the output can be adjusted relatively independently of the envelope characteristics of the input.

Electronic Reverberation

Even utilizing all of the modification techniques mentioned so far, many purely electronic sounds have a "lifeless" quality that is often undesirable. Live sounds from an orchestra, on the other hand, have a depth and richness that cannot be easily explained in terms of frequency, amplitude, and spectrum.

The concert hall itself adds considerably to the texture of orchestra music. In fact, an otherwise "dry" recording of electronic sounds is considerably enhanced by playing through loudspeakers scattered around the stage of a good concert hall. The difference, of course, is the presence of reverberation in the hall in which a combination of direct and reflected sound reaches the listener. The reflected sound can come from any direction and with different time delays with respect to the direct sound. Reflection can also occur several times, each with diminishing amplitude.

Because of the multitude of delay times, concert hall reverberation and tape reverberation are considerably different. The latter consists of distinct echoes, while the former has no perceivable echo at all. A multitude of techniques and devices has been developed to electronically simulate concert hall reverberation in tape recording.

The earliest attempt was an extension of the tape reverberation method. Rather than having just one playback head, several were used, all spaced at irregular intervals from the single recording head. This was fairly effective in suppressing distinct echoes, since so many echoes were produced. However, sharp transients such as a hand clap still resulted in an initial chain of echoes.

Most other reverberation schemes are really electromechanical in nature. Objects such as special springs, metal plates, stretched gold foils, and even empty chambers with hard walls were fitted with transducers for signal input and output. The reverberation effect is created when sound waves from the input transducer reflect from the ends or other boundaries of the object. The "reverberation chamber" approach yields good results but must be quite large in order to achieve natural results. The other devices are considerably smaller due to slower propagation of sound in them as compared to air. Spring units typically utilize two or three different springs and are most popular for lower-quality work. The metal plate and gold foil units produce a more spacious effect with less evidence of echo due to two-dimensional propagation of the sound waves.

One problem with such electromechanical devices is *coloration* of the reverberated sound, meaning a fairly gross modification of the spectrum of the reverberated sound. Typically, frequencies below 500 Hz and above 5 kHz are attenuated, and response to middle frequencies is irregular. Springs are worst in this respect and gold foils are best.

Recently, the plummeting costs of digital logic and memory have made all-electronic reverberation devices practical. Digital techniques make possible a very high-quality audio delay line that when combined with feedback and mixing networks gives excellent reverberation results. Analog delay lines capable of handling audio signals directly may also be used in reverberation networks, although background noise can be a problem in exacting applications. Although echo density and coloration can still be problems, they are a function of the quantity and arrangement of the component parts and not the physical characteristics of some specialized material. Design details of digital reverberation simulators will be covered more thoroughly in Section III.

Chorus Synthesizers

The other "life-giving" element typically missing in electronic sounds is multiplicity of sound sources. A single trumpet playing a nice little solo has one effect, while a hundred trumpets playing the same passage in four-part harmony has quite a profoundly different effect. Who has not thrilled to the sound of thousands of voices singing the National Anthem prior to a football game?

The effect of a number of players performing the same passage is called a *chorus* effect. What has been desired for a long time is a device or process that would accept a sound signal as an input and generate an output that resembles a large number of copies of the input signal. An obvious control parameter for such a device is the multiplicity factor.

Looking more closely at the physical chorus effect, it is seen that the difference between two separate players and one player playing twice as loud is that the two sounds being combined are not exactly alike. For example, the fundamental sound frequencies will be slightly different, resulting in a slight beating effect. Unlike beating sine waves, the resultant amplitude of two beating complex waves remains relatively constant, but individual harmonics may momentarily cancel. Also vibrato, which is not synchronized between the players, may cause even greater momentary frequency differences. The end result is a slight, random, spectrum modulation of the resulting sound. As more players are added, changes in the amplitude and phase of the component harmonics become more pronounced and random. A spectral plot of 100 trumpets playing the same note would show broad peaks at each of the harmonic frequencies rather than narrow lines. Note that the overall spectral envelope is unchanged, which allows one to distinguish 100 trumpets from 100 violins.

Research into construction of the chorus box mentioned earlier has been in two different directions. One attempts to directly simulate multiple sound sources with a number of audio delay lines, whose delay is constantly changing over a narrow range. The theory is that a second sound is exactly like the first except that the vibrations are occurring at different points in time. The variation in delay times prevents a constant echo effect. Multiplicity can be controlled fairly well with such a setup by changing the number of delay lines. Digital signal processing techniques are well suited for implementation of this scheme.

The other approach works on the basic parameters of the input sound attempting to simulate the effect rather than the actual chorus itself. Accordingly, it uses filters to separate the input spectrum into bands and amplitude and phase modulators plus spectrum shifters to randomly manipulate the individual bands. Finally, the sound is put back together and sent out. Although not particularly good for simulating a small group of players, the technique is apparently very effective for simulating a large number. A taped demonstration witnessed at the Spring 1977 Audio Engineering Society convention made a cheap portable synthesizer sound like a whole auditorium full of synthesizers.

Analysis–Synthesis Methods

It should now be well established that the synthesis of sound can be controlled to the tiniest of details by appropriate manipulation of the fundamental parameters. The basic problem, then, is in determining exactly how these parameters should be varied to get the desired effect. One possibility, of course, is experimentation so that the relation between parameter change and audible effect becomes familiar. If this is adequately accomplished, then the composer can readily specify what is required for the desired effect. There are many practical difficulties, however. One is that such extensive experimentation is quite time consuming even with entirely real-time equipment. A related problem is documenting the results of such experimentation. Cataloging of desirable or unusual effects discovered during such experimentation for later recall is possible with a computer-based system, however.

One approach to the problem begins with realizing the frequency of requests such as, "I want something that sounds like (some natural sound) except for . . ." Thus, if one could determine the exact parameter variation of the prototype sound, then the desired parameter manipulation for the desired result might be more easily determined. Such a procedure is called analysis–synthesis because a prototype sound is analyzed into its component parameters, which may then control a synthesizer to reproduce a similar sound.

Envelope Tracking

The first step in the process is an accurate determination of the parameters of interest in the prototype sound. Overall amplitude is perhaps the easiest to extract. A device for doing this is usually called an *envelope follower*. Although rms amplitude is probably the most desirable measure, it is much easier to determine average amplitude. Another tradeoff that must be considered in the design of an envelope follower is speed of response versus the ability to accurately determine the amplitude of low-frequency signals. The reason is that the device will start to follow the slow waveform of a low-frequency sound itself rather than the overall average amplitude.

Pitch Tracking

Determining the fundamental frequency or *pitch tracking* is considerably more difficult. Relatively constant-frequency simple (not a lot of harmonics) sounds isolated from all other sounds and background noise can be readily processed. However, rapidly varying, complex, or insufficiently isolated sounds are much more difficult to follow. Semipitched sounds such as the chime mentioned in Chapter 1 are better handled with formant tracking, which will be discussed. The most common error made by pitch tracking equipment is a momentary false output that is a multiple or submultiple of the correct value. Multiples of the correct value are the result of mistaking one of the harmonics for the fundamental that might actually be very weak or absent. Submultiples can result when the waveform undergoes substantial change of parameters other than fundamental frequency. Thus, any successful pitch tracker for a variety sounds generally looks at periodicity of waveform peaks, or in the case of sophisticated computer processing, looks at every frequency component and determines the highest common divisor.

Spectrum Tracking

Generalized spectrum tracking can be done in several ways. For definitely pitched sounds, the amplitude envelope of each individual harmonic can be determined with computer-processing techniques. A somewhat simpler technique involves a bank of 10 to 30 bandpass filters and an amplitude envelope follower connected to the output of each filter. Any sound can be passed through such a *filterbank analyzer,* and its rough spectrum shape as a function of time can be determined.

Another method that also involves a computer is *formant tracking.* The spectrum of many interesting sounds such as speech can be fairly well described by the frequency, height, and width of peaks in their spectrum shape. Frequently, even the height and width parameters are ignored. The resulting small number of parameters describing the time varying spectrum shape is quite attractive for analysis–synthesis purposes. For example, tracking of just the frequency of the two lowest formants of voiced speech sounds is adequate for intelligible speech reconstruction.

Unfortunately, accurate formant following is as difficult as accurate pitch tracking. For example, there need not necessarily be a constant number of formants in the sound being analyzed. As a result, the analyzer must recognize when two formants merge into one or when one just decreases in amplitude and disappears. If the overall spectrum shape contains a long downward slope, the ear will often recognize a local flattening in that trend as a subdued formant, even though no real peak occurs.

Use of Analysis Results

It should be obvious from the foregoing that really accurate analysis of sound into the simple parameters that have been discussed is not always possible. However, the accuracy that is attainable is generally quite acceptable for analysis–synthesis experiments. Occasionally, some hand editing of the data obtained is necessary to correct gross errors or fill in missing data caused by nearly inaudible "defects" in the prototype sound.

Generally, the data obtained from the analysis can be represented as a number of curves showing how the parameters vary with time. Such a set is shown in Fig. 2–11. On a computer-based system, these curves would actually be available to the user to study and modify as desired. In a real-time system, these parameters would really be just varying voltages generated by the analysis equipment. In either case, some, if not all, of the parameters would be processed and then they would pass to synthesis equipment, which generates the modified sound.

The analysis–synthesis technique can be applied in a number of ways. One intriguing possibility is transferral of certain characteristics from one type of sound to another. For example, let's assume that a short trumpet solo

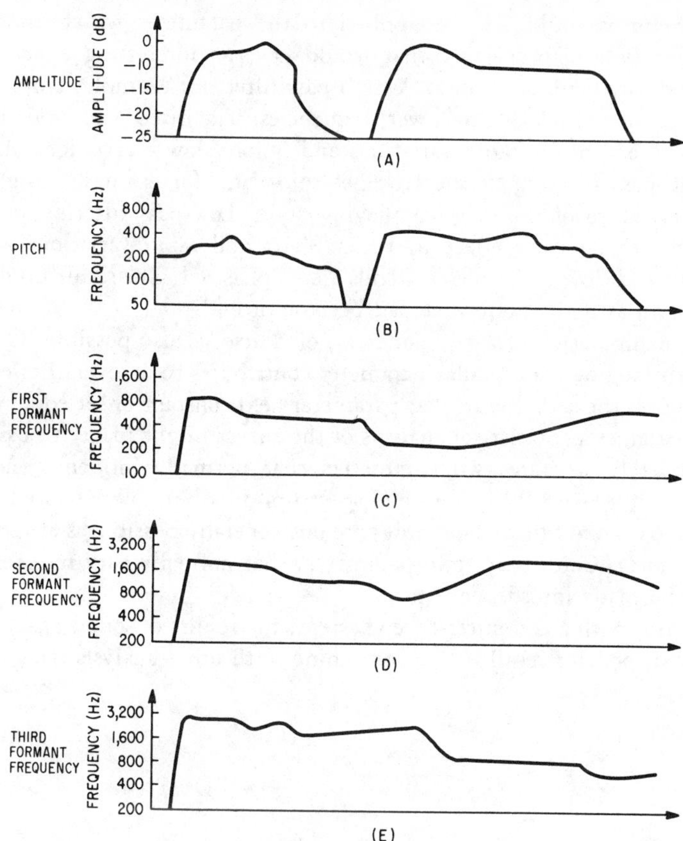

Fig. 2-11. Parameter variation of a typical natural sound. (A) Amplitude. (B) Pitch. (C) First formant frequency. (D) Second formant frequency. (E) Third formant frequency.

passage has been analyzed into amplitude, frequency, and rough spectrum shape parameters. Let's further assume that the passage is a lively one indicative of the performer's playing style. With resynthesis, these particular parameters could control a tone that more resembled that of a clarinet. Since the spectral analysis was very rough, the exact timbre of the trumpet would not have been captured, but the general trend that reflects changes in the overall tone would have been. The result would be that many of the characteristics of the trumpet playing style would have been transferred to the clarinet sound. Note that in a real situation it may not even be possible to actually play a clarinet in such a manner.

Besides simple transferral of parameters, modification of the curves is also possible. Since a parameter when converted to a varying voltage is just another signal, many of the processing techniques that applied to sound pressure waveforms could also be applied to the parameter waveform or envelope. One type of processing that would have an interesting effect is *filtering* of the parameter envelopes. A high-pass filter, for example, emphasizes high frequencies relative to lower frequencies. The direct effect on the waveform is to emphasize rapid variations and ignore slower variations and trends. High-pass filtering of the trumpet solo data, for example, might produce a caricature of the original playing style. Low-pass filtering of a parameter has an opposite effect in which short and rapid variations are smoothed out and slow variations or trends are emphasized. The result might very well sound as if the performer had become drunk!

Hand manipulation of the parameters, of course, is also possible. One way to determine how a particular parameter contributes to an overall effect is to resynthesize the sound with that parameter held constant or set equal to some other parameter. Statistical analysis of the curves might make it possible to completely separate two parameters that normally influence each other. For example, overall loudness and spectrum distribution are related in trumpet sounds. Loud but mellow notes are not generally possible as are soft but blaring notes. Conversely, two parameters that normally vary independently may be made interdependent.

Of course, with a computer-based system, the results of sound analysis may be stored for later recall or for combining with other analysis data.

3

Voltage Control Methods

As briefly mentioned in Chapter 1, the development and use of voltage-controlled sound synthesizers was an important milestone in the history of electronic music synthesis. More than any other single development, it served to popularize synthesis methods not only with the listening public but also with composers and performers.

Voltage control is really a fundamental concept. For the first time there has been established a one-to-one correspondence between an easily manipulated physical variable, a voltage level, and each of the important parameters of sound. Thus, manipulation of a voltage would actually be manipulation of a frequency, amplitude, formant position, waveform distortion parameter, etc. Frequently, voltage-controlled techniques are characterized as *continuous* or *analog* techniques because one physical variable (the signal or control voltage) represents another physical variable (amplitude, frequency, etc.).

Also of importance is the *modularity* of voltage-controlled synthesizers. The synthesizer itself is nothing more than a package for holding a number of *independent modules* that may be interconnected in literally an infinite variety of ways. The number of simultaneous sounds and their complexity is dependent mainly on the type and number of modules available and the means available for controlling them. Only a very few modules are required to produce single simple electronic sounds. More are required for implementation of subtle variations and multipart harmony. If a given complement of modules is insufficient for a particular application, more are easily added at moderate cost.

Compatibility is another key characteristic of voltage-controlled synthesizers. All inputs are compatible with all outputs, meaning that any physically possible permutation of interconnections is also electrically safe and potentially useful. Furthermore, in some instances outputs are compatible with each other. In such cases, two outputs plugged into the same input (with a "Y" connector, for example) actually results in mixing of the two signals involved in equal proportions. Compatibility often extends to the point that different manufacturers' modules may be easily interconnected.

Finally, the modules of a modern voltage-controlled synthesizer offer good *accuracy* in the relationship between a control voltage and the value of the sound parameter being controlled. Thus, two modules with the same control input can be expected to produce nearly identical results. Although it is relatively simple to design and produce devices that respond to control voltages, designing one that accurately and consistently responds to them is considerably more difficult. Even so, accuracy is one characteristic that could benefit from improvement.

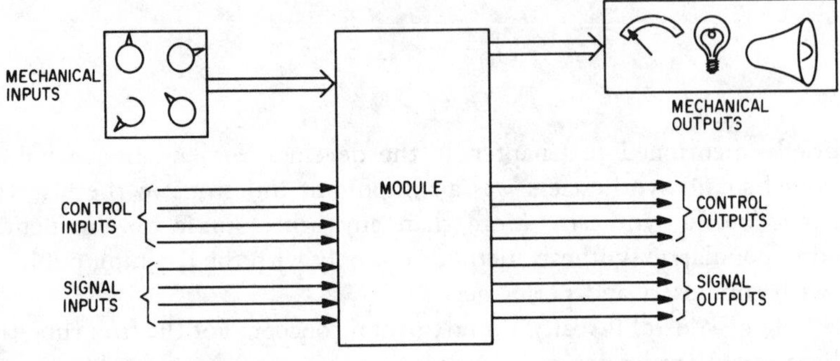

Fig. 3–1. General voltage-controlled module

Typical Module Characteristics

In examining these points more closely, let's look first at the general characteristics of a typical module such as diagrammed in Fig. 3–1. This module has three classes of inputs and three classes of outputs. It is rare that a single module would actually have all six classes of input/output (I/O), but it is possible.

A *mechanical input* is a parameter that is physically supplied by the user. Examples are the positions of knobs, levers, the amount of pressure on a plate, the state of switches, or other nonelectronic inputs to the system. There may be none, one, or several such inputs on a single module. In the case of knobs or levers, two are often used to precisely control one variable: a coarse adjustment and a fine adjustment. Switches usually set particular operating modes and may have several positions each. With the exception of *transducer* modules such as keyboards, the mechanical inputs are usually set up ahead of time and then changed only infrequently during the actual production of sound. Thus, except for transducers, mechanical controls influence operating parameters that stay relatively constant.

Mechanical outputs are less common and consist of lights, meters, speaker cones, and similar indications to the user. Except for speakers, mechanical outputs are just user aids and do not directly participate in the synthesis process.

A *signal input* normally expects to see an ordinary audio signal in the 20-Hz to 20-kHz frequency range. However, the signal inputs of any properly designed module are perfectly capable of responding to dc voltage levels and ultrasonic frequencies up to 50 kHz and higher. This broad range allows signal inputs to also handle slowly varying control voltages, which is a very important capability.

A *signal output* normally supplies an ordinary audio signal to other modules. Like the signal input, it is usually capable of supplying dc and very-low-frequency signals as well for control purposes.

The function of a *control input* is to accept a control voltage whose instantaneous value controls some parameter of the signal output. The presence of control inputs is the factor that distinguishes voltage-controlled modules from ordinary laboratory equipment, which usually has only mechanical inputs. Control inputs are used for those parameters that change rapidly, usually within the course of a single sound or note.

A *control output* is similar to a signal output except that it normally supplies control voltages to other modules. However, if the voltage at a control output varies rapidly enough, it may also be used directly as an audio signal.

From the foregoing it should be apparent that the distinction between audio signal voltages and control voltages is in their use and not necessarily in their physical properties. Although control voltages typically vary slowly compared to audio signals, there are applications for rapidly varying control voltages and slowly varying audio signals. It is this lack of physical distinction between parameters and signals that is responsible for much of the power of voltage-control methods.

There is, however, one more class of signals used in the voltage-controlled synthesizer. These are digital on–off control signals and timing pulses. Only a few specialized modules, which will be discussed later, use them. Although it is safe to mix these digital signals with the others, the effects are seldom useful. Any useful effect can also be obtained through more "correct" interconnection procedures.

General Module Types

Modules can be grouped according to their primary functions. There is, of course, some overlap among groups, but for the most part the distinctions are clear.

Transducers function primarily as sources of control voltages but are directly dependent on some form of input for determining what the control voltage output should be. Perhaps the best example is an organ-type keyboard specially designed to produce a control voltage that is a function of the particular key being pressed. Besides the control voltage output, the keyboard also produces two digital timing signals whenever a key is pressed. The first is called a *trigger,* which is a pulse that is generated on the initial depression of a key. Its primary function is to mark the *beginning* of a note. The other signal is called a *gate* and is used to mark the *duration* of the note. The gate signal is present as long as a key is pressed. Thus, these two timing signals qualify the control voltage output from the keyboard.

Generators are similar to transducers but generally produce a predefined type of output signal that can be influenced with mechanical and control inputs but not completely determined in detail as with a transducer. A good example of an audio signal generator is a voltage-controlled *oscillator*. Typically, several outputs are provided, each one supplying a different but fixed waveform at a fixed amplitude. The voltage level at the control input directly affects the *frequency* of the multiple waveform outputs, but the waveshape and amplitude, which are fixed by design, remain constant. A good example of a control voltage generator is the *envelope generator*. This device supplies a predetermined voltage contour in response to the trigger and gate signals mentioned earlier. Mechanical controls generally specify details about the contour generated, although rarely a control voltage might be able to specify some of these.

Modifiers typically accept signal inputs and control inputs and produce a signal output. Modification of one or more parameters of the input signal is performed in accordance with the voltage levels at the control inputs. A voltage-controlled amplifier is a good example of a modifier. Typically, the signal input is of constant amplitude, but the amplitude of the output is determined by the control input.

Interconnections

In order to perform a useful function, the synthesizer modules must be interconnected. A true general-purpose synthesizer provides only mechanical mounting and operating power to the modules; otherwise they are completely independent. Probably the most popular connection method involves the use of patch cords similar to those found in old telephone switchboards but with both ends free. The cords and standard 1/4-inch phone plugs are quite flexible and rugged and allow fully shielded connections that minimize noise pickup. A particular arrangement of patch cords is called a *patch*. A complex patch may involve so many cords that a rat's-nest appearance results that may even obscure the front panel of the synthesizer. In such a situation, it may become difficult to follow a particular cord through the maze without pulling on one end of it. Even so, most users love the patch cord concept and on occasion can be seen to point proudly at the "jungle" that represents the creation of a new sound.

Another popular interconnection technique uses a pinboard matrix. The matrix is divided into rows representing module outputs and columns representing module inputs. Each row and column is clearly labeled with module number, type, and signal name. A connection from an output to an input is made by inserting a pin at their point of intersection. An output may drive multiple inputs by having pins at multiple column positions along the row corresponding to the output. Multiple outputs may also be connected together for equal mixing without the use of Y adaptors simply by inserting pins at multiple row positions along a single column. A complex pinboard matrix patch is, of course, much neater than the equivalent using patch cords. Furthermore, documentation of the patch is much easier. However, pinboard synthesizers tend to be less easily expanded due to the subpanel wiring between the modules and the pinboard. Also, if the row or column capacity of the pinboard should be exceeded, either another matrix will have to be added (and provisions for patching from one matrix to the other) or the entire matrix will have to be replaced with a larger one. Thus, pinboards are usually only found in "standard" models of prepackaged synthesizers.

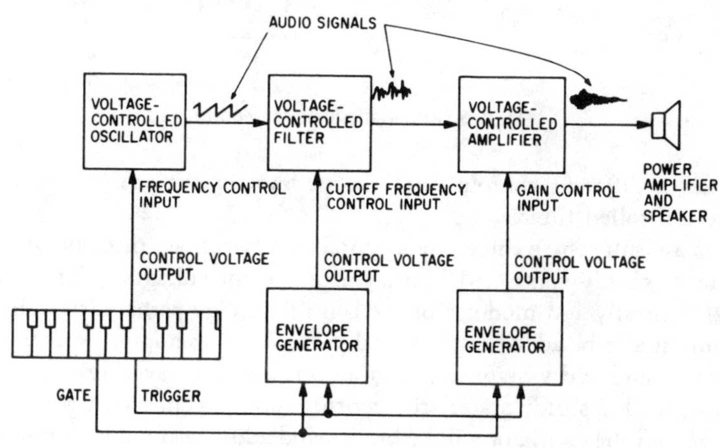

Fig. 3–2. A simple voltage-controlled module patch

A Simple Patch

Regardless of the method of patching, the important point is that the user thinks in terms of the basic parameters of sound when a patch is being designed. Figure 3–2 shows a very simple patch for producing individual notes under the control of an organ-type keyboard. One of the keyboard outputs is a voltage level proportional to the key *last* struck. This voltage determines the *frequency* of the voltage-controlled oscillator. The trigger and gate outputs from the keyboard then enter the first envelope generator, which produces a voltage contour in response to these timing signals. This voltage enters the control input of the voltage-controlled amplifier, where it impresses the contour shape onto the *amplitude* of the output signal from the oscillator, thus giving it an envelope. Finally, the second envelope generator

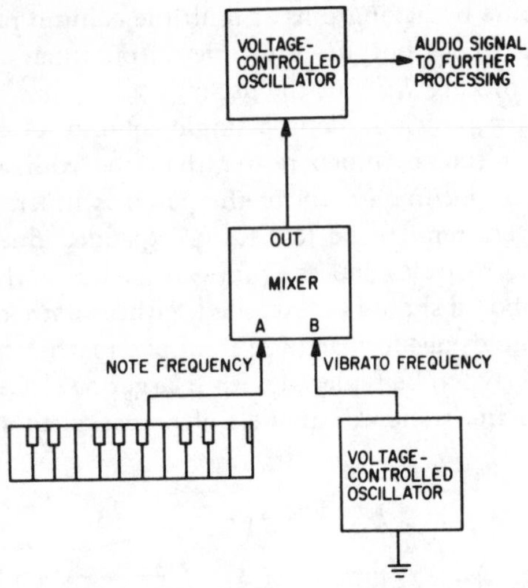

Fig. 3–3. Added modules for vibrato

impresses a different contour onto the *spectrum* of the sound through the voltage-controlled filter.

As a result, these three fundamental parameters are directly, and most important, visibly controlled by the three control voltages. More complex patches generally add modules in the control voltage paths, although a few more might also be added to the signal path. As an example, let us take this basic patch and add vibrato. Since vibrato is a small wavering of frequency during extended steady states, the control voltage connection between the keyboard and the oscillator will be broken and additional modules inserted as in Fig. 3–3. First, another oscillator is added, which is the source of the low-frequency vibrato waveform. For this example, no control voltage is supplied to the oscillator; its mechanical controls are used to set the vibrato frequency. The vibrato voltage is combined with the keyboard output with the *mixer* module shown. Mechanical controls on the mixer determine the proportion of each input signal that appears at the output. For natural-sounding vibrato, the controls are set for only a small contribution from the vibrato oscillator. The resulting control voltage is then sent to the original oscillator and the remainder of the system as before.

It is easy to imagine further growth of the patch, since the vibrato produced by the example patch is rather crude. Typically, one might want short notes and the beginnings of long ones to be free of vibrato. After a delay period on long notes, vibrato should commence gradually. Addition of another voltage-controlled amplifier and envelope generator in the frequency control voltage path will allow this effect to be produced. Similar additions may also be made in the amplitude and spectrum control paths. Once a good understanding of the parameters of sound has been developed, most patches are obvious. Note that more modules may actually be tied up in processing control voltages than audio signals!

Signal Levels in the Synthesizer

So far the value of voltage control has been established and the desirability of an accurate relationship between control voltage magnitude and sound parameter magnitude has been mentioned. However, now the exact form of this relationship needs to be established. Although there is considerable agreement in the industry on the control relations to be discussed, there are a few manufacturers of smaller systems that do things differently.

Frequency-Control Relation

Of all the parameters of sound, frequency is probably the most important. The ear is considerably more sensitive to small changes in frequency than any other parameter. Also, music theory is significantly more concerned with intervals, chords, and other pitch-related topics than it is with other areas. Thus, the choice of a relationship between a frequency-control voltage and the resulting output frequency should be chosen carefully.

The range of human hearing can be considered to be 10 octaves, which is a 2^{10} or 1,024:1 or 20 Hz to 20 kHz range. Within this range, a relative error of 1% is a minimum goal with considerably less being desirable in the middle four octaves. A relative error of 1% means that an intended frequency of 20 Hz cannot actually be less than $20 - 20/100 = 19.8$ Hz or greater than 20.2 Hz. Likewise, any frequency between 19.8 kHz and 20.2 kHz would be acceptable for an intended value of 20 kHz. Note that the absolute magnitude of error at the high end is a whopping 200 Hz, while at the low end it is only 0.2 Hz. Expressed as a full-scale accuracy, a specification method almost universally used by the measuring-instrument industry, the requirement would be 0.2 Hz/20 kHz = 0.001%. Laboratory voltage-measuring instruments with this kind of accuracy are almost nonexistent, exceedingly expensive, and fragile, yet this and more is being asked of a voltage-controlled oscillator module for a synthesizer!

The most obvious relationship between control voltage and frequency is a linear one, that is, a *direct* relationship between voltage and frequency. For the sake of argument, let us assume the relationship $F = 1{,}000V$, where F is the output frequency in hertz and V is the control voltage in volts. With this relation, the audio range would be covered with a control voltage range of 20 mV to 20 V. The 1% error alluded to earlier would amount to 200 μV at the low end of the range and 0.2 V at the upper end.

Actually, 20 V is a little high for convenient use of modern linear ICs. A maximum of 10 V would be more reasonable. The 100-μV error now allowed would be quite difficult to deal with. Typical sources of error in this range are thermoelectric voltages, voltages induced from stray magnetic fields, and thermal noise in resistors. What is worse, we expect these voltage levels to travel freely through patch cords without degradation. Thus, it is apparent that directly proportional voltage control is impractical for a wide control range and great relative accuracy.

Exponential Relation

Another relationship that makes more sense from a lot of viewpoints is an *exponential* one. Stated first in musical terms, such a relationship could be something like a 1 V/*octave*. In mathematical terms, this would be $F = 2^V F_0$, where F is the output frequency, V is the control voltage in volts, and F_0 is the basis frequency for this relative scale. For a basis frequency of 20 Hz, a voltage range of 0 to 10 V would cover the audible range. An interesting property of such a scale is that the 1% relative accuracy desired corresponds to about 14.5 mV *independent* of the frequency range. Thus, rather than a liberal error allowance at high frequencies and a stingy one at low frequencies, the margin for error is a constant, manageable value.

This property alone would be sufficient persuasion for adopting the exponential relationship, but there are many more desirable characteristics. In Chapter 1, it was noted that the sensation of pitch was an approximately exponential function of frequency. Using an exponential voltage-controlled oscillator, a linear increase in control voltage of, say, 1 V/sec would result in a reasonably steady rise of pitch. A linear VCO, on the other hand, would very rapidly sweep through all of the low frequencies and then seem to require a considerable amount of time to complete the upper end of the sweep.

Even if the ear's response did not resemble an exponential curve, the equally tempered musical scale is precisely exponential. One octave, of course, corresponds to 1 V and a half-step corresponds to 1/12 V or about 83.3 mV. Likewise, a fifth corresponds to 7/12 V and a major third is 1/3 V. Thus, if some arbitrary voltage level produces a particular pitch, a voltage 1/12 V higher produces a pitch one half-step higher.

One application of this property is in transposition from one key to another. Consider a melody played in the key of C on a keyboard that outputs control voltages. If a constant voltage of 1/6 V is *added* to the keyboard output, the melody would actually sound in the key of D. The constant voltage may be injected with a mixer between the keyboard and the oscillator, although most VCO modules have a basis frequency knob that does the same thing.

Injection of vibrato is also considerably simplified with an exponential VCO. A 1% vibrato, for example, would require a 15 mV peak-to-peak vibrato voltage independent of what note was played. With a linear VCO, the vibrato would be excessive on the low notes and nearly inaudible on the high ones. Thus, the vibrato amplitude would have to be made proportional to frequency through the use of a voltage-controlled amplifier.

Although exponential control of frequency at the rate of 1 V/octave is an industry-wide standard, the best VCO modules do have a linear control voltage input available. Its primary use is in using rapid and deep frequency modulation as a method of altering the spectrum of the oscillator's output waveform without incurring an undesirable *average* frequency shift due to the modulation.

Amplitide Relation

Amplitude is the other parameter of primary importance that needs a control voltage relationship established. Whereas the audible frequency range is a 1,000:1 ratio, the audible amplitude range is 1,000 times greater yet or 10^6:1. This 120-dB range might be a nice goal for live listening in a soundproof room but certainly could not be utilized in a normal environment. Furthermore, recording equipment is limited to a 60-dB to 70-dB range at best. Thus, a 10,000:1 or 80-dB range on voltage-controlled amplifiers would be a reasonable requirement.

The accuracy requirement for amplitude control is not nearly as stringent as frequency control accuracy. A 10% error, which corresponds to about 0.8 dB, would be barely audible. However, if the voltage-controlled amplifier were being used in a control voltage path processing frequency-related control voltages, considerably better accuracy would be desirable. Without going through the linear versus exponential argument again, it is clear that the control voltage relationship should be exponential.

A common setup would be such that 8 V would specify unity (0 dB) gain and lesser voltages would decrease gain at the rate of 10 dB/volt. Typically, as the control voltage approaches zero and the gain is decreasing toward −80dB, a squelch circuit comes into play, which actually cuts the signal completely off. Control voltages greater than +8 V can provide some positive gain in the circuit. With such a setup, the gain expression would be $AV = 10^{(V-8)/2}$, where AV is the voltage gain and V is the control voltage in volts. Like the oscillator, an added linear mode control input is helpful for special applications using amplitude modulation for timbre modification.

Most parameters used in other modules are related to either frequency or amplitude and thus usually have an exponential relationship. However, any time that a variable is required to cover a wide range, the exponential relationship is useful.

Standard Voltage Levels

Signal levels in a voltage-controlled synthesizer, both audio and control, are generally kept at a constant amplitude except when amplitude control is actually being performed. The standardization of signal levels from transducer and generator modules enhances the compatibility of signals throughout the system.

It has already been alluded to that control voltages range from 0 V to 10 V in magnitude. The polarity of control voltages is usually positive, although some module designs will perform as expected with negative control voltages as well. An oscillator, for example, can be coaxed into producing subaudible frequencies for vibrato use by giving it negative control voltages. Although the accuracy usually deteriorates, it is still quite useful. Audio signals are usually 20 V peak to peak in amplitude and swing equally negative and positive.

Actually, these voltage levels and amplitudes are fixed by what is convenient to use with IC operational amplifiers. These circuits are usually operated from positive and negative 15-V power supplies and start to distort severely if signal levels exceed 13 V in magnitude. These levels are considerably higher than the 1-V rms (2.8 V peak to peak) typically encountered in high-fidelity audio systems. One reason is to minimize the effect of noise and voltage offsets that may be encountered when a signal travels through a dozen or more IC amplifiers before it even leaves the synthesizer. Occasionally, it is desirable to cut all signal levels in half to ±5 V to allow the use of inexpensive CMOS switching elements, which are limited to ±7-V power supplies. Sometimes the control voltage sensitivity is doubled to compensate, so a little more care in minimizing noise and error voltages is required. In other cases, negative control voltages are used instead to get a reasonable control range.

Some Typical Modules

Let us now take a closer look at the most often used modules in a voltage-controlled system. The descriptions to be given are not those of any particular manufacturer's line but are representative of the input, output, and control complement on many commercial units. Home-brew synthesizer modules can easily have all of the features to be discussed, since the incremental cost of adding most of them is insignificant compared to the "heart" circuitry of the module. Detailed design and circuit descriptions will be given in Chapter 6, in which module designs will be optimized for computer control of many of the operating parameters.

Voltage-Controlled Oscillator

The voltage-controlled oscillator, usually abbreviated VCO, is the most fundamental module of the system. Usually more VCOs are present than any other module type. An actual VCO module has a number of control inputs, signal outputs, and mechanical inputs.

The last waveform is a sine wave whose characteristics need not be reiterated. Generally, the actual oscillator portion of a VCO generates one of these waveforms and the others are derived from it by use of simple nonlinear circuits. The most popular type of oscillator inherently produces a very precise sawtooth wave with the ramp portion linear to within a fraction of a percent and a very short "flyback" period on the order of a microsecond or less. A triangle wave is obtained by taking the absolute value of the sawtooth voltage with a full-wave rectifier circuit. Actually, the resulting triangle has a little notch during the sawtooth flyback period, but it is usually inaudible. The rectangle wave may be derived either from the sawtooth or the triangle by use of an infinite clipper circuit. Variations in the duty cycle are accomplished by shifting the clipping threshold away from the zero voltage point. The sine wave is, oddly enough, created by passing the triangle wave through a "soft clipping" circuit. The circuit rounds the peaks of the triangle and produces a sine wave with 0.2 to 2% total harmonic content, quite low enough to get the sugary sweet timbre characteristic of sine waves. The waveforms are usually sent out at fixed amplitudes such as 10 V positive and negative, although it is conceivable that output level controls might be provided.

Voltage-Controlled Amplifier

A voltage-controlled amplifier, abbreviated VCA, in many respects resembles the VCO in the way that control inputs are handled. However, since it is a modifier module, it has signal inputs. Usually, several signal inputs are provided. Depending on the sophistication (and expense) of the module, the signals may either be added together in equal proportions, have a mechanical gain control to determine the contribution of each input, or really be equivalent to several VCAs and have a control voltage determine the gain of each signal input. The second-mentioned case with front panel gain controls is probably the most common. Occasionally, one of the signal inputs may be equipped with a phase inversion switch, which allows harmonic cancelling when synchronized, but differently shaped waves are fed in or special effects when processing control voltages. In any case, the VCA also functions as a mixer, since several signals may be combined into one. Mixing is the same as algebraic summation so if control voltages are processed with the VCA, they will add up just like the control voltage input circuitry of the VCO.

The control input arrangement is similar to that of the VCO. Often fewer control inputs are summed together, since elaborate multisource modulation of amplitude is less common. A decibels per volt panel control can be expected as well as an overall gain control. The latter is often inserted in the signal path after the signal inputs have been mixed together but before the actual VCA circuit. This is done to minimize distortion in the VCA circuit if the input levels are unusually high. The VCA signal output is quite

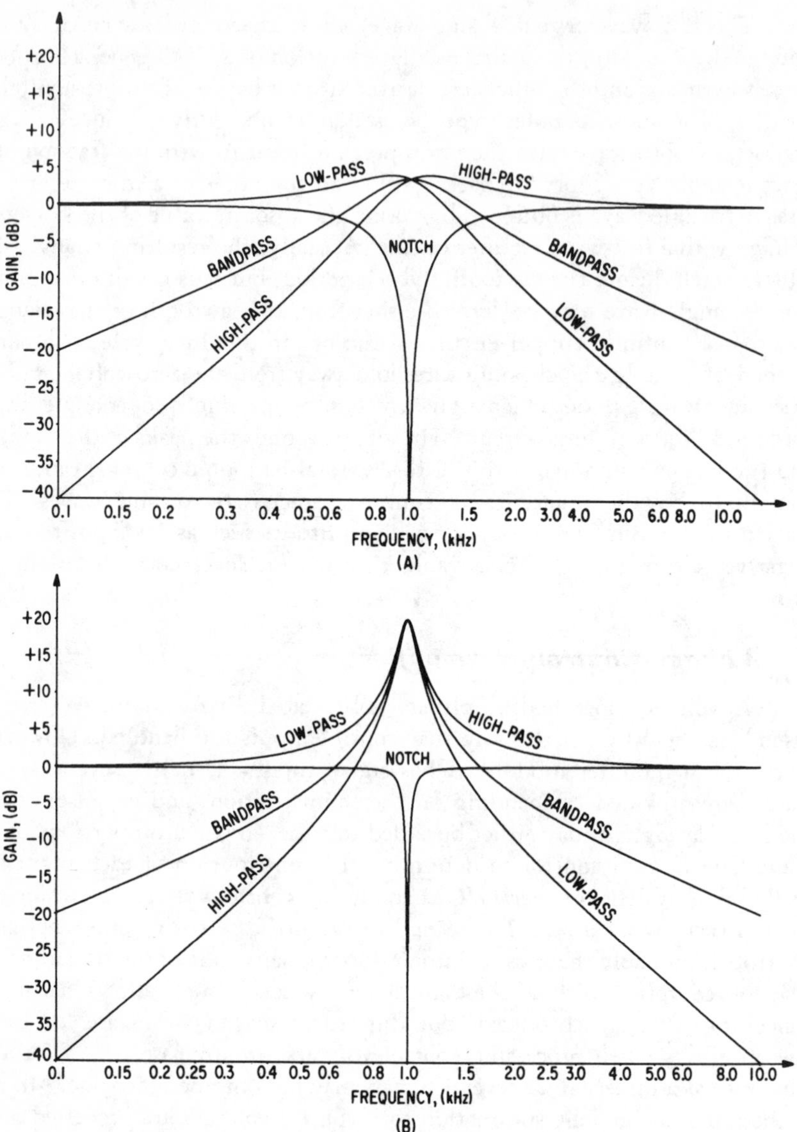

Fig. 3–5. Common voltage-controlled filter response shapes. (A) Low *Q* factor (1.5). (B) High *Q* factor (10).

straightforward with one or two provided. If two are present, they are independent and the second is often the inverse of the first.

Voltage-Controlled Filter

The voltage-controlled filter (VCF) is the most complex and costly "common" module in the synthesizer. One is indispensable but more than two is rare in the smaller systems. Voltage-controlled filters of adequate performance are a recent development, and there is still considerable room for improvement.

The signal inputs and controls are similar to those of the VCA, although there may be only one or two provided. There are usually several signal outputs, however, each corresponding to a different filter *mode.* The most popular filtering circuit simultaneously generates a low-pass, high-pass, and bandpass output from a single input. A band-reject output may also be provided at very little additional cost. Sometimes the multiple outputs are applied to a tapped potentiometer, and the user selects a mixture of these filtering functions to be sent to a single output.

Although there are multiple outputs, there is only one frequency parameter. Under the proper operating conditions (low Q factor) the low-pass and high-pass −3-dB frequencies and the center frequencies of the bandpass and band-reject outputs are all the same. At higher Qs, the low-pass and high-pass filtering functions undergo a phenomenon called *corner peaking,* which is illustrated in Fig. 3–5. At very high Qs, the corner peaking becomes excessive, and the audible filtering effect of low-pass, bandpass, and high-pass outputs becomes similar. The notch output under these conditions becomes so narrow that its effect on the sound is hardly noticeable.

Since the Q factor has such an important effect, it must be variable. The most common configuration is a single panel control for Q. It is desirable, however, to have a voltage-controlled Q probably with an exponential relationship, since the useful range for Q is from 0.5 to several hundred at least. One common imperfection in existing filters is that high Q factors lead to instability and may even cause the filter to break into intermittent oscillation. If this was not such a problem, Qs up in the thousands would be useful for generating slowly decaying ringing sounds in response to a short input pulse.

Normally, the frequency control inputs are straightforward and essentially identical to the frequency control inputs on the VCO. However, there is an interaction between frequency and Q that must be considered. Taking the bandpass output as an example, there are two things that may happen when the center frequency is varied. In a *constant* Q filter, the Q factor remains constant as center frequency is changed. This is desirable if one is filtering white noise to give it a sense of pitch, since the same degree of "pitchedness" will be retained regardless of the center frequency. However, if the filter is used to create ringing sounds, the ringing *time* will be much longer at lower frequencies than it will be at high frequencies. This is because Q is really related to the rate of ringing decay in terms of number of cycles rather than seconds. A *constant bandwidth* filter actually has a Q that is proportional to center frequency. Thus, if the bandwidth is set to 100 Hz and the center frequency to 300 Hz, the effective Q is low, but if the center frequency is 5 kHz, the 100-Hz bandwidth represents a relatively high Q. Although there are applications for both types of frequency control, most

VCF modules are constant *Q*. The ideal case would have two sets of frequency control inputs, one set with constant *Q* response, and the other set with constant bandwidth response.

From the response curves in Fig. 3–5 it is apparent that the cutoff slopes of the filter responses are essentially constant regardless of *Q* once the attenuation reaches 6 dB or so. Steeper slopes are possible by cascading filters and driving each member of the cascade with the same control voltage. However, there is a growing interest in variable-slope filters, preferably voltage-controlled variable slope. The reason is that detailed analysis of mechanical instruments, particularly the trumpet, reveals that the changes in spectrum caused by changes in emphasis closely approximate the effect of a filter with fixed cutoff frequency but variable slope. Actually, implementing such a filter turns out to be a nontrivial task. In particular, variable mixing of the intermediate outputs of a cascade of ordinary filters does not work very well because of phase shifts through the individual filters. Reasonable approximations are possible, however, if suitable phase correctors are used.

Clippers

Although the VCF is the primary spectrum modification device in the synthesizer, occasionally clipping and other nonlinear waveshaping functions are integrated into a module. About the simplest useful setup would be a sharp clipper with upper and lower thresholds variable by means of panel controls or control voltages. A somewhat more flexible circuit would allow independent gain for positive and negative portions of the waveform and optional inversion of the negative portion. A very general nonlinear waveshaping module might have a dozen or more panel controls that together specify an arbitrary transfer function as a multisegment approximation using straight line segments. The effects available with nonlinear shaping devices generally cannot be duplicated with filters, but they are not as dramatic either. Thus, nonlinear shapers are usually found only on larger synthesizers.

Envelope Generators

The modules discussed so far can generate just about any steady or repetitively changing sound that can be desired. However, in order to even synthesize ordinary musical notes, a source of control voltages shaped like a common amplitude envelope is needed. The envelope generator module is specifically designed to perform this function.

A simple envelope generator produces the general shape shown in Fig. 3–6 in response to trigger and gate digital control inputs. Note that the envelope voltage output is zero under quiescent conditions. When the gate rises, the envelope rises toward a steady-state value during the attack period. The slope and thus the duration of the attack is usually determined by a

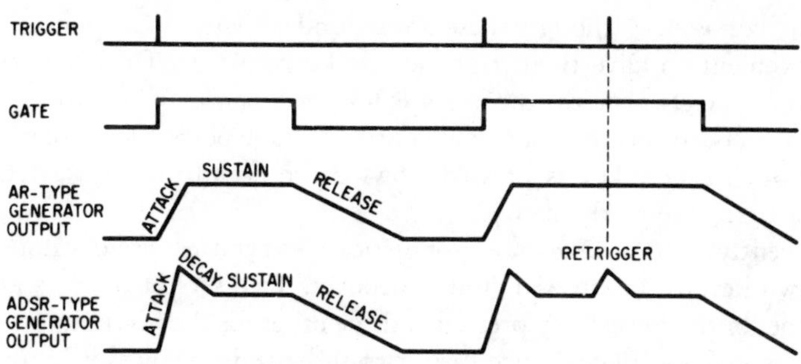

Fig. 3–6. Typical envelope generator outputs

mechanical control. As long as the gate is held high, the envelope remains in its steady state. When the gate turns off, the envelope makes a decay transition back toward zero. Again, the decay period is adjustable with a panel control. Note that the trigger signal is not really needed, since it has no influence on the envelope output. Such a simplified envelope generator is called an attack–release (AR) generator.

A more sophisticated envelope generator is the attack–decay–sustain–release (ADSR) type. Four parameters define its shape. The slope of the initial attack and the final decay are adjustable as with the AR type. However, the initial attack *overshoots* above the steady-state sustain level. Thus, the additional parameters are the amount of overshoot and the duration of the initial decay from the overshoot level to the sustain level. Note that the trigger pulse can reinitiate the overshoot cycle even if the gate remains high. The ADSR shape is preferred, since the initial overshoot resembles the action of many musical instrument types. Also, because of its retriggering capability, rapidly repeated notes at the same frequency are readily distinguished. If desired, the controls can be set to simulate the simpler AR shape. Although the transitions are shown as linear ramps, typical circuit implementations of envelope generators usually result in a decaying exponential shape.

Music Keyboard

The most common manual input to a synthesizer is through a standard organ-like keyboard with a three- to five-octave range. Outputs from the keyboard are a control voltage and trigger and gate digital signals. The control voltage output always corresponds to the key last pressed. Depending on the design, the output voltage with two keys pressed is equal to the lowest key, the highest key, or some intermediate value. The trigger pulse is generated on the initial depression of a key, and the gate is on as long as a key is pressed.

Most keyboards have three mechanical controls. One is for adjusting volts per octave and another is for adjusting the voltage level of the lowest key (basis voltage). Although these are redundant with VCO controls, it is very convenient to have them right at the keyboard itself particularly if it feeds several VCOs. The third control is for portamento. When rotated away from its zero position, the change in control voltage output from one level to another when a new key is pressed slows down, resulting in a pitch glide from the first note to the second.

Recently, a somewhat more sophisticated keyboard was developed that allows two keys to be pressed simultaneously. Two sets of outputs are provided, one for the lowest key pressed and the other for the highest key. When properly scored and played with care, two independent voices with different characteristics may be played on one keyboard. Another simple and often employed scheme is to simply use several keyboards such as with theater organs. Digital scanning techniques have also been applied to synthesizer keyboard design such that truly polyphonic playing is possible. One decision that has to be made in the design of such a keyboard is the assignment of keys to control voltage–trigger–gate output groups. If the voices controlled by the keyboard are not all the same, the assignment of voices to keys may vary greatly according to playing technique or even random chance. Digital keyboards will be studied in greater detail in Chapter 9.

Other Modules

The modules that have been described so far are those that can be expected to be present in any synthesizer, often in multiples. There are also a number of specialized module types for special effects, to perform functions normally requiring a number of interconnected modules, and "utility" versions of the standard modules already discussed. Utility modules, particulary VCOs and VCAs, are less flexible, less accurate, and therefore quite a bit less expensive than their standard counterparts. They arė used freely in complex patches where their characteristics are adequate for the task.

Sequencer

One specialized module that adds a measure of automation to the synthesis process is called a *sequencer.* Interesting repetitive effects can be created with one or more VCOs set to their very-low-frequency range and used as sources of control voltages. However, if a specific sequence such as a short melody is desired, it is not normally obvious how a group of oscillators might be set up to generate it. A sequencer allows the user to directly determine and easily modify specific, arbitrary sequences of control voltages.

The sequencer is usually designed to simulate a keyboard; thus, it has trigger and gate outputs as well as the control voltage output. The simplest sequencers might have 16 potentiometer knobs and a "speed" control that determines the frequency of a clock oscillator. Each cycle of the clock causes a scanning circuit to look at the next potentiometer in sequence and generate a control voltage according to its setting. Also trigger and gate pulses would be generated. The final result, if the sequencer is connected to a VCO, is that a sequence of 16 notes of uniform duration would be generated and repeated. Usually there is some way to short cycle the unit in order to produce shorter sequences. Frequently, the speed control has sufficient range such that the voltage sequence output repeats fast enough to become an audio signal. Thus, the sequencer becomes an arbitrary waveform generator for simple waveforms.

The next step up consists of adding a duration control under each pitch control so that irregular rhythms can be easily handled. From this point sequencers can get increasingly sophisticated all the way up to computer systems and music languages. Digital sequencers can easily have up to 256 and more steps in the sequence. Sequences may be entered and edited with a small digital keyboard much like those found on calculators. Sometimes a sequencer may act as a memory unit on a music keyboard allowing the user to "play" in the sequence and then edit it in memory. Microprocessor application as a "supersequencer" is discussed in Chapter 11.

Sample-and-Hold Module

One fairly simple device that in many ways sounds like a sequencer is a sample-and-hold module. Like the sequencer, it has an internal clock oscillator and possibly provisions for an external oscillator. It also has a signal input and an output. Every cycle of the clock causes the circuit to "look" at the input voltage at that instant and remember it. The remembered voltage appears at the output as a constant value until the next clock cycle. If the input waveform were a slow sawtooth, for example, the output would resemble a staircase with the number of steps dependent on the ratio of clock frequency to input frequency. If the output voltage were connected to a VCO, the result would be a scale of individual pitches. More complex waveforms would produce sequences of notes that would either repeat, evolve, or be seemingly random depending on the exact ratio of sampling (clock) frequency to input signal frequency.

White Noise Generator

The white noise generator module is perhaps the simplest in the system, at least on the front panel. Usually there is a single output jack for the white noise signal. Occasionally, there might be a "pink" noise jack also. The difference between the two is that white noise has a constant spectral power *per hertz* of bandwidth, while pink noise has constant power *per octave.* Thus, pink noise actually sounds whiter (better balance between low- and high-frequency components) because of the exponential pitch response of the ear.

Specialized Modifiers

Other specialized modules are based on the sound modification techniques described in Chapter 2. Reverberation simulators, usually of the spring type, are quite popular for enlarging the synthesized sound. Generally, the only control present determines the mixture of straight and reverberated sound. Ring modulators are also popular because of their low cost and distinctive effect. Typically, there are just two signal inputs with level control knobs and a single output. Frequency shifters are found rarely due to their very high cost and specialized application.

One "module" (it is usually a free-standing unit) that has recently become available is a digital implementation of the speed-changing tape machine described earlier. In one of its modes, it has the ability to change the frequency of sounds passing through it without altering the harmonic structure or overall speed of the sound. When connected in a feedback mode, a single note comes out as an ascending or descending series of notes.

A Typical Patch

Although the evolution of a relatively simple patch was described earlier, let us look at how a more complex patch might be designed, given a particular set of requirements. Throughout the discussion, the proportionality and symmetry properties of exponential voltage-controlled synthesis will be emphasized. This will also be used as an opportunity to introduce the technique of FM timbre synthesis, a simple yet powerful method of producing quite a wide variety of timbres under the control of only two parameters.

The first step in designing a complex patch, as opposed to fiddling around and discovering one, is to develop a physical understanding of the desired effect. In this case, we are trying to develop a timbre (spectrum) modification technique that can produce as wide a variety of effects as possible under the control of a minimum number of parameters. In Chapter 1, while describing frequency modulation for the production of vibrato, it was mentioned that if the vibrato frequency became high enough and the vibrato depth (percent modulation) became great enough, the unmodulated sound would be completely altered into metallic clangs and breaking glass. However, there are numerous intermediate conditions that produce useful musical tones. Since there are only two parameters involved, the modulation frequency and amplitude, and since the range of effects is so great, the situation bears further investigation.

Frequency Modulation Terminology

Before continuing, some terms must be defined to avoid confusion. Two signals are involved, the *modulating* signal, which was the vibrato waveform, and the *modulated* signal, which is the tone being modified. The following terms are really defined only if the modulating signal waveform and the modulated signal waveform are both sine waves and a *linear* VCO (or linear input to an exponential VCO) is used for the modulation. The *modulating frequency* is the frequency of the modulating signal. The *deviation* is the magnitude of the difference between the modulated signal's unmodulated frequency (center frequency) and the highest or lowest instantaneous frequency it attains when frequency modulation is performed. Thus, the deviation is proportional to the *amplitude* of the modulating signal. Finally, the *modulation index* is the ratio of the deviation to the modulating frequency. Thus, the modulation index is also proportional to the modulating signal's amplitude when the modulating signal's frequency is constant.

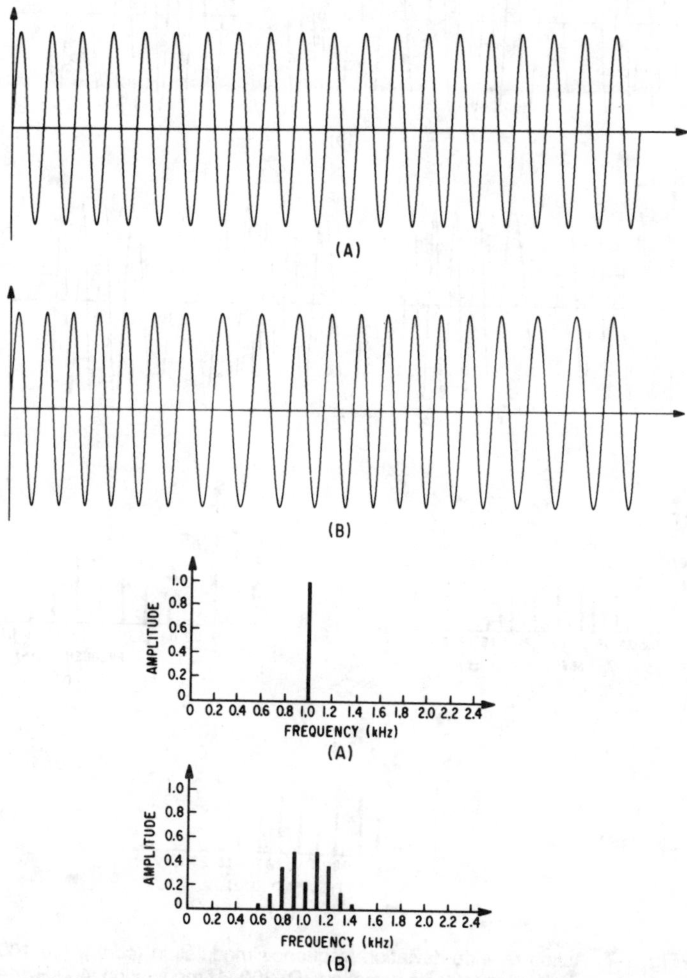

Fig. 3–7. Action of wide-deviation frequency modulation. (A) Unmodulated 1-kHz carrier. (B) 100-Hz modulation, 200-Hz deviation.

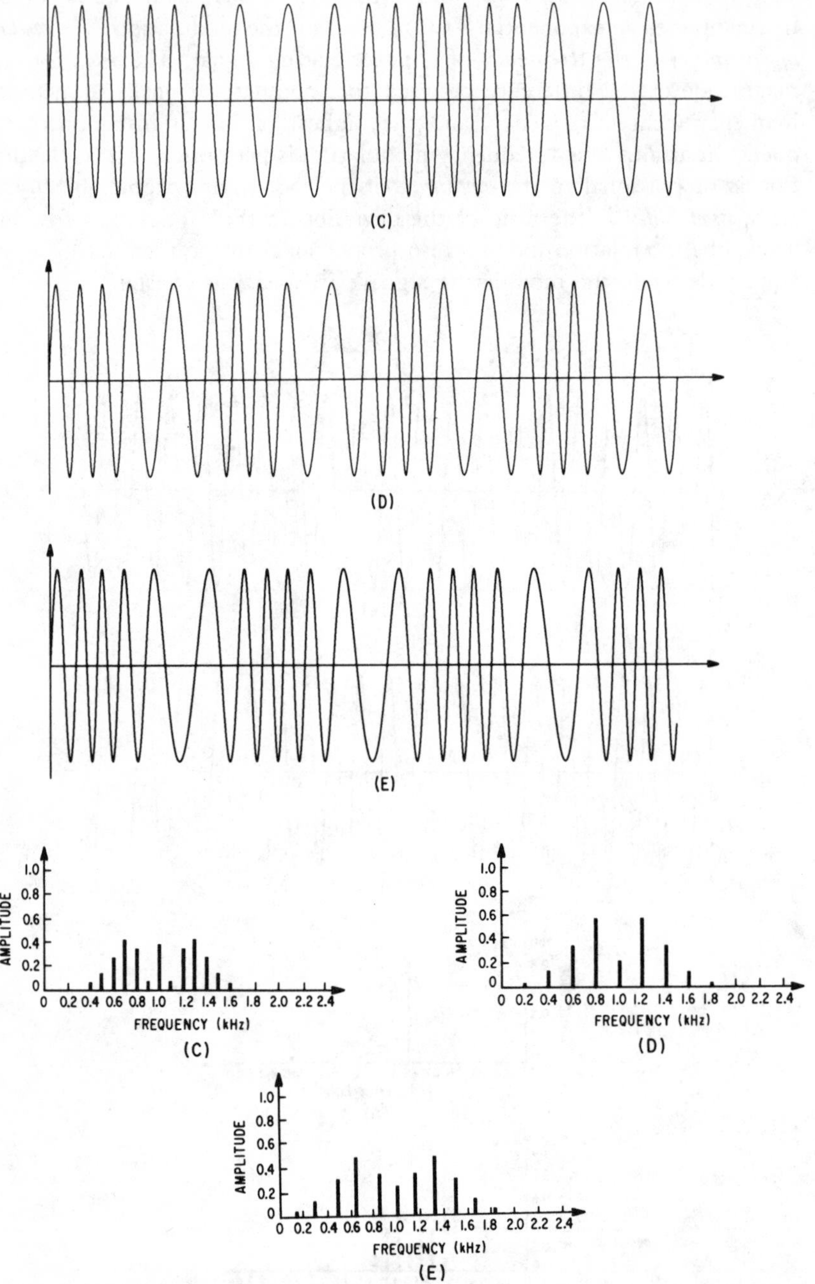

Fig. 3–7. Action of wide-deviation frequency modulation (*cont.*). (C) 100-Hz modulation, 400-Hz deviation. (D) 200-Hz modulation, 400-Hz deviation. (E) 171-Hz modulation, 513 Hz deviation.

Perhaps a concrete example will help to clarify these terms. Figure 3–7A shows an unmodulated signal at 1,000 Hz and its spectrum, which, of course, consists of a single line, at 1 kHz. In Fig. 3–7B, a modulating signal of 100 Hz has been imposed, and its amplitude is such that the original unmodulated signal now swings between 800 Hz and 1,200 Hz for a deviation of 200 Hz. Now, one would probably expect the spectrum to spread out and fill the area between 800 Hz and 1,200 Hz, but as the spectral plot shows, such is not the case. Instead, individual sine wave component lines have been added, some of which are even outside of the 800-Hz to 1,200-Hz range. These added frequencies are often called *sideband* frequencies, a term borrowed from radio transmission jargon. Actually, a close look at the modulated signal's waveform reveals that its shape repeats exactly 100 times/sec. So according to Fourier's theorem, component frequencies of this waveform can only exist at multiples of 100 Hz as the spectral plot indeed shows. To the ear, the result is a 100-Hz tone with a rather thin, horn-like timbre.

In the situation just described, the modulating frequency is 100 Hz, the deviation is 200 Hz, and the modulation index, therefore, is 200 Hz/100 Hz = 2. Figure 3–7C shows the result of increasing the amplitude of the modulating signal such that the modulation index increases to 4. Additional spectrum lines are visible, and those that were present with the lower index have changed somewhat in amplitude. The audible pitch is still 100 Hz due to the continued harmonic spacing of 100 Hz, but the timbre is thicker, due to more low-frequency content, and less horn-like due to greater spreading of the spectrum.

A continued increase in the modulation index causes the formation of an even wider spectrum to the point that the lower sideband frequencies try to go negative. What actually happens, though, is that they are reflected back into the positive frequency domain where they mix with other sideband frequencies already present. The resulting amplitude of a mixed sideband frequency (also a harmonic in this case) is dependent on the exact phase between the modulating frequency and the modulated frequency.

Effect of Deep Frequency Modulation

If the modulating frequency is increased to 200 Hz and its amplitude is adjusted so that the modulation index is equal to 2, then the waveform and spectrum of Fig. 3–7D results. Note that the relative amplitudes of all of the spectral components are the same as they were in Fig. 3–7B except that they are spread out to 200 Hz spacing. The ear now interprets this as a 200-Hz tone. Thus, it seems that the apparent pitch of the frequency-modulated tone is equal to the modulating frequency. Before jumping to this conclusion, however, consider what happens if the modulating frequency is *not* a submultiple of the modulated frequency, such as 171 Hz. The result in Fig. 3–7E shows the expected 171-Hz spacing between the sideband components, but these frequencies are *not* harmonics of a common fundamental unless 1 Hz is

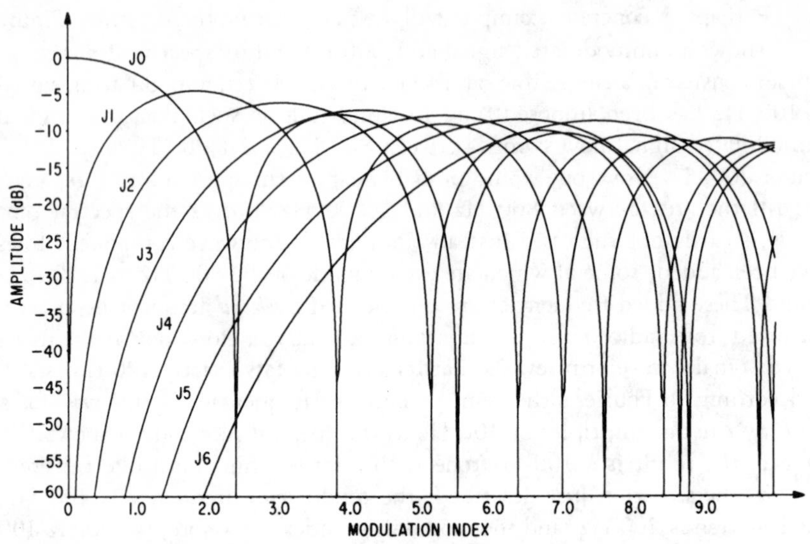

Fig. 3–8. Bessel functions plotted in decibels

considered a fundamental. The resulting inharmonic tone is still pleasant to hear but the timbre is bell-like rather than horn-like. With larger modulation indices, sideband reflection, and nonsubmultiple modulating frequencies, a reflected sideband would typically not fall on the same frequency as a nonreflected sideband. The result is a proliferation of spectrum lines and the shattering glass sound mentioned earlier.

It should be apparent from the examples in Fig. 3–7 that the relation between modulation index and sideband amplitudes is not a simple one. It is predictable, however, with the aid of *Bessel functions,* some of which are plotted in Fig. 3–8. If one wished to determine the amplitudes of the sidebands of the Fig. 3–7B example, the first step would be to find the horizontal position corresponding to the modulation index of 2.0. The J_0 curve at that position is the amplitude of the zeroth sideband, which is the 1,000-Hz center frequency, J_1 corresponds to the first sideband pair at 900 Hz and 1,100 Hz, and so forth. Note that these amplitudes are with respect to the unmodulated 1,000-Hz signal, which is given a reference amplitude of 0 dB.

Thus, if the modulating and modulated frequencies remain constant and the modulation index changes, the spectrum undergoes a complex evolution. This can be a very useful musical effect and is called *dynamic depth FM* timbre synthesis. With a voltage-controlled synthesizer, it is an easy technique to apply and produces dramatic effects with relatively few synthesizer modules.

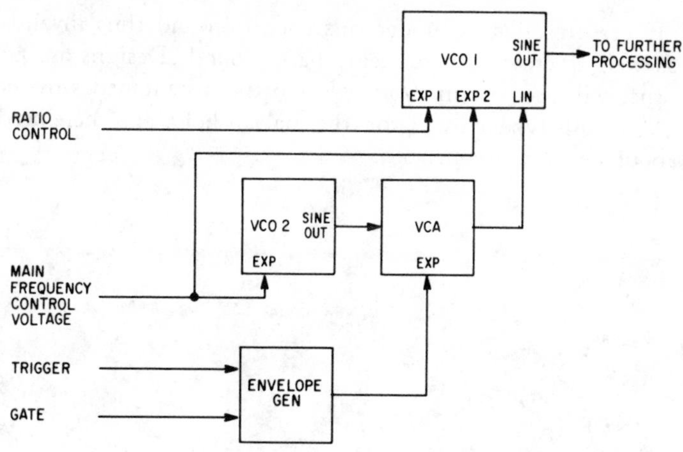

Fig. 3-9. Patch for dynamic depth FM

Patch for Dynamic Depth FM

Figure 3–9 shows a possible patch for dynamic depth FM. VCO 1 is the primary VCO, which provides the modulated signal. VCO 2 supplies the modulating signal. VCO 1 is modulated by VCO 2 through an auxiliary *linear* control input. This is necessary for the preceding analysis to be valid. Note that the main frequency control voltage is connected to *both* VCOs. Since these control inputs are exponential, the "ratio" voltage level determines the ratio between the modulated signal's center frequency and the modulating frequency. If, for example, it was set to 2 V, then VCO 1 (unmodulated) would track VCO 2, but two octaves higher. The modulation depth is set by a VCA controlled by an envelope generator.

Thus, if this setup were connected to a keyboard, for example, the keyboard output voltage would control the frequency of both oscillators, but VCO 1 would always be four times higher in frequency than VCO 2. The apparent pitch of the generated tones would be equal to the frequency of VCO 2. The trigger and gate signals from the keyboard would be connected to the envelope generator, which, in turn, produces the control voltage that determines the modulation index, and thus the spectrum of the tone. For producing actual notes, the output of VCO 1 would at the very least pass through another VCA controlled by the same or another envelope generator in order to apply an amplitude envelope.

Changing the ratio voltage also affects the modulation index and, if not set for a simple ratio, results in inharmonic spectra. This voltage could even be set so that the modulated signal's center frequency is *less* than the modulating frequency. One point should be kept in mind as the parameters in the system are varied. With the linear input to VCO 1, it is possible to specify a *negative* instantaneous frequency. The most popular VCO designs will simply cease oscillating under this condition and thus invalidate the analysis as well as creating a suddenly harsh sound. Designs are possible, however, that will oscillate in *opposite phase* if the instantaneous frequency is negative. With this type of oscillator, the analysis holds and there need be no concern about negative frequencies.

4

Direct Computer Synthesis Methods

Although voltage-controlled synthesis methods are very flexible and very popular, they are not the last word. Even though much work with direct computer synthesis predates widespread application of the voltage-control concept, it will be described here as an alternative to voltage control. As a matter of fact, the earliest extensive direct computer synthesis program actually used imaginary "modules" that corresponded closely to the voltage-controlled modules described in Chapter 3.

Direct computer synthesis and digital synthesis in general runs the gamut in sophistication from buzzy one-voice "toy" programs to serious professional program packages. Of course, this is not a unique situation, since analog synthesizers and even standard musical instruments find the same range of application. Throughout this chapter and indeed in all of Sections II and III, emphasis will be on techniques suitable for high-quality synthesis. The application of simplified versions of these as well as other very elementary techniques in low-cost music systems will be addressed in Section IV.

Limitations of Voltage Control

Let us first describe some of the very real limitations of voltage-controlled equipment and techniques. Accuracy is one problem. Although it has been shown that extreme accuracy in the *final result* may be undesirable, accuracy in the intermediate stages, which may then be degraded in a controlled manner, is very desirable. For example, in the FM patch just described, if the spectrum is harmonic and frequency components are reflected, they mix with unreflected frequency components, and the resulting amplitude is a function of the phase relationship between modulating and modulated signals. However, since the oscillators are not exact, they will not be at exactly the frequency ratio desired. The result is that the phase between the two is drifting continuously, and thus the spectrum is changing continuously when it should be standing still. Although this shifting spectrum may often be desirable, it would be nice if the speed and degree of shift could be controlled rather than left to chance. Even if the frequency ratio were exact, there is generally no way to control the actual phase with voltage-controlled equipment. If nothing else, precise control of impreciseness is useful for creating contrast among mechanical, rich, and sloppy effects.

Historically, voltage-controlled oscillators and filters have had the most serious accuracy problems. The reason is that the exponential converters used are not ideal devices. They are highly sensitive to temperature, and "parasitic" physical defects also reduce their accuracy at the extremes of the audio range. Tremendous improvements in accuracy and stability have been made over the years, however, so that today it is possible to make a VCO that is adequately accurate at a reasonable cost. However, even small improvements beyond this come at a great increase in cost and complexity. Voltage-controlled amplifiers had been less of a problem in the past, but the complex patches of today routinely use VCAs to process control voltages in the frequency control paths of patches. The result is that inaccuracy in the VCA will translate into frequency errors that are easily heard.

With a microprocessor in a *hybrid* voltage-controlled system, it becomes possible to automatically compensate for inaccuracies to a great extent. In such a system, the microprocessor can address each module in the system with several "test" control voltages and measure the response to each. Using this information, it can then compute a correction function that is saved in a table in memory. Subsequently, all control values are modified by the respective correction function before being sent to a module. Such an *automatic tuning* routine would be performed whenever the equipment is turned on and then occasionally thereafter as it warms up.

One of the characteristics of direct computer synthesis is that extreme accuracy is inherent. The "standard precision" arithmetic in most computer systems is good to about seven decimal digits or one part in 10 million. If improved accuracy is desired, the "cost" of obtaining it is fairly small. Thus, the question of accuracy in the control of sound parameters generally need not even be raised.

Simultaneous Sounds

The maximum number of simultaneous sounds available is another voltage-controlled synthesizer limitation. One aspect of this limitation is that a fairly large number of modules is needed to generate and control a single sound. To even simulate a small chamber orchestra all at once with a synthesizer would be out of the question. The other aspect is the limitation of the performer in controlling a number of sounds with a number of parameters each. Thus, almost all synthesizer music is produced with the aid of a multitrack tape recorder. Only one part or voice of the music is performed and recorded at a time, and the parts are later combined by mixing the tracks together.

The multitrack recorder would seem to be a complete solution to the simultaneous sound problem with the only disadvantage being that the synthesis process is taken out of real time. However, this is not the case. As a simple example, consider a rapid run (fast series of notes) on an instrument with the amplitude envelope characteristics of a piano. Assuming initial silence, the envelope of the first note struck would rise rapidly and then fall slowly. Shortly afterward, the second note would be struck, but, since the first note has not yet died away, there are now two simultaneous sounds. The third note would increase the number to three and so forth. At some point, the first note would be so faint that it could be ignored, but it is not clear exactly how many simultaneous sounds were built up, although it is certainly not more than the number of notes in the run.

A similar run on a synthesizer keyboard would create a very different result even if the timbre and envelope of a single note was identical to the previous instrument. In this case, the first note struck would start an envelope identical to the previous case, but, when the second note was struck, the pitch of the tone would immediately be updated to the second note's frequency and a new envelope segment would be started. Thus, simultaneous sounds are not created, which should be obvious since only one tone oscillator was involved.

Theoretically, this could be corrected with the multitrack tape recorder by recording each note of the run on a separate track, although such a procedure would not really be practical. The problem could also be partially solved by using a digital scanning polyphonic keyboard and enough modules to create up to, say, eight simultaneous independent tones. Even if in the ideal case there were more than eight simultaneous sounds, the effect of abruptly terminating the first when seven others are still sounding would probably go unnoticed. The important point is that such a need for large numbers of simultaneous sounds may occur only rarely in a composition. Either all of the equipment or effort needed for the worst case must be available or the problem must be ignored.

In direct computer synthesis, a virtually unlimited number of simultaneous sounds may be built up when circumstances dictate. The cost of this capability is borne only when the event occurs. During other times, when the sound is simpler, the ability to handle large numbers of simultaneous sounds is free! This applies to other capabilities as well. The effect is like being able to rent additional synthesizer modules by the minute from a company with an essentially infinite inventory.

Programmability

The difficulty in controlling a number of simultaneous sounds to a great degree by a single performer is also overcome in direct computer synthesis systems. The control problem is actually one of time: during real-time performance, there is simply not enough time available for the performer to attend to very many variables. In the typical direct computer system, the control functions are *programmed* to any degree of detail desired and without time constraints. An intricate passage of only 10 sec duration may be fussed over for hours to get all the parameter variations right and then be immediately followed by a long solo requiring very little effort to specify. In a nutshell, the limits of complexity are determined by the imagination and patience of the composer and not the equipment or technique of the performer.

Sequencer modules are one attempt to add a programming capability to the conventional voltage-controlled synthesizer, although they typically have a small capacity and only control a few variables. However, more sophisticated sequencers based on microprocessors or minicomputers can extend voltage-controlled system programmability to the point of rivaling direct computer techniques.

Experimentation in new sound generation and modification *techniques* is much easier in a direct computer synthesis system than designing, building, and troubleshooting precision electronic circuits. A "module" or processing element is nothing more than a subprogram in the direct computer systhesis system. A severe modification may amount to nothing more than typing in a few dozen words of program code. A disastrous error requiring complete redesign of the process wastes only the *time* spent on the faulty design, not numerous precision electronic components. Also, many of the modification techniques now under development are simply not possible with conventional analog techniques.

Direct Computer Synthesis Problems

Lest the preceding seem as if direct computer synthesis is faultless, let us look at some of its limitations given the present state of the art.

Direct computer synthesis is presently not a real-time technique except in limited circumstances with fast computers. This means that once the sound has been specified and programmed, the computer must "crunch" on it for awhile before the sound is actually heard. The amount of time involved depends on a great many factors. Obviously, computer speed has a great influence, since a large campus mainframe may easily be 100 times faster than a personal microcomputer. Sound complexity is another important factor with the more complex sounds taking a greater amount of time. Finally, operational methods of the computer make a big difference. When using a campus mainframe, the delay between program submission and resulting sound can be many times greater than the actual computation time because other people are using the machine. A personal system, on the other hand, does not have this problem. The net result is that the time delay can actually reach 1,000 times the duration of the sound being synthesized, although common values are 10 to 100 times.

Programmability is simultaneously an advantage and a disadvantage of direct computer synthesis. Many people see it as a disadvantage because the "immediacy" of direct experimentation and improvisation is not present. Instead, programmability requires considerable preplanning and foreknowledge of the audible effects of various specifications and variations. A related problem is an unwillingness to learn the basic programming concepts required to effectively use the technology.

Most people, including musicians and many engineers, view the computer as a very complex device that is equally complex to use. In particular, a complete lab manual for a large voltage-controlled synthesizer is usually not very thick and covers most aspects of usage from how to turn it on to the most advanced techniques possible with the equipment. In contrast, a manual for a particular direct synthesis program may not be any thicker but contains little or no background material and does not attempt to explore the limits of the program. If the potential user asks for applicable background material, he may be handed a hundred pounds of books and manuals, or worse yet, told that nothing suitable exists.

A very practical difficulty with direct computer synthesis is that a critical mass with respect to expenditures of money for equipment and time for programming exists before "significant" results can be obtained. Significant here means musically useful output as opposed to trite little demonstrations. With voltage-controlled techniques and some imagination, only a few hundred dollars worth of equipment and a stereo tape recorder are needed to get a good start. Reasonable sounding results are obtained almost from the beginning and improve from there. A computer system capable of equivalent results with a direct synthesis program may cost from $4,000 on up. At this time, a considerable amount of programming effort is also necessary to get the "basic system" running. It should be noted, however, that once the critical mass is reached, the *full power* of direct computer synthesis is available with any extra expenditure going toward increased speed and convenience of use.

Overcoming the Problems

Until now the preceding limitations have severely restricted the use of direct computer synthesis, particularly following the commercial introduction of voltage-control equipment. However, many of these are now being overcome.

The time factor is being improved substantially through the use of very fast logic dedicated to the specific calculations needed for sound synthesis. Personal computer systems, used only by the composer himself, eliminate waiting time at large computer centers. The increased speed in conjunction with improved man–machine interfaces and personal systems now means that programmed control of the system can be supplemented with direct, interactive control. Programmed control is still desirable for the final output, but rapid interactive control can also be used for experimentation. The perceived complexity of computers in general and programming in particular is being overcome by easier to use computer systems and early introduction of programming concepts. It is not unusual for elementary school students to become very adept at programming using simplified languages. Hopefully, books such as this will take some of the mystery out of the theoretical aspects of direct computer synthesis. Even the critical mass problem is decreasing in severity as the performance/price ratio of digital electronics seems to double every year.

These improvements in technology coupled with inherent limitless capability would seem to indicate that direct computer synthesis will eventually oust all other methods in serious electronic music applications.

Sound in Digital Form

Computers deal with numbers and sound consists of continuously varying electrical signals. Somehow the two have to be accurately linked together in order for direct computer sound synthesis to work at all. Fortunately, this is possible with fewer limitations than might be expected.

The first problem to be solved is how to represent a waveform that can wiggle and undulate in a seemingly infinite variety of ways with a finite string of numbers having a finite number of digits. Intuitively, one would probably suggest dividing the time axis up into a large number of segments, each segment being a short enough time so that the waveform does not change very much during the segment. The average amplitude of the waveform over each segment could then be converted into a number for the computer or vice versa. It would seem that the accuracy of the approximation could be made as good as desired by making the segments small enough.

Let us take an example and see how small these segments must be for high-fidelity sound-to-numbers and numbers-to-sound conversion. Figure 4–1A shows a 1-kHz sine wave that has been chopped into 100 segments per cycle of the wave. The segment time is thus 10 μsec. Assuming that the desire is to generate the sine wave given the string of 100 numbers repeated continously, the problem is to determine how good it will be.

Digital-to-Analog Converter

First, however, a device to do the conversion is needed. Such a device is called a *digital-to-analog converter,* which is usually abbreviated DAC. Such a device accepts numbers one at a time from a computer or other digital source and generates one voltage pulse per number with a height proportional to the number. Thus, a DAC that is calibrated in volts would give a voltage pulse 2.758 V in amplitude if it received a numerical input of 2.758. The width of the pulses is constant but varies with the type of DAC. For now, the pulse width will be assumed to be very small compared to the spacing between pulses.

Figure 4–1B shows the output from a DAC fed the 100 numbers representing a 1-kHz sine wave. As expected, it is a string of very narrow

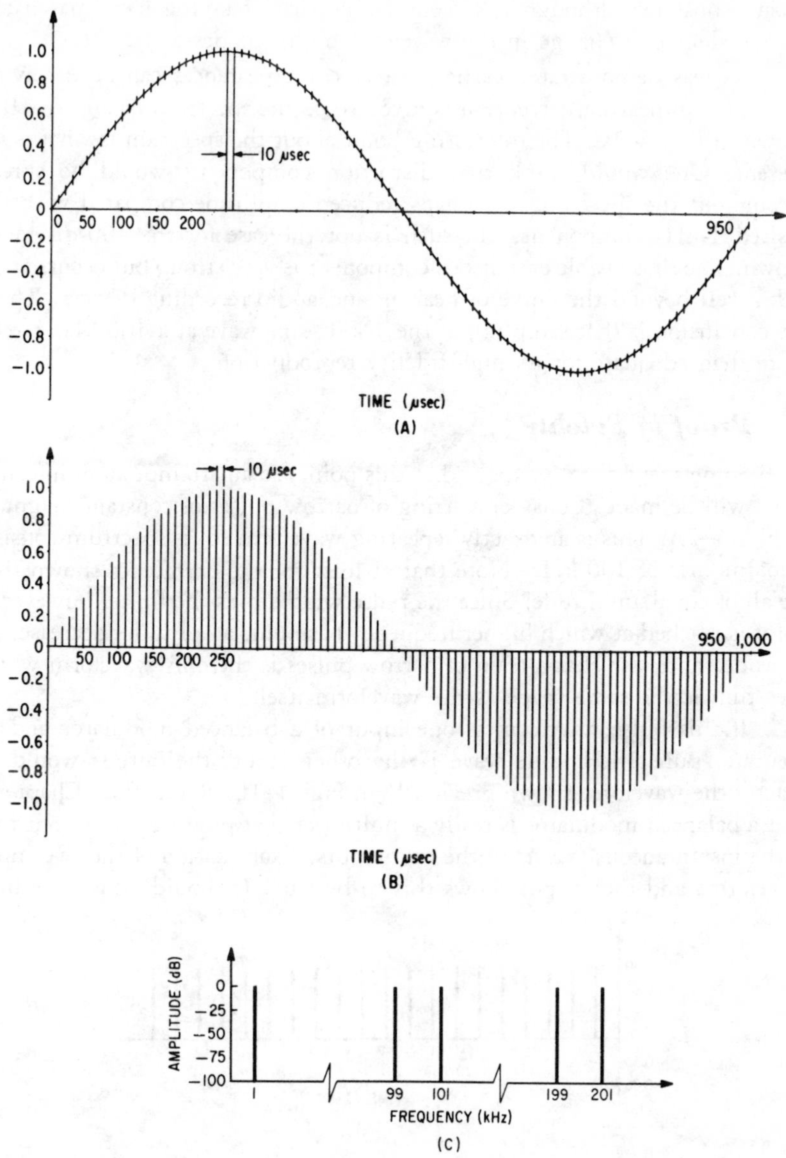

Fig. 4–1. (A) 1-kHz sine wave divided into 100 10μsec portions. (B) Sine wave approximation from DAC. (C) Spectrum of B.

pulses spaced at 10-μsec intervals. Each individual pulse or the number it represents is called a *sample* because it gives the waveform amplitude at a sample point in time. The frequency of the pulses is called the *sample rate* and in this case it is 100 ks/s (kilosamples per second). The sample rate is almost always constant, although it is conceivable that changing it to match the current degree of change in the waveform might be desirable.

As was demonstrated earlier, waveform appearances can be deceiving when human hearing perception is involved so the spectrum of Fig. 4–1B is shown in Fig. 4–1C. The interesting point about the spectrum is what is *not* present. One would think that distortion components would be spread throughout the spectrum at perhaps reduced amplitude compared with the desired 1-kHz component, but such is not the case for the 100-dB range shown. The first visible extraneous component is very strong but occurs at 99 kHz, well beyond the range of hearing and audio recording devices. Thus, the conclusion is that sampling of the 1-kHz sine wave at a 100-kHz rate is more than adequate for its high-fidelity reproduction.

Proof of Fidelity

Some skepticism is expected at this point, so an attempt at an informal proof will be made. Consider a string of narrow pulses of constant height as in Fig. 4–2A. This is an exactly repeating waveform so its spectrum consists of harmonics of 100 kHz. Note that at least for the harmonics shown they are all of equal amplitude. Since the pulse widths must be finite, however, a point is reached at which higher frequency harmonic amplitudes decrease. As an aside, note also that a train of narrow pulses is the only waveform whose spectrum is the same shape as the waveform itself.

If this pulse waveform is one input of a balanced modulator and an accurate, pure 1-kHz sine wave is the other input, the output would be exactly the waveform shown previously in Fig. 4–1B. Recall from Chapter 2 that a balanced modulator is really a multiplier that produces an output that is the instantaneous *product* of the two inputs. Examination of the two input waveforms and the output shows this to be true. It should also be recalled

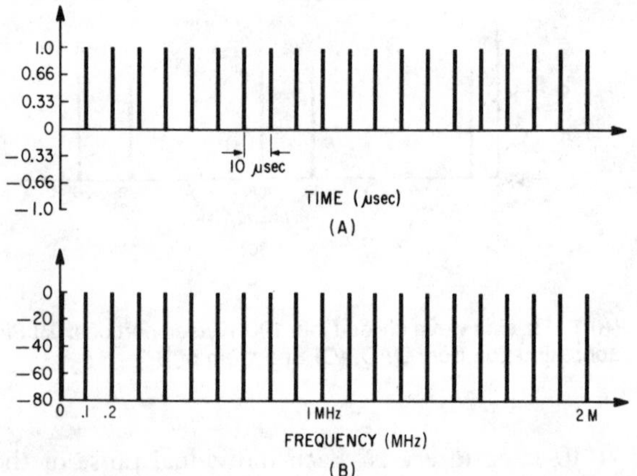

Fig. 4–2. Properties of a string of pulses. (A) String of narrow pulses. (B) Spectrum of A.

that if one input to the balanced modulator is a complex signal and the other input is a sine wave, then each component of the spectrum of the complex signal is split in half with one-half moving up and the other half moving down in frequency an amount equal to the sine wave input's frequency. This in fact is exactly what happened in Fig. 4–1C to produce pairs of components at 99 and 101 kHz, 199 and 201 kHz, and so on. The component at 1 kHz is due to the fact that the pulse train had a dc (zero frequency) component that was also split in half. The upper half moved up to 1 kHz and the lower half reflected through zero up to 1 kHz.

If desired, the spectrum of the sampled 1-kHz sine wave can be cleaned up with a low-pass filter. It is not very difficult to construct a filter that has essentially no effect at 1 kHz but that attenuates 99 kHz and higher frequencies so much that they can be ignored. If the sampled waveform of Fig. 4–1B were passed through such a filter all that would escape through the output would be the single 1-kHz frequency component, which would, of course, appear on an oscilloscope screen as a pure 1-kHz sine wave.

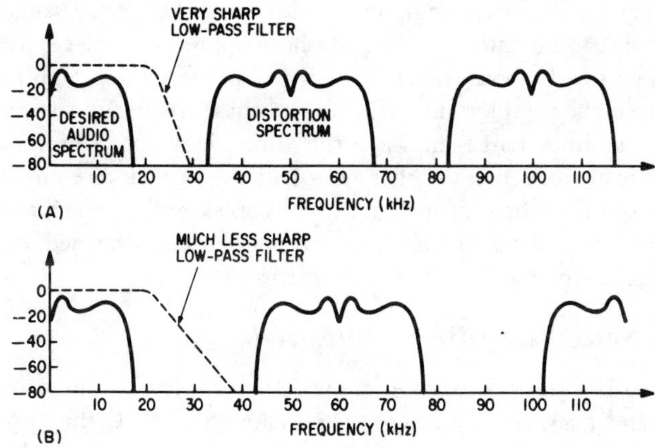

Fig. 4–3. Spectrum of sampled audio signals. (A) 50-ks/s sample rate. (B) 60-ks/s sample rate.

Setting the Sample Rate

Since reproduction of the 1-kHz wave was so satisfactory, how low can the sampling frequency be made before the results are unsatisfactory? If, for example, the sample rate was lowered to 50 ks/s, then the preceding analysis would predict a spectrum with a 1-kHz component, 49-kHz component, 51-kHz, 99-kHz, and so forth. Other than the need for a better filter, the situation is just as satisfactory as before. In fact, if a very good low-pass filter is available, the sample rate could be as low as a shade above 2 ks/s or only a little more than two samples per cycle of the sine wave. Obviously, the assumption that the wave did not change very much from sample to sample is not necessary.

Of course, for sound and music a whole spectrum of frequencies must be reproducible, not just single sine waves. Fortunately, a sampled arbitrary waveform behaves just the same as a sampled sine wave. The spectrum of the waveform is reproduced unaltered and then symmetrical pairs of copies around each harmonic of the sampling frequency are also introduced. Figure 4–3 shows the result of a full 20-Hz to 20-kHz audio spectrum sampled at a 50-ks/s rate. Since there is no overlap between the desired spectrum and the copies, a low-pass filter can once again be used to eliminate the copies.

The preceding argument is equally valid for conversion of sound waveforms into numbers. The waveform is first sampled with a balanced modulator or its equivalent and then the sample pulse amplitudes are measured with an analog-to-digital converter (ADC),which is nothing more than an ultrafast digital voltmeter. Each sample thus becomes a number that may then be processed by the computer. No information about the curves and undulations of the waveform is lost *provided* that the spectrum of the waveform has no frequency components above one-half of the sampling rate. Unfortunately, some natural sounds do have appreciable energy beyond the audible range so a low-pass filter is needed to prevent these high frequencies from reaching the sampler and ADC. Since these frequency components are beyond the audible range anyway, the filter does not audibly affect the sound. If signal frequencies higher than half the sample rate are allowed to enter the sampler, their offspring in the copies will overlap the original spectrum and will cause distortion. Such a situation is termed *aliasing* and the resulting distortion is called alias distortion.

Any Sound Can Be Synthesized

Figure 4–4 shows a block diagram of a complete computerized audio-to-digital and back to audio again conversion system. If the two low-pass filters are matched and have infinite attenuation beyond one-half of the sample rate, the waveforms at points A and B are *exactly* alike! Since the waveform at point A is not audibly different from the input, this is truly a high-fidelity system. The computer could also be programmed to supply its own stream of numbers to the DAC, and it therefore follows that the computer can produce *any* sound. Note also that the system has no low-frequency limitation, thus allowing signals down to dc to be reproduced.

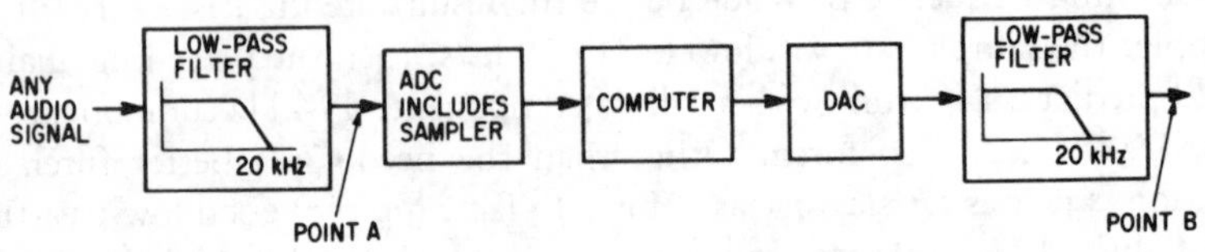

Fig. 4–4. Computerized digital audio system.

Recently, variations of the system shown in Fig. 4–4 have been used in ordinary sound record/playback applications. The "compact disk" digital audio playback system, for example, breaks the block marked "computer" in half but is otherwise the same. The left half becomes a digital modulator (to encode digital information onto an RF carrier wave) and laser scriber to produce a modified type of video disk. The right half becomes a laser scanner to recover the modulated RF carrier wave and a demodulator to recover the digital information, which is then passed on as before. Similar systems using a video cassette recorder in place of the laser disk are also available. Such systems far surpass regular analog disks and tapes in reproduction fidelity, thus further emphasizing the fact that *any* sound can be synthesized by a direct synthesis system.

The foregoing has all been an application of Nyquist's theorem, which states in mathematical terms that an ADC or a DAC can handle signal frequencies from zero up to a little less than one-half the sample rate with absolutely no distortion due to the sampling process whatsoever. The low-pass filters employed to separate the desired signal from the spectrum copies determine how close to the theoretical one-half limit one can get. The main requirement of the filter is that it attenuate spurious signals above one-half the sample rate enough to be ignored while leaving desired signals below one-half the sample rate unaltered. For high-fidelity applications, this means that very little attenuation of frequencies up to 20 kHz is allowed and that 50 dB or more attenuation above 30 kHz is desirable, assuming a 50-ks/s sample rate. A filter that sharp is fairly difficult to construct but is in the realm of practicality. Thus, a rule of thumb is that the sample rate should be 2.5 or more times the maximum signal frequency of interest with the larger figures allowing simpler filters to be used. This is shown in Fig. 4–3B, in which an increase in sample rate from 50-ks/s to 60-ks/s has reduced the filter cutoff slope requirement by half!

The sample rate may also be reduced for lower fidelity applications. The laser-disk- and videotape-based digital audio systems mentioned earlier operate at slightly over 44 ks/s. Broadcast FM quality may be obtained at 37.5 ks/s and ordinary AM radio quality (which can be surprisingly good through decent equipment) could be done at 15 ks/s to 20 ks/s. The advantage of lower sample rates, of course, is a reduction in the number of samples that must be computed for a given duration of sound.

Signal-to-Noise Ratio

Of course, frequency response is not the only measure of sound quality. Background noise is actually a much worse problem with standard analog audio equipment. Figure 4–1C clearly indicated that the sampling process itself did not introduce any background noise. However, when the samples are in numerical form, only a finite number of digits is available to represent them, and this limitation does indeed introduce noise. Such roundoff error is termed *quantization error* because a sample pulse, which can be any amplitude whatsoever, has been quantized to the nearest available numerical representation. Background noise due to quantization error is termed quantization noise.

An actual ADC or DAC usually has a definite maximum signal amplitude that it can handle. A typical value is from −10 to +10 V. Inputs to an ADC beyond this range are effectively clipped, and numerical inputs to a DAC beyond this range are converted into a value that fits. The 20-V range is then broken up into a large number of *quantization levels,* which is usually a power of two, since DACs and ADCs are typically binary devices. The number of quantization levels generally ranges from 256 to 65,536, which corresponds to 2^8 and 2^{16} or 8 and 16 bits, respectively.

Let us try to estimate the amount of background noise present in a 12-bit (4,096 level) DAC output so that the number of levels necessary for high-fidelity reproduction can be determined. Twenty volts divided by 4,096 equals 4.88 mV per level. Thus, the 500th level would be 2.44141 V and would have to be used for all desired voltages between 2.43895 and 2.44384 V. It is reasonable to assume that if the desired voltage level falls in this range, it is equally likely to be anywhere in the range and the same should be true for any other quantization level. Thus, the *average* error (difference between desired level and the nearest quantization level) is one-quarter of the difference between quantization levels. This works out to an average error amplitude of 1.22 mV. The maximum signal amplitude without distortion is 10 V. Therefore, the maximum signal-to-noise ratio is 10/0.00122 = 8,192. Expressed in decibels, this is about 78 dB. Actually, due to an oversimplified analysis, the average noise amplitude is really one-third of the quantization interval; thus, a more accurate figure is 76 dB.

If the number of quantization levels were doubled (one bit added to make 13), the denominator of the previous equation would be halved, resulting in an increase in the signal-to-noise ratio of 6 dB. Eliminating a bit would subtract 6 dB from the signal-to-noise ratio. In real DACs and ADCs, the quantization levels are not perfectly spaced or perfectly equal in size. Such imperfections add about 4 dB to the noise level. Thus, the signal-to-noise ratio that can be expected is approximately 6 dB times the number of bits in the DAC or ADC.

Compared with analog audio equipment, the 72 dB available from a 12-bit DAC is quite good, in fact better than any program source available to consumers and better even than much professional recording equipment. An increase to 16 bits, which is achieved by the newer direct synthesis installations, and one has dynamic range far exceeding any available analog recording device!

As a result, direct computer synthesis utilizing a 50-ks/s to 60-ks/s sample rate and 16-bit DACs is capable of unsurpassed audio quality. At the other end of the spectrum, 15 ks/s to 20 ks/s with 10 to 12 bits gives AM radio quality that is quite sufficient for experimentation. Rates as low as 8 ks/s to 10 ks/s with 8 bits are suitable for demonstrations and telephone quality but with the bass present.

A Typical Direct Computer Synthesis Installation

Until recently, very few of the computer installations used for music synthesis were used exclusively for that purpose. Most of them were just large campus or corporate computer centers with the added equipment necessary for digital-to-analog conversion and occasionally analog-to-digital conversion. One property of classic direct synthesis is that only a small portion of the expense and size of the equipment necessary is specialized for sound generation; the rest is standard computer gear that would be present anyway. Thus, in such cases in which the computer center already existed, the initial investment in sound synthesis was small. However, as we shall see later, the calculations necessary to produce the millions of samples needed for even a short musical piece can eat up large blocks of computer time, which, on the large machines, is priced by the second. Thus, as a practical matter, usage of the installation was budget limited after all.

Today it is possible for a music or electrical engineering department to have its own minicomputer installation with the hardware necessary for direct computer synthesis. Furthermore, these small, inexpensive computers have as much if not more power than the large mainframes of a few years ago. Although these systems are less convenient to program for sound synthesis, they are much more convenient to use because the computer's resources are not shared with hundreds of other users. Also, the cost of maintaining such a facility is no longer directly related to the running time of direct synthesis programs. It is perfectly feasible to allow a program to run all night computing another iteration of the 2-min finale to a 20-min piece.

Microcomputers and personal computers are also at the point where it is practical to consider their use in small direct synthesis systems for the purpose of experimentation and increasing flexibility. The power of these machines is surprisingly good with newer models equaling the power of minicomputers three or four years ago. Microcomputers are easily interfaced with conventional synthesis equipment for computer control applications such as automatic patching or sequencer use. With the proper peripheral equipment, they can do as good a job of direct synthesis for unique or otherwise impossible effects as more expensive systems although at a slower speed. The personal computer user, however, has only himself to please, so program running time is even less of a factor than with dedicated minicomputer installations.

Minimum System

Figure 4–5 shows the minimum hardware complement necessary for direct computer synthesis. Note, however, that the only device limiting the quality and complexity of the sound is the DAC and audio tape recorder for

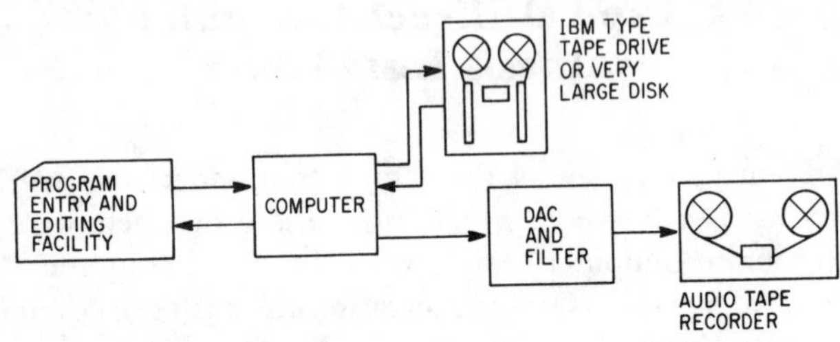

Fig. 4–5. Minimum system for direct computer synthesis.

recording the results. Otherwise the *full power* of the technique is available on this system. More elaborate setups can materially improve speed and convenience of use but do not directly improve the sound itself.

The program entry and editing facility is probably the most crucial in providing an easy to use system. Music of significant complexity requires dozens and even up to hundreds of pages of typed sound specifications, music notation adapted for computer use, and other instructions. The ability to easily enter and edit this information is of great importance. Perhaps the least desirable medium for this task is the old punch-card and printer listing approach. Use of a CRT terminal is probably the most desirable of all standard computer input techniques. Dedicated and personal installations may use any technique that is appropriate or affordable, although the CRT terminal approach is still the most likely.

The computer itself is not really very important. If one of the "canned" direct synthesis programs is to be used, the computer must be able to accept the language it was written in and have sufficient memory to hold the program. Speed is important, since it directly affects the running time of a synthesis program. The computer also should have "automatic multiply and divide," a feature that increases the effective speed of most synthesis programs by a factor of five or more.

Storage of Samples

It is safe to say that any serious direct synthesis program computing nontrivial music will not run in real time. This means that the 10,000 to 50,000 samples needed for each and every second of sound simply cannot be computed as fast as they are used. Also, without a great deal of difficulty and loss of efficiency, the rate that can be computed varies erratically according to sound complexity and other factors. Thus, the universal approach is to compute the samples at whatever rate the program runs and save them on a mass storage device capable of holding at least a couple million samples. An IBM-type computer tape drive is probably the most economically suitable device. A single $20 reel of tape can easily hold in excess of 10 million 16-bit samples, giving an uninterrupted running time of over 3 min at 50 ks/s. Large computer centers can also be expected to have enough disk capacity to hold a sizable number of samples, which offers several advantages over tape. Even the floppy disks commonly used in microcomputers can be a practical storage medium in experimental systems, although lower sample rates must be used and a single diskette can only hold 15–30 sec of sound.

After the samples have been computed and stored away, they must be passed through the DAC at the final intended sample rate. The obvious way to do this is to read the samples back from the mass storage device and transfer them at a constant rate to the DAC. For high fidelity, however, the sample rate must be rock steady; even a few nanoseconds jitter will increase the background noise level substantially. Thus, the DAC would typically have its own crystal clock and at least one sample buffer. The computer servicing the DAC for playback must be able to provide the next sample before the current one is finished. What this all means is that the computer must usually be totally dedicated to the task of reading samples and sending them to the DAC. Unfortunately, the operating systems of most large computers are unable to insure uninterrupted execution of a single program so music playback must be done in a stand-alone mode.

Often the expense of monopolizing the resources of a large computer cannot be borne so the disk or tape containing the samples is played through a DAC connected to a minicomputer. In the past, it was fairly common practice to build a specialized hardware device for reading sample tapes. The design of such a device was complicated by the fact that data on computer tape is grouped into records of perhaps 3,000 samples each with gaps of several hundred samples equivalent between. The playback device thus required a substantial buffer memory to insure the uninterrupted flow of data to the DAC. Of course, mini- or microcomputer installations for direct synthesis should not experience any of these problems.

Sometimes the tape or disk drives available on smaller systems may not be fast enough to provide the desired sample rate. This limitation may be compensated for by running the DAC at half of the desired sample rate and operating the audio tape recorder at half of the intended tape speed. Then when the audio tape is played at full speed, the desired sample rate will have been attained. One difficulty with this approach is that the high-frequency equalization of the audio recorder is switched according to tape speed, which would be expected to alter the high-frequency response somewhat. A more severe problem is that during recording bass frequencies down to 10 Hz will be generated but may not record. When played back at double speed, a distinct loss of bass is the result. Also, any power line hum in the recording will be reproduced at a much more audible 120 Hz.

As mentioned earlier, the low-pass filter following the DAC is critical. One might think that if the sample rate is above 40 ks/s a filter is not needed at all, since all unwanted frequencies are above the audible range anyway. However, since these frequencies are so strong, they can easily mix with the bias oscillator in an audio tape recorder and result in audible beat notes. Thus, a filter of at least moderate effectiveness is required with high sample rates. The filter becomes more critical at the lower sample rates used for experimentation because these unwanted frequencies are audible and sound terrible. Sharp cutoff low-pass filter design will be discussed in detail in Chapter 12.

Computation of Sound Waveforms

Now that it has been established that computers can generate sound of the highest quality directly, the next topic of interest is the techniques used for computing sound waveforms. Although one could theoretically sit down at a computer console and type in sample values, just about anything that could be done without recourse to a pocket calculator would sound like white noise on playback. The problem is similar to the one experienced when drawing waveforms directly onto movie film. Of course, this does not even address the difficulty of providing tens of thousands of samples for every second of sound output.

In this section, a general overview of practical methods of sound waveform computation will be presented. A more detailed description of these techniques and others along with example programs will be given in Section III.

Sin and Other Built-in Functions

An obvious method of generating a single sine wave with a computer is to use the sin function found in nearly all high-level programming languages. The general expression for the Nth sample of a sine wave of frequency F and the amplitude A is $Sn = A\sin(2\pi FT/Fs)$, where T is time in seconds and Fs is the sample rate in samples per second. Since time and sample number are directly proportional and the sample rate is constant, considerable computer time may be saved by defining a constant $K = 2\pi/Fs$ and using the form $Sn = A\sin(KnF)$. Samples for the sine wave are computed simply by defining values for the variables A and F and then evaluating the expression for sample numbers 0, 1, 2, up to M, where M/Fs is the duration in seconds desired for the wave.

Of course, during the calculations the values of A and F can change. Often separate expressions that are also evaluated every sample time determine the value of A and F to be used in the "tone generation" expression given above. Thus, amplitude envelopes, amplitude modulation, and frequency modulation are all very easily accomplished.

Other waveshapes may be easily computed even though a built-in function for the desired shape is not provided by the computer's programming language. A sawtooth wave, for example, is defined by the expression

$$Sn = A\left[2\left(\frac{nF}{Fs} \text{ MOD } 1.0\right) - 1\right]$$

where the mod function gives only the remainder when the expression to its left is divided by the expression to its right. A triangle wave may be formed from sawtooth samples by applying

$$Sn_{TRI} = 2A_{TRI}\left(\left|Sn_{SAW}\right| - \frac{A_{SAW}}{2}\right)$$

One must be careful when directly computing complex waveshapes with sharp corners and vertical lines because alias distortion can occur. When these waves are computed, they are computed perfectly with all of their harmonics up to infinity. However, those harmonics that exceed half the sample rate will be reflected back down into the audible spectrum and cause distortion. The problem is generally not severe as long as these waveforms are held to low frequencies, but it does prevent use of these shapes as fundamental basis waves such as is done in the voltage-controlled synthesizer.

Fourier Series

Probably the most flexible method of generating waveshapes by computer is to use the Fourier series. Individual sine wave harmonic (or specific nonharmonic) frequencies can be computed at selected phase angles and amplitudes and summed together to produce a composite waveform. Any problem with alias distortion due to high harmonics is circumvented by simply omitting those that exceed half the sample rate from the calculation. Of course, the amplitudes of individual components may be continuously varied for a changing spectrum shape. The effect of a filter with any arbitrary frequency response may be simulated by multiplying each harmonic amplitude by the filter response curve amplitude at the corresponding frequency.

Simultaneous Sounds

Simultaneous sounds are easily done by computing the string of samples for each sound and then simply *adding* the strings of samples together to get one string for the composite sound. Fortunately, the same effect is realized if one sample for each sound is computed and then the samples are added producing a single sample for the composite sound, thus greatly reducing storage requirements. The loudness of each sound in the combination can be easily controlled by multiplying its samples by a gain factor for the sound. It is a typical practice to compute all waveforms at the same amplitude level and then adjust their relative amplitudes when the sounds are mixed.

Since the DAC, which will eventually receive these composite samples, can only handle a limited range of values, it is usually convenient to define this range as being between −1.0 and +1.0 and then scale the samples immediately before being sent to the DAC. This allows the sound generation programming to be independent of the actual DAC that will be used for playback. The amplitudes of the individual samples being summed up is kept considerably below 1.0 so that there is no possibility of overflow and distortion.

Updating of Parameters

The computation methods described so far are completely flexible and allow the parameters of sound to be changed at will at any speed and in any manner. Unfortunately, they are also very expensive in terms of the computation time required. A particulary bad case is the sin function, which is usually very slow compared with the overall speed of the computer. In order to improve speed, it is necessary to impose some restrictions so that simplifying assumptions may be made. Of course, if a particular situation demands full flexibility, it may be invoked for the particular sound or time under consideration without affecting the computation efficiency of other sounds or portions of the piece.

One simplifying assumption is that amplitudes, frequencies, spectra, and other parameters of the sounds being synthesized do not change rapidly. Thus, the programming that computes these parameters from other data can be done at a slower rate than the waveform computation itself. For a 50-ks/s sample rate, it may be convenient to evaluate these slow-moving parameters every 25 samples rather then every sample. This, of course, reduces the computational load of these calculations by a factor of 25 but still gives a half millisecond timing resolution—a factor of 10 to 20 better than hearing perception. Since it is these slower variations that add most of the interest to sounds, they may now be made more complex without appreciably extending the total computation time for the piece.

Table Lookup

Another assumption is that waveforms change little, if any, from one cycle to the next. Thus, one cycle of the waveform may be placed in a table and then table lookup techniques applied to quickly retrieve the samples. Most computers can perform a table lookup in considerably less time than even a simple sample computation. Unfortunately, implementation of the technique is complicated somewhat by the fact that, for most frequencies, there is a nonintegral number of samples per cycle of the waveform. The problem is solved by tabulating the waveform at a frequency for which there *is* an integral number of cycles per sample. When table lookup is required at a different frequency, the table lookup routine, for example, might be requested to "find the 8.763rd entry" in the table. Interpolation between the 8th and 9th sample may be performed or, if the table is large enough, the nearest tabulated entry, which would be the 9th, would be used. There is thus a tradeoff between table size, lookup time, and sound quality, since errors result in background noise being added to the waveform. Since the costs of memory are declining faster than the speed of memory or computers is increasing, table lookup without interpolation is a frequently used technique. In fact, completely table-driven synthesis programs are possible. Note that the table method can also be applied to envelopes and any other curve that is likely to be used more than once. Table lookup methods will be studied in detail in Chapter 13 and again in Chapter 20.

Hardware Aids

Another way to increase computation speed is to connect some specialized hardware to the computer that is designed to be especially efficient in the calculations typically needed for music. For the microcomputer user, a hardware multiplier would be of great benefit if his microprocessor chip does not have multiply and divide built in. The difference in processing speed can easily be 10:1 over multiplication in software and might result in a three- to fivefold increase in overall music program speed. The multiplier could be expanded into a multiplier-summer, which would speed up sum-of-products calculations such as a Fourier series. A full array processor normally performs high-speed operations on matrices and vectors such as multiplication, addition, and even inversion. In sound synthesis, it could be used to compute several samples of several sounds at once and thus greatly speed things up. A device known as a "fast Fourier transform processor" is specifically optimized for computing Fourier transforms. Although normally used to rapidly compute the spectrum of a waveform for sound and vibration analysis, most can also compute a waveform given the spectrum. Although there are limitations in using a Fourier transform processor for generating changing waveforms, its availability can be a great asset.

Digital Sound Modification

Nearly all of the sound modification techniques described in Chapter 2 can be easily implemented in a direct computer synthesis system. Spectrum modification by means of filtering can be accomplished with *digital filters.* Actually, a digital filter is nothing more than an equation that specifies the Nth output sample as a function of several previous input samples and some filter response parameters. A special case is the *recursive* digital filter, which only uses the previous output sample and the current input sample along with response parameters to produce an output sample. All of the common filter amplitude response shapes such as low-pass, bandpass, and high-pass are easily done with recursive digital filters. Arbitrary response shapes can also be done in a straightforward manner with nonrecursive digital filters. Calculation time is longer with these, since several up to several hundred previous input samples are evaluated to produce the output but the response shapes produced would be very difficult to duplicate with recursive digital or analog filters. As with all other direct synthesis techniques, there is no real limit to the number of digital filters that may be in use simultaneously. Usually the programming is done with a small group of routines for the different general types of filters and then the characteristics of specific filters in use at the time are simply numbers stored in a table in memory.

Reverberation and chorus effects previously described are also easily done. One of the simplest operations in a direct synthesis system is delay. All that is required for delay is a memory buffer and a simple program for storing current samples into and withdrawing delayed samples from the buffer. Very little computation time is required for a delay function, although the buffer memory could become substantial for long or multiple delays. Delay times are easily varied in whole sample increments and interpolation may be used for even finer increments. Thus, all methods for reverberation and chorus may be applied directly and even refined considerably. If time is no object, the characteristics of a particular concert hall may be duplicated using only the waveform of a spark discharge (or other repeatable sharp sound) recorded in the actual hall for input.

The tape-splicing methods covered earlier can be done also and with great efficiency. Generally, the computer system should have a large disk storage facility for quick access to a library of recorded natural and synthetic sounds. The largest part of such a sound-editing system is simply the bookkeeping needed to keep track of sound fragments in various stages of completion. The actual cutting and splicing operations could be done at a graphic display console showing actual waveforms or spectra with a light pen to specify the cut or splice points.

One modification technique that does not always work well when done digitally is nonlinear waveshaping. Since clipping and other waveshape distortions are likely to generate strong high-frequency harmonics, alias distortion can become a problem. If necessary, the distortion operation can be done at a much higher sample rate at which the alias distortion is less of a problem, then digitally low-pass filtered to less than half of the system sample rate, and finally resampled. Fortunately, such gross distortion techniques are seldom needed when more refined techniques are available.

Music Programming Systems and Languages

Although most of the calculations required for direct computer synthesis are fairly simple, it is not very practical to create a piece of music by programming the equations one by one as needed and then assembling everything as one large, highly specialized program. Instead, general-purpose music programming systems are used. Besides reducing redundant programming effort, a music programming system provides the framework necessary for the orderly utilization of the infinite flexibility of direct computer synthesis. Also such programming systems make it possible for users with little computer background to effectively, if not optimally, utilize the system.

Two fundamental kinds of music programming systems can be readily identified. A tightly structured system is planned from the start with specific goals in mind. In it are all of the elements and functions necessary for the specification and computation of all sounds falling within the system goals. A distinguishing feature of tightly structured systems is the presence of a specification or *music language* for controlling the system. A loosely structured system basically consists of a central data base and a collection of programs for processing information into or out of the data base. The individual programs in the collection are essentially independent and new programs may be written at any time. Systems of this type are usually the product of evolution. Note that the programs comprising a tightly structured system could easily be part of a larger loosely structured system.

Tightly Structured System

The *music* programming languages found in tightly structured systems are entirely different from typical *computer* programming languages. One type, which will be discussed in detail in Chapter 18, has a simplified structure and therefore limited goals. NOTRAN, for example, was designed for playing organ music. Due to this very narrow subset of possibilities a great many simplifying assumptions could be made. For example, musical conventions of pitch, duration, rhythm, and in fact conventional music notation itself could all be utilized to simplify the structure and language of the system. The calculations involved in computing the waveforms, envelopes, and other parameters were narrowed to specific types. The programming necessary for these calculations was all done by the system implementor and need not concern the user. In fact, the user need only translate the written score for a piece into the NOTRAN language and then define a number of parameters for each organ voice used in the piece. The NOTRAN processor then interprets the translated score and voice parameters and sends this interpreted information to the "prefabricated" sound computation routines that actually compute the samples.

Statements within the NOTRAN language are placed in strict time sequence from beginning to end. Program flow and music flow are identical and linear from one statement to the next. Statements are of two basic types, control and sound specification. Control statements make no sound and take no time themselves but do influence events occurring *after* their appearance up until another control statement of the same type redefines the control function. Voice statements (which describe the timbre or "stops" of a specified voice) and tempo statments (which determine the speed of playing) are of this type.

Sound specification statements, on the other hand, do cause the generation of sound and take time in a musical sense. A single note statement, for example, may consist of many separate note specifications, each corresponding to an individual note in the score and all starting simultaneously. Consecutive notes each have their own note statements. Thus, notes in NOTRAN are specified in two dimensions: horizontally for different pitches at the same time (harmony) and vertically for sequencing. A note specification specifies a voice, a pitch, a duration, and an articulation (such as staccato). Additional parameters describing the timbre of the specified voice are taken from the last encountered corresponding voice statement. After a piece has been coded in the NOTRAN language, the job is essentially over. The complete specification of the sound is contained in the resulting string of NOTRAN statements, and all that remains to be done is to run the program and record the results.

As can be seen, NOTRAN is highly structured and very limited. This does not mean, however, that enhancements would not be possible. For example, a couple of years after it was first defined and implemented, percussion sounds were added. A percussive voice definition statement type was added and percussive note specifications were formulated. This feature was added, however, in a manner completely consistent with the existing structure of the system. With such a constraint, there are definite limits to expansion.

Maximum Flexibility System

A second type of structured music system is similar but has as a goal maximum usable flexibility. Even with such a goal it is still necessary to make simplifications although not nearly as severe. The MUSIC V system, for example, retains the concept of a note that is best described as an event. A piece consists of a quantity of events, each starting at specified points in time independent of their durations or other events. Another simplification is that the system actually simulates an idealized, modular synthesizer similar in concept to the voltage-controlled equipment described previously. For the most part, sounds are generated by specifying the inputs and interconnections of imaginary modules that themselves must be specified. In most cases, the user can actually think in terms of standard voltage-controlled modules but with functions, accuracy, range, and quantity impossible to achieve with real modules.

The actual music language associated with MUSIC V is quite different from that of NOTRAN. In particular there is no parallel with standard music notation. Instead, all of the information is in terms of physical sound parameters such as frequency in hertz, amplitude in volts or decibels, time in milliseconds, etc. Often tables of values are used to specify how each of these parameters are to change with time during an event.

The MUSIC V processor is actually configured into three *passes* or scans of the input data. During pass one, the services of a macroprocessor program are available to allow certain repetitive statements to be generated under the control of higher-level parameters. Also done during pass one is instrument definition as a combination of predefined modules called *unit generators*. Integration of parameters in graphic form into the score is also possible. One unique feature of the MUSIC V system is that during pass one the statements describing instruments and notes do not have to be in time order. This feature makes the macroprocessor more flexible and easily applied.

Pass two is a sorting program that sequences the output from pass one into strict time sequence. At this point, some additional processing of parameters that influence a number of sequential notes can be performed, since the statements are in time sequence. For example, time scale shifts for retards or fine frequency ratio control among simultaneous notes would normally be done during pass two.

Pass three is the actual language interpreter and sound generation program. It works much like the NOTRAN interpreter just described except that it is much more sophisticated. One or two streams of samples may be produced for monophonic and stereophonic sound, respectively.

Extending the MUSIC V system is much less restricted than with NOTRAN. Most desirable expansions amount to writing additional processing programs for pass one. For example, it would be possible to write a processor that would convert a NOTRAN score into equivalent MUSIC V complete with equivalent voices constructed from available unit generators. Additional unit generators or even entire instruments that are not conveniently described in terms of unit generators could also be added to pass three.

Loosely Structured Systems

Looking again at loosely structured systems, the data base is seen to be the most important component of the system, in fact, the only link that holds it all together. Several different kinds of data can be kept in the data base. Using a hypothetical system as an example, it is obvious that sample data representing a previously computed piece or sampled natural sounds would be present. Curves of all sorts such as amplitude envelopes, spectrum shapes, and actual waveforms would also be present. Finally, text representing perhaps statements in one or more music languages or just lists of instructions would be there too.

The purpose of a program in the loosely structured system is to either convert data from the data base into sound; take data out, process it, and put it back in a different form; or convert external information into a suitable form and enter it into the data base. A sound output program is an example of the first type because it would take sample data from the data base and convert it to sound through the DAC. A reverberation simulator would take sample data and perhaps a list of instructions from the data base and return reverberated samples to the data base. A synthesizer program would take language statements and curves out and produce samples. A macroprocessor could take statements in a very powerful, structure-oriented rather than note-oriented music language and convert them into statements (probably much more numerous) in a lower music language. This would circumvent the immediate necessity of an interpreter for the new language. An input processor program might look at a keyboard interfaced to the system and convert the key action it sees into music language statements or other suitable form. A sound analysis program could take sample data and produce curves representing the changing parameters of the sound analyzed. Nearly an infinite variety of possibilities exist for programs in such a system.

Using a loosely structured system is not unlike tape-editing methods for producing electronic music. Initial sound material or language statements are taken through a sequence of steps using various programs until the final result is obtained. At intermediate points, the piece may exist as a number of fragments at various stages of processing. Contrast this to a highly structured system in which the entire specification for the piece is self-contained in a string of language statements.

Because of its very nature, the loosely structured system is easily and almost infinitely expandable. The only limitation is the structure of the data base itself. Even that can be expanded by adding more data types, but a proliferation of conversion programs could develop if many were added.

5

Microprocessors

The development of microprocessors and the subsequent refinement of semiconductor memories to go with them will undoubtedly become the most important technological breakthrough of this half-century. Even now they are finding their way into all kinds of products from microwave ovens to music synthesizers. Eventually, it will become so cheap to apply computer intelligence to products that it will be done almost automatically if even the slightest need exists. However, such widespread application is still in the future, although nobody really knows if that means 2 years or 10.

Returning to the present, the significance of microprocessors in music synthesis is that the cost of doing things with computers is now much less than it was a few years ago. For the most part, computer music techniques, both direct and synthesizer controlled, were hypothesized and developed years ago by well-backed institutions. So although no really new techniques are made possible by microprocessors, the existing ones can now, or soon be, utilized by individuals at a reasonable cost. Also, the low cost of components makes practical the implementation of some of the grander schemes that have only been hypothesized in the past.

Sequencers, for example, have been very expensive (compared to other modules in a voltage-controlled system) and highly specialized devices. Their innards consisted of dozens to a couple of hundred digital integrated circuits, and their front panels had several dozen controls. Even with all of this, it took only a few minutes of use to discover just how limited those devices were. Now a microprocessor in conjunction with a few integrated circuits can perform all of the functions of even the most sophisticated sequencers and still be grossly underutilized. Panel control action and quantity can be designed more for the convenience of the user rather than for the simplification of logic circuitry. The microprocessor is inherently reprogrammable for altered or enhanced function, although sequencer manufacturers may not always encourage this. In fact, microprocessors today are often designed into a product (not just musically oriented ones) as a cost-saving or performance-improving measure and are not even mentioned in advertising literature or the user's manual. The reason given for such behavior is that users are not yet sophisticated enough to handle the increased flexibility offered by programmability.

The forces necessary to change this attitude are already at work, however, because the increasing number of computers in use also brings on increased public awareness of their nature, and most importantly, programmability. In the 1960s, computers were so expensive that only large corporation accounting departments and well-financed research organizations could afford them. Consequently, there were very few people working with and knowledgable about computers and programming. Now with inexpensive business and school computers and particularly millions of home and hobby computers, many more people are being exposed to programming concepts. It has been proven many times with elementary school children that programming itself is an easy skill to acquire, and what's more, is nearly intoxicating when introduced properly. Thus, a more aware public will encourage designers of all microprocessor products, not just synthesis equipment, to make available full flexibility through programming.

In this chapter, a cursory review of the history of microprocessors will be given and the important characteristics of three microprocessor chips that will be exemplified in Sections II and III will be outlined. Unfortunately, a tutorial overview of microprocessor hardware and software fundamentals would require an entire book this size to cover. For those unfamiliar with computers in general, there are indeed several such volumes, at least one of which should be read in conjunction with the remaining text of this book. Those only familiar with a high-level computer language such as BASIC or FORTRAN should also study the sections of those books devoted to machine code programming. The discussion to follow will therefore assume some familiarity with fundamental hardware and software concepts so that we may concentrate on the specifics of music synthesis with microprocessors.

Microprocessor Terminology

The terminology that will be used *very* frequently in the discussions to follow needs to be defined. A *microprocessor* is the central processing unit (CPU) of a computer system built with a small number of integrated circuits. Most microprocessors are single IC chips, although the more powerful ones may be a *set* of highly specialized ICs specifically designed to work together. Standard logic components have also been put on a single printed circuit board and marketed as "microprocessors," but they do not fit the present definition.

A *microcomputer* is a microprocessor with program memory, data storage memory, and input and output means added. It is functionally equivalent to the contents of conventional minicomputer cabinets. Recently, single-chip microcomputers have become available. Although they satisfy the definition, the size of the memories and I/O system provided and the difficulty or impossibility of expansion make them special-purpose devices unsuited for most general-purpose computer applications. However, they do have significant potential in music synthesis, which will be shown later.

A microcomputer *system* is a microcomputer with actual I/O devices added. The ease of use and ultimate potential of the system is strongly related to the speed and type of I/O equipment present. Also, the majority of the cost of the system is due to I/O gear. A *general-purpose* system is one with a sufficient software and I/O complement to be easily used for many types of applications. For most work, this simply means that the system has program development capability, program assembly or compilation capability, and program execution capability. For many of the musical applications of microprocessors that will be discussed, a general-purpose system is a necessity.

Brief History of Microprocessors

Although the history of microprocessors has been short, it has been very interesting. Reviewing their history here is relevant because it gives an idea of what to expect for the future. This is important in music synthesis because today's large computer techniques will be implemented on tomorrow's personal microcomputer. The dates given in this synopsis are not the manufacturer's official introduction dates but rather the approximate dates of availability of the devices to individuals and small businesses. Larger companies undoubtedly had access to information and prototype chips well before general availability.

The microprocessor started out as just an ordinary calculator chip that was documented well enough by the manufacturer so that customers could program it. Its initial use was simply to expedite the development of specialized hand-held calculators and business machines such as cash registers. Shortly thereafter, the semiconductor manufacturers realized that, whenever a microprocessor chip was sold, memory ICs to hold the programs were also sold. In fact, it was often the case that more money was spent on memory than the microprocessor. Thus, the expense of developing ever more sophisticated microprocessor chips was justified on the expectation of increased profits from memory device sales!

The First True Microprocessor

The first well publicized *true* microprocessor was the 4004 from Intel, first available in early 1972. "True" here means a device that works primarily in the binary number system; is at least theoretically infinitely expandable in program memory size, data memory size, and I/O capability; and can handle text characters as easily as numbers. Such a device could, if the necessary effort were expended, be programmed to handle *any* kind of computer task except at a slower speed. Intel marketed the 4004 strictly as logic replacement where speed was not important but logic decision complexity was high such as in traffic light controllers or automatic bowling pin setters. The 4-bit word size, instruction set, and data memory-addressing method utilized by the 4004, however, seemed quite strange to those already familiar with mini- and maxicomputers, so they did not show much interest in using the device for conventional computer applications. Another inhibition to its use by individuals and small enterprises was the virtual requirement that specialized, mask-programmed[1] memory components from Intel be used.

The First Popular Microprocessor

Several months later, Intel made available the 8008 microprocessor. This 8-bit machine overcame many of the problems of the 4004. It was designed to be usable with standard memory components from a variety of manufacturers. Its method of addressing memory was much more conventional with program and data memory being identical. Also, it could directly address without bank switching 16K bytes, an amount considered ample at the time. Its instruction set was definitely limited but conventional enough to be identified with the instruction sets of the smaller minicomputers. The major limitations of the 8008 were slow speed and a rudimentary interrupt capability.

This air of conventionality and familiarity, however, was the key to its success and, in the opinion of some, the cause of sooner-than-expected use of microprocessors as minicomputer replacements in many applications. What was actually being offered was not a cheaper way to make traffic light controllers but a *computer,* with all of the capabilities and potential of other much more expensive computers. People knowledgeable about computers realized this and acted on it. University electrical engineering, chemical engineering, and computer science departments launched microcomputer projects so that each student could work with a real computer in lab sessions. Entrepreneurs dreamed up small microcomputer-based systems and immediately set out to develop them. Hard-core hobbyists started building their own computers around the 8008. The semiconductor manufacturers found customers writing huge, complex programs and adding extra outboard logic to the microprocessor to overcome the weaknesses that still remained.

The Dawn of Personal Computing

One event of major significance was the publication in one of the major hobby electronics magazines in March 1974 of an article describing a build-

[1]A mask-programmed memory device incurs a tooling charge of $750 to $2,000 and a minimum order of 25 copies or more. Any change to the program requires a new mask. Thus, such a technique is only suitable for large-quantity production.

it-yourself computer based on the 8008. Although a handful of dedicated hobbyists had been constructing computers from surplus parts as much as 6 years earlier, this was the first public exposure of the concept that computers can make a fascinating hobby. Immediately, significant interest in the MARK-8 arose along with three newsletter-type publications devoted to the computer hobby. Hundreds of machines were eventually built, which may seem small until compared to only a couple dozen hobby computers in existence prior to that article.

Toward the end of 1974, Intel made available its successor to the 8008: the 8080. This machine was indeed an enhancement of the 8008 and was influenced heavily in its design by what people were coaxing the 8008 to do. Among its improvements were a tenfold increase in speed, quadrupled memory-addressing capability, unlimited stack length, and a number of added convenience instructions to perform tasks that were found to be subroutines in nearly all 8008 programs. A few months earlier, National Semiconductor introduced its IMP-16 microprocessor. This device (actually a set of five ICs) was not just similar to a minicomputer, it was a full 16-bit minicomputer CPU with multiple addressing modes and optional multiply/divide (a sixth IC). For some unknown reason, probably related to the marketing approach, it never caught on like the 8080.

In the 1975 time frame, every major semiconductor company introduced a microprocessor. Motorola, for example, entered their 6800 into the race at this time. Its organization philosophy was very different from the 8080 in emphasizing efficient addressing of memory over numerous on-chip registers. Its bus timing protocol was also much simplified and, in the author's opinion, was more effective. The 6800 was also the first microprocessor to operate entirely from a single 5-V power supply.

Shortly thereafter, MOS Technology offered the 6501, which was plug-in compatible with the 6800. Its instruction set was entirely different, however, and in many ways substantially superior. It was the first microprocessor to use *pipelining* to speed up internal operations. Most significant, however, was its price, which, at $25, was 8 to 10 times less than the prevailing price of microprocessors. This was more in line with true manufacturing costs, thus rapidly forcing the other suppliers to adjust their pricing structure accordingly. A lawsuit by Motorola subsequently forced slight changes (actually improvements) to the 6501's electrical interface so that it was not compatible with the 6800, and the model's number was changed to 6502.

Also during this time, Signetics offered their 2650, while RCA introduced their COSMAC, and General Instruments announced the 1600 (technically a 16-bit unit). National Semiconductor simplified their IMP-16 into the PACE (another 16-bit unit) and then further simplified it into the 8-bit SCAMP (later SC/MP). Other manufacturers opted to copy existing architectures, with Texas Instruments making the 8080 and Intersil offering a 12-bit microprocessor that was Digital Equipment PDP-8 software compatible. A new company called Zilog was formed to make a substantially improved 8080 called, appropriately enough, the Z-80. All of these companies ultimately offered complete computers built around their microprocessors, but none was ever successful in the general microcomputer market.

The Altair 8800 Microcomputer

The next milestone in the popularization of microprocessors has to be the *announcement* in January 1975 of the Altair 8800 microcomputer kit by MITS as a feature article in another major hobby electronics magazine. Announcement is emphasized because machines were not delivered until several months later. Nevertheless, tremendous excitement and quite a bit of confusion was created by the announcement. The excitement was due to the microprocessor chip used: the yet to be generally available, exceedingly powerful (compared to the 8008) 8080. Also, the availability of a kit interested many more people who were not skilled enough to acquire parts and etch printed circuit boards themselves. One confusing factor was the price of the kit; $60 less than the current price of the microprocessor IC itself, and the kit contained cabinet, power supply, and several dozen additional ICs and other parts necessary to support the microprocessor. Most could not believe that the $360 8080 chip was actually included! This time thousands of machines were ordered and delivered, and real magazines sprang up to meet the tide of interest created.

MITS itself was completely overwhelmed with thousands of orders, which explains the delivery delays that have since become commonplace in the industry. Had they been able to deliver immediately, the subsequent evolution of the hobby computer industry may have been entirely different with one manufacturer in a position of complete dominance. As it was, the market was thrown wide open to dozens of small companies that materialized to meet the demand.

Since the Altair used a parallel bus structure with sockets for plugging in extra memory and peripheral equipment interfaces, these same companies were able to effectively compete in the add-on market even after MITS started delivering machines. This bus structure, now called the S-100 bus, has become a defacto standard in 8080 (and later Z-80) systems because such a variety of CPU, memory, and peripheral interface boards are available. Keen competition in the S-100 marketplace kept prices low and innovation high.

The First Wave

The original Altair, and later Imsai and some others, were strictly "hobby" computers. They were nearly always built from kits and expanded piecemeal as time and resources permitted. In most cases, software consisted of little more than what the owner could write and perhaps copy from magazine articles or friends at computer club meetings. The mass storage hardware and operating system software that makes a computer easy and efficient to use was not often seen on these machines.

Then in 1976–77, three *integrated* microcomputers were introduced, two by relatively large companies, and each gained a large following. The PET (Personal Electronic Transactor) computer manufactured by Commodore was the first. Actually, Commodore had already made a name for itself in the pocket calculator business but at the time was struggling. The PET was truly integrated with a keyboard, display monitor, and tape cassette storage all in the same cabinet. Most important, a large amount of software was built-in as a ROM, including a highly sophisticated (at the time) and speedy BASIC interpreter and rudimentary operating system for controlling the cassette storage. One weakness in comparison to S-100 computers was the lack of a convenient expansion facility. The $600 asking price (which later proved to be a teaser) was an incredible shock, being much less than what a similarly equipped S-100 type computer would cost. One reason for the low price was that Commodore, who had earlier acquired MOS Technology, manufactured most of the key ICs themselves, including the 6502 microprocessor, the masked ROM, and the memory ICs. The 6502 in fact had been invented by MOS Technology while they were independent and had many advantages over the then popular 8080 in an integrated computer product.

Shortly thereafter, Radio Shack introduced its TRS-80 computer. The name was simply an abbreviation of the manufacturer (Tandy Radio Shack), while the 80 referred to its Z-80 microprocessor, which was a substantially improved 8080. Radio Shack packaged their machine differently than Commodore did. The computer and keyboard were combined into a single, somewhat overgrown keyboard case, whereas the display, cassette storage, and power supply were each separate units. All were connected to the keyboard unit by cables and each was separately priced. The ROM software was similar with an operating system and BASIC, although the latter was a greatly simplified version of the language. Expansion was better provided for in that larger-capacity-memory ICs could simply be plugged in, and a separate expansion box having even more memory and a disk controller was later offered. Pricing for a comparable system turned out to be somewhat less than the PET's, which had risen to $800. This, coupled with Radio Shack's thousands of already existing electronics stores, made the machine an instant hit with sales that quickly outstripped the PET's early lead.

The third popular computer of the period was not designed in the engineering department of a large company. Instead it evolved from an earlier model in the California basement of two entrepreneurs, Steve Wozniak and Steve Jobs. The Apple II was packaged much like the TRS-80 but had a built-in power supply and used a 6502 microprocessor like the PET. Its ROM operating system was more advanced than the other two, however, but, like the TRS-80, the BASIC interpreter was a simplified integer-only version. Two features set it apart, however, and, in the author's opinion, were responsible for its ultimate success. One of these was its much superior display, which offered full color (when used with a color monitor) and, for the first time in a microcomputer, true bit-mapped graphics at a moderately high resolution (280 wide × 192 high). The other was the presence, right in its keyboard enclosure, of eight unused printed circuit board edge connectors where expansion boards could be easily plugged in. Because of the designers' background as hobbyists, the Apple's hardware and software were thoroughly documented, which further accelerated support by other hardware and software manufacturers and user groups.

During this time, S-100 computers were also being improved. The early practice of entering "bootstrap loader" programs through the front panel switches was replaced by ROM boards, while video display boards displaced teletypewriters as the primary user interface. Most important, however, was the increased use of floppy disks for mass storage in place of tape cassettes. This was made possible by the introduction of the CP/M operating system in a generic form, which could be easily adapted to the wide and somewhat disjointed variety of S-100 systems available. As would be expected due to their inherently expandable and modular nature, it was possible to build an S-100 computer that was much more powerful than the PET, TRS-80, Apple, and other similar but less well-known machines. With memory capacities as large as 64K, S-100 computers could start being used for serious business, engineering, and research purposes.

The Second Wave

The introduction and success of these three microcomputers and others during 1976–77 caught the attention of numerous entrepreneurs, venture capitalists, and, to a lesser extent, larger established companies. During the 1978–80 time period, many, many more integrated microcomputers were introduced. Simultaneously there was an explosion of computer clubs, computer stores, computer magazines, and both regional and national computer shows to support the marketing needs of this sudden increase in available machines. The split between home/hobby/educational usage and business applications that barely showed up earlier widened considerably.

The business side showed the most growth probably because, at the time, the business market was seen to be larger and more immediate than the home/hobby/educational market. The basic S-100 hardware architecture and CP/M operating system dominated the design of second-wave business microcomputers. In nearly all cases, the microprocessor was a Z-80, memory was 64K bytes, and the display was a separate 24-line × 80-character terminal. Floppy disk mass storage was obligatory, but many shifted from 8-inch diskettes to the less expensive and lower capacity 5-inch size. Costs were further reduced by integrating all of the standard circuitry onto one motherboard to which was added several S-100 bus sockets for memory and I/O expansion. Several of these machines even omitted the sockets (and the power supply capacity needed to drive them), opting instead for a minimum-cost "standardized" computer.

Dozens of computers of this type were developed and introduced to the marketplace. The lack of diversity and in many cases virtual identity led to the first use of "clone" in magazine reviews of many of these systems. Ultimate success became largely a matter of who could manufacture machines at the lowest cost and market them most effectively. As a result, most of these computers had relatively short lifetimes, many only a few months, and some never went beyond the announcement stage.

Also during this time, the "original three" were upgraded to meet business needs but still retained their architectural identity. Commodore offered floppy disk drives for the PET and later upgraded its display from 40 to 80 characters per line. Apple also offered a disk drive and much improved BASIC, although the display was kept at 40 characters. Interestingly enough, independent companies developed Apple-compatible plug-in boards to expand the display to 80 characters and changed the microprocessor to a Z-80, thus allowing the CP/M operating system and associated business software to run. Radio Shack also offered disks for the TRS-80, but nothing was ever done about the display, which was 16 lines of 64 characters. Also, the architecture was not compatible with CP/M, even though a Z-80 microprocessor was used. However, since TRS-80s outnumbered other microcomputers at the time, much business software was written specifically for it.

There was also much activity in the home/hobby/education arena where participation was more by established companies rather than new startups. Atari, who had established themselves with arcade video games, offered their model 400 and 800 computers. Packaged much like an Apple and even using the same 6502 microprocessor, these machines were intended for a somewhat less sophisticated audience. One new feature they offered was a *ROM cartridge slot* that could be accessed without removing the cover or even turning the power off. The idea was that software packages could be offered on ROM in enclosed "cartridges" that could be changed in the computer as easily as cassette tapes are changed in a stereo system. Texas Instruments introduced their 99/4 computer, which was intended for the same audience. Technologically, it was a quantum leap past anything else at the time and included a 16-bit microprocessor (the TI 9900), very sophisticated color graphics IC, and four-voice sound (one might hesitate to call it music) generator. Its sophistication was largely wasted, however, because the machine's complex architecture was kept secret and TI software obscured its inherent power. Amid much speculation about dominating the market, Heath introduced a Z-80-based kit computer called the H-8. Although bus-organized much like the S-100 machines, it turned out to be incompatible with them. In spite of the speculation, it never was very successful. Mattell also introduced a 6502-based machine that never became popular.

Not all of the companies were established, however. Exidy offered their 8080 based Sorcerer, which was best known for its programmable character generator approach to graphics. Another was the Superbrain, remembered for its flashy ad campaign. Micro Technology Unlimited, previously a small add-on board manufacturer, offered their 6502-based MTU-130 near the end of this period. It had many advanced hardware and software features, such as an independent (from the CPU) disk controller and very fast, device-independent disk-operating system, which were fully appreciated only by advanced hobbyist and research users.

Strangely enough, the original three continued to fare well in the hobby/education arena. The TRS-80 benefitted from its low price, ready availability, and extensive coverage in new TRS-80-specific magazines. Also some schools had started using it in courses. The PET also found significant acceptance in schools, largely due to its all-in-one packaging and an educational "3-for-2" promotion by Commodore. In Canada and Europe, however, the PET did extremely well being the dominant computer in those areas. Apple made the biggest gains during this period. A great variety of add-on boards became available, perhaps even exceeding the number of S-100 add-ons in the marketplace. Software support mushroomed as programmers began to realize the power of its architecture and learned to make it perform. Of all of the machines introduced during the first two waves, the Apple II is the only one that has survived, essentially unchanged.

More Microprocessor Advancements

During the 1976–80 period, things were also changing in the microprocessor and memory markets. The winners of the early microprocessor race became apparent, and thus many manufacturers opted instead to second-source (copy) the more popular chips, although virtually none discontinued their own proprietary entries. In terms of number of *different* microprocessor-based products using it (so-called "design wins"), the Z-80 was victorious. In terms of actual numbers of ICs sold (most in a few very high-volume products), the 6502 was the clear leader. The 6800 placed a distant third, while the others barely showed up on the charts regardless of the measuring method.

Simultaneously, the semiconductor manufacturers were readying their next generation of higher-performance, 16-bit microprocessors. Although 16-bitters had been introduced in 1974 (IMP-16) and again in 1976 (9900 and PACE), designers tended to ignore them. The reasons are obscure, but perhaps one was that the expense of building a 16-bit system outweighed the relatively small performance increase these early entries offered.

The earliest high-performance 16-bit microprocessor beyond those mentioned above was the LSI-11 from Digital Equipment. The microprocessor was actually designed by Western Digital and was a set of three large ICs. DEC only offered it on a board with memory and bus interface and at a relatively high price too. It could run most software written for the PDP-11, which is probably the most popular minicomputer ever. Not to be outdone, Data General came out with their MicroNova, which *was* available as a chip as well as a board and executed the Nova minicomputer instruction set. Its electrical characteristics were highly unorthodox, however. Fairchild also introduced a Nova-compatible microprocessor called the Microflame, which was faster and more conventional in its interfacing. None of these minicomputer emulator microprocessors was ever successful, however. The seemingly valid approach of solving the software problem by making the microprocessor execute already written minicomputer software likely failed because nobody really wanted to run old minicomputer software.

Intel moved next in 1979 and introduced their 8086, which was the first 16-bit offering from a company with an already successful 8-bit microprocessor. Compared to some that immediately followed, the 8086 was not really very sophisticated, but it was faster than earlier offerings and, most significantly, could run 8080 software after being processed with an automatic translator program and reassembled. Not much later, Zilog announced the Z-8000 and Motorola their 68000. These two were incredibly sophisticated, having large register complements, rich instruction sets, and very high-speed potential. The 68000 in particular surpassed all but the biggest minicomputers in its potential power. It actually looked like a 32-bit computer to a programmer with 16 32-bit general-purpose registers but with a 16-bit data bus! It could also address up to 16 *mega*bytes of memory *directly* without the bank switching (segmentation) the 8086 and Z-8000 required. Although there was much hope and speculation about a 16-bit version of the 6502 during this time, it never materialized. Much later in 1982, National Semiconductor tried a new 16-bit design called the 16032. Like the 68000, it had 32-bit internal architecture but was more oriented toward high-level language execution and efficient use in time-sharing systems.

As this is being written (late 1984), Intel has had the greatest success with the 8086 and its variations in terms of both design wins and units sold. The 68000 is the prestige winner, however, being preferred in systems where high computation speed and large memory-addressing capacity is important. The Z-8000 and 16032 are clearly behind with the former suffering from a lack of promotion and the latter from its late start. True 32-bit versions of all of these plus new entries from AT&T (the Bellmac-32) and NCR are being worked on now and can be expected to be generally available in a couple of years.

Memory Advances

In many ways, the availability and pricing of memory ICs drive microcomputer development almost as much as the microprocessor chips do. The key component is the random-access memory IC, or "RAM chip" for short. The first RAM chip large enough to do anything significant with was the 1101. Its capacity was 256 bits, and typical cost was about $4 in 1971. Shortly thereafter, at about the same time as the 8008 microprocessor was introduced, the 1103 1K bit RAM became available for $7. This was the first *dynamic RAM,* which meant that each row of memory cells had to be read periodically to refresh and maintain the stored information. Dynamic RAMs are inherently denser and cheaper to make than static RAMs and thus led the way in increased RAM chip capacity.

While 1K RAM chips were adequate for dedicated applications of microprocessors, it was expensive and space-consuming to make memories large enough for a general-purpose microcomputer from them. For example, an 8K byte memory board required 64 of the 18-pin 1103 RAMs plus a nontrivial amount of drive circuitry. Microprocessor applications got a good boost in 1974, however, when 4K bit RAM chips made their appearance. Most of the industry settled on a 22-pin package with full address decoding that was known generically as the 2107. Mostek, however, pioneered a 16-pin version (the MK4096) in which the full 12-bit address was entered into the IC sequentially as two 6-bit halves on only 6 pins. This allowed packing densities almost twice as high as the 22-pin version, although many engineers were reluctant to use them because of greater circuit complexity. Prices on both versions dropped to the $10 level by 1976 and ultimately to about $2.50 near the end of their lifespan in 1978. It was now possible to build a 32K byte memory board for about the same cost as 8K bytes would have cost 3 years earlier.

The 16K RAM chips made their appearance in 1977 and became really practical to use in 1979. By then, the wisdom of 16-pin packaging and address multiplexing was fully realized, and, as a result, only the 16-pin package style was offered. The availability of these RAM chips is what really fueled the second wave of CP/M business computers described earlier. One could actually build the maximum addressable 64K byte memory for a Z-80 microprocessor in a small 3.5-inch × 3.5-inch area in the corner of the computer's motherboard. Interestingly enough, both the Radio Shack and the Apple II computers were designed to use the 4096 type of 4K RAM with provisions to also allow use of the 16K chips. When 16K prices fell to the $12 range in 1979, 16K upgrade kits were offered by dozens of firms for less than $100. Within a year, Apple and Radio Shack computers with less than maximum memory (48K bytes) were a rarity indeed.

The 64K RAM chips appeared in 1981 and quickly came down to a practical price level of about $8 by 1982. Besides the greater bit capacity, a significant difference was that only +5-V power was necessary rather than the +12, +5, and −5 voltages needed by earlier RAMs. This change also freed up two pins on the package, thus allowing continued use of a 16-pin package with one pin left over! Now full memory for an 8-bit microprocessor was a single row of 8 chips, which could easily get lost among the other circuitry. Thus, the issue of addressing much larger memories to allow more sophisticated applications became more urgent. While some companies tacked bank switching logic onto 8-bit Z-80s and 6502s, most switched to 16-bit microprocessors that had large memory-addressing capability built in. To a great extent, the 64K RAM drove the third wave of microcomputers that will be described shortly.

As this is being written, 256K-bit RAM chips are becoming available, still in a 16-pin package, at a price of about $35. Meanwhile, 64K RAMs are selling for about $4.50. Price crossover with 64Ks is expected in 1986 and, by then, 1M-bit RAMs will probably be visible on the horizon. Whether the 16-pin package will be retained is unknown (it could be by combining the data-in and data-out pins), but one thing seems certain: memory capacity for a given cost will continue to double every 2 years for the remainder of the 1980s. The future effect this will have on microcomputer architecture is uncertain, but it can be nothing but good for programmers and users.

The Third Wave

The third wave of new microcomputers had a very definite starting date: August 17, 1981. This was the date that IBM introduced their "IBM Personal Computer." While some were disappointed and others were pleased about the level of technology it utilized, all were surprised. For a microprocessor, it used the Intel 8088, which was an 8-bit bus version of the 16-bit 8086 mentioned earlier. Thus, it potentially had greater power than Z-80-based computers but could not run the CP/M operating system. Instead, it ran a somewhat improved operating system that came to be known as MS-DOS. The biggest surprise to this writer, however, was its reasonable price compared to existing CP/M-based business computers.

The "PC," as it was nicknamed, was an instant hit and immediately garnered the software support that has become crucial to the long-term success of a new computer. Since it included several sockets for expansion boards, a whole new add-on industry has sprung up. Its immense popularity and initial supply shortage also spawned a flood of "workalikes," "compatibles," and outright clones from over two dozen new companies. The PC architecture (8086 instruction set and MS-DOS operating system) has in fact so thoroughly dominated that any new business microcomputer today simply must be able to run IBM PC software. Conversely, the Z-80 and CP/M type of machine has virtually dropped out of sight in the business arena. The S-100 bus, in the meantime, became an official IEEE standard but now seems to have retreated to use in industrial microcomputers.

The home and hobby type of microcomputer became even more differentiated from the business type. This was the era of the mass-produced, incredibly cheap, throwaway computer. The race was started by Sinclair, who introduced a machine about the size of a textbook that used a Z-80, could run BASIC, and connected to a color television set—for $100. Although it had its shortcomings (it couldn't compute and display at the same time, for example), it sold well. Commodore followed with their 6502-based VIC-20 and later Commodore-64. The latter was unique in that it provided 64K bytes of memory for the same price others were charging for 16K and less. Texas Instruments repackaged their 99/4 and trimmed its price substantially. Atari also cut the price of their 400 and 800 machines to be competitive, but Apple held firm on the Apple II. During 1983, a raging price war broke out, which saw the Commodore-64 price fall as low as $180 with the other contenders proportionally less. By early 1984, only Commodore and Apple remained in the high-volume home market. Since then, Coleco and IBM have attempted to enter the market but with limited success.

With the great power of recent 16-bit microprocessors, a third class of microcomputer became possible: the scientific/engineering workstation. These typically used a 68000, had memory from 256K to 1M bytes or more, a very-high-resolution graphic display, and disk storage of 5M bytes and up. The operating system was typically UNIX, a very large and complex operating system originally developed for PDP-11 minicomputers. Unfortunately, along with their great power and capacity came prices that started at nearly $10,000 and went up from there. While only a tiny number (compared to business and home microcomputers) have been sold, their mere existence has influenced engineers, programmers, and product planners greatly.

Apple Computer, in designing a successor for their aging Apple II, used the 68000/large-memory/graphics-display theme of the engineering workstations, scaled it down a little, and combined it with intuitive, graphics-oriented software to create their Lisa and later MacIntosh computers. The former was intended for business use and is more expensive, whereas the latter seems appropriate for almost any application and costs less than $3,000. Strangely enough, neither machine has any expansion slots nor significant program development support and thus has not been attractive to hobbyists and independent add-on manufacturers at all.

As you can see, the history of microcomputers has been tumultuous indeed, and the immediate future is not likely to be less so. But use in complete computers is just one application of microprocessors. Outside of the swirling computer mainstream, microprocessors are used extensively in dedicated applications to simply replace logic or increase circuit capability. Since the primary purpose of this book is to explore the *musical* applications of microprocessors, further discussion of specific computers will be held until Chapter 20.

Microcomputer Peripheral Devices

Although any peripheral device that can be used with a large computer can theoretically be connected to a microcomputer, only a small subset is commonly used in general-purpose microcomputer systems. This subset has been found to give the maximum convenience of system use consistent with performance and cost requirements. However, as we shall see later, certain big system peripherals may be desirable for some musical applications.

Main Memory

In a microcomputer system, main memory is often considered as a peripheral. Usually additional memory is available from several manufacturers, and it may be freely purchased and plugged into the system when needed. Main memory comes in two flavors, *read-only* memory, usually abbreviated ROM, and *read/write* memory, usually abbreviated RAM. ROM is not affected by loss of operating power and cannot be overwritten; thus, it is generally used for unchanging system programs such as a monitor or language translator. Pure ROM is completely unalterable, having had its bit pattern frozen in during manufacture. Although masked ROM is by far the cheapest type, much of the ROM used in general-purpose microcomputers today is of the erasable and reprogrammable type. This type can have its bit pattern erased with a strong ultraviolet lamp and a new pattern entered with special programming equipment. This capability is a valuable asset because virtually all programs are subject to some change as the system expands or program "bugs" are uncovered.

RAM may be freely written into and therefore may hold different programs at different times. RAM is required for the storage of programs under development and the data they use. Large computers have always used RAM exclusively for main memory. However, the core memories used by earlier computers did not lose their contents when power was shut off so operating system programs loaded into them could be expected to remain until specifically overwritten. The RAM used in microcomputers, on the other hand, is highly volatile and subject to complete data loss within milliseconds of a power failure. Thus, operating software kept in RAM must be reloaded whenever the system is turned on for use. Appropriate peripheral equipment such as a disk can reduce this task to a few seconds duration or even allow its automation. Although programs frozen into ROM are convenient, there is sometimes a tendency to spend too much money on ROM when the more flexible RAM would be a better choice, particularly when the needed peripheral equipment for efficient reloading is available.

The amount of main memory in a microcomputer varies widely. Amazing things have been done with a 6502-based system having only 1.1K of user RAM and 2K of system ROM. At the other extreme, the Apple

Macintosh computer was just recently expanded to 512K of memory because its original 128K was deemed inadequate for the needs of its extremely complex software. Since the cost of memory is so low and continues to decline, there is less interest now in space-efficient programming techniques and more in time-efficient ones, both for the programmers and for the machines.

The amount of memory actually needed is largely determined by the application. In later discussion, three broad classes of microprocessor applications in music will be explored. These are *logic replacement* in actual synthesis and control circuitry, *general-purpose computers* that control external synthesis circuitry, and very powerful general- and special-purpose computers that perform *direct computer synthesis*. Accordingly, the logic replacement application requires the least amount of memory, often only a few thousand bytes, while additional memory can always be put to effective use in a direct computer synthesis system.

Mass Storage

Next to main memory, external mass storage is the most reliable indicator of overall system capability. Further, the type of external storage used has a great influence on typical system operating procedures. A system with no external storage at all is extremely limited in general-purpose applications.

The earliest microcomputers, if they had any mass storage at all, often used punched paper tape. This was the natural result of using a teletype machine for text input and output, but it was very slow (10–50 bytes/sec), noisy, and the tape was nonreusable. Another often-used early storage peripheral peculiar to microcomputers was an audio tape recorder. It turned out to be fairly easy to program a microcomputer to generate audio signals dependent on the data to be saved and then recognize them on playback to recover the data. Generally, the encoding/decoding circuitry was simple, and cheap portable cassette recorders were adequate, which meant that audio cassette storage could be implemented for less than $50. While faster, quieter, and cheaper to run than paper tape storage, the recorder still had to be manually operated and the stored data could not be edited in a straightforward manner. In the late 1970s, some experimental products using program-controlled cassette decks were introduced in an attempt to overcome the manual operation and editing problems, but none was successful. Even now, one occasionally hears of a new low-priced microcomputer that uses some kind of tape cartridge for low-cost storage, but then invariably the manufacturer offers or completely switches to disk storage instead.

Floppy Disk

The flexible or "floppy" disk is a relatively new mass-storage device that seems custom made for microcomputer systems. Introduced by IBM in 1970 as a fast method of loading control programs into their big computers, the floppy disk is considered by most microcomputer users to be the ultimate mass storage device when cost is considered. The storage disk itself, called a diskette, is square, moderately stiff like a piece of cardboard, and sells for two to five dollars. Three physical sizes are in common use: the original 8-inch size, the 5-inch size, which was introduced around 1977, and the 3-inch size, which came out in 1983. Data on the diskette is divided into a number of concentric (not spiral) *tracks,* each of which is divided into a number of *sectors.* Each sector typically holds 128, 256, 512, or 1,024 bytes depending on the computer. Some disk drives record data on both sides of the disk. A record/play head is mounted on a carriage that can be quickly moved in and out to access any track on the disk just as a cut on a record can be quickly accessed by moving the pickup arm. After positioning to the correct track, timing circuitry waits for the desired sector to rotate by. Any sector may be randomly located and read or written in less than a second, making the floppy disk a truly random access device. This and the fact that individual sectors may be very quickly updated by reading and rewriting gives the floppy disk complete editing capability.

Original 8-inch floppy disks held 77 tracks, each of which had 26 sectors of 128 bytes on one side for a total capacity of about 250K bytes. Data could be written or read at the rate of 31K bytes per second after the sector had been found. Later improvements doubled the recording bit density and data transfer rate, and, even later, double-sided drives with a separate head for each side appeared, upping the total capacity to just over a million bytes per disk. With more efficient sectoring schemes (8 sectors of 1,024 bytes each per track), up to 1.26 million useful data bytes could be stored.

The first 5-inch diskettes had only 35 tracks and 8 or 9 sectors of 256 bytes each for a total of about 80K bytes. Also, the rotational speed was reduced to 300 rpm from 360 rpm, which, with the shorter track length, reduced the data transfer rate by half to about 16K bytes/sec. Nevertheless, 5-inch disk systems became very popular because they were less expensive, software could replace hardware in encoding and decoding the slower bit stream, and smaller sizes simplified packaging. These too have been improved in several stages. First, the bit density was doubled as in 8-inch systems and then both sides of the disk were used. Later, slightly more of the disk surface was utilized, thus increasing the number of tracks to 40, and finally the track density itself was doubled to provide 80 tracks. At that point, 720K bytes of useful data could be recorded on a 5-inch disk, although the read/write speed was still half that of an 8-incher. Very recently, the bit density has been increased again, and the rotational speed stepped back up to 360 rpm to produce a 5-inch disk drive that has the same attributes as an 8-inch drive. Experimental products with even higher capacities up to 5M bytes on a 5-inch diskette have appeared but so far have not caught on.

Three-inch diskettes and drives are still quite new but already have equalled the most popular 5-inch formats in storage capacity and speed. Their main attractions are even smaller size and lower power consumption than 5-inch units, although at this time 3-inch drives and the diskettes themselves are more expensive. Another feature that is often important when inexperienced people use them is that some types of 3-inch diskettes are packaged in a rigid plastic case with a door that automatically closes when the diskette is removed from the drive. Ultimately, it is expected that 3-inch disks will replace 5-inch ones just as 5-inchers have now largely replaced 8-inchers.

Winchester Disk

Floppy disks have two inherent limitations, however, that prevent them from operating faster and storing truly large amounts of data. First, the plastic-based media are not dimensionally stable with temperature and humidity changes so the track density is limited to about 100 tracks per inch. Also, since the recording head actually contacts the surface during reading and writing, the rotational speed is limited to minimize wear. Even before microcomputers and floppy disks, large mainframe computers used *rigid media* disk drives to store tens or hundreds of megabytes with data transfer rates of 1M byte per second or more. This was accomplished by using magnetically coated metal disks that were spun so fast (up to 3,600 rpm) that the read/write heads floated on a cushion of air. Besides being large (the disk platters were commonly 15 inches in diameter) and heavy (drives often weighed several hundred pounds), prices started at several thousand dollars and went up from there, making them clearly impractical for microcomputer use.

One reason for the high cost and storage capacity still far below theoretical levels was the need for removability. Just as diskettes are frequently changed in a floppy disk drive, disk packs are often changed in a mainframe installation. Allowing for removability requires a complex mechanical arrangement to align the disk within the drive, means to purge dust particles from the new disk, and wide mechanical tolerances (which translate into reduced capacity) to allow for drive-to-drive and disk-to-disk differences. In the early 1970s, the *Winchester* project at IBM discovered that, by permanently sealing the disk within the drive, much lower costs and higher capacities could be obtained. When applied to microcomputers in the late 1970s, the tremendous capacity of these mainframe *fixed disk* units (often over 1,000M bytes) was traded off for a smaller disk platter size and even lower cost. Additionally, the expensive, high-speed, servo-driven access arm was replaced with a simpler but slower stepper motor driven mechanism. Initial units were still 15 inches in diameter (only one platter, however), but that was quickly reduced to 8 inches and later to 5 inches. With each size reduction, the typical capacity range remained about the same, which means that the bit and track density figures of current 5-inch units are truly remarkable.

Today, miniature 5-inch Winchester disk drives (sometimes called "mini-winnies") are fairly common on high-end microcomputers. The most popular capacities are 5 and 10M bytes on one and two sides, respectively, of a single platter, and the data transfter rate is typically 625K bytes/sec. Greater capacities up to 40M bytes are possible by stacking up additional platters, while experimental units have attained up to 160M bytes by increasing the bit and track density. Although the 5- and 10M-byte drive prices have gradually declined to under $500, the real impetus to their increased use was availability of controller ICs. Prior to that, a rigid disk controller board might have 50-100 IC packages and could easily cost in excess of $1,000.

One fundamental problem with any kind of Winchester disk drive is that the recording medium is fixed in place within the drive. Archiving and keeping backup copies of data (in case of computer or disk drive failure) required that it be read off the Winchester disk and rewritten onto a different, removable medium. Although special cartridge tape drives are often promoted for this purpose, in most cases the floppy disk drive (which still must be present to get new software loaded into the machine) is used instead. Another problem is that when the application fills up the Winchester disk, one does not have the option of just changing the medium and continuing; another drive or a capacity upgrade is necessary. Attempts have been made to retain the high bit and track densities of Winchester technology while offering removable media and still keeping the cost reasonable. After several false starts, it appears that this goal will ultimately be reached.

One unique approach that is creating quite a bit of interest is "Bernouli technology" pioneered by IoMega Corporation. The floppy medium is fixed to a simple metal hub and packaged in a rigid plastic case. When inserted into the drive, the disk is spun at high speed, typically 1,500 rpm, which makes it rigid due to centrifugal force. The speed is also high enough to make the disk pull toward yet float over the head on an air cushion (Bernouli effect). The real advantage is that momentary contact between the disk and head (called a "crash" in rigid disk terminology) is not detrimental, which makes the units rugged and reliable. Problems with dimensional stability of the medium are solved by using a servo positioner (rather than stepping motor), which does tend to increase the drive cost. The removable cartridges, however, are potentially very inexpensive. This feature makes a Bernouli technology system very attractive in direct computer synthesis applications in which the media cost for storing digitized audio data must be minimized.

Text Keyboard

The most fundamental microcomputer input device is a typewriter-like "text" keyboard. Typically, it is also the most used peripheral device because the operator spends most of the time interacting with the system by typing. Unfortunately, quality keyboards with full-sized keys having the proper surface contour and desirable mechanical feel are relatively expensive. More than a few manufacturers have attempted to skimp on the keyboard only to be forced to offer an improved model later with a "real" keyboard or have the computer fail in the marketplace.

Text keyboards are interfaced to a microcomputer in one of three ways. The S-100 and CP/M type of computer popular in the late 1970s typically used a CRT terminal and thus its keyboard for input. This was a particularly inflexible interface technique, since it was the terminal that actually operated the keyboard and determined how it functioned rather than the microcomputer's program. Many quirks and inconveniences in CP/M's operation can be traced to this limitation.

Most low-priced computers have a built-in keyboard that is directly, and often minimally, interfaced to the microprocessor. Typically, the program actually scans the keyswitch array, that is, constantly monitors the status of each individual key. This approach give the programmer much more flexibility in determining exactly how the keyboard functions. For example, some keys could be programmed to automatically repeat if held down, while others would have single action in a word-processing program. A game program might have a different action altogether. A simple music input program could be able to tell how long a key was pressed and perhaps even track simultaneous keypresses.

The IBM Personal Computer made the third interface method, a detached keyboard, popular. The keyboard becomes a physically separate peripheral device connected to the computer through a cable. Logic (often a single-chip microcomputer itself) on the keyboard does the scanning and reports the results to the main system using a serial bit stream format. In order to retain much of the flexibility of the directly interfaced keyboard, the scanning logic usually sends one keycode when a key is pressed and another when it is released. This information then allows the program to be aware of the status of each key without having to constantly look at all of the keys.

Computer system designers are constantly looking for ways to input information that do not involve a text keyboard. This is particularly important for "casual" users who may be unfamiliar with computer operation. Direct voice input is, of course, a natural suggestion and some limited success has been realized in special function systems. Most other alternate schemes are graphic in nature and will be described in Chapter 11.

CRT Display

In the early days of computing, even before microcomputers became commonplace, users interacted with the system via punched cards and printed listings. If they were lucky, a teletype-like terminal could be used for interactive computing rather than waiting hours or overnight for results. CRT display screens were a luxury usually reserved for the computer center operator. Today, it is safe to say that virtually all microcomputers are equipped with a CRT display, either built-in or through a connection to an external monitor or TV set.

The vast majority of such displays form their image by illuminating dots in a large, fixed array of dots. Thus, text characters as well as graphic elements such as lines, curves, and symbols are formed from dot patterns. Text characters, for example, are typically formed from a matrix of dots either 5 or 7 dots wide × 7 or 9 dots high and either can produce a highly readable, though stylized, type font. Horizontal, vertical, and 45° diagonal graphic elements are also formed well from a dot matrix, but other angles and shapes such as circles show noticeable and often objectionable distortions due to the fixed dot matrix construction. Chapter 11 details these and other considerations in displaying music-synthesis-related information.

The capacity of a CRT display for showing text and graphics varies widely. Inexpensive microcomputers intended to connect to a home television are severely limited to as few as 23 lines of 22 characters each or a 176 wide × 184 high display matrix, although color is usually available. The popular Commodore-64 home computer extends the capacity to 25 lines of 40 characters or 320 wide × 200 high graphics, about the limit for most TVs due to blurring. More sophisticated systems and all business microcomputers have a text display capacity of at least 24 lines of 80 characters up to 66 lines of 132 characters, although many do not have any graphics capability. Those that do have graphics offer matrix sizes up to 640 wide × 400 high, although most are less. The Apple Macintosh, for example, is 512 wide × 342 high. Even higher resolutions up to 1,280 × 1,024 are found on engineering workstation type of systems. A color display is seldom seen on business microcomputers because their typically blurred and misregistered images are hard on the eyes after hours of use.

Printers and Plotters

Even with easily operated computer systems and high-speed displays, there is no escape from the need for printed output. Standard file folders of printed text and graphics will always be required for effective communication with others.

The most commonly available and least expensive printers are of the dot matrix type. In these, characters are formed from a fixed matrix of dots just like on a CRT display screen. Mechanically, the print head consists of a column of seven or nine small, stiff, magnetically driven wires that press an inked ribbon against the paper on command, often within a millisecond or less. As the head scans across the printed line horizontally, the wires are driven in a precisely timed sequence to produce the dot matrix characters. Print quality is not one of the strong points of dot matrix printers, but generally it is easily readable.

Recently, a technique called multipass printing has been developed that improves the print quality substantially. The idea is to overprint the line twice up to as many as eight times with the dots displaced slightly on each pass so they overlap and produce smoother, more continuous lines. The technique is indeed successful in hiding the dot structure of the characters and produces results comparable to a standard typewriter with a cloth ribbon. One model produced by Sanders Technology, however, uses precision mechanics and a carbon film ribbon to produce results comparable to typesetting. Dot matrix printer speeds range from about 40 to 50 characters per second up to 300 and more, while prices range from well under $300 to well over $1,000. Naturally, the more expensive models are faster and may have the multipass capability.

Most dot matrix printers can also accept arbitrary binary patterns from the computer and print them as corresponding dot patterns on the paper. This then allows the printer to reproduce exactly any kind of graphics the CRT can display in a process often called a "screen dump." Common dot densities are 80 dots per inch horizontally × 72 dots per inch vertically up to as high as 240 × 288. Because the printers must reproduce traditional horizontal and vertical spacings when printing characters, the graphics dot density is seldom equal in both directions. Even at the lower density, a standard printed page can typically hold many more dots than the standard screen can display, although uniformity of dot placement is not as good as the display's. Such graphics printing capability is very important in most musical applications.

"Daisy wheel" printers are normally used when office typewriter print quality is desired. Characters are printed by rotating a wheel with characters embossed on its spokes into position and then magnetically hammering it against the ribbon and paper. The print wheels are interchangeable for different type sizes and styles. These machines are also capable of producing general dot graphics but typically at lower densities from 60 × 48 up to 120 × 96 dots per inch and at much lower speeds than dot matrix printers. Graphics is accomplished by positioning the paper and print head under program control then printing the period. In fact, most of the drawings of waveforms, response curves, etc., in this book were produced with a printer of this type on 17 × 22-inch paper and then photographically reduced.

The best device for printed graphics output is a plotter. These produce drawings as well as text by inking smooth lines between designated endpoints using an X-Y coordinate system. Drawing pens are easily interchangeable for different colors or even different line widths. Quality is usually high, since only the endpoints need be on the fixed grid and no dot structure is evident in the lines. Some models show irregularities and wiggles in plotted lines at certain angles, however, due to the stepper motor drive system employed. Also the X-Y grid itself is fairly fine with 200 and 254 (metric) grids per inch being common densities. Unlike a dot matrix printer in which the print time depends only on the image size, plotting time depends on the image complexity. For most images, plotters come out being substantially slower than dot matrix printers. Only recently have plotters become inexpensive enough to be practical to connect to a microcomputer. It is now possible to get a unit capable of 8.5 × 11-inch plots for under $500, while a unit with extra features such as automatic circle drawing and an 11 × 17-inch plotting size can be under $1,000. Larger sizes are available but at sharply higher prices.

Miscellaneous Devices

Many other miscellaneous peripheral devices are found on microcomputers but not as frequently as those mentioned above. One of these is a telephone *modem*. The word is actually a contraction of "*mod*ulator" and "*dem*odulator." In essence, it allows a computer to send binary digital information over telephone lines by modulating an audio carrier tone with data to be sent and also demodulating the received tone signal to recover received data. This then allows a microcomputer to call up a mainframe and exchange data with it or call another microcomputer and exchange program or data files. Computer "bulletin boards" operated by clubs or hobbyists can also be accessed by any computer equipped with a modem. Data transmission speeds are moderately high with common values being 30 and 120 bytes per second. Prices range from under $200 for a 30-byte/sec unit up to $400–500 for a 120-byte/sec unit. Transmission accuracy for modern units is remarkably good, even over long-distance telephone circuits.

Another common convenience item is a computer-readable clock and calendar. Besides allowing the operating system to automatically keep track of creation and update dates for data files, such a clock can be useful in keeping track of time for real-time music input or synthesis applications. Actually, one would think that with three-dollar stick-on electronic clocks everywhere, they would be built into all computers, regardless of price. Such is not the case, however, and in fact such a capability is usually either a moderately expensive add-on board or a highly promoted standard feature.

Speech input and output capability is also occasionally seen. Of these, speech output has been much more successful, although speech input is beginning to show potential. Both have a long way to go before computers can be used by conversing with them. Speech synthesis devices will be briefly described in Chapter 20.

Microcomputer Software

Software, of course, is the key to a useful microcomputer system regardless of the amount of memory or other peripheral devices available. While much of the software that will be discussed in succeeding chapters is specialized for music synthesis, a considerable amount of standard support software is used in all general-purpose microcomputer systems. Although the term "standard" is used, there is considerable variation in implementaion and use details according to the individual manufacturer's philosophy. Most of the discussion will be centered around the support software required for program development in assembly language, although much of it applies equally well to compiler languages. Conversely, the vast body of business software such as word processors, spreadsheets, databases, and "business" graphics packages that has been developed for microcomputers recently is of little interest here and will not be considered further.

System Monitor

The most fundamental piece of support software is the system monitor. With very few exceptions, microcomputers are unlike minicomputers in that the traditional "programmer's console" with dozens of toggle switches and lights is absent. Instead, a system monitor program is used to allow equivalent console functions to be performed through the primary interactive I/O device, such as a keyboard/display. All system monitors have the capability of reading memory, modifying memory, examining the microprocessor registers, and controlling the loading, dumping, and execution of programs. More comprehensive monitors have debugging functions such as search memory and breakpoints or program trace. Sometimes these and other debugging functions are part of a separate debugger program.

Systems using a floppy disk term their monitors "disk-operating systems," or DOS. In addition to the basic console and debugging functions outlined above, DOS controls the allocation of disk space, finds and creates files given a mnemonic name, and does other disk housekeeping chores. Through DOS, the user may request a disk index listing, delete an unwanted file, copy files from one disk to another, specify programs to be loaded by name, and read or write data files a character at a time. DOS handles all of the blocking or unblocking of characters to make full disk sectors. An important DOS feature is the ability to do all of these tasks on command from a user program as well as with console commands.

Text Editor

Much of the actual time a user spends with a microcomputer system is probably spent with the text editor program. Even if he or she is a perfect typist and never needs to actually edit, the editor is necessary to create text files for the assembler or compiler or even music interpreter. However, since people are seldom perfect typists and are never perfect programmers, the editor is also used to add, delete, change, and move program text. Most editors are limited to editing files that are small enough to fit into main memory. Thus, large programs must be broken into acceptably small segments and edited separately. Typically, a file would be read into a text buffer in memory, edited as required, and a new file would be created. The old file can then be deleted if desired. If large insertions that might cause the file to exceed available memory are anticipated, a portion of the text buffer contents may be written as one file, deleted from memory, and the remainder along with the insertion would be written as another file. The assembler or compiler can link the segments together into a single program. Having a large amount of memory available is obviously a benefit when using this type of editor.

Highly sophisticated editors supplied as part of some disk-operating systems are able to handle any size file by *scrolling* the text through memory forward and backward in response to user commands. Insertions and deletions may be made in any order by scrolling the text on the screen to the desired point and then keying in the change. The inherent editing capability of the disk allows long files to be edited directly without creating unnecessary copies. Less advanced editors may still allow unlimited file size and insertions but can only scroll forward, thus requiring that editing be done in sequence to some extent.

Assembler

The purpose of an assembler is to convert program *source* text statements into binary machine language *object* code and a printed listing. Assemblers work in a variety of ways according to the size of system they were designed for and level of sophistication.

Today, good assemblers work with a disk-operating system in a general way that is much more convenient than the early cassette-based ones were. Before being run, the assembler is given the name of the source file, which already exists, and the names of two new files that it will create; one to hold the object code and the other to hold the listing. The assembler then scans the source file two or three times and produces the object and listing files. Before printing the listing file, the user can quickly scan it using the editor to see if any errors were flagged by the assembler. Assuming there were few or none, the editor can be commanded to print the listing if one is actually desired. The operating system may either load the object file into memory itself or a loader program may be used for that purpose. After loading, the user may specify the data files, if any, and execute the program. With such a setup, program size is limited only by the capacity of the diskette and the amount of memory available for the assembler's symbol table. Most of the preceding comments also apply to compiler languages such as FORTRAN or the new structured microcomputer languages such as C and Pascal.

High-Level Language

By far the most popular high-level language for microcomputers is BASIC. Originally developed at Dartmouth University for student use on a large time-sharing computer, it has evolved well beyond its design goals into a general-purpose programming language. Although its strengths and weaknesses in music programming will be detailed in Chapter 18, it can be said here that it is an excellent one-shot problem-solving language but not especially suited for large or complex programs. As a matter of fact, most of the waveforms and plots in this book were done using simple BASIC programs. BASIC will also be used periodically to illustrate program algorithms. One unique feature present in nearly all microcomputer BASIC is the PEEK and POKE functions. These allow a BASIC program to directly address and read or write any memory location in the microcomputer. If the system utilizes memory-mapped I/O[2], then BASIC programs may be written to operate any I/O device on the system!

On microcomputers, BASIC is almost exclusively implemented as an interpreter and is permanently stored in read-only memory. Thus, BASIC programs exist in memory as character strings in the same form as they appear in print except for perhaps the substitution of single, normally unprintable, bytes for keywords. Part of the BASIC interpreter is a simple, line-number-oriented text editor. When the "run" command is given, the interpreter scans each program line, extracts the meaningful information from the line, acts upon it, and then goes to the next line. As a result, BASIC programs tend to run very slowly compared to the inherent capability of the microcomputer. Nevertheless, BASIC is very easy to learn and use and for any but highly repetitive calculations its speed is adequate. Most disk-based microcomputers also have a BASIC *compiler* available, which greatly speeds up execution at the expense of losing the interpreter's interactive program development feature.

Another commonly used language on microcomputers is simply called C. It was developed at Bell Laboratories to run on PDP-11 minicomputers and has efficiency features that make it suitable for system programming as

[2]Memory-mapped I/O is peculiar to the PDP-11 line of minicomputers and most microprocessors. Essentially all I/O device status, control, and data registers are addressed like memory locations with all memory reference microprocessor instructions available for I/O register manipulation.

well as application programming. For example, an often-required program function is incrementing a variable. Most languages require a whole statement of the form $A = A + 1$, which when compiled will almost invariably result in at least three machine instructions: load from A, add constant 1, store into A. In C, a variable can be incremented by writing $A+$ in an expression, which would normally compile into a single "increment memory" machine instruction. There is also an excellent facility for handling addresses (pointers), often lacking in other languages. Because of its efficiency, C is often used in direct synthesis applications and in fact is recommended for that application. The only real drawbacks to C are its sometimes cryptic appearance and lack of direct support for sophisticated data structures.

Many other languages are used as well. Pascal is becoming a very popular teaching language in formal computer science courses. FORTRAN, a very old language, is often available to make the task of converting mainframe scientific software to microcomputers straightforward if not easy. Other specialized mainframe languages such as COBOL (business) and LISP (artificial intelligence) have microcomputer versions. A very large and comprehensive language developed for the Department of Defense called Ada is being implemented on large microcomputers and shows a promising future.

As microprocessors become faster and microcomputers incorporate more memory, there is more interest now in writing *all* software in high-level languages, not just specialized applications or one-shot problem solutions. In many cases (but certainly not all!), the system's greater power hides the inefficiencies that can occur when system programs such as editors, compilers, and even disk-operating systems are written in a high-level language.

Example Microprocessor Descriptions

The first edition of this book, completed in 1979, selected three major musical application areas of microprocessors and then described the characteristics of the "best" microprocessor for each. These were logic replacement, synthesizer control, and direct synthesis for which the 6502, 8080, and LSI-11, respectively, were recommended. Besides the apparent one-for-three shooting performance (the 8080 became obsolete and the LSI-11 was never popular), most microprocessor applications now seem better divided into just two areas: general-purpose systems and dedicated-function systems. General-purpose systems, in which the user is aware of the operating system and often does programming, are extensively used to control synthesizers and do direct synthesis. Dedicated-function systems, in which the microprocessor is "hidden" from the user, certainly cover logic replacement but also synthesizer control and, to a growing extent, even direct synthesis.

Since there is now almost total overlap between microprocessor types and typical applications, the real distinctions have become performance (speed and ease of assembly language programming) and cost (total hardware cost of a typical system). Accordingly, only two microprocessors, one at each end of the spectrum, will be selected for detailed description here.

In the comparative discussions to follow, two areas of difference among microprocessors will be concentrated upon. These are its machine language instruction set, since that directly influences assembly language programming, and its bus structure and timing, which influences system hardware design, particularly in the logic replacement application. Only the most important points that distinguish the subject microprocessor from others will be covered. More detail can be found in the wealth of manufacturer's literature and microprocessor design books available.

The 6502 for Logic Replacement and Low Cost

The original notion behind development of microprocessors was to provide a standard LSI chip that, when combined with standard memories, could perform the functions of a custom LSI chip. The reasoning was that, since semiconductor cost is nearly inversely proportional to production volume, the lower cost of standard parts would outweigh any cost advantages of an optimized custom chip. Although things did not quite work out like that, quite a lot of microprocessors are used for logic replacement instead of building microcomputers.

Of all the 8-bit microprocessors now on the market, the 6502 comes closest to filling all logic replacement needs. Its price, although not the absolute lowest on the market, is low enough to replace even relatively small logic systems. Its raw speed, which is the highest of all 8-bit MOS microprocessors, is high enough to replace all but the most speed-sensitive logic systems. Its instruction set, although not a programmer's dream, is powerful and straightforward, unlike the obscure and convoluted sets of many other logic replacement microprocessors. Its bus structure, which is a model of simplicity, is very easily interfaced while at the same time allowing some very sophisticated direct memory access and multiprocessor schemes to be implemented with a minimum of effort. Although not nearly as popular as the Z-80, there is a sizable core of users who swear by it for general-purpose computer applications also.

In music, there are numerous jobs that might normally be done with conventional logic that can also be done by a 6502 cheaper, simpler, faster, smaller, or just plain better. For example, a digitally scanned music keyboard with velocity sensing on both press and release is one possibility. Another is a universal multichannel envelope generator with the envelope shapes programmable by the user. A supersequencer is another obvious application. The 6502 is fast enough to even generate tones with programmable waveforms using simplified direct synthesis techniques. Many of these applications will be detailed in later chapters.

The 6502 requires a single +5-V power supply, making it directly compatible with TTL logic systems. A 16-bit address bus, 8-bit bidirectional data bus, and numerous control signals are provided. Incredibly, there are three unused pins on the package! The on-chip clock oscillator/driver requires only a TTL inverter, a crystal (or R-C network), and a few passive components to generate a two-phase nonoverlapping clock. Although the standard frequency is only 1.0 MHz, a complete machine cycle is executed in just one clock cycle.

According to the manufacturer's literature, there are no fewer than nine different package and pin configurations of the basic 6502. Two of these are the typical 40-lead dual-in-line package with all features available and the other seven are smaller and cheaper 28-lead packages with different mixes of omitted functions and intended for small configurations. The primary difference between the two 40-lead versions is that the 6502 has a built-in clock oscillator and driver, whereas the 6512 requires an external two-phase clock oscillator and driver. The advantage of an external clock is that timing and waveshapes can be precisely controlled, although the oscillator pins of 6502 can also be externally driven. Thus, the 6502 will be the model for further discussion.

Bus Structure and Timing

Figure 5–1 shows a 6502 read cycle that is about as simple as one can get. The 1-μsec machine cycle is divided into Phase 1, which is the first 500 nsec, and Phase 2, which is the last 500 nsec. Actually, when using the on-chip oscillator, the cycle may not be split exactly 50-50, but the signal relationships are still valid. During Phase 1, the address bus and read/write line settle to valid indications, and near the end of Phase 2 the microprocessor reads the data bus. Static read-only devices can actually be connected to the address and data buses without any other control signals at all; if they see their address, they drive their data. Approximately 600 nsec is allowed for memory access, although typically greater than 850 nsec can be tolerated before malfunction.

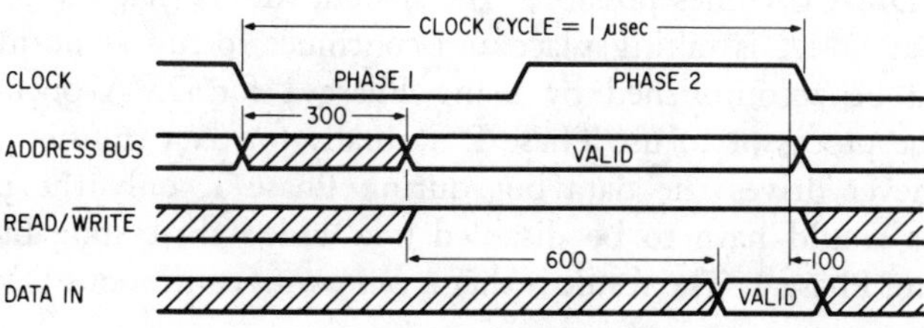

Fig. 5–1. 6502 read cycle timing

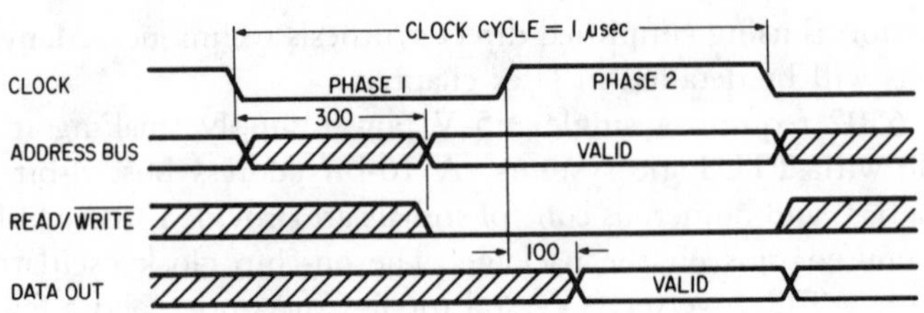

Fig. 5–2. 6502 write cycle timing

The write cycle in Fig. 5–2 is quite similar. The address and write indication settle during Phase 1, and the data to be written is put onto the data bus by the processor at the beginning of Phase 2 and held until the start of the next Phase 1. Devices written into will, therefore, have to look at Phase 2 and read/write to decode a valid write operation. These are the only cycle types; all input and output is memory mapped.

Being so simple, there must be limitations and indeed there are a couple. A ready line is available for slow memories to request additional time for access. If the 6502 sees a low level on this line at the beginning of Phase 2, it will delay reading the data bus until the next cycle. The catch is that write cycles cannot be extended with this signal.[3] Actually, at the present state of the art, there is little if any cost advantage in using such slow memory. In fact, if only a couple hundred extra nanoseconds are needed, it would be better to reduce the clock frequency anyway. The other catch is that if "transparent latches" (level clocked) are used for output registers and the clock is Phase 2, then glitches at the outputs are likely when written into. The problem can be solved by either using edge-triggered registers (trigger at end of Phase 2) or by generating a delayed Phase 2 that does not become active until the data bus is stable.

One unusual property of the 6502 is that the address bus *cannot* be disabled for direct memory access operations. This and the fact that there is no hold pin like on other microprocessors and write cycles cannot be stopped would seem to make DMA difficult, if not impossible. Actually, a little study of the bus timing reveals that if three-state buffers are added to the address lines and 400-nsec memory (or a slight clock slowdown) is used, then *transparent* DMA becomes possible. Transparent means that the processor is unaware that DMA is taking place and continues to run at normal speed. This would be accomplished by using Phase 1 for DMA operation and allowing the processor to use Phase 2 normally for data transfer. Since the processor never drives the data bus during Phase 1, only the processor's address bus would have to be disabled (via added three-state buffers) for DMA during Phase 1. The result is that a *guaranteed* continuous DMA rate of

[3] A new 6502 version constructed with CMOS transistors that became available in 1984 does honor the ready signal during write cycles.

1 million bytes/sec is available for dynamic memory refresh, DMA displays, and other uses without any effect on the microprocessor at all. Most other microprocessors would be stopped cold using conventional DMA techniques at this speed. Even another 6502 may be connected to the same bus with oppositely phased clocking (external clock operation would be required) for a dual-processor system. Clearly, then, the 6502 bus is actually one of the most flexible available.

Interrupts

Interrupts on the 6502 at first seem somewhat limited but on closer examination are seen to be extremely flexible. Two priority levels of interrupt are built in, the standard maskable (can be disabled by program instructions) interrupt and a nonmaskable interrupt, which has a higher priority. The maskable interrupt request line into the 6502 is level sensitive and will continue to interrupt the CPU as long as it is enabled and active. Unwanted multiple interrupts are prevented, however, because the CPU disables them after the interrupt sequence until the program enables them again. The nonmaskable interrupt is edge sensitive. Whenever the logic level at this input goes from high to low, the nonmaskable interrupt sequence is unconditionally executed. These two different interrupt actions are very useful in logic replacement applications and in fact avoid a serious problem[4] the 8080 has in general-purpose applications.

The interrupt sequence itself consists of executing a "jump to subroutine indirect" through dedicated addresses in high memory. These addresses are called *vectors* and are FFFC-FFFD (hexadecimal notation) for maskable and FFFE and FFFF for nonmaskable interrupts. Any number of vectored interrupt levels may be implemented for each interrupt type by having the interrupting device respond to read cycles at those addresses with the address of the service routine.

Registers

The 6502 has possibly fewer bits of on-chip registers than any other microprocessor. Besides the program counter, there is an 8-bit accumulator and two 8-bit index registers. The stack pointer is also 8 bits and the stack is thus limited to 256 bytes and is always in Page 1. The status register has the usual negative, carry, and zero flags but also has overflow, interrupt disable, and decimal mode flags. When the decimal mode flag is on, the arithmetic instructions assume two-digit BCD data. As we will see later, what is lacking in register count is made up double in memory-addressing flexibility.

[4] If an 8080 program gets caught in a loop with the interrupt disabled, it is impossible to interrupt the program and return to the monitor. Reset is the only way out, which destroys the program counter and other registers, making straightforward isolation of the loop impossible.

6502 instructions may be either one, two, or three bytes in length. The first byte is always the op code and the second and third bytes, if present, are either immediate operands or addresses. The first 256 bytes of memory (0000-00FF) are termed the *base page* and can be addressed by many instructions with a single address byte. However, the base page is indispensable for most programming and is not merely a convenient way to save on memory.

The 6502 CPU is unusually efficient in executing instructions. Many require only as many machine cycles as memory cycles and nearly all of the remainder require only one extra cycle. Average execution speed may often exceed 350,000 instructions/sec due in part to extremely fast conditional jumps (2.5 μsec average) and immediate mode instructions (2 μsec). For even higher speed, selected CPUs with clock frequencies as high as 4.0 MHz are available, which can approach speeds of 1.5 million instructions/sec (MIPS) when combined with bipolar memory.

Addressing Modes

Like most minicomputers, the strength of the 6502 is its memory-addressing modes. Easy access to memory and a number of in-memory operations reduce the need for registers. Although the manufacturer boasts 13 addressing modes, only 10 are sufficiently differentiated to be listed here:

1. Register, the operand is the designated register.
2. Immediate, the operand is the byte following the instruction.
3. Relative, the operand address is formed by adding the following byte to the location counter (signed add). Used only by conditional branch instructions.
4. Zero page, the address of the operand is contained in the single following byte.
5. Absolute, the address of the operand is contained in the two following bytes.
6. Zero page indexed, the address of the operand is formed by adding the following byte to the specified index register discarding the carry if any.
7. Absolute indexed, the address of the operand is formed by adding the following two bytes to the specified index register (unsigned add).
8. Indirect, the address of a byte pair containing the address of the operand is in the following two bytes. Used only by the unconditional branch instruction.
9. Indexed indirect, the zero page indexed sequence is used to locate a byte pair on the base page containing the address of the operand.
10. Indirect indexed, the second byte of the instruction points to a byte pair on the base page, which is added to the Y index register (unsigned add) to form the address of the operand.

A close examination of a detailed instruction set listing immediately reveals that no instruction is legal in all of these modes and that most can use half or fewer of them. In particular, instructions using one index register for an operand cannot use the same register in forming the address of the other operand. Also, the unqualified indirect mode would be very useful generally, but the same effect can be achieved with either of the other indirect forms if the index register contains zero.[5] Other than these, the selection seems to be well thought out, since the need for an unavailable combination is not frequent. Note that the base page *must* be used to perform variable addressing of any possible memory location; the indexed modes only have a range of 256 bytes due to the 8-bit size of the index registers.

A full instruction set listing is shown in Table 5-1 along with the allowable addressing modes and execution time. One unique feature is that shift and rotate instructions can work directly in memory and with indexed addressing to boot! Note that the condition codes are set even when something is merely loaded. Both the LSI-11 style bit test and compare any register instructions are also included, although the immediate form of bit test is mysteriously absent.[5]

There are some weak points too. For example, the arithmetic instructions always include the carry in the calculation. For the more common single-byte or subtract, it is necessary to first clear or set the carry flag, respectively (if its current state is unknown). Conditional branches are limited to true and complement testing of individual condition flags, although the inclusion of an overflow indicator makes it easy to simulate all of the combination forms also. One perennial headache is that index registers must pass through the accumulator on the way to or from the stack.[5]

Interfacing Tricks

Although not obvious from the foregoing description, the 6502 lends itself well to individual bit control functions. For individual testing of external conditions such as key closures, a standard digital multiplexor can be connected to respond to a range of addresses and gate the addressed input onto the most significant bit of the data bus. A shift or rotate memory left instruction can then copy the addressed condition into the carry flag for testing without disturbing any of the registers. Inexpensive addressable latches can be used for individual control of output bits, again without disturbing any registers. If the addressable latches are wired to respond to a group of addresses and take their data from the least significant bit of the data bus, then a shift memory left will clear the addressed bit and a shift

[5] The CMOS 6502 mentioned earlier does have an unindexed indirect addressing mode added as well as several new instructions including bit test immediate and direct push and pop of the index registers.

Table 5–1. 6502 Instruction Set Listing

Instruction	*Addressing Modes*[1] IMM	ABS	ZPG	Z,X	Z,Y	A,X	A,Y	I,X	I,Y	ACC[2]	REL	I	Function	Flags
LDA	2	4	3	4		4	4	6	5				Load A	N Z
STA		4	3	4		5	5	6	6				Store A	
LDX	2	4	3		4		4						Load index X	N Z
LDY	2	4	3	4		4							Load index Y	N Z
STX		4	3		4								Store index X	
STY		4	3	4									Store index Y	
ADC	2	4	3	4		4	4	6	5				Add to A with carry	N Z V C
SBC	2	4	3	4		4	4	6	5				Subtract from A w/carry	N Z V C
AND	2	4	3	4		4	4	6	5				And to A	N Z
ORA	2	4	3	4		4	4	6	5				Logical or to A	N Z
EOR	2	4	3	4		4	4	6	5				Exclusive or to A	N Z
CMP	2	4	3	4		4	4	6	5				Compare with A	N Z C
CPX	2	4	3										Compare with X	
CPY	2	4	3										Compare with Y	
INC DEC		6	5	6		7							Increment, decrement	N Z
INX INY										2			Increment X and Y	N Z
DEX DEY										2			Decrement X and Y	N Z
ASL LSR		6	5	7		6				2			Shift left or right	N Z C
ROL ROR		6	5	7		6				2			Rotate left or right	N Z C
BxS BxC										2			Branch conditionally on any flag	
CLx SEx										2			Set or clear any flag	Note[3]
JMP		3								5			Jump unconditionally	
JSR		6											Jump to subroutine	Note[4]
RTS RTI										6			Return from subroutine	Note[5]
PHA PHP										3			Push A, push status	
PLA PLP										4			Pull A, pull status	Note[6]
TXA TXA										2			Transfer index to A	N Z
TAX TAY										2			Transfer A to index	N Z
TXS										2			X to stack pointer	
TSX										2			Stack pointer to X	N Z
NOP										2			No operation	

Notes:

1 Numbers in this column are execution times with a 1-MHz clock.
2 Accumulator addressing mode also covers implied addressing.
3 Flags that may be set or cleared directly are: carry, overflow, interrupt enable, decimal mode.
4 Jump to subroutine does not save the flags; however, an interrupt does save them.
5 Return from interrupt restores the flags.
6 PLA sets N and Z flags; PLP loads status from the stack.

right will set it. Since indexed addressing is available with the shifts, very efficient bit testing and control loops are possible.

Besides logic replacement, the 6502 can be used quite successfully for general-purpose applications. The main factor inhibiting this besides the course of history is its reliance on a base page and its limited indexed addressing range. The base page complicates a relocating linking loader considerably because both base page and regular memory relocation are required. Although the 6502 is a model of efficiency when processing tables less than 256 bytes in length, bigger lists cannot be handled using straightforward indexed addressing. Instead, pointers must be formed on the base page and address calculation done with normal arithmetic instructions.

Direct synthesis can be done significantly faster with the 6502 than with other 8-bit processors. The addressing modes are quite efficient in handling the waveform and other tables involved provided they do not exceed 256 bytes in length. Properly programmed, translation of a byte via table lookup may add as little as 4 μsec to execution time. An 8 × 8 unsigned multiply can be performed by software in as little as 92 clock cycles average for a full 16-bit product. These figures make the idea of using a 6502 microprocessor for each voice in a direct synthesis system at least worth considering.

The 68000 for General Purpose and High Performance

Of the existing 16-bit microprocessors available for use by anyone in 1984, the Motorola 68000 is clearly the best performer in musical applications. It is inherently fast with speeds as high as 3 million register-to-register instructions per second. It has a rich register complement of 16 32-bit general-purpose registers, which makes that speed claim meaningful. And it can handle big applications using very large data arrays because of its unsegmented addressing range of 16M bytes. These factors together allow an instruction set that is *very* easy to program in assembly language and has the power necessary for efficient code generation by high-level language compilers.

Whereas an 8-bit microprocessor can be thoroughly documented in a 16- or 24-page brochure, Motorola needs a 200-page paperback book to do the same for the 68000. Much of this bulk concerns usage in very complex, multiuser, time-sharing computer systems for which it has been highly promoted. In fact, the performance of the 68000 is comparable to that of large minicomputers typically used in time-sharing systems and beats the pants off the room-sized IBM 360/40 the author used in 1970. However, it is possible, even easy, to use the 68000 in small single-user systems or even logic-replacement-dedicated applications as well, which is the case for most musical applications. These are the usage modes that will be covered here with emphasis on those features that make the 68000 unusually effective in high-performance *single-user* applications.

The 68000 family is actually available in four different configurations and three different clock speeds. The "standard" 68000, upon which this discussion is based, comes in a very large 64-lead dual-in-line package that measures about 1 inch × 3.5 inches. This version has a separate 16-bit data bus and 24-bit address bus that together account for 40 of those pins. The 68008 is an 8-bit data bus version with 20 address lines (1M byte addressing range) that fits into a more petite 40-lead package. It is absolutely instruction-set-compatible with the standard 68000 but costs substantially less (under $20) and runs about 60% as fast. The 68010 is essentially the same as the 68000 but has hardware enhancements that are valuable in multiuser applications. Due to more efficient internal operation, it is slightly faster for most programming as well but costs twice as much as a 68000. The standard clock speed for these three versions is 8 MHz, although 10 MHz and 12.5 MHz are available at extra cost and 16 MHz may ultimately become available.

The 68020 is the newest family member with a full 32-bit data bus and separate 32-bit address bus. That gives it a linear, unsegmented addressing range of more than 4 *giga*bytes! It is packaged in a small, difficult-to-use, 112-lead "pin grid array" that is less than 1.5 inch square. Because of the 32-bit data bus and incredibly efficient internal operation, it is 3 to 10 times faster than the 68000, particularly for short loops, common in most direct synthesis algorithms. The standard clock speed is projected to be 16 MHz. It is interesting to note that the initial price of $487 is actually less than the 8080's initial price of $360 in 1974 if inflation is taken into account.

Bus Structure and Timing

The 68000 is really a 32-bit microprocessor with a 16-bit data bus. Only 24 of the potential 32 address bits are available externally, and 32-bit operands are transferred 16 bits at a time. All addresses are *byte addresses,* which makes byte manipulation software easy. Since the registers and data bus are more than 1 byte wide, a property known as "byte sex" becomes important. In essence, this specifies how multiple byte operands such as 16- and 32-bit numbers are stored in memory. The 68000 uses *positive byte sex* in which the most significant bytes (leftmost in registers) are stored at lower byte addresses. Thus, reading values from a memory dump listing is easy because they are listed in the same order one would write them on paper or visualize them in registers. The address of a 2- or 4-byte operand is the address of its most significant byte, which in the 68000 must always be even.

In order to simplify hardware handling of individual 8-bit bytes on a 16-bit data bus, the lowest address line on the 68000 is replaced by a lower data strobe line and an upper data strobe line. For 16-bit (word) transfers, both strobes are activated, whereas for byte transfers, only one is pulsed: upper for even addresses and lower for odd addresses.

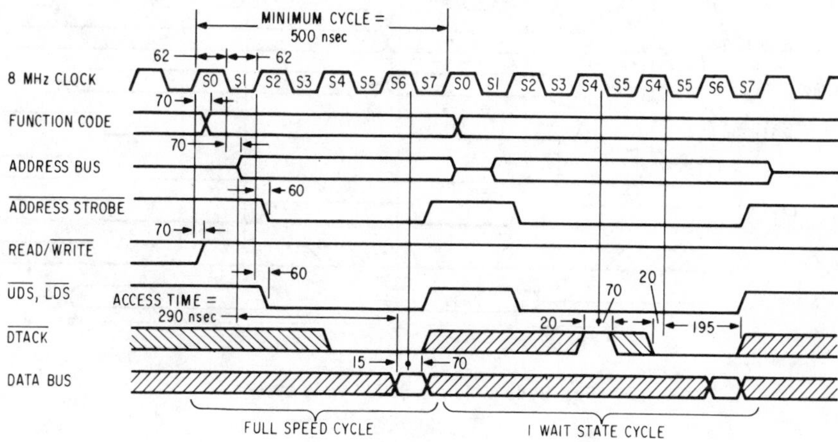

Fig. 5–3. Motorola 68000 read cycle (8-MHz operation)

Besides address and data strobe lines, the 68000 has three additional lines that specify a *function code.* The function code acts like an address modifier and identifies where the associated address came from as a 3-bit code. Five of the possible combinations are used as follows: 001, user data; 010, user program; 101, supervisor data; 110, supervisor program; and 111, interrupt acknowledge. In complex 68000-based systems, distinction between operating system and user programs and also between program code and data can be implemented using the function codes. In simpler single-user implementations, the function code is normally used only to identify interrupt acknowledge bus cycles.

Virtually all normal 68000 program execution involves just two kinds of bus cycles: a read cycle and a write cycle. Each of these requires *four* clock cycles to execute (assuming no wait states); thus, the maximum bus cycle rate is 2 MHz with the standard 8-MHz clock frequency. In addition to read and write, there is a very rarely used read-modify-write cycle, a "68000-compatible" cycle, and an interrupt acknowledge cycle.

Figure 5–3 shows a simplified 68000 read cycle. Each half-cycle of the clock is given a "state number" of 0 through 7. The bus cycle begins with State 0, during which the three *function code* lines are updated. Next, during State 1, the address lines are activated with the correct address. Note that the address lines are disabled and float between bus cycles, a feature that requires careful address decoder design and can be confusing when address signals are examined on an oscilloscope. After this addressing setup, the cycle proper starts in State 2 when Address Strobe is asserted. For read cycles, the Read/Write line remains high to specify a read. Also during State 2, the Lower Data Strobe and Upper Data Strobe lines are driven low according to the type of data transfer and remain along with Address Strobe until the end of the cycle in State 7.

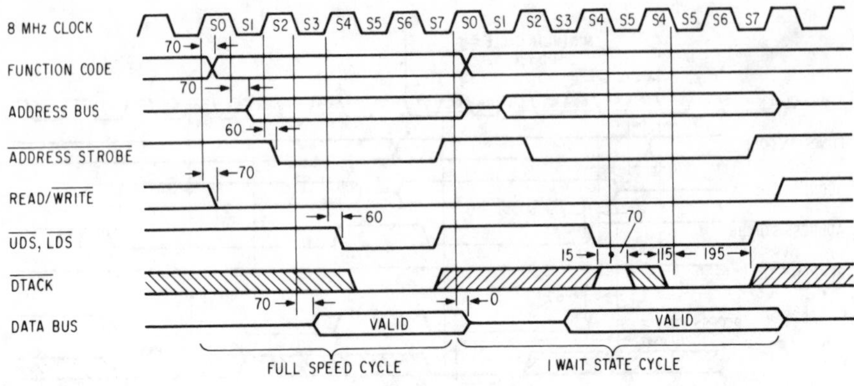

Fig. 5–4. Motorola 68000 write cycle

Like all microprocessors, the 68000 has provisions for waiting on slow memories, dynamic RAM refresh, and so forth. The others, however, have a wait signal, which must be activated to cause such a wait; ignoring the wait signal will allow full speed operation. The 68000 instead uses a data transfer acknowledge signal (DTACK), which must be driven to cease waiting and allow the cycle to complete. Motorola literature, which is geared toward large-system implementation, devotes a great deal of space to how this signal should be driven, which makes 68000 bus cycles appear to be much more complex than they really are. In reality, DTACK can be treated as simply the inverse of wait in a simple system. In systems with all static memory requiring no wait states, DTACK can simply be tied to ground, and the bus cycles will proceed at full speed.

In any case, DTACK is sampled at the beginning of State 5. If it is low, the cycle proceeds, and read data is latched in the microprocessor at the beginning of State 7. If DTACK is high when sampled in State 5, States 4 and 5 are repeated indefinitely until it is seen to be low. Thus, waiting is in increments of 125 nsec (assuming an 8-MHz clock), a much smaller penalty than with the 6502. For static memories (such as ROM), the allowable read access time is about 290 nsec, whereas, for dynamics (which are triggered by address strobe rather than an address change), it is about 235 nsec. Neither requirement puts much stress on modern memory components, so zero wait state operation should generally be possible.

Figure 5–4 shows a write cycle, which is quite similar to the read cycle just discussed. During State 2, simultaneously with Address Strobe, Read/Write goes low to signal a write cycle. The data strobes are not activated until State 4, at which time data on the data bus is guaranteed to be stable. When a word is written, both data strobes are activated to cause writing into both halves of the word. However, only one is activated when a byte write is to be performed. Memory must be organized into two 8-bit halves such that writing only occurs when the corresponding data strobe is activated in conjunction with read/write being low. All signals remain stable until State 7 when the address and data strobes are removed. Address and data themselves remain for one additional half-clock. Since valid data and address completely overlaps read/write and the data strobes, there is no problem in using transparent latches for output registers as there is in the 6502.

The read-modify-write cycle is shown in Figure 5–5. Most high-performance minicomputers and mainframes use this type of cycle, which is shorter than separate read and write cycles because the address is sent out only once, to speed up certain instructions such as "increment memory." In the 68000, it is actually longer (10 clock cycles instead of 4 + 4) and used only for interprocessor communication in a multiprocessor shared-memory system. The idea is to link the testing (read) and setting (write) phases of memory flag manipulation such that no other processor can test or change that same flag between the two phases. Only one 68000 instruction, called appropriately enough Test And Set, uses the read-modify-write cycle. Its distinguishing feature is that Address Strobe remains active during both the read and write halves of the cycle, which should prevent the bus arbitrator in a multiprocessor system from giving control to another processor between the halves. Since the Test And Set instruction does very little (other instructions are much more useful for single-processor flag manipulation), its use can be avoided and this type of bus cycle ignored in a simple system design.

Most of the time, 68000 bus cycles are executed back-to-back with no dead time between State 7 of the previous cycle and State 0 of the next cycle. This is due in part to pipelined internal operation in which the next instruction is often read from memory while the previous one is still executing. There can, however, be any number of idle clock cycles between bus cycles, which causes problems when interfacing to I/O chips designed for the 6800 (Motorola's original 8-bit microprocessor) and the 6502, which require uniformly spaced bus cycles. The 68000 thus offers a "6800- (6502) compatible bus cycle" option. At all times while power is applied and the clock is running, the 68000 will generate a uniform rectangular wave called

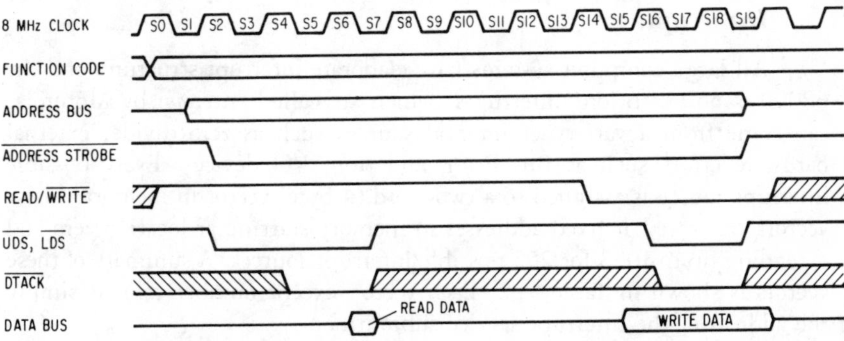

Fig. 5–5. Motorola 68000 read-modify-write cycle

Enable, which is equivalent to the 6502's Phase 2. The frequency of this signal is one-tenth the clock frequency and has a 60% low, 40% high duty cycle. Any normal 68000 bus cycle can be converted into a synchronous 6800 cycle by driving the Valid Peripheral Address (VPA) line low before the beginning of State 4. This would normally be done by a decoder recognizing the address of an I/O chip on the address lines. The 68000 will then wait until Enable goes low, drive Valid Memory Address low, and then transfer data when Enable goes high and low again. Since Enable is a uniform frequency rectangular wave and 68000 bus cycles can start at any time, the amount of time required to execute a 6800-compatible cycle can vary from 10 clocks to 18 clocks. One could in fact make all bus cycles 6800-compatible by grounding the VPA line, but then system speed would be less than half of its potential.

Several other bus control signals are available for more complex systems. One of these is Bus Error, which will abort a bus cycle in progress and generate an interrupt if activated. In a small system, its main use is to flag attempted access of nonexistent memory as an error condition and return to the operating system. In a large system using virtual memory, this signal would come from the memory manager and would indicate that the area of memory just addressed is on disk and needs to be swapped in. In such cases, bus cycles can actually be *retried* by proper use of the Halt signal. A simple system would just tie Halt and Reset together and use the result as the system reset signal.

Three signals are used for direct memory access (DMA) applications. These are Bus Request, Bus Grant, and Bus Grant Acknowledge. They operate in a complex two-phase handshake sequence that will not be detailed here. The 68000 is quite efficient in releasing the bus for DMA with as little as one clock cycle of overhead involved. As is traditional with microprocessors, once the 68000 has released control of the bus (which includes data, adddress, and most of the controls), it is the responsibility of the DMA device to generate all of the timing signals needed for data transfers.

Interrupts

All large computer systems have elaborate interrupt structures and the 68000 is no exception. Interrupts, which are called *exceptions* by Motorola, can come from a variety of internal sources such as zero divide, external hardware errors such as Bus Error, and from I/O devices. Every possible interrupt source is assigned to a two-word (4-byte) vector in memory. These vectors are stored at fixed addresses in memory starting at location zero and extending up to 1023 for 255 possible interrupt sources. A summary of these vectors is shown in Table 5–2. Each vector, except number zero, is simply the address of the interrupt service subroutine.

When an interrupt occurs, the processor status and a return address are pushed onto the supervisor stack. Next, the corresponding vector is read to

Table 5–2. 68000 Interrupt Vectors

Address (Hex)	*Description*
000000	Reset, initial stack pointer
000004	Reset, initial program counter
000008	Bus error
00000C	Address error
000010	Illegal instruction
000014	Zero divide
000018	CHK instruction failed
00001C	TRAPV instruction saw overflow
000020	Privilege violation
000024	Trace interrupt
000028	Unused op-codes beginning with hex A
00002C	Unused op-codes beginning with hex F
000030–000038	Reserved vectors
00003C	Uninitialized interrupt
000040–00005C	Reserved vectors
000060	Spurious interrupt
000064	Level 1 autovector I/O interrupt
—	
00007C	Level 7 autovector I/O interrupt
000080	TRAP 0 instruction
—	
0000BC	TRAP 15 instruction
0000C0–0000FC	Reserved vectors
000100–0003FC	Available for I/O-device-generated vectors

determine where the service routine resides. It is the responsibility of the service routine to save any registers it might use and restore them when it returns. When complete, a Return From Interrupt instruction is used to restore the status register and return to the interrupted program.

System reset is actually vector zero but is handled differently. Nothing is saved on reset; instead, locations 0–3 are loaded into the supervisor stack pointer and locations 4–7 give the address of the initial program code. Thus, a 68000 system must always have read-only memory for these eight locations. Typically, all of low memory will be ROM, and the interrupt/ vectors will point to a prearranged area of RAM that contains a modifiable jump table to the actual interrupt service subroutines. Since low memory must be ROM, most 68000 operating systems reside in low memory and put user programs in high memory, the exact opposite of 6502-based systems.

The 68000 has a wealth of internally generated interrupts. The simplest of these flag software error conditions such as division by zero, accessing a word at an odd address, and illegal instructions or addressing modes. When in user mode, some instructions are privileged and will cause an interrupt when executed. Actually, illegal instructions are divided into three groups and each group interrupts through a different vector. One group is truly illegal and will remain so even with future incarnations of the 68000. The other two groups comprise "emulator" instructions and each has potentially 4,096 variations. In the future, some of these may do something useful such as floating-point math. For now, the subroutine that services the emulator instructions can decode and "execute" them in software. Beyond these, there are 16 more trap instructions, each with its own interrupt vector. The traps are typically used to call operating system routines (as many as 16) without the user program needing to know where in memory the routines are stored. Finally, there is a trace interrupt that is generated after every instruction execution if the trace bit is on in the status register. This feature makes it very easy to implement software tracing of program execution.

There are eight separate interrupt priority levels in the 68000. The highest are internally generated and external hardware error indications that cannot be disabled. The other seven levels are normal I/O-type interrupts. A 3-bit level number in the status register determines which levels are allowed to generate interrupts. When this register contains seven, all I/O interrupts except Level 7 are inhibited. When it contains lower numbers, lower level interrupts are allowed. A zero level number allows all interrupts. When an interrupt is recognized, the current level number in the status register is changed to match the level number being serviced, thus inhibiting further interrupts on that or a lower level. Higher-priority interrupts, however, can still interrupt the lower-priority service routine, thus providing a true multilevel nested operation.

I/O interrupt hardware can be either simple or complex. For a simple system, the 68000 can be instructed to generate a vector number based on the priority level being serviced, thus providing up to seven possible interrupt sources. This *autovector* mode is activated by driving the VPA signal during interrupt acknowledge bus cycles. Using this approach does not preclude having multiple interrupt sources on each level, but then the level service routine would have to poll devices on its level to determine which was interrupting. With more complex hardware, each interrupting device can drive a unique 8-bit vector number onto the data bus during interrupt acknowledge bus cycles. This would provide for direct, automatic entry into each device's service subroutine with no polling or status testing necessary.

Registers

Whereas the 6502 offers a spartan set of four working registers but very flexible memory addressing to compensate, the 68000 offers the most registers coupled with the most useful addressing modes. There are in fact eight *data registers* and eight *address registers,* each of which is a full 32 bits in length. All eight of the data registers (D0–D7) and seven of the address registers (A0–A6) can be used however the program sees fit. Address Register 7 is normally reserved as a stack pointer, since the interrupt, subroutine linkage, and privilege hardware assume that. There are, in fact, two A7 registers, one for Supervisor Mode and one for User Mode. The present privilege mode selects which one is active. Actually, any of the address registers can be used as a stack pointer with equal ease, a valuable feature for many high-level languages.

Data registers act essentially like accumulators and all are equivalent; none have dedicated functions. All of the standard arithmetic operations including shifts and multiply/divide operate on data registers. Some of the addressing modes can use values in the data registers as offsets and indices. Since data registers are 32 bits long, they are often called upon to hold shorter 8- and 16-bit values. In general, when a shorter value is loaded into or created in a data register, it is put at the lower (rightmost) end and the remainder of the register *is not changed.* This action can lead to program bugs but is very useful when needed.

Address registers most closely resemble the index registers of classic computers. Limited arithmetic such as add/subtract, compare, and increment/decrement can be performed but not shifts or logical operations. Address registers always contain 32-bit values; if a word value is loaded or generated, it is *sign extended* to 32 bits. Byte-sized operations are not allowed on address registers.

Addressing Modes

Historically, as small computers became more sophisticated, the greatest improvement was in the variety of memory-addressing modes available. For example, the Digital Equipment PDP-11 became the most popular minicomputer largely because of its many and varied addressing modes. Likewise, the 6502, Motorola 6809, and 68000 have reached the heads of their respective classes because of flexible memory addressing.

Addressing modes are important because, when manipulating common data structures, the availability of a single instruction with an appropriate addressing mode can replace several time- and space-consuming address calculation instructions. This is doubly important in music synthesis applications, which typically manipulate large, moderately complex data structures. A particularly strong point of the 68000 is that these addressing modes work for data arrays as large as the addressing range, i.e., up to 16M bytes. Other processors using segmented memory, such as the 8086 series, may have nearly as many addressing modes as the 68000, but they are useless when array sizes exceed 64K bytes. In fact, a considerable amount of segment register swapping is usually necessary when the total size of all arrays exceeds 128K bytes.

Table 5–3 is a summary description of the addressing modes offered by the 68000. Keep in mind that, whenever an address register or a data register participates in an address mode calculation, the full 32 bits (or optionally 16 bits) of the register is used. Also, the result of an addresss calculation is always a 32-bit integer of which the lower 24 are sent out to the address bus on the 68000. The 68020, with its 4G-byte addressing range, merely sends out all 32-bits of the result; the addressing modes still work the same way.

Table 5–3. 68000 Addressing Modes

Coding	Name	Function
000DDD	Data register direct	Operand is content of data register DDD
001AAA	Address register direct	Operand is content of address register AAA
010AAA	Address register indirect	Operand is content of memory at address in address register AAA
011AAA	Address register indirect with postincrement	Operand is content of memory at address in address register AAA; after the instruction, the operand length (1, 2, or 4) is added to register AAA
100AAA	Address register indirect with predecrement	Before the instruction, the operand length is added to address register AAA; the operand is content of memory at address in register AAA
101AAA O O	Address register indirect with offset	Operand is content of memory at address in address register AAA plus the 16-bit offset in the word following the instruction
110AAA R O	Address register indirect with offset and index	Operand is content of memory at address in address register AAA plus the content of register R (either A or D, either 16 or 32 bits) plus an 8-bit offset; both specified in the word following the instruction
111000 a a	Absolute short (16-bit)	Operand is content of memory at address in the 16-bit word following the instruction
111001 a a a a	Absolute long (32-bit)	Operand is content of memory at address in the 32-bit long word following the instruction
111010 O O	Relative with offset	Operand is content of memory at address in program counter plus the 16-bit offset in the word following the instruction
111011 R O	Relative with offset and index	Operand is content of memory at address in program counter plus the content of register R (either A or D, either 16 or 32 bits) plus an 8-bit offset; both specified in the word following the instruction
111100 I I	Immediate short	Operand is the content of the word following the instruction
111100 I I I I	Immediate long	Operand is the content of the long word following the instruction
111101 111110 111111	Unused Unused Unused	These are reserved for future expansion of the addressing modes; the 68020 uses two of them
	Quick immediate short	A 3-bit field in some instructions specifies an operand between 1 and 8 inclusive
	Quick immediate long	An 8-bit field in some instructions specifies an operand between −128 and +127.

Notes: 1. The first line under "coding" is the 6-bit address mode specification field found in all instructions using generalized address modes. Each symbol represents a single bit in this field.

2. The second line under "coding," if any, represents additional bytes following the instruction that contains additional addressing information. Each symbol represents a complete byte.

3. The "move" instruction contains two generalized address mode fields. If each requires additional following words, the source address word or words come first.

Instruction Set

The 68000 instruction set is best described as simple and straightforward. Although there are only 56 distinct instruction types (just a few more than the 6502), there are thousands of variations when one takes into account the addressing modes and other instruction "modifiers." The instruction set is claimed to be highly "orthogonal" or "symmetrical," which in the limit means that any instruction could use any addressing mode for both source and destination operands. Since actual achievement of this ideal would require a very large number of bits in the operation code and lead to many nonsense instructions, most 68000 instructions have some kind of addressing mode restrictions. Occasionally, these are severe, for instance, the program counter relative mode can never be used to address a destination.

Besides one or two addressing mode specifications, most instructions have a *size* modifier that specifies the length of the operands (Table 5–4). The available sizes are byte (8 bits), word (16 bits), and long word (32 bits). Some instructions may have an implied size or may operate only on words or long words. When either a data or an address register is used as a source operand, the size modifier specifies how much of the lower part of the register to read. When a data register is used as a destination, only the lower part is changed. All 32 bits of an address register, however, receive the sign-extended result of any instruction using it as a destination.

One reason for so few instruction types for such a powerful processor is the presence of a generalized "Move" instruction. This instruction can use any addressing mode or register for the source and almost any addressing mode for the destination. So important is Move that nearly one-quarter of the possible combinations of the 16 operation code bits are used by it. With appropriate addressing modes, Move replaces the myriad loads, stores, pushes, pops, etc., of other instruction sets. One of the variations of Move uses what is known as a "quick immediate" source operand. In a single 16-bit instruction word, any value between −128 and +127 can be loaded into any data register. A "move multiple registers" instruction can move any combination of the general registers to or from any memory location using any of the memory-addressing modes. The combination of registers desired is specified using a one-word bit map where each bit corresponds to a register. This instruction really makes saving and restoring registers in subroutines easy, and it executes at full bus-limited speed.

Add and subtract binary arithmetic can be performed on 8-, 16-, and 32-bit quantities. Not only can a register be the recipient of the result, but a register can be added to memory with the result stored in memory. There is no provision in the 68000 for pairing up data registers to hold 64-bit operands or results so multiply is restricted to 16 × 16 and divide to 32/16. Both signed and unsigned binary arithmetic is possible as well as binary-coded-decimal add and subtract. "Add quick" and "subtract quick" allow any register or memory location to be incremented or decremented by 1 to 8 with

Table 5–4. 68000 Instruction Set Summary

Opcode	*Size*	*Source*	*Destination*	*Operation*
ABCD	B	D	D	Binary coded decimal add source to destination with extend
	B	M	M	
ADD	BWL	Gs	D	Twos complement binary add source to destination with result stored in destination
	BWL	D	Gm-R	
ADDA	WL	Gs	A	"
ADDI	BWL	I	Gd-A	"
ADDQ	BWL	Q3	Gd	"
ADDX	BWL	D	D	Twos complement binary add source to destination with extend
	BWL	M	M	
AND	BWL	Gs-A	D	Logical AND source to destination
		D	Gm-R	"
ANDI	BWL	I	Gd-A	"
ANDI xx	B	I	xx	Logical AND to condition code or status register; status register is privileged
ASL	BWL	Q3	D	Arithmetic shift left data register; shift count is in source
	BWL	D	D	
	W		Gd-R	Shift memory left one bit position only
ASR	BWL	Q3	D	Arithmetic shift right data register; shift count is in source.
	BWL	D	D	
	W		Gd-R	Shift memory right one bit position only
Bcc	BW	O8,16		Branch relative if condition is true
BCHG	L	I	D	Test the bit number specified by the source and set the zero condition according to its state; then change the bit to the opposite state
	B	I	Gd-R	
	L	D	D	
	B	D	Gd-R	
BCLR	L	I	D	Test the bit number specified by the source and set the zero condition according to its state; then clear the bit to zero
	B	I	Gd-R	
	L	D	D	
	B	D	Gd-R	"
BSET	L	I	D	Test the bit number specified by the source and set the zero condition according to its state; then set the bit to one
	B	I	Gd-R	
	L	D	D	
	B	D	Gd-R	"
BSR	BW	O8,16		Branch relative to subroutine; 32-bit return address pushed onto stack
BTST	L	I	D	Test the bit number specified by the source and set the zero condition according to its state
	B	I	Gd-R	
	L	D	D	
	B	D	Gd-R	"
CHK	W	Gs-A	D	Destination compared against zero and content of source; trap if less than 0 or greater than source
CLR	BWL		Gd-A	Clear the destination to zero
CMP	BWL	Gs	D	Subtract source from destination and set condition codes
CMPA	BWL	Gs	A	"
CMPI	BWL	I	Gd-A	"
CMPM	BWL	M+	M+	"
DBcc	W	O16	D	Continue if condition is true; if false, decrement destination and branch relative if not zero
DIVS	W	Gs-A	D	Divide 32-bit destination by 16-bit source and store 16-bit quotient and remainder in the destination; signed and unsigned
DIVU	W	Gs-A	D	
EOR	BWL	D	Gd-A	Logical exclusive-or source to destination
EORI	BWL	I	Gd-A	"
EORI xx	B	I	xx	Logical exclusive-or to condition codes or status register; status register is privileged

Table 5-4. **68000 Instruction Set Summary** *(Cont.)*

Opcode	*Size*	*Source*	*Destination*	*Operation*
EXG	L	D	D	Exchange source register with destination register
	L	A	A	
	L	A	D	
EXT	WL		D	Sign extend next size shorter operand to the designated length
JMP			Gj	Jump unconditionally to effective address
JSR			Gj	Jump to subroutine at effective address, 32-bit return address pushed onto stack
LEA	L	Gj	A	Load effective address into address register
LINK		O16	A	The 32-bit destination content is pushed onto the stack; next, the stack pointer is loaded into the destination; finally the source is added to the stack pointer
LSL	BWL	Q3	D	Logical shift left data register, shift count is in source
	BWL	D	D	
	W		Gd-R	Shift memory left one bit position only
LSR	BWL	Q3	D	Logical shift right data register, shift count is in source
	BWL	D	D	
	W		Gd-R	Shift memory right 1 bit position only
MOVE	BWL	Gs	Gd-A	Move from source to destination and set condition codes
MOVE xx	W	Gs-A	xx	Move to/from condition codes, status register, or user stack pointer; status register and user stack pointer are privileged
	W	xx	Gd-A	
MOVEA	WL	Gs	A	Move from source to destination
MOVEM	WL	RL	Gd-R-+	Move designated registers sequentially to memory
	WL	Gm− −	RL	Move memory sequentially to designated registers
MOVEP	WL	D	Mo	Transfer data between a register and alternate bytes in memory
	WL	(A)+O	D	
MOVEQ	L	Q8	D	Move source to destination sign extended
MULS	W	Gs-A	D	Multiply 16-bit destination by 16-bit source and store 32-bit product in the destination; signed and unsigned
NBCD	B		Gd-A	Binary coded decimal negate with extend
NEG	BWL		Gd-A	Binary negate destination
NEGX	BWL		Gd-A	Binary negate destination with extend
NOT	BWL		Gd-A	Ones-complement destination
OR	BWL	Gs-A	D	Logical "or" source to destination
		D	Gm-R	"
ORI	BWL	I	Gd-A	"
ORI xx	B	I	xx	Logical "or" to condition code or status register; status register is privileged
PEA	L	Gj	Stack	Push effective address onto stack
RESET				Pulse the reset signal (privileged)
ROL	BWL	Q3	D	Logical rotate left data register, rotate count is in source
	BWL	D	D	
	W		Gd-R	Rotate memory left 1 bit position only
ROR	BWL	Q3	D	Logical rotate right data register, rotate count is in source
	BWL	D	D	
	W		Gd-R	Rotate memory right 1 bit position only
ROXL				Same as ROL except uses extend bit
ROXR				Same as ROR except uses extend bit
RTE				Status register and program counter restored from the stack, privileged
RTR				Condition codes and program counter restored from the stack

Table 5–4. 68000 Instruction Set Summary (*Cont.*)

Opcode	*Size*	*Source*	*Destination*	*Operation*
RTS				Program counter restored from the stack
SBCD	B	D	D	Binary coded decimal subtract source from destination with extend
	B	M	M	
Scc	B		Gd-A	Set all bits in destination equal to specified condition (false = 0, true = 1)
STOP		I16		Load source into status register and stop until interrupted, privileged
SUB	BWL	Gs	D	Twos complement binary subtract source from destination with result stored in destination
	BWL	D	Gm-R	
SUBA	WL	Gs	A	
SUBI	BWL	I	Gd-A	"
SUBQ	BWL	Q3	Gd	"
SUBX	BWL	D	D	Twos complement binary subtract source from destination with extend
	BWL	M	M	
SWAP	W		D	Swap 16-bit halves of destination
TAS	B		Gd-A	Set negative and zero condition code according to destination and then set bit 7 of destination; uses special read-modify-write bus cycle
TRAP		I4		Generate internal interrupt to trap vector specified by 4-bit immediate field
TRAPV				Generate internal interrupt if overflow condition is set
TST			Gd-A	Set condition codes according to destination
UNLK	L		A	The stack pointer is loaded from the specified address register; a long word is then popped from the stack and loaded into the address register

Addressing mode key:

Gs	General source address, any of the coded address modes in Table 5-3.
Gd	General destination address, any of the coded address modes except the immediate and relative modes.
Gm	General memory address, any of the coded address modes except register direct.
Gj	General jump address, any of the coded modes except register direct, predecrement, postincrement, and immediate.
−A	Address register direct not allowed.
−R	Neither address nor data register direct allowed.
−+	Address register indirect postincrement not allowed.
−−	Address register indirect predecrement not allowed.
−±	Neither postincrement nor predecrement is allowed.
A	Any address register.
D	Any data register.
M	Address register indirect addressing mode.
Mo	Address register indirect with offset addressing mode.
I	Any of the immediate addressing modes, length equal to operation length or a following number.
Q	Quick immediate, either 3 bits (range 1–8) or 8 bits (range −128 to +127).
O	Offset (displacement) following the instruction, either 8 or 16 bits.
RL	Register list coded as a 16-bit word following the instruction. Each bit corresponds to a register and a 1 bit means process the register.
xx	Specialized source or destination as listed in instruction description.

a single 16-bit instruction. Along with arithmetic, the usual And, Or, and Exclusive-Or operations are available with either a data register or memory as the destination.

The 68000 maintains five condition code bits that are set after most instructions. Four of these are Negative, Zero, Carry, and Overflow, which are used by the conditional branch instructions. The fifth is called Extend and is set the same as Carry on arithmetic instructions but is not affected by moves. The Extend bit is used instead of carry by the multiple-precision instructions Add Extended and Subtract Extended. Conditional branch instructions have a 4-bit field that is coded for useful combinations of the condition codes. For example, the "greater than" jump condition is determined by a complex logical combination of the Negative, Zero, and Overflow bits such that it works even after comparing two signed numbers that were large enough to cause overflow when subtracted in the comparison process. Explicit branch conditions are available for all seven possible relations between two operands, both signed and unsigned, plus an always true and an always false condition to make a total of 16. The conditional branch instruction itself can test for a condition and jump up to 126 bytes away in a one-word instruction. A two-word format can jump up to 32K bytes away while an unconditional jump instruction can use any addressing mode to jump anywhere.

Other unusual or specialized instructions include test any bit by bit number in either a register or memory and optionally set, clear, or flip it. The bit number itself can either be specified in the instruction or in a data register. Check is a single word instruction that simultaneously compares a data register with zero and a value specified using any addressing mode. If the register content is out of bounds, an interrupt is generated. This instruction can be liberally sprinkled in sensitive code without significantly increasing its space or time requirements. Another time-saver is the Decrement and Branch instruction. As usual, it will decrement the content of a register and simultaneously branch if the result is not yet negative. However, it also tests a specified branch condition and will not branch if it is met. Thus, there are two possible exits from a loop constructed using this instruction. Link and Unlink instructions are used to conveniently reserve space on the stack when a subroutine is entered and then freeing it upon return. Load-Effective Address simply performs an addressing mode calculation and puts the result into a specified address register or it can be pushed onto the stack.

Speed

Computing the exact execution time of a particular 68000 instruction is difficult because the effect of each addressing mode for both the source and destination operands as well as the size specification must be considered. In general, however, all of the simple instructions require time equal to the sum of their memory cycles plus perhaps two to four more clock cycles for internal computation. Shifts require two clock cycles per position shifted. Multiply requires approximately 70 clocks, whereas divide needs 150, which translates into 9 and 19 μsec, respectively, at 8 MHz. Interrupt response takes about 44 clocks, which, when added to the longest possible instruction (a divide), gives a worst case response time of 24 μsec. In order to obtain this level of performance, the 68000 often "looks ahead" in the instruction and data stream. Thus, there is some uncertainty in timing, and occasionally (such as when a branch is successful) extra words are read from memory that are never used.

As the foregoing figures show, the 68000 and indeed all current 16-bit microprocessors are a little weak on math in relation to its strength in other operations. Floating-point subroutines, which would be needed by most high-level languages, are slower yet with typical times of 100 μsec for multiply and 40 μsec for add/subtract (single precision). The universal solution to this problem is the addition of a separate math "co-processor" IC connected in parallel with the microprocessor, which in effect adds hardware floating-point instructions to its repertoire. Such chips bring the floating-point multiply-divide times down to the same range as the corresponding integer operations and greatly simplify programming. At the time of writing, Motorola had announced such a co-processor for the 68020 but was far from actually having it available. Instead, applications needing high-performance arithmetic, such as music synthesis, have utilized the National Semiconductor math co-processor intended for their 16000 microprocessor, which can be easily driven by a 68000 as a peripheral.

Software

From the preceding, it should be obvious that the 68000 is exceedingly easy to program in assembly language when compared with other microprocessors, both 8- and 16-bit. Inexplicably, usable and affordable 68000 software for single-user systems has been very slow in materializing. Operating systems, such as UNIX, are typically very large, complex, and expensive, with pricetags exceeding $1,000 *per CPU* not uncommon. OS-9 is more reasonable but still much more complex and expensive than operating systems for 8-bit processors were. Languages seem to suffer from the same problem, with pricetags for good compilers equally as high as the operating systems. Most of the problem stems from the 68000's historical use in large and expensive time-sharing computers. Use of the 68000 in Apple's MacIntosh computer was expected to quickly remedy the situation and may ultimately do so, although not nearly as fast as expected. Hopefully, as more low-cost single-user 68000-based computers are introduced with *open architectures,* low-cost software optimized for single-user applications will become available.

SECTION II

Computer Controlled Analog Synthesis

As was often pointed out in Section I, computers can be involved in electronic music synthesis in one of two distinctly different ways. A computer may be interfaced to either standard or specialized sound-synthesizing equipment and thus perform as a *controller* of this equipment. Or, with suitable programming, the computer may merely *simulate* such equipment and thus generate sound *directly*. Of these two means of involvement, the application of microprocessors to control functions seems more straightforward. In addition, the weight of current interest seems to be toward computer-controlled synthesizers. Accordingly, Chapters 6 to 11 will be devoted to describing more fully the types of circuits and equipment that must be controlled, the interfacing techniques that may be used to allow such control, and the programming and human interface techniques needed to actually effect the control. In these chapters, the emphasis will be on the control of *analog* synthesizing equipment using *digital* techniques. Analog in this context refers specifically to the entire gamut of voltage-controlled equipment whose general function and usage was described in Chapter 3. Digital refers to the use of microprocessors both as general-purpose control computers and as special-purpose logic replacements in interface equipment.

6

Basic Analog Modules

Probably the most important idea in the history of analog music synthesis is that of a *modular* synthesizer. Prior to the conception and implementation of this idea by Robert Moog, numerous special-purpose synthesizers and, according to their designers, "general-purpose" synthesizers were built and used. Music synthesis, however, is such a large and complex problem that even the most ambitious general-purpose machines had serious shortcomings. The major shortcomings were in the *structure* of the machines, not the capability of the various oscillators, amplifiers, and filters that did the work.

In a modular system, the structure is largely unspecified. The *user* defines the structure appropriate to the requirements at the time and interconnects the available modules to realize that structure. When that requirement has passed, the modules are readily reconfigured to meet the next requirement. The idea is roughly akin to the concept of movable type in printing.

Analog System Standards

There must be some consistency among the modules, however, in order to insure compatibility when they are connected. Before continuing, a few system-wide "standards" that typically apply to a broad range of commercial analog modules will be outlined. Standard power supply voltages are +15 V, +5 V, and −15 V with respect to system ground. The 5 V supply is used by digital logic elements in the system and the ±15 V is used by analog circuits, such as operational amplifiers. All supplies are tightly regulated, usually to better than 1%, although some high-frequency noise can be expected on +5. The standard power supply voltages are generated and regulated at a central location and distributed to all of the modules in the system. Other voltages used by some digital and analog ICs such as +12 V, −5 V, and −12 V are conveniently derived from the standard voltages with IC voltage regulators (some of which are less than 50 cents each) or zener diodes or even resistive voltage dividers.

Although the +15 V and −15 V supplies may be regulated well enough for use as reference voltages, it can be difficult to keep them noise free in large systems with many modules drawing varying load currents. Thus, it may be advantageous to distribute a very carefully regulated reference voltage also. Any board that uses the reference can then buffer it with a simple op-amp voltage follower for load currents up to 20 mA. For maximum ease of use, the reference should be set equal to the standard signal amplitude.

Signal and Control Voltages

Signal and control voltage levels are customarily standardized to either ±5 V or ±10 V. Either level is comfortably below the clipping level of around 13 V exhibited by linear ICs operated on ±15 V. With the almost universally accepted VCO control sensitivity of 1 octave/V, a 5 V system will have to use both positive and negative control voltages to cover an acceptably wide frequency range. Ten-volt systems, on the other hand, have adequate range with only positive control voltages, although negative values are often desirable for further increasing the low end of the frequency range.

When used in a strictly computer-controlled system, it is attractive to consider "binary scaling" of signal levels and control sensitivities. One very nice set of numbers would be a signal amplitude of 8.192 V and a control sensitivity of 0.9766 octaves/V (1.024 V/octave). If potentials are expressed in millivolts, then these are very "round" binary numbers. Positive control voltages would therefore span eight octaves, which is quite adequate musically (32 Hz to 8 kHz) but could also be extended by the use of negative control voltages. Furthermore, the 8-V levels would be more easily handled (translation: less costly) by analog-switching elements than full 10-V levels while still having substantially better noise immunity than 5-V levels. Using these round binary values in a computer-controlled analog system will considerably ease the transition to purely digital modules or direct synthesis at some later date. In any case, virtually any voltage-controlled module, whether scratch built or purchased, is readily converted (or simply readjusted) to any of these standards. The VCO to be described later, which is designed to a 10-V standard, can be converted to 8 V simply by reducing the system reference voltage to 8.192 V and touching up a few trim pots.

Digital control signals such as an envelope generator trigger can be any amplitude but for compatibility with digital logic should swing between ground and +5 V. The switching threshold level of digital inputs should be around 1.5 V, again for compatibility with digital logic.

Signal and control inputs of modules usually have a fixed impedance of 100K resistive. Although output impedances are sometimes set at 1,000 ohms to allow mixing of parallel-connected outputs, the author prefers a zero output impedance level. This actually provides the most flexibility, particularly in a precalibrated computer-controlled system, because the output voltage remains constant regardless of load. Mixing of outputs is much better accomplished with a multiple-input voltage-controlled amplifier or mixer module anyway. Internal current limiting in nearly all IC op-amps prevents damage if two outputs should be accidently paralleled or an output is shorted to ground. If resistive output protection is required, the 1K output resistor can be placed inside the feedback loop of the output amplifier to eliminate loading errors.

Mechanical Considerations

Standard synthesizer modules are usually designed to mount into a rack with an attractive front panel exposed. The height of the panel is usually fixed at around 6 inches and the width varies upward from 1½ inches according to the number of I/O jacks and panel controls included. The actual circuitry is usually contained on a small printed circuit board mounted to the panel and connected to the jacks and controls with hookup wire.

Interfacing a standard modular system to a computer would probably involve the construction of a "computer interface box," which would be a patch panel with a few up to a hundred or more jacks installed. The interface box would then be patched into the synthesizer just like any other module. Pinboard-patched systems would be handled in the same way conceptually but, of course, would be much neater in appearance. The advantages of such an interfacing approach are that the synthesizer can still be used in the conventional manner and that hybrid systems (conventional manual control combined with computer control) are possible (and even probable).

However, a totally computer-controlled synthesizer need not require any direct manual access to the analog modules. Instead, all patching and operating parameters should be under the control of the computer. Furthermore, the operating programs and procedures in an ideal system should make it considerably *easier* for the user to set up patches and operating parameters through the computer. In such a system, panel-mounted modules and scores of knobs would be superfluous. Internal calibration adjustments would still be necessary, however, to compensate for gradual drift of important parameters as the circuitry ages.

A preferable packaging arrangement then would be printed circuit boards that plug into a backplane; essentially the same method used for logic modules in microcomputer systems. These boards may either be small, each being a one-for-one equivalent of the typical panel-mounted module, or they may be large multichannel or multifunction boards.

The latter approach is quite feasible, since the number of parts needed for a single module function is typically small. Also, large boards can be more cost effective because some circuit elements, particularly computer interface elements, may be shared among the channels. Examples of such boards might be an eight-channel VCO or a completely general quadraphonic "pan pot" consisting of a four-by-four array of VCAs.

Another method of partitioning functions is the "voice per board" concept. The modules that would typically be patched together for a musical voice are all present on the same board, already interconnected. Although not nearly as flexible as a standard functionally modular system, the voice modular approach can be thought of as and controlled like an orchestra with a limited, fixed complement of instruments. Also, much of the cost and complexity of computer-controlled patching is eliminated because patching itself is minimized.

Regardless of board construction and organization philosophy, the backplane and card file housing the boards should be separate from the computer packaging to eliminate possible pickup of digital noise. Also, it may be necessary to shield the boards from each other with perhaps a steel cover plate to minimize crosstalk. Backplane wiring of audio signals may also need to incorporate twisted pairs or shielded cable.

The active analog circuits on such boards either could be built up from scratch using the circuits about to be described as a foundation or may be purchased as "epoxy modules" from several sources. The scratch method is becoming much easier as linear ICs designed specifically for voltage-controlled modules are becoming available. Either way, the per module cost of the computer-controlled system should be substantially less than that of panel-mounted commercial modules. The disadvantage of the total computer-oriented system is, of course, that the computer must be used to "get into" the system at all.

Analog Components

Since a significant portion of the expense of an overall computer-controlled analog synthesizer is in the analog modules, it is appropriate to become familiar with the circuitry in such modules even if the reader intends to use an existing commercial synthesizer. In the following material, actual circuitry[1] of the three most used analog modules will be described. These are tested, practical circuits using a minimum of specialized components. Their performance is excellent and well suited for use in computer-controlled analog-synthesizing systems. The circuit discussions to follow will assume a basic familiarity with linear transistor circuits and IC operational amplifiers. If the reader is unfamiliar with these topics, several excellent references are listed in the bibliography.

The most common active element in these circuits is the ubiquitous operational amplifier. These devices have improved greatly with the introduction of truly low-cost field-effect transistor (FET) input stages. The semiconductor technology used to accomplish this goes by names such as "BIFET" and "BIMOS" because junction FETs and MOSFETs, respectively, are integrated with bipolar transistors on the same chip.

[1]The original source of these circuits is *Electronotes Newsletter*.

Op-amps made with these technologies possess an almost ideal combination of desirable properties such as low cost, wide bandwidth, fast slew rate, and vanishingly small bias currents. It is now quite reasonable to choose one of these amplifiers as a personal "standard" to be used in all applications and forget about specialized "high-speed," "low-bias," or "economy" devices. Even duals and quads are available at very attractive prices. The only real shortcoming of this breed of amplifiers is generally poorer initial offset voltage and drift with respect to equally priced bipolar input types. The appendix gives a listing of the more popular FET input op-amps as well as several conventional bipolar types for comparison.

In spite of the convincing arguments just given, a variety of op-amps will often find their way into circuit diagrams given in this book. The author is reluctant to specify such premium performance devices when a common garden variety 741 or LM301 will suffice. Also many circuits are not original with the author, and, therefore, the originally specified components are shown. The reader can freely substitute the newer types (designated as "general replacement" in the appendix) wherever these are used with no detrimental effect on circuit operation. Occasionally, really high performance in one specification may be neeeded, which would require the use of a specialized device. Most likely this would be an ultra-high-speed or really low offset voltage or drift requirement.

Voltage-Controlled Oscillator

The VCO is simultaneously the most important and most critical module in the system. The circuit topology chosen must, as much as possible, be "inherently accurate" with any practical shortcomings being due to less than ideal components rather than the circuit configuration. The waveform from the basic oscillator should be readily shaped with frequency-independent networks into several additional shapes with distinctly different harmonic spectra containing both even and odd order harmonics. Finally, of course, the circuit should meet the usual goals of low cost, minimum use of specialized components, and operation from standard voltages.

Fundamental Types

Two fundamentally similar oscillator types are popular. One type normally produces triangle and square waveforms, while the other generates a sawtooth and a narrow pulse. Either pair of waveforms can be readily shaped into sawtooth, triangle, rectangle, and sine waveshapes with simple, frequency-independent (containing no inductors or capacitors in the signal path) networks.

A block diagram for either type of oscillator is shown in Fig. 6–1. Note that the oscillator itself is actually a *current*-controlled oscillator. The control voltages are combined by the input-processing block into a single, properly scaled control voltage but still in exponential (actually logarithmic) form.

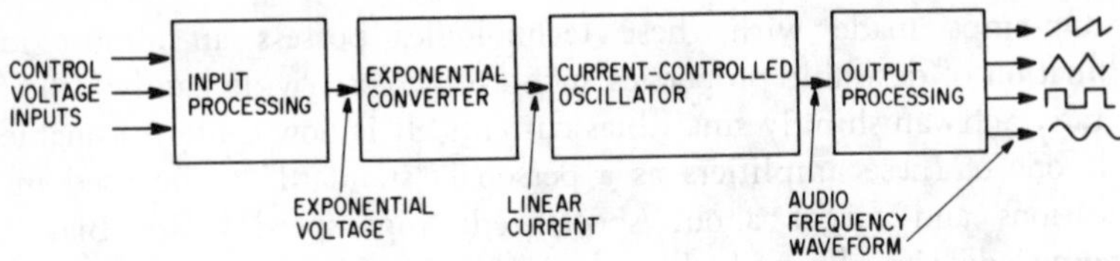

Fig. 6–1. Elements of a VCO module

The exponential converter block simultaneously takes the exponential of the scaled control voltage and converts it into a current, thus exponentially converted *voltages* never occur. The reasons for this are the same as those that forced us to go to an exponential control relationship in the first place; small voltages are extremely susceptible to noise, thermoelectric voltages, and other errors. Small currents, on the other hand, are less readily polluted. Furthermore, practical, accurate exponential conversion elements are inherently voltage-to-current converters.

The oscillator block uses the control current to charge a capacitor. The greater the control current, the faster the capacitor charges (or discharges for a negative current) from one voltage level to another. The triangle-square type of oscillator, for example, uses the positive control current from the exponential converter to charge the capacitor from lower voltage "A" to higher voltage "B" as shown in Fig. 6–2A. When the capacitor voltage reaches B, a level sensor operates a current reverser, which negates the control current, causing the capacitor to discharge toward A again at the same rate. When A is reached, the level sensor reverses the current again and the cycle repeats. Thus, it can be seen that the capacitor voltage assumes a triangular shape. The square wave available is actually the control signal for the current-reversing switch.

The sawtooth-pulse oscillator is similar in that the capacitor is charged from A to B by the control current. The discharge cycle, however, is made as rapid as possible by shorting out the capacitor with a switch when B is reached. The capacitor voltage, then, is a sawtooth shape as in Fig. 6–2B. The advantage is that no current-reversing device is needed, but a very fast shorting switch is necessary for good high-frequency performance. Note that, if the current and voltage levels are the same, the sawtooth circuit will oscillate at twice the frequency of the triangle circuit. In either case, the greater the control current the faster the cycle repeats and the higher the frequency. This relation is theoretically linear for either type of oscillator, assuming that the reversing switch is perfect or the discharge switch has zero resistance and zero on time.

The output-processing block converts the naturally occurring waveforms in either circuit into those waveforms that are customarily used in voltage-controlled synthesizers. Besides shaping, it scales the amplitude and average dc level of the waveforms to match standard signal levels in the system.

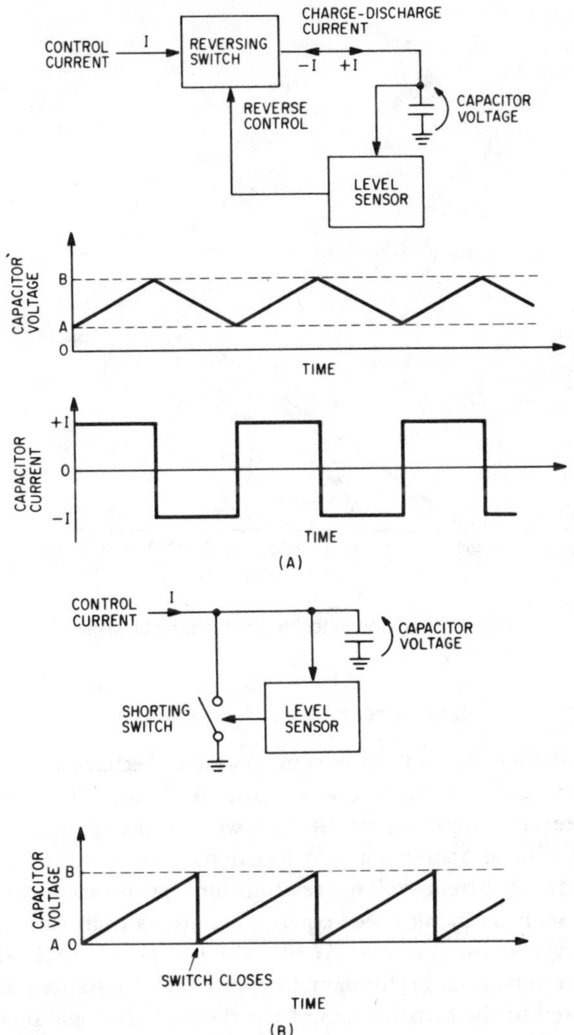

Fig. 6–2. Current-controlled oscillators. (A) Triangle-square oscillator. (B) Sawtooth-pulse oscillator.

For purposes of illustration, the sawtooth type of oscillator will be described more fully. The author feels that the difficulties in rapidly discharging the capacitor are significantly less severe than those encountered in finding a "perfect" reversing switch. Also, a digital equivalent of the sawtooth oscillator, to be described in a later chapter, is substantially simpler to implement than the triangle oscillator equivalent. We will start in the middle with the exponential converter, which is the singular most critical part of the circuit, and work out in both directions.

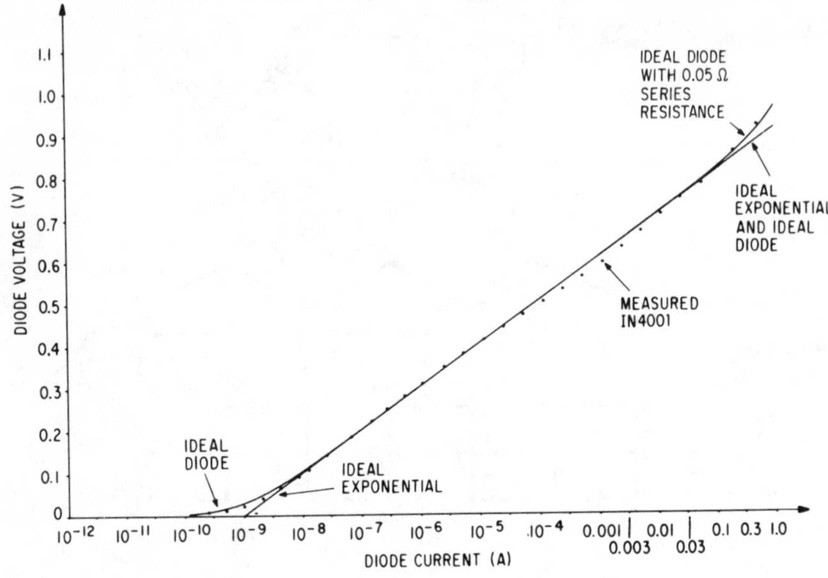

Fig. 6–3. Silicon junction diode characteristics

Exponential Converter

Before the widespread use of semiconductor technology, accurate nonlinear transfer functions were very difficult to obtain. Those that could be obtained were only approximations that were imperfect even with perfect components. Silicon semiconductor junctions, however, are predicted by theory to possess a current–voltage relationship that is exponential in nature. The classical semiconductor diode equation relates current through the diode with the voltage across it as $I = AI_s e^{BT} (e^{CV/T} - 1)$, where A, B, and C are constants (combinations of fundamental physical constants), I_s is another constant related to the construction of the diode, T is the absolute temperature in degrees Kelvin, and V is the applied voltage. Thus, it can be seen that the current is an exponential function of voltage if $e^{CV/T}$ is much greater than unity.

Fortunately, available real diodes are of sufficient quality to very closely conform to theory. The graph in Fig. 6–3 shows the current–voltage relationship of a 1N4001 diode, a very common 10-cent item. The graph is on semilog coordinates to make exponential behavior readily apparent. Also shown is a plot of an absolutely ideal exponential response, a theoretically perfect diode, and a perfect diode with a fixed series resistance of 0.05 ohms, a typical value for the 1N4001. Note the extremely close correspondence between the actual diode and the ideal diode with series resistor model over a current range of better than 10^9 to 1. In fact, the range of close conformity with an ideal exponential response exceeds 10^6 to 1. Obviously, this diode or something similar is worth considering for the exponential converter.

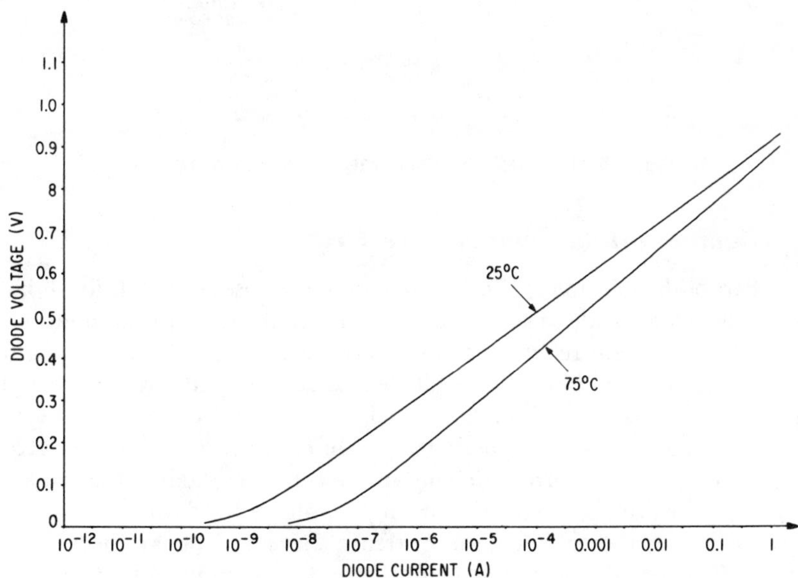

Fig. 6–4. Temperature dependence of diode characteristics

All is not rosy, however, as the graph in Fig. 6–4 shows. The diode characteristic is adversely affected by temperature! Not only does the curve shift to the right with increasing temperature, its slope changes somewhat. This behavior, of course, was predicted by the diode equation, since both exponential terms are dependent on temperature. Variation of the first term is responsible for the right shift, and the magnitude of B is such that the diode current doubles for every 10°C increase in temperature, assuming everything else remains constant. Variation of the second term with temperature is much less, since T is alone in the denominator and is responsible for the change in slope.

A voltage-controlled oscillator based on this diode would have drifted over five octaves upward in frequency and would respond at the rate of 1.16 octaves/V relative to initial tuning and 1 octave/V at 25°C (equivalent to room temperature of 77°F). Drifts with smaller temperature changes would be proportionally less but still a 1°C change in temperature would cause nearly a half-step pitch drift. This temperature dependence is clearly unacceptable unless the diode is kept in a very precise temperature-controlled chamber!

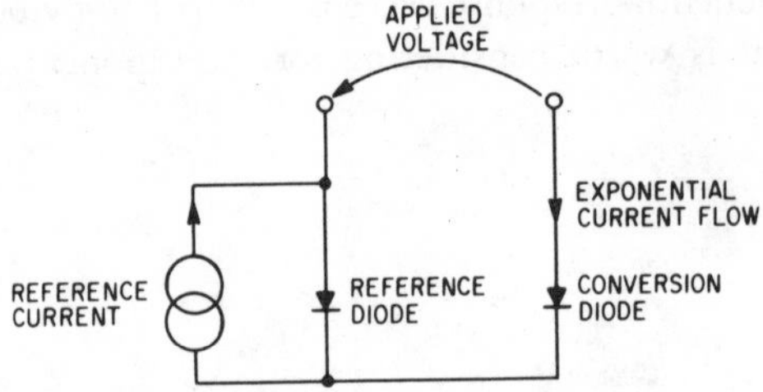

Fig. 6–5. Temperature compensation with a second diode

Compensating Temperature Drift

Part of the solution to this problem lies in the use of an additional diode with characteristics identical to the first one and the circuit configuration of Fig. 6–5. A constant reference current is applied to this added diode with a magnitude about midway in the range of usable output currents from the converter. The voltage to be converted is now applied between the two diodes (in practice from an operational amplifier so that the reference current is not upset), and the current flowing in the converter diode is the exponentially converted current. Note that the input voltage must swing positive and negative to get the full range of currents above and below the reference current. This circuit completely compensates for the right shift of the diode characteristic with increasing temperature because a similar shift occurs for the voltage across the added compensation diode. The change in slope is not corrected, but it is a much smaller effect than the horizontal shifting.

In a practical application, matched transistors are used for exponential conversion partly because matched diodes are rare but mostly because the three terminals on a transistor allow the circuit paths for voltage application and current output to be separated. For good-quality transistors (constant, high current gain), the collector current is proportional to the exponential of the base to emitter voltage according to the equation, $I_c = A\alpha I_{es}e^{BT}(e^{11627V_{be}/T} - 1)$, where I_c is the collector current, α and I_{es} are transistor-construction-dependent constants (common base current gain and emitter saturation current, respectively), and V_{be} is the base-emitter voltage. This equation is essentially identical to the diode equation given earlier.

Figure 6–6 shows a practical configuration with the input voltage referenced to ground and an op-amp-regulated reference current source. The op-amp maintains a constant reference current independent of changes in the exponential output current by adjusting its own output voltage to carry away the sum of the reference and output currents. The only real constraint on reference current magnitude is that it not be so large as to cause internal transistor resistances to come into play or be so small that leakages become significant. Therefore, the reference current is ideally set to 1 μA, about midway in the range of useful currents (1 nA to 1 mA) but, due to finite

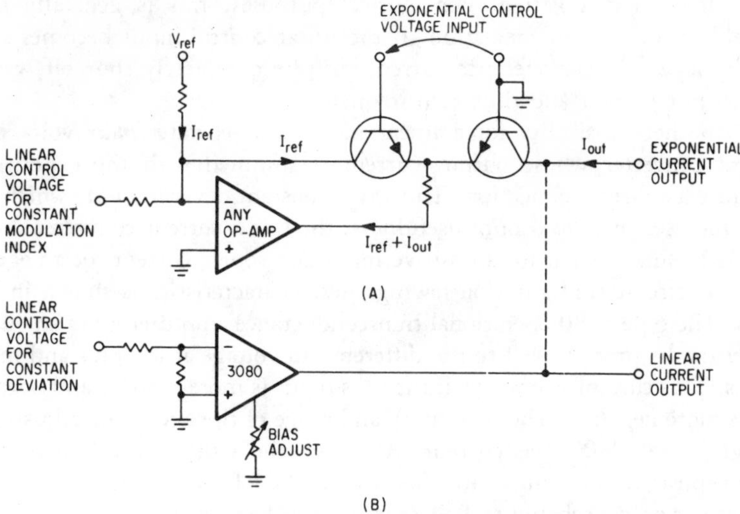

Fig. 6–6. Practical exponential converter. (A) Exponential voltage to current converter. (B) Linear voltage to current converter.

op-amp bias currents, is typically set to around 10 μA. When connected to the oscillator to be described later, a current range from about 0.25 μA to 0.25 mA will cover the audible range. The resistor in series with the amplifier output serves to limit the maximum output current to a safe value. Like the two-diode circuit, the matched transistors cancel the major temperature dependence of the exponential converter. The output current flows *into* this exponential converter and the voltage-compliance range is from roughly ground to the positive collector breakdown voltage. Note that *negative-going* input voltages result in increasing magnitudes of output current. The polarity may be reversed simply by swapping connections to the bases of the two transistors. This circuit performs well but still has two remaining imperfections, which will be remedied later.

Linear Control Input

A linear control input for the dynamic depth frequency modulation described in Chapter 3 can easily be added to this exponential converter. One possibility is to simply modulate the reference current by summing the linear control voltage with the reference voltage in the reference current regulator. The effect can be understood by noting the overall I/O relation for the exponential converter: $I_{out} = I_{ref}e^{39V_{in}}$. Thus, the linear control voltage input *multiplies* the oscillator frequency by factors greater than unity for positive inputs or less than unity for negative inputs. Linear frequency modulation implemented through this input will be such that the modulation index (ratio of frequency deviation to center frequency) will be constant as the center frequency is varied. For musical purposes, this is generally more desirable than constant deviation. If the linear control input becomes sufficiently negative, the reference current may be completely shut off, giving zero output current and thus zero frequency.

Another possibility for a linear input is a separate *linear* voltage-to-current converter whose output current is summed with the exponential current via a direct connection. This gives constant deviation FM, which also has some uses. For maximum usefulness, the linear current converter should be able to sink current for a positive input and source current for a negative input. A circuit configuration having these characteristics is shown in Fig. 6–6B. The type 3080 operational transconductance amplifier gives an output *current* that is proportional to the difference in voltage at the plus and minus inputs. This current is positive if the plus input is more positive and negative if it is more negative. The sensitivity and range of the circuit are adjusted by changing the 3080's bias current. Although the actual control current can become positive (sourcing) with this circuit, the following current-controlled oscillator would probably stall if that were to happen.

The 3080 is described more fully in the next section on voltage-controlled amplifiers.

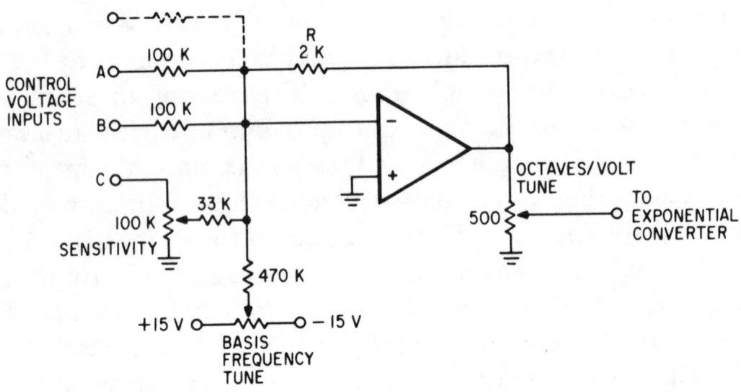

Fig. 6–7. Input voltage processor

Input Processor

The exponential converter transistors are driven by the input-processor block. Typically, several control voltages are summed together to form a composite control voltage with two or three of the control inputs coming directly from the front panel of the module. The sensitivity of one or more of these front-panel inputs is usually adjusted by front-panel controls. Another one or two voltages come from additional panel controls used to adjust the tuning of the module.

The ideal circuit configuration for combining these together with complete isolation is the inverting op-amp summer as shown in Fig. 6–7. In this example, inputs A and B would have a fixed sensitivity, usually of 1 octave/V (or 0.9766 for a binary-calibrated system) and C could be varied from zero up to perhaps 3 octaves/V. The "tune" control determines the basis frequency (frequency with all inputs at zero) by feeding a variable dc voltage directly into the summer. A fine-tuning control and more inputs can be added to this structure essentially without limit. Note that *algebraic* summation of the input voltages is inherent; thus, a negative voltage at one of the inputs will counteract a positive voltage at another input.

The output voltage from the input processor is scaled by adjusting the value of R relative to the input resistors. Since this circuit will drive the base of an exponential converter transistor directly, the transistor equation must be solved to determine the range of output voltages needed. It turns out that a 0.018-V increase in base voltage will double the collector current at room temperature. It is common practice to set R to 2,000 ohms when 100K input resistors are used which would scale a 1-V input down to 0.020 V. An internal trimming potentiometer between the op-amp output and the exponential converter base is then used to adjust to the exact value needed around 18 mV. Note that the polarity inversion (positive-going input voltages produce negative-going outputs) precisely matches the requirements of the exponential converter.

Assuming that the tuning control is set to midrange (no net effect on the control voltage sum) and all control inputs are zero, the output of this circuit would also be zero. The exponential converter would then produce a current equal to the reference current, which is typically set to 10 μA. Positive control voltage sums (more negative input to exponential converter) give higher currents from the exponential converter, while negative sums give lower currents. For normal operation, the tuning control would be set negative so that 0 V from the other inputs would produce the lowest normal audio frequency. Then positive control voltages from 0 V to 10 V would cover the audio range. Negative control inputs in addition to the negative contribution of the tuning control could produce even lower frequencies, useful as control voltages themselves.

Sawtooth Oscillator

The current from the exponential converter could be used to charge (actually discharge since it is a negative current) a capacitor directly. Greater accuracy is obtained, however, if the exponential converter collector remains at a constant voltage near ground, since then the collector-base voltage is near zero and leakages are minimized. This desire is satisfied by feeding the current directly into the summing node of an integrator as shown in Fig. 6–8. The negative current is integrated and inverted by the op-amp and appears as a positive-going ramp at its output. The op-amp used for the integrator must have low bias current yet high speed for optimum low- and high-frequency performance, respectively, which usually means a FET op-amp.

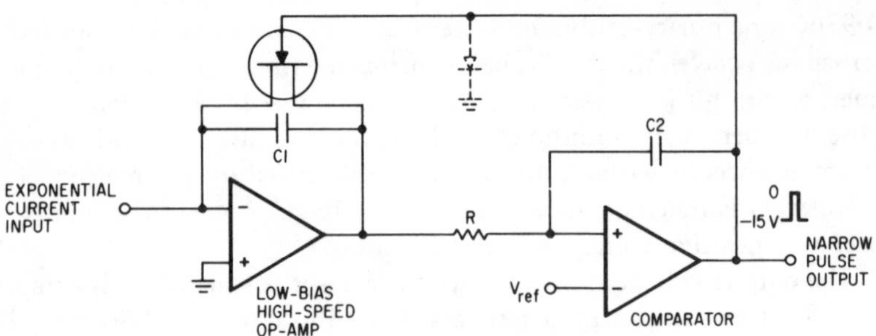

Fig. 6–8. Sawtooth oscillator

The comparator compares the integrator output with a positive reference voltage, V_{ref}. As long as the integrator output is less than V_{ref}, the comparator output is negative, which keeps the FET switch across the integrating capacitor off, allowing it to charge. As soon as the integrator voltage reaches V_{ref}, the comparator output starts to go positive. As it does, the positive comparator input is forced even more positive through C2 giving positive feedback and causing the comparator to snap on. The comparator output is constrained to rise no further than ground, but this is enough to fully turn on the high-threshold-voltage FET switch, which discharges C1 and brings the integrator output back to ground potential in preparation for another cycle. The comparator is prevented from responding instantly to the drop in integrator voltage by the charge accumulated on C2 when the comparator switched high. In effect, a one-shot is formed with a time constant of RC2, which is arranged to be long enough for the FET to completely discharge C1. Even though every reasonable effort is made to speed the discharge, the control current still loses control for a finite time each cycle. This will cause the higher oscillator frequencies to be flat, that is, lower than expected from the control current magnitude. This error can be compensated for as will be shown later.

The value of C1 is chosen to provide the required range of output frequencies given the 0.25 μA to 0.25 mA range of current input. The expression for frequency is $F=I/CV_{ref}$ and the expression for capacitance is $C=I/FV_{ref}$ where V_{ref} is the reference voltage in volts, F is frequency in hertz, C is capacitance in farads, and I is the exponential current in amperes. The easiest way to calculate C is to first determine the highest frequency of interest and then solve the second equation for I = 0.25 mA. The lowest frequency for really accurate response (and zero control voltage if the highest frequency corresponds to a +10-V control voltage) is 1,024 times lower. Much lower frequencies are possible with good components and moisture-proofed circuit boards, as much as 1,000 times lower yet for a total range of over a million to one. For a nominal audio range of 20 Hz to 20 kHz and V_{ref} of +5 V, C1 would be about 2,500 pF. For optimum performance over a 32-Hz to 8-kHz range in an 8-V system with V_{ref} of 4.096 V, C1

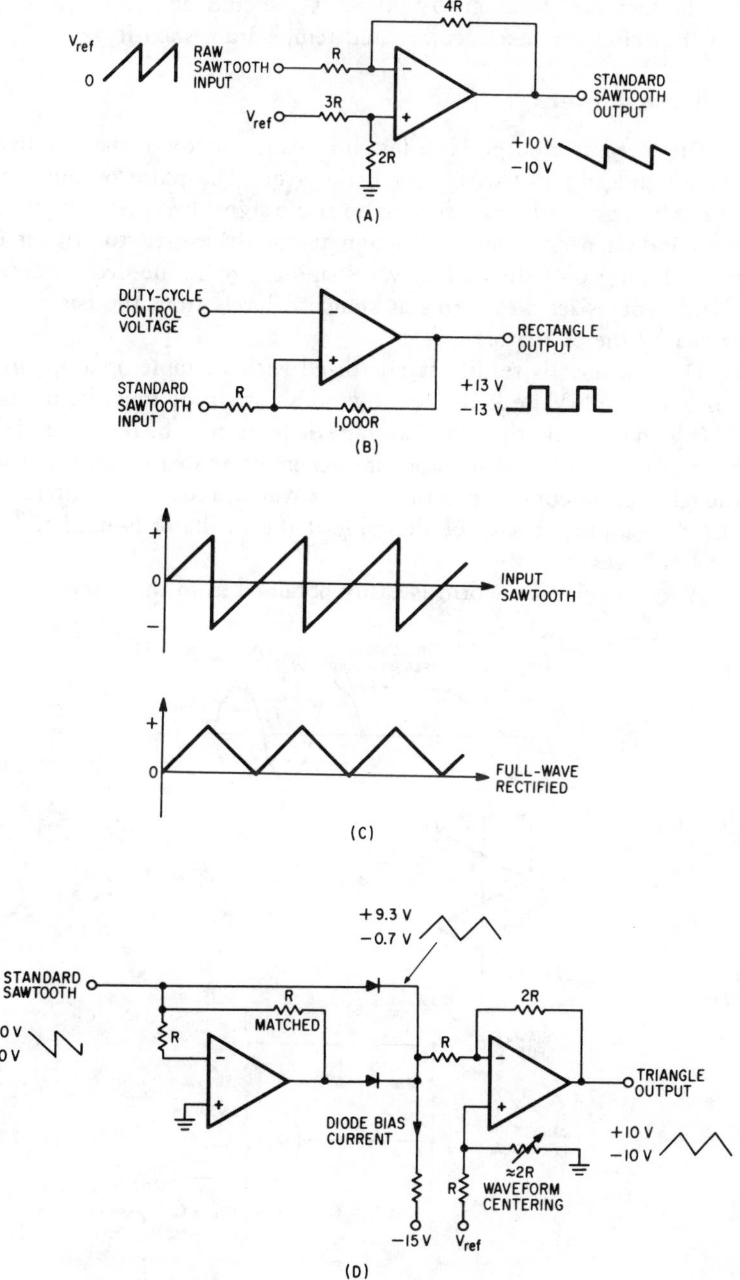

Fig. 6–9. Waveshapers. (A) Sawtooth standardizer. (B) Rectangle shaper. (C) A sawtooth into a triangle. (D) Practical sawtooth-to-triangle converter.

should be increased to about 5,000 pF. C1 should be a high-quality polystyrene capacitor for best accuracy and temperature stability.

Waveshapers

The integrator output is a low-impedance sawtooth that oscillates between ground and V_{ref} with very little error. The pulse output from the comparator is generally not useful as an audio signal because its width is only a few hundred nanoseconds, although it could be used to trigger digital circuits. Figure 6–9 shows the waveshaping circuits needed to derive the standard synthesizer waveforms at standard levels from the basic sawtooth provided by the oscillator.

The sawtooth is readily standardized with a simple op-amp circuit. If V_{ref} is 5 V, the 5-V peak-to-peak sawtooth amplitude must be increased to 20 V (a gain of 4) and the 2.5-V average dc level must be removed. Trimmer pots or precision (0.1%) resistors are generally needed to do this job well. Although this amount of precision is not really necessary for straight audio use of the output, it may be desirable if the oscillator is used to generate control voltages.

A rectangular waveform is easily obtained from the standardized saw-

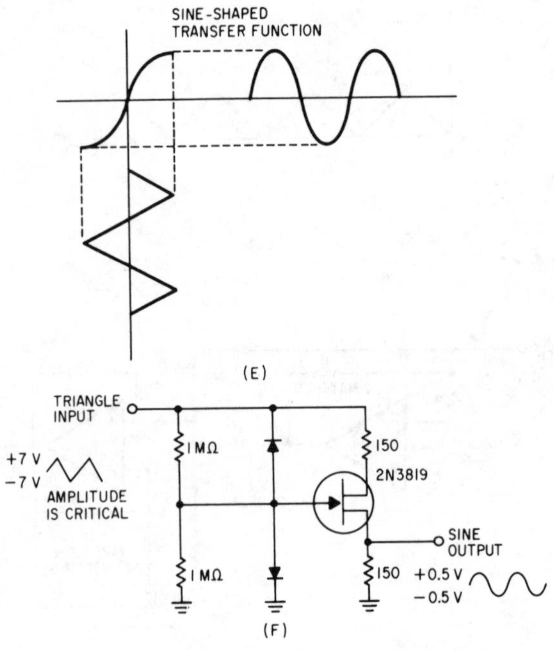

Fig. 6–9. Waveshapers (*cont.*). (E) Triangle-to-sine conversion. (F) Triangle-to-sine converter.

tooth with an op-amp connected as a comparator. The sawtooth is fed into one side of the comparator and a dc width control voltage is fed into the other side. The comparator output will be high whenever the instantaneous sawtooth voltage is higher than the dc comparison voltage and low otherwise. Thus, the duty cycle of the output varies between 100% and 0% as the dc comparison voltage varies between −10 V and +10 V. A small amount of positive feedback gives a Schmidt trigger action to the comparator, which maintains fast rise and fall times even though the sawtooth frequency may only be a fraction of a hertz. The amplitude of the rectangular wave is set by the saturation voltage of the op-amp's output in the circuit shown, although precise standard voltage levels may be easily obtained if desired.

Deriving a triangle waveform from a sawtooth is interesting but relatively simple. The basic idea is to full-wave rectify the sawtooth, which gives the required shape, and then remove the dc component and rescale it back to standard levels. The first step is to obtain a standardized sawtooth opposite in phase to the one already generated with a simple unity gain inverter. The two out-of-phase sawtooths are then fed into a classic two-diode full-wave center-tap rectifier. A resistor to the negative power supply keeps some current flowing through one of the diodes at all times. This simple, open-loop rectifier is far superior to the usual closed-loop rectifier found in op-amp application notes at the higher audio frequencies. Finally, the triangle output amplifier removes the dc (a portion of which is the rectifier diode's forward voltage) and scales the triangle to standard levels. Although the shaping is essentially perfect, there is a small glitch in the triangle when the sawtooth is resetting. This may be minimized by injecting a pulse of opposing polarity at this time or by using a low-pass filter to smooth over the glitch.

A good sine wave may be obtained from the triangle wave by distorting it with a nonlinear circuit. Figure 6–9E shows how a sine-shaped transfer function can round the pointed peaks of a triangle wave into an approximate sine shape. Although several types of nonlinear circuits can be used, the FET-based circuit in Fig. 6–9F works well and is inexpensive. Note that the amplitude of the triangle input must be very carefully matched to the nonlinear transfer function for minimum sine wave distortion. This would normally be accomplished with two trim adjustments, one for amplitude, and the other to compensate for asymmetry. Total harmonic distortion can usually be trimmed to less than 1% with this circuit. Lower distortion is possible by following the sine shaper with a tracking low-pass filter.

Practical Schematic

A complete, practical schematic of the VCO is given in Figs. 6–10 and 6–11. All input structures are resistive (100K) to an op-amp summing junction and can be expanded to fit individual needs. Trimming adjustments are provided so that input sensitivities and output amplitudes can be adjusted to precisely match the system standards for use in a precalibrated computer-controlled system. The existence of +10 and −10 system reference voltages is assumed. Also, several refinements beyond the basic circuit blocks just described have been incorporated.

The input circuit for exponential control voltages has been refined by

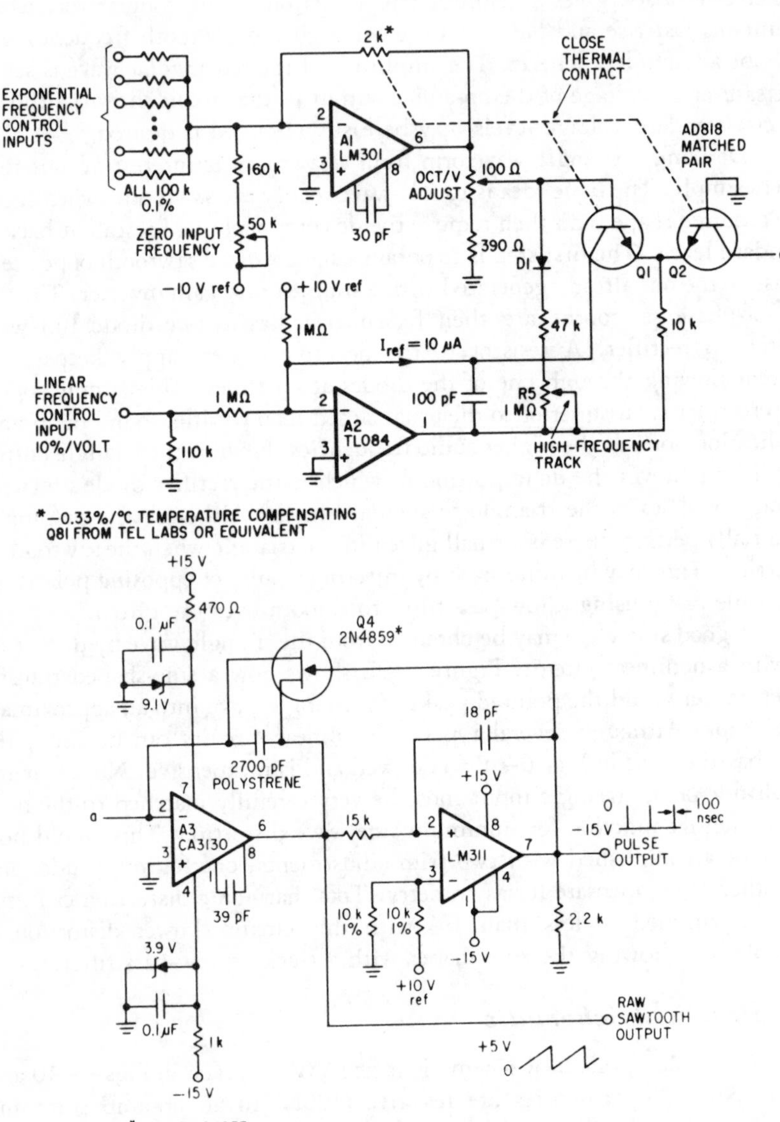

Fig. 6–10. Practical VCO input processor and oscillator

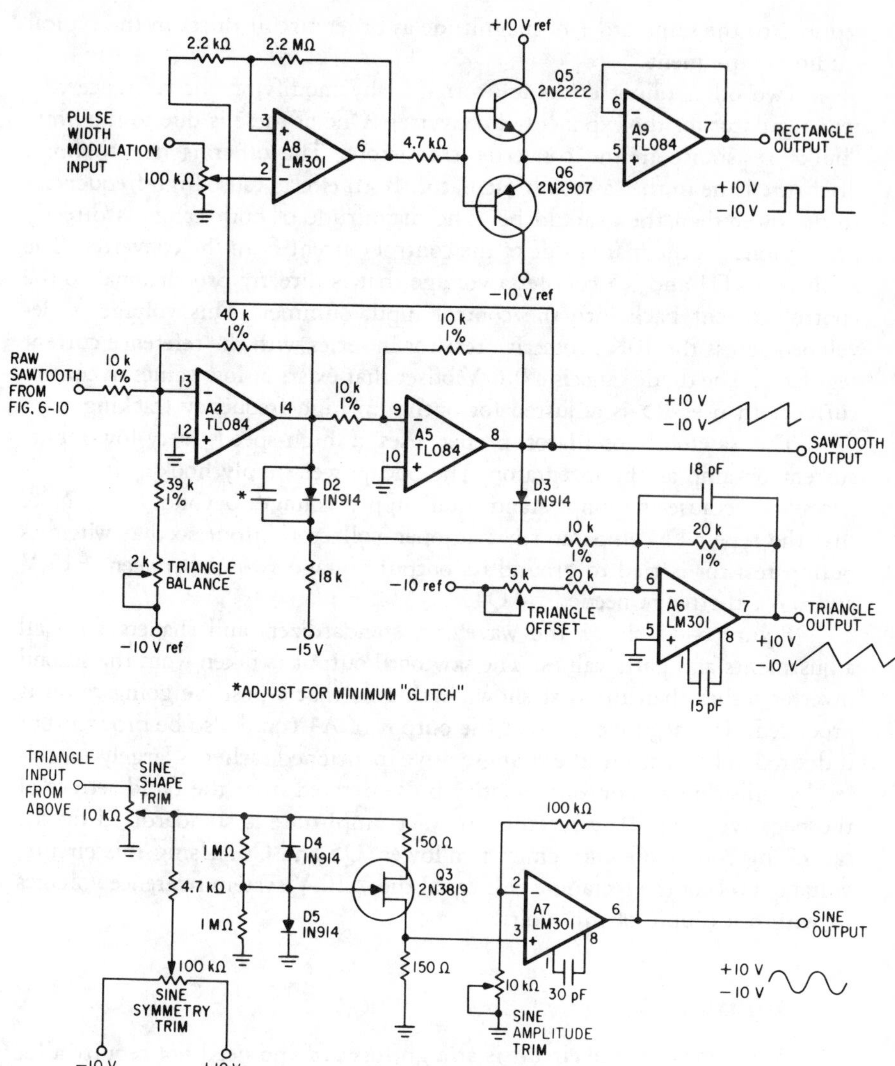

Fig. 6–11. Practical VCO output waveshapers

using a thermistor in the feedback network to cancel out the remaining exponential converter temperature coefficient. At room temperature, this coefficient is about −3,300 parts per million (ppm) per °C; thus, a resistor with a +3,300 ppm temperature coefficient is required. Note that the compensation is exact only at 27°C because the exponential converter temperature dependence goes as $1/T$ rather than as KT, which the resistor provides. Nevertheless, temperature drift due to the exponential converter is reduced to the same order of magnitude as other circuit drifts in the typical studio environment.

Two other minor errors are corrected by modifying the reference current regulator for the exponential converter. One of these is due to the finite "bulk" resistance in the converter transistors. The other is due to finite discharge time in the sawtooth oscillator. Both effects cause high frequencies to be lower than they should be. The magnitude of both errors is directly proportional to the magnitude of the control current from the converter. The addition of D1 and R5 couples a voltage that is directly proportional to the control current back into the control input summer. This voltage is developed across the 10K protective resistor in series with the reference current regulator. The diode cancels a 0.6-V offset that exists at low values of control current. In use, R5 is adjusted for optimum high-frequency tracking.

The sawtooth oscillator proper uses a high-speed, very-low-input-current op-amp as the integrator. The odd power supply hookup for A3 is necessary because it cannot stand total supply voltages beyond 15 V. Note that the type 311 comparator has an open-collector output so that when its pullup resistor is tied to ground its output voltage swings between −15 V and 0 V, the range needed by Q4.

Figure 6–11 shows the waveform standardizers and shapers with all adjustments and parts values. The sawtooth output is taken from the second inverter rather than the first shown earlier so that a positive going ramp is produced. The negative ramp at the output of A4 could also be brought out if desired. The glitch in the triangle wave mentioned earlier is largely cancelled by injecting an opposite polarity pulse derived from the rapid retrace of the negative ramp. The rectangular-wave amplitude is standardized by the saturating complementary emitter follower, Q5 and Q6. Using this circuit, voltage levels of the rectangle will equal the ±10-V system reference voltages to within a couple of millivolts.

Adjustment

Adjustment of the circuit is straightforward and need not require a lot of test equipment, although a frequency counter, accurate digital voltmeter, and oscilloscope are helpful. For use in a precalibrated computer-controlled system, the adjustments should be made to the values listed in Table 6-1. These values offer the most logical control relationship and widest possible range in a precalibrated system. Ideally, they should be set as accurately as possible and then rechecked every few months of operation. This will allow programming of the system to proceed with minimal concern over analog errors in the system. Also shown in the calibration table are performance parameters obtained from a breadboard of the circuit. As can be seen, the performance is excellent in nearly all respects and certainly much better than could be obtained just a few years ago at 10 times the cost.

Table 6-1. Adjustment of Voltage-Controlled Oscillator

Oscillator adjustment

1. Set "zero input frequency" pot for 60 Hz (use power line sync on oscilloscope) with no control voltages applied
2. Apply 1.000 V to an exponential control input and adjust "oct/v adjust pot" for 120 Hz output
3. Remove the control voltage and adjust the "zero input frequency" pot for 16.3525 Hz
4. Apply +10 V to a control input and adjust "high-frequency track" pot for 16745 Hz

Waveshaper adjustment

1. Using a moderate frequency (1 kHz) adjust "triangle balance" pot for best triangle waveshape
2. Adjust "triangle offset" pot for equal positive and negative peaks
3. Vary the capacitance across D2 for minimum "glitch" on the positive peak of the triangle
4. Alternately adjust "sine shape trim" and "sine symmetry trim" for lowest harmonic distortion
5. Adjust sine amplitude for 20 V p-p output. Sine symmetry may have to be touched up for equal positive and negative peaks

Performance of breadboarded unit

Control voltage	*Frequency (Hz)*	*Error (%)*
0.000	16.35	0
1.000	32.71	0
2.000	65.44	+0.05
3.000	131.1	+0.21
4.000	261.9	+0.10
5.000	524.3	+0.19
6.000	1048.0	+0.14
7.000	2096.0	+0.13
8.000	4190.0	+0.09
9.000	8379.0	+0.08
10.000	16745.0	0

Average temperature coefficient at 1 kHz from +25°C to +35°C is 0.11%/ °C.

Voltage-Controlled Amplifier

The VCA is the second of the "basic three" modules. For many applications, its performance is not nearly as critical as the VCO just described. This is because VCAs are normally utilized to control the *amplitude* of an *audio* signal, and the human ear is much less sensitive to inaccuracies in amplitude control than it is to imperfect frequency control. The typical VCA module used in a "manual" synthesis system, therefore, is seldom very precise or carefully calibrated. For a critical application, the user is expected to calibrate the VCA using the several panel controls that are normally available.

In the precalibrated computer-controlled system, however, the use of VCAs to process *control* signals, which may eventually control a VCO, is more likely. For example, the control inputs to a precalibrated VCO will have a fixed but precisely known octave/volt control sensitivity. If one wishes a variable (by the computer) control sensitivity, then a VCA with the control input driven by the computer is inserted in the control path to the VCO. Depending on the design, a VCA may be used as a multichannel mixer with the gain of each channel set by an individual control voltage. When used to mix control voltages, its accuracy again becomes important. Thus, it is apparent that for maximum usefulness attention should be given to accuracy and temperature drift in the design of the VCA.

Controlled Gain Block

The heart of the VCA is the controlled gain block. Actually, a multiplication of one signal (the signal voltage) by another (the control voltage or a function thereof) is being performed. Full four-quadrant multiplication where the output is the true algebraic product of the instantaneous voltages, either positive or negative, at the control and signal inputs is certainly acceptable if not desirable. Note that if this were true, there would be no distinction between control and signal inputs to the block. Actually four-quadrant circuits are fairly difficult and less accurate than two-quadrant circuits. The two-quadrant circuit restricts the control voltage to positive values, while both positive and negative signal voltages are acceptable.

In the past, virtually any scheme that would electrically vary the gain of a circuit was a candidate for the controlled-gain block. Really ancient methods include the use of a photoresistive cell (cadmium sulfide type) illuminated by a neon lamp and remote cutoff pentode vacuum tubes that were designed for variable-gain applications. Even servo motor-driven potentiometers were used when cost was no object. More modern methods include the use of a junction FET as a voltage-variable resistor or recognition of the fact that the dynamic resistance of a diode decreases with increasing forward current. Variation in the gain of a transistor amplifier with bias-current variation was another popular method.

The two standards of comparison that have been used in the past for gain-control techniques are control-to-signal isolation and signal distortion. Control feedthrough into the signal generally results in high-amplitude, low-frequency thumping noises whenever the gain is rapidly changed. Even a moderate amount of such feedthrough is completely unacceptable in modern voltage-controlled equipment usage. Signal distortion, if present, is usually worst at low-gain settings where it is least likely to be noticed. Besides these, speed and accuracy of response are now of great importance also.

Using the first two performance standards, the lamp-photocell approach is essentially perfect. The FET voltage-variable resistor has no control feedthrough but does distort the signal some unless its amplitude is quite small. All other methods (except servo pots) suffer from both maladies to some extent. Unfortunately, a lamp-photocell variable-gain block is impractical for an electronic music VCA because it is very slow, having time constants in the tens of milliseconds range, and is very unpredictably nonlinear in its control relationship. Response of the FET is instantaneous, but it too possesses a nonlinear control response, although somewhat more predictable. Varying the bias in a transistor amplifier, which is the worst method from an inherent control isolation standpoint, is the one that is normally used now to build a VCA. Such a controlled-gain block is called a *transconductance* two-quadrant multipler.

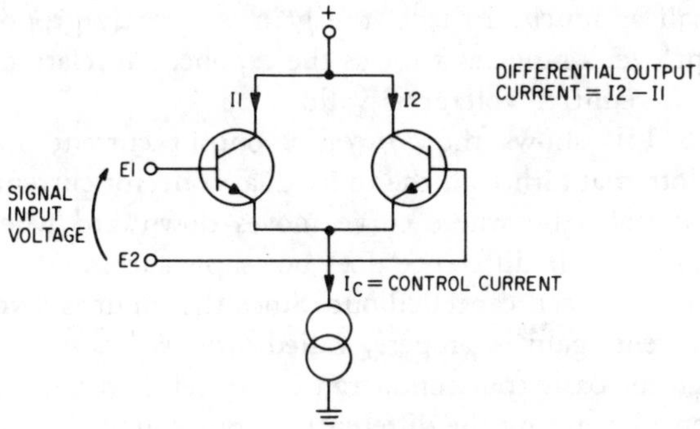

Fig. 6–12. Basic transconductance gain block

Transconductance Gain Block

The basic transconductance gain block is the differential transistor amplifier stage shown in Fig. 6–12. For normal two-quadrant operation, the signal voltage is applied *differentially* between the two transistor bases, and a control *current* applied to the emitters determines the gain. The output signal is the difference in collector *current* of the transistors, which may be converted into a differential voltage by use of equal-value collector load resistors. Normally, the two transistors are assumed to be carefully matched. Important parameters that must be matched are current gain, which should be high (over 100), and the base-emitter voltage versus collector current relationship.

Basic operation is easily understood if a few observations are made. First, the sum of the two collector currents is always equal to the control current. Regardless of the individual base voltages (within reason), the common emitter voltage will adjust itself to make this fact true. Since the transistors are matched, if the differential input voltage is zero, meaning that the base-emitter voltages are equal, then the two collector currents are equal and the differential output current is zero.

Now, recalling the transistor equation given earlier, it was learned that at room temperature a transistor's collector current will double for every 18-mV increase in base-emitter voltage. Therefore, if the differential input voltage became 18 mV, that is E1 = E2 + 0.018, then I1 would be twice as great as I2. Since the sum of the currents must equal the control current, it can be concluded that I1 = 2/3Ic and I2 = 1/3Ic. Increasing the input to 36 mV would shift the ratios to 4/5 and 1/5. Further increases in the input voltage will cause essentially all of the control current to flow through Q1. Reversing the polarity of the input would favor I2.

Figure 6–13A is a plot of the collector currents as a function of differential input voltage for two different control currents. For the reasonably linear portions of the curves in the ± 10 mV range, it is apparent that the slope of the 1-mA curve is *half* that of the 2-mA curve, which means that the *gain* is also half as much. In fact, the gain is directly proportional to the control current over a range as wide as the exponential relation between base current and base-emitter voltage is valid.

Figure 6–13B shows the *differential* output current under the same conditions. Note that although the individual collector currents show severe control feedthrough (the whole curve moves downward when the control current decreases), their difference does not show such a shift meaning that the feedthrough has been cancelled out. Since the input is a voltage and the output is a current, gain is properly called *transconductance.*

Although the basic transconductance gain cell is very simple, driving it properly is not. Generating the differential input voltage is not difficult, but sensing the differential output would require one or more op-amps and excellent common-mode rejection in order to obtain decent control isolation. A variable-current sink, which is required for the control input, requires additional circuitry also.

Operational Transconductance Amplifier

Fortunately, variable-transconductance gain-controlled blocks are available in IC form at prices under a dollar. The 3080 type of *operational transconductance amplifier* (OTA), for example, has the diff-amp gain cell, an output differential amplifier, and a current-controlled current source for the control all-in-one package. Figure 6–14 shows the symbol for an OTA and a highly simplified internal schematic. The device operates on standard ±15-V supplies and has a fairly high-impedance differential-voltage input. Since the common-mode voltage range is quite large (nearly equal to the supply voltages), in practice one of the inputs can be grounded and the signal applied to the other input. The control current is fed *into* the I_C terminal and is absorbed at a constant voltage of about −14.4 when using 15-V supplies. The output is single-ended and is a *current.* Although this takes some getting used to, it usually proves to be an advantage. At room temperature, the output current is equal to $19.2 \times E_{in} \times I_C$, where E_{in} is the differential input voltage in volts, I_C is the control current in milliamperes, and the output is in milliamperes. Note that this relation is accurate only for input voltages less than 10-mV peak and that the output current can never be greater than I_C. The allowable range of I_C for accurate operation is from

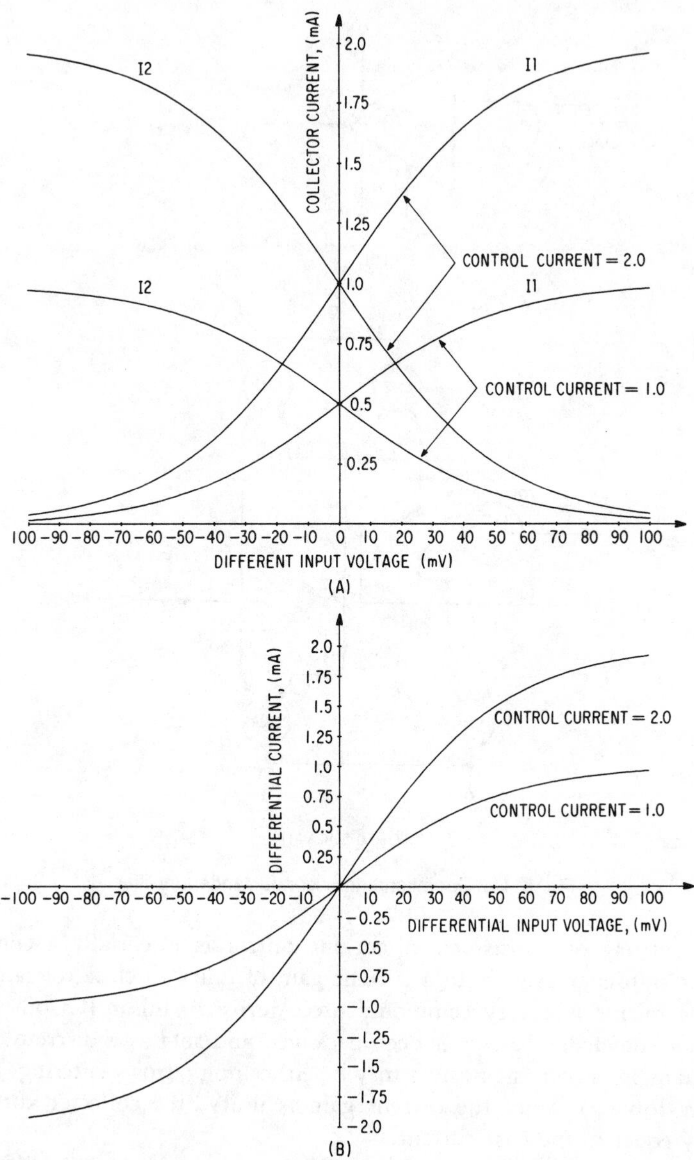

Fig. 6–13. (A) Individual transistor currents for two control currents. (B) Differential output current for two control currents.

0.0005 mA to 0.5 mA with range extension to even lower currents allowable at moderate temperatures.

Internally the 3080 is composed entirely of transistors and *current mirrors* (shown as circles labeled "CM" in Fig. 6–14), which in turn are com-

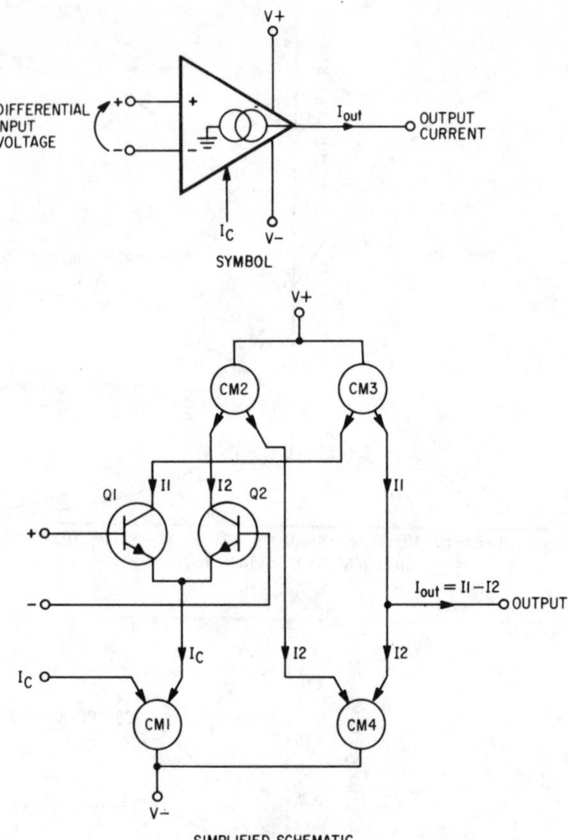

Fig. 6–14. Operational transconductance amplifier

posed entirely of transistors. A current mirror is essentially a common-emitter transistor stage with a current gain of unity to close tolerances. A current mirror is a very commonly used device in linear ICs but to the author's knowledge has never been packaged and sold as a discrete device. Like transistors, current mirrors may be either npn (arrows entering) or pnp (arrows leaving). Since the current gain is unity, the collector current is exactly equal to the base current.

The controlled-gain cell of the 3080 is a two-transistor differential amplifier. Tracing the simplified 3080 schematic will reveal that the differential gain cell emitter current is equal to *Ic* by virtue of CM1. Q1's collector current, I1, gives a positive contribution to the output current via CM3, while Q2's collector current I2, is inverted by CM4 and gives a negative output contribution. The net output current is therefore I1–I2, which means that the current mirrors have performed a differential to single-ended *current* conversion. Since the output is connected only to transistor

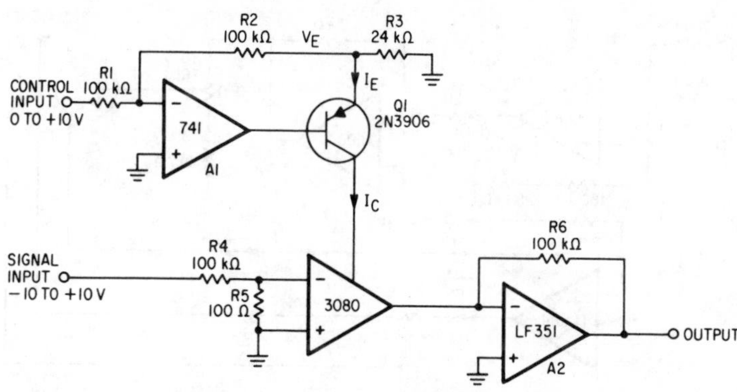

Fig. 6–15. Linear VCA using 3080

collectors, the output impedance is very high and is typically several megohms for the 3080.

Application of the 3080 OTA

Figure 6–15 shows an application of the 3080 as a simple yet accurate linear VCA. The gain of the circuit is given by $A = E_{in}/10$, which means that unity gain is obtained for a +10-V control and zero gain for zero control. Signal input voltages may range between −10 V and +10 V, while the control input is operable over a range of 0 V to +10 V. Negative control inputs completely shut off the signal.

Note that the signal input is attenuated by a factor of 1,000 by R4 and R5 before it is applied to the 3080. This is necessary in order that the ±10-mV linear range of the 3080 input not be exceeded and cause excessive distortion. The control current for the 3080 is generated by A1 in conjunction with Q1. If the current gain of Q1 is high, then I_E is nearly equal to I_C. The precise value of I_E is monitored by R3 to create V_E and is fed back to A1's input via R2. In operation, A1 will adjust its output voltage to make $V_E = -V_{in}$, which is perfectly normal inverting amplifier operation. Actually, the effective current-sensing resistance is R3 in parallel with R2 (A1's inverting input is at virtual ground) so the output current with a +10 control voltage will be approximately 0.5 mA.

The output current from the 3080 is converted into an output voltage by A2, which functions as a current-to-voltage converter. With the control current set at 0.5 mA and a 10-V input signal, evaluation of the transconductance equation for the 3080 reveals that the output current amplitude will be approximately 0.1 mA. R6 therefore should be approximately 100K for unity gain through the entire circuit when the control voltage is +10 V. The value of R3 may be trimmed to adjust the control sensitivity. For use in

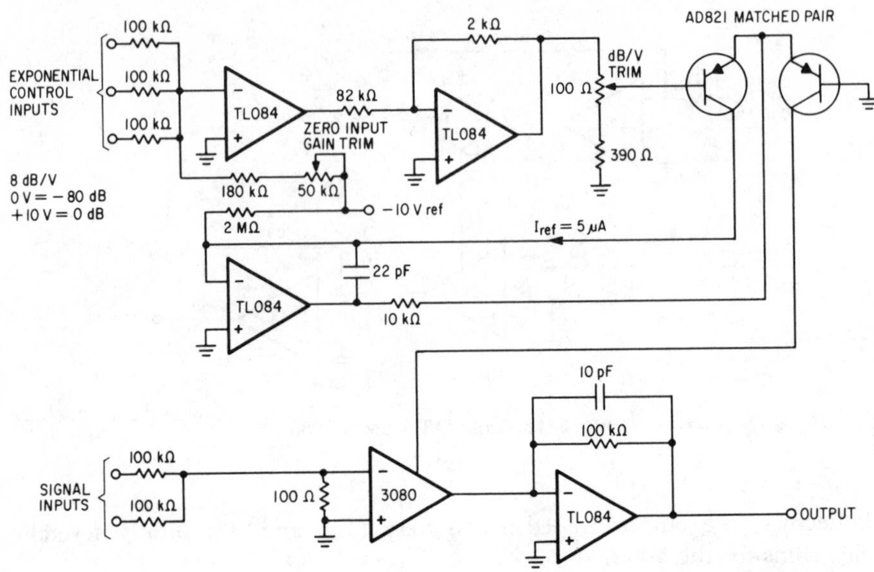

Fig. 6–16. Voltage-controlled amplifier with exponential gain control

a 5-V system one could either select a −5 to +5 control range or a 0 to +5 control range. In the former case, the input to A1 would have to be offset by connecting an additional 100K resistor to the + 5 system reference voltage. In the latter case, the control sensitivity would have to be doubled by reducing R3 to about 12K.

For maximum accuracy, the offset voltages of both op-amps should be nulled. Offset voltage in the 3080 should also be nulled for minimum control feedthrough. This may be accomplished by using an attenuator on the noninverting input similar to that on the inverting input and feeding it with a variable dc voltage. The offset null will have to be a compromise value, however, since it changes somewhat with control current.

Exponential Gain Control

As outlined in Chapter 3, an exponential relation between amplifier gain and control voltage is quite desirable. Since the 3080 is a current-controlled device, it would seem that the exponential converter used in the voltage-controlled oscillator could be used directly. Unfortunately, a close look reveals that the 3080 requires a *positive* control current (current enters the 3080) and the exponential converter used earlier supplies a *negative* current.

The most straightforward solution to the problem is to use a pnp matched transistor pair in the exponential converter, which reverses the output current polarity—and everything else. Input polarity reversal, therefore, must be cancelled with another op-amp inverter in the control-current input processor. A complete circuit for an exponential response VCA is shown in Fig. 6–16.

Improving Linearity

There are still several problems that limit the overall accuracy of a transconductance gain-control element. Probably the most serious is the remaining nonlinearity of the device. A related problem is the marginal signal-to-noise ratio created by the necessity of very small signal amplitudes at the gain element's input. Proper shielding can reduce coupled noise, but the signals are so small that semiconductor device noise is significant. With the 10-mV peak levels used by the preceding circuits, nonlinearity will cause about 1.3% harmonic distortion and give a signal-to-noise ratio of about 66 dB. Used as a control voltage processor, nonlinearity is nearly 5% of full scale and rms noise is 0.05% of full scale. Tradeoffs are possible, that is, less distortion but more noise or vice versa, but neither parameter changes dramatically with input signal level. Clearly, much improvement is necessary if the VCA is to be useful in the control path to a VCO! A final problem is that the gain drifts with temperature according to the semiconductor junction equation. The magnitude of this drift is the same as the control voltage sensitivity drift in a VCO, about 0.33%/°C.

Concentrating on linearity first, it is seen that the linearity error is independent of the control current. This means that a 10-mV input will produce the same percentage of distortion at a low-gain setting as it will at a high-gain setting. Furthermore, the effect of the nonlinearity is always a *reduction* in the actual instantaneous output below what it ideally should be. It should therefore be possible to *predistort* the input signal with an opposite nonlinearity to compensate for the gain cell nonlinearity and therefore improve things considerably.

Figure 6–17 shows a simple predistorter that can be added directly to the 3080-based circuits given earlier. Analysis of the circuit is rather in-

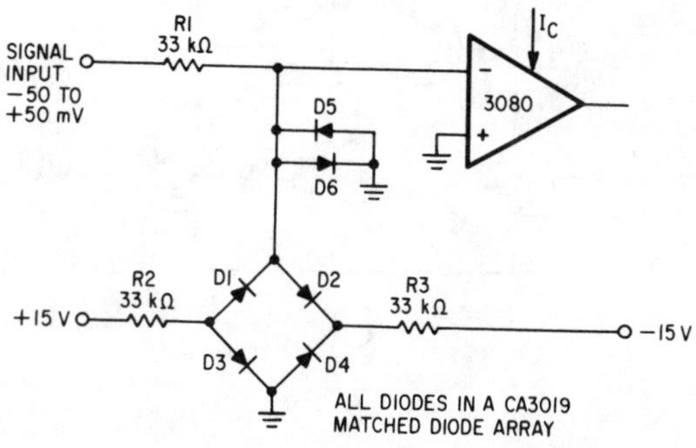

Fig. 6–17. Diode bridge predistortion circuit

volved but a few observations can be made with little effort. D5 and D6 are protective diodes that normally do not conduct; thus, they can be ignored. Resistors R2 and R3 in conjunction with the supply voltages act like current sources and bias the diode bridge. Since the diodes are all matched, equal currents flow in each one and in turn give equal dynamic impedances of about 100 ohms each. The dynamic impedance of the bridge acts with R1 to form a voltage divider for the signal voltage. With zero signal input, the impedance of the overall bridge is also 100 ohms so the attenuation is about 330, one-third that used in uncompensated circuits.

For positive input voltages, the current through D1 decreases and increases through D2. Because of the constant bias current, the current through D4 must therefore decrease, while that through D3 increases. Since the dynamic impedance of the diodes is inversely proportional to their currents, the bridge impedance will change also. For small signals, the impedance decreases are closely matched by the increases and the bridge impedance remains constant. As the signal voltage rises, the diodes with increased impedance dominate (since they are in series with a decreased impedance diode) and the bridge impedance rises. The input voltage to the 3080 is therefore boosted to counteract its tendency to flatten the waveform peaks. The circuit runs away when the signal current exceeds the bridge bias current so D5 and D6, which are in the diode array IC anyway, prevent any possible damage to the 3080.

The improvement offered by this circuit is impressive. With a 50-mV peak voltage into the 3080, the harmonic distortion is only 0.25%. The increased signal amplitude also improves the signal-to-noise ratio by nearly 14 dB to a total of 80 dB. Resistors R2 and R3 should be carefully matched as well as the 15-V power supplies to prevent even order harmonic distortion.

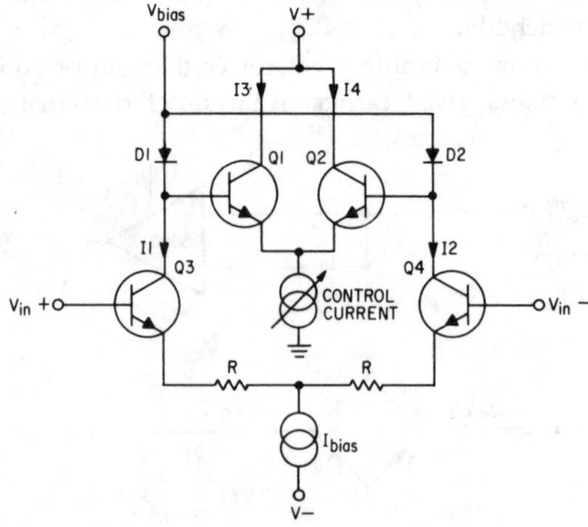

Fig. 6–18. Gilbert multiplier

For peak performance, it may be necessary to trim the resistors to better match the diode array characteristic to the 3080 input characteristic.

Essentially this same predistortion circuit can also be found inside a CA3280 *dual* OTA. The diode predistortion network is connected directly between the + and − inputs and is floating; thus, it is not necessary to ground one of the inputs as in the previous circuit. The output and control structures are the same as the 3080, and the diode circuit has a *variable* bias current control. This is accomplished by adding a terminal called I_D, which sinks current into the negative supply the same as I_C. In practice, the magnitude of I_D determines the average impedance of the diode network, which, when combined with a series input resistor, determines the signal level applied to the variable gain cell. The diode network impedance is $70/I_D$ ohms where I_D is given in milliamps and is usually set in the 0.1 mA range. Note that the input series resistor value should be at least 20 times the diode network impedance for best predistortion action. Since all of the input components are inherently matched in the 3280, adjustment of the predistortion circuit is not required, and output distortion can be expected to be less. Noise level has also been reduced (the original 3080 was not specifically designed for audio use) to less than 2 μV rms, which makes signal-to-noise ratios over 80 dB possible.

Gilbert Multiplier

Another predistortion circuit is shown in Fig. 6–18. This circuit is termed a Gilbert multiplier after its inventor. Diodes D1 and D2 actually do the predistortion and receive the input signal as *currents*, I1 and I2. For greater convenience of use, transistors Q3 and Q4 convert a conventional differential input voltage to the differential current required by the rest of the circuit. The two resistors set the input voltage range, which can be made as large as standard 5-V signal levels. The output is a differential current as before. Performance is even better than the diode bridge predistorter, offering an additional 6-dB improvement in noise level and distortion reduction to 0.1%. Last but not least, the circuit automatically temperature compensates the gain cell, making it essentially ideal.

Unfortunately, all of the components must be carefully matched to obtain such good performance, normally a difficult task with discrete circuitry. Recently, however, a linear IC having two of these circuits along with 3080-style differential-to-single-ended converters has been introduced by a company appropriately named Solid State Music. Unlike the 3080, this IC was designed specifically for audio VCA applications. Figure 6–19 shows a simplified schematic of the IC, which at the time of writing is known by the type number SSM 2020. The inputs can accept signals up to 5-V peak directly, while the output is a current up to 1-mA peak. Note the inclusion of two pairs of exponential converter transistors and even a temperature-compensating resistor for them.

VCA Using the 2020

Rather than describe the IC itself in detail, let's look instead at a complete VCA circuit using it in Fig. 6–20. The 10-V signal input is first attenuated to 5 V by R1 and R2. In a 5-V system, R1 may be omitted and R2 increased to 100K. The input impedance of the 2020 itself is tens of megohms with a bias current requirement of about 500 nA. The current output, which at 5 V signal input will have a peak value roughly one-third of the control current, is converted into a 10-V peak output by A1, which is connected as a current to voltage converter. R3 should be adjusted for unity gain through the circuit with 1 mA of control current. The offset trim circuit at the 2020 noninverting signal input is necessary to cancel the device's offset voltage and minimize control feedthrough.

The control circuitry shown provides simultaneous linear and exponential gain control. Study of the configuration of A2 and the transistor pair in the 2020 should reveal that it is exactly the same exponential conversion structure as used in the VCO circuit. In normal operation, one control input would be at zero, while the other is exercised over the full control range. With both inputs at zero, a reference current of 0.1 μA flows into the 2020. This gives a gain of 0.0001 (−80 dB) relative to the 1-mA value which,

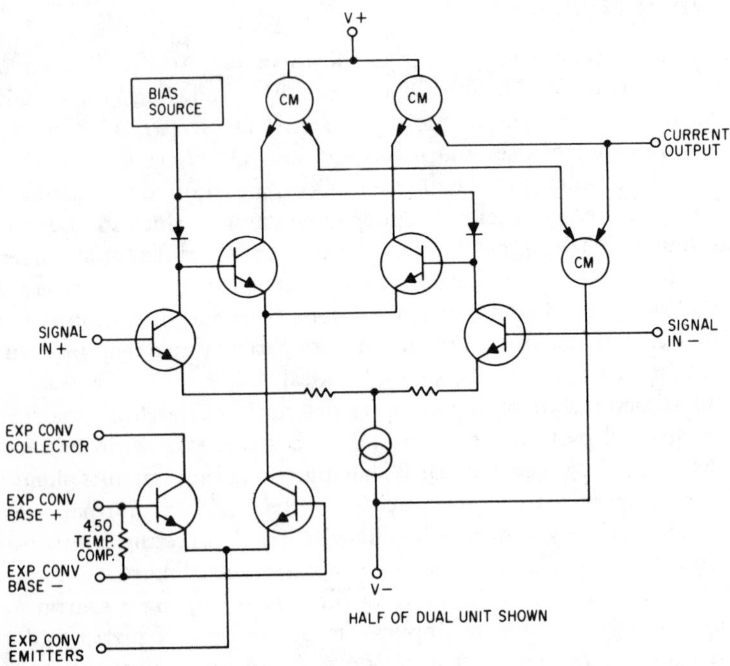

Fig. 6–19. Simplified schematic of SSM 2020 VCA IC

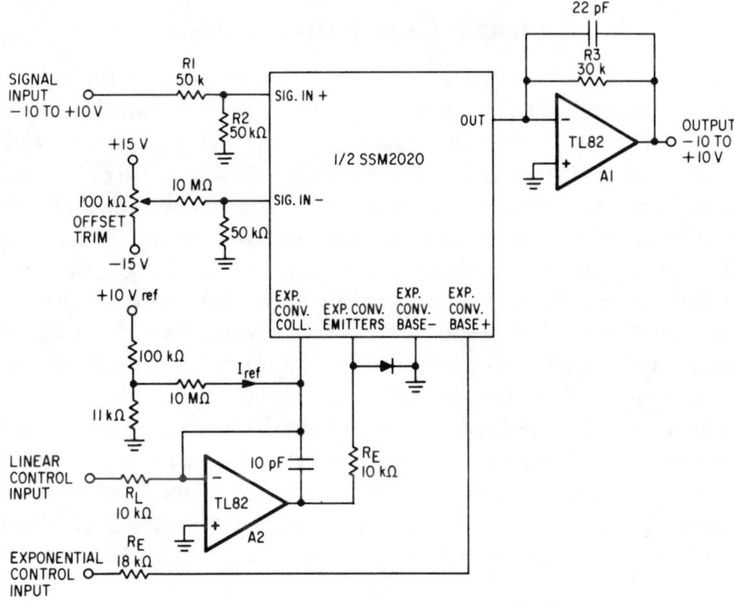

Linear = 0 Exponential = 0, Ic = 0.1 μA
Gain = − 80 dB
Linear = +10, Exponential = 0, Ic = 1.0 mA,
Gain = 0 dB
Linear = 0, Exponential = +10, Ic = 1:0 mA,
Gain = 0 dB 8 dB/V

Fig. 6–20. Practical VCA using the SSM 2020

although not precisely zero, is sufficient to audibly silence the unit. Raising the linear control input to +10 V while maintaining the exponential input at zero will increase the control current to 1 mA and provide unity gain. The expression for gain, therefore, is $G = 0.1E1$, where G is the gain and E1 is the voltage applied to the linear input.

With the values shown, the exponential input has a sensitivity of 8 dB/V. Thus, +10 at this input would raise the gain 80 dB above the zero input value and give unity gain. *RE* can be adjusted to provide exactly 8 dB/V, which incidently is quite close to the increase in amplitude necessary for a doubling of perceived loudness. The nonstandard impedances of the control inputs may be easily corrected with additional op-amp buffers. Note that a TL-82 dual FET amplifier was used for A1 and A2. The high slew rate is necessary at high audio frequencies and the low bias current is needed for predictable operation with the extremely low reference current used in the exponential converter transistors.

Voltage-Controlled Filter

Of the basic three modules, filters have historically been the most difficult to voltage control. Traditional L-C filters were tuned by changing reactive components, either the capacitor or the inductor. Later, with the widespread use of operational amplifiers and R-C active filters, the resistor was varied for fine tuning purposes and the capacitor was changed for different ranges. With careful design, however, the tuning range available through variable resistance alone can be made wide enough for electronic music applications. Thus, the requirement for a wide-range voltage-variable resistance similar to that needed for a VCA is seen. As a result the FETs, photocells, and biased diodes that were used in early VCAs were also used in VCFs along with all of their attendant drawbacks.

Unfortunately, the final solution of the VCA problem, the transconductance variable-gain stage, does not directly involve a variable resistance. Therefore, application to tuning a VCF is not at all obvious. Before giving up and resuming the search for a wide-range accurate voltage-variable resistor, let's see if a variable-gain function can be used to tune a filter.

Variable Gain Tunes a Filter

The single-pole passive R-C low-pass filter shown in Fig. 6–21A will be used as an example. With a high-impedance load, the circuit has unity gain at very low frequencies and a 6 dB/octave attenuation slope at high frequencies. The cutoff frequency (frequency for a gain of 0.707) is 1/6.283RC. If the circuit is driven from a low-impedance source, the cutoff frequency can be tuned over a wide range by varying R alone without affecting the passband gain or attenuation slope.

The active circuit shown in Fig. 6–21B has exactly the same characteristic if R1 = R2 except that its output is capable of driving a finite impedance. For other cases, $Fc = 1/6.283R2C$ and $Ao = R2/R1$, where Fc is the cutoff frequency and Ao is the dc or passband gain. As before, tuning can be accomplished by varying R2 alone. Although this also affects Ao, we will ignore that for a moment.

The point of this discussion is that the *effect* of changing R2 can be exactly simulated with a *variable-gain* amplifier and a *fixed R2* as in Fig. 6–21C. Since the inverting input of the op-amp is at virtual ground, only the feedback *current* through R2 is important. Thus, the effect of doubling R2 in circuit B can be obtained by setting the VCA gain to one-half and leaving R2 alone in circuit C. Generalizing, $R_{eff} = R_{act}/G$, where R_{eff} is the effective value of the feedback resistor, R_{act} is its actual value, and G is the VCA gain. Substituting into the cutoff frequency equation, $Fc = G/6.283R2C$, it is seen that the cutoff frequency is directly proportional to the VCA gain.

The last step is to eliminate variation of passband gain with cutoff frequency. With the present setup, $Ao = R2_{eff}/R1 = R2/R1G$ and therefore as the cutoff frequency goes up, Ao decreases. Actually, the output of the

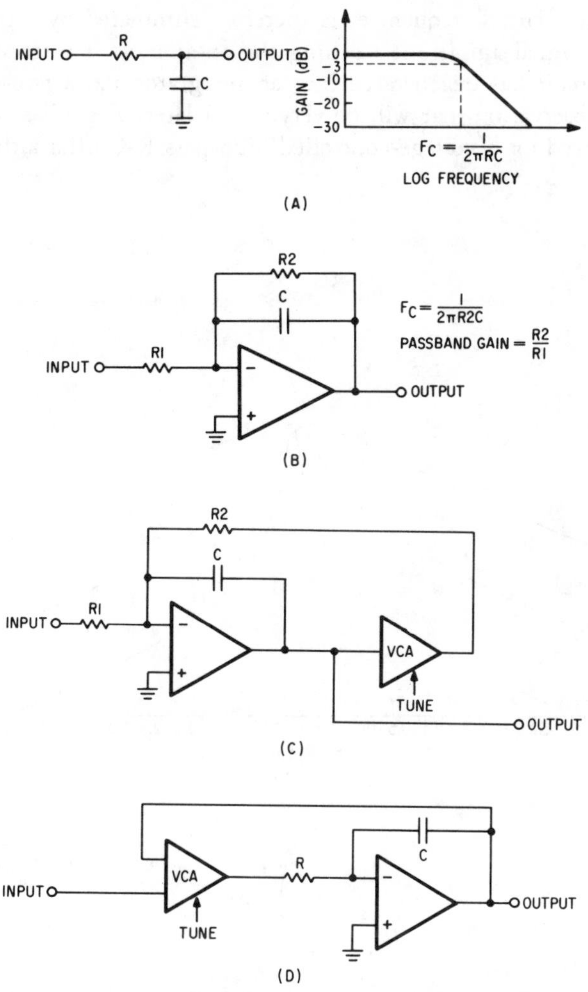

Fig. 6–21. Steps toward a voltage-controlled low-pass filter. (A) Single-pole R-C low-pass filter. (B) Active version of A. (C) Tunable version of B using a VCA. (D) Improved version of C with constant gain.

VCA in Fig. 6–21C has a constant passband gain because the previous expression is multiplied by G, which then cancels the G in the denominator, leaving $Ao = R2/R1$. It would seem that the problem is solved, but closer analysis reveals that at low cutoff frequencies the input signal level to the VCA may become extremely large to offset its corresponding low gain and therefore will be subject to severe distortion.

In Fig. 6–21D, the same elements have been rearranged to overcome the signal level problem. Essentially, both the input signal and the feedback signal go through the VCA. The tendency for the op-amp output amplitude to rise at low cutoff frequencies is therefore eliminated by a proportionate decrease in signal amplitude reaching the op-amp. It is interesting to note that the circuit has degenerated into an integrator and a two-signal input VCA; an observation that will be very useful later. A similar configuration can be derived for a voltage-controlled high-pass R-C filter although not as easily.

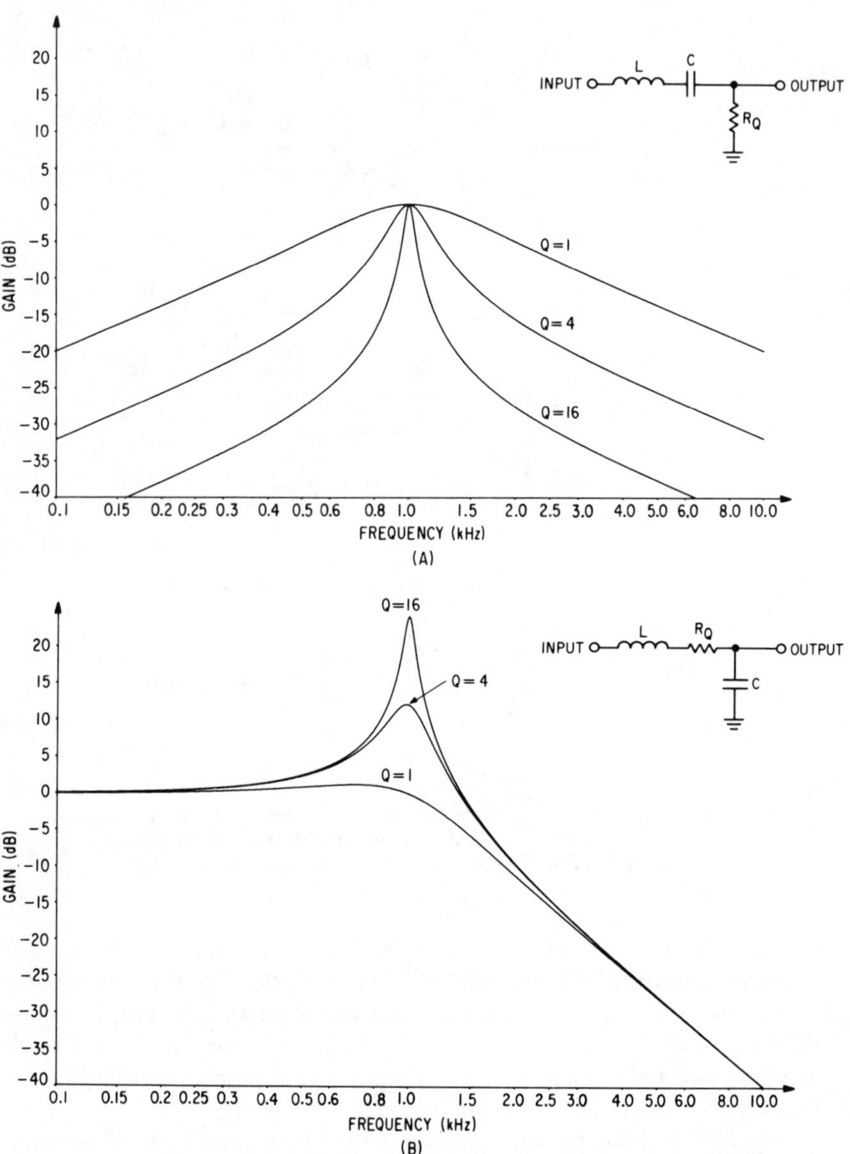

Fig. 6–22. Four fundamental R-L-C filters. (A) Bandpass. (B) Low-pass.

Voltage-Tunable Bandpass Filter

The most dramatic uses of filters in electronic music require a high Q (hopefully voltage-controlled as well) bandpass function. Cascading low-pass and high-pass sections together and having them track a common control voltage is not a practical solution mainly because quite a few would be

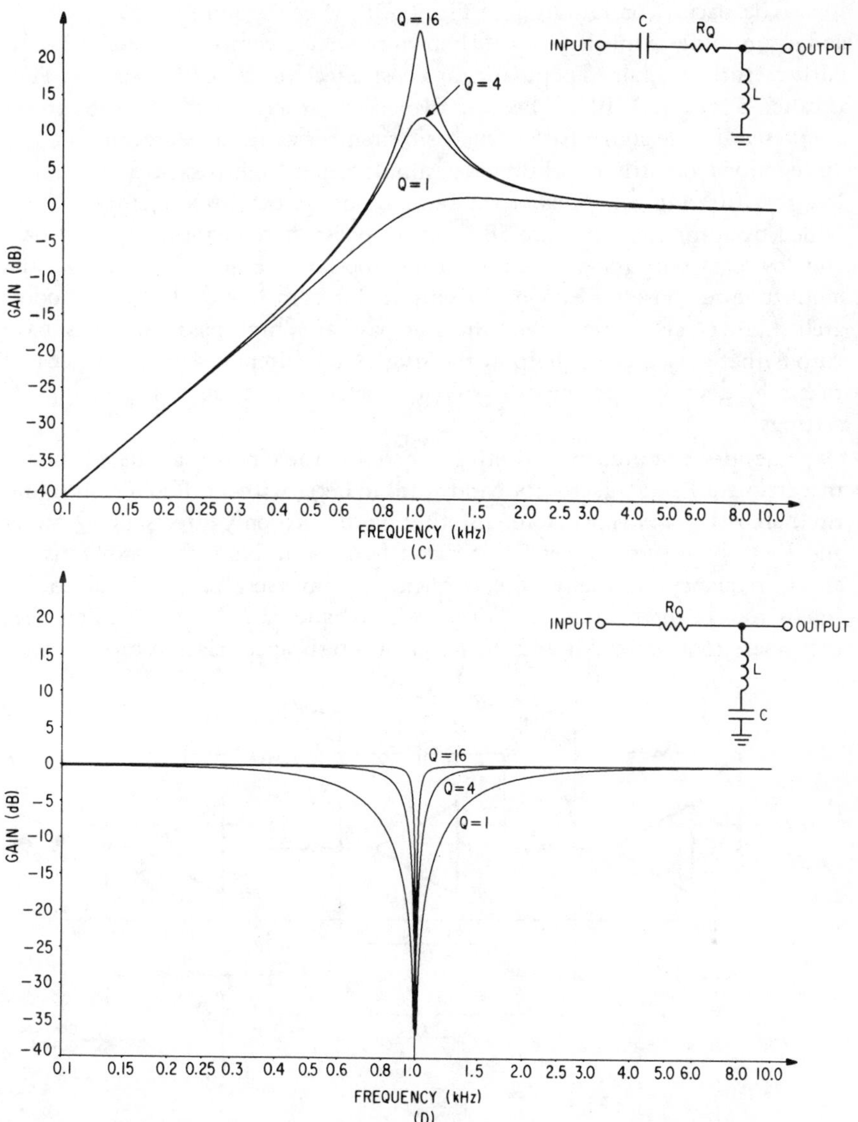

Fig. 6–22. Four fundamental R-L-C filters (*cont.*). (C) High-pass, (D) Band-reject.

required for any degree of sharpness. There exists, however, a very versatile filter structure that not only simulates exactly an R-L-C filter in the resonant (bandpass) mode but *simultaneously* simulates the other three possible filtering functions that could be built with one resistor, one inductor, and one capacitor as shown in Fig. 6–22. The family of amplitude response curves represents low, medium, and high Q cases corresponding to high, medium, and low values of R_Q.

The circuit configuration in Fig. 6–23, which requires two integrators and a summing amplifier, is well known to analog computer users but only fairly recently has gained popularity as a cost-effective active filter circuit. This is called a "two-pole filter" because two energy storage elements (capacitors) are present in the signal path. The basic circuit is called a "state-variable" or "integrator-loop" filter and provides simultaneous high-pass, bandpass, and low-pass filtering functions of the same input. A band-reject output is obtained by summing (they are 180° out of phase at resonance) the high-pass and low-pass outputs with an additional op-amp. Figure 6–24 shows the amplitude responses of each of the outputs for both low Q (1.5) and moderately high Q (15). Note that the low-pass and high-pass functions have cutoffs that are twice as sharp as the single-pole filters discussed earlier and that they develop a prominent peak just before the cutoff point for high Q settings.

Besides simultaneous filtering functions, the circuit has the advantage that frequency and Q factor (or bandwidth in hertz with a different configuration) are *independently* variable. In other words, R_Q only affects the Q factor and R_F only affects the center or cutoff frequency. Note that two resistors affect frequency. Actually, the frequency is inversely proportional to the square root of their product. If they are equal and varied together, however, the square root drops out and the frequency–resistance relationship is linear.

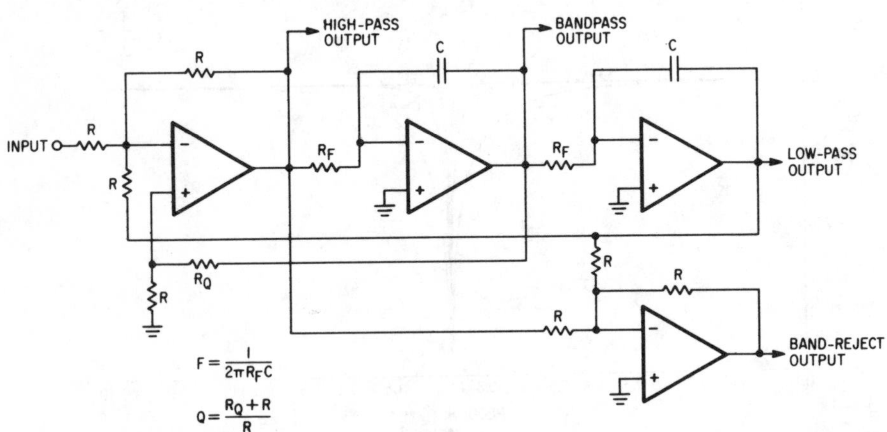

Fig. 6–23. Two-pole tunable active filter

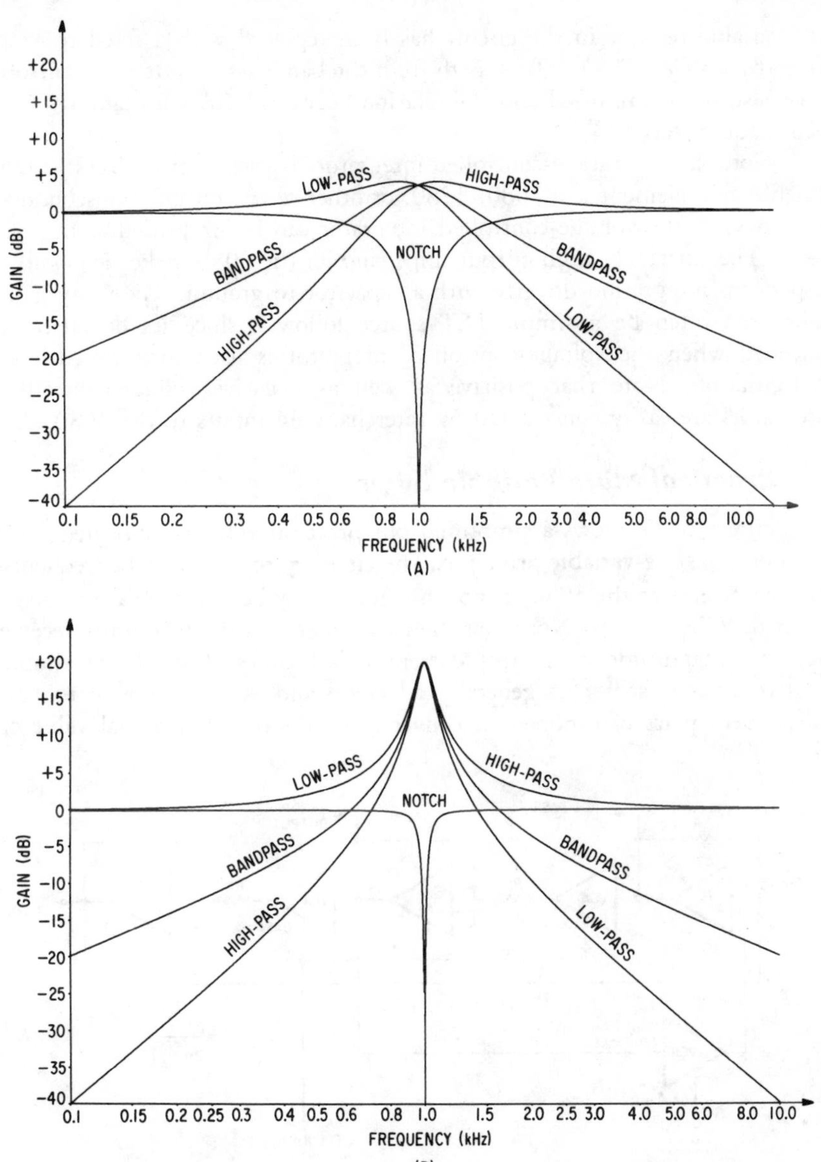

Fig. 6–24. Amplitude response of circuit in Fig. 6–23. (A) $Q = 1.5$. (B) $Q = 15$.

Although the relation between R_Q and Q is nonlinear in the circuit shown, the addition of another op-amp can make it perfectly linear.

Tuning the filter with voltage-controlled amplifiers should now be almost self-evident but for convenience is shown in Fig. 6–25. Essentially each variable resistor in the circuit has been replaced with a fixed resistor driven by a VCA. The feedback path from the bandpass output that controls Q has also been simplified and the relation between VCA gain and $1/Q$ has been made linear.

Note that a "voltage-controlled integrator" is used in two places. If the variable-gain element is a 3080, 3280, or other *current* output transconductance device, the voltage-controlled integrator can be simplified as in Fig. 6–26. The extremely high output impedance of the 3080 makes it possible to perform integration directly with a capacitor to ground. The unity gain buffer can often be a simple FET source follower, since its dc offset is cancelled when the voltage-controlled integrator is used in a closed-loop configuration. Note that positive as well as negative voltage-controlled integrators are easily constructed by interchanging inputs to the 3080.

Practical State Variable Filter

Figure 6–27 shows a simplified but practical voltage-controlled filter based on the state-variable principle. The circuitry to generate the frequency control currents to the 3080s is not shown but may be the same as that used earlier in VCA circuits. Note that the two integrators should ideally receive the same magnitude of control current at all times. Use of the simple resistive current sharer is generally adequate and even preferable to two independent pairs of exponential converter transistors. The actual value of

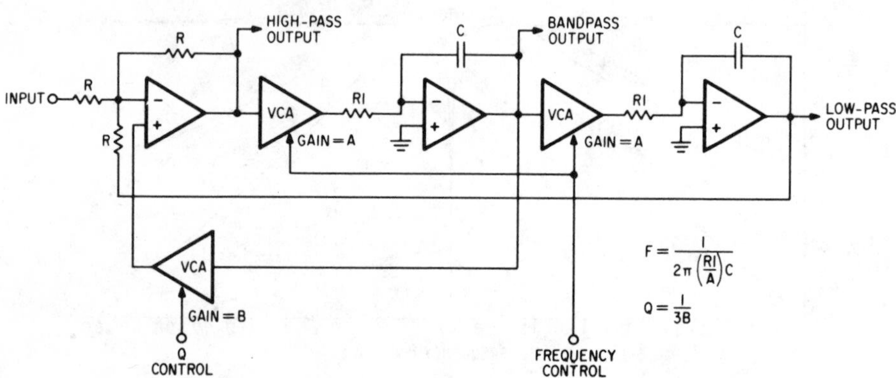

Fig. 6–25. Voltage-controlled version of Fig. 6–23.

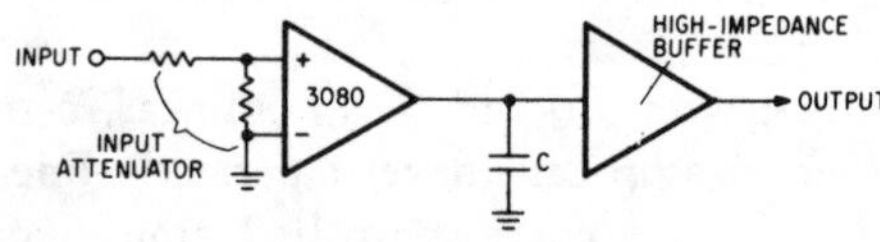

Fig. 6–26. Voltage-controlled integrator using 3080

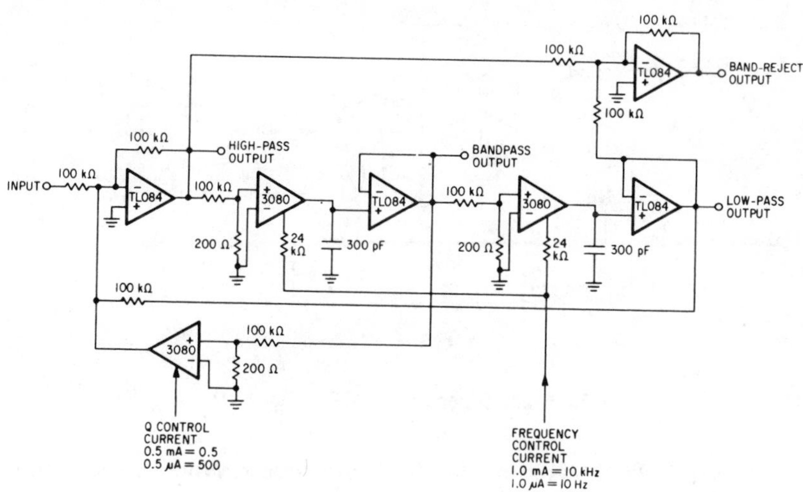

Fig. 6–27. Practical state-variable filter

these resistors is not critical as long as they are matched (1% is fine) and not so large that the compliance range of the control current source is exceeded. The 3080s may, however, have to be matched somewhat by hand and held in good thermal contact for optimum results. The two halves of a 3280 would be an ideal solution in this case. Another alternative is the use of a matched trio of transistors for exponential conversion. The third transistor is connected in parallel with the usual exponential output transistor except for the collector, which becomes a second output terminal. The harmonic distortion introduced by the 3080 gain elements is much less than in the VCA application, since the filter is a closed-loop, negative-feedback network.

Controlling Q

Proper control of *Q* is an interesting problem. First, it is desirable that *Q* be an exponential function of control voltage, since it has a useful range from 0.5 to over 500. This 1,000-to-1 range is best handled by having a 1-V change in *Q* control voltage correspond to doubling or halving of *Q*. Also, it is probably desirable that high *Q* correspond to a high control voltage. Since high *Q* corresponds to low control currents in this circuit, the polarity of the *Q* control voltage will have to be inverted somewhere in the exponential converter circuit. Finally, there may be occasions when constant *bandwidth* is desired as the filter is tuned rather than constant *Q*. If the *Q* control is exponential at "1 V per double" and two *Q* control inputs are provided, constant bandwidth operation is achieved by feeding the frequency control voltage into one of the *Q* control inputs as well as a frequency input. This causes the *Q* to increase in direct proportion to center frequency and thereby provide constant bandwidth.

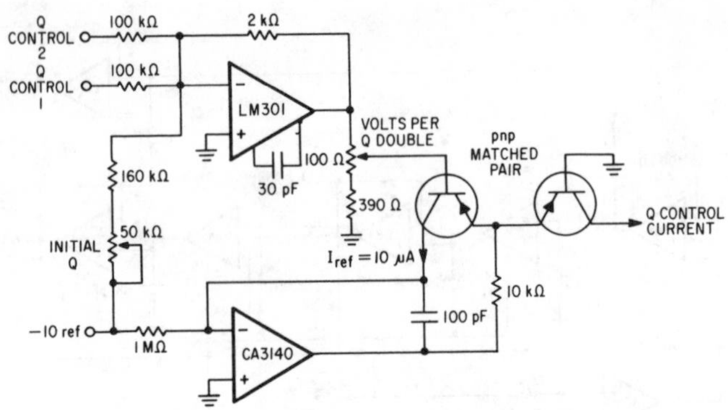

Fig. 6–28. *Q* control for VCF in Fig. 6–27

Figure 6–28 shows a suitable *Q* control circuit. Note that it is similar to the VCO frequency control circuit except that a pnp matched pair is needed to satisfy the control current needs of the 3080. The reversal in transistor polarity also reverses the control sense as required for *Q* control.

Quad Voltage-Controlled Integrator IC

Besides use in the state-variable filter, voltage-controlled integrators can actually be used in any kind of active filter circuit, even the simple one-pole low-pass discussed earlier. Since any filter function that can be done with resistors, capacitors, and inductors can also be done with combinations of one- and two-pole RC active filters, it follows that voltage-controlled integrators can be used to make any of those filters voltage controlled. As a result, a quad voltage-controlled integrator IC has been developed, also by Solid State Music, for use in voltage-controlled filters.

Figure 6–29 shows a block diagram of the type 2040 voltage-controlled filter IC. Basically, four transconductance gain cells driving four high-

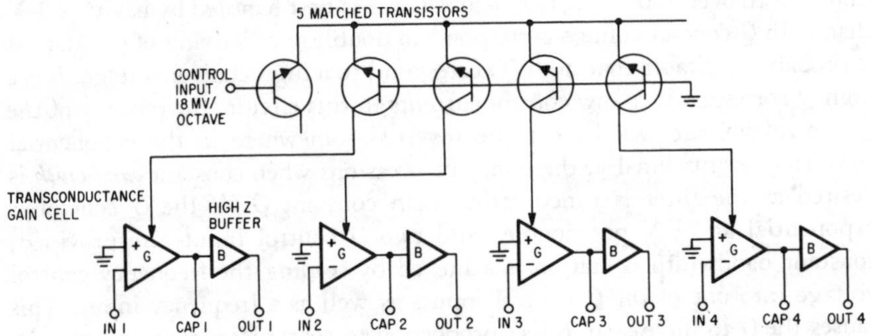

Fig. 6–29. Block diagram of SSM 2040 quad voltage-controlled integrator IC

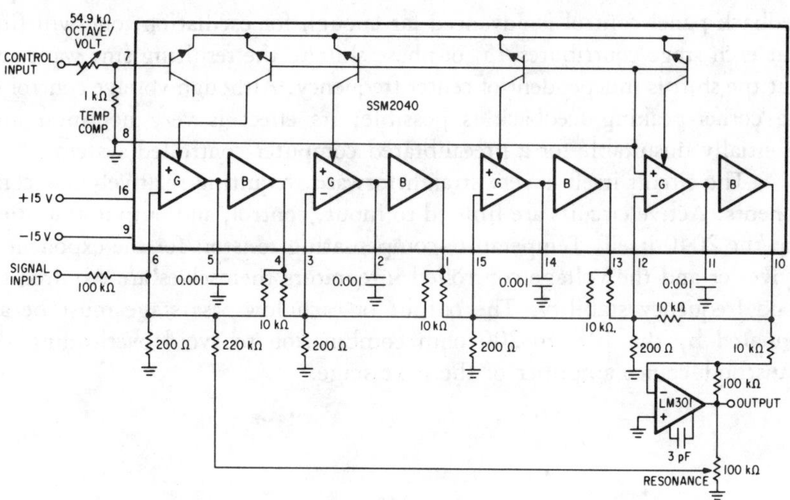

Fig. 6–30. Voltage-controlled four-pole low-pass filter with corner peaking

impedance buffers are provided. The gain cells have a predistortion circuit and therefore can accept input signals as large as 80 mV and still generate less than 1% distortion. The four gain cells are fed equal control currents from a built-in multioutput exponential converter. The integrating capacitors are supplied by the user, however, and should be 1,000 pF or larger. One limitation to keep in mind is that the buffer amplifiers are only capable of a 1-V peak output swing and can only supply 500 μA of load current.

Figure 6–30 shows a voltage-controlled filter circuit using the 2040. This is properly termed a "four-pole low-pass filter with corner peaking" and is quite popular, although not as much so as the state-variable type described earlier. The main difference is that the low-pass cutoff of 24 dB/octave is much sharper than the state-variable cutoff of 12 dB/octave. A bandpass function is obtained by feeding a portion of the filter's output back to its input to create a resonance. Enough of this feedback will cause a pure sine wave oscillation at the center frequency. Note that a true bandpass response is not produced by the feedback because there is appreciable very-low-frequency gain. This resonance technique is often called *corner peaking* to distinguish it from true bandpass filtering, which has zero response at both frequency extremes. At moderate to high Q settings, however, the audible difference can be quite subtle.

The filter is really four identical single-pole low-pass sections in cascade all tracking the same control voltage. Each low-pass section is functionally equivalent to the VCF in Fig. 6–21D discussed earlier. When cascaded as shown, each section contributes a cutoff slope of 6 dB/octave; thus, simultaneous outputs of 6, 12, 18, and 24 dB/octave are available. When the feedback panel control is advanced far enough for oscillation, one will find that each stage contributes 45° of phase shift to the resulting sine wave and that the shift is independent of center frequency. Although voltage control of the corner-peaking feedback is possible, its effect is very nonlinear and essentially unsuitable for a precalibrated computer-controlled system.

The circuit itself is very straightforward, requiring relatively few components. Active circuits are limited to input, control, and output amplifiers and the 2040 itself. Temperature-compensating resistors for the exponential converter and the voltage-controlled integrators themselves are required for good frequency stability. The output of each low-pass stage must be attenuated by the 10K to 200 ohm combination to avoid overloading the transconductance amplifier of the next stage.

7

Digital-to-Analog and Analog-to-Digital Converters

The primary interface element between the digital logic found in a microcomputer system and the analog modules of a voltage-controlled system are digital-to-analog converters (DACs) and analog-to-digital converters (ADCs). For synthesizer control, only DACs are needed to convert numbers from the computer into control voltages. However, ADCs are used in some of the human interface techniques to be described later. Fortunately, the two devices are very closely related, and, in fact, most ADC circuits utilize a DAC as a key element.

The purpose of these "data-conversion" devices is to translate between the electrical quantities of current or voltage and digital quantities. For analog synthesizer control with a microprocessor, voltage is the preferred analog representation and twos-complement fixed-point binary is the preferred numerical representation. We can further specify that analog voltages in the range of −10 V to +10 V, and logic voltages compatible with TTL should be acceptable to the converter.

A number of terms are used to describe and specify data-conversion devices. Most all of them are equally applicable to DACs and ADCs so the discussion will focus on DACs. Although converters that work with binary-coded decimal numbers are available, their variety is extremely limited. Also, since BCD arithmetic is inconsistent with maximum utilization of microprocessor speed, the discussion will be restricted to binary converters.

Data Conversion Terminology

Resolution

The most important and most quoted converter specification is its *resolution* measured in terms of *bits*. Resolution is essentially a measure of the number of different voltage levels that a DAC can produce. A 3-bit DAC, for example, accepts 3-bit binary numbers as input and can produce no more than eight different voltage levels as its output. With an ideal DAC, these eight levels would be equally spaced across the range of output voltages. If the output is to span the range of −10 V to +10 V, for example, these eight levels might be assigned as:

Binary	*Analog*	*Binary*	*Analog*
000	−10.00	100	+ 1.42
001	− 7.14	101	+ 4.29
010	− 4.29	110	+ 7.14
011	− 1.42	111	+10.00

Actually, since twos-complement binary inputs are usually desirable, the eight levels should probably be assigned instead as:

000	+ 0.00	100	−10.00
001	+ 2.50	101	− 7.50
010	+ 5.00	110	− 5.00
011	+ 7.50	111	− 2.50

Unfortunately, neither assignment is ideal. The first has no code for a zero output and puts out rather odd voltages anyway. The second has a zero point and nice round levels but falls short of the full ±10-V range desired. Actually, practical DACs have considerably more resolution than this example so that last missing level on the positive side is generally of no consequence. Using the twos-complement assignment, the resolution of this 3-bit DAC would be a very coarse 2.5 V. The maximum error in converting an arbitrary number (with rounding) to a voltage would be only half of this or 1.25 V.

Moving up to an 8-bit DAC improves things considerably. The resolution now would be $20/(2^8-1)$ or 0.078 V. The largest negative output would still be −10 V, but the positive limit would be one step short of +10.0 or +9.922 V. Even with 8 bits, the step size of 0.078 V controlling a voltage-controlled oscillator with a sensitivity of one octave per volt would yield a pitch step size of about one semitone. A 12-bit DAC would have a step size of 0.00488 V, which would give a nearly inaudible 1/17 semitone increment. Even higher resolutions are available, but the expense would limit extensive use.

Usually it is convenient to consider the binary input to a DAC as being a signed binary fraction between −1.000 . . . and +0.9999 . . . . The output voltage of the DAC then is the binary fraction (rounded or truncated to the DAC's resolution) times 10 V. This representation has the advantage that calculations leading up to the value to be converted are not affected by the actual resolution of the DAC used. For example, if a 16-bit computer is being used, it would be convenient to perform all calculations using 16-bit fractional arithmetic. (Fractional arithmetic is really the same as integer

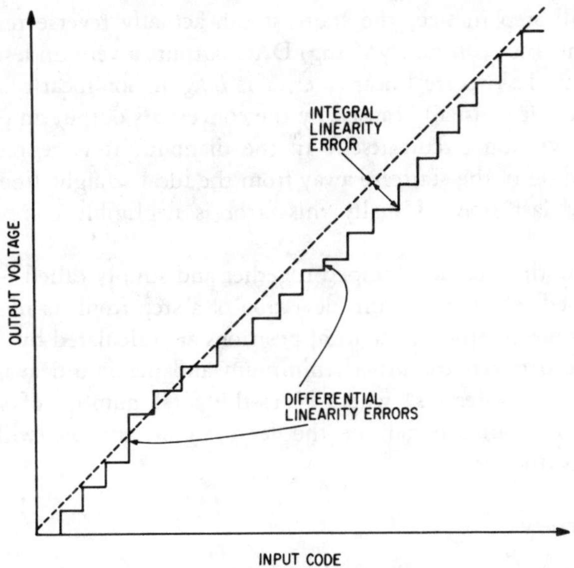

Fig. 7–1. DAC linearity errors

arithmetic and is just as fast on microcomputers. This topic will be discussed in Chapter 18.) When a number is sent to the DAC to be converted, all 16 bits are sent out. The DAC in turn is interfaced so that it sees the most significant *N* bits of the word, *N* being the DAC's resolution. An ADC likewise would connect to the most significant bits of the word and supply zeroes for the unused low order bits. The ultimate resolution implied by 16 bits is an astounding 305 μV. An 8-bit microcomputer would probably handle things in a similar manner unless converter resolutions of 8 bits or less are being used.

Linearity

Another term used in specifying DACs is *linearity*. Linearity is related to accuracy but is definitely not the same thing. Although the voltage levels of an ideal DAC are perfectly equally spaced, real DACs have severe difficulty even approaching the ideal for reasonably high resolutions. The most common linearity error is called *differential* linearity error. Although the physical reason for this will become clear later, Fig. 7–1 illustrates this error. The stepped plot shown represents the output that would occur if the DAC were driven by a binary counter. Differential linearity refers to the actual difference in step position between any two adjacent steps compared to the ideal difference. When a differential linearity error occurs, it is because one step is either higher or lower than it should be. The diagram shows a differential linearity error of one-half of the ideal step size, which is equivalent to one-half of the least significant bit (LSB) of the digital input. If the error exceeds a full step in size, the staircase can actually reverse resulting in a nonmonotonic (not constantly rising) DAC output, a very undesirable error.

Another, less severe linearity error is *integral* nonlinearity. Unlike the previous error, it is usually caused by the converter's output amplifier rather than the conversion circuit itself. In the diagram, it is represented by a gradual bending of the staircase away from the ideal straight line connecting the first and last steps. Usually this error is negligible compared to the differential error.

Often both errors are lumped together and simply called nonlinearity. This is defined as the maximum deviation of a step from its ideal position. For linearity measurement, the ideal positions are calculated by dividing the analog range between the *actual* minimum and maximum analog outputs into $N-1$ equal intervals, where N is the total number of steps. Nonlinearities less than one-half of the least significant bit will guarantee monotonic performance.

Accuracy

Accuracy is very similar to lumped linearity but uses the ideal endpoints instead of the actual endpoints of the converter's range. Thus, for a −10 V to +10 V 12-bit converter, the ideal endpoints would be −10 V and +9.99512 V (+10 less one LSB). Accuracy may be specified as either percent of full scale or in terms of the least significant bit. A converter with accuracy better than one-half LSB would not only be monotonic but also as accurate as the resolution and linearity characteristics allow.

Assuming perfect linearity, inaccuracy can be due to *gain* and *offset* errors as illustrated in Fig. 7–2. A 5% pure gain error would cause the converter output to range between, for example, −9.5 V and +9.495 V rather than the intended −10-V to +9.995-V endpoints. A 0.5-V pure offset error might result in an output between −10.5 V and +9.495 V. Fortunately, both of these errors are easily trimmed out, leaving ultimate accuracy a function of the linearity. Some applications of converters, such as direct audio signal conversion, are little affected by inaccuracy as long as the linearity is adequate. When purchasing a converter, one can usually expect the accuracy, after trimming, as well as the linearity to be better than one-half LSB unless it is an unusually high resolution (16 bits) unit or it is clearly marked as being a gradeout from a more expensive line.

Settling Time

When the digital input to a DAC changes, the analog output does not instantly move to the new value but instead wanders toward it and oscillates around it for awhile. The time required from when the digital input changes until the output has stabilized within a specified tolerance of the new value is called the *settling time*. The specified tolerance is usually one-half LSB, which is

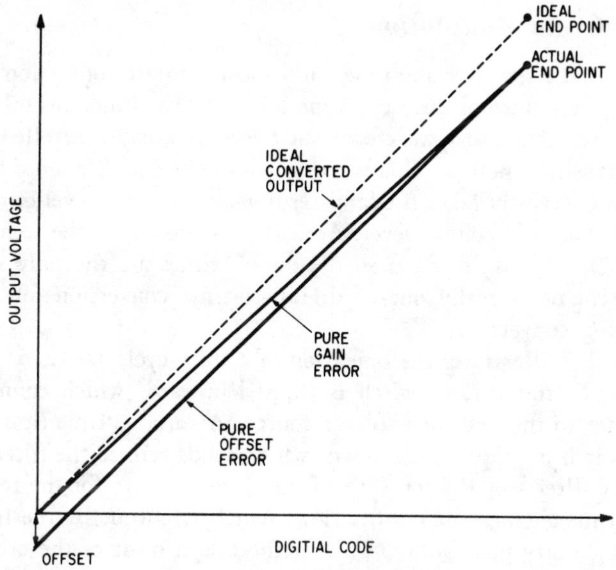

Fig. 7-2. Offset and gain errors

the only tolerance that really makes sense. The settling time is nearly always much longer for a big change in output voltage than for a small one. Typical values are 30μsec for a full scale (−10 V to +10 V) change and 2 to 5 μsec for a 0.1 V or less change, which is quite adequate for any synthesizer control application. Five to ten times greater speed is available without a great price increase for direct conversion of audio.

Unfortunately, the DAC output does not always make the transition smoothly from one level to another. Even when counting up one level at a time, the output can be seen to *glitch* by a large fraction of a volt between certain adjacent levels. Besides extending the settling time between these particular levels, the momentary incorrect output may create an improper response or excessive noise in the controlled circuit. Although some specialized DACs may be designed for minimum glitch energy (voltage spike height squared times its duration), in most cases the user must suppress the glitches if they cause problems. This is generally accomplished with a low-pass filter when speed is unimportant or with a sample-and-hold circuit.

DAC Techniques

Over the years, dozens of methods of digital-to-analog conversion have been conceived and utilized. What we are interested in for synthesizer control are methods suitable for 8 to 16 bits of resolution having good inherent accuracy and stability and a speed in the low millisecond range. Actually, higher speed can be a great benefit because it allows *multiplexing* of one converter among several tasks.

Duty-Cycle Modulation

Probably the simplest and inherently most accurate conversion method is based on pulse-width or duty-cycle modulation. The fundamental concept is to generate a rectangular waveform with very precisely controlled voltage levels and transition points. This waveform is then sent through a low-pass filter, which effectively takes the long-term *average* voltage level of the wave and outputs it as a dc voltage level. Actually, the beauty of the technique is that the voltage levels are fixed so the on–off times are the only variable. Thus, the scheme is really one of digital-to-time conversion followed by time-to-analog conversion.

Figure 7–3 illustrates the operation of a duty-cycle DAC. At integral multiples of T, the analog switch is flipped upward, which connects the low-pass filter to the reference voltage source. A variable time (less than T) later, the switch is flipped back down, which sends zero to the filter. In the example, the filter sees V_{ref} for 25% of the time and zero for the remaining 75%. The time average then is $0.25V_{ref}$, which is output by the filter and load isolating unity gain buffer. This method (and most of the others that will be studied) gives a *multiplying* DAC because the output voltage is proportional to the *product* of a reference voltage and the digital input expressed as a binary fraction.

A simple digital counter can be used to control the analog switch in response to a digital input. At the beginning of a T interval, the counter would be preset to the digital value to be converted. A stable, high-frequency clock causes the counter to count down toward zero. As long as the counter is nonzero, the switch would be up, but as soon as it reaches zero, the switch would be thrown down until the next cycle.

For high conversion speed, the frequency of the clock should be as high as possible but not so high that analog switching time becomes a major portion of a clock cycle. A realistic figure might be 10 MHz. The frequency

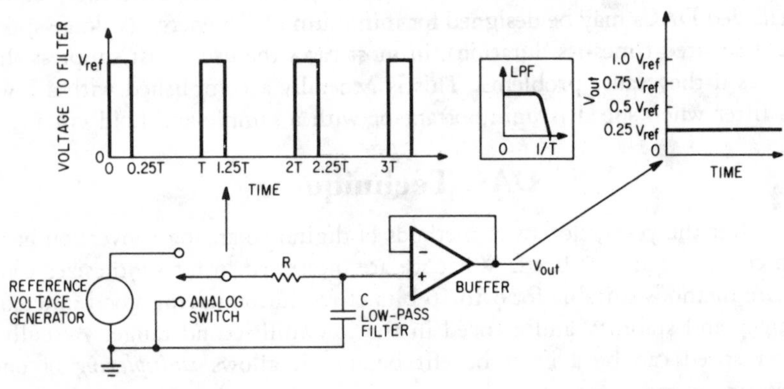

Fig. 7–3. Digital-to-analog conversion via pulse-width modulation

of the rectangular wave into the filter is the clock frequency divided by the number of counter states, which is equivalent to the resolution of the DAC. Thus, a 4096 level (12-bit) resolution would give a frequency of 10 MHz/4096 or 2,441 Hz, which is a period of about 410 μsec.

The output of the low-pass filter will have some ripple superimposed on top of the average dc level, since its cutoff is not infinitely sharp. It would be reasonable to desire a ripple amplitude of less than one-half the least significant bit. With the simple RC filter shown, the cutoff frequency would have to be roughly 1/8,000 of the rectangular wave input frequency to have an acceptable ripple. The cutoff frequency in this example then would have to be around 0.3 Hz, which is equivalent to an RC time constant of over 0.5 sec. Even though this sounds slow, the worst-case settling time of the filter to one-half LSB would be roughly nine times the time constant or nearly 5 sec! Adding a bit of resolution to this DAC would multiply the settling time by slightly greater than four. Although more complex filters and switching sequences may reduce the response time to tens of milliseconds, this clearly is not a high-speed technique. Differential linearity, however, is essentially perfect regardless of resolution, and integral linearity is limited only by the regulation of the reference voltage under a varying load. Accuracy can also be excellent, limited primarily by the reference and the difference between switch turn-on and turn-off times.

Resistor String DAC

Another approach to D-to-A conversion that is inherently much faster is to use various combinations of resistors and switches along with a stable reference voltage. The idea is to use the digital code to operate the switches such that the resistors are connected in various configurations to produce the desired fraction of the reference voltage at the output.

Conceptually, the simplest arrangement of switches and resistors is shown in Fig. 7–4. This 3-bit example uses seven equal-value resistors connected in series between the reference voltage source and ground. Eight analog switches, only one of which is on at a time, select the desired fraction of the reference voltage according to the 3-bit digital input to the 3-to-8 decoder and connects it to the analog output. One drawback to the circuit should be immediately clear; for every added bit of resolution, the number of resistors and switches doubles. An 8-bit converter, therefore, would require 255 resistors and 256 switches! In the past, such a circuit was completely impractical beyond 4 or 5 bits. Its advantages, however, actually make it attractive in integrated form where the repeated resistor-switch chain structure can be laid out inexpensively on a chip. National Semiconductor, for example, has a line of D-to-A and A-to-D converters that use this structure at the 8-bit level. Another drawback is that the output must be buffered by an op-amp voltage follower. Connecting a finite load resistance to the output will greatly affect the circuit's linearity because its output impedance changes with the digital code.

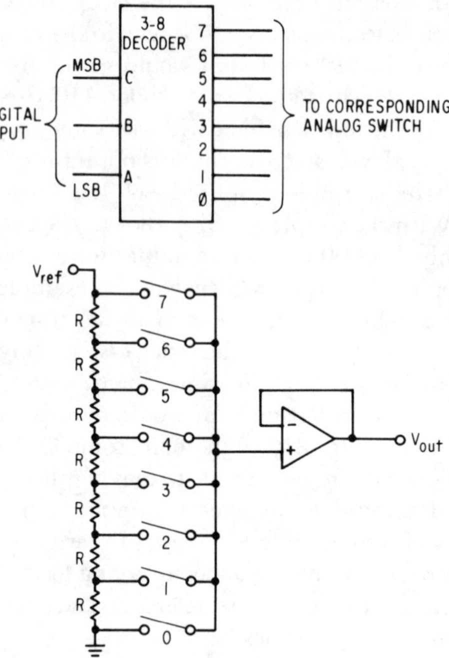

Fig. 7–4. Resistor string DAC

The most significant advantage is that all of the resistors are of the same value, and each resistor corresponds to one and only one step in the input code-output voltage graph in Fig. 7–1. Differential linearity can be made very good even with fairly inaccurate resistors. For example, if 5%-tolerance resistors were used, the worst differential linearity error would be only one-tenth of the step size—very good performance indeed. Better yet, this level of differential linearity can be maintained even at very high resolutions of 12 bits and more using the same 5%-tolerance resistors, just a whole lot more of them.

Integral linearity can be a problem, however. Imagine building one of these DACs at the 8-bit level. For the 255 resistors required, you would buy three bags of 100 5% resistors and connect them in the series string using all of the resistors from one bag before going to the next. Although all of the resistors are within 5% of their marked value and will be fairly randomly distributed throughout this range, it is entirely possible that bag 1 might average a couple of percent lower than bags 2 and 3 because they were made on a Monday. When the DAC is complete and tested, it will be found that the first 100 steps will be a couple of percent smaller than the others on the average, which makes the overall stair-step curve bow down and to the right very significantly. Of course, in a real manufacturing situation or on a chip, the errors are likely to be more evenly distributed, but, when they are not, the unit will have to be rejected. The point is that, with any DAC circuit using resistors and switches, overall linearity and accuracy cannot be better than the accuracy of the components.

Resistive Divider

The most common technique and the one on which nearly all commercial DACs are based is the resistive divider technique. Figure 7–5 shows a simple 2-bit resistive divider type of DAC. Each switch is controlled by a bit of the digital input. If a bit is a one, the switch is up connecting its resistor to the reference voltage; for zero bits it is down and the resistor is grounded. It is instructive to calculate the output voltage for each of the four possible combinations of 2 bits. Clearly, 00 would give zero output and 11 would give V_{ref}. The case of 10 gives an R-2R voltage divider, which results in $2/3 V_{ref}$ output, while 01 gives a 2R-R divider and $1/3 V_{ref}$. Once again the circuit is a multiplying DAC with an output proportional to the product of a reference voltage and a binary fraction input.

The scheme is readily expanded to more bits by adding one switch and resistor for each new bit. The third bit, for example, would use a resistor value of 4R and the new voltage levels would be from $0/7 V_{ref}$ to $7/7 V_{ref}$ in steps of $1/7 V_{ref}$. Each new bit would use a resistor twice as large as the previous bit. Note that the output range stays the same (0 to V_{ref}) but that each added bit halves the size of the steps.

This network is often called a *weighted resistor* voltage output network because the value of each resistor is weighted in inverse proportion to the significance of the bit controlling it, and the output is inherently a voltage level. The performance of the circuit is, in general, good. Differential linearity is determined largely by the accuracy of the resistors used. If the resistors are not in the proper ratio and the resolution is high, grossly unequal step sizes or even nonmonotonic behavior is possible. As an example, assume an 8-bit converter with perfect 1R, 2R, . . . 128R resistors but the 1R resistor is 1% too large, that is, 1.01R. The table below shows the voltage output of the network for some possible digital inputs:

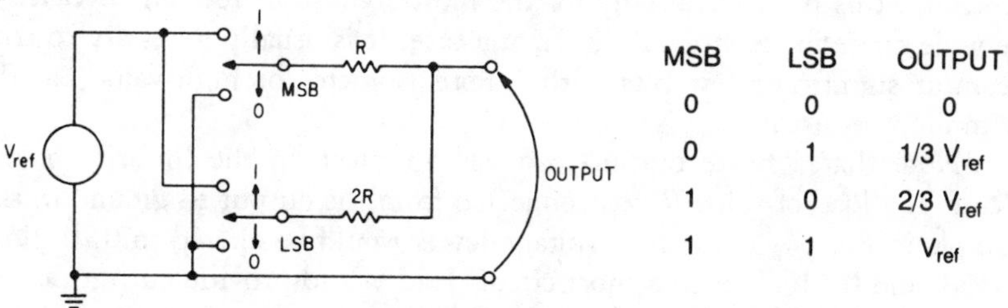

MSB	LSB	OUTPUT
0	0	0
0	1	$1/3\ V_{ref}$
1	0	$2/3\ V_{ref}$
1	1	V_{ref}

Fig. 7–5. Weighted resistor DAC

Digital	Analog × Vref
00000000	0.000000
00000001	0.003941
00000010	0.007882
—	—
01111110	0.496586
01111111	0.500527
10000000	0.499473
10000001	0.503414
—	—
11111110	0.996059
11111111	1.000000

As can be seen, an increase in the digital input from 01111111 to 10000000 results in a slight *decrease* in analog output, a classic manifestation of nonmonotonicity. Except for this step, the rest are $0.003941V_{ref}$ high. Some additional calculation will reveal that the maximum allowable value of 1R for monotonic performance is (1+1/128)R, at which point the voltage levels for 01111111 and 10000000 are the same. If 1R were too small by the same amount, this step would be twice the size of the others, which still gives a 1LSB differential linearity error but preserves monotonicity. It can also be easily determined that the allowable percentage error for less significant resistors doubles for each bit toward the least significant end. In general, though, all of the resistors will have some error, so individual resistors will have to be more precise to guarantee differential linearity better than 1LSB. A rule of thumb that will always work is that the resistor corresponding to bit N should have a tolerance better than $1/2^{N+1}$. Thus, the most significant resistor of a 12-bit DAC should have a tolerance of ±0.024% or better.

Even if the resistors were perfect, the analog switches used have a finite on resistance, which adds to the effective resistance of each bit. If all switches have the same internal resistance, proper ratios are destroyed and linearity suffers again. The effect of switch resistance can be minimized by making the weighted resistors very large but then speed suffers. Also, stable, tight tolerance resistors in the megohm range are difficult to find. Sometimes the switches are scaled in size, and therefore resistance in proportion to the bit significance to maintain proper ratios in spite of high switch resistance. Generally, this is practical only for the most significant few bits because of the wide range in resistor values. In any case, it is usually necessary to trim the most significant few bits with a potentiometer or high-value parallel "trimming" resistors.

Note that a finite output load has no effect on the linearity of the circuit. If a load of value R was connected from the output to ground in the example in Fig. 7–5, the four voltage levels would be altered to 0, $0.2V_{ref}$, $0.4V_{ref}$, and $0.6V_{ref}$. Even a short circuit load would provide output *currents* of 0, $0.5V_{ref}/R$, $1.0V_{ref}/R$, and $1.5V_{ref}/R$. Thus, the equivalent circuit of the converter can be represented as a variable-voltage generator in series with a resistor equal to the parallel combination of all of the weighted resistors. For reasonably high-resolution converters, this equivalent resistance is essentially *R*/2.

Speed

Unlike the previous scheme, the speed of this circuit is quite good. The only limitation on speed is the switching time of the switches and the load capacitance at the output node where all of the resistors are tied together. Even with a slow switching time of 1 μsec, a node capacitance of 10 pF, and an *R* value of 50K, the settling time for 12 bits of resolution would be 1 μsec + 9 (25K × 10 pF) = 3.25 μsec. With this kind of speed, the limiting factor is often the buffer amplifier usually connected to the output. For even higher speeds, the current output configuration (output "shorted" to the input of a current-to-voltage converter op-amp circuit) can be used to eliminate the 2.25-μsec contribution of output capacitance.

Although the speed is high, this circuit (in fact all resistive divider networks) is subject to glitches when moving from one level to another. The root cause of large glitches is nonsymmetrical switching time of the analog switches. Assume for the moment that a 3-bit DAC is moving up one step from 011 to 100 and that the switches go from 1 to 0 faster than from 0 to 1. The resistor network will actually see a switch state of 000 during the time between 1-0 switching and 0-1 switching. This momentary zero state creates a large negative glitch until the most significant switch turns on. Even if switching times are identical, the less significant bits may be slower than the more significant ones because they handle much lower signal currents. Unequal switching may be largely overcome in some circuit configurations, but small glitches can still be generated during finite switching times when a fraction of the reference voltage is still passing through a partially off switch. Thus, although some DAC glitching is a fact of life, a simple low-pass filter that may even be above the audio range is usually sufficient to eliminate the effect of glitches in synthesizer control applications.

R-2R Ladder

Figure 7–6 shows a different resistance divider network that is the basis for most modern DACs. Although somewhat more difficult to analyze than the weighted resistor network, the output voltages are 0.0, 0.25, 0.5, and 0.75 times V_{ref} corresponding to codes of 00, 01, 10, and 11. Bits are added by inserting a switch, series 2R resistor, and 1R resistor to the next lower bit between the MSB and LSB. Note that the resistor to ground from the LSB is 2R rather than 1R. This is called a *terminating* resistor because it simulates the equivalent impedance of an infinite string of less significant bits all in the zero state.

The advantages of this configuration are numerous. One is that only two different values of precision resistors are needed. Although about twice

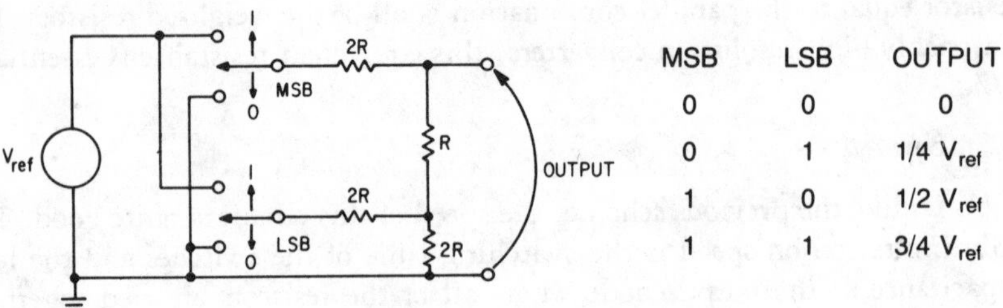

MSB	LSB	OUTPUT
0	0	0
0	1	1/4 V_{ref}
1	0	1/2 V_{ref}
1	1	3/4 V_{ref}

Fig. 7–6. Resistor ladder DAC

as many resistors are used, the ease of matching their characteristics (remember only the *ratio* accuracy is important) leads to better DAC performance with varying temperature. In fact, all resistors could be of the same value if 2R is actually two 1R resistors in series. Another advantage is that the load impedance of all of the switches is about the same. This eliminates the need for scaling switch size; instead the switch resistance can simply be subtracted from the 2R series resistor (or a large resistor placed in parallel with 2R). Speed can be better because the node capacitances are spread out rather than concentrated into one node as with the weighted resistor circuit. Analysis of the effect of an error in a single resistor is considerably more complicated, although the same resistor accuracy rule for guaranteed monotonic performance still holds. Also, the linearity of this circuit is not affected by load resistance or a direct short either. The equivalent output impedance is essentially *R*.

Other variations of the resistance ladder are also used. The most popular is the current-switching structure shown in Fig. 7–7. Essentially the circuit has been turned upside down with *Vref* driving the ladder at what was the output point and an op-amp current to voltage converter connected to what was *Vref*. Speedwise, this circuit is probably the best. The reason is that voltage levels on the resistor network nodes do not change, since the ladder current is simply switched between true ground and "virtual ground" at the op-amp summing junction. Likewise, voltage levels at the switches do not change. When voltage levels are constant, stray capacitances are not charged so there is no RC time constant slowdown. The result is inherently high overall speed nearly equivalent to the individual switch speed. Settling times of less than 0.5 μsec (neglecting the effect of the output amplifier) are routine, and 20 nsec is possible in low-resolution designs.

Segmented DAC

One recently discovered circuit essentially combines the resistor string method described earlier with the resistor ladder method to get the major advantages of each. In order to understand how it works, refer back to Fig.

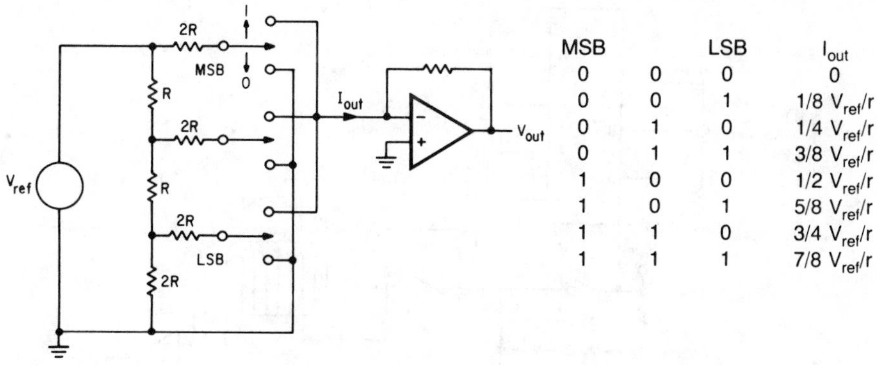

MSB		LSB	Iout
0	0	0	0
0	0	1	1/8 V_{ref}/r
0	1	0	1/4 V_{ref}/r
0	1	1	3/8 V_{ref}/r
1	0	0	1/2 V_{ref}/r
1	0	1	5/8 V_{ref}/r
1	1	0	3/4 V_{ref}/r
1	1	1	7/8 V_{ref}/r

Fig. 7–7. Inverted current ladder DAC

7–6 and note that, as drawn, the digital code essentially *interpolates* between ground and the reference voltage according to the binary fraction operating the switches. In fact, the circuit will interpolate between *any* two voltages if the ground terminal is freed and connected instead to the second voltage. Figure 7–8 shows a 3-bit example, in which the lower ladder terminal is connected to +1 V and the upper terminal is connected to +2 V. The 3-bit digital code then selects eight voltage levels ⅛V apart starting at *and including* the voltage at the lower ladder terminal (+1 V) and ending one step short of the voltage at the upper ladder terminal (+2 − ⅛ V).

To form a segmented DAC, a modified resistor string DAC is first constructed using two sets of switches so that two output voltages are produced, the second always one step higher than the first (Fig. 7–9). These voltages are then buffered by op-amps and applied to the ends of a resistor ladder DAC, which in turn interpolates the large step into much smaller ones. The most significant bits of the digital code drive the resistor string DAC, while the remaining less significant bits drive the resistor ladder DAC.

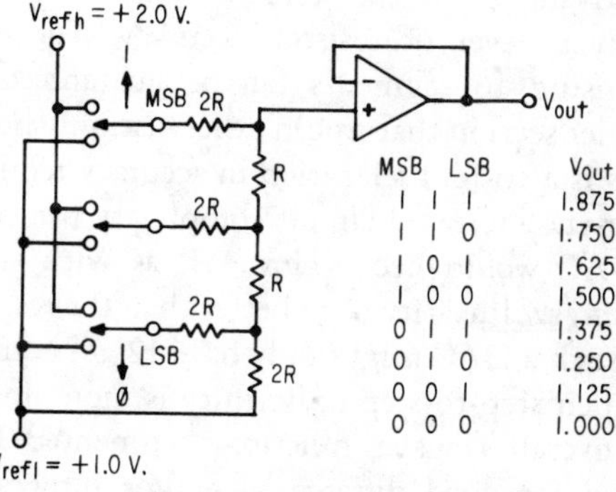

MSB		LSB	Vout
1	1	1	1.875
1	1	0	1.750
1	0	1	1.625
1	0	0	1.500
0	1	1	1.375
0	1	0	1.250
0	0	1	1.125
0	0	0	1.000

Fig. 7–8. Ladder DAC interpolating between +1 and +2 V

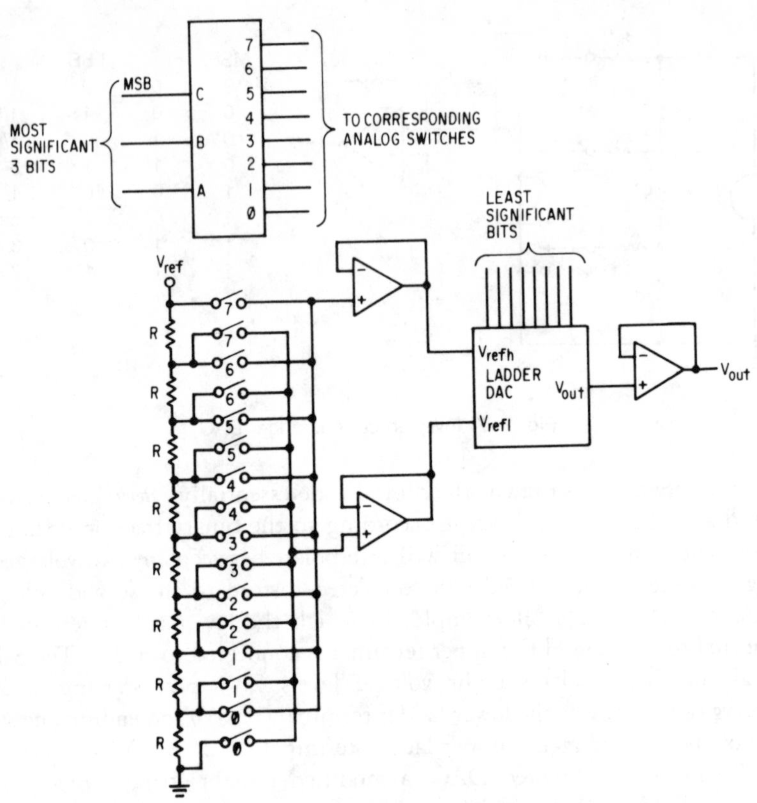

Fig. 7–9. Segmented DAC

The split can be made anywhere, but the incentive is to apply most of the bits to the ladder. Commercial units typically apply the most significant 3 or 4 bits to the resistor string DAC. Other circuit structures using *current* division and interpolation are also possible.

The main advantage of this circuit is much improved differential linearity for a given level of resistor accuracy. For example, a 16-bit segmented DAC using 16 segments can be guaranteed monotonic using resistors in the ladder section that would otherwise only be precise enough for a 12-bit unit. This is a 16-fold relaxation in accuracy requirement that much more than pays for the increased circuit complexity over what a straight 16-bit ladder-type DAC would need. However, as with the original resistor string DAC, the *integral* linearity is no better than the resistor accuracy in the string section, so such a DAC might only have 12-bit equivalent accuracy. In applications in which step-to-step uniformity is more important than slight curvature of the overall transfer function, segmented DACs can be very valuable. The need for good differential and/or integral linearity will be discussed in the DAC applications described in succeeding chapters.

Exponential DAC Circuits

The preceding DAC circuits were all linear, that is, the output voltage was a linear function of the input digital word. Nonlinear DACs are also possible using only resistors, switches, and op-amps. In sound synthesis, an exponential DAC would be of particular interest. Using such a device, an exponential response to a digital word could be obtained from a linear analog circuit without a separate analog exponential converter. Figure 7–10 shows a conceptual circuit for an exponential DAC. Essentially the circuit is a chain of switchable attenuators that may have a gain of either 1.0 (switch on, bit = 0) or a specific gain of less than 1.0. The output voltage is equal to the *product* of the individual stage gains rather than the sum as with linear converters. The buffer amplifiers prevent switching of succeeding stages from affecting the attenuation ratios. For the values shown, the output is $V_{ref} \times 2^{-N/4}$, where N is the input expressed as a binary integer. Thus, the I/O table would be as follows:

Binary	*N*	*Output* × V_{ref}
000	0	1.000
001	1	0.841
010	2	0.707
011	3	0.594
100	4	0.500
101	5	0.421
110	6	0.353
111	7	0.296

Bits may be added at the left end of the circuit for increased range (toward zero) or at the right end for increased resolution. The accuracy of exponential conversion is limited only by resistor accuracy and the characteristics of the op-amps. Other circuit configurations are possible using an amplifier per 2 bits or even fewer at the expense of more switches. Since the

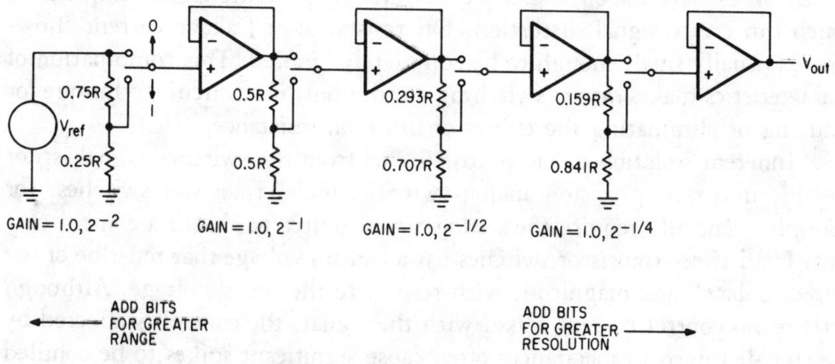

Fig. 7–10. Exponential DAC

network is a multiplying DAC, one obvious application is an audio attenuator with response directly in decibels, where the audio signal replaces the reference voltage source. Or with some rescaling of resistor values, the transfer function, $V_{out} = V_{ref} \times 2^{-N/12}$, can be realized, which would give the 12-tone equally tempered musical scale directly with a linear VCO.

While the circuit in Fig. 7–10 gives a perfect exponential transfer function (assuming perfectly accurate resistor values and op-amps), one can also construct a circuit that gives a *straight-line approximation* to an exponential curve. This may be done by modifying the resistor string section of the segmented DAC described earlier. The lower resistors are reduced in value, while the upper resistors are increased such that the segments follow a true exponential curve. The ladder section then linearly interpolates between the segment endpoints. The DAC-86 is a commercial example that uses 8 segments and 16 steps per segment to convert a 7-bit code. The primary application for this type of DAC is in telephone quality speech reconstruction from a digital signal. This will be described more fully in Chapter 12.

Analog Switches for DACs

Several different kinds of semiconductor switches are typically used in DACs as well as general analog signal switching. The latter application will be of great interest later when computer-controlled patching of synthesizer modules is considered. The ideal switch, of course, would act like a relay with nearly zero contact resistance, complete isolation between control and signal circuits, and high-signal-voltage capability but with submicrosecond switching times and essentially unlimited life. Practical semiconductor switches fall rather short on the first three points but are still quite usable if the limitations are understood.

Switch "on" resistance, for example, is certainly more than ideal. Depending on the switch type, it may range from just a few ohms to well over a thousand ohms with typical values in the 50-ohm to 500-ohm range. Some switch types have an on resistance that varies with the signal amplitude, which can create signal distortion. Off resistance or leakage current, however, is usually small enough to be completely ignored. This combination of characteristics makes *current* switching a commonly used circuit technique for reducing or eliminating the effects of finite on resistance.

Inherent isolation of the control signal from the switched signal is not possible in a fast, precision analog switch. Bipolar transistor switches, for example, generally require the analog signal source to absorb a control current. Field-effect-transistor switches use a control voltage that must be of the correct polarity and magnitude with respect to the signal voltage. Although little or no control current mixes with the signal, the control is affected by the signal. Internal capacitances often cause significant spikes to be coupled from the control circuit into the signal circuit. Feedthrough capacitance also

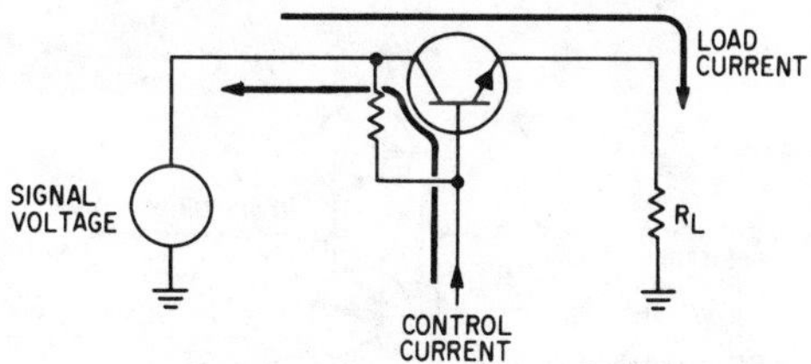

Fig. 7–11. Basic bipolar transistor analog switch

reduces the off isolation of high-frequency signals or lets input spikes that are intended to be gated off by the switch through to the output anyway. Limits on signal amplitude that can be switched are imposed by breakdown voltages of the switch itself and, in the case of FET switches, the power supply voltages available for switch control. These limitations are such that ±10-V analog signals are not always easily handled.

Bipolar Transistor Switch

The bipolar transistor is one of the oldest analog switches in use. Presently it is used in discrete form whenever low-voltage, moderately accurate, very inexpensive switching is to be performed. Bipolar transistors are also used extensively in monolithic DACs, where their errors are easily cancelled through the use of matched transistors.

The basic bipolar transistor switch is shown in Fig. 7–11. Note that the role of the collector and the emitter have been reversed. This reduces greatly the inherent *offset voltage* of the transistor switch. For small signal currents (less than 1 mA), the inverted connection provides saturation voltages in the low-millivolt range as opposed to 60 mV or more for the normal common-emitter connection. The required control current is the same order of magnitude as the signal current due to the very low current gain of the inverted connection.

Note that the control current flows through the signal source. This need not cause much of a problem if the source has a low impedance such as an op-amp output. Note also that, although the switch can actually pass small amounts of negative current when on, it cannot block a signal voltage more negative than half a volt when off. Positive signal voltage blocking is limited to about 5 V because of the 6-V base-to-emitter breakdown of nearly all silicon transistors. Greater breakdowns up to 25 V are available in transistors designed for analog switching, however.

One advantage of this switch is low control glitch feedthrough to the output. All analog switches have capacitance between the control element and the signal elements. Charging and discharging of these capacitances during switching can create sizable glitches at the load. Since a bipolar transistor switch is current activated, the voltage swing at the base is very small and therefore the glitch is small.

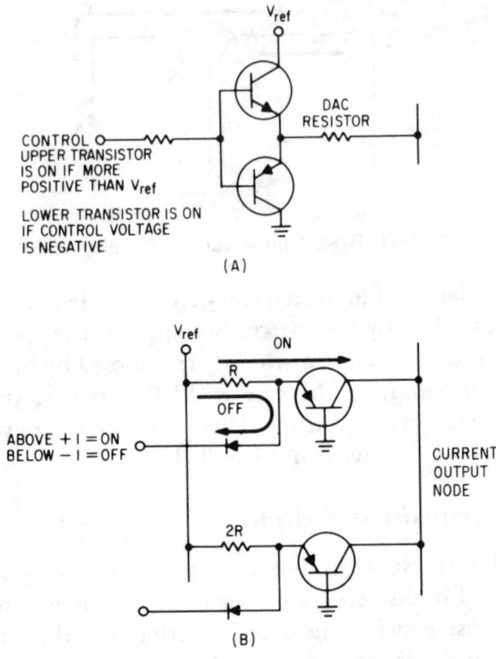

Fig. 7–12. Bipolar transistor switches for DACs. (A) Voltage switch. (B) Current switch.

Figure 7–12 shows two possible configurations of transistor switches in DACs. The first circuit is a double-throw voltage switch that switches its output between V_{ref} and ground with very little error. With the simple resistive-voltage-to-control-current converter shown, the control logic swing for this switch must be from a negative voltage to a positive voltage greater than V_{ref}. An inherently bipolar (+ and − output voltages) DAC may be made if the bottom transistor is connected to $-V_{ref}$ instead of ground and the control swing is increased. Note that the V_{ref}s can change over a wide range as long as the drive is sufficiently greater than either and that they do not cross (V_{ref} on npn more negative than V_{ref} on pnp). Total voltages ($V_{ref}+$ $-$ $V_{ref}-$) up to the *collector* breakdown can be accommodated with this circuit.

The second circuit is often used in monolithic DACs. Weighted resistors are used to establish binary-weighted currents. The current either flows through the common-base-connected switching transistor into the output line or through the steering diode into the switch driver. If the current gain of the transistors is high, very little signal current is lost through the base. Note that this is strictly a current output DAC and that the current must be sunk at ground or negative potentials. The temperature dependence of output current caused by changing emitter-base drop in the switching transistors may be cancelled by a matched transistor in the V_{ref} source.

Junction FET Switch

The field effect transistor is the most commonly used analog switch for general-purpose applications. FETs have the desirable characteristic that little or no control current flows in the signal circuit. They are also blessed with a zero offset voltage (for zero load current), which contributes greatly to accuracy with low-level signals. The on resistance is higher than bipolar transistors, but proper circuit design can generally overcome that difficulty.

Junction field-effect transistors (JFET) are well suited for general switching in music synthesis systems because their on resistance is constant regardless of signal level. An N-channel FET, for example, behaves essentially as a pure resistance between source and drain when the gate-to-source voltage is zero. The switch is off when the gate is more negative with respect to the source than the pinchoff voltage. Most JFETs are symmetrical (source and drain interchangable), so if there is a voltage drop across the switch when it is off, the gate must be more negative than the most negative source/drain terminal. The gate must never be allowed to become positive with respect to the source or drain because the gate-channel diode will become forward biased and control current will flow into the signal path. P-channel JFETs work similarly, but all voltage polarities are reversed.

Figure 7–13 shows a basic JFET analog switching circuit. A large resistor (100K to 1M in practice) between the gate and source keeps the JFET normally on. The control voltage is applied to the gate through a blocking diode. When the control is more positive than the positive peaks of the signal, this diode is reverse biased (preventing positive gate-channel potential) and the conducting JFET is essentially isolated from the control. To turn the JFET off, the control voltage must be made $V_{pinchoff}$ more negative than the negative peaks of the signal. The signal voltage range thus is determined by the control voltage swing and the pinchoff voltage. With ±15-V power supplies and ±10-V signals, the pinchoff cannot exceed 5 V. Note that a small current flows through the now forward-biased blocking diode and the gate-source resistor into the signal source. Fortunately, this current can usually be ignored if the signal source is a low impedance.

The P-channel switch is essentially the same except that the positive swing of the control voltage must exceed the positive signal peak by the pinchoff potential. P-channel FETs are generally slower and have higher on resistance than N-channel FETs by a factor of two to three. One fact of life is that really low on resistance is incompatible with low pinchoff voltages. The best switching JFETs have on resistances in the range of 20 ohms and pinchoff voltages close to 10 V. Thus, standard ±15-V power supplies would not be able to switch ±10-V signals when using such high-performance devices.

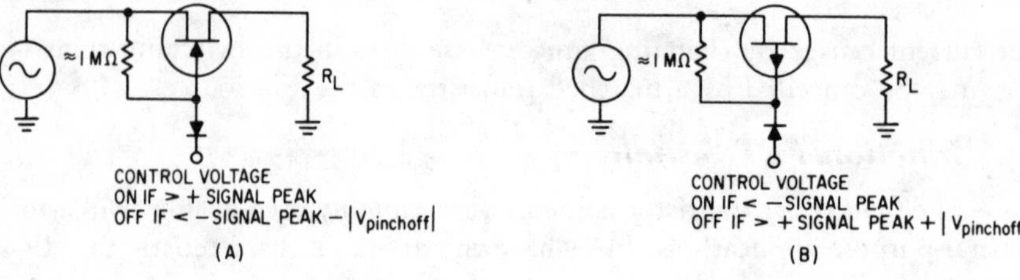

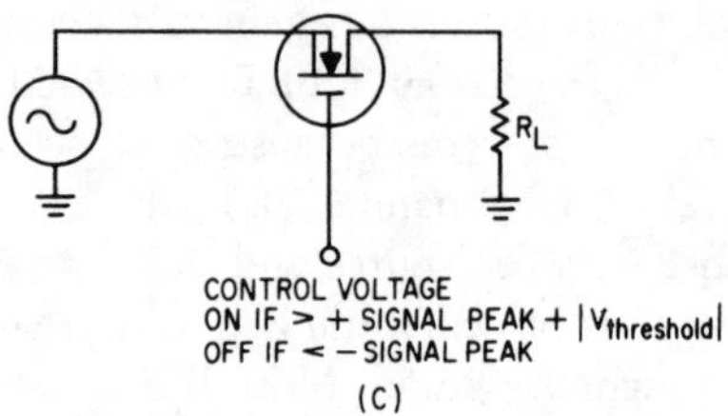

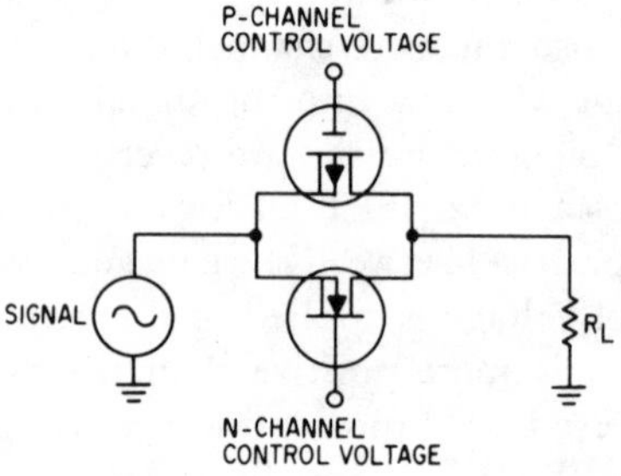

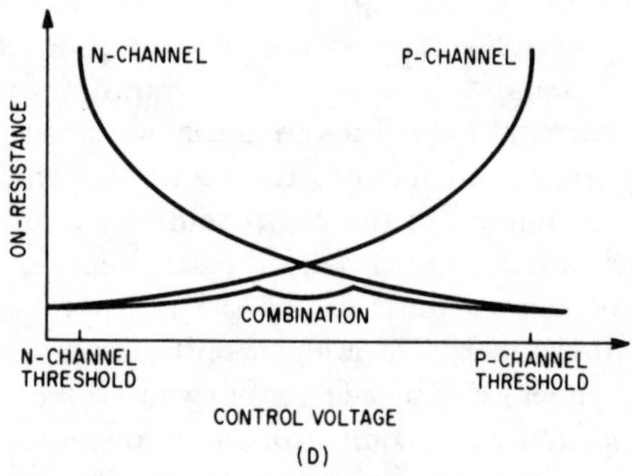

Fig. 7–13. Basic FET analog switches. (A) N-channel junction FET. (B) P-channel junction FET. (C) N-channel MOSFET. (D) Complementary MOSFET switch.

MOSFET Switch

Metal-oxide gate FETs (MOSFET) are also frequently used for switching. The MOSFET is the most nearly perfect switching transistor available from the standpoint of control-to-signal isolation. Basic operation is the same as with a JFET except that the gate is *insulated* from the channel and all voltages are shifted up somewhat. An N-channel MOSFET, for example, is normally off with a zero gate-to-source voltage. The gate must become more positive than a *threshold voltage* before the switch turns on. The gate may also swing negative with no effect other than driving the device deeper into cutoff. In fact, the gate voltage swing is limited only by internal breakdown voltages; it is otherwise isolated (except for a small capacitance) from the channel.

One difficulty with MOSFETs is that the on resistance is indefinite; the more positive the gate the lower the resistance. If the MOSFET is carrying an audio signal into a finite load resistance, the channel resistance will be modulated by the signal itself, causing nonlinear distortion. This happens because the gate- (fixed drive voltage) to-source (varying audio signal) voltage will be changing. Since there is a saturation effect at large gate-to-source voltages, distortion will be minimized by suitable control overdrive. Distortion is also reduced by using larger load resistances. A typical switching N-channel MOSFET might have a nominal on resistance of 100 ohms that may vary from 75 ohms to 150 ohms with ±15-V drive and ±10-V signals. Newer MOS technologies such as DMOS and VMOS can actually attain on resistances as low as 1 ohm and carry ampere level currents!

A very nice analog switch may be constructed from two MOSFETs of opposite polarity connected in parallel. To turn on, both switches must be driven on by opposite polarity control voltages, which can reverse to drive both switches off. The major advantage of this circuit is that signal voltage levels as large as the drive voltages may be handled. Although each individual switch is highly nonlinear and even cuts off for part of the signal cycle, the parallel combination is always on. In fact, when the on resistance of the N-channel unit is increasing with positive-going signals, the P-channel resistance is decreasing to compensate. The result is considerably less signal distortion. This structure is called a CMOS (complementary MOS) transmission gate and is available in integrated form as quad switches and eight-channel analog multiplexors at very low cost. The disadvantage of most integrated transmission gates is a ±7.5-V signal and drive-voltage limitation. Recently, "B-series" CMOS has become available and can handle up to ±9-V signals, adequate for an 8-V standard system, although some care in use will have to be exercised. Specialized units with even higher voltage ratings are available but at a much higher cost.

Figure 7–14 shows a good general-purpose driver for both JFETs and MOSFETs that can in turn be driven by TTL logic. The driver output swings

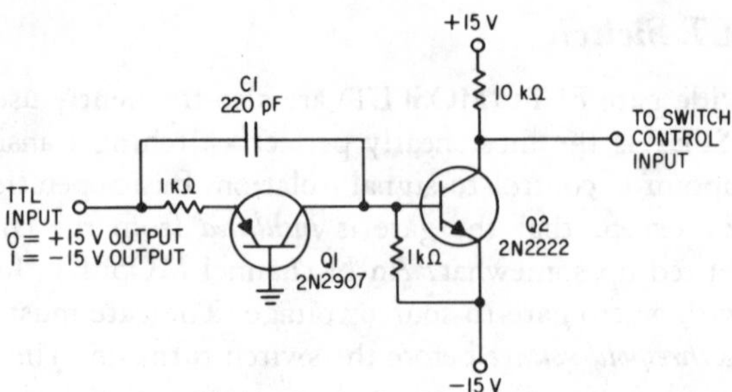

Fig. 7–14. FET switch driver

between whatever positive and negative supply voltages are connected. The output is negative for a logic high input, which would drive N-channel FET switches off. In operation, Q1 performs as a level shifter by feeding the approximately 3-mA logic input current through to the base of Q2. The 220-pF capacitor speeds up the turnoff of Q2 (turnon of N-channel FETs) by removing its stored base charge. As shown, the circuit will provide switching times of around 200 nsec. Without C1 this deteriorates to around 1 μsec. Much faster operation (down to 20 nsec or less) can be obtained by changing C1 to 100 pF, Q2 to a 2N3646, and reducing its collector load resistor to the 1–2.2K Ω range.

Recently, completely integrated analog switches have appeared on the market. These "BIFET" devices accept normal logic levels and analog supply voltages of ±15 V and provide several NFET switching functions per package. Each switch in a typical array of four can handle ±10-V analog signals and switching time is about 0.5 μsec. These are perfect for most applications not requiring really high speed or exceptionally low on resistances.

Current-to-Voltage Conversion

Returning to DACs, it is often the case that the output amplifier limits many performance parameters, particularly settling time. The purpose of the amplifier, of course, is to isolate the DAC resistor network from load variations so that accuracy is maintained. By far the simplest output buffer is simply a voltage follower op-amp connected to a voltage output DAC network. Although simple, it is relatively slow when general-purpose op-amps are connected as voltage followers because of the heavy frequency compensation required. Specialized voltage-follower amplifiers such as the LM310 are so fast, however, that overall speed may be dominated by the DAC output capacitance.

Nearly all commercial DACs are inherently current-output devices. Many of these can actually generate small voltages across small load resistors with no loss of linearity. A non-inverting amplifier with gain can amplify the

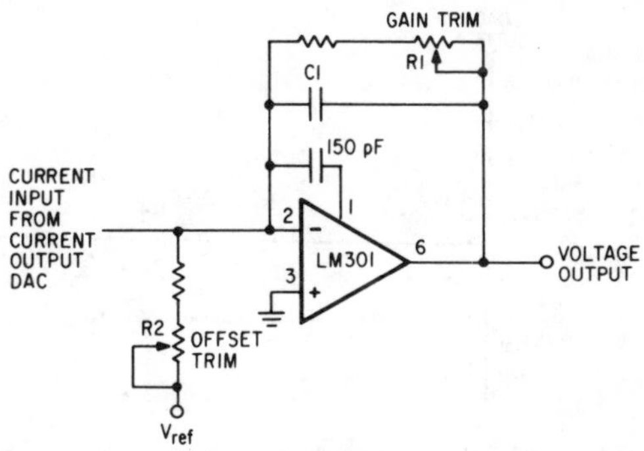

Fig. 7–15. Fast, inexpensive current-to-voltage converter

resulting fractional volt signal to standard levels with good speed, since less frequency compensation is needed. Noise pickup could be a problem, though, if this technique is used with high-resolution DACs.

The current-to-voltage converter configuration shown in Fig. 7–15 is probably the best, really inexpensive circuit available for most applications of current-output DACs. The "three-for-a-dollar" LM301 op-amp using feed-forward compensation easily gives under 3-μsec settling times, normally obtainable only with more costly "high-speed" op-amps. Although the effective zero impedance of the amplifier summing node eliminates output capacitance slowdown, in practice C1 is usually needed to keep the DAC output capacitance from making the op-amp unstable. Gain and offset errors are also easily trimmed out in this circuit because the adjustments do not interact. Some types of CMOS DACs are affected by output amplifier bias current, which is approximately 100 nA for the LM301. FET-type op-amps, such as the LF356, are then required and C1 is mandatory with a value in the 10–30 pF range. These also require that the amplifier's own offset be trimmed to zero in order to minimize differential linearity errors.

Number Coding

Several different binary codes are in common use with DACs. All of the example circuits given previously were unipolar, that is, gave output voltages between zero and a V_{ref} or output currents between zero and I_{ref}. One way to obtain a bipolar voltage output would be to use the dual emitter-follower bipolar transistor switch shown in Fig.7–12 with a bipolar reference supply. The result would be a voltage output DAC that would swing between $-V_{ref}$ and $+V_{ref}-$ 1LSB (switches connected to R-2R ladder). For example, all zeroes would give $-V_{ref}$, 10000 . . . would give zero volts, and 11111 . . . would give one step less than $+V_{ref}$. Such a code is called *offset binary* because it is equivalent to a plain unsigned binary (positive output only) DAC output between zero and $+2V_{ref}$ shifted down by V_{ref} as in Fig.

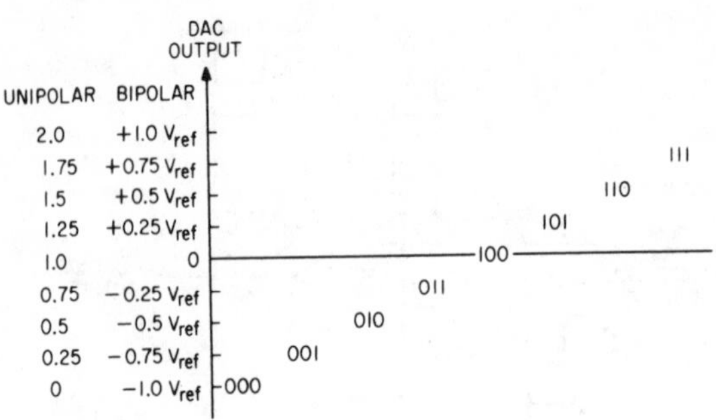

Fig. 7–16. Offset binary coding.

7–16. In fact, inherently bipolar output DAC networks are not usually built. Instead, a unpiolar DAC is used and half of the reference voltage is *subtracted* from the DAC output in the output amplifier. With a current output DAC connected to a current-to-voltage converter, the offset can be accomplished by drawing a current equal to one-half the full-scale DAC current out of the amplifier summing node.

Most computers use twos-complement representation for bipolar numbers, however. Fortunately, conversion of twos-complement binary to offset binary is very simple; the most significant bit (the "sign" bit) is simply inverted! No other logic or corrections are needed. This, of course, is extremely simple to do in the computer program, the DAC interface, or the most significant DAC switch itself.

There is a practical disadvantage to offset binary coding for bipolar output. Recall that the effect of a slight error in the weight of the most significant bit showed up as an odd-sized step in the exact middle of the output range and nowhere else. Also, since the most significant bit has the most stringent accuracy requirement, this type of error would be the most difficult to avoid. With offset binary, this midscale error would show up at the zero output level, precisely where it would be most noticed.

Sign magnitude is another coding scheme that eliminates this error. An N-bit sign-magnitude number has a sign bit and $N-1$ magnitude bits, which form an unsigned binary fraction. A sign-magnitude DAC would send the magnitude value to a conventional unipolar DAC and then use the sign bit to control the output amplifier. When the sign bit is zero, the amplifier would pass the DAC output unaltered. When it is one, the amplifier would become an inverter and give negative outputs for positive inputs. Such a "sign-bit amplifier" is shown in Fig. 7–17. Although this circuit can have a gain error if the two resistors are not equal, any error around zero is small and can be easily trimmed out by zeroing the op-amp's offset voltage. Another advantage is that this circuit effectively adds a bit of resoluton to the overall DAC without doubling the resistor network accuracy requirement.

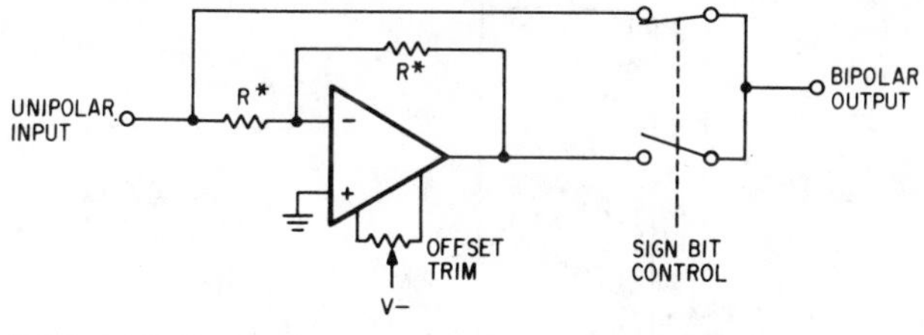

Fig. 7-17. Sign-bit amplifier

Conversion of twos complement, which would still be the preferred internal computer code, to sign magnitude is fairly simple. The function needed would pass the twos-complement value bits unaltered if the sign bit were zero and invert them if it were one. The conditional inversion is easily accomplished with exclusive-or gates in the interface or can be done by software.

Some Commercial DACs

For most applications requiring resolutions greater than 5 or 6 bits, the expense and difficulty of finding precision resistors outweighs the cost of a commercial prepackaged DAC. Most modern 8- and 10-bit units are monolithic and packaged in standard 16-pin IC packages. Twelve-bit and higher resolutions until recently were invariably hybrid devices usually packaged in small epoxy modules. Now several 12-bit monolithic units are on the market at prices under $20 for the commercial temperature grade. Segmented DACs up to 16 bits are also available as monolithic ICs, but none have true 16-bit integral linearity and accuracy. In this section, the most widely used inexpensive devices in the 8-, 10-, and 12-bit resolution range will be briefly described. There are, of course, a large number of similar devices on the market that will perform just as well in computer-controlled synthesizer applications.

1408 and DAC-08 Type for 8 Bits

One of the earliest 8-bit monolithic DACs was developed by Motorola and bears the generic type number 1408/1508. The 1508 is an expensive military temperature range device, but the 1408 performs nearly as well in room temperature environments and costs less than $5. The 1408 is offered in 6-, 7-, and 8-bit *linearity* grades, although all have 8 bits of resolution. The linearity grade is indicated by an "-X" following the type number. For this discussion, use of the 8-bit grade is assumed.

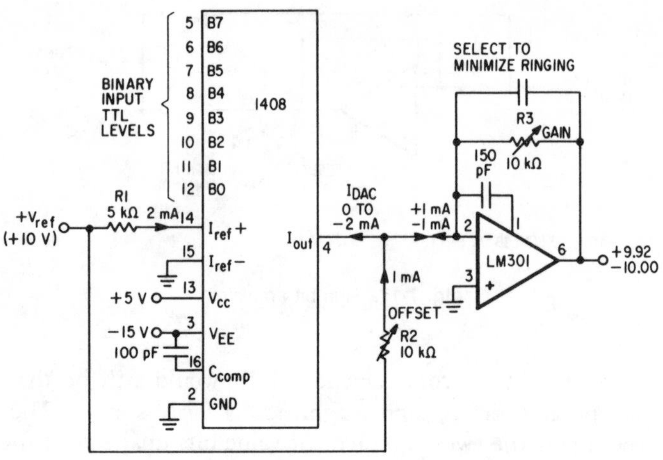

Fig. 7–18. Application of 1408-type IC DAC

Like most inexpensive monolithic DACs, the 1408 is a bare-bones device incorporating little more than the analog switches and R-2R ladder network. An external reference source and output amplifier are required for a complete DAC. The 1408 is basically a current-activated device; the reference is a current and the output is a current. It is also a multiplying DAC. The output current, I_{out}, is equal to the reference current, I_{ref}, times the binary input expressed as an unsigned binary fraction between 0 and 0.994. The reference current may range from 0 to about 4 mA, although below 0.5 mA linearity errors increase such that monotonicity cannot be guaranteed. The reference current must always be positive and the output current is actually negative, meaning that the DAC output *sinks* current. Standard power supply voltages of +5 V and −15 V are used.

Figure 7–18 shows a typical hookup for the 1408. Although other methods of supplying the reference current exist, the one shown is the simplest. The $I_{ref}+$ input sinks the reference current at a voltage equal to the voltage at $I_{ref}-$. For a reference voltage of +10 V with respect to ground, $I_{ref}-$ is tied to ground and $I_{ref}+$ receives a reference current of 2 mA (the optimum value) through a 5K resistor (R1) tied to the reference voltage. A compensation capacitor of 100 pF is required to frequency compensate the internal reference current circuitry.

An output voltage range of −10 to +10 is developed from the 0 to −2 mA output current with a current-to-voltage converter. A +1.0 mA current from the reference voltage source through R2 offsets −1.0 mA of the DAC output, giving a net current swing into the amplifier of −1.0 to +1.0 mA. This current is then converted into a −10-V to +10-V swing as a function of R3. The current output settling time is about 0.3 μsec, which is extended to approximately 3 μsec by the amplifier. R2 and R3 may be made adjustable over a small range (low value trim pot in series with a slightly reduced resistor) to precisely calibrate the scale factor and offset.

The digital input is offset binary coded but may be converted to twos complement by placing an inverter in the path to B7. Standard TTL logic levels are acceptable and the loading is less than one-half unit load.

A similar type of device is the DAC-08, invented by Precision Monolithics but made by several companies. Besides a much higher speed than the 1408 (85 nsec current settling time), it has *two* current output terminals. Both outputs sink current, but one is the complement of the

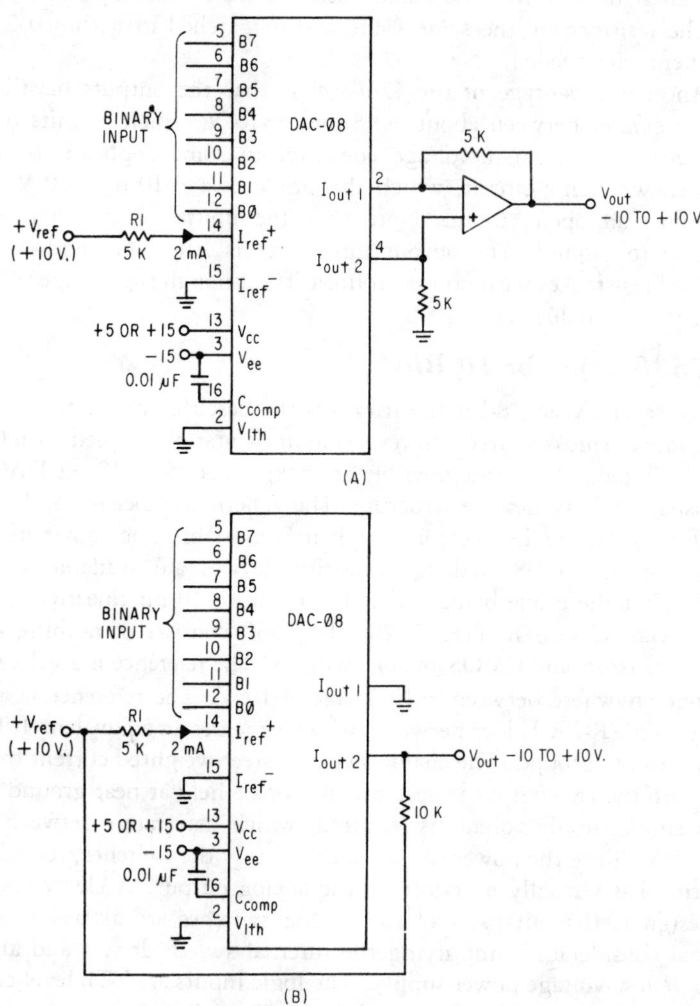

Fig. 7–19. (A) Application of DAC-08 IC DAC. (B) Use of simple resistor current-to-voltage converter with DAC-08.

other. For example, for a digital input of 01000000, I_{out1} will be one-quarter of the reference current and I_{out2} will the three-quarters of the reference current. Thus, the full reference current magnitude is effectively divided between the two outputs according to the digital code. Availability of the two outputs is an advantage in a bipolar output DAC as shown in Fig. 7–19A. Here the I_{out1} output is connected to the op-amp summing junction as before, but the I_{out2} output is connected to the noninverting input of the same amplifier. The op-amp thus effectively subtracts I_{out1} from I_{out2} and converts the difference into a voltage. The parts values given produce an output range of −10 to +10 V and a settling time under 2 μsec. Note that all of the resistors are the same value and if matched to within 0.2%, no adjustments are needed.

Another advantage of the DAC-08 is that the outputs have a large *voltage compliance* between about +18 and −10 V, which permits use of a simple resistor current-to-voltage converter in some applications. Figure 7–19B shows such a circuit, which also produces a −10 to +10 V output swing into an open circuit. Note that the unused output terminal is connected to ground. The output impedance is 10K ohms and can drive finite load resistances with no loss in linearity, although the voltage swing, of course, will be reduced.

7530 Type for 10 Bits

For several years, 8-bit linearity was the best that could be done with bipolar monolithic circuitry. However, ion implantation coupled with CMOS switch technology has made possible an inexpensive ($10) 10-bit DAC with an unusual but very flexible structure. The generic number is 7530 and the originator is Analog Devices, although it is available from other manufacturers. Like the 1408, reduced linearity devices are available so check carefully that the grade being ordered is rated for 10-bit linearity.

As can be seen in Fig. 7–20, the 7530 consists of nothing except precision resistors and CMOS analog switches! The reference is a voltage that can range anywhere between −10 V and +10 V. The reference is applied directly to the R-2R ladder network, which provides an equivalent 10K pure resistive load to ground. The analog switches steer weighted current from the ladder into the two output buses, which *must* be held at near ground potential. A single supply voltage is required, which may range between +5 V and +15 V. Since the power supply operates only the switches, its value and regulation has virtually no effect on the analog output. A clever feature of this design is that all parts of the analog switches are always at ground potential considerably simplifying the internal switch drivers and allowing the single low-voltage power supply. The logic inputs are TTL level compatible regardless of supply voltage and draw essentially zero input current. A precision feedback resistor is provided for an external current-to-voltage converter.

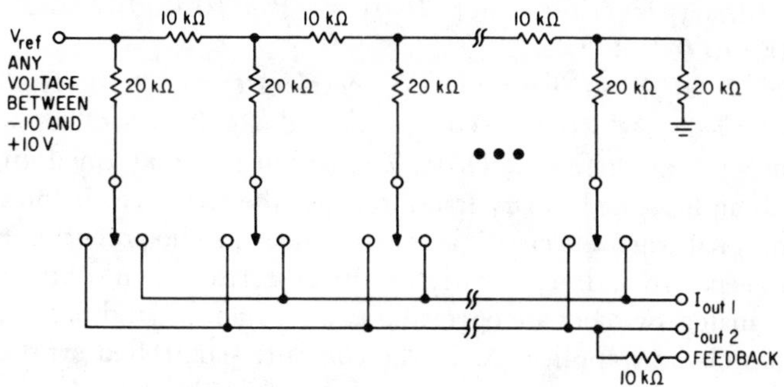

Fig. 7–20. 7530-type 10-bit IC DAC

By far the most important feature of this circuit is its ability to handle *bipolar* reference inputs. In fact, there is nothing to prevent audio signals up to 10 V in amplitude from being applied to the reference input. The two output buses are complements of each other. With all switches in the zero state (shown), the entire reference current (less 1LSB) is directed to the I_{out2} bus and none goes to I_{out1}. The converse is true for all switches in the one state. In the intermediate states, the sum of the two currents equals the reference current less 1LSB. Thus, if the input, D, is considered to be an

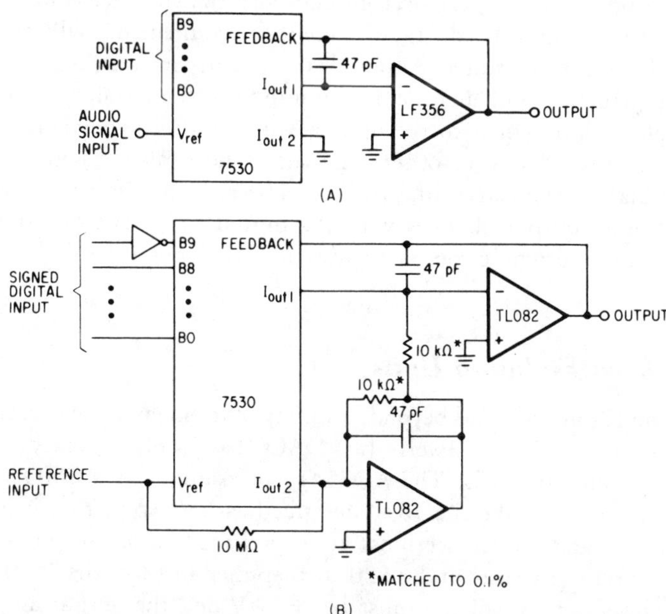

Fig. 7–21. Applications of the 7530 10-bit DAC IC. (A) Digital potentiometer. (B) Four-quadrant multiplying DAC.

unsigned binary fraction, then $I_{out1} = (V_{ref}/10{,}000)D$ and $I_{out2} = (V_{ref}/10{,}000)(0.999 - D)$.

Figure 7–21 shows two typical connections of the 7530. The first is a *digital potentiometer,* which is useful as an audio gain control as well as a general-purpose fixed-reference DAC. The output is simply the digital input expressed as an unsigned binary fraction times the reference. If the reference is an audio signal, then the circuit acts as a standard audio potentiometer with a gain between zero and very nearly unity. Distortion should be zero, since the CMOS analog switches are operating at a constant ground potential. Such a circuit has obvious application in the computer-controlled synthesizer.

The second circuit is a full *four-quadrant* multiplying DAC. Four quadrant means that the final output voltage is the correct algebraic product of a *signed* reference voltage and a *signed* digital input. This normally highly complex function is obtained with the addition of nothing more than one op-amp and two matched resistors. The extra op-amp negates the current from I_{out2} and combines it with the current from I_{out1} in the output amplifier. The effect is that the two currents are subtracted, giving a result that can be either positive or negative. An inherent offset of 1/2LSB exists, however, which can be cancelled by connecting a 10M resistor between the reference input and the I_{out2} terminal of the 7530. The digital input is offset binary, which can be converted to twos complement with a logic inverter.

Two details often overlooked in using CMOS DACs such as the 7530 is that the outputs must be very near ground potential and that amplifier bias current must be minimized. Ignoring either requirement will cause the differential linearity to suffer. Although the circuits in Fig. 7–21 keep the outputs at virtual ground (an op-amp summing junction), they will in reality be at a voltage level equal to the op-amp's input offset voltage. For 10-bit DACs, more than 2 mV of offset can cause a noticeable loss of linearity. Amplifier bias current causes linearity errors because the effective impedance of the converter output changes with the digital code. The easiest way to avoid such bias current errors is to use an FET input type of op-amp as shown.

Higher-Resolution Units

At the 12-bit level and beyond, a variety of technologies and packaging techniques are available. Twelve-bit DACs have only recently become available as monolithic ICs. The AD7541, for example, is a CMOS switch and resistor type just like the 7530 described earlier except that it has two more switches and ladder sections. It is packaged in an 18-pin DIP IC package and typically costs under \$20. It is applied just like the 7530 except that the power supply voltage must be +15 V and the output amplifier's offset voltage must be trimmed to under 0.5 mV in order to achieve 12-bit linearity. FET-type amplifiers are mandatory to avoid bias current errors. One pitfall in the device's application is that its output capacitance is nearly 200 pF as the result of large junction analog switches needed for 12-bit performance. Although the current settling time is specified at 1.0 μsec, and most FET amplifiers have a 2-μsec settling time, it is difficult in practice to get an overall voltage output settling time under 6 μsec because of the output capacitance.

The DAC-312 is another 12-bit device that uses the segmentation technique to provide low cost (under $12) and 12-bit differential (10-bit integral) linearity in a monolithic IC. It uses current segmentation with a 3-bit segment generator (eight segments) and a 9-bit interpolator. It is connected just like the DAC-08 described earlier, but the output current (up to 4 mA) is four times the reference current. Being a bipolar transistor device, its current settling time is very fast at 250 nsec. Figure 7–22 shows a circuit using a DAC-312 and an LM318 high-speed op-amp to produce a voltage output settling time in the 1-μsec range.

Hybrid modules are also common at the 12-bit level, and, while they tend to cost more than the monolithic ICs do, they are usually complete voltage output units that require no additional components. The Hybrid Systems DAC349 is an example that is packaged in a standard 24-pin ceramic DIP and looks like any other IC. For under $30, it includes a precision-regulated voltage reference and an output amplifier. Varying connection patterns among several of its pins select unipolar or bipolar output and 5- or 10-V output ranges. Perhaps the only disadvantage of this unit is the slow internal amplifier, which can take as long as 20 μsec to settle after a full-scale output change.

Even higher resolution is available at a proportionate increase in cost. Fourteen-bit linearity (16-bit resolution) costs about $50, true 16-bit linearity is around $200, and an unbelievable 18-bit (1 part in a quarter

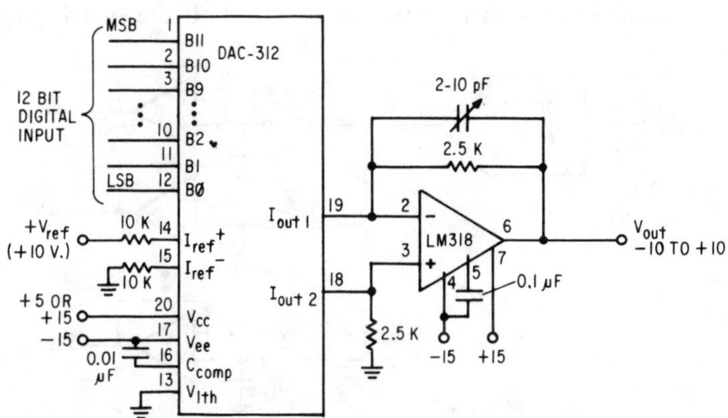

Fig. 7–22. Application of DAC-312 12-Bit DAC

million) unit goes for nearly $1,000. With this kind of precision, one no longer casually connects ordinary op-amps with solder on ordinary circuit boards. The various gain and offset errors of the amplifiers and thermocouple voltages in the wiring can easily wipe out the advantage of 16- and 18-bit accuracy. Fortunately, 12-bit accuracy is generally sufficient for producing control voltages in a computer-controlled analog synthesizer system.

Many DACs are now available with input registers to hold the binary value being converted. These are often promoted as being "microprocessor-compatible," since they can be connected right across the system's data bus and strobed when the DAC is addressed by the program. Unfortunately, their extra cost is often much more than equivalent external latches would be. Also, at the 12-bit level, it can be very difficult to keep noise from the data bus, which is flipping about wildly all the time, out of the analog circuitry connected to the same IC. Noise isolation is much easier with external latches.

Multiplexing DACs

Even though DACs have decreased dramatically in size and cost from earlier units, it is still far too expensive to use a 12-bit DAC every time a computer-generated control voltage is needed. Fortunately, it is possible to *multiplex* the output of a single fast converter and make it look like several identical but slower converters.

Figure 7–23 shows the fundamental concept of DAC multiplexing. Each multiplexed output consists of an analog switch, storage capacitor, and a voltage-follower op-amp. The idea is to store the output voltage for each channel in the capacitor rather than a separate register-DAC combination. For example, when output 1 must be updated the single DAC is given the corresponding digital input, a delay for DAC settling is taken, and S1 is closed momentarily to update the charge on C1. Following this, other channels could be updated with no effect on output 1. If the switch, capacitor,

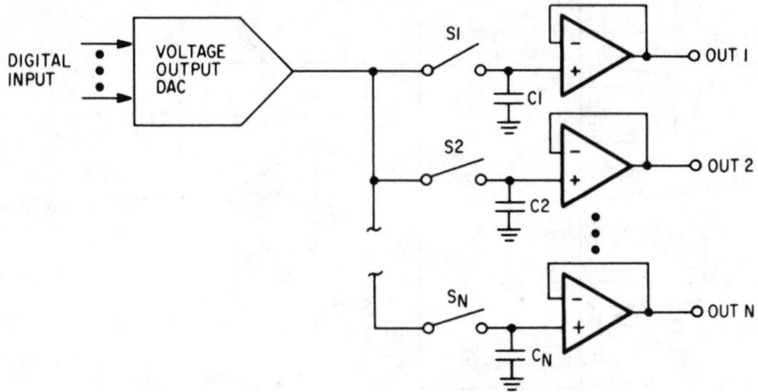

Fig. 7–23. DAC multiplexing

and voltage follower have no leakage, the new voltage level would persist indefinitely until a further update was required. Thus, one could visualize a multiple-channel DAC board for a microcomputer in which the program would supply a channel number and corresponding voltage level whenever an output voltage needs to be changed. The board would have only one DAC and numerous sample-and-hold (SAH) channels of the type just described, but it would look like a board with possibly dozens of individual 12-bit DACs.

Of course, in the real world several factors combine to give less than ideal performance. Since there are finite leakages, it is necessary to *refresh* the storage capacitors periodically to prevent output drift, not unlike refreshing a dynamic microcomputer memory. The main limitation of the number of channels that can be driven from one DAC is the ratio of channel-drift time to channel-update time. With constant-leakage currents, the holding capacitor should be large to minimize the drift rate. However, it should be small to minimize the update time. In a practical music application, update times beyond 50 μsec could limit the speed with which the channels could be manipulated. As a result, the requirement for adequate speed places an upper limit on the capacitor size and consequently refresh interval.

When developing a practical circuit for DAC multiplexing, several factors must be considered. The main DAC is an important contributor to overall performance and, of course, determines the resolution of the system. Since this one DAC will control a large number of channels, its cost will be divided N ways. A good-quality, stable unit carefully trimmed for minimum error should be used, since any errors here will affect all channels. High speed is definitely a benefit so a couple of extra bucks spent on a high-speed output amplifier for the DAC would be worthwhile.

Several analog switch characteristics are important in DAC output multiplexing applications. "On" resistance, for example, greatly affects the time necessary for updating but does not contribute to inaccuracy. This is because the capacitive load acts as an infinite load resistance after it has charged to the DAC voltage through the switch. Likewise, signal-dependent on resistance would not be expected to distort the signal. A very important parameter is the "feedthrough glitch" from the switch when it turns off. This glitch will cause an output error because it slightly alters the capacitor voltage at the moment of turnoff. This error may be made as small as desired by increasing the hold capacitor but then update time is increased. A good switch then would have low on resistance and low glitch energy, normally conflicting requirements.

Since a large number of analog switches will be used, the required drive circuitry becomes important. With individual FET switches, the digital-decoding and level-shifting circuits would probably dominate a board with more than a few channels. A 16-channel unit using individual JFETs, for example, would require a 1-of-16 TTL decoder and 16 driver circuits like the one in Fig. 7–14. Integrated switch-driver circuits would still require the decoder.

Analog Multiplexors

Integrated circuit *analog multiplexors,* however, are ideal for the application. An eight-channel multiplexor, for example, contains a 1-of-8 decoder, eight switch drivers, and eight analog switches. One side of each switch is connected to eight individual package pins and the other sides all connect to a ninth pin. Three *address* inputs select the desired switch and a fourth *chip-enable* input controls operation of the selected switch. Although these circuits were intended to select one of eight *inputs* and connect it to a single *output,* they work just as well in reverse for output multiplexing a DAC. Two eight-channel multiplexors are easily combined into a 16-channel equivalent as shown in Fig. 7–24. The scheme can be readily expanded to additional channels not unlike expanding a microcomputer memory.

The 4051 is a very inexpensive CMOS eight-channel analog multiplexor that can be had for less than $1.50. Its main limitation, as with all low-cost CMOS, is a restricted signal-voltage capability of 15 V peak to peak. One application that could use the 4051 directly is a multichannel 0 to +10 DAC for generating unipolar control voltages. Since the voltages being switched are between 0 V and +10 V, the 4051 could be powered from the +15-V system supply. Logic inputs to the 4051 must swing between V_{ss} (connected to ground along with V_{ee} in this case) and V_{dd} (+15), which is easily accomplished with high-voltage open-collector TTL drivers such as 7406, 7407, 7426, 7445, etc., and a pullup resistor to +15. The 4051 could also be used to switch ±5-V analog levels if it were connected to +5-V and −5-V power supplies. An internal level shifter allows the digital inputs to retain a positive only swing of 0 V to +5 V. The resulting ±5-V signal on the hold capacitor could be boosted to ±10-V standard levels in the buffer amplifier or used directly in a 5-V system.

A "B-series" 4051 (4051B) can be used in the bipolar configuration to switch ±8-V signals and thus directly handle the full voltage range of an 8-V system. In order to do this, well-regulated supply voltages of +8 V and −8 V (buffered system reference voltage is ideal) must be used to power the CMOS. Logic swings between ground and +8 V are required. Although often no more expensive, the 4051B is likely to be harder to purchase than the standard 4051.

BIFET analog multiplexors handling a ±10-V signal range without strain are also available. These are easier to use, require standard ±15-V power, utilize TTL logic levels but have a higher on resistance (350 ohms as compared to 100 ohms for the 4051), and are much more expensive. Another advantage of these circuits is their immunity to static discharge, since JFETs rather than MOSFETs are used internally.

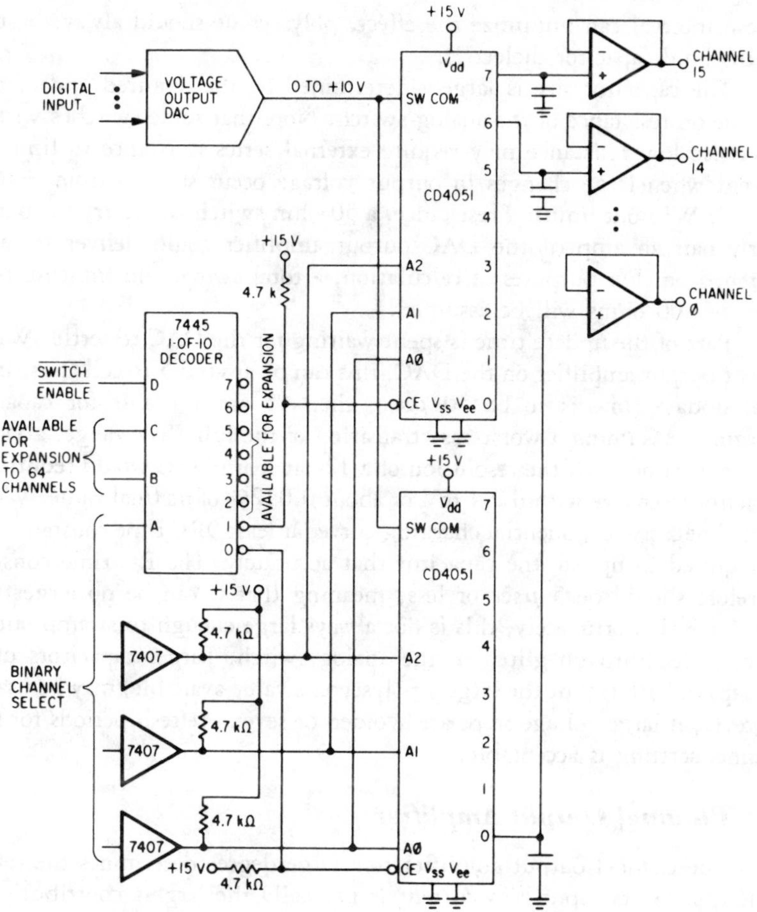

Fig. 7–24. 16-channel multiplexed DAC using CD4051

Hold Capacitors

The hold capacitor also influences performance greatly. Not only does its value determine the update speed and required refresh interval, its dielectric material determines the accuracy of the held voltage. All capacitors have a "memory" effect to some degree, which becomes apparent when the voltage on the capacitor is suddenly changed after having been constant for a long time. The result is that the new voltage level gradually creeps toward the old level with a time constant on the order of 20 msec. The final amount of creep may range from over 1% for ceramic disk capacitors to less than 0.01% for polystyrene or polypropylene capacitors. Although a decreased refresh interval can minimize the effect, polystyrene should always be used for the hold capacitor dielectric.

The capacitor size is largely determined by the required update time and the on resistance of the analog switch. Note that some switches with an otherwise low resistance may require external series resistance to limit the current when large changes in output voltage occur such as from −10 to +10 V. Without limiting resistance, a 50-ohm switch would try to conduct nearly half an amp (if the DAC output amplifier could deliver it) when switched on. For purposes of calculation, a total switch and limiting resistance of 400 ohms will be assumed.

Part of the update time is spent waiting for the DAC to settle. With a decent output amplifier on the DAC, this can be around 5 μsec. Thus, if the total update time is to be 50 μsec, then 45 are available for capacitor charging. Assuming a worst-case transition of the full 20-V range, a worst-case error of one-half the resolution of a 12-bit main DAC would require the capacitor to charge within 2.4 mV or about 0.012% of its final value. With a normal negative exponential charging curve, at least 9RC time constants will be required to update the capacitor that accurately. The RC time constant therefore should be 5 μsec or less, meaning that C can be no larger than 0.016 μF. Unfortunately, this is not always large enough to swamp out the effect of feedthrough glitch in the analog switch. Larger capacitors up to perhaps 0.1 μF (about the largest polystyrene value available) may be usable, however, if large voltage steps are avoided or several refresh periods for final channel settling is acceptable.

Channel Output Amplifier

The channel output amplifier to a large degree determines the refresh period, since its input bias current is normally the largest contribution to leakage from the storage capacitor. This problem may be easily circumvented by using one of the newer FET input op-amps that have vanishingly small bias currents. However, these tend to have larger offset voltages than bipolar input stage devices and cost more. So, as an exercise, let us determine just how bad the situation would be with a standard bipolar op-amp.

The LM324A is a popular quad op-amp with an unusually low bias current of 45 nA and a typical offset voltage of 2 mV, a little less than one-half the step size of a 12-bit, ±10-V DAC. With a hold capacitor of 0.016 μF calculated previously, the drift rate due to bias current will be 2.8 V/sec. Thus, if drift is to be held to less than one-half the DAC step size (2.5 mV) between refreshes, the refresh interval should be less than 880 μsec. A refresh operation could be expected to take considerably less time than a full update operation, since the capacitor voltage change is normally very small. A 20-μsec refresh time, for example, would allow 5 μsec for DAC settling and a liberal three time constants for capacitor recharge. With these numbers, it should be possible to keep 880 μsec/20 μsec=44 channels refreshed, and it would be realistic to support as many as 64 with a 2-time constant recharge period. Larger capacitors (to minimize switch glitch error) yield a slightly increased channel capacity because, although the longer drift time is cancelled by longer recharge time, the DAC settling time becomes less of a factor. Thus, it would be worth considering the LM324 as the channel output amplifier in a system with 64 or fewer channels.

Refresh Logic

As with dynamic memory in a microcomputer system, refreshing the multiplexed DAC presents some problems that partially offset the lower cost. One method of handling the refresh requirement would use the microcomputer system's interval timer to interrupt the program periodically. The interrupt service routine would then update all of the DAC channels from a table in memory and return. Whenever the main program actually wanted to change a DAC channel output, it would directly update both the output and the corresponding table location.

Although easily implemented, this scheme has two serious difficulties. One is the time stolen from the main program for the refresh operation. With 64 channels and bipolar channel amplifiers, all available time would be used to refresh the DAC. Even with FET amplifiers, a substantial amount of time may be stolen. Also, if the microcomputer is stopped or a nonmusic-playing program is executed, such as the system monitor, the DAC refreshing stops and the channel output voltages drift away to undefined levels. If the synthesizer were not shut down, the drifting voltages could produce a really raucous racket! Thus, it is advantageous to perform the refresh automatically with some scanning logic—or a logic replacement microprocessor dedicated to the refreshing operation.

An Intelligent DAC?

A 6502 and three additional support chips would make a superb multiplexed DAC controller. Figure 7–25 outlines such a unit that could support up to 128 channels. The 6532 interface chips simultaneously provide two 8-bit I/O ports, 128 bytes of read/write memory, and one interval timer each. These provide all of the interfacing needed between the control processor and the using system, DAC, and analog multiplexor. The 2716 PROM provides nonvolatile program storage for up to 2048 bytes, ample for a very sophisticated refresh routine indeed. These four ICs could be expected to cost less than $50 total, which is less than 40 cents per channel.

Using a microprocessor for refresh control offers a lot more advantages than a low package count, however. The using system, for example, can communicate the 12 bits of data and 7-bit channel address on a byte basis

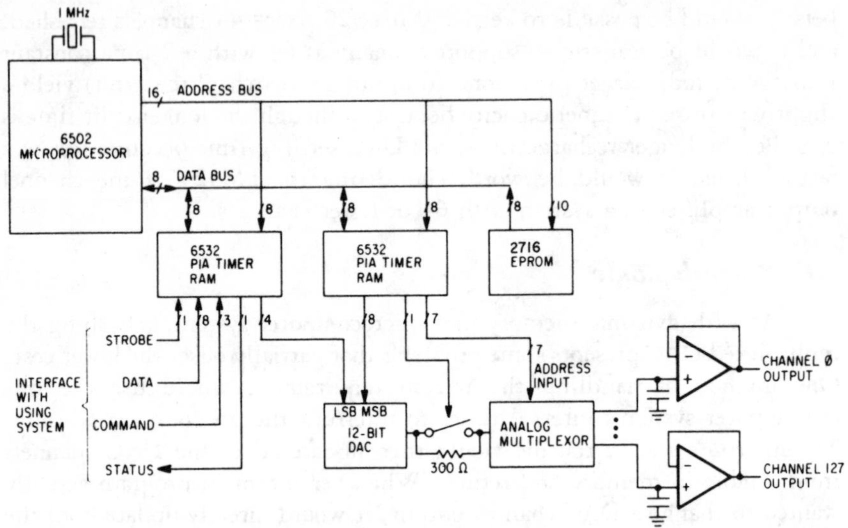

Fig. 7–25. An intelligent 128-channel multiplexed DAC

with full request/acknowledge handshaking. After the data is transferred, it can go on about its business, while the DAC micro goes through the gyrations of updating the channel. With proper programming of the DAC micro, burst rate updating much faster than is directly possible could be accommodated by storing the data away for later action. The micro could be cognizant of the magnitude of voltage change on the storage capacitors and decrease the "wait for settle" delays when the change was small. Average throughput could be further increased by shorting out the 300-ohm protective resistor except when a large voltage step occurred. With the timers available on the 6532 chips, some higher-level commands such as "linearly ramp channel 43 from −2.5 V to +1.6 V over the next 700 msec" could be implemented right in the DAC, relieving the host system of that sort of task.

Analog-to-Digital Converters

In a computer-controlled analog synthesis system, ADCs are used mostly for the input of manual data. Control knobs, slide pots, joysticks, and existing synthesizer keyboards are all sources of voltage that need to be converted into numbers for use by the system. In some cases, the output of analysis devices such as envelope followers, pitch trackers, filter banks, or even a raw audio signal must also be converted into digital form at medium (100 samples/sec) to high (10K to 50K samples/sec) speeds.

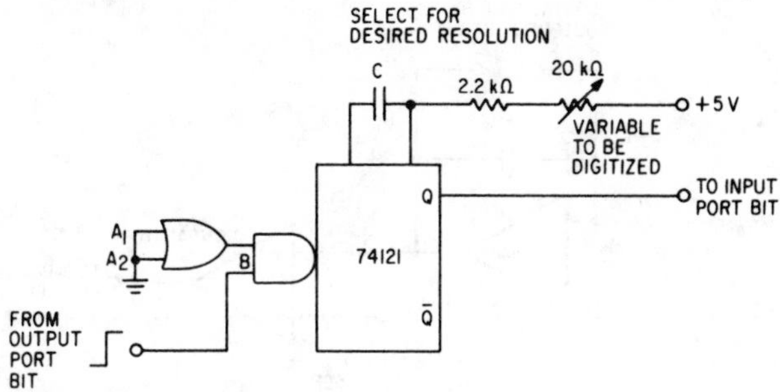

Fig. 7–26. Single-shot method of analog-to-digital conversion

Single-Shot Method

The simplest ADC method, which is often used in microprocessor-based games, utilizes a *single-shot* or monostable multivibrator. Effectively, the quantity to be digitized, which must usually be a resistance but can be a dc voltage, is made to vary the pulse duration of a single-shot circuit. The variable to be digitized is now time, which can be easily measured by a counting loop in the microprocessor or an external hardware counter.

Figure 7–26 shows how a variable resistance such as a rotary or slide pot can be digitized directly by the microcomputer. To perform a measurement, the digitizing routine would first pulse an output bit connected to the trigger input of the single-shot IC. Following application of the trigger, the microcomputer would enter a routine that looks at the state of the single-shot via an input-port bit and counts a register up from zero every loop that it remains on. When the single-shot times out, an exit is taken from the loop and the content of the register is the converted value.

The shortest loop possible in 6502 machine code is 8 μsec and is in the same range for most other 8-bit micros. An 8-MHz 68000 can do such a test loop in 2.25 μsec. For 8-bit equivalent resolution (1 part in 256) using a 6502, the single-shot time would have to be 256 times 8 μsec or 2.05 msec for maximum resistance. In a 68000-based system, this time is reduced to 0.58 msec. Unfortunately, the time cannot go to zero for minimum resistance so before the converted value is used, the time corresponding to minimum resistance (one-tenth the maximum time in the example) will have to be subtracted out. This method is capable of higher resolutions by further extending the maximum single-shot period; however, 8 bits is usually quite sufficient for digitizing single-turn or short travel slide potentiometers.

This technique is also readily extended to measuring voltages with the circuit in Fig. 7–27. Normally, the analog switch is closed and the integrator output voltage is therefore zero. To make a measurement, the

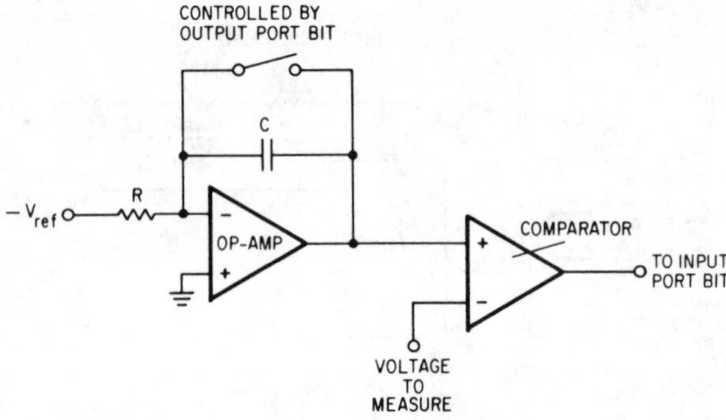

Fig. 7–27. Single-slope integration method

microcomputer opens the switch and monitors the output of the comparator as before. The integrator output now starts going positive at a constant rate determined by the reference voltage magnitude. When it finally becomes more positive than the unknown voltage, the comparator switches low and the accumulated count is the converted value. As before, the resolution attainable is dependent on the speed of the microcomputer and the time available for conversion.

Dual-Slope Method

One problem with both of the preceding circuits is that accuracy and stability depend on the quality of a capacitor. The circuit in Fig. 7–28 overcomes this difficulty by *comparing* the input voltage with a reference voltage, using the capacitor only as a comparison medium. A measurement cycle consists of two phases. Normally S2 is on, forcing the integrator output to zero. During phase 1, S1 selects the unknown voltage for the integrator input, and S2 is opened to allow the integrator to charge negative at a rate dependent on the unknown voltage. The amount of time spent in phase 1 is constant and carefully controlled by a counting loop similar to that used for measurement. At the beginning of phase 2, S1 is flipped so that the negative

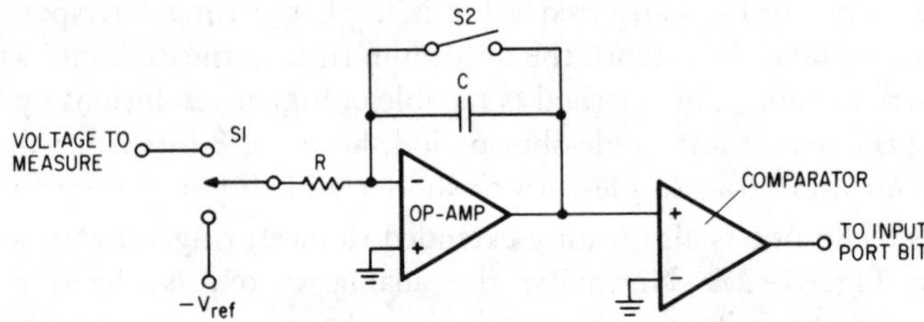

Fig. 7–28. Dual-slope integration method

reference voltage is connected to the integrator. Being of opposite polarity, the integrator starts to recharge toward zero again. The time necessary to reach and cross zero is monitored by the microcomputer as before. If a similar loop is used in each phase, the converted value will be in fractional terms of the reference voltage and the value of the capacitor is no longer critical.

Accuracy in excess of 12 bits is readily obtained with this *dual-slope* circuit, although long conversion times would still be necessary with the microcomputer doing the timing and control. Every additional bit of resolution would double the time required for conversion. Dual slope takes about twice as long as the single-slope or single-shot method because both the reference and the unknown are, in effect, digitized. A hardware counter could be used instead to increase the speed, but these techniques still remain relatively slow.

Integrated circuit dual-slope ADCs are available with resolutions as high as 20,000 steps. Unfortunately, most of these are intended for digital panel meters and therefore have decimal outputs. The MM5863 from National Semiconductor, however, provides 12-bit binary output and conversion times as short as 20 msec when used with an LF11300 "analog front end" circuit. This is adequately fast for digitizing most slowly changing voltages.

Linear Search and Tracking ADC

The better techniques for analog-to-digital conversion work by comparing the unknown analog voltage with the output of a DAC using the basic configuration in Fig. 7–29. In practice, the DAC output is systematically varied until it matches the unknown as closely as possible as determined by the comparator. When this is accomplished, the input to the DAC is the digital equivalent of the unknown voltage. The key to high speed is an efficient search algorithm and a fast DAC and comparator.

The simplest search method is the linear search. The DAC is set to zero (or negative full scale if it is bipolar) and then incremented one step at a time

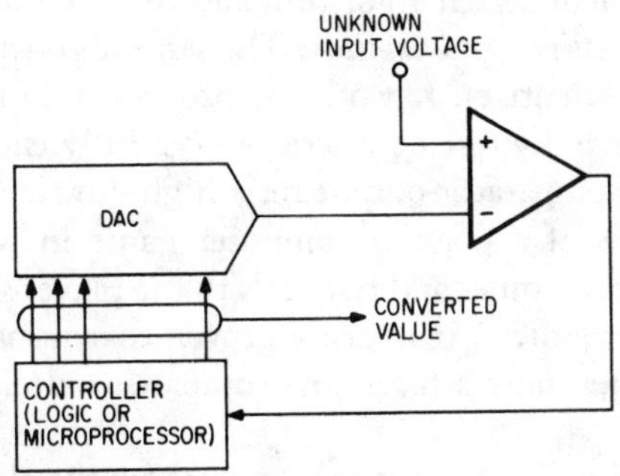

Fig. 7–29. Analog-to-digital conversion using a DAC

until the comparator switches from high to low, indicating that the unknown input voltage has just been crossed. Of course, this is not likely to be any faster than the voltage-to-time methods described earlier. However, if the unknown voltage has not changed much since the last reading, the search could be started at the last value rather than zero.

A refinement of the linear search is the *tracking* ADC. In operation, the comparator output is constantly monitored. If the comparator output is high, the DAC output is increased one step. If it is low, the DAC is backed off one step. The result is that the DAC always contains the digital equivalent of the input voltage within one step, provided the unknown voltage changes slowly. The inherent one-step oscillation around the correct value may be suppressed by use of a *window* comparator, which has an "equals" output as well as a greater-than and less-than output. If the equals window is set to be a little over one step wide, the oscillation is stopped. A window comparator is simply two ordinary comparators with different reference voltages—the difference being the window width.

The control circuit for a tracking ADC is exceptionally simple, just a high-frequency oscillator and an up–down counter. The comparator output is connected to the direction control input of the counter and the clock makes the counter count in the indicated direction. The clock period must be longer than the settling time of the DAC. Usually in a microcomputer system, the clock can be a microprocessor clock phase chosen such that the counter never changes when it might be read by the microprocessor. As long as the rate of input voltage change does not exceed the counting speed, the tracking ADC has a "zero" conversion time. The slew rate limitation can be very real, however. For example, a 12-bit tracking ADC with 1-MHz clock would require over 4 msec to slew from one end of the range to the other. If used for direct digitizing of audio, such a converter could not handle full-scale sine waves higher than 77 Hz without serious errors.

Successive Approximation Search

The most efficient search algorithm and the one used by all high-speed ADCs is termed *successive approximation*. The same algorithm is called a *binary search* by computer scientists. It works by progressively narrowing in on the unknown voltage level by testing a series of carefully chosen "trial" voltages and looking at the comparator output for a high–low indication. (This same problem is the basis of a popular computer game in which the computer "thinks" of a random number and responds to the player's guesses with a "too high" or "too low" verdict.) It is easily proven that no more efficient search algorithm exists when only a high–low comparison decision is available for each trial.

Referring to Fig. 7–30, it is easy to see how the algorithm works. The example is one of homing in on an unknown voltage of +3.253 V using a

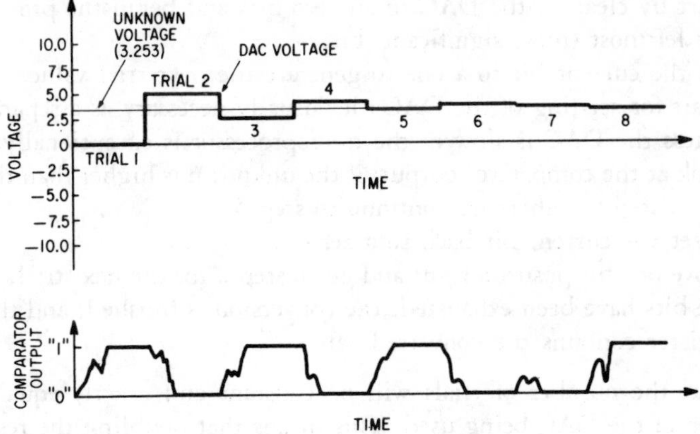

Fig. 7–30. Successive approximation search method

DAC with a range of − 10 V to + 10 V in the ADC system. The first trial is used to determine the polarity of the unknown voltage. The DAC is set to 0 V output and the comparator is read after sufficient delay for settling. In this case, the comparator output would be high, indicating that the unknown is higher than the trial, which is indeed the case. The next trial value should be +5 V. This time the comparator output would be low, indicating that the trial was too high.

At this point it is known that the unknown is somewhere between 0 V and +5 V. The rule is that the next trial value should always be set midway in the range that the unknown is known to occupy. The result of the trial will be a new range, half the size of the previous one, that is also known to surround the unknown. Proceeding, the next trial would be midway between 0 and +5, namely +2.5. The sequence would continue: low, try 3.75; high, try 3.125; low, try 3.437; high, try 3.281; high, etc. Note that after only seven trials the unknown has been pinned down to within 30 mV, better than 0.15% of full-scale accuracy. Eventually the voltage range surrounding the unknown becomes as small as the step size of the DAC used to generate the trial voltages, and the conversion is declared to be complete. The last trial value is the converted result.

Now if the reader is observant he may have noted that the trial values are nice round numbers—in the binary sense. Assuming the use of an 8-bit offset binary DAC, the sequence of trials expressed in binary would be: 10000000 (0), 11000000 (5), 10100000 (2.5), 10110000 (3.75), 10101000 (3.125), 10101100 (3.437), 10101010 (3.281), etc.

It turns out that computation of the next trial value is really no computation at all. It is simply a bit manipulation that any microprocessor is quite adept at. If the binary input to the DAC is treated as a register, the manipulation is as follows:

1. Start by clearing the DAC to all zero bits and begin the procedure at the leftmost (most significant) bit.
2. Set the current bit to a one to generate the next trial value.
3. Wait for settling of the DAC (not usually necessary as a separate step unless the DAC is slow or the microprocessor is exceptionally fast).
4. Look at the comparator output: if the unknown is higher than the trial, go to step 6, otherwise continue to step 5.
5. Reset the current bit back to a zero.
6. Move one bit position right and go to step 2 for the next trial. If all of the bits have been exhausted, the conversion is finished, and the DAC register contains the converted value.

Note that the number of trials will be constant and exactly equal to the resolution of the DAC being used. This means that doubling the resolution by adding a bit will only lengthen the conversion time slightly, unlike previous methods in which conversion time would also be doubled.

```
                  ;        "DAC" IS DAC OUTPUT PORT ADDRESS
                  ;        MOST SIGNIFICANT BIT OF "CMP" IS COMPARATOR, 1 IF INPUT IS
                  ;        GREATER THAN DAC OUTPUT, 0 OTHERWISE
                  ;        RETURNS WITH CONVERTED VALUE IN A, TWO'S COMPLEMENT NOTATION
                  ;        USES INDEX REGISTER X AND ONE TEMPORARY MEMORY LOCATION
                  ;        25 BYTES, AVERAGE OF 199 MICROSECONDS  EXECUTION TIME

0000 A980         ADC:     LDA   #X'80      ; INITIALIZE TRIAL BIT REGISTER
0002 8580                  STA   TRLBIT     ; LOCATION TRLBIT ASSUMED TO BE IN PAGE 0
0004 A900                  LDA   #0         ; INITIALIZE TRIAL VALUE
0006 0580         ADC1:    ORA   TRLBIT     ; SET TRIAL BIT IN A
0008 8D0017                STA   DAC        ; SEND TRIAL VALUE TO DAC
000B AE0217                LDX   CMP        ; TEST COMPARATOR OUTPUT
000E 3002                  BMI   ADC2       ; LEAVE TRIAL BIT ON IF INPUT .GT. DAC
0010 4580                  EOR   TRLBIT     ; TURN TRIAL BIT OFF IUF INPUT .LT. DAC
0012 4680         ADC2:    LSR   TRLBIT     ; SHIFT TRIAL BIT RIGHT ONE POSITION
0014 90F0                  BCC   ADC1       ; LOOP IF BIT NOT SHIFTED OUT OF TRLBIT
0016 4980                  EOR   #X'80      ; FLIP SIGN BIT TO GET TWO'S COMPLEMENT
0018 60                    RTS              ; RETURN
```

Fig. 7–31. Successive approximation analog-to-digital conversion routine for the 6502

Successive Approximation Logic

Just to show how efficient this algorithm is and how practical it is to execute in software on a microprocessor, it has been coded into assembly language for the 6502 microprocessor in Fig. 7–31. In this subroutine, the DAC is considered to be an 8-bit offset-binary-coded unit at the symbolic address DAC, and the comparator is assumed to be connected to the most significant bit (sign bit) of the input port addressed symbolically by CMP. A one from the comparator indicates that the unknown is *higher* than the trial. The output from the subroutine is an 8-bit signed twos-complement number; however, removing one instruction will preserve the natural binary coding when a unipolar ADC is being implemented.

First, the program is exceptionally short: only 25 bytes long. It is also very fast (199 μsec for a 1-MHz clock rate) compared to the figures that were discussed earlier. With this kind of inherent speed, the microcomputer system could easily digitize several manual controls 100 times/sec with little impact on the time available for other tasks.

Resolutions beyond 8 bits are readily handled by 8-bit microprocessors, but the program size and conversion time increase substantially because of the double precision operations now required. A 12-bit subroutine coded for the 68000 (Fig. 7–32) reveals the power and speed of this processor. The routine is 46 bytes long (assuming that the DAC and CMP registers can be reached with a 16-bit address) and requires only 107 μsec at 8 MHz. Note that the sequence of operations has been rearranged somewhat to maximize the amount of time allowed for the DAC and comparator to settle. If this were not done, the comparator would be tested just 1 μsec after the trial value was written into the DAC register. Also, the DAC register can be write-only, an advantage when the hardware is built.

A hardware successive approximation controller is also easy to build and, in fact, now can be purchased as a single IC good for up to 12 bits. With a hardware controller, the final limit on conversion speed is the settling time of the DAC and the delay of the comparator. Since even a mediocre 75-cent comparator responds in 200 nsec (LM311 type), the challenge is

```
000000           *      "DAC" IS DAC OUTPUT PORT ADDRESS, 12 BITS LEFT JUSTIFIED
000000           *      "DAC" MAY BE A WRITE-ONLY REGISTER.
000000           *      BIT 7 OF "CMP" (8-BIT REGISTER) IS COMPARATOR OUTPUT, 1 IF
000000           *      INPUT IS GREATER THAN DAC OUTPUT, 0 OTHERWISE.
000000           *      RETURNS WITH CONVERTED 12 BIT VALUE LEFT JUSTIFIED IN D0.W,
000000           *      TWOS COMPLEMENT.  USES ONLY D0 (SAVES OTHERS).
000000           *      46 BYTES, AVERAGE OF 107uS EXECUTION TIME @ 8MHZ.
000000
000000 48E740C0 ADC     MOVEM.L D1/A0/A1,-(SP)     SAVE WORK REGISTERS USED
000004 307CFF00         MOVE.W  #DAC,A0            KEEP ADDRESS OF DAC IN A0 AND ADDRESS
000008 327CFF02         MOVE.W  #CMP,A1            OF CMP IN A1 FOR FAST ACCESS
00000C 4240             CLR.W   D0                 CLEAR THE TRIAL VALUE REGISTER
00000E 720F             MOVEQ   #15,D1             SET INITIAL TRIAL BIT NUMBER
000010 6008             BRA.S   ADC3               JUMP INTO SUCCESSIVE APPROXIMATION LOOP
000012 4A11     ADC1    TST.B   (A1)               LOOK AT THE COMPARATOR OUTPUT
000014 6B02             BMI.S   ADC2               SKIP IF INPUT IS GREATER THAN DAC OUTPUT
000016 0380             BCLR    D1,D0              CLEAR THE CURRENT TRIAL BIT NUMBER IF LESS
000018 5341     ADC2    SUBQ.W  #1,D1              DECREMENT THE TRIAL BIT NUMBER
00001A 03C0     ADC3    BSET    D1,D0              SET THE CURRENT TRIAL BIT
00001C 3080             MOVE.W  D0,(A0)            SEND CURRENT TRIAL VALUE TO DAC
00001E 0C410003         CMP.W   #3,D1              TEST IF 12 BITS DONE
000022 6CEE             BGE.S   ADC1               LOOP UNTIL BIT NUMBER BECOMES 3
000024 0A408008         EOR.W   #$8008,D0          CONVERT RESULT TO TWOS COMPLEMENT & KILL
000028                                             * LAST SPURIOUS TRIAL BIT
000028 4CDF0302         MOVEM.L (SP)+,D1/A0/A1     RESTORE REGISTERS USED
00002C 4E75             RTS                        AND RETURN
```

Fig. 7–32. Successive approximation analog-to-digital conversion routine for the 68000

presented by the DAC. Because the speed of most DACs is determined by the output amplifier, it would be nice if it could be eliminated. This, in fact, can be done easily if the connection to the comparator is slightly altered. Rather than using a *voltage* comparator with a voltage output DAC and an unknown input voltage, what is desired is a *current* comparator that can be connected directly to a current-output DAC. The unknown voltage can be converted to a current by use of an accurate series resistor.

True current comparators with sufficient accuracy are not generally available but the configuration shown in Fig. 7–33 is virtually as good and uses the same LM311-type voltage comparator. A mismatch between the DAC current output and the unknown current will tend to pull the 311 inverting input away from ground, thus switching the comparator according to the direction of the mismatch. The two diodes across the comparator inputs limit the voltage swing for large mismatches, thereby maintaining high speed (small voltage swing minimizes effect of stray capacitances) and keeping the current output DAC happy.

Figure 7–34 shows a complete 12-bit ADC circuit that is easy and inexpensive to build and is very fast. A DAC-312 current output DAC is combined with a DM2504 successive approximation register (made by National Semiconductor and others) and the comparator circuit just described to yield a conversion time of only 6 μsec. The 2-MHz clock sequences the successive approximation at the rate of one trial per clock cycle. A conversion is started by a negative-going pulse at the START input and completion is signaled by EOC going low. The analog input impedance is 5K but varies somewhat during the conversion and should be driven by a high-speed op-amp output. If a 12 μsec conversion time is acceptable, a 74C905 CMOS successive approximation register can be used in place of the DM2504 and the clock slowed to 1 MHz.

Complete Hybrid module ADC circuits using the successive approximation technique have been available for many years, but their cost has always been much higher than an equivalent circuit constructed from a DAC, a comparator, and a successive approximation register. Until recently, all monolithic IC ADCs were of the much slower dual-slope type. Even now, 8 bits is the highest resolution offered in an integrated circuit ADC.

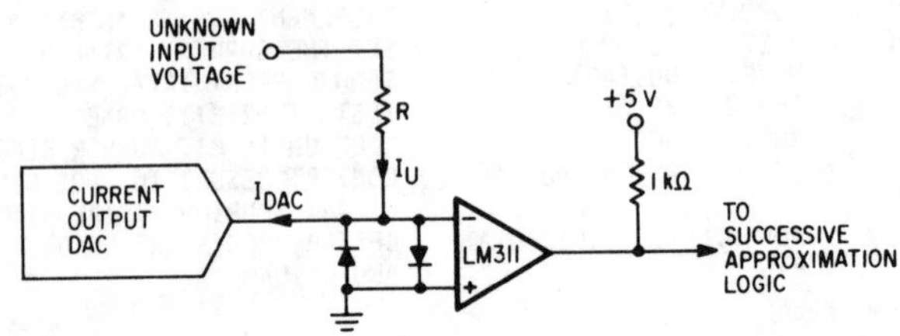

Fig. 7–33. Analog circuitry for a high-speed ADC

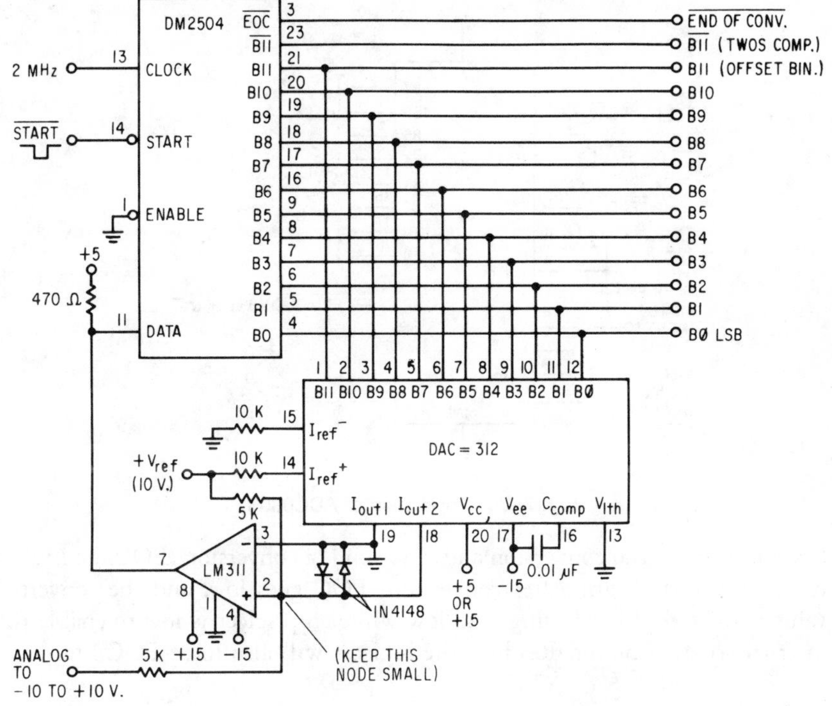

Fig. 7–34. 6-μsec 12-bit ADC using DAC-312

One very reasonably priced (under \$5 for ½ LSB linearity) unit is the ADC0801 series from National Semiconductor. It uses a resistor string DAC internally along with CMOS circuitry and is capable of conversion times in the 60–100-μsec range. It operates entirely from a +5 V power supply and accepts analog input voltages from 0 to +5 V as well. The 8-bit output value goes through an internal tri-state buffer and thus can be connected directly to the microprocessor data bus in a small dedicated system. Figure 7–35 shows a typical hookup for the ADC0803, which is the ½ LSB grade unit. Although the analog input is a very high impedance when the unit is idle, it becomes finite and variable during conversion and therefore should be driven from an op-amp output. Internally, a 2-to-1 voltage divider provides a +2.5-V reference from the +5-V power input, but an external reference can be connected to the V_{ref} pin if desired. The analog input range is twice the reference voltage but must not be larger than the supply voltage or negative.

The sequencing clock is generated by a built-in RC oscillator and a conversion requires from 66 to 73 clock cycles to complete. The components shown will produce approximately 1 MHz or an external clock can be connected to pin 4. A negative pulse on the start input while chip select is

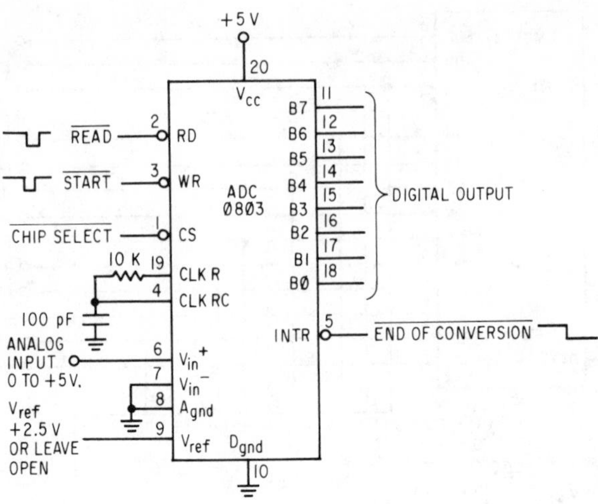

Fig. 7–35. Application of ADC0803

low will initiate the conversion and make end of conversion (EOC) go high if it is not already high. After conversion, EOC goes low, and the converted value may be read by driving read low while chip select is low to enable the internal tri-state buffer. Reading the register will also force EOC high.

Sample and Hold

There is one practical difficulty, however, with the successive approximation algorithm; it assumes that the unknown voltage input does not change during the course of the conversion. If it does change, significant conversion errors can occur, although their magnitude will not exceed the total amount of change over the conversion interval. Even though successive approximation ADCs are quite fast, signals one might think are slow moving can still change enough in a few microseconds to create an error of several resolution steps in a high-resolution converter. A 20-Hz full-scale sine wave "moves" at rates above one step (12-bit ADC) every 4 μsec. If the conversion time was a speedy 16 μsec, random errors as large as four steps would result, giving an effective resolution of only 10 bits. Such a "raw" ADC would be worthless for converting audio signals.

The same sample-and-hold setup that was used to multiplex a DAC can also be used to sample a fast-moving signal and then hold its instantaneous value at a predictable point in time for accurate conversion. The performance requirements of the sample and hold can be substantially greater than for DAC multiplexing, however. When in the sample mode (switch closed), the on resistance and holding capacitor size must be small enough so that a large difference between input voltage and capacitor voltage does not develop due to the rapidly changing input. Ideally, this difference amounts to a slight low-pass filtering of the signal, but if the multiplexor on resistance is nonlinear, it can also introduce distortion. Of course, low on resistance and small hold capacitors contribute to larger switching transient errors. With a good sample and hold, full-range audio signals can be converted with ADCs as slow as 25 μsec. This topic will be discussed more fully in Chapter 12.

Multiplexing ADCs

Like DACs, ADCs are generally too expensive to use for each signal to be digitized. Again, however, *multiplexing* can be used to make one fast ADC look like several slower ones. Even the speed tradeoff is not really necessary with techniques such as the single-slope integrator in Fig. 7–27. To add more channels, one simply adds more comparators (type 339 quad comparators work well) with the plus inputs all connected to the single integrator and the minus inputs connecting to individual unknown voltages. The comparator outputs go to individual input-port bits of the microcomputer. The microprocessor counting loop can be modified to actually perform eight analog-to-digital conversions simultaneously! Although the simultaneous conversion loop will be slower than a single-channel loop, it will not be eight times slower, which results in *increased* per channel conversion speed as well as hardware savings. A similar parallel conversion approach could also be used with the linear-search ADC method in which a DAC replaces the integrator.

Although simultaneous conversion is not possible with the successive approximation search method, multiplexing by adding comparators is a very simple and effective method. A digital multiplexor such as a 74150 16-channel unit can accept a binary channel number and effectively connect the addressed comparator to the successive approximation logic or input-port bit. Thus, duplication of the expensive trial DAC is avoided. Note that this is restricted to slowly moving signals unless a sample-and-hold circuit is added to each channel.

Analog multiplexing several inputs into one sample-and-hold/ADC combination is probably the most used ADC multiplexing technique. The same analog multiplexors that were suitable for DACs are equally good for ADCs; the roles of input and output are simply interchanged. Two members of the ADC0801 series described earlier have built-in analog multiplexors. The ADC0808, for example, has an 8-input multiplexor, whereas the ADC0816 has a 16-input multiplexor. These are still quite reasonably priced, with the ADC016 being in the $10 range. A dedicated microprocessor makes an excellent ADC multiplex controller as well. For continuous sampling of several changing signals, the dedicated micro allows each channel to have its own sample rate matched to the signal to be digitized. Even compensation for known errors in the signal source could be handled on a per-channel basis by the micro.

8

Signal Routing

In the previous two chapters, the sound-synthesizing elements that are part of a computer-controlled analog synthesizer were studied in detail. First, voltage-controlled circuits such as oscillators, amplifiers, and filters that do the actual sound waveform generation and modification were discussed. This was followed in Chapter 7 by a discussion of interface elements such as DACs and analog switches that allow the computer to control the analog synthesis circuits. The final step in the synthesis portion of the system is interconnection of these synthesis and interface elements into a useful system. Of course, there are almost as many ways to do this as there are system designers, but an attempt will be made to group these into three different organizational philosophies, all of which have been hinted at in previous discussion.

The first organization, which we shall call "Type 1," is really no organization at all. The analog elements are simply mounted in rows on a front panel, each independent of the others except for power. The computer interface elements are likewise grouped together and are also logically independent. Interconnection is done *manually* by means of patch cords or pinboards, just as on a conventional synthesizer. In fact, most systems of this type incorporate a standard analog synthesizer or a collection of standard synthesizer modules. Interface elements may be standard multichannel DACs with nothing more added than a jack panel to accept standard patch cords. In such a system, the computer automates such tasks as sequencing, generation of arbitrary envelope shapes, smooth manipulation of several parameters simultaneously, and controlling polyphony. Note that these are the most difficult tasks to perform on a classic manual synthesizer system. Since off-the-shelf components can be utilized and the overall organization does not differ greatly from conventional systems, this approach would be expected to be the most popular, at least for the near future.

The Type 2 organization is like Type 1 except that the computer is in complete control of the interconnections among elements as well. In its most elementary form, it is a Type 1 system with a computer-controlled switching matrix added to replace the manual patch cords. A completely general switching matrix very quickly becomes prohibitive in size, but fortunately there are ways to reduce it without undue sacrifice in flexibility. If the analog modules are precalibrated, the synthesizer may be packaged as a black box with perhaps four signal outputs representing final quadraphonic sound. Essentially, such a system is a low-cost analog approach to the capabilities of totally digital synthesizers, which will be described in Section III. The advantage of this organization, of course, is that every aspect of sound production can be specified, edited, stored, and retrieved automatically by the computer. A side benefit is more efficient module use because the interconnection patterns can be dynamically changed.

The Type 3 approach is a "voice-oriented" or "instrument-oriented" organization. The fundamental idea here is that extreme interconnection flexibility is not required because most synthesis work utilizes a small number of standard patches for most sounds. Thus, these standard configurations can be prepatched as part of the design of an *instrument module*. Several different kinds of instrument modules would be used in a typical setup, each corresponding, more or less, to a traditional orchestral instrument. All inputs to the modules would be digital from the control computer's I/O bus, while the module's output is mixed onto an analog "channel bus" corresponding to a channel in the final sound. Such a setup is extremely modular because of the parallel buses. To add a voice module, one simply plugs it in. When all sockets are filled, additional ones are simply connected in parallel with the same buses. Another advantage is that this organization is conceptually simple, since interconnection is not a variable to be considered. The user composes for and controls the system much like a typical orchestra but with a wider range of timbres to choose from and freedom from human player limitations.

Of course, any real system is unlikely to be a pure case of any of these three organizations. A fundamentally Type 1 system, for example, is quite likely to have some kind of rudimentary interconnection control. One technique is the use of additional VCAs in some signal paths to enable and disable control signals at various times. In addition, Type 3 concepts may be used to reduce the number of computer control channels needed. A pure Type 2 system can become too large to be practical unless some Type 1 and Type 3 concepts are incorporated as well. A Type 3 system might have a small portion devoted to uncommitted elementary modules for special effects use, or the voice modules may have several selectable interconnection patterns available. Thus, an actual system is likely to incorporate some aspects of all three organizational types. Nevertheless, it is seldom difficult to classify a computer-controlled analog system into one of these three categories.

The remainder of this chapter will be devoted to a more detailed look at some of the techniques that can be used in each organizational philosophy. An understanding of this material should enable the reader to evaluate the various approaches and develop his own personal bias.

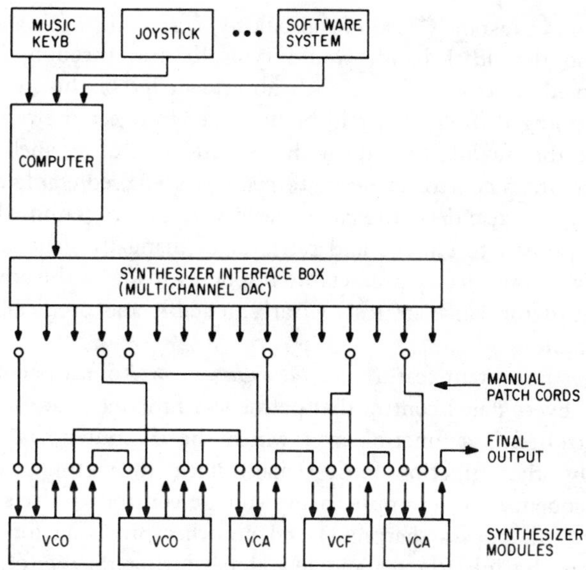

Fig. 8–1. Type 1 manually patched system

Manually Patched Computer-Controlled System

As mentioned previously, the manually patched system is really nothing more than a box of DACs added to an otherwise conventional synthesizer as shown in Fig. 8–1. Since use of standard off-the-shelf components (including the computer system) is one of the attractions of this organization, most comments will be made with this in mind. This, of course, should not discourage home construction of the needed modules (which can easily cost one-quarter as much as purchased modules), but most hobbyists would probably be interested in one of the more sophisticated organizations.

The synthesizer is obviously an important part of the system. In many cases, one must make do with an existing available synthesizer. If a synthesizer or a collection of modules is being purchased for the system, however, attention to a few key characteristics will insure success with a minimum of effort.

Synthesizer Requirements

Overall quality of the modules should be moderate to high. One should not accept poorer performance from a synthesizer that is to be computer controlled than would be acceptable for manual control. In fact, the computer is usually much *less* able to correct for deficiencies in the analog modules than a human player is. For example, a person using a ribbon controller or other proportional control device hears the sounds as they are produced and can instantly (and unconsciously) correct for tuning errors. The computer, on the other hand, would typically run through a stored or preprogrammed control sequence with no knowledge of the sound coming out. If the tuning drifted, it would be necessary to reject the recording and either retune the module (usually with a slight twist of a panel control) or edit the computer's control sequence to compensate. Predictable response to control voltages is also desirable particularly with preprogrammed computer control (as opposed to storage and retrieval of manually generated control functions). Without clearly predictable response, many of the advantages of programmed performance are lost. Clearly, a stable and predictable synthesizer is desirable.

Another important feature is *total voltage control* of all parameters that are variable. Every panel control that performs a function that cannot also be voltage controlled is a function over which the computer has no control. Consequently, that function must remain static throughout a computer-controlled sequence. For example, many voltage-controlled filters have panel controls for *Q* (bandpass sharpness) and no other provision for varying *Q*. Thus, *Q* must be initially set and left alone during the performance or a cueing system devised whereby the computer can signal the operator to twist the control! Another example would be the duty-cycle control for the rectangular-wave output on many voltage-controlled oscillators. Rotary switches used to select one of several operating modes rather than simultaneous output of all modes such as with state-variable filters is another "feature" of some modules that limits their usefulness in a computer-controlled system.

A final requirement is consistent control characteristics. This is not normally a problem with prepackaged synthesizers or modules from a single manufacturer but can become a real problem in a mixed system. For example, if some modules work on a 10-V standard and others work with 5 V, it is necessary to keep track of which modules are patched to what computer interface channels. This is normally a greater problem than mixing modules in a purely manual system, since in the latter case panel controls can often be set for acceptable performance and the operator can adapt to the somewhat changed characteristics. Likewise, signal level differences may cause gross errors in tonal balance unless the computer is informed or the necessary adjustments are made when the patch is set up.

Control Computer Requirements

The control computer, of course, is the heart of the system and should also be selected with some care. Again, however, one may be forced to use an existing computer. Fortunately, virtually any computer can be made to work well given sufficient programming effort, but a couple of computer characteristics greatly simplify the implementation of a Type 1 system, particularly if all subsystems are purchased. The first question to ask is: What digital/analog interface boards are available to plug into my computer and are they cost effective? Probably the best system from this standpoint is the S-100 type closely followed by the Apple- and IBM PC-compatible computers. Unfortunately, many analog interface boards emphasize analog-to-digital conversion more than the digital-to-analog, which is needed for synthesis work. At the time of writing, there was at least one cost effective 16-channel DAC board available for S-100 systems. As microcomputer-controlled synthesis gains momentum, boards with more channels at a much lower cost per channel are sure to become available.

Another feature that is virtually mandatory in a control computer is a so-called real-time clock or interval timer. This hardware feature allows the computer to be cognizant of the passage of time without regard for the execution time of the software. This capability is necessary for accurate and, above all, repeatable timing of the music performance. If multitrack recordings of the music are being made, it may be desirable to have a real-time clock that can be externally driven or synchronized. Since many systems use the ac power line as the timing reference, it is not difficult to record power line hum when the first music track is recorded and then use playback of that track to synchronize subsequent recordings. The 6522 type of parallel I/O interface IC found on most 6502- and some 68000-based computers can easily be programmed to generate a timing reference signal output and later accept it as input to drive one of the two timers on the chip.

As anybody who has done real-time control programming knows, it is not possible to have too much speed. An adequately fast computer simplifies programming and allows many otherwise important time factors to be ignored. An amply fast machine allows normally inefficient but convenient programming techniques such as high-level languages to be used for many of the control functions. Use of a 16-bit computer would certainly be desirable.

Computer Interface Box

The biggest variable in the system, however, is the computer interface box itself. This would be expected to consist of a number of DAC channels, each connected to a standard jack.

The first question that arises naturally is: How many DAC channels are required? A maximum number is easily arrived at by totaling the *control* inputs on all of the modules in the synthesizer. Thus, it would be possible for the computer to manipulate every control input in the system, which would be the ultimate in flexibility. Of course, many modules have two or more control inputs connected essentially in parallel so computer control of multiple parallel inputs would be redundant. For example, many VCOs have three control inputs: a primary frequency control input, a secondary one for injection of vibrato, and a third normally used for a constant transposition voltage. Typically, the computer would supply the primary and transposition controls and another oscillator would supply the vibrato signal. However, rather than using two DAC channels and doing the combining (addition) in the VCO, one channel can be used and the addition done in the computer. Thus, a practical maximum channel count would be the total number of voltage-controlled *functions* available in the synthesizer.

Next, it is necessary to decide what the resolution and accuracy of the DACs should be. If 16-bit DACs were cheap, they would probably be used exclusively and the question of resolution could be ignored. However, the cost of the DAC is important in nearly all cases except very large multiplexed systems where one DAC (and its cost) might serve over 100 output channels. As was mentioned many times in the previous chapter, 12 bits for a DAC is a good compromise between resolution and cost. The 4096 output levels of such a DAC are close enough together so that any stepping effect, such as when the DAC is controlling the frequency of a VCO, is virtually inaudible.

Although 12-bitters are relatively cheap ($30), output multiplexing is still necessary to obtain an acceptable per-channel cost figure. Commercial analog output subsystems seldom multiplex more than 16 outputs from a single DAC and therefore cost in the neighborhood of $10 to $25 per channel. The main reason for small multiplex factors in these units is the manufacturer's desire to retain high update speeds, much higher than necessary to control a synthesizer. Sticking with off-the-shelf modules, it may be possible to purchase collections of sample-and-hold amplifiers at less cost and further expand a 16-channel board. The home builder, on the other hand, can utilize the techniques already discussed and add over 100 channels to a single inexpensive DAC at a parts cost of little more than a dollar per channel.

Another factor to consider is the update (sample) rates to be used in controlling the synthesizer. Required update rates are highly application dependent. For example, in synthesizing speech, 100 updates of the parameters per second are usually ample for producing speech of high quality. In music synthesis, one of the key questions is whether the computer will generate envelope shapes through the analog interface or whether envelope generator modules will be used with the computer controlling just the *parameters* of the envelopes. If the computer generates envelopes directly, update rates up to 500/sec may be necessary for accurate rendition of fast envelopes. Most other control functions get along nicely on 100 updates/sec.

Finally, it may be desirable to incorporate a low-pass filter in the DAC outputs, particularly if a dedicated DAC is used for each channel. The filter prevents the control voltages from changing at an excessively high rate when an update is performed. This can be important because fast transients on control inputs may couple audibly into the controlled signal path as clicks. The cutoff frequency of the filter is best determined by experiment but a good starting value is the reciprocal of the shortest update interval to be used. This is usually low enough to be effective, yet high enough to avoid

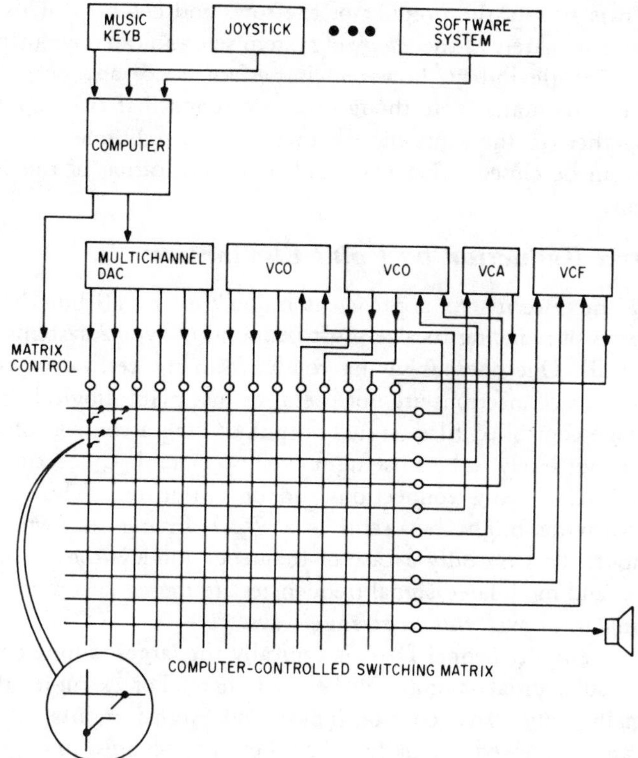

Fig. 8–2. Type 2 automatically patched system

distortion of the control voltage contours. Most multiplexed DACs, however, provide sufficient filtering in the channel sample-and-holds themselves.

Automatically Patched Computer-Controlled System

An automatically patched system in its elementary form is a Type 1 system with the jacks and patch cords replaced by an electronic switching matrix that is under the computer's control. Such a system is represented in Fig. 8–2 but in practice the switching matrix may be organized differently from the two-dimensional matrix shown. Comments about the synthesizer and the computer made earlier are just as valid in a Type 2 system. Therefore, let us proceed directly to a discussion of the switching matrix.

The simplest type of patching matrix, at least conceptually, is the straight rectangular array of single-pole switches as in the drawing. All subsystem outputs, including the DACs, drive the columns, and all of the subsystem inputs are connected to rows. The final synthesizer output is considered as an input to a speaker subsystem. The number of switches in the matrix then is simply the product of the rows and columns. This number increases approximately as the *square* of system size and can obviously become very large. The flexibility, however, is perfect, since any output can be connected to any input. Note though the restriction that two *outputs* cannot be tied together (to the same input); in this case, only one switch on any given row can be closed. This may lead to simplification of the switching arrangement.

Matrix Reduction by Point Elimination

Since the pure matrix approach is impractical for all but the smallest systems, ways of reducing its size must be found if Type 2 systems are to be practical at all. One obvious saving results from the realization that some output-to-input connections are not useful or just plain illogical. For example, a voltage-controlled filter signal output driving a control input on the *same* filter is not likely to be a useful or even predictable connection. In fact, virtually all self-driving connections can be eliminated. The one case in which self-driving might be useful is a VCO driving its own frequency control input. This is really a case of frequency modulation, in which the modulating and modulated signal frequencies are the same and has the effect of distorting the waveforms in strange ways.

Since the multichannel DAC is typically the largest single contributor of outputs, substantial savings can be made here. For example, the DACs will normally only drive control inputs, not signal inputs; thus, those switches can be removed. Actually, a few should be retained in the event that a signal input does need to be driven. Savings can also be made by dedicating DAC outputs to narrow ranges of control inputs. This can be done with little if any flexibility loss because all DAC outputs are normally equal; thus, it makes no difference which one is used to drive a particular input. If two widely separated control inputs must be driven by the same DAC, two DAC channels may be utilized and the computer can be responsible for giving both the same data.

Other connection restrictions can be built in to further reduce the switch count. Flexibility may be retained for special cases by adding extra rows and columns with each added row connected to a column. Then, if a special case requires a connection for which there is no path because of omitted switches, the signal may be routed through one of the extra rows and columns to make the connection. There is a clear tradeoff between interconnection restriction and extra circuits to retain flexibility. If too many switches are omitted, it may require more added circuits to maintain flexibility than were saved by the omissions.

Reduction by Subgroup Organization

One way to organize and formalize interconnection restrictions is to consider the overall patching matrix as a set of independent submatrices.

First, the set of modules in the system, including outputs from the interface DACs, are divided into groups. The modules chosen to form a group should form a compatible set, that is, in a real patching situation the interconnections among elements of the group would be a maximum and "outside" connections to other groups would be a minimum. Since the matrix size is proportional to the square of the number of modules in the group, the size of the individual submatrices can be dramatically reduced. In fact, it is easy to show that the theoretical reduction in overall matrix size is proportional to the number of subgroups it is broken into if the subgroups are equal in size. For example, if a matrix were broken into five equal-sized subgroups, then the total number of switches would be one-fifth as large.

Of course, in a practical system one subgroup must be able to connect to another. Therefore, "communications" input columns and output rows for the subgroup must be added as in Fig. 8–3. The limit on subdivision is reached when the quantity of switches devoted to communications exceeds that saved by the subdivision.

Other methods are available for reducing switch count and are, of course, widely used in very large switching matrices such as a telephone central office. The basic idea in all of these is to concentrate the myriad of inputs into a few "buses" with one set of switches and then distribute the buses to the desired outputs with another set of switches. If the number of buses remains constant, then the number of switches increases *linearly* with increases in input and output count rather than exponentially. The difficulty with such schemes in patching a synthesizer is that their fundamental assumption, that a *small* number of inputs are connected to outputs, is not valid. One will generally find that a large fraction of available inputs, outputs, and modules are used in a significant number of patches.

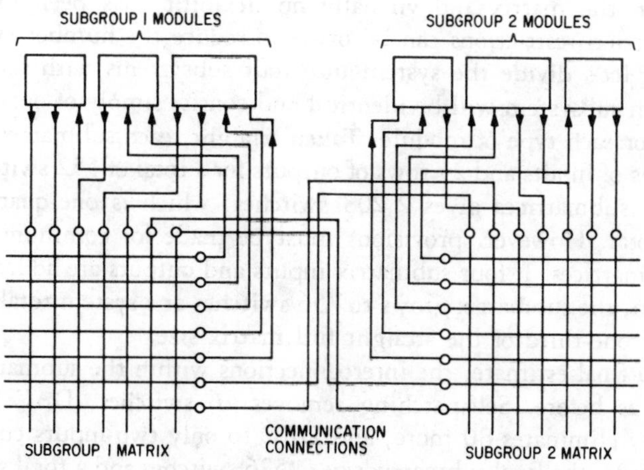

Fig. 8–3. Subgroup organization of switching matrix

Assuming that a suitable submatrix organization and set of interconnection restrictions has been established, it becomes apparent that going from a block diagram of a patch to a pattern of matrix switch closings is no longer straightforward. Things can become so complex that a given patch might not seem possible when in fact it is. Of course, this is an excellent job for the control computer, which can be programmed to accept the patching specification directly and then search for an interconnection pattern that implements it.

Reduction Example

A concrete example should serve to illustrate these points. Let's assume that a moderately large system is to be automatically patched and that the maximum practical amount of flexibility is desired. The system to be patched is as follows:

1. 8 VCO 3 control in, 4 signal out
2. 16 VCA 1 control in, 2 signal in, 1 signal out
3. 4 VCF 2 control in, 1 signal in, 3 signal out
4. 4 special modules, 1 signal in, 1 control in, 1 signal out
5. 32-channel DAC

A little arithmetic will reveal that there is a total of 92 inputs and 96 outputs, giving no fewer than 8,832 crosspoints in the matrix.

If the system is to be organized as one large matrix, the first reduction step is to eliminate self-patching paths, which amounts to a 184-switch reduction. If DAC outputs are only allowed to drive the 52 control inputs, then 32(92−52) = 1,280 more switches are eliminated. Finally, if each individual DAC is only allowed to drive one of two control inputs, then 30 × 52 = 1,664 switches can be removed. There are now only 5,704 switches in the matrix and virtually no flexibility has been lost. Other interconnection restrictions can be made to reduce the number even more.

Now let's divide the system into four subsystems with four submatrices. Each subsystem will be identical and consist simply of one-quarter of the total for each type of module. Taken straight, each submatrix will have 24 columns of inputs and 23 rows of outputs for a total of 552 switches. This times four submatrices gives 2,208 switches, which is one-quarter of the original total. However, provisions must be made for communication between submatrices. If four submatrix inputs and outputs are added for communication, the submatrix grows to 756 switches or a system total of 3,024, still about one-third of the straight full matrix size.

For a final estimate, the interconnections within the submatrix can be restricted as before. Self-patching removes 46 switches, DAC to control inputs only eliminates 80 more, and DAC to only two inputs cuts another 104 off. Thus, the final submatrix size is 526 switches and a total system size of a little over 2,000 switching points. This is obviously large but not completely impractical. The only real sacrifice in flexibility so far has been the limit of four signals connecting one subsystem with the others. Further reductions can be made by further restricting interconnections, requiring some manual patching, such as among subsystems, or permanent patching of those connections that are nearly always made. Properly planned and backed by an automatic signal routing program, these additional restrictions can have a minimal effect on the utility of the system.

Mechanical Relays

In actually implementing a switching matrix, a number of switching methods can be used. The primary split is between mechanical switches, such as relays, and solid-state analog switches. The main advantage of relay switching is the essentially zero contact resistance and total immunity to signal overload conditions. Disadvantages besides bulk and cost are slow response times and excessive noise if a circuit is switched live.

One type of relay specifically made for matrix switching is the telephone crossbar switch. These consist of contact assemblies arranged into rows and columns. A relay coil is needed for every row and column rather than every crosspoint, making the device very cost effective in the larger sizes such as 50 × 50 or 100 × 100. Unfortunately, they are highly specialized devices, generally only available to telephone equipment manufacturers. The true hobbyist experimenter may be able to occasionally find them in scrap yards, however.

A related device, also used in telephone switching systems, is the stepping relay. The simplest type functions as a 10- or 20-position solenoid-driven rotary switch that may be stepped into any position by pulsing the coil. Another type has two coils and two-dimensional movement. With proper pulsing of the coils, the armature may be connected to any of 100 points. One advantage of stepping relays is their inherent memory; they will stay put until moved to a different position. The disadvantages are very slow speed (1 to 2 sec to step to the desired position) and extremely noisy operation.

One type of relay that is practical is the magnetically latched reed relay. The contacts are sealed in glass, operation takes 1 to 2 msec, and they are essentially inaudible. A permanent bias magnet (or separate bias winding) gives a latching action. The bias field is insufficient to cause closure of the relay but can hold it closed. A current pulse that aids the bias field will close the relay, while one that opposes it will open the relay. The coils can be wired in a matrix array just like the contacts. Thus, to establish a connection between, say, column 31 and row 17, one would pulse coil column 31 positive and coil row 17 negative for a millisecond to turn that relay on. Reed relays designed for matrix operation may even have two coils in addition to the bias coil, which eliminates the need for diodes when connected in a matrix.

Semiconductor Analog Switches

Semiconductor switches are likely to be of more interest. The "contact" resistance of the switch can become a problem, however, because the voltage drop across this resistance will have an effect on the apparent sensitivity of control inputs. For example, a 300-ohm switch resistance and 100K control input impedance will cause an error of 30 mV on a 10-V control signal or nearly half a semitone. Op-amp buffers at some outputs of the switching matrix can easily eliminate this error. Signal overload may be a problem with analog switches. The most inexpensive CMOS switches are limited to 8 V peak and severely distort any signals beyond that.

Several common analog switch ICs are useful in switching matrix construction. For maximum flexibility in organizing the matrix, the 4066 type of CMOS analog switch offers four independent switches in a single 16-pin DIP package. The on resistance is in the 50-ohm range, and the "B" version can handle ±8-V signal swings with a ±8-V power supply. The 4051 1-of-8 analog multiplexor mentioned earlier gives eight switches in a package, of which only one at a time may be on, also with a 50-ohm resistance. These can be very effective in small matrices such as 4 x 8 or 8 x 8 in which a 4051 is used for each row. Also available is the 4052, which is a dual 1-of-4 multiplexor, and the 4053, which is a triple 1-of-2 unit. One significant advantage of the 405X series is that the control voltage to the switches need swing only between ground and the positive supply voltage; it need not go negative as required by the 4066. Although these switches are inexpensive (less than $1.50), all will require external latches to keep them in the desired state and will require logic level shifters to be driven from TTL logic levels. When a number of them are used in a large switching matrix, these latches and level shifters can easily constitute half the circuitry.

A more recent IC that is tailor-made for switching matrices is the MC142100 (Motorola) or CD22100 (RCA). This is an array of 16 CMOS analog switches that is internally arranged into a 4 x 4 matrix and costs under $3.00. Besides getting 16 switches from a 16-pin IC package, there is an internal flip-flop to control each switch. The device interfaces to the driving logic or computer just like a 16-bit write-only memory. There are four address inputs that are used to identify one of the 16 switches and a data and write pulse input. To turn the addressed switch on, a one would be placed on the data line and a positive pulse delivered to the write line. To turn a switch off, the data would be zero instead. Any on-off combination is possible and a special internal circuit turns all the switches off when power is first applied. The on resistance is somewhat higher (100 ohms) than the 405X series, but the error incurred (1/6 semitone for a 100K load) may be small enough to ignore. About the only drawback of this device is the need for level shifters on the address and control inputs than can swing between the negative and positive supply voltages.

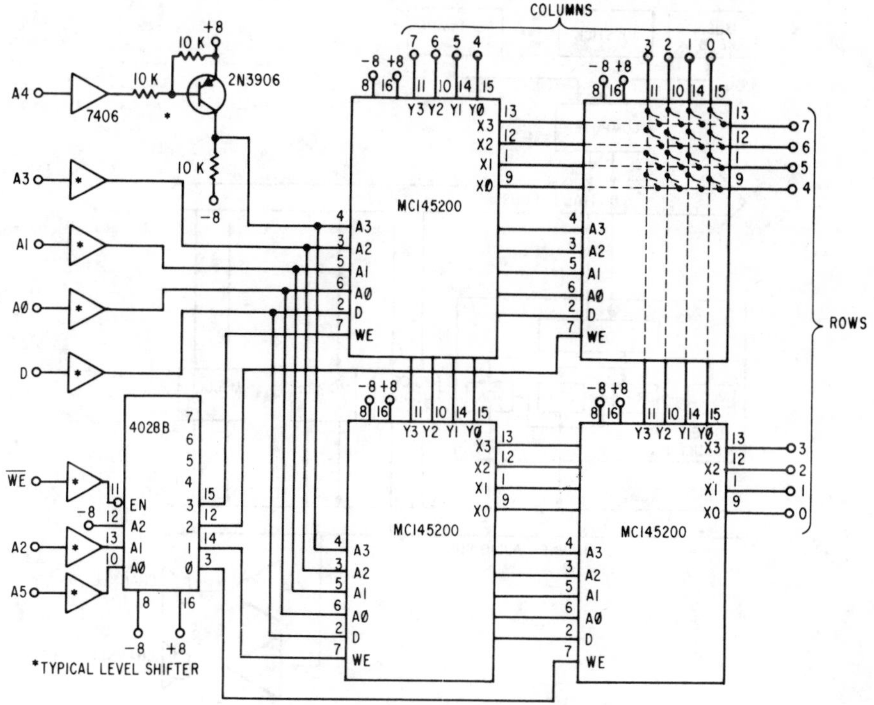

Fig. 8–4. 8 x 8 analog switching matrix

Figure 8–4 shows an 8 x 8 switching matrix using the CM142100. Level shifters on all inputs convert TTL levels to that needed by the switches and CMOS decoder. The six address inputs select one of the switches (least significant 3 bits select the column and most significant 3 select the row), the data input determines the switch state, and the *negative-going* strobe triggers the switch's flip-flop. The 4028 decoder is used to select one of the 4 x 4 matrices according to two of the address bits, and the four unused outputs allow easy expansion to a 16 x 8 array size.

The example system mentioned earlier could be quite effectively patched using a similar matrix. Each of the four submatrices could fit on a single board with about 60 pins needed for analog I/O connections and as few as 16 digital signal pins for control. The 526 switching points would be handled by approximately 35 of the matrix ICs plus a few packs of miscellaneous logic and the level shifters for a total parts cost of less than $200. Note that to take advantage of the matrix reduction discussed earlier that many crosspoints in the overall matrix will be empty. One of the design challenges is to organize the row and column assignments so that the empty positions are combined, thus allowing elimination of full 4 x 4 matrix

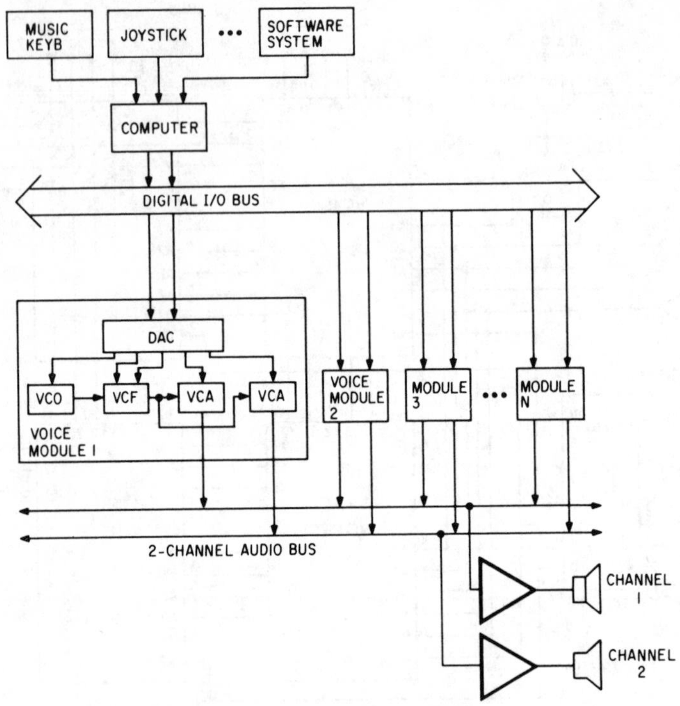

Fig. 8–5. Fixed-patched system

packages. While not a one-evening project, an automatic patching system can certainly be practical when compared with the rest of the system.

Fixed-Patched Computer-Controlled System

An instrument-oriented synthesizer is really a radical departure from the function-oriented synthesizer discussed up to this point. The system "building blocks" are now entire sounds or "voices" rather than low-level signal-processing functions. Thus, a typical synthesis setup should require fewer modules and interconnections as well as being easier to understand. The price paid for this simplicity is flexibility, since many decisions have been made by the module designer rather than the user. For clarity we will refer to the usual voltage-controlled functions such as VCOs, VCAs, etc., as "function modules" and the others as "voice modules."

An analogy to logic ICs is easily drawn. The typical function modules are like fundamental logic elements such as gates, flip-flops, and single-shots. Voice modules, on the other hand, are more like MSI circuits such as decoders, counters, multiplexors, and read-only memories. In modern logic design, one often uses these sophisticated MSI functions to perform mundane functions that earlier might have been done with discrete gates merely because the interconnections are simpler. Likewise, since computer-controlled interconnection between synthesizer function modules can become complex, a higher-level building block can be used to reduce the complexity.

Figure 8–5 gives an idea of how a fixed-patched system might be put together. Although a single-voice module configuration is shown, both less flexible and more flexible modules can be imagined. As in a Type 2 system, the computer can be in complete control of the system with all user inputs passing through it. A digital bus connecting all of the module inputs together is driven by the computer. Each module has a unique set of addresses and each control function in the module is a member of the set. The module outputs are mixed onto one or more analog channel buses, which correspond to stereo or quad audio channels. With proper design of the digital and analog buses, an essentially unlimited number of modules may be added to form very large systems.

Voice Module Design

Since the user is forced to live with them, the design of the voice modules is very important. The major design variables are flexibility and sophistication. At one extreme of flexibility we have very specific modules that are not unlike a rank of organ pipes. At the other extreme is flexibility equivalent to a small submatrix of function modules discussed earlier. A simplistic module may be little more than a simple tone source combined with a gain control amplifier (an IC sound generator chip for electronic games would fall into this category), while a sophisticated one may go to great lengths to duplicate the sound of a particular instrument.

Specific function modules are probably the most difficult to design but are the easiest to use. Typically, the goal might be to emulate a particular instrument at least well enough to be convincing when played in combination with other instruments. Figure 8–6 gives a general structure for such a module. The initial signal is generated by a VCO driven by a DAC. If the instrument to be emulated has fixed tuning (such as a piano or organ), the

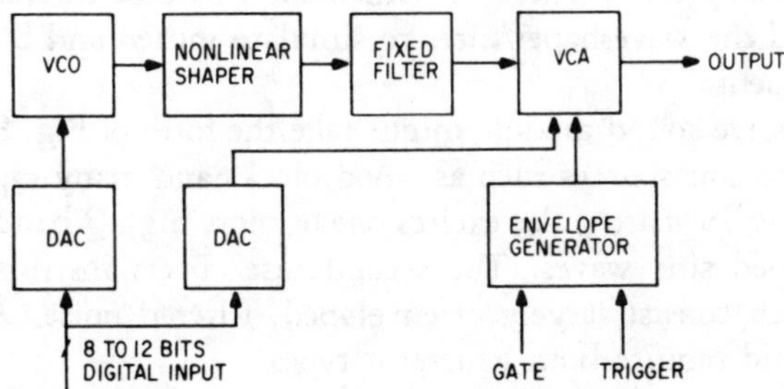

Fig. 8–6. Fixed-instrument voice module

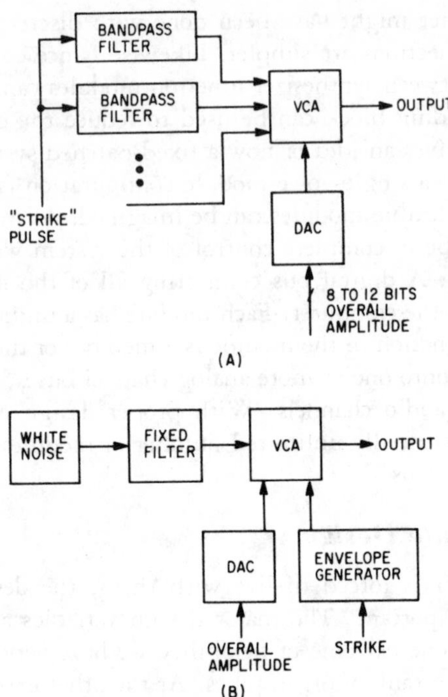

Fig. 8–7. Basic percussion instrument generators. (A) Resonant percussive sound generator. (B) Noisy percussive sound generator.

DAC may have as few as 6 bits of resolution. The combination of nonlinear waveshaper and fixed filter produces the characteristic timbre of the instrument. The shaper provides spectral characteristics that track the frequency of the VCO, whereas the filter provides formants (peaks in the spectrum) that remain constant. The VCA, its DAC, and envelope generator complete the sound processing and produce the final output at the desired amplitude.

Additional circuitry may be added to enhance realism. One example would be the use of a noise generator to introduce small random variations in frequency and amplitude. Another refinement would be interaction between amplitude and the waveshaper/filter to simulate muted and blaring timbres of the instrument.

A percussive sound module might take the form of Fig. 8–7. The first case covers resonant sources such as wood blocks and many types of pitched drums. Basically, a sharp pulse excites one or more high *Q* bandpass filters to produce damped sine waves. The second case covers instruments such as cymbals, which consist largely of enveloped, filtered noise. A snare drum generator would require both generator types.

Increasing Flexibility

A synthesizer based on such specific fixed function modules is little more than a computer-controlled organ with a wider than normal selection of stops. More flexibility can be had by making the previously fixed elements variable under computer control. For example, the fixed filter could be made variable as could the waveshaper. Some or all of the envelope parameters could also be made variable. With these changes, a single module type could cover a range of instrument types with appropriate control from the computer.

An even more generalized module could be imagined. A selector might be added to the VCO so that any of the standard VCO waveshapes could be selected. Ultimately, a programmable waveform generator (in which a small memory loaded by the computer contains the waveform) driven by the VCO would be used. The filter could be expanded to a full VCF with selection of the filtering function as well as the cutoff frequency and Q factor. The envelope generator could also have a programmable envelope shape like the waveform generator.

Even with voice modules of the type shown in Fig. 8–6 in which every parameter can be controlled, there are still serious flexibility limitations. For example, a sound may require two independently tunable formants, which requires two bandpass filters. FM synthesis is not possible because only one VCO is present. In fact, the majority of special effects is just not available with the example module.

The situation can be improved markedly, however, by expanding the module somewhat and allowing perhaps a half-dozen different configurations through a simple switching arrangement. Commercial voice-modular synthesizers typically include two independent VCOs, two variable filters, several VCAs, and several envelope generators, the latter usually implemented in software. Available interconnection patterns range from two parallel voices, to various intertwined combinations of the elements, even to FM connections where one VCO modulates the other or one of the filters. In particular, the two VCOs have been found to be very flexible, often eliminating the need for a generalized waveshaper (the second oscillator can be tuned to provide a prominent harmonic, for example). A moderately effective chorus effect can be obtained by having the VCOs *almost* track each other. A specific example of a voice modular synthesizer using these techniques can be found in Chapter 19.

While these measures are typically more than adequate for a performance-oriented synthesizer, flexibility for special cases is still limited. Thus, a few independent function modules and processor modules (like frequency shifters, chorus generators, and reverberation devices) are needed to supplement the voice modules if a flexible, comprehensive system is the goal.

Direct Digital Interface

The interface between digital signals from the computer and control inputs of the signal-processing components can often be simplified. The reason is that standard voltage levels and response functions are not needed, since all control paths are *local* to the module. Thus, a current output DAC might feed directly into a current-controlled oscillator without conversion to standard voltage levels, exponential conversion, etc. A multiplying DAC could be used to directly control gain without transconductance gain cells and so forth. The result is that a voice module will cost considerably less than

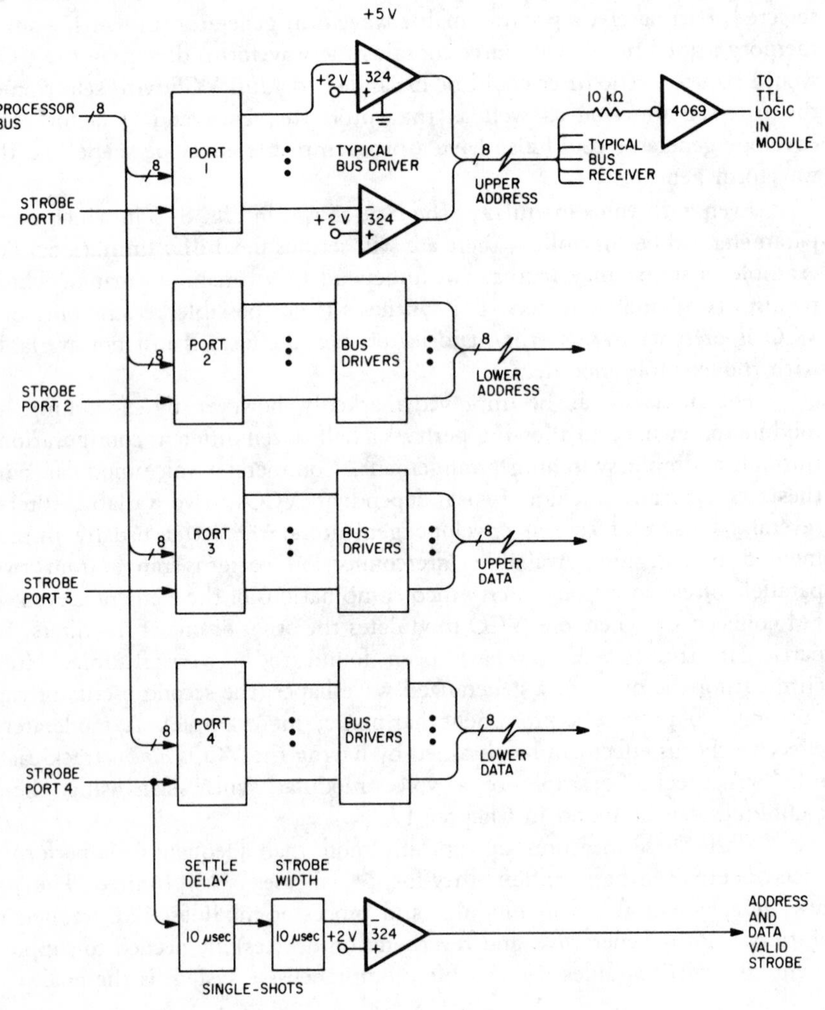

Fig. 8–8. Voice modular synthesizer digital bus

the equivalent collection of standard voltage-controlled modules and companion multichannel DAC.

As mentioned earlier one strength of the fixed-patched approach is the possibility of easy, nearly infinite expandability. This is made possible by totally parallel buses, both digital and analog, connecting the modules together. Proper design of the buses, however, is necessary to realize this potential.

The usual microcomputer bus is not at all acceptable for the digital control bus of the synthesizer. For one, its speed requirement severely limits the length and load allowable on the bus. Also, its high-speed signals, which flip around wildly all the time, are a source of noise that can easily get into the audio circuitry. The solution is a bus used only for transmitting data to the voice modules. Since the microcomputer program that will be sending data to the modules over the bus cannot go much faster than a word every 10 to 20 μsec, the bus can be slowed considerably, thus allowing long lengths and minimizing noise generation. One technique that works well for controlling rise times is to use op-amp voltage followers for bus drivers! An LM324 quad op-amp, for example, provides nice clean ramps with a 6- to 10-μsec transition time for TTL levels. Slow switching CMOS logic on the modules themselves provides virtually no load to the bus and tolerates slow rise times without oscillation.

Figure 8–8 shows the implementation of an example synthesizer bus. For simplicity, the bus is capable of output only, that is, data cannot be read back from the synthesizer modules. For maximum flexibility and expandability, 16 address lines and 16 data lines are defined. The interface between the bus and the computer consists simply of four 8-bit output ports, or if a 16-bit processor is used, two 16-bit ports. With up to 65,536 addresses available, an addressing standard can be defined whereby the most significant 8 bits define a particular module and the least significant 8 bits address a function within that module allowing up to 256 modules and 256 functions per module to be addressed.

To perform a data transfer, one merely sets up the address and data output ports. When the last port has been written into by the microcomputer, a pair of single-shots times out the data transfer to the synthesizer over the next 20 μsec. A CMOS gate and latches on the module board decode the register address and latch the data in response to data on the bus. Series resistors on the CMOS inputs protect against mishaps on the bus.

Because of the slow speed of the bus and inherent noise immunity of CMOS, several feet of open backplane wiring can be easily driven without perceptible signal degradation. If the bus must be run some distance in a cable, the 32 data and address lines can be individual conductors with no special shielding. The write-enable signal, however, should be run as a twisted pair with ground to minimize noise pickup from the other signal lines. Combined with an overall shield, cable lengths up to 50 feet can be easily accommodated.

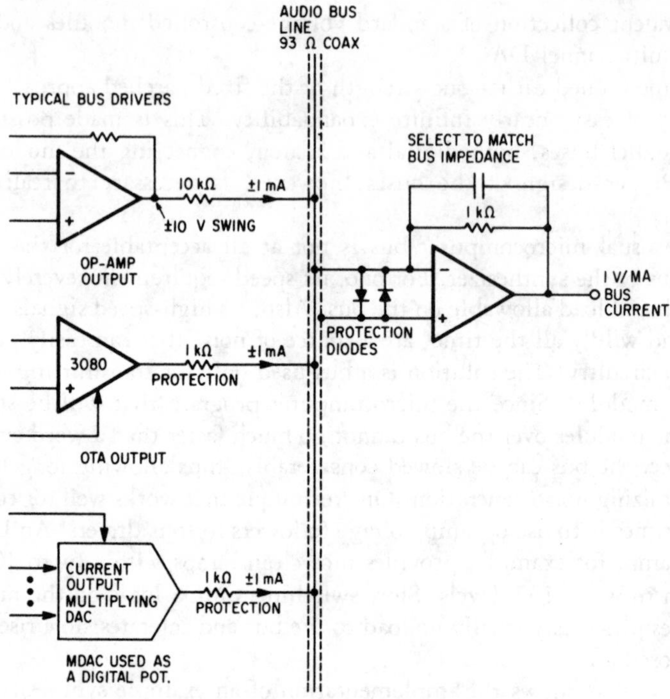

Fig. 8–9. Voice modular synthesizer audio bus

Audio Bus

The audio bus in Fig. 8–9 is a bit unusual. One line is used for each audio channel in the final synthesizer output; therefore, from one to four would be typical. Analog switches and/or programmable gain amplifiers determine which audio channel a particular module drives, thus setting the voice's position in acoustic space. To minimize noise pickup from the backplane and allow a virtually unlimited number of modules to combine their outputs, the audio lines are *current* sensitive. This means that each audio bus line is terminated with an amplifier with near-zero input impedance. The modules pump audio *current* up to 1 mA peak into the bus lines either from a voltage source with series resistor or directly from current output devices such as transconductance gain cells or multiplying DACs. The zero impedance amplifier is simply an op-amp current-to-voltage converter. The capacitor across the feedback resistor is chosen to cancel the bus capacitance. Even though the digital bus is optimized for minimum noise generation and the audio bus is relatively immune to noise pickup, it should be kept away from the digital bus and run as a twisted pair with ground around the backplane. When outside the backplane area, the audio signals should be run in low-capacitance (93 ohms) coax cable.

9

Organ Keyboard Interface

After a suitable synthesizer for output and a computer for control have been found, the final and ultimately most important subsystems are the devices used to communicate musical ideas to the system. The next three chapters will discuss devices for original input of musical material as well as equipment useful for displaying and editing the material. These input techniques are equally valid for real-time computer-controlled synthesizers and direct computer synthesis, which will be discussed at length in Section III. Most of them are fairly standard and were originally developed for computer applications other than music. One exception is the music keyboard, which is the subject of this chapter.

Undoubtedly the most popular musical input device will be a standard organ keyboard. Most new users will prefer it, at least initially, because of familiarity and because for most reasonably conventional music it is simply the most efficient method for getting musical data into the computer. Also, being a mass-produced item, the typical purchase price for a keyboard mechanism is quite reasonable compared with construction from scratch.

Even so, the usual organ keyboard leaves a lot to be desired. For example, the only "information" available about a key closure is which key was struck and for how long. This is just as well, since the typical organ would not be able to utilize additional information anyway. However, a music synthesizer, particularly a computer-controlled one, can and should utilize every bit of information available. To this end, special keyboards that also sense the speed of key depression, variations in pressure while it is down, and other variables have been constructed. Fortunately, some of these features are easily retrofitted to standard keyboards or in some cases may be merely a function of the interface circuitry used to connect the keyboard to the system.

One final keyboard characteristic, which piano and organ players usually take for granted, is polyphony, i.e., simultaneous sounds in response to simultaneous key closures. Whereas in an organ or piano there is one tone generator per key, such is not the case in a synthesizer. Furthermore, the

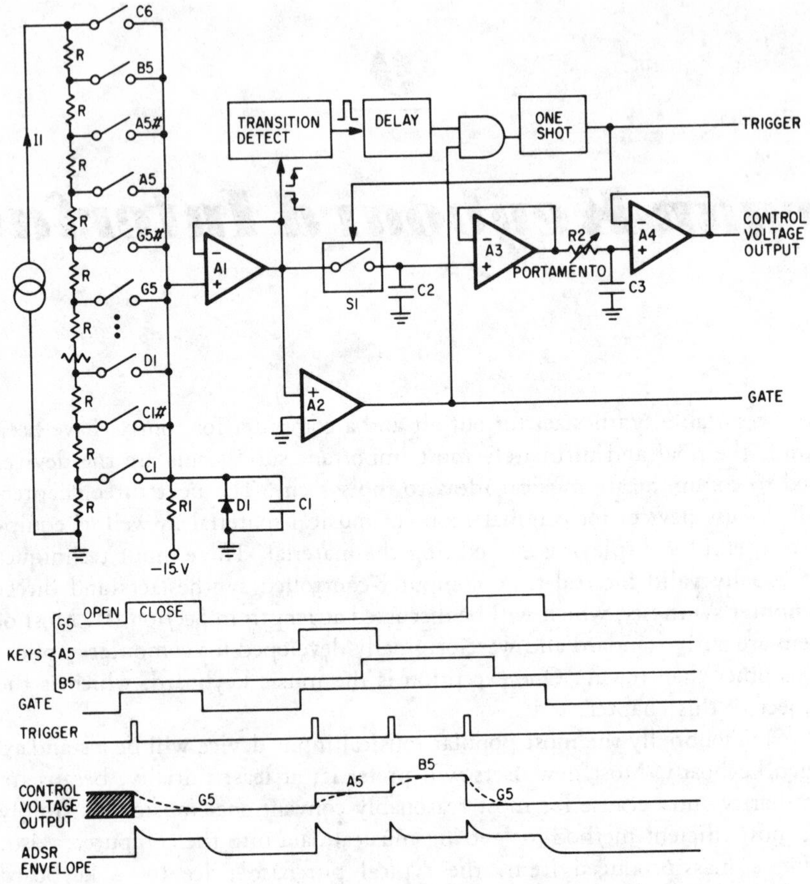

Fig. 9–1. Typical synthesizer keyboard

multiple synthesizer voices may be quite different from each other. Thus, the major tasks for a polyphonic synthesizer keyboard are not only orderly connection of a voice to a depressed key but assignment of the "correct" voice to the key.

Adapting a Standard Synthesizer Keyboard for Computer Input

Since most standard synthesizers contain one or more keyboards already, it might be useful to consider interfacing such a keyboard to a microcomputer. The standard synthesizer keyboard usually provides three outputs; digital trigger and gate and an analog control voltage proportional to the key last depressed. The gate output is high (logic 1) whenever any key is depressed. The trigger output is a short pulse that signals the exact instant that a key is pressed. Typically, these two outputs would go to an envelope generator, which in turn controls a VCA to shape the amplitude envelope of the notes.

Figure 9–1 is a simplified schematic diagram of such a keyboard. The heart of the unit is the keyboard itself. Organ keyboards are usually constructed with a straight gold-plated spring wire attached to each key. When a key is pressed, this wire contacts a stationary gold-plated rod running the length of the keyboard. This rod is called a "keyboard bus" in organ-builder's terms. For the synthesizer interface, the spring wire on each key connects to a tap point on a series string of resistors designated R in the diagram. A current source sends a constant current through the string, creating an equal voltage drop across each resistor. For 100-ohm resistors (a common value) and $^{1}/_{12}$ V/resistor (12-tone scale and 1 V/octave output) the current would be 0.83 mA. Thus, the keyboard bus picks up a definite voltage when a key is pressed against it. If two or more keys simultaneously contact the bus, the voltage corresponding to the *lowest* key pressed appears on the bus due to the action of the constant current source. The remainder of the interface circuit essentially looks at the bus voltage and produces proper gate, trigger, and control voltage outputs.

Gate and Trigger

The gate output is the easiest to generate. If no keys are pressed, R1 (in the megohm range) tends to pull the bus down toward −15 V. D1, however, limits the fall to about −0.5 V. When any key is pressed, the bus is immediately pulled up to a positive voltage dependent on the key pressed. The gate voltage then may be taken from a comparator referenced to ground, which will produce a logic one for positive bus voltage and a zero for negative bus voltage. C1 is a noise filter in the range of 200 pF, while A1 is a unity gain buffer, which prevents loading of the keyboard bus.

The trigger circuit must provide a short (1 to 10 msec) pulse at the *beginning* of each key closure. In all cases but one, this occurs when there is a sudden change in keyboard bus voltage. In the circuit shown, a transition detector generates a pulse whenever such a sudden change happens. This pulse would be the trigger output if it were not for the case that occurs when a single contacting key is lifted. In this case, the trigger pulse should be suppressed. To solve the problem, the transition detector output is delayed slightly and logically anded with the gate signal. The result triggers a one-shot, which provides the actual trigger output. Thus, when the transition to no keys is detected it is blocked from producing a trigger. The delay need only be long enough for the gate comparator to respond.

The control voltage output from the keyboard normally follows the bus voltage. However, when no keys are pressed, it should reflect the voltage level of the last key released. This is necessary because most envelope generators do not begin their decay until the gate voltage has gone away. In effect, a sample-and-hold function is needed. S1 and C2 form the sample-and-hold, which is updated whenever a trigger is generated. C2 should be a low-leakage low-dielectric absorption type (polystyrene) and A3 should be a low-bias type so that the control voltage output does not audibly drift during long decays. R2 and C3 provide adjustable portamento, which is a gliding effect between notes.

The timing diagram illustrates a typical playing sequence on the keyboard. For an isolated key closure, the gate goes high during the closure time and the trigger is coincident with the rising edge of the gate. The control voltage output goes from whatever it was to the level corresponding to note G5. The next case is a three-note sequence in which the key closures overlap somewhat. The first note (A5) starts the gate and trigger as before. When B5 is initially struck, nothing happens because A5, being lower than B5, takes precedence and no voltage change occurs on the keyboard bus. When A5 is finally released, the change in bus voltage is detected and another trigger is generated and updates the control voltage output. Response to the following G5 is immediate, however, since it is lower than B5. At the end of the sequence, when G5 is released, the trigger is suppressed and the control voltage output remains at the G5 level. Also shown is a typical ADSR envelope that might be generated in response to the illustrated gate and trigger sequence.

Computer Interface

Interfacing such a keyboard to a computer is fairly simple. Basically, all that is needed is an ADC connected to the control voltage output and two input port bits connected to the trigger and gate signals. Whenever a trigger occurs, an analog-to-digital conversion would be initiated. If keyboard operation is restricted to the 12-tone equally tempered scale, then the ADC need only be accurate enough to determine which key is pressed. Thus, a 6-bit ADC is sufficient for a five-octave keyboard provided that the voltage step from key to key is matched to the ADC step size.

Once interfaced, it is a simple matter to write a program loop that looks at these inputs and controls the synthesizer in response to them. If keyboard activity is to be stored for later editing and recall, a real-time clock is needed. The program would then note the time and the keyboard voltage whenever a trigger occurred or the gate changed. Maximum program flexibility is attained if triggers and gate changes are connected to the interrupt structure on the computer. Then the program may do other tasks and still respond to the keyboard quickly when necessary.

Figure 9–2 is a simplified diagram of a suitable interface. The gate, trigger, and ADC output data enter through an input port. The flip-flop is set whenever a trigger pulse or trailing gate edge occurs, which signifies a significant keyboard event. When set, this flip-flop may request an interrupt via the 7405 open-collector inverter. The interrupt service routine can de-

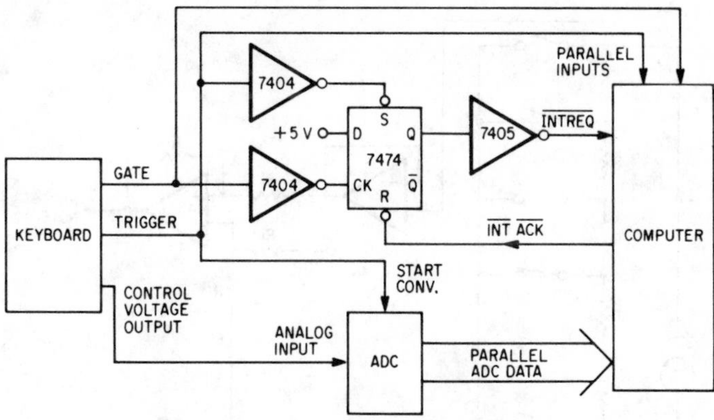

Fig. 9–2. Analog keyboard-to-computer interface

termine if the keyboard is requesting by examining the trigger and gate signals. After reading the ADC output, the request flip-flop can be reset through an output port bit. If a 6-bit ADC is used, the entire interface only requires 8 input port bits and 1 output port bit. The interface is equally applicable to software ADC methods. Once the interrupt service routine determines that the keyboard caused the interrupt, the ADC subroutine can be entered to read the keyboard voltage.

Polyphonic Keyboards

In spite of its vast audio-processing power, most analog synthesizers are inherently monophonic (one note at a time) instruments. In fact it is usually the keyboard that causes this limitation. One can always use multiple keyboards with a voice for each but an increasingly popular musical application of microprocessors is as *polyphonic* keyboard controllers that allow a synthesizer player to become a real-time one-man band. Before discussing such a keyboard controller, let's examine a fairly common analog technique used to obtain two simultaneous independent notes from a single keyboard.

Two-Note Keyboard

Figure 9–3 shows the idea behind a two-note analog keyboard using a single-keyboard bus. As mentioned in the single-note interface, when more than one key is pressed, the bus voltage will correspond to the *lowest* key pressed. What is needed is an additional circuit to generate a voltage proportional to the *highest* key pressed as well. Examining the situation with two keys down, it is seen that all of the resistors between the two keys are shorted out (three resistors in the example). Since the string is driven by a constant-current source, the voltage at the top of the string, E2, will *decrease* by an amount equal to the voltage that would normally appear across the shorted

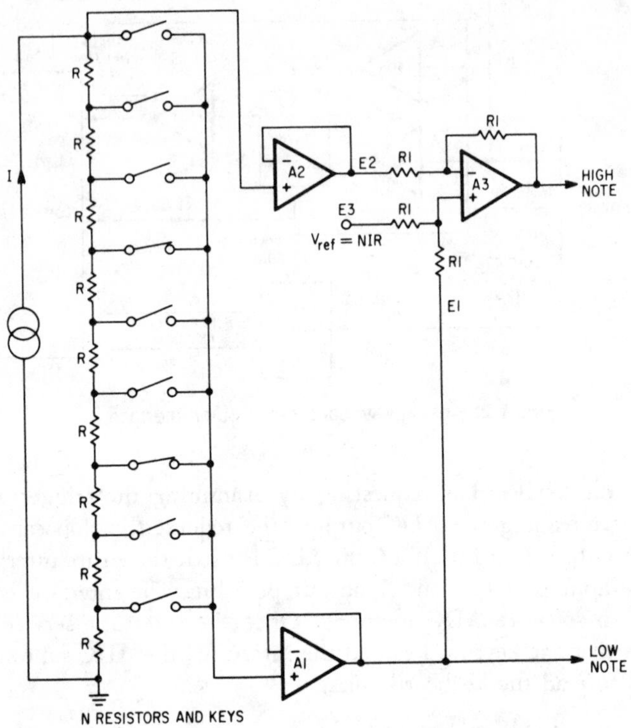

Fig. 9–3. Two-note analog keyboard

resistors. This decrease, when added to the low-note voltage that is already available, will yield a voltage proportional to the highest key pressed. The voltage decrease may be determined by subtracting E2 from a reference voltage, E3, which has been adjusted to be equal to the normal top-of-string voltage with no keys depressed. Thus, the highest note output is equal to E1 + (E3 − E2), where E1 is the low-note output. Op-amp A3 in conjunction with four matched R1 resistors performs this calculation, while A1 and A2 buffer the bus and top point from loading.

Before discussing trigger and gate circuitry, let's think a little about how the keyboard *should* respond to various playing situations. For convenience, the low note will be called Voice 1 and the high note will be called Voice 2. With no keys pressed, the two gates should be down, and the two voltage outputs should be held at their previous values. If two keys are pressed simultaneously, then both gates should rise, both triggers should fire, and the control voltages should move to their respective values. So far no problem, but what happens if only one key is pressed? Ideally, only one voice would respond while the other remains idle. If one does remain idle, which should it be? Likewise, if two keys are down initially and one is lifted, ideally one of the gates would go away and the corresponding voltage output would not change. Which one should it be? These problems would be particularly important if the voices were different, such as a rich timbre for the low notes and a thin timbre for the high notes. If the answer is consistent such that the high note always takes precedence when only one key is down, the circuitry can be designed easily enough. But then the question becomes whether that choice is appropriate for all music that will be played. In a nutshell, this defines the assignment problem that is difficult for two voices and purely a matter of compromise for more than two.

Ultimate Limitations

If the trigger and gate circuitry used on the one-voice keyboard is applied to each channel of the two-voice case, the behavior will be far from ideal. First, the two gates would be identical because both would be looking for a positive bus voltage. In addition, if only one key is pressed, both voices would trigger and both would output the same control voltage. If a second key is struck, one voice will retrigger and update its output depending on whether the second note is lower or higher than the first.

So far the problems are not particularly bad if both voices have the same timbre. The real difficulty occurs when two keys are down and the player attempts to release them simultaneously, expecting the two-note chord to die out during the envelope decay. What will almost surely happen instead is that one of the keys will release first, and the voice that was assigned to that key will trigger and update itself to the other key. The end result will be that the two voices will decay while playing the same note and it is not even predictable which note it will be!

Obviously, logic and delay circuits can be added to obtain performance closer to the ideal. The most important element would be a circuit to specifically detect when only one key is down and modify the gate and trigger action according to the chosen set of rules. Since one set of rules may not be appropriate for all playing situations, a selector switch might be added to allow changing the rules. Even with its limitations, the two-voice analog keyboard is an inexpensive feature often found in prepackaged synthesizers and used primarily as a selling point.

Beyond two voices, it is necessary to return to the digital domain. Actually, an all-digital keyboard interface would make the most sense for musical input to a computer, since a digital-to-analog operation (series resistor string and keyswitches) and an analog-to-digital operation can both be bypassed. It should be intuitively obvious that a suitable digital circuit can constantly *scan* all of the keyswitch contacts, *track* the state of each one, and *report* significant events to the computer. Assignment of keys to voices would then be done in the control computer, where as little or as much intelligence as necessary can be applied to the task.

A Microprocessor-Based Keyboard Interface

Not only can digital logic solve the polyphonic keyboard problem and thereby effect an efficient, completely general interface to a microcomputer, but also a dedicated microprocessor can replace the logic. In this section, a five-octave *velocity-sensitive* keyboard interface will be described, which uses a 6502 microprocessor to perform all of the needed logic functions. Using a dedicated microprocessor results in an interface that uses a minimum of parts, is easy to build, is flexible in that the operational characteristics may be altered by reprogramming, and is actually inexpensive.

Velocity Sensing

Before delving into the actual circuitry and programming, let's develop a set of specifications for the unit. First, what is velocity sensing and how is it implemented? Basically, velocity sensing is a very inexpensive way to obtain additional information about keystrokes beyond simple duration. The keys on a piano, for example, are velocity sensitive. The actual speed of key travel downward at the exact instant of key "bottoming" solely determines the force with which the hammer strikes the string. In fact, the hammer "coasts" a finite distance from the point of key bottoming to actual contact with the string. Thus, *variations* in velocity or pressure *while* the key is going down do not affect the sound! Unfortunately, a velocity-sensitive organ keyboard will not feel at all like a piano keyboard because the inertia of the hammer is absent, but the same kind of information will be available. Note that since we are using a synthesizer the velocity information need not necessarily control the amplitude of the note. It could just as well control timbre, vibrato, or the envelope.

The mechanical modification necessary to allow velocity sensing on an organ keyboard is really quite simple. All that is required is a second keyboard bus spaced a fixed distance above the standard bus and positioned such that the keys' spring wires make contact with it when in the *up* position. Now, when a key travels down, the wire will first break contact with the upper bus after a short distance, float freely between the buses for the majority of the travel, and then finally contact the lower bus just before the key bottoms. The average downward velocity of the wire and thus the key may be determined by measuring the time interval between breaking the upper contact and making the lower one! If desired, the speed of release at the end of a note may also be determined, which might indeed be used to vary envelope decay. For monophonic keyboards, it is relatively easy to design analog timing circuits that will produce a control voltage output proportional to velocity. For polyphonic keyboards, however, only digital scanning logic can cope with the problem.

The actual characteristics of standard two-bus commercial keyboards are not quite ideal but can be lived with. Contact resistance, for example, is quite low and perfectly suitable for carrying any kind of logic signal. The contact time differential used for velocity sensing varies from a minimum of around 5 msec to a reasonable maximum of 50 msec. Attempting to pound the key for shorter times results in severe bounce of the key itself as well as possible damage. Gently easing the key down for longer times requires so much care that it is unlikely to be done. Variations in the differential from key to key and even the same key from stroke to stroke are in the range of 20% up or down. The very light touch characteristic of organ keyboards is probably responsible for much of the variation.

Contact bounce is a problem that must be dealt with if spurious outputs are to be prevented. Bounce on contact make is generally 1 msec, although it can be as long as 3 msec. Bounce on break, however, can be as long as 5 msec which normally occurs for the slower velocities. Thus, to retain any degree of accuracy in velocity timing the keyboard controller logic must define the time differential as being between the *last* bounce of contact break on one bus to the *first* bounce of contact make on the other bus. With a microprocessor doing the work, such sophistication is relatively simple. Another option sometimes used by synthesizer manufacturers who also make their own keyboards is to dispense with contacts altogether and use other types of position sensors such as light source-photocell combinations, which do not bounce.

Keyboard Events

The real purpose of the keyboard interface is to report all *significant* keyboard activity to the using system. With velocity sensing, this requires five pieces of information about each keystroke:

1. A number defining the key
2. When it was pressed
3. A number defining the depression velocity
4. When it was released
5. A number defining the release velocity

If the time of depression and release are defined as elapsed time from an arbitrary point such as the beginning of the song, then the time relationship among all keystrokes is retained and the keyboard activity can be stored and reproduced exactly or edited.

For a real-time playing situation, each piece of information should be reported as soon as it is available. It is possible to break each keystroke into two parts, which will be called *events*. A depression event would therefore consist of a key identification, its depression velocity, and the "time of day" that it was depressed. Similarly, a release event would specify which key, its release speed, and when it was released. With information in this form, it becomes easy for the system control computer to operate the synthesizer in immediate response to the keyboard and/or record the playing sequence.

For convenience in this design example, each keyboard event will consist of four 8-bit bytes. The first byte will be the key identification, which will be a binary number between 0 and 60 with 0 corresponding to C1 and 60 corresponding to C6 on the five-octave 61-note keyboard. The most significant bit of this byte will distinguish press events from release events with a 1 signifying depression. The second byte will be a velocity value in which small numbers correspond to high velocities (short "float" times). The third and fourth bytes will be the time of day in 1-msec increments. Although this only pins down the time to within 65 sec, that should be quite close enough to avoid confusion. If desired, a fifth byte could extend unique timing information to over 4 hr.

The keyboard interface will present these four bytes as 32 parallel bits that can be read by the using system in any way it sees fit. However, it is extremely important that a *handshake protocol* be defined so that there is no risk of an event becoming lost because another event occurred before the using system could read the first one. This can be accomplished with a request/response flip-flop similar to the one used with the analog keyboard. When the keyboard has an event ready, it updates the 32-bit parallel output and sets the request flip-flop. The using system seeing the request on, reads the 32 bits and resets the request flip-flop. The keyboard is prevented from outputting new data while the flip-flop is on. If another event does occur

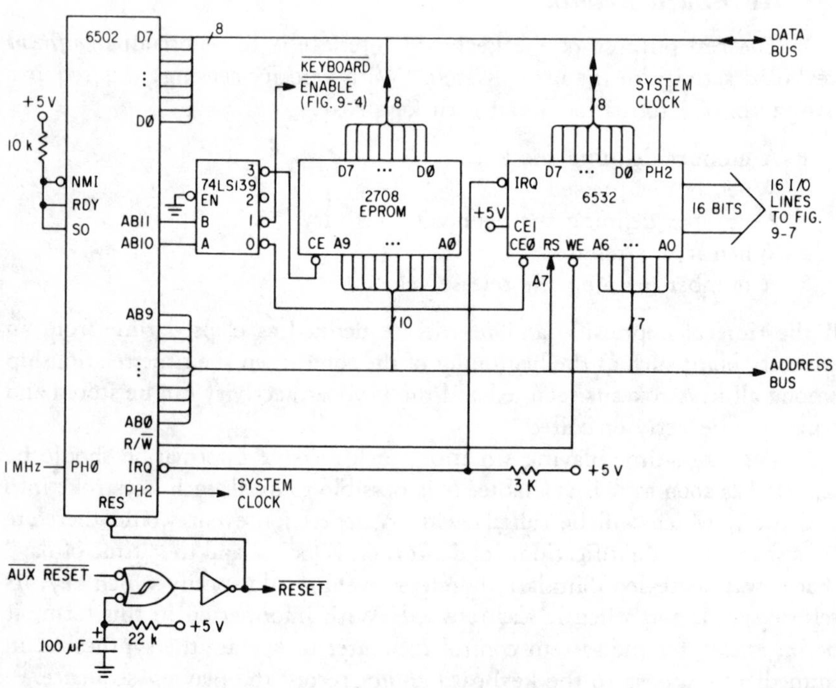

Fig. 9–4. Keyboard interface microprocessor

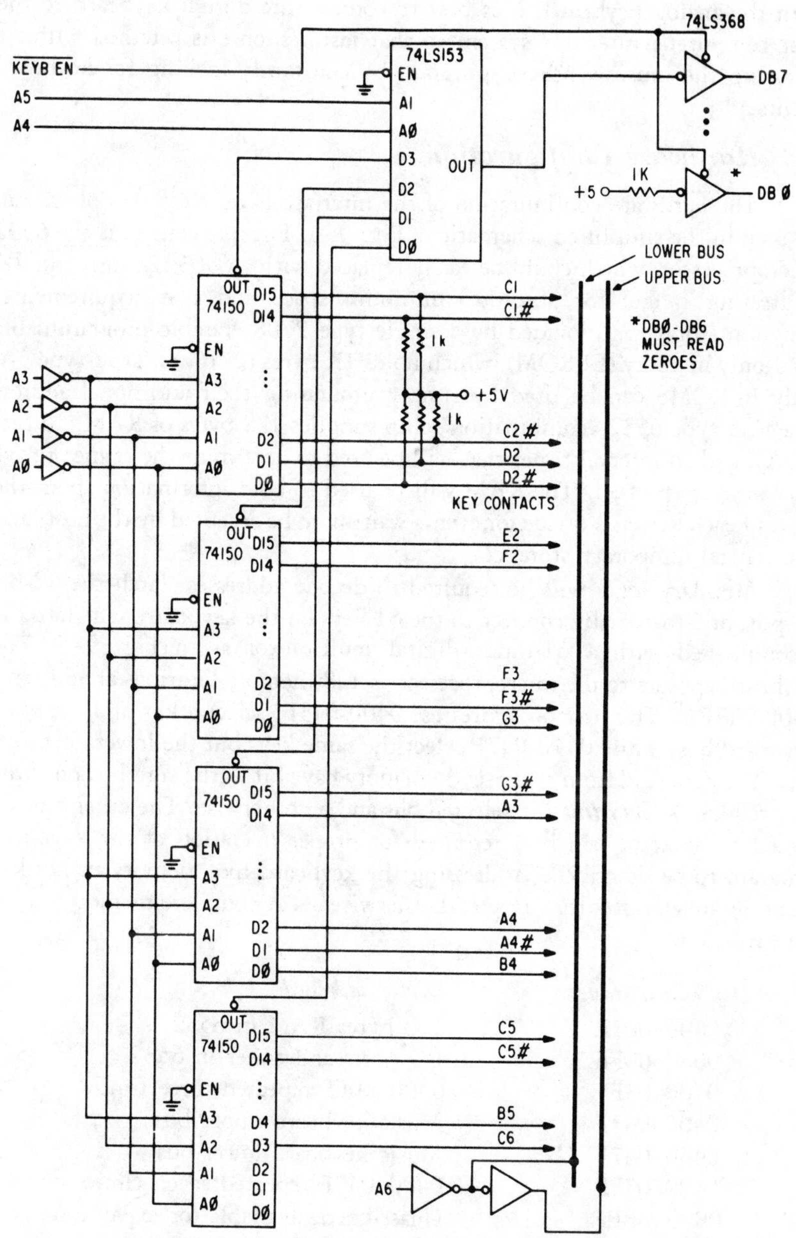

Fig. 9-5. Keyboard multiplexor

before the using system reads the previous one, the keyboard can save it in a first-in-first-out queue. In hard-wired logic, such queues are expensive, but with a microprocessor-based interface, they are virtually free. If the time of the event is ascertained when it occurs rather than when it is read by the using system, such queuing has no effect on keystroke timing accuracy. As with the analog keyboard, it is best to connect the digital keyboard to the host computer's interrupt system so that fast response is retained without tying up the music-synthesis program by constantly looking for keyboard events.

Hardware Configuration

The hardware configuration of the interface is relatively simple as can be seen in the simplified schematic of Fig. 9–4. First, of course, is the 6502 microprocessor, which could be easily replaced with a 6503 (28 pins and 4K addressing range) for absolute minimum space and cost requirements. Program storage is provided by a single type 2708 erasable programmable read-only memory (EPROM), which holds 1K bytes (2716- or 2732-type 5-V only EPROMS can be used by simply grounding their additional address lines). A type 6532 "combination" chip supplies 128 bytes of RAM, 16 bits of I/O, and an interval timer that will be used to determine the "time of day" that keys are pressed. The RAM will be used to hold information about the state of each key, as a queue for events waiting to be accepted by the host, and for general temporary storage.

Auxillary logic will be required to decode addresses, latch the 32-bit output, and to actually connect to the 61 keys on the keyboard. The latter is accomplished with a 61-input digital multiplexor as in Fig. 9–5. The keyboard appears to the microprocessor as 128 memory locations at addresses 0400-047F$_{16}$. The first 64 addresses, 0400-043F, select a key and the *upper* keyboard bus, while 0440-047F select the same keys but the lower keyboard bus. The data read from this pseudomemory have bit 7 (the sign bit) off if the selected key is *contacting* the selected bus and on otherwise. The other bits are forced to be zero, which is required for proper operation of the keyboard program to be described. Addressing the keyboard like memory makes key scanning much faster than it would otherwise be. A complete memory map is shown below:

Hex address range	*Device addressed*
0000–007F	128 bytes RAM in 6532
0080–00FF	I/O ports and timer in 6532
0100–03FF	0000–00FF repeated three times
0400–043F	Music keyboard upper bus
0440–047F	Music keyboard lower bus
0480–07FF	0400–047F repeated seven times
0800–0BFF	Unassigned, available for expansion
0C00–0FFF	1K bytes EPROM 2708 type
1000–FFFF	000–0FFF repeated 15 times

Note that since address decoding is incomplete a variety of addresses will refer to the same device. In particular, the EPROM can be reached by addresses between FC00 and FFFF, which include the interrupt vectors. The

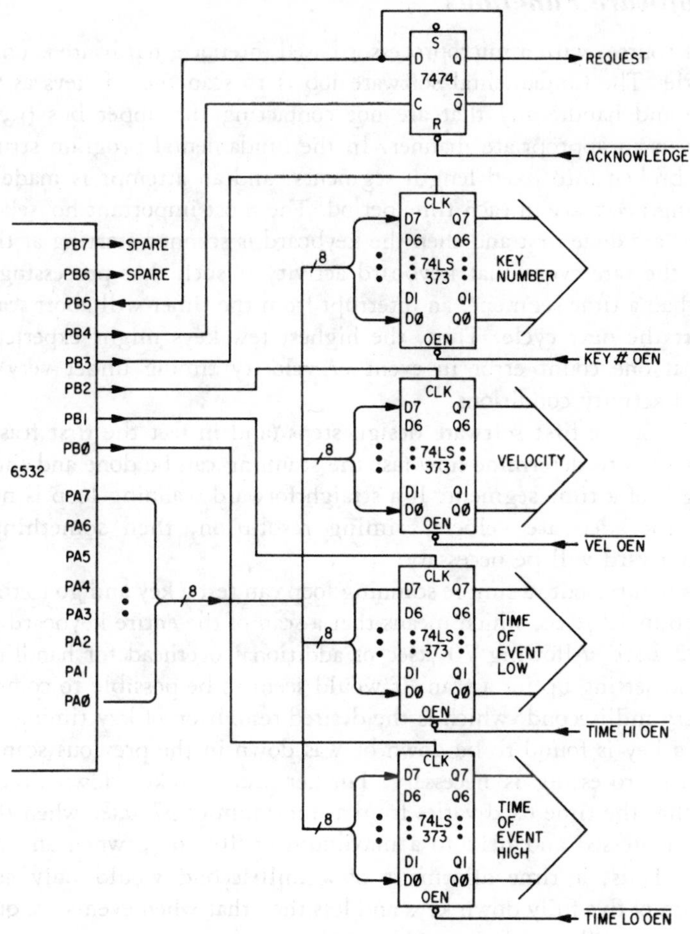

Fig. 9–6. Using system interface

128 bytes of RAM in the 6532 can be reached by both page zero and page one addresses, which allows both stack usage and convenient page zero addressing.

The remaining logic is shown in Fig. 9–6. The four-latch ICs are wired to 12 of the port bits on the 6532 as a simple output expansion (12 bits to 32 bits). The keyboard program can manipulate the data and clock inputs to the latches and thus exert complete control over their contents. The four groups of three-state outputs from the latches allow flexible and convenient interfacing to the using system. Two more of the port bits are used to control and sense the handshake flip-flop. The remaining 2 bits are available for expansion.

Software Functions

Of course, with a microprocessor-based interface, hardware is only half the battle. The fundamental software job is to scan the 61 keys as fast as possible and handle any that are not contacting the upper bus (i.e., depressed) in an appropriate manner. In the fundamental program structure, time is broken into fixed length segments, and an attempt is made to do everything necessary in each time period. The most important housekeeping functions are done first and then the keyboard is scanned starting at the low end. In the rare event that keyboard activity is such that processing takes longer than a time segment, an interrupt from the timer will abort scanning and start the next cycle. Thus, the highest few keys might experience an occasional one count error in event or velocity timing under very heavy keyboard activity conditions.

One of the first software design steps (and in fact the first feasibility study step) is to determine how fast the scanning can be done and therefore the length of a time segment. If a straightforward scanning loop is not fast enough for adequate velocity timing resolution, then something less straightforward will be necessary.

As it turns out, a simple scanning loop can test a key and go to the next if it is up in 12 μsec, which means that a scan of the entire keyboard would take 732 μsec. Allowing 70 μsec of additional overhead for handling the timer and setting up for a scan, it would seem to be possible to complete a scan every millisecond, which is the desired resolution of key timing. However, if a key is found to be down or was down in the previous scan, then additional processing is necessary. Further study of key-down processing reveals that the time used varies from a minimum of 37 μsec when the key is fully depressed and held to a maximum of 100 μsec when an event is queued. Thus, a time allotment of a millisecond would only cover a maximum of five fully down keys and less than that when events are queued, which is not really satisfactory. Although several courses of action are possible (2-MHz version of 6502 or external hardware to make key scanning faster), for this example the scan period will be increased to 1.28 msec. Velocity timing will therefore have a resolution of 1.28 msec, which is adequate when compared with normal variation in the velocity time differential.

Software Flowchart

An overall program flowchart is given in Fig. 9–7. When power is first applied or after a reset, all of the important program variables are initialized and then the main loop is entered. In the loop, the "time of day" is updated first taking into account the 1.28-msec update interval and 1.0-msec time of day units. Next the queue of events is checked. If an event is in the queue, then a check is made to determine if the previous event is still awaiting

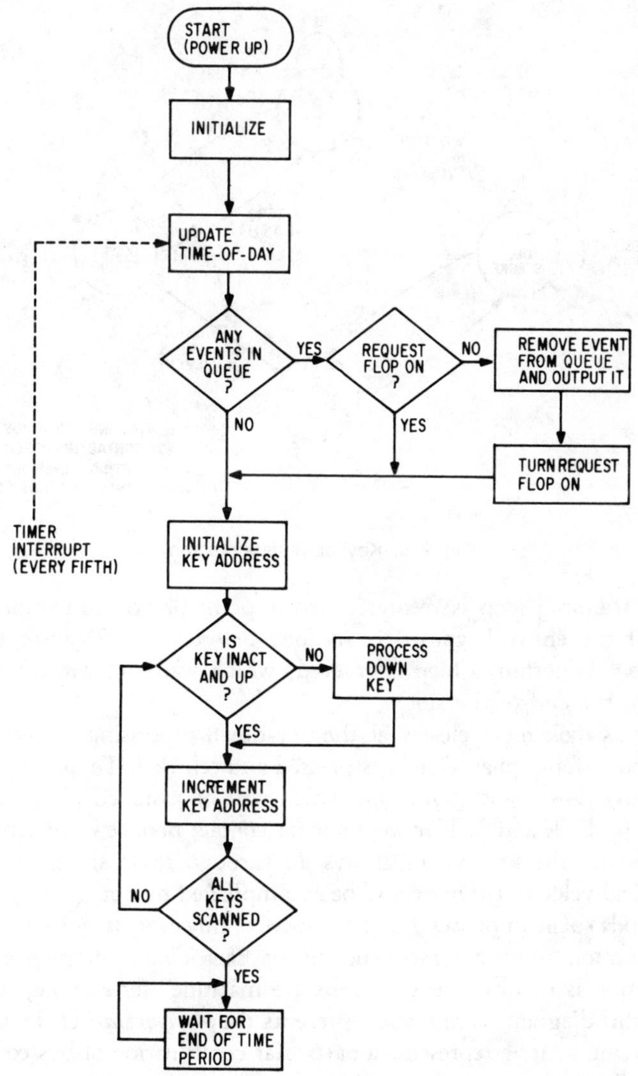

Fig. 9-7. Overall program flow

action by the host system. If so, the event is left in the queue and the program continues. Otherwise, the event is removed from the queue, put into the output ports, and deleted from the queue.

Key scanning is next. Each key is tested to determine if it is contacting the upper bus and had been previously as well. If not, an exit from the scanning loop is taken to process the active key. Key-down processing looks at the previous "state" of the key and decides whether to start or continue a velocity count, queue an event, or just do nothing. After key-down process-

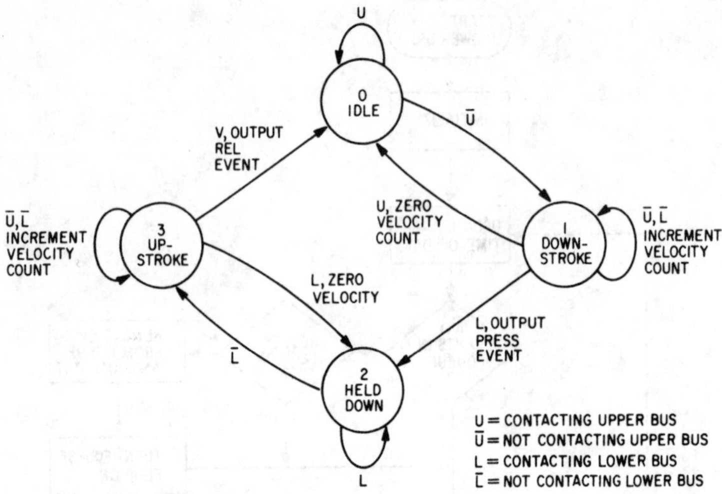

Fig. 9–8. Keyboard state diagram

ing, the scanning loop is reentered at the point of exit and scanning continues. If the entire keyboard is scanned before the 1.28-msec time slot elapses, a "do-nothing" loop is entered, which waits for a timer interrupt signifying the end of the slot.

Let us look more closely at the key-down processing. A key actually goes through four "phases" as it is pressed and released. These are up, going down, fully down, and going up, which will be assigned phase or "state" numbers 0, 1, 2, and 3. If it were not for contact bounce or possible sloppy playing style, the key would always go through these states in strict sequence, and velocity timing could be accomplished by noting the number of scan periods spent in phases 1 and 3. Bounce, however, is quite real, so it is not uncommon for the state sequence to "backtrack" and complicate matters. The solution is to simulate a "finite state machine" for *each* key as in Fig. 9–8. In this diagram, each circle represents the *previous state* of the key. Each arrow leaving a circle represents a particular combination of bus contacts for the key. Every possible combination of previous state and bus contact has such an arrow, which points to what the *next* state of the key will be. Some arrows also specify an action to be performed. For example, State 1 has three outgoing arrows even though one of them reenters the same state. If the previous state was 1 and the lower bus is contacted by the key under consideration, then the next state is 2 and a press event is generated. Likewise, if neither bus is contacted, then the next state is also 1 and the velocity count is incremented.

It is easy to see how contact bounce is taken care of by studying the diagram. Bounce while the upper contact is opening on the downstroke may cause the traversal from 0 to 1 and back to 0 several times. Each time contact with the upper bus is remade the velocity count is reset. Finally, however, the bouncing stops and the State 1 looparound increments the velocity counter on each scan cycle. The very first time contact with the lower bus is seen, a press event is generated using the accumulated velocity count. Thus, the desired timing from *last* upper bounce to *first* lower bounce is implemented. An exactly analogous sequence occurs when the key is released. Note that simultaneous contact with both upper and lower buses is physically impossible and therefore not accounted for in the diagram.

Program Description

A complete, assembled program listing for the keyboard is given in Fig. 9–9. Looking at RAM memory allocation first, it is seen that nearly half of it is devoted to saving information about the state of each key. The low 2 bits of each byte are used to hold the state number, while the upper 6 bits are used as a velocity counter. The entire state byte is 0 if a key is inactive. Thirty-two more bytes are used to implement an event queue, which allows up to seven events to be stacked up before overflow. Five bytes are used to

```
0000          ;         MUSIC KEYBOARD CONTROL PROGRAM
0000          ;         THIS EXAMPLE PROGRAM SCANS A 61 NOTE VELOCITY SENSITIVE MUSIC
0000          ;         KEYBOARD AND FORMATS THE SIGNIFICANT EVENTS INTO 4 BYTE GROUPS
0000          ;         FOR USE BY A HOST MICROCOMPUTER SYSTEM.
0000
0000          ;         DEVICE AND MEMORY ADDRESSES
0000
0000  =   PORAM   =      $0000          ; FIRST PAGE 0 RAM LOCATION
0080  =   PAREG   =      $0080          ; 6532 I/O PORT A DATA REGISTER
0081  =   PADIR   =      $0081          ; 6532 I/O PORT A DIRECTION REGISTER
0082  =   PBREG   =      $0082          ; 6532 I/O PORT B DATA REGISTER
0083  =   PBDIR   =      $0083          ; 6532 I/O PORT B DIRECTION REGISTER
009C  =   TMWRI   =      $009C          ; 6532 TIMER WRITE, /1, ENABLE TIMER INTERRUPT
008C  =   TMRD    =      $008C          ; 6532 TIMER READ, LEAVE INTERRUPT ENABLED
0100  =   P1RAM   =      $0100          ; FIRST PAGE 1 RAM LOCATION (IS SAME 128
0000                                    ; BYTES AS PORAM
0400  =   MKYBU   =      $0400          ; BASE ADDRESS OF MUSIC KEYBOARD UPPER BUS
0440  =   MKYBL   =      $0440          ; BASE ADDRESS OF MUSIC KEYBOARD LOWER BUS
FC00  =   ROM     =      $FC00          ; FIRST LOCATION IN 1K EPROM
0000
0000          ;         RAM MEMORY ALLOCATION
0000
0000                    *=   PORAM
0000      MKYBST        *=*+ 61         ; SPACE FOR THE CURRENT STATE OF 61 KEYS
003D      QUIP          *=*+ 1          ; EVENT QUEUE INPUT POINTER
003E      QUOP          *=*+ 1          ; EVENT QUEUE OUTPUT POINTER
003F      EVQU          *=*+ 32         ; SPACE TO QUEUE UP TO 7 EVENTS
005F      TIME          *=*+ 3          ; ELAPSED TIME IN MILLISECONDS SINCE TURNON
0062      TIMEF         *=*+ 2          ; FRACTIONAL PART OF ELAPSED TIME
0064      TIMCNT        *=*+ 1          ; 5 COUNTER FOR TIMER INTERRUPTS
0065      VCJPPT        *=*+ 2          ; INDIRECT POINTER FOR VECTOR JUMP
0067
0067          ;         INITIALIZATION
0067
0067                    *=   ROM        ; START AT BEGINNING OF ROM
```

Fig. 9–9. Listing of keyboard control program

```
FC00 D8      INIT   CLD                  ; SET BINARY ARITHMETIC MODE
FC01 A280           LDX  #$80            ; INITIALIZE STACK POINTER TO END OF PAGE 1
FC03 9A             TXS                  ; RAM
FC04 A9FF           LDA  #$FF            ; SET DATA DIRECTION REGISTERS ON 6532
FC06 8581           STA  PADIR           ; PORT A TO ALL OUTPUTS
FC08 A91F           LDA  #$1F            ; PORT B BITS 0-4 TO OUTPUTS, REMAINDER TO
FC0A 8583           STA  PBDIR           ; INPUTS
FC0C A9FF           LDA  #VCJPTB/256     ; INITIALIZE UPPER BYTE OF VECTOR JUMP
FC0E 8566           STA  VCJPPT+1        ; POINTER
FC10 A905           LDA  #5              ; INITIALIZE TIMER INTERRUPT COUNT
FC12 8564           STA  TIMCNT
FC14 A9FF           LDA  #255            ; START TIMER, SET FOR 255 MICROSECONDS
FC16 859C           STA  TMWRI           ; AND ENABLE TIMER INTERRUPT
FC18 58             CLI                  ; ENABLE INTERRUPT SYSTEM
FC19
FC19         ;      MAIN PROGRAM LOOP
FC19
FC19 A562    MLOOP  LDA  TIMEF           ; ADD 1+18350/65536 MILLISECONDS TO ELAPSED
FC1B 18             CLC                  ; TIME
FC1C 69AE           ADC  #18350&$FF      ; FIRST DO FRACTIONAL PART
FC1E 8562           STA  TIMEF
FC20 A563           LDA  TIMEF+1
FC22 6947           ADC  #18350/256
FC24 8563           STA  TIMEF+1
FC26 A55F           LDA  TIME            ; THEN INTEGER PART
FC28 6901           ADC  #1
FC2A 855F           STA  TIME
FC2C 9006           BCC  QUCK
FC2E E660           INC  TIME+1          ; CARRY THROUGH HIGH TWO BYTES
FC30 D002           BNE  QUCK
FC32 E661           INC  TIME+2
FC34 A63E    QUCK   LDX  QUOP            ; TEST IF ANYTHING IN THE EVENT QUEUE
FC36 E43D           CPX  QUIP
FC38 F03E           BEQ  KYSCN           ; GO TO KEY SCAN IF NOT
FC3A A582           LDA  PBREG           ; TEST IF I/O WAITING ON HOST
FC3C 2920           AND  #$20
FC3E D038           BNE  KYSCN           ; GO TO KEY SCAN IF SO
FC40 A000           LDY  #0              ; DEQUEUE AN EVENT AND OUTPUT IT IF NOT
FC42 B53F           LDA  EVQU,X          ; KEY ID
FC44 8580           STA  PAREG
FC46 A908           LDA  #$08            ; STROBE IT INTO I/O REGISTER
FC48 8582           STA  PBREG
FC4A 8482           STY  PBREG
FC4C B540           LDA  EVQU+1,X        ; VELOCITY
FC4E 8580           STA  PAREG
FC50 A904           LDA  #$04
FC52 8582           STA  PBREG
FC54 8482           STY  PBREG
FC56 B541           LDA  EVQU+2,X        ; TIME OF EVENT LOW
FC58 8580           STA  PAREG
FC5A A902           LDA  #$02
FC5C 8582           STA  PBREG
FC5E 8482           STY  PBREG
FC60 B542           LDA  EVQU+3,X        ; TIME OF EVENT HIGH
FC62 8580           STA  PAREG
FC64 A901           LDA  #$01
FC66 8582           STA  PBREG
FC68 8482           STY  PBREG
FC6A A910           LDA  #$10            ; SET THE REQUEST FLIP-FLOP
FC6C 8582           STA  PBREG
FC6E 8482           STY  PBREG
FC70 8A             TXA                  ; MOVE QUEUE OUTPUT POINTER UP 1 NOTCH
FC71 18             CLC
FC72 6904           ADC  #4
```

Fig. 9–9. Listing of keyboard control program (*cont.*)

```
FC74 291F                AND  #$1F           ; WITH WRAPAROUND FOR 32 BYTES OF QUEUE
FC76 853E                STA  QUOP
FC78
FC78          ;          SCAN THE KEYBOARD. SCAN LOOP IS EXPANDED BY 4 FOR GREATER SPEED
FC78
FC78 A03C     KYSCN      LDY  #60            ; INITIALIZE KEY ADDRESS
FC7A D01B                BNE  KYSCN4         ; ENTER EXPANDED LOOP AT PROPER PLACE
FC7C B90004   KYSCN1     LDA  MKYBU,Y        ; GET UPPER BUS CONTACT INDICATION
FC7F 190000              ORA  MKYBST,Y       ; COMBINE WITH PREVIOUS KEY STATE
FC82 D020                BNE  KYPROC         ; BRANCH IF ACTION REQUIRED
FC84 88       KYSCNA     DEY                 ; DECREMENT KEY ADDRESS
FC85 B90004   KYSCN2     LDA  MKYBU,Y        ; REPEAT FOR NEXT KEY
FC88 190000              ORA  MKYBST,Y
FC8B D017                BNE  KYPROC
FC8D 88       KYSCNB     DEY
FC8E B90004   KYSCN3     LDA  MKYBU,Y        ; REPEAT FOR NEXT KEY
FC91 190000              ORA  MKYBST,Y
FC94 D00E                BNE  KYPROC
FC96 88       KYSCNC     DEY
FC97 B90004   KYSCN4     LDA  MKYBU,Y        ; REPEAT FOR NEXT KEY
FC9A 190000              ORA  MKYBST,Y
FC9D D005                BNE  KYPROC
FC9F 88       KYSCND     DEY                 ; DECREMENT KEY ADDRESS AND TEST IF DONE
FCA0 10DA                BPL  KYSCN1         ; GO SCAN MORE KEYS IF NOT FINISHED
FCA2 30FE     KYSCN5     BMI  KYSCN5         ; WAIT FOR TIMER INTERRUPT
FCA4
FCA4          ;          BASED ON PREVIOUS KEY STATE DISPATCH TO CORRECT KEY PROCESSING
FCA4
FCA4 2903     KYPROC     AND  #$03           ; ISOLATE STATE NUMBER
FCA6 0A                  ASL  A              ; SET UP VECTOR JUMP
FCA7 0A                  ASL  A
FCA8 8565                STA  VCJPPT
FCAA 6C6500              JMP  (VCJPPT)       ; DO THE VECTOR JUMP
FCAD
FCAD          ;          RE-ENTER THE SCAN LOOP AT THE PROPER PLACE BASED ON KEY ADDRESS
FCAD
FCAD 98       SCNREN     TYA                 ; GET LOW 2 BITS OF KEY ADDRESS IN CARRY
FCAE 6A                  ROR  A              ; AND SIGN FLAGS
FCAF 6A                  ROR  A
FCB0 1004                BPL  SCNRE1         ; REMAINDER OF (KEY ADDRESS)/4
FCB2 B0EB                BCS  KYSCND         ; 3
FCB4 90D7                BCC  KYSCNB         ; 1
FCB6 B0DE     SCNRE1     BCS  KYSCNC         ; 2
FCB8 90CA                BCC  KYSCNA         ; 0
FCBA
FCBA          ;          KEY STATE PROCESSING ROUTINES
FCBA
FCBA A901     STAT0      LDA  #1             ; SET THE STATE TO 1 AND ZERO THE VELOCITY
FCBC 990000              STA  MKYBST,Y       ; COUNT
FCBF D0EC                BNE  SCNREN         ; RE-ENTER SCANNING LOOP
FCC1
FCC1
FCC1 B90004   STAT1      LDA  MKYBU,Y        ; TEST KEY CONTACT WITH UPPER BUS
FCC4 3005                BMI  STAT1A         ; JUMP IF NOT CONTACTING IT
FCC6 990000              STA  MKYBST,Y       ; CLEAR KEY STATE TO 0 (INACTIVE) IF
FCC9 F0E2                BEQ  SCNREN         ; CONTACTING IT AND RE-ENTER SCAN LOOP
FCCB B94004   STAT1A     LDA  MKYBL,Y        ; TEST KEY CONTACT WITH LOWER BUS
FCCE 100F                BPL  STAT1C         ; JUMP IF CONTACTING IT
FCD0 B90000              LDA  MKYBST,Y       ; IF NOT, GET KEY STATE AND INCREMENT THE
FCD3 18                  CLC                 ; VELOCITY COUNT
FCD4 6904                ADC  #4
FCD6 9002                BCC  STAT1B         ; SKIP IF NO OVERFLOW
FCD8 E904                SBC  #4             ; RESTORE MAX VELOCITY COUNT IF OVERFLOW
FCDA 990000   STAT1B     STA  MKYBST,Y
```

Fig. 9–9. Listing of keyboard control program (*cont.*)

```
FCDD DOCE           BNE  SCNREN        ; RE-ENTER SCAN LOOP
FCDF 98     STAT1C  TYA                ; OUTPUT A KEY PRESS EVENT
FCE0 0980           ORA  #$80          ; FIRST BYTE = KEY ID NUMBER, DEPRESS
FCE2 78             SEI                ; DISABLE TIMER INTERRUPT WHILE QUEUEING
FCE3 A63D           LDX  QUIP          ; GET QUEUE INPUT POINTER
FCE5 953F           STA  EVQU,X        ; STORE FIRST BYTE
FCE7 B90000         LDA  MKYBST,Y      ; GET KEY STATE
FCEA 4A             LSR  A             ; ISOLATE AND RIGHT JUSTIFY VELOCITY COUNT
FCEB 4A             LSR  A
FCEC 9540           STA  EVQU+1,X      ; OUTPUT AS SECOND BYTE OF EVENT
FCEE A55F           LDA  TIME          ; GET LOW BYTE OF TIME
FCF0 9541           STA  EVQU+2,X      ; OUTPUT AS THIRD BYTE
FCF2 A560           LDA  TIME+1        ; GET HIGH BYTE OF TIME
FCF4 9542           STA  EVQU+3,X      ; OUTPUT AS FOURTH BYTE
FCF6 8A             TXA                ; MOVE QUEUE INPUT POINTER UP 1 NOTCH
FCF7 18             CLC
FCF8 6904           ADC  #4
FCFA 291F           AND  #$1F          ; WITH WRAPAROUND
FCFC 853D           STA  QUIP
FCFE 58             CLI                ; RE-ENABLE INTERRUPTS
FCFF A902           LDA  #2            ; SET KEY STATE TO 2
FD01 990000         STA  MKYBST,Y
FD04 D0A7           BNE  SCNREN        ; RESUME SCANNING
FD06
FD06
FD06 B94004 STAT2   LDA  MKYBL,Y       ; TEST KEY CONTACT WITH LOWER BUS
FD09 10A2           BPL  SCNREN        ; RESUME SCANNING IF IN CONTACT
FD0B A903           LDA  #3            ; SET THE STATE TO 3 AND ZERO VELOCITY
FD0D 990000         STA  MKYBST,Y      ; COUNT IF NO CONTACT
FD10 D09B           BNE  SCNREN        ; AND RESUME SCANNING
FD12
FD12
FD12 B94004 STAT3   LDA  MKYBL,Y       ; TEST KEY CONTACT WITH LOWER BUS
FD15 3007           BMI  STAT3A        ; JUMP IF NOT CONTACTING IT
FD17 A902           LDA  #2            ; SET STATE TO 2 AND CLEAR VELOCITY COUNT
FD19 990000         STA  MKYBST,Y      ; IF CONTACTING LOWER BUS
FD1C D08F           BNE  SCNREN        ; RE-ENTER SCAN LOOP
FD1E B90004 STAT3A  LDA  MKYBU,Y       ; TEST KEY CONTACT WITH UPPER BUS
FD21 1010           BPL  STAT3C        ; JUMP IF CONTACTING IT
FD23 B90000         LDA  MKYBST,Y      ; IF NOT, GET KEY STATE AND INCREMENT THE
FD26 18             CLC                ; VELOCITY COUNT
FD27 6904           ADC  #4
FD29 9002           BCC  STAT3B        ; SKIP IF NO OVERFLOW
FD2B E904           SBC  #4            ; RESTORE MAX VELOCITY COUNT IF OVERFLOW
FD2D 990000 STAT3B  STA  MKYBST,Y
FD30 4CADFC         JMP  SCNREN        ; RE-ENTER SCAN LOOP
FD33 78     STAT3C  SEI                ; DISABLE TIMER INPURRUPT WHILE QUEUEING
FD34 A63D           LDX  QUIP          ; OUTPUT AN EVENT, GET QUEUE INPUT POINTER
FD36 943F           STY  EVQU,X        ; STORE FIRST BYTE = KEY ID NUMBER, RELEASE
FD38 B90000         LDA  MKYBST,Y      ; GET KEY STATE
FD3B 4A             LSR  A             ; ISOLATE AND RIGHT JUSTIFY VELOCITY COUNT
FD3C 4A             LSR  A
FD3D 9540           STA  EVQU+1,X      ; OUTPUT AS SECOND BYTE OF EVENT
FD3F A55F           LDA  TIME          ; GET LOW BYTE OF TIME
FD41 9541           STA  EVQU+2,X      ; OUTPUT AS THIRD BYTE
FD43 A560           LDA  TIME+1        ; GET HIGH BYTE OF TIME
FD45 9542           STA  EVQU+3,X      ; OUTPUT AS FOURTH BYTE
FD47 8A             TXA                ; MOVE QUEUE INPUT POINTER UP 1 NOTCH
FD48 18             CLC
FD49 6904           ADC  #4
FD4B 291F           AND  #$1F          ; WITH WRAPAROUND
FD4D 853D           STA  QUIP
FD4F 58             CLI                ; RE-ENABLE INTERRUPTS
FD50 A900           LDA  #0            ; SET KEY STATE TO 0 (INACTIVE)
```

Fig. 9–9. Listing of keyboard control program (*cont.*)

```
FD52 990000          STA  MKYBST,Y
FD55 4CADFC          JMP  SCNREN         ; RESUME SCANNING
FD58
FD58        ;        PROCESS TIMER INTERRUPT
FD58
FD58 C58C   TIMINT   CMP  TMRD           ; CLEAR THE TIMER INTERRUPT REQUEST
FD5A C664            DEC  TIMCNT         ; TEST IF FIFTH TIMER INTERRUPT
FD5C F001            BEQ  TIMIN1         ; SKIP AHEAD IF SO
FD5E 40              RTI                 ; IF NOT, RETURN FROM INTERRUPT
FD5F A905   TIMIN1   LDA  #5             ; RESET 5 INTERRUPT COUNTER
FD61 8564            STA  TIMCNT
FD63 68              PLA                 ; CLEAN OFF STACK FROM INTERRUPT SEQUENCE
FD64 68              PLA
FD65 68              PLA
FD66 4C19FC          JMP  MLOOP          ; GO TO MAIN LOOP FOR ANOTHER TIME PERIOD
FD69
FD69        ;        INDIRECT JUMP TABLE FOR STATE PROCESSING
FD69
FD69                 *=   $FF00          ; TABLE MUST START ON A PAGE BOUNDARY
FF00 4CBAFC VCJPTB   JMP  STAT0          ; GO TO STATE 0 PROCESSING
FF03 00              .BYTE 0             ; 1 BYTE PAD SO THAT VECTOR ENTRY ADDRESSES
FF04                                     ; ARE DIVISIBLE BY 4
FF04 4CC1FC          JMP  STAT1          ; GO TO STATE 1
FF07 00              .BYTE 0
FF08 4C06FD          JMP  STAT2          ; GO TO STATE 2
FF0B 00              .BYTE 0
FF0C 4C12FD          JMP  STAT3          ; GO TO STATE 3
FF0F
FF0F        ;        MACHINE INTERRUPT AND RESET VECTORS
FF0F
FF0F                 *=   $FFFA
FFFA 0000            .WORD 0             ; NON-MASKABLE INTERRUPT, NOT USED
FFFC 00FC            .WORD INIT          ; RESET, GO TO INITIALIZATION ROUTINE
FFFE 58FD            .WORD TIMINT        ; MASKABLE INTERRUPT, GO TO TIMER SERVICE
0000                                     ; ROUTINE
0000                 .END
  0 ERRORS IN PASS 2
```

Fig. 9–9. Listing of keyboard control program (*cont.*)

store the time of day in such a format that the most significant three bytes give it in units of milliseconds. The remainder is used for miscellaneous temporary storage and the processor stack.

A word should be said about how the timer is actually handled in the program. The timer in the 6532 is really intended for use as an *interval* timer and what is needed for the keyboard program is an interrupting *oscillator* with a 1.28-msec period. Fortunately, the timer can be set up as an oscillator, but the only period available in that mode is 256 μsec. Thus, the timer service routine maintains a counter and on every *fifth* interrupt a new scan starts and the time of day is updated. In order for the time of day to be in exact millisecond units when the update interval is 1.28 msec, binary fractional arithmetic is utilized to add $1.476E_{16}$ to the time of day, which is equal to 1.28_{10} to an accuracy of 0.0005%. Thus, timing is as accurate as the crystal used to clock the 6502.

The event queue is a classic circular queue, which is quite simple to handle. An *input pointer* always points to the first available queue slot, while an *output pointer* designates the first slot that contains valid data. If both pointers point to the same slot, the queue is empty and no data is available. After a deposit or withdrawal from the queue, the pointers are incremented by four, since each event requires four bytes. Wraparound of the circular queue from end to beginning is implemented by masking the queue pointers so that they can never contain a value larger than 31. No test is made for a full queue so if more than seven events are stacked up due to nonresponse from the host, they will be lost. Timer interrupts are disabled during queue operations, but since the timer is an oscillator, no timing errors accumulate.

Actual scanning of the keyboard is slightly unconventional due to the need for high speed. Since the vast majority of keys will be inactive, the scan loop is made as efficient as possible for that case. Also the scanning loop is *expanded* by a factor of four to decrease the time per key from 15 μsec to an average of 12.25 μsec for a total savings of 167 μsec. Any key that is not both in State 0 and contacting the upper bus causes a *vector jump* to the appropriate processing routine, which is based on the 2-bit state code kept for each key. Since a vector *jump* is used to get to the processing routine, returning to the proper point in the expanded scan loop is a little tricky but quite fast. The state processing routines themselves simply implement the state diagram of Fig. 9–8. Note the convenience of indexed addressing where the key number currently being considered is always kept in the Y register and can be used to *directly* access contact status as well as the state byte for the current key.

MIDI

One of the central issues raised by the use of a separate keyboard microprocessor is the communication of keystroke data between the keyboard and the synthesizer's processor. The method just described is highly efficient and cost-effective when both ends of the interface (the keyboard and the synthesizer) are under the builder's control. The same would be the case with a manufacturer of keyboard-driven, microprocessor-controlled synthesizers who makes both the keyboard and the synthesizer. Of course, in these cases, each interface and data format design would probably be different as the designer attempts to optimize cost and performance to the problem at hand.

Recently, however, users of commercial keyboard synthesizers have shown increased interest in connecting them together so that keystrokes on one synthesizer could also trigger sounds in another synthesizer from a *different manufacturer*. Additionally, a demand has developed for keyboards purchasable separately from the synthesizer and keyboardless "expander" synthesizers that can increase the number of voices available from a stock synthesizer. Separate digital sequencers capable of recording a sequence directly from a keyboard and later playing it through a synthesizer have also become available. Many owners of personal microcomputers would like to

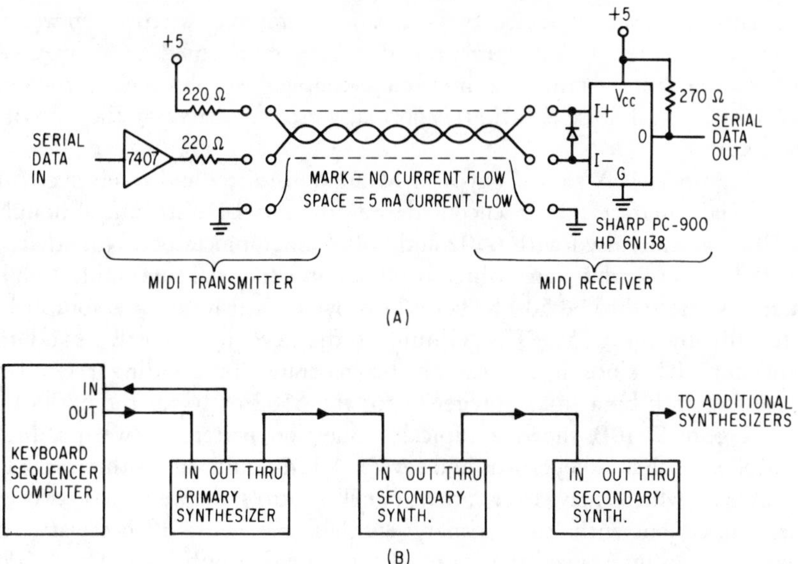

Fig. 9–10. (A) MIDI electrical interface. (B) Typical MIDI chained network

drive an external commercial synthesizer without designing and building an interface. Realization of these and other connection possibilities requires some sort of standard way of communicating keyboard information among units.

Enter MIDI, which is an acronym for Musical Instrument Digital Interface. Unlike most computer standards, which are "defacto" (i.e., what the largest manufacturer does becomes the standard by default), it is a synthesizer industry-wide cooperative standard that was developed before there was a pressing need for it. In its basic form, it allows the transmission of keystroke information from a keyboard, sequencer, or personal computer ("MIDI controller") to a group of synthesizers with relatively few problems. The standard also provides for transmission of panel control information (such as slidepot positions for various parameter settings) and even synthesizer setup and configuration information, although serious data compatibility problems are often encountered with these advanced functions due to synthesizer structural differences.

Electrically, data are transferred as a serial bit stream rather than by parallel transfer of whole bytes as in the previous example. The standard data rate is 31.25K bits/sec. which is very fast for serial data but much slower than parallel transfer. Ten bit times (32 μsec per bit) are required to transmit a byte including the usual start and stop bits but without parity so the total byte time is about ⅓ msec. Standard serial interface ICs easily handle the parallel-to-serial and serial-to-parallel conversion required. The signal itself is usually sent over a shielded twisted-pair of wires as a switched *current* with a one represented by no current and a zero represented by 5 mA. An optoisolator (a light-emitting diode close-coupled to a photocell in the same case for electrical noise isolation) is normally used for detecting the current at the receiver.

Figure 9–10A shows a typical MIDI transmitter and receiver circuit. Any serial interface IC can encode/decode the serial bit stream, although a 6850 is typically used with 6502 and 68000 microprocessors. Note that the 31.25 K bits/sec. data rate, which is not a standard serial communication bit rate, was selected to be 500 KHz divided by 16, which can be accomplished internally by the 6850. This eliminates the need for a costly "baud rate generator" IC, since it can usually be generated by dividing the microprocessor clock by a small integer (2 for the 6502 or 16 for the 68000).

Figure 9–10B shows a typical connection pattern between a MIDI controller, such as a keyboard, and several MIDI-equipped synthesizers. The controller, which may have other panel controls as well, has two-way communication with the primary synthesizer. Thus, if necessary, the controller can interrogate the status of the primary synthesizer. The "MIDI-thru" connection on each synthesizer simply provides a buffered copy of the signal received by the "MIDI-in" connector. Thus, data sent from the controller to the primary synthesizer can also be "heard" by the other synthesizers. Addressing information in the data bytes (called "channels" in MIDI terminology) determines which synthesizer acts on the data to produce sound.

The complete MIDI communication protocol is rather complex and subject to revision, so only its most basic provisions will be covered here. Readers desiring the full, current specification should check the Bibliography at the back of the book.

MIDI-equipped synthesizers operate in one of three communication *modes*. In "mono" mode, the 4 address bits associated with commands address actual oscillators or voices in the synthesizer. If one synthesizer has fewer than 16 voices, then two or more can be used up to a total of 16 voices. This mode offers the most flexibility because the MIDI controller can refer directly to voices, which may be patched quite differently, by number. "Poly" mode, which is most useful for live performance keyboard playing, generally assigns each synthesizer in the chain to one channel addresses. Each synthesizer will then only respond to MIDI commands addressed to its channel. If the synthesizer is indeed polyphonic (has several voices), then it is capable of receiving several keystrokes at once, which *it* assigns to internal voices according to whatever its key assignment algorithm would be if a keyboard was connected directly. A synthesizer in "omni" mode in effect ignores the channel address and responds to everything in the MIDI command stream.

The MIDI data format itself is much like an 8-bit microprocessor instruction; there is an operation or *command* byte (inexplicably called a

Table 9–1. MIDI Command Summary

Command Bytes	*Description*
1001cccc 0kkkkkkk 0vvvvvvv	NOTE ON EVENT. cccc = 4-bit channel number. kkkkkkk = 7-bit key number where 60 (decimal) is middle C. vvvvvvv = 7-bit key-down velocity where 0 is slow and 127 is fast. Use 64 if the keyboard is not velocity sensitive.
1000cccc 0kkkkkkk 0vvvvvvv	NOTE OFF EVENT. cccc and kkkkkkk fields are as for NOTE On. vvvvvvv = 7-bit key-up velocity.
1010cccc 0kkkkkkk 0ppppppp	NOTE PRESSURE UPDATE. cccc and kkkk fields are as for Note On. ppppppp = 7-bit pressure value for key kkkkkkk, 0 is light and 127 is heavy. This command is sent every 10–50 msec. It need not be sent if the keyboard has no pressure sensors.
1101cccc 0ppppppp	CHANNEL PRESSURE UPDATE. Used in mono mode. Updates the pressure parameter in voice cccc. ppppppp is as for Note Pressure Update.
1011cccc 0ddddddd 0vvvvvvv	CONTROL CHANGE. Used to change internal variables of synthesizer listening to channel cccc. ddddddd is 7-bit device (control) number as follows: 0-31 vvvvvvv is most significant 7 bits of value for control numbers 0-31. 32-63 vvvvvvv is least significant 7 bits of value for control numbers 0-31. 64-95 vvvvvvv is state (0=off, 127=on) of switch numbers 0-31. 96-127 miscellaneous synthesizer commands including mode (mono/poly/mono) select. vvvvvvv is ignored but must be present.
1110ccc 0hhhhhhh 01111111	PITCH WHEEL CHANGE. Used to change internal pitch wheel variable of synthesizer listening to channel cccc. hhhhhhh is most significant 7 bits of the new value and 1111111 is least significant 7 bits.
1100cccc 0ppppppp	PATCH CHANGE. Specifies that synthesizer listening to channel cccc should change to "patch" ppppppp. This is of course highly synthesizer dependent.

"status byte" in the standards document) followed by zero or more *data* bytes (Table 9–1). The command byte is always identified by having its most significant bit set to a one, while data bytes always have a zero there. Although this convention limits data values to 0–127 or −64 to +63, it completely prevents a permanent "out-of-sync" condition if a byte should be lost somewhere or an erroneous command code is received. In cases in which increased resolution is needed, two data bytes can be used to express values up to 16,383 or −8,192 to +8,191. Table 9–1 gives a brief summary of the commands and data formats useful in a keyboard interfacing situation. Note that in most cases, the most significant 3 bits of the command give the command code, while the least significant 4 bits is the channel address. The F command, which is not listed, provides for the transmission of system-dependent data that vary for different manufacturers.

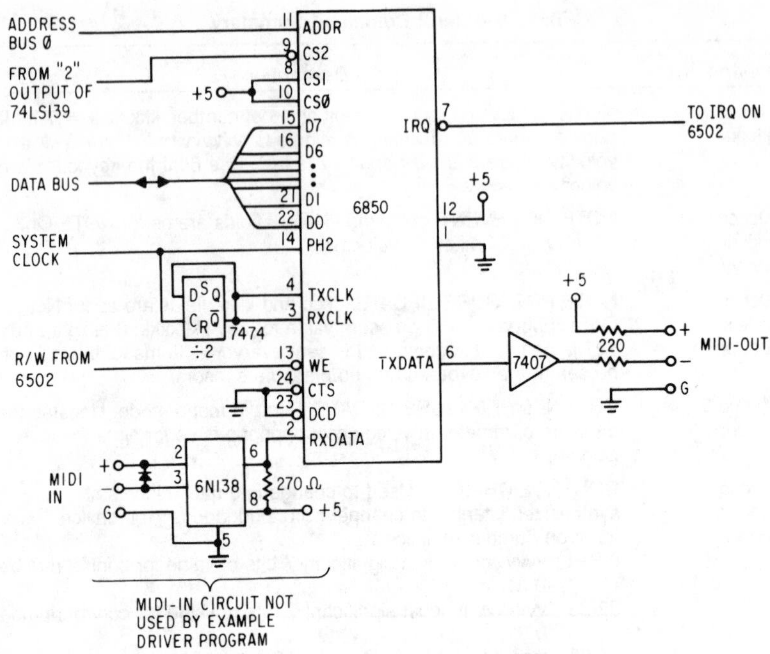

Fig. 9–11. Keyboard addition for MIDI

Figure 9–11 shows a circuit that may be added to the music keyboard interface example to implement a MIDI interface. It uses a 6850 serial I/O chip, which costs substantially less than $5. Its three internal registers (one read-only, one write-only, and one read/write) are addressed at 0800 and 0801 hexadecimal, which were previously unused.

Softwarewise, it is relatively easy to modify the keyboard program to output MIDI keyboard data instead of the parallel format described earlier. The STAT1C routine would be modified to output a MIDI "press" event and STAT3C would output a "release" event. Since MIDI does not use time of press and release information, the code at MLOOP for updating the time of day can be omitted. For maximum speed in outputting MIDI data, the timer-interrupt service routine, which is entered every 256 μsec, should check the serial I/O chip and queue instead of the main loop at QUCK as before. The affected code has been rewritten in Fig. 9–12.

Improvements

The keyboard just described is not the last word by any means. Another fairly easily obtainable contact arrangement is called a "second-touch" keyboard. With normal playing pressure, it behaves just like a conventional keyboard. However, additional pressure at the end of the stroke causes the

```
SERCTL  =    $0800           ; 6850 SERIAL I/O CHIP CONTROL REGISTER
SERSTS  =    $0800           ; 6850 STATUS REGISTER
SERDTA  =    $0801           ; 6850 TRANSMIT AND RECEIVE DATA REGISTER

------------------------------

INIT    LDA  #$17            ; INITIALIZE 6850 SERIAL I/O CHIP
        STA  SERCTL
        LDA  #$15
        STA  SERCTL

------------------------------

STAT1C  SEI                  ; DISABLE INTERRUPTS WHILE STORING EVENT
        LDX  QUIP            ; OUTPUT AN EVENT, GET QUEUE INPUT POINTER
        LDA  #$90            ; KEY DOWN EVENT ON MIDI CHANNEL MIDICH
        ORA  MIDICH
        STA  EVQU,X          ; STORE IN QUEUE
        INX                  ; INCREMENT QUEUE POINTER
        CPX  #$20            ; WRAPAROUND THE POINTER IF NECESSARY
        BNE  STAT1D
        LDX  #0
STAT1D  TYA                  ; GET KEY NUMBER
        CLC                  ; ADJUST TO MIDI STANDARD OF 60=MIDDLE C
        ADC  #60-24          ; THIS GIVES 2 OCTAVES BELOW AND 3 ABOVE
        STA  EVQU,X          ; STORE RESULT IN QUEUE
        INX                  ; INCREMENT AND WRAPAROUND QUEUE POINTER
        CPX  #$20
        BNE  STAT1E
        LDX  #0
STAT1E  STX  QUIP            ; SAVE QUEUE POINTER TEMPORARILY
        LDA  MKYBST,Y        ; GET VELOCITY COUNT, RANGE 0-63
        LSR  A
        LSR  A
        TAX                  ; LOOKUP APPROPRIATE MIDI VELOCITY
        LDA  VELTAB,X        ; IN A TABLE
        LDX  QUIP            ; RESTORE QUEUE POINTER
        STA  EVQU,X          ; STORE THE VELOCITY IN THE QUEUE
        INX                  ; INCREMENT AND WRAPAROUND QUEUE POINTER
        CPX  #$20
        BNE  STAT1F
        LDX  #0
STAT1F  STA  QUIP            ; STORE THE UPDATED QUEUE POINTER
        CLI                  ; RE-ENABLE INTERRUPTS
        LDA  #2              ; SET KEY STATE TO 2
        STA  MKYBST,Y
        JMP  SCNREN          ; RESUME SCANNING

------------------------------

STAT3C  SEI                  ; DISABLE INTERRUPTS WHILE STORING EVENT
        LDX  QUIP            ; OUTPUT AN EVENT, GET QUEUE INPUT POINTER
        LDA  #$80            ; KEY UP EVENT ON MIDI CHANNEL MIDICH
        ORA  MIDICH
        STA  EVQU,X          ; STORE IN QUEUE
        INX                  ; INCREMENT QUEUE POINTER
        CPX  #$20            ; WRAPAROUND THE POINTER IF NECESSARY
        BNE  STAT3D
        LDX  #0
STAT3D  TYA                  ; GET KEY NUMBER
        CLC                  ; ADJUST TO MIDI STANDARD
        ADC  #60-24
        STA  EVQU,X          ; STORE RESULT IN QUEUE
        INX                  ; INCREMENT AND WRAPAROUND QUEUE POINTER
        CPX  #$20
        BNE  STAT3E
        LDX  #0
STAT3E  STX  QUIP            ; SAVE QUEUE POINTER TEMPORARILY
        LDA  MKYBST,Y        ; GET VELOCITY COUNT, RANGE 0-63
        LSR  A
        LSR  A
        TAX                  ; LOOKUP APPROPRIATE MIDI VELOCITY
        LDA  VELTAB,X        ; IN A TABLE
        LDX  QUIP            ; RESTORE QUEUE POINTER
        STA  EVQU,X          ; STORE THE VELOCITY IN THE QUEUE
        INX                  ; INCREMENT AND WRAPAROUND QUEUE POINTER
        CPX  #$20
        BNE  STAT3F
        LDX  #0
STAT3F  STA  QUIP            ; STORE THE UPDATED QUEUE POINTER
        CLI                  ; RE-ENABLE INTERRUPTS
        LDA  #0              ; SET KEY STATE TO 0 (INACTIVE)
        STA  MKYBST,Y
        JMP  SCNREN          ; RESUME SCANNING
```

Fig. 9–12. Modified code segments for MIDI

```
------------------------------

TIMINT  CMP  TMRD          ; CLEAR THE TIMER INTERRUPT REQUEST
        PHA                ; SAVE A ON THE STACK
        LDA  SERSTS        ; CHECK 6850 TRANSMITTER STATUS
        AND  #$02
        BEQ  TIMIN1        ; JUMP AHEAD IF BUSY
        LDA  QUOP          ; IF FREE, TEST IF ANYTHING TO TRANSMIT
        CMP  QUIP
        BEQ  TIMIN1        ; JUMP AHEAD IF NOT
        TXA                ; IF SO, SAVE X
        PHA
        LDX  QUOP          ; AND GET THE QUEUE OUTPUT POINTER
        LDA  EVQU,X        ; GET NEXT BYTE TO TRANSMIT
        STA  SERDTA        ; AND TRANSMIT IT
        INX                ; MOVE QUEUE OUTPUT POINTER
        CPX  #$20          ; AND WRAPAROUND IF NECESSARY
        BNE  TIMIN0
        LDX  #0
TIMIN0  STX  QUOP          ; SAVE UPDATED QUEUE OUTPUT POINTER
        PLA                ; RESTORE X FROM THE STACK
        TAX                ; AND CONTINUE
TIMIN1  PLA                ; RESTORE A FROM STACK
        DEC  TIMCNT        ; TEST IF FIFTH TIMER INTERRUPT
        BEQ  TIMIN1        ; SKIP AHEAD IF SO
        RTI                ; IF NOT, RETURN FROM INTERRUPT
TIMIN1  LDA  #5            ; RESET 5 INTERRUPT COUNTER
        STA  TIMCNT
        PLA                ; CLEAN OFF STACK FROM INTERRUPT SEQUENCE
        PLA
        PLA
        JMP  MLOOP         ; GO TO MAIN LOOP FOR ANOTHER TIME PERIOD

------------------------------

VELTAB  .BYTE 127,127,127,127,127,117,96,81  ; MIDI VELOCITY TRANSLATE
        .BYTE 69,61,53,48,43,39,35,32        ; TABLE
        .BYTE 30,27,25,23,22,20,19,18        ; PREPARED FROM EQUATION:
        .BYTE 16,15,14,14,13,12,11,10        ; TABLE=(635/N)-10
        .BYTE 10,9,9,8,8,7,7,6               ; WILL PROBABLY NEED CHANGE
        .BYTE 6,5,5,5,4,4,4,4                ; TO BEST MATCH THE
        .BYTE 3,3,3,2,2,2,2,2                ; VELOCITY CONTROL OF THE
        .BYTE 1,1,1,1,1,0,0,0                ; SYNTHESIZER BEING USED
```

Fig. 9–12. Modified code segments for MIDI (*cont.*)

key to travel a bit more and make contact with a third bus. It should even be possible to couple the second-touch mechanism with the velocity-sensing mechanism just discussed and end up with a very versatile keyboard indeed.

Recently, *pressure-sensitive* keyboards have become available for the more sophisticated live-performance synthesizers. These typically use the same dual-contact arrangement to detect key-down and measure velocity but replace the usual felt bottoming pad with a conductive rubber pad. As key pressure increases, the area of contact between a ball-shaped metal protrusion on the key and the pad increases, thus reducing the contact resistance. A current source and multiplexed A-to-D converter scanned along with the keys then gives continuous pressure readings for all keys that are down. Typically, for every key that is down, the keyboard computer will send pressure reading updates to the host every 10–50 secs. Note that the MIDI protocol requires 3 byte times or 1 msec to send a single pressure update command so the impetus is toward longer update periods.

Most keyboard synthesizers (even if they don't have velocity and/or pressure sensing) also have a footpedal, which is usually rigged to control overall volume plus pitch and modulation "wheels" immediately to the left of the keybed. The latter are really just unusually smooth-acting slide pots that

Fig. 9–13. The Notebender™ keyboard in action

have a spring return to center feature. The pitch wheel simply detunes the instrument sharp or flat as it is moved, and the modulation wheel changes some other sound parameter according to how the synthesizer is set up. These controls are moderately useful but have the drawback of affecting all of the notes at once, and the two wheels tie up one of the playing hands.

To the players of nonkeyboard conventional instruments such as the violin or trumpet, a keyboard seems to be very restrictive in its expressive capability even when coupled with the most sophisticated synthesizer available. This problem has, in fact, been recognized for years, probably from the time of Bach when keyboard instruments really started to be used extensively. In the past, all kinds of alternate keyboard arrangements have been proposed to solve this problem including keys that move in more than one dimension. Although actually building the mechanics of such keyboards was not too difficult, only recently has electronic and microprocessor technology made it possible to translate each mechanical motion into a variation of a particular sound parameter. Velocity and pressure sensing are simple refinements that go a long way toward offering a live-keyboard player the control over dynamics taken for granted by players of nonkeyboard instruments.

One recent example of a multidimensional keyboard is design work being done by Robert Moog, inventor and popularizer of the modular analog synthesizer. The keyboard "keys" are actually just printed patterns on a plastic sheet overlay. The keys are pressure sensitive but do not actually move. The innovation is that the keyboard controller not only knows which key or keys are being pressed and how hard, but also *where* on the key surface in X and Y dimensions. Each key, in effect, becomes a tiny graphic digitizer pad. These three variables plus the key number can then be patched to control any three sound parameters desired on an individual, per key basis. The device is inherently inexpensive and can be extremely effective for those willing to relearn their keyboard technique. In fact, it is probably most attractive to instrument players without keyboard experience.

Another group doing similar work is Key Concepts. Their Notebender™ keyboard looks, acts, and plays like a high-quality conventional keyboard (Fig. 9–13). However, each key has the ability to independently slide forward (toward the player) and backward ¾ inch on a frictionless rocker mechanism with a spring return to center. The only visible clue to this action is an undercut notch on the black keys to prevent interference with the white keys. A special friction surface allows the player to move the keys without finger slippage. Besides this new key "displacement" variable, the keyboard uses a highly uniform velocity and pressure-sensing technique that does not rely on switch contacts or conductive rubber pads. As the name implies, the displacement variable is usually patched to modify the pitch of the note that key is playing. By means of panel controls right on the keyboard, the bend direction, range, and programmed nonlinearities in the transfer function (to aid in bending the pitch by specific amounts such as half-steps) can be selected and controlled. A 68000 microprocessor is used to control the keyboard and process information from its sensors. At the current stage of development, the Notebender keyboard is handmade to very high-quality standards and is therefore quite expensive. The sensing technology, however, is inexpensive for the level of precision achieved so costs should come down when production volume increases.

10
Other Input Methods

Quite a number of other input methods are useful in the computer-controlled synthesis system. These can be broken down into four major categories. The first is manual real-time input such as the keyboard just discussed. This method is characterized by the user physically manipulating a mechanical device of some sort that is directly interfaced to the system. The second is source-signal analysis, which has already been discussed somewhat. Depending on the circumstances, it may be simply an extension of manual input methods such as using the *sound* of a conventional musical instrument (which the user is physically manipulating) as input to the system. In other cases, it may involve analysis of some signal that the user did not generate and over which direct control is not exercised. The third method, which may not be considered to be a valid input method by some, involves the evaluation of mathematical equations or simple random chance to control some or all aspects of a piece. Finally, we have music languages, which might be considered as the physical manipulation of a typewriter keyboard. The difference, however, is that the manipulation is not in real time so the user has an unlimited amount of time to consider what the input will be.

In this chapter methods one and three will be emphasized. Source-signal analysis will be covered in Chapter 17, while music languages will be detailed in Chapter 18.

Manual Input Devices

Just about anything that can be moved, bent, twisted, or banged on and can accommodate contacts or a transducer has probably been used as an input source to a synthesizer. Of course, if a device can generate a control voltage for a synthesizer, then an ADC can interface the device to a computer.

Ribbon Controller

One of the more unique and interesting devices is the ribbon controller. In many ways, the ribbon controller resembles the resistor string analog

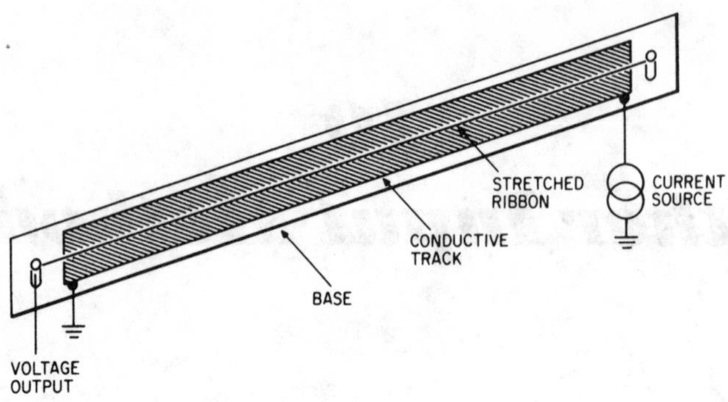

Fig. 10–1. Ribbon controller

keyboard described earlier. The device is constructed from a conductive (resistive) strip of material placed under a length of stretched wire or metal ribbon as in Fig. 10–1. Typical lengths of the conductive track may be as much as 3 feet, while the spacing between the wire and the track when not in use is on the order of 1/4 inch.

In operation, a constant current is passed through the resistive track, and the output of the device is taken from the ribbon itself. To use, the player merely presses the ribbon against the track wherever desired and an output voltage proportional to distance from the point of contact to the ground end of the track is produced. Proper selection of ribbon and track materials allows the user to easily slide a finger along the ribbon to create smoothly varying output voltages. An interface circuit similar to that for the resistor string keyboard can be used to generate trigger and gate signals from the raw voltage output. Even the dual voice analog keyboard scheme is applicable for controlling two nearly independent voices (they cannot cross each other) from a single ribbon controller.

Although most often used as a "free-form" controller, it is easy to add calibration markings so that the general location of the various notes can be instantly determined. The player's ear, however, is the final judge of proper playing position. This brings up an important point about this and most other manual controllers. Immediate audible feedback is necessary to use these devices at all even if the application is strictly input to the computer for later use.

It is also possible to add "frets" to the resistive track simply by affixing pieces of fairly large wire at desired locations along the track. For a dedicated fretted controller, the track itself may be replaced with a string of equal-valued resistors with each junction terminating at a fret wire glued to a nonconductive backing. At this point, the ribbon controller becomes a keyboard without the keys. It would not be difficult to set up devices with multiple ribbons that would resemble the fingerboard of a guitar.

Related direct input devices are rotary and linear slide potentiometers. The slide pot, which is a fairly recent development, is of particular interest, since it is actually a miniature ribbon controller with the ribbon in constant contact with the track and a handle to simplify the sliding. Their most common application is in fancy consumer audio equipment and sound studio control boards but long travel units (3 1/2 inches) also make good direct input devices. Their low cost (as little as 50 cents each) means that quite a number can be provided and used simultaneously. Rotary pots, especially if fitted with a large knob and calibrated scale, have also been shown to be effective direct input devices.

Joysticks

One limitation of ribbon controllers and various types of potentiometers is that essentially only one degree of movement freedom is available, which in turn implies that only one output from the device is present. The human hand, on the other hand, is capable of several degrees of freedom in its movement. Devices for direct hand manipulation are called *joysticks*, a name derived from a similar, but much larger, device used as an aircraft control. Joysticks may have only one or several degrees of freedom but the term usually applies to a two-axis (two degrees of freedom) device.

A joystick usually takes the form of a handle poking through a hole in the top of the joystick cover. The handle may be 2 to 5 inches long and can be moved forward and back or sideways or any combination of these motions always pivoting about the hole in the cover. The joystick produces two outputs, one proportional to the X component (sideways) of the handle position and the other proportional to Y (forward to back). The cheap "joysticks" often seen on electronic games merely close switch contacts when the handle is moved. Ideally, the unit should offer the same resistance to motion in any direction but some inexpensive ones may favor motion along the principal axes. For some applications it is desirable for the handle to remain in its last position when released, while for others a spring return to center (X = 0, Y = 0) is appropriate.

A variety of mechanical arrangements is used to separate lever movement into X and Y components, but the most ingenious is shown in Fig. 10–2. The arrangement of brackets does the separation, while two standard rotary pots are used to convert the motion into output voltages. Note that only a fraction of the pots' rotary range is utilized so some postprocessing of the output voltage will probably be necessary.

Joysticks of reasonable quality are commonly available for about $5.00. Although these may not be quite as smooth acting as one constructed according to the figure, they are small and convenient. One nice feature is that each axis often consists of *two* pots ganged together. Connecting the two pots *differentially* can provide a bipolar output voltage that may not require additional processing to utilize.

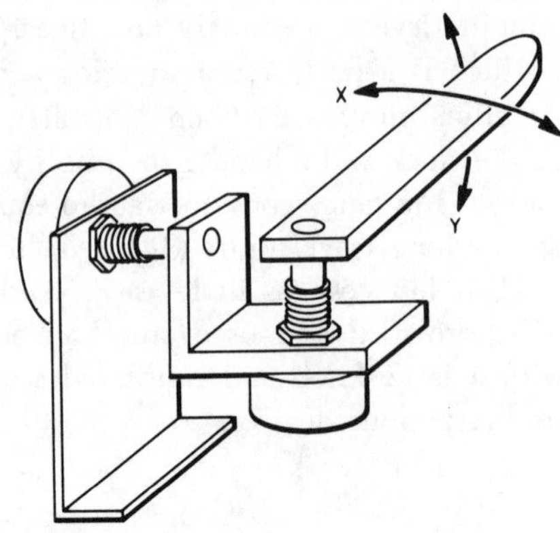

Fig. 10–2. Two-axis joystick construction. Source: *Electronotes Musical Engineers Handbook*, 1975.

Joysticks can be readily extended to three or more degrees of freedom. The third axis can simply be *twisting* of the handle as it is moved left and right, forward and back. To add such a capability to Fig. 10–2, one merely replaces the handle with a third pot whose shaft becomes the handle. The fourth axis could be a mechanism for sensing up and down motion of the handle. One might even conceive of a fifth output that would be proportional to squeezing pressure on the handle!

Graphic Digitizer

Although not a new input device, *graphic digitizers* have recently been reduced in cost sufficiently to suggest their use as a dynamic input device. The digitizer acts somewhat like a two-dimensional ribbon controller and typically consists of a flat padlike surface perhaps a foot square and a special stylus that the user holds like a pen. When near the surface, the device outputs the X and Y coordinates of the pen tip position to an accuracy of 0.01 inch or better. In one mode of operation, X and Y are sent out 50 or more times/sec, allowing the host system to determine not only the pen position but its velocity. In another mode, ouputs are only generated when the user presses the pen on the pad, thus allowing precise coordinates to be entered. A sheet of paper may be placed on the pad surface and anything printed on it entered into the system. Digitizers are also available that simply respond to finger or pencil pressure. These can be very inexpensive (under $100) but are generally not as precise as those that use an electromagnetic pickup stylus. The possibilities in a music system are endless, ranging from a two-dimensional keyboard to a quick method of inputing sheet music. Even three-dimensional digitizers are available. The position of a pen point in three-dimensional space (as large as 36 inches on a side) is output as X, Y, and Z coordinates!

Another novel input method is the *breath control* transducer. Essentially these are nothing more than pressure transducers with a tube that can be inserted into the user's mouth. Variations in breath pressure, which may be positive or negative, are converted into output variations. Such devices are most useful when the user's hands and feet are already tied up manipulating other input devices.

Modified Musical Instruments

Many potential users of a computer-based synthesis system may have spent years perfecting playing techniques on various instruments such as the guitar or clarinet. Accordingly, it has become common to fit contacts and other sensors to these instruments for easy input into a synthesizer or computer. For example, it is relatively simple to install contacts under the keys of a clarinet. This coupled with a rough amplitude analysis of the actual clarinet sound gives the functional equivalent of a keyboard. Translating key closure patterns into equivalent notes is not so simple because it is the *pattern* of keys that are pressed that is important. When going from one pattern to another, it is unlikely that all of the keys will make or break simultaneously so some intelligence is required to prevent spurious note outputs. Also many notes have "alternate fingerings." Thus, even if the clarinet is to be used to control a synthesizer directly, a microprocessor would be useful as part of the interface.

Guitar controllers are another popular item. These are actually an application of source-signal analysis, but the guitar and associated pickups are usually modified to simplify the analysis task. For example, since simultaneous tones are very difficult to separate, an independent magnetic pickup is provided for each string. Also, since strong harmonics can lead to pitch errors when the signal is analyzed, the pickups are placed near the center of the string length. If such a guitar were simply connected to a conventional amplifier, the sound would be quite dull and lifeless.

Typically, the guitar's audio signal is analyzed into amplitude and frequency parameters for each of the six strings. Often the amplitude channel is used merely as a trigger source for an envelope generator; thus, the synthesized sound may have any amplitude envelope desired. One of the attractions of guitar controllers is the fact that they are inherently polyphonic. Not only can up to six nearly independent tones (each string has a somewhat different frequency range) be simultaneously controlled, there is no problem in the assignment of notes to voices; the string corresponds to the voice.

Algorithmic Input

Certainly everyone has been exposed in one way or another to the often beautiful images created from mathematical equations. The spiragraph, which is a machine for drawing cycloids, and its output is such an example.

In fact, much computer art is done by evaluating various equations. Often "random-number generators" are used to set the parameters of the equations and then the computer takes off and generates an image. The "artistic" part of the process is the knowledge of what equations make good "material" and the judgment to modify or reject unsuitable results.

The same concepts can be applied to sounds and music. In fact, many purely analog synthesizers have the means for automatically generating sequences of control voltages that may be highly ordered, totally random, or anything in between. Likewise, a computer user has at his disposal the ability to evaluate equations of any complexity for ordered sequences and a random-number generator for disordered sequences. Algorithms for averaging and selecting random data can also be easily set up. Since this whole discussion crosses the line between music performance and music composition, it will be kept brief and no value judgments will be made about the various techniques.

A complete electronic music performance involves many sequences of events and dozens of time-varying parameters. On the other hand, a simple melody really only requires two parameters, the pitches and durations of the notes. Since conventional music starts with a melody and adds accompaniment, algorithmic composition efforts usually concentrate on generating melodies. Depending on the application, the "melody" may be as simple as a repeating sequence of notes or a genuine attempt at automatically composing a true melody.

Sample-and-Hold Module

One very useful device for sequence generation that is present on many analog synthesizers is a sample-and-hold (SAH) module. Functionally, it is the same device that was discussed in the section on analog-to-digital conversion. For synthesizer use, it has a signal input, a trigger input, and a signal output. When a trigger occurs, the output is immediately updated to match

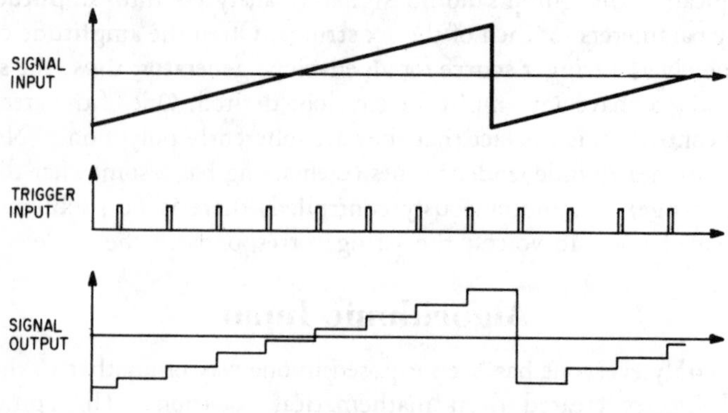

Fig. 10–3. Sampling a low-frequency sawtooth wave

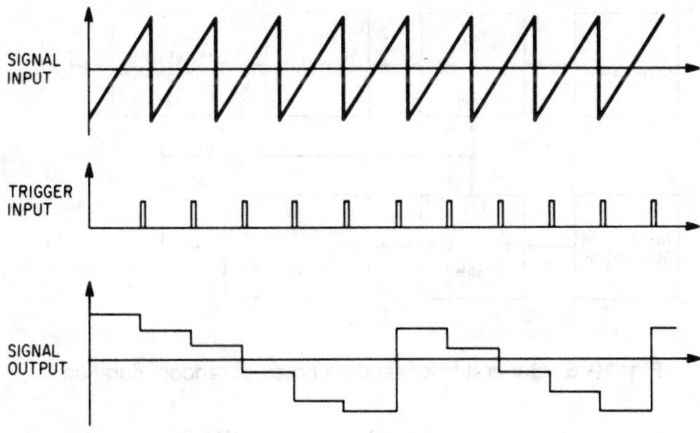

Fig. 10–4. Sampling a high-frequency sawtooth wave

the input. Between triggers, the output remains constant at its last value. The trigger input is usually designed so that any kind of waveform can drive it with perhaps the positive-going zero crossings of the wave being the trigger points. In essence, the SAH module accepts a continuously varying input and produces a stepwise output where the trigger initiates each step. Thus, if the SAH output drives a VCO and the trigger also drives an envelope generator, then a distinct "note" is produced for each trigger.

One of the simplest applications of the SAH module is in producing arpeggios. If a very-low-frequency (0.2 Hz) sawtooth wave is fed into the signal input and a 2 Hz pulse is fed into the trigger input, the output will be a staircase wave as in Fig. 10–3. When controlling a VCO, the staircase will produce an ascending sequence of 10 notes that repeats indefinitely. The actual notes depend on the amplitude of the sawtooth and the VCO settings.

If the pulse and sawtooth frequencies are not in a precise integral ratio, then each repetition of the sequence will be different. It is not difficult to adjust things to produce a scale of fifths that increases (or decreases) a half-step each iteration for six iterations and then repeats. If the sawtooth frequency is increased so that it is slightly higher than the trigger frequency, a *descending* series of notes is produced as illustrated in Fig. 10–4. Note that a slight change in the relative frequencies of the two waves can have a profound effect on the output sequence. This sensitivity increases as the sawtooth frequency increases. In the kilohertz range, interesting patterns of sequence evolution are produced as the sawtooth frequency drifts slightly due to imperfections in the VCO generating it. One can become completely absorbed in knob twiddling using a such a setup.

For truly random sequences, the SAH module can be set up to sample white noise. One would feed white noise into the signal input and a constant frequency into the trigger input. The output then would be a random series of steps. When using a typical analog white noise generator (diode junction

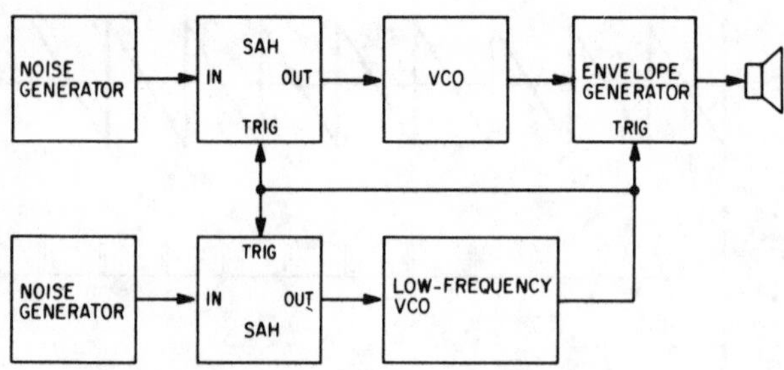

Fig. 10–5. Generator for random notes of random duration

noise), the steps are completely random and will never repeat. When this signal drives a VCO (use the sine wave output), the resulting series of random pitches of identical duration is the typical Hollywood conception of a computer hard at work.

Two SAH modules set up according to Fig. 10–5 will produce a random pitch sequence with random durations. Essentially, the first SAH determines the pitches, while the second determines the durations by controlling the VCO that provides the trigger pulses. The result is more interesting but still completely disordered.

Statistics

Although random sequences are unpredictable, they do have definite statistical properties. The most important ones are the mean or average value, the standard deviation, and the probability density function. The output of virtually any noise generator will have an average value of zero. If a mean of +5 V is desired, all that is necessary is to add a dc voltage of that magnitude. The standard deviation is equivalent to the rms voltage of the noise; thus, it may be changed with a simple gain control. Most noise sources also have a gaussian (bell-shaped normal curve) density function, which is not quite as easy to change. Even though a SAH module converts white noise into a random series of steps, the sampling process does not change any of these statistical properties.

The probability density function can be changed by using the SAH module differently. The idea is to *randomly* sample a *periodic* waveform. The resulting probability density function depends only on the shape of the sampled waveform, not on the properties of the noise source. Figure 10–6 shows a setup to do this. If the waveform to be sampled is in the kilohertz range, then only slight random variations in the sampling interval are needed. Thus, for practical purposes the step durations can still be controlled as desired.

Fortunately, the standard synthesizer waveforms give desirable density functions. Both the sawtooth and the triangular wave give a *uniform* (flat-

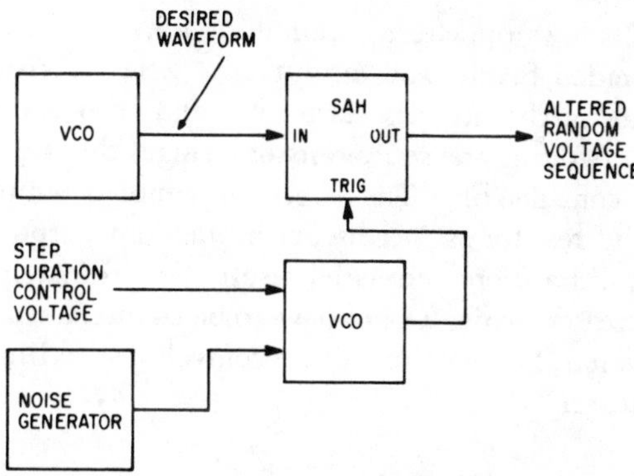

Fig. 10-6. Altering the probability density function

topped) distribution. A sine wave gives a reasonable likeness of a normal distribution, which might be useful for cleaning up the output of an otherwise poor noise source. Note that unlike a true normal distribution, there is an upper limit on peak deviation from the mean. A square wave gives two spikes, which means that only two different output voltages are possible and there is a random selection between them. (Actually this only applies to perfect square waves and SAHs; in a real situation one would occasionally get an intermediate output.) A rectangular wave gives similar results, but one value will be more probable than the other according to the duty cycle of the wave.

So far the SAH module was assumed to be perfect, that is, the input was instantly sampled and held. In a real SAH module, each occurrence of the trigger fires a single shot, which closes the sampling switch long enough for the hold capacitor to charge up to the instantaneous input signal voltage. Typically, this time is in the low microsecond range and is constant. If a resistance is inserted in series with the analog switch then the output will move *toward* the input during the sample interval but will not reach it. The effect is sometimes called "slew limiting" of the SAH.

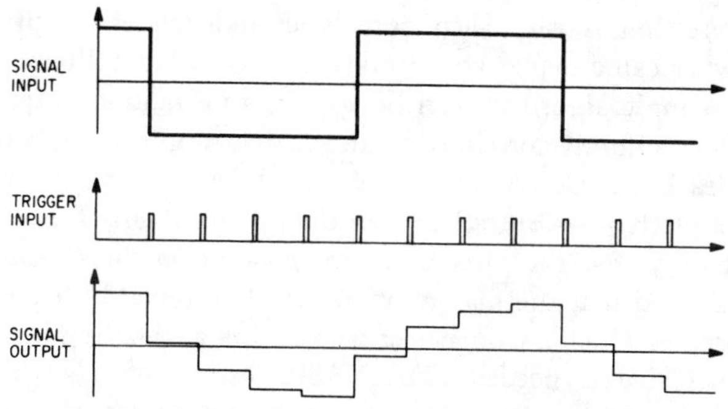

Fig. 10-7. Slew-limited sampling of square wave

Figure 10–7 shows the effect of sampling a low-frequency square wave with such a degraded SAH. The output is a series of rising and falling arpeggios, but the pitch intervals start large and then decrease after each direction reversal. Altering the series resistor changes the step size and rate of interval decrease considerably. The effect on sampled white noise is also interesting. As the resistor is increased, the random output changes from total disorder toward a more correlated result. Unfortunately, the standard deviation also decreases, which would have to be counteracted with a VCA in a practical application. Obviously, voltage control of slew limiting would be a useful SAH feature.

Controlling Randomness

As was mentioned, a slew-limited SAH module is capable of imparting a degree of order in random sequences. Actually, it is possible to get exactly the same results by passing the signal to be sampled through a single-pole R-C low-pass filter first. If white noise is to be sampled, then this amounts to filtering the noise. The slew-limited SAH module is actually a discrete-time low-pass filter, which is the first step toward a digital filter!

A sequence of random numbers is actually sampled white noise. Thus, one can easily write a program to simulate analog sampling of white noise by using the RND (random number) function available in the BASIC programming language. If a synthesizer is interfaced to the computer, then random numbers can be fed to an oscillator to produce the same kinds of note sequences available with analog setups. One point to be aware of is that most random number generators have a *uniform* probability distribution, generally between 0.0 and 1.0. A good approximation to a gaussian distribution may be had by adding up 12 random numbers (distributed uniformly between 0.0 and 1.0) and subtracting 6.0 from the sum. The mean of the result will be 0 and the standard deviation will be 1.0.

The name "stochastic music" refers to music (melodies) that orginates from sequences of random numbers. It should be apparent that raw random numbers, regardless of the probability distribution function, would create rather uninteresting music. Each note is an independent entity, with no relation to what came before and no influence on what follows.

A very simple algorithm can be applied to a random sequence, however, to produce a highly correlated sequence that might be more interesting. The basic idea is to use random numbers to determine the direction and magnitude of pitch *movement* rather than the pitches themselves. As a simple example, let's say that the pitches are to be notes on the chromatic equal-tempered scale and that the maximum allowable interval between successive notes is an octave. Thus, a sequence of random integers falling between −12 and +12 inclusive is needed. The BASIC expression INT(25*RND(1)) −12 will produce such a sequence. To produce a note sequence, numbers would first be assigned to the notes on the scale. Next, a starting point, such as middle C, must be selected. To determine what the next note should be, one simply evaluates the above expression and *adds* the random number to the numerical equivalent of the previous note.

One undesirable side effect of this process is that the notes can run off the ends of the scale. One solution is to treat the ends of the keyboard as "reflecting barriers," which would "bounce" the sequence back toward middle C. For a gentle reflecting action, one might alter the split of up/down probabilities to favor down when the current note is high and vice versa.

In any case, the resulting "melody" is highly correlated because the pitch of the current note depends on *all* of the preceding notes as well as a random input. Likewise, the current note will influence all future notes. The audible effect of such a sequence (particularly if the maximum allowed interval is small) can be described as an aimless wandering with few surprises. Most listeners would say that the sequence is too correlated to be really interesting.

Various schemes have been tried to produce sequences that are more correlated than raw random numbers but less correlated than the method just described provides. Just as white noise has a flat spectrum, the sampled white noise associated with raw random numbers also has a flat spectrum. The algorithm just discussed is actually a simple digital filter; an integrator to be exact. An integrator is simply a low-pass filter with a 6-dB/octave cutoff slope. Unlike the typical low-pass filter, however, the response curve continues to increase as frequency decreases without limit. The random numbers emerging from the process then have a filtered spectrum that increases by 6 dB for each octave of frequency decrease. Thus, it would seem that other digital filters would be useful for modifying random sequences.

More Sophisticated Techniques

One such filter that has been studied is a so-called "pink noise" or "1/F" filter, which has a slope that rises *3 dB/octave* as frequency decreases. The 1/F designation is used because the spectral *power* per hertz of bandwidth is inversely proportional to frequency. Since this is midway between 0 dB and 6 dB, the degree of correlation should also be intermediate. Listening tests bear this out; most people rate 1/F sequences as more pleasing than raw or integrated sequences. Unfortunately, a good 1/F digital filter is quite complex.

Another idea is to provide a mechanism whereby the influence of past events either ceases or diminishes as the sequence continues. For example, one might specify that the next note will depend on the previous three notes and a random input. One implementation method involves a large table that lists every possible combination of the three previous notes. Each entry in the table specifies a percentage probability for the next note. The random-number generator is used to select the next note based on the specified probabilities. The character of the music generated thus depends on the table entries and the number of prior notes considered.

One method for filling the table is analysis of existing music. For example, one might perform a statistical analysis of all four note sequences in the most popular Bach organ fugues. The data obtained could be compiled into a table like the one just described. There would probably be numerous combinations that did not occur in the music analyzed, so one might have to add a "back-tracking" capability to the program. One problem with extending the technique to consider longer sequences of notes is the tremendous increase in table size. The analysis of most conventional music, however, would result in a large proportion of empty (zero probability) table entries. Thus, it may be more compact to formulate the data into a set of rules. Besides memory savings, it is usually easier to experiment with the rules than thousands of probability table entries.

The results of such efforts have been mildly successful in producing interesting sequences. Pieces produced by analyzing Bach's music, for example, may sound Bach-like for a short run of a few notes. However, after listening for awhile, it becomes apparent that the music is just drifting aimlessly and getting nowhere. Overanalysis is likely to result in whole phrases from the analyzed material appearing in the output.

Analog Feedback Techniques

Another method of producing sequences is to use the principle of *feedback*. The sequences produced, while definitely not random, are complex and often unpredictable. The basic idea is to set up a collection of devices or modules, each of which has an input, an output, and performs some processing function. The modules are strung together and the output of the last module is fed back into the input of the first. Multiple-feedback paths can also exist. A simple sequence, even a single event, is then fed into the chain and gets processed over and over changing some on each trip. With multiple feedback paths, the sequence may be split and duplicated on each evolution.

One of the simplest setups is a series of SAH modules, all driven by the same trigger as in Fig. 10–8. A multiple-input VCA is used to selectively mix an input from outside and one or more feedback loops. With only the input enabled, the final output from the system is simply a delayed, sampled version of the input. Outputs taken from intermediate states would be identical but with differing delays. This might be useful in creating sequence echo effects or even have a sequence play a "round" with itself.

With the end-around feedback path enabled, many possibilities exist. One could, for example, fill the SAH chain with a short sequence of notes (five SAHs could hold a five-note sequence), disable the input, and recircu-

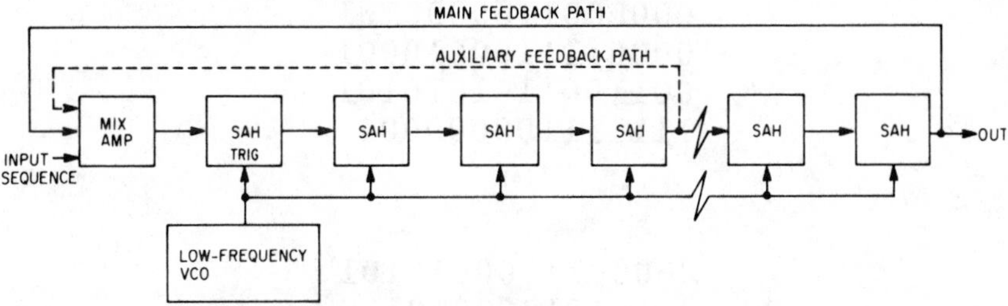

Fig. 10–8. SAH module feedback sequence generator

late the same sequence. If the SAH modules were perfect, the sequence would repeat indefinitely, but in reality analog errors would accumulate and the sequence would evolve in perhaps interesting ways. If, instead of removing the external input, it were fed a constant 1/12 V, the sequence would shift upward a half step on each interaction. If the feedback gain were greater or lesser than unity, the pitch intervals in the sequence would progressively increase or decrease, respectively. Enabling a second feedback path would create such complex patterns that they may be difficult to predict beyond the first repetition. The use of slew-limited SAH modules adds yet another dimension of possibilities.

Digital Feedback Techniques

A digital feedback system can be set up using flip-flops connected as a shift register. Figure 10–9 shows such a system. The input summer that drives the register is a parity generator that actually computes the "modulus 2 sum" of all its inputs. The switches enable a particular feedback path if closed. A low-frequency VCO provides trigger pulses to drive the system.

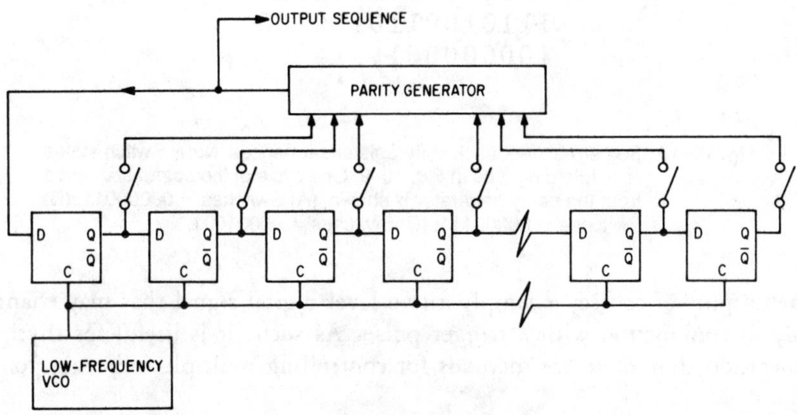

Fig. 10–9. Feedback shift register sequence generator

```
0000001100000101
0000111100010001
0011001101010101
111111100000001
```

(A)

```
0000011100010101
0110101000010110
0110001100101001
1101110100010011
0111100001101001
0001111101011100
1001011111100111
101101100000001
```

(B)

```
0000100101000011
0101100110010101
0011110011011010
0000101001011000
1001110001111111
1000001110011111
0110010001000110
0111010111011011
0000001100011011
1100010111101010
1011111101000101
0110111000011110
1110100110100100
100000001
```

(C)

Fig. 10–10. Some 8-bit feedback shift register sequences. Note: Switch states read left to right as in Fig. 10–9. One cycle of the output sequence from the parity generator is shown. (A) Switches = 00000011. (B) Switches = 00000111. (C) Switches = 00001001.

The output, of course, is simply a two-level digital signal that may change only in conjunction with a trigger pulse. As such, it is useful for rhythm generation, but there are methods for controlling multiple-frequency tones also.

The sequence generated depends entirely on the configuration of open and closed switches. Since there are 2^N possible switch combinations, a fairly

1111111010101011
0011001000100011
1100001010000011
000000100000001

(D)

0001110001001011
1000000110010010
0110111001000001
0101101101011001
0110000111110110
1111010111010001
0000110110001111
0011100110001011
0100100010100101
0100111011101100
1111011111101001
1001101010001100
0001110101010111
1100101000010011
1111110000101111
000110100000001

(E)

Fig. 10–10. Some 8-bit feedback shift register sequences *(cont.)* (D) Switches = 10000001. (E) Switches = 00011101. This is the longest possible sequence using an 8-bit register (255 bits).

small number of stages can create a nearly infinite number of different patterns ranging from highly structured to virtually random. The sequence length (number of clock cycles necessary to cause the sequence to repeat) varies from just 2 to $2^N - 1$, where N is the number of shift register stages. From this vast array of sequences, Fig. 10–10 shows a few of those possible with an 8-bit register.

The Muse

At least one interesting device has been marketed that is based on the feedback shift register principle. It is called the "Muse" and is advertised as a music composition machine with which the user, by setting several levers and switches, controls a sequence generator, which in turn controls a single oscillator to produce notes.

A simplified block diagram of the device is shown in Fig. 10–11. Thirty-eight different digital signals are generated by several counter stages and a 31-stage shift register. These signals along with constant 0 and 1 are

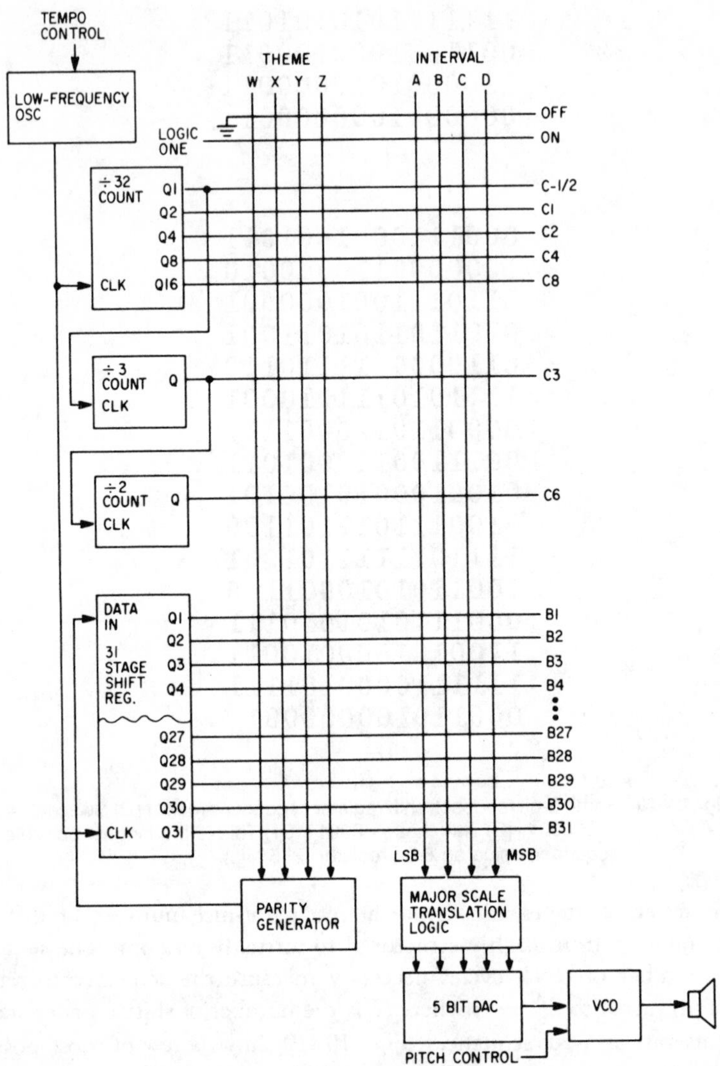

Fig. 10–11. Block diagram of Muse

connected to 40 signal rows. Eight 40-position slide switches divided into two groups of four switches act as columns and can select any individual row signal. Four of the switches, which are called "theme" controls, feed a parity generator whose output feeds the 31-position shift register. The other four switches, designated "interval" controls, are connected through some translation logic to a 5-bit DAC, which drives a VCO tone generator and output speaker. The VCO and DAC are adjusted so that the step size is a semitone on the equally tempered scale and the translation logic converts its 4-bit input into a 5-bit output according to the conventions of the major musical scale. An adjustable low-frequency oscillator clocks the counters and shift register.

In the Muse, the rows driven by the counters and constant 0 and 1 are designated as the "C" (counter) region. Five of these rows are connected to a simple 5-bit counter, while two more connect to a divide-by-6 and divide-by-12 counter. The outputs of the various counters are normally used for short, highly ordered sequences. For example, if the "A" switch is set to row "C1", B to C2, C to C4, etc., the device will generate an ascending major scale. Essentially, a binary counter has been connected to the DAC, which would be expected to generate an ascending staircase waveform. If switch A is moved to the C1/2 position, the scale will still ascend but by alternate intervals of one note and three notes. Moving B and D back to the off position (constant 0 row), results in a pair of trills: C-D-C-D-G-A-G-A-C-D . . . Many other combinations, of course, are possible, but the sequence length will never be more than 64 notes using the C6 row or 32 notes otherwise.

The 31 rows in the "B" (binary) region are driven by the 31 stage shift register, which shifts downward from row 1 to 2 to 3, etc. The four "theme" switches are used to control the shift register by determining what will be shifted into the register's first stage input. If they are set in the C region, then the register acts merely as a delay line. This can be useful in creating cannon effects. However, if one or more are set in the B region, then a feedback path into the shift register is created and some complex sequences indeed can result. One possibility is to set the theme switches for a complex sequence, set three of the interval switches in the C region for a repetitive tone pattern, and set the fourth somewhere in the B region. The result is that the repetitive pattern is modified according to the shift register pattern. Although one can think through what the effects of a particular switch setting might be, there are so many degrees of freedom that one usually succumbs to random tinkering. The number of unique combinations is for all practical purposes infinite.

Obviously, the concept can be easily expanded to more stages, more notes, more voices, rhythm control, and even scale changes. Of all the algorithmic "composition" methods discussed thus far, the author feels that this one holds the most promise and is the most fun to use. It is obvious that the Muse can be easily simulated on any microcomputer system using any language desired. Although user interaction may not be as convenient as the many slide bars and switches on the real thing, it becomes easy to expand or restructure the device with minor program changes. Also, with the user interaction techniques discussed in the next chapter, even the user interface can be improved upon.

11
Control Sequence Display and Editing

One of the unique capabilities of a computer-controlled synthesizer is meaningful graphic communication with the user. Many of the normally abstract ideas about sound parameter variation become concrete objects when visualized through a computer-driven graphic display. As such, they become much easier to manipulate as well as comprehend. Imagine for a moment reading the text of this book without the benefit of illustrations. The notions of waveshape, spectrum shape, parameter variation contours, etc., would be difficult to visualize regardless of the quality of exposition. With figures to illustrate ideas, understanding of the point being illustrated as well as its relation to other points is made easy, almost natural. "Dynamic" illustrations in which variables actually move is better yet for understanding relationships. A graphic display device provides these aids to the music system user who must constantly conceptualize a myriad of interrelated parameters and effects in the evolving composition.

Not very long ago one interacted with a computer music system solely through punched cards. The keypunch machine in the computer center was the only means available for editing the sound material, which consisted of music language statements and an occasional tabulated curve. Alphanumeric display terminals for on-line editing of text were rare, while graphic display consoles were exceedingly expensive luxuries. Now an interactive alphanumeric display is expected even on small, inexpensive home systems and reasonably adequate graphic capability costs less than $500.

Whereas the previously discussed musical input methods concentrated on getting data into the system in an initial good form, this chapter will discuss methods for building up a composition from little or nothing through *editing*. Editing is a process whereby a body of initial material is modified or rearranged in response to commands by the user. It also covers the addition of new material and the deletion of old or unwanted material. An ideal computer music-editing system should be able to accept input in a variety of forms, such as keyboard activity, source signal analysis, algorithmic sequence generation, and music language statements. It should be able to "show" the material to the user in several ways, such as music language statements, standard or specialized music notation, graphs of parameter variation, and actual synthesized sound. The editing commands should be simple yet powerful and correspond to the method chosen for showing the material to be edited. Composition by editing is a uniquely interactive method for producing the kind of music the user really has in mind rather than the best approximation that human dexterity or music language restrictions allow.

Types of Display Devices

Historically, computer data displays have been divided into two types, alphanumeric and graphic. The former is so named because it is designed to display strictly letters and numbers, whereas the latter is more generalized, being capable of displaying line drawings or in some cases gray scale images. Theoretically, the alphanumeric display is a proper subset of graphic displays because, after all, characters are nothing more than graphic shapes. However, the very generality of graphic display means that character display quality or quantity is likely to be less for equivalently priced devices. Because of this, many computer users have the mistaken idea that a graphic display can never do as good a job on text as can the alphanumeric type. A good-quality graphic display, however, can certainly equal the performance of commonly used, less expensive text-only displays with the added convenience of a single-display device for both types of information.

Many display technologies have been used to display characters and graphics. Although other methods have claimed to be superior to the cathode ray tube in one way or another, the CRT remains the undisputed leader and likely will continue to be until the late 1980s. CRT hardware is cheap because of heavy usage in television, radar, and oscilloscopes. Display resolution can be very high; a million resolvable points is routine and upward of 20 million can be done. The most commonly used CRT displays are fast, capable of being completely updated in milliseconds. Although other capabilities such as gray scale and color presentations are important for some applications, the following discussion will focus on monochrome displays capable of line drawings and alphanumerics.

A graphic CRT display can be thought of as a two-dimensional rectangular surface. Any point on the surface can be specified by giving X and Y coordinates. However, since digital logic drives the display, there is a limit to the number of discrete X and Y coordinate values. The smallest increment possible in either direction is commonly called a *raster unit*. A low-resolution display may have as few as 200 raster units in each direction, whereas a high-resolution display might have 4,000 or more. The electron beam that creates the spot of light on the screen does have a finite size, however. In fact, it is often larger than the raster unit size in a high-resolution display. Herein

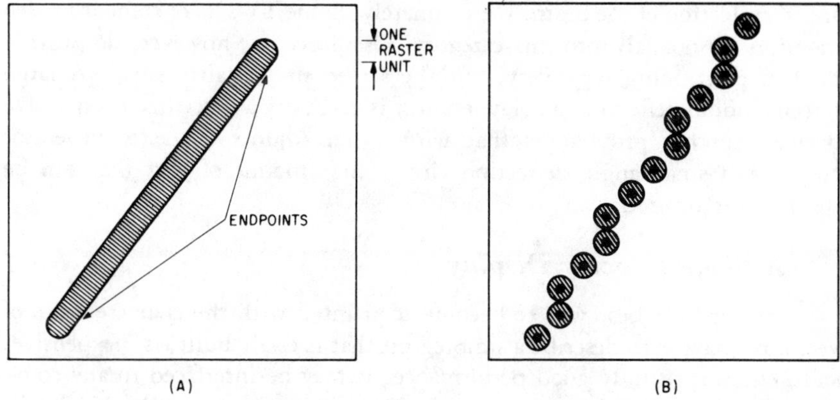

Fig. 11–1. Methods of displaying a line. (A) Line-plotting display. (B) Point-plotting display.

lies the difference between *addressable* points, which are the product of X and Y raster unit counts, and *resolvable* points, which refer to the quantity that can theoretically be displayed without merging into a continuous sheet of light.

Graphic Display Classifications

Graphic displays are classified by whether the fundamental display element is a *line* or a *dot* (point). A line drawing display is capable of drawing a smooth continuous line from any X,Y coordinate (X and Y are integers in terms of raster units) to any other on command. A point display is capable of illuminating any combination of dots at X and Y raster unit intersections. Figure 11–1 shows the difference in appearance between the two presentations in which all other factors such as number of raster units and beam size are equal. Clearly, the line display provides a superior image. This is because only the endpoints are constrained to be at grid points in the line display.

Line drawing displays are usually called *vector* displays because the lines satisfy the mathematical definition of a vector. Such displays have a number of important advantages besides better-looking images. The most important is that they are easy to program. The display accepts data in essentially the same form that it is likely to be manipulated and stored in. Another advantage is that interactive editing of the image is fairly easy to implement and large data buffers in memory are generally not required. Resolution of the image (number of horizontal and vertical raster units) can be made quite high for a moderate increase in cost and memory usage.

There are, however, disadvantages that prevent vector from being the dominant CRT display technology. Perhaps most serious is the required CRT *monitor*, which consists of the tube, high-voltage power supply, and X and Y deflection amplifiers. It must be capable of *random* (on command) X and Y deflection of the beam. Unfortunately, home TV sets or standard video monitors do not fall into this category. Oscilloscopes, however, do provide random positioning capability, but the screen size is fairly small. A large screen random deflection display monitor is currently a specialized, expensive device. Another problem is that without an adjunct character generator circuit and small-angle deflection circuit the amount of text that can be displayed is limited.

A Simple Vector Display

Perhaps the best way to become acquainted with the characteristics of vector displays is to describe a simple unit that is easily built, is inexpensive, and gives surprisingly good performance. It may be interfaced to any computer that has two 8-bit output ports. The output consists of X, Y, and Z (beam on–off control) voltages that can use any oscilloscope having dc-coupled amplifiers as a display monitor. The resolution is 256× 256 raster units, but the quality is equivalent to much larger dot-type displays.

One fact of life is that the image on the tube must be rewritten continuously. This is called *refreshing* the display and is necessary to prevent it from fading away within a fraction of a second. For most display monitors, the image must be refreshed at least 40 times/sec to avoid flicker. Maximum image complexity is directly proportional to the number of lines that may be drawn in one refresh interval. Very detailed, complex drawings are possible, however, if some flicker is allowed. It is also sometimes possible to obtain an oscilloscope with a *long-persistence* phosphor in which the image does not fade so quickly. These are usually yellow or orange in color as opposed to green and are commonly used in medical applications. The display to be described requires about 50 μsec to draw a line. Thus, about 500 lines may be drawn in the 25-msec interval allowed for a 40-Hz refresh rate.

Two 8-bit output ports are used to control the display. Port one is used for specifying X and Y coordinates. The coordinates are unsigned numbers in the range of 0 to 255 with zero corresponding to the bottom and left edges of the screen. Only 4 bits of the other port are used. The "save X" bit when a logic one causes the content of port one to be interpreted as an X coordinate and stored in an internal register. The "move X" bit causes the previously saved X to be sent to the X DAC, which then immediately moves the CRT beam to the new X position. "Move Y" immediately transfers port 1 to the Y DAC and moves the beam. The fourth bit is called "draw," which turns the beam on for 50 μsec and sets up for controlled movement so that straight lines are drawn. For proper operation of draw, move X and move Y should be set simultaneously with draw.

A typical sequence for drawing a line between two arbitrary endpoints, X_1,Y_1 and X_2,Y_2 would be as follows:

1. Initially port 2 (the control port) is zeros.

2. Store X_1 into port 1 (the coordinate port).
3. Set "store X" and "move X" bits to ones and then zeros to cause an immediate move to X_1.
4. Store Y_1 into port 1.
5. Set "move Y" bit to a one then a zero to cause an immediate move to Y_1.
6. Store X_2 into port 1.
7. Set "store X" bit on then off to store X_2 in the display generator without affecting the X DAC.
8. Store Y_2 into port 1.
9. Set "move X," "move Y," and "draw" bits on.
10. Wait 50 μsec for the line to be drawn.
11. Clear the control port to zeros.

Usually the majority of an image is formed by line segments joined end-to-end. In this case, each additional segment after the first only requires Steps 6 to 11 to be executed.

Display List Interpreter

In actual use, a display subroutine would be written that would display all of the line segments needed for the desired image once and then return. A *display list* in memory can specify the line segments in a form that allows rapid retrieval and display yet easy manipulation of the list for editing. The display subroutine then becomes a *display list interpreter* executing commands from the list not unlike a BASIC interpreter. Although considerably more sophisticated list formats are possible, let us describe one that is simple yet well suited for this display.

The display list consists of individual "list elements" strung end to end. Each element contains an "operation code" byte followed by "operand" bytes. Code 01_{16}, for example, will specify a move with the beam off; therefore, it will be followed by two bytes specifying X,Y coordinates of the destination. Code 02 specifies an isolated line segment; thus, X_1,Y_1 and X_2,Y_2 will follow as four bytes. For drawing connected line segments, it is most efficient if they are drawn consecutively. Accordingly, code 03 indicates that a count byte and a series of coordinates follows. A move will be done to the first coordinate of the series and thereafter lines will be drawn from point to point through the series. The count byte specifies up to 255 lines in the series.

In music synthesis applications, it is common to display graphs in which one axis, usually X, simply increments for each line in the graph. Considerable space saving is therefore possible by defining a "graph" segment type. Code 04 is used to specify a graph. It is followed by a count byte, an increment byte, the initial X coordinate, and then a series of Y coordinate bytes. The count byte is as before, while the increment byte specifies the amount that X is incremented for each graph point. The initial X byte is needed to specify where the graph begins horizontally. For completeness, one could specify code 05 as being a graph with Y being automatically incremented. The end of the entire display list is specified by a code of 00.

Many other element types can be defined to make image editing easier and faster. If one desired to move a set of lines vertically by 10 raster units it would be necessary to alter the Y coordinates of every one of the lines individually. The idea of *relative* coordinates overcomes this problem. With relative coordinates, the position of all line endpoints are relative to a specified point. By changing the coordinates of the specified point (origin), one can change the position of all lines that are relative to that point. To implement this, code 06 will specify an origin segment and will be followed by X,Y of the new origin. Codes 07 to 0B correspond to 01 to 05 except that all coordinates are relative.

It is also useful to be able to skip portions of a display list or reuse parts of it for similar subimages. Code 0C is used to specify an unconditional jump. It is followed by two bytes that specify where in memory the remainder of the list is located. The jump simplifies editing because a deletion, for example, can simply insert a jump that skips around the unwanted list elements. Code 0D is similar except it specifies "jump to subroutine." The address of the next list element is saved and a jump to another display list is taken. When a "return" (code 0E) is seen in the secondary list, a jump back to the saved address is taken. If the display list interpreter is written so that return addresses are saved on the processor's stack, the sublists may be nested.

Relative coordinates make such "image subroutines" very useful. A common subroutine, such as the shape of an object, can be used to draw the object at different positions on the screen. One would have a "set relative origin" element followed by a "jump to subroutine" element for each copy of the object desired. This technique would also be useful for displaying characters.

To facilitate compact storage of text, code 0F will specify an ASCII mode. It is followed by the X,Y coordinate of the first character and then the text itself as normal ASCII character codes. The ASCII "ETX" character is used to indicate end of text and a return to graphics mode. One could define a variety of control characters in the text to allow formating without going to graphic mode and changing coordinates for each line of text. Note that graphic text display is quite capable of proportional spacing (different letters are different widths such as the text of this book) and superscripts or subscripts or even varying point (character) size. Unfortunately, with this simple display example only a few dozen characters can be drawn in a 25-msec refresh interval.

Keeping the Image Refreshed

To maintain the image on the screen without flicker, the list interpreter would have to be called at least 40 times/sec. An easy way to keep the display refreshed and do other work as well is to have an interval timer interrupt 40 times/sec. The interrupt service routine would refresh the display once and return. If priority interrupts are available, the display should probably be the lowest priority. If more than 25 msec is required to display the list, the system would revert to a state in which the list size determines the refresh rate, which would be less than 40 Hz.

Obviously, the system can become completely tied up refreshing the display if the image is complex. Often this is not a problem if the application

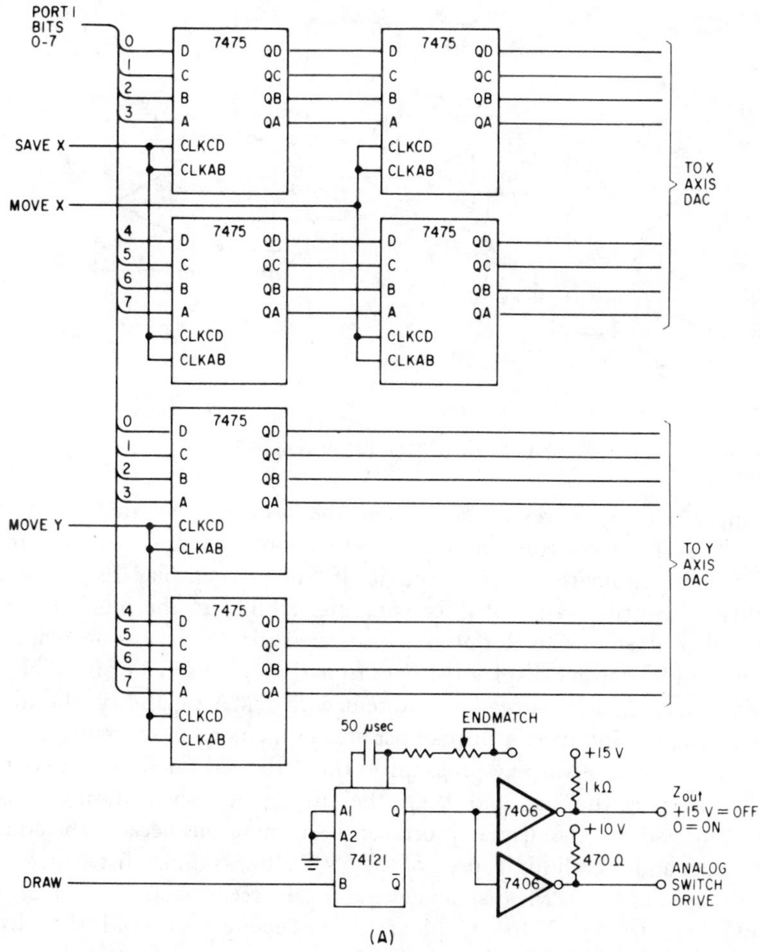

Fig. 11-2. (A) Simple vector graphic display interface—digital portion.

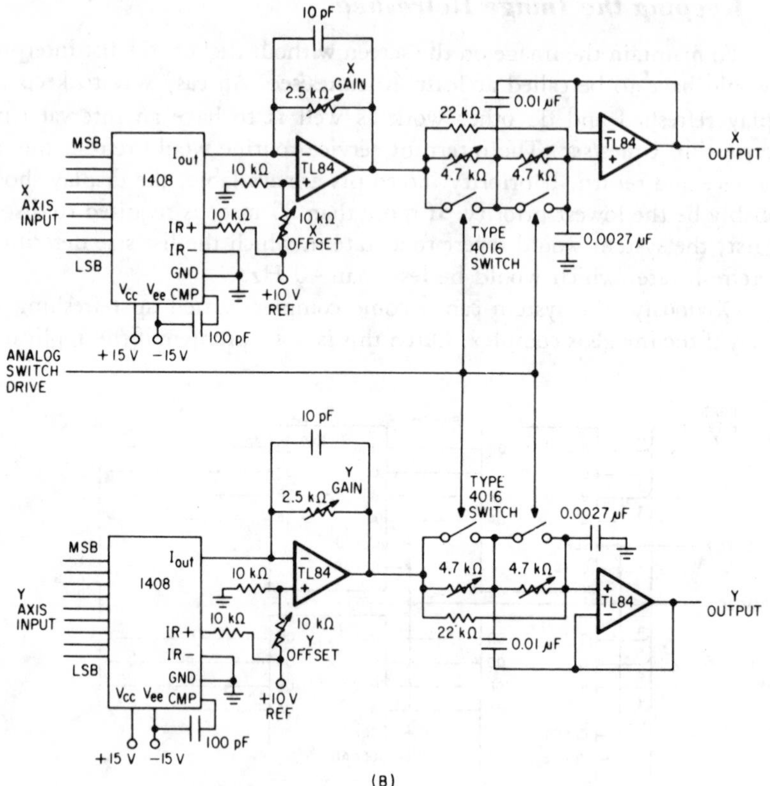

Fig. 11–2 (*Cont.*). **(B) Analog portion.**

is simply editing curves or text where the system is waiting on the user virtually 100% of the time anyway. For other applications, it would be nice if the display automatically refreshed itself from the display list. One possibility is to utilize a small microcomputer similar to the music keyboard driver described in Chapter 9 as a dedicated display processor. The main system would transfer display list data to it through a serial or parallel port. Alternatively, in a bus-organized system with DMA capability, the display processor could interpret a display list area of memory shared with the main system processor. A display program in the dedicated micro would continuously interpret the list and keep the display refreshed. Using a 6502 microprocessor for the display processor is advantageous because the addressing modes and overall high speed of the 6502 allow complex list structures to be processed as fast as the display generator can accept data. A 1K or 2K byte EPROM (2708 or 2716) is plenty large enough to hold the display interpreter and fundamental list-editing software. One to four 2K byte static RAM chips (6116 type) can easily hold display lists larger than the display's ability to refresh them at a reasonable rate. A 6522 parallel I/O chip provides

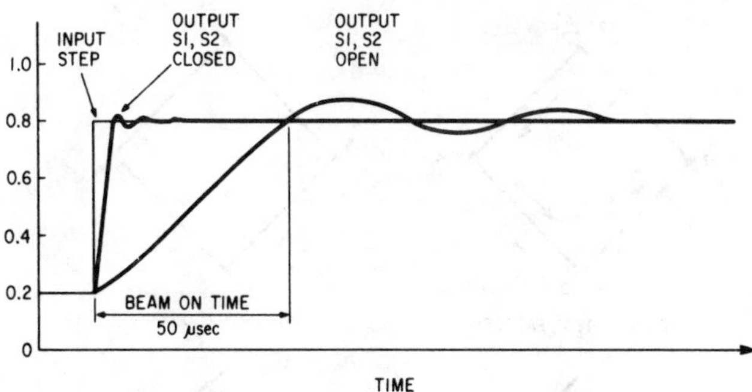

Fig. 11–3. Step response of vector generator

a convenient interface to the vector generator about to be described and also includes a timer that can be used to control the refresh rate.

Vector Generator Circuit

Figures 11–2A and B show a schematic of the vector display generator. The digital portion of the interface is quite simple, consisting mostly of type 74LS75 quad *transparent* latches. The latches are necessary because the same port is used for both X and Y coordinates and to insure that the X and Y DACs are updated *simultaneously* when a line is to be drawn. The term transparent means that as long as the clock input is high, the input data passes straight through to the output. Thus, a move X operation, which calls for setting both "save X" and "move X" control bits high, enables the clocks on both sets of X latches allowing data to pass through the leftmost set and be latched into the rightmost set. The single shot is used to carefully control the beam on time independent of program timing when a draw is executed. This prevents bright dots at the ends of lines. The Z axis output is boosted to 15 V, since most oscilloscopes require high-level drive to control the beam.

The heart of the analog section is the X and Y DACs. Type MC1408L8 DACs are used in a circuit similar to that in Fig. 7–18. The offset circuit has been modified, however, to provide a voltage output (from current-to-voltage converter op-amp) of +2.5 for a digital input of 0 and +7.5 for an input of 255. The type TL0084 is a very convenient quad FET input op-amp selected here for its speed.

Unfortunately, generating the X and Y voltage contours necessary for drawing a smooth, uniformly bright line between arbitrary endpoints on a CRT is not as simple as it sounds. The task is called *vector generation* and circuits that do it are called *vector generators*. An ideal vector generator would move the beam at a constant, uniform *velocity* regardless of the line length or orientation, would be free of wiggles and other distortions at the endpoints, and would have good matching of lines sharing the same endpoint. To make matters worse, the necessary analog computations must be done accurately at high speeds. The vector generator used in this simple display sacrifices

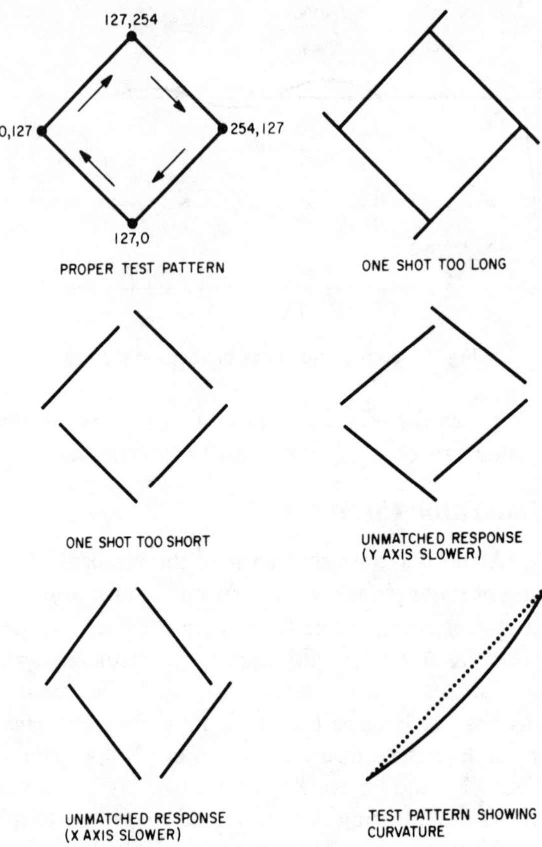

Fig. 11–4. Adjustment of vector generator

constant velocity in the interest of simplicity. The effect of varying beam velocity is that short lines will appear to be brighter than long lines and the portion toward the endpoints may also be brighter than the middle. To the eye, the effect is not objectionable but it does create difficulty if one wishes to photograph the screen.

Vector generation is accomplished by using a portion of the step response of a resonant low-pass filter. Figure 11–3 shows the step response of the filter used. Note that the filter output rises from its previous value fairly linearly, *overshoots* the final value, and then oscillates around it for a time before settling. Since the time from the input step to the output first crossing the final value is constant and the curve during this time is reasonably linear, it is suitable for use as a vector generator. Note that line straightness on the screen depends on *matching* the X and Y curves, not on the straightness of the curves themselves. S1 and S2 have been added to quickly damp out the oscillation around the final value after the line has been drawn and to allow fast moving with the beam off. Their effect is to raise the cutoff frequency of the filter about 20-fold. The switches themselves are inexpensive CMOS transmission gates. Since the voltages being switched are between +2.5 V and +7.5 V plus some margin for overshoot, the CMOS is powered between +10 V and ground. This also allows simple open-collector TTL gates to drive the switches.

Adjustment of the circuit is fairly simple. First the gain and offset pots on each DAC must be adjusted so that 00 gives +2.5 V output and FF gives +7.5 V. Next, using an oscilloscope, the low-pass filters in the vector generator should be adjusted for identical step response shape and time to first final value crossing. If the capacitors are initially matched to within 1% or so, then shape matching should not be a problem and the two pots in the X axis circuit can be adjusted for time matching. Finally, using a test pattern consisting of a diamond (all lines at 45°), the end match pot should be adjusted so that the lines just meet. If one line passes the other before meeting, then the step response balance should be touched up a bit. Any curvature of the lines due to the vector generator can be ascertained by displaying a 45° angle line and then a series of points (lines with zero length) along the path that should have been traversed by the line.

Note that very little additional expense is involved in improving the resolution of the display. For example, the number of addressable points may be increased 16-fold merely by using 10-bit DACs and a couple of extra latch packages. With 12-bit DACs, the raster unit size becomes so small that X and Y coordinates become essentially "continuous" quantities. The significance of this is seen by considering the display of, say, an arbitrary number of *equally* spaced lines in a fixed area of, say, one-half the screen width. With 256 raster units, one-half of the screen would be 128 raster units. If 47 lines need to be displayed, the space between lines should be 128/47 = 2.723 raster units. On the screen some lines would actually be three units apart while others are only two, obviously not equally spaced. With a 4096 raster-unit display, however, the lines would be 43 and 44 units apart and thus appear quite equally spaced on the screen.

Raster Scan Displays

The other major CRT display type is commonly called a *raster scan* display. This is because the deflection circuits in the CRT monitor constantly scan a rectangular area in a set pattern consisting of numerous parallel horizontal lines. As the beam scans, it may be turned on and off at controlled times to show a dot pattern representing the desired image. Since the deflection amplifiers always handle the same waveform (normally a sawtooth) at a constant frequency, they may be made quite inexpensively even for the high power levels required for large-screen magnetic deflection tubes. This and the fact that our national television system works on the same principle are key advantages of raster scan displays. Note that since time is the only variable required to control dot position, the raster scan display is inherently a digital device.

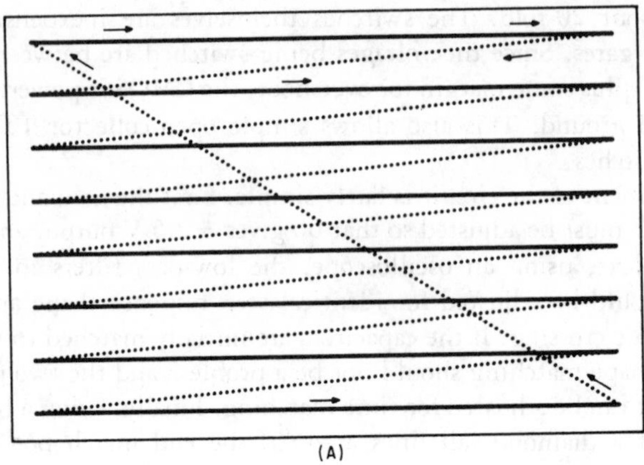
(A)

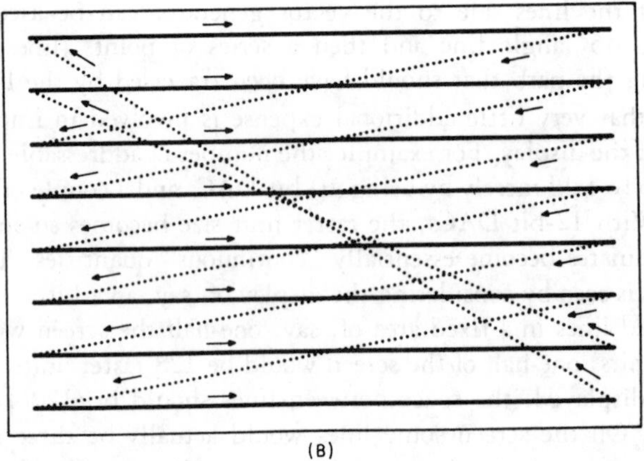
(B)

Fig. 11–5. Simple (A) and interlaced (B) raster scanning

The maximum resolution of a raster scan display is fairly well defined by the scanning frequencies used. Since television receivers and TV standard video monitors are so common, the low-cost raster display maker is essentially locked into standard TV frequencies, which are 15,750 Hz horizontal and 60 Hz vertical. For a normal scanning pattern, this yields 262 horizontal scan lines of which roughly 240 are usable (the others are wasted during vertical retrace). There is no hard limit on horizontal resolution, but there is little reason to have more points per inch than the vertical axis. With a 4:3 aspect ratio (screen width:height), this gives a horizontal resolution of 320 points.

A technique called *interlacing* effectively doubles the vertical resolution to 480 lines. It does this by vertically shifting odd-numbered screen scans one-half the scan line spacing with respect to even-numbered scans. Although effective for moving pictures viewed at a distance which is typical of television, an expensive precision monitor is required for an acceptable stationary image when viewed at close range, which is more typical of computer displays. Higher horizontal rates of 30 kHz or 60 kHz and/or slower vertical rates of 30 Hz are other methods of achieving up to 2,000 scan lines per frame, which is the practical limit of real-time raster display technology.

Nevertheless, 240 × 320 resolution is quite usable for music applications. Although the image appears much coarser, a 256 × 256 raster display gives just as accurate a picture as a 256 × 256 vector display would for waveform plots. The difference would really show up, however, if a number of lines at different angles pass through a small portion of the screen. With a raster display, the lines may just merge into a patch of light making it difficult to trace an individual line through the maze. A vector display, on the other hand, would retain good line identity in such a situation.

Unlike the vector display just described, automatic screen refresh by external hardware is inherent in raster displays. The overwhelming reason for this is the blazing speed with which data must be read from the display list and sent to the display to keep up with the scanning. As an example, consider that the horizontal sweep period of standard TV is roughly 64 μsec. In practice, at least 15 μsec must be subtracted to allow for horizontal retrace, leaving about 50 μsec for the image. For a horizontal resolution of 320 points, no fewer than 320 bits must be sent to the display during this time. This gives a bit rate of 6.4 MHz or a byte every 1.25 μsec, much too fast for directly programmed output. Thus, in practice an exact screen image is stored in a display buffer that may either be part of the display interface or may be main microcomputer memory with direct memory access (DMA) used to rapidly read the data for display.

Display Buffer

The display buffer required for a raster display can become quite large indeed. A full 320 × 240 display would be 76,800 bits or 9.6K bytes, which is comparable to the total memory capacity of many microcomputer systems. Note that even if scanning frequency limitations did not exist doubling the resolution would increase the display buffer size (and therefore cost) *four* times. Commercial display designers have devised numerous ways to reduce this, but all of them involve trading off either display generality or programming ease or both. The two most common schemes also attempt to combine text display and graphic display functions by adding special *graphic symbols* to the character set of an otherwise normal text display. One method divides the character cell into three rows of two squares each and assigns 64 character codes to cover all of the possible combinations of light and dark squares. The resulting graphic resolution ranges from 128 × 48 for hobbyist-level 16-line 64-character displays to 160 × 72 for commercial 24-line 80-character units. This is obviously quite coarse but is at least completely general within the limited resolution.

The other method that is often found in alphanumeric display terminals adds various graphic character shapes such as horizontal, vertical, and diagonal lines and corners, junctions, arcs, etc., to the character set. The user can then select line segments from this set and piece images together that appear to be of high resolution. While excellent for images such as game boards, bar charts, and other highly structured material, the technique is quite limited on arbitrary lines and curves such as music-control functions and waveforms.

Bit-Mapped Display Interfaces

Thus, for any kind of serious graphics work a true *bit-mapped* or *pixel* display is a necessity. The term bit-mapped means that every point on the display literally corresponds to a bit in the display memory, whereas pixel refers to the fact that individual *pic*ture *el*ements can be manipulated.

Most integrated personal computers today have some form of bit-mapped graphics display capability. Integrated here means that the display generation circuitry is part of the computer as opposed to a separate display terminal. Even the under-$200 Commodore-64 has a 320 × 200 pixel resolution in its two-color mode. The Apple II line typically provides 280 × 192, although the newest members also have a 560 × 192 mode, which is quite a resolution mismatch. Pixel graphics is not really standard on the IBM PC, but most users purchase the option (usually to run "business graphics" software), which offers an even more mismatched 640 × 200 resolution in the monochrome mode. Many IBM "clones" offer better graphics capability as a standard feature; the Tandy 2000, for example, has 640 × 400 resolution even in the eight-color mode. The Apple MacIntosh is currently the best-known low-cost graphics-oriented computer. Its 512 × 342 resolution, although not the highest around, is well balanced and backed up by a microprocessor (68000) that is ideally suited to graphics manipulations. Unfortunately, its "closed" architecture makes connection to synthesis equipment and user programming of signal-processing-oriented graphics software much more complex than necessary, although its built-in software can be of some use.

Larger bus-oriented and multiuser computers typically use separate display terminals rather than integrated display generators. Usually, such terminals are alphanumeric with perhaps some line segment character shapes available. Full graphics terminals are available, however, as are graphics retrofit kits for some of the more popular alphanumeric units. Graphics programming, particularly graphics editing, which will be described, of such a terminal is difficult and slow due to the serial communication link between terminal and computer.

Bus-oriented computers using the S-100 bus, Multibus (Intel), Versabus and VME bus (Motorola), or Q-bus (DEC), have available plug-in raster graphics display boards that can offer much higher resolutions than integrated computers. A resolution of 640 × 400 is common and up to 1,280 × 1,024 is available with from 2 to 2^{24} colors. Of course, costs can be quite high, but such units have the resolution required for nearly any conceivable musical application. For example, three-dimensional spectral plots, which often look like mountain ranges, need high display resolution to be useful. Likewise, a conventional score editor benefits greatly from resolution high enough to permit seeing an entire page of music rather than just one line at a time.

Color

As with home televisions, color is expected on home computer displays and, in fact, most connect to color TV sets. A color television, even an expensive one, makes a very poor computer display because the three color signals are *multiplexed* onto one 4-MHz band-limited video signal. The result is that the *displayable* (as opposed to addressable) color resolution is often no better than 100 pixels across the screen due to blurring. Add to that artifacts of the multiplexing process, such as ghosts and "worms" at sharp edges in the image, and the result is a very unpleasant display to watch at close range. The better personal computers provide separate red-blue-green color signals to specialized monitors, which gives a much more satisfactory image.

With current color picture tube technology, there are still substantial defects that make color displays tiring to use for long periods. One of these is poor convergence, in which the three color images do not perfectly line up, an effect often seen in the Sunday comics. For example, when white characters are shown against a dark background, obvious color fringes are seen around the edges, or in extreme cases, entire characters may be a rainbow of color. Another problem is moiré patterns of "beating" between the tube's color dot or stripe pattern and individual display pixels. Very expensive color monitors (upward of $2,000) can minimize these problems by using a more precise "sectorized" convergence system and fine pitch shadow masks that may have dot or stripe density up to three times that of entertainment grade monitors.

Perhaps the best way to appreciate the clarity difference between monochrome and color displays is to compare them side-by-side showing the same image. The higher the resolution of the display generator, the more dramatic the difference is. Monochrome images can be enhanced in many ways, such as providing gray scale and rippling dashed lines, to highlight parts of images. If the resolution is high enough, an almost endless variety of shading patterns can be used when gray scale is not available. Apple MacIntosh software uses this technique extensively.

Editing the Display List

Unfortunately, a pixel display is difficult and space consuming to program. Whereas one can simply specify the coordinates of the endpoints of a line with a vector display, all of the points in between must be specified with the pixel display. This in itself is an interesting problem: define an algorithm that illuminates the *best* set of points possible on a fixed grid between two endpoints, also on the grid. In any case, a graphic subroutine package is a necessity when using a pixel display. Routines for point plotting, line drawing, and character generation are all necessary.

The real problem with pixel displays, however, lies in the fact that the display buffer does not contain data in a format that can be edited in general; it is just a mass of bits. As was mentioned earlier, a vector display list can be organized by *objects*, making it easy to locate an object, move it, delete it, or add a new one without regard to other objects on the screen. In contrast, the data in a pixel display buffer is organized by *position* in the display field. From looking at the data itself it is practically impossible to delineate objects and determine their exact size and orientation.

Direct editing of a pixel list is of necessity very limited. As an example, consider a pixel display showing a number of lines in which some of the lines may cross. If the user wants to delete a line it would not be difficult for him (using human eyes) to recognize the line on the display and supply its endpoints to the editing program. The program would then simply trace through the line and turn the pixels off, thus erasing it. Adding a new line would be simply a matter of specifying it and setting the appropriate pixels on. Thus, one would think that moving a line could be accomplished by first deleting it and redrawing it elsewhere. A very serious problem occurs, however, if the line of interest crosses another because a little gap will be left in the second line when the first is deleted. If interactive line movement using perhaps a joystick is to be implemented, large portions of the second line may be erased as the first moves around.

The only way to overcome the editing problem in general is to maintain *two* display lists, one in pixel format for the display and the other in vector format for editing and saving results. The easiest way to handle the two lists is to execute all editing operations on the vector list and then call a routine to interpret the vector list and create an updated pixel list whenever anything has changed. In many cases, this would call for erasing the pixel list and regenerating it completely from the vector list. In other cases, it may be possible to regenerate only a portion of the pixel list, or in the case of additions, simply do similar operations to both lists. When editing is complete, it is the vector list that should be stored.

Applications of Graphic Displays in Music

The term "interactive graphics" is commonly used to refer to the activities about to be described. Three fundamental subsystems are required in an interactive graphics application. First, of course, is the computer and graphic display device. Second is the array of input devices used by the operator to communicate with the system. Last is the software necessary to tie it all together. In a well-implemented interactive graphics application, the user sits with eyes glued to the screen, hands manipulating input devices, and mind closing the feedback loop. The effect is as if the image on the screen is an extension of the user's consciousness. To meet this goal, a highly effective human interface, both input devices and software, is required.

Many of the music input devices described previously are suitable for and in fact some were orginally developed for interactive graphics work. A joystick, for example, is typically a two-dimensional device, thus mating perfectly with a two-dimensional display. When connected to the computer through an ADC and suitable programming, one can point to objects or literally draw curves on the face of the display. As a practical matter, however, it is fairly difficult to control a joystick precisely; thus, intended straight lines are crooked and pointing is somewhat of a trial-and-error procedure.

Graphic Input Techniques

A *mouse* is a related device that overcomes the awkwardness of a joystick. Typically, it is about the size and shape of an orange half and is equipped with orthogonal wheels that allow it to roll around easily on a table top. The wheels are connected to transducers and provide X and Y outputs. Essentially, the position of the mouse corresponds to the joystick's handle, but a much larger movement range allows more precise control. Another device called a *trackball* consists of a smooth ball about the size of a baseball sitting nearly frictionless in a stationary socket. The user can roll the ball in any direction and thus provide X and Y outputs. Since the range may encompass one or more complete revolutions, control is more precise. Its major advantage is conservation of table space.

The graphic digitizer mentioned earlier is the most precise of all. Since the pen or stylus is completely frictionless, one may input to the system as accurately as drawing on paper can be done. In fact, because of their precision and repeatability, a screen outline may be taped to the digitizer surface and used as a guide in the interaction process. If real ink is used in the digitizer pen, then a permanent record of the input is produced as a by-product.

It would seem though that the ideal situation would be drawing directly on the display screen itself and in fact devices called *light pens* actually accomplish this—almost. A light pen consists of a high-speed photocell and a lens system that makes its angle of acceptance very small and localized. If placed on the surface of the CRT directly above an *illuminated* portion of the image, a pulse is generated whenever the beam refreshes that part of the image. With the software-refreshed vector display described previously, the pulse can be connected to interrupt the CPU while the line "seen" by the pen is drawn. With a pixel display, additional hardware is generally necessary to determine the X and Y positions of the beam when the pulse occurs. In either case, one can easily point to an object on the screen and the program can ascertain which object it is or its location.

Drawing on the screen where nothing currently exists is a little more difficult. In practice, a *tracking pattern* is displayed, which the user can point to and move around. The path followed by the pattern then becomes the drawn line. Various types of tracking patterns are used, but the circle type is easiest to understand. A circle of dots is displayed that has a diameter slightly larger than the acceptance area of the light pen. As long as the pen points to the center region, no light is seen and the pattern remains stationary. Pen movement in any direction, however, will put one of the dots in sight of the pen. The tracking program in the computer will respond by moving the entire pattern such that the new pen position is in the center. Besides drawing lines, interactive graphics software can provide for "attaching" the tracking pattern to an object, which can then be positioned as desired. Unfortunately, a vector display or extremely fast computer is just about mandatory for this degree of interaction.

Light pens do have their problems, however. In general, they must be carefully tuned to the display used such as by adjusting the focus length to match CRT faceplate thickness. For tracking applications, the CRT brightness needs to be tightly controlled to avoid the effects of light scattering within the CRT faceplate and ambient light. Short persistence phosphors are necessary for good pulse resolution, although long persistence visible short persistence infrared types exist. Obtaining the necessary speed at low light levels is a design problem that increases cost. Nevertheless, a properly functioning light pen is a joy to use and probably the best interactive graphics input device available short of mind reading.

Finally, most interactive graphics setups use a standard typewriter keyboard and a special *function keyboard*. Each function key is set up to instruct the interactive program to perform a specific function each time the key is pressed. The actual function of a particular key is entirely dependent on the particular interactive software in use at the time. For example, six keys may be reserved to control the display. One might expand the image 5% when pressed and a second could shrink it 5%. Four more could move the entire display left, right, up, or down. Other often-used interactive functions may be assigned to other keys. A function keyboard works just like an alphanumeric keyboard but is usually limited to 16 to 32 keys and constructed so that the key legends may be easily changed. In fact, legend overlay sheets are commonly used and one would typically have a sheet for each interactive program available. In sophisticated systems the sheets may actually be punched or otherwise coded so that the program can verify that the operator has actually inserted the correct one!

Most personal computers, however, don't have the luxury of a separate function keyboard, but many do have from 4 to 10 *function keys* added to the standard layout. These are typically placed in a single- or dual-column to the left or a single row above the main key array. The latter arrangement allows for displaying *legends* at the very bottom of the screen that line up with the function keys when the keyboard is positioned right. The interactive graphics program (or text editor or just about any kind of interactive program) can then dynamically change the legends as the program changes modes. This has proven very effective in the Micro Technology Unlimited line of computers and others.

A similar option that works well with a light pen, mouse, or other pointing device, is to display a *menu* of function options that the user then "points" to. In a complex program, only a few such *soft keys* may normally appear in a dedicated area of the display, but, when more are temporarily needed to qualify an earlier selection, part of the screen image can be saved and overwritten with the temporary menu. These are often called *pull-down menus* because of their appearance when the normal menu is at the top of the screen. In systems with sufficient display resolution, interactive programs designed for first-time users may even dispense with words for the legends and substitute little pictures called *icons*. Extensive use of such conventions was first popularized by the Apple McIntosh computer and has since become relatively common.

Composition by Editing

Now that the tools used in interactive graphics have been described, let's look at how these can be used to communicate musical and acoustical ideas to a computer-based synthesis system.

First, consider a case in which direct control of several sound parameters simultaneously is desired. Further assume that the exact shape of the variation contours and their interrelation is critically important in creating the desired audible result. To make matters more difficult, the shape of the required contours is only roughly known. Finally, the rapidity of the variations is such that real-time manual control is out of the question. What has been described is a perfect example of synthesizing a realistic singing voice, although the concepts apply to any complex, rapidly changing sound.

Composition by editing is best done if one starts with some approximation, no matter how coarse, of the desired results. In realistic speech synthesis one might start by analyzing natural speech into the parameters of interest. Even if the goal is a female singing voice and the input is a gravel-throated male voice, the set of parameter variations that results is close enough to the final result so that the necessary editing changes are somewhat apparent. One might also use a "speech synthesis by rule" program, which accepts a phonetic spelling and produces a first cut at the values needed.

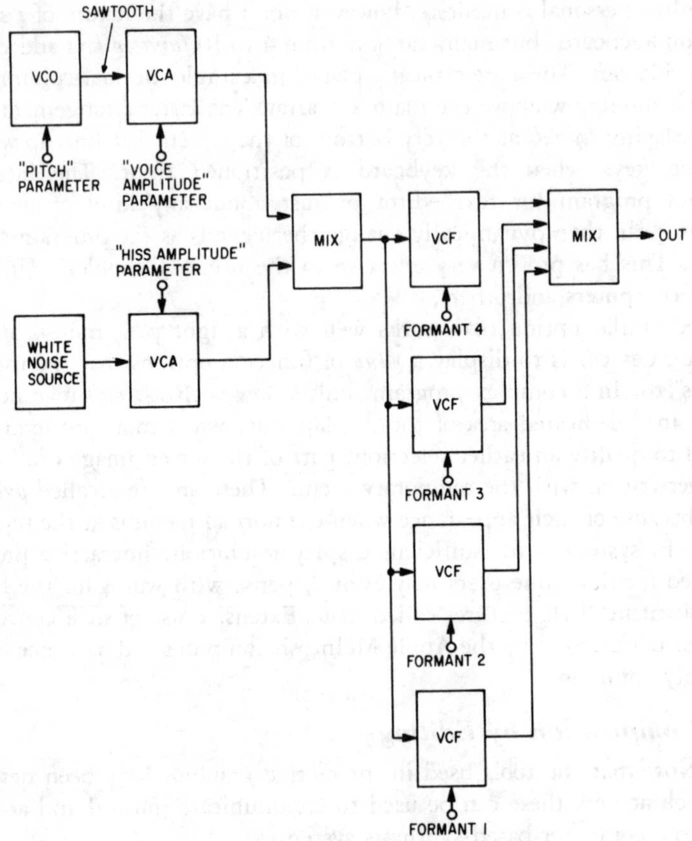

Fig. 11–6. Singing voice synthesis patch

Again, even though the initial values are crude, a starting point is established from which improvements may be made.

With an interactive graphics editing system, the task of determining magnitude and direction of necessary changes and then actually accomplishing the changes is considerably simplified. An editing function is distinguished from an input function by the fact that its action depends on what is already there. Some editing functions may be *reversible*. This means that two functions with opposite effect are available and that anything done by one can be undone by applying the other. Nonreversible functions can only be undone by retrieving a copy of the data made prior to execution of the nonreversible function. Examples of both types of functions will be given later in this discussion.

Figure 11–6 shows the configuration of analog-synthesizing equipment used in this example. The application is speech (singing) synthesis, and seven independent parameters are to be controlled. Four of these are the center frequencies of the four bandpass filters used to simulate the first four formants of speech. Two more are used to control the amplitude of the voice (buzz) and noise (hiss) sources. The last determines the pitch of the voice. It is assumed that a multiple-channel DAC has been connected to the computer so that the synthesizer modules can be controlled. For an application such as this, 50 to 100 updates of the parameters per second should be sufficient.

While experts in the field might argue the completeness of this model for producing a convincing singing voice, it is the author's belief that precise control of the parameters available is often more important than the number of parameters being controlled. The purpose here is to understand how interactive graphics can be utilized to quickly determine how these seven parameters should be varied to obtain the desired result. Further details concerning speech synthesis theory and practice are abundantly available in the references.

Figure 11–7 shows what a graphic display representation of a portion of these seven control functions might look like. The horizontal axis is time and the vertical axes depend on the particular curve. With all seven functions shown at once, it is easy to see the relationships that exist among the functions. When more detail is required, such as when actually editing one

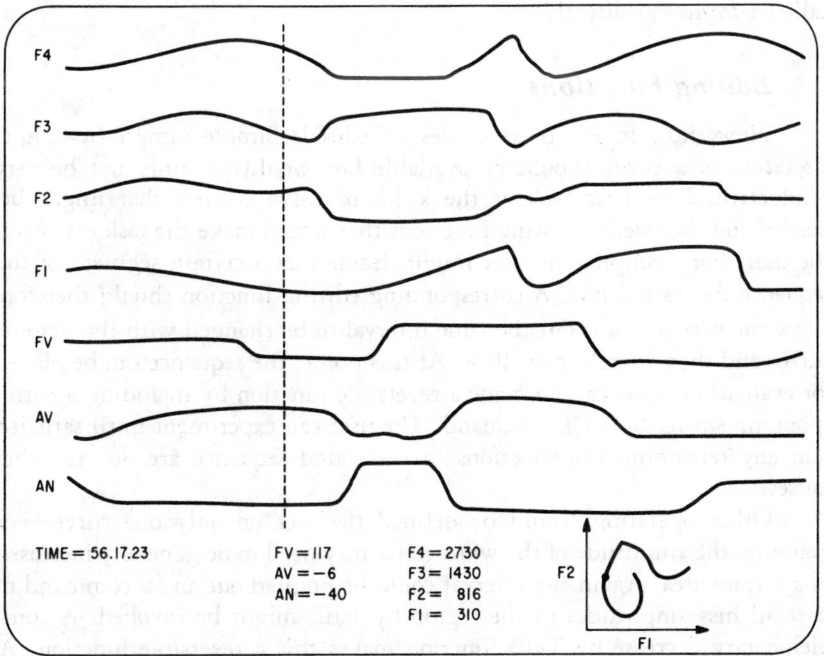

Fig. 11–7. Typical display of portion of speech synthesis sequence

of the curves, a command or function key would be available to suppress display of all but one or two of the curves.

Also shown is a cursor that can be used to designate a specific point in time on the functions. The cursor can be easily moved back and forth to find the area of interest. Any of the input devices mentioned earlier could be used to move the cursor, even the function keyboard. To aid the user in finding the audible area of interest, the program could be set up to actually send the corresponding data to the synthesizer as the cursor is moved.

Each of the seven parameter values, of course, has some kind of physical units, such as hertz for the formant and pitch frequencies. While the exact value of a parameter may not be as important as its relationship to other parameters, it is often necessary to know the value more precisely than the display shows it. Accordingly, the values of each parameter at the current cursor position is displayed at the bottom of the screen.

For critically comparing two parameters, it is useful to be able to plot one against another as is done in the bottom right corner. Commands, of course, would be available to select the parameters being compared. The curve shown represents the time interval spanning the screen and the emphasized point represents the current cursor position. One thing the curve does not show is the time scale, but the user can get a good feel for it by moving the cursor and noting the corresponding movement of the emphasized point. It is even possible to have editing functions that operate on this curve (often called a *trajectory*) directly.

Editing Functions

Now, how might these curves be edited? Simple sample-by-sample alteration of a curve should be available but would certainly not be very productive. Let's first look at the kinds of curve editing that might be needed and then define editing functions that would make the task easier for the user. For example, the user might decide that a certain segment of the sequence moves too fast. A corresponding editing function should therefore allow the user to point out the time interval to be changed with the graphic cursor and then stretch it by 10%. At this point, the sequence can be played for evaluation. This can be made a reversible function by including a corresponding shrink by 10% command. The user can experiment until satisfied that any remaining imperfections in the sound sequence are due to other causes.

Other operations could be defined that act on only one curve. For example, the amplitude of the white noise may need to be generally increased in a certain area. Again the interval could be pointed out and a command to raise all hiss amplitudes in the region by 1 dB might be invoked. A complementary decrease by 1-dB function makes this a reversible function. A copy function might be imagined whereby the contour of one curve could be

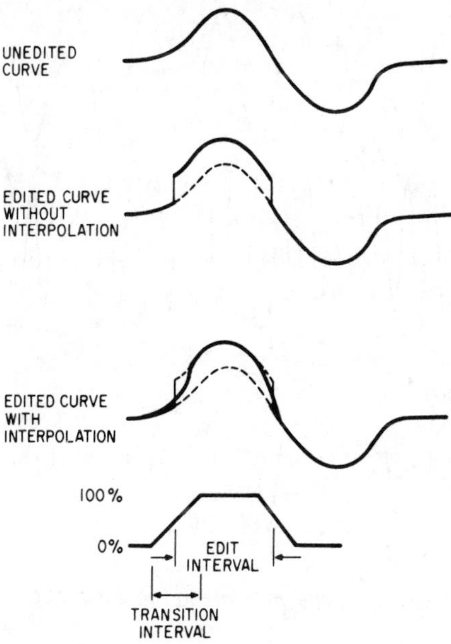

Fig. 11–8. Interpolation window

copied to another curve over a specified interval. Contours could also be swapped or even called up from a library of contours that had been successfully used earlier. Note that these are nonreversible functions. The editing software should have provisions for saving the status of things before a nonreversible function is performed.

At this point, a potential problem is seen. These editing changes can result in a discontinuity at the boundary between edited and unedited portions of the curves. What is needed is a method of *interpolation* so that the boundary transitions are smooth. Figure 11–8 should be helpful in visualizing how such interpolation might be done. A key concept is the idea of an *interpolation window*. An interpolation window is itself a curve that varies between 0% and 100%. In use, it is applied to two curves; the original unedited curve and the edited but not interpolated curve. The result is a third, interpolated curve that actually consists of a weighted sum of the first two curves. In effect, the interpolation window specifies how to weight the sum. At the 0% points, the result is equal to the unedited curve. At the 50% points, the result lies midway between unedited and edited curves. At the 100% point, it is all edited curve. As can be seen, interpolation considerably smooths the transition between unedited and edited segments.

In use, no single interpolation window shape is ideal for all situations. One variable is the width of the transition interval relative to the edit interval. Another is the shape of the transition interval itself. Although the

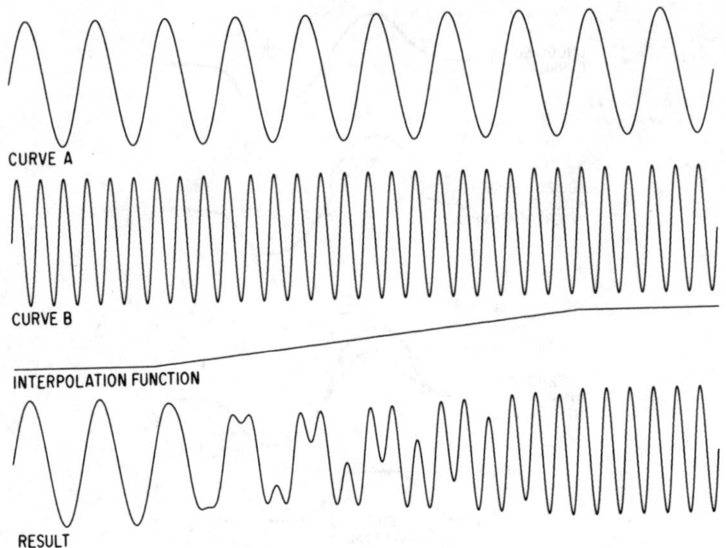

Fig. 11–9. Interpolation between two different curves

window is continuous at the beginning and end of the transition interval, its *slope* is not. A smooth fillet at these points might be more desirable for many applications.

The concept of interpolation and variable interpolation windows can be useful for other functions as well. For example, rather than interpolating unedited and edited curves, one might want to interpolate between two completely different curves. Figure 11–9 shows how two curves, A and B, are combined using an interpolation curve. The result starts out the same as A but then gradually acquires an increasing proportion of B's characteristics. Eventually, it is all B. Like the interpolation windows, various shapes and durations for the interpolation curve are possible.

Another possibility is interpolation between a varying curve and a constant. The effect is a "pulling" of the varying curve toward the constant and a reduction in the degree of variation. From these examples, it should be obvious that interpolation is a very powerful technique not only for editing but for building up control functions from nothing.

Noncontinuous Curves

Not all synthesis control functions are continuous curves; some are discrete on–off functions. A good example would be rhythm instruments. Some of these, such as drums, have no "duration" per se, so the only variable to represent on the screen is discrete points in time. Others may have a controllable duration, so initiation and conclusion points are needed. Figure 11–10 shows how a complex rhythm might be represented on a graphic

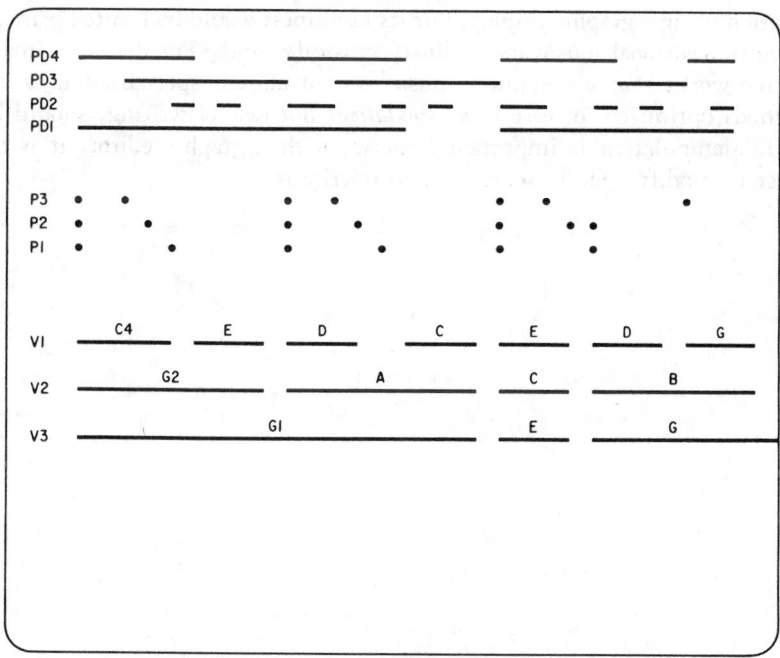

Fig. 11–10. Typical display of portion of rhythm sequence

display screen. Each line of symbols represents a different percussion instrument. For those with initiation points only, a simple point is plotted when the sound starts. For those with duration, a line connecting initiation and conclusion points is drawn. In the general case, percussion sounds are combined with notes of a definite pitch, which themselves have a duration and can be represented by lines as well but with an identifier, perhaps a small letter or number over the line, to specify the note's pitch, amplitude, or other information. Parameter curves for complex sounds could be mixed in as well.

Editing functions for on–off controls are much simpler than for parameter curves, since time is the only significant variable. Essentially, all that can be done is to move initiation and conclusion points forward and back, delete events, and add events. In the case of identified events, the identification can be changed. It would also be desirable to be able to reassign a string of events to a different instrument.

Note that all of this is starting to approach a method of computer music notation but with a heavy graphic orientation. Actually, standard music notation is somewhat graphic, at least in the representation of note pitches and to some extent note sequencing, but beyond that it is strictly symbolic. A system could certainly be set up to conveniently enter and edit music notation using a graphic display, but its usefulness would be limited primarily to conventional music and ordinary musical sounds. For the more imaginative works that a computer music system allows, specialized notation methods optimized for ease in *manipulation*, not ease of writing, should be used. Manipulation is important because, with a graphic editor, it is far easier to modify a faulty score than to rewrite it.

SECTION III

Digital Synthesis and Sound Modification

In the previous section, the application of microcomputers to the control of external synthesis equipment was examined in detail. In this section, we will discuss methods of having digital logic or the computer itself merely *simulate* such equipment. As was mentioned briefly in Chapter 4, this is by far the most powerful synthesis technique known because *any* computer can simulate *any* quantity of conventional or special-purpose synthesis equipment. Although the full benefit of such flexibility usually requires operation outside of real time, the concepts are useful in designing real-time digital synthesis systems as well.

12
Digital-to-Analog and Analog-to-Digital Conversion of Audio

One of the most important components of a digital sound synthesis system is the DAC used to convert digital data into an analog audio signal. Conversely, sound modification by digital methods requires an ADC of high quality. Unfortunately, one cannot simply buy a DAC or ADC module from a converter company, interface it to a computer or other digital device, connect it to an audio system, and expect good results. Although the modules do indeed convert between analog and digital domains, additional hardware and signal processing is necessary before they can handle audio well. Since synthesis is of greatest interest here, this discussion will be concerned primarily with digital-to-analog conversion of audio signals.

In Chapter 4, it was learned that at least in theory the audio quality possible with a DAC is dependent on only two factors. The *sample rate*, which is the speed at which numbers are fed to the DAC, determines the upper frequency response limit of the system, while the *resolution*, which is related to the number of possible output voltage steps, determines the signal-to-noise ratio. Unfortunately, however, there are other sources of error that tend to degrade the signal-to-noise ratio. In Chapter 7, it was noted that when the digital input to a DAC is changed the output may not move smoothly to the the new value. Instead, it can glitch momentarily to a voltage far removed from either the previous or the new voltage. Such glitching produces distortion that may be severe. Even if glitching was absent, the DAC's output amplifier will contribute to distortion if it ever *slews* between voltage levels. Inexpensive, slow amplifiers can generate a large amount of high-frequency distortion this way.

Figure 12-1 shows what a practical, high-performance audio DAC system would consist of. First, a rock-steady sample rate is essential, since any variation increases noise and distortion. For example, even a 10-nsec random jitter in the sample-to-sample time can create a noise floor just 66 dB below the signal level at a 50-ks/s sample rate. This in effect negates the benefit of using DACs with more than 11 bits of resolution. Generally, a fixed-frequency crystal oscillator driving a programmable (or fixed) modulus

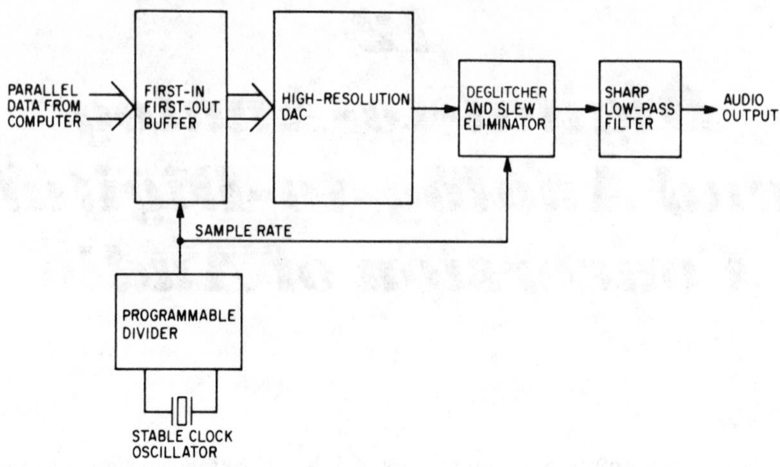

Fig. 12–1 High-quality audio DAC system

counter is used for the time base. Such a setup can be expected to exhibit a jitter of less than 1 nsec if the oscillator is shielded from electrical noise. Also, the higher crystal frequencies such as 10 MHz tend to reduce jitter even further.

Because of the stability requirement, connecting the DAC directly to an output port and then using the computer's interrupt system to time the samples is unsuitable for anything other than initial experimentation. The same applies to the direct memory access facility of most computers. Instead, a first-in, first-out buffer is inserted between the computer and the DAC. With the buffer, sample pulses from the time base cause an immediate (or with constant delay) transfer of data to the DAC while the computer has additional time to provide the next sample to the buffer. Often only one stage of buffering, which makes it a simple register, is sufficient. In other cases, FIFO IC chips containing 40 or so stages can bridge gaps in the data flow up to nearly a millisecond at 50 ks/s. In fact, the computer itself will tyically be acting as a large FIFO if the data is coming from a mass storage device.

Other elements in the chain are the high-resolution DAC, low-pass filter, and combination deglitcher/antislew device. Each of these will be described in detail in the following sections.

Increasing Dynamic Range

The most difficult and hence most expensive requirement of a high-fidelty audio DAC is the high-resolution DAC module. Earlier it was shown that the maximum signal-to-noise ratio that can be expected from an N bit DAC is 6N dB. Note the importance of the word *maximum*. This refers to the ideal condition in which the signal exactly fills the full-scale range of the

DAC. A signal level higher than this will increase distortion (which is the same as noise if the signal is a complex waveform) due to clipping, while a lower-level signal will reduce the S/N ratio because the noise level is independent of the signal level. The graph in Fig. 12–2 shows this effect. Also shown is the S/N ratio characteristic of a typical professional audio tape recorder rated at 60 dB S/N. Note that these curves represent unweighted, wideband signal/(noise + distortion) and do not take into account the fact that the tape recorder's mostly high-frequency noise may be less audible than the white noise typical of DACs.

The most obvious feature of the graph is the very sudden onset of overload (clipping) distortion in the DAC curves. The tape recorder, on the other hand, has a more gradual overload characteristic. At the 40-dB point, which represents 1% overload distortion (the minimum amount audible to most people), the tape recorder is handling about 10 dB more signal than a 10-bit DAC can. This is called "headroom" and is valuable for handling momentary peaks and overloads without excessive distortion. For the 10-bit DAC to have the same amount of headroom, the average signal it handles must be reduced by 10 dB. Thus, a 12-bit DAC would probably be needed to equal the tape recorder's noise performance with any real signal containing momentary peaks.

In the following discussion, it is assumed that 16-bit sample words are available from the synthesis process. This level of precision fits the word size of 8- and 16-bit computers and is generally regarded as the ultimate in an audio DAC system. However, the discussion applies equally well to other sample sizes both more and less than 16 bits.

Brute Force

It is clear from the foregoing that a high-resolution DAC will be needed in a high-fidelity DAC system. Even with a 12-bit DAC and 10 dB of headroom, signal levels must be carefully monitored to maintain an overall high S/N while at the same time avoiding overload. The additional dynamic range afforded by 14- and 16-bit DACs not only improves the sound (in live performance anyway) but reduces the effort required to control signal levels.

Whereas a suitable 12-bit DAC module can be purchased for about $30, additional resolution comes at a high price. Fourteen bits, for example, command $150 or more while 16 bits go for about $300. These prices are for units with guaranteed monotonicity and linearity errors of less than one-half of the least significant bit over a reasonably wide temperature range.

The price also pays for a super precise and stable reference voltage source so that the full-scale accuracy is comparable to the linearity. In audio work, full-scale accuracy is of little concern, since its only effect is a shift in signal amplitude. For example, a 1% shift in reference voltage, which would be intolerable in normal applications of these DACs, would amount to only a

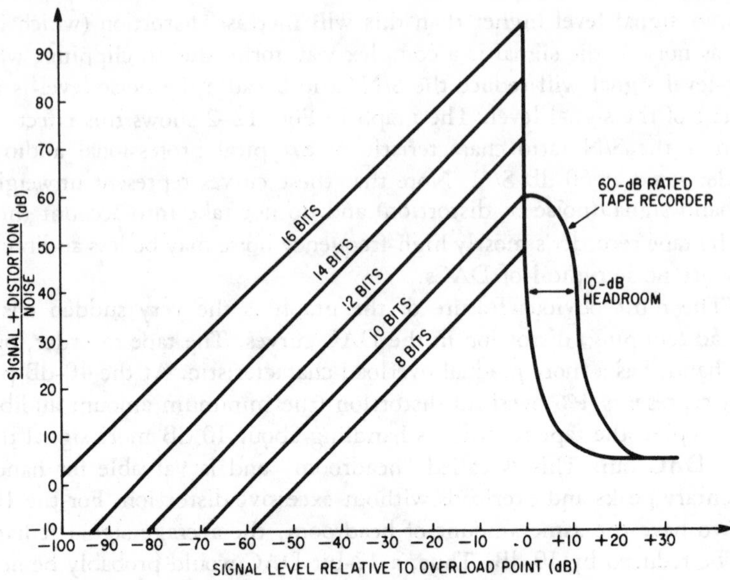

Fig. 12–2. Noise performance of several DACs and a professional tape recorder

0.08-dB shift in level. Fortunately, with the increased interest in digital audio equipment, lower-cost DAC modules without such overkill in the reference voltage source are becoming available.

Another potential complication is that the manufacturers of these units recommend periodic (monthly) "recalibration" in order to continuously meet their specifications. This should not be surprising, since one-half of the least significant bit on a 16-bitter is a mere 0.0008% or 8 parts per million. Any ordinary resistor or zener diode would drift that much from the heat of a cigarette 3 feet away! Even the precision, low-drift components used in these DACs can experience a small but permanent shift if exposed to extremes in temperature.

Fortunately, though, nearly all of the long-term drift is due to the zener reference source having no audible effect. Amplifier offset shifts may also contribute but again there is no audible effect. The ladder resistors that determine the linearity and therefore the noise level are matched and normally drift together. Thus, a yearly check is probably all that is required if temperature extremes are avoided.

In the final analysis, if one wants better than 12-bit performance and a minimum of trouble, and an extra couple of hundred dollars is not really significant, then a true 14- or 16-bit DAC is probably the best choice. Note also that this is the only way to attain the noise performance suggested by the curves in Fig. 12–2 without compromise. The cost-cutting techniques that will be studied next all sacrifice something in order to avoid using a true high-resolution DAC.

Sign-Magnitude Coding

Looking again at the curves in Fig. 12–2, it is seen that the maximum S/N ratio of 96 dB for a 16-bit DAC occurs right at the point of overload. In a real listening situation, this would correspond to the peak of the loudest crescendo in the piece. At the ear-shattering volume this might represent, one is highly unlikely to notice a noise level scarcely louder than a heartbeat. On the other hand, during extremely quiet passages when the noise would be noticed most, the noise level remains unchanged meaning that the S/N ratio has degraded.

It would be nice if some of the excess S/N at high signal levels could be traded off for a cheaper DAC without affecting or even improving the S/N at lower signal levels. This, in fact, is possible and can be accomplished in at least three different ways.

Although not specifically mentioned previously, an audio DAC must be connected so that both positive and negative voltages can be produced. Normally, this is accomplished by offset binary coding and shifting the normally unipolar DAC output down by exactly one-half of full scale. In audio applications, a dc blocking capacitor is sufficient for the level shifting.

Low signal levels imply that the *net* DAC output hovers around zero. An offset binary DAC, however, sees this as one-half scale. In Chapter 7, it was determined that the most significant bit of the DAC had the greatest accuracy requirement; therefore, it is logical to assume that the greatest linearity error would occur when the MSB switches. Unfortunately, this occurs at half scale also so this kind of DAC imperfection would directly subtract from the S/N ratio at *low* signal levels as well as high. Thus, with offset binary coding, one *must* use a highly linear DAC.

The sign-magnitude method of obtaining a bipolar DAC output does not suffer from this problem. Using the basic circuit configuration that was shown in Fig. 7–17, small signal levels will only exercise the lesser significant DAC bits, thus eliminating the noise caused by errors in the most significant bits. As a side effect, the sign-bit amplifier provides the equivalent of one additional bit of resolution making a 16-bit DAC act like a 17-bitter!

The significance of all this is that inexpensive DACs with 16 bits of resolution but only 13 or so bits of *linearity* are available. When linearity is less than resolution it means that the most significant bits are off enough to make the DAC nonlinear at the points where the affected bits change. A 16-bit DAC with 13-bit linearity could have nearly an eight-step gap or backtrack right at 1/2 scale, lesser errors at 1/4 and 3/4 scale, and an even smaller error at 1/8, 3/8, 5/8, and 7/8 scale. If connected in an offset binary circuit, it would perform no better than a 13-bit DAC. But when connected in a sign-magnitude circuit, we have just the tradeoff that we have been looking for as the curve in Fig. 12–3 shows.

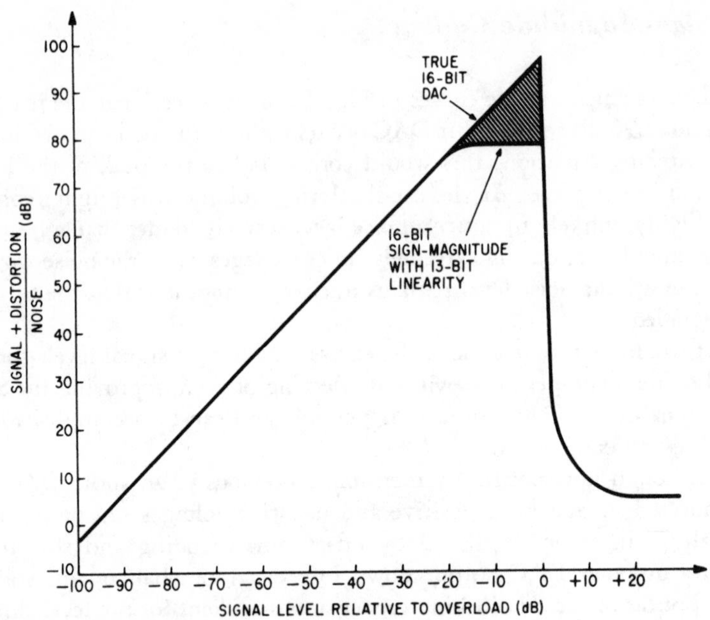

Fig. 12–3. Performance of degraded linearity sign-magnitude DAC

At low levels, the signal has insufficient amplitude to even reach the nonlinearities at ⅛ scale. Thus, at these levels the S/N ratio is what would be expected from a true 16-bit DAC. At higher levels, the little glitches at ⅛, ¼, etc., tend to raise the noise level to what a 13-bit DAC would provide. But since the sound is so loud at this point anyway the increased noise will be totally inaudible. In effect, the shaded area is what is given up when a $50–$100 pseudo-16-bit DAC is substituted for the $300 true 16-bit unit.

In using the sign-magnitude circuit, it is mandatory that the two resistors be accurately matched. If they are not, an unpleasant even order harmonic distortion is generated. The two analog switches required to switch between normal and inverted DAC output are not much of a problem, since one of them would be used anyway in the deglitcher to be described.

Some logic is required to convert normal twos-complement integers to sign-magnitude integers. This consists of a set of N-1 exclusive-or gates inserted in series with the 15 low order bits to the DAC. When the input is negative, the gates invert the twos-complement negative number back into a positive magnitude. The DAC output should be offset by +1/2 the step size to retain a distinction between 0 and −1, which is translated to −0.

Note that this method could be extended to additional bits, since the most significant bits no longer must be precisely calibrated. As a practical matter, though, personal computers are unlikely to have words longer than

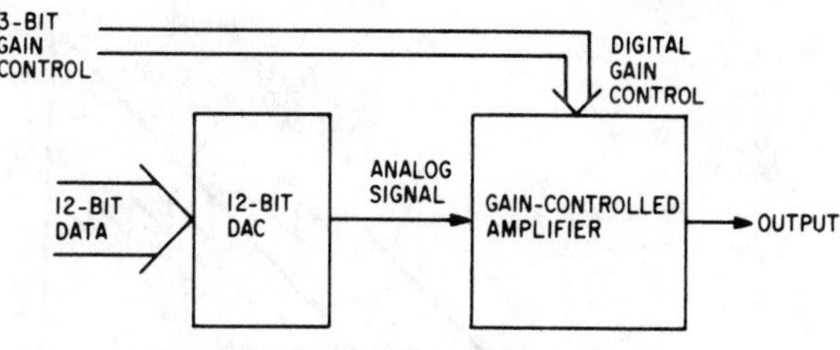

Fig. 12–4. Floating-point DAC

16 bits for quite some time, and the difference would probably be inaudible anyway.

Segmented DAC

The sign-magnitude DAC just described is really a special case of the *segmented* DAC discussed in Chapter 7 with two segments: one from minus full scale to just under zero and the other from just over zero to plus full scale. Use of a real segmented DAC with the usual 8 or 16 segments in fact provides the same benefits as sign magnitude coding with the advantage of having the code conversion logic and sign-bit stage built into the DAC module itself. There are in fact 16-bit DACs on the market designed for audio applications that use the segmented architecture. Note that, although the *differential* linearity at zero (and elsewhere) may be essentially perfect, if the spec sheet reads 13-bit *integral* linearity (0.006%), then at high signal levels the distortion due to that nonlinearity will be the same as a 13-bit DAC. In practice, the distortion generated by a segmented DAC with 13-bit integral linearity will be mostly low-order harmonics that tend to be less audible than the sharp spikes caused by localized nonlinearities in an equivalent all-ladder DAC. Interestingly, a harmonic distortion analyzer's typical rms readout would lead one to the opposite conclusion.

Floating-Point DACs

A method commonly used in analog audio equipment to improve apparent S/N ratio is to "ride the gain." Strong signals are made stronger by increasing the gain, while weak signals are made even weaker by reducing the gain. Since the noise is most audible at low signal levels, the act of reducing the gain also reduces the noise and so improves the S/N ratio. The main problem encountered in this scheme is knowing when and how much to change the gain setting.

In an audio DAC application, it should be possible to apply the same concept to a 12-bit DAC to improve its S/N ratio at low signal levels. Consider the setup in Fig. 12–4. Twelve-bit samples operate the 12-bit DAC in the normal way. However, three additional bits control a variable-gain

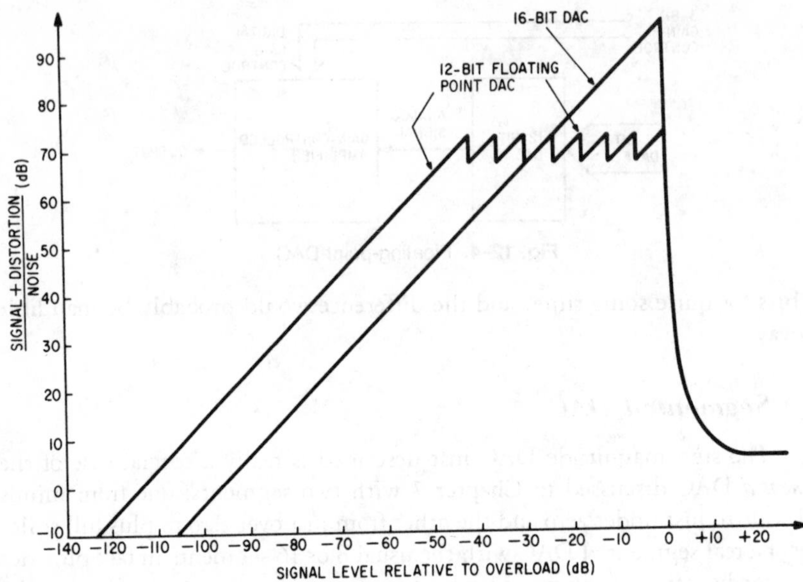

Fig. 12–5. Floating-point DAC performance

amplifier, which the DAC drives. Low signal levels are created by programming the amplifier for a low gain rather than reducing the digital sample values going to the DAC. Thus, the DAC's noise is also reduced and the resulting S/N ratio tends to be constant at low signal levels.

Let us assume for a moment that the programmable gain amplifier has eight possible gain settings, each a factor of two apart. Thus, gains of 1.0, 0.5, 0.25, . . . , 0.0078 are possible. The corresponding S/N ratio graph for the system is shown in Fig. 12–5. The *maximum* S/N ratio is no more than that of an ordinary 12-bit DAC, but at low signal levels it is actually better than a true 16-bit unit! Furthermore, only 15 bits are used for the samples. Note that these are theoretical figures, since retaining a noise level 115 dB below the overload point in subsequent circuitry is quite a feat indeed.

Since the gain data are carried along with the signal data in each sample, there is no problem in handling transients as there is in an analog audio system. The data format is actually very much like the floating point number format in computer arithmetic. The 12 bits going to the DAC are the "fraction" part, while the 3 bits going to the gain control circuit are the "exponent." The base of 2 is set by the design of the gain control circuit.

A floating-point DAC can also be viewed as having a variable step size. In the region close to zero, the step size is quite small, which minimizes quantization noise. As the signal level increases, the step size becomes twice as large, four times, etc., until at levels near overload the steps are 128 times larger than at low levels. Of course, every time the step size is doubled the quantization noise increases by 6 dB, but the signal has also increased by 6 dB; thus, the S/N ratio is nearly constant.

One problem in using this setup is that the sample data must be converted from their typical 16-bit signed integer format into the floating point format, which can be time consuming. A relatively simple hardware translator, however, can be placed between the computer and the DAC to accomplish this on the fly. Essentially, the translator must determine which of several "ranges" each sample lies in. The range determination then controls the amplifier and a parallel shifter, which insures that the most significant 12 bits in the particular sample are sent to the DAC. Operation would be as follows:

Digital sample values	*Bits to DAC*	*Gain selection*
0000–07FF	0–11	0.0625
0800–0FFF	1–12	0.125
1000–1FFF	2–13	0.25
2000–3FFF	3–14	0.5
4000–7FFF	4–15	1.0

A similar table can be constructed for negative sample values. Note that the lowest gain used is 0.0625. If the input samples are normal 16-bit integers, it is not possible to get the extra dynamic range that floating-point format allows.

Aside from the parallel shifter, constructing a floating-point DAC is fairly simple. For the DAC part, one would use a standard 12-bit DAC module set up for offset binary coding with an inverter in the most significant bit to make it twos complement. The gain-controlled amplifier must be accurate, at least to the 0.012% level to retain 12-bit performance. If the gains are not accurate, there can be a nonlinearity at points where the gain switches such as in Fig. 12–6. Simple analog switches with precision gain-setting resistors can be used for the amplifier. A multiplying DAC could also be used if it can accept a bipolar reference. The main DAC output would be connected to the reference input of the multiplying DAC. The 3-bit "exponent" would be sent to a 1-of-8 decoder whose outputs would be connected to the most significant 8 bits of the MDAC. The MDAC output then becomes the final system output.

Exponential DACs

Just as exponential control voltages in analog synthesizers allow accurate, noise-free representation of parameters having a wide range, exponential DACs, which are also called *companding* DACs, can increase audio dynamic range with a limited number of sample bits. For use with audio signals, which are inherently linear, one would first take the logarithm of the sample value.

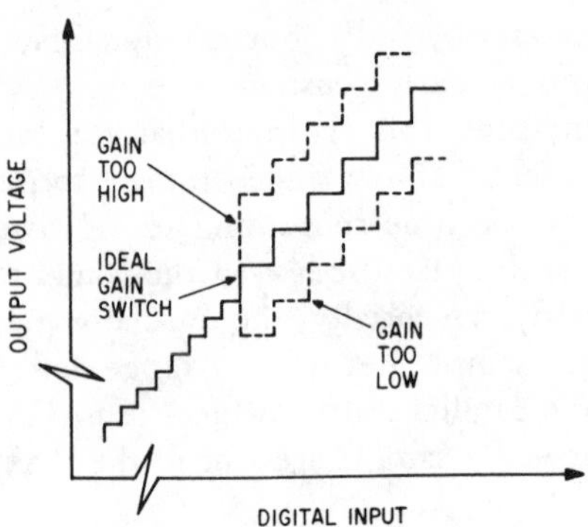

Fig. 12–6. Effect of gain accuracy

When fed to an exponential DAC, the output becomes a linear function again. One could also view an exponential DAC as having a continuously increasing step size as the output voltage increases. Thus, the step size is a constant *percentage* of the *output* voltage rather than just a constant voltage.

Exponential DACs are ideal for absolutely minimizing the number of bits in each sample without unduly sacrificing dynamic range. An 8-bit scheme used extensively in long-distance telephone circuits, for example, maintains a nearly constant S/N ratio of 35 dB over a 35-dB signal level range, a feat that would otherwise require a 12-bit DAC.

Actually, a floating-point DAC is the first step toward an exponential DAC. Their drawback is the 6-dB ripple in S/N ratio that is apparent in Fig. 12–5. A true exponential DAC would have no ripple in the S/N curve at all.

One possibility for an exponential DAC circuit was shown in Fig. 7–10. For use as a DAC rather than an attenuator, one would simply apply a constant dc input voltage. A nice property of this circuit is that dynamic range and maximum S/N ratio can be independently adjusted. Each added bit on the left *doubles* the dynamic range measured in decibels. Each added bit on the right increases the S/N ratio by about 6 dB. Note, however, that there is no escaping resistor accuracy requirements; they still must be as accurate as a conventional DAC with an equivalent S/N rating. One problem with the circuit is the large number of amplifiers required, one per bit. Besides the possible accumulation of offset errors and amplifier noise, such a cascade tends to have a long settling time.

Another approach to the construction of an exponential DAC is essentially an extension of the floating-point approach using a smaller conventional DAC and greater-resolution gain-controlled amplifier. Rather than the base being 2.0, it could be $\sqrt{2}$. The gains available would therefore be 1.0, 0.707, 0.5, 0.353, 0.25, etc. The S/N ripple then would be about 3 dB. Smaller bases such as $\sqrt[4]{2}$ or $\sqrt[8]{2}$ would cut the ripple to 1.5 dB and 0.75

dB, respectively. What this actually amounts to is a piecewise linear approximation of a true exponential curve.

Segmented DACs using unequal segment slopes can also be used to make a piecewise linear-approximate exponential curve. The DAC-86 is a 7-bit plus sign unit that does this using a 4-bit fraction, a 3-bit exponent, and a base of 2. Its application is in digital telephone systems and occasionally speech synthesizers. To the author's knowledge, nobody has yet manufactured a high-fidelity (12 to 16 bits) exponential DAC module.

Which Is Best?

The logical question, then, is: Which technique is best for high-fidelity audio? Using a true 16-bit DAC is unmatched for convenience and does the best job possible on 16-bit sample data. It is expensive, however, and may require maintenance. Actually, the other techniques were developed years ago when a true 16-bit DAC was considered an "impossible dream."

Next in convenience is the use of any of the several "designed-for-audio" 16-bit converters currently on the market. While noise and distortion at high signal levels fall somewhat short of ideal 16-bit performance, it is doubtful if anyone could ever hear the difference. Architectures range from brute-force ladders with the differential linearity errors ignored to segmented units to sign-magnitude units. Burr-Brown, for example, offers both a ladder (PCM-51) and a segmented (PCM-52) 16-bit audio DAC in a 24-pin IC package for about $40. Analog Devices has a nice 40-pin CMOS segmented DAC (AD7546) in the same price range that will be used later in an example audio DAC circuit. Analogic sells a somewhat more expensive sign-magnitude hybrid module that probably comes closer to true 16-bit performance than any other "shortcut" unit currently available.

Floating-point and exponential DACs have the lowest potential cost for a wide-dynamic-range audio DAC. They are also suitable for expansion beyond the dynamic range of a true 16-bit unit if other audio components can be improved enough to make it worthwhile. However, the gain-controlled amplifier settling time and overall coding complexity make it a difficult technique to implement with discrete logic.

Reducing Distortion

As was mentioned earlier, glitching of the DAC can contribute to distortion that is unrelated to the resolution of the DAC itself. Actually, there would be no problem if the glitch magnitude and polarity were independent of the DAC output. Unfortunately, however, the glitch magnitude depends heavily on both the individual DAC steps involved and their combination. Typically, the largest glitch is experienced when the most significant bit of the DAC changes during the transition. Proportionally smaller glitches are associated with the lesser significant bits because, after all, their influence on the output is less.

If the DAC is offset binary encoded, the largest glitch, therefore, occurs right at zero crossing. Unfortunately, even low-amplitude signals are going to cross zero so the distortion due to glitching can become absolutely intolerable at low signal levels. The distortion also becomes worse at higher frequencies, since more glitch energy per unit time (power) is being released. Sign-magnitude coding can have the same problem because of switching transients from the sign-bit amplifier. Floating-point DACs, however, attenuate the zero-crossing glitch along with the signal at low levels.

Glitch magnitude and duration are not often specified on a DAC data sheet. When they are, the units are very likely to be volt-seconds because of the unpredictable nature of DAC glitches. Unfortunately, this alone is insufficient information to even estimate the distortion that might be produced in an audio application. What is needed is the rms voltage of the glitch and its duration so that the energy content can be determined.

Low-Glitch DAC Circuits

The two primary causes of glitching in DAC circuits are differences in the switching time of the various bits (skew) and differences between the bit turn-on and turn-off times. In some DAC circuits, the most significant bit switches carry considerably more current than the least significant bits, thus contributing to differences in switching times. Some R-2R designs, however, pass the same current through all of the bit switches, thus eliminating this cause of skew. Even the digital input register can contribute to skew, since it will undoubtedly span two or more ICs that may have different propagation times. The use of high-speed Schottky registers, which are verified to have equal delay times, will minimize this source of skew. Any sign-magnitude or floating-point translation logic should be in front of the input register as well.

Nonsymmetrical turn-on/turn-off time is an accepted fact of life among TTL logic designers. The reason is storage time in the saturated bipolar transistor switches, which also applies to many DAC analog switch designs. The digital input registers often accentuate the problem for the same reason. There are, however, low-glitch DACs on the market that use emitter-coupled logic internally for the register and nonsaturating current steering analog switches.

Typically, these are only available in 12-bit versions, since they are designed primarily for CRT deflection circuits. One type that is available has a maximum glitch amplitude of 40 mV, a duration of 60 nsec, and a full-scale output of ±5 V. With a 1-kHz full amplitude output, the glitch distortion would be about−78 dB with respect to the signal, about 6 dB below its 12-bit quantization noise. At 10 kHz, however, the glitch distortion rises by 10 dB, making it the dominant noise source.

Sample-and-Hold Deglitcher

The usual solution to DAC glitching at the sample rates used in audio applications is the incorporation of a sample-and-hold module at the output of the DAC. In operation, it would be switched to the hold state just prior to loading the next sample into the DAC and would not be switched back into the track mode until the DAC has settled at the new level. In this way, glitches from the DAC are not allowed to reach the output.

As a practical matter, however, even SAH modules glitch when switched from one state to another. This is alright, however, *if* the magnitude and polarity of the glitches are constant and independent of the signal level. In that case, the glitches contain energy only at the sample rate and its harmonics, which will eventually be filtered out. Most commercial SAH modules are fairly good in this respect. A linear variation of glitch magnitude with the signal level can also be acceptable, since the only effect then would be a slight shift in the dc level of the output.

Another SAH parameter that must be constant for low distortion is the switching time from hold to sample mode. If this varies nonlinearly with signal voltage level, then harmonic distortion is produced. Unfortunately, the switching time of most analog switches is signal voltage dependent. The reason is that they cannot turn on (or off) until the switch driver voltage crosses the switch threshold voltage which, as was discussed in Chapter 7, is relative to the signal voltage. Since the driver voltage does not have a zero rise time, the time to cross the threshold voltage will vary with the signal level. A linear variation would be alright, but a perfectly linear drive voltage ramp is unlikely. However, if the drive voltage is of sufficiently large amplitude and centered with respect to the signal, reasonably linear variation can be obtained.

Slew-Limiting Distortion

There still exists a subtle yet quite significant distortion mechanism in the typical SAH module that is unrelated to glitching or switching time variation. The mechanism is slew limiting of the amplifiers in the SAH module when switching from hold mode to sample mode. Figure 12–7 shows a typical SAH module. When the sampling switch is closed, the circuit acts as a simple voltage follower. When open, A2 buffers the capacitor voltage

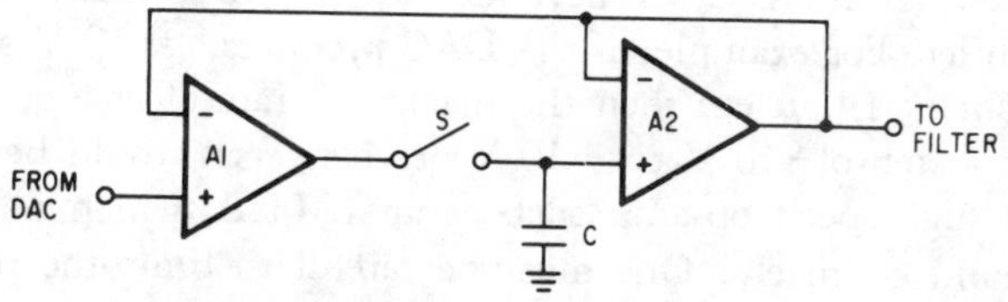

Fig. 12–7. Typical feedback SAH circuit

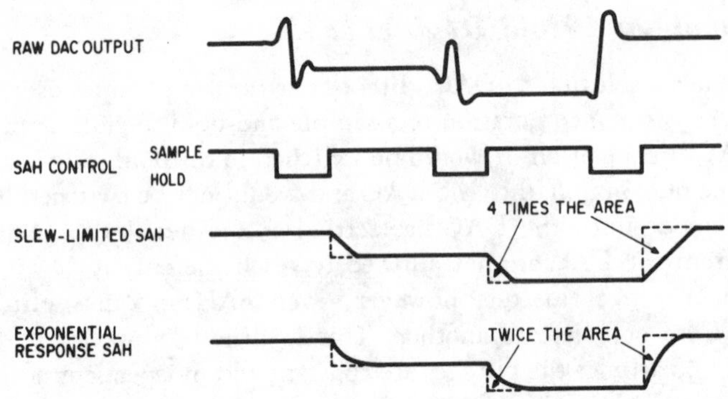

Fig. 12–8. Mechanism of slew-limiting distortion

and produces the output voltage. The effective offset voltage is dependent only on the characteristics of A1. This is normally important, since A2 is optimized for low-bias current and typically has a high offset voltage (A2 could even be a simple FET source follower, which, in fact, is often done).

The problem occurs when the input voltage changes while the circuit is in hold mode. When this occurs, A1 goes into saturation, since its feedback is from the previous input voltage. When S recloses, the capacitor is charged at a nearly constant rate from the saturated output of A1 through the switch resistance until its voltage essentially matches the new input voltage. At this point, A1 comes out of saturation and the output settles.

Figure 12–8 shows how linear charging of the hold capacitor contributes to distortion. For a one-unit change from one sample to the next, the shaded error is one-half square unit. But for a two-unit change, the error is two square units. Thus, the error is proportional to the *square* of the difference between successive samples. It's not difficult to see how this can generate a great deal of distortion, especially since slew times can easily reach 20% of the sample interval with this type of circuit.

If the step response is a normal inverse exponential instead of a linear ramp, the error is directly proportional to the step size. This situation does not cause any distortion, although it can affect the apparent overall signal amplitude from the DAC when the steps are large (high signal frequency).

Figure 12–9 shows a simple SAH that can be designed not to slew under any circumstances. If the values of R and C are properly chosen, then the voltage change across C will never exceed (or even approach) the slew rate of the amplifier. For example, if the DAC produces ± 10 V and the R-C time constant is 1.0 μsec, then the maximum rate of change of capacitor voltage (for a step of −10 V to +10 V or vice versa) would be 20 V/μsec. A standard high-speed op-amp such as an LM318, which is rated at 50 V/μsec, would do nicely. One must be careful to limit the peak current through the analog switch to a value less than its saturation current or a

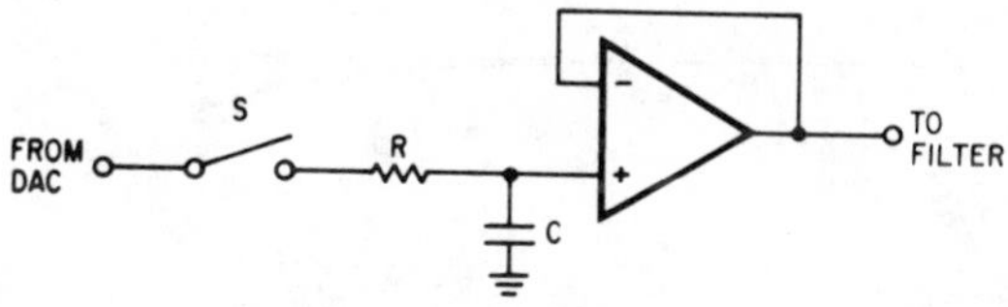

Fig. 12-9. Simple nonslewing SAH

secondary slewing effect may be introduced. The offset cancellation and low drift of the previous SAH circuit are simply not needed in audio applications where dc cannot be heard and maximum hold times are around 10 μsec.

Track-and-Ground Circuit

Another type of deglitcher that is suitable for audio DACs is called a track-and-ground circuit. Essentially, it uses one or possibly two analog switches to disconnect from the DAC and ground the filter input during the period that the DAC is glitching. In doing so, problems with SAH slewing, hold capacitor nonlinearity, and even part of the switching transient are neatly bypassed.

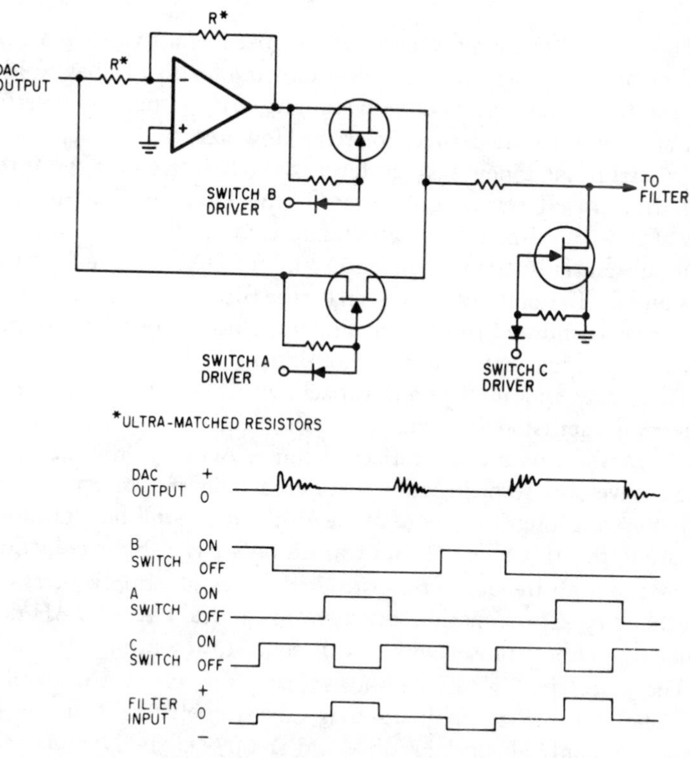

Fig. 12-10. Track-and-ground circuit

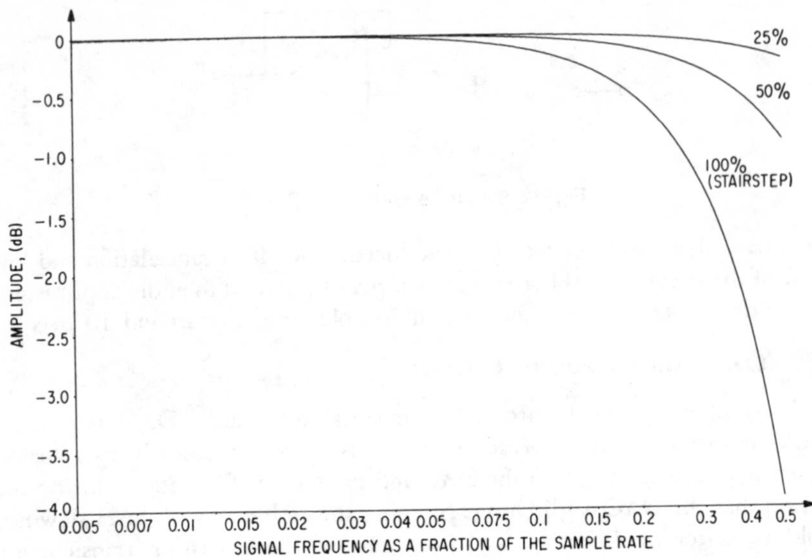

Fig. 12–11. Effect of finite DAC pulse width on high-frequency amplitude

Figure 12–10 shows a simplified schematic of a two-switch track-and-ground circuit integrated with a sign-bit switch for a sign-magnitude DAC. The A and B switches select between straight DAC output and inverted DAC output according to the desired polarity. However, both are open while the DAC is settling at a new voltage level. Switch C grounds the filter input during the turn-off transient of A or B, the DAC settling time, and the turnon of A or B. Although the grounding is not perfect due to on resistance of C, it substantially attenuates feedthrough of DAC glitches and transients from A and B. The only transient seen by the filter is from switch C itself and most of that is shunted to ground. Finally, since there are no amplifiers in the switching signal path, there is nothing to slew.

There does appear to be a drawback with the circuit, however. Rather than getting a stairstep approximation of the audio waveform, the filter gets pulses of constant width and variable height. Actually, the mathematics of sampled waveform reconstruction are derived on the assumption that the samples entering the filter are of *zero* width and varying but infinite height. Fortunately, the only effect of finite width pulses is a slight reduction in the amplitude of high-frequency reconstructed waves, or simply a loss of treble. A pure stairstep approximation such as from an ideal DAC or SAH deglitcher is actually a train of pulses with width equal to the sample period.

The graph in Fig. 12–11 shows that even this is a relatively minor effect. The stairstep approximation is down nearly 4 dB at the Nyquist frequency but only about 1.32 dB down at 60% of the Nyquist frequency, which represents a 15-kHz signal at a 50-ks/s sample rate. With pulses half as long as the sample period, a reasonable value for the previous track-and-ground circuit, the corresponding figures are 0.912 dB and 0.323 dB. In any case, the high-frequency droop can be compensated for in the low-pass filter.

Low-Pass Filter

The final component of the audio DAC system is the low-pass filter, which removes the sampling frequency and unwanted copies of the signal spectrum. Not all audio DAC/ADC applications require the same degree of filter sophistication, however. A DAC application at a 50-ks/s sample rate, for example, really needs a filter only to avoid burning out tweeters and interfering with the bias frequency of tape recorders. The ear itself is quite capable of filtering everything above 25 kHz. DAC applications at substantially lower sample rates need a reasonably good filter because the alias frequencies are audible. A sample rate of 15 ks/s, which would give good AM radio quality, would produce quite a harsh sound if frequencies above 7.5 kHz were not attenuated at least 30 dB to 40 dB. Audio-to-digital conversion at low to medium (10 ks/s to 30 ks/s) sample rates requires the best filters because high-frequency program content, which usually cannot be controlled, may transform into quite audible lower frequencies upon digitizing.

Low-Pass Filter Model

Figure 12–12 shows a model low-pass filter shape that all real low-pass filters resemble to some extent. The passband is the set of frequencies that the filter passes with little or no attenuation and extends from dc to the cutoff frequency. The stopband extends from the cutoff frequency to infinity and is the set of frequencies that the filter attenuates substantially. The cutoff slope is a measure of how sharply the filter distinguishes between passband and

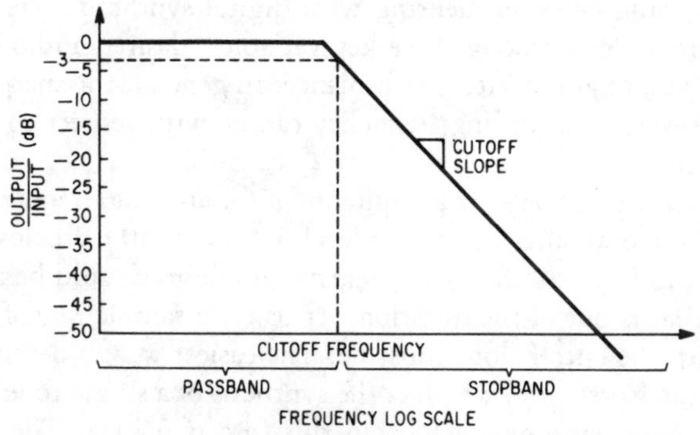

Fig. 12–12. Model low-pass filter shape

stopband regions. An ideal low-pass filter would exhibit a perfectly flat passband, an infinite cutoff slope, and complete signal attenuation in the stopband.

Cutoff frequency is not always a consistently defined term. For simple filters, it is usually given as the frequency at which the signal is attenuated by 3 dB or to about 70% of its low-frequency amplitude. For more sophisticated filters, it is the lowest frequency at which cutoff becomes evident. In either case, the cutoff frequency merely marks the *beginning* of *noticeable* attenuation and certainly should not be set equal to one-half the sample rate in audio DAC applications.

In many cases, the cutoff slope of the filter is reasonably linear when frequency is plotted on a log scale and the filter attenuation is plotted in decibels (as is done in Fig. 12–12). On such a scale, frequency decades, which are tenfold increases, and octaves, which are frequency doublings, are of consistent length anywhere on the scale. Since the cutoff slope is approximately linear, it is convenient to specify it in terms of "decibels per decade" or "decibels per octave" with the latter being the more common term. In cases in which the cutoff slope is not constant, it is almost always steeper close to the cutoff frequency than further out. In these cases, either the maximum and ultimate slopes are both given or a composite figure, which is the average slope over the first octave beyond cutoff, is given.

Sometimes the *pole count* is used to characterize the steepness of the cutoff slope. In simple filters, the ultimate cutoff slope is always equal to the number of *effective* reactive elements in the filter circuit times 6 dB/octave. A reactive element is either a capacitor or inductor directly in the signal path that is not performing a coupling, bypass, or suppression function. More complex filters may have an initial cutoff steepness greater than this but will always end up with 6N slopes well beyond cutoff.

Actual Filter Requirements

In designing or experimenting with digital synthesis, one must make an intelligent tradeoff among three key variables: desired audio bandwidth, sample rate, and required filter performance. In general, the sharper the filter cutoff, the lower the sampling frequency can be with respect to the highest signal frequency.

As an example, consider a requirement for an audio frequency response flat to 5 kHz and an alias distortion level of at least 50 dB below the signal level. For an infinite cutoff slope filter,the sample rate could be as low as 10 ks/s. Since that is out of the question, let us try a sample rate of 12 ks/s and see how sharp the cutoff slope must be. The easiest way to determine this is to consider the worst case, which is the synthesis of a single tone right at the top of the frequency range, which in this case is 5 kHz. The lowest alias frequency with the 12-ks/s sample rate is 12 − 5 or 7 kHz and the filter must attenuate this by at least 50 dB. Assuming the cutoff frequency is 5

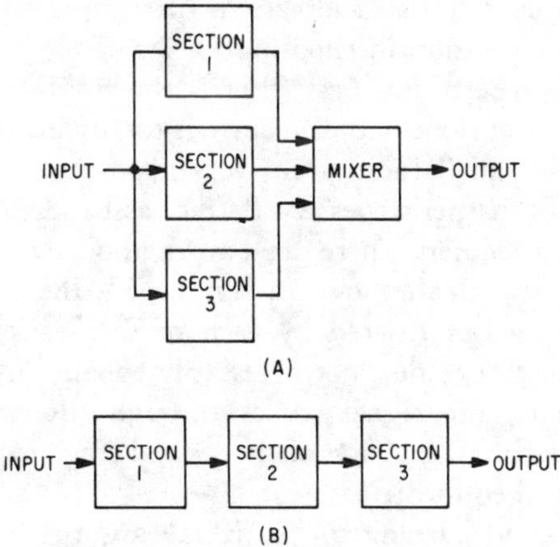

Fig. 12–13. Methods of filter section combination. (A) Parallel method. (B) Cascade method.

kHz, the interval from 5 kHz to 7 kHz is just short of one-half an octave using the formula: Octaves = 1.443LN(*Fh*/*Fl*), where *Fh* and *Fl* are the upper and lower frequencies, respectively. Thus, the cutoff slope would have to be 95 dB to 100 dB/octave, a very high figure indeed. If the sample rate were raised 25% to 15 ks/s, the filter could go all the way to 10 kHz before it must attenuate 50 dB. This gives a cutoff slope of only 50 dB/octave, a much, much easier filter to implement. In most cases, these requirements could be relaxed somewhat. It is unlikely that one would want to shatter glass with a maximum-amplitude, maximum-frequency tone and then worry about small fractions of a percent of alias distortion.

Both of the preceding examples assumed that the digital synthesis system never tried to *generate* frequencies higher than 5 kHz. As will be seen later, it may be difficult to meet that constraint and still make good use of frequencies close to 5 kHz. If a 6-kHz tone was actually synthesized in the 15-ks/s system, the simple filter would pass its *alias* at 8 kHz with an attenuation of only 33 dB. On the other hand, if one used the filter designed for a 12-ks/s system with a 15-ks/s sample rate, it would be permissible to synthesize frequencies as high as *8 kHz* without exceeding the −50-dB alias rejection requirement. Note that 8 kHz is actually *above* one-half the sample rate. Its alias frequency is therefore *lower* than the signal frequency, but since that is 7 kHz, the filter attenuates it adequately. The conclusion, then, is that a good filter can either reduce the required sample rate, simplify the synthesis computations, or some of both.

Sharp Low-Pass Filter Design

Sharp low-pass filter design is itself an interesting topic that has filled many books, usually with quite a bit of mathematics. Here we will just discuss the general characteristics of various filter types so that the reader can make an intelligent decision in choosing one.

The simplest type of low-pass filter is the single-pole R-C. Unfortunately, its gentle cutoff slope of 6 dB/octave is totally inadequate for an audio DAC. Also its passband flatness is not very good.

In order to get sharper slopes and flatter passbands, several filter *sections* may be combined together. There are two methods of combination called *parallel* and *cascade,* which are shown in Fig. 12–13. In the parallel setup, the same raw input signal is filtered by each of the sections and then their outputs are combined together, not necessarily equally, in the mixer. In the cascade arrangement, the signal passes through filter sections one after another. Thus, any filtering action of the second stage is in addition to that of the first stage and so forth.

With the cascade arrangement, it is easy to determine the total amplitude response if the amplitude response of each section is known. The filter gain at any given frequency is simply the *product* of the section gains at that frequency. If gains are expressed in decibels (usually negative, since a filter is designed to *attenuate* certain frequencies), then the overall decibel gain is simply the *sum* of the section decibel gains.

The overall response of the parallel arrangement is considerably more difficult to determine, since the *phase* response of the sections must also be known. If the section outputs are out of phase, which is the usual case, then their sum in the mixer will be *less* than the sum of their gains. Nevertheless, there are certain advantages of the parallel arrangement. Also, for the types of filters that will be discussed, any response curve that can be obtained with one arrangement can be precisely duplicated using the same number of sections of the same complexity wired in the other arrangement, although the individual section responses will be different. Thus, for convenience, the examples will use the cascade arrangement.

Iterative R-C Low-Pass Filter

Returning to the simple R-C filter, Fig. 12–14 shows what can be done by cascading these simple sections using a unity-gain buffer amplifier between each section for isolation. The curves are all normalized so that the −3-dB frequency is the same for each curve. For any individual curve, all of the sections are identical. However, each curve requires sections with a different cutoff frequency. As can be seen, adding more sections improves cutoff slope, although passband flatness is affected only slightly. However, even 32 sections does not give a very sharp cutoff for the first 50 dB, which is the most important region for sample filtering. Using the 32-section filter, the sample rate must be 5.45 times the −3-dB frequency to be assured of −50-dB alias distortion. This type of filter is termed "iterative R-C" and is used primarily where overshoot and ringing cannot be tolerated in the step response.

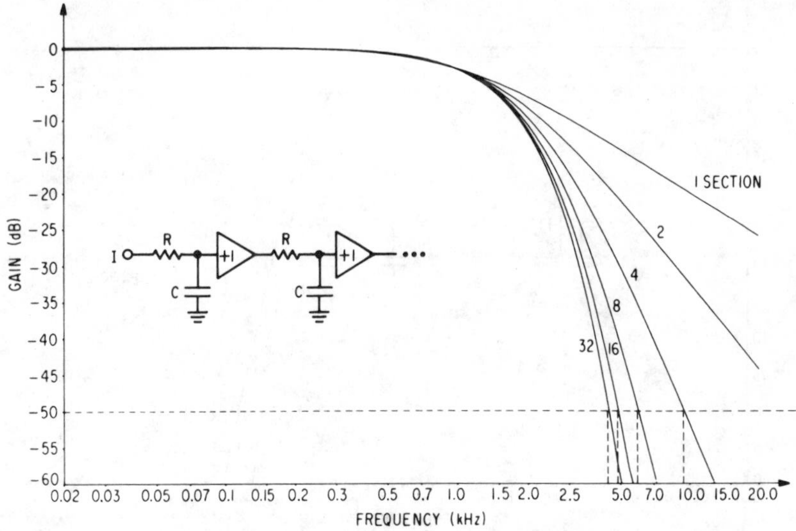

Fig. 12–14. Iterative R-C filter performance

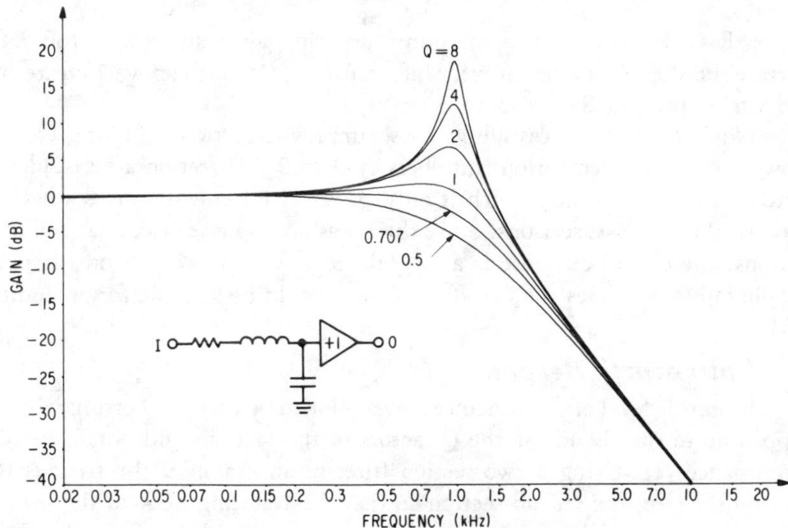

Fig. 12–15. Two-pole R-L-C filter section performance

R-L-C Filters

Another basic type of low-pass filter section is the two-pole R-L-C resonant type. This filter has an ultimate slope of 12 dB/octave/section. What makes it interesting is that a response *shaping* parameter, Q, is available. Figure 12–15 shows the response of this type of filter section with different values of Q. When $Q = 1/2$, the response degrades to that of a two

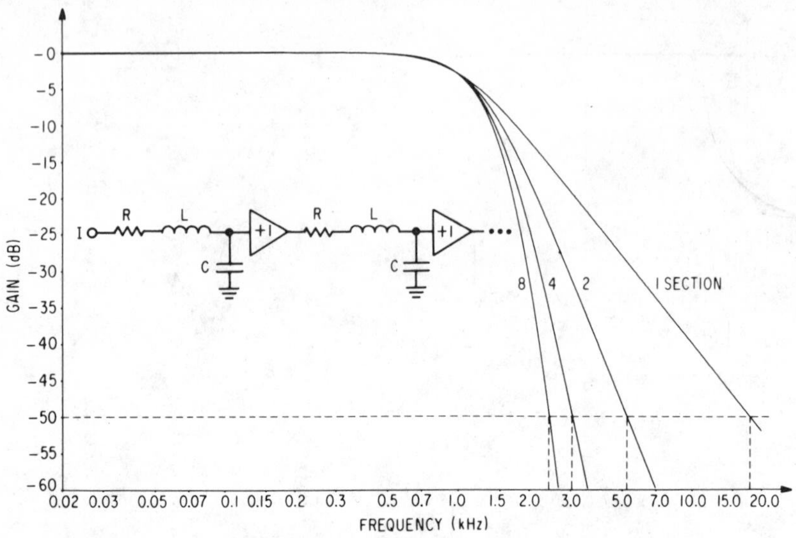

Fig. 12–16. Cascaded two-pole R-L-C filter performance. $Q = 0.707$.

section R-C. Higher *Q*s tend to "pump up" the gain just below cutoff and increase the slope just after cutoff. Unfortunately, *Q*s much above 1 create an undesirable peak in the response.

Now, how about cascading these improved sections? Figure 12–16 shows the result when various numbers of $Q = 0.707$ section are cascaded. Note that just 8 sections, which is only 16 reactive elements, gives a better response than 32 R-C sections. Since there was no response peak in any of the sections, the overall response is also peak-free. With the 8-section filter, a sample rate 3.44 times the cutoff frequency would be suitable for an audio DAC.

Butterworth Response

Even this level of performance leaves a lot to be desired. Fortunately, it is possible to merely adjust the *Q* factors of the sections and obtain better performance yet. Using a two-section filter as an example, the trick is to increase the *Q* of the second section so that the resulting peak in the *section* response tends to fill in the rounded area just beyond cutoff of the first section response. The result in Fig. 12–17 shows that this scheme is indeed successful in improving the passband flatness just short of cutoff as well as reaching the ultimate slope of 24 dB/octave soon after cutoff. Shown in Fig. 12–18 is the response of three-, four-, six-, and eight-section cascades. With this level of performance, an eight-section filter allows a sample rate just 2.43 times the cutoff frequency.

One little detail that was not mentioned is how to calculate what the section *Q*s should be to get the optimum benefit of this technique. First,

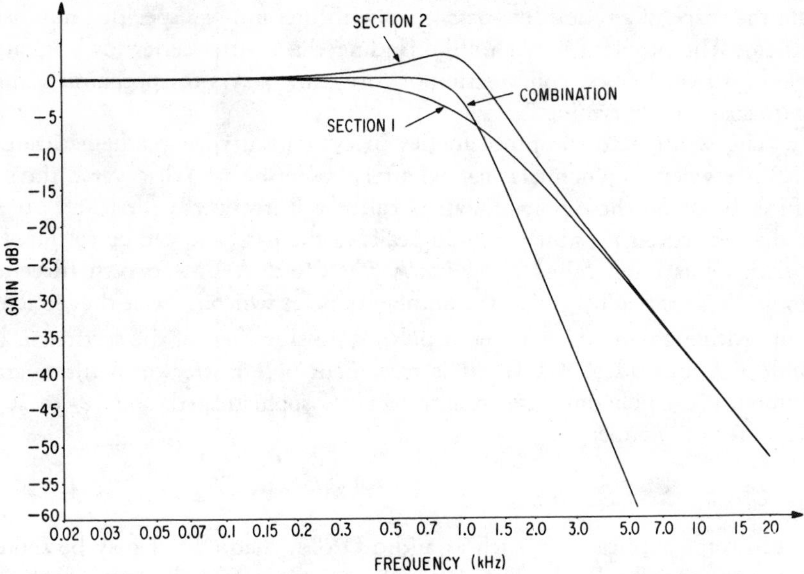

Fig. 12-17. Individual section response of two-section Butterworth

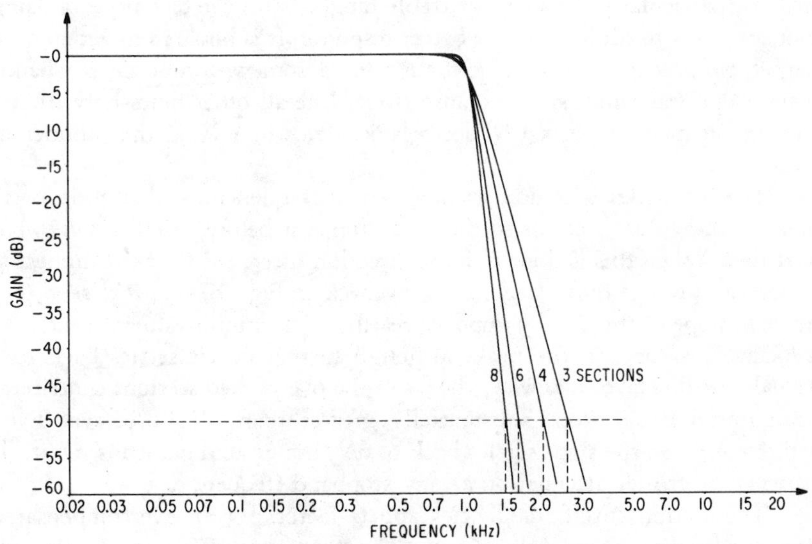

Fig. 12-18. Butterworth filter performance

however, one must define rigorously what is meant by optimum. For the curves in Fig. 12–17, optimum was taken to mean the *flattest response* possible before cutoff and the *steepest slope* as soon after cutoff as possible. The job is to take the set of realizable response curves for the R-L-C section and approximate the shape of an ideal low-pass filter with the sum of a specified number of them. The problem is not unlike finding the Fourier series for a square wave in which the best combination of curvy sine waves to approximate the square shape is determined.

The solution to the problem lies in evaluating what mathematicians call Butterworth polynomials, named after the person who discovered them. A filter based on these polynomials is called a Butterworth filter and gives the sharpest cutoff possible when no peaks in the passband can be tolerated. As such, it is often called a *maximally flat* filter. A Butterworth filter is completely specified by giving the number of poles which is twice the section count. Although an odd number of poles is possible (one of the sections is a simple R-C instead of R-L-C), it is rare. Four-pole Butterworth filters are common, eight-pole units are considered fairly sophisticated, and 12- to 16-polers are really super!

Chebyshev Response

In some applications, such as audio DACs, sharp cutoff may be more important than absolutely flat passband response. After all, even the best speaker systems have frequency response unevenness that can reach several decibels, particularly in the upper treble range. With the technique of using resonant peaks to fill in holes for better response, it is possible to get an even sharper *initial* cutoff slope in exchange for a somewhat uneven passband. Initial slope was emphasized because these, like all other poles-only filters, have an ultimate slope of $6N$ decibels/octave, where N is the number of poles.

The basic idea is to adjust the resonant frequencies and slightly overpeak the individual sections so that the drop just before cutoff is somewhat overfilled. When this is done to a multisection filter, the Q of the highest Q section can become quite large. Looking back to Fig. 12–15, it is seen that the downslope of the $Q = 8$ response reaches a maximum value of nearly 54 dB/octave just beyond the peak, although further out it settles back to a normal 12 dB/octave. Likewise, the Qs of the overpeaked sections contribute to an initial cutoff slope substantially greater than $6N$ dB/octave. Even further out when the slope settles back to $6N$, the ground gained is retained, resulting in greater attenuation at any stopband frequency.

The section cutoff frequencies and Q factors for an overcompensated filter can be determined using *Chebyshev* polynomials. Whereas the Butterworth filter has only one shape parameter, the Chebyshev filter has two: the number of poles and the passband *ripple*. The ripple figure specifies how uneven the passband is allowed to be in terms of decibels. Thus, a 0.5-dB Chebyshev filter has a maximum peak just 0.5 dB above the minimum valley in the passband. As it turns out, the optimum arrangement of peaks and valleys results in all of them being equal in amplitude; thus, the filter is said to have *equiripple* in the passband.

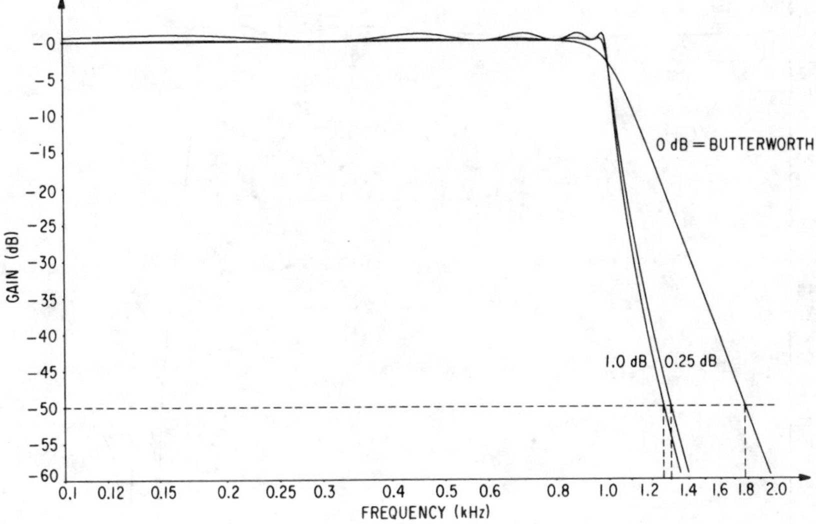

Fig. 12–19. Five-section Chebyshev filter response

Figure 12–19 shows two five-section Chebyshev filters with differing amounts of ripple allowed plus a Butterworth, which can be considered to be a Chebyshev with zero ripple, for comparison. Note that by merely allowing 0.25 dB of ripple, a reasonable amount for high-fidelity audio, that a 50-dB attenuation is achieved at 1.30 times the cutoff frequency rather than 1.62. This in turn would allow a sample rate as low as 2.3 times the cutoff frequency.

Elliptical Response

Believe it or not, there is still something that can be done to improve cutoff slope. The idea is to follow the basic low-pass filter with a band-reject (notch) filter tuned just a little beyond the cutoff frequency in an attempt to make the cutoff sharper. Essentially, the notch depresses the response just after cutoff in much the same way that peaks improve the flatness just before cutoff.

Unfortunately, to be effective the notch must be narrow. Thus, on the other side of the notch, the response curve starts back up toward what it would have been without the notch filter. At this point, another notch can be inserted to press the curve back down again. This is continued until the original filter curve has dropped low enough to be satisfactory without further help. Figure 12–20 shows the response curve of a 7th order (it is no longer meaningful to give section or pole counts) elliptical filter. With such a filter, the sample rate could be a mere 2.19 times the cutoff frequency, the best yet.

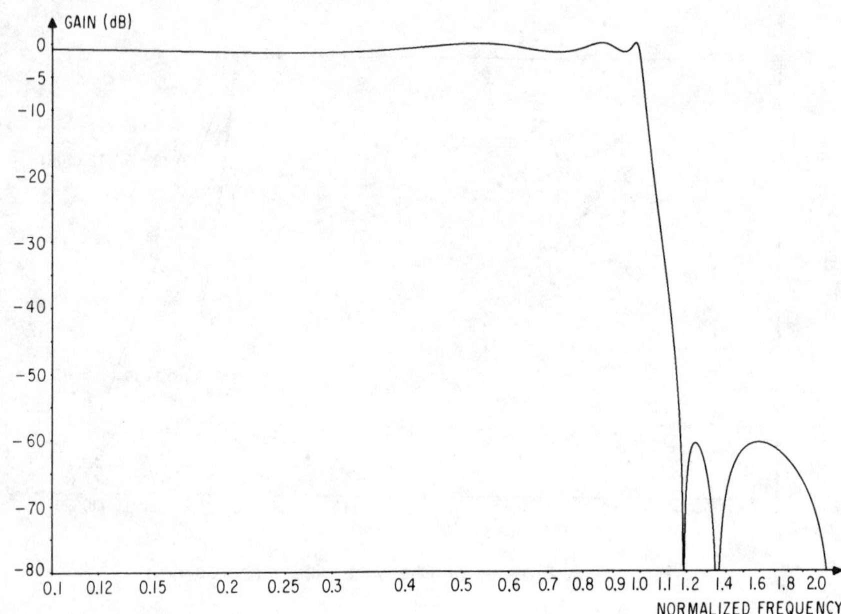

Fig. 12–20. Seventh order, 1.25-dB-ripple, 60-dB-attenuation elliptical filter amplitude response

Such filters are called elliptical (also Cauer) filters after the mathematical functions that describe them. Three parameters are necessary to specify an elliptical filter: the *order*, which is related to the number of reactive components, the allowable passband ripple, and the minimum allowable stopband attenuation, also called stopband ripple. The latter figure is needed in order to determine how closely the notches must be spaced. With such a large number of variables, design tables for elliptical filters are almost impossible to find and their design procedure is quite complex. Later in this chapter, however, an abbreviated design table will be given along with sample circuits.

Although an elliptical filter provides the sharpest cutoff with the fewest number of reactive elements, these elements all *interact* with each other (there are no discrete "sections" with isolating amplifiers between them) making precise (1% or better) element values mandatory. In contrast, the sections of Butterworth and Chebyshev filters are independent because of isolating amplifiers and, when necessary, can be tuned independently. Therefore, it is probably better for the individual experimenter/designer to stick with the latter types, at least, initially.

Phase Shift

So far in this discussion the *phase* response of the low-pass filters has been ignored. Regretfully, it is a fact of life that the sharper a filter cuts off,

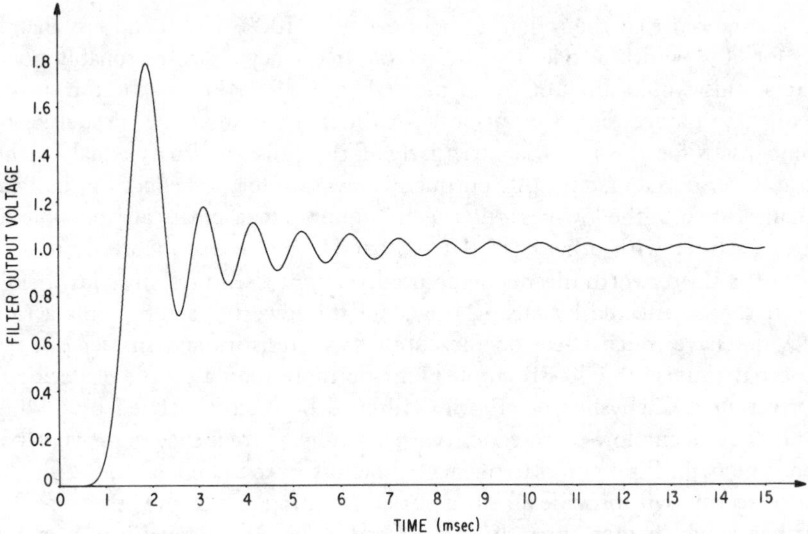

Fig. 12–21. Step response of five-section 0.25-dB Chebyshev filter (1 kHz cutoff)

the worse its phase shift will be right before cutoff (the phase after cutoff is not important, since the signal is greatly attenuated). Poor phase response in a filter also means poor transient response, which is evident in Fig. 12–21, which shows the response of the five-section 0.25-dB Chebyshev to the leading edge of a square wave.

The ringing waveform is due to the four peaked low-pass sections that make up the filter. Since they are sharper, elliptical filters are even worse, while Butterworth types, although much better, are still far from perfect. It is important to realize, however, that, while this might be characterized as poor transient response for a filter, it is quite good compared to normal audio standards, particularly for speakers. The majority of the ringing is right at the top edge of the passband, and, while it appears to imply a large peak in the response, we have seen that it only amounts to 0.25 dB. Also note that such an isolated step function should never come from the DAC, since it implies the synthesis of frequencies far beyond one-half the sample rate.

Thus, this filter characteristic should not be confused with what hi-fi critics term poor transient response, which is usually a mid- and low-frequency phenomenon. In any case, a decision must be made between a sophisticated filter and low sample rate or a simpler filter with better transient response and a higher sample rate.

Finite Sample Width Compensation

Earlier it was mentioned that if the DAC output was actual steps or pulses of finite width a slight high-frequency rolloff was inevitable. Figure

12–11 showed that the rolloff is about 4 dB for 100% width and less than 1 dB for 50% width at one-half the sample frequency. With reasonably good filters, this would amount to no more than 2 dB of loss at the top of the frequency range. For the utmost in fidelity, it may be desirable to compensate for the rolloff, particularly if the pulse width is equal to the sample period (stairstep DAC output). Correction for this effect can best be accomplished in the low-pass filter. Although it is mathematically possible to design a filter with other than flat passbands, it is a very involved process.

If a Butterworth filter is being used, a slight rise in response just before cutoff can be effected by raising the *Q*s of the lowest *Q* stages. This action does not have much effect on the cutoff characteristics and in fact can be expected to raise the 50-dB cutoff point no more than a couple of decibels. Correcting a Chebyshev or elliptical filter is best accomplished by adding another resonant low-pass section with a resonant frequency somewhat beyond the main filter cutoff frequency. *Q* factors in the range of 1 to 2 for the added section will provide a gentle but accelerating rise in the otherwise flat passband, which then abruptly cuts off as before. Any resonant peak in the extra section will occur so far into the main filter stopband that its effect will be completely insignificant.

Figure 12–22A shows the typical performance of such a compensation stage. The frequency scale has been normalized so that 1.0 represents the cutoff frequency of the main low-pass filter; thus, compensation accuracy above 1.0 is of no concern. Curve A shows the amplitude response of a DAC with stair-step output (100% pulse width) at a sample rate 2.5 times the main filter cutoff frequency and followed by a deglitcher with a time constant that is 10% of the sample period. Since a finite deglitcher time constant also represents a slight high frequency loss, it is appropriate to compensate for it at the same time. Curve B is the amplitude response of the compensation stage, and curve C is the composite, compensated response.

The short BASIC program in Fig. 12–22B can be used to iteratively design compensation filters. The variables *F*0 and *Q*0 are the frequency and *Q* parameters of the compensation filter normalized to the main filter cutoff frequency. *F*1 is the sample rate, also normalized. *T*0 is the DAC output pulse width, and *T*1 is the time constant of the deglitcher, both as fractions of the sample period. For track-and-ground deglitchers, set *T*1 to zero. To use the program, set the *F*1, *T*0, and *T*1 variables to match the DAC operating conditions and "guess" at values for *F*0 and *Q*0. Then run the program and note the shape of the compensated curve either by manually plotting it or adding plotting statements to the program. The goal is accurate compensation up to 1.0 with a gradual rolloff for higher frequencies as in Fig. 12–22A. Good starting values are those used to produce the curves in A; *F*1 = 2.5, *T*0 = 1.0, *T*1 = 0.1, *F*0 = 1.58, and *Q*0 = 1.45.

Fig. 12–22. (A) Two-pole sin(X)/X compensator performance. (B) BASIC program to evaluate compensation filters.

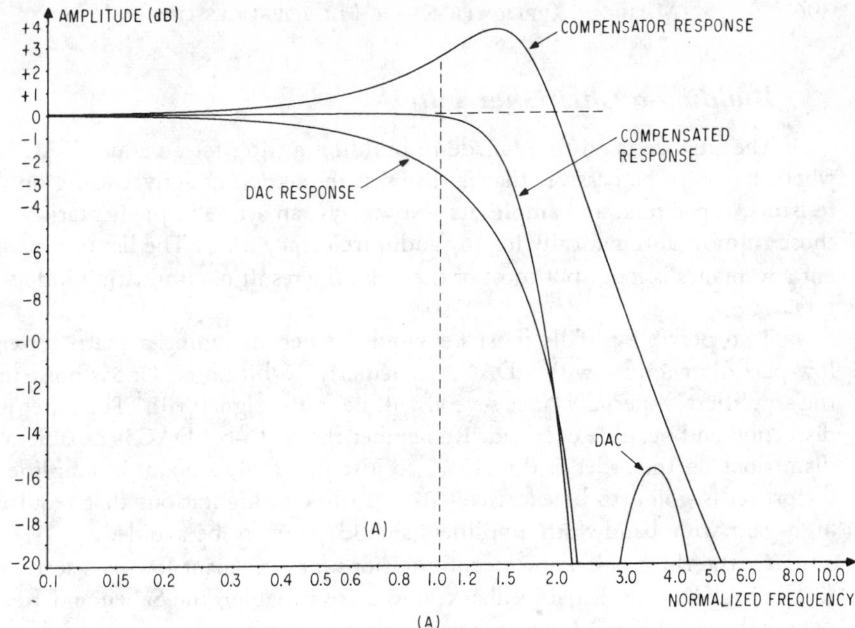

(A)

```
10 REM  PROGRAM TO AID IN THE DESIGN OF 2-POLE COMPENSATION FILTERS FOR DACS
11 REM  USING FINITE OUTPUT PULSE WIDTHS AND TIME CONSTANT LIMITED DEGLITCHERS.
20 REM  IN STATEMENTS 101-105, SET THE VARIABLES AS FOLLOWS:
21 REM  F1 = SAMPLE RATE AS A MULTIPLE OF THE MAIN FILTER'S CUTOFF FREQUENCY
22 REM  T0 = DAC OUTPUT PULSE WIDTH AS A FRACTION OF THE SAMPLE PERIOD
23 REM  T1 = DEGLITCHER TIME CONSTANT AS A FRACTION OF THE SAMPLE PERIOD
24 REM  F0 = RESONANT FREQUENCY OF PROPOSED COMPENSATION FILTER
25 REM  Q0 = RESONANT Q OF PROPOSED COMPENSATION FILTER
26 REM  N = NUMBER OF FREQUENCY POINTS TO EVALUATE AND PRINT
30 REM  WHEN RUN, THE PROGRAM PRINTS THE NORMALIZED FREQUENCY BETWEEN 0.1 AND
31 REM  10 TIMES THE MAIN FILTER CUTOFF FREQUENCY ON A LOG SCALE AND THEN FOR
32 REM  EACH FREQUENCY, THE RAW DAC OUTPUT AMPLITUDE INCLUDING SIN(X)/X AND
33 REM  DEGLITCHER TIME CONSTANT LOSSES, THE COMPENSATION FILTER GAIN, AND THE
34 REM  PRODUCT OF THE TWO WHICH IS THE COMPENSATED DAC OUTPUT.
101 F1=2.50
102 T0=1.0
103 T1=0.1
104 F0=1.58
105 Q0=1.45
106 N=100
200 F2=F1/(6.283*T1): REM NORMALIZED 3DB DOWN POINT OF DEGLITCHER
201 F3=F1/T0: REM NORMALIZED FREQUENCY OF FIRST SIN(X)/X NULL
210 F=0.1: REM INITIAL STARTING FREQUENCY
220 PRINT "FREQUENCY";TAB(15);"DAC OUTPUT";TAB(30);"COMP. GAIN";TAB(45);
221 PRINT "COMPOSITE"
230 F=0.1: REM INITIAL FREQUENCY
300 A=ABS(SIN(3.14159*F/F3)/(3.14159*F/F3)): REM SIN(X)/X LOSS
301 A=A*((F2/F)/SOR(1+(F2/F)↑2)): REM DEGLITCHER ADDITIONAL LOSS
310 G=SQR(1/((F/F0)↑4+(F/F0)↑2*(1/Q0↑2-2)+1)): REM COMP FILTER GAIN
320 R=A*G: REM COMPOSITE CORRECTED OUTPUT
400 PRINT F;TAB(15);A;TAB(30);G;TAB(45);R
500 F=F*10 (2/N)
510 IF F<10.0 THEN GOTO 300
999 STOP
```

(B)

Building a Chebyshev Filter

The first decision to be made in building a filter for an aduio DAC is whether it is to be passive, that is, use real inductors, or active, using only resistors, capacitors, and amplifiers. Nowadays, an active implementation is chosen almost automatically for any audio-frequency filter. The list of apparent advantages is long, but most of them are the result of eliminating inductors.

Two possible pitfalls must be avoided when designing a sharp active low-pass filter for use with a DAC, particularly 16-bit units. One is noise in the amplifiers, especially since several will be in the signal path. The other is distortion and possible overload. Remember that a 16-bit DAC is capable of distortions on the order of 0.0015%, so just about any amount of amplifier distortion is going to be excessive. Active filter configurations that require high-gain wide bandwidth amplifiers should therefore be avoided.

Of the three best-known configurations for a resonant low-pass section (Sallen and Key, multiple feedback, and state variable), the Sallen and Key circuit shown in Fig. 12–23 has many important advantages. First, it is hard to imagine a circuit using fewer components. Also, the filter characteristics are relatively insensitive to component variations. Most important, however, is the amplifier requirement, a simple unity-gain buffer with ideally infinite input impedance and zero output impedance. Such an amplifier is very easily constructed with an ordinary op-amp, special voltage-follower op-amp, or discrete components. Since the gain is unity, the output noise amplitude is nearly the same as the input referred noise level, which is what appears on the amplifier spec sheet. Also, the frequency-independent 100% feedback minimizes the amplifier distortion. About the only negative aspect of the circuit is that high Q factors require a large spread in capacitor values.

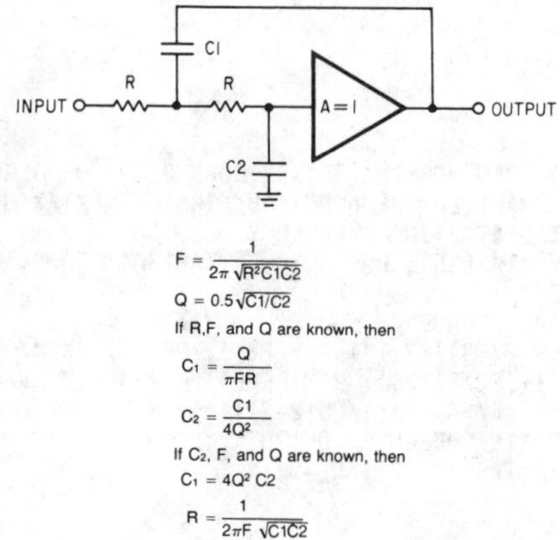

Fig. 12–23. Sallen and Key resonant low-pass section

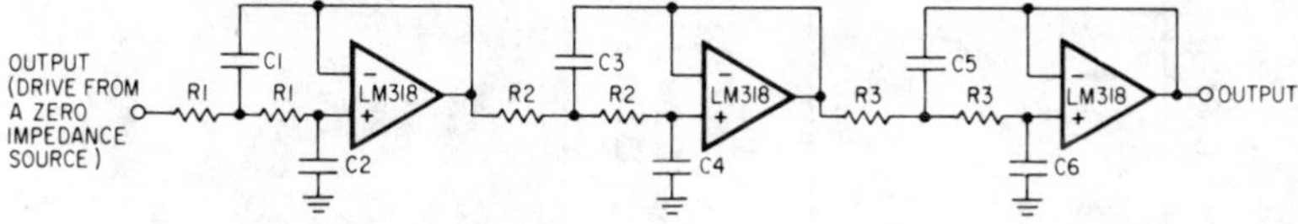

Sample Rate* (kHz)	3-dB Cutoff (kHz)	R1 (kΩ)	C1 (pF)	C2 (pF)	R2 (kΩ)	C3 (pF)	C4 (pF)	R3 (kΩ)	C5 (pF)	C6 (pF)
8	2.67	15.2	17,380	7,500	14.9	24,200	1,250	15.4	64,190	250
10	3.33	15.2	13,900	6,000	14.9	19,360	1,000	15.4	51,353	200
12	4.0	15.2	11,590	5,000	14.9	16,133	833	12.8	51,353	200
15	5.0	12.2	11,590	5,000	14.9	12,910	667	10.3	51,353	200
20	6.67	9.14	11,590	5,000	14.9	9,680	500	7.70	51,353	200
25	8.33	7.31	11,590	5,000	11.9	9,680	500	6.16	51,353	200
30	10.0	6.09	11,590	5,000	9.93	9,680	500	5.13	51,353	200
40	13.3	4.57	11,590	5,000	7.45	9,680	500	3.85	51,353	200

*Filter response is down 40 dB at 1/2 sampling frequency

(A)

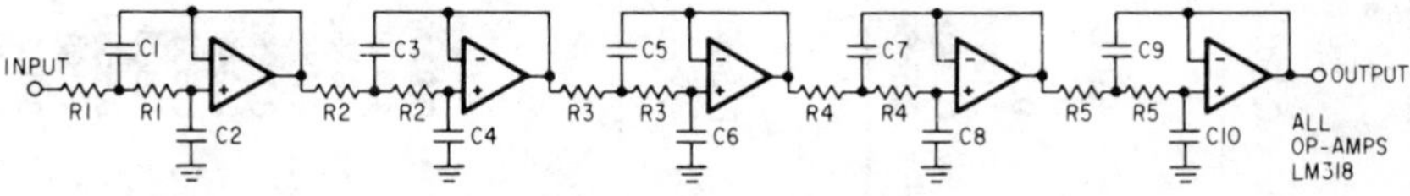

Sample Rate* (kHz)	3-dB Cutoff (kHz)	R1 (kΩ)	C1 (pF)	C2 (pF)	R2 (kΩ)	C3 (pF)	C4 (pF)	R3 (kΩ)	C5 (pF)	C6 (pF)	R4 (kΩ)	C7 (pF)	C8 (pF)	R5 (kΩ)	C9 (pF)	C10 (pF)
8	3.08	12.74	19,700	12,500	15.99	17,400	2,500	15.61	22,450	937	13.57	40,250	450	15.84	100,000	109
10	3.85	12.74	15,760	10,000	15.99	13,918	2,000	15.61	17,960	750	13.57	32,200	360	13.82	91,680	100
12	4.62	12.74	13,130	8,330	15.99	11,600	1,667	15.61	14,970	625	13.57	26,836	300	11.52	91,680	100
15	5.77	12.74	10,500	6,667	15.99	9,280	1,333	15.61	11,975	500	10.85	26,836	300	9.21	91,680	100
20	7.69	12.74	7,880	5,000	15.99	6,959	1,000	11.71	11,975	500	8.14	26,836	300	6.91	91,680	100
25	9.62	10.19	7,880	5,000	12.79	6,959	1,000	9.37	11,975	500	6.51	26,836	300	5.53	91,680	100
30	11.5	8.49	7,880	5,000	10.66	6,959	1,000	7.81	11,975	500	5.43	26,836	300	4.61	91,680	100
40	15.4	6.37	7,880	5,000	8.00	6,959	1,000	5.85	11,975	500	4.07	26,836	300	3.45	91,680	100

*Filter response is down 50 dB at 1/2 sampling frequency

(B)

Fig. 12–24. Design data for active Chebyshev filters. (A) Three-section 1-dB ripple. (B) Five-section 0.25-dB ripple.

Table 12-1. Design Data for Chebyshev Filters

Ripple = 0 dB (Butterworth) Cutoff frequency = section frequency = 1.0

Number of sections	F_{50}/F_3	*Q Sct 1*	*Q Sct 2*	*Q Sct 3*	*Q Sct 4*	*Q Sct 5*	*Q Sct 6*	*Q Sct 7*	*Q Sct 8*
1	17.79	0.7071							
2	4.22	0.5411	1.305						
3	2.61	0.5176	0.7071	1.932					
4	2.05	0.5098	0.6014	0.8999	2.563				
5	1.78	0.5062	0.5612	0.7071	1.101	3.196			
6	1.61	0.5043	0.5412	0.6302	0.8213	1.307	3.831		
7	1.51	0.5032	0.5297	0.5905	0.7071	0.9401	1.514	4.466	
8	1.43	0.5024	0.5225	0.5669	0.6468	0.7882	1.061	1.722	5.101

Ripple = 0.1 dB Cutoff frequency = 1.0

Number of sections	F_{50}/F_3	*F Sct 1* / *Q Sct 1*	*F Sct 2* / *Q Sct 2*	*F Sct 3* / *Q Sct 3*	*F Sct 4* / *Q Sct 4*	*F Sct 5* / *Q Sct 5*	*F Sct 6* / *Q Sct 6*	*F Sct 7* / *Q Sct 7*	*F Sct 8* / *Q Sct 8*
1	16.59	0.9321							
		0.7674							
2	3.36	0.6491	0.9491						
		0.6190	2.185						
3	1.95	0.4688	0.7628	0.9717					
		0.5997	1.333	4.639					
4	1.52	0.3623	0.6129	0.8493	0.9828				
		0.5934	1.184	2.456	8.092				
5	1.32	0.2940	0.5065	0.7292	0.8984	0.9887			
		0.5906	1.128	2.046	3.926	12.54			
6	1.22	0.2469	0.4296	0.6314	0.8038	0.9275	0.9920		
		0.5890	1.100	1.883	3.123	5.733	17.98		
7	1.16	0.2126	0.3723	0.5539	0.7187	0.8523	0.9459	0.9941	
		0.5881	1.084	1.798	2.794	4.403	7.871	24.40	
8	1.12	0.1866	0.3280	0.4920	0.6463	0.7796	0.8852	0.9582	0.9955
		0.5875	1.074	1.748	2.619	3.850	5.883	10.34	34.82

Ripple = 0.25 dB Cutoff frequency = 1.0

Number of sections	F_{50}/F_3	F *Sct 1* / Q *Sct 1*	F *Sct 2* / Q *Sct 2*	F *Sct 3* / Q *Sct 3*	F *Sct 4* / Q *Sct 4*	F *Sct 5* / Q *Sct 5*	F *Sct 6* / Q *Sct 6*	F *Sct 7* / Q *Sct 7*	F *Sct 8* / Q *Sct 8*
1	16.00	0.8993							
		0.8093							
2	3.20	0.5893	0.9424						
		0.6575	2.539						
3	1.88	0.4174	0.7467	0.9700					
		0.6373	1.557	5.527					
4	1.48	0.3201	0.5958	0.8438	0.9822				
		0.6307	1.385	2.935	9.729				
5	1.30	0.2588	0.4906	0.7224	0.8961	0.9884			
		0.6277	1.319	2.447	4.729	15.14			
6	1.21	0.2169	0.4153	0.6243	0.8005	0.9264	0.9919		
		0.6261	1.287	2.252	3.763	6.928	21.749		
7	1.15	0.1865	0.3594	0.5470	0.7151	0.8052	0.9453	0.9941	
		0.6251	1.268	2.151	3.367	5.323	9.531	29.56	
8	1.11	0.1636	0.3164	0.4855	0.6425	0.7775	0.8842	0.9578	0.9955
		0.6245	1.256	2.091	3.158	4.656	7.125	12.53	38.58

Ripple = 0.5 dB Cutoff frequency = 1.0

Number of sections	F_{50}/F_3	F *Sct 1* / Q *Sct 1*	F *Sct 2* / Q *Sct 2*	F *Sct 3* / Q *Sct 3*	F *Sct 4* / Q *Sct 4*	F *Sct 5* / Q *Sct 5*	F *Sct 6* / Q *Sct 6*	F *Sct 7* / Q *Sct 7*	F *Sct 8* / Q *Sct 8*
1	15.44	0.8672							
		0.8637							
2	3.08	0.5425	0.9376						
		0.7055	2.944						
3	1.82	0.3793	0.7357	0.9689					
		0.6839	1.812	6.520					
4	1.45	0.2894	0.5844	0.8403	0.9819				
		0.6769	1.612	3.469	11.54				
5	1.28	0.2334	0.4801	0.7179	0.8946	0.9882			
		0.6737	1.536	2.894	5.618	19.01			
6	1.19	0.1954	0.4060	0.6198	0.7984	0.9257	0.9918		
		0.6720	1.498	2.664	4.472	8.249	25.91		
7	1.14	0.1679	0.3510	0.5426	0.7127	0.8494	0.9449	0.9940	
		0.6710	1.477	2.545	4.002	6.340	11.36	35.25	
8	1.11	0.1472	0.3089	0.4813	0.6401	0.7762	0.8835	0.9576	0.9955
		0.6703	1.463	2.474	3.753	5.546	8.495	14.95	46.03

Table 12-1. *(Cont.)*

Ripple = 1.0 dB Cutoff frequency = 1.0

Number of sections	F_{50} / F_3	F *Sct 1* / Q *Sct 1*	F *Sct 2* / Q *Sct 2*	F *Sct 3* / Q *Sct 3*	F *Sct 4* / Q *Sct 4*	F *Sct 5* / Q *Sct 5*	F *Sct 6* / Q *Sct 6*	F *Sct 7* / Q *Sct 7*	F *Sct 8* / Q *Sct 8*
1	14.77	0.8295							
		0.9563							
2	2.95	0.4964	0.9332						
		0.7850	3.562						
3	1.77	0.3432	0.7261	0.9679					
		0.7613	2.200	8.012					
4	1.42	0.2608	0.5746	0.8373	0.9815				
		0.7535	1.958	4.270	14.26				
5	1.26	0.2099	0.4712	0.7142	0.8934	0.9881			
		0.7499	1.867	3.564	6.944	22.29			
6	1.18	0.1755	0.3980	0.6160	0.7966	0.9251	0.9918		
		0.7480	1.820	3.281	5.530	10.22	32.11		
7	1.13	0.1507	0.3439	0.5389	0.7108	0.8485	0.9446	0.9940	
		0.7469	1.794	3.134	4.949	7.853	14.08	43.71	
8	1.10	0.1321	0.3025	0.4779	0.6381	0.7751	0.8830	0.9574	0.9954
		0.7461	1.777	3.047	4.642	6.870	10.53	18.54	57.10

Therefore, one must be careful not to let C2 get so small that amplifier input capacitance becomes a significant factor.

Figure 12–24 and Table 12–1 give design data for Butterworth and Chebyshev filters using Sallen and Key sections. In Fig. 12–24, complete data including component values is found for a five-section 0.25-dB and a three-section 1-dB Chebyshev. The former is recommended for ultra-high-fidelity applications, while the latter is quite suitable for experimentation. In fact, it is common practice to utilize two different sample rates in computer music applications. The lower rate would be used for experimentation and fast turnaround where quality is not overly important, while the higher rate would be used for the final performance. Thus, one good filter would be constructed for the higher rate and one or more of the simpler types would satisfy experimental needs. Table 12–1 provides data that can be used to design a filter with nearly any number of sections, ripple amplitude, and cutoff frequency. When selecting components for the filter, be sure to use 5% or better polystyrene capacitors and 1% film resistors, particularly with four or more sections. A good amplifier to use is, believe it or not, an LM318 high-speed op-amp, which gives acceptably low noise and total freedom from slewing distortion. The dual NE5532 from Signetics also works well and has even less noise.

The last concern is the order of the sections in the cascade. Mathematically, the order is not significant but in real life it can make a substantial difference. The problems are most acute with the highest Q section. The high Q means that internal amplifier noise frequencies in the vicinity of the resonant peak will be amplified. It also means that large-amplitude signals right at the peak frequency can be amplified to the point of overload. To minimize noise, the highest Q section should be placed first, right after the DAC. Here, noise at the resonant frequency will be considerably attenuated by subsequent stages. Unfortunately, since it sees raw DAC output, certain data patterns could severely overload it. Thus, if an op-amp buffer is used in the filter sections, the *lowest* Q section should connect to the DAC with successively higher Q sections following toward the output.

Building an Elliptical Filter

Although elliptical filters are more difficult to understand, design, and successfully build than Butterworth or Chebyshev types, their sharper cutoff characteristic for a given number of reactive circuit components is attractive. Elliptical filters are normally implemented as ladder type L-C circuits or the direct active equivalent rather than individual sections isolated by amplifiers. The reason for this is also responsible for the circuit's small number of reactive components. Below the cutoff frequency, the inductors and capacitors interact to provide a series of closely spaced resonant peaks like the Chebyshev filter. Above cutoff, these *same* elements interact differently to produce anti-resonant notches. Figure 12–25A and B shows two possible

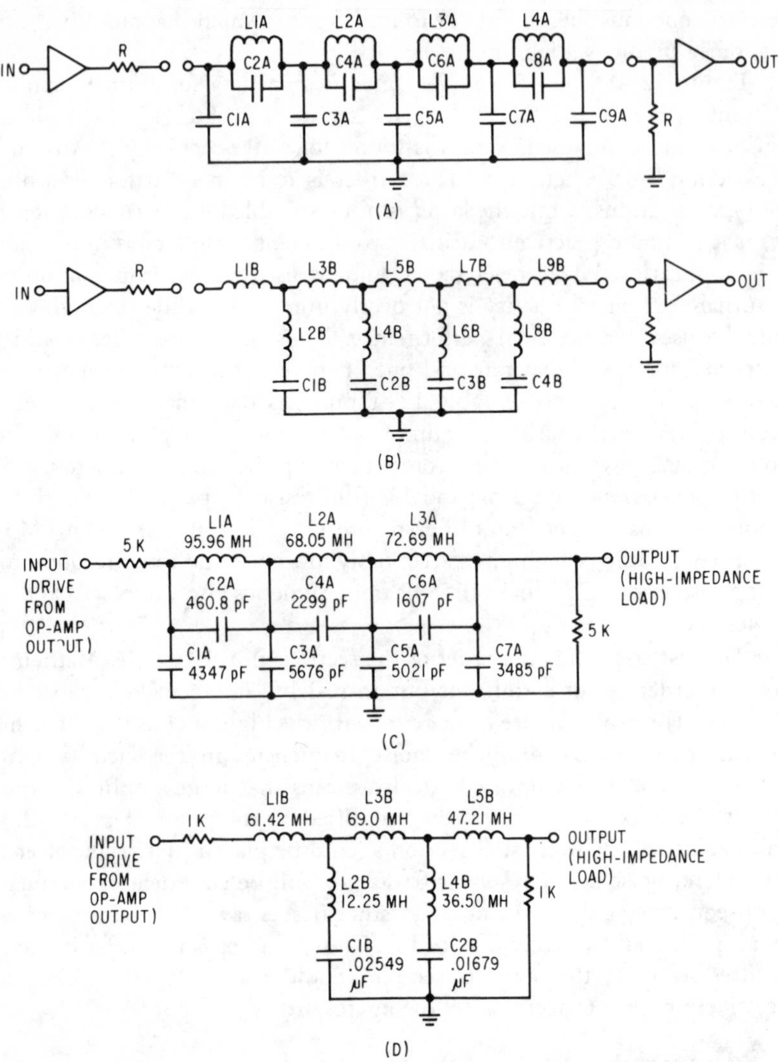

Fig. 12–25. L-C ladder implementation of elliptical filter. (A) Parallel resonant form. (B) Series resonant form. (C) Seventh-order, 0.28/60-dB, 10-kHz cutoff elliptical filter. (D) Fifth-order, 1.25/40-dB, 5,180-Hz cutoff elliptical filter.

passive L-C implementations of a ninth order elliptical filter. In fact, when the source and load impedances (represented by R in the figure) are equal, the two forms are equivalent with A favoring capacitors and B favoring inductors. Note that, at low frequencies, the filter's *insertion loss* will be 6 dB because of the voltage divider effect between the source and load resistors.

Table 12–2 gives design data for elliptical filters of this form. Fifth, seventh, and ninth order types with passband ripples of 0.28 and 1.25 dB

Table 12–2. Design Data for Elliptical Filters

Order	Passband Ripple	Stopband Attenuation	Cutoff Ratio	L1A C1B	L2A C2B	L3A C3B	L4A C4B	C1A L1B	C2A L2B	C3A L3B	C4A L4B	C5A L5B	C6A L6B	C7A L7B	C8A L8B	C9A L9B
5	0.28	40	1.325	1.106	0.7859			1.275	0.2288	1.752	0.6786	0.9789				
5	0.28	50	1.556	1.177	0.9543			1.340	0.1430	1.923	0.4008	1.139				
5	0.28	60	1.887	1.225	1.079			1.383	0.0879	2.050	0.2390	1.253				
5	0.28	70	2.281	1.253	1.155			1.408	0.0567	2.128	0.1519	1.322				
5	1.25	40	1.206	0.8304	0.5469			2.001	0.3992	2.248	1.189	1.538				
5	1.25	50	1.390	0.9030	0.6993			2.114	0.2467	2.551	0.6900	1.790				
5	1.25	60	1.624	0.9471	0.8031			2.183	0.1603	2.754	0.4359	1.956				
5	1.25	70	2.000	0.9812	0.8891			2.236	0.0964	2.922	0.2577	2.092				
7	0.28	50	1.155	1.158	0.7013	0.7893		1.323	0.2000	1.618	1.044	1.366	0.7233	0.9741		
7	0.28	60	1.252	1.207	0.8560	0.9143		1.367	0.1449	1.785	0.7231	1.579	0.5055	1.096		
7	0.28	70	1.390	1.245	0.9960	1.022		1.401	0.1033	1.931	0.5017	1.771	0.3516	1.197		
7	0.28	80	1.556	1.271	1.103	1.101		1.424	0.0753	2.041	0.3603	1.917	0.2525	1.270		
7	1.25	60	1.167	0.9254	0.5843	0.6739		2.153	0.2315	2.327	1.199	1.990	0.8004	1.746		
7	1.25	70	1.287	0.9591	0.6964	0.7622		2.206	0.1675	2.543	0.8404	2.276	0.5669	1.891		
7	1.25	80	1.440	0.9858	0.7972	0.8378		2.248	0.1186	2.733	0.5837	2.530	0.3956	2.012		
9	0.28	60	1.086													
9	0.28	70	1.143													
9	0.28	80	1.221													
9	0.28	90	1.305													
9	1.25	60	1.052													
9	1.25	70	1.095													
9	1.25	80	1.167													
9	1.25	90	1.236													

and stopband attenuations of 50 to 90 dB are given. These should cover the range of application for audio filters from minimum cost experimental units to very sharp professional application units. The element values are given in henries and farads for a cutoff frequency of 0.159 Hz and impedance level of 1 ohm. To compute actual practical component values, use the formulas below:

$$L' = \frac{0.159RL}{F} \qquad C' = \frac{0.159C}{RF}$$

where L' and C' are the practical component values, L and C are from the table, R is the source and termination impedance, and F is the cutoff frequency. Figure 12–25C shows a practical seventh order parallel resonant filter design having 0.28 dB ripple, 60 dB attenuation, a cutoff frequency of 10 kHz (25 ks/s sample rate), and an impedance of 5,000 ohms. Figure 12–25D shows a fifth order series resonant filter with 1.25 dB ripple, 40 dB attenuation, 5,180 Hz cutoff (12.5 ks/s sample rate), and 1K impedance.

Even considering the advantages of small size, inexpensive components, etc., of active implementation, actual passive implementation of the filter, just as shown in Fig. 12–25, does have some advantages. For one, there are only two amplifiers in the signal path to contribute noise and distortion, and these can often be part of surrounding circuitry and not specifically "charged" to the filter. The L-C networks can be easy to tune, which may be necessary with the higher-order filters. Finally, the component values tend to be similar in magnitude unlike the active Chebyshev filter described earlier. On the minus side, the inductors are susceptible to hum pickup from stray magnetic fields and therefore should be of torroid or pot core construction and kept away from power transformers. Also, it is conceivable that nonlinearities in the magnetic core could contribute a slight amount of distortion, so relatively wide air gaps within the core should be used. Inductor size and Q are not much of a problem because the section resonant frequencies will be in the high audio range.

In actually building such a filter, accurate element values are crucial; 2.5% for fifth order, 1% for seventh order, and 0.5% or better for ninth order. This is normally accomplished with an impedance bridge, a bunch of polystyrene capacitors, and a supply of ferrite pot cores and magnet wire. The pot cores usually have tuning slugs that simplify the task of getting exactly the right inductance, and appropriate parallel combinations of two or three capacitors can usually be determined easily. Typically, the parallel resonant form will be preferred since it has fewer inductors.

An active implementation of the filter using only op-amps, resistors, and capacitors is also possible and straightforward to derive from the passive L-C circuit. Whereas the Sallen and Key circuit studied earlier is a contrived form that just happens to have the same response as a resonant R-L-C low-pass section, *impedance converters* are normally used for active elliptical filters. An impedance converter is an active circuit that in effect converts one type of passive component, such as a capacitor, to another type, such as an inductor, by means of phase shifting. A *gyrator*, for example, does just that; connect a capacitor across its output terminals and its input terminals have the frequency-phase characteristic of an equivalent inductor. A *negative impedance converter* shift things just 90° instead of 180° and thus can make a resistor act like an inductor in a suitably designed circuit. While these circuits are interesting to study, their theory is beyond the scope of this discussion.

The negative impedance converter (NIC) is very easy to apply to the L-C elliptical filter circuits given earlier, however. Figure 12–26A shows the series resonant form of a seventh-order elliptical filter adapted to a NIC active circuit. In effect, the phase of everything has been shifted 90° so every inductor becomes a resistor, every resistor becomes a capacitor, and every capacitor becomes a "frequency-dependent negative resistor" implemented with a negative impedance converter and two capacitors. Fig. 12–26B shows the same circuit with "practical" element values included. These were calculated for a 10-kHz cutoff from the Table 12–2 entries for a seventh-order, 0.28/60-dB filter. First, an impedance scale factor is determined using $Z = 1/6.283FC$, where F is the cutoff frequency and C is a convenient capacitor value in farads. For best results, choose C so that Z is in the 5K to 20K range. For this example, 2,200 pF gave an impedance scale factor of 7,235. Values for the remaining components are simply the impedance scale factor times the corresponding element values from the filter table. Figure 12–26C shows the actual active filter circuit. Most of the resistor values are simply copied from the element values in Fig. 12–26B. The two 499K resistors are included to provide a path for the amplifier bias current and also give the circuit accurate response down to dc. The 4.99K resistors in the negative impedance converters merely need to be matched; their actual value does not affect the response.

One of the big advantages of this circuit is that all of the capacitors are the same value! Of course, the resistors turn out to be strange values, but it is much easier to find precision resistors with strange values than capacitors. In practice, the circuit impedance is usually adjusted so that the capacitors are some standard value (such as 2,200 pF here) which is easy to get. One would typically purchase several dozen 5% capacitors of this value and select those that fall within 1% of 2,200 pF for use. One pitfall of this circuit is that at certain frequencies, the output swings of the NIC op-amps will be three times the input signal amplitude. Thus, the input signal amplitude should be restricted to 3 V peak to avoid severe distortion. Also, there is a 6 dB passband loss that is made up for somewhere, usually in the output amplifier. Amplifier noise is not much of a problem because the NICs don't tend to amplify noise at the resonant peaks. Note that the bias current for amplifiers A1, A3, and A5 plus that of the output amplifier passes through the two

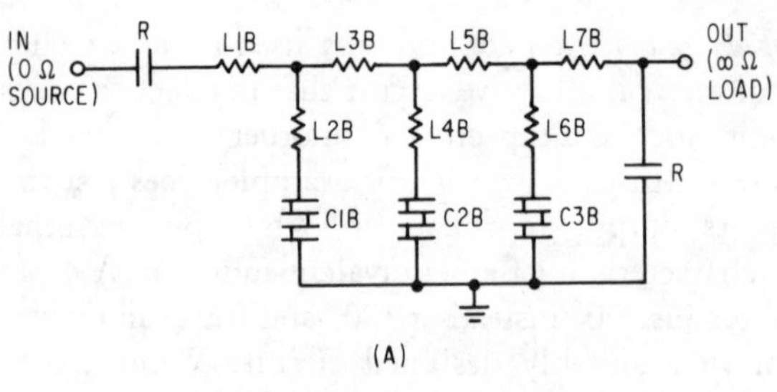

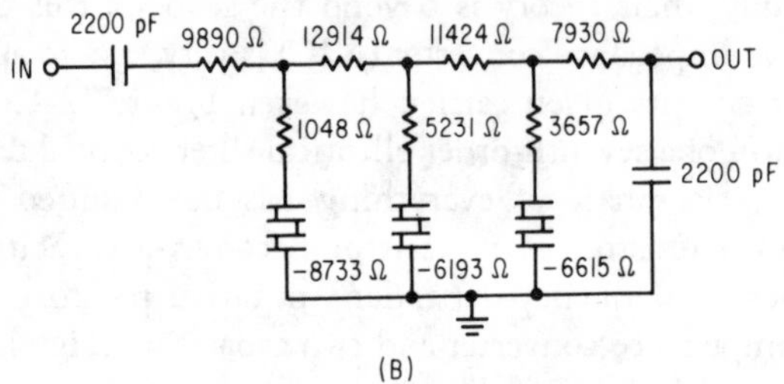

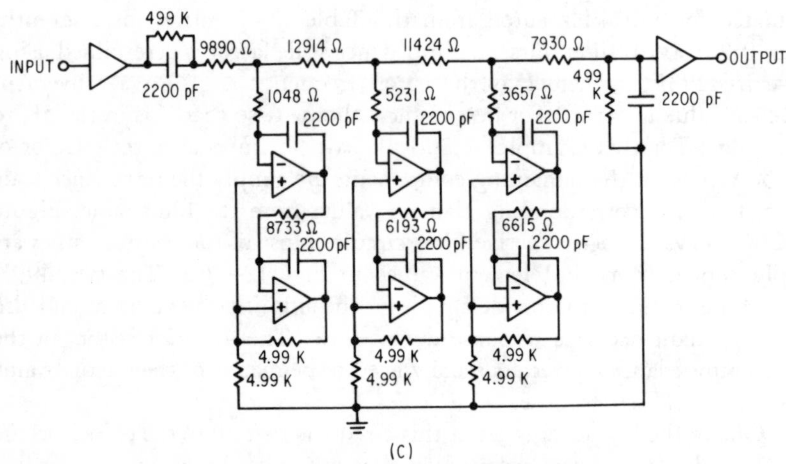

Fig. 12–26. Active elliptical filter design. (A) Active filter form using negative impedance converter. (B) Element values for 0.28/60-dB, 10-kHz cutoff, 7,235-ohm impedance. (C) Complete active elliptical filter circuit.

499K resistors. To avoid large offsets, all of the amplifiers should be FET types. Singles, such as the LF356, should be used for the input and output amplifiers, while duals, such as the TL072, are convenient for the negative impedance converters.

Digital Anti-Alias Filters

From the foregoing, it is obvious that very sharp cutoff analog filters for digital audio applications can become quite complex, costly, and just plain

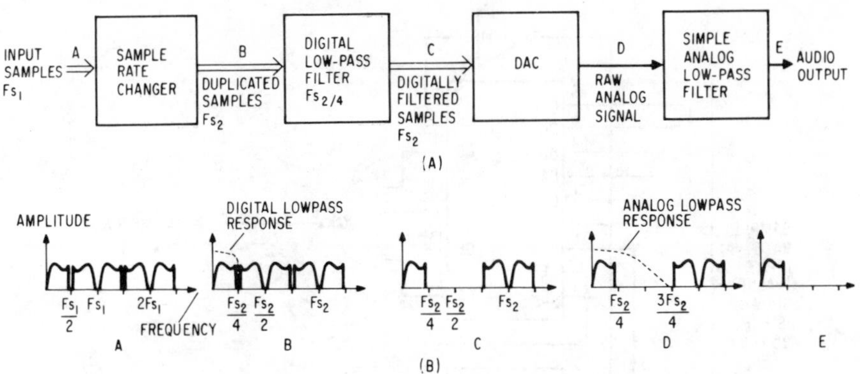

Fig. 12–27. Digital anti-alias filter. (A) Block diagram. (B) Signal spectra at indicated points.

messy to work with. It seems strange to have to deal with complicated, precision analog circuits in what might otherwise be an all-digital system. Actually, use of a *digital filter* right before the DAC can greatly simplify the analog filter by substantially increasing the sample rate to the DAC without increasing the sample rate from the source. The analog filter can then be less sharp and still adequately separate the signal spectrum from its alias copies. Figure 12–27 shows how this would be accomplished in principle.

The source sample stream is presented at a rate of Fs_1 to the sample rate changer block, which, in this example, multiplies the sample rate by 2 to produce sample rate Fs_2. This is accomplished by simply duplicating each input sample to produce two identical output samples. Below these blocks is shown the spectral equivalents of the original signal A and the multiplied rate signal B. Of course, this duplication of samples has not really accomplished anything in the frequency domain so the overall spectra are the same.

However, the 2X increased rate can now be *digitally filtered* by the digital low-pass filter block to just below $Fs_2/4$ to produce signal spectrum C. Sample stream C is then D-to-A converted at sample rate Fs_2 to produce analog signal D. Note that there is a very large frequency gap between the desired signal spectrum, which extends up to $0.25Fs_2$, and its first alias copy, which extends down to only $0.75Fs_2$. This gap, which is nearly 1.6 octaves wide, provides plenty of room for a *simple* analog low-pass filter to perform the final filtering. In fact, a three-section Butterworth filter can provide 56-dB suppression of alias distortion in this example. Greater multiplication factors are also possible. A 4X increase, for example, would allow use of a two-section analog filter yet provide 67-dB alias suppression.

What the sample rate changer and digital low-pass filter blocks do, in effect, is to *interpolate* an intermediate output sample point between each input sample point. Unfortunately, "sin(X)/X" interpolation, which is much more complex than linear interpolation, is needed. Sample rate conversion

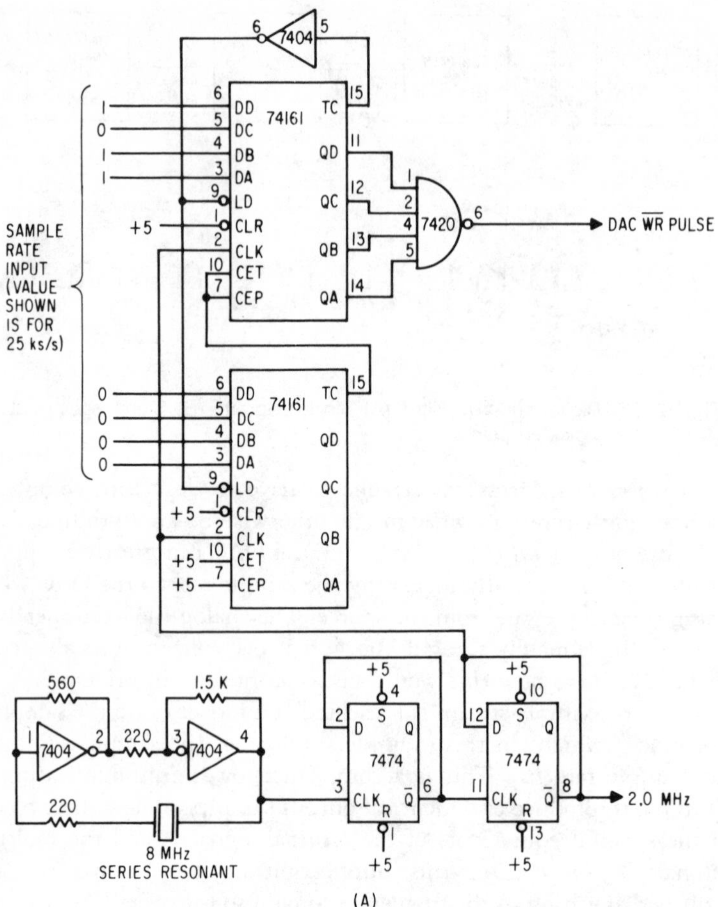

Fig. 12–28. Sixteen bit audio DAC. (A) Timing generator. (B) Data register and DAC. (C) Sin(X)/X compensator and filter.

and *interpolating filters* will be described in more detail in Chapter 14. Besides replacing a complex analog filter with a stable digital one, this technique can eliminate much of the phase distortion of a high-order analog filter. Whereas in the digital domain it is easy to design a very sharp low-pass filter with virtually zero phase distortion, it is nearly impossible to accurately phase compensate a high-order analog low-pass filter. Phase distortion in the simple analog filter that remains here is of little consequence, since it occurs at the top of *its* passband where there is now no signal energy.

Of course, the entire scheme depends on a sharp cutoff, linear phase, digital filter which, until recently, was much more complex and costly even than a high-order compensated analog filter. However, such filters (for a 2X

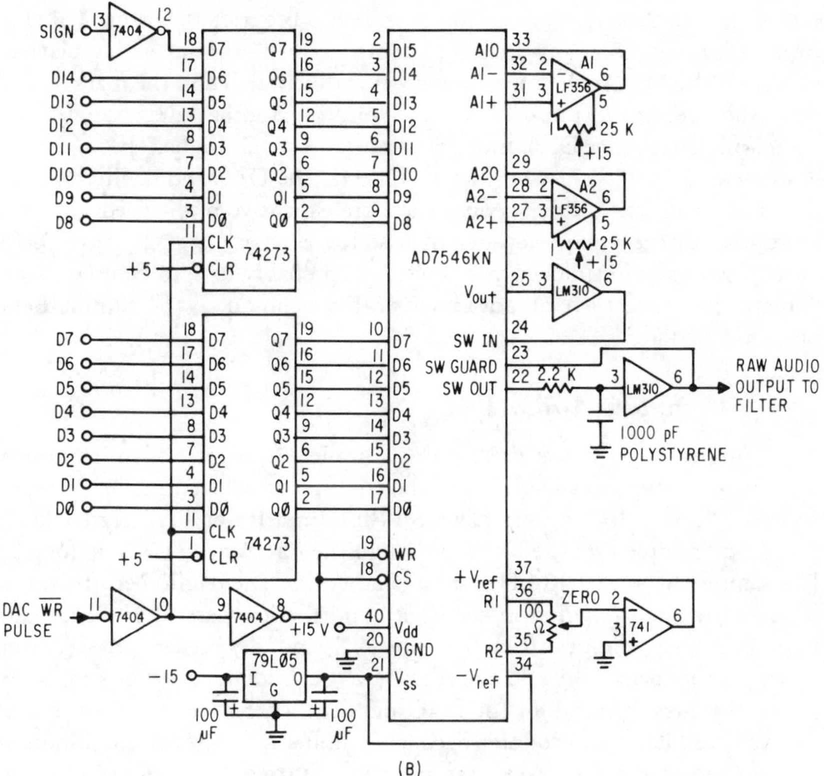
SIGN
7404
D14
D13
D12
D11
D10
D9
D8
74273
CLK
CLR
+5
D7
D6
D5
D4
D3
D2
D1
DØ
DAC WR PULSE
AD7546KN
A10
A1−
A1+
LF356
25 K
+15
A20
A2−
A2+
Vout
LM310
SW IN
SW GUARD
SW OUT
2.2 K
RAW AUDIO OUTPUT TO FILTER
1000 pF POLYSTYRENE
WR
CS
+15 V
Vdd
DGND
Vss
+Vref
R1
R2
−Vref
ZERO
100 Ω
741
79L05
−15
100 μF
(B)

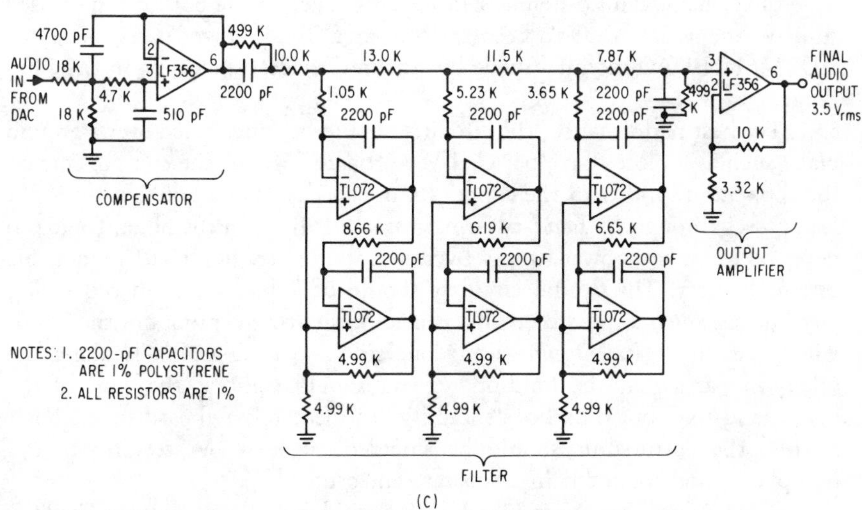
4700 pF
AUDIO IN FROM DAC
18 K
4.7 K
LF356
510 pF
499 K
2200 pF
10.0 K
13.0 K
11.5 K
7.87 K
1.05 K
5.23 K
3.65 K
TL072
8.66 K
6.19 K
6.65 K
4.99 K
499 K
10 K
3.32 K
FINAL AUDIO OUTPUT 3.5 Vrms
COMPENSATOR
FILTER
OUTPUT AMPLIFIER
NOTES: 1. 2200-pF CAPACITORS ARE 1% POLYSTYRENE
2. ALL RESISTORS ARE 1%
(C)

sample rate increase) have been integrated onto proprietary custom LSI chips by at least one company making "compact disk" digital audio playback systems. Although such chips are not generally available in the marketplace, they show exciting promise for the future. Another drawback of this technique is that the DAC must now run at a much higher speed. For the example in Fig. 12–27, where Fs_1 is 40 kHz, the DAC and deglitcher must now run at 80 ks/s, which requires a more expensive high-speed DAC and more care in the circuit layout. In a stereo playback system, two DACs, rather than one multiplexed two ways, will probably have to be used. Thus, perhaps the greatest overall advantage of this technique is the elimination of phase distortion.

A Complete Audio DAC

Figure 12–28 shows a reasonably complete schematic of an inexpensive yet high-quality audio DAC using the concepts developed in the preceding sections. It is a 16-bit unit having 14-bit linearity at high signal levels. Maximum sample rate is 50 ks/s, although the filter shown is set up for a 25-ks/s sample rate and a 10-kHz audio bandwidth. The deglitcher utilizes the handy extra analog switch in the 7546, and the low-pass filter incorporates high frequency compensation for sin(X)/X and deglitcher time constant losses. Component values in the filter have been rounded to the nearest 1% standard values. Timing for the DAC and deglitcher is derived from a built-in crystal oscillator and counter-decoder combination. The counter inputs are shown connected for a 25-ks/s sample rate (40 μsec, 80 counts) but can be reconnected for any rate from 7.8 to 50 ks/s. They could also be connected to a port on the host for a programmable sample rate. Note that the filter will need to be changed for different sample rates. The 2-MHz output can be used to drive the audio ADC to be described later. Total cost of parts using the AD7546KN DAC module (made by Analog Devices) should be in the $100 range.

For best performance, the circuitry should be constructed over a ground plane such as a piece of copper-clad Vectorboard. Mount the components on the copper side and trim the copper from the edge of any hole a component lead passes through by hand-twisting a small drill bit in the hole. There can never be too many power-supply bypass capacitors of the 0.1-μf monolithic ceramic variety. The digital circuitry should be kept away from the analog elements as much as possible. This is made easier by the pinout of the 7546, which has all digital signals along one side and analog signals along the other. In particular, the holding register should right at the edge of the board, and its input data lines should go immediately offboard to the host. Finally, the entire unit should be shielded, at least by steel front- and backplates, and mounted in a separate enclosure.

The timing diagram in Fig. 12–29 should be self-explanatory. The WR pulse to the DAC can be used to inform the host system that a sample has

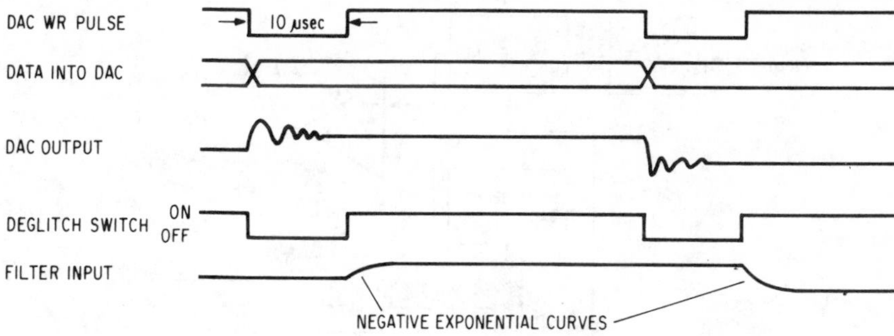

Fig. 12–29. Audio DAC timing diagram

been latched from the data-in lines and that a new sample should be made available. The data could be supplied directly by a running audio-output program, direct memory access circuit, or FIFO buffer logic. The DAC output signal is 10 V peak-to-peak in amplitude but is reduced to 5 V by the filter compensation stage. The filter itself reduces it further to 2.5 V but then is amplified back to 10 V (3.5 V_{rms}) by the output amplifier, a level sufficient to overcome minor ground-loop noise. Ground-loop concerns may be completely eliminated in exchange for dc response by incorporating a standard 600-ohm line transformer into the unit (use a 25-μF nonpolarized dc blocking capacitor in series with the transformer primary). The output amplifier can drive a primary impedance as low as 600 ohms.

Only three adjustments are necessary after the unit is built. For best linearity in the DAC, the offset voltage of A1 and A2 must be nulled. Do this by removing the 7546, temporarily shorting both amplifier inputs to ground, and turning the offset null pot to the point where the amplifier output switches between − 14 and + 14 V. The dc offset at the final output is zeroed with the potentiometer in the 7546 reference circuit. Perform the adjustment with the DAC running and outputting a string of zero samples. This is important because control feedthrough capacitance in the deglitcher contributes to the output offset.

Audio Digitizing

At this time, let us take a brief look at analog-to-digital conversion of audio. In a synthesis application, the major reason for digitizing audio is for modification or source-signal analysis. Consequently, there is not as much need for superdynamic range and distortion figures as with the audio DAC.

Like the DAC, an off-the-shelf ADC alone is not suitable for audio. A block diagram of an audio ADC is shown in Fig. 12–30. The low-pass filter considerations are not the same as those with the DAC except that high sample rates do *not* eliminate the need for a filter. The DAC used for

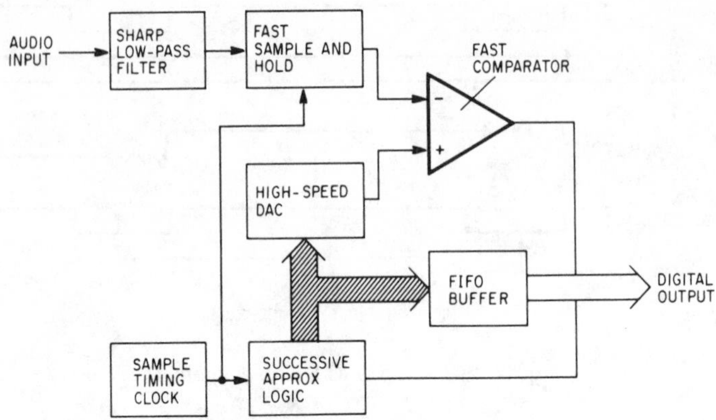

Fig. 12–30. Audio ADC

successive approximation must be reasonably fast in order to attain the higher audio sample rates. For example, the settling time of the DAC plus the response time of the comparator must be less than 2 μsec if 12-bit conversions are to be done at 40 ks/s. This can be a very strict requirement if a fast sample rate and high resolution for audio recording/playback is desired. The successsive approximation logic is as described in Chapter 7. The FIFO buffer holds the last sample value converted until the host can accept it. As with the DAC, the buffer may be as simple as a single register or a true multilevel hardware FIFO. Uniformity of sample rate is just as important as before and therefore should come from a crystal-controlled timing generator.

The sample-and-hold, however, performs a completely different function. Rather than gating out glitches, its job is to capture the input signal at an instant in time and hold it long enough to be digitized. Slewing and glitching are not important, but aperture time and aperture uncertainty are critical for low noise and distortion in the converted results.

Figure 12–31 illustrates the job to be done by the SAH module. *Acquisition time* specifies the interval between the sample command and the time when the SAH is adequately following the signal. This time usually varies with signal level but need not cause concern unless it becomes longer than the sample period minus the ADC conversion time. Even when the signal is being followed, there is a finite lag in the tracking called *tracking error*. As long as the lag time is constant, its only effect is a very slight reduction in high-frequency response, but if it varies with signal amplitude, distortion can be introduced.

When the hold command is given, there is a finite delay before the sampling switch *starts* to turn off, which is called *aperture delay*. Once the switch begins to turn off, there is an additional delay before it is completely turned off, which is called *aperture time,* and is a critical audio SAH parame-

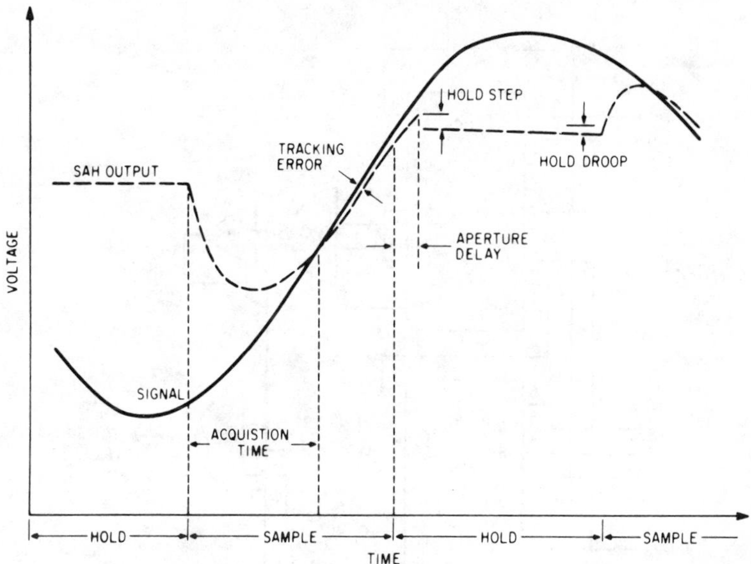

Fig. 12–31. SAH errors

ter. It is critical because the partially off switch is highly nonlinear and contributes to distortion. *Aperture uncertainty* is a variation in aperture delay usually caused by variations in signal amplitude. It has the same distortion-causing effect as variation in the sample rate. Both of these aperture errors create distortion proportional to frequency and amplitude. Essentially, then, the aperture is the effective time width over which the signal voltage is measured and, much like a camera lens, a small aperture gives sharper focus over a wider range of conditions.

Hold step usually is not important unless it varies with signal level. One must wait until the turn-off transient decays before starting the conversion cycle, however. Hold droop is almost never a problem, since the hold time is a few dozen microseconds at most.

Often, it is helpful to have an automatic gain-control (AGC) circuit in the signal path before the SAH and ADC to keep signal levels consistently high. In order to retain information about the dynamics of the input, it would be a simple matter to digitize the gain-control voltage in the AGC circuit with an inexpensive 8-bit ADC module. Since this voltage changes slowly, its sample rate could be as low as tens of hertz. Internally, the AGC information could multiply the samples from, say, a 12-bit ADC into full 16-bit samples and restore the dynamic range. Note that the response speed of the AGC circuit has no bearing on the accuracy of reconstruction provided it is fast enough to suppress sudden, high-amplitude transients below the ADC clipping point.

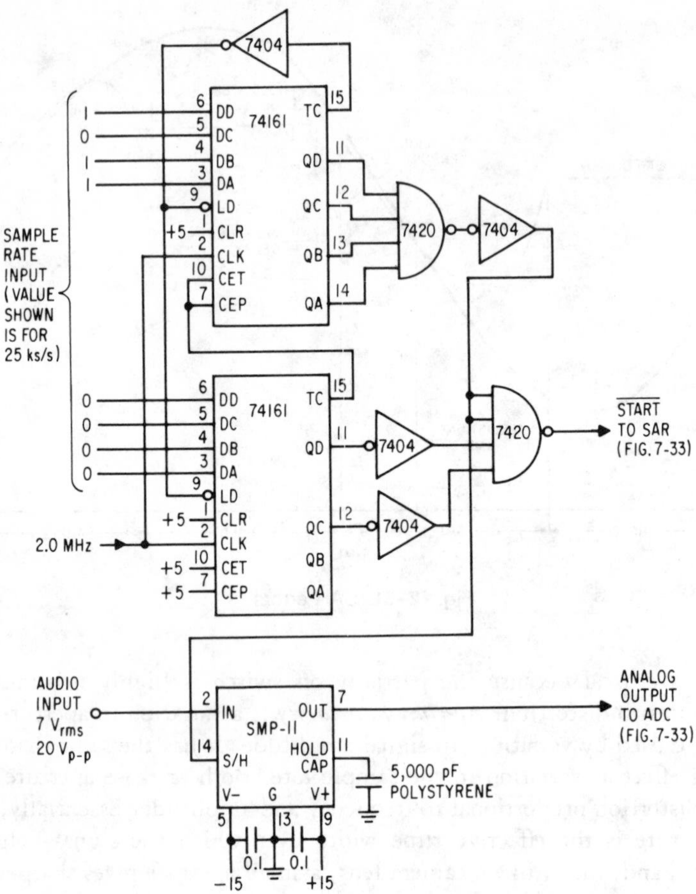

Fig. 12–32. Front-end for 12-bit audio ADC

A 12-Bit Audio A-to-D Converter

Although the last few years have seen a very large price decrease in 16-bit DAC modules suitable for audio use, the same has not been true for ADC modules. This is even true at the 12-bit level where a converter fast enough for audio use still costs $100 or more. Figure 12–32 shows a timing generator and sample-and-hold circuit that may be added to the fast ADC circuit in Fig. 7–33 to allow sampling audio signals at rates up to about 80 ks/s. The SMP-11 (Precision Monolithics) in the SAH circuit normally has dynamic characteristics unsuitable for deglitchers but it performs well in ADC sampling. The 2-MHz clock for the successive approximation register also operates the timing generator, which properly sequences SAH and successive

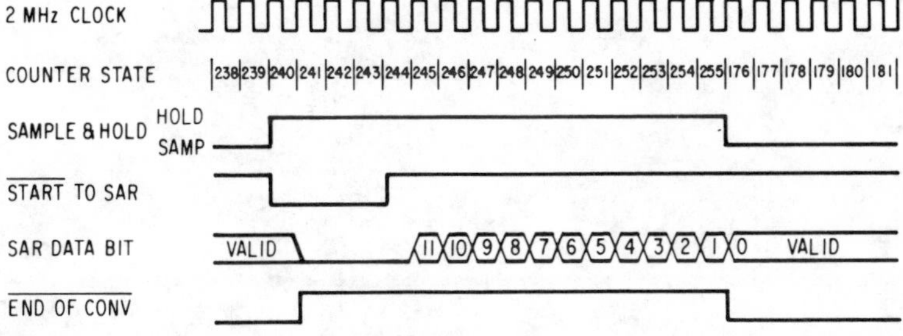

Fig. 12–33. Timing diagram for 12-bit audio ADC

approximation register operation. Total parts costs should be under $30. Of course, a suitable filter must be added to these two circuits.

A timing diagram of the unit is shown in Fig. 12–33. A sampling cycle starts with the 8-bit counter reaching the 240 (11110000) state, which switches the SMP-11 into its hold mold and resets the successive approximation register. Four counts later at 244 (11110100), the SAR is allowed to run. Conversion is complete after 12 additional counts and the counter reloads for the next cycle. The SAH is also switched back to sample mode to reacquire the input signal. The host system can look at the end of conversion output signal, which holds for the sample period minus 8 μsec, to determine when valid data is present. By inserting a 12-bit latch between the SAR and host, the data valid time is extended to a full sample period. The counter inputs are shown connected for a 25-ks/s sample rate (40 μsec, 80 counts) but can be reconnected for any rate from 7.8 to 80 ks/s. If both the DAC from Fig. 12–28 and this ADC are being constructed, the sample rate counter can be shared between the two.

13
Digital Tone Generation Techniques

Because of its total generality, there can be difficulty in knowing where to start in designing a direct digital synthesis system. Most often, though, the fundamental concepts of analog synthesis, which have been proven through years of use, form the basis for a digital synthesis system. Thus, digital equivalents of tone generators, sound modifiers, and control mechanisms are incorporated into the system, hopefully with improved characteristics and flexibility. In fact, some direct synthesis software systems simulate a complete "voltage"-controlled synthesizer along with provisions for simulated patch cords! In this chapter, the digital equivalents of analog tone generators will be described followed later by other tone-generation techniques that are practical only in the digital domain.

One of the many strengths of digital tone generation is that the frequency and amplitude of the resulting waveforms are extremely accurate and stable with time. The user need have no concern whatever about the unpredictable results that frequency and amplitude errors can create. Also, the exact phase between two or more digitally generated tones can be controlled to an equal degree of precision. Of course, if slight relative errors are desired for, say, an ensemble effect, they will actually have to be added in.

Although the previous chapter may have seemed to be preoccupied with vanishingly low noise and distortion figures for the overall sound, *individual* tones need not be of such high quality. For example, a slight amount of harmonic distortion on a single tone is completely inaudible, while even the effect of a larger amount is simply a slight change in timbre. The equivalent amount of distortion in an ensemble of sounds would be very objectionable because of the accompanying intermodulation distortion. Also, super-signal-to-noise ratios for a single tone are not needed because subsequent signal processing, which is what would change the amplitude, also processes the noise, thus retaining whatever the tone's S/N ratio is *independent* of signal level. These are important points because, as will be shown later, extra effort and computation time are necessary for ultra-low-distortion tone generation.

One of the big problems with the generation of tones of arbitrary frequency and waveform is the avoidance of alias distortion. As it turns out, it is quite possible, sometimes unavoidable, to digitally generate a tone having frequency components above one-half the sample rate. When this occurs, the higher frequencies are reflected down as lower frequencies that then sail right through the DAC's low-pass filter, no matter how sophisticated. The audible effect is usually harsh distortion or excessive noise, and it occurs even with single tones. The only way to positively avoid this source of alias distortion is to avoid generating significant amounts of excessively high frequencies.

Direct Waveform Computation

One of the easiest ways to generate tones digitally is to simulate the operation of an analog voltage-controlled oscillator. In an actual synthesis program, the "oscillator" would probably be a subroutine that accepts some arguments (control "voltages") such as one or more frequency parameters and returns one or more results representing samples on one or more output waveforms. The subroutine would probably also require some carryover storage from one sample to the next.

The analog VCO that was described in Chapter 6 consisted of three major parts: control input acquisition, the sawtooth oscillator proper, and waveshaping circuits. A digital equivalent will require the same setup. Concentrating on the oscillator part, it was seen to consist of a current source, an integrator, a comparator, and a discharge (reset) circuit. Fortunately, the digital equivalents to all of these are exceptionally simple and, most important, require very little computation time.

Digital Sawtooth Oscillator

An integrator is an accumulator, somewhat like a bucket that integrates the flow rate of water entering it. A computer accumulator is also an integrator; it accumulates discrete-sized "pieces" represented by numbers added to it via the "add" instruction. When a bucket overflows, it remains full and only the excess water is lost. When an accumulator overflows, its entire contents are dumped and integration starts anew. Thus, it should be apparent that if one considers a number that is repeatedly added to a computer's accumulator to be a "current," the accumulator contents to be the integrator's output, and the overflow phenomenon of binary arithmetic to be a combination comparator/discharge circuit, one has a sawtooth oscillator just like the analog one.

This can be clarified by examining the program segment below, written in 6502 assembly language:

```
LOOP CLC           CLEAR CARRY FLAG              2
     ADC  B        ADD B TO ACCUMULATOR          3
     STA  DAC      WRITE ACCUMULATOR TO DAC      4
     NOP           WAIT 16 CLOCKS FOR A          2
     NOP           TOTAL LOOP TIME OF            2
     NOP           25 μSEC WHICH GIVES           2
     NOP           A 40-ks/s SAMPLE RATE         2
     NOP                                         2
     JMP  *+3                                    3
     JMP  LOOP     REPEAT                        3
                                                25
```

Assuming that the A register was initially 0 and that B contains 1, the sequence of numbers that would be sent to the DAC would be 1, 2, 3, 4, . . . 125, 126, 127. Now, assuming twos-complement arithmetic, the next addition would try to produce 128, which, of course, overflows the 6502's 8-bit accumulator, producing instead a result of −128. The sequence would continue −127, −126, . . . , −2, −1, 0, 1, etc., and a full sawtooth cycle has been completed. The overflow from +127 to −128 is simply the sawtooth flyback.

In a typical 6502, this loop would execute in 25 μsec, giving a sample rate of 40 ks/s. Since 256 times around the loop are required for a single sawtooth cycle, the sawtooth frequency will be 40 ks/s/256 = 156.25 Hz, essentially D-sharp below middle C. Now, what if B has the value 2 in it? Register A, starting at zero would be 0, 2, 4, . . . , 124, 126, −128, −126, . . . , −2, 0, 2, etc. It would take only 128 iterations for a complete cycle, so the tone frequency would be 312.5 Hz, precisely twice what it was. Other frequencies can be had by setting B to other values. Thus, continuing the analog sawtooth analogy, the content of B represents the current into the integrator, although it will be called the *increment* in the discussion to follow.

Improving Frequency Resolution

Obviously, only a very limited number of frequencies is available with this basic loop. Another way to change the sawtooth frequency is to change the loop time and thus the sample rate, perhaps by changing the number of NOP instructions. However, this would violate the holy dogma of direct computer synthesis, which decrees that the sample rate shall remain constant throughout the system.

Actually, the numbers in the accumulator and B should be considered as *fractions* between −1 and +1. Thus, the accumulator starts at 0, increments in units of 1/128 to 127/128, overflows to −128/128, continues to 0, and repeats. B can hold values of 1/128, 2/128, 3/128, etc. The sawtooth frequency is given by $F = 40{,}000I/2$, where I is the fraction stored in B, the 40,000 is the sample rate, and the 2 is because the sawtooth traverses a range of 2 units; from −1 to +1. In order to get finer frequency resolution, it is simply necessary to specify the increment with more precision.

Increasing the accumulator and increment word length to 16 bits improves frequency resolution considerably. A modified loop to do this is:

```
LOOP  LDA  L     GET LOWER BYTE OF 16-BIT
                 "ACCUMULATOR"                  3
      ADC  C     ADD LOWER BYTE OF INCREMENT    3
      STA  L     SAVE LOWER BYTE OF RESULT      3
      LDA  H     GET UPPER BYTE OF
                 "ACCUMULATOR"                  3
      ADC  B     ADD UPPER BYTE OF INCREMENT
                 WITH CARRY                     3
      STA  H     SAVE UPPER BYTE OF RESULT      3
      STA  DAC   ALSO OUTPUT IT TO THE DAC      4
      JMP  LOOP  REPEAT                         3
                                               --
                                               25
```

Here memory locations H and L function as the accumulator with H being the most significant byte, while B and C hold the increment with B being most significant. The formula for frequency is the same as before, but now the frequency resolution is 256 times better or about 0.61 Hz. Thus, if it is desired to generate middle C, which has a frequency of 261.625 Hz, the value of the increment should be $I = 2F/40{,}000$, which evaluates to 0.01308. Converted to fractional form with a denominator of 32,768, it would be closest to 429/32,768 and therefore locations B and C would contain 429 or the hex equivalent, 01AD. The important point is that the frequency resolution has been improved from an unacceptable 156 Hz to a mere 0.61 Hz. Extending the fractions to 24 bits gives a resolution of 0.0024 Hz (1 cycle/7 min), which for practical purposes makes frequency a continuous variable.

One interesting property of the digital sawtooth generator is that the increment can be *negative* as easily as it is positive. With negative increments, the sawtooth slopes downward and underflows upward, just the opposite of positive increments. This behavior satisfies the mathematical requirements for a negative frequency, which is a handy property if dynamic depth frequency modulation is being performed because then one does not need to worry about possible negative frequencies.

Other Waveforms

Just as an analog sawtooth can be easily converted into other waveforms, some simple computations are all that is necessary to transform digital sawtooths. Programming for the conversion would simply accept a sample from the sawtooth generator and return a sample of the converted waveform. Perhaps the simplest is conversion into a square waveform. Sawtooth samples are merely tested to determine if they are positive or negative. If positive, a value equal to positive full scale is produced, otherwise negative full scale is sent out. Rectangular waves with the width specified by a parameter are nearly as easy; simply compare the sawtooth samples with the parameter rather than with zero.

Conversion to a triangular waveform requires a little more manipulation, although it still parallels the analog operation. Full-wave rectification is equivalent to an absolute value function, thus the first step is to test the sawtooth sample and negate it if it is negative. A potential problem exists, however, because there is no positive equivalent of negative full scale in twos-complement arithmetic. If this value is seen, simply convert to the largest positive number which results in an ever so slightly clipped triangle wave. The next step is to center the triangle, which is accomplished by subtracting one-half of full scale from the absolute value. The result now is a triangle wave but with one-half of the normal amplitude. A final shift left by 1 bit doubles the amplitude to full scale.

Conversion to a sine wave is most difficult. The analog-rounding circuits used to do the job have as their digital equivalent either the evaluation of an equation representing the rounding curve or a table lookup. Of these two, table lookup is far faster but does require some memory for the table. The brute-force way to handle table lookup is to simply take a sawtooth sample and treat it as an integer index into a table of sines. The table entry would be fetched and returned as the sine wave sample. Memory usage can be cut by a factor of four by realizing that the sine function is redundant. Thus, if the sawtooth sample, S, is between zero and one-half full scale use the table entry directly. If it is between one-half and full scale, look into the table at $1.0 - S$. If S is negative, negate the table entry before using it.

Still, if the sawtooth samples have very many significant bits, the table size can become quite large. One could truncate S by just ignoring the less significant bits and looking up in a smaller table. Rounding is another possibility that is implemented simply by adding the value of the most significant bit ignored to the sample before truncation. As we shall see later, rounding has no effect on the *audible* portion of the error. Generally, truncation is accurate enough if a reasonable size table is used. For example, a 256-entry table, which would require 512 bytes, using symmetry would be the equivalent of 1,024 entries. The distortion incurred by using this table would be approximately 54 dB below the signal level, or the equivalent of 0.2% distortion. Actually, the kind of distortion produced will sound more like noise so a S/N ratio is the more appropriate measure. At very low frequencies, the noise amplitude will appear to be modulated by the signal.

Linear Interpolation

The most accurate approach, however, is *interpolation* between the sine table entries. Linear interpolation gives good results for very gentle curves such as sine waves and, if done perfectly, could be expected to reduce the noise level to −103 dB based on a 256-entry table with symmetry, which is the limit of 16-bit samples anyway. Figure 13–1 shows generalized linear

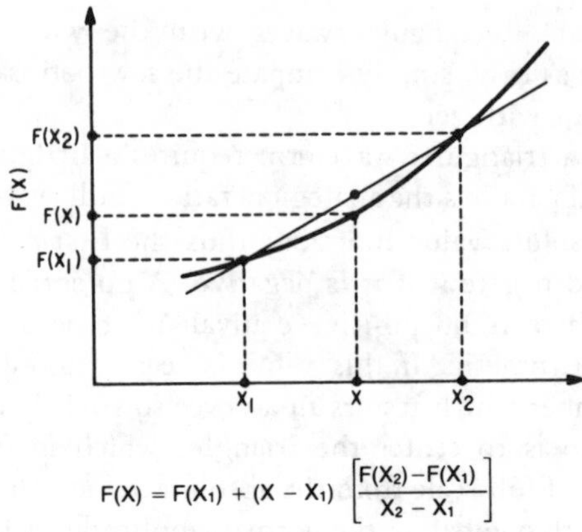

Fig. 13–1. Linear interpolation

interpolation and some important information about it. Essentially, the job is to compute the correct value of $F(X)$ given an arbitrary X, where X is the sawtooth sample and $F(X)$ is the sine sample. X_1 and X_2 are tabulated arguments, while $F(X_1)$ and $F(X_2)$ are the tabulated sines of those arguments.

Due to the nature of the table and binary arithmetic, the computation is actually simpler than it looks. Since the table is tabulated in equal increments of X, the quantity $X_2 - X_1$ is a constant. If the table has a power of two number of entries, then even the division by $X_2 - X_1$ is a simple shifting operation. As a result, the overall computation is reduced to two subtractions, an addition, and one multiplication.

As an example, consider linear interpolation in a sine table of only 64 entries using a 16-bit argument and assuming that the table entries are signed 16-bit values. Let's further assume that a separate table giving $F(X_2) - F(X_1)/(X_2 - X_1)$ is also available, which will be called the *first derivative table* and that its entries have been scaled to make the following operations possible. Figure 13–2 illustrates binary linear interpolation.

The first step is to save the most significant 2 bits of the argument and transform the remaining 14 bits into a positive, first-quadrant value. Next, using only the 6 bits left in the upper byte, access the function table to get $F(X_1)$ and the derivative table to get $F(X_2) - F(X_1)/(X_2 - X)$. Finally, multiply the lower byte of the argument, which is $X - X_1$, by the derivative and add the product (possibly shifted for scaling) to $F(X_1)$ fetched earlier. The derivative table entry need be only one byte long; therefore, the multiply is an 8 x 8-bit operation, which can be quite fast even in software on an 8-bit machine. Before returning, the two saved bits, which identify the quadrant, should be examined and the function value adjusted accordingly. The linear interpolation is so effective that this 192-byte table gives a sine wave with 30 dB less noise than a 512-byte table using the brute-force method. In practice, it would be up to the programmer to decide if the memory savings and

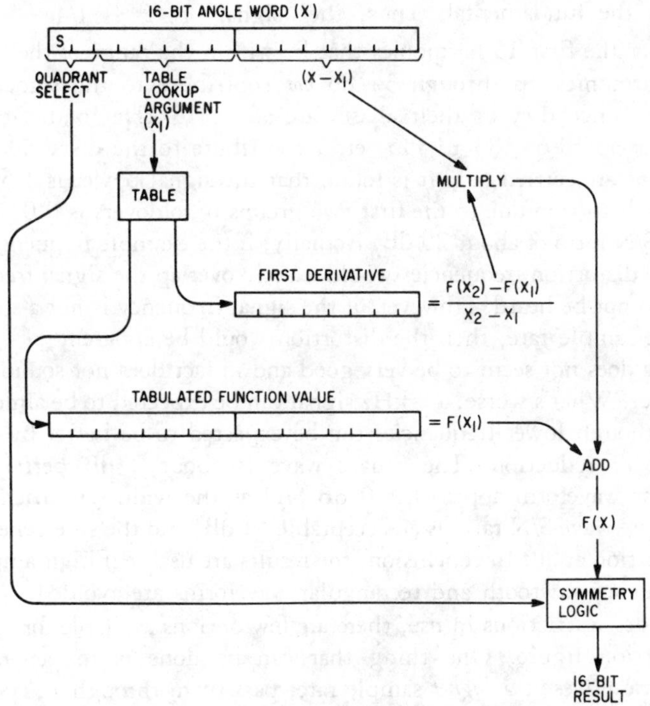

Fig. 13–2. Linear interpolation in a sine table

improved noise level are worth the extra computation time, particularly if hardware multiply is not available.

Alias Distortion

So far everything sounds great; all of the normal analog synthesizer waveforms are available in digital form with adequate frequency resolution and are just waiting to be processed further. There exists, however, one problem that can only be minimized and that is alias distortion from the upper harmonics of most of these waveforms. When the algorithms just described are used to generate samples on a waveform, the samples generated are exactly the same as would have come from an ADC sampling the equivalent analog waveform *with no low-pass filter!* Thus, one would expect the higher harmonics to fold back into the audio range and create distortion.

Before deciding what to do about the problem, its severity should be determined. As a "best-case" example, let us assume a sample rate of 50 ks/s, the use of a sharp 15-kHz low-pass filter in the output DAC, and a 1-kHz sawtooth wave. The idea is to add up the power in all of the unaliased harmonics in the 15-kHz range and compare this with the sum of the aliased harmonics that are *in the 15-kHz range*.

The power spectrum of a sawtooth wave is well known and is $Pn = P_1/n^2$, where Pn is the power in the nth harmonic relative to the power in the fundamental. Thus, the "signal" is 1 + 1/4 + 1/9 . . . + 1/225 for the first 15 harmonics that lie within the range of the low-pass filter. Harmonics 16 through 34 do *not* contribute to the signal or the distortion, since they or their aliases are above 15 kHz in this example. Harmonics 35 to 65, 85 to 115, etc., contribute to the distortion. If the calculations are carried out, it is found that the signal power is 1.58 units, while the distortion due to the first-two groups of foldovers is 0.01717 unit giving a S/N ratio of about 20 dB. Actually, if the example frequencies were exact, the distortion frequencies would exactly overlap the signal frequencies and would not be heard. However, if the signal frequency is not a submultiple of the sample rate, then the distortion would be apparent.

This does not seem to be very good and in fact does not sound all that good either. What's worse, a 2-kHz signal can be expected to be almost 6 dB worse, although lower frequencies can be expected to be better by about 6 dB/octave of reduction. The square wave is about 2 dB better, but a rectangular waveform approaches 0 dB S/N as the width approaches zero. The triangle wave S/N ratio is an acceptable 54 dB, and the sine generates no alias distortion at all. In conclusion, the results are usable if high-amplitude, high-frequency sawtooth and rectangular waveforms are avoided.

Besides restrictions in use, there are few options available for lowering the distortion figure. One thing that can be done is to generate the troublesome waves at a *higher* sample rate, pass them through a *digital* low-pass filter operating at the higher rate, and then *re-sample* the filter output at the lower system sample rate. For example, the sawtooth might be generated at 400 ks/s, which is eight times the system rate and then fed to a simple digital low-pass filter that cuts off at 15 kHz. Only every eighth sample emerging from the filter would actually be used. With this setup, the S/N ratio for the 1-kHz sawtooth would be improved to 38 dB. While the computation time necessary to do this in software is much greater than that required for some of the more sophisticated tone generation techniques, it can be a viable *hardware* technique whereby simplicity of the algorithm often outweighs computation time considerations because the digital hardware is so fast.

Table Lookup Method

If direct computer synthesis is to live up to its promise of nearly infinite flexibility and very high sound quality, then better tone-generation techniques than the simulation of analog synthesizer oscillators will have to be used. One of these involves scanning of precomputed waveform tables. An important advantage is that the sample values stored in the table can in many instances be selected so that alias distortion is not a problem. Another is that microprocessors are far more efficient in looking up waveform samples than in computing them from scratch.

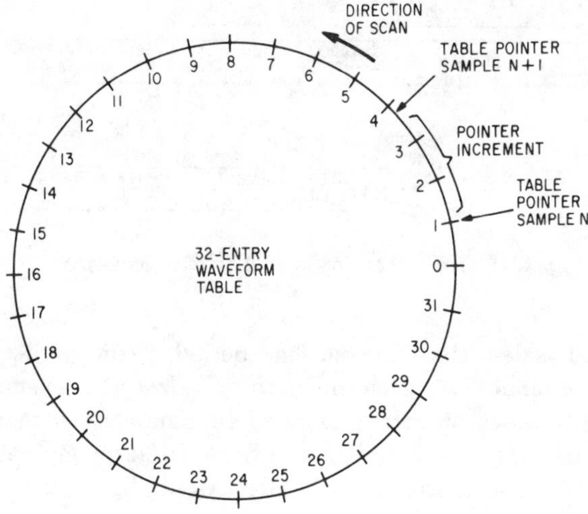

Fig. 13–3. Waveform table scanning

Elementary tone generation by table scanning is just what the terms imply: a simple loop is programmed to fetch the table entries one at a time and send them to the DAC. When the end of the table is reached, scanning should continue uninterrupted at the beginning. Each time through the table is one cycle of the waveform. Figure 13–3 shows graphically a generalized table-scanning process. Since the beginning follows the end, the table can be imagined to be circular. The table pointer points to an entry and the pointer increment specifies how far the pointer is to advance between samples.

If the number of table entries is a power of two, the "wraparound" can be simplified. Essentially, an I-bit counter is programmed, where $I = \log_2 N$, and N is the number of table entries. The value of the counter is used as a pointer into the table. When the counter overflows from maximum count to zero, the pointer automatically starts at the beginning of the table. Thus, tables of 256 entries are extremely convenient in an 8-bit microcomputer, since the lower byte of the address pointer can be used as the counter and the upper byte, which is the "page number" (block of 256 memory addresses starting at an address divisible by 256) of the table, is left alone.

Controlling Frequency

As with sawtooth oscillator simulation, the frequency of the tone may be changed by altering the time between lookups, but this amounts to changing the sample rate. Thus, frequency control is achieved by changing the increment from 1 to 2 to 3, etc. Note that this means that table entries are skipped as the scanning proceeds. However, as long as the number of

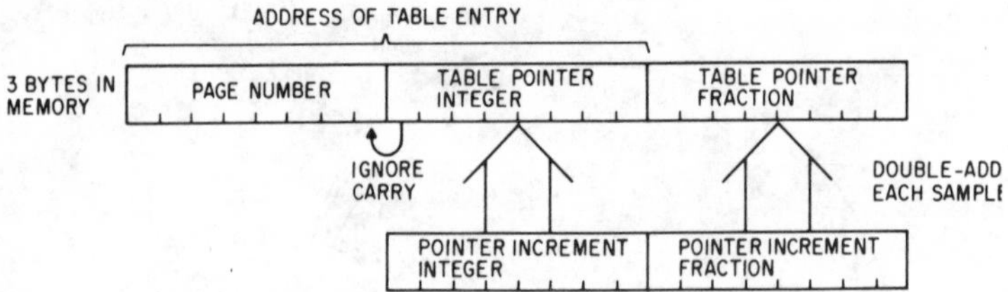

Fig. 13–4. Table scanning in an 8-bit microprocessor

entries skipped is less than one-half the period of the highest significant harmonic in the tabulated waveform, nothing is lost and no audible noise is added. If the number of entries skipped becomes larger than this, alias distortion occurs. Also, the fact that each trip around the table is likely to be different is of no significance, since the effect would be the same as sampling a waveform at a rate that is not an exact multiple of its frequency.

As before, only a very few frequencies can be generated with integer increments, so it will be necessary to extend the precision of the increment by adding a *fractional part*. Now, the pointer increment and the table pointer are *mixed numbers* having an integer part and a fractional part. Note that the fractional part of the pointer implies some kind of interpolation between adjacent table entries. For maximum speed, however, the fractional part of the pointer can be ignored and the integer part used to select the table entry as before.

A simple example should clarify this some. Let us assume a moderate-performance direct synthesis sytem with a sample rate of 15 ks/s and waveform tables having 256 entries of 8 bits each. If a tone frequency of 220 Hz (A below middle C) is desired, the pointer increment should be 3.75466 according to the formula: $I = NF/Fs$, where I is the increment, N is the number of table entries, F is the tone frequency, and Fs is the sample rate. In an 8-bit machine, it is convenient to make the pointer and the increment double-byte mixed numbers with the upper byte being the integer part and the lower byte being the fractional part. Thus, the decimal mixed number, 3.75466 would have an integer part of 3 and a fractional part of 193, the latter being 0.75466 multiplied by 256.

To get the next sample from the table, the increment would be double-precision added to the pointer with overflow from the integer parts ignored. Then the integer part of the pointer would be used to access the table. If the microprocessor has an indirect addressing mode through memory like the 6502, then Fig. 13–4 illustrates how utterly simple these operations are. A three-byte vector in memory is used for each tone. The most significant byte gives the page address of the waveform table, while the remaining two bytes are the pointer. An indirect load through the leftmost two bytes of the vector are all that is necessary for the table lookup! In the 6502, the entire operation of adding the increment and getting the next sample from the table takes a mere 23 clock cycles, which for the standard machine is 23 μsec. While other 8-bit microprocessors will be slower, this is a highly efficient operation on all of them. The 68000 can perform the identical operation (table pointer in a data register, increment in memory) in 44 clock cycles, which, at 8 MHz is only 5.5 μsec, sufficiently fast to synthesize several tones in real time!

It is perfectly feasible to gradually change the pointer increment in order to gradually change the frequency. Thus, glides, vibrato, and even dynamic depth FM can be accomplished by changing the increment as required. The only limit to the speed and magnitude of increment variation is the FM sidebands that result. If they become broad enough, a portion may spill over the Nyquist frequency and begin to generate alias distortion.

Table Size

A natural question at this point is, "How large should the table be for an acceptable noise and distortion level?" Actually, there are two sources of error in samples derived by table lookup. One is simply *quantization error* of the stored samples, which can be made vanishingly small (− 100 dB) simply by using 16 bits to store a table entry. The other error is the *interpolation error* that occurs when the fractional part of the table pointer is nonzero. This error, which is worst with no interpolation at all, can be made small only by using a large table and linear, quadratic, or higher order interpolation between the tabulated points. Thus, interpolation noise is likely to completely dominate, and if it does not, the precision of the table entries should be increased until it does.

Unfortunately, the average magnitude of the error, and hence noise, is dependent on the waveform stored in the table. If the waveform can be exactly described by a simple formula, a mathematician can always take the formula and other parameters such as size of table, interpolation method, sample rate, and DAC LPF cutoff and derive an exact S/N ratio.

A much simpler way to get a noise estimate is to simulate an ideal tone generator and a table-driven tone generator and look at the *difference* in the sample values generated. What is desired is the rms average of the *ac component* of the difference, which represents the noise power. The ac component of the difference is simply the actual difference samples with the long-term average of the difference, which represents the inaudible dc component of the error, subtracted out. It is also important that the two tone generators be precisely in phase (truncating rather than rounding the table pointer introduces a phase shift of π/N radians where N is the number of table entries) otherwise the noise estimate will be excessively pessimistic.

The simulation is best done by choosing an irrational number such as π for the pointer increment and obtaining several hundred to a thousand samples from each generator and their differences. The rms average difference is found by squaring the adjusted difference samples and adding them up. The ideal signal samples are also "ac coupled," squared, and added up. The

```
1000 REM   TABLE NOISE CALCULATE PROGRAM
1001 REM   N=NUMBER OF TABLE ENTRIES    P=PHASE SHIFT DUE TO TRUNCATION
1010 N=256: P=1/(2*N)
1100 REM   GET THE MEAN OF THE IDEAL SAMPLE STREAM AND THE MEAN OF THE
1101 REM   DIFFERENCE BETWEEN IDEAL AND TABLE LOOKUP SAMPLES
1110 REM   M1=MEAN OF IDEAL, M2=MEAN OF DIFFERENCE
1120 M1=0: M2=0: T1=0
1130 FOR I=1 TO 1000
1140 T1=T1+.314159
1150 IF T1>=1 THEN T1=T1-1
1160 T=T1
1170 GOSUB 2000
1180 M1=M1+S
1190 S1=S
1200 T=(INT(N*T1)/N)+P
1210 GOSUB 2000
1220 M2=M2+(S1-S)
1300 NEXT I
1310 M1=M1/1000
1320 M2=M2/1000
1330 PRINT "MEAN OF IDEAL SAMPLES = ";M1
1340 PRINT "MEAN OF DIFFERENCE = ";M2
1400 REM   GET THE AUDIBLE IDEAL SIGNAL POWER AND AUDIBLE NOISE POWER
1401 REM   V1 IS SIGNAL POWER   V2 IS NOISE POWER
1410 V1=0: V2=0: T1=0
1420 FOR I=1 TO 1000
1430 T1=T1+.314159
1440 IF T1>=1 THEN T1=T1-1
1450 T=T1
1460 GOSUB 2000
1470 V1=V1+(S-M1)*(S-M1)
1480 S1=S
1490 T=(INT(N*T1)/N)+P
1500 GOSUB 2000
1510 V2=V2+(((S1-S)-M2)*((S1-S)-M2))
1520 NEXT I
1600 REM   PRINT RESULTS
1610 PRINT "SIGNAL POWER = ";V1
1620 PRINT "NOISE POWER = ";V2
1630 PRINT "NOISE LEVEL IS ";4.3429*(LOG(V1)-LOG(V2));" DB DOWN."
1999 STOP
2000 REM   SIMPLE WAVEFORM SUBROUTINE, INPUT IS T, 0<=T<=1, OUTPUT IS S
2100 S=SIN(6.283186*T)
2200 RETURN
3000 REM   COMPLEX WAVEFORM SUBROUTINE, INPUT IS T, 0<=T<=1, OUTPUT IS S
3010 REM   CHANGE GOSUBS IN LINES 1170, 1210, 1460, 1500 TO USE
3100 A=6.283186*T
3110 S=SIN(A)+SIN(2*A)+SIN(3*A)+SIN(5*A)+SIN(8*A)+SIN(11*A)+SIN(14*A)
3120 S=SIN(17*A)+S
3130 RETURN
9999 END
```

Fig. 13–5. program to calculate table lookup interpolation noise

two sums, which represent noise and signal *energy* over the same test period, are divided to obtain the S/N ratio.

Figure 13–5 is a program written in BASIC for estimating the S/N ratio of the table lookup method with specified parameters. The subroutine starting at statement 2,000 should look at the variable T, which represents time, and return the corresponding ideal tone sample by storing it in S. T will always be between 0 and 1 but will never equal 1. The range of Ss returned is not important but should be reasonable. The effect of a table lookup tone-generation routine is simulated by quantizing T according to the specified number of table entries and calling the ideal tone-generator subroutine.

The program executes in two parts. The first part runs 1,000 samples through and accumulates the mean of the ideal samples and the mean of the difference. The second part runs another 1,000 samples to compute the rms difference as described earlier. Phase shift due to truncation in the table lookup is also corrected. When complete (the program may run for several minutes on many systems) it prints a single number, which is the S/N ratio in decibels. Note that this is an absolute worst case, since all noise frequencies including those that would be stopped by the DAC's filter are included. A figure in better agreement with actual audible noise would be about 5 dB better.

Figure 13–6 gives some results from running the program. Table sizes of 256, 512, and 1,024 were tried with no interpolation and with linear interpolation. Two waveforms were also tried, one being a simple sine wave and the other being a fairly rich waveform having an equal mix of fundamental, 2, 3, 5, 8, 11, 14, and 17th harmonics.

A. NO INTERPOLATION
1. Sine waveform
   a. 256 points 42.99 dB
   b. 512 points 49.03 dB
   c. 1024 points 55.05 dB
2. Complex waveform
   a. 256 points 23.56 dB
   b. 512 points 29.55 dB
   c. 1024 points 35.41 dB

B. LINEAR INTERPOLATION
1. Sine waveform
   a. 256 points 85.19 dB
   b. 512 points 97.23 dB
   c. 1024 points 109.28 dB
2. Complex waveform
   a. 256 points 42.75 dB
   b. 512 points 54.76 dB
   c. 1024 points 66.82 dB

Fig. 13–6. Worst case table noise for various combinations of table length, stored waveform, and interpolation. (A) No interpolation. (B) Linear interpolation.

Filling the Table

Once a suitable table size and interpolation method has been determined, the remaining task is to fill the table with waveform samples. Since the table is seldom, if ever, filled in real time, a variety of techniques is applicable.

Probably the simplest method conceptually is drawing a waveform by hand on a piece of graph paper (or a graphic digitizer) and then entering the sample values into the table. Although simple in concept, there are a number of constraints that should be kept in mind. One is that the table must contain exactly one cycle of the waveform; therefore, the first and last samples are the same as any other adjacent pair and must be *continuous*. When drawing, some forward planning is necessary to complete the cycle exactly at the end of the scale. Alternatively, the cycle can be drawn freehand and the grid lines added afterward in the proper scale.

This same constraint applies if one desires to capture a musical instrument sound in a table. When digitizing the waveform, one possibility is to simply adjust the sample rate and the tone frequency until one cycle exactly fills *N* samples. Another alternative is a sample rate conversion program that in effect does superinterpolation in order to adjust the sample rate *after* several cycles of the waveform have been digitized.

When drawing by hand, it is very easy to come up with waveforms with such strong upper harmonics that alias distortion and noise can be a problem when the table is scanned with pointer increments larger than 1.0. Thus, one should be careful to draw reasonably smooth curves rather than sharp angles or discontinuous jumps. Note that if a perfect sawtooth waveform were placed in a table, the result when scanned would be identical to the sawtooth oscillator studied earlier.

Table Filling by Fourier Series

One of the best ways to fill the table is to specify the amplitudes and optionally the phases of the harmonics desired in the waveform and then use a Fourier series or Fourier transform program to compute the table entries. The result when the table is scanned is a tone with the exact harmonic makeup specified. Since the timbre of the tone has a much stronger relation to the harmonic structure than to the appearance of the waveform, experimentation to find the desired timbre will be easier with the Fourier series approach.

Another advantage is that alias distortion can be positively controlled. Since the exact harmonic makeup of the table content is known, one simply avoids having the highest harmonic of the highest frequency tone generated using the table ever get high enough to produce an audible alias. In practice, this means that tables used for the higher register voices should have a more restricted spectrum than those used for the lower-pitched voices. For example, if the sample rate is 30 ks/s, the DAC filter cuts off at 10 kHz, and the highest note played is C6 (two octaves above middle C, 1,046 Hz), the highest harmonic present in the table should be about the 18th. This would alias to about 11.2 kHz, which would be attenuated. Any harmonics higher than the 18th would alias to frequencies lower than 11 kHz and would be attenuated little if any. For a bass voice with an upper limit of middle C, one could go to about the 70th harmonic with no problems.

Actually computing the waveform that corresponds to a particular set of harmonic amplitudes is quite simple in BASIC, although slow. Essentially one computes sine waves at the fundamental and harmonic frequencies, multiplies each by its corresponding amplitude specification, and adds them up. For example, assume that a waveform with 1 unit of fundamental, 0.5 unit of second harmonic, and 0.15 unit of third harmonic is desired. Assume further that the table size is 256 and the table entries are 8-bit twos-complement numbers. Since the sin function in BASIC expects angles in radians, the *angle increment* that corresponds to a table increment of 1.0 is $2\pi/256$ or 0.024544. Thus, we will start the angle, A, at 0, compute the first table entry, increment A by 0.024544, compute the second entry, and so on until the 256th entry is done. The *preliminary* value of a table entry, therefore, is equal to $\sin(A)+0.5\sin(2A)+0.15\sin(3A)$. This assumes that all of the phase angles are zero. If a 90° phase angle is desired for the third harmonic, the third term of the expression above should be changed to $0.15\sin(3A+1.5708)$, where $1.5708=(90)(2\pi)/360$.

After the preliminary table entries are computed, they must be adjusted and converted into binary integers for use by the table-scanning routine, which will undoubtedly be written in assembly language. The first step is to *normalize* the existing entries so that there is no overflow when conversion is done but at the same time the full-scale range is used in order to minimize quantization noise. This is done by scanning the table and finding the entry with the *largest absolute value*, which will be called M. Then each entry in the table is multiplied by $127/M$ and "poked" into memory at the locations reserved for the table. The poke function available in many microcomputer BASICs converts the adjusted entry from floating point to the single-byte twos-complement integer desired.

Figure 13–7 implements these operations in an easy-to-use form. The A array holds the harmonic amplitudes and the P array holds the phases. N is a variable that specifies the highest harmonic to process. Ideally, amplitude-array elements should be between 0 and 1.0 for ease in visualizing relationships between harmonics, although the normalization process allows virtually anything. The phase entries range from 0, which represents zero phase shift, to 1.0 which is a 360° shift. Therefore 0.5 is 180°, 0.25 is 90°, etc. If phase of the harmonics is not important (it usually is not for audio waveforms), the variable Q should be set to zero. This instructs the program to set the phases *randomly*, since zero phase for all of the components

```
1000 REM PROGRAM TO UTILIZE THE FOURIER SERIES TO FILL A WAVEFORM TABLE
1010 REM ARRAY A HOLDS THE AMPLITUDES OF THE HARMONICS
1020 REM ARRAY P HOLDS THE PHASES OF THE HARMONICS
1030 REM THE ZEROTH ELEMENT OF A AND P CORRESPONDS TO THE DC COMPONENT
1040 REM VARIABLE N HOLDS THE NUMBER OF THE HIGHEST HARMONIC TO PROCESS
1050 REM VARIABLE M HOLDS THE SIZE OF THE TABLE TO GENERATE
1060 REM VARIABLE Q IF 0 SELECTS RANDOM PHASES, IF 1 USES ARRAY P
1070 REM ARRAY T IS THE GENERATED TABLE WITH ALL ENTRIES BETWEEN BUT NOT
1080 REM INCLUDING -1 AND +1
1100 REM AMPLITUDE DATA
1110 DATA 0,.8,.6,.2,.55,1.0,.7,.3,.2,.1,.05
1120 REM PHASE DATA
1130 DATA 0,0,.2,.4,.7,.45,.1,.5,.85,.9,0
1140 LET N=10
1150 LET M=256
1160 LET Q=1
1200 REM SET UP THE AMPLITUDE AND PHASE ARRAYS
1210 FOR I=0 TO N
1220 READ A(I)
1230 NEXT I
1240 FOR I=0 TO N
1250 IF Q=0 GOTO 1270
1260 READ P(I)
1270 GOTO 1280
1270 LET P(I)=RND(1)
1280 NEXT I
1300 REM MAIN LOOP TO COMPUTE PRELIMINARY TABLE CONTENTS
1310 FOR I=0 TO M-1
1320 LET T(I)=0
1330 LET A1=6.28318*I/M
1340 FOR J=0 TO N
1350 LET T(I)=T(I)+A(J)*COS(J*A1+6.28318*P(J))
1360 NEXT J
1370 NEXT I
1400 REM SCAN RESULTING TABLE FOR MAXIMUM ABSOLUTE VALUE
1410 LET A1=0
1420 FOR I=0 TO M-1
1430 IF ABS(T(I))½A1 THEN LET A1=ABS(T(I))
1440 NEXT I
1500 REM NORMALIZE THE TABLE
1510 FOR I=0 TO M-1
1520 LET T(I)=T(I)/A1*.99999
1530 NEXT I
1600 REM ADD CODE HERE TO OUTPUT THE TABLE IN SUITABLE FORM
1700 STOP
1800 END
```

Fig. 13–7. Program to optimally fill waveform tables

almost always produces waves with a single high-amplitude peak and low average amplitude elsewhere, which is less than optimum for low noise. The array T is the waveform table containing values between -1 and $+1$ when the program returns. Additional code to convert the values into integers with the appropriate range and to store them in the final waveform table is easily added.

Assembly language can also be used to construct the table in 1% to 10% of the time required by a BASIC program. Part of the improvement is due to more efficient program execution, while the rest is due to the use of fixed-point rather than floating-point arithmetic. Only the sin function poses any computational difficulty and that can bypassed through use of a sine table with a length equal to the waveform table being filled. Chapter 18 will describe the use of integer and fractional arithmetic to maximize the speed of digital synthesis computation.

Dynamic Timbre Variation

In a voltage-controlled synthesizer, the tone generators usually put out an unchanging waveform that is dynamically altered by processing modules. Although the same can be done in direct synthesis with digital filters, the table method of tone generation lends itself well to types of timbre variation not easily accomplished with filters.

One technique that is quite practical involves two waveform tables and interpolation between them. The idea is to start with the waveform in Table A and then *gradually* shift to a different waveform in Table B. The arithmetic is actually quite simple. First, a mixture variable ranging between 0 and 1.0 is defined, which will be called M. The contribution of waveform B to the resultant waveform is equal to M and the contribution of A is $1.0 - M$. The actual resultant samples are computed by evaluating $Sr=(1-M)Sa+MSb$, where Sr is the result sample, Sa is a sample from the A table, Sb is the B-table sample, and M is as before. Thus, as M changes from 0 to 1.0, the mixture changes in direct proportion.

In actual use, M should be updated frequently enough so that it changes very little between updates. Also the same table pointer should be used on both tables to insure that they are in phase. If these rules are followed, the transition is glitch- and noise-free even for very fast transitions. The technique is not limited to two tables either. One could go through a whole sequence of tables in order to precisely control a very complex tonal evolution.

Speaking of evolution, it would be desirable to know exactly what the spectrum of the tone does during the transition. If each harmonic has the same phase in the two tables, then the amplitude evolution of that harmonic will make a smooth, monotonic transition from its amplitude in tone A to its new amplitude in tone B.

Things get quite interesting, however, if they are *not* in phase. Depending on the phase and amplitude differences between the two tables, any number of things can happen as shown in Fig. 13–8. The graph shows amplitude and phase variations of an arbitrary harmonic during a linear transition from wave A, where this harmonic has an amplitude of 0.4 units, to wave B, where its amplitude is 0.9 units. Its phase in wave A is taken as a zero reference and its phase in wave B is the parameter for the curves. When the phase of this harmonic in wave B is also zero, the amplitude transition is linear. It becomes progressively nonlinear and even dips momentarily along its rise as the phase difference approaches 180°.

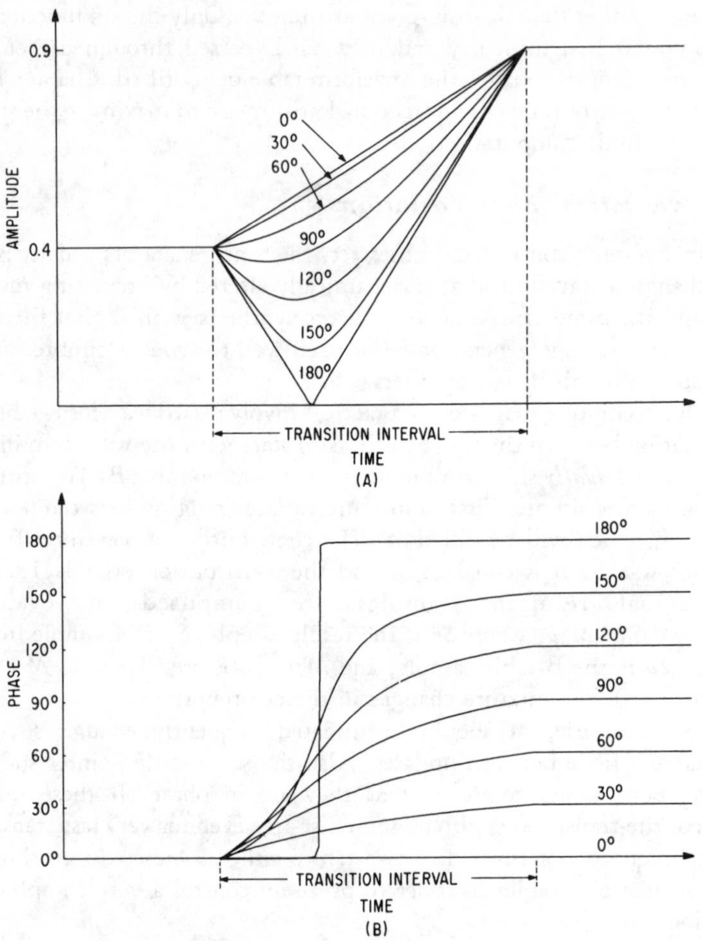

Fig. 13–8. Time-variable interpolation between two sine waves. (A) Amplitude contours; phase difference is parameter. (B) Phase contours; phase difference is parameter.

Note on the phase curve that the phase of the resultant shifts during the transition as well. This dynamically shifting phase means that the harmonic *frequency* is actually shifting during the transition region! The magnitude of apparent frequency shift is proportional to the instantaneous slope of the phase curve. Thus, at the beginning and end of the transition region, the frequency is unchanged, but it may momentarily increase or decrease in the middle.

The preceding applies to each harmonic in the two waves independently. Thus, a complex harmonic evolution in which some change linearly, some nonlinearly, and some undershoot is easily set up merely by altering the harmonic phases in one of the waveforms. It is important to realize that, while there is a great variety of possible transitions, the technique is not general enough so that any arbitrary transition can be realized. One could piecewise approximate an arbitrary transition by using a sequence of tables, however.

Another method of dynamic spectrum variation using the table lookup method actually amounts to a continuous Fourier series evaluation. One would have a single table, which is actually a sine table, and program several table pointers with pointer increments that are integer multiples of the smallest increment. Then, using each pointer in sequence, the corresponding samples would be fetched from the table, multiplied by a corresponding amplitude factor, and the products added together to produce the output sample. This is equivalent to treating each harmonic as a separate tone and controlling its amplitude independently. Relative phase can be controlled by temporarily adding a phase parameter to the pointer when table access is performed but using the original pointer value when the increment is added.

The technique is not limited to exact harmonic frequencies either, since the set of pointer increments need not be integer multiples. Most stringed musical instruments in which the string is plucked or struck have upper harmonics that are somewhat sharp with respect to the fundamental. Bells and chimes have spectra that are decidedly inharmonic. For these and other similar sounds, this is the only general technique available. Although dynamic depth FM can also produce inharmonic spectra, only gross control is possible; the details of the spectrum are pretty much left to chance.

While this technique can be time consuming for a large number of harmonics, it is quite effective for a small number. Its primary strength over faster Fourier techniques to be discussed is that amplitudes and phases of the harmonics may be changed at *any* time and as rapidly as desired without glitches and discontinuities in the composite waveform. In particular, a hardware implementation of the technique can be extremely flexible and effective as well as adequately fast for real-time tone generation.

Fourier Transformation

Fourier transforms are the cornerstone of many modern signal-processing techniques. They have a list of desirable mathematical properties that seems never to end as well as many useful physical properties for synthesis and analysis work. The main attractive feature about any kind of Fourier operation is that it is a bridge between the *time domain*, which is concerned with waveforms and sample values, and the *frequency domain*, which is concerned with the amplitudes and phases of frequency components. The primary need for such a bridge is that the human ear hears in the frequency domain, while sound waves are stored, synthesized, and observed (via an oscilloscope) in the time domain.

As we shall see, a block of samples representing a segment of sound can be transformed into the frequency domain via Fourier transform and appear as a bunch of harmonic amplitudes and phases. This data can then be transformed *back* into a block of samples unscathed and indistinguishable (within round-off error) from the original block via an inverse Fourier transform! Thus, Fourier transformation is a reversible operation. However, while in the frequency domain, we can manipulate the spectrum *directly* by altering individual frequency component amplitudes as desired; no filters to design and tune are necessary. After the manipulation has been accomplished, the inverse transform returns the data to the time domain. This is one way to implement a filter with a completely arbitrary amplitude response.

One can also synthesize a spectrum directly and convert it to the time domain for output. This can be valuable, since most sounds are more easily described in terms of their spectrum rather than in terms of their waveforms. Although a method was just discussed for Fourier *series* synthesis, the Fourier transform can require far less computation if the required spectral detail is great.

In source-signal analysis using digital techniques, the first step is nearly always Fourier transformation of the input into spectral form. Since the ear hears in the frequency domain, it is logical that audible features of the source signal will be much more apparent than when in the time domain. In most cases, transformation greatly reduces the quantity of data to be processed as well.

Characteristics of the Discrete Fourier Transform

Fourier transforms applied to sampled data are usually called *discrete* Fourier transforms, since the time domain data are at discrete instants of time and the frequency data are likewise at discrete frequencies. One very important property of the discrete transform is that the waveform data are specific-sized chunks called *records*, each consisting of a specified number of samples. The discrete transform *assumes* that the samples in the record represent exactly one cycle of a *periodic* waveform. This assumption must be made regardless of whether or not it is actually true, as in Fig. 13–9. The transform then gives all of the harmonic amplitudes and phases of the assumed periodic waveform.

This *record-oriented* property has several important ramifications when constantly changing arbitrary sounds are to be synthesized or analyzed. For most applications, the record size is fixed and often is a power of two. Thus, even if a periodic waveform were being analyzed, it is unlikely that a record would exactly span a single cycle. In order to reduce the resulting error, the record size is chosen to be great enough to span *several* cycles of the lowest frequency expected. Then the partial cycle at the beginning and end of the

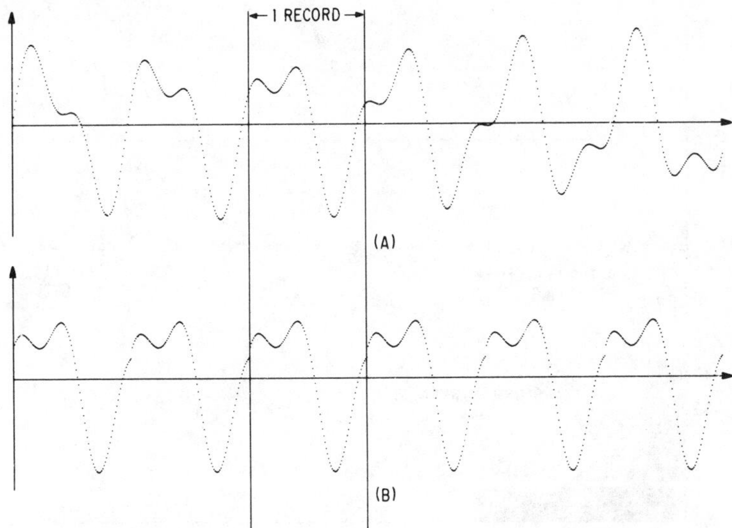

Fig. 13–9. Actual and assumed waveforms used with discrete Fourier transform. (A) Actual wave to be analyzed. (B) Assumed wave that will be analyzed.

record is of less consequence. Techniques are available to "tail out" the ends of the record to minimize the error even further.

When a large but nonintegral number of cycles of a truly periodic waveform is transformed, each harmonic of the actual waveform becomes a *group* of harmonics of the assumed waveform. An example of this is shown in Fig. 13–10 in which 5.31 cycles of a waveform containing fundamental, second, and third harmonics in equal proportions was made into a record and Fourier transformed. The three clusters of transform harmonics correspond to the individual harmonics of the actual waveform. High-frequency energy above the third waveform harmonic is due to the discontinuity caused by the nonintegral number of cycles in the record.

When a section of *changing* sound is marked off into a record, the spectrum reported by the Fourier transform is the *average* spectrum during the time interval represented by the record. Thus, if one wishes to use Fourier transformation to track a changing spectrum, the variation contours will themselves be sampled curves with the sample period equal to the record period. As a result, there is a tradeoff between long record size for minimum "periodicity error" and maximum frequency resolution, and a short record size for following rapidly changing sounds. One technique that is often useful is to *overlap* successive records rather than arrange them end to end. This way one can obtain a high "spectrum sample rate" while using adequately long records.

Fourier transform synthesis is also complicated by record orientation. There are actually two problems. One is that an integral number of cycles of

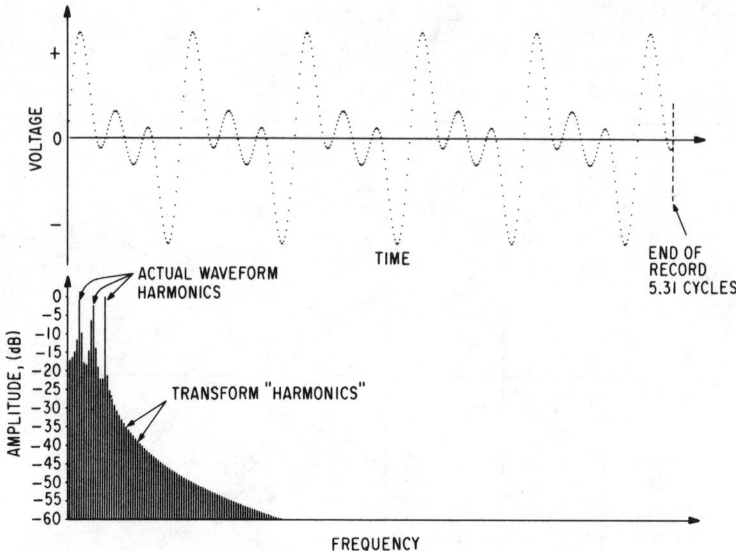

Fig. 13–10. Discrete Fourier transform of 5.31 cycles of a waveform containing equal proportions of fundamental, second, and third harmonics

the synthesized waveform is just as unlikely to span the record as in the analysis case. The other problem is that if the spectrum changes significantly from one synthesized record to the next, there is likely to be a discontinuity between the two records when they are spliced together. These synthesis problems may be overcome by record overlapping and time-variable interpolation between the overlapping records.

The frequency domain data produced and used by the discrete Fourier transform bear a very specific relationship to the corresponding sample record. In particular, the number of harmonics (including the zeroth or dc component) in the frequency domain representation is exactly one-half the number of samples in the time domain record plus one. It is easily seen that any more than this would not make any sense. For example, let's assume a record size of 200 samples taken at a sample rate of 10 ks/s. The record duration, therefore, is 20 msec, which is also the period of the assumed periodic waveform. A 20-msec period is a 50-Hz frequency for the assumed wave, so harmonics would fall at 50 Hz, 100 Hz, 150 Hz, etc. It is easy to determine, then, that there are 100 harmonics at or below one-half the sample rate and, when the dc component is included, the total becomes 101, which is one-half the record size plus one. This also shows that the *frequency resolution* of the analysis is 50 Hz or simply the reciprocal of the record duration.

Each harmonic in turn consists of two components. Although harmonics have been characterized by amplitude and phase so far, the Fourier transform normally deals in *sine* and *cosine* components of the harmonic, which can be negative as well as positive. Conversion between the two forms is actually quite simple. The overall harmonic amplitude, A, is given by $A=\sqrt{S^2+C^2}$, where S is the sine component value and C is the cosine component. The effective phase angle (in radians) is listed in the following table:

C	S	*Phase angle*
+	+	$\mathrm{Tan}^{-1}(S/C)$
−	+	$\mathrm{Tan}^{-1}(S/-C)$
−	−	$\mathrm{Tan}^{-1}(S/C)$
+	−	$\mathrm{Tan}^{-1}(-S/C)$

Note that these formulas always give a positive amplitude and phase angle. Also, C will have to be tested for zero before calculating the phase angle to avoid division overflow. When C is zero, the phase is $\pi/2$ if S is positive and $3\pi/2$ if S is negative. When translating from amplitude and phase to sine and cosine the formulas are: $C=A\cos(P)$ and $S=A\sin(P)$. Thus, conversion from one form to the other is fairly simple.

The dc and Nyquist frequency components of the wave are a special case, however. The cosine part of the zeroth harmonic is the actual dc component, while the sine part would be expected to be zero, since a zero frequency wave cannot have a phase angle other than zero. For mathematical completeness, it is also necessary to consider the harmonic at exactly one-half the sample rate. As it turns out, the Nyquist frequency harmonic must have a zero sine part also. Note that if this Nyquist frequency component is very strong, it is an indication of serious aliasing in the data. Thus, in a real audio signal application, its existence can usually be ignored.

Now, if the harmonic components are counted up, we find that there is exactly the same quantity of *numbers* forming the frequency domain representation as are in the time domain representation. Actually, this is a requirement if the transformation is to be precisely reversible for any arbitrary sample set as was stated earlier. Fourier transformation is exactly what the name implies, a data *transformation*. It alone is not a magic data compression technique.

Slow Fourier Transform

Before delving into the fast Fourier transform, it is necessary to understand how the straightforward but slow version works. A few pages ago there was some discussion about filling a waveform table by evaluating a Fourier series. By making a couple of modifications to the procedure, the inverse (frequency domain to time domain) slow Fourier transform results. The first modification is that the number of samples generated in the output record will be exactly twice the number of harmonics in the input record. The other modification is for the sine and cosine form of the harmonic data. Thus, when filling a waveform table of 256 entries, 128 harmonics must be specified, although many if not most of the higher ones may be zero to avoid aliasing problems when the table is used for synthesis.

The program segment below illustrates the inverse slow Fourier transform. The "*C*" and "*S*" arrays hold the cosine and sine harmonic data, respectively. The dc component uses subscript 0, the fundamental uses subscript 1, etc. Thus, the cosine component of the eighth harmonic would be stored in *C*(8) and the sine component would be in *S*(8). During execution, the time samples will be stored in the *T* array, which also starts at subscript 0 and is assumed to initially contain zeroes. The constant *N* is simply the number of samples in the record and should be even.

```
1000 FOR I=0 TO N/2-1
1001 FOR J=0 TO N-1
1002 LET T(J)=T(J)+C(I)*COS(6.28318*I*J/N)
1003 NEXT J
1004 NEXT I
```

The outer loop steps through the harmonics starting at the zeroth and ending one short of *N*/2. The inner loop steps through all of the time samples for each harmonic adding the specified cosine and sine components to the current content of the samples.

The "forward" transform, which converts time samples into harmonic components, however, is what most people have in mind when they speak about a Fourier transform. Unfortunately, its computation is not intuitively obvious, although it turns out to be no more complex than the inverse transform. The basic approach for determining the amplitude of a component with a particular frequency and phase is to *generate* samples of the sought component, *multiply* them by corresponding samples of the signal to be analyzed, and then *add* up the products. The sum, after being divided by one-half the record size for averaging and mathematical anomalies is the amplitude of the signal component having that frequency and phase! (The dc component will be twice its correct amplitude, however.)

The truth of this can be comprehended by remembering that multiplying two sinusoidal signals is equivalent to balanced modulation and produces a signal having only sum and difference frequency components. The reader should also recall that any sinusoidal wave averaged over an integral number of cycles is zero. It is easily seen then if the two signals being multiplied have *different* frequencies, that the product consists of two sinusoidal waves that, when averaged over a duration having an integral number of periods for both, gives zero. If the frequencies being multiplied are the same, the difference frequency is zero, which is dc and results in an average value equal to the product of the signal amplitudes if they are perfectly in phase. When not in phase, the average is proportional to the cosine of the phase difference. Fortunately, this procedure works even when one of the signals has many frequency components; if one component matches it will contribute a dc component to the product samples. Thus, by using two "probe" waves 90° apart in phase at all of the possible harmonic frequencies of the data record, one may determine its complete harmonic amplitude and phase makeup.

The program segment below, which is remarkably similar to the inverse transform segment, performs discrete Fourier analysis. The *C, S,* and *T* arrays and *N* are as before and *C* and *S* are assumed to be initially zeroes.

```
1000 FOR I=0 TO N-1
1001 FOR J=0 TO N/2-1
1002 LET C(J)=C(J)+T(1)*COS(3.14159*I*J/N)/(N/2)
1003 LET S(J)=S(J)+T(I)*SIN(3.14159*I*J/N)/(N/2)
1004 NEXT J
1005 NEXT I
```

The outer loop in this case scans the time waveform, while the inner loop accumulates running averages of cosine and sine components of each harmonic. Note that the Nyquist frequency component is not computed. Therefore, if one transforms arbitrary random data and then transforms it back, the result will not be exactly equivalent. However, practical, unaliased data will be returned with only a slight roundoff error. Note also that in both of these program segments that the inner and outer loops may be interchanged with no real effect on the results.

Fast Fourier Transform

Examination of the preceding two program segments reveals that N^2 *useful* multiplications and additions are required for the transformation. Useful is emphasized because a well-thought-out assembly language implementation of the programs could eliminate multiplications within the cosine and sine arguments by proper indexing through a sine table. Likewise, subscript calculations can be eliminated by use of index registers. The division by $N/2$ in the forward transform may still be required, but it can be deferred until the computation is completed and then need only be a shift if the record size is a power of two. In the case of the inverse transform, the number of multiplications may be cut in half by using the amplitude-phase form for the harmonics rather than cosine-sine.

Even with the world's most efficient assembly language program, a tremendous amount of computation is needed for even a moderate number of samples. For example, 20-msec blocks taken at a 25 ks/s sample rate would be 500 samples that, when squared, implies about a quarter of a million operations for the transform. Upping the sample rate to 50 ks/s quadruples the work to a million operations. An efficient assembly language program on a minicomputer with automatic multiply would require about a minute for such a transform, while a BASIC equivalent running on a microcomputer might crunch on it overnight, and that is just one record!

Like many topics in computer science, the real key to speed lies in an efficient algorithm rather than an efficient program. In the case of the discrete Fourier transform, such an algorithm was first publicized in 1965 and results in an enormous reduction in computation at the expense of a longer and rather difficult-to-understand procedure. The fast Fourier transform algorithm requires approximately $N\log_2 N$ multiplications and additions instead of N^2. This means that 512 samples need only about 4,500 operations, while 1,024 samples need about 10,000 operations. This is a savings of 100-to-1 for the 1,024-sample case!

Redundancy

The key to the fast Fourier transform (FFT) algorithm is identification and systematic elimination of redundancy in the calculations executed by the slow Fourier transform (SFT). From looking at the two program segments, it is obvious that every possible product of samples (forward) or amplitudes (inverse) and sine/cosine values is formed. Figure 13–11A shows how the sine and cosine multipliers for each harmonic can be arranged in a square array. The horizontal axis represents time, while the vertical axis represents frequency. The number at each intersection is a sample of the sine/cosine wave for the row at the time designated by the column.

For the forward transform, one would first write the waveform sample values as a row of numbers above the top of the coefficient array. Then each sample would be multiplied by every coefficient in the corresponding column with the product written just below the coefficient. Finally, the products would be added up by row and the sums written as a column at the right side of the array. This column then represents the spectrum of the waveform. For the inverse transform, the process would be reversed by starting with the spectrum column, forming products by row, and adding by column to get a row of time samples. Parts B and C of Fig. 13–11 show these operations for a record size of 16 samples. Note that the row for the sine of the dc component, which would otherwise be all zeroes, has been replaced by the sine of the Nyquist frequency component.

Examination of the array reveals considerable redundancy in the products, however. For example, the product of sample number 2 and the cosine of $\pi/2$, which is 0.707, occurs four times. If in the computation, multiplication by a negative number is replaced by subtracting the product of the corresponding positive number, then the product of sample 2 and 0.707 can be reused eight times. Further computational savings are possible by skipping multiplication altogether when the cosine or sine values are zero or unity. Doing all of this reduces the actual number of unique products to a

Sample Number / Harm. No.	0	1	2	3	4	5	6	7	8	9	10	11	12	13	14	15	Spectrum
C 0	1.000	1.000	1.000	1.000	1.000	1.000	1.000	1.000	1.000	1.000	1.000	1.000	1.000	1.000	1.000	1.000	______
C 8	1.000	−1.000	1.000	−1.000	1.000	−1.000	−1.000	−1.000	1.000	−1.000	1.000	−1.000	1.000	−1.000	1.000	−1.000	______
C 1	1.000	.924	.707	.383	.000	−.383	−.707	−.924	−1.000	−.924	−.707	−.383	.000	.383	.707	.924	______
S 1	.000	.383	.707	.924	1.000	.924	.707	.383	.000	.383	.707	.924	−1.000	.924	.707	.383	______
C 2	1.000	.707	.000	−.707	−1.000	.707	.000	.707	1.000	.707	.000	.707	−1.000	.707	.000	.707	______
S 2	.000	.707	1.000	.707	.000	.707	−1.000	.707	.000	.707	1.000	.707	.000	−.707	−1.000	−.707	______
C 3	1.000	.383	−.707	−.924	.000	.924	.707	−.383	−1.000	−.383	.707	.924	.000	−.924	−.707	.383	______
S 3	.000	.924	.707	−.383	−1.000	−.383	.707	.924	.000	−.924	−.707	.383	1.000	.383	−.707	−.924	______
C 4	1.000	.000	−1.000	.000	1.000	.000	−1.000	.000	1.000	.000	−1.000	.000	1.000	.000	−1.000	.000	______
S 4	.000	1.000	.000	−1.000	.000	1.000	.000	−1.000	.000	1.000	.000	−1.000	.000	1.000	.000	−1.000	______
C 5	1.000	−.383	−.707	.924	.000	−.924	.707	.383	−1.000	.383	.707	−.924	.000	.924	−.707	−.383	______
S 5	.000	.924	−.707	−.383	1.000	.383	−.707	.924	.000	−.924	.707	.383	−1.000	.383	.707	−.924	______
C 6	1.000	−.707	.000	.707	−1.000	.707	.000	−.707	1.000	−.707	.000	.707	−1.000	.707	.000	−.707	______
S 6	.000	.707	−1.000	.707	.000	−.707	1.000	−.707	.000	.707	−1.000	.707	.000	−.707	1.000	−.707	______
C 7	1.000	−.924	.707	−.383	.000	.383	−.707	.924	−1.000	.924	−.707	.383	.000	−.383	.707	−.924	______
S 7	.000	.383	−.707	.924	1.000	.924	−.707	.383	.000	−.383	.707	−.924	1.000	−.924	.707	−.383	______

Fig. 13–11. (A) Slow Fourier transform worksheet.

Sample Number Harm. No.	0	1	2	3	4	5	6	7	8	9	10	11	12	13	14	15	Spectrum[1]
	.310	.694	.473	.515	.339	.334	.171	.142	−.013	−.060	−.209	−.277	−.419	−.517	−.652	−.830	
C 0	1.000	1.000	1.000	1.000	1.000	1.000	1.000	1.000	1.000	1.000	1.000	1.000	1.000	1.000	1.000	1.000	.000
	.310	.694	.473	.515	.339	.334	.171	.142	−.013	−.060	−.209	−.277	−.419	−.517	−.652	−.830	
C 8	1.000	−1.000	1.000	−1.000	1.000	−1.000	1.000	−1.000	1.000	−1.000	1.000	−1.000	1.000	−1.000	1.000	−1.000	.000
	.310	−.694	.473	−.515	.339	−.334	.171	−.142	−.013	.060	−.209	.277	−.419	.517	−.652	.830	
C 1	1.000	.924	.707	.383	.000	.383	−.707	−.924	−1.000	−.924	−.707	−.383	.000	.383	.707	.924	.000
	.310	.641	.334	.197	.000	−.128	−.121	−.131	.013	.055	.148	.106	.000	.198	.461	.767	
S 1	.000	.383	.707	.924	1.000	.924	.707	.383	.000	−.383	−.707	−.924	−1.000	−.924	−.707	−.383	.500
	.000	.266	.334	.476	.339	.309	.121	.054	.000	.023	.148	.256	.419	.478	.461	.318	
C 2	1.000	.707	.000	−.707	−1.000	−.707	.000	.707	1.000	.707	.000	−.707	−1.000	−.707	.000	.707	.037
	.310	.491	.000	−.364	−.339	−.236	.000	.100	−.013	−.042	.000	.196	.419	.366	.000	−.587	
S 2	.000	.707	1.000	.707	.000	−.707	−1.000	−.707	.000	.707	1.000	.707	.000	−.707	−1.000	−.707	.247
	.000	.491	.473	.364	.000	−.236	−.171	−.100	.000	−.042	−.209	−.196	.000	.366	.652	.587	
C 3	1.000	.383	−.707	−.924	.000	.924	.707	−.383	−1.000	−.383	.707	.924	.000	−.924	−.707	.383	.049
	.310	.266	−.334	−.476	.000	.309	.121	−.054	.013	.023	−.148	−.256	.000	.478	.461	−.318	
S 3	.000	.924	.707	−.383	−1.000	−.383	.707	.924	.000	−.924	−.707	.383	1.000	.383	−.707	−.924	.159
	.000	.641	.334	−.197	−.339	−.128	.121	.131	.000	.055	.148	−.106	−.419	−.198	.461	.767	
C 4	1.000	.000	−1.000	.000	1.000	.000	−1.000	.000	1.000	.000	−1.000	.000	1.000	.000	−1.000	.000	.054
	.310	.000	−.473	.000	.339	.000	−.171	.000	−.013	.000	.209	.000	−.419	.000	.652	.000	
S 4	.000	1.000	.000	−1.000	.000	1.000	.000	−1.000	.000	1.000	.000	−1.000	.000	1.000	.000	−1.000	.113
	.000	.694	.000	−.515	.000	.334	.000	−.142	.000	−.060	.000	.277	.000	−.517	.000	.830	
C 5	1.000	−.383	−.707	.924	.000	−.924	.707	.383	−1.000	.383	.707	−.924	.000	.924	−.707	−.383	.056
	.310	−.266	−.334	.476	.000	−.309	.121	.054	.013	−.023	−.148	.256	.000	−.478	.461	.318	
S 5	.000	.924	−.707	−.383	1.000	−.383	−.707	.924	.000	−.924	.707	.383	−1.000	.383	.707	.924	.083
	.000	.641	−.334	−.197	.339	−.128	−.121	.131	.000	.055	−.148	−.106	.419	−.198	−.461	.767	
C 6	1.000	−.707	.000	.707	−1.000	.707	.000	−.707	1.000	−.707	.000	.707	−1.000	.707	.000	−.707	.057
	.310	−.491	.000	.364	−.339	.236	.000	−.100	−.013	.042	.000	−.196	.419	−.366	.000	.587	
S 6	.000	.707	1.000	.707	.000	−.707	1.000	−.707	.000	.707	−1.000	.707	.000	−.707	1.000	−.707	.061
	.000	.491	−.473	.364	.000	−.236	.171	−.100	.000	−.042	.209	−.196	.000	.366	−.652	.587	
C 7	1.000	−.924	.707	−.383	.000	.383	−.707	.924	−1.000	.924	−.707	.383	.000	−.383	.707	−.924	.056
	.310	−.641	.334	−.197	.000	.128	−.121	.131	−.013	−.055	.148	−.106	.000	.198	−.461	.767	
S 7	.000	.383	−.707	.924	−1.000	.924	−.707	.383	.000	−.383	.707	−.924	1.000	−.924	.707	−.383	.044
	.000	.266	−.334	.476	−.339	.309	−.121	.054	.000	.023	−.148	.256	−.419	.478	−.461	.318	

Note 1: Entries are the true sum divided by 8

Fig. 13–11. (*Cont.*). (B) Worksheet filled in for forward Fourier transform.

Sample Number / Harm. No.	0	1	2	3	4	5	6	7	8	9	10	11	12	13	14	15	Spectrum
	.310	.694	.473	.515	.339	.334	.171	.142	−.013	−.060	−.209	−.277	−.419	−.517	−.652	−.830	
C 0	1.000	1.000	1.000	1.000	1.000	1.000	1.000	1.000	1.000	1.000	1.000	1.000	1.000	1.000	1.000	1.000	.000
	.000	.000	.000	.000	.000	.000	.000	.000	.000	.000	.000	.000	.000	.000	.000	.000	
C 8	1.000	−1.000	1.000	−1.000	1.000	−1.000	1.000	−1.000	1.000	−1.000	1.000	−1.000	1.000	−1.000	1.000	−1.000	.000
	.000	.000	.000	.000	.000	.000	.000	.000	.000	.000	.000	.000	.000	.000	.000	.000	
C 1	1.000	.924	.707	.383	.000	−.383	−.707	−.924	−1.000	−.924	−.707	−.383	.000	.383	.707	.924	.000
	.000	.000	.000	.000	.000	.000	.000	.000	.000	.000	.000	.000	.000	.000	.000	.000	
S 1	.000	.383	.707	.924	1.000	.924	.707	.383	.000	−.383	−.707	−.924	−1.000	−.924	−.707	−.383	.500
	.000	.192	.353	.462	.500	.462	.353	.192	.000	−.192	−.353	−.462	−.500	−.462	−.353	−.192	
C 2	1.000	.707	.000	−.707	−1.000	−.707	.000	.707	1.000	.707	.000	−.707	−1.000	−.707	.000	.707	.037
	−.037	.026	.000	−.026	−.037	−.026	.000	−.026	−.037	−.026	.000	−.026	−.037	−.026	.000	.026	
S 2	.000	.707	1.000	.707	.000	−.707	−1.000	−.707	.000	.707	1.000	.707	.000	−.707	−1.000	−.707	.247
	.000	.175	.247	.175	.000	−.175	−.247	−.175	.000	.175	.247	.175	.000	−.175	−.247	−.175	
C 3	1.000	.383	−.707	−.924	.000	.924	.707	−.383	−1.000	−.383	.707	.924	.000	−.924	−.707	−.383	.049
	.049	.019	−.035	−.045	.000	.045	.035	−.019	−.049	−.019	.035	.045	.000	−.045	−.035	−.019	
S 3	.000	.924	.707	−.383	−1.000	−.383	.707	.924	.000	−.924	−.707	.383	1.000	.383	−.707	−.924	.159
	.000	.147	.112	−.061	−.159	−.061	.112	.147	.000	−.147	−.112	.061	.159	.061	−.112	−.147	
C 4	1.000	.000	−1.000	.000	1.000	.000	−1.000	.000	1.000	.000	−1.000	.000	1.000	.000	−1.000	.000	.054
	.054	.000	−.054	.000	.054	.000	−.054	.000	.054	.000	−.054	.000	.054	.000	−.054	.000	
S 4	.000	1.000	.000	−1.000	.000	1.000	.000	−1.000	.000	1.000	.000	−1.000	.000	1.000	.000	−1.000	.113
	.000	.113	.000	−.113	.000	.113	.000	−.113	.000	.113	.000	−.113	.000	.113	.000	−.113	
C 5	1.000	−.383	−.707	.924	.000	−.924	.707	.383	−1.000	.383	.707	−.924	.000	.924	−.707	−.383	.056
	.056	−.021	−.040	.052	.000	−.052	.040	.021	−.056	.021	.040	−.052	.000	.052	−.040	−.021	
S 5	.000	.924	−.707	−.383	1.000	−.383	−.707	.924	.000	−.924	.707	.383	−1.000	.383	.707	−.924	.083
	.000	.077	−.059	−.032	.083	−.032	−.059	.077	.000	−.077	.059	.032	−.083	.032	.059	−.077	
C 6	1.000	−.707	.000	.707	−1.000	.707	.000	−.707	1.000	−.707	.000	.707	−1.000	.707	.000	−.707	.057
	.057	−.040	.000	.040	−.057	.040	.000	−.040	.057	−.040	.000	.040	−.057	.040	.000	−.040	
S 6	.000	.707	−1.000	.707	.000	−.707	1.000	−.707	.000	.707	−1.000	.707	.000	−.707	1.000	−.707	.061
	.000	.043	−.061	.043	.000	−.043	.061	−.043	.000	.043	−.061	.043	.000	−.043	.061	−.043	
C 7	1.000	−.924	.707	−.383	.000	.383	−.707	.924	−1.000	.924	−.707	.383	.000	−.383	.707	−.924	.056
	.056	−.052	.040	−.021	.000	.021	−.040	.052	−.056	.052	−.040	.021	.000	−.021	.040	−.052	
S 7	.000	.383	−.707	.924	−1.000	.924	−.707	.383	.000	−.383	.707	−.924	1.000	−.924	.707	−.383	.044
	.000	.017	−.031	.041	−.044	.041	−.031	.017	.000	−.017	.031	−.041	.044	−.041	.031	−.017	

Fig. 13–11. (*Cont.*) (C) Worksheet filled in for inverse Fourier transform.

mere 28 instead of the original 256! Although it is not immediately apparent how the redundancies can be identified in a general algorithm, one can use matrix theory and trigonometric identities and derive the FFT algorithm from this type of table.

A completely different way to look at the redundancy involves the concept of *decimation*. As an example, consider a sample record with N samples where N is even. Using the SFT, one could perform N^2 operations and wind up with the spectrum. Now consider splitting the record into two smaller records with $N/2$ samples in each such that the even numbered samples go to one record and the odd numbered ones to go the other. If an SFT is performed on each record, it will require $N^2/4$ operations for a total of only $N^2/2$ operations. The trick is to combine the two resulting spectrums into one representing the true spectrum of the original record. This can be accomplished by duplicating the even sample spectrum of $N/4$ harmonics and adding with a progressive phase shift the odd sample spectrum, also duplicated, to yield $N/2$ harmonics total. The combination requires N extra multiplications and additions.

If N is divisible by 4, the decimation operation could be repeated to give four records of $N/4$ samples each. The SFT can be performed on each, requiring only $N^2/4$ operations, and the four resulting spectrums combined in two stages to form the final spectrum. In fact, if N is a power of two, decimation can be repeated until there are $N/2$ subrecords, each having only two samples as in Fig. 13–12. Note the resulting scrambled order of the samples. This is called *bit-reversed* order because if the binary representation of the scrambled sample numbers is observed in a mirror, it will appear to be a simple ascending binary sequence.

Since the discrete Fourier transform of two samples is trivial (the cosine component of the single harmonic is the sum of the sample values, while the sine component is the difference), most of the computation is combining the subspectra together in stages to form the final spectrum. The essence of the FFT, then, is complete decimation of the time samples followed by recombination of the frequency spectra to form the exact spectrum of the original sample set.

Complex Arithmetic

At this point in the description of the FFT we will be forced to commit a mathematical "copout" that is customary in such a discussion. In any case, it will not only simplify the discussion but will facilitate the development of an FFT program. The first step is to treat each harmonic, which has a cosine and a sine component, as a single *complex number*. Although the cosine component is normally called the "real" part and the sine component the "imaginary" part, both are quite real as far as a physical waveform is concerned. Therefore, it is best to forget about "real" and "imaginary" and

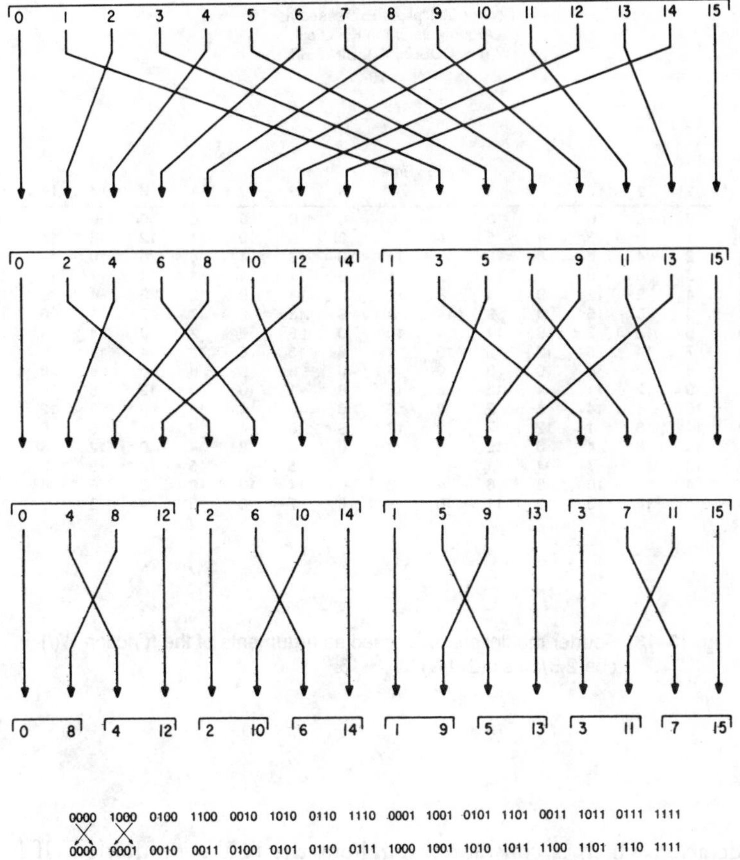

0000 1000 0100 1100 0010 1010 0110 1110 0001 1001 0101 1101 0011 1011 0111 1111

0000 0001 0010 0011 0100 0101 0110 0111 1000 1001 1010 1011 1100 1101 1110 1111

Fig. 13–12. Stages in decimation of a 16-sample record

consider the complex number as a compact method of representing a pair of closely related but independent numbers. Accordingly, complex numbers will be represented here as two ordinary numbers, real part first, separated by a comma in a manner much like the two-dimensional coordinates of a point.

The cosine and sine multipliers used in the computation are also considered to be complex numbers. Previously we used the cosine and sine of an angle that incremented by $2\pi/N$ for the fundamental, $4\pi/N$ for the second harmonic, etc. Now the cosine and sine of the angle will be treated as a single complex number. Since the angles are always an integer times $2\pi/N$, we can define a complex function, W, such that $W(I)=\cos(2\pi I/N),\sin(2\pi I/N)$, where I is any integer and N is the number of points in the record under

Fourier Multipliers Expressed as
Arguments of the Function
W(I) = COS(2πI/N), SIN(2πI/N)
N = 16

Time

	0	1	2	3	4	5	6	7	8	9	10	11	12	13	14	15	
0	0	0	0	0	0	0	0	0	0	0	0	0	0	0	0	0	
1	0	1	2	3	4	5	6	7	8	9	10	11	12	13	14	15	
2	0	2	4	6	8	10	12	14	0	2	4	6	8	10	12	14	
3	0	3	6	9	12	15	2	5	8	11	14	1	4	7	10	13	
4	0	4	8	12	0	4	8	12	0	4	8	12	0	4	8	12	F
5	0	5	10	15	4	9	14	3	8	13	2	7	12	1	6	11	r
6	0	6	12	2	8	14	4	10	0	6	12	2	8	14	4	10	e
7	0	7	14	5	12	3	10	1	8	15	6	13	4	11	2	9	q
8	0	8	0	8	0	8	0	8	0	8	0	8	0	8	0	8	u
9	0	9	2	11	4	13	6	15	8	1	10	3	12	5	14	7	e
10	0	10	4	14	8	2	12	6	0	10	4	14	8	2	12	6	n
11	0	11	6	1	12	7	2	13	8	3	14	9	4	15	10	5	c
12	0	12	8	4	0	12	8	4	0	12	8	4	0	12	8	4	y
13	0	13	10	7	4	1	14	11	8	5	2	15	12	9	6	3	
14	0	14	12	10	8	6	4	2	0	14	12	10	8	6	4	2	
15	0	15	14	13	12	11	10	9	8	7	6	5	4	3	2	1	

Fig. 13–13. Fourier multipliers expressed as arguments of the function $W(I) = \cos(2\pi I/N), \sin(2\pi I/N)$. $N = 16$.

consideration which is constant throughout the FFT computation. If I ever exceeds the range of 0 to $N-1$, it is customary to use the principal value, which is simply I mod N. Finally, as if nothing is sacred, even the time samples are considered to be complex numbers with a real part and an imaginary part.

As a result of going complex, the number of harmonics is *equal* to the number of complex samples. Thus, the forward FFT takes a set of N *complex* time samples and generates a set of N complex harmonics. As we will see later, all of the intermediate arithmetic in the FFT algorithm is also complex.

In the real world, which includes audio, the time samples are, of course, real, which means that the imaginary parts are zero. The corresponding spectrum has only $(N/2)+1$ *unique* harmonics; the remaining $(N/2)-1$ are simply the *complex conjugate* (the signs of the sine components are reversed) of the others less dc and Nyquist frequency components. Thus, in actual use with audio samples, one has N samples and $(N/2)+1$ harmonics, just as before. Although the preceding implies considerable waste in the computation, a method of eliminating it will be described later.

With these conventions for representing everything as complex numbers, the SFT coefficient matrix can be rewritten as in Fig. 13–13. The numbers listed in the matrix are *arguments* to the *W* function mentioned earlier needed to generate the proper complex multiplier. The operations involved in going from time to frequency and back are the same as before, except all arithmetic is now complex. In case one has forgotten (or never knew), the basic arithmetic operations on two complex numbers, A,B and C,D, are given below:

$$A,B + C,D = A+C,B+D$$
$$A,B - C,D = A-D,B-D$$
$$A,B \times C,D = AC-BD,AD+BC$$

$$\frac{A,B}{C,D} = \frac{AC+BD}{C^2+D^2}, \frac{BC-AD}{C^2+D^2}$$

The nice thing about the complex form of the SFT is that it is completely symmetrical. There are no special cases for dc or Nyquist components, and the form of the output is exactly the same as the form of the input.

The FFT Algorithm

At this point, we are ready to look at the FFT algorithm itself. Actually, there are many different algorithms, each with an edge over the others in certain applications. They all, within roundoff error, give the same result, however. The one that will be described here is one of the most straightforward and has the desirable property that sines and cosines (the *W* function) are used in ascending order. In technical terms, it is a radix 2 FFT using time decomposition and input bit reversal. Radix 2 means that the record size must be a power of two. Other radices are possible, but two is the most efficient, particularly in a binary computer.

The first step in the FFT is to completely decompose the input samples, which means that they are scrambled in bit-reversed order as in Fig. 13–12. Fortunately, the scrambling can be accomplished without need for a second array. One simply programs two counters, one normal and one bit-reversed, and iterates them from 0 to $N-1$. Whenever the bit-reversed counter is numerically greater than the normal counter, the corresponding samples are swapped. This is illustrated in Fig. 13–14 for $N=16$, but the procedure applies for any record size as long as it is a power of two. In assembly language on a microprocessor, one could use just one counter and write a bit-reversal function, which would take a binary number and return its bit-reversed equivalent.

Step	Normal Counter	Bit Reverse Counter	Action
1	0000	0000	NONE
2	0001	1000	SWAP 1 & 8
3	0010	0100	SWAP 2 & 4
4	0011	1100	SWAP 3 & 12
5	0100	0010	NONE
6	0101	1010	SWAP 10 & 5
7	0110	0110	NONE
8	0111	1110	SWAP 14 & 7
9	1000	0001	NONE
10	1001	1001	NONE
11	1010	0101	NONE
12	1011	1101	SWAP 13 & 11
13	1100	0011	NONE
14	1101	1011	NONE
15	1110	0111	NONE
16	1111	1111	NONE

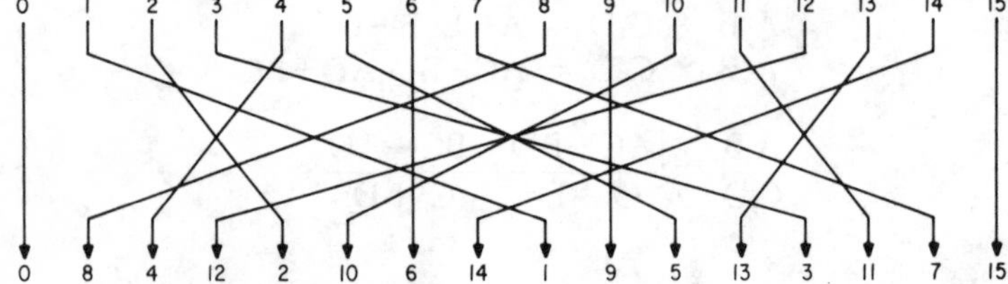

Fig. 13–14. In-place bit-reverse scrambling

The second part of the procedure takes the scrambled sample set, massages it using the *W* function with various arguments, and produces the spectrum as output in natural ascending order. The computation is done *in place*, which means that the sepctrum *replaces* the sample data with no intermediate storage required! Thus, the FFT is literally a transformation of the data in the record.

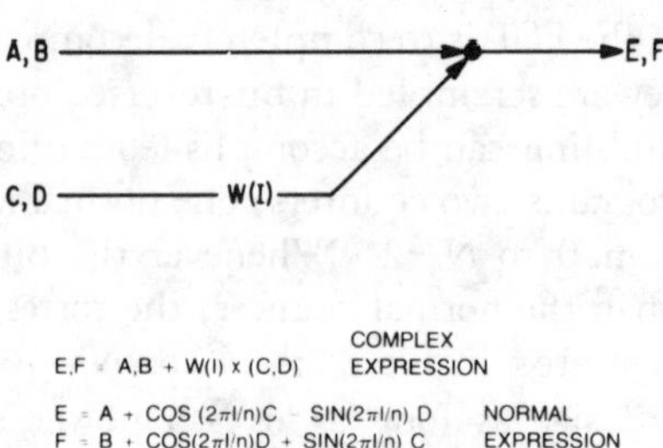

Fig. 13–15. Nodes used in FFT butterfly diagram

The massaging is best described using a special flowchart called a *butterfly diagram* because of its appearance. The fundamental element of a butterfly diagram is the *node*, which is illustrated in Fig. 13–15. There are always two inputs to the node. One goes straight in, while the other is multiplied by the *W* function of a specified argument before entering. In the node, the two inputs are added together to form a single number, which may then become the source for further computations. A node therefore implies one *complex* multiplication and one *complex* addition. In a computer program, this would be accomplished with four normal multiplications and additions.

Figure 13–16 shows the butterfly diagram for a 16-point ($N=16$) FFT. Note that there are N rows and $\log_2 N$ columns of nodes. The rows correspond to storage locations that are initially filled with the scrambled time samples and later become loaded with the spectrum harmonics. The computation proceeds one column at a time starting from the time samples at the left. In order to retain the in-place computation property of the algorithm, the nodes are evaluated in *pairs*. Each member of the pair uses the same inputs and produces outputs on the same rows as the inputs. Furthermore, these inputs are not used by any of the other nodes in the column. Thus, after the node pair is evaluated, the node outputs can be stored in place of the values used as their inputs. Careful examination reveals that the two values of the *W* function used in each pair of nodes are always the negative of

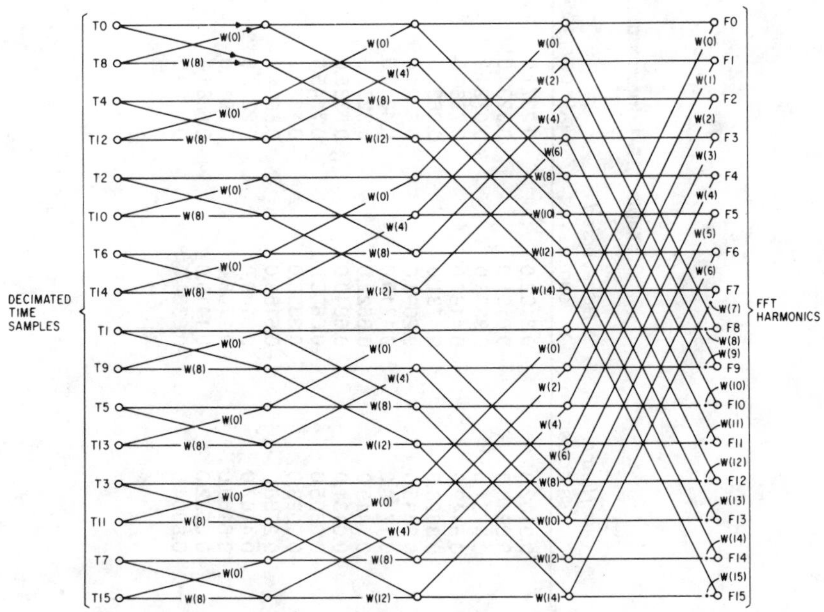

Fig. 13–16. $N = 16$ FFT butterfly

Table 13—1. Intermediate Results of a 16-Point FFT

I	*Normal samples*	*Bit-reversed samples*	*Node column 1*	*Node column 2*	*Node column 3*	*Node column 4*
0	0.3102,0	0.3102,0	0.2971,0	0.2176,0	0.0002,0	0.0003,0
1	0.6940,0	−0.0131,0	0.3233,0	0.3233,.7580	0.2238,1.823	0,4.000
2	0.4731,0	0.3393,0	−0.0794,0	0.3765,0	0.3765,.7449	0.2987,1.978
3	0.5149,0	−0.4187,0	0.7580,0	0.3233,−0.7580	0.4229,0.3066	0.3940,1.274
4	0.3393,0	0.4731,0	0.2637,0	−0.2174,0	0.4351,0	0.4351,0.9004
5	0.3336,0	−0.2093,0	0.6824,0	0.6824,0.8232	0.4229,−0.3066	0.4518,0.6604
6	0.1710,0	0.1710,0	−0.4812,0	0.7449,0	0.3765,−0.7449	0.4543,0.4879
7	0.1419,0	−0.6522,0	0.8232,0	0.6824,−0.8232	0.2238,−1.823	0.4476,0.3551
8	−0.0131,0	0.6940,0	0.6335,0	0.4503,0	0.0001,0	0,0
9	−0.0605,0	−0.06051,0	0.7545,0	0.7545,0.8504	0.6266,2.098	0.4475,−0.3553
10	−0.2093,0	0.3336,0	−0.1832,0	0.8167,0	0.8167,0.9267	0.4543,−0.4879
11	−0.2766,0	−0.5168,0	0.8504,0	0.7545,−0.8504	0.8824,0.3968	0.4517,−0.6605
12	−0.4187,0	0.5149,0	0.2383,0	−0.4501,0	0.9004,0	0.4351,−0.9004
13	−0.5168,0	−0.2766,0	0.7914,0	0.7914,0.9723	0.8824,−0.3968	0.3940,−1.274
14	−0.6522,0	0.1419,0	−0.6884,0	0.9267,0	0.8167,−0.9267	0.2987,−1.978
15	−0.8304,0	−0.8304,0	0.9723,0	0.7914,−0.9723	0.6266,−2.098	0,−4.000

each other. This is important because the actual number of multiplications required to evaluate the node pair can then be cut in half.

After the first column of nodes has been processed, everything is back in storage in a partially transformed state, and processing of the next column of nodes can begin. When the rightmost column has been evaluated, the array contains the N complex harmonics. Note that for the first column the nodes that should be paired for calculation are adjacent. In the next column, the pair members are two apart, in the third column four apart, and so forth. Also note that the mass of crossing lines forms a group of two nodes in the first column, four nodes in the next column and so forth until there is only one mass in the final column. These and other symmetries discovered by examining the diagram should make the progression sufficiently clear so that generalization for other values of N can be understood. Since the progression is consistent from column to column, it is clear that a general FFT subroutine can be written for any value of N that is a power of two.

Table 13–1 shows the actual sequence of intermediate results corresponding to the diagram. The example time samples are of a seven-harmonic approximation to a sawtooth wave with a few degrees of phase shift included to make life interesting. Note that the spectrum output starts with the dc component in the zero array position, fundamental in position 1, etc. up to the seventh harmonic in position 7. The Nyquist component is in position 8 (the sine part is always zero), while higher array positions contain the first through the seventh harmonics again but in descending sequence and with the sign of the imaginary components (sines) flipped. Also note that the correct amplitudes of the frequency components have been multiplied by $N/2$ except for the dc component, which is N times too large.

An FFT Subroutine in BASIC

Figure 13–17 is an FFT program written in BASIC. Although BASIC and fast are contradictory terms, the program serves to illustrate the algorithm and to allow the reader to become familiar with it. The array of complex input samples is actually stored and handled as two arrays of normal numbers; $D1$ being the real part and $D2$ being the imaginary part. Note that the array subscript starts at zero. When the transformation is complete, the spectrum is stored in the same two arrays. To insure that N is a power of two, the record size is specified by K, which is $\log_2 N$ and must be a positive integer.

In the program itself, statements 3110 to 3125 scramble the naturally ordered time samples into bit-reversed order using the method illustrated earlier. $N3$ being the "for" loop index counts naturally from 1 to N. $N1$ in conjunction with statements 3114 to 3117 acts like a bit-reversed counter taking on successive values of 0, 8, 4, 12, 2, etc. (for the $N=16$ case). Whenever $N1$ is greater than $N3$, the samples pointed to by $N1$ and $N3$ are swapped.

```
3000 REM   FAST FOURIER TRANSFORM USING TIME DECOMPOSITION WITH
3001 REM   INPUT BIT REVERSAL
3002 REM   COMPLEX INPUT DATA IN ARRAY D1 (REAL PART) AND D2 (IMAGINARY
3003 REM   PART).
3004 REM   COMPUTATION IS IN PLACE, OUTPUT REPLACES INPUT
3005 REM   K SPECIFIES NUMBER OF POINTS, K=LOG(2)N
3100 REM   SCRAMBLE THE INPUT DATA INTO BIT REVERSED ORDER
3110 N=2**K
3111 N1=0
3112 N2=N-1
3113 FOR N3=1 TO N2
3114 N4=N
3115 N4=N4/2
3116 IF N1+N4>N2 GOTO 3115
3117 N1=N1-INT(N1/N4)*N4+N4
3118 IF N1<=N3 GOTO 3125
3119 T1=D1(N3)
3120 D1(N3)=D1(N1)
3121 D1(N1)=T1
3122 T2=D2(N3)
3123 D2(N3)=D2(N1)
3124 D2(N1)=T2
3125 NEXT N3
3200 REM   DO THE COMPLEX TRANSFORM
3210 N4=1
3211 N6=2*N4
3212 FOR N3=0 TO N4-1
3213 A=N3*3.1415927/N4
3214 C=COS(A)
3215 S=SIN(A)
3216 FOR N7=N3 TO N-1 STEP N6
3217 N8=N7+N4
3218 T1=C*D1(N8)-S*D2(N8)
3219 T2=C*D2(N8)+S*D1(N8)
3220 D1(N8)=D1(N7)-T1
3221 D2(N8)=D2(N7)-T2
3222 D1(N7)=D1(N7)+T1
3223 D2(N7)=D2(N7)+T2
3224 NEXT N7
3225 NEXT N3
3226 N4=N6
3227 IF N4<N GOTO 3211
3228 RETURN
```

Fig. 13–17. FFT subroutine in BASIC

Statements 3210 to 3227 implement the butterfly diagram and consist of three nested loops. The outer loop, which spans lines 3211 to 3227, is executed for each column of nodes. The next loop starts in line 3212 and is iterated for each different principal value of the W function. The innermost loop starting at 3216 covers all of the pairs of nodes using a particular principal value. In the $N=16$ example, the outer loop will be executed four times for the four columns of nodes. The middle loop will be executed one time for column 1, twice for column 2, four times for column 3 and eight times for the final column. The inner loop count is the inverse of the middle loop and is executed 8, 4, 2, and 1 time for each iteration of the middle loop.

Innermost in the nest of loops is the useful calculation for a pair of nodes. The complex numbers that form the node inputs, outputs, and W function are handled one part at a time according to the rules of complex arithmetic. Note that only the lower argument value (principal value) of W is explicitly evaluated, since the upper argument value gives the same result with opposite sign. A count of useful operations for the node pair gives four multiplications and six additions. These statements are evaluated $(N\log_2N)/2$ times, which gives a total of $2N\log_2N$ multiplications and $3N\log_2N$ additions.

So far the FFT has been described in terms of transforming a set of time samples into a frequency spectrum. Because of the symmetry of the W coefficient array, transforming a spectrum into a sample record requires only a trivial change in the FFT subroutine. All that is necessary is to place a minus sign in front of $N3$ in statement 3213. When this is done, the spectrum to be transformed is stored in the D arrays in the same format that it appears after a forward transform (be sure to store both the normal and the conjugate spectrum) and the modified FFT subroutine is called. The time samples will then appear in the $D1$ array in natural sequence with the first one at the zero subscript position. No amplitude adjustment is necessary after the inverse transform.

Modification for Real Data

As was noted earlier, the complex formulation of the FFT tends to be wasteful when the time samples are real. The multiplication count turns out to be twice the promised value, which is due to the assumption of complex data and the redundant set of computed harmonics. Fortunately, it is possible to eliminate the wasted storage and redundant spectrum by the addition of a real/complex conversion subroutine.

For the forward FFT, the idea is to store the even-numbered time samples in the real part of the data array and the odd-numbered samples in the imaginary part, thus doubling the number of samples stored. Next, the FFT is performed as described previously. The spectrum that emerges is no longer redundant and typically looks like a list of random numbers. At this point, a *complex-to-real* conversion is performed on the spectrum, which results in a complete, conventional spectrum of $N+1$ harmonics for the $2N$ data points. For convenience, the Nyquist component is stored as the sine part of the dc component which would otherwise always be zero.

For an inverse FFT, the spectrum is first entered into the data array normally with no duplication required. Next a *real-to-complex* conversion is performed that transforms the set of real harmonics into a complex set. Finally, the inverse FFT is executed to generate a list of $2N$ time samples stored in even–odd order as before.

Figure 13–18 is a diagram of the computations involved in the complex-to-real conversion. First the dc and Nyquist components are both

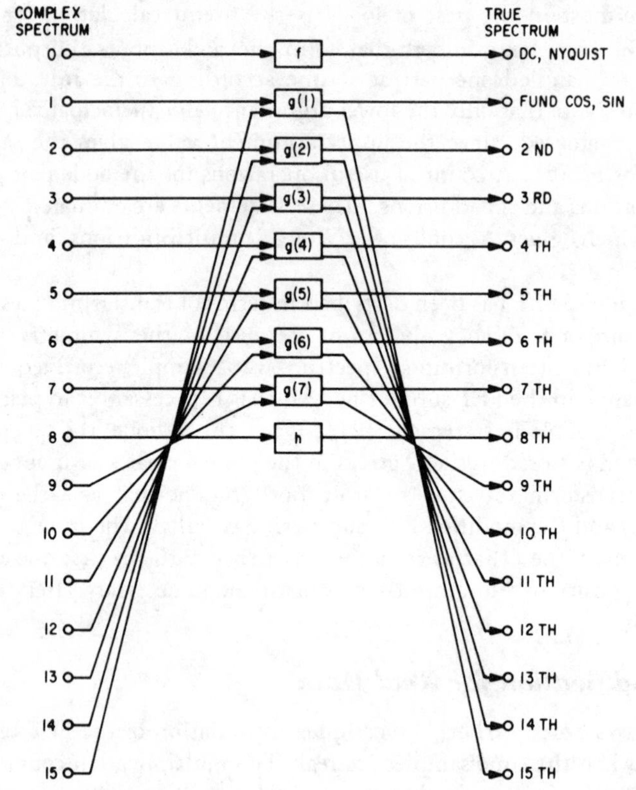

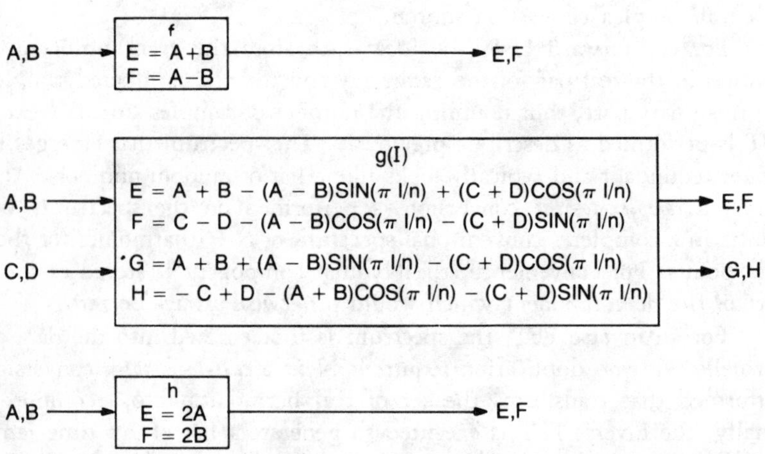

Fig. 13–18. Complex-to-real transformation for $N = 16$

derived from the dc term in the complex spectrum according to the "*f*" function. Next the pairs of harmonics that would have been conjugates if the even–odd storage arrangement were not done are combined according to the "*g*" function to produce a pair of real harmonics. Finally, the "*h*" function is applied to the remaining $N/2$th spectral component. Note that cosines and sines of angle increments half the size of the smallest increment used in the FFT are utilized in evaluating *g* much like an extra step in the FFT. In fact, the whole procedure can be regarded as an extra column of nodes in the FFT algorithm.

Figures 13–19 and 13–20 are BASIC subroutines for complex-to-real and real-to-complex conversion, respectively. The complex-to-real routine also scales the spectrum output so that all of the harmonics, including the dc component, are of the correct amplitude. Except for scaling, the real-to-complex routine undoes what the complex-to-real routine does.

The conversion adds essentially $2N$ multiplications to the FFT, which gives a total of $2N+2N\log_2 N$ for $2N$ data points. If $M = 2N =$ the number of real data points, this is equal to $M\log_2 M$ multiplications, which is the

```
4000 REM   COMPLEX TO REAL TRANSFORMATION FOR FOURIER TRANSFORM
4001 REM   IF REAL DATA POINTS ARE ALTERNATELY STORED IN D1 AND D2
4002 REM   ARRAYS, I.E.  T0->D1(0), T1->D2(0), T2->D1(1), T3->D2(1), ...
4003 REM   THEN THIS ROUTINE CONVERTS THE COMPLEX SPECTRUM INTO A
4004 REM   REAL COSINE-SINE SPECTRUM.
4005 REM   THE ROUTINE ALSO DOES AMPLITUDE CORRECTION ON THE DC
4006 REM   COMPONENT AND THE HARMONICS SO THAT THE FINAL SPECTRUM OUTPUT
4007 REM   IS THE TRUE SPECTRUM OF THE WAVE.
4008 REM   THE SINE PART OF THE DC COMPONENT IS SET EQUAL TO THE NYQUIST
4009 REM   COMPONENT AND SHOULD BE NEAR ZERO IF THE SAMPLE RATE OF THE
4010 REM   DATA WAS ADEQUATE.
4011 REM   THIS ROUTINE USES THE SAME INPUT AS THE FFT ROUTINE
4100 N=2**K
4200 REM   COMPUTE DC AND FOLDOVER COMPONENTS
4201 T1=D1(0)
4202 T2=D2(0)
4203 D1(0)=(T1+T2)/(2*N)
4204 D2(0)=(T1-T2)/(2*N)
4300 REM   COMPUTE REMAINDER OF FREQUENCY COMPONENTS
4301 FOR N1=1 TO N/2
4302 N2=N-N1
4303 C=COS(-3.1415927*N1/N)
4304 S=SIN(-3.1415927*N1/N)
4305 T1=(D1(N1)+D1(N2))/2
4306 T2=(D1(N1)-D1(N2))/2
4307 T3=(D2(N1)+D2(N2))/2
4308 T4=(D2(N1)-D2(N2))/2
4309 T5=T2*S-T3*C
4310 T6=T2*C+T3*S
4311 D1(N1)=(T1-T5)/N
4312 D1(N2)=(T1+T5)/N
4313 D2(N1)=(T4-T6)/N
4314 D2(N2)=(-T4-T6)/N
4315 NEXT N1
4316 RETURN
```

Fig. 13–19. Complex-to-real spectrum transformation routine in BASIC

```
5000 REM   REAL TO COMPLEX TRANSFORMATION FOR INVERSE FOURIER TRANSFORM.
5001 REM   THIS ROUTINE CONVERTS A REAL COSINE-SINE SPECTRUM INTO A
5002 REM   COMPLEX SPECTRUM THAT WHEN INVERSE FOURIER TRANSFORMED WILL
5003 REM   PRODUCE REAL DATA POINTS STORED SUCH THAT EVEN NUMBERED
5004 REM   POINTS ARE IN THE REAL PART OF THE DATA ARRAY AND ODD
5005 REM   NUMBERED POINTS ARE IN THE IMAGINARY PART OF THE ARRAY.
5006 REM   THIS ROUTINE IS THE INVERSE OF THE COMPLEX TO REAL ROUTINE
5007 REM   EXCEPT FOR SCALING WHICH HAS BEEN SET FOR THE PROPER OUTPUT.
5008 REM   THIS ROUTINE FOLLOWED BY AN INVERSE FOURIER TRANSFORM IS THE
5009 REM   EXACT INVERSE OF A FORWARD FOURIER TRANSFORM FOLLOWED BY THE
5010 REM   COMPLEX TO REAL ROUTINE.
5011 REM   THIS ROUTINE USES THE SAME INPUT AS THE FFT ROUTINE
5100 N=2**K
5200 REM   RESTORE DC AND FOLDOVER COMPONENTS
5201 T1=D1(0)
5202 T2=D2(0)
5203 D1(0)=T1+T2
5204 D2(0)=T1-T2
5300 REM   COMPUTE REMAINDER OF FREQUENCY COMPONENTS
5301 FOR N1=1 TO N/2
5302 N2=N-N1
5303 C1=COS(-3.1415927*N1/N)
5304 S1=SIN(-3.1415927*N1/N)
5305 T1=(D1(N1)+D1(N2))/2
5306 T4=(D2(N1)-D2(N2))/2
5307 T5=(D1(N2)-D1(N1))/2
5308 T6=(-D2(N1)-D2(N2))/2
5309 T2=T5*S1+T6*C1
5310 T3=T6*S1-T5*C1
5311 D1(N1)=T1+T2
5312 D1(N2)=T1-T2
5313 D2(N1)=T3+T4
5314 D2(N2)=T3-T4
5315 NEXT N1
5316 RETURN
```

Fig. 13–20. Real-to-complex spectrum conversion routine in BASIC

promised value. With clever programming to avoid multiplication by zero and one in the FFT and real conversion routines (especially in the first column of the FFT), one can ultimately reach a lower limit of $M\left[(\log_2 M)-2\right]$ multiplications, which is a significant reduction when M is small.

Using the FFT for Synthesis

Although the greatest value of the FFT is in sound analysis and modification, it is covered in this chapter because it is also a powerful "synthesis-from-scratch" technique. Unfortunately, its record-oriented properties complicate application to changing spectra with arbitrary frequency components. However, if the required spectral detail is great, the FFT can be much more efficient in computing samples than a direct Fourier series evaluation in spite of these complications.

In all FFT-based synthesis procedures, the general idea is to compute a sequence of sample records using the FFT and then combine them sequen-

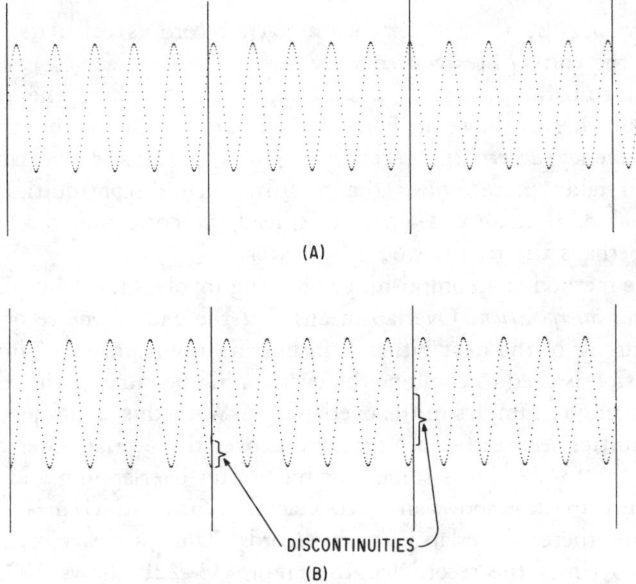

Fig. 13–21. Generating an arbitrary frequency sine wave with the FFT. (A) Record boundaries with a 256-Hz wave. (B) Phase correction between records.

tially in time to produce a continuous string of samples suitable for further processing or output to a DAC. Generally, the record size is chosen once and remains constant throughout the synthesis but a dynamically variable record size is conceivable. If the synthesis result is intended for human consumption, record sizes in the 10-msec to 50-msec range provide the best tradeoff between frequency and time resolution consistent with human perceptual capabilities.

In order to get acquainted with some of the problems and their solution, let's first consider the task of generating a sine wave of an arbitrary but constant frequency using the FFT. For the purpose of illustration, we will assume a sample rate of 10 ks/s = 0.1 msec/sample, a record size of 256 = 25.6 msec, and a sine wave frequency of 200 Hz. The first problem that will be noted is that 200 Hz is not an exact harmonic of 1/25.6 msec = 39.0625 Hz. The closest harmonic is the fifth, which is 195.3 Hz, an error of about one-third semitone. If FFT synthesis is to be useful, a way must be found to produce such intermediate frequencies accurately.

Figure 13–21A illustrates the problem. Shown is an exact sampled 200-Hz waveform and the record boundaries for 256-sample records. Obviously, the *phase* of the desired wave with respect to the record boundaries is different for each record. In fact, the phase advances by (200 − 5 × 39.0625)/39.0625 = 0.12 cycle every record period. Since the spectrum fed to the FFT includes phase, one can increment the phase of the fifth harmonic by 0.12 × 2π before each record is calculated and thus generate the correct *average* frequency.

Unfortunately, there is a substantial glitch where the records are spliced together as shown in Fig. 13–21B. This is due to the fact that the wave frequency *within* the records is still 195 Hz and the entire phase correction takes place *between* the records. Such discontinuities are quite objectionable. If there was a way to spread the correction throughout the record, perhaps the results would be better.

One method of accomplishing spreading involves the concepts of record *overlap* and *interpolation*. Overlap means that the end of one record overlaps the beginning of the next rather than butting up against it. Time-variable interpolation is used to combine the overlapping portions of the records into a single string of samples in the overlap area. With this technique, the sharp discontinuities seen earlier are spread out over the overlap interval.

Figure 13–22 shows some possibilities for overlapping and interpolation. Figure 13–22A shows an overlap factor of 50%, which means that 50% of the time there is overlap between records. Thus, a new record is started every 0.75 times the record length. Figure 13–22B shows 100% overlap where a new record is started when the previous one is only half complete. Even higher orders of overlap are possible. Obviously, overlapping results in more computation, since more records are needed per unit time.

The interpolation needed in the overlap areas is accomplished with the same method described earlier regarding interpolation between two waveform tables. One requirement is that the "weighting curves" always sum up to 1.0 during the overlap interval. A linear curve is the simplest that

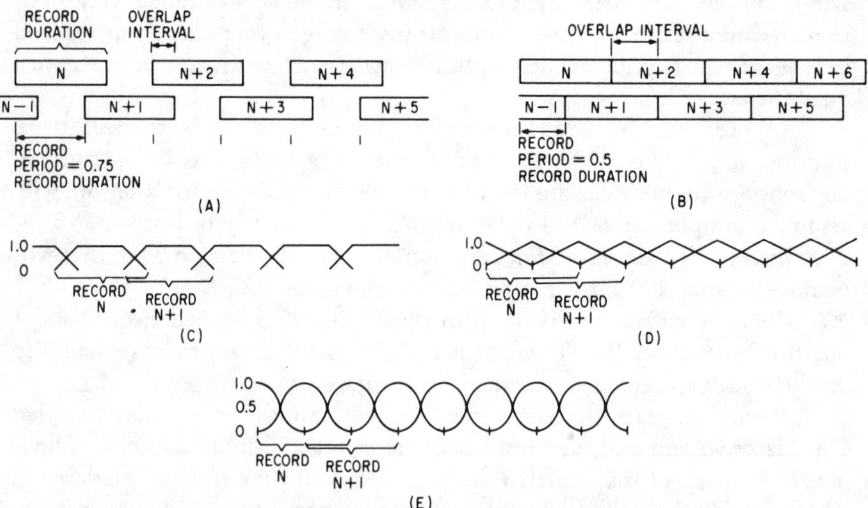

Fig. 13–22. Record overlap and interpolation. (A) 50% overlap. (B) 100% overlap. (C) Interpolation curves for 50% overlap. (D) Linear interpolation for 100% overlap. (E) $\sin^2$ interpolation for 100% overlap.

satisfies this requirement. A better curve for 100% overlap is the $\sin^2$ curve, which also gives a sum of 1.0 (remember that $\sin^2 A + \cos^2 A = 1$).

Now, how does overlap and interpolation affect the job of creating a 200-Hz tone with the FFT? Taking the case of 100% overlap, it is immediately obvious that the phase shift per record of the fifth harmonic needs to be only one-half of its previous value or 0.06 cycle because there are now twice as many records per unit time. A general expression for the phase shift per record period with 100% overlap is: $P = D(F - H)/2$, where P is the phase shift in terms of cycles/record period, F is the desired frequency in hertz, H is the nearest harmonic frequency of the record duration, and D is the record duration. A little study will reveal that the largest possible phase shift, 0.25, occurs when the desired frequency falls midway between harmonics.

How well does overlap and interpolation work in smoothing out distortions in the synthesis? Figure 13–23 was prepared using a "worst-case" situation of synthesizing a 214.8-Hz wave (halfway between fifth and sixth harmonics) with a record duration of 25.6 msec, 100% overlap, and a $\sin^2$ interpolation function. The waveform itself in Fig. 13–23A seems to be essentially perfect when compared to the ideal below but shows 34% or about 3 dB of amplitude modulation, which is due to partial phase cancellation during the interpolation. Such amplitude modulation is not always objectionable for musical applications, since it occurs at the relatively slow record frequency.

A more sensitive analysis was performed in Fig. 13–23B by taking the FFT of 51.2 msec of the synthesized waveform, which, ideally, would show an 11th harmonic component and nothing else. In fact, there is a small amount of distortion clustered around the signal frequency that is caused by the amplitude modulation. With arbitrary frequencies, the phase shift per record averages only half the maximum, which corresponds to about 7.9% or 0.7 dB of modulation. Higher overlap factors and multiway interpolation in the synthesis can reduce the distortion dramatically. A four-to-one overlap, for example, exhibits 0.6% worst-case amplitude modulation, which is only about 0.05 dB and therefore quite inaudible.

The Phase-Derivative Spectrum

At this point, let's examine the best way to represent an arbitrary spectrum for use with FFT synthesis. First, we will assume that the arbitrary spectrum, which will be called the *source spectrum*, is given as a list of sinusoidal components with each component characterized by an *amplitude* and a *frequency* parameter. If the spectrum is dynamically changing, there will be such a list for each record period, which means that the amplitude and frequency parameters are sampled functions but at a relatively low sample rate.

The first step toward an FFT-compatible representation is to specify frequencies in terms of the reciprocal of the record duration. Thus, with a

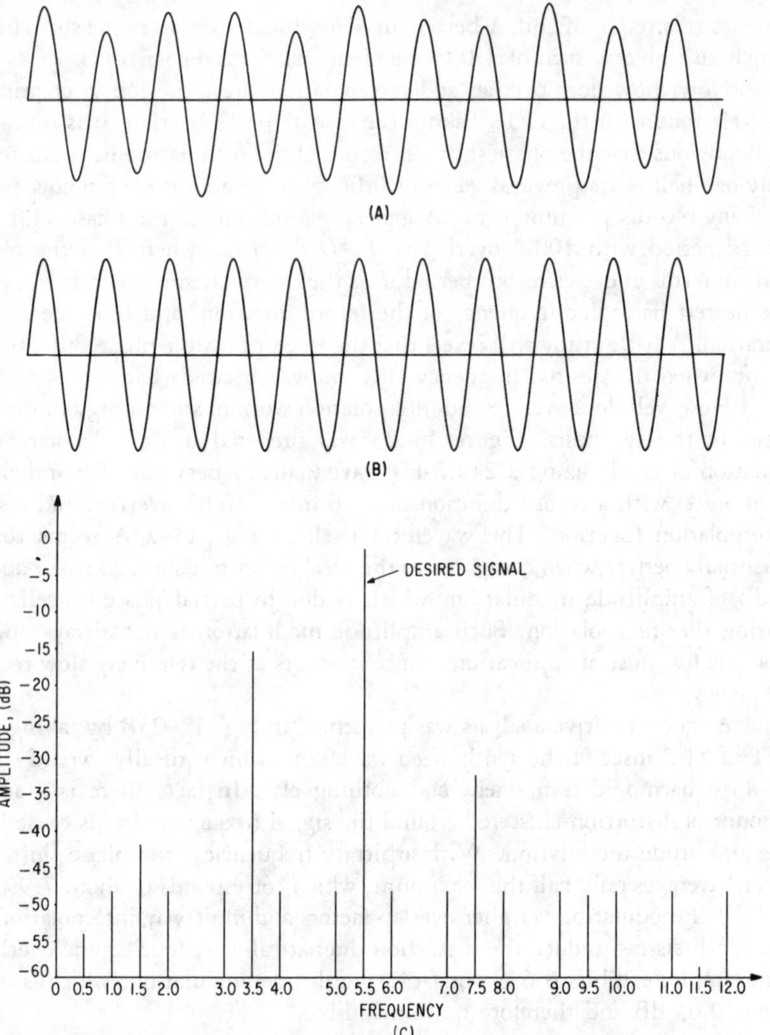

Fig. 13–23. FFT synthesis of 5.5 harmonic using 2:1 overlap. (A) FFT-synthesized waveform. (B) Reference-perfect waveform. (C) Spectrum of synthesized waveform.

record duration of 25.6 msec = 1/39.0625 Hz, a 100-Hz component would have a frequency of 2.56 units. The integer part of the *rounded* frequency parameter is the harmonic in the FFT that this particular frequency component will affect.

Next, we define the *current FFT spectrum*, which for convenience will be in the amplitude-phase form. This spectrum, after conversion into cosine–sine form, is what is Fourier transformed to produce a record. After each record is computed, the current FFT spectrum is updated according to the source spectrum. Note that the current spectrum will have to be copied before the FFT is executed.

Updating the current spectrum from the source spectrum is simple if the source spectrum components are far enough apart such that no more than one affects any given FFT spectrum harmonic. First, each source frequency is rounded to an integer and the amplitude simply copied to the corresponding FFT harmonic number. Next the rounded value is subtracted from the unrounded value and the difference is divided by two (for two-to-one overlap factor) to yield a number between -0.25 and $+0.25$. This number is *added* to the *current phase* (in units of 2π mod 1.0) of the corresponding FFT harmonic to give a new phase. After all of the source spectrum is processed, another FFT sample record is computed and the process is repeated. Note that even a very-low-frequency source spectrum component, which may correspond to the dc component of the FFT, comes out alright by virtue of the amplitude–phase to cosine–sine conversion.

Problems occur, however, when two or more source components map into the same FFT harmonic. In real life, two such closely spaced frequencies would slowly beat together giving an apparent frequency equal to the stronger of the two (or the average if substantially equal) and a periodic varying amplitude envelope with a frequency equal to the difference between the component frequencies. While not exact, it is possible to replace the two closely spaced components with one component and some tremolo in the amplitude parameter for the new component.

A more exact method that works for any number of closely spaced frequencies is to keep track of the current phase of *each* in a separate array. When the FFT harmonic affected by the cluster is updated, the contents of this array are combined according to:

$$P_r = \tan^{-1}\left[\frac{\sum_{i=1}^{N} A_i \sin(P_i)}{\sum_{i=1}^{N} A_i \cos(P_i)}\right]$$

$$A_r = \sqrt{\left[\sum_{i=1}^{N} A_i \cos(P_i)\right]^2 + \left[\sum_{i=1}^{N} A_i \sin(P_i)\right]^2}$$

where N is the number of frequencies in the cluster, A_i and P_i are the amplitude and phase, respectively, of the ith array element, and A_r and P_r are the amplitude and phase of the resultant that are entered into the FFT spectrum.

Table 13–2 shows these methods applied to a short segment of sound. It is a sequence of source spectrums, spaced 12.8 msec apart. Frequency is

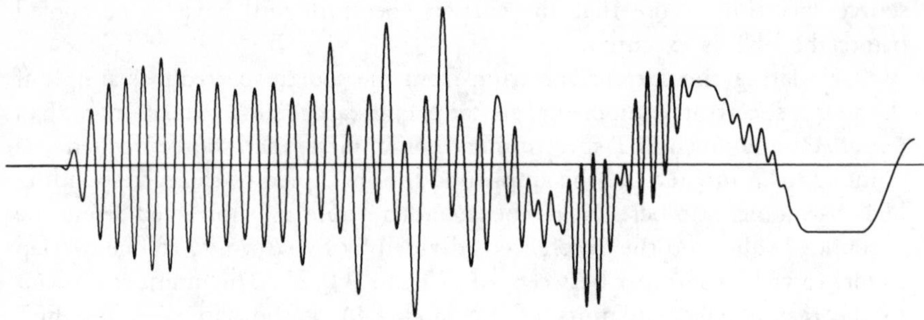

Fig. 13–24. Waveform computed from sequence of object spectrums from Tables 13–2 and 13–3.

expressed as multiples of the inverse of the record size (39 Hz for 10-ks/s sample rate and 256 record size) and amplitude is in arbitrary units. Table 13–3 is a listing of the nonzero portion of the corresponding FFT spectrum sequence.

Figure 13–24 is the actual waveform (with line segments connecting the sample points for easier visualization) created by this sequence. Note that ultrasharp attacks are simply not possible with FFT synthesis. In fact, no event shorter than a record period can be resolved. This drives home the primary assumption of FFT synthesis that the record size must be shorter than the limits of human time perception yet longer than the limits of human frequency perception for simultaneous tones.

Table 13–2. FFT Synthesis Example: Source Spectrum Sequence

Record number	*Freq.*	*Amp.*	*Freq.*	*Amp.*	*Freq.*	*Amp.*	*Freq.*	*Amp.*	*Freq.*	*Amp.*
1	0	0								
2	5.7	1.0								
3	6.0	1.3								
4	6.3	1.0								
5	6.3	1.0								
6	6.3	1.0	2.1	0.5						
7	6.3	1.0	2.1	0.75						
8	6.3	1.0	2.1	1.0						
9	6.1	0.75	2.4	0.6	8.7	0.2	9.3	0.2	0.4	0.3
10	5.9	0.2	2.7	0.1	8.7	0.5	9.3	0.5	0.4	0.7
11	8.7	0.5	9.3	0.5	0.4	1.0				
12	8.7	0.5	9.3	0.5	0.4	1.0				
13	8.7	0.3	9.3	0.3	0.4	1.0				
14	8.7	0.1	9.3	0.1	0.4	1.0				
15	0.4	1.0								
16	0.4	1.0								

Table 13–3. FFT Synthesis Example: Sequence of Object Spectrums

Record number	*Hrm.*	*Amp.*	*Phase*	*Hrm.*	*Amp.*	*Phase*	*Hrm.*	*Amp.*	*Phase*	*Hrm.*	*Amp.*	*Phase*
1	—	All 0										
2	6	1.0	0.85									
3	6	1.3	0.85									
4	6	1.0	0.00									
5	6	1.0	0.15									
6	6	1.0	0.30	2	0.5	0.05						
7	6	1.0	0.45	2	0.75	0.10						
8	6	1.0	0.60	2	1.0	0.15						
9	6	0.75	0.65	2	0.60	0.35	9	0.235	0.00	0	0.30	0.20
10	6	0.20	0.60	3	0.10	0.20	9	0.309	0.50	9	0.70	0.40
11	9	0.951	0.50	0	1.0	0.60						
12	9	0.809	0.50	0	1.0	0.80						
13	9	0.000	0.00	0	1.0	0.00						
14	9	0.162	0.00	0	1.0	0.20						
15	0	1.0	0.40									
16	0	1.0	0.60									

Note that all harmonics not specifically listed are assumed to have zero amplitude.

Other Digital Tone Generation Techniques

The tone-generation techniques described up to this point have all been *direct*, that is, a straightforward application of digital technology to generating very precise arbitrary waveforms (table lookup) or very precise arbitrary spectrums (Fourier synthesis). Either, with allowance for smooth parameter changes, is theoretically capable of synthesizing any kind of tone. While these methods are therefore completely general, a lot of "data" must be "input" to the generator to produce what often seem to be simple changes in a tone's timbre.

Recall from Chapter 3 that analog FM synthesis was capable of producing a wide variety of tone colors by manipulating only two synthesis parameters: the modulation index and the ratio of modulating to carrier frequencies. Since only two variables were being controlled, the "data rate" needed by FM synthesis to produce dramatic timbre variations was very low. FM, however, is not a direct technique, since there is no simple relationship between the "data" (modulation index and frequency ratio) and either the waveform or the spectrum. It is also not a general technique, at least in its pure form, because it cannot synthesize any arbitrary waveform or spectrum. For the remainder of this chapter, we will look at FM and other indirect digital synthesis techniques that in many applications have substantial advantages over direct techniques.

FM Synthesis

FM synthesis is as easily implemented in digital form as it is in analog form. Furthermore, it is efficient in its use of memory space and computing

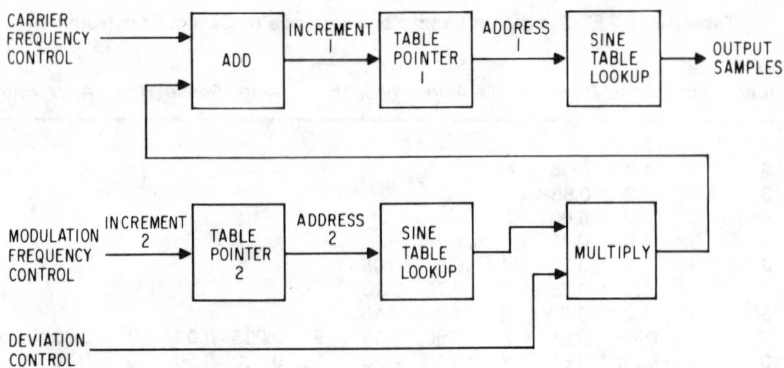

Fig. 13–25. FM synthesis calculations

power relative to table lookup and Fourier synthesis techniques. In its pure form, only one table, which contains a sine wave, is required. For each sample, as few as three additions, two table lookups, and one multiplication are required. This remains true even when the modulation index is changed for dynamic timbre variation.

Figure 13–25 is a "block diagram" of these calculations, which can easily be translated into a program or dedicated hardware. Note that, unlike the analog case, controls for the three variables (carrier frequency, modulation frequency, and deviation amount) are kept separate rather than combined to provide the more useful pitch frequency, ratio, and modulation index controls. Otherwise, the combination calculations would be done for every output sample, which substantially increases computing effort. Typically, the more useful "source" controls would be translated into these "object" controls at a slower *control sample rate*, which may be one-tenth of the audio rate or less. Flexibility is also increased because the same synthesis routine could serve for constant deviation or constant modulation index synthesis as the pitch frequency is varied.

Note that if the carrier frequency is relatively low and the deviation amount is large, it is possible for table pointer 1 to have a negative increment specified, i.e., a negative frequency. This is no problem for digital synthesis, provided signed arithmetic is being used, and simply results in the sine table being scanned backward. In actual use, it has been found that interpolation noise in the sine table lookups is much more detrimental in FM synthesis than in direct table-scanning synthesis. This is because errors in lookup of the modulating wave are compounded when they modulate the carrier wave. Therefore, either the sine table must be large or linear interpolation in a smaller table used. One should shoot for at least 16-bit accuracy in the table lookup results, which means effective table sizes of 64K points for no interpolation or 0.5 to 1K for linear interpolation. Since the table content is fixed as 1 cycle of a sine wave, symmetry can be used to reduce table size by a

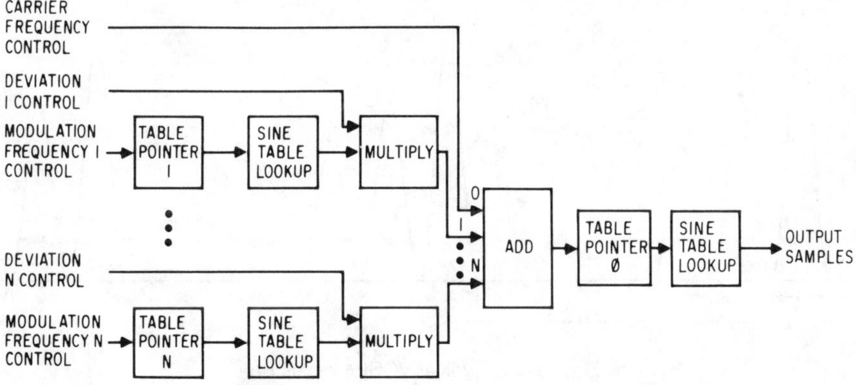

Fig. 13–26. FM synthesis using a complex modulating wave

factor of 4. One potential drawback of digital FM synthesis is the possibility of aliasing when the carrier frequency becomes too high or the modulation index becomes too large. To avoid the sudden harsh sound of aliasing, some intelligence may have to be applied to the synthesis process.

More complex forms of FM synthesis are also possible when implemented digitally, which can largely overcome its otherwise limited range of timbres. One possiblity is to use a complex *carrier* wave and a sine-modulating wave, which produces a duplicate set of modulation sidebands around each harmonic of the carrier. A more interesting technique is to use a complex *modulating* waveform while retaining a sinusoidial carrier waveform. For example, using a modulating waveform with just two frequency components, i.e., two harmonics, results in a final spectrum with sidebands around the carrier due to each frequency component and its associated modulation index alone plus additional sidebands due to all possible sums and differences of multiples of the frequency components. If the carrier frequency and each component of the modulating signal are all harmonically related, all of the sidebands are also harmonics and many of them will overlap at equal frequencies. The resulting amplitudes at these frequencies are determined by relative amplitudes and phases of the equal-frequency sidebands. Thus, complex spectra with wide local variations in harmonic amplitudes are possible. It may in fact be possible to approximate arbitrary spectral shapes closely enough for practical synthesis applications with just a few harmonics in the modulating wave, although determining these would not be a simple task.

Only a slight modification of Fig. 13–25 is necessary to implement complex modulating-wave FM. The table used in table lookup number 2 is simply replaced by a table containing the complex modulating wave. Note that with this approach, the deviation control will affect the modulation

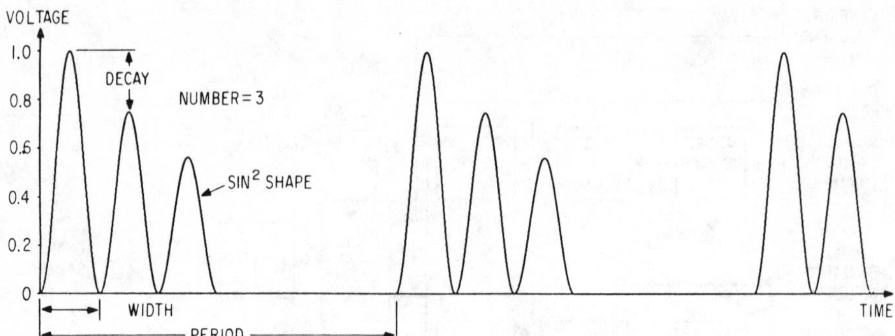

Fig. 13–27. Typical VOSIM waveform

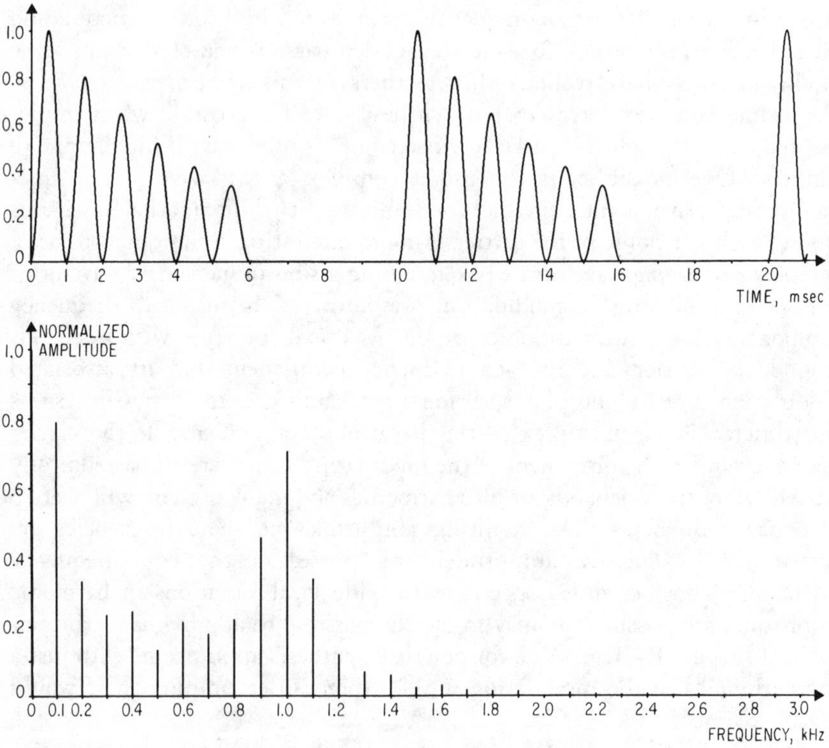

(A)

Fig. 13–28. (A) Reference VOSIM waveform: decay = 0.8; width = 1.0 msec; number = 6; and period = 10 msec. (B) Same as (A) except period = 20 msec. (C) Same as (A) except width = 0.67 msec. (D) Same as (A) except decay = 0.5. (E) Same as (A) except number = 2.

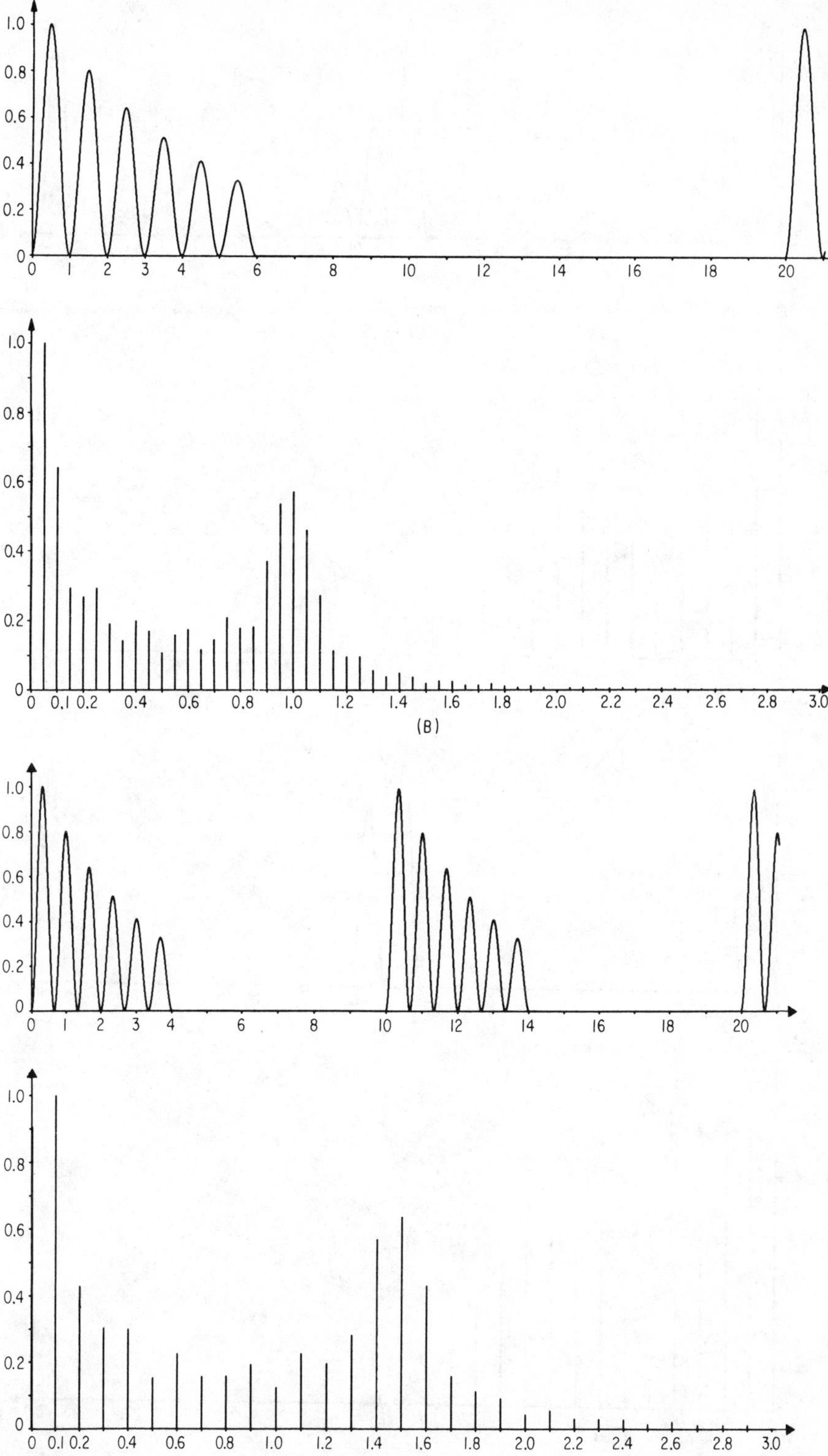
1.0
0.8
0.6
0.4
0.2
0
0 1 2 3 4 6 8 10 12 14 16 18 20
0 0.1 0.2 0.4 0.6 0.8 1.0 1.2 1.4 1.6 1.8 2.0 2.2 2.4 2.6 2.8 3.0
0 1 2 3 4 6 8 10 12 14 16 18 20
0 0.1 0.2 0.4 0.6 0.8 1.0 1.2 1.4 1.6 1.8 2.0 2.2 2.4 2.6 2.8 3.0

(B)

(C)

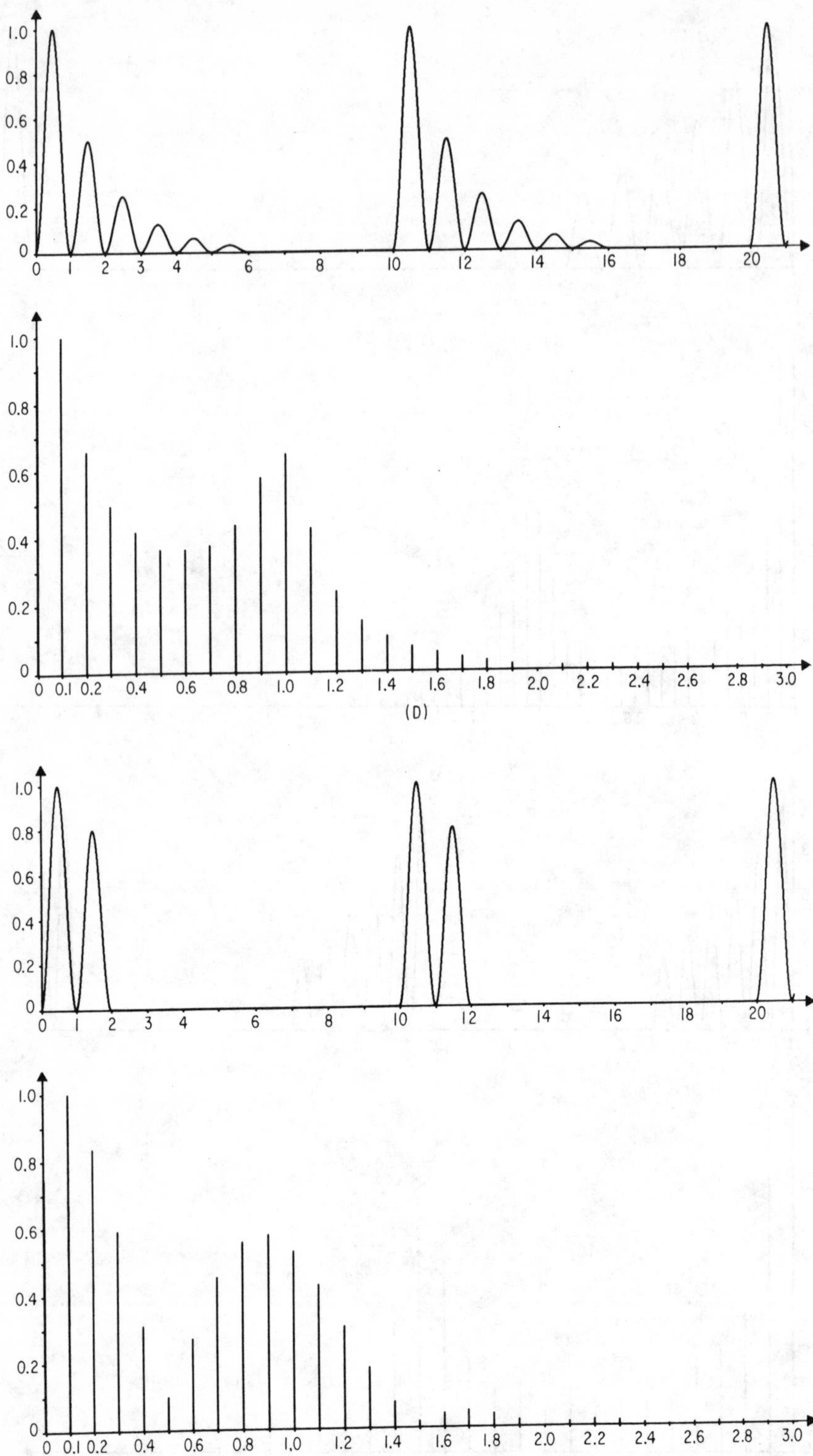
1.0
0.8
0.6
0.4
0.2
0
0 1 2 3 4 6 8 10 12 14 16 18 20
1.0
0.8
0.6
0.4
0.2
0
0 0.1 0.2 0.4 0.6 0.8 1.0 1.2 1.4 1.6 1.8 2.0 2.2 2.4 2.6 2.8 3.0
1.0
0.8
0.6
0.4
0.2
0
0 1 2 3 4 6 8 10 12 14 16 18 20
1.0
0.8
0.6
0.4
0.2
0
0 0.1 0.2 0.4 0.6 0.8 1.0 1.2 1.4 1.6 1.8 2.0 2.2 2.4 2.6 2.8 3.0

(D)

(E)

index of all components of the complex modulating wave simultaneously. If instead the calculations are restructured as in Fig. 13–26, the modulation indices as well as the frequencies of each modulating component can be separately controlled. Also, all table lookups remain into the same, easily interpolated, sine table. As few as two modulating frequency components have been found to dramatically improve the utility of FM synthesis. In one experiment, piano tones (which are normally not well synthesized with FM techniques) were quite successfully approximated using one modulating frequency equal to the carrier frequency and another four times the carrier frequency. The slightly inharmonic partials of piano tones were then simulated by slightly detuning these ratios.

"VOSIM"

Other "minimal-parameter" synthesis techniques besides FM are possible, although none seem to be quite as flexible. One of these, which is quite efficient in synthesizing a wide range of vocal-like sounds, is called VOSIM, from the words VOcal SIMulation. VOSIM uses a very simple waveform described by three parameters that is periodically repeated at the desired fundamental frequency. Figure 13–27 shows the VOSIM waveform, which consists of one or more bell-shaped pulses. A single *width* parameter specifies the baseline widths of the pulses. The first pulse has unity amplitude, while succeeding ones are smaller according to a *decay* parameter that ranges between 0 and 1. Finally, a *number* parameter specifies how many pulses there are in each period. Any time left over between the end of the pulse group and the beginning of the next period is filled with zeroes. The pulses themselves are sine-squared curves, which is equivalent to one cycle of a negative cosine wave raised up to the axis. After the pulse group is specified, it is simply repeated at the desired frequency and multiplied by an amplitude envelope. Note that the time occupied by the group is in absolute terms independent of the period. Thus, the "blank" time between pulse groups will vary with the period, but the pulse group itself will remain constant. If the period becomes smaller than the group width, the group is simply truncated and restarted, although this is normally kept from happening.

Figure 13–28 illustrates some of VOSIM's properties. Figure 13–28A shows a reference VOSIM waveform (decay = 0.8, width = 1 msec, number = 6, period = 10 msec = 100 Hz), along with its normalized harmonic spectrum and spectral envelope. Figure 13–28B shows a wave with the same parameters but with its period increased to 20 msec. Note that the overall spectral envelope is essentially unchanged; there are just more harmonics filling the space under it. Thus, the position in frequency of major spectral envelope features remains constant as fundamental frequency is varied, a desirable property not possessed by the digital synthesis techniques discussed so far. Figure 13–28C shows that reducing the width parameter to 0.67 msec increases the frequency of the broad spectral peak to about 1.5 kHz. In Fig. 13–28D, the decay parameter is reduced to 0.5, which makes the spectral

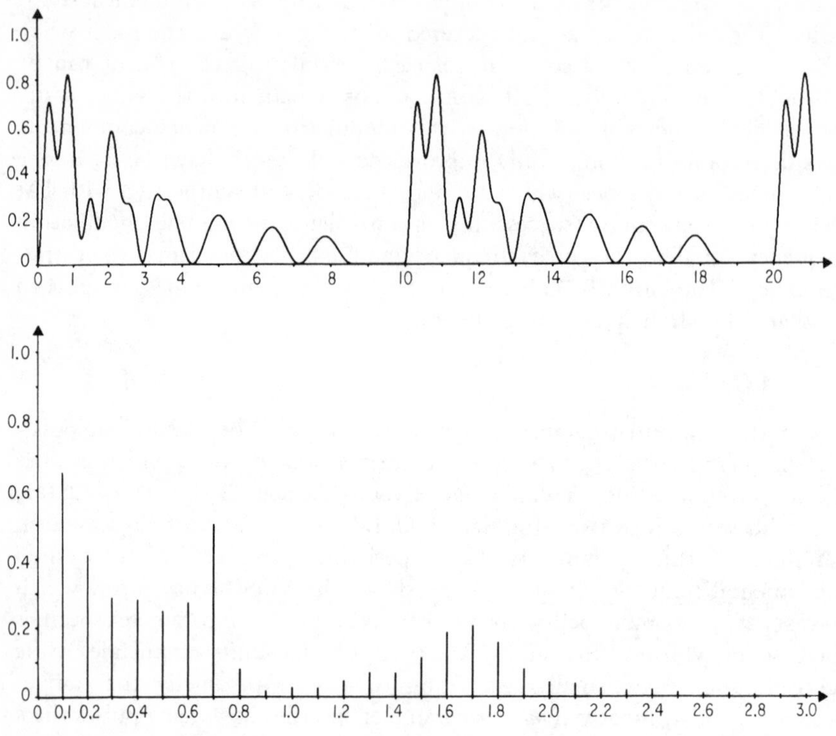

Fig. 13–29. Combination of two VOSIM generators

peak broader, whereas in Fig. 13–28E the number of pulses is reduced to two, which also broadens the peak but in a different way. All of these sounds have a strange vocal-like timbre, although it is unrecognizable in terms of specific vowels.

It is also possible to combine two or more VOSIM generators to produce two or more prominent peaks in the spectrum as was done in Fig. 13–29. Here, two prominent peaks, one at about 700 Hz and the other at 1,700 Hz, have been produced by adding the outputs of two VOSIM generators with identical parameters except for the pulse width. With suitable selection of values, specific vowel sounds can in fact be produced. Of course, any or all of the parameters are easily manipulated while the tone is sounding for dynamic timbre effects. In fact, if the width parameter is made to vary randomly at a rapid rate, the effect of filtered noise is produced with center frequency roughly equal to the reciprocal of the average width.

As with FM, implementation of the VOSIM algorithm is straightforward and efficient. In the simplest case, a single table-lookup routine using a *one-shot* table scanner into a table containing the raised-cosine shape is sufficient. At the beginning of a period, a pulse counter is reset, an

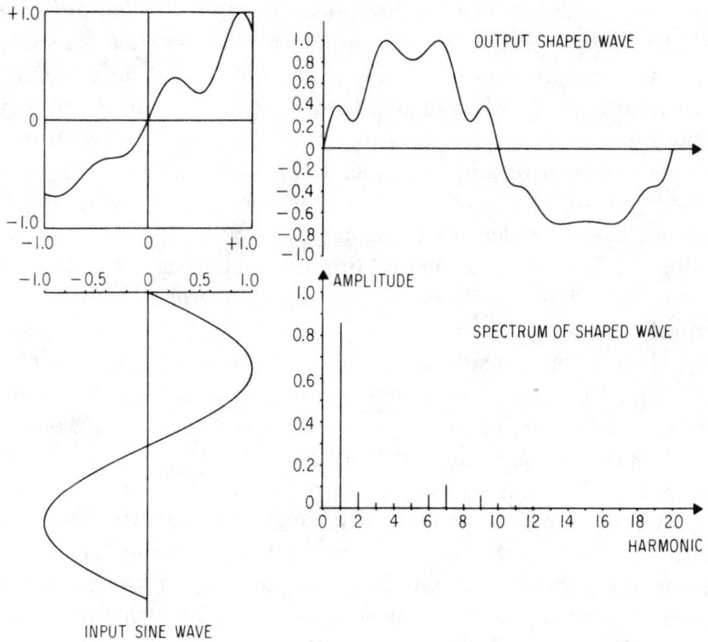

Fig. 13–30. Nonlinear transfer function standard form

amplitude factor is set to unity, and the table pointer is reset to zero. The pointer is then allowed to advance through the table at a rate determined solely by the pulse-width parameter. After the pointer has advanced completely through the table, the pulse counter is incremented and the current value of the amplitude factor is multiplied by the decay parameter. Then, if the pulse counter is still less than the number parameter, the table pointer is reset and allowed to run another scan. If all pulses have been generated, the table pointer is left at the end, thus producing zeroes until the beginning of the next period. Accuracy requirements are not severe for any of these calculations including the table lookups. The actual algorithm is complicated somewhat if the pulse widths are not a multiple of the sample period and even more if the total period is not a multiple. Even so, the technique remains a highly efficient means of producing tones with stationary spectra as the pitch is varied.

Waveshaping

This technique is somewhat of a misnomer when applied in a digital context because any waveshape desired can be produced in a straightforward manner simply by placing it into a waveform table. However, *dynamic* variation of the waveform is difficult and requires either constant rewriting of the table content or time-varying interpolation along a sequence of waveform tables. The more specific term, "nonlinear waveshaping synthesis," is actually nothing more than subjecting a sine wave to a nonlinear distortion process such as that described in analog form at the beginning of Chapter 2. By simply varying the amplitude of the input sine wave, the spectrum of the output waveform will vary in a complex fashion. What makes the technique much more useful in digital form is that very precise arbitrary transfer functions are easily implemented, using, guess what, a table. By contrast, the analog equivalent is generally limited to clipping and rectification operations or, at best, piecewise-linear approximations to curves using a small number of segments.

Fig. 13–30 shows a standardized representation of a nonlinear transfer function. As with Fig. 2–1, the input sine wave is applied in the X direction, and corresponding Y points on the curve represent the output. For easy and consistent application in digital circuitry, the input signal is restricted to the range of -1 to $+1$, and the output signal is similarly restricted. Since the input is always a sine wave, it is usually not shown while the output and its spectrum are shown. It is not necessary for the curve to pass through the origin, but, if it doesn't, there will be an output dc offset for no input, which could lead to audible envelope thumps and other problems in subsequent processing. Thus, it may be desirable to shift the curve up or down so that it does pass through the origin. Using this representation, it becomes easy to put the shape into a table with the X values representing successive table entries and the Y values representing the value of the entries. Although this requires the curve to be a single-valued function, analog hysteresis effects could probably be simulated by using two tables and keeping track of the slope of the input sinusoid.

While any kind of curve can be used for a distorting function, even one drawn by hand, mathematicians like to use polynomials to describe arbitrary curves. With such a description, they can then predict what the output spectrum will be without actually simulating the process on a computer and then using the Fourier transform. Explaining that process here won't be attempted, but some of the properties of polynomial curves are easily understood. One desirable property is that the highest harmonic present in the output is equal to the highest power of X used to construct the curve. This aids tremendously in predicting and avoiding alias distortion.

One specific class of polynomials that has other desirable acoustic properties when used to construct nonlinear distorting functions is called *Chebychev polynomials of the first kind*. Figure 13–31A–H shows equations for these polynomials up to the eighth order, their corresponding distortion curve, the output waveform when the input is a sine wave of unity amplitude, and the harmonic spectrum of the output. Note that, in effect, each of these polynomials multiplies the frequency of the input sine wave by a factor equal to its order. Or, in other words, a Chebychev polynomial of order

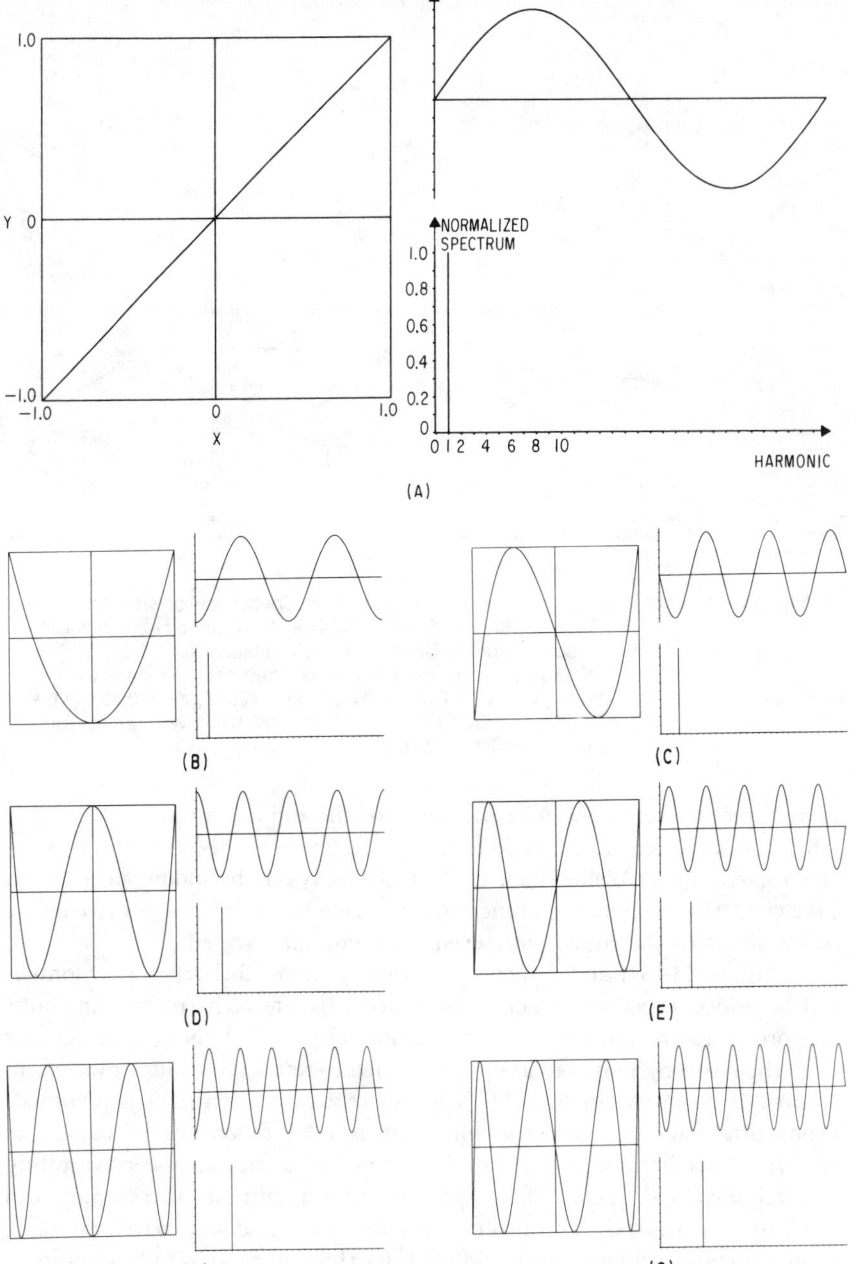

Fig. 13–31. Example nonlinear transfer function. (A) First-order Chebyshev polynomial, $Y = X$. (B) Second-order Chebyshev polynomial, $Y = 2X^2 - 1$. (C) Third-order Chebyshev polynomial, $Y = 4X^3 - 3X$. (D) Fourth-order Chebyshev polynomial, $Y = 8X^4 - 8X^2 + 1$. (E) Fifth-order Chebyshev polynomial, $Y = 16X^5 - 20X^3 + 5X$. (F) Sixth-order Chebyshev polynomial, $Y = 32X^6 - 48X^4 + 18X^2 - 1$. (G) Seventh-order Chebyshev polynomial, $Y = 64X^7 - 112X^5$

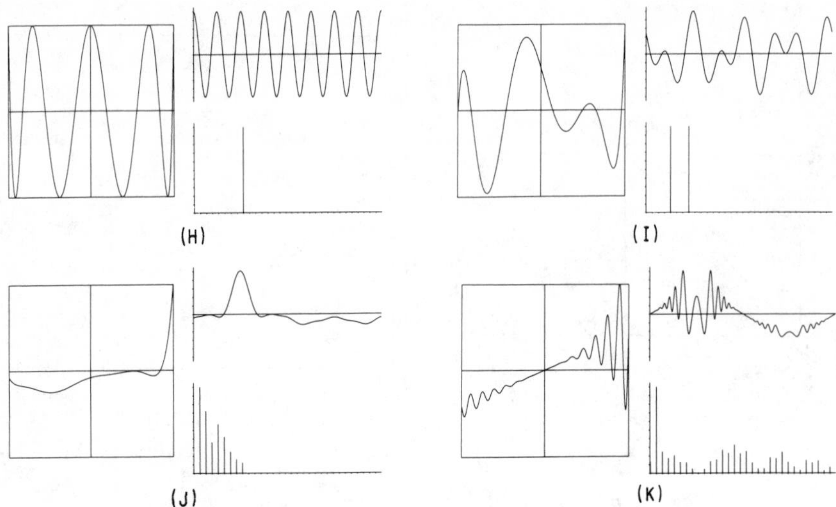

Fig. 13–31. (*cont.*) + $56X^3 - 7X$. (H) Eighth-order Chebyshev polynomial, $Y = 128X^8 - 256X^6 + 160X4 - 32X^2 + 1$. (I) Combination of fourth- and seventh-order Chebyshev polynomials, $Y = 0.5\,[T_4(X) + T_7(X)]$. (J) Combination of first eight Chebyshev polynomials, $Y = 0.28\,[T_1(X) + 0.72T_2(X) + 0.36T_3(X) + 0.57T_4(X) + 0.42T_5(X) + 0.25T_6(X) + 0.16T_7(X) + 0.12T_8(X)]$. (K) Contrived transfer function, $Y = 0.42X + X^3 \exp(X - 1) \sin(14\,\pi X)$.

N will produce only the *N*th harmonic of the input sine wave. Note that when the curve describes an odd function (the shape to the left of the Y axis is the negative image of the shape to the right) only odd harmonics are created. Likewise, when it is an even function (the shape to the left is a positive image of the shape to the right), only even harmonics are created.

Figure 13–31I and J shows that two or more Chebychev polynomials can be added together to get a controlled mixture of harmonics in direct proportion to the amount of each polynomial included. Note that, in this case, the resulting polynomial must be scaled to restrain the output waveform amplitude to unity. In Fig. 13–31K, an arbitrary mixture of polynomial, exponential, and trignometric functions is used to create the curve. Its spectrum has harmonics out to the 30th and a desirable gently rolling spectral envelope. Thus, it is apparent that nonlinear waveshaping can produce any arbitrary amplitude spectrum just as direct waveform table scanning could. In fact, one could consider the process as simply scanning a waveform table with a sine wave rather than a sawtooth wave as in the direct procedure.

The preceding analysis only holds when the input sine wave is of unit amplitude. If the amplitude is reduced, the spectrum will change. Generally, the upper harmonics will decline more rapidly than the lower ones as the

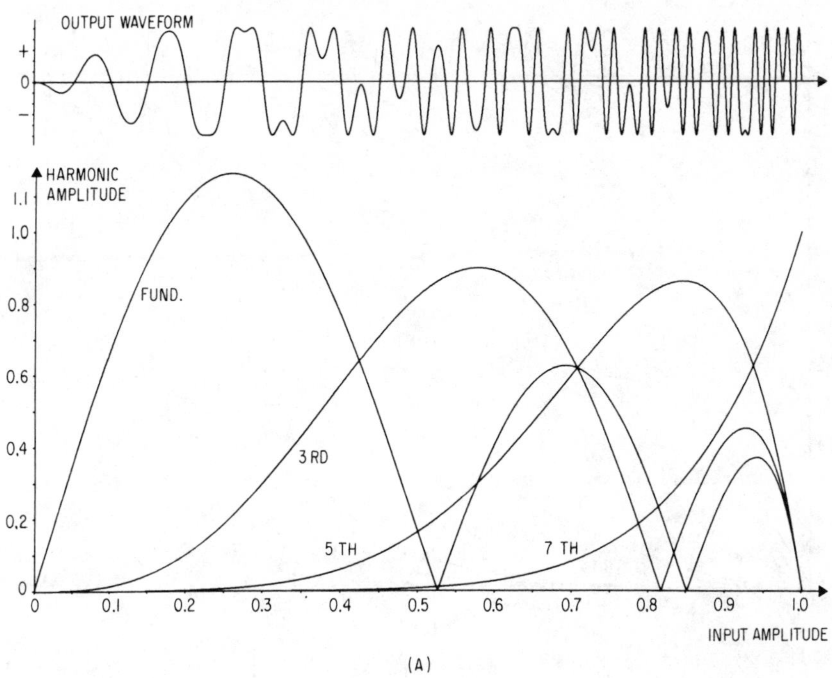
OUTPUT WAVEFORM
+
0
−
HARMONIC AMPLITUDE
1.1
1.0
0.8
0.6
0.4
0.2
0
FUND.
3 RD
5 TH
7 TH
0 0.1 0.2 0.3 0.4 0.5 0.6 0.7 0.8 0.9 1.0
INPUT AMPLITUDE

(A)

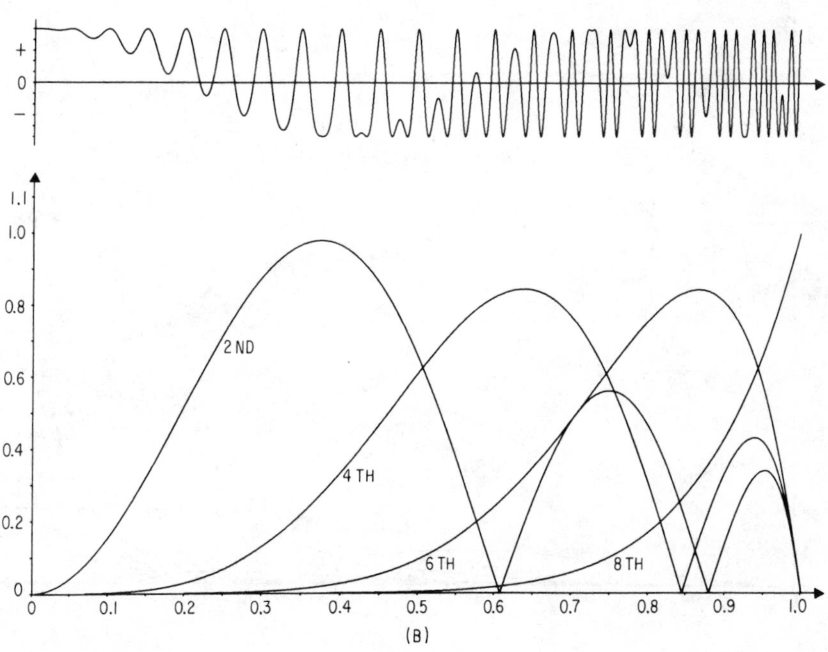
+
0
−
1.1
1.0
0.8
0.6
0.4
0.2
0
2 ND
4 TH
6 TH
8 TH
0 0.1 0.2 0.3 0.4 0.5 0.6 0.7 0.8 0.9 1.0

(B)

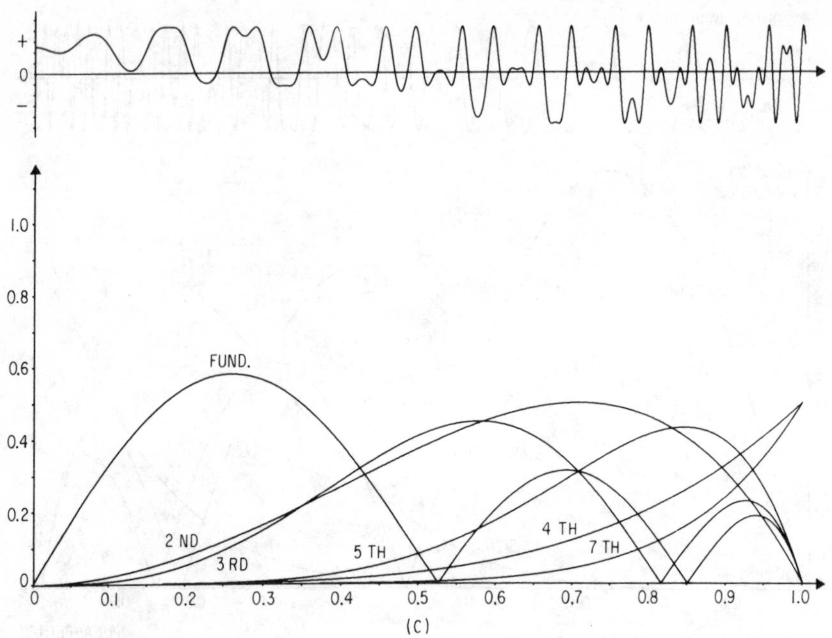
+
0
−
1.0
0.8
0.6
0.4
0.2
0
FUND.
2 ND
3 RD
5 TH
4 TH
7 TH
0
0.1
0.2
0.3
0.4
0.5
0.6
0.7
0.8
0.9
1.0
(C)

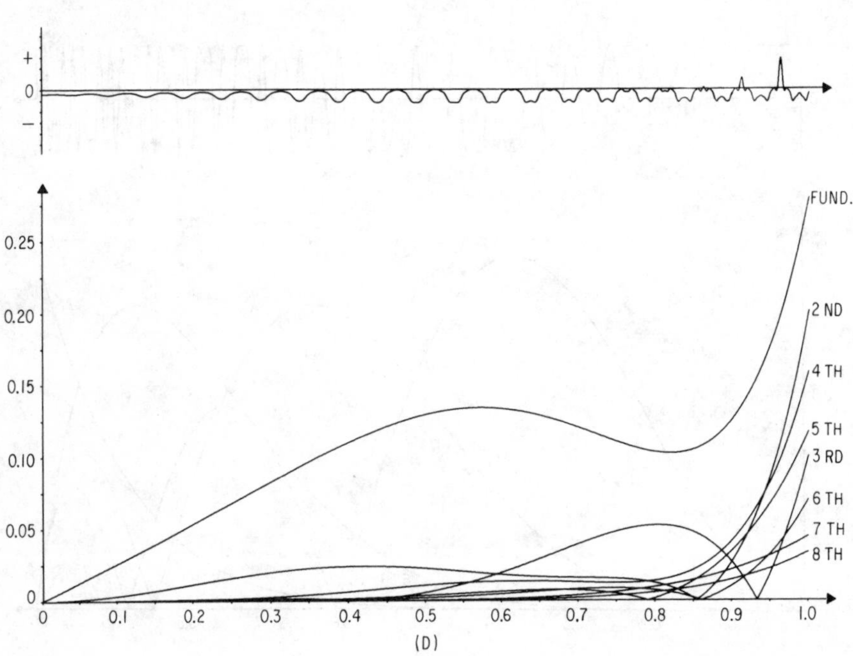
+
0
−
0.25
0.20
0.15
0.10
0.05
0
FUND.
2 ND
4 TH
5 TH
3 RD
6 TH
7 TH
8 TH
0
0.1
0.2
0.3
0.4
0.5
0.6
0.7
0.8
0.9
1.0
(D)

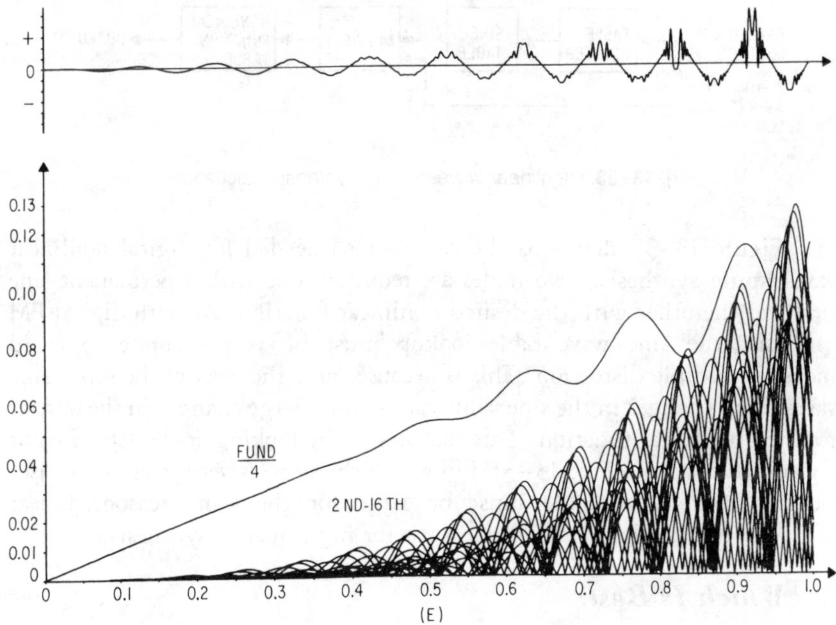

Fig. 13–32. (A) Spectrum of Fig. 13–31G as input amplitude varies. (B) Spectrum of Fig. 13–31H as input amplitude varies. (C) Spectrum of Fig. 13–31I as input amplitude varies. (D) Spectrum of Fig. 13–31J as input amplitude varies. (E) Spectrum of Fig. 13–31K as input amplitude varies.

input amplitude is reduced, which is exactly how most conventional musical instruments operate. A trumpet played softly, for example, has weaker upper harmonics than one played loudly. A plucked string's high harmonics decay more quickly than the fundamental and lower harmonics. Thus, a relatively realistic simulation can often be obtained simply by applying the amplitude envelope *before* the nonlinear shaping operation. It will usually also have to be applied again afterwards if Chebyshev polynomials are used, since the output amplitude may not begin to decline until the input amplitude is quite small. Figure 13–32A–E illustrates this effect using the nonlinear functions given in Fig. 13–31G–K, respectively. The graphs show the changing waveshape and how the amplitude (on the Y axis) of each harmonic varies as the input amplitude (on the X axis) varies. Note the extremely complex, although definitely structured, harmonic evolution pattern in Fig. 13–32E. For the patterns to show up, it was necessary to plot the fundamental at one-quarter of its true amplitude and also show only the first 16 harmonics. Using an interactive program in which transfer curves can be drawn with a digitizer or light pen should be exciting to say the least.

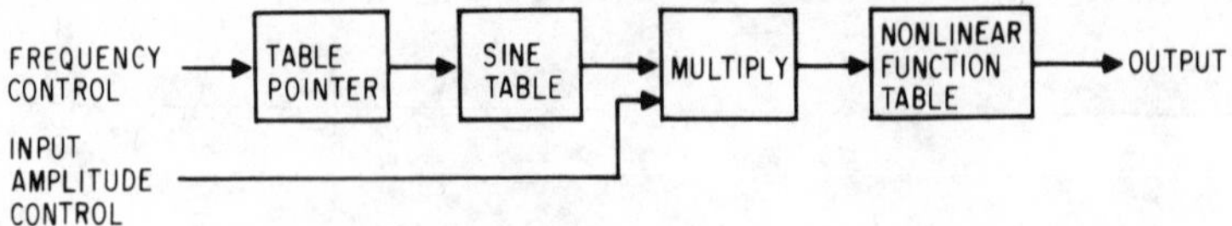

Fig. 13–33. Nonlinear waveshaping synthesis calcuations

Figure 13–33 diagrams the calculations needed for digital nonlinear waveshaping synthesis. Two tables are required; one with a permanent sine wave and the other with the desired nonlinear function. As with digital FM synthesis, the sine wave table lookup must be very accurate to avoid undesired audible distortion. This is because, near the peak of the input sine wave, small changes in the sine value can produce large changes in the output from the nonlinear function. This can be seen by looking at the left or right edges of the curve in Fig. 13–31H in which the slope is very steep. Likewise, the nonlinear curve table must be large for the same reason. Linear interpolation into both tables is a must for high-quality synthesis.

Which Is Best?

In this chapter, five distinctly different methods of synthesizing sound digitally have been covered. Also available are several less well-known and generally less-useful techniques that have been described in research papers. There is, of course, no "best" technique for all purposes. Direct waveform and spectrum synthesis methods are the most general but are difficult to control and require a lot of computing power to implement. The reduced parameter methods are easy to control but can be difficult or impossible to adapt to specific arbitrary requirements. In fact, it is usually advantageous to simply play with the variables to see if a sound adequately close to the desired result can be obtained and then either go from there or try a different technique. Another advantage of reduced parameter methods is that computational effort, at least theoretically, is reduced. However, the theoretical advantage may not necessarily be true in practice due to increased accuracy requirements. In the final analysis, if a synthesizer or program is to rely on just one technique, it should be one with greater generality such as waveform table scanning. A really comprehensive synthesis system would ideally provide for *all* of those discussed in this chapter plus provision for easily adding others as they are discovered.

14
Digital Filtering

In analog synthesis, filtering is used almost exclusively for modification of the severely limited oscillator waveforms available. However, as was just discussed, digital oscillators and tone generators are considerably more flexible and are themselves capable of virtually any spectral effect desired. Nevertheless, tone modification by filtering is still an important technique if for no other reason than convenience. In the digital domain, such modification may be achieved directly by giving each harmonic its own amplitude envelope, thereby simulating the effect of a varying filter. However, use of an actual filter may require far fewer varying parameters to achieve the desired result. This is particularly true if the user has had experience with analog systems because the desired result will usually be thought of in terms of filtering.

Also, some types of sounds require the use of filters in their synthesis. For example, it is difficult to generate "random" noise with a specified frequency spectrum directly; however, one or more filters can easily shape a flat noise spectrum into what is required. Also, in sound modification applications in which one has no direct control over the source material, filtering is the only reasonable way to modify the spectrum. Frequency-sensitive time delay (dispersion) and frequency-sensitive phase shift are functions that are useful in chorus and reverberation simulators and that are normally regarded as "all-pass" filtering. Finally, as we shall see in the next chapter, digital filter ringing is a very convenient method for generating percussive sounds.

Just as a digital oscillator can generate any waveform subject to the constraints of sampling, a digital filter can be designed to have any frequency and phase characteristic desired with only two limitations. One is the high-frequency limit imposed by sampling. For example, a digital high-pass filter cannot be expected to provide a high-pass characteristic up to infinity like an ideal analog filter would. Instead, the response is undefined beyond one-half the sample rate and may be distorted somewhat just below one-half the sample rate. Another limitation is that filters cannot be expected to predict the future! While this may seem obvious, a low-pass filter specification with

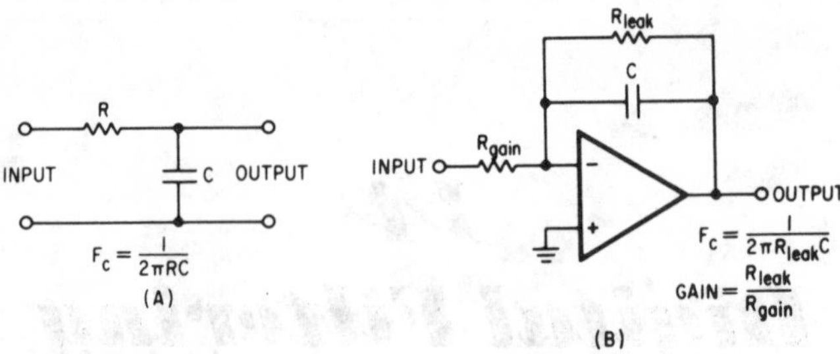

Fig. 14–1. Analog R-C filters. (A) Passive implementation. (B) Active implementation.

zero phase shift at all passband frequencies is asking exactly that. For example, if the filter were presented the first three samples of a low-frequency yet high-amplitude wave, it would have no way of "knowing" whether it really was part of a low-frequency cycle or part of a high-frequency but low-amplitude cycle without further data. Zero phase shift implies that such a decision is made immediately and the samples either pass to the output or are blocked. *Linear* phase shift, which implies *constant time delay* independent of frequency, however, is readily available. Note that for filtering outside of real time this constraint can be effectively overcome by delaying everything else to match.

Digital filtering, like other aspects of digital signal processing, can be highly mathematical. After all, a digital filter is nothing more than a mathematical function that accepts a string of input numbers and provides a string of output numbers. In this chapter, however, digital filters will be discussed as a natural outgrowth of fundamental analog filtering circuits. Later, an intuitive approach will be used to discuss filters with an arbitrary amplitude response shape. It should be noted that many of the filtering concepts mentioned here are equally applicable to analog filtering and some in fact were not mentioned in the sections on analog filtering.

Digital Equivalents of Analog Filters

The simplest analog filters consist of just two components: a resistor and a capacitor. These can be configured in two ways to provide single-pole (6 dB/octave) low-pass or high-pass filters. For the moment, we will concentrate on the low-pass circuit.

Back in Chapter 6, it was shown that the exact same R-C low-pass response could be obtained with an op-amp and an R-C feedback circuit such as in Fig. 14–1. Careful examination of this circuit reveals a standard analog integrator with a "leak" resistor placed across the capacitor. The resistor causes the capacitor charge to leak away and thereby puts an upper limit on the very low frequency and dc gain of the circuit. In fact, the 3-dB attenuation point is the frequency at which the capacitive reactance equals the leak

Input Samples	*Output Samples*
.000	.000
.309	.309
.588	.897
.809	1.706
.951	2.657
1.000	3.657
.951	4.608
.809	5.417
.588	6.005
.309	6.314
.000	6.314
−.309	6.005
−.588	5.417
−.809	4.608
−.951	3.657
−1.000	2.657
−.951	1.706
−.809	.897
−.588	.309
−.309	.000
.000	.000
.309	.309
.588	.397
.809	1.706

(A)

Input Samples	*Output Samples*
.000	.000
.588	.588
.951	1.539
.951	2.490
.588	3.078
.000	3.078
−.588	2.490
−.951	1.539
−.951	.588
−.588	.000
.000	.000
.588	.588
.951	1.539

(B)

Fig. 14–2. Filtering action of a digital integrator. (A) Response to sine wave samples at 0.05 Fs. (B) Response to sine wave samples at 0.1 Fs.

resistance. The dc gain is simply the leak resistance divided by the input-gain-determining resistor.

In the previous chapter, it was mentioned that a digital accumulator acts like an integrator when numbers are repeatedly added to it. This is just as true when the numbers being accumulated are samples of some arbitrary waveform as when they represent a constant "current" in a digital oscillator.

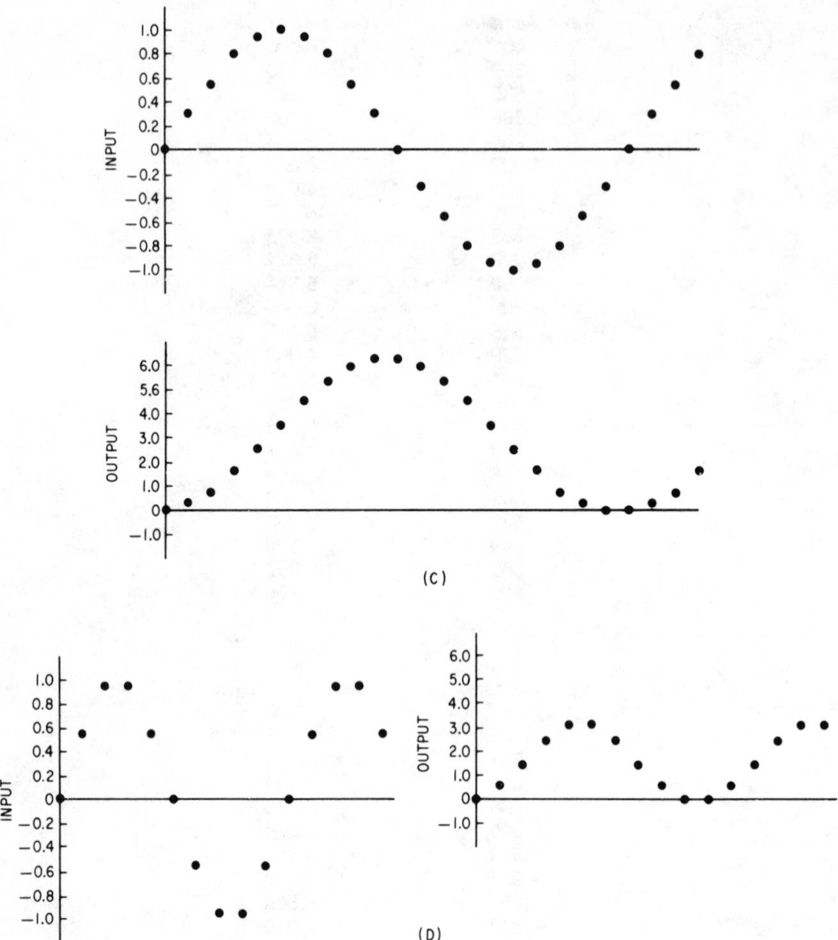

Fig. 14–2. Filtering action of a digital integrator (*cont.*). (C) Graphs for Fig. 14–2 (A). (D) Graphs for Fig. 14–2 (B).

Therefore, inasmuch as an integrator is a type of analog low-pass filter, an accumulator is a type of digital low-pass filter.

As an example, consider the tables and plots of Fig. 14–2. A digital integrator is implemented by simply adding input samples to an accumulator and providing output samples that are the present content of the accumulator. As an experiment, two different strings of sine wave samples are tried. The first string represents a sine wave with a frequency 1/20 of the sample rate, while the second string has a frequency of 1/10 F_s. The amplitudes of both input waves are identical. The resulting tables and graphs give the response of the digital integrator to these strings of samples. Note that the lower frequency wave comes out with approximately twice the amplitude of the higher-frequency wave. Also note that the output wave lags the input wave by 90°. This behavior is just what would be expected of a real analog integrator. Even the dc offset at the output would be expected, since the input was suddenly applied at zero-crossing time. Although not apparent in the figure, the integrator does not contribute any noise or distortion to the signals passing through but may alter the signal-to-noise ratio due to its filtering effect.

Digital R-C Low-Pass Filter

Returning to the leaky integrator equivalent of an R-C low-pass filter, let us see how the same effect can be accomplished digitally. It should be obvious that the magnitude of the leakage current is proportional to the voltage across the capacitor and the direction is such that the capacitor is discharged. Since the capacitor voltage is the same as the output voltage (the capacitor lead connected to the op-amp's inverting input is at virtual ground), the leakage current is proportional to the instantaneous output voltage. This *same* discharging effect can be simulated by *subtracting* a constant *proportion* of the accumulator's content from the accumulator every sample period. In fact, the percentage of accumulator "charge" that should be subtracted is exactly equal to the percentage that would have leaked through the leakage resistor *during one sample period* in the analog filter.

It is well known that the capacitor voltage during discharge follows an inverse exponential curve: $E=E_0\exp(-T/RC)$, where E is the voltage after time T, E_0 is the initial voltage, and R and C are the component values in ohms and farads. Since the cutoff frequency is $1/2\pi RC$, a substitution can be made in the equations, and it is found that $E=E_0\exp(2\pi F_cT)$, where F_c is the cutoff frequency of the filter. Converting the sample period, T, to the sample rate, F_s, makes the final result: $E=E_0\exp(-2\pi F_c/F_s)$. Thus, the proper percentage to subtract from the accumulator each sample period is: $1-\exp(-2\pi F_c/F_s)$ which can be designated K. A BASIC statement for implementing the digital filter then would be:

```
1000 LET A=A-K*A+I
```

where A is the accumulator content, K is the leakage constant, and I is the input sample. This statement is executed for each input sample and successive values of A are the output samples.

One could also simply *multiply* the accumulator contents by $1-K$, which can be called L, and put the product back into the accumulator with the input added in. In BASIC, the result would be:

```
1000 LET A=A*L+I
```

which is about as simple as one can get. Note that L can never be greater than 1.0. If it were, the filter would be unstable and eventually overflow even-floating-point arithmetic. (Imagine, a universe full of energy circulating in this little filter!)

Note that the expression for finding K or L depends on the *ratio* of cutoff frequency to sample frequency. This should have been expected, since the same string of sample values can represent entirely different signal frequencies if the sample rates are different. Thus, it is customary in digital filter work to always specify frequency as a fraction of the sample rate rather than in hertz. Amplitude response plots, therefore, have the frequency axis calibrated from zero (or some lower limit if a log scale) to 0.5.

There is still one undesirable effect in the digital filter. It has a substantial amount of passband gain. In fact, as K is adjusted for lower cutoff frequencies, the gain increases in inverse proportion to K. This is of no immediate concern with the floating-point arithmetic in BASIC but later, when the filter arithmetic is converted to integers for increased speed, it can become a real headache. The amount of dc gain is easily determined by noting that for a constant input of 1.0 the output will rise until the amount removed from the accumulator each sample period via leakage is equal to the amount added via the input. Thus, the dc gain is $1/K$ or $1/(1-L)$. The best way to counteract the gain is to multiply the input samples by the inverse, K, before adding. The final filter statement therefore is:

```
1000 LET A=A*L+K*I
```

Note that two multiplications and one addition are required for each sample processed. By rearranging constants and allowing large numbers in the *accumulator*, one of the multiplications can be eliminated:

```
1000 LET O=K*A
1001 LET A=A-O+I
```

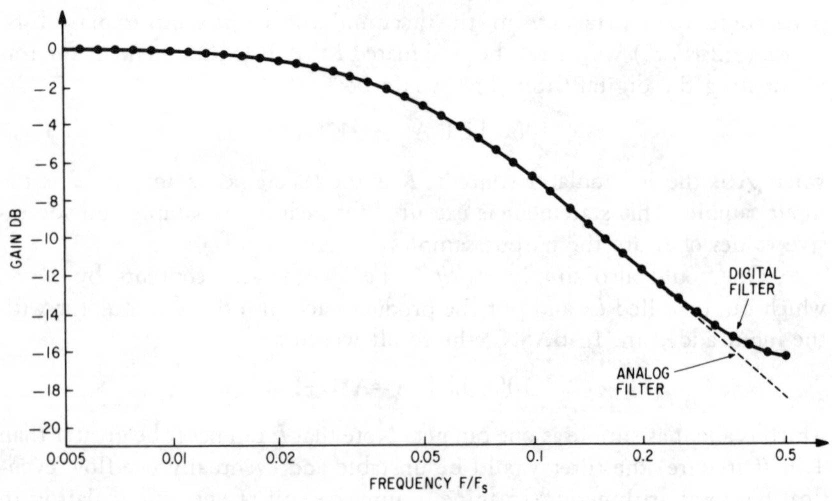

Fig. 14–3. Measured response of digital low-pass filter

where O is now the output of the filter. Although this is certainly slower in BASIC because of the extra statement, it is likely to be much faster in assembly language because of the elimination of a multiplication operation.

At this point one can repeat the Fig. 14–2 experiment with several different frequencies to observe the typical R-C low-pass characteristic, which was done to create Fig. 14–3. Note that near the $0.5F_s$ point the −6 dB/octave cutoff slope decreases somewhat. This is due to actual aliasing of the filter response, since it is not zero at or beyond $F_s/2$. As digital filters are studied, it will be found that their amplitude response always tends to depart from the ideal as the Nyquist frequency is approached.

One can also apply digital square waves to the filter and observe that the output samples show the same kind of leading edge rounding that the analog filter exhibits. In fact, the samples of the square-wave response (step response in general) are *exactly* the same as ADC samples from the response of an analog R-C low-pass filter would be. A digital filter having this property is said to be *impulse invariant*, which for our purposes means that the time domain response is the same as the corresponding analog filter.

Signal Flow Graphs

Although the calculations involved in a digital filter can be represented as equations or program fragments, they do not give a very clear picture of the

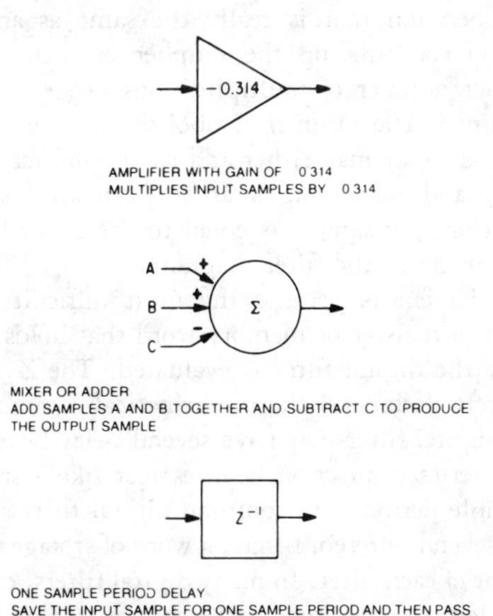

−0.314
AMPLIFIER WITH GAIN OF 0.314
MULTIPLIES INPUT SAMPLES BY 0.314
A
B
C
+
+
−
Σ
MIXER OR ADDER
ADD SAMPLES A AND B TOGETHER AND SUBTRACT C TO PRODUCE THE OUTPUT SAMPLE
z^{-1}
ONE SAMPLE PERIOD DELAY
SAVE THE INPUT SAMPLE FOR ONE SAMPLE PERIOD AND THEN PASS ON TO THE OUTPUT

Fig. 14–4. Symbols used in signal flow graphs

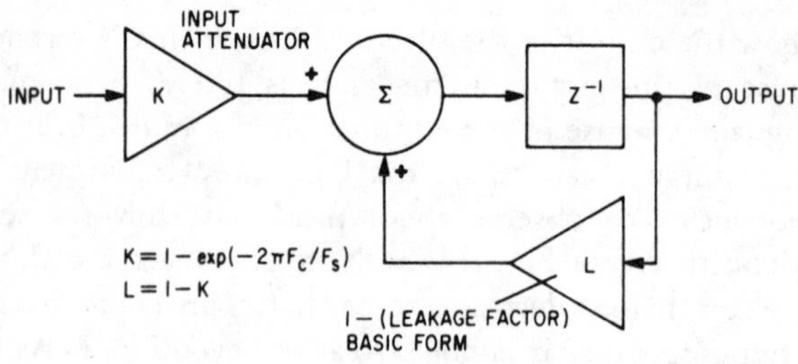

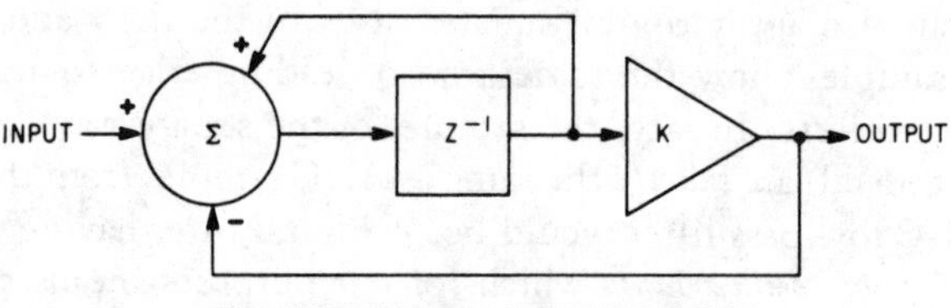

Fig. 14–5. R-C low-pass digital filter diagram

"structure" of the filter. Signal flow graphs give such structural information and at the same time are readily converted into program segments. The three symbols used to construct such graphs are shown in Fig. 14–4 and with them any kind of digital filter can be represented. The amplifier symbol represents a *multiplication* operation that is really the same as an amplifier with a specified gain. By counting up the number of such symbols in a filter diagram, the exact number of multiplications needed to process an input sample is determined. The summer symbol can have any number of inputs, and each individual input may either add to or subtract from the output as denoted by plus and minus signs at the arrowheads. The number of additions/subtractions per sample is equal to the count less one of summer inputs for all summers in the filter diagram.

The delay element is perhaps the most difficult to understand. In essence, the box is a register or memory word that holds a sample value for use the *next* time the digital filter is evaluated. The Z^{-1} symbol inside is optional and merely designates the mathematical meaning of a one sample delay. A typical digital filter may have several delay boxes, often connected in series. Such a series connection behaves just like a shift register that is shifted every sample period. If a common digital filter subroutine is being used to simulate several different filters, a word of storage will be required for each delay element of each filter. In many digital filters, each delay operation is roughly equivalent to a reactive element in an analog filter.

Figure 14–5 shows the R-C low-pass filter drawn in signal flow graph form. Converting such a diagram into a series of program statements consists of two major steps. In the first step, the input sample and the outputs of all

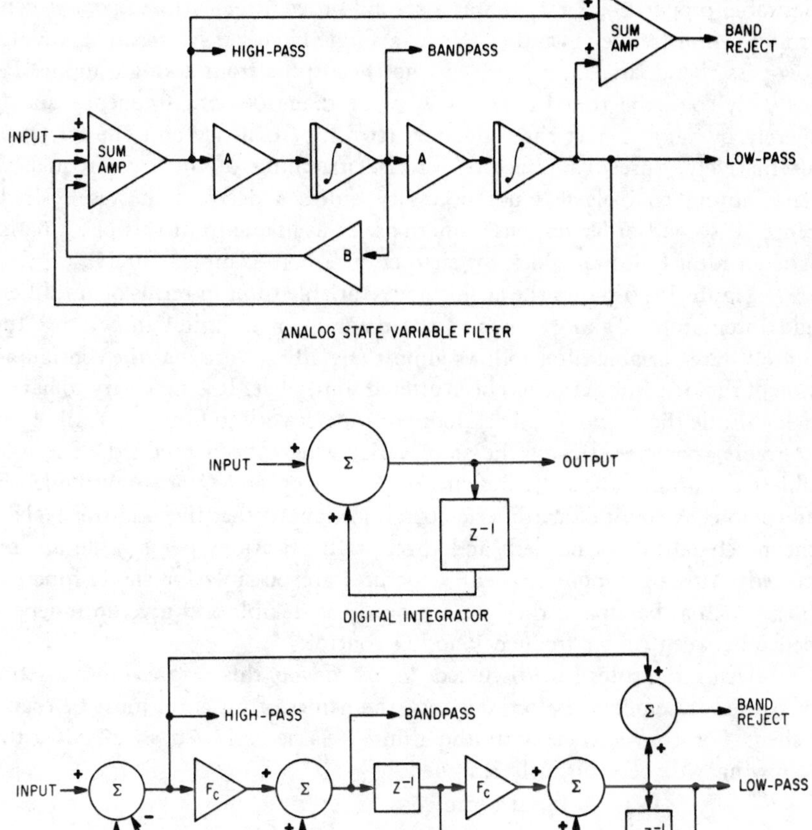

Fig. 14–6. Analog and digital state-variable filter

delays are multiplied by the specified constants and added/subtracted in the indicated ways to produce the output sample and inputs to the delays. In the second step, the delay block inputs that were just computed are stored into the registers corresponding to the delays. When the next input sample is to be processed, the values just stored in the delays become the new delay outputs.

State-Variable Digital Filter

The analogy between analog and digital filters can be extended to cover the state-variable type as well. Recall from Chapter 6 that the state-variable or integrator loop filter was exceedingly versatile because of a number of desirable properties. First, it was a second-order filter with *independent* control of center frequency and *Q*. Next, a single circuit *simultaneously* provides low-pass, bandpass, high-pass, and notch outputs from a single input. Finally, it could be tuned over a very wide range of both frequency and *Q* merely by varying just three resistors (two for frequency and one for *Q*) or alternatively, three gain factors. Precise matching of the two frequency-determining controls was not necessary unless a deep notch was desired. Since all second-order response functions are available from this one circuit, it is an ideal building block for sharper and more complex filters.

Figure 14–6 shows the analog state-variable filter in terms of amplifiers and integrators. Taking this and the diagram of a digital integrator, the digital state-variable filter follows almost trivially. (Note that the configuration of the first integrator has been altered somewhat. It is necessary to have a delay inside the overall feedback loop for the network to function.) All of the desirable characteristics of the state variable have been retained. The four different outputs are still present and frequency and *Q* are independently adjustable. A count of arithmetic operations reveals that five additions (six if the notch output is needed) and three multiplications per sample are required. Although more efficient structures are possible for single-function filters such as bandpass, they are not nearly as flexible and give up independence between center frequency and *Q* control.

Using the rules just discussed, let us convert this diagram into a series of BASIC statements. Before starting, the names of variables must be established. For convenience with the limited names allowed in BASIC, the following will be arbitrarily assigned:

I	Input sample
L	Low-pass output sample
B	Bandpass output sample
H	High-pass output sample
N	Notch output sample
F1	Frequency control parameter
Q1	*Q* control parameter
D1	Delay associated with bandpass output
D2	Delay associated with low-pass output

The first task is to compute all of the outputs. The sequence of computation is important in order to minimize the statements and to avoid having a variable depend on itself in the same time period. Careful examination of the diagram reveals that if the low-pass output is evaluated first, everything else falls into place. Thus, the first step is accomplished by the following statements:

```
1000 LET L=D2+F1*D1
1001 LET H=I-L-Q1*D1
1002 LET B=F1*H+D1
1003 LET N=H+L
```

Next the inputs to the delays must be computed and stored:

```
1004 LET D1=B
1005 LET D2=L
```

This completes the computation for the sample period. Note that two statements may be saved by realizing that the current content of the two delays is the same as the bandpass and low-pass outputs.

Tuning Relationships

In order to use the filter, it is necessary to know the relationship between the frequency- and Q-determining factors, $F1$ and $Q1$, and the corresponding actual physical parameters. The first logical step is to look at these relationships in the analog filter. Referring back to Fig. 6–25, the Q of the state-variable filter is seen to be simply the inverse of the R_Q gain path from the bandpass output through the input summing amplifier to the high-pass output. The same behavior can also be expected from the digital state-variable. Thus, $Q1=1/Q$ which has a useful range from 2, corresponding to a Q of 0.5, to zero which corresponds to infinite Q.

In fact, infinite Q is a reasonable situation with most digital filters. When excited by a pulse, the infinite Q filter will ring forever with a perfect digital sine wave neither gaining nor losing amplitude for as long as one wishes to let the program run! Actually, the roundoff errors in integer and some floating-point computer arithmetic cancel out each cycle so that there is no net accumulation of error. Thus, a ringing infinite Q digital filter is one way to obtain high-quality sine waves without interpolating in a sine table. Only two multiplies and two adds per sample generated are required, since $Q1$ is zero and there is no input. Thus, it is a highly efficient method as well.

The center frequency relation is a little more difficult and a little less ideal. For the analog state-variable filter, it was given as $F=1/(2\pi R_F C)$ where R_F was the integrator input resistor and C was the feedback capacitor. It is interesting to note that at this frequency the gain of each analog integrator is 1.0, since $R=X_C=1/(2\pi FC)$. Thus, we would expect that resonance would occur in the digital equivalent at the frequency at which the integrator gain cancels the loss due to the $F1$ amplifiers thereby producing a net path gain of 1.0. The gain of the digital integrator alone is approximately $F_s/2\pi F$, where F is the test frequency and F_s is the sample rate. Thus, the frequency of unity integrator gain is $F_s/2\pi$. Factoring in the F1 parameter, the unity-gain frequency becomes $F=F1F_s/2\pi$ and conversely $F1=2\pi F/F_s$, where F is the filter's center frequency.

Unfortunately, this relationship is not exact with the error getting worse as the center frequency approaches one-half the sample rate. The root cause is the digital integrators whose gain at high frequencies is greater than it should be. This is one manifestation of amplitude response aliasing that

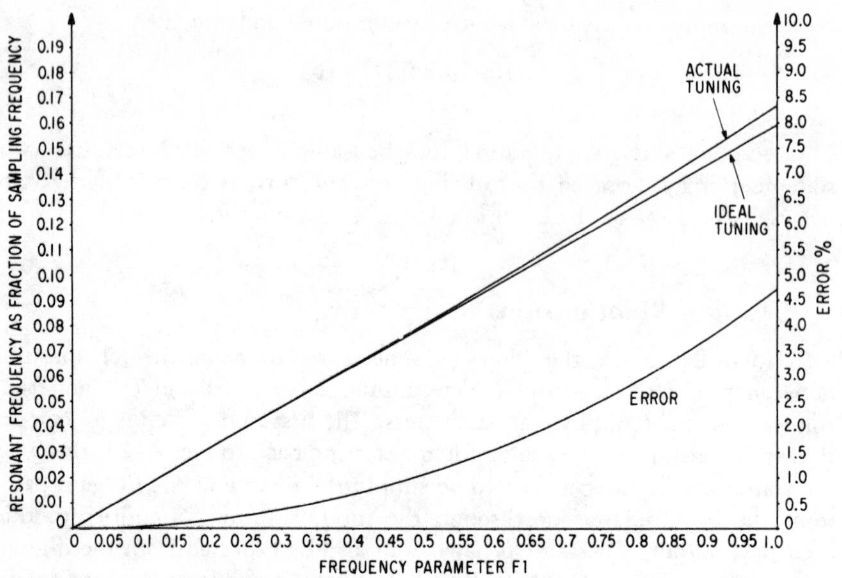

Fig. 14–7. Tuning error of digital state-variable filter

was mentioned earlier. Figure 14–7 gives an idea of the magnitude of the error for different center frequencies. For use at less than one-tenth the sample rate, which is 5 kHz in a 50-ks/s system, the tuning error is about 1.6% or about one-quarter semitone.

One can derive a frequency correction factor, however. The ideal gain of the digital integrators is $F_s/2\pi F$ but the actual gain is greater than this by a factor of $\pi F/\sin(\pi F)$. The frequency correction factor, therefore, is the reciprocal or $\sin(\pi F)/\pi F$. This factor varies from 1.0 at low frequencies to 0.6366 at one-half the sample rate. When combined with the approximate center frequency formula, the result becomes: $F1=2\sin(\pi F/F_s)$, where F is the center frequency and $F1$ is the exact value of the frequency parameter for that center frequency. Since the correction is relatively small and a fairly smooth monotonically rising curve, a correction table with linear interpolation between the entries is an alternative to evaluating a sine function. In fact, one could simply use the sine table that is almost certainly incorporated somewhere in the synthesis program that is using the digital filter.

Multiple Feedback Digital Filters

With active analog filters, there are circuits available that perform a specific low-pass, bandpass, or high-pass second order filtering function with fewer components than the state-variable type. In exchange for their simplicity, Q and center frequency are tied together and related to circuit components by complex, usually nonlinear equations. Furthermore, the circuits make great demands on the amplifier and component characteristics and consequently are limited to low Q factors. It seems only proper that digital filters with the same mix of characteristics exist.

Figure 14–8 shows low-pass, bandpass, and high-pass versions of the multiple-feedback digital filter along with design equations and program segments. Like their analog counterparts, the best application is in fixed filter banks for spectrum shaping. However, they can be retuned as often as desired by recomputing the constants. Note that for low center frequency and high Q that the A and B constants get quite close to 2.0 and 1.0, respectively. Small errors in the constants can therefore have a great effect on the filter's characteristics. It is important to realize, however, that only the amplitude response curve is distorted; no harmonic or intermodulation distortion is ever added to the signal because of inaccurate multiplying constants.

The alert reader may have noticed a degree of similarity among the various multiple-feedback designs. There exists in fact a single digital filter structure that can be used to implement *any* second order filtering function merely by altering the constants; something difficult if not impossible to do with analog circuitry. The structure in Fig. 14–9 is called a *cannonical* second order filter because of its generality. The structure requires only five multiplications and four additions per sample and uses just two storage locations.

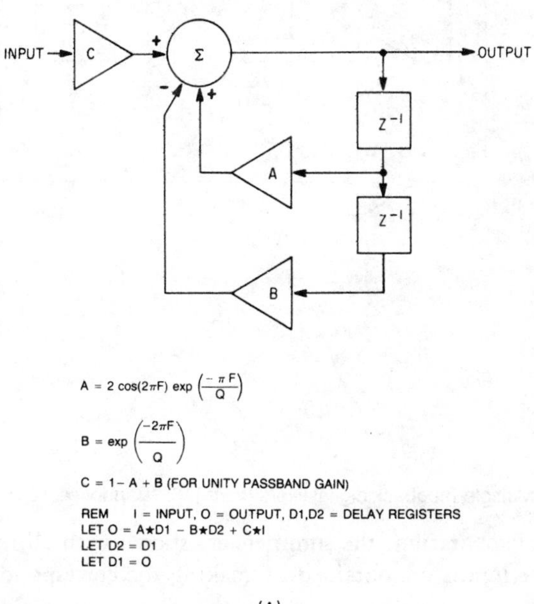

Fig. 14–8. Multiple-feedback digital filters. (A) Low-pass.

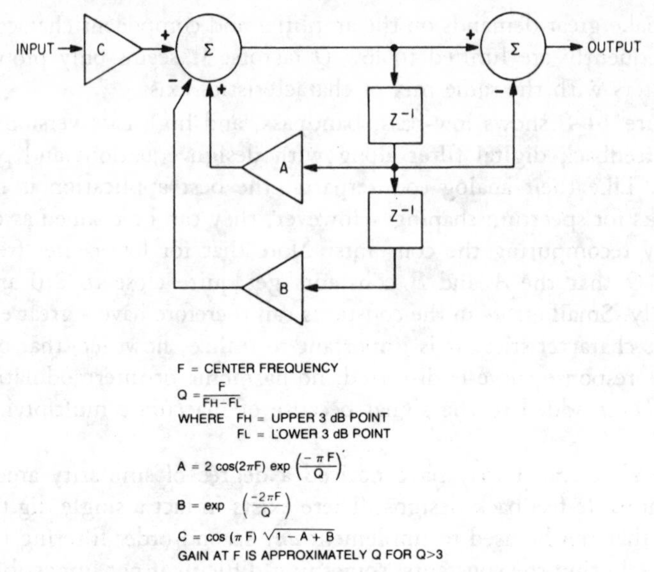

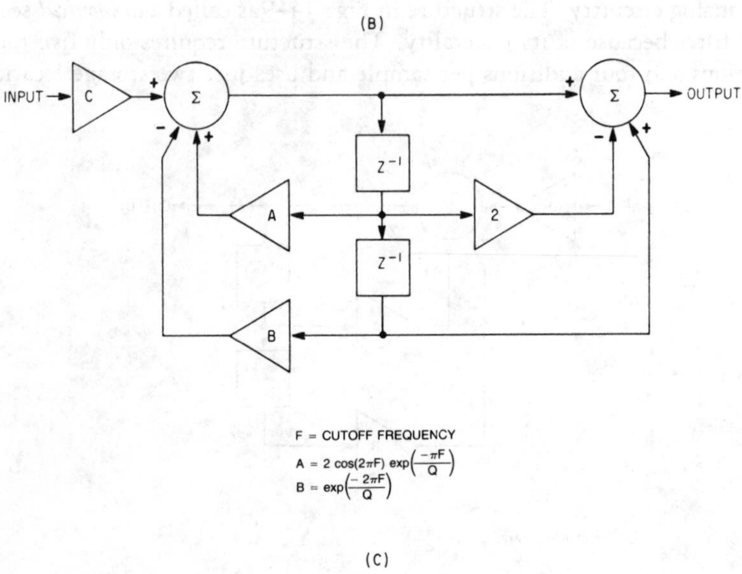

Fig. 14–8. Multiple-feedback digital filters (*cont.*). (B) Bandpass. (C) High-pass.

For ease of implementation, the summers are shown with all inputs positive acting; negative inputs are obtained by making the corresponding constants negative.

Examination reveals two *feedback* paths and two *feedforward* paths. Generally, the feedback paths are responsible for any peaks or poles in the

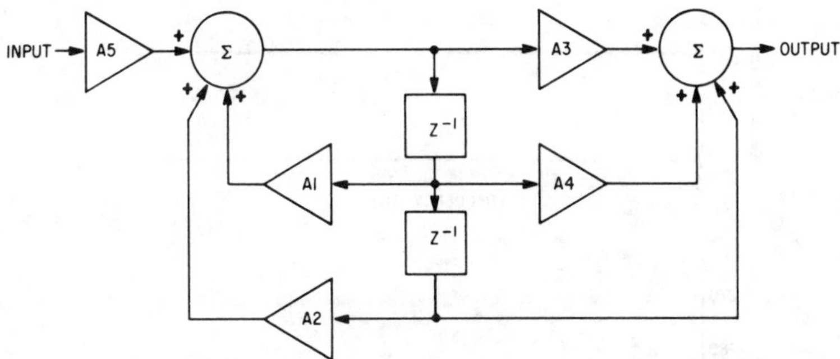

Fig. 14–9. Cannonical second order digital filter

amplitude response curve, while the feedforward paths cause response dips or zeroes. Note that the same design equations for the filters given earlier can be applied to the cannonical form with any unused constants set to zero. Because of its generality, this structure is ideal for use in a general-purpose filtering subroutine or hardware implementation as a digital filter module.

All-Pass Digital Filter

One important type of filter that has not yet been discussed is the *all-pass* filter. As its name implies, it is not a frequency-discriminating filter and in fact passes all frequencies equally well with unity gain. Instead, its purpose is frequency-sensitive *phase shift*. All filters shift phase in varying amounts as a natural consequence of frequency discrimination, but the all-pass filter exhibits phase shift alone. Consequently, an all-pass network can be used to correct for the phase shift of a regular filter without disturbing its amplitude response. In synthesis applications, however, it is used to introduce a time-varying, frequency-sensitive phase shift to otherwise stationary sounds, thereby imparting added richness to the sound.

Before looking at the filter itself, the relation between phase shift and time delay should be understood. Either parameter can be plotted as a function of frequency as in Fig. 14–10. One type of all-pass filter is a simple delay line. As shown in Fig. 14–10A, an ideal delay line has *constant* delay independent of frequency. Its phase shift, however, is a *linear* function of frequency as shown in Fig. 14–10B. This can be explained by noting that at very low frequencies the 500-μsec delay is only a small fraction of a cycle. At 500 Hz, which is a 2,000-μsec period, the 500-μsec delay becomes a quarter cycle phase lag or −90°. At 1 kHz, the delay becomes a half cycle and so on. At higher frequencies, the phase-shift magnitude continues to increase, but it is customary to plot the principal value of the shift. Thus, the curve shifts up to 180° leading and continues its decline from there.

In mathematical terms, the delay curve is the derivative (proportional to slope) of the phase curve or, conversely, the phase curve is the integral

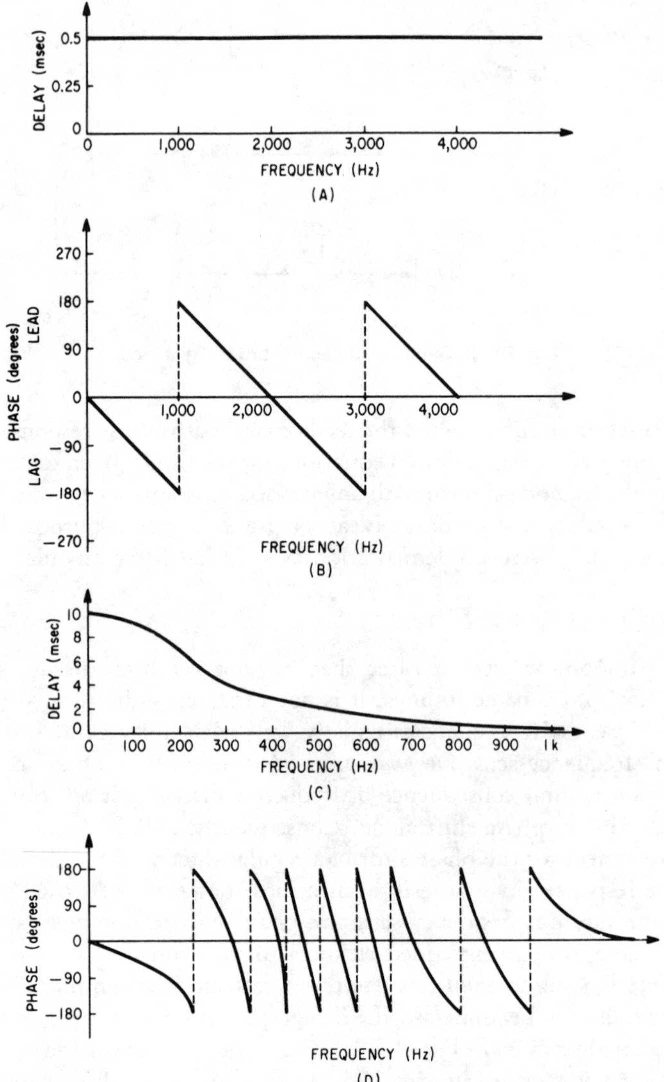

Fig. 14–10. Phase and delay graphs. (A) Delay versus frequency of 500-μsec delay line. (B) Phase versus frequency of 500-μsec delay line. (C) Delay of a highly dispersive filter. (D) Phase of a highly dispersive filter.

(proportional to area under a curve) of the delay curve. As a result, only one curve is needed to fully characterize the delay/phase behavior of the filter.

For musical purposes, the most useful all-pass filters exhibit nonlinear phase shifts and therefore time delays that vary with frequency. This means that a sharp transient, which contains a wide range of frequency components, will exit from the filter with the frequency components separated and

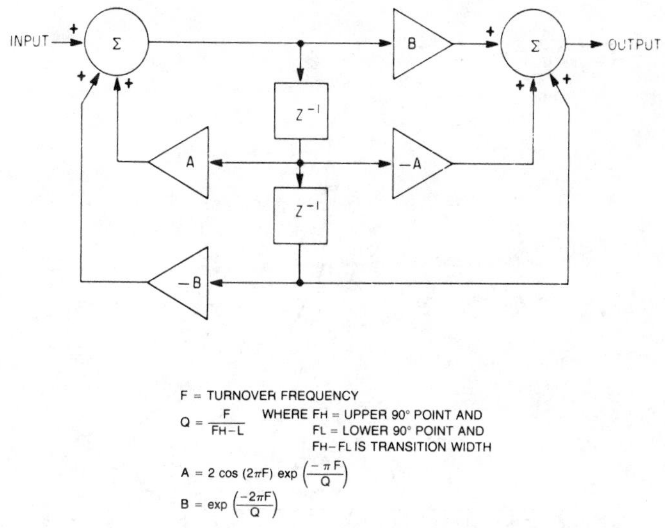

Fig. 14–11. Digital all-pass filter

smeared out in time. The effect is called *dispersion* and is quite analogous to the effect of a prism on white light. Figures 14–10C and D illustrate an extreme case of dispersion. Usually, high frequencies are delayed least, which means that the transient is converted into a quickly descending frequency sweep having a "thunk"-like sound. Such an extreme case gives the auditory illusion of the sound being sent over a 100-foot stretched wire and in fact is heard frequently on long-distance telephone circuits. Such a large amount of dispersion requires many filter sections in combination to emulate.

Figure 14–11 shows a second order all-pass filter that is a useful building block. Like all other second order digital filters, it is an adaptation of the cannonical form; however, due to symmetry of the constants and unity gain, three of the five multiplications can be bypassed. Examination of the constants reveals that the feedforward and feedback paths are completely complementary. Essentially, the zeroes cancel the poles to produce a flat amplitude response, but since phase shifts add rather than multiply, the frequency-sensitive phase shift is reinforced.

The phase and delay characteristics of the basic second order all-pass filter section are shown in Fig. 14–12. At low frequencies, the phase shift is near zero and at high frequencies it is 360° with a monotonic, though nonlinear, transition between. Two parameters describe the filter. One is the "turnover frequency" at which the phase shift is 180°. The other is called the "transition width" and is related to the sharpness of the transition from 0° to 360° shift, quite analogous to the Q of a bandpass filter. The edges of the transition zone are where the phase shift is 90° and 270°. The delay curve

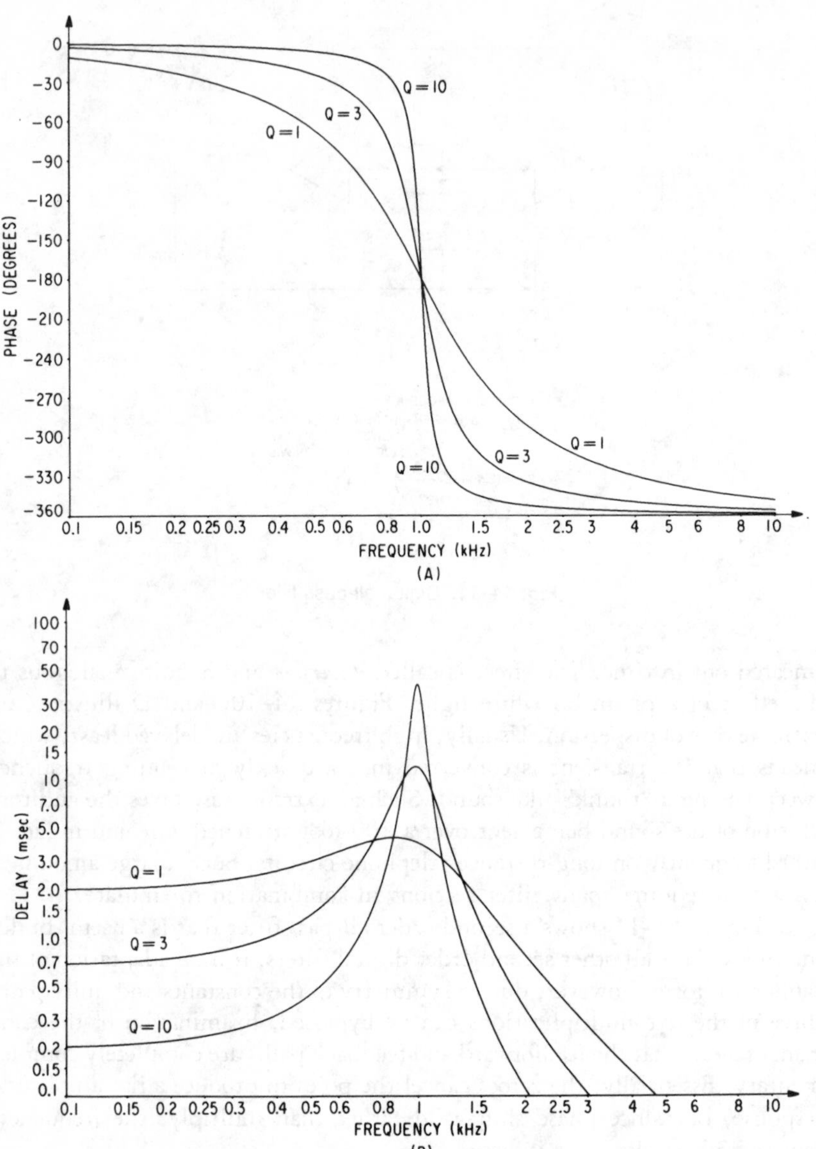

Fig. 14–12. (A) Phase response of two-pole all-pass filter. (B) Delay response.

shows near zero delay at the frequency extremes and maximum delay at the turnover frequency.

More complex phase and delay characteristics may be created by cascading all-pass sections. The dispersive filter mentioned earlier may be simulated by cascading a number of all-pass sections with successively higher turnover frequencies. Since the maximum time delay is inversely related to the turnover frequency (at a constant "Q" value), the delay of the cascade is inversely proportional to frequency.

The audible effect of fixed all-pass filters is generally subtle, but dynamic variation of the filter parameters can have a dramatic effect. Consider, for example, a cascade of four all-pass filters each with the same turnover frequency and a relatively broad transition width. Next, assume a 1-kHz sine wave tone fed through the filters. If the filter turnover frequencies are high, such as 10 kHz, the tone will be phase shifted very little. If the turnover frequency is allowed to rapidly decrease, the tone will experience a constantly increasing phase shift up to a maximum of 1,440° or four cycles when the turnover frequency has decreased to 100 Hz or so.

During the turnover frequency transition, however, the tone coming out of the filter had a lower instantaneous frequency! Reversing the sweep will produce a momentary higher frequency. The speed of the transition determines the peak frequency deviation. If the signal entering the filter has numerous harmonics, the temporary frequency shift will "ripple" audibly through the harmonics as the turnover frequency shifts. By driving the turnover frequency parameter with a low-frequency periodic or random signal, a chorus-like effect can be obtained.

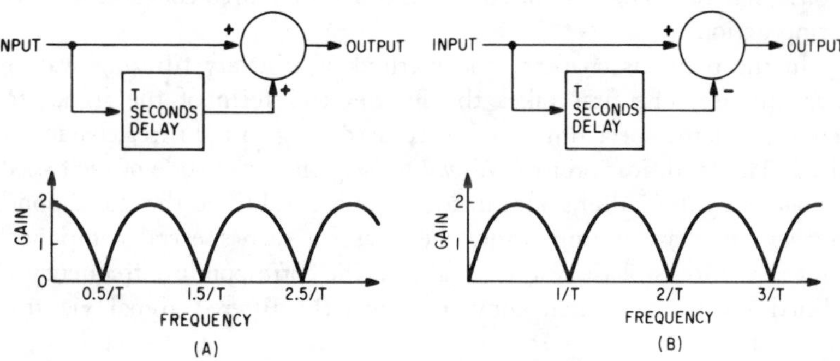

Fig. 14–13. Cosine (A) and sine (B) comb filters

Digital Notch Filters

Although a standard notch filter response can be created by suitable setting of the cannonical digital filter constants, other more interesting and useful variations are possible. The comb filter mentioned in Chapter 2 is one of these that is very simple to produce in a digital synthesis system. The filter is constructed by splitting the signal into two paths, inserting a time delay in one of the paths, and mixing the signals together in equal proportions as shown in Fig. 14–13. The filtering effect is produced by phase cancellation between the delayed and undelayed signals. At very low frequencies, the delay line in Fig. 14–13A has essentially no effect on the phase of the signal so it reinforces the undelayed signal in the mixer. When the frequency increases such that the delay introduces a 180° phase shift, the delayed signal cancels the undelayed signal in the mixer producing zero output. Higher frequencies are passed in varying amounts until the phase shift through the delay reaches 3 × 180° which produces another cancellation and so forth. The filter in Fig. 14–13B works the same way except that the first notch is at zero frequency.

If the delay time is slowly varied while filtering a broadband signal source, the distinctive sound of flanging is produced. In a digital synthesis system, the delay is very easily produced with a small memory buffer, the size of which determines the delay. Such a technique can only give delays that are a multiple of the sample period, which results in some choppiness in the flanging effect. This may be overcome, at some sacrifice in noise level, by interpolating between adjacent samples at the end of the simulated delay line to provide essentially continuous delay variation.

Filters with an Arbitrary Response

One of the advantages of digital signal processing is that *any* filter response can be obtained in a straightforward manner. Furthermore, the response may be changed as often and as much as desired concurrent with the filtering action.

In the previous chapter, one method of arbitrary filtering was mentioned. In use, one first takes the Fourier transform of the signal to be filtered. Next the spectrum is modified according to the filter characteristic desired. The modification involves *multiplying* the amplitude of each spectral component by the filter's amplitude response value at the corresponding frequency. If phase is important, the phase of each spectral component is *added* to the filter's phase response value at the corresponding frequency. The modified spectrum is then converted into the filtered signal via inverse transformation.

Of course, with the FFT, the continuous stream of samples to be filtered must be broken into records, processed, and the results spliced together again. This indeed can be accomplished without the distortions that were encountered in direct FFT synthesis, but the process is complex and can be time consuming. Another method that works continuously, sample by sample, is called *direct convolution*. With this method, one can write a subroutine that accepts a table of numbers describing the filter's *time domain* response along with *individual* input samples to produce individual output samples. The routine is exceedingly simple and can be quite efficient when written in assembly language or implemented in hardware.

Before describing the algorithm, it is necessary to become familiar with a filter's *impulse response* because that is the table of numbers used by the filter subroutine. The transient response of high-fidelity components is usually characterized by noting their response to square waves. If the square-wave frequency is low, the result is essentially the step response of the component. Although few manfacturers care to admit it, hi-fi components act like bandpass filters and the step response reveals a lot (in fact, everything) about the "filter's" characteristics.

The same idea applies to the impulse response, but the test signal is a very narrow pulse rather than a voltage step. In theory the pulse should have zero width, infinite amplitude, and finite energy content. In practice, an analog impulse has a width that is small in comparison to the fastest responding element of the filter under consideration and a height small enough to avoid distortion. In a digital system, the impulse is quite simple: just a single 1.0 sample surrounded by a sea of zeroes. The spectrum of an isolated

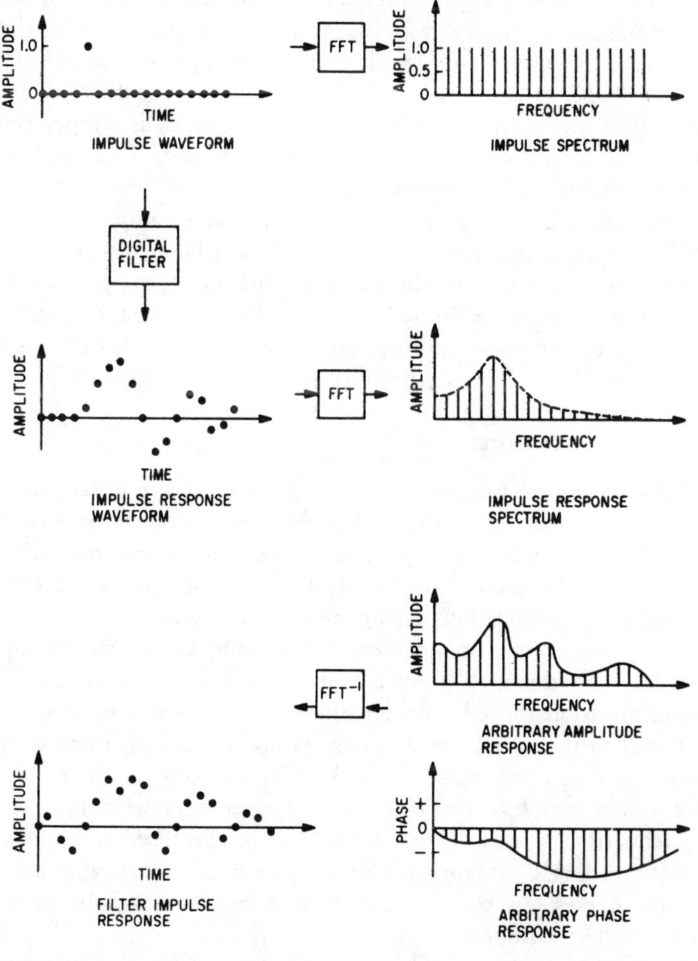

Fig. 14–14. Impulse response relations

impulse is equally simple: an infinite number of frequency components all of equal amplitude and all with zero phase angles.

The filter's output in response to an impulse input tells everything about its amplitude and phase response but in an easy to use form. Since the input spectrum is flat and has zero phase, the output spectrum will *directly* represent the amplitude and phase response of the filter under test! This means that the characteristics of a digital filter can be plotted merely by taking the Fourier transform of its impulse response. This, in fact, is how many of the filter response curves in this book were plotted. Conversely any amplitude and phase response may be inverse Fourier transformed to get the corresponding impulse response. These are very important points and are illustrated in Fig. 14–14.

If two widely separated impulses are fed to a filter, one would expect to see two copies of the impulse response. If the first impulse is twice the height of the second, the first response will have twice the amplitude as well but the same basic shape. If the impulses are moved closer together, they start to overlap. Since filters are linear, the composite output is simply the point-by-point sum of the responses due to each impulse. This applies to any number of impulses at any spacing.

Although it is already being taken for granted, sampled analog signals are really strings of impulses, the height of each being proportional to the sample values. According to the previous paragraph, the output of a filter receiving such impulses as input is equal to the sum of the responses to each individual sample impulse as illustrated in Fig. 14–15. This then is the crux of direct convolution digital filtering.

Implementation

The first step in implementing the algorithm is to obtain the impulse response in usable form. For digital filtering, *samples* of the impulse response are needed. The samples must be taken at the same sample rate as the signal to be processed. If the rate is different, all filter response frequencies will be altered in direct proportion to the ratio of the sample rates. Any stable impulse response will be bounded on both sides by zeroes, which can then be discarded. Unfortunately, most responses do not suddenly cut off, so a truncation decision must be made. Since the computation time is directly proportional to the number of response samples retained, there is an incentive to retain as few as possible. Very broadly speaking, if all of the response samples omitted are less than 0.01 of the largest response sample, then only filter attenuation beyond 40 dB is likely to be disturbed to any significant degree. Accordingly, retaining samples down to 0.001 will not disturb attenuation curves less than 60 dB. In any case, the impulse response becomes a string of numbers.

The calculations involved are quite simple. Assuming that some data has already gone through the filter, the Ith output sample is equal to the Ith

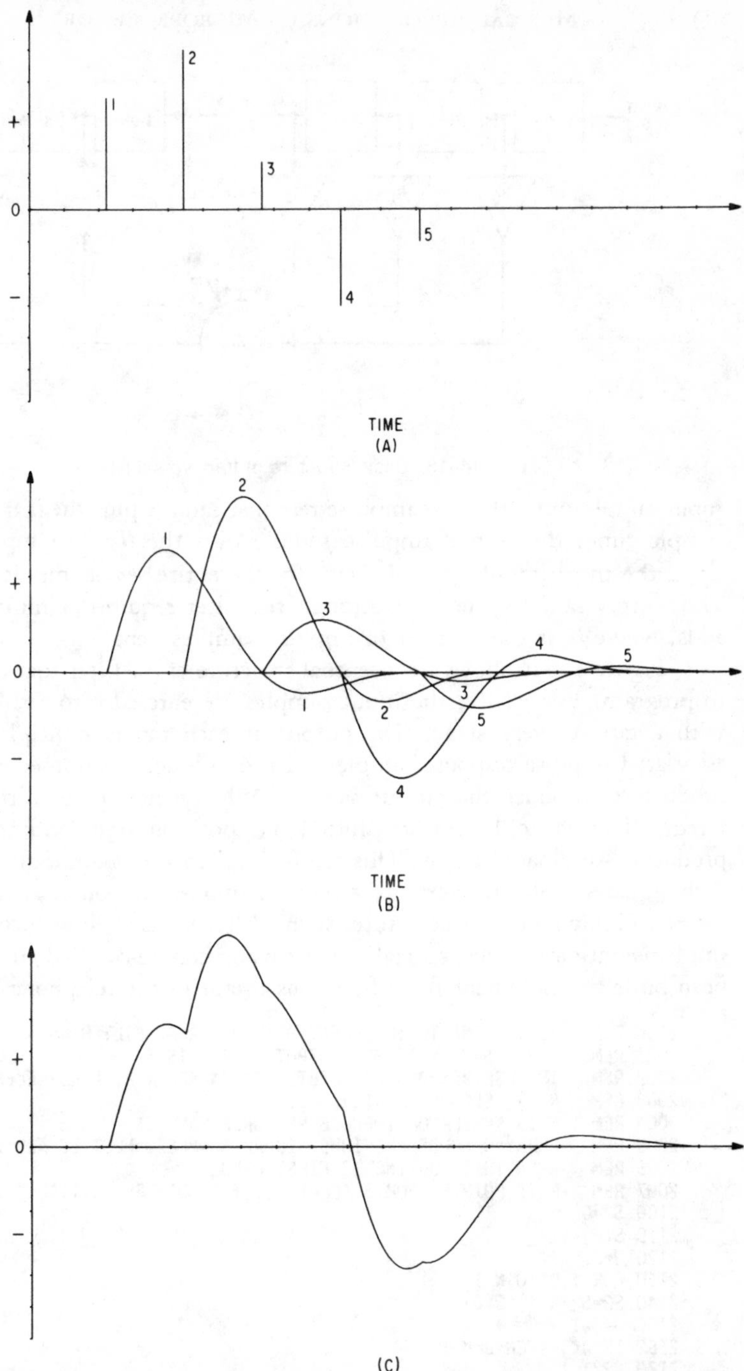

Fig. 14–15. How filter impulse responses combine to produce an overall response. (A) Input impulses. (B) Individual impulse responses. (C) Sum of impulse responses.

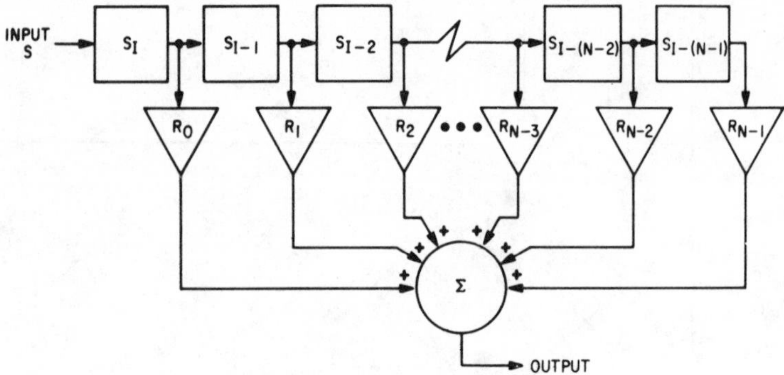

Fig. 14–16. Basic structure of transversal filter

input sample times the first impulse response sample plus the $(I-1)$th input sample times the second impulse sample plus the $(I-2)$th input sample times the third impulse sample, etc. for the entire set of impulse samples. Thus, every sample processed through the filter requires N multiplies and adds, where N is the number of impulse samples kept.

Figure 14–16 shows a conceptual structure of the filter that is very easy to program. Essentially, the input samples are entered into a shift register with a tap at every stage. The output at each tap is multiplied by the associated impulse response sample and the product is summed with other products to produce the output sample. When a new input sample is entered, all of the old ones are shifted one position right and the sum of products is evaluated again. This is often called a *transversal* filter because each signal sample traverses the tabulated impulse response. Because of its simple, highly repetitive structure, such a filter lends itself well to hardware implementation. In fact, specialized ICs using charge-coupled circuitry have been built to implement filter functions useful in the telephone industry.

```
2000 REM   SUBROUTINE TO IMPLEMENT A TRANSVERSAL FILTER
2001 REM   INPUT SAMPLE IS S1, OUTPUT SAMPLE IS S2
2002 REM   IMPULSE RESPONSE OF FILTER IN IN ARRAY R, FIRST ELEMENT IN
2003 REM   R(0), SECOND IN R(1),....
2004 REM   N IS NUMBER OF IMPULSE RESPONSE SAMPLES
2005 REM   ARRAY S HOLDS PREVIOUS SIGNAL SAMPLES, MUST BE ALL ZEROES
2006 REM   WHEN THIS ROUTINE IS FIRST USED
2007 REM   P IS POINTER FOR S ARRAY, IT TOO MUST BE INITIALLY ZERO
2100 S2=0
2110 S(P)=S1
2120 J=P
2130 FOR I=0 TO N-1
2140 S2=S2+R(I)*S(J)
2150 J=J-1
2160 IF J<0 THEN J=N-1
2170 NEXT I
2180 P=P+1
2190 IF P=N THEN P=0
2200 RETURN
```

Fig. 14–17. Transversal filter subroutine in BASIC

When programming according to the diagram, actually shifting the data is very inefficient. Instead, a *pointer* to the current sample is maintained and references to stored previous sample values are made relative to the pointer. Figure 14–17 is a program in BASIC that implements the transversal filter. The *R* array contains the impulse response, the *S* array contains previous signal samples, and *N* is the number of impulse response samples. The input sample is *S*1 while the output sample is *S*2.

In order to make maximum use of the algorithm, it is helpful to know some additional impulse response properties. First, if the filter has zero or linear phase its impulse response will always be perfectly symmetrical. If such a phase response is acceptable, the number of multiplications needed per sample can be essentially cut in half by adding the symmetrical parts together *before* multiplication as shown in Fig. 14–18.

There are limits to the technique too. Filters with low-frequency discrimination, sharp cutoff slopes, or narrow peaks and dips in their amplitude response tend to have long duration impulse responses and therefore will require a lot of calculation. Thus, a simple bandpass or low-pass function is better performed with one of the previous techniques. On the other hand, if the amplitude response has a lot of peaks and dips, only the narrowest or

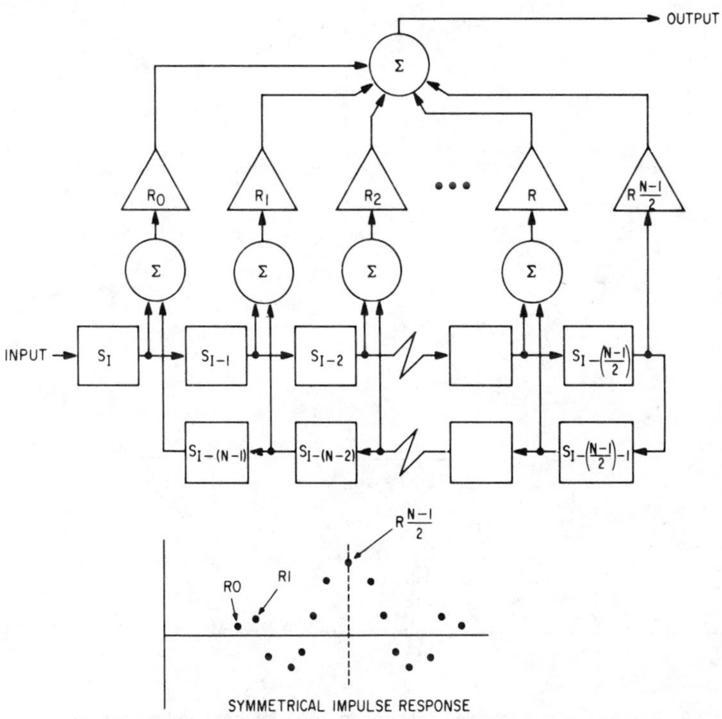

Fig. 14–18. Simplification of Fig. 14–16 for symmetrical impulse response

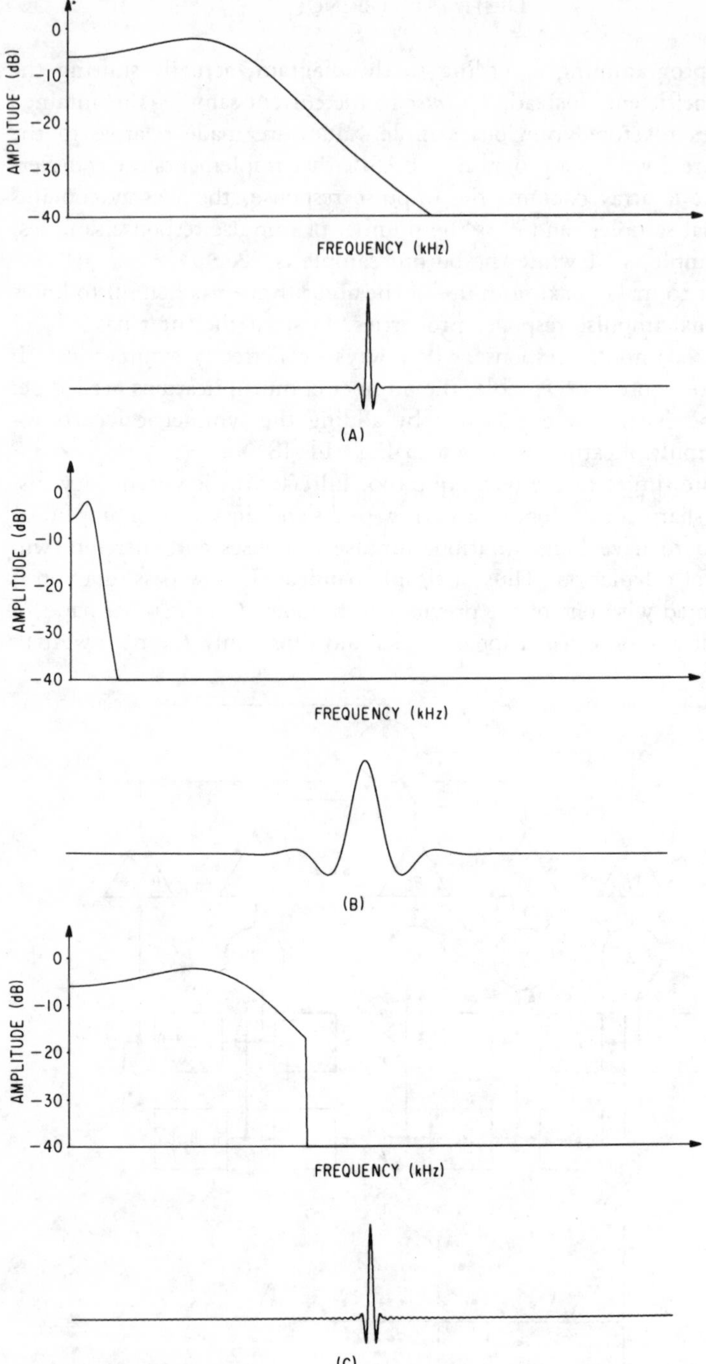

Fig. 14–19. Some example impulse responses. (A) Well-behaved response. (B) Low-frequency feature lengthens response. (C) Sudden cutoff lengthens response.

lowest frequency "feature" significantly affects the duration of the impulse response. This means that the other features essentially ride along free. Figure 14–19 shows several response curves and their associated impulse responses, which should aid in understanding these properties. Note in particular that, while an ideal low-pass or bandpass filter characteristic can be achieved with this technique, the extremely long, slowly decaying impulse response makes its application impractical. Any attempt to shorten the response by truncation or smoothing off destroys the ideal cutoff shape. Because of the long impulse response, the FFT filtering method should be used when such idealized filtering functions are needed.

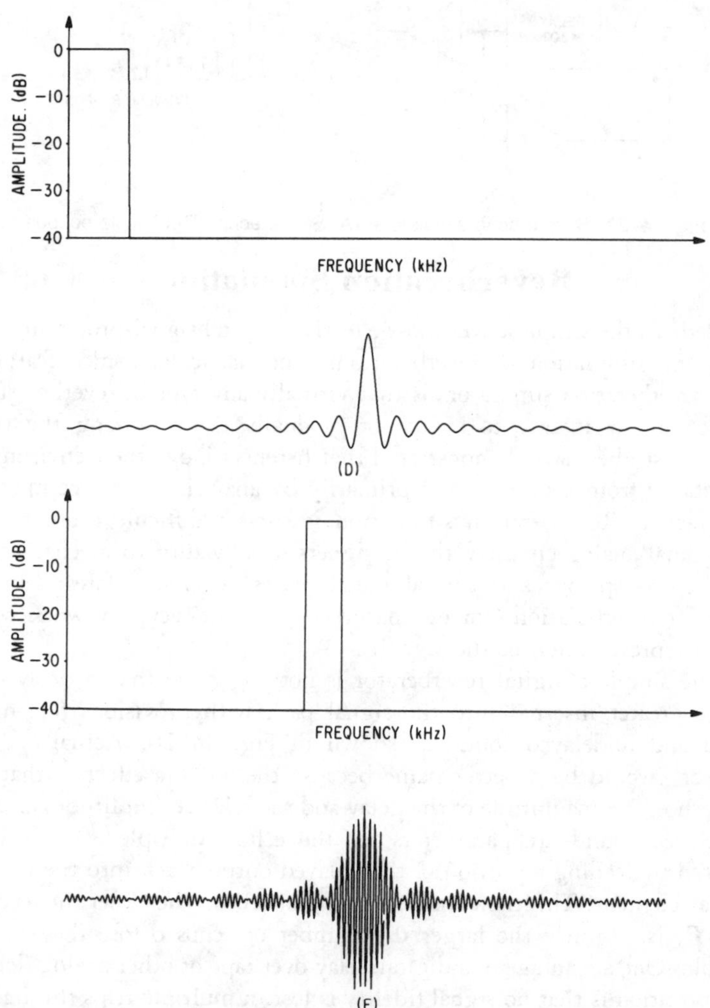

Fig. 14–19. Some example impulse responses (*cont.*). (D) Ideal low-pass filter response. (E) Ideal bandpass response.

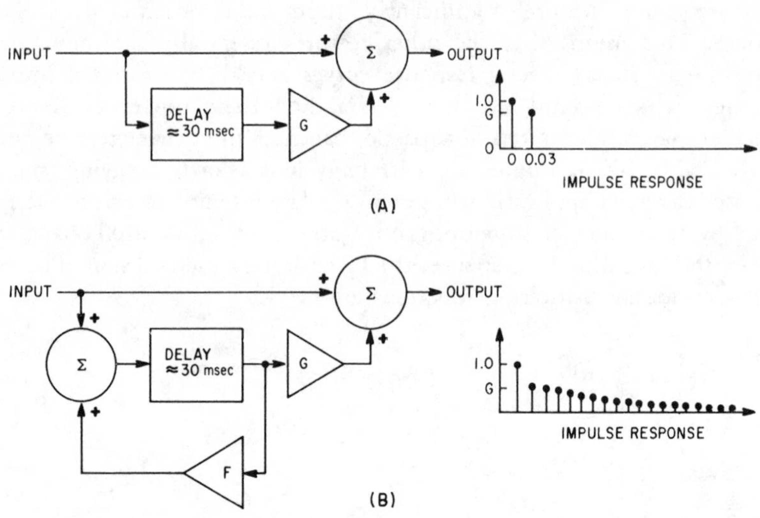

Fig. 14–20. Simple echo simulators. (A) Single echo. (B) Multiple echoes.

Reverberation Simulation

Perhaps the simplest, yet most effective, digital signal-processing function is the simulation of reverberation. One particularly nice feature of digital reverberation simulators is that virtually any type of reverberation is possible, and it is easy to switch or gradually evolve among the types. Perceptual studies have demonstrated that listeners judge their environment and distance from sound sources primarily by analyzing the accompanying reverberation. Reverberation simulation is such a difficult problem with conventional analog circuitry that designers usually turn to mechanical devices such as springs and special metal plates. Even the latest "analog" devices for reverberation (analog charge coupled ICs) actually work with a sampled representation of the signal.

The simplest digital reverberator is nothing more than a delay of 30 msec or greater inserted into the signal path with provisions for mixing delayed and undelayed sound as shown in Fig. 14–20. Actually, "echo simulator" would be a better name because the audible effect is that of a single echo. The magnitude of the delay and the relative amplitudes of direct and delayed sound are parameters for the echo. Multiple echos may be simulated by feeding a portion of the delayed output back into the input of the delay element. This then creates a string of echos. The closer the feedback factor, F, is to unity the larger the number of echos before they become inaudible. One advantage of a digital delay over tape or other analog delay in this application is that no signal fidelity is lost in multiple trips through the delay line. Thus, feedback factors close to 1.0 are possible without fear of some minor amplitude response peak exceeding unity feedback and causing oscillation.

Even with a perfect delay line, the string of equally spaced echos produced is not at all like concert hall reverberation. In an empty concert hall a clap of the hands produces not a series of echos but what sounds like white noise with a smoothly decreasing amplitude. The amplitude decrease approximates an inverse exponential function, which if plotted in decibels would be a constant number of decibels per second. The rate of decrease is generally specified by stating the time required for a 60-dB reduction in reverberation amplitude. This figure is used because under normal circumstances the reverberation has become inaudible at that point. Typical reverberation times for concert halls are in the 1.5-sec to 3-sec range, although values from near zero to somewhat more than this may be useful in electronic music.

Echo density is another parameter that can be used to characterize a reverberation process in general terms. The single delay line reverberator suffers from a low (and constant) echo density of 0.03 echos/msec. In a concert hall, the echo density builds up so rapidly that no echos are perceived. One measure of the quality of artificial reverberation is the time between the initial signal and when the echo density reaches 1/msec. In a good system, this should be on the order of 100 msec. Furthermore, there should be a delay of 10 msec to 20 msec between the signal and the very first echo if a sense of being far away from the sound is to be avoided. Finally, if the reverberation amplitude decrease is not smooth, a somewhat different yet distinct echo effect is perceived. A plot of the impulse response of the reverberator is a good way to visualize the buildup of echos and the overall smoothness of amplitude decrease.

A natural consequence of any reverberation process is an uneven amplitude response. For example, if the amplitude response of the single-echo generator described earlier were measured, it would be found to rise and fall with a period (in frequency) equal to the reciprocal of the delay time. In fact, examination of the signal flow reveals that it is the same as that of a comb filter! However, since the ratio of delayed to direct signal is normally less than unity, the notch depth is relatively shallow. The feedback delay line has the same properties except that the feedback results in a series of resonances. As the feedback factor approaches unity, the *Q*s of the resonances get quite high, producing a very uneven amplitude response.

Concert hall reverberation also has an uneven amplitude response, but the peaks and valleys are closely spaced, irregular, and not excessively high or deep. It is not unusual to find several peaks and valleys *per hertz* of bandwidth with an average difference between peak and valley of 12 dB. It is possible to have high echo density combined with a low *resonance* density. An excellent example is an empty locker room or even a metal garbage can. The small size of the reverberant chamber precludes resonant modes spanning a large number of wavelengths of moderate frequency sound. The converse situation, a high resonance density but low echo density, can be produced by the feedback delay line reverberator with a very long delay time, which does not sound like reverberation at all.

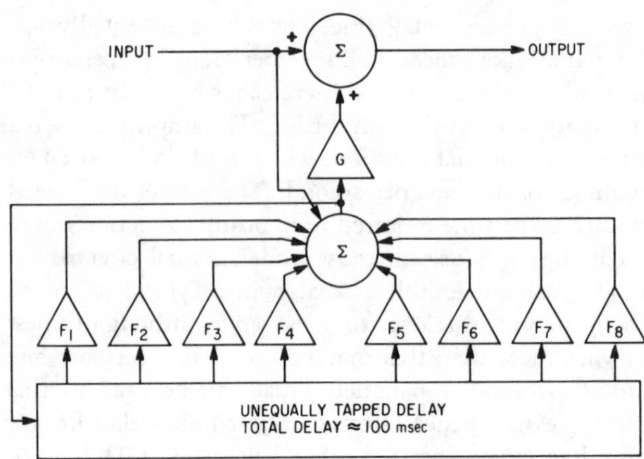

Fig. 14–21. Tapped delay line digital reverberator

A Practical Filter for Concert Hall Reverberation

In theory, it is possible to exactly duplicate the acoustics of a particular concert hall by recording its impulse response and then applying the transversal filter technique to the sound to be reverberated. Typical reverberation times of 2 sec, however, mean that the filter is 50K to 100K samples long, which is clearly impractical. On the other hand just about any assemblage of delays, summers, and multipliers will produce some kind of reverberation if it doesn't oscillate instead. Some, of course, are much better at simulating convincing concert hall reverberation than others.

In order to increase the echo density, it is necessary to use several delays of unequal length. The structure in Fig. 14–21 is the digital equivalent of the multiple-head tape reverberation simulator mentioned in Chapter 2. The placement of the taps and the values of the feedback constants are very important in determining the sound of the system. Generally, the taps should be approximately exponentially distributed but placed at prime number locations. This insures a maximum rate of echo buildup. The feedback constants strongly interact with each other and in fact there is no easy way to tell if a particular set will not cause sustained oscillation. Typical values are around 0.8 with the long delay taps being somewhat more and the short taps somewhat less. In any case, experimentation with the number, placement, and gain of the taps is necessary to achieve the type of reverberation required.

Another approach is based on the concept of cascading simple reverberation modules. One could use the Fig. 14–20B setup as a module and cascade two or more of them in order to improve the echo density. One problem that can arise is that at certain frequencies the peaks and valleys in the individual

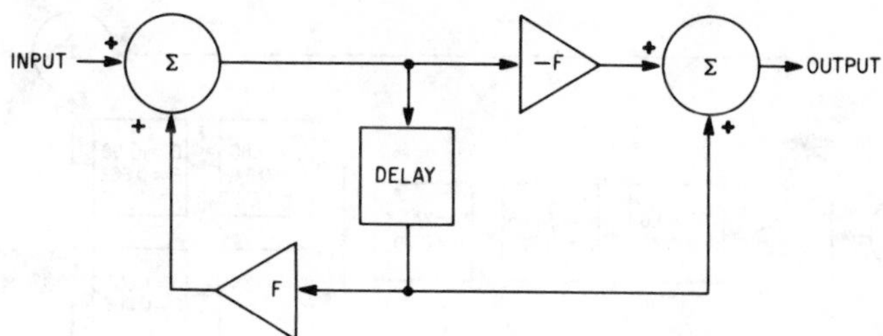

Fig. 14–22. All-pass reverberation module

amplitude responses may coincide to produce an exceptionally strong peak or valley. One way to avoid the problem is to very carefully choose the delays of the modules so that peaks or valleys do not coincide. However, doing this while also scrambling the delays for good echo density would probably require an iterative search program, and the results would not allow very much adjustment flexibility.

A better way is to modify the multiple-echo module so that it has a uniformly flat amplitude response. Actually, all of these reverberation diagrams are equivalent to familiar digital filters, the only difference being that the delay is hundreds or thousands of samples long rather than one. A slight rearrangement of the summers can convert the multiple echo diagram into the equivalent of an all-pass filter. Since the notches introduced by the feedforward path cancel the resonances created by the feedback path, the overall amplitude response is flat.

Figure 14–22 shows an all-pass reverberation module. Two parameters characterize the module. The delay, D, determines the echo spacing for the module, while the feedback factor, F, determines the reverberation time for the module. Cascades of as few as three modules can give a reasonable simulation of concert hall reverberation, although upwards of seven give noticeably better results. As with the tapped delay line reverberator, the delay parameters should be approximately exponentially distributed but in all cases must be a prime number of samples. An easy way to come up with a first approximation is to give the first stage the longest delay, which is in the 50-msec range, and then successively multiply it by a constant somewhat less than 1.0 such as 0.78. Thus, if the longest delay were 50msec, then the succeeding ones would be close to 39, 30.4, 23.7, etc. The shortest delay should not be much less than 10 msec if a distant, hollow sound is to be avoided.

Appropriate values of the feedback factor tend to be similar for all stages, although they should not be identical. The feedback factors and the delays combine to determine the reverberation time. The reverberation time of a single stage is the number of delay recirculations required to attenuate the signal 60 dB times the delay time. Thus, $R_t = -6.9D/\mathrm{Ln}(F)$, where R_t is the reverberation time in seconds, F is the feedback factor, and D is the delay

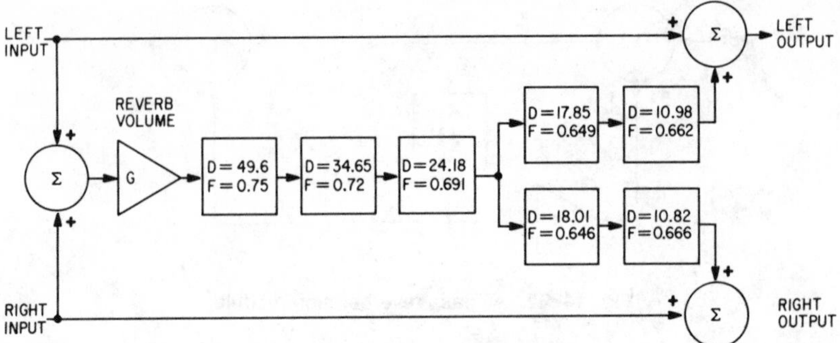

Fig. 14–23. High-quality stereo reverberator

in seconds. For practical purposes, the reverberation time of a cascade of sections is equal to the longest section time. Thus, if the delays get successively shorter and the feedback is approximately constant, the longest delay section determines what the feedback factors should be.

After the initial values for each stage are determined, further refinement can be performed by plotting the impulse response and making slight adjustments to maximize the echo density and minimize any periodicity or unevenness in the decay envelope. Figure 14–23 shows a stereo reverberator. The subtle but significant differences between the channels insures that the reverberation will be perceived as coming from all directions, while the original signal retains its normal directivity.

Chorus Effect

In some ways, a chorus effect is similar to reverberation. Both are very helpful in adding complexity and realism to simple (relative to natural) synthesized sounds. As was detailed in Chapter 2, there are two different approaches to implementing a chorus effect. One attempts to directly simulate *N* instruments all playing the same notes. The other seeks to simulate the acoustic effect of a number of players. The first is most successful for relatively small multiplicity factors, while the latter, with sufficient effort, can give the impression of thousands of sound sources.

Direct simulation of multiple sources is the simplest. The premise is that the basic sound of each instrument is identical to the others, but slight differences in timing, intonation, and vibrato are what contribute to the chorus effect. Figure 14–24 shows a diagram of a chorus simulator suitable for a moderate multiplicity. Each of the parallel delay lines has a different, randomly varying delay. In addition, each delayed channel undergoes a small amount of amplitude modulation, again randomly. The varying delays introduce phase and frequency modulation, which simulates differences in timing and intonation. The amplitude modulation is of secondary impor-

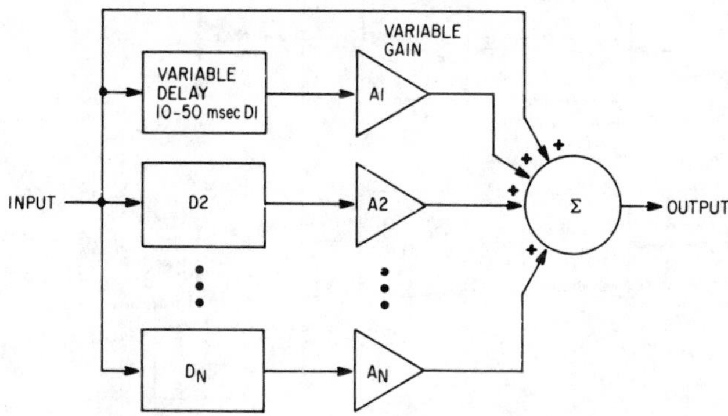

Fig. 14–24. Direct chorus simulator

tance but tends to emphasize momentary enhancements and cancellations of the multiple sources.

The random control signals are white noise that has been low-pass filtered with a cutoff in the range of 10 Hz to 20 Hz. It is important that the noise used for each channel be uncorrelated (taken from a separate generator), which is easily done with a digital noise generator (to be discussed in Chapter 15). If naturalness is desired, it is important that the peak frequency modulation caused by changing delay times be held to 1 Hz or less for midfrequencies. Because of the numerous variables, adjustment is best done by ear.

The system shown with a half-dozen delays is remarkably effective in simulating a small chorus. Although a fair amount of computer memory is necessary for the delay lines (much of it can be shared by programming a single long line and variable taps), very little computation is required relative to the results obtained. Because of the numerous parameters available for experimentation, many weird and whacky effects should also be possible.

The other method of chorus simulation is considerably more involved but much simpler than hundreds of the sections just discussed. Basically, the idea is to use a collage of randomly varying delays, phase shifters, frequency shifters, and frequency selective filters. Figure 14–25 is a block diagram[1] of the system that was originally implemented with purely analog circuitry. Because of its complexity, it is a good candidate for digital implementation.

This system differs from the one described earlier in that the input spectrum is split into several bands and that differences in intonation are simulated primarily with spectrum (frequency) shifters rather than phase or delay shifters (although these too are used extensively). As was mentioned in Chapter 3, a spectrum shift destroys harmonic relationships among components of the shifted spectrum, whereas a delay shift does not.

[1]The block diagram was taken from notes gathered from a technical paper delivered by Robert Orban at the 55th convention of the Audio Engineering Society.

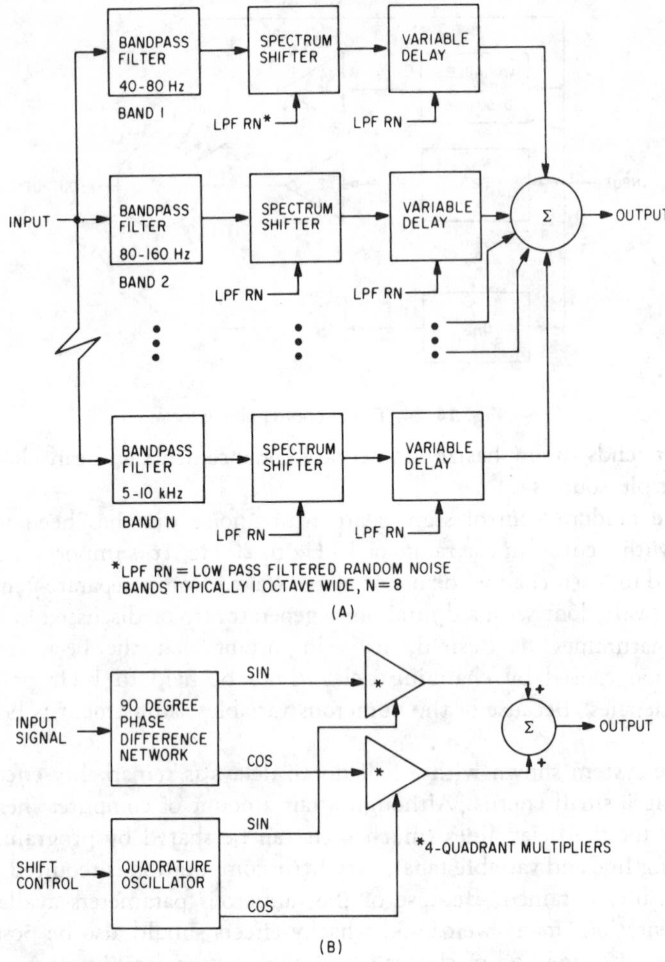

Fig. 14–25. (A) Parametric chorus simulator. (B) Spectrum shifter block diagram.

Figure 14–25B diagrams a spectrum shifter consisting of three major parts. The first and most critical is a 90° *phase difference network*. The purpose of the network is to produce two output signals from a single input such that the phase *difference* between the outputs is 90° *independent* of frequency. Such a network is constructed from two multisection all-pass filters as shown. Although the input-to-output phase shift of each filter alone varies considerably with frequency, the phase difference is reasonably constant over a fairly wide frequency range. More sections in the filters broaden the frequency range of accurate 90° phase difference. Phase errors generally cause incomplete suppression of the unwanted spectrum copy. Note that since the input spectrum is split into fairly narrow bands that the 90° phase difference network can be simpler than it would otherwise be.

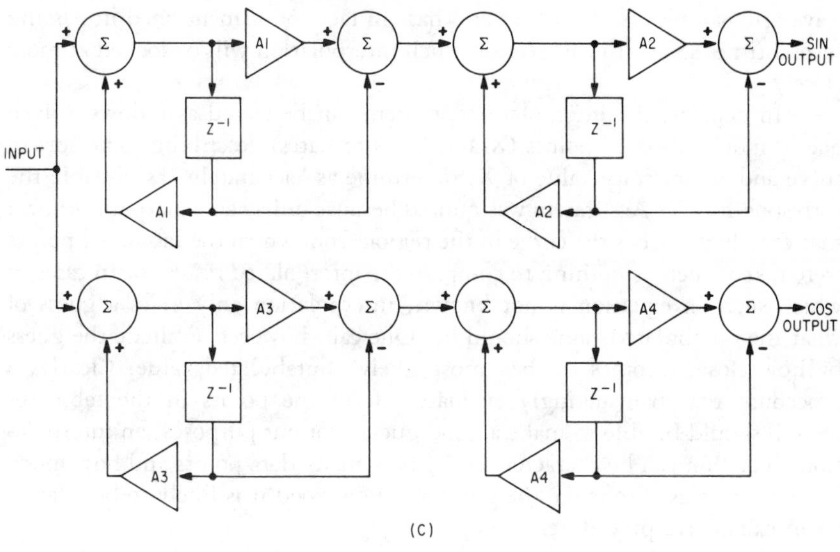

$A_1 = e^{-(.9511Fc/Fs)}$ $A_3 = e^{-(3.751Fc/Fs)}$

$A_2 = e^{-(10.52Fc/Fs)}$ $A_4 = e^{-(41.50Fc/Fs)}$

WHERE:
Fc = CENTER FREQUENCY OF BAND
Fs = SAMPLE RATE

Fig. 14–25. (*Cont.*). (C) 90 degree phase difference network detail.

The other elements are exceptionally easy to implement in digital form. The frequency of the sine and cosine waves entering the multipliers determines the amount of spectrum shift hertz for hertz. As shown, the spectrum is shifted up, but inversion of the driving oscillator phase will cause a downshift instead. The oscillator is easily implemented with a sine table and two pointers one-quarter the table length apart. Smooth transitions from upshift to downshift are accomplished by letting the table increment go negative, thereby generating "negative" frequencies.

The entire system is operated much like the simpler chorus synthesizer. Essentially, all of the variable elements are fed independent, slowly varying random signals. Again, adjustment is best done by ear, although many strange effects are possible by misadjustment.

Interpolation

Virtually everyone was taught in junior high school (before the advent of pocket calculators anyway) how to interpolate in a table of logs or trig functions in order to get an extra digit or two of precision. However, in digital music synthesis, interpolation between waveform table entries or waveform samples is of interest and has, in fact, been mentioned in passing several times so far. In this section, such interpolation will be looked at more closely.

In general, the interpolation problem can be stated as follows: Given one or more tabulated points (X and Y coordinates) describing some sort of curve and an arbitrary value of X, determine as "accurately" as possible the corresponding Y. Accurately was quoted because unless an equation is known that exactly describes the curve in the region from which the tabulated points were taken, there is nothing to compare the interpolated result to. In cases in which such an equation is not known, interpolation only gives a guess of what the untabulated value should be. One can, however, evaluate the guess by how close it comes to the "most likely" untabulated value. Clearly, a procedure that painstakingly evaluates all of the points in the table (or record) should be able to make a good guess. For our purposes, an interpolation algorithm can be characterized by how many data points and how much calculation is used to make the guess and how good it is likely to be relative to an exhaustive procedure.

The general approach to performing interpolation is to first find an equation that "fits" the data, that is, a plot of the equation would pass through the data points being considered. After this is done, the X for which a value is needed is plugged into the equation and out comes its corresponding Y. The accuracy of this Y depends entirely on how well the "interpolation function" models the physical process that created the data points in the first place. This is important because there are many different equations that will pass through the tabulated data points. Note that in the general case the tabulated points need not be equally spaced. In synthesis applications, however, they usually are, which simplifies the calculations.

Generally speaking, the interpolation will be most accurate when the unknown point is in the middle of the cluster of known points. If it is completely outside the tabulated points, the process is known as *extrapolation*, which is sheer speculation as to what the point might be if the curve continued to behave as it did in the tabulated interval.

One class of equations that can be used in interpolation is the standard algebraic polynomials. In general an $N-1th$ degree polynomial can be found that will exactly pass through N data points. Once found, the polynomial can be easily evaluated at the unknown point. The higher the degree of the polynomial, that is the more data points that are considered, the better the interpolation results.

The simplest example, which is what most people call interpolation, is linear interpolation. Here, a first-degree polynomial, which is a straight line, is fit to two data points; one on each side of the unknown point. The procedure for doing this was described in detail in the previous chapter. One could also fit a quadratic curve through three points and so forth. When a

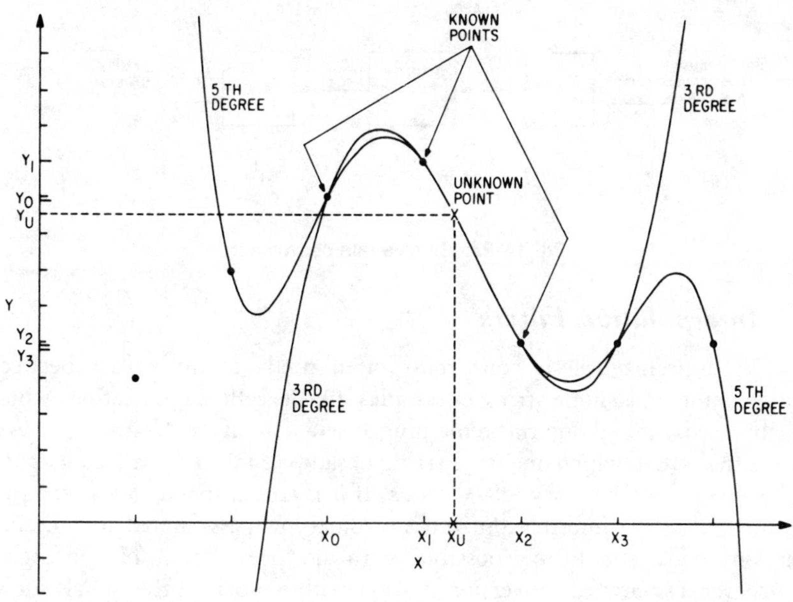

NOTE: X_1, Y_1 X_2, Y_2 X_3, Y_3 X_4, Y_4
GIVEN FOR 3rd DEGREE
POLYNOMIAL INTERPOLATION

CUBIC FORMULA FOR X SPACING = 1.0

$$
\begin{aligned}
Y_u = & - 1/6\, Y_0[(X_u - X_1)(X_u - X_2)(X_u - X_3)] \\
& + 1/2\, Y_1[(X_u - X_0)(X_u - X_2)(X_u - X_3)] \\
& - 1/2\, Y_2[(X_u - X_0)(X_u - X_1)(X_u - X_3)] \\
& + 1/6\, Y_3[(X_u - X_0)(X_u - X_1)(X_u - X_2)]
\end{aligned}
$$

X_u, Y_u = UNKNOWN POINT

X_0,Y_0 X_1,Y_1 X_2,Y_2 X_3,Y_3 = FOUR TABULATED POINTS SURROUNDING THE UNKNOWN POINT

GENERAL POLYNOMIAL INTERPOLATION FORMULA

$$Y_u = \sum_{K=0}^{N} Y_K \prod_{\substack{I=0 \\ I \neq K}}^{N} \left[\frac{X_u - X_I}{K - I}\right]$$

WHERE N = DEGREE OF POLYNOMIAL = NUMBER OF POINTS TO CONSIDER MINUS 1

X_I, Y_K = TABULATED POINTS (X_I SPACING = 1.0)

X_u, Y_u = UNKNOWN POINT

Fig. 14-26. Third- and fifth-degree interpolation polynomials

cubic is used with four data points, the procedure is called a *cubic spline*, which is detailed in Fig. 14–26 and compared with a fifth-degree interpolation polynomial.

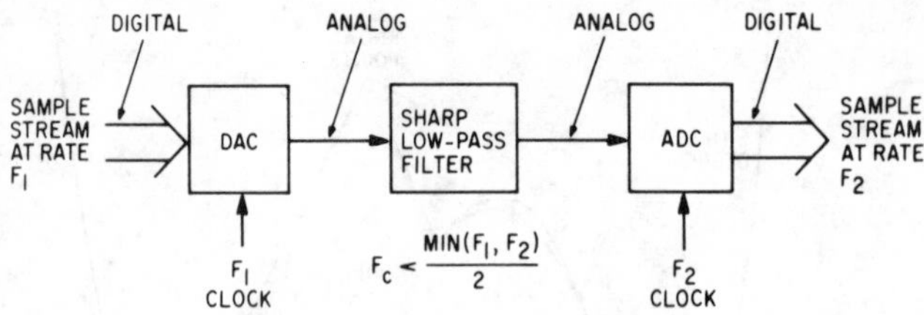

Fig. 14–27. Sample-rate conversion

Interpolation Filters

In digital synthesis, one most often needs to interpolate between sample points in a single string of samples. One excellent application, which will be used throughout the remaining discussion, is *sample-rate conversion*. This is the case in which one has a string of samples taken at, say, 25 ks/s and wishes to convert it to, say, 28.371 ks/s. If it is true that the 25 ks/s samples captured all of the information in the original low-pass-filtered signal, then the conversion should be possible with no degradation of the signal whatsoever. Downward conversion is also possible provided the signal is low-pass filtered to less than one-half the new sample rate.

Probably the first inclination in solving the rate-conversion problem is to linearly interpolate between the input samples as required to obtain the output samples. Unfortunately, this simple method generates an unacceptably large amount of noise. Cubic and quintic splines are better, but the noise is still excessive when high-frequency signals are being converted. These simple procedures fail primarily because the sample points are sparse compared with the variability of the curve before it was sampled, even though we know that they are dense enough for accurate reconstruction of the curve by a low-pass filter.

Figure 14–27 illustrates another sample-rate-changing process based on reconstruction of the original waveform and resampling at a different rate. The digital sample stream is converted into analog form at the original sample rate by the DAC and filtered by the low-pass filter. The filtered waveform is then resampled at the converted sample rate to provide the result. The low-pass filter cutoff should be less than one-half of the *lower* of the two sample rates. By studying the diagram, it is apparent that the *filter* actually does the interpolation and the digital–analog–digital conversion is just overhead. What is desired is a way to simulate this sample-rate-conversion system completely in the digital domain.

Earlier it was learned that the output waveform of a filter is actually the superposition of impulse responses, one for each input sample. Figure 14–28 shows the ideal low-pass impulse response, where the cutoff frequency is exactly one-half of an arbitrary sample frequency. Note that the response is zero at all sample times except the one that corresponds to the input impulse!

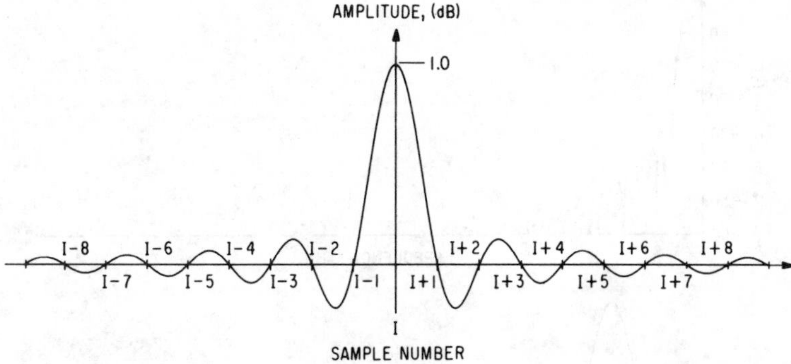

Fig. 14–28. Impulse response of ideal low-pass interpolating filter

Figure 14–29 shows in detail how the impulse responses to a string of samples combine to produce a very smooth curve that exactly passes through the sample points that are being low-pass filtered. In this respect, the filter output satisfies the requirements for an interpolation function of the sample points.

At this time, we can write the equation of the smooth curve connecting the data points. If we ignore the filter's delay and call the point at the center of the cluster point 0 ($X=0$, $Y=Y_0$) and scale the X axis in units of the sampling period, the impulse response, I_0, due to point X_0, Y_0 is: $I_0=Y_0\sin(\pi X)/\pi X$. Continuing, the response due to the point X_1, Y_1 is: $I_1=Y_1\sin(\pi(X-1))/\pi(X-1)$, where the $(X-1)$ accounts for shifting the impulse response right one unit so that it is centered about X_1. In fact the response due to a general point X_i, Y_i is: $I_i=Y_i\sin(\pi(X-i))/\pi(X-i)$. The

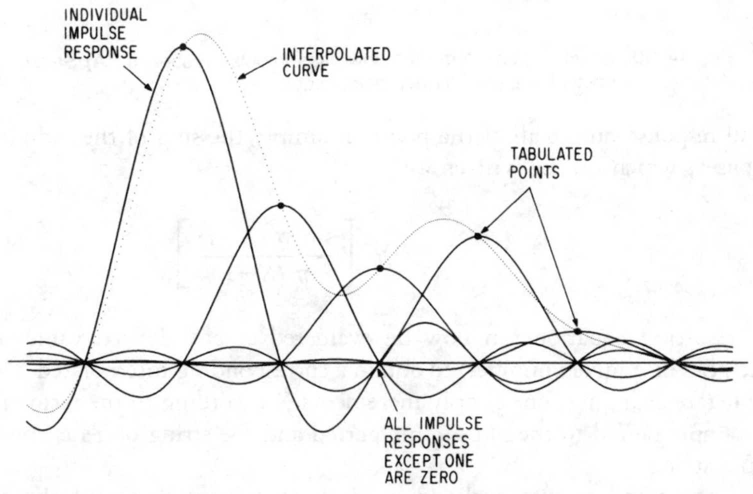

Fig. 14–29. Action of low-pass interpolating filter

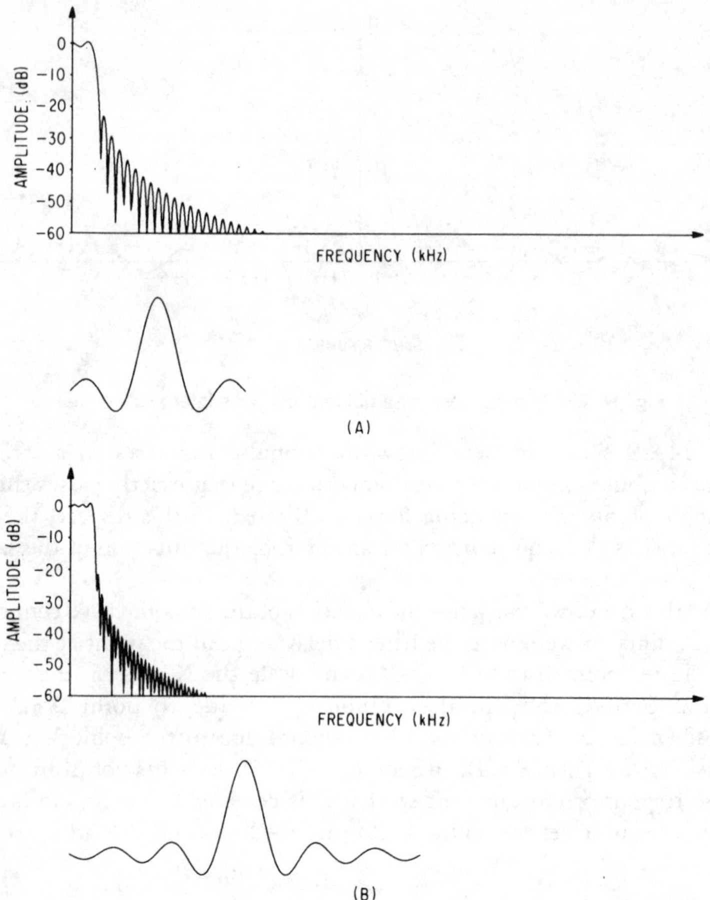

Fig. 14–30. Effect of truncating ideal low-pass impulse response. (A) Seven points kept. (B) Thirteen points kept.

overall response due to all of the points is simply the sum of the individual responses, which can be written as:

$$Y = \sum_{i=-\infty}^{+\infty} Yi \left[\frac{\sin \pi (X-i)}{\pi (X-i)} \right]$$

This resulting equation can now be evaluated at any desired value of X (which can be a mixed number) to obtain a corresponding interpolated Y. For sample rate changing, one simply increments X according to the ratio of the new sample period to the old sample period and the string of Ys is the new sample string.

The procedure just outlined is ideal, that is, it will give the same sample values that would have been obtained if the signal was originally

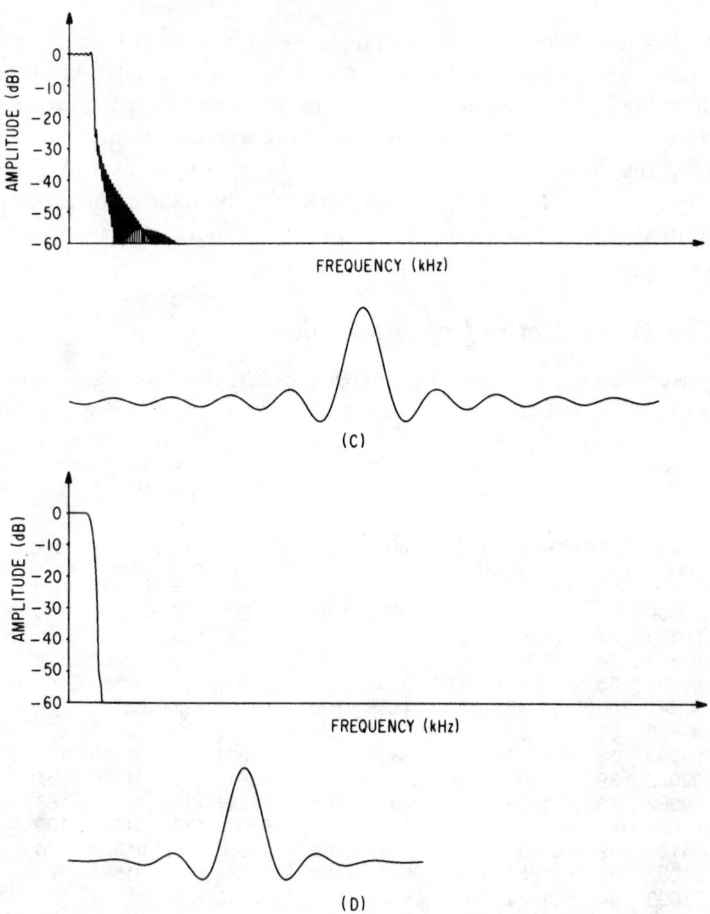

Fig. 14–30. Effect of truncating ideal low-pass impulse response *(cont.)*. (C) Twenty-one points kept. (D) Thirteen points kept and tailing function used.

sampled at the new rate. Unfortunately, the infinity signs in the interpolation function make it completely impractical. Since the individual impulse response curves decrease fairly rapidly on either side of zero, it is possible to simply cut them off at some point. If this is done, the limits on the summation become finite such as -10 to $+10$ (they should be symmetrical), which means that a cluster of 21 points is examined to determine the interpolation function. When the summation is truncated like this, it is important that the unknown point be close (within an input sample period) to the center of the cluster.

The truncated impulse response no longer corresponds to an ideal low-pass filter. Instead, the degraded filter exhibits a finite cutoff slope and a finite maximum attenuation as shown in Fig. 14–30. The finite cutoff slope means that the data being converted must be somewhat oversampled if serious alias distortion is to be avoided. The finite maximum attenuation means that some noise will be introduced by the interpolation. It is also possible to "tail off" the ends of the impulse response rather than truncate it. The effect of this is to increase the maximum attenuation at the expense of decreasing the cutoff slope. This means that if the input data is adequately oversampled, either the interpolation noise may be reduced or fewer points may be used in the interpolation. Tailing off will be discussed further in Chapter 16.

The Table Method of Interpolation

Even when the number of points is reduced to a reasonable value, the sine functions and divisions necessary to apply the method are very time

SECTION 1		SECTION 2		SECTION 3		SECTION 4		SECTION 5		SECTION 6	
ADDR	DATA	ADDR	DATA	ADDR	DATA	ADDR	DATA	ADDR	DATA	ADDR	DATA
0	.00000	32	.00000	64	.00000	96	.00000	128	.00000	160	.00000
1	.99833	33	−.02819	65	.01157	97	−.00527	129	.00211	161	−.00062
2	.99333	34	−.05422	66	.02247	98	−.01023	130	.00407	162	−.00119
3	.98504	35	−.07801	67	.03263	99	−.01483	131	.00587	163	−.00169
4	.97349	36	−.09952	68	.04198	100	−.01905	132	.00748	164	−.00213
5	.95878	37	−.11870	69	.05047	101	−.02286	133	.00891	165	−.00251
6	.94099	38	−.13554	70	.05805	102	−.02624	134	.01015	166	−.00282
7	.92022	39	−.15004	71	.06470	103	−.02918	135	.01120	167	−.00308
8	.89662	40	−.16220	72	.07039	104	−.03167	136	.01206	168	−.00328
9	.87032	41	−.17207	73	.07511	105	−.03371	137	.01274	169	−.00343
10	.84150	42	−.17968	74	.07887	106	−.03530	138	.01322	170	−.00353
11	.81032	43	−.18510	75	.08165	107	−.03644	139	.01354	171	−.00358
12	.77698	44	−.18840	76	.08349	108	−.03715	140	.01368	172	−.00358
13	.74168	45	−.18967	77	.08441	109	−.03744	141	.01366	173	−.00355
14	.70464	46	−.18902	78	.08444	110	−.03732	142	.01350	174	−.00348
15	.66607	47	−.18654	79	.08364	111	−.03684	143	.01320	175	−.00339
16	.62621	48	−.18237	80	.08203	112	−.03599	144	.01277	176	−.00326
17	.58528	49	−.17663	81	.07967	113	−.03482	145	.01224	177	−.00311
18	.54354	50	−.16956	82	.07663	114	−.03336	146	.01161	178	−.00295
19	.50121	51	−.16099	83	.07297	115	−.03163	147	.01090	179	−.00276
20	.45854	52	−.15138	84	.06875	116	−.02967	148	.01012	180	−.00257
21	.41577	53	−.14077	85	.06404	117	−.02751	149	.00928	181	−.00237
22	.37312	54	−.12931	86	.05891	118	−.02519	150	.00841	182	−.00216
23	.33084	55	−.11716	87	.05344	119	−.02273	151	.00751	183	−.00194
24	.29814	56	−.10446	88	.04769	120	−.02019	152	.00660	184	−.00173
25	.24824	57	−.09137	89	.04174	121	−.01757	153	.00568	185	−.00151
26	.20834	58	−.07801	90	.03565	122	−.01493	154	.00477	186	−.00129
27	.16964	59	−.06455	91	.02951	123	−.01229	155	.00388	187	−.00107
28	.13232	60	−.05111	92	.02337	124	−.00967	156	.00302	188	−.00085
29	.09655	61	−.03781	93	.01728	125	−.00711	157	.00219	189	−.00063
30	.06248	62	−.02479	94	.01132	126	−.00463	158	.00141	190	−.00042
31	.03026	63	−.01215	95	.00555	127	−.00255	159	.00068	191	−.00021
										192	.00000

Fig. 14–31. Interpolation table

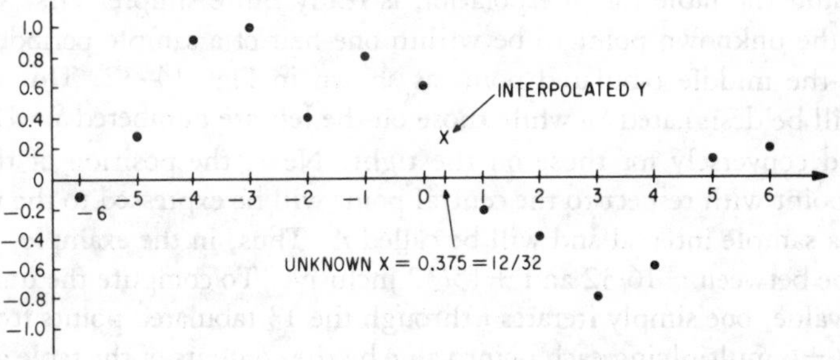

Known X	Known Y	Table Address	Table Entry	Y × Table Entry
−6	−.1	204	.0	.0
−5	.3	172	−.00358	−.00107
−4	.9	140	.01368	.01231
−3	1.0	108	−.03715	−.03715
−2	.4	76	.08349	.03340
−1	.8	44	−.18840	−.15072
0	.6	12	.77698	.46619
1	−.2	20	.45854	−.09171
2	−.4	52	−.15138	.06055
3	−.8	84	.06875	−.05500
4	−.6	116	−.02967	.01780
5	.1	148	.01012	.00101
6	.2	180	−.00257	−.00051
				.25510 = Interpolated Y

Fig. 14–32. Interpolation table use example

consuming, particularly on a microcomputer. Applying a tailing function (instead of truncating) takes even longer. The answer to this dilemma is the maxim: When in doubt use tables! As it turns out, a very simple table lookup algorithm can be derived that requires N multiplications, table lookups, and additions, where N is the number of points considered. These numbers are the same even if a tailing function is used to reduce interpolation noise.

The basic idea is to store the impulse response in a table. Since the impulse response is symmetrical, the table needs to be only half the size it would otherwise be. Fig. 14–31 shows how the data is placed in the table. First, we will assume that N is odd. The table area is then divided into $(N - 1)/2$ sections and, for convenience on a binary computer, each section contains a power of two number of points. The time span of a section is the same as the input stream sample period. In the example, $N = 13$ and there are six sections with 32 entries each for a total of 192 entries. It is also necessary to include or imagine 16 zeroes preceding the first and following the last section.

Using the table for interpolation is really quite simple. First we will restrict the unknown point to be within one-half of a sample period, either side, of the middle tabulated point as shown in Fig. 14–32. This middle point will be designated S_0 while those on the left are numbered $S-1$, $S-2$, etc., and conversely for those on the right. Next, the position of the unknown point with respect to the central point will be expressed to the nearest 1/32 of a sample interval and will be called A. Thus, in the example, A will always be between $-16/32$ and $+15/32$ inclusive. To compute the unknown sample value, one simply iterates i through the 13 tabulated points from -6 through $+6$ multiplying each point value by the contents of the table at $A+i$ and adding up the products. The sum is the interpolated value! When looking into the table the sign of the argument is ignored, which implements the symmetry. If the argument is greater than 6 or less than -6, zero should be returned.

Note that the location of the unknown point is quantized to 1/32 of a sampling interval. Abiding by this restriction limits the variety of sample-rate ratios. One could reduce this restriction by increasing the size of the table or by linear interpolation in the table, which is now allowable because the tabulated function is densely sampled. One could also apply the table to compute two interpolated samples, one on either side of the arbitrary unknown sample and linearly interpolate between them, thus reducing interpolation effort. This is permissible because now the waveform is grossly oversampled (by a factor of 32 in the example) and linear interpolation will not add nearly as much noise as before. The two methods are in fact exactly equivalent but the second only requires one linear interpolation rather than 13.

Actually writing a sample-rate-conversion program is somewhat tricky because both "future" and "past" input samples are needed and because of the different input and output sample rates. The problem is generally solved by using an input buffer, an output buffer, and a simulated shift register for the samples used in the interpolation. The routine would also accept a sample rate ratio, R, which would be a mixed number either greater than or less than unity.

In practice, the routine would initially be given a full input buffer, an empty output buffer, and a shift register full of zeroes. It would also keep track of a time variable, A, which corresponds to the A used in the interpolation example and which is constrained to the range of -0.5 to $+0.5$. To generate the next output sample, R is added to A. If the sum is between -0.5 and $+0.5$, an interpolation is performed and the computed sample is put into the output buffer. If the sum is greater than $+0.5$, the shift register is shifted one position, the next input sample is taken from the input buffer and put into the vacant shift register slot, and 1.0 is subtracted from A. This is repeated if necessary until A is less than $+0.5$, at which point an interpolation is performed generating another output sample and so forth.

When the output buffer becomes full, a dump routine is called to transfer it someplace. Likewise, when the input buffer becomes empty, a load routine is called to refill it.

Note that, if the sample rate is being converted downward ($R > 1$), the data must be separately low-pass filtered (or have been adequately oversampled in the first place) prior to the sample-rate conversion. The interpolation filter described cuts off at one-half the input sample rate and therefore does no bandlimiting itself.

15 Percussive Sound Generation

Up to this point, discussion has concentrated on the synthesis of basically periodic tones. Percussive sounds, however, are quite important as well and may in fact have even more variety than periodic types of sounds. Whereas tones can be fairly well described by giving a few parameters, many percussive sounds defy simple description. As is the case with tones, direct digital techniques offer considerably more freedom in the synthesis of percussive sounds than do analog techniques. Percussive sound generation is such a large topic that only a brief introduction can be offered here. Nevertheless, the techniques discussed should be suitable for a wide variety of percussive sounds.

Types of Percussive Sounds

Out of the infinite variety of percussive sounds, it is possible to define roughly four categories. Type 1 sounds are those that are basically sine wave tones with a suitable amplitude envelope. Any of the synthesis techniques covered previously are quite adequate for generation of the tone component of the sound, while direct computation or table lookup is suitable for the envelope. Nearly all sounds in this group have a moderate to strong sense of pitch due to the periodic foundation. Familiar instruments producing sounds in this group are wood blocks, clavés, orchestral bells, and bongo drums.

Type 2 is similar, but the underlying "tone" consists of several, nonharmonically related sine wave components. Most free (without snares) drums produce sounds in this category when struck with moderate force by a padded drumstick. Unlike strings and metal bars, the various vibration modes of a drumhead do not correspond to integrally related frequencies. Again, the previous synthesis methods can be used to produce the basic tone to which an amplitude envelope is added.

Type 3 sounds are best described as filtered, enveloped noise. In many cases, the instrument physics are basically the same as for Type 2, but the number of frequency components is so large that the sound resembles random noise. In other cases, the instrument operates by means of scraping or rattling, thus producing random noise directly. Synthesizing such sounds basically amounts to determining the amplitude response of the filter and the shape of the amplitude envelope. Cymbals, drums with snares, and sand blocks produce sounds that are excellent examples of this type of percussion.

The last class most resembles the first but has great potential for a wide variety of distinctive percussive sounds. These are sounds made by a nonlinear vibrator such as a ruler held over the edge of a table. The difference is that the basic parameters of the vibration such as frequency and waveform change as the amplitude of the vibration changes. In the case of the ruler, the nonlinearity arises from the fact that the effective vibrating length is less on the downstroke, where it bears against the table edge, than on the upstroke, where it is restrained by the player's hand. The relative time spent in each of the two states varies with amplitude, until at low amplitude the table edge becomes dominant and the vibration expires with a Type 1 characteristic.

Damped Sine Wave Generation

Most sounds in the first two categories can be quite adequately simulated with one or more exponentially damped sine waves. Although a sine wave tone generator can be given an amplitude envelope for this purpose, the very fast attack characteristic of these sounds requires that the attack begin at the zero crossing of the sine wave. Otherwise, audible clicks may be generated, particularly when the wave being enveloped is of low frequency.

A convenient way of obtaining damped sine waves with the required attack phase continuity is to ring a high *Q* filter! The center frequency determines the wave frequency and the *Q* determines the decay rate. Because of the precision and stability of digital filters, even very slow decay rates are easily handled.

The filter-ringing technique is very common in the analog world for simulating the sounds of all kinds of percussive instruments. Its use is most popular in electronic organs, where up to a dozen different percussion "instruments" are driven by digital logic to provide rhythm accompaniment to the standard organ sound. For example, a fairly high-frequency (1–2 kHz), high-*Q* (50) ringing filter is used to simulate clavés. A lower-frequency (500 Hz), lower-*Q* (10–20) filter makes a convincing wood block sound. Even lower frequencies (100–250 Hz) and moderate *Q*s do a surprisingly good job of simulating tom-tom's even though a real tom-tom is a Type 2 percussive sound. Much lower frequencies (50 Hz) have all of the oomph of a bass drum when played through a good speaker system.

To these rather common-sounding percussion "instruments," one may add many others by manipulating the frequencies and *Q*s. In particular, if a number of clavé-like instruments with pitches on a musical scale are defined, a tune can be played that the average person almost invariably associates with falling raindrops. And who has not heard a melody "played" by a coffee

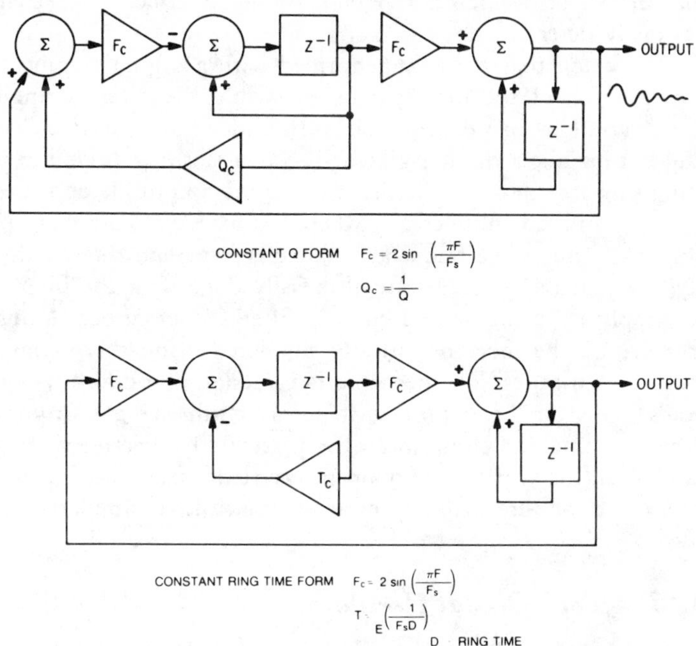

Fig. 15–1. Digital ringing filter

percolator or corn popper? The tuned percussive sounds in this case are in the wood block frequency range but with somewhat lower Qs. And then we can have all kinds of tuned thuds, bottle pops, and little pings to work with as well.

Although any resonant digital filter of the recursive type (one that has feedback paths) can be rung, probably the digital state-variable type is the easiest to work with because of the essentially linear relation between the filter parameters and digital constants. Since no input signal is required, the structure can be simplified to one of the two shown in Fig. 15–1. To start the filter ringing, one *initializes* the left delay element with a value of A and the right delay element with zero. Following this, every iteration of the filter will produce an output sample on a damped sine wave starting at zero and initially going positive. The first positive peak amplitude will always be slightly less than A depending on the Q parameter. Since the filter is a state variable, the center frequency may be varied without affecting the Q. This means that the damping time increases as the center frequency is reduced.

The second form of the filter shown has a ringing time that is constant as the ringing frequency is changed. Besides being a trifle simpler in structure, the constant ring time may be more useful musically. The equation given in the diagram gives the time required for the ringing amplitude to decay 8.7 dB or to about 37% of its original value. Since the decay is a constant number of decibels per second, the decay time to other endpoint values is easily determined.

One function that is easily performed with a digital ringing filter is dynamic variation of the filter parameters while the filter is ringing. In particular, variations in frequency can turn a nice "ding" into a "doioing" that sounds a lot like a ringing glass with water sloshing around in it. One interesting property, however, is that the ringing amplitude decreases when the frequency is raised and increases when it is lowered. This is not particularly noticeable unless the frequency change is large and the Q is high.

Type 2 percussive sounds are also easily done with the filter-ringing method simply by using several ringing filters. The various drums mentioned earlier can be more realistically simulated using the method along with published figures for the vibration modes of uniformly stretched drumheads. This can be important if one is synthesizing a drum solo in which the instrument is clearly heard. A particularly effective ringing-filter application is in the synthesis of tympana (kettledrums). The ability to tune the filters while they are sounding means that a realistic simulation is possible.

A "Perfect" Digital Oscillator

When the Q is allowed to go to infinity, the two filter structures become identical and one has a digital oscillator. If integer arithmetic is used, the resulting sine wave will run forever with no noticeable amplitude increase or decrease. In fact, such an oscillator using only 8-bit arithmetic was set up and allowed to run overnight with no change in amplitude. This was particularly interesting because there was a nonintegral number of samples per cycle of the waveform. Apparently, because of the circular nature of the oscillation, the roundoff errors cancel after a number of iterations leaving *exactly* the same two numbers in the delay registers as an earlier iteration. The perfection of the waveform is limited only by the noise inherent in the N-bit representation of the samples generated.

The content of the other delay also describes a "perfect" sine wave but out of phase with the first wave. In fact, the phase angle is nearly 90° depending on the oscillator frequency. For very low frequencies (relative to the sample frequency), it is quite close to 90°. Often a *quadrature* oscillator whose outputs are exactly 90° apart is useful. The simple modification of the infinite Q filter shown in Fig. 15–2 makes the phase difference exactly 90° independent of frequency at the expense of two additional multiplications per sample. Still this is much faster than computing a sine and cosine from a series approximation and is much more accurate than looking in a sine table. The restriction, of course, is that the sine/cosine values are generated in sequence and at equal spacing. An application of the oscillator is in a FFT program, particularly for a large number of points. Examination of the FFT butterfly reveals that the calculation sequence is easily arranged such that the W function uses equally spaced sines and cosines in ascending order.

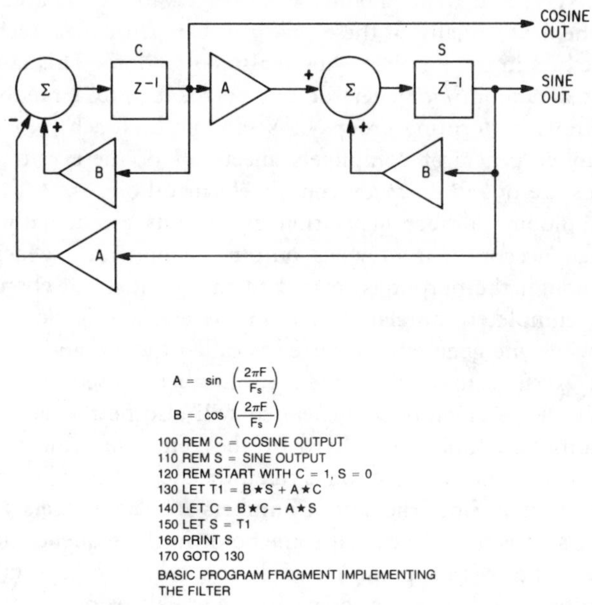
COSINE OUT
C
S
Σ
Z^-1
A
Σ
Z^-1
SINE OUT
B
B
A
A = sin (2πF / Fs)
B = cos (2πF / Fs)
100 REM C = COSINE OUTPUT
110 REM S = SINE OUTPUT
120 REM START WITH C = 1, S = 0
130 LET T1 = B★S + A★C
140 LET C = B★C − A★S
150 LET S = T1
160 PRINT S
170 GOTO 130
BASIC PROGRAM FRAGMENT IMPLEMENTING
THE FILTER

Fig. 15–2. Modification of infinite Q filter for 90° phase angle

Digital Noise Generation

Type 3 percussive sounds are primarily based on filtered random noise. Therefore, to generate such sounds digitally, a source of sampled white noise is needed. The filtering then can be accomplished with the same filters used in other applications.

If one were to connect an ADC to an analog white noise generator, the resulting samples would appear to be random numbers with a gaussian amplitude probability distribution. Actually, if the ADC included an antialias low-pass filter, the noise samples would be somewhat correlated. However, for noise sampling the filter is not really needed, since the alias noise will also be white and indistinguishable from the rest of the signal.

Fortunately, it is not necessary to sample analog white noise if the goal is a string of samples that sounds and behaves like white noise. Instead, one simply uses a random number generator with each number from the generator being a noise sample. There are numerous random number algorithms available but only two will be discussed here.

In general, a random number generator provides an N-bit binary number every time it is called. Each of the 2^N possible combinations should be equally likely, and there should be no perceivable correlation from one number to the next. Finally, if these conditions are truly met, each bit or any subset of the bits in the numbers should also be random. This last condition implies that a random *bit* generator can be made into a random number generator simply by forming groups of N random bits each. No algorithmic random number generator completely meets all of these criteria but any imperfections are or can be made completely inaudible.

Most random number generation algorithms are actually numerical functions that accept their previous output as input and generate a new output. Although the output is related to the input in an obscure way, it seems to be completely unrelated to it in the end application. The initial input used when the generator is started is called the *seed* and can usually be any number except zero. If the same seed number is used on two different occasions, the series of numbers generated will also be the same.

The numerical function utilized by the generator almost always uses integer arithmetic, and the function is carefully chosen according to the word size of the computer. Since the output numbers are also integers with a finite number of bits, it is obvious that at some point in the sequence the seed will pop up again. From this point forward, the sequence repeats itself. An efficient random number generator will generate all or nearly all of the 2^N different numbers that can be represented by an N-bit word before repeating. Thus, in a 16-bit computer, about 65,000 random numbers can be generated with single-precision arithmetic. Even at a 50-ks/s sample rate, which gives a repetition period of a little over 1 sec, such a generator produces perfectly acceptable white noise for human consumption.

Linear Congruential Method

One of the most popular random number algorithms is called the *linear congruential* method. The basic function is: $R_{new}=(A \times R_{old}+B) \bmod M$, where A and B are carefully chosen constants and M is the largest possible number plus one for the chosen word length. The arithmetic is assumed to be unsigned integer and ignoring overflow neatly implements the mod function. The generator is completely specified by giving values for A, B, and the word length. For any given word length, there are values for A and B (besides the trivial ones $A=1$ and $B=1$) that give M values before repeating. One of the references gives an extremely detailed analysis of how to determine good values for these parameters for general random number use. The following table summarizes A and B values that are suitable for white noise generation with different word lengths.

The method is quite efficient if the computer has an unsigned multiply instruction. It does have one important shortcoming, however; the less significant bits are not very random. If random bits or short random words are desired, the most significant bits should always be used.

Word length	*Sequence length*	*A*	*B*
8	256	77	55
12	4096	1485	865
16	65536	13709	13849
24	16777216	732573	3545443
32	4294967296	196314165	907633515

Shift Register Method

Another method that is superior to the linear congruential method in some respects can be called the feedback shift register random bit generator. As the name implies, the method generates random *bits* that are grouped to form random numbers. A feedback shift register similar to that discussed in Chapter 10 is used. By proper selection of the taps to be exclusive or-ed and fed back, the register can generate a sequence of 2^N-1 bits before repeating. To form an *N*-bit random integer, where *N* is equal to or less than the register length, one simply iterates the register at least *N* times and then reads the result directly from the register.

One advantage of the method is that all of the bits are random and therefore can be used indiscriminately for random control functions. Another advantage is that only logical operations are needed. On the other hand, the method as presently formulated is not as efficient at generating numbers with large *N* compared with the previous method even if the computer does not have a multiply instruction. Also, when set up for iterating *N* times to get an *N*-bit number, it fails some statistical randomness tests. This fault may be minimized by iterating somewhat more than *N* times. On the other hand, quite satisfactory white noise samples are generated with only a few iterations, such as five, for full 16-bit noise samples.

The shift register method is ideally suited for hardware implementation. With very little logic (three IC packages costing less than three dollars), one can set up a random number peripheral that will pass anyone's test for randomness including nonrepeatability of results. The circuit in Fig. 15–3 shows a 26-stage shift register with feedback logic that would be iterated by the microcomputer's clock. Up to 14 (8 are shown) of the register bits are available for connection to an input port. If the clock phase used to trigger the register is chosen properly, there is no danger of the register changing while the computer is reading it. The 2^{26} sequence length would run over 30 sec alone, but variations in program execution time make it highly unlikely that any repetition could ever be detected. Skeptics can substitute a type 4031 64-bit register for the type 4006 18-bitter and have a period of nearly 150 million years at 1 MHz.

Digressing for a moment, such a circuit makes an excellent analog noise generator as well. One simply clocks it at 400 kHz or more (an R-C oscillator

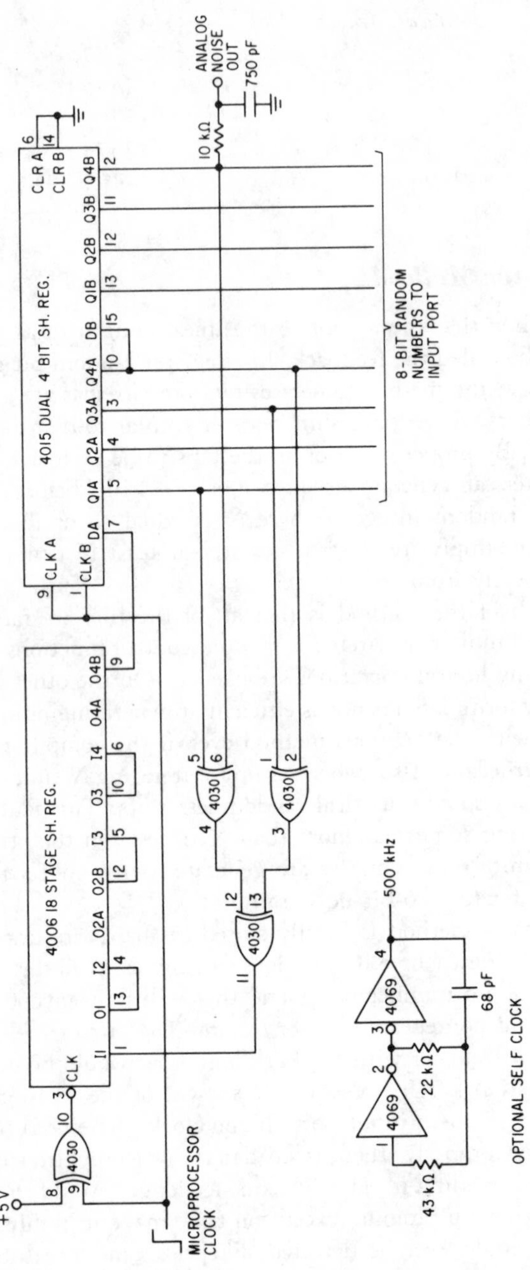

Fig. 15–3. Random-number peripheral

is fine) and runs one of the register bits through an R-C low-pass filter with a cutoff around 20 kHz. The output sound and waveform are indistinguishable from diode noise sources and are much less susceptible to hum pickup. Also, the output amplitude is repeatable and stable, a virtue not shared by diodes.

A modification to the shift register method will greatly increase its efficiency as a white noise subroutine. Essentially, the register and exclusive-ors are turned inside-out, which results in several of the register bits changing in an iteration rather than one. Assuming that the register length is the same as the word length, the following steps are performed for an iteration:

1. Shift the register left bringing in a zero on the right and putting the overflow bit into the carry flag.
2. If the carry flag is off, the iteration is complete.
3. If the carry flag is on, flip selected bits in the register. This may be accomplished by exclusive-oring a mask word with the register contents. The iteration is now complete.

In a 16-bit machine, these steps may require as few as three instructions to generate a sample of quite acceptable, if not statistically perfect, white noise. The table below lists mask words for common computer word lengths.

Word length	*Sequence length*	*Mask in hexadecimal*
8	265	1D
12	4095	1D9
16	65535	1D87
24	16777215	1D872B
32	4294967295	1D872B41

Using the Random Numbers

The output of the random number generators just discussed is a string of unsigned integers. However, since they are random, one can interpret them as standard twos-complement numbers as well or even as binary fractions. Since twos complement is slightly asymmetrical (there is one more possible negative value than possible positive values), the mean of the sequence will be −0.5 of the least significant bit rather than 0. This almost never causes problems unless the sequence is integrated for long periods of time.

Although the output of a random number generator when sent through a DAC sounds like white noise and in fact gives a white Fourier transform, it does not look at all like natural white noise. The difference is its probability density function, which is uniform rather than gaussian. As was mentioned in Chapter 10, one can easily convert uniformly distributed random numbers into near-gaussian distributed numbers by adding up 12 of them (assuming a range of 0 to 1.0) and subtracting 6.0 from the sum. The mean of the result will be 0 (except for the error described above) and the standard deviation will be 1.0. The simulation is not exact because the probability of a result greater than 6 standard deviations from the mean is 0 when it should be about 2×10^{-9}. Actually, since uniformly distributed and gaussian-distributed numbers sound the same and even may look the same after filtering, there is little reason to perform the gaussian conversion.

In many synthesis or modification applications, one may need several uncorrelated sources of white noise simultaneously. If the random number generator is reasonably good, one can simply distribute successive numbers to the separate processes requiring them. Thus, one random number generator can be used to simulate any number of random processes.

Type 3 Percussive Sounds

Now that we have a source of white noise lets discuss how it can be used to synthesize Type 3 percussive sounds. A pure Type 3 sound may be generated by filtering the noise and applying a suitable amplitude envelope. Very simple filters are adequate for many common sounds. For example, a quite deadly sounding gunshot may be produced by high-pass filtering the noise with a 300 Hz to 500 Hz cutoff and applying an envelope with zero attack time and decay to −30 dB in 100 msec to 200 msec. Conversely, a cannon boom is noise low-pass filtered at 100 Hz to 200 Hz with a somewhat longer attack and decay than the gunshot. Returning to musical instruments, high-pass filtering above 1 kHz with a 50 msec to 100 msec attack and decay simulates brushes (lightly on a snare drum) quite well. Maracas sound best with a little lower cutoff frequency and shorter attack and decay. Cymbal crashes have about the same frequency distribution as maracas but a fast attack and long decay in the 0.5-sec to 1-sec range as well as high overall amplitude.

Some sounds are not pure Type 3. A standard snare drum beat is the best example and consists of a burst of virtually white noise (only the very lowest frequencies are missing) combined with a Type 1 or Type 2 drum sound. A very realistic close range (remember how it sounded when one passed just 5 feet away in a parade?) bass drum sound can be produced by amplitude modulating 500-Hz low-pass filtered noise with the primary 50 Hz damped sine wave and mixing the two together.

Noise may also be bandpass filtered to simulate other classes of sounds. Many types of drums are more easily synthesized with filtered noise than several damped sine waves and sound just as good if not better. The bass drum, for example, can be done by bandpass filtering in the 50-Hz range as in Fig. 15–4. Pitched drums such as tom-toms also come out well if somewhat higher center frequencies are used. Sometimes it may be necessary to cascade two bandpass filters to provide greater attenuation of frequencies far removed from the center frequency, which would otherwise detract from the naturalness. It should be noted that bandpass filters not only take time to die out after the input is removed but also take time to reach full output if the input is suddenly applied. In some cases, the filter itself may generate a suitable envelope simply by turning the noise input on and off. Single-pole R-C low-pass filters also have a finite build-up time, but it is relatively short.

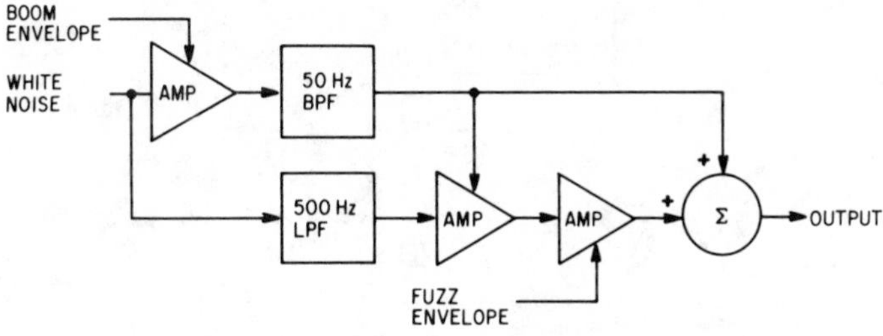

Fig. 15–4. Bass drum simulator

Nonlinear Vibrator Simulation

Many interesting percussive sounds fall into the Type 4 category. The vibrating ruler mentioned earlier is one example, while a strongly plucked rubber band is another. To these everyday examples can be added any number of artificially contrived examples.

Such sounds involve one or more nonlinear vibrating members. One characteristic of nonlinear vibrators is that the waveform and frequency of vibration depend to some degree on the amplitude of the vibration. A linear vibrator, on the other hand, is totally independent of amplitude. While every natural (and electrical analog) vibrator is nonlinear to some extent, the effect at normal amplitude levels is small enough to ignore.

The object here is to simulate the behavior, that is, plot the vibration waveform, of an excited nonlinear vibrator given certain vital statistics about its components and an expression or a table describing the nonlinearity. Figure 15–5 shows a standard spring-mass vibrator, just as it would appear in a physics textbook. The *position* of the mass relative to its stable or neutral position as a function of time is the variable of interest.

The classic first step in analyzing the vibrator is to note all of the forces acting on the mass and then apply the conservation principle that requires these forces to balance out, that is, sum to zero. There are three forces at work (gravity will be ignored, since it is a static force that has no effect on the vibration dynamics): the spring-restoring force, the force of friction, and the force of inertia. The restoring force is normally proportional to the difference between the present position and the neutral position and always pulls toward the neutral position. The force-versus-position relation is what will be made nonlinear later. The friction force can either be due to sliding friction, in which case its magnitude is constant (as long as there is movement) or due to viscous friction with magnitude proportional to velocity. Viscous friction will be used, since it is better behaved and more "natural." In either case, the direction is opposite to the direction of movement. The inertia force is proportional to the mass of the vibrator and the acceleration (rate of speed

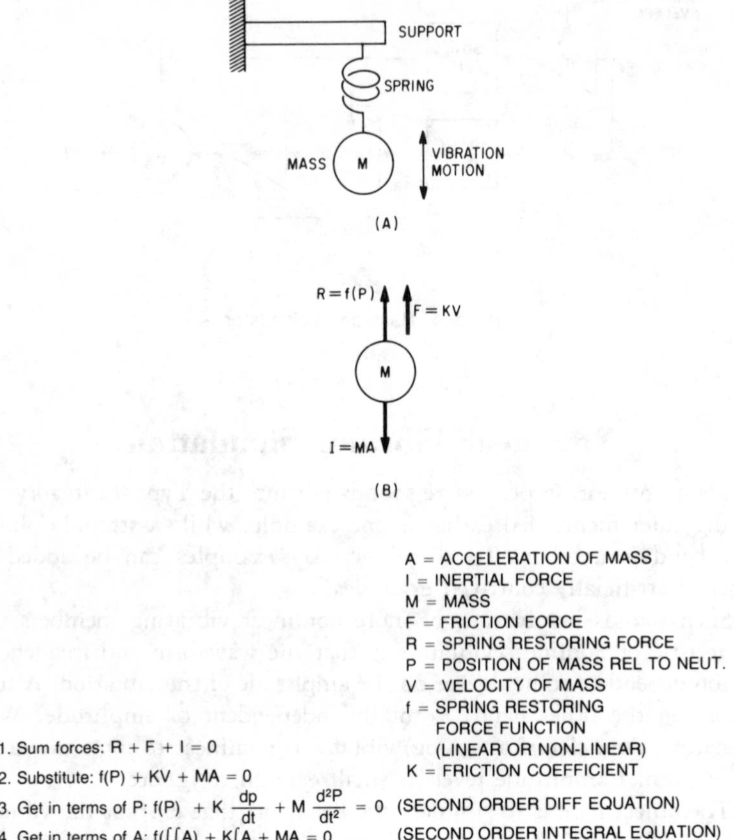

Fig. 15–5. (A) Spring-mass vibrator. (B) Forces on the mass. A, acceleration of mass; I, inertial force; M, mass; F, friction force; R, spring-restoring force; P, position of mass relative to neutral; V, velocity of mass; f, spring-restoring force function (linear or nonlinear); and K, friction coefficient.

change) it is experiencing. Its direction opposes the sum of the other two forces.

After the various forces are identified and written in equation form, it is customary to rewrite the equation in terms of the primary variable, P (position), instead of velocity and acceleration. This is easily done, since velocity is the *time derivative* of position and acceleration is the time derivative of velocity. The result is a standard second order differential equation.

Our goal, however, is to *simulate* the physical process described by the equation, not "solve" it in the mathematical sense. In order to get the equation into an easily handled form for simulation, it is better to write it in terms of acceleration, A, rather than position. If this is done, velocity is

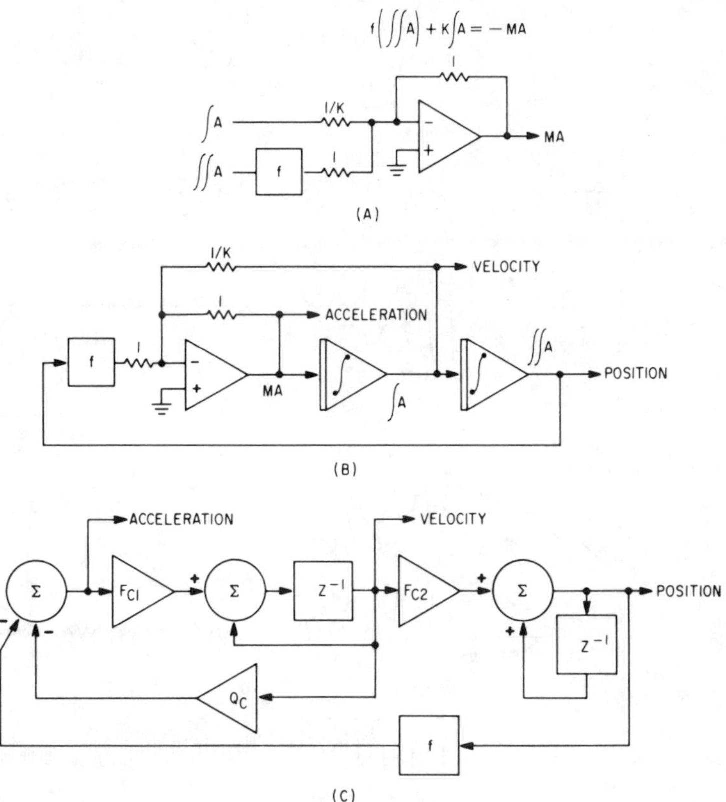

Fig. 15–6. (A and B) Electrical analog of spring-mass vibrator. (C) Digital implementation.

replaced by the *time integral* of acceleration, and position is replaced by the double time integral of acceleration. The resulting equation then is a second order integral equation.

At this time, we are ready to construct an electrical analog of the mechanical vibrating system. The first step is to move the *MA* term to the right side of the equation and assign it to the output of an op-amp summer as in Fig. 15–6. The left side of the equation now specifies the input to the summer, which is also shown. The remaining task is supplying $\int A$ and $\int\int A$. This can be accomplished neatly by passing the summer output, *MA*, through two integrators in series and making the indicated connections as in Fig. 5–15B. This looks strangely similar to the state-variable filter and, in fact, is exactly the same if the input is removed and the noninverting integrators are replaced by inverting ones with the friction-feedback term flipped to compensate.

Thus, a nonlinear vibrator may be simulated by inserting a nonlinear transfer function in the feedback path from the low-pass output and then

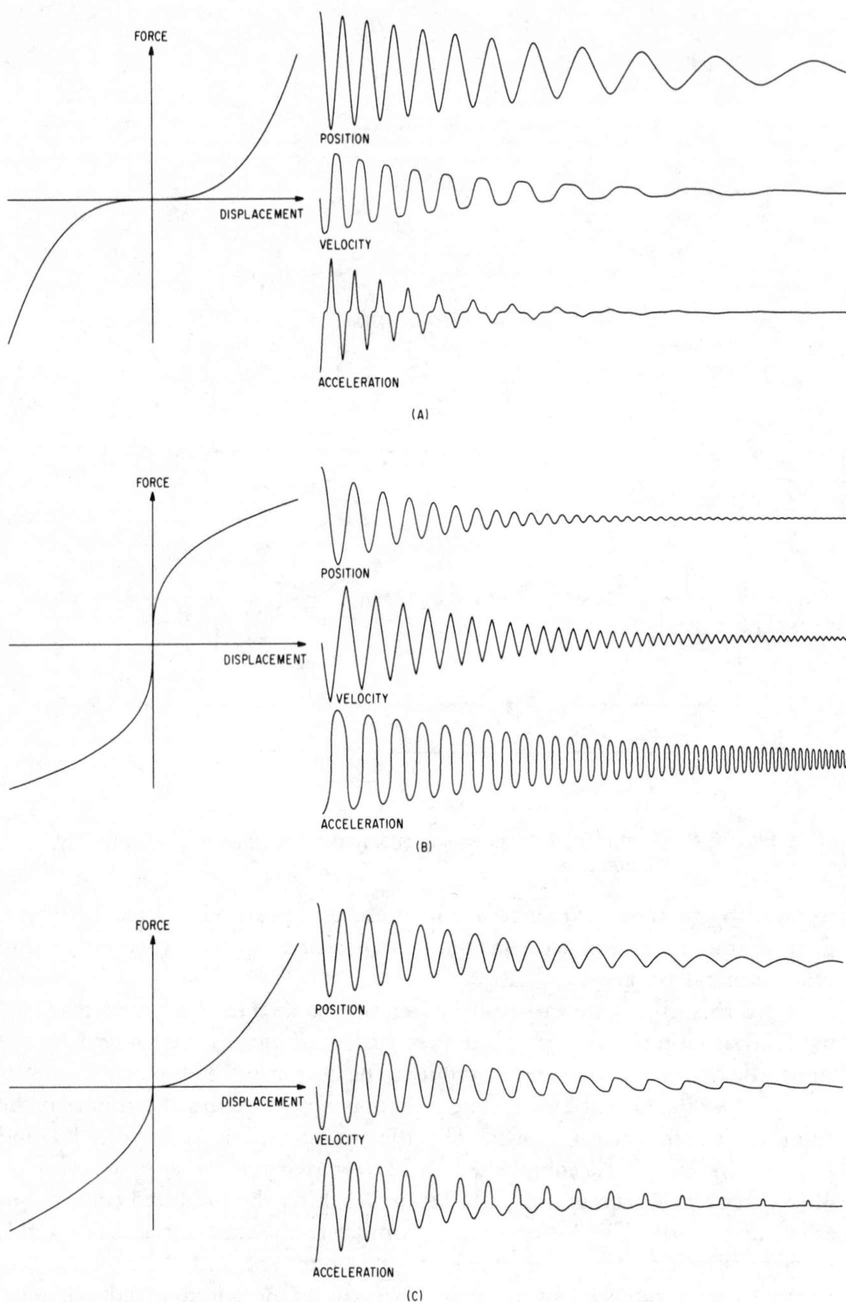

Fig. 15–7. Nonlinear vibrator simulation. (A) Increasing slope. (B) Decreasing slope. (C) Non-symmetrical slopes.

exciting the filter for results. Although an analog nonlinearity using diodes is quite possible (and an interesting experiment), with the digital equivalent an equation or table describing the transfer function can be used instead.

Not just any randomly chosen curve will work for the transfer function, however. In order for the oscillation to die out completely, the slope of the curve must always be positive. If the slope tends to *increase* away from zero as in Fig. 15–7A, the oscillation frequency will *decrease* as it dies out and vice versa. Symmetrical transfer functions lead to odd harmonics only while nonsymmetrical ones give all harmonics. The position (low-pass) output of the vibrator tends to have a very strong fundamental relative to the harmonics. The velocity (bandpass) and acceleration (high-pass) outputs have greater harmonic content.

The position feedback path is not the only one that can be made nonlinear. The velocity path may also be nonlinear with the general effect of distorting the decay envelope. Any of the amplifiers in the vibrator structure can also be made nonlinear. For example, making the value of Fc_1 dependent on position means that the vibrating mass depends on position such as in the vibrating ruler case. (The reader should be aware that the ruler sound cannot be duplicated with just the nonlinear oscillator; the impact of the ruler hitting the table excites additional resonances in the ruler that require additional filters to simulate.) It is important to note that digital simulations of nonlinear vibrators can easily generate frequencies above one-half the sample rate. Thus, experiments should be done at fairly low resonant frequencies and without sharp discontinuities in the nonlinear transfer functions.

16
Source-Signal Analysis

One of the great strengths of digital techniques lies in the ability to thoroughly analyze already existing sounds. These may either be "natural" sounds such as musical instruments, speech, animal sounds, etc., or they may be synthesized sounds. In either case, the goal of analysis is to determine values of the fundamental parameters that characterize the sound and how they vary with time.

When the ultimate purpose is synthesis, one may do analysis simply for education. Certainly, a good understanding of the parameters of existing sounds will aid in the specification of parameters for similar synthetic sounds. Often, published literature will have the necessary information, but it may be obscurely presented or applicable only to generalized or overly specialized cases. Even when published literature is adequate initially, most synthesis applications can be expected to gradually specialize beyond its scope. In either situation, firsthand analysis experience is quite helpful.

The most common application of analysis, however, is in sound modification in which one obtains data from a natural sound and uses it to direct the synthesis of an artificial sound. Sometimes the distortions introduced by the analysis/synthesis process alone are sufficient for the desired results. Usually, though, the analysis data are modified before the synthesis is performed. Digital processing of the analysis data can usually be performed such that the useful information is in an easily usable form. For example, if one wishes to apply the overall spectral *envelope* of a particular sound to another sound, a standard spectral analysis can be *smoothed* so that details about the individual harmonics are suppressed but the overall envelope is preserved.

Digital signal analysis is a very broad, very complex topic that keeps research staffs at many universities busy continuously. It is typically highly mathematical as well and most literature on the subject is quite obscure without the necessary training. Although one cannot completely escape such complexities, an attempt will be made in this chapter to discuss the most important and easily implemented analysis techniques. While these may not always be the most efficient or most accurate techniques, they get the job done. It is much more important for the beginner to actually do some analysis programming and see the results than to have a thorough mathematical understanding of the underlying principles. Only two types of analysis will be described in detail. The first is generalized spectrum analysis in which the time-varying spectrum of the source sound is determined. The second concentrates on extracting and following the frequency parameter of a changing sound, a very useful function.

Spectrum Analysis

Most source-signal analysis begins with spectral analysis, since virtually everything that is audible and important about a sound shows up vividly in a spectral analysis. The results of the analysis may then be plotted, passed directly to a synthesis process, or undergo further processing.

A time-variable spectral plot, which is also called a *short-time spectral analysis*, is actually a three-dimensional "surface" that shows the relation between time, frequency, and amplitude variables. Time and frequency are the independent variables, while amplitude is the dependent variable. When spectra are computed digitally, all three variables are quantized and two of them, amplitude and frequency, are also sampled. In effect the "volume" represented by the allowable ranges of these variables is filled with discrete points and the spectral surface is defined only at point intersections.

Plotting Methods

Obviously, most computer graphic displays and plotters cannot directly show a three-dimensional surface. This shortcoming has resulted in at least five distinct methods of representing the data on paper or a CRT screen. Perhaps most obvious is an isometric drawing of the surface such as illustrated in Fig. 16–1A. The surface is drawn in a horizontal position with peaks and valleys much like a land area relief map. Typically, time runs north/south, while frequency runs east/west, although they may be interchanged. Height always represents amplitude. Such a representation gives a "spectacular view" of the spectrum to say the least but is very difficult to draw, since hidden line removal (the surface is opaque instead of transparent) is necessary to avoid clutter.

A somewhat easier-to-draw representation consists of a stack of standard two-dimensional curves such as illustrated in Fig. 16–1B. Each curve represents a standard amplitude-versus-time plot at a particular frequency. Therefore, the horizontal axis is time and the vertical axis is amplitude. Each graph is displaced vertically upward as well so the vertical axis is also frequency. Sometimes the curves are skewed to the right as well as upward to give an isometric effect.

A third method, which is particularly applicable to digital spectra, approaches a true three-dimensional representation more closely. With a

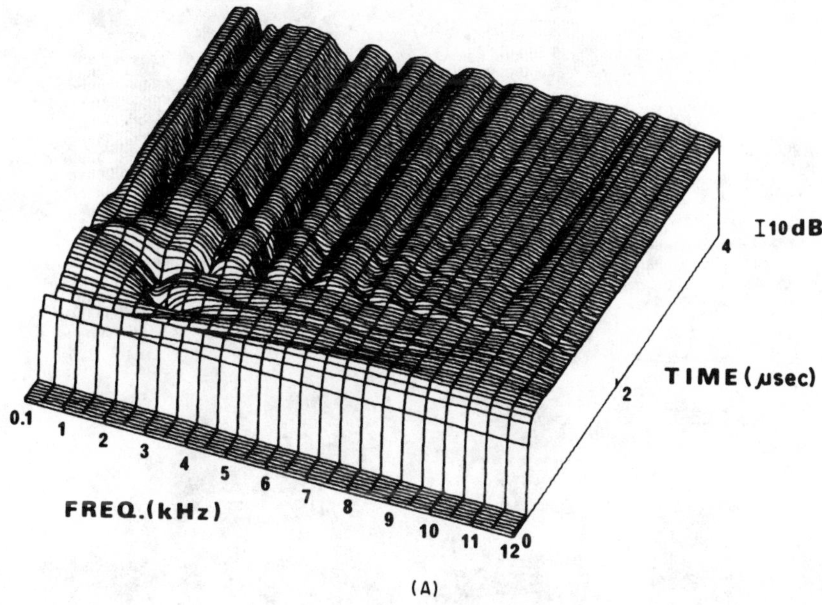

(A)

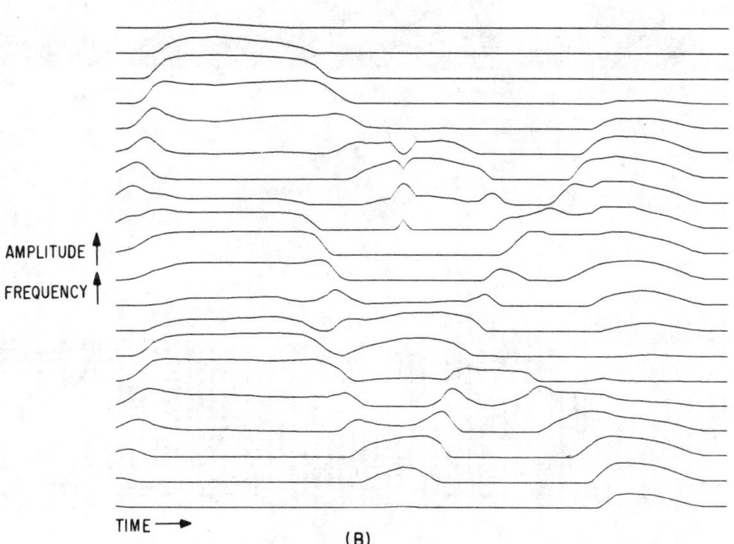

(B)

Fig. 16–1. Methods of representing three-dimensional spectral data in two dimensions. (A) Isometric projection. Source: Audio Engineering Society Preprint No. 1139, "Three-Dimensional Displays for Demonstrating Transient Characteristics of Loudspeakers," 1976. (B) Stack of two-dimensional curves.

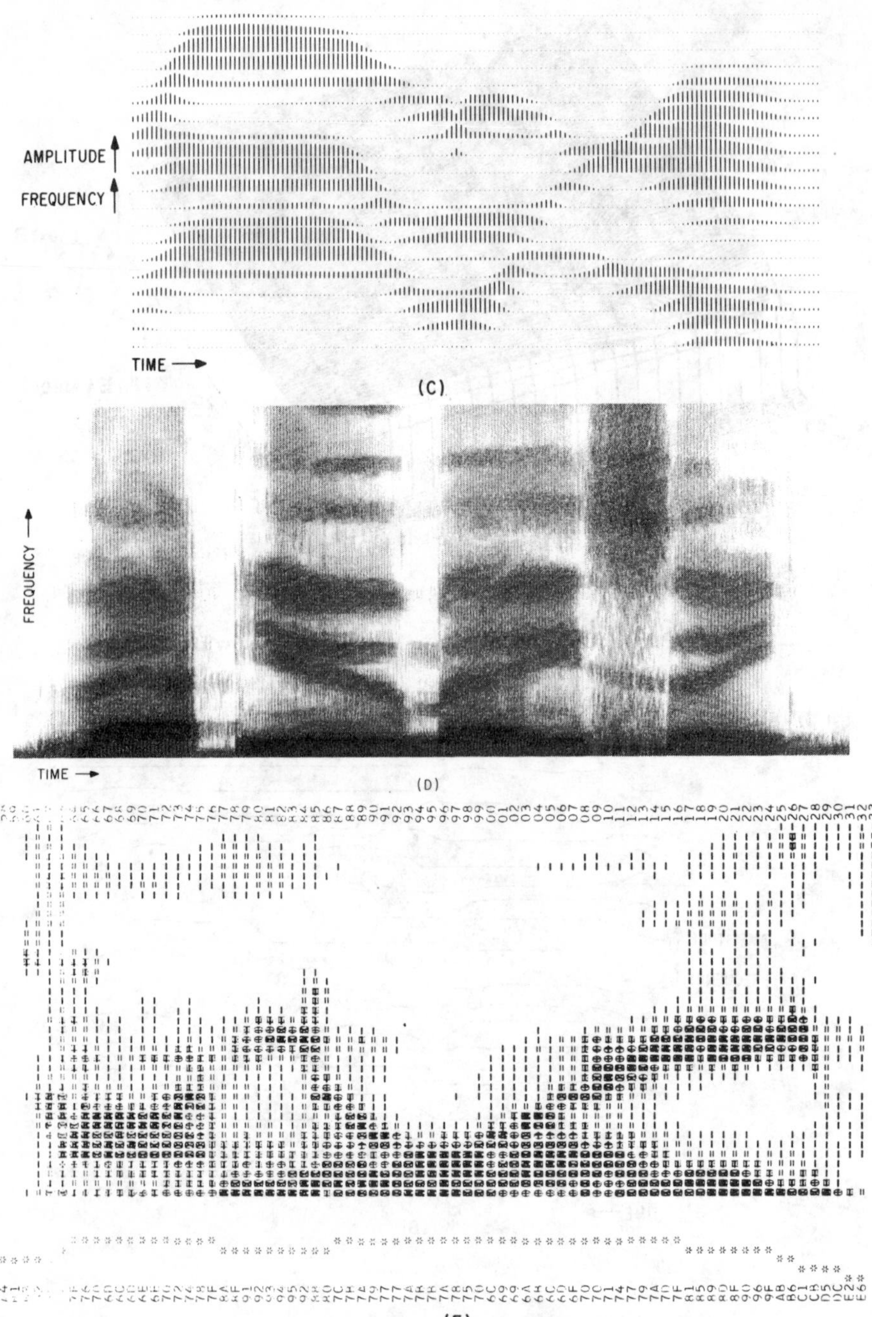

Fig. 16-1. Methods of representing three-dimensional spectral data in two dimensions *(cont.)* (C) True 3-D using bar lines for Z axis. (D) Gray scale (Kay sonagram). (E) Gray scale (line printer).

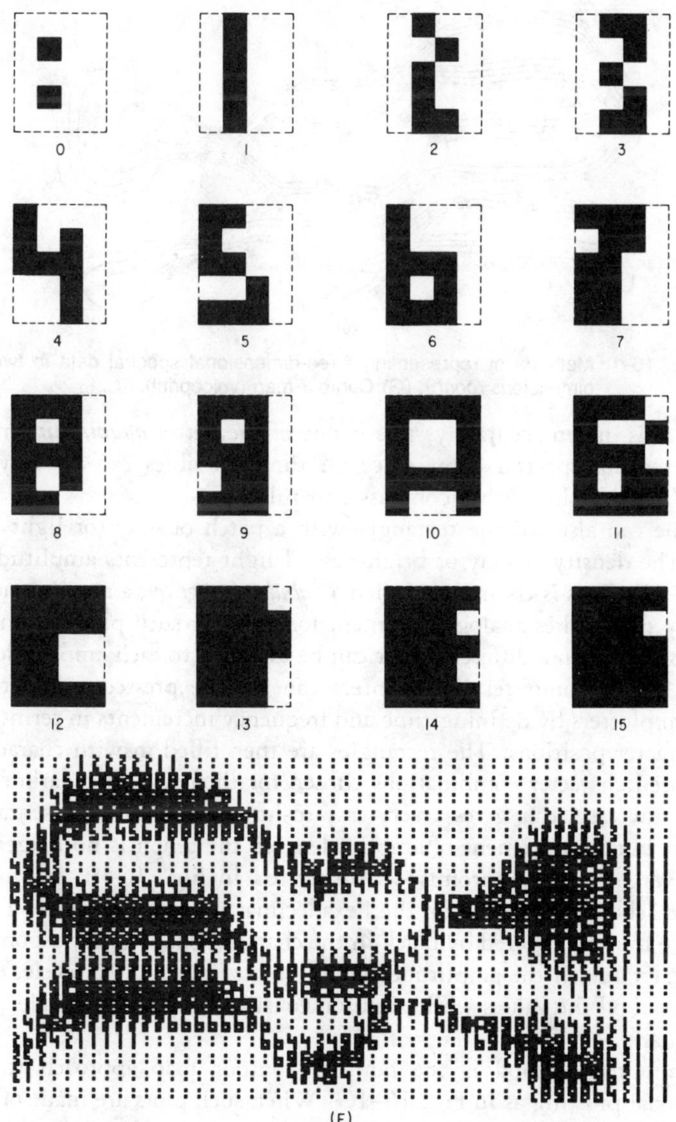

Fig. 16–1. Methods of representing three-dimensional spectral data in two dimensions *(cont.)*. (F) Optically weighted character set. Spectral plot using optically weighted characters.

sampled spectrum, amplitude data values are only known at specific increments of time and frequency. Thus, if the two dimensions of a sheet of paper correspond to time (horizontal) and frequency (vertical), then the area has been divided into an array of rectangles, much like graph paper. What is drawn within the confines of a particular rectangle represents amplitude at that time and frequency intersection. One could simply draw a bar line in the rectangle such that the length corresponds to amplitude as in Fig. 16–1C. If

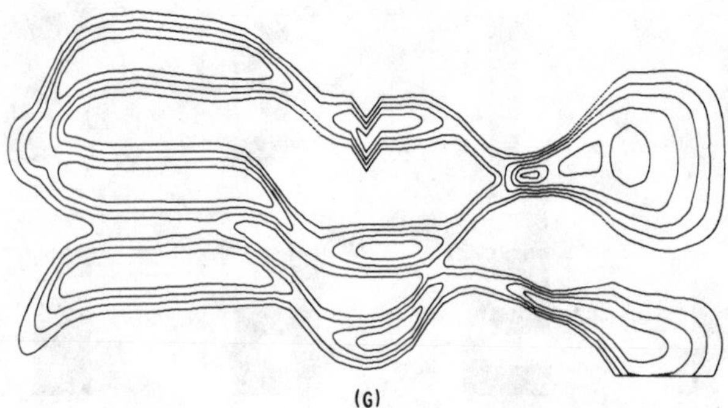

Fig. 16–1. Methods of representing three-dimensional spectral data in two dimensions *(cont.)*. (G) Contour map (voiceprint).

the figure is drawn accurately, this is one of the better *quantitative* methods of representing spectral data, since all three variables can be very easily *measured* on the plot with a compass and ruler.

One can also fill the rectangle with a patch of gray (or light if on a CRT). The density of gray or brightness of light represents amplitude as in Fig. 16–1D. This is commonly called a *sound spectrogram*, a name coined by a company that makes analog equipment for drawing such plots. If one has a color display, then a different color can be assigned to each amplitude quantization level. Computer line printers can also be pressed into service as spectrum plotters by defining time and frequency increments in terms of line and character positions. The rectangles are then filled in with characters or overprinted character combinations chosen for their apparent darkness.

In any case, this gives a very-easy-to-interpret visual representation of the data, but measurement of amplitude from the graph is no longer possible. A very clever compromise is illustrated in Fig. 16–1F in which 16 different "characters" based on the hexadecimal digits are defined. The idea is to have the area covered by black in the character shape to correspond to its numerical value. If the amplitude values are quantized to 16 levels, one can merely read off the values while simultaneously having a "gray-scale" plot to scan visually.

The final method is the familiar contour map approach to three-dimensional plotting as in Fig. 16–1G. When such plots are made of speech spectra, they are often called "voiceprints" because of the resemblance in form to fingerprints (there is some controversy over whether they are nearly as distinctive as fingerprints). This is perhaps the most accurate method of representation, particularly if changes in the spectrum are slow. Unfortunately, visual interpretation in terms of features valuable for synthesis is difficult.

Time–Frequency Resolution

In a spectral plot, good frequency resolution is desirable so that individual harmonics of the sound are clearly distinguishable. Good time resolution is also desirable so that the exact time of significant spectral events can

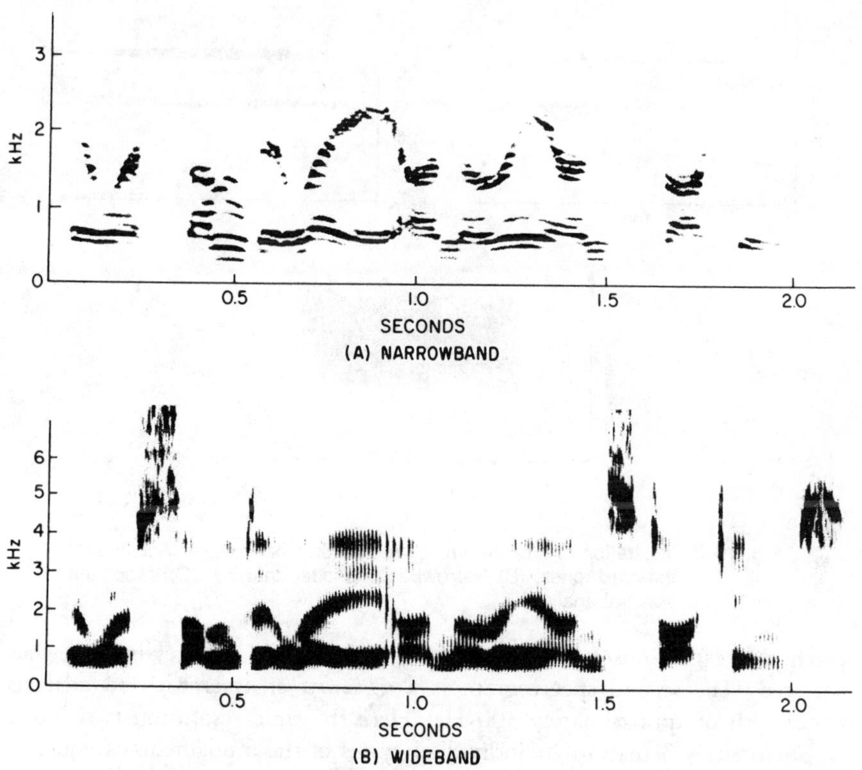

Fig. 16–2. Wideband and narrowband spectrograms. (A) Narrowband (45 Hz). (B) Wideband (300 Hz). Source: *Applications of Digital Signal Processing,* Alan V. Oppenheim, Editor, Prentice-Hall, 1978.

be determined. Unfortunately, spectral analysis is limited in the frequency and time resolution that it can show. This is not due to any particular shortcoming in the computation or the plotting method but instead is due to a fundamental law of physics. Since the unit of frequency is "events per second" and the unit of time is seconds, it should be intuitively obvious that precise measurement of the amplitude of a frequency *component* in the presence of other components will take a finite amount of time. In fact, if frequency resolution of X hertz is desired, a segment of sound lasting a minimum of $1/X$ sec must be analyzed. Even the human ear is subject to this limitation. As tone bursts are made shorter, there is greater difficulty in identifying exactly what the pitches are.

The two spectrograms in Fig. 16–2 illustrate the time–frequency tradeoff. The first spectrogram is called a *narrowband* analysis because the analysis bandwidth is about 45 Hz. This allows individual harmonics of the sound (a human voice) to show clearly. The waving up and down of the horizontal lines, which are the harmonics, is the result of changing voice

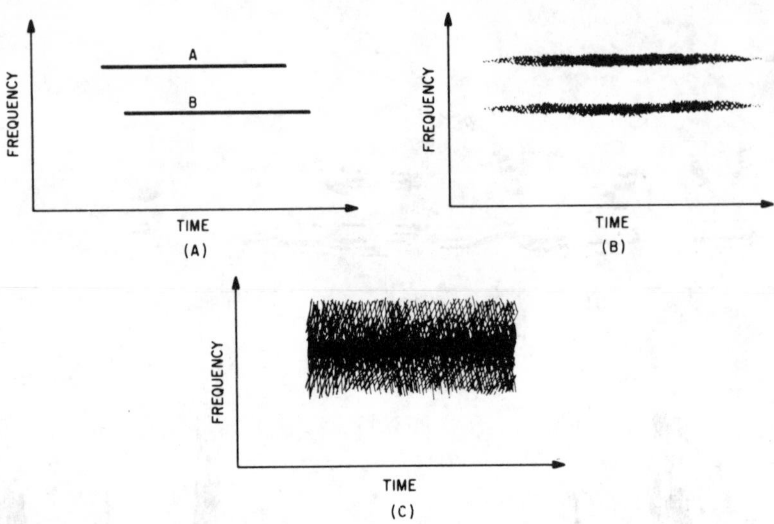

Fig. 16–3. Illustration of time–frequency resolution limitation. (A) Actual synthesized tones. (B) Narrowband spectral analysis. (C) Wideband spectral analysis.

pitch. Note that onset and termination of the major features is somewhat smeared. The second spectrogram is a *wideband* analysis with an analysis bandwidth of approximately 300 Hz. Here the time resolution is so good (approximately 3 msec) that individual cycles of the fundamental frequency are resolved, which causes the vertical bands. However, only the formants show up; the harmonics are too closely spaced relative to 300 Hz to be resolved.

Returning to the array of rectangles that makes up a digital sound spectrogram, one can consider a narrowband analysis to correspond to rectangles that are wide and short, while a wideband analysis uses narrow and tall rectangles. The *area* covered by a rectangle remains constant and is equal to approximately unity (hertz times time). The actual surface area covered on the plot depends on the scale factor chosen for frequency and time axes. An analog spectrogram is subject to the same limitation except that the rectangles become somewhat diffuse, overlapping ellipses. By using interpolation in two dimensions, a digital spectrogram can be made to appear identical to an analog one.

Although it would seem that the narrowband and wideband plots could be combined into a single figure with both good frequency and time resolution, it is not possible to do so unambiguously. This is illustrated in Fig. 16–3 in which two nearly simultaneous tone bursts are analyzed. The narrowband analysis easily separates the two tones but smears the leading and trailing edges such that it is impossible to tell which occurred first. The wideband analysis has very sharp leading and trailing edges, but now the two tones are merged together so it is still not possible to say which came first.

Data Representation

Most of the spectral plotting methods that have been discussed have a limited dynamic range for indicating amplitude. This is particularly true in the gray-scale representation. Usually, it is the changes and ratios of amplitude that are important rather than the absolute amplitude itself. Therefore, it is customary to at least partially *normalize* the amplitude scale so that overall low-amplitude portions of the signal show up as well as the high-amplitude portions. The normalizing effect can be achieved either with an automatic gain control mechanism (which can be applied after the signal is digitized) or by expressing the amplitude of each frequency component as a *percentage* of the total spectral power for that time slot. In either case, it is helpful to know the true overall amplitude which can be plotted as a conventional graph below the spectrogram. When pitched sounds are being analyzed, it is also nice to have a fundamental frequency plot as well, since this information may be difficult to determine accurately from either a narrowband or wideband analysis.

Although spectral plots are instructive to look at and, in fact, may be the goal of educational spectral analysis, the associated data must often be stored for later use. The most straightforward method of storing spectral data is in *frames*. Each frame represents spectral data at a point in time. Within the frame there is a byte or word for every frequency band used in the analysis. There may also be one or two additional elements for the overall amplitude and fundamental frequency if these data are available. With narrowband analysis data, the frames would be spread far apart in time and each frame would have a large number of elements. An example would be a frame every 30 msec with 165 elements per frame representing 30-Hz bands up to 5 kHz. Frames for wideband analysis data would occur more often, but each frame would have fewer elements. The corresponding example would be 7.5-msec frames with 40 elements, which gives 130-Hz resolution up to 5 kHz. Note that the amount of data to be stored per second is roughly the same.

With many types of spectral data it may not be necessary to retain full frequency resolution in the higher frequencies. For example, a frequency change from 60 Hz to 90 Hz is interpreted by the ear as an interval of a fifth; however, a similar shift from 5,000 Hz to 5,030 Hz is a mere 10-cent (0.1 semitone) shift, which is marginally audible if at all. As a result, the analysis bandwidth can often be widened above a kilohertz or so without loss of audible spectral features, thereby reducing the amount of data per spectral frame.

Filtering Methods of Spectral Analysis

The most obvious method of performing spectral analysis is by means of bandpass filtering. The general idea is to feed the time-varying input signal to a large number of bandpass filters, each with a different center frequency.

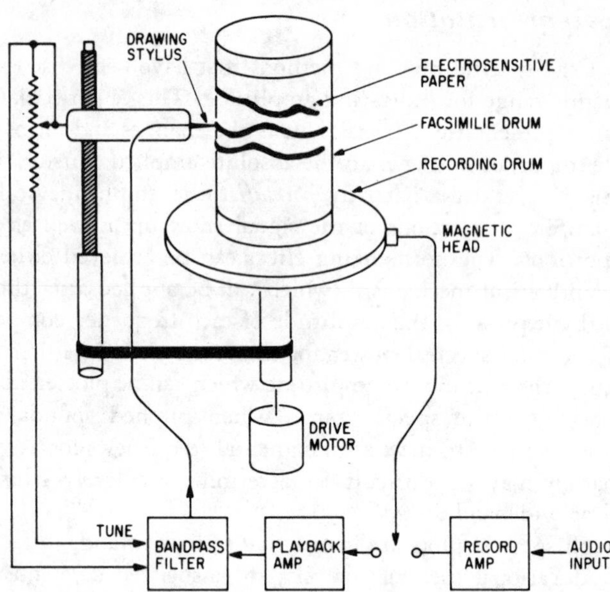

Fig. 16–4. Kay electric sound spectograph

The amplitude of the filter outputs is sampled periodically to provide the spectral data. If the center frequencies and *Q* factors of the filters are chosen properly, all possible frequencies in the band of interest will excite at least one filter.

Any number of analog methods for directly realizing or simulating such a structure have been devised. Probably the most interesting is that utilized by Kay Electric Company in their Sound Spectrograph. The basic parts of the machine shown in Fig. 16–4 are the magnetic recording drum, the facsimile image drum, and a single tunable bandpass filter. The recording drum is mechanically coupled to the facsimile drum such that they rotate in unison.

In use, up to 2.4 sec of sound can be recorded on the surface of the magnetic drum. To plot a spectrogram, a piece of electrosensitive paper (turns dark when current is passed through it) is wrapped around the facsimile drum and the machine is started in playback mode. The audio signal from the drum goes through the bandpass filter and then directly to the writing stylus. High-amplitude filter outputs create a darker trace than low-amplitude outputs. A leadscrew causes the writing stylus to gradually move along the length of the drum and at the same time increase the center frequency of the filter. Thus, the audio signal is serially analyzed at a large number of center frequencies outside of real time. An amplitude-quantizing attachment is also available to replace the gray-scale plot with a contour plot.

Most analog spectrum analyzers, however, use a bank of bandpass filters so that the spectrum analysis is performed in parallel in real time. The

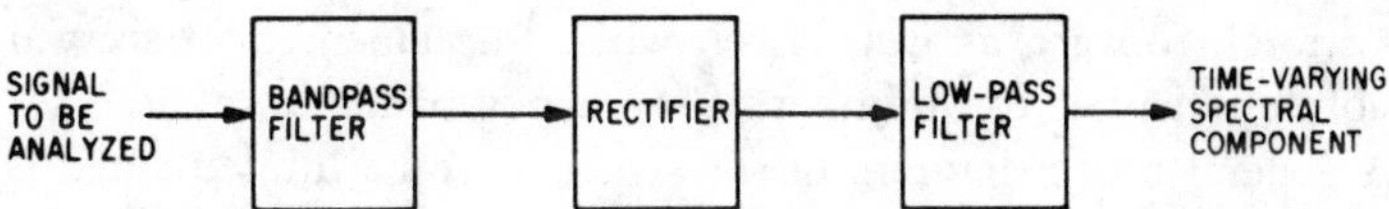

Fig. 16–5. One channel from a filterbank spectrum analyzer

structure of each channel of such an analyzer is shown in Fig. 16–5. First the signal is bandpass filtered with a center frequency corresponding to the channel under consideration. The output of the filter, which is still an ac signal but with a limited frequency range, is rectified as the first step in determining its amplitude. This is best accomplished with a full-wave rectifier so that the ripple frequency will be high. A final low-pass filter removes the ripple, giving the short time *average* of the bandpass filter output. For the lowest couple of bands, the design of this filter is critical, since too much filtering means a slow response, while inadequate filtering lets the ripple through, effectively adding noise to the channel output.

A Digital Filterbank Spectrum Analyzer

Let's now discuss a digital implementation of the analog filterbank analyzer. The main advantage of the filterbank method over the Fourier transform method that will be described later is its simplicity and ease of understanding. Because of its simplicity, dedicated hardware implementa-

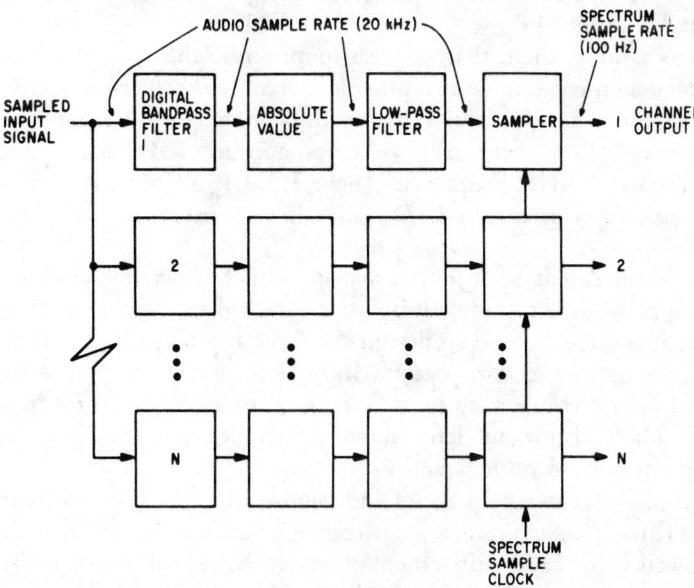

Fig. 16–6. Digital filterbank spectrum analyzer

tion is straightforward as well. Even when implemented in software, it is reasonably efficient if the number of frequency bands is small.

A general block diagram of the structure to be implemented is shown in Fig. 16–6. This is essentially an extension of the analog channel diagram into digital form. The input signal is a string of samples at the normal audio sample rate, which will be assumed to be 20 ks/s in this discussion. The sampled signal passes through a bandpass filter, rectifier, and low-pass filter in succession, all of which operate at the audio sample rate. The *output* of the low-pass filter, however, changes very slowly and therefore can be resampled at a much lower frequency to provide spectral frames at a reasonable rate such as 100/sec. As a computer program, the analyzer would essentially accept samples continuously and return a spectrum frame for every 200 input samples.

The first element to consider is the bandpass filter. Since only a bandpass response is needed and the center frequencies are fixed, the cannonical form will be used because it requires only two multiplications per sample.

The next task is to select the center frequencies of the filters. The spectrum sample period of 10 msec suggests that 100-Hz bands are optimum, although wider or narrower bands can be used as well. A bandwidth narrower than 100 Hz simply means that the bandpass filter will respond slowly to signal changes and, as a result, the channel output will be oversampled. A bandwidth greater than 100 Hz means that the low-pass filter and sampler following the rectifier will limit the channel response speed rather than the bandpass filter.

Let's assume, then, that we wish to minimize the number of frequency bands yet retain enough data to provide a good representation of significant audible features. For illustration there will be 30 frequency bands scaled on a quasiexponential scale with bandwidths ranging from 50 Hz at the low end to 500 Hz at 7.5 kHz. Frequencies above 7.5 kHz are not considered, since the low-pass filter used in *A*-to-*D* conversion has probably attenuated them anyway.

It is convenient to specify lower and upper cutoff frequencies for the filters, especially when using a mixture of bandwidths. The center frequency, however, is what is needed to design the filter and it is *not* exactly midway between the upper and lower cutoff points. It is, in fact, the geometric mean of F_h and F_l and is given by $F_c = \sqrt{F_l F_h}$, where F_c is the center frequency. This formula holds for any definition of cutoff frequency as long as the same definition applies to both F_l and F_h.

Given the center frequencies and bandwidths, the last task is to compute the filter *Q* factors. Since the percentage bandwidths vary from band to band as well as the bandwidths themselves, each filter will have a different *Q*. But before the *Q*s can be determined, the inevitable *overlap* between bands must be considered. Overlap is bound to occur because the cutoff slope at the band edges is finite. If the *Q*s are made high in order to minimize overlap as

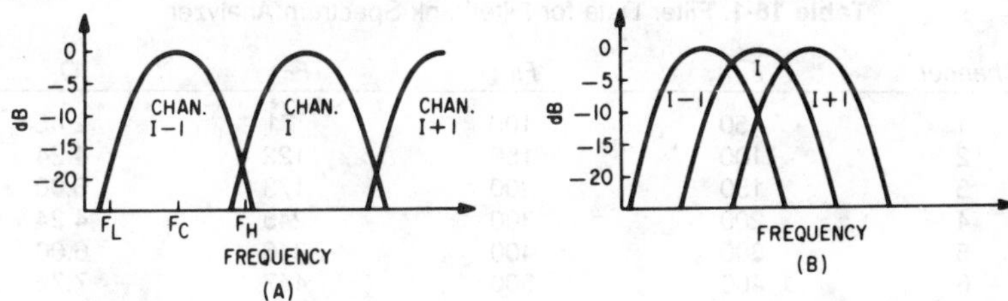

Fig. 16–7. Overlap between analyzer filters. (A) Insufficient overlap. (B) Excessive overlap.

in Fig. 16–7A, there will be large frequency gaps that none of the filters respond very strongly to. On the other hand, excessive overlap degrades frequency resolution. Overlap can be characterized by noting at what attenuation adjacent amplitude responses cross. A good number for the single-section bandpass used here is −6 dB or the 50% *voltage* response points. The formula for Q based on a 6-dB bandwidth is: $Q = 1.732F_c/(F_h - F_l)$.

Table 16–1 and Fig. 16–8 show the 30-channel bandpass responses with overlap at the 6-dB points. What is plotted in Fig. 16–8 is the *gain* versus frequency for each filter after it has been normalized for unity gain at the center frequency. This would seem to be the only reasonable way to normalize filter gains, but a peculiar thing happens if one feeds white noise into the analyzer. Some channels, notably the high-frequency wide bandwidth ones, report a higher amplitude than others even though the input sound has a flat spectrum!

The uneven response is due to the fact that white noise has constant power *per hertz* of bandwidth, and the wider bandwidth filters therefore absorb more power. A typical complex music spectrum would show the same results. On the other hand, a sound having only a few widely spaced harmonics would be analyzed correctly! The only way to avoid this dilemma is to use equal bandwidths for all of the filters. If wider bandwidths are desired at the higher frequencies, two or more bands can be *averaged*, which does not create problems. Even though the spectral data are reduced, computation time soars. The filterbank analyzer, therefore, is best suited for rough analysis of dense (lots of frequency components) spectra, in which case the channel gains are normalized for equal response to white noise.

The low-pass filters following the rectifiers must also be specified. As was mentioned earlier, their primary job is to smooth ripple from the rectifier without unduly slowing response to sudden spectrum changes. However, one must be careful to avoid multisection sharp cutoff filters because their step response includes a lot of ringing, which would distort the analysis. A reasonable compromise is a resonant low-pass with a Q of around 0.8. Since the spectrum sample rate is 100 Hz, a cutoff frequency of 30 Hz or so is indicated. Acceptable ripple rejection in the lowest band may require a

Table 16-1. Filter Data for Filterbank Spectrum Analyzer

Channel	*Fl*	*Fh*	*Fc*	*Q*
1	50	100	71	2.45
2	100	150	122	4.24
3	150	200	173	6.00
4	200	300	245	4.24
5	300	400	346	6.00
6	400	500	447	7.75
7	500	600	548	9.49
8	600	700	648	11.22
9	700	800	748	12.96
10	800	900	849	14.70
11	900	1,000	949	16.43
12	1,000	1,200	1,095	9.49
13	1,200	1,400	1,296	11.22
14	1,400	1,600	1,497	12.96
15	1,600	1,800	1,697	14.70
16	1,800	2,000	1,897	16.43
17	2,000	2,200	2,098	18.17
18	2,200	2,400	2,298	19.90
19	2,400	2,600	2,498	21.63
20	2,600	2,800	2,698	23.37
21	2,800	3,000	2,898	25.10
22	3,000	3,300	3,146	18.17
23	3,300	3,600	3,447	19.90
24	3,600	4,000	3,795	16.43
25	4,000	4,500	4,243	14.70
26	4,500	5,000	4,743	16.43
27	5,000	5,500	5,244	18.17
28	5,500	6,000	5,745	19.90
29	6,000	6,500	6,245	21.63
30	6,500	7,500	6,982	12.09

lower cutoff for that band, however. Note that aliasing is a secondary concern when the channel outputs are sampled, since the *waveform* of the channel output is of interest.

Improving the Analyzer

Before advancing to Fourier transform analysis, let's discuss some ways of improving the performance of the filterbank analyzer. The most obvious improvement is bandpass filters with flatter passbands and steeper cutoffs to improve analysis accuracy and reduce overlap. In particular, attenuation far from the center frequency could stand considerable improvement. Such filters can be realized by cascading simple bandpass filters as was done to get a supersharp low-pass in Chapter 12. Note, however, that sharp cutoffs increase filter ring time just as surely as narrow bandwidths, so minimizing overlap will incur a penalty in time resolution.

Another improvement is in the rectifier and low-pass filter area. If the bandwidth is fairly small compared to the center frequency, the bandpass filter output waveform will appear to be a pure sine wave with a varying

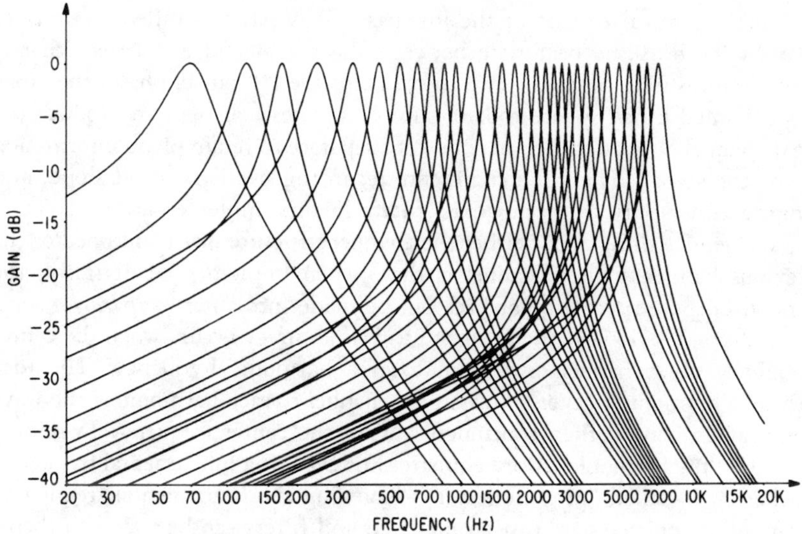

Fig. 16–8. Individual filter amplitude response curves

amplitude. If instead of the cannonical form, the state-variable bandpass filter form is used, the filter output and a 90° phase-shifted copy at the same amplitude are available. The amplitude of the waves can then be determined instantly without rectification or filtering simply by taking the square root of the sum of their squares! This then would eliminate the rectifier and low-pass filter at the expense of a more complex bandpass filter.

The converse is also possible, that is, the *bandpass* filter can be eliminated as in Fig. 16–9. Here, the input signal is split and balanced modulated (multiplied) by the two outputs of a quadrature oscillator running at the *center frequency* of the channel. Recall that balanced modulation produces sum and difference frequencies but suppresses the original signals. The following low-pass filter allows only sufficiently low *difference* frequencies through. Thus, the modulator–filter combination acts like a bandpass filter with a bandwidth *twice* the low-pass cutoff frequency and a cutoff shape either side

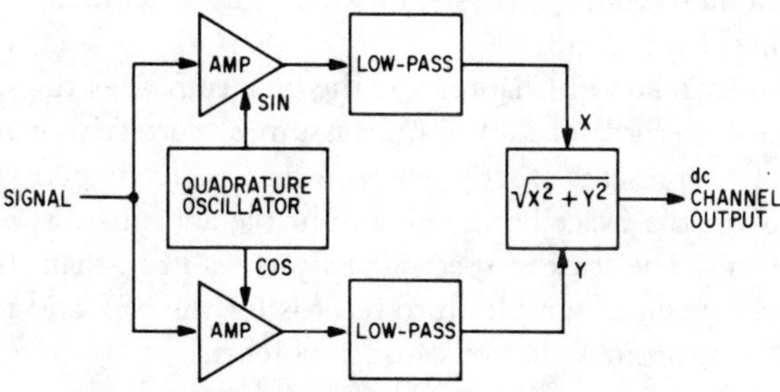

Fig. 16–9. Heterodyne filterbank channel

of center identical to that of the low-pass. This setup is called a *heterodyne filter,* since it is the beat note between the signal and a "carrier" that is actually measured. Since the two signal paths are 90° out of phase, they may be combined by a "square root of sum of squares" element to produce the final channel output or they may be kept separate to retain phase information about the signal. The same comments regarding overlap, cutoff slope, and ringing time apply to the low-pass filters in this implementation.

One nice thing about either the channel structure just mentioned or the previous bandpass filter channel is that, when implemented digitally, the general-purpose spectrum analyzer can be made into a *harmonic tracker* with little effort. Obviously, the greatest analysis accuracy occurs when the center frequency of a channel exactly matches a harmonic frequency. The idea behind a harmonic tracker is to assign a channel to each harmonic of the wave being analyzed and then continuously vary the center frequency to remain locked on the harmonic. A prerequisite, however, is a fundamental frequency tracker or so-called "pitch follower." Knowing the fundamental frequency, harmonic frequencies are easily calculated and filters can be tuned to them. The channel output then gives a time history of the actual *harmonic* spectrum of the tone, which is then directly applicable to Fourier series or FFT synthesis methods.

Spectrum Analysis Using the FFT

Almost as obvious as bandpass filtering is spectral analysis by means of Fourier analysis. After all, Fourier and his theorem is what the whole idea of a frequency spectrum is all about. Applying Fourier analysis to exactly one cycle of a periodic waveform in order to determine its harmonic makeup is a theoretically simple task that, for practical purposes, yields an exact result. On the other hand, applying it to a complex changing sound with arbitrary frequency content is not as simple and can be far from exact as well. The computational efficiency of the fast Fourier transform, however, makes Fourier analysis such an attractive method of high-resolution spectral analysis that users often go to great lengths to overcome its problems. Spectrum analysis by digital filtering is attractive only for low-resolution (few bands) analysis, harmonic-tracking analysis, or where the "intelligence" necessary to implement the FFT is lacking.

As was mentioned in Chapter 13, the FFT computes the spectrum of a finite-sized *block* (record) of samples. It assumes, correctly or not, that the block of samples represents exactly one *period* of a perfectly periodic waveform and in turn gives the exact harmonic amplitude and phase spectrum of the *assumed* waveform. The trick in spectral analysis via FFT, then, is to break up the continuous stream of samples into records for the FFT and to insure that the necessary assumptions do not cause problems.

The first practical task is to decide the record size, which in turn determines the maximum frequency and time resolution of the analysis.

Since the spectrum is averaged over the duration of a record, the time resolution can be no better than the record duration. And since the FFT gives harmonic frequencies that are integral multiples of the reciprocal of the record duration, the frequency resolution can be no better than this either. Thus, time resolution multiplied by frequency resolution can be no less than unity. Another consideration is that for maximum efficiency and ease of programming, the record size should be a power of two.

Continuing the example used earlier (20-ks/s signal sample rate, 50-Hz frequency resolution, 100-s/s spectrum sample rate), we see that the record size must be at least 400 samples to obtain the required frequency resolution. The corresponding time resolution is 20 msec, which means that the 100-s/s spectrum sample rate oversamples the changing spectrum by a factor of two. We will see later that overlap between successive records is often desirable and that it results in spectral oversampling as well. After rounding up to the next power of two, the FFT example used in the following discussion will assume a record size of 512, which gives a frequency resolution of 39 Hz, and a spectral sample rate of 78 s/s.

Equivalent Bandpass Filter

Since the filterbank and the FFT methods of spectral analysis yield similar results, it makes sense to talk about an *equivalent bandpass filter* corresponding to each of the "harmonics" computed by the FFT. As an example, let us study the 10th FFT harmonic. Ideally, it should act as a bandpass filter with a lower cutoff of 9.5 × 39 Hz = 370 Hz and an upper cutoff of 10.5 × 39 Hz = 409 Hz. Conceptually, it is simple to plot the

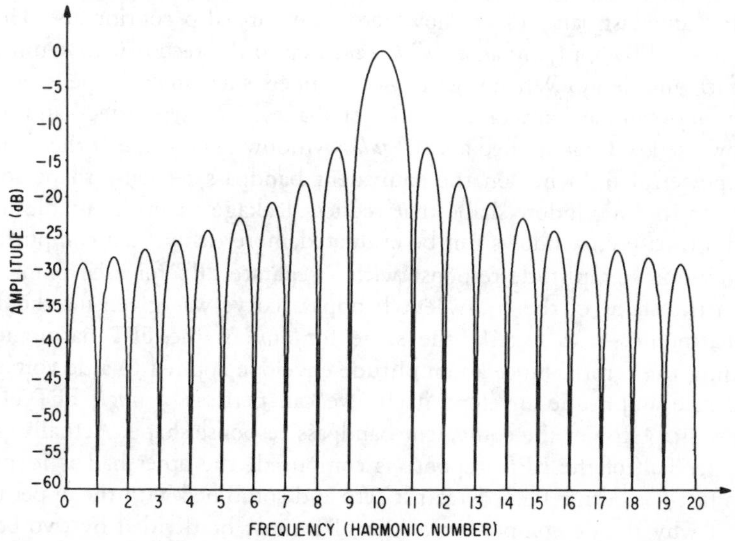

Fig. 16-10. Equivalent bandpass filter response of 10th FFT harmonic

equivalent bandpass curve. One simply generates a large number of pure sine waves of different frequencies (much more closely spaced than 39 Hz), performs an FFT (512-sample record) of each one, and plots the amplitude of the 10th FFT harmonic as a function of sine wave frequency (the phase has no effect). One might think that the equivalent bandpass filter would be ideal, that is, have a flat top and vertical sides. However, the actual plot in Fig. 16–10 is quite the opposite. If one purchased an analog bandpass filter exhibiting such a response curve, it would probably be returned for warranty repairs!

Close examination of the curve, however, reveals that the response is zero at all *integral multiples* of 39 Hz except 390 Hz, where the response is unity. Corresponding curves for the other FFT harmonics are similar except for being shifted up or down by a multiple of 39 Hz. Thus, the analysis of a periodic waveform having a fundamental frequency of 39 Hz (or an integral multiple of 39 Hz) will be exact. This should be expected because the FFT *assumes* that the sample block is periodic at 39 Hz and, conversely, one should expect some error if this is not true. The real problem with the response curve is not its curved top or sloping sides but its poor attenuation at frequencies far removed from the center frequency. This phenomenon is termed *leakage*, which must be reduced to the −40-dB to −80-dB range if the spectral analysis results are to be meaningful.

The primary cause of leakage is the discontinuity between the beginning and the end of the record when the test frequency is not an integral multiple of 39 Hz. If there were some way to adjust the ends of the record so that they are continuous, then perhaps the leakage would be reduced. One way to force continuity is to taper both ends of the record toward zero. Since the first and last samples are now zero, they are also continuous. This is accomplished by applying an *amplitude envelope* to the record with symmetrical attack and decay. When used in this manner, such an envelope is called a *window* and can have any of a number of shapes. The zero attack-and-decay window used so far is termed a *rectangular* window. The shape of the window has a powerful influence on the equivalent bandpass response shape so the goal is to find a window shape that reduces leakage to an acceptable level.

Fortunately, windows can be evaluated more easily than computing a point-by-point amplitude response with a separate FFT for each point. Although the shape of the equivalent bandpass curve was given for the 10th FFT harmonic, it is exactly the same for any of the FFT harmonics—including the zeroth. Since an amplitude envelope applied to a dc voltage is simply the amplitude envelope itself, we can perform a *single* FFT of the window shape to get the equivalent bandpass response shape. Actually, only the upper half of the BPF response is computed, the other half is identical and in fact has been reflected against zero and combined with the upper half. (This is why the dc component of the FFT must be divided by two before use.)

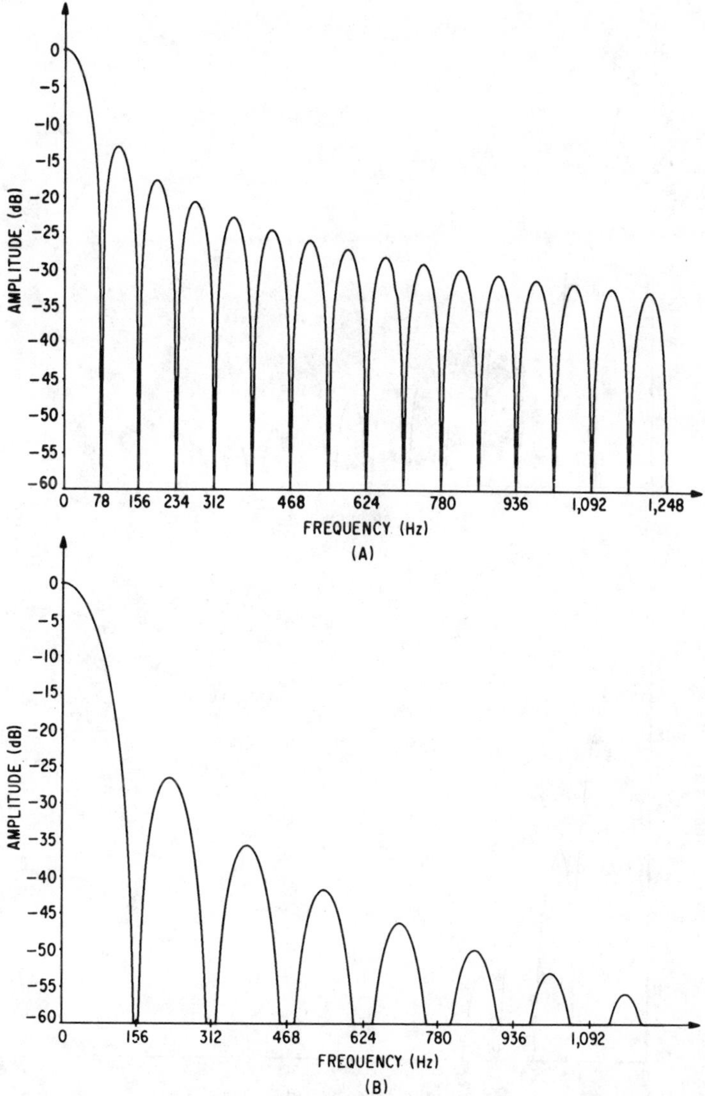

Fig. 16–11. Equivalent half-bandpass filter shapes of common windows. (A) Rectangular window. (B) Triangular window.

Of course, an FFT of the window shape will only evaluate the equivalent BPF at certain discrete frequencies. To get an accurate plot of the curve *shape*, a very large FFT must be performed with the window occupying a small portion at the beginning and zeroes occupying the remainder. For example, to check the response at eight different frequencies between each null point, an FFT eight times the window length will have to be computed. In our example, this means a 4,096-point FFT. On the other hand, most all

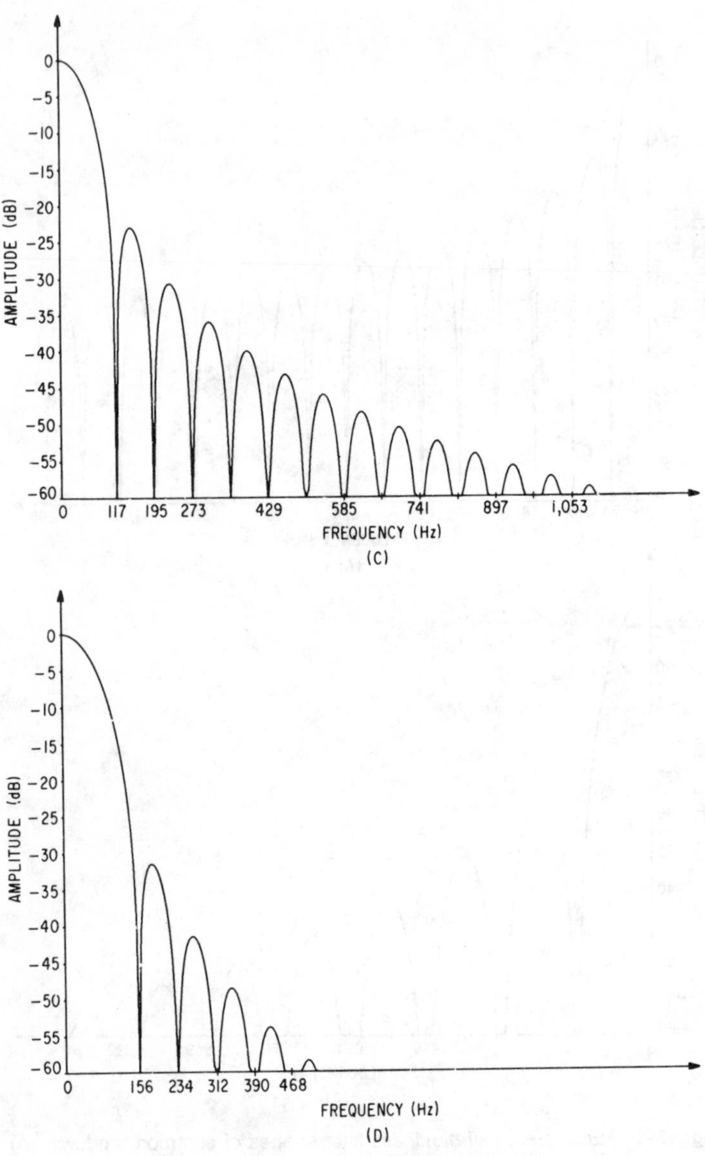

Fig. 16–11. Equivalent half-bandpass filter shapes of common windows *(cont.).* (C) Half-sine window. (D) Hanning window.

useful windows have the same basic bandpass shape; a large central lobe with ripples on both sides. The peak of the ripples and therefore the points of worst leakage occur midway between the nulls, that is, at frequencies halfway between the original FFT harmonics. Thus, the peaks of the leakage can be plotted by evaluating an FFT only twice as long as the window.

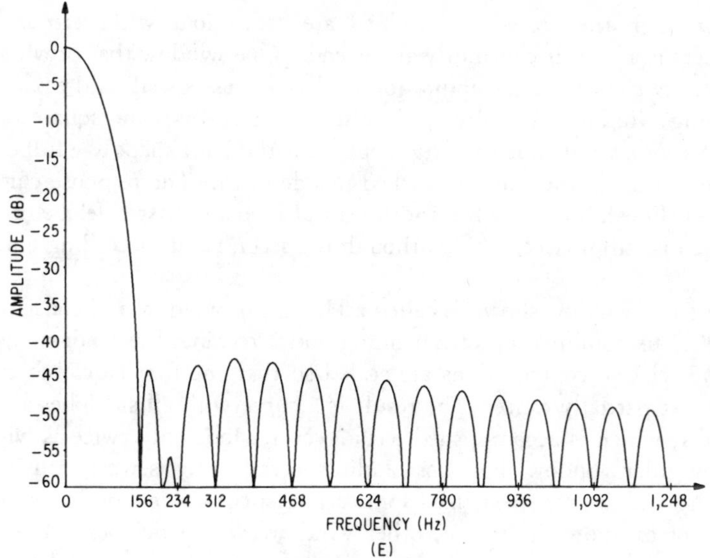

Fig. 16–11. Equivalent half-bandpass filter shapes of common windows (*cont.*). (E) Hamming windows. $HM(X) = 0.54 - 0.46(\cos(2\pi X)), 0 \leq X \leq 1$.

Some Example Windows

Now that they can be easily plotted, let's evaluate some windows. Perhaps the simplest is a linear rise and fall, which is called a triangular window. This window, along with the upper half of its equivalent bandpass response shape, is plotted in Fig. 16–11B. Two characteristics are immediately apparent. First, the leakage attenuation is much better than that of the rectangular window shown for reference. Second, the apparent width of the central lobe, which is the primary bandpass response, is double that of the rectangular window. This is the price that is paid for low leakage, and the lower the leakage, the broader the bandpass. Thus, one must decide how much leakage can be tolerated and choose a window that meets but does not greatly exceed that figure. For our example, a figure of −40 dB will be chosen and none of the secondary lobes, even the one closest to the center lobe, will be allowed to exceed it. According to this criterion, the triangular window is not suitable, since the first sidelobe is at −27 dB. Nevertheless, the third and higher sidelobes are less than −40 dB, a figure that seemingly even the 100th lobe of the rectangular window cannot meet.

A similar window is the half sine wave. It has the advantage of a flat rather than pointed top. Its characteristics are shown in Fig. 16–11C. Its central lobe is only 1.5 times as wide as the rectangular window, yet has even better sidelobe attenuation (beyond the first) than the triangular window. Its second sidelobe, which is at the same frequency as the first triangular window sidelobe, is about −32 dB.

Although the preceding windows are continuous with zero at both ends, there is a *slope* discontinuity at the ends. One window that provides for continuity of slope (and continuity for *all* derivatives as well) is the *cosine bell* or hanning window. Actually, it is just the point-by-point square of the half-sine window but, due to a trig identity, is the same shape as a full cosine cycle shifted up to the axis and turned upside down. The response curve in Fig. 16–11D exhibits a double width central lobe and first sidelobe of −32 dB, which is still unacceptable, although the second and succeeding ones are fine.

The last window shown is called a Hamming window and consists of a very judicious combination of a hanning and a rectangular window. Essentially the relative contributions are scaled so that the first sidelobes cancel and the rest partially cancel. The result is a curve with all sidelobes at −42 dB or less, which is accomplished with a central lobe only twice as wide as the rectangular window. For most audio spectral analysis work, this is the optimum window. For specialized applications such as signal detection in the presence of overpowering noise, other windows with sidelobes of −80 dB and better are available at the expense of an even wider central lobe.

Performing the Analysis

At this point, we are ready to outline the procedure necessary to go from an indefinite-length sample string to a sequence of spectral frames using the FFT. For illustration purposes, the example of a 20-ks/s sample rate, 512-point FFT, 39-Hz frequency resolution, and 78-s/s spectral sample rate will be continued. The crux of the analysis procedure is how the continuous stream of samples will be broken up into 512 sample records for the FFT. One possibility is to simply take the 512 samples from the input, transform them, take the next 512, transform, etc. If this is done, windowing of the records may greatly attenuate or miss significant waveform details that occur when the window amplitude is near zero. Furthermore, only 39 spectrums will be computed per 20,000 samples (1 sec).

Overlap can be used to insure that all parts of the waveform are seen and increase the spectral sample rate as well. The general idea is the exact inverse of the method outlined in Chapter 13 in which direct FFT synthesis was discussed. For two-to-one overlap, one would only take 256 samples from the string for each spectral frame. The other 256 in the record would be left over from the previous frame. The process can be likened to a 512-sample shift register. Each frame time 256 new samples would be shifted in and the oldest 256 would be shifted out and thrown away. Other overlap factors (which need not be integers) for both higher- and lower-spectrum sample rates are possible simply by altering the number of samples shifted in.

There are a couple of complications in the computation that can lead to a lot of partially redundant data arrays. When a window is applied to overlapped sample data, it must not alter the data itself because some of it will be needed for overlapping purposes in the next spectral frame. Likewise, the FFT will destroy the sample data unless a copy is made and the copy transformed. For maximum efficiency, one can combine copying, windowing, and bit-reverse decimation into one program loop that takes little more time than windowing alone. If memory space is tight, the samples that are not needed in the next frame may be destroyed.

In summary, the procedure for converting a string of samples into a string of spectra is as follows (512-point FFT and 2:1 overlap):

1. Discard 256 signal samples from the right half of the analysis record.
2. Copy (or equivalent) the remaining 256 samples from the left to the right half of the analysis record.
3. Accept 256 new signal samples from the input string and put them in the left half of the analysis record.
4. Make a copy of the analysis record.
5. Apply the chosen window to the copy.
6. Do a 512-point real FFT.
7. The 256 sine and cosine components represent one spectral frame. They may be stored as is or processed further.
8. Go to step 1 for the next spectral frame.

Note that twice as much output data is generated as input data if phase information is retained. This is a result of oversampling (overlapping), but as will be seen later such oversampling simplifies subsequent spectral processing. In fact, for analysis–resynthesis applications, it may be necessary to further oversample the sequence of spectra to obtain good resynthesis quality after modification.

Spectral Processing

In the previous section, two methods of obtaining the time-varying spectrum of a sound were presented. We can now assume that the spectrum is in the form of a sequence of frames at the spectral sample rate and each frame contains samples (in frequency) of the spectral curve at a point in time.

Three primary applications exist for the spectral data. The first is direct modification of the spectrum and immediate FFT resynthesis as sound. The second, which may be considered an extension of the first, is the extraction of one or more time-varying parameters, such as fundamental frequency or gross spectral shape. These data may then be used to control conventional synthesis equipment such as oscillators, filters, etc., rather than direct reconstruction with the FFT. The third application is display and subsequent study in an effort to learn more about the processes that created the original sound.

Often, it is convenient to perform some translation of the spectral data before it is modified. If the FFT was used for analysis, each time–frequency sample of the spectrum is represented by a cosine magnitude and a sine magnitude. We have already seen how this form can be converted into amplitude and phase form. The amplitude, which is always positive, can be further converted into decibels if desired. Since the human ear has difficulty in distinguishing amplitude differences much less than 1 dB, the decibel amplitude data can be quantized to as few as 6 bits without serious degradation.

There may be an inclination to discard the phase data, since they have little audible effect on the sound. However, the phase data give valuable information about a sound parameter that is quite important—frequency. The fundamental and harmonics of an arbitrary tone are unlikely to fall precisely at the center frequencies of the analysis bands. The results of this mismatch are twofold. First, since the bandwidth of the Hamming window is four times the frequency spacing of the analysis, a given signal component will show up strongly in as many as four adjacent frequency bands. Second, the exact frequency of the signal is unknown. Even though the analysis seems imperfect, resynthesis will yield a result essentially equal to the original signal. It is the phase information that allows accurate reconstruction. We will see later how phase can be utilized to precisely determine the component frequencies.

Direct Spectral Modification

Spectral analysis, modification, and resynthesis via FFT comprise the easiest method of implementing a filter with arbitrary amplitude and phase characteristics. Often, it is the most efficient method as well, since the computation effort is independent of the filter's response shape. Another advantage is that time-varying filters are handled as easily as fixed ones, a virtue not shared by the transversal method of arbitrary filter implementation. Basically, one takes the sequence of spectral frames and multiplies the amplitude of each spectral component by the amplitude response of the filter at the corresponding frequency. The resulting sequence of spectral frames is then converted back into sound via FFT synthesis. When the spectral data is in sine–cosine form, both components must be multiplied by the filter's amplitude response.

One can also *add* two or more spectra together. Since the FFT used in synthesis is a linear process, the result should be equivalent to individual resynthesis and conventional mixing of the results. However, there are two advantages to mixing in the frequency domain. First, there is no phase cancellation among the combined spectra if just amplitude spectra are used. Directly combining sine–cosine spectra, however, gives the typical amount of interference among harmonics of the combined tones. The other advantage of spectral combination is that only one resynthesis is necessary, thus reducing computation effort.

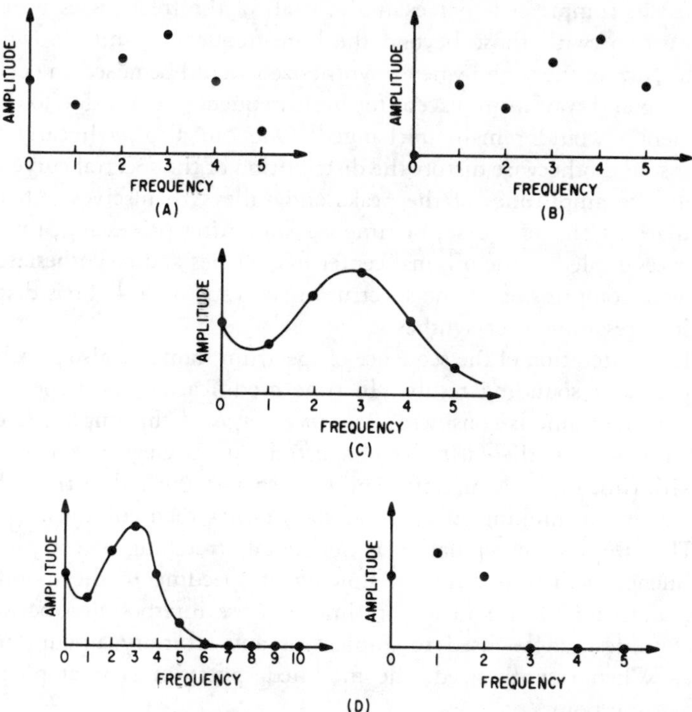

Fig. 16–12. Spectrum frequency manipulations. (A) Unmodified spectral data. (B) Spectrum shift upward. (C) Frequency interpolation. (D) Left: Linear compression of interpolated spectrum. Right: Resampling at original center frequencies.

Besides amplitude modification of the spectral components, many weird and wonderful things can be accomplished by altering their *frequencies* as in Fig. 16–12. If, for example, the spectral frequency resolution is 39 Hz, an upward spectrum shift of 39 Hz can be accomplished simply by shifting the numbers in each frame upward one slot. The dc frequency band would be replaced by zero and the highest band would be discarded. Likewise, the spectrum may be shifted downward *without* the reflection around zero that analog frequency shifters suffer from. Circular shifting and spectral inversion are also easily accomplished.

For maximum flexibility in frequency alteration, it is necessary to interpolate between the tabulated frequencies. The same techniques used for *time* interpolation in Chapter 13 can be used for *frequency* interpolation in a spectral frame. With suitable interpolation, the spectral curve can be regarded as continuous (infinite sample rate in frequency) and frequency shifts of any arbitrary amount may be performed.

Instead of shifting all frequencies by an equal amount, which usually converts harmonic tones into inharmonic ones, the spectrum can be linearly stretched or compressed. For example, if all of the frequencies were multiplied by two (with those beyond the high-frequency limit thrown away), then the *pitch* of the sound when resynthesized would be raised an octave, but the timing and waveform (except for high-frequency rolloff due to discarded components) would remain unchanged! One can also *non*linearly stretch, compress, and otherwise distort the distribution of the spectral curve without affecting the amplitudes of the peaks and valleys themselves. All of these manipulations can, of course, be time varying. After processing, the spectral curve is resampled at the original center frequencies and resynthesized. Note that severe compression of the spectrum may lead to local "alias distortion" when it is resampled for synthesis.

Time alteration of the sequence of spectrum frames is also possible with equally strange-sounding results. In time modification, each spectral component in the frame is considered as a *time sample* of the amplitude curve of that component. If the entire set of spectral data is viewed as a rectangular array with time in the X direction and frequency in the Y direction, then this is equivalent to thinking in terms of rows rather than columns.

The simplest manipulation is horizontal stretching or compression of the sequence, which amounts to slowing or speeding of the sound events *without* affecting the frequency or timbre. *Time* interpolation between the spectral values can be used to implement any arbitrary amount of speed change. When resynthesized, the modified spectrum is resampled at the original time points.

The dispersive filter mentioned earlier may be simulated by shifting the rows of spectral data with respect to each other such that the lower-frequency rows are delayed more than the higher-frequency rows. Reverse dispersion in which high frequencies are delayed more is also possible as well as nonlinear dispersion. Small amounts of dispersion are most effective with percussive sounds, while larger amounts affect all but the most steady of tones. Vocals in particular are given strange accents by dispersion.

Since the spectral data are being considered as a set of simultaneously varying waveforms, it is obvious that these waveforms may themselves be filtered. Uniform low-pass filtering of all of the bands simply blurs rapid changes in the spectrum, thus making vocals, for example, sound drunk. High-pass filtering, on the other hand, emphasizes rapid changes and may produce a "caricature" of the original sound. Resonant low-pass filtering with moderate Q factors preserves the steady states of the spectrum but gives any rapid changes a "twangy" quality due to the overshoot and ringing of the filter. Of course, each frequency band can be filtered differently, which tends to combine filtering and dispersion effects.

Resynthesis

In Chapter 13, direct synthesis from amplitude and frequency data using the FFT was described. Basically, the procedure consisted of conversion from an amplitude–frequency "source" form into an amplitude–phase and ultimately sine–cosine "object" form that was compatible with the FFT. However, most of the spectrum modifications that have just been discussed can be performed directly on the sine–cosine or amplitude–frequency form of the spectrum. Resynthesis should therefore be simplified over the method given in Chapter 13.

One desirable property of an analysis–synthesis system is *transparency*, that is, no signal distortion in the absence spectral modification. Distortionless reconstruction can, in fact, be done very simply using unmodified spectral data from the analysis. First, each spectral frame is inverse transformed to recover the windowed sample record that created the frame. Next, the window is divided out giving the original sequence of samples. Finally, the overlap is removed to obtain the original continuous stream of samples. Any difference between the original and reconstructed data is due to roundoff error in the arithmetic, most of it probably from the window removal (division by small numbers at the edges of the window) step.

However, if modifications are made, two things are likely to happen. First, the inverse-transformed modified records cannot be expected to butt together nicely and continuously like unmodified records do. Second, the inverse transform of a modified frame may show little if any evidence of a window because the precise amplitude and phase relations necessary for the window-shaped envelope will have been altered. Inverse windowing, therefore, is likely to distort the record and actually emphasize discontinuities between the records.

Thus, the problem of eliminating interrecord discontinuities is similar to that encountered in FFT synthesis from scratch. The same solution, that is, windowing and synthesis overlap, used for direct synthesis is reasonably adequate for resynthesis. The disadvantage of applying this method is that an unmodified spectrum will no longer provide precisely the original data, since the resynthesis manipulation itself amounts to a modification. Methods are available to reduce resynthesis error to zero but they are complex and amount to essentially infinite overlapping (overlap factor=record length) of the synthesis. As mentioned in Chapter 13, a four-to-one synthesis overlap provides results clearly superior to two-to-one overlap and therefore is preferred in conjunction with four-to-one analysis or careful time interpolation of two-to-one analysis data.

Parameter Extraction

Instead of immediate resynthesis, one may wish to further analyze the spectral data in an effort to extract one or more of the fundamental parameters of sound. These parameters may then be used to direct a conventional synthesis process or may be stored for later recall with the advantage that a handful of fundamental parameters can often replace hundreds of spectral components without loss of information significant to the application.

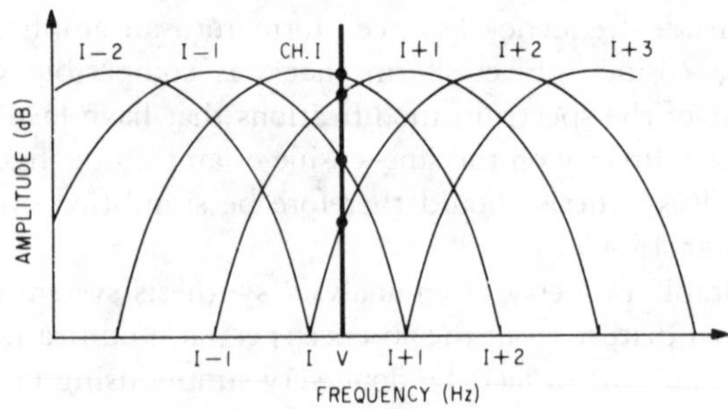

Fig. 16–13. Response of spectrum analysis with Hamming window to a single frequency component

Variations in overall amplitude are most easily extracted. One simply sums the amplitudes of all of the frequency bands to get the total amplitude for the frame. This neatly overcomes problems with rectifier ripple experienced in analog envelope followers, although the signal processing involved is certainly much more complex. Another advantage is that some frequency bands may be weighted more heavily than others. For example, if a result with good correlation to subjective loudness is desired, the spectrum can be weighted according to the Fletcher-Munson loudness curves described in Chapter 1. Since the weighting curve itself depends on amplitude, some intelligence is needed to select the proper curve anyway.

Frequency Analysis

True frequency analysis, in which the sound being analyzed is broken down into a list of components in which the exact frequency and amplitude of each is tabulated, is another useful form for analysis data. Note that this is the "source-spectrum" form used for direct FFT synthesis in Chapter 13. The process described there of updating the phase of the object spectrum to obtain arbitrary frequencies can be reversed to determine what an arbitrary frequency is from analysis data. One simply looks at the *phase* of successive analysis frames and ascertains the magnitude and direction of shift from one frame to the next. This then gives the difference between the band's center frequency and the signal frequency. For example, if the phase in band I advances 45° ($\pi/4$) every frame, it can be concluded that the signal frequency is equal to the band's center frequency plus one-eighth of the spectral sample rate.

With a Hamming analysis window, a single frequency component will excite as many as four adjacent analysis bands as shown in Fig. 16–13. One could compute frequency from the channel with the strongest response (channel I in the diagram) and ignore the others and get good results. However, if the spectrum sample rate is sufficiently high, the frequency can be computed from *any* of the responding channels. If a good, clean frequency component is actually being seen (as opposed to random noise), then all of the frequency measures will yield the same value. A high spectral sample rate is necessary because otherwise the phase shift for a distant band such as $I+2$ in the diagram may exceed 180° per frame and give a false result. For the Hamming window, an analysis overlap factor of four or more would give a sufficiently high spectral sample rate.

Another constraint is that frequency resolution must be high enough so that every component of the signal is completely resolved. If the components are not completely separated, serious errors in frequency and amplitude measurement are likely. For a Hamming window, this means that frequency components can be no closer than four times the reciprocal of the analysis record duration. In our analysis example (20-ks/s F_s, 512-sample analysis record), this evaluates to about 150 Hz. The only reasonable way to improve frequency resolution is to use longer analysis records, which, of course, degrade time resolution. Alternatively, if all of the frequency components are nearly equal in amplitude, a rectangular window having one-half the bandwidth of the Hamming window can be considered.

Once the frequency of a component has been determined, its amplitude must be calculated to complete the analysis. The simplest method is to note the band with the greatest response to the component and use its response amplitude. The error incurred when doing this is small enough (1.5 dB maximum for a Hamming window) that it can be ignored in many applications. For greater accuracy, the curved top of the equivalent bandpass filter can be considered and a correction factor derived based on the difference between the dominant band's center frequency and the actual signal frequency. One could also rms sum (square root of the sum of squares) the responding bands to get a single amplitude measurement for the component. Of course, all of the analysis bands will show some response due to noise or leakage. However, only those with sufficiently high outputs and reasonable frequency correlation among adjacent bands should actually be considered as detecting a valid signal component.

Spectral Shape Analysis

Many natural sounds can be modeled as an oscillator driving a filter as in Fig. 16–14. The oscillator's waveform is called the *excitation function* and is normally rich in harmonics. The filter is called the *system function* and is typically rather complex having several resonant peaks and possibly some notches as well. The spectrum of the output sound is the point-by-point product of the excitation function spectrum and the amplitude response of the filter as in Fig. 16–14B. In musical applications, the frequency of the excitation function is the primary variable, since it determines the pitch of the resulting tone. The waveform may also change some, typically acquiring additional upper harmonic amplitude as its overall amplitude increases. Al-

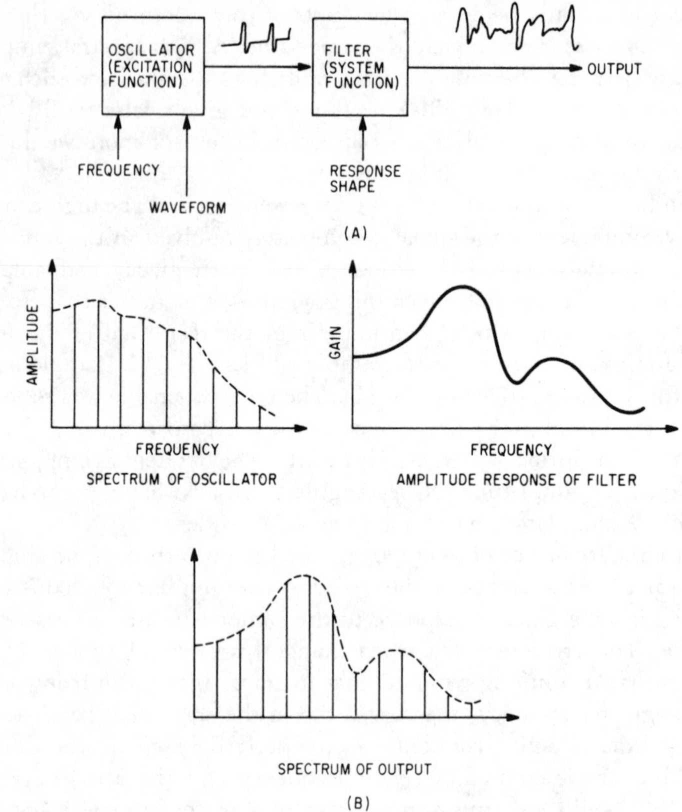

Fig. 16–14. Natural sound modeling. (A) Simple model of natural sound process. (B) Spectral interpretation of simple model.

ternatively, the excitation function can be white noise, which does invalidate the pitch parameter but has no effect on anything else. The system function may be either fixed or variable depending on the sound being modeled.

The range of natural sounds to which this model is applicable is actually very large. Most wind instruments, such as the bassoon, and bowed string instruments, such as the violin, are well described by this model. The human voice is a prime example. In these examples, a harmonic-rich excitation function is generated by a vibrating element such as a reed, sticky string, or flapping folds of flesh. Resonators in the instruments, such as the folded tube of the bassoon, wood panels with odd-shaped cutouts, or oral and nasal cavities filter the excitation function before it actually escapes into the air. Musical instruments usually have fixed resonators (notable exceptions are muted brass instruments), whereas the human voice depends on a highly variable resonator for its expression. All of these resonators may have a number of distinct resonant frequencies (peaks in the amplitude response) and some, such as the violin, can have significant antiresonant valleys as well.

In technical terms, the resonant peaks are called *poles* of the system function while the notches, if present, are termed zeroes. In speech and music work, the zeroes are frequently ignored and the poles are called *formants*. The goal of formant estimation is determination of the number of formants, their resonant frequencies, and possibly their bandwidth or Q factors. This information represents the characteristics of the filter, which is usually a majority portion of the analyzed sound's timbre. Musical applications of formant analysis seek the design of a filter with the same formant structure as the analyzed sound. Different synthesized excitation functions are then modified by the filter. The resulting sound has the most prominent characteristics of both. For example, if vocal vowel sounds are used for the formant analysis and the resultant filter is driven with a square-wave excitation function, the vowel quality would be retained but with the characteristically hollow timbre of square waves!

Perhaps the most straightforward method of formant analysis is to scan the *amplitude* spectrum and find the center points of high-amplitude *clusters* of harmonics. The center points are the formant frequencies. The bandwidths may be estimated by noting the 3-dB points on either side of each peak. This method works well only if the harmonics are dense compared to the bandwidths of the formants, which means a low excitation frequency. This is because the excitation function harmonics effectively *sample* the filter response curve and insufficiently dense sampling leads to aliasing and incorrect conclusions regarding the response curve. Even if the sampling is theoretically dense enough, interpolation may have to be used to increase it further so that the center point and 3-dB points of the peaks can be accurately determined. Note that the original spectral analysis need not resolve the harmonics themselves to be useful for this method of formant analysis.

Linear Prediction

A more refined method of formant analysis is called *linear prediction* because, by specifying the filter involved in the original sound generation, one is able to *predict* what future time samples of the sound are likely to be. Although originally developed for the efficient transmission of speech signals over limited bandwidth channels, linear prediction is useful in music synthesis because it results in an actual *design* of the filter represented by the system function. Unfortunately, the calculations are too involved to be covered here in simple terms but the general characteristics of linear prediction can be discussed. Additional reference material is listed in the bibliography.

In linear prediction, the actual filter used to generate the sound being analyzed is *approximated* by a filter having a specified number of poles and zeroes. Often, because of computational difficulties encountered in handling the zeroes, an *all-pole* model is used. The filter resulting from all-pole linear prediction analysis gives the "best" (least-square error) approximation possible when constrained to the specified number of poles (twice the number of resonances). Often, the appropriate number of resonances to use can be determined from a physical knowledge of the natural sound source. In such cases, the linear prediction model can be expected to give excellent results. In cases in which the filter is arbitrary, a balance between resonance count and result quality will have to be determined by experiment. If vocals are being analyzed, three or four resonances are quite sufficient to capture the *intelligence* of the words. Many more are necessary to characterize the timbre in sufficient detail for recognition of the singer's identity. Figure 16–15 shows the results of linear prediction analysis of a vowel sound with different resonance counts.

An all-poles digital linear prediction calculation usually results in the set of *multiplier coefficients* necessary for implementation of the filter in cannonical form. These coefficients apply only to the feedback paths; the feedforward coefficients, which implement zeroes, are zero for an all-poles model. The number of coefficients from the calculation will be $2N+1$, where N is the number of resonances. The extra coefficient is an overall gain factor. The cannonical form of the filter can be converted into cascade form with N sections. The conversion is desirable because multiplier accuracy requirements of the cascade form are much less than the cannonical form.

Note that linear prediction just gives the filter design, not the actual formant frequencies and bandwidths. Although the latter can be determined by analyzing the filter, they are not needed to utilize the filter for synthesis with an arbitrary excitation function.

Homomorphic Analysis

In digital music synthesis using the natural sound model of Fig. 16–14, all that is really needed is a plot of the filter's amplitude response. With such a plot, the methods of arbitrary filter implementation discussed in Chapter 14 can be used to apply the filter to a different excitation function. However, a typical spectrum plot such as the one in Fig. 16–16A shows effects due to discrete harmonics of the excitation function as well as general trends due to the system function. In homomorphic analysis, the goal is to obtain an amplitude response curve of the system function independent of the characteristics of the excitation function.

From examination of the overall spectrum, it is obvious that what is desired is a "smoothed" plot of the spectrum that retains the general spectral shape but suppresses the individual harmonic "noise." This smoothing may be accomplished by a moving average, which is actually a digital low-pass transversal filter, or by other low-pass filters applied to the frequency sample sequence just like they would be normally applied to a time sample sequence.

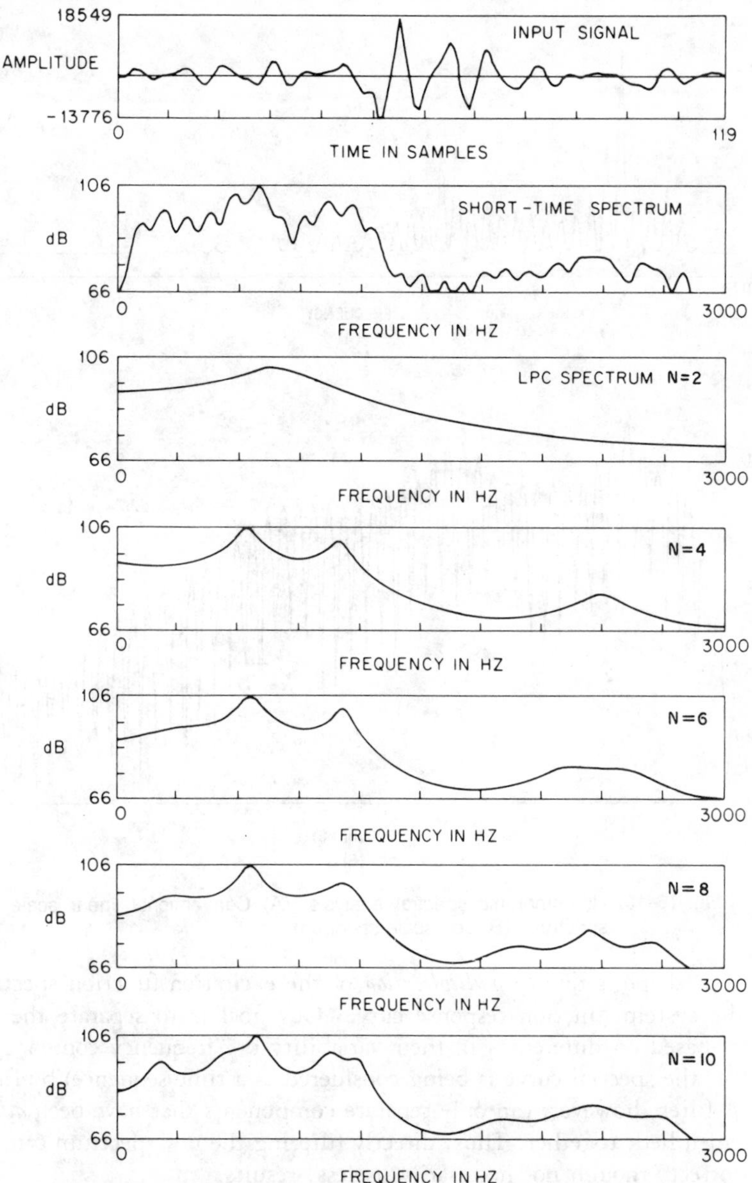

Fig. 16–15. Effectiveness of linear preditive spectral analysis. Source: *Digital Processing of Speech Signals*, L.R. Rabiner and R.W. Schafer, Prentice-Hall, 1978.

In the following discussion, the spectrum will in fact be considered as a time sequence and terms relating to time-sequence processing will be used.

Unfortunately, applying a linear filter to a raw amplitude spectrum is not really mathematically correct. In the natural sound model, the final

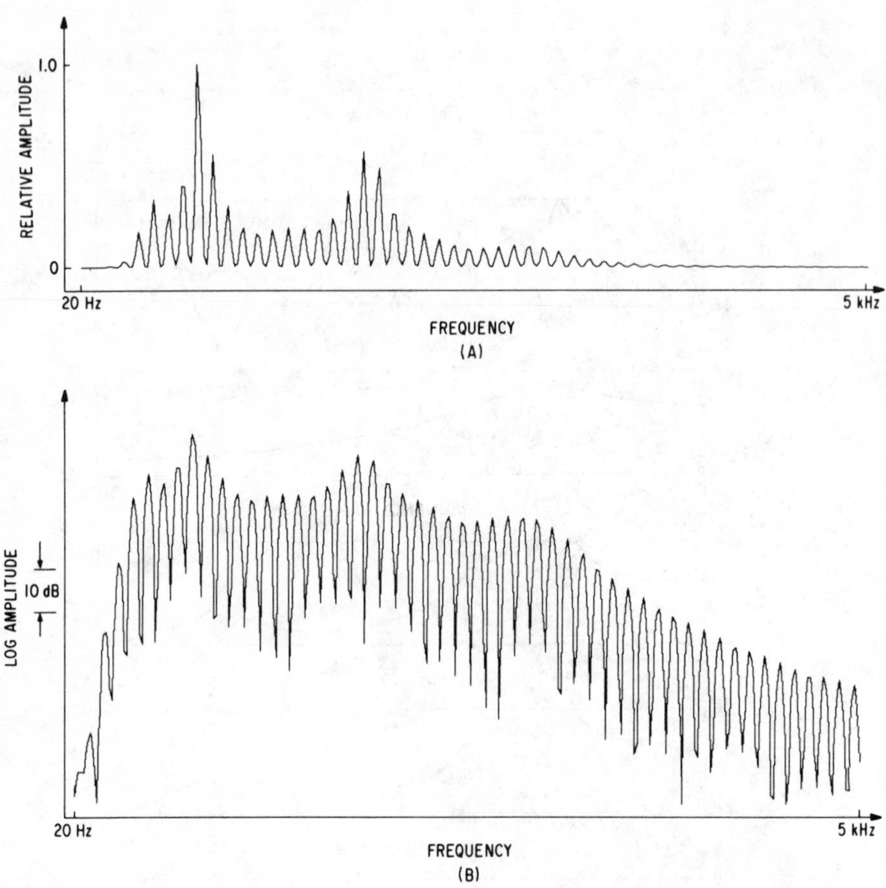

Fig. 16–16. Homomorphic spectral analysis. (A) Conventional linear scale spectrum. (B) Log scale spectrum.

spectrum shape is due to *multiplication* of the excitation function spectrum and the system function response curve. Our goal is to separate the two spectra based on differences in their variability or "frequency content" (remember the spectral curve is being considered as a time sequence) by filtering. A filter, however, can only separate components that have been *added*, not multiplied, together. Thus, directly filtering the raw spectrum can lead to incorrect, though not necessarily useless, results.

The problem is solved by remembering from high school math that the *product* of two numbers is equal to the antilog of the *sum* of their logarithms. Thus, if the amplitude spectrum is converted to decibels as in Fig. 16–16B, then the resultant shape is the sum of the excitation decibel spectrum and the filter response curve in decibels. The two curves may now be separated by filtering using a high-pass to recover the excitation spectrum and a low-pass to obtain a clean system function response shape. In music synthesis, the

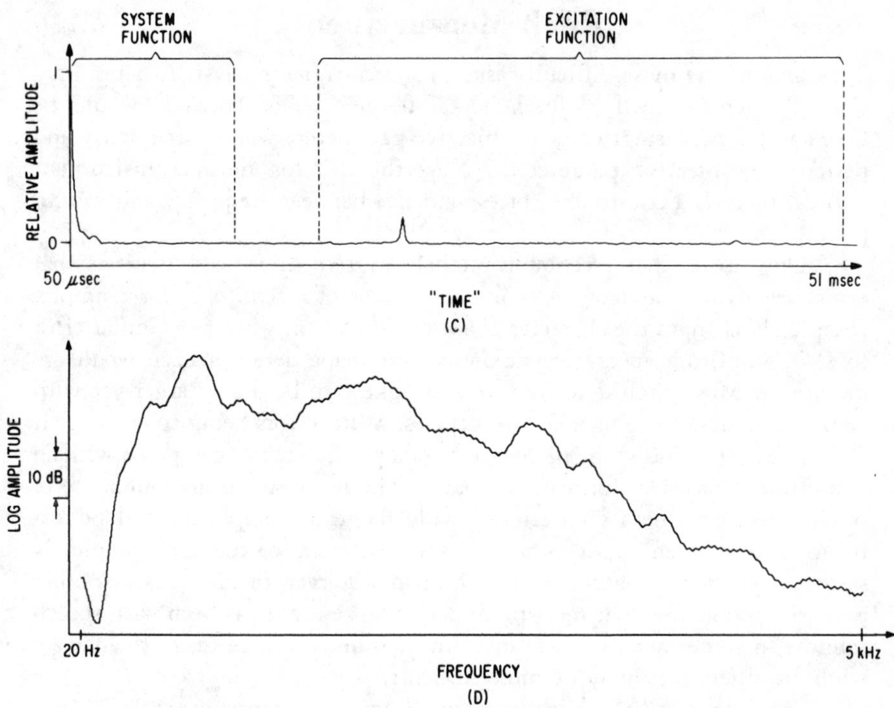

Fig. 16–16. Homomorphic spectral analysis *(cont.)*. (C) Magnitude of the cepstrum. (D) Smoothed log spectrum.

recovered excitation function is usually discarded, except for its fundamental frequency, and the recovered system function is utilized.

Of course, the Fourier transform can also be used to implement the separation filter with the advantage of zero phase shift. Phase shift (delay) in the separation filter is undesirable because it shifts all of the recovered frequencies upward (or downward depending on the direction of filtering). The forward Fourier transform of a decibel spectrum, however, is a mathematical absurdity and so the word *cepstrum* was coined to refer to it. The word is formed by reverse spelling of the first half of the word "spectrum" and tacking on the last half. It is only fitting, then, to call the independent variable of a cepstral plot, which has the dimension of time, *quefrency*! A cepstral plot is shown in Fig. 16–16C.

Low-quefrency values in the cepstrum are due to the system function shape, while high-quefrency values are due to the excitation function. To recover the system function shape, all quefrency values above a certain cutoff point are set to zero and the inverse Fourier transform is taken. Figure 16–16D shows a cepstrally smoothed spectrum. To recover the excitation function, low-quefrency values are omitted and the inverse transform is taken.

Pitch Measurement

One of the most difficult tasks in source-signal analysis is determination of pitch. Actually, "fundamental frequency" or "period" would be better terms because pitch is a subjective parameter, whereas frequency and period are objective parameters. Nevertheless, for musical instrument sounds, there is a one-to-one correspondence between frequency and *musical* pitch.

One reason that acceptable pitch measurement is so difficult is that errors are acutely obvious. A momentary error of a semitone, for example, completely changes the character of a musical phrase, whereas a similar error (6%) in amplitude measurement or spectral shape determination would go unnoticed. Most pitch detector errors are likely to be much larger yet with common values of one or even two octaves. With errors being so obvious, it is much easier to judge the performance of a pitch detector compared with an amplitude detector or formant estimator. The net result is an abundance of pitch detection schemes covering a wide range of complexity and performance levels. Even so, it is safe to say that none of them is completely satisfactory, that is, agree with a human observer in all cases. Another potential problem is that most pitch detection research has been with speech sounds. In some ways, musical instrument sounds will be easier to analyze, while in others they may be more difficult.

Typical accuracy specifications for a frequency counter are 0.001% or 1 Hz, whichever is greater. However, anyone who has purchased such a device and then tried to use it to tune a musical instrument knows that a very clean, smooth waveform is necessary to avoid gross errors. The reason, of course, is that the frequency counter responds to *zero crossings* (a zero crossing is said to occur when the signal voltage changes sign from plus to minus or minus to plus) of the waveform and complex musical instrument waveforms may have any even number of zero crossings per cycle.

Figure 16–17 shows a number of unquestionably periodic waveforms. The human ear has no problem in determining their pitch, but all of the pitch detection schemes that will be discussed will fail miserably on at least one of them. Although the waveforms are contrived, it is reasonable to expect something like each of them to occur occasionally in musical instrument tones. The last waveform, which is just white noise, can be a problem as well because a pitch detector should also give an indication that the sound is unpitched.

If a pitch detector output is to agree with a human observer, it is reasonable to first ask how the human performs the task. Unfortunately, that is not known for sure, but two distinctly different theories have evolved. The first proposes that pitch is judged by detecting the *periodicity* of the waveform. The example waveforms are certainly periodic, and, in fact, careful visual determination of their period of repetition would give an accurate result in all cases. Changing waveforms would give a little more trouble because the waveshape repetition would not be precise every period. Pitch

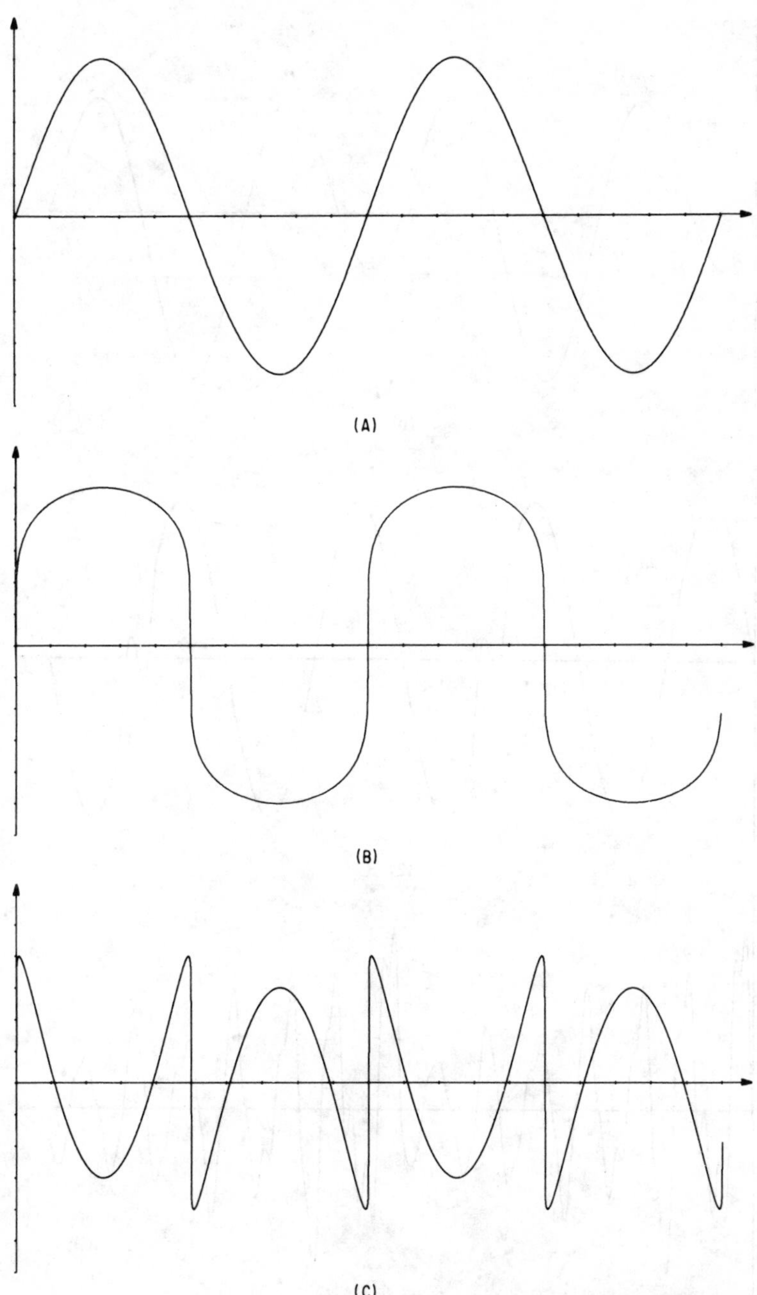

Fig. 16–17. Troublesome waveforms for pitch detectors. (A) Sine wave (only one frequency component). (B) Flattened sine wave (rounded peak is hard to detect accurately). (C) Missing fundamental.

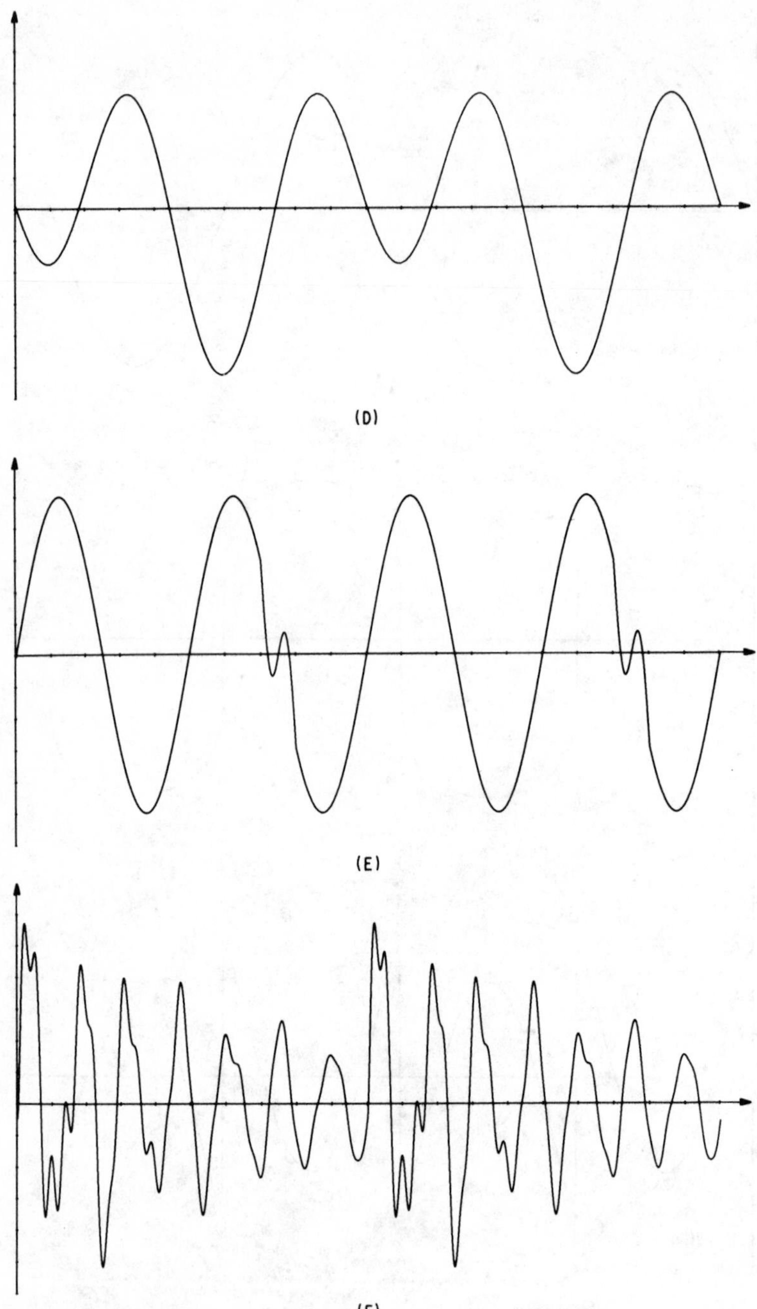

Fig. 16–17. Troublesome waveforms for pitch detectors *(cont.)*. (D) Strong harmonic. (E) Contrived wave in which peak detection is useless. (F) Speech sounds.

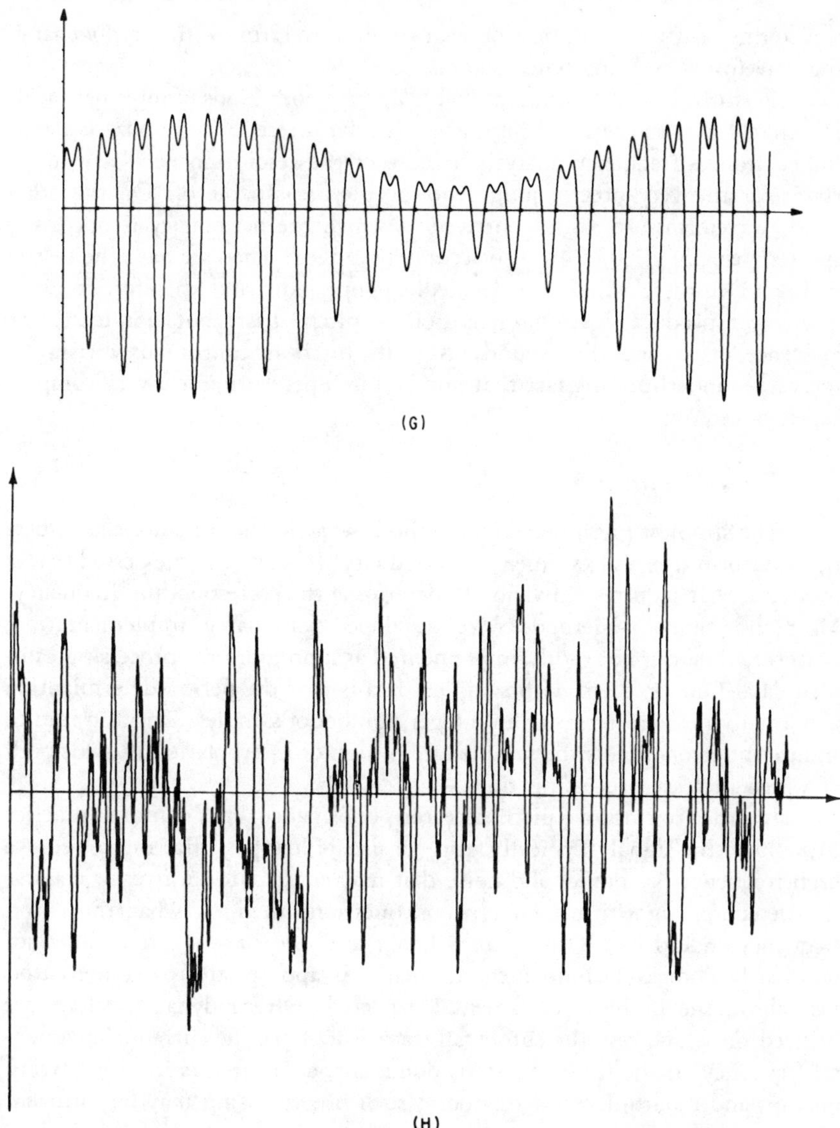

Fig. 16–17. Troublesome waveforms for pitch detectors *(cont.)*. (G) Rapidly changing amplitude. (H) White noise (has no pitch)

detector designs based on finding the period of repetition are *time domain* methods, since they directly examine the time waveform.

The second theory maintains that the ear performs a frequency analysis of each harmonic and then computes the "lowest common divisor" to determine what the fundamental frequency is even if the fundamental component itself is missing. Such an analysis method also works well for the example waveforms, but blind application of it can lead to errors with rapidly changing waveforms and unpitched sounds.

In truth, human hearing probably utilizes both kinds of information. It is unlikely that the pitch of high-pass (1-kHz) filtered 60-Hz buzz is determined from a frequency analysis because of the resolution necessary to account for the very precise judgments people are capable of. On the other hand, waveforms are easily contrived in which the periodicity is not easily spotted visually yet they are also accurately judged. Then we have the case of bells and chimes, which are decidedly nonperiodic and therefore nonharmonic yet produce a strong sensation of pitch. Last, but not least, the existence of a tone that sounds as if its pitch is continuously rising—forever[1]—underlines the fact that human pitch perception is a very complex topic indeed.

Time-Domain Methods

The simplest pitch detection methods work in the time domain, where the waveform itself is examined for periodicity. In fact, it is the period that is measured that requires a division to determine the corresponding frequency. Most time-domain methods were developed for analog implementation; however, they can be readily implemented as a program for processing sampled data. One problem with sampled data is that the period determination is normally made in terms of an integer number of samples. This can lead to significant errors unless the sample rate is high or interpolation is used, both of which increase processing time.

In order to improve pitch detector performance, it is common practice to *preprocess* the signal. Typically, this consists of low-pass filtering to remove high-frequency harmonics and noise that may contribute to jitter or confuse the detection algorithm. An obvious question, then, is what the cutoff frequency should be. If the sounds being analyzed have a strong (but not necessarily dominant) fundamental, then it is appropriate to set the cutoff just above the highest fundamental expected. Often, dynamic filters are utilized, in which case the cutoff can track just above the current fundamental frequency. If the fundamental is dominant, as it often is in direct string pickups and mouthpiece microphones, such preprocessing may be sufficient to allow a simple zero-crossing detector to do the actual period detection. Even if the fundamental is not dominant, repeated *integration* can make it dominant. Unfortunately, the integrators emphasize low-frequency transients and may actually blank out the zero-crossing detector for hundreds of

[1]This is usually demonstrated as a continuous upward sweep or an ascending musical scale that never stops. In reality, the effect is much like the stripes on a barber pole, and, in fact, a spectrogram of the former example is an endless series of upward sloping diagonal bars. For a scale, the continuous rise is simply quantized at musical scale pitches.

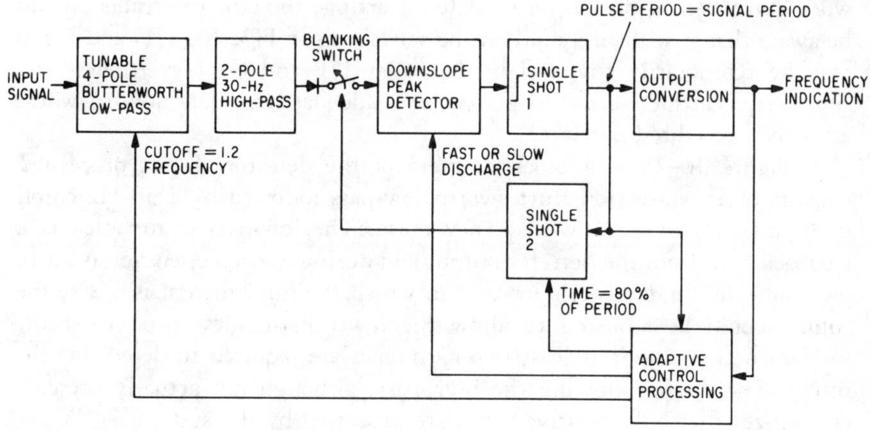

Fig. 16–18. Simple time-domain pitch detector. Source: *Electronotes Newsletter # 55*, July, 1975.

milliseconds following a transient. Of course, if the fundamental is absent as in Figs. 16–17C and F, low-pass preprocessing may filter out the entire signal and leave nothing to process further. Thus, with more sophisticated pitch detectors, the preprocessing filter cutoff should be fairly high, such as 1 kHz, and used primarily for reducing noise.

Experience with typical instrument waveforms and examination of Fig. 16–17 reveals that in all cases but one the location of waveform *peaks* contains sufficient information for determining periodicity. In fact, a simple positive peak detector with dynamic threshold performs infinitely better than a zero-crossing detector. A dynamic threshold is implemented by setting the threshold for peak detection to some fraction of the amplitude of the last detected peak. The trick is to make this fraction small enough so that sounds of decreasing amplitude, such as Fig. 16–17G, are followed properly yet high enough to avoid double peaks from waveforms such as Fig. 16–17F. When double peaks are unavoidable, the detector can be *blanked* for some fraction of the currently measured period. Peaks would not be detected during the blanking interval. Of course, any peak detector scheme will fail on the waveform in Fig. 16–17D, which has two equally spaced positive peaks of equal amplitude. However, Fig. 16–17D has only one negative peak so perhaps two detectors, one for positive and one for negative peaks, would work better. Where there is disagreement between the two, the one reporting the longest period would be selected for output.

Let's examine a fairly simple pitch detector based on peak detection[2] that has been reasonably successful as an analog implementation and should

[2]This pitch detector was designed by B.A. Hutchins and was described in Electronotes 53–55.

work quite well in digital form. Before starting, though, the reader should be aware that it will surely fail on the waveforms in Fig. 16–17D and E and may be temporarily confused by Figs. 16–17F and G. Nevertheless, its simplicity is attractive and its performance adequate for "data taking" where errors can be edited out later.

Figure 16–18 is a block diagram of the detector. Input processing consists of a two-section Butterworth low-pass followed by a 30-Hz cutoff high-pass to suppress low-frequency noise. The low-pass is tunable via a feedback path from the detector output and during normal operation is set to pass only the fundamental. In cases in which the fundamental is weak, the tuning could be adjusted to allow the lower harmonics through (if the fundamental is absent at least two harmonics are required to determine the pitch). The diode following the high-pass, although not actually present, emphasizes that only positive peaks are processed by the system.

The downslope peak detector is an improvement over the standard type in that dynamic thresholding is automatic. Figure 16–19 is a simplified schematic of the detector with typical analog waveforms. The ideal diode and storage capacitor form a peak-holding circuit that holds the highest voltage reached by the input. The leakage resistor serves to slowly discharge the peak holder to allow proper response to changing input signals. A buffer amplifier followed by slight (1% to 5%) attenuation passes a large fraction of the most recent peak voltage to a comparator, which compares this voltage to the raw input. When the peak reverses and starts back down, the comparator output goes positive. When the input re-reverses and crosses the (decayed) held peak

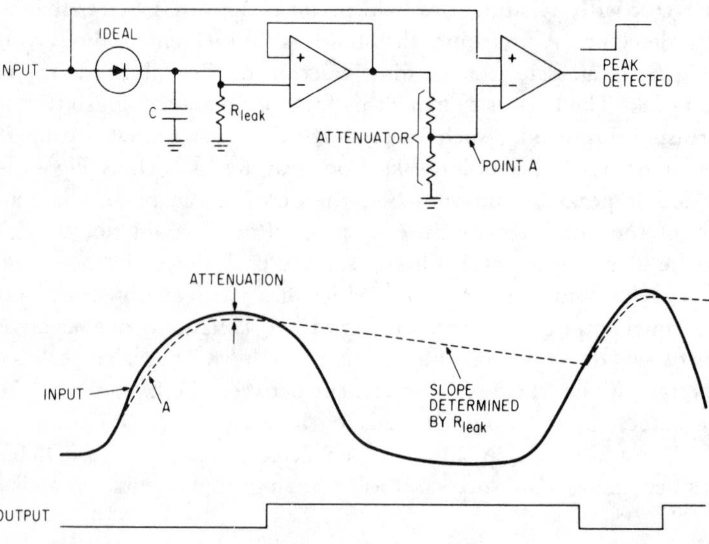

Fig. 16–19. Downslope peak detector

again, the comparator goes negative. If the leakage current is low, the circuit is capable of responding exclusively to the highest peak in the presence of other peaks of nearly equal height. However, too little leakage inhibits response to decaying signals entirely. In a digital implementation, the precise point of comparator switching can be determined by interpolation at the switching point only, thus avoiding a significant increase in computation elsewhere.

In an analog implementation, single-shot number 1 simply indicates the beginning of a new period. The output converter is a period-to-voltage converter followed by a reciprocal element. In a digital implementation, one would simply count samples between peak detections for the period and do a digital division or table lookup.

The adaptive control processor looks at the current frequency and sets three detection parameters accordingly. The preprocessor filter cutoff is set at about 1.2 times the current frequency, while the blanking single shot is set for 80% of the current period. The peak detector discharge rate is normally set fairly high to allow tracking of decaying signals. During startup from silence, however, it is set for little or no discharge. Startup also requires that the low-pass filter revert to a high cutoff frequency and that the blanking time be set to a low value. As soon as two peaks are detected, which then gives a preliminary period estimate, the parameters are set accordingly. If the first estimate is erroneous due to multiple peaks, the filter cutoff and blanking will continue to favor high frequencies until the peak detector has charged to the absolute highest peak in the signal. At this point, a longer period would be found and the feedback would adjust to favor it. The processor also detects long dead periods and resets to the startup mode in response.

One way to improve the performance of the detector is to construct a duplicate that processes negative peaks. As before, if the two disagree, the final pitch output should the lower of the two estimates. With this improvement, about the only waveforms that it would consistently fail on would be Fig. 16–17E and a backward version of Fig. 16–17F, the latter of which is unlikely to occur unless the speech had been subjected to severe dispersion.

The idea of using multiple detectors and taking a majority vote has been carried to the limit in a scheme proposed by Gold and Rabiner. The general idea is to make several (six) estimates of the period using individual peak and valley (negative peak) amplitudes as well as differences between peak and valley and peak and previous peak. These six estimates along with the preceding two estimates for each are combined in a decision tree to obtain the final estimate. If there is a significant lack in consistency among the 18 values, no decision is made and the sound is declared to be unpitched. A full explanation of the algorithm is quite involved and would require too much space to reproduce here. Although seemingly complex, the programming is straightforward and efficient.

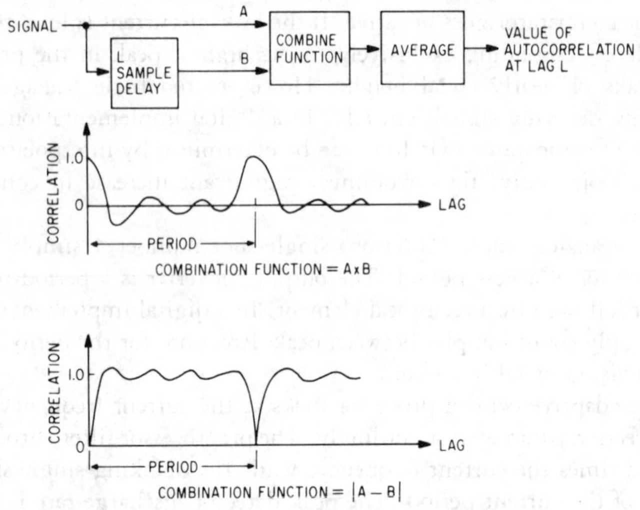

Fig. 16–20. Autocorrelation analyzer

The algorithm actually settles on the correct period for each of the sample waveforms and flags the noise as well. There is a potential problem with the waveform in Fig. 16–17B whose very broad, nearly flat peak would make any kind of pitch detection based on peak analysis susceptible to noise. Also, if the amplitude of the crook in Fig. 16–17E was reduced so that the peaks around zero disappeared, the method would fail. The interested reader is referred to the bibliography for references giving exact implementation details.

Autocorrelation

The most sophisticated of time-domain techniques is termed *autocorrelation* analysis. Autocorrelation means literally that a section of the waveform spanning several cycles is compared with a time-delayed version of itself as in Fig. 16–20. In practice, the delay starts at zero and is increased until the correlation reaches a high peak, which, in theory, indicates a full-cycle delay.

In true autocorrelation, the raw and delayed signal samples are combined by taking their sample-by-sample product, adding up the products for enough samples to cover at least two pitch periods, and dividing by the number of samples processed to get the value of the autocorrelation function for a particular delay value or *lag*. This process is repeated for different lags until the largest peak is found. If none of the peaks is very large, then the sound is unpitched.

A related technique combines the two signals by adding up the sample-by-sample magnitude of their difference. When the signals remesh at a lag equal to the period, the differences will tend toward zero, which means that a large *dip* in the correlation function is being sought.

Quite obviously, either method involves a lot of calculation, approximately $M \times N$ operations, where M is the number of samples in the waveform section being analyzed and N is the number of lags tried in the peak/dip search. It can be reduced substantially by only evaluating lags that are close to the last measured pitch period.

In theory, true autocorrelation is guaranteed to produce maximum-height peaks only at multiples of the true period. Thus, any perfectly periodic waveform will be correctly analyzed by the autocorrelation method. A changing waveform, however, is a different story. When the waveform changes, the peak corresponding to the pitch period is smaller than it would otherwise be because of the inexact repetition. There are also additional peaks that may be due to strong harmonics, formants, etc. If the pitch peak attenuation due to waveform change is great enough, these secondary peaks will cause an error.

Frequency-Domain Methods

Pitch detection in the frequency domain is fairly simple to understand but does imply a lot of computation to obtain the spectrum. However, if the spectrum is used for formant analysis, then the additional processing necessary for pitch detection is relatively minor.

The most straightforward frequency-domain pitch-detection scheme is an extension of frequency analysis mentioned earlier. The idea is to take the measured frequency of each significant component found and determine the greatest common divisor. For example, if components were found at 500 Hz, 700 Hz, 1,100 Hz, and 1,500 Hz, the fundamental would be 100 Hz because it is the highest possible frequency for which all of the measured frequencies are harmonics. In real life, though, the frequency measurements will not be exact because of noise, a changing spectrum, etc. Thus, classic greatest-common-divisor algorithms will have to be extensively modified to allow some slop. Also, confining attention to the strongest half-dozen or fewer components will lessen the likelihood of confusion. If the least common multiple turns out to be a ridiculous number such as 20 Hz (any value less than the spectrum analysis bandwidth is suspect), then an unpitched sound should be assumed.

The primary difficulty with the frequency-analysis method is the restriction on harmonic spacing so that accurate analysis is assured. When low fundamental frequencies are to be analyzed, this leads to very long analysis records and the possibility of significant frequency content changes over the duration of the record, which in turn can lead to errors.

Homomorphic spectral analysis leads to a very good pitch detector, in fact one of the best available for speech sounds. In a cepstral plot, the low-quefrency values correspond to the spectrum shape, while high-quefrency values correspond to the excitation function. For harmonic-rich tones, there will be a single sharp peak in the upper part of the cepstrum that corresponds to the fundamental frequency of the sound. The reciprocal of the quefrency of the peak is the fundamental frequency. This peak will be present even if the actual fundamental and several lower harmonics of the analyzed tone are missing, a situation that confuses pitch detectors using low-pass preprocessing.

However, confusion is possible in certain cases. For example, if the excitation function has only odd order harmonics such as a square or triangular wave, the cepstrum will give a fundamental frequency twice its correct value. This is because the cepstrum essentially responds to periodicity of harmonic *spacing*, and the spacing of odd order harmonics is twice the fundamental frequency. A pure sine wave, which all other schemes discussed handle beautifully, gives a pitch estimate equal to the reciprocal of the record length used in analysis! These failures could be a problem with certain kinds of musical instrument sound such as a clarinet or a flute. Thus, cepstral pitch detection should be augmented by other pitch-detection schemes for maximum accuracy.

17
Digital Hardware

At this point, we are ready to start discussing actual implementation and use of some of the digital sound synthesis and modification techniques that have been described. There is, however, a natural division between hardware and software implementation techniques. Either can perform any of the functions that have been studied. A hardware approach performs the data movement and calculations considerably faster than software. In fact, the usual goal of hardware implementation is real-time operation. Software, on the other hand, is cheaper, easier, and more flexible but much slower. Finally, the $5 MOS microprocessor and high-speed bipolar microprocessors make possible a third category that behaves in a system like a hardware implementation but is designed, and for the most part, built like a software implementation.

Hardware implementation and real-time operation seem to be of greatest interest to most people at this time. Digital synthesis hardware can be integrated into an overall computer-controlled system in several ways, however. At the lowest level, one can build modules that on the outside act just like analog modules but offer greater precision, more flexibility, and perform functions impossible to do with analog hardware. Along the same lines, the voice-per-board method of system organization can be done entirely with digital hardware and with the same advantages. One may define and construct a modular *digital* synthesizer that conceptually acts like a modular voltage-controlled synthesizer but is all digital, including the signal-routing system. It is also practical to consider an actual programmable "computer" specialized for ultra-high-speed execution of synthesis algorithms in an effort to combine the flexibility of software with the speed necessary for real-time operation. Special-purpose "black boxes" that perform certain useful but time-consuming operations such as the FFT can also be added as a peripheral to general-purpose computers in order to enhance the speed of software-based synthesis.

Unfortunately, a complete discussion of all of these options is well beyond the scope of this chapter. However, those suitable for implementation by individuals will be described in detail, while the others will only be surveyed.

Analog Module Replacement

In many cases, digital techniques and circuitry can replace analog circuitry with the substantial advantages that have been described earlier. One of the biggest potential advantages in this role, however, is the ability of digital logic to *multiplex* itself among numerous channels. Modern logic is so fast that in many cases it would just be loafing when used to implement a single function. The surplus speed along with a small amount of memory can instead be used to simulate *several* independent modules using only one set of somewhat more complex logic. The per-function cost is then reduced, often considerably below that of an equivalent quantity of analog modules. Digital oscillators, which will be discussed extensively in the following paragraphs, lend themselves well to multiplexed operation. It is not difficult to have one logic board perform the function of 16 or more functionally independent oscillators!

Simple Digital Oscillator Module

Enhanced frequency accuracy and greater waveform variety are the leading advantages of a digital oscillator over a conventional voltage-controlled type. The oscillator we will be discussing initially accepts a single-word digital input that controls frequency and produces a single analog output. The oscillator may be used as a stand-alone oscillator module or may be part of a larger voice module.

The most fundamental part of the oscillator is the variable-frequency source. Basically, all digital oscillators share one common trait in this area: they take a fixed, crystal-controlled, high-frequency clock and divide it down to a useful range under the control of a digital word. There are at least four distinct ways of doing this, each with a set of advantages and disadvantages. For the purposes of illustration, we will assume that the goal is to generate frequencies in the audio range with infinite frequency resolution and perfect short-term as well as long-term frequency stability.

Divide-by-N Frequency Generator

The most obvious frequency generator is the divide-by-N counter. The circuit merely accepts the fixed frequency reference, F, a digital number, N, and produces an output frequency of F/N Hz. Any number of logic schemes can be used to implement the divide-by-N, and they are all quite inexpensive and easy to understand. Figure 17–1 shows one that requires only counter blocks (plus one two-input gate) and is indefinitely expandable. The idea is to load N into the counter at the beginning of an output cycle and count up to all ones on successive clock pulses. When the counter overflows, N is loaded again and the cycle repeats. The actual division factor is 2^M-N, where M is the number of counter bits. If the twos complement of N is supplied, however, the circuit indeed divides by N.

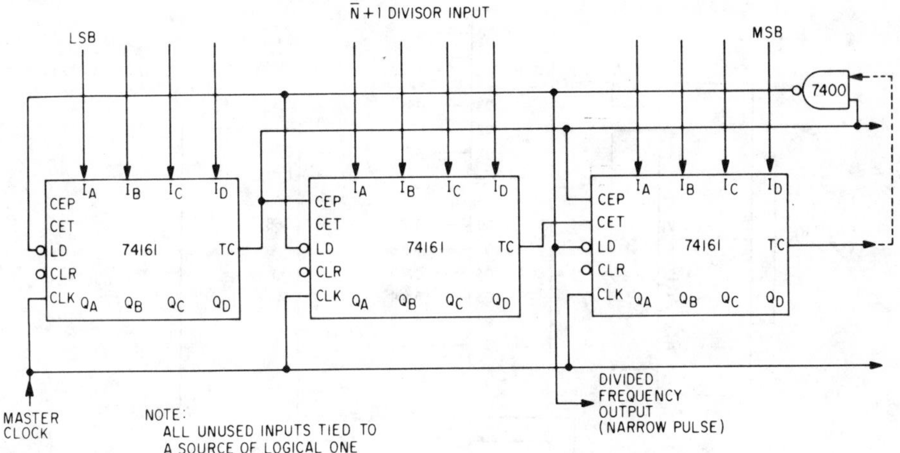

Fig. 17–1. Simple, high-speed divide-by-*N* counter

The master clock may be as high as 15 MHz (30–40 MHz if "S" or "F" series TTL logic is used), and the output frequency consists of pulses with a length of one clock period. *N* may be changed at almost any time, but if it is changed within 10 nsec of the end of an output pulse, an incorrect value may be loaded into the counters and cause a momentary glitch (click) in the output frequency.

The assumption behind the divide-by-*N* approach is that, if the clock frequency is high enough, the frequency increment between adjacent values of *N* will be small enough to be inaudible. Let's determine how high the master clock must be to get a resolution of 5 cents (1/20 of a semitone or 0.3%) throughout the audio range. Taking the low end first, we seek a clock frequency, F, such that $F/N=20.0$ and $F/(N-1)=20.06$, where N is the division factor for a 20-Hz output. Using the standard procedure for solving simultaneous equations, F and N are found to be 6.68 kHz and 334, respectively. Solving the same equations at the upper end of the audio range gives an F of 6.68 MHz and N the same as before.

Since the clock frequency must remain fixed, we are forced to use the 6.68 MHz value of F, since using lower values will not provide the required amount of resolution at high frequencies. Thus, with a master clock of 6.68 MHz, the division ratio varies from 334 for a 20-kHz output to 334,000 for a 20-Hz output. The counter circuit in Fig. 17–1 will therefore require 20 bits or five 4-bit counters, which could then provide frequencies as low as 6.4 Hz. While the resolution at high frequencies barely meets specification, the resolution at low frequencies is 1,000 times better than required. Note that the high-frequency resolution can only be improved by a factor of two before counter speed limitations become a factor. Clearly, the divide-by-*N* method of frequency generation performs best when generating low frequencies.

One advantage of the divide-by-*N* method is that the output frequency is pure, that is, there is no jitter in the period other than that of the master

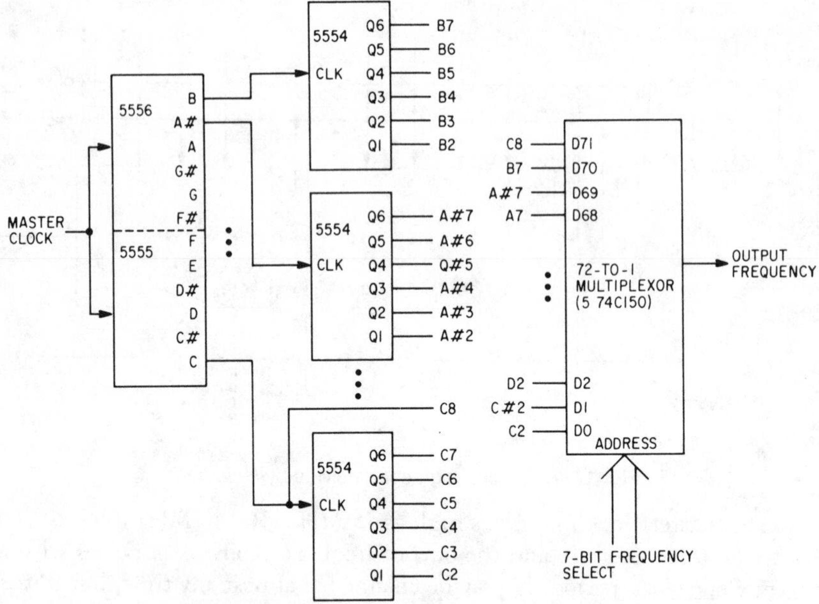

Fig. 17–2. Equal-tempered scale frequency generator

clock. The circuit merely passes every *N*th input pulse to the output. A potential problem with the method, however, is the highly nonlinear, reciprocal relation between *N* and output frequency.

Modern electronic organs use dividers to produce all of the notes on the 12-tone equally tempered scale *simultaneously*. The heart of these instruments is an IC called a "top octave divider." This IC (sometimes a set of two) accepts a high-frequency clock input and produces 12 different output frequencies, which correspond to the 12 equally tempered notes in the highest octave of the organ. Associated with each output internally is a simple divide-by-*N* counter with appropriate *N*s wired in. Each output in turn drives a 6-bit binary counter, which provides the lower notes in precise octave increments as shown in Fig. 17–2.

One example is the MM5555 family from National Semiconductor. The type 5555 and 5556 ICs accept an input frequency of 2.12608 MHz and produce outputs from C8 (four octaves above middle C) to B8 (4,186 Hz to 7,902 Hz) plus a C9 output. By judicious selection of the clock frequency, the maximum output frequency error has been made less than 0.66 cent with respect to ideal equal temperment. The 5554 hex flip-flop divides these down as low as C2, which is about 65 Hz. For a programmable oscillator, a multiplexor (it should be CMOS to match the weird logic levels used by the 5555 family) can be added to select one of the 72 output frequencies under control of a digital address input. Thus, if only 12-tone equally tempered note frequencies are desired, they can be selected with a simple 7-bit number

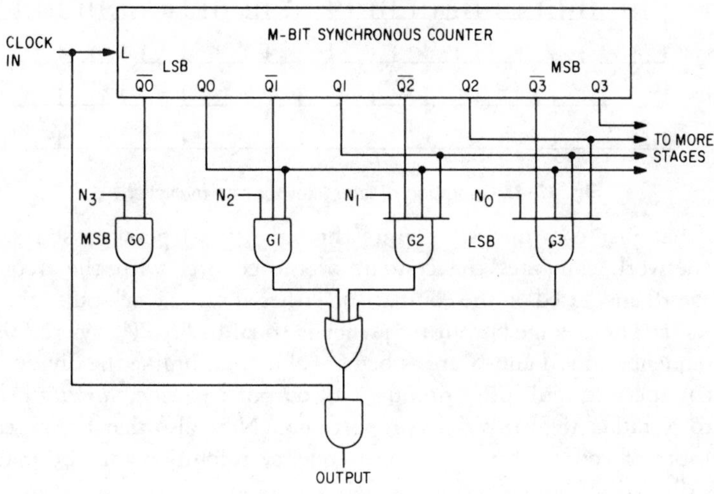

$M = 4$

$2^M = 16$

$N = 11$

$$F_{out} = \frac{F_{in} .11}{16} = 0.6875\ F_{in}$$

				N_0	N_1	N_2	N_3	
Q3	Q2	Q1	Q0	G3	G2	G1	G0	OUT
0	0	0	0	0	0	0	1	1
0	0	0	1	0	0	0	0	0
0	0	1	0	0	0	0	1	1
0	0	1	1	0	1	0	0	1
0	1	0	0	0	0	0	1	1
0	1	0	1	0	0	0	0	0
0	1	1	0	0	0	0	1	1
0	1	1	1	1	0	0	0	1
1	0	0	0	0	0	0	1	1
1	0	0	1	0	0	0	0	0
1	0	1	0	0	0	0	1	1
1	0	1	1	0	1	0	0	1
1	1	0	0	0	0	0	1	1
1	1	0	1	0	0	0	0	0
1	1	1	0	0	0	0	1	1
1	1	1	1	0	0	0	0	0

Fig. 17–3. Rate multiplier

that directly corresponds to the note rather than a 20-bit number that would have to be looked up in a table. Also, multiple simultaneous outputs can be implemented by adding multiplexors only.

Rate Multiplier

The rate multiplier is a combination counter and logic network specifically designed for variable-frequency generation. Its basic form is illustrated in Fig. 17–3. The fixed-frequency clock is fed to a standard binary counter of

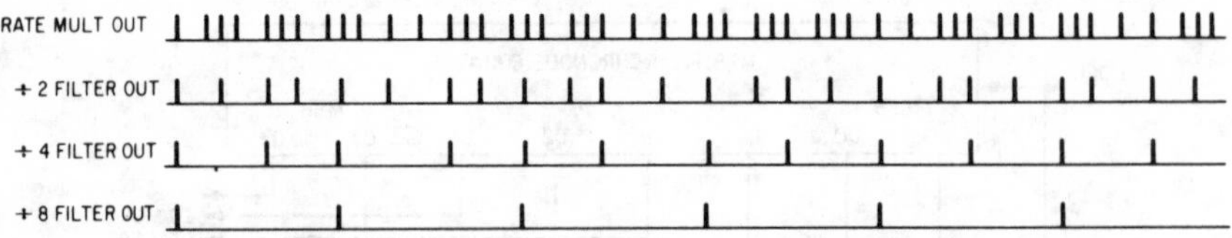

Fig. 17–4. Operation of jitter filter for rate multiplier

M bits that just continuously counts through its 2^M possible states. The gating network compares the content of the counter with the frequency control word and based on the comparison either allows a clock pulse through or blocks it. The average output frequency is equal to $FN/2^M$, where *F* is the clock frequency and *M* and *N* are as before. Note that unlike the divide-by-*N* approach, the rate multiplier produces an output frequency *directly* proportional to *N* rather than inversely proportional. Note also that by increasing the number of counter bits that the frequency resolution may be made as high as desired without altering the clock frequency.

So far this sounds ideal but there is a catch. Examining the gating structure and truth table for $N=11$, it is seen that the output pulses are erratically spaced, although there are indeed 11 of them per 16 input pulses. A little further study of the effect of different *N*s reveals that the *instantaneous* output frequency never varies over a range greater than two to one, although it is never less than that either unless *N* is a power of two, in which case it does not vary at all. The audible effect of such frequency jitter is a very rough sound to say the least. Thus, it is clear that a rate multiplier alone is unsuitable as an audio tone source.

One can, however, "digitally filter" the jittery output with a simple binary counter and reduce the percentage of frequency modulation. Figure 17–4 shows how a divide-by-8 counter smooths the frequency jitter substantially from 100% to about 12%. Unfortunately, the clock frequency must be increased by a factor of 8 to compensate for the frequency division of the jitter filter. By adding stages to the filter counter, the jitter may be made as small as desired, subject only to the clock-frequency limit of the rate-multiplier counter. A divide-by-256 filter counter, which leaves only a trace of roughness in the sound, is probably adequate in most cases. Thus, if the rate multiplier is to be used to produce frequencies up to 20 kHz, the clock frequency must be 5.12 MHz, about what it was with the divide-by-*N* approach.

With an overall output frequency relation of $FN/2^{M+J}$, where *J* is the number of bits in the jitter filter, it is seen that frequency is a linear function of the digital word, *N*. Thus, frequency resolution is poorest at *low* frequencies rather than at high frequencies. If one wishes to experiment with rate multipliers, the 7497 is a 6-bit cascadable unit that functions up to 20 MHz. Four of these, an 8-bit filter counter (74393), and a 5-MHz crystal oscillator are sufficient to build a frequency source with good resolution at all but the very lowest audio frequencies (1.5% at 20 Hz).

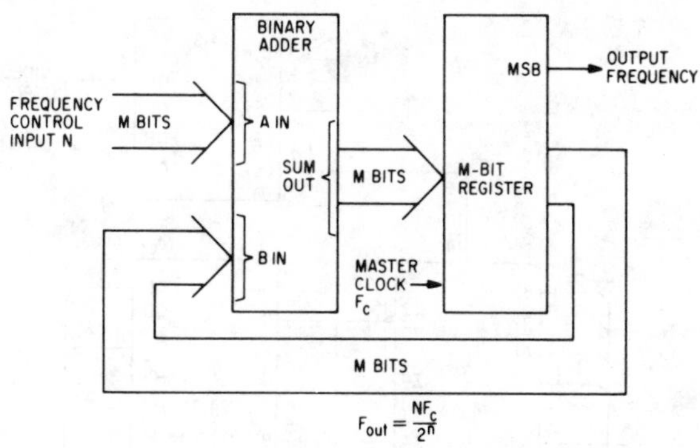

Fig. 17–5. Accumulator-divider structure

Accumulator Divider

The accumulator-divider method is based on the digital sawtooth generator discussed in Chapter 13. The basic structure shown in Fig. 17–5 consists of a set of binary adders and a D-type register. The adders sum the current register contents and the frequency control word together and feed the result back to the register, which latches it up on the next clock pulse. Thus, N is repeatedly added to the M-bit register, which overflows whenever the accumulated sum exceeds 2^{M-1}. The overflow frequency is the output frequency which can be conveniently detected by monitoring the most significant register bit. As with the sawtooth generator, the output frequency is $FN/2^M$, the same as the rate multiplier. Note that the division ratio must be two or greater in order to use the MSB as the output.

The circuit can be considered to let every $N/2^M$th clock pulse through to the output. When this ratio is an integer, which only occurs when N is a power of two, the output pulse train is jitter-free. When it is not an integer, it alternates between the integer values on either side such that the long-term average is exactly equal to the fractional value. For example, if M is 16 (2^M is 65,536) and N is 384, the ratio $2^M/N$ is 65536/384 or 170.66667. The circuit will alternate dividing by 170 and by 171 with the latter occurring twice as often as the former. Thus, the peak *time* jitter is never more than one clock period. The peak-to-peak *frequency* jitter in percent is simply the reciprocal of N. Thus, at low output frequencies the jitter is very small but gets worse as the output frequency is increased. Contrast this with the rate multiplier, which has an essentially constant jitter regardless of output frequency.

The absolute frequency resolution of the accumulator divider is dependent entirely on the register length, M, and can be increased without theoretical limit. The relative resolution as a fraction of a particular output frequency is simply $1/N$ for the N required to produce the frequency of interest. The lowest possible output frequency is $F/2^M$, while the highest is $F/2$ if the most significant register bit is the output. The master clock frequency determines the time jitter, which is one clock period peak to peak.

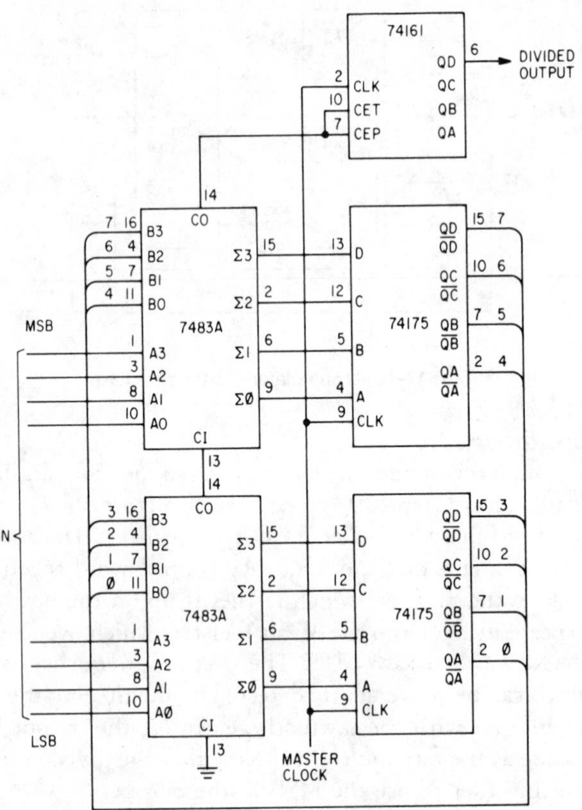

Fig. 17–6. Experimental accumulator divider

As an example, let's assume that an oscillator with 1-cent (0.06%) resolution over a 20-Hz to 20-kHz frequency range and inaudible jitter is desired. Under normal conditions, 0.5% frequency shift is about the minimum audible for single tones of moderate frequency. It is reasonable to assume that this much jitter at 20 kHz would be completely inaudible, while at midfrequencies the jitter is far less anyway. At 1 kHz, for example, it would be a mere 0.025%, which is much lower than the wow and flutter figures for most audio equipment.

The first step is to determine the clock frequency from the jitter requirement. The period of the highest frequency is 50 μsec and 0.5% of this is 250 nsec. Thus, the clock frequency must be at least 4 MHz to meet the jitter specification. To meet the resolution requirement at 20 Hz, N must be 1/0.0006 or about 1,600. If the output frequency equation is rewritten as $F=6.4 \times 10^9/2^M$, M can be found by applying $M=\log_2(6.4 \times 10^9/20)$, which yields a figure of 28.2. Thus, the adder and register must be 28 bits long. Note, however, that N will never be greater than 1,342,178, which means that only about 20 bits are needed to represent N. The remaining

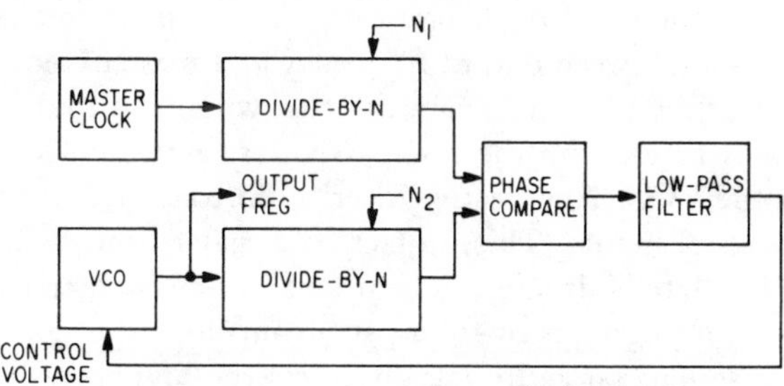

Fig. 17–7. Phase-locked-loop frequency synthesizer

adder B inputs should be grounded. In fact, the upper eight adder and register bits can actually be replaced by a simple counter that is enabled to count when the most significant remaining adder generates a carry out. In this respect, the "extra" 8 bits in M function as a jitter filter!

If one wishes to experiment with the accumulator divider, the general circuit structure shown in Fig. 17–6 is suggested. The A version of the type 7483 adder has a high-speed carry generation circuit internally, which becomes important when several are used for long words. The 74161 is a synchronous counter that is easily enabled to count when an adder carryout is present. If, however, the most significant A input to the most significant adder is zero, then the most significant register bit is guaranteed to flip, which can then be used to trigger a ripple counter such as a 74393 instead.

Phase-Locked Loop

When using the preceding methods, an output could only be produced coincident with a clock pulse. Therefore, the frequency resolution and time resolution (jitter) is limited by how finely time can be divided up by the clock. The phase-locked-loop (PLL) method, however, uses a tunable oscillator, which generates the output frequency, and a feedback mechanism that keeps it locked on the correct frequency relative to a second fixed frequency clock.

The structure of the PLL frequency synthesizer is shown in Fig. 17–7. Two independent divide-by-N counters are used along with independent inputs, N_1 and N_2. The N_1 counter reduces the master clock frequency to some convenient value. The N_2 divider likewise divides the voltage-controlled oscillator output to, when the circuit is stabilized, the same convenient value. The phase comparator looks at the two frequencies and produces a dc correction voltage that tends to adjust the VCO to equalize the comparator inputs. In effect, the upper counter divides the clock to an intermediate frequency, while the lower counter and VCO multiplies this up to the desired output frequency. The output frequency is therefore equal to $F(N_1/N_2)$ with no theoretical restriction on the values of N_1 and N_2. Thus, any rational output frequency may be produced.

The circuit should also, theoretically, have a jitter-free output regardless of the relation between output frequency and master clock frequency. In reality, however, the phase-comparator error voltage output has significant ripple, which is filtered by the low-pass filter. Any remaining ripple will tend to jitter the VCO. An effective filter, unfortunately, slows the response to changing digital inputs. This, in fact, is a major limitation of the circuit as a musical oscillator, although it is useful in precision test equipment in which frequency changing is by front panel controls and is done infrequently. There is also a serious range limitation unless the low-pass filter and certain VCO parameters are altered as a function of final output frequency.

Which is Best?

Of these four techniques, which comes closest to the goals of infinite resolution and freedom from short-term frequency jitter? The divide-by-*N* is the only technique with a totally clean output and, given a suitably high clock frequency, can have excellent resolution at low- and midaudio frequencies as well. As we shall see later, it does not lend itself well to multiplexing, however. The rate multiplier has no resolution limitation but does exhibit significant frequency jitter at all frequencies, which must be filtered. Its main advantage is the availability of specialized rate multiplier ICs, which reduce parts count. It does, however, multiplex well. The accumulator divider has no resolution limit either, and its jitter decreases with output frequency. It is the most complex, however, but it does multiplex quite well. The PLL divider was included for completeness; it is not recommended as a music oscillator except in very limited situations.

The accumulator divider seems to have more good features than the others, although it is more complex. We will see later how multiplexing can actually make it the simplest in terms of parts count. The divide-by-*N* is probably the best for a dedicated oscillator, where its nonlinear control characteristic can be tolerated.

Waveshaping the Oscillator Output

The frequency-generation circuits that have been discussed thus far either put out narrow pulses or square waves at the desired frequency. For use as a practical analog oscillator replacement, other output waveforms are necessary. A pulse output is readily converted to a sawtooth wave by the circuit in Fig. 17–8. The pulse, which may only be 100 nsec wide, is stretched by the single shot and discharges the capacitor through a transistor switch. The current source (which can be just a resistor for audio applications) then recharges the capacitor during the remainder of the cycle. Square waves, such as from the accumulator divider, can also operate the circuit.

There is a problem, however: the amplitude decreases as frequency increases. While not objectionable for a limited range of two octaves or less, it must be compensated over a wider range. The charging current could be

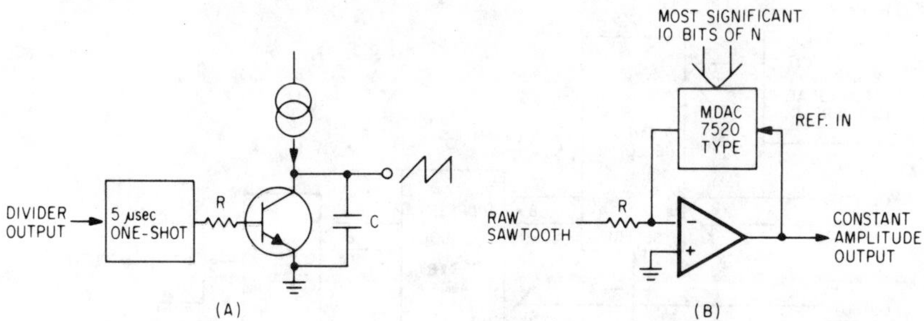

Fig. 17–8. Digital divider waveshaping circuits. (A) Generating a sawtooth wave. (B) Compensating a sawtooth from a divide-by-*N* oscillator.

increased at higher frequencies by deriving it from a DAC connected to the most significant frequency control bits. For a divide-by-*N* frequency source, a multiplying DAC could be placed in the feedback path of an op-amp to provide reciprocal compensation.

Along these same lines, a square-wave output can be integrated into a triangle wave, and a multiplying DAC can be used to raise the integrator gain at high frequencies. Two variable integrators in a state-variable low-pass configuration can filter a square wave into a reasonable sine wave as well. The 2040 integrated voltage-controlled filter can do both of these jobs quite well and can be driven directly from a current output DAC.

Although these essentially analog methods do work, they seem to defeat the whole purpose of going digital in an oscillator module. Much more flexible waveshaping can be had by implementing some of the techniques discussed in Chapter 13. In the example of accumulator division given earlier, the most significant 8 bits of the register were implemented as a binary counter, which counted through every one of its states every cycle. If an 8-bit DAC is connected to the counter, a sawtooth wave with amplitude *independent* of frequency would emerge. One could also construct logic to implement all of the direct waveform computation methods detailed in Chapter 13 such as triangle and sine conversion as well.

Another possibility is table lookup shaping followed by digital-to-analog conversion and filtering to get an analog output. In hardware, this is accomplished by placing a *read-only memory* (ROM) between the accumulator divider and the DAC as in Fig. 17–9. The ROM functions exactly like a

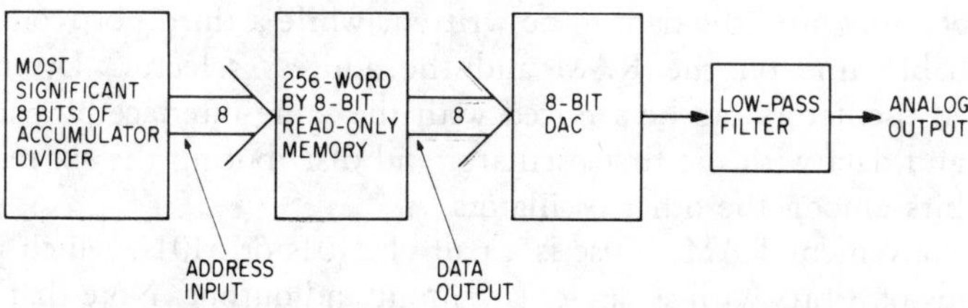

Fig. 17–9. Digital waveshaping of digital oscillator

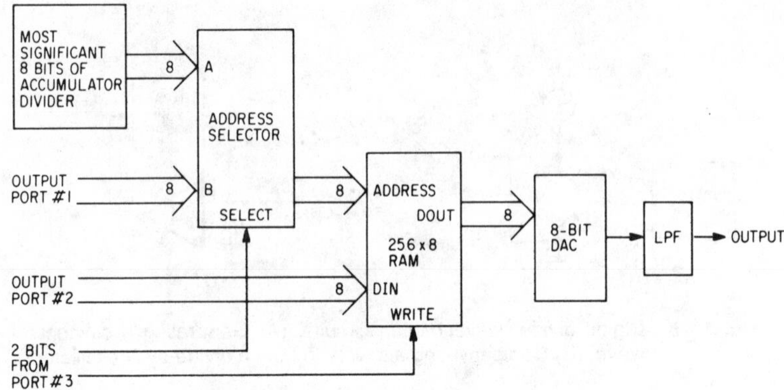

Fig. 17–10. Digital waveshaping using RAM

waveform table and simply transforms sawtooth input samples into samples on any waveform desired.

A particularly convenient type of ROM to use is the erasable and reprogrammable variety (EPROM) such as the 1702, which is organized as 256 8-bit words. Since this type of EPROM is virtually obsolete for microprocessor program storage, it can be purchased for $3 or less. The type 2708 EPROM is four times larger with 1,024 8-bit words. A digital oscillator with four different waveforms may be constructed by connecting the lower 8 address bits to the frequency divider and using the remaining 2 address bits to select one of four waveforms. Even larger EPROMs such as the 2716, 2732, or 2764 with 2K, 4K, and 8K words, respectively, can be used for up to 32 different waveforms at very little additional cost. An EPROM programmer connected to the user's microcomputer would allow the waveforms to be computed in BASIC and then written into EPROM for use in the oscillator module.

Obviously, read/write memory can also be used to hold the waveform. If this is done, the control computer can set the oscillator output waveform and even change it during the course of the music. Figure 17–10 shows how the RAM is connected between the divider and the DAC. The main item of interest is the address selector. During normal operation, the accumulator divider is selected as the source of addresses for the RAM. When a new waveform is to be written into the RAM, the selector allows addresses from the first microcomputer output port to reach the RAM instead. A second output port provides the data to be written, while a third port controls the write enable line on the RAM and the address selector. Up to three additional oscillators can be serviced with the same interface by paralleling address and data with the first oscillator and distributing the six remaining control bits among the other oscillators.

A convenient RAM to use is a pair of 2101s or 5101s, which provides 256 words of 8 bits with separate data input and output. Note that gradual waveform changes during a note are not really possible because addressing the RAM for writing thoroughly scrambles the read data going to the DAC. This can be overcome somewhat by using a larger RAM, such as a 2K x 8-bit 6116 or 8K 6164, which can hold 8 and 32 waveforms, respectively, at once. All of the waveforms can be written ahead of time and then instantly selected as desired without glitching the output. Note that data input and output of the 6116 are the same pins, so an 8-bit tri-state buffer and an 8-bit latch will have to be added to separate them.

Variable and Constant Sample Rate

The oscillator and ROM/RAM waveshaper just discussed is an example of *variable sample rate* digital synthesis. Earlier, it was strongly suggested that the sample rate should remain constant in a digital synthesis system. This in fact is true if the system is handling several unrelated signals at once. However, a dedicated oscillator is handling only one signal so the rule can be relaxed somewhat with important advantages.

Using the Fig. 17–10 system as an example, we ignore for a moment the fact that the count-up rate of the most significant 8 bits of the accumulator divider is not exactly constant. Therefore, if the raw DAC output is examined, it is found to consist of exactly 256 steps per cycle of the waveform and each cycle is *identical* to the previous one. As the division ratio and hence synthesized wave frequency is changed, the stepped wave is merely stretched or compressed, but its step-by-step shape remains constant. The spectrum of such a wave is exactly harmonic, including all of the alias copies of the intended spectrum. Thus, the alias distortion is purely *harmonic* distortion rather than intermodulation distortion and white noise. Furthermore, and this is the crux of the matter, the quantization noise is also harmonic distortion! This means that perfectly clean sounding tones can be produced with 8 and even fewer bit DACs.

Since the reader is not really expected to believe the previous paragraph immediately, let's discuss the meaning of harmonic distortion. In audio equipment, the most prevalent measure of quality is harmonic distortion. Literally, this means that any tone entering the equipment will leave with its harmonic amplitude relationships altered. Even large amounts (several percent) of such distortion are inaudible *provided* the distortion is pure, that is, no other type of distortion is present, and that the amplitude alteration is spread out evenly among the harmonics.

However, the mechanism that causes harmonic distortion in audio equipment does not meet either criteria when several tones are present simultaneously. First, intermodulation (IM) distortion is inevitable, which causes easily heard nonharmonic frequencies to occur. In fact, an amplifier with *pure* harmonic distortion would be quite an interesting device indeed. Second, the harmonic portion of the distortion tends to concentrate at high frequencies,

Table 17–1. Performance of a 64-Word 6-Bit Waveform Table

Harmonic number	*Desired amplitude*	*Actual amplitude*
0	−100	−48.67
1	−3	−3.14
2	−5	−5.13
3	−10	−10.28
4	−8	−8.27
5	−2	−2.02
6	0	−0.16
7	−4	−4.27
8	−10	−10.29
9	−15	−14.88
10	−19	−19.45
11	−10	−10.15
12	−5	−5.09
13	−1	−1.12
14	−6	−6.2
15	−12	−12.14
16	−20	−21.06
17–32	−100	−52.24 best −36.72 worst

Ideal sample values	*Actual sample values*	*Ideal sample values*	*Actual sample values*	*Ideal sample values*	*Actual sample values*
−0.051854	−0.0625	−0.181621	0.1875	−0.005724	0.0
0.249919	0.25	−0.182356	0.1875	0.243738	0.25
0.353100	0.34375	−0.174635	−0.1875	0.470721	0.46875
0.150009	0.15625	−0.383177	−0.375	0.463172	0.46875
0.072522	0.0625	−0.224204	−0.21875	0.248244	0.25
0.460679	0.46875	−0.106272	−0.09375	−0.028076	−0.03125
0.909300	0.90625	−0.463232	−0.46875	−0.353254	−0.34375
0.745635	0.71875	−0.999997	−0.96875	−0.720503	−0.71875
0.068102	0.0625	−0.990784	−0.96875	−0.903528	−0.875
−0.280506	−0.28125	−0.335606	−0.34375	−0.654850	−0.65625
0.090172	0.09375	0.217383	0.21875	−0.086723	−0.09375
0.536646	0.53125	0.136746	0.125	0.389132	0.375
0.334821	0.34375	−0.134930	−0.125	0.526439	0.5
−0.255813	−0.25	0.0744874	0.0625	0.424187	0.40625
−0.407391	−0.40625	0.585016	0.5625	0.319185	0.3125
0.058757	0.0625	0.643670	0.625	0.248252	0.25
0.452688	0.4375	0.0782302	0.0625	0.158014	0.15625
0.213340	0.21875	−0.486549	−0.46875	0.084257	0.09375
−0.364094	−0.34375	−0.559661	−0.5625	0.082703	0.09375
−0.584477	−0.5625	−0.330236	−0.3125	0.070032	0.0625
−0.244755	−0.25	−0.151069	−0.15625	−0.058026	−0.0625
				−0.177100	−0.1875

where it is easily heard. Historically, harmonic distortion ratings were used because they were easy to measure and correlate well with IM readings, which are a much better measure of subjective distortion. Although direct IM measurements are now easily performed, tradition requires that harmonic distortion still be quoted on spec sheets.

As an example, consider the synthesis of a tone having the exact harmonic makeup (chosen at random) listed in Table 17–1. For the sake of argument, let's assume that only 64 words of memory (64 samples per cycle) are available and that each word is a paltry 6 bits long, which means that a 6-bit DAC can be used. Also shown in Table 17–1 are the corresponding sample values to 16-bit (5-digit) accuracy and rounded to 6-bit accuracy. The final column shows the actual harmonic spectrum that would emerge from this low-budget tone generator.

The first surprise is that the difference between desired and actual harmonic amplitudes expressed in decibels is not very great, at least for the significant high-amplitude ones. Lower-amplitude harmonics do suffer greater alteration but are more likely to be masked by the higher-amplitude harmonics. The real difference is that no harmonic can be entirely absent because of the quantization "noise." In actual use with a fairly "bright" harmonic spectrum, the approximation errors would be audible but would be characterized as a slight timbre alteration rather than distortion; much like the audible difference between two presumably excellent speaker systems of different manufacture. The use of 8 bits and 256 steps for the waveform of a digital oscillator is therefore well justified.

Although the alias frequencies are also harmonic, they should be filtered if a high-pitched "chime" effect is to be avoided. Unfortunately, the filter cutoff must track the tone frequency as it changes. This used to be an expensive proposition but a 2040 VCF driven by an 8-bit DAC connected to the frequency control word can now solve the problem for under $15. In many cases, it may be possible to omit the filter. For example, when using a 256-entry waveform table, only fundamental frequencies below 150 Hz require filtering, since otherwise the alias frequencies are entirely beyond 20 kHz. In fact, mellow tones containing few harmonics can be generated filter-free down to 80 Hz.

A dedicated digital tone generator can, of course, be based on the constant sample rate approach too. The structure is basically the same as Figs. 17–9 and 17–10 except for the following:

1. The master clock (sample rate) is much slower, such as 50 ks/s.
2. The most significant bits of the accumulator divider will be actual register bits, since the slow clock eliminates the "jitter-filter" counter (the jitter now becomes interpolation error).
3. The waveform memory will require more words (1,024) and more bits per word (10–12), since interpolation and quantization error will now be white noise instead of pure harmonic distortion.

The constant sample rate tone generator is, in fact, a precise hardware implementation of the software table-scanning technique described in Chapter 13. In exchange for additional hardware complexity, one has a structure that can use a fixed low-pass filter (probably no filter at all for 50-

ks/s sample rate), operates at a much lower clock rate, and can be easily multiplexed. There is one serious problem that the variable sample rate approach did not have and that is "harmonic overflow" or alias distortion caused by generating frequencies beyond one-half the sample rate. This may be controlled only by cutting back on stored waveform complexity when high-frequency tones are being generated.

Multiplexed Digital Oscillator

Digital circuitry has the unique ability to be *time multiplexed* among several, possibly unrelated, tasks. Although a large time-sharing computer is the epitome of this concept, quite small amounts of very ordinary logic can be multiplexed among several similar tasks and made to act like many copies of itself. Probably the best way to illustrate time multiplexing is to describe a specific example and then generalize from it. Since digital oscillators have been under discussion, let's examine the design and implementation of a multiplexed digital oscillator module having the following general specifications:

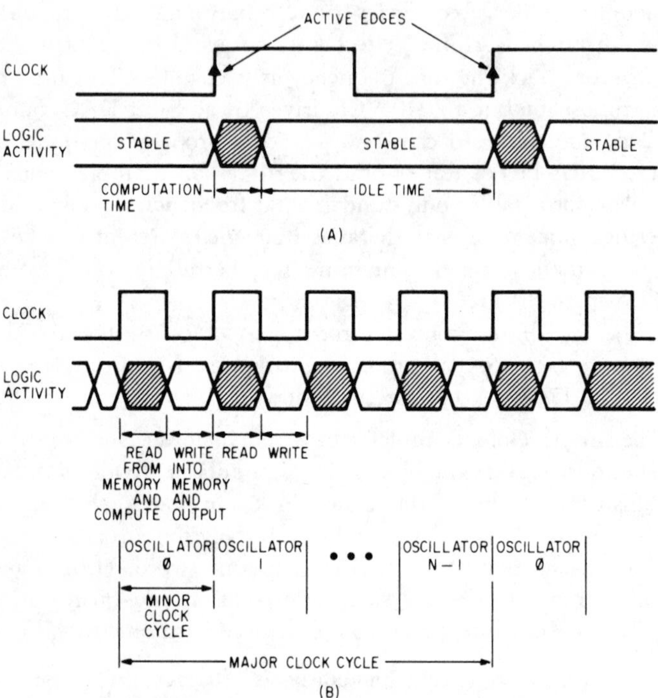

Fig. 17–11. Timing of generalized digital oscillators. (A) Nonmultiplexed oscillator timing. (B) Multiplexed oscillator timing.

1. Sixteen independent oscillators are simulated.
2. Each oscillator has an independently programmable waveform.
3. Moderately high tonal quality (50 dB S/N) is desired.
4. Waveforms may be dynamically updated *without* glitching the output.

Although the last feature may be impractical in a single-channel oscillator, its cost is divided by 16 when multiplexed.

A typical nonmultiplexed digital oscillator has a timing diagram something like Fig. 17–11A. Immediately following the active clock edge, things happen and signals change. A finite time later, everything settles down and remains stable until the next active clock edge. The time between settling and the next clock is "wasted" because nothing is happening.

Multiplexing utilizes this idle time by assigning it to the "data" for one or more additional oscillators as illustrated in Fig. 17–11B. Such data consist of the frequency control word, the state of the counter in the frequency divider, and the waveshaping table. Essentially, the data are read from a memory, the next state is determined by the logic, and the result is written back into the memory and an output circuit. The entire sequence for a particular oscillator takes place during one *minor clock cycle*. A *major clock cycle* consists of N minor clock cycles, where N is the number of oscillators simulated. There will, in fact, be a minor clock cycle counter that identifies minor cycles within a major cycle. Thus, the *sample rate* for each oscillator is the major clock frequency, while the *throughput rate* for the computation logic is N times the sample rate or the minor clock frequency.

Before proceeding further, the implementation technique for the oscillator must be determined. One thing to keep in mind is that the minor cycle frequency is N times the effective clock frequency for a particular oscillator. This eliminates the variable sample rate techniques described earlier because they all require a clock frequency on the order of 5 MHz. To multiplex these according to the specs above would require a throughput rate of 16 x 5 or 80 MHz, somewhat beyond the capabilities of standard logic. Thus, a fixed sample rate approach will be used. In the example system being

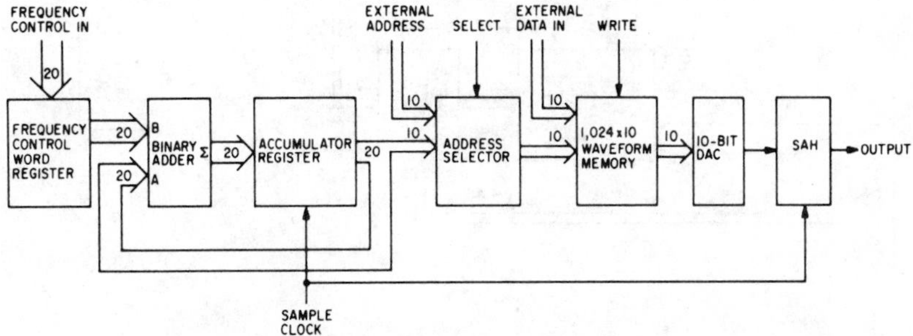

Fig. 17–12. Nonmultiplexed oscillator organization

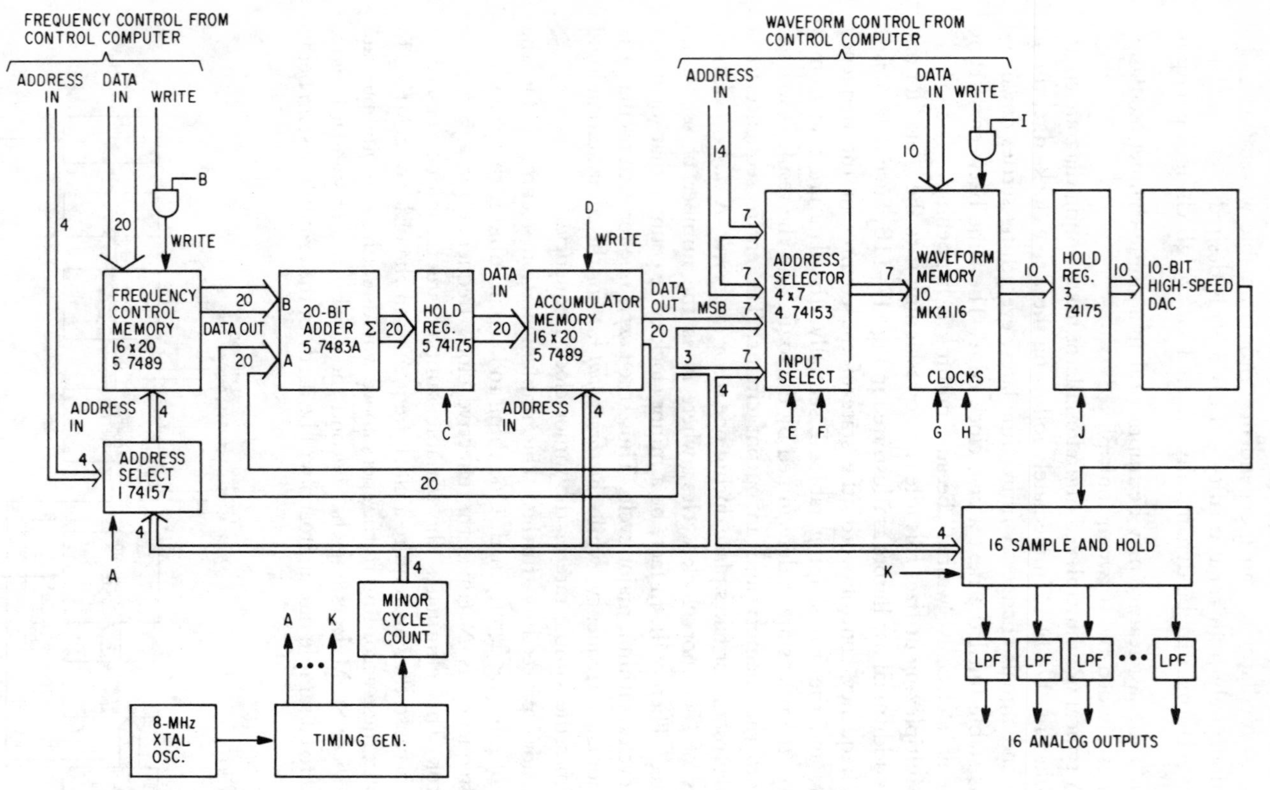

Fig. 17–13. Multiplexed oscillator organization

discussed, the sample rate will be set at 62.5 ks/s, which when multiplied by 16 yields a throughput rate of 1.0 MHz. This equates to a major cycle time of 16 μsec and a minor cycle time of 1.0 μsec.

Hardware Structure

The first step in designing the multiplexed oscillator is to draw a detailed block diagram of the equivalent nonmultiplexed oscillator as in Fig. 17–12. Note that the data input to the oscillator logic comes from a register and that the DAC output goes to a sample-and-hold, which acts like an analog register. The 20-bit word length chosen for the accumulator allows a frequency resolution of 0.3% at 20 Hz and 0.005% (equal to typical crystal oscillator accuracy) at 1 kHz. The 10-bit word length for waveform address and data gives a S/N ratio of greater than 50 dB for the tone.

In converting to the multiplexed oscillator shown in Fig. 17–13, one replaces all registers with memories, each consisting of *N* words and addressed by the minor clock cycle counter. In the case of the waveform tables, an *N* times larger memory holds all of the waveforms, and a particular section is addressed by the minor cycle counter. Thus, the frequency control word becomes the *frequency control memory*, which is 16 words of 20 bits, and the accumulator register becomes the *accumulator memory*, which is the same size. The waveform memory grows to 16K by 10 if each oscillator is to have a different waveform. The final outputs now come from 16 SAH circuits, which are addressed like a 16-position analog memory.

Before determining the timing diagram, components must be selected for the various blocks. Such a selection must be made on the basis of speed and cost. Obviously, memories that require a 2 μsec cycle time cannot be used, but, on the other hand, a 50-nsec bipolar memory would be overkill for the waveform tables. For this example, the waveform memory will use 10 type 4116 MOS dynamic RAMs, which are organized as 16,384 words of 1 bit each. Although dynamic RAMs are the cheapest form of memory available, they require periodic *refreshing* to retain data. Refreshing is accomplished simply by reading at least one location in each of the 128 blocks of 128 addresses every 2 msec. Since the oscillators are constantly scanning through the waveform memory, it will be automatically refreshed provided that zero frequency (or an exact multiple of 7.8125 kHz) is not programmed for all of the oscillators simultaneously.

Frequency control words and accumulators will be stored in 10 type 7489 bipolar memories, which are conveniently organized as 16 words of 4 bits each. The address selector for the waveform memory uses four type 74153 dual one-of-four multiplexors, which simultaneously select between accumulator and external addresses and between lower and upper 7-bit halves

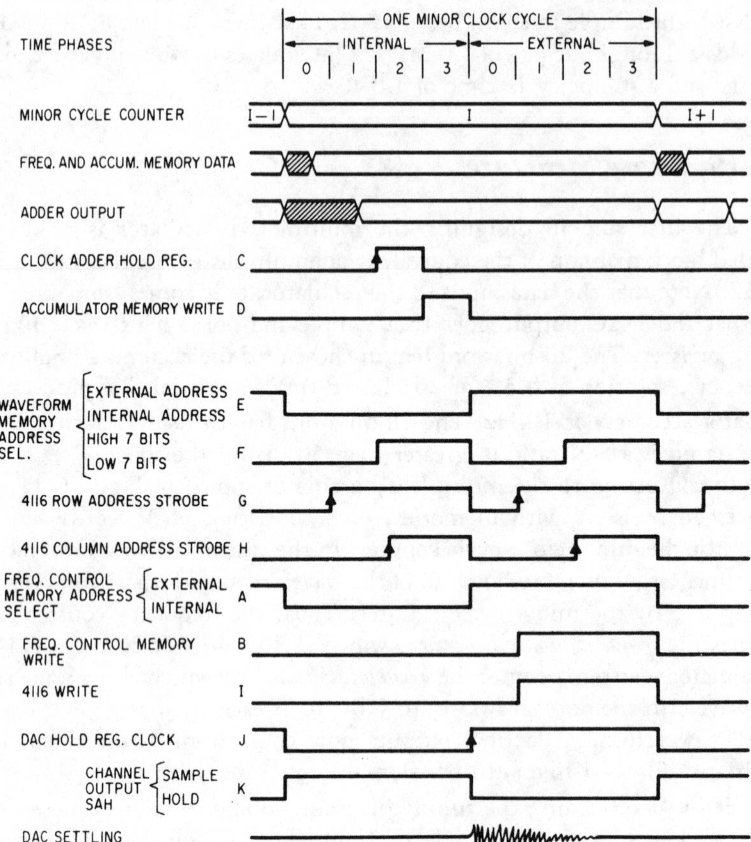

Fig. 17–14. Multiplexed oscillator timing diagram

as required by the 4116s.[1] The frequency control memory address must also pass through a selector to allow the control computer to write frequency control words into the memory. This may be implemented with a single 74157. The 20-bit adder will use five cascaded type 7483A 4-bit adders.

Unfortunately, there are a few timing and design details that require additional latches to correct. One problem is that the 7489 memories do not have an edge-triggered write. This means that a race condition is possible when writing, which can be corrected by inserting a 20-bit holding register between the adder output and the accumulator memory input. Another problem is that the 4116 waveform memory only activates its data output for a short time at the end of a memory cycle. Thus, another holding register

[1]The type 4116 RAM actually time multiplexes 14 address bits on 7 address pins. Two clock inputs called row address strobe (RAS) and column address strobe (CAS) trigger internal latches, which then reconstruct the full 14-bit address. The reader should consult the manufacturer's data sheet (Mostek Corporation) for full details.

between the 4116s and the DAC is required. Almost any edge-triggered latch can be used for the holding registers but the type 74175 will be specified because of its low cost and ready availability. Figure 17–13 shows a block diagram of the complete multiplexed oscillator. Excluding the timing generator and interface to the control computer, the total digital IC package count is approximately 40.

Timing

Figure 17–14 shows a timing diagram for the events that take place during one *minor* clock cycle. The only difference from one minor cycle to the next is the content of the minor cycle counter, which addresses the various memories involved. Each minor clock cycle consists of two subcycles that are termed *internal* and *external* subcycles. During the first subcycle, the required internal oscillator calculations are performed. The second subcycle is available to the external control computer for writing in new frequency control words or new waveforms if it so desires. Each subcycle is further divided into four "phases," each 125 nsec in duration. These phases are used to sequence the various events that take place. All of the necessary timing signals (except CAS, which utilizes a 30-nsec delay element) can be generated by a 3-bit counter driven by an 8-MHz crystal-controlled clock.

At the beginning of a minor cycle, which is also the beginning of an internal subcycle, the minor cycle counter is incremented, which causes an address change to the frequency control memory and the accumulator memory. Since these are bipolar memories, the newly addressed contents emerge about 50 nsec later. The adder, which sees a stable input about midway through Phase 0, produces a stable output by the middle of Phase 1. At the beginning of Phase 2, the adder output is latched in the adder holding register and during Phase 3 the sum is written back into the accumulator memory. While all of this is going on, the *previous* contents of the accumulator memory are used to address the waveform memory in conjunction with 4 bits from the minor cycle counter, which identifies which stored waveform to use. The address selector switches between low 7-bit mode and high 7-bit mode as required by the 4116s at the beginning of Phase 2. The RAS spans Phases 1 to 3 while the CAS spans Phases 2 and 3 but with a 30-nsec turn-on delay to allow address switching to complete. At the end of Phase 3, data from the waveform memory is available and is latched into the DAC register.

The DAC is allowed to settle during the second subcycle and the appropriate SAH channel is updated during the first half of the *next* minor cycle. Thus, SAH channel I will actually contain the signal from oscillator I-1 which is corrected simply by relabeling the analog outputs.

This time skew from one minor cycle to the next is an example of *pipelining*, which is a very powerful logic throughput enhancement technique. It is applicable whenever a repetitive sequence of operations is to be done by logic (or sampled analog) blocks connected in series. Rather than making the logic fast enough to do all of the operations in one clock period, only one operation per clock is performed. The data words shift down the chain one position per cycle and are operated on in assembly line fashion. Since a given block has a full cycle to "do its thing," slower logic can be used. Conversely, the throughput rate can be speeded up, often by several times compared with a nonpipelined approach. Pipelining is very easy to implement when strictly repetitive tasks are performed. Fortunately, nearly all hardware implementations of digital synthesis techniques are sufficiently repetitive.

Returning to the oscillator timing diagram, the external subcycle is used to allow the control computer to access the frequency control and waveform memories without interfering with the oscillator operation. Following address settling in Phase 0, Phases 1 to 3 are available for writing into the frequency control memory. An and gate connected to the RAM's write enable input inhibits actual writing unless the control computer specifically allows it. A similar arrangement is used for writing into the waveform memory. The waveform memory can also be read externally if desired. If write enable is not exercised, read data is available during Phase 3.

Interfacing to the Control Computer

The simplest method of interfacing the oscillator is direct connection of the 50 external input signals to 50 output port bits and suitable software manipulation of the bits to effect the desired results. Timing requirements for writing into the frequency control memory are very simple. First, the write enable pulse must be at least 1 μsec in duration. Also the 4-bit address must be set up and stable 30 nsec before write enable is turned on and must remain stable for 30 nsec after it is removed.

The waveform memory is a little more difficult to handle. Essentially, none of its inputs are allowed to change during an external subcycle. This requirement may be satisfied by inserting latches between the computer and the waveform memory inputs and clocking the latches at the beginning of minor cycles.

The number of output port bits required may be cut in half by realizing that simultaneous writing into both memories is not likely to be done. Since each memory requires 24 bits of information (address + data), only 24 port bits are needed plus two more for the write enables. Since registers are required anyway for operating the waveform memory, one may fill the registers 8 bits at a time with only 8 bits needed for the data and 5 bits used for control as shown in Fig. 17–15.

Fourier Series Tone Generator

The oscillator module just described is certainly quite versatile but does suffer one shortcoming: dynamic variation of the waveform, that is, smooth

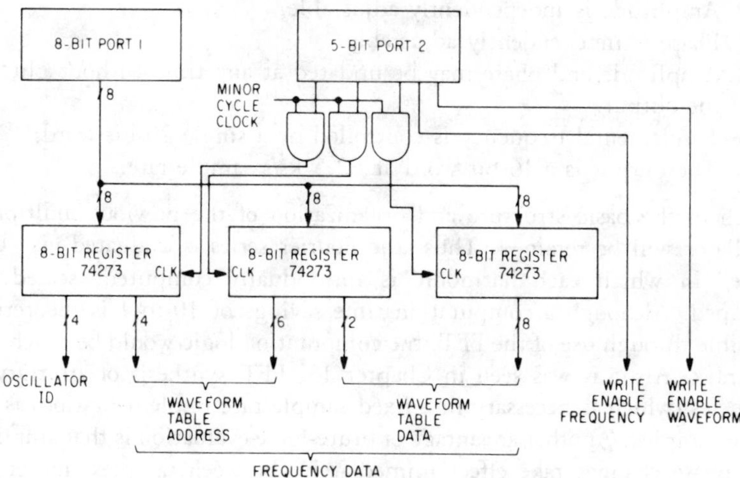

Fig. 17–15. Minimal microcomputer interface

changes during the duration of a single note, is not really practical. Although the logic timing is such that a new waveform can be written without interfering with waveform scanning, it would be very difficult to rewrite a waveform on the fly and insure that discontinuities due to half-old/half-new waveform scanning did not occur. One could possibly use two oscillator channels along with variable-gain amplifiers to alternately interpolate between successive versions of the waveform. In any case, variable filters would probably be used for dynamic variation.

What is needed is a Fourier transform or Fourier series tone generator, which is set up for continuous variation of the harmonic amplitudes and possibly the phases as well. When one realizes that such a tone generator is really nothing more than a bank of sine wave oscillators operating at harmonically related frequencies and having independent amplitude control, it becomes obvious that a multiplexed oscillator could do the job. Although the previous oscillator could provide up to 16 harmonic (and inharmonic as well) frequencies, external gain control elements would be necessary to control relative amplitude. Thus, an optimized Fourier series tone generator will be briefly described. Note that, although the unit is multiplexed in order to generate numerous harmonics, it can only generate a single composite tone, whereas the previous oscillator could generate 16 tones. Many musical situations, however, call for a solo instrument of great expressiveness with accompaniment in the background. The solo could therefore be played by the Fourier series generator, while the less critical accompaniment could be played by the oscillator bank described earlier.

The unit that will be described has the following general specifications:

1. Up to 64 harmonics in an unbroken series from 0 to 63.

2. Amplitude is independently adjustable.
3. Phase is independently adjustable.
4. Amplitude and phase may be updated at any time without glitching the output.
5. Fundamental frequency is controlled by a single 20-bit word.
6. The output is a 16-bit word at 62.5 ks/s sample rate.

Much of the basic structure and organization of the previous multiplexed oscillator will be retained. Thus, the Fourier series is evaluated via "brute force" in which each harmonic is individually computed, scaled, and summed. Although a computation time savings of 10-to-1 is theoretically possible through use of the FFT, the computation logic would be much more complex. Also, as was seen in Chapter 13, FFT synthesis of arbitrary frequencies (which is necessary in a fixed sample rate implementation) is even more complex. Another advantage of brute-force evaluation is that amplitude and phase changes take effect immediately, between samples, rather than between FFT records.

Hardware Structure

Following the same development as before, Fig. 17–16 shows the conceptual block diagram of a single harmonic channel without multiplexing. The first obvious feature is that three control variables are involved: frequency, amplitude, and phase. Another feature is the inclusion of two multiplier blocks, one for multiplying the frequency parameter by the harmonic number and the other for multiplying the sine table content by the amplitude variable. Phase control is implemented by adding the phase shift parameter to the accumulator contents in a separate *phase adder* before feeding it to the sine table. Finally, we have a *harmonic accumulator*, which sums the output of this channel with that of the other harmonic channels to provide the final output, which is then sent to the DAC.

Before continuing further, a few things should be said about the word lengths of the various blocks. When the 20-bit frequency control word is multiplied by the 6-bit harmonic number, a 26-bit product is expected. However, in order to use the same accumulator frequency generator and sample rate as before, only the *low order* 20 bits of the product are used. Thus, product overflow is possible when high fundamental frequencies are used. While this may seem to be an operational restriction, a little thought will reveal that product overflow is indicative of serious alias distortion in the tone anyway. When using the tone generator, the amplitudes of all harmonics that exceed 31 kHz will have to be made zero. The word lengths in the sine lookup blocks are 10 bits, the same as before. When 64 individual sine waves are added up, the result is a 16-bit final output word.

Let's now look at these blocks and see how they would be implemented in the multiplexed case. Since there are 64 harmonics, the amplitudes and

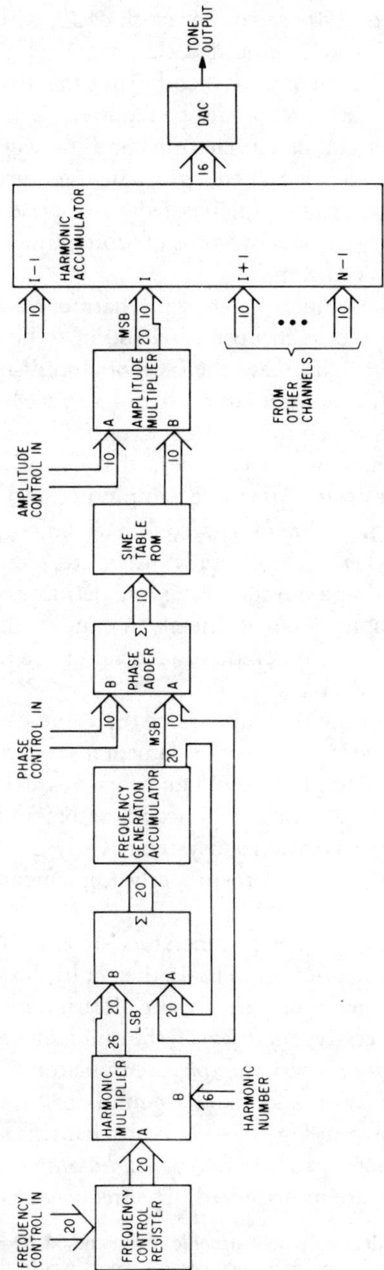

Fig. 17–16. Block diagram of a single-harmonic channel

phases can be stored in two 64-bit by 10-bit memories. The throughput rate is 64 × 62.5 kHz=4 MHz or 250 nsec minor clock cycle, which means that bipolar or fast MOS memories will be needed. Unfortunately, 64 words is a somewhat nonstandard size for memory ICs and using the 16- × 4-bit type 7489 memory means that 20 packages would be required. Other possibilities are the 2101A-1, which has a 200 nsec cycle time, and the 93422, which is a 50 nsec bipolar device. The latter is fast enough to be used directly, whereas the MOS 2101A-1 would have to be pipelined. Both of these have identical pin connections and are organized as 256 words of 4 bits; thus, three-quarters of their capacity will not be utilized.

When considering 64 channels, each with harmonically related frequencies,[2] the leftmost four blocks in Fig. 17–16 seem to be redundant. In particular, it would be nice to eliminate the harmonic multiplier as well as individual frequency generation accumulators. In order to see how this might be done, consider the case in which the frequency control word has a value of 1 and the entire module had just been reset, that is, all 64 frequency generation accumulators set to 0. After one sample period (16 μsec), the fundamental accumulator has a value of 1, second harmonic 2, third 3, etc. After a second sample period cycle, they are 2, 4, 6, etc., and after a third cycle they are 3, 6, 9, etc. After a number of sample periods, overflow of the highest harmonic is inevitable. This is merely an indication that it has completed a full cycle and can be ignored. In fact, all of the harmonics will overflow as they complete full cycles.

These same relationships hold regardless of the value of the frequency control word. Thus, the content of the fundamental's *accumulator* can be multiplied by the harmonic number to obtain what *would* be in the harmonics' accumulators if they had their own accumulators and adders! This then eliminates 63 frequency generation subsystems. Only the low 20 bits of the 26-bit product should be retained to properly implement the overflow phenomenon mentioned earlier.

Now that the redundant frequency generators are eliminated, let's see about getting rid of the multiplier as well. If the multiplexing is done in order of increasing harmonic numbers, then multiplication by 2, 3, 4, etc., can be accomplished by successive *addition* of the fundamental's frequency generation accumulator into a second *indexing* accumulator. Thus, the harmonic multiplier is replaced by an adder and accumulator. The substructure that accomplishes this is shown in Fig. 17–17. Note that this substructure is *not* multiplexed, but it does provide *multiplexed data* to the 64 sine generators, which, of course, are multiplexed. The frequency-control register

[2]If one wishes to generate decidedly nonharmonic tones, the 64 frequency generation subsystems may be retained. The frequency control words would then come from a 64-word × 20-bit memory rather than a harmonic multiplier. Thus, one has essentially 64 independent sine wave generators and a 64-channel mixer with independent gain control for each channel. The phase control adders are useless in such an application and therefore can be omitted.

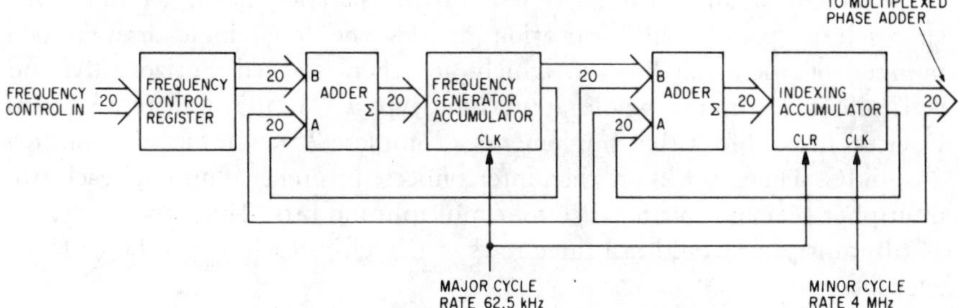

Fig. 17–17. Harmonic-frequency generator

and the two accumulators are therefore actual registers rather than memories. In operation, the frequency-generation accumulator is clocked at the 62.5-kHz major cycle rate, while the indexing accumulator is clocked at the 4-MHz minor cycle rate. Note that the indexing accumulator must be cleared at the beginning of every major cycle for proper operation.

Amplitude Multiplier

The amplitude multiplier is much more difficult to eliminate so let's see what is involved in hardware multiplication. There are a multitude of hardware multiplication techniques that would require an entire chapter to describe in detail. There are, however, basically two ways of multiplying in hardware. The first is the serial shift and add algorithm or *serial multiplication*. When an M-bit multiplier is being multiplied by an N-bit multiplicand, the basic approach is to examine the M bits one bit at a time and based on the result either add the multiplicand to a product accumulator followed by a shift or just do the shift (either the accumulator can move right or the multiplicand can move left). This approach is economical of hardware requiring just an N-bit adder, an $M + N$-bit shift register, and an N-bit latch but is slow, since M clock cycles are necessary to compute the product. With Schottky TTL logic, shift and add can be done at about a 20-MHz rate, which means that a 10×10 multiplication requires 500 nsec to perform, too slow for the Fourier series generator as currently specified, although possibly adequate for a 32-harmonic implementation.

The second approach is called *parallel multiplication*. Essentially, a large number of adders and gates is combined to form a massive combinational logic network that accepts the factors as static inputs and eventually produces the product output after the logic states have stabilized. For short word lengths, it may even be practical to use a ROM as a multiplication table. Besides much higher speed, the parallel multiplier is much easier to use, since no clocks or timing signals are necessary. Settling time from when operands are applied to when the result is stable is in the 150-nsec range for 10-bit operands and a 20-bit product.

Each IC manufacturer has its own pet parallel multiplier line. One approach to parallel multiplication divides the large logic array into a number of identical blocks, which are then stacked horizontally and vertically to form the whole array. One type (AM2505, Advanced Micro Devices) uses a block that implements a complete 2 × 4 multiplication in a 24-pin IC. These blocks are then interconnected using a column for each two multiplier bits and row for each four multiplicand bits. Thus, the needed 10 × 10 multiplier would use three rows of five chips each for a total of 15 IC packages.

A variety of complete parallel multipliers all on a single chip are also available. One example, the MPY1616 from TRW, includes a 16 x 16-bit multiplier array and a 35-bit adder/accumulator on the multiplier's output all in a 64-pin IC package. The total multiply–add time is about 150 nsec. In spite of the large (1 inch × 3 inch) ceramic package, the unit's 3–5 W power dissipation requires that a heatsink be glued to its top surface, although it is still substantially less than what 32 AM2505s would require. Other organizations such as 12 × 12 and 8 × 8 are also available, and a couple of recent units even use high-speed CMOS technology to reduce heat dissipation to more manageable levels. Unfortunately, all parallel multiplier ICs seem to be expensive ($50 to $100 or more), probably because usage volume is quite low compared to other IC types. In any case, a parallel multiplier is indicated for the Fourier series tone generator.

Before continuing, let's briefly investigate a method for eliminating the amplitude multiplier. It is well known that if two sine waves of exactly the same frequency and unity amplitude but of different phase are added, that the amplitude and phase of the resultant depends on the phase difference according to:

$$A = 2\cos\frac{P_1 - P_2}{2} \qquad P = \frac{P_1 + P_2}{2}$$

where A is the resultant amplitude, P is the resultant phase, and P_1 and P_2 are the phases of the individual waves. Thus, the two parameters P_1 and P_2 can be manipulated to give the effect of A and P parameters. The advantage, of course, is that multiplication by A and addition to the harmonic accumulator is replaced by two additions to the accumulator. There are disadvantages, however. One is that the throughput rate of the phase adder and sine table is doubled; another is the highly nonlinear relation between P_1, P_2 and A, P, which would probably require a translation table to overcome. The most serious disadvantage, however, is that greatly increased resolution in the sine table is necessary for good control at low-amplitude levels where the two waves nearly cancel. This means both more words in the

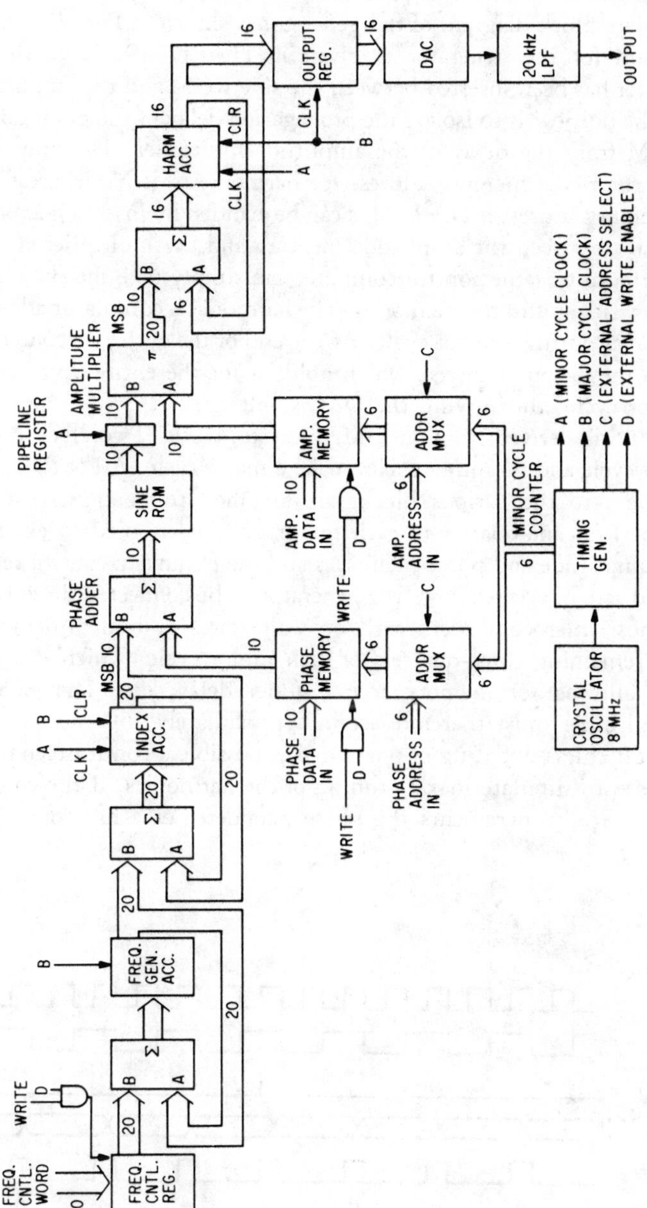

Fig. 17–18. Complete Fourier series tone generator

sine table as well as greater word length. To equal the dynamic range and noise performance of the 1024 × 10-bit sine table with a true multiplier, one would have to go to a 4,096 entry sine table with 16 bits per entry.

A complete block diagram of the generator is shown in Fig. 17–18. A timing diagram for the generator is given in Fig. 17–19. Note that a pipeline register has been inserted between the sine ROM and the amplitude multiplier. The purpose is to isolate the propagation delay of the phase adder and sine ROM from the delay of the amplitude multiplier. The only side effect is that the phase memory address for harmonic N is N, whereas the amplitude memory address is $N+1$. This can be avoided by inserting another pipeline register between the amplitude memory and the multiplier. However, for minimum cost the control computer can simply take the skew into account when writing into the memories. The harmonic accumulator adds up the 64 sine waves during a major cycle. At the end of the cycle, its content is transferred to the output register, which holds it for the entire duration of the next major cycle, thus giving the DAC stable data.

All timing is derived from an 8-MHz crystal clock. Two clock cycles make a minor cycle and 64 minor cycles make a major cycle. All of the clock and clear inputs to the various blocks are assumed to be positive edge triggered. The first one-quarter of each minor cycle is devoted to external access to the amplitude and phase memories and the frequency-control register. This rapid rate of access allows the generator to be connected directly to the bus of most microcomputers with no wait states or buffer memories needed. The remaining three-quarters of each minor cycle, which is about 190 nsec, is allowed for memory access, adder delay, etc. The parallel amplitude multiplier must therefore act in approximately 150 nsec.

Rapid, glitchless updating of phase makes possible a control technique that can be used to simulate inexact tuning of the harmonics. If the control computer periodically increments the phase parameter of a harmonic, the

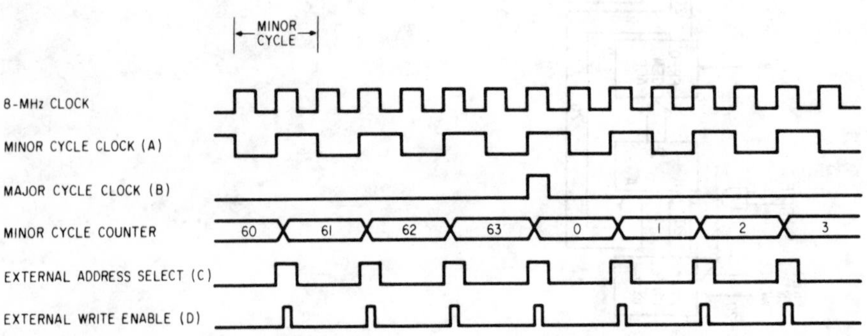

Fig. 17–19. Timing diagram for Fourier series tone generator

effective frequency of that harmonic will be increased somewhat. Although the magnitude of frequency shift is restricted to a few hertz, the technique is useful in simulating a real vibrating string with slightly sharp upper harmonics.

An Intelligent Oscillator?

The best method of interfacing either of the previously described oscillators to a system is the use of a dedicated microprocessor. Actually operating such an oscillator bank with frequency glides and dynamic waveform changes to worry about, not to mention other modules in the system such as amplifiers and filters, may pose a very heavy load on the control computer. It would be much nicer if the oscillator bank could be given high-level commands such as "increase frequency of channel 7 from C4 to G4 linearly over a period of 300 msec starting at time point 1230," or "change the harmonic content smoothly from what it is currently to the following specification over the next 150 msec."

A dedicated processor to perform such functions would actually add very little to the module cost. Two-thousand bytes of program ROM should be sufficient for a moderately sophisticated command interpreter. Read/write memory is only necessary for miscellaneous programming use and the storage of parameters; thus, it can be 256 or at most 1K bytes in size. Memory and I/O interfacing would involve about five additional ICs. A simple logic replacement microprocessor such as a 6502 suffices quite well for the intelligence. The net result is that less than $50 worth of extra parts can be added to make an intelligent oscillator.

Speaking of the 6502 microprocessor, the observant reader may have noticed that the 16-channel multiplexed oscillator timing diagram exactly parallels the 6502's bus timing. In fact, one could drive the 6502 clock with the internal/external address selector signal. Since the 6502 does nothing during the first half of its 1-μsec bus cycle, that half would be the oscillator's internal half cycle. The external half cycle would be devoted to the microprocessor, which could then *directly* write into the frequency and waveform memories. In fact, with some attention to detail, these memories could appear to the micro as regular read/write memory and thereby eliminate interface ports and registers altogether!

Communication between the control computer and the oscillator can now be more casual. This allows techniques such as serial asychronous (RS-232),[3] which are normally useless in real-time control applications, to be effectively utilized. In turn, this means that digital modules can be designed

[3]This is the method most often used to talk to "normal" peripherals such as terminals, printers, etc. It is a serial by bit technique that is inherently slow (compared with microprocessor speed) and usually implemented with little or no busy/done feedback or error checking. Its main virtue is standardization and minimal wiring complexity (3 wires are sufficient for bidirectional communication).

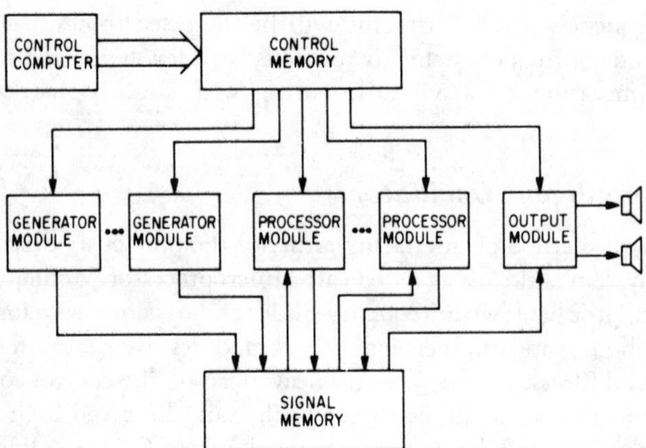

Fig. 17–20. Digital synthesizer organization

with a "universal interface" that can easily connect to any kind of control computer. Furthermore, interpretive high-level languages, such as BASIC, can be used to control the oscillators and other intelligent digital music modules.

Modular Digital Synthesizer

Up to this point, we have been discussing the digital implementation of analog modules in which an analog output is retained. These outputs are then interconnected and processed further in the *analog* domain just as if they had originated in an analog module. In a modular *digital* synthesizer, all signal generation, processing, and interconnection are done in the digital domain. Only the final two- or four-channel audio output is in analog form. One advantage of an all-digital synthesizer is the elimination of vast quantities of DACs. Another is that multiplexed operation of the component modules makes available very large numbers of module functions at an attractive per-module cost. The biggest advantage in the author's mind, however, is complete *interconnection* flexibility. As we saw in Chapter 8, a generalized analog-switching matrix for even a moderate number of modules can become very large indeed. An equivalent digital matrix using read/write memory is compact and economical. At this point in history, there are as many different digital synthesizer organizations as there are digital synthesizers in existence. The organization in Fig. 17–20, however, represents an ideal that most of all them approach to some degree. The entire system revolves around two major memories. The control memory contains all operation parameters for all of the modules, including interconnection information. The control computer writes into the control memory, while the modules read from it.

The signal memory contains sample words of all signals in the system. Essentially, every module *output* is associated with a word in the memory. During each system sample period, the content of the signal memory is updated by the modules according to their current output samples. Every module *input* represents a read access to an address specified by the control memory. Interconnection then is accomplished simply by specifying read addresses for module inputs! The modules themselves are normally highly multiplexed so a single "oscillator board" might actually represent 16 oscillator functions. In a truly modular system, one can easily add multichannel modules simply by connecting them to the memory buses.

A Hard-Wired Digital Synthesizer

Probably the best way to introduce the basic concepts of a digital modular synthesizer is to briefly describe one fairly simple unit that has been proposed. The basic idea is to emulate the operation of a large modular analog system with the advantages of direct computer control, programmable interconnection matrix, and, of course, extreme accuracy, freedom from drift, etc. Analog module terminology will be used to describe the digital modules, since from the control computer's point of view, the whole system looks just like a multitude of DACs driving analog modules coupled with a signal routing matrix.

The system as it was originally proposed has the following modules, although there is certainly room for expansion:

16-way multiplexed oscillator
16-way multiplexed mixer/controlled amplifier
16-way multiplexed state-variable filter
16-way multiplexed contour (envelope) generator
16-way multiplexed universal filter
16-way multiplexed multiinput mixing amplifier
32 "pseudo"-DACs
4 final output DACs
2 white noise generators (uniform and gaussian)
1 reverberation element

The system sample rate is 62.5 ks/s and all signals are 16-bit twos-complement values. Full scale is considered to be 12 bits, however, with the extra bits used to provide substantial "headroom" in the signal processing.

Figure 17–21 shows the general structure of a module. Up to seven classes of digital words are handled by the module. "Fixed" controls are values fetched from the control memory that act just like adjustment knobs on analog modules. They are called fixed because only the control computer can alter their values, not other modules in the system. Addresses for signal memory read accesses are also read from the control memory. One address is

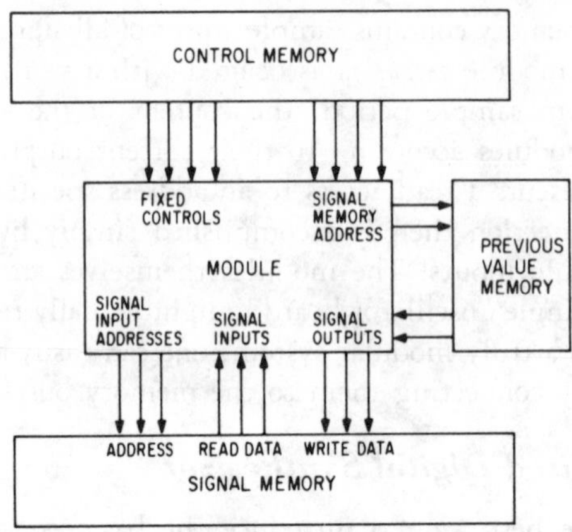

Fig. 17–21. Typical digital synthesizer module

read for each of the module's signal inputs and is sent to the signal memory, which returns a signal input. Since a unique location in the signal memory is associated with every module output, these addresses serve to define intermodular connections. Signal output words from the module are written into the control memory at locations defined when the module is built. Many modules require temporary storage from one sample to the next. In multiplexed modules, this is a small memory, which is called the "save memory." Usually, the save memory is not a system resource, but rather it is part of the module itself.

In most respects, the module functions parallel the equivalent analog modules. The oscillator module, for example, has two signal inputs that are summed and control frequency just like a VCO. The tuning relationship is exponential with a resolution of 3 cents. In the original proposal, the oscillator provided the "basic four" waveforms (sawtooth, triangle, rectangle, sine) to four locations in the signal memory, but the present low cost of memory would make a programmable waveform equally practical. Fixed controls for "octaves per unit" and zero offset would also be included, although they were not originally present.

The mixer/controlled amplifier acts just like an analog VCA. Although the control computer is capable of generating slow contours for envelopes and so forth, a 16-way multiplexed contour generator with four different curve segment shapes is provided to relieve it of that function. Virtually any contour shape can be constructed from the linear, concave, convex, and "S" curves available.

The universal filter module consists of 16 general second order cannonical digital filters in which each of the five multiplying factors is read from the control memory. Since the input and output of each filter communicates with the signal memory, they can be cascaded, paralleled, and even made into a filter bank spectrum analyzer by suitable setting of control words and signal memory addresses. The pseudo-DAC module simply serves as a method for the control computer to write directly into the signal memory.

As might be expected, the system is performance limited by the two memories. Although the control memory is shown as a system-wide resource, in reality it is part of the individual modules. Only the control computer requires access to all of the control memory. Modules need only access the portion that holds their own control words. Control memory design, then, is equivalent to that employed in the multiplexed oscillators described earlier. Thus, the control memory does not limit performance as modules are added.

The signal memory is a different story, however. Every module must be able to access any part of it at random. In fact, the total number of read accesses per sample period is equal to the total number of signal inputs in the system. Likewise, the number of write accesses per sample period is equal to the number of signal outputs in the system. The total number of words in the memory is also equal to the number of outputs. Thus, at first glance, $N + M$ memory cycles must be performed in a sample period, where N is the number of inputs and M is the number of outputs. The proposed system had provisions for 288 inputs and 288 outputs. A straightforward time-multiplexed signal memory would need a cycle speed of 27 nsec to get all 576 accesses accomplished in a 16-μsec sample interval.

The cycle rate can be nearly cut in half if writing is performed in an orderly fashion. This is quite reasonable, since every word is written each sample period and write addresses are preassigned to the modules. In order to save time when writing, the memory array is organized such that several write ports are formed that can be written into simultaneously. In the proposed system, the signal memory consisted of 18 blocks of 16 words each. Only 16 write cycles were therefore necessary to update the entire memory. By using the block write, the number of memory accesses per 16μsec is cut down to 304, which allows a 50-nsec read cycle and a 100-nsec write cycle; a practical figure for conventional logic.

The number of signal inputs in the system is therefore limited by signal memory speed. The only way to overcome that limitation without sacrificing interconnection flexibility is to completely duplicate the memory so that two real read access ports are available. The same data would be written into the same addresses in both memories simultaneously. Reading would be independent with half of the modules reading from one memory, while the remainder read from the other half. The memory throughput capability would therefore be doubled. Memory splitting without duplication is also possible if a *communication module* is defined that can transfer selected signals from one-half of the system to the other.

Signal-Processing Computer

In spite of the flexibility of a modular digital synthesizer, nothing matches the generality of an ordinary computer in sound synthesis and modification. However, only the largest general-purpose computers are fast enough for really significant real-time synthesis, not to mention their enormous cost. A specialized signal-processing computer, however, is less general than a standard computer but more general than the collection of hard-wired modules described earlier. The primary benefit of a signal-processing computer is that the computations, their sequencing, and their eventual disposition can all be specified by programming.

Speed is gained by taking advantage of repetition and using "macroinstructions," both of which allow a high degree of parallelism and pipelining. Speed is also enhanced by the virtual absence of conditional branch-type instructions, which normally bog down a pipelined machine. One simple type of macroinstruction can be represented by the expression A = A + B + CD, where A is an accumulator register and B, C, and D are variable operands. This single instruction replaces two adds, a multiply, and several data move instructions in a typical computer yet requires little if any extra hardware to implement because of the nature of multiplication. Such an instruction is useful in implementing digital filters and performing the fast Fourier transform. As a matter of fact, an instruction to perform the calculations involved in evaluating an FFT node pair is well within the realm of practicality. Other macroinstructions might perform linear interpolation, maximum-value selection, or table lookup (including argument scaling and table origin offset), again with a single instruction.

Repetition is denoted by arranging data in blocks and then executing a particular instruction on the entire block. In this manner, a long, highly efficient pipeline can be kept filled with data a high percentage of the time. For example, a parallel multiplier array can be pipelined by placing a set of registers between each level of 2 × 4 multiplier blocks. Although the overall input-to-output delay is increased substantially, the throughput rate is increased dramatically. It is not unreasonable to obtain a new product every 40 nsec with TTL logic. This is possible because in a nonpipelined parallel multiplier the top levels settle out first and become idle, while the lower levels continue to settle. Pipelining allows new data to be given to the top levels as soon as they settle.

More recently, special *signal-processing microprocessors* have become available. These differ from conventional microprocessors, such as the 6502 or 68000, in several important respects. First, their internal structure is comparatively simple, consisting of a program memory, data memory, a couple of registers, an adder, and a parallel multiplier. Program instructions are even more primitive than a conventional processor's machine language. They typically consist of several bit fields that together specify exactly what each internal element should do during the instruction cycle. Thus, it is possible, after careful study of the problem, to keep most of the elements busy doing parallel computation on every instruction. Often the program instructions must be organized into a single long loop where each trip through the loop processes one sample of the input signal. Decisions are made using conditional execution, in which the instruction either does the indicated operation or does nothing so that the loop time is constant. Program memory is usually *masked ROM* right on the chip, although some models allow for external program memory, often with a speed penalty. Data memory is also on-chip and typically rather small, such as 256 words or less. Processing accuracy ranges from 12 to 16 bits, although multiple precision operations are possible. Speed is respectable with instruction times of 200–300 nsec being common. Each processing element, including the multiplier, can perform an operation in one instruction time. In general, signal-processing microprocessors are usually limited to special function modules, and use of the on-chip ROM requires high-usage volume to justify the masking cost.

A special case of the signal-processing computer is the *array processor*. These are normally hard-wired or microprogrammed to perform a limited variety of operations on blocks of numbers at very high speed. Normally they are interfaced to a host computer as a direct memory access I/O device. In operation, one or more arrays of numbers are transferred to the array processor followed by a sequence of operation commands. Often, these operations are at a very high level such as computation of the autocorrelation function, conversion of an array of complex numbers from polar form to rectangular form and vice versa, or even a complete FFT. It is not unusual for an array processor optimized for FFT computation to compute a 1,024-point FFT in *15 msec* using 16-bit arithmetic! Such a device can require an entire rack full of logic, however.

Much sound synthesis computation can be effectively performed by an array processor. For example, one block of samples can be an audio signal, while a second block can be an amplitude envelope. An array multiplication (computes element-by-element product) operation will then return an array of enveloped samples. Transversal digital filtering is another array-oriented operation that can be performed efficiently on an array processor.

Even with the tremendous speed improvement offered by signal-processing computers and array processors, there is no guarantee that real-time operation can be sustained during highly complex portions of the score. Nevertheless, such devices are very useful in composing a complex piece where subsets of the final score can be performed in real time. They are also valuable in the final run where what might be hours of computation is reduced to minutes.

Digital Voice-Per-Board System

The voice modular concept of synthesizer organization is also well suited to digital implementation. In general terms, a voice module is nothing more than a frequency generator, static waveshaper, optional dynamic waveshaper (variable filter), and amplitude controller connected in a series string as in Fig. 17–22. A one or more channel envelope generator controls

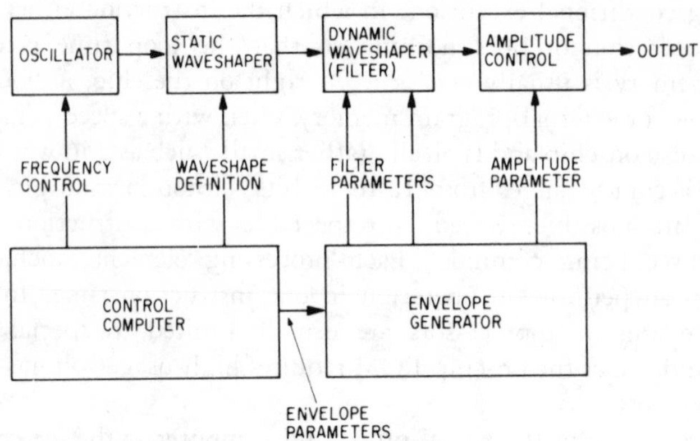

Fig. 17–22. General voice module

the amplitude and dynamic waveshaper. A very wide variety of new and existing musical instruments can be simulated by suitable setting of parameters.

We have seen how digital circuitry does an excellent job implementing the oscillator and static waveshaper and, when multiplexed sufficiently, does so at low cost. The dynamic waveshaper can be implemented via Fourier series (in which case the static waveshaper is not needed) or with a digital filter. The amplitude-control element is simply a multiplier, whereas envelope generation can be done by the using system or a dedicated microprocessor.

When cost is an overriding factor, the Fourier series approach is out (remember that the entire unit diagrammed in Fig. 17–18 is just one voice). A digital filter and amplitude multiplier would only be practical in a highly multiplexed voice module and even then the hardware for such "simple" signal processing would dominate the module's cost, mainly because of the multiplications required. At this time, analog-variable filters and controlled amplifiers can do the job cheaper, while their inaccuracies are not significant in this application. Thus, in a voice module, digital techniques are most effective for frequency- and static-waveform generation, while analog techniques are best for economical processing of the tone.

When hybrid techniques are used in a voice module, multiplexing of the frequency generator and waveshaper becomes less attractive because the analog portion of the module cannot be multiplexed. In fact, much current work in this area is with nonmultiplexed "voice-per-board" modules that can be built, or purchased, one at a time as need (or budget) dictates. This does not mean that some logic functions cannot be profitably shared. The crystal frequency standard, for example, can be shared among modules as can the interface to the control computer.

A Hybrid Voice Module

Figure 17–23 is a block diagram of a hybrid voice module that is practical for an individual to build. Very little is present that has not been discussed in detail previously. The most interesting feature is a "floating-point" method of specifying the frequency parameter. The method allows a frequency resolution of better than 1 cent throughout the audio range with a single 15-bit parameter. The idea is to use the most significant 3 bits of the parameter to specify an octave and 12 additional bits to specify a frequency within the octave.

The frequency and waveform generator utilizes variable-sample-rate techniques to minimize the size and resolution required in the waveform memory. Waveforms as coarse as 4-bit resolution and 16 steps have been successfully used in similar generators, and while a wide variety of timbres

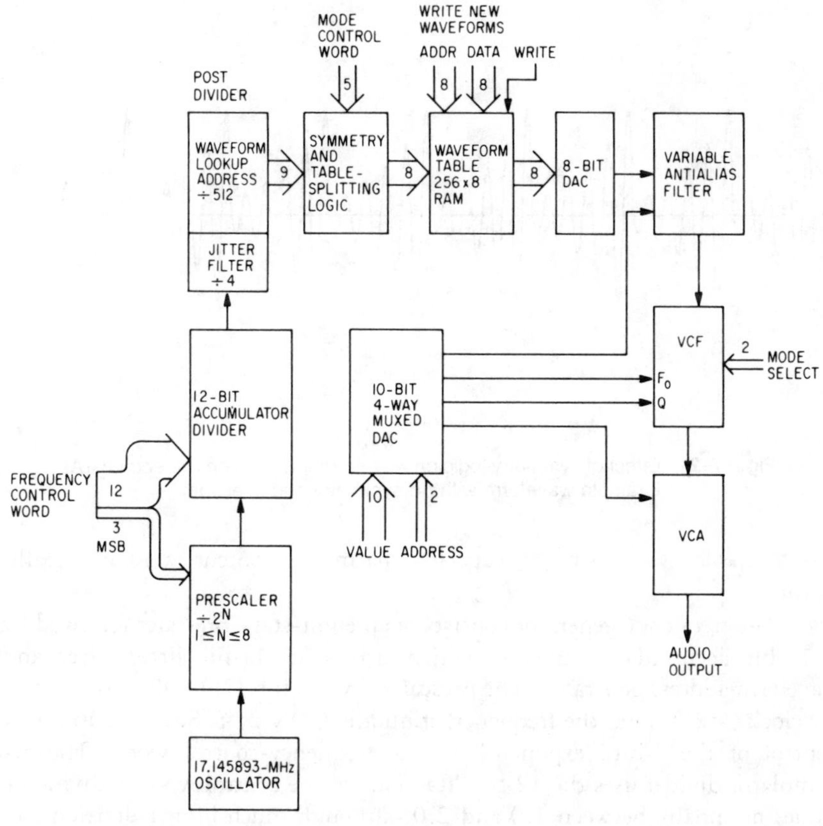

Fig. 17–23. Hybrid voice module

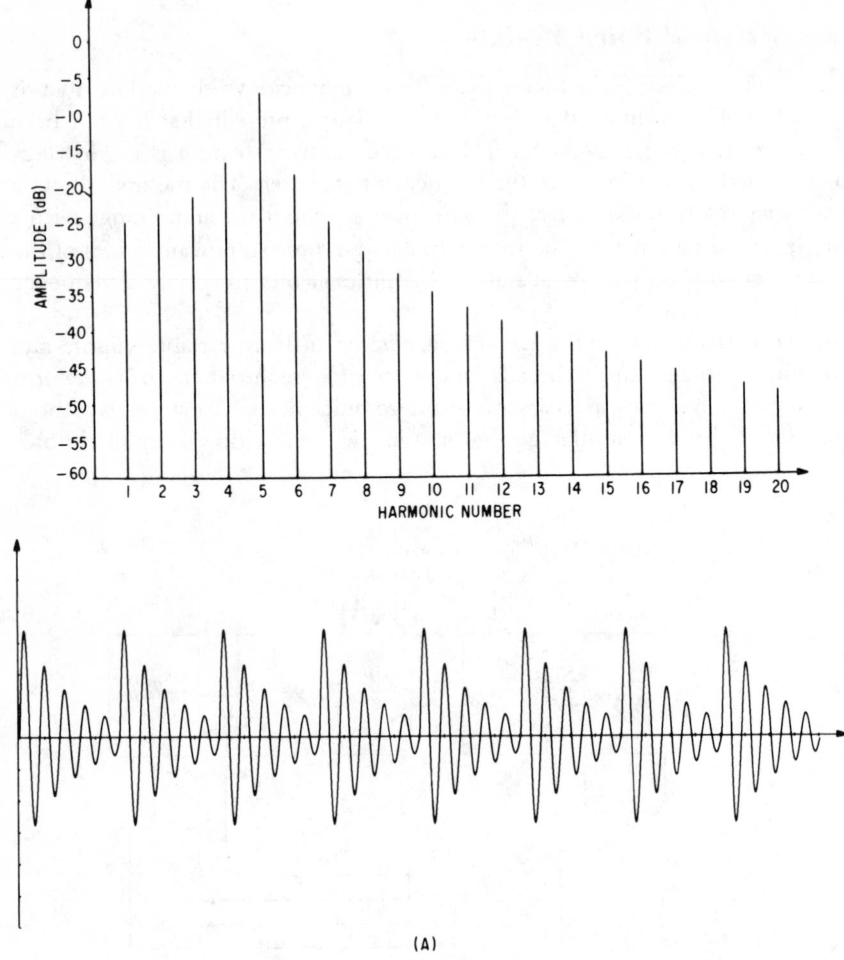

Fig. 17–24. Effect of symmetry logic on waveform and harmonic spectrum. (A) Example waveform with no symmetry and spectrum.

was available, waveforms of very low harmonic content were not really possible.

The frequency generator consists of an eight-stage prescaler followed by a 12-bit accumulator divider, which drives an 11-bit jitter filter and waveform address generator. The prescaler divides the 17.145893-MHz master clock ($=2^{16}$ times the frequency of middle C) by 2, 4, 8, . . . 256 under control of the 3-bit "exponent" in the frequency-control word. The accumulator divider uses the 12-bit "fraction" of the control word to divide by values nominally between 1.0 and 2.0, although much higher division factors are possible with a loss in resolution. The first 2 bits of the postdivider function as jitter filter, while the remaining 9 bits participate in waveform table lookup. The highest fundamental frequency that can be generated is 33

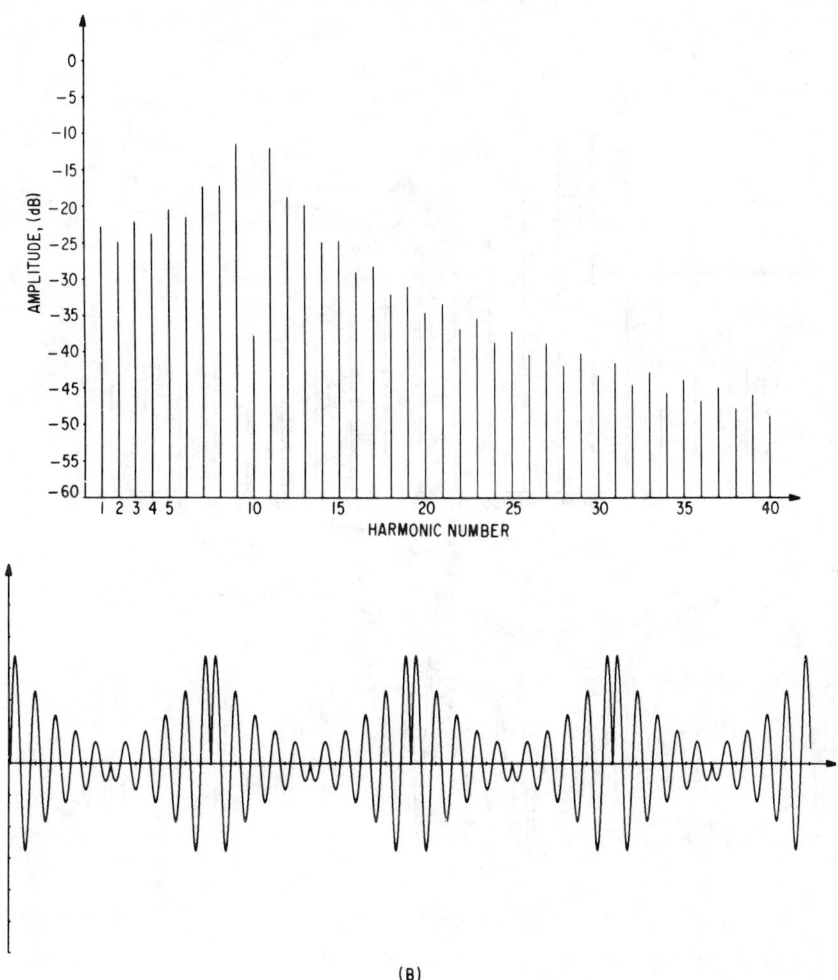

Fig. 17–24. Effect of symmetry logic on waveform and harmonic spectrum *(cont.)*. (B) Waveform with even symmetry added and spectrum.

kHz, whereas the lowest frequency for full resolution is 65.4 Hz, although much lower frequencies are possible with less frequency resolution.

The basic waveform generator is a 256-word × 8-bit read/write memory. It may hold either four different 64-point waveforms, two 128-point waves, or a single 256-point waveform. To increase flexibility and partially overcome the small size of the waveform memory, particularly when the four-waveform mode is selected, *symmetry* logic has been added. Under the control of a mode word, normal operation plus 4 degrees of symmetry can be imposed on the tabulated waveform without changing the memory contents. Figure 17–24 illustrates the symmetry options and their effect on the shape and harmonic spectrum of the tabulated wave. Option 1 is called *even symmetry* and consists of alternately playing the waveform forward for a cycle and

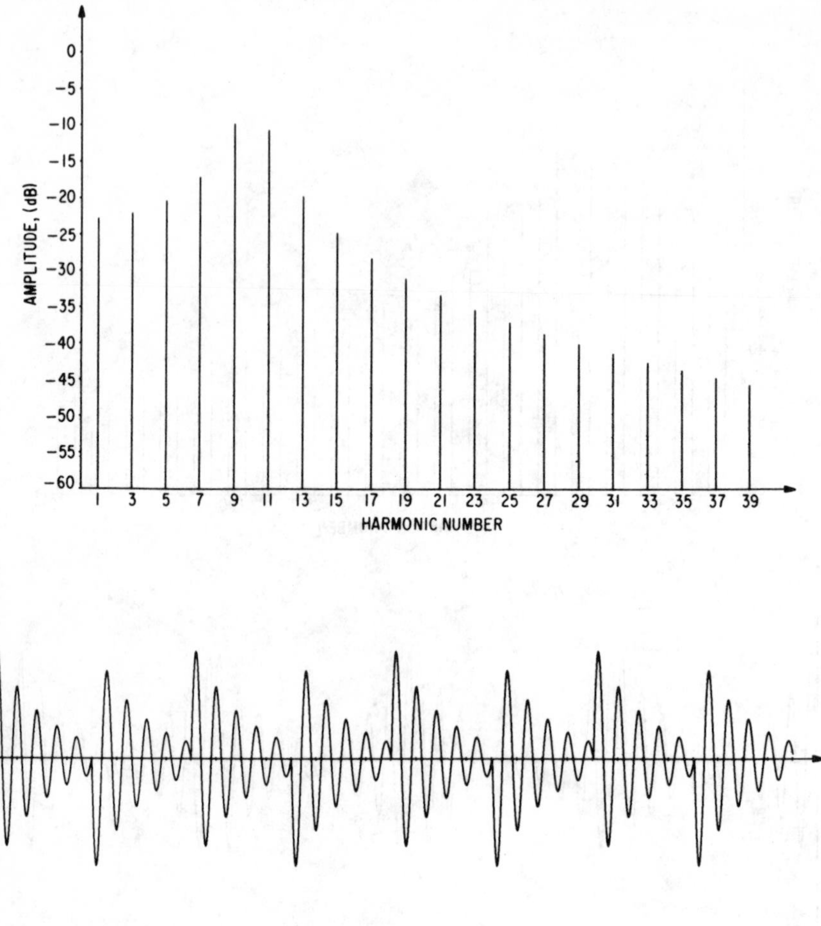

Fig. 17–24. Effect of symmetry logic on waveform and harmonic spectrum *(cont.)*. (C) Waveform with odd symmetry added and spectrum.

backward for a cycle. The audible effect is a tone with substantially the same timbre and brillance but an octave lower in pitch. *Odd* symmetry is created when the waveform is alternately played right-side-up for a cycle and upside-down for a cycle. The resulting tone has the same degree of brilliance and other characteristics as the original but also has the distinctive hollow quality of odd order harmonics plus octave-lowered pitch. Even symmetry may be followed by odd symmetry, which gives a two-octave pitch reduction, odd order harmonics, and a weird timbre reminiscent of balanced modulation or spectrum shifting. Finally, odd symmetry followed by even symmetry retains the two-octave drop but removes the hollow quality from the timbre.

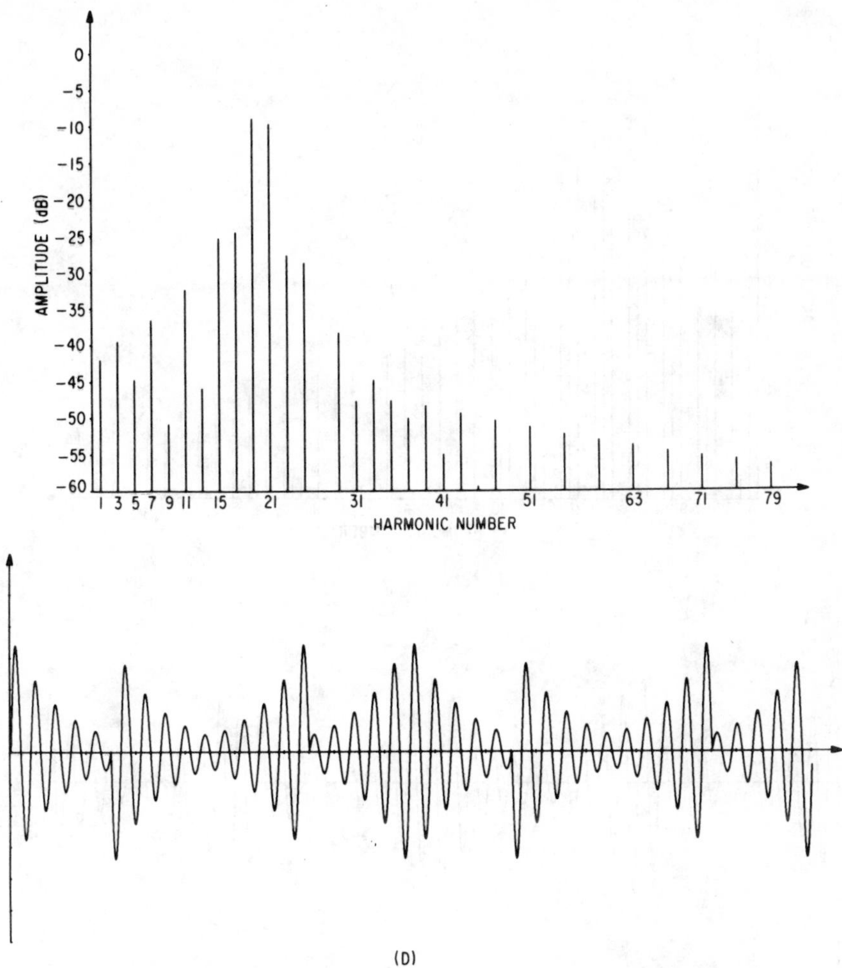

Fig. 17–24. Effect of symmetry logic on waveform and harmonic spectrum *(cont.)*. (D) Waveform with even symmetry followed by odd symmetry and spectrum.

Fortunately, this kind of symmetry logic is quite simple. Even symmetry is created by conditionally inverting the 8 address bits entering the waveform memory. On even scans though the waveform memory, the address bits pass unaltered, while on odd scans they are inverted by exclusive-or gates, thus addressing the table backward. Odd symmetry is similarly implemented by conditionally inverting the 8 data bits leaving the memory, which are assumed to be offset binary encoded. The most significant 2 bits of the postdivider in conjunction with the symmetry selection determines when address or data should be inverted.

Figure 17–25 shows a logic schematic of the frequency generator and static waveform generator. The 17.14-MHz frequency standard is sent to an

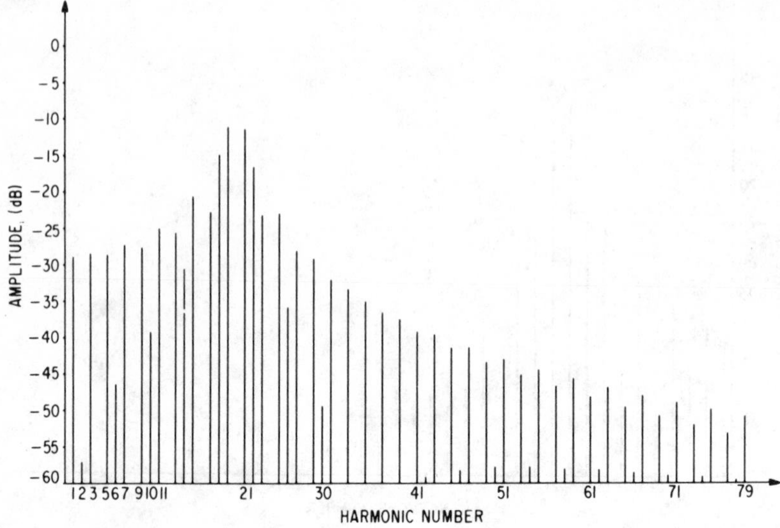

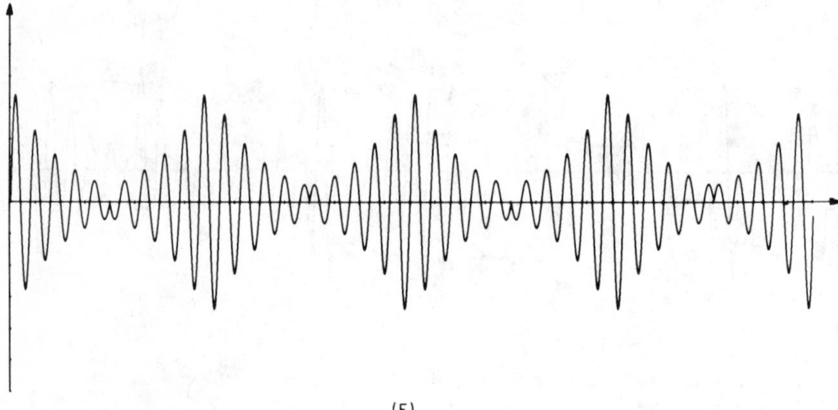

(E)

Fig. 17–24. Effect of symmetry logic on waveform and harmonic spectrum *(cont.)*. (E) Waveform with odd symmetry followed by even symmetry and spectrum.

8-bit prescaler counter built with 74LS161 counters. The "LS" version is necessary because a timing anomaly of the standard 74161 prevents operation at high clock frequencies. An eight-input multiplexor (74151) selects one of the eight divided outputs under the control of three frequency control bits. The multiplexor output is strobed by a D-type flip-flop to suppress glitches when the frequency control register is changed.

The prescaler output clocks both the accumulator and the postdivider. The latter is enabled to count only when the adder in the accumulator divider generates a carry output. Note that the frequency and mode control registers

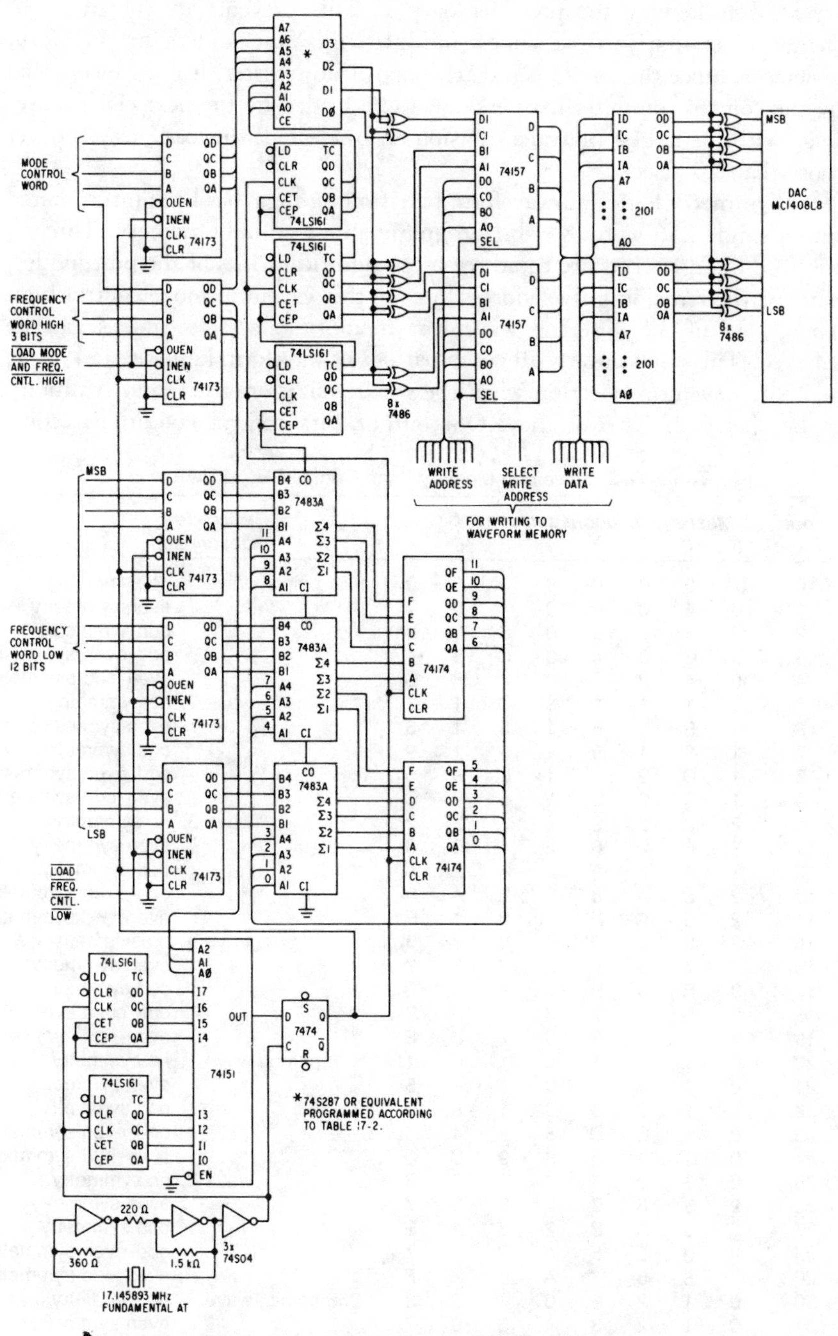

Fig. 17–25. Digital portion of hybrid voice module

are also clocked by the prescaler output. This prevents its content from changing at inopportune times and glitching the adders or waveform generator. Since the 74173 is a synchronous load register, it must be enabled by the control computer long enough to be loaded by the next clock pulse. Even with the largest prescaler division ratio selected, the load delay is never more than 15 μsec.

Symmetry logic and waveform partitioning logic has been incorporated into a single 256-word × 4-bit programmable read-only memory. Three of the ROM address bits are the three most significant bits of the postdivider, whereas the remaining five address bits are the waveform mode control bits. Thus, one of 32 different waveform memory operating modes can be selected. This allows nearly all combinations of waveform table size (64, 128, or 256), waveform selection when the smaller sizes are used, and symmetry to be specified. Two of the ROM output bits control conditional com-

Table 17-2. Waveform Memory Scan Control PROM Pattern

Mode Number[1]	*Most significant accumulator bits*[2] *0*	*1*	*2*	*3*	*4*	*5*	*6*	*7*	*Mode description*
0	0[3]	0	0	0	0	0	0	0	64 points, wave 1, no symmetry
1	0	4	0	4	0	4	0	4	even symmetry
2	0	8	0	8	0	8	0	8	odd symmetry
3	0	C	8	4	0	C	8	4	odd–even symmetry
4	0	4	8	C	0	4	8	C	even–odd symmetry
5	1	1	1	1	1	1	1	1	wave 2, no symmetry
6	1	5	1	5	1	5	1	5	even symmetry
7	1	9	1	9	1	9	1	9	odd symmetry
8	1	D	9	5	1	D	9	5	odd–even symmetry
9	1	5	9	D	1	5	9	D	even–odd symmetry
10	2	2	2	2	2	2	2	2	wave 3, no symmetry
11	2	6	2	6	2	6	2	6	even symmetry
12	2	A	2	A	2	A	2	A	odd symmetry
13	2	E	A	6	2	E	A	6	odd–even symmetry
14	2	6	A	E	2	6	A	E	even–odd symmetry
15	3	3	3	3	3	3	3	3	wave 4, no symmetry
16	3	7	3	7	3	7	3	7	even symmetry
17	3	B	3	B	3	B	3	B	odd symmetry
18	3	F	B	7	3	F	B	7	odd–even symmetry
19	3	7	B	F	3	7	B	F	even–odd symmetry
20	0	1	0	1	0	1	0	1	128 points, wave 1, no symmetry
21	0	1	4	5	0	1	4	5	even symmetry
22	0	1	8	9	0	1	8	9	odd symmetry
23	0	1	C	D	8	9	4	5	odd–even symmetry
24	0	1	4	5	8	9	C	D	even–odd symmetry
25	2	3	2	3	2	3	2	3	wave 2, no symmetry
26	2	3	6	7	2	3	6	7	even symmetry
27	2	3	A	B	2	3	A	B	odd symmetry
28	2	3	E	F	A	B	6	7	odd–even symmetry
29	2	5	6	7	A	B	E	F	even–odd symmetry
30	0	1	2	3	0	1	2	3	256 points, wave 1, no symmetry
31	0	1	2	3	4	5	6	7	even symmetry

Notes: [1]Most significant 5 PROM address bits expressed in decimal.
[2]Least significant 3 PROM address bits expressed in decimal.
[3]PROM contents expressed in hexadecimal.

plementers on the waveform memory, while the other two are the most significant waveform memory address bits. The other six waveform memory address bits are taken directly from the postdivider.

Although the exact ROM contents will depend on personal preference, Table 17–2 shows one possibility that works well. The chosen combinations of waveform size, symmetry, etc., are simply arranged sequentially and assigned mode numbers from 0 to 31, which corresponds to the 5-bit mode control input. The only omitted waveform combinations are odd, even–odd, and odd–even symmetry with 256-point waveforms.

Final values from the waveform memory are sent directly to an inexpensive 8-bit DAC. From this point forward, the tone will be processed by the voltage-controlled analog circuitry in Fig. 17–26. The four control voltages required are generated by a 10 bit DAC that is multiplexed four ways using sample-and-hold circuits. Note that writing into the waveform memory will generate intolerable noise and therefore must be done while the amplitude is set to zero. This is one reason for multiple-waveform capability.

One problem with all variable-sample-rate techniques is the need for a tracking antialias filter. Without the filter, low-frequency waveforms with little harmonic content will exhibit a "chime-like" effect due to the high alias frequencies that are unmasked by the absence of strong high-frequency harmonics (remember that with variable sample rate, the alias frequencies themselves are harmonic). The filtering requirement is simplified considerably by using one channel of the 10-bit multiplexed DAC to drive a 2050 VCF IC connected as a two-section Butterworth filter. Although the filter control could be slaved to the frequency control word, the latter's floating point format complicates matters. Thus, for simplicity and maximum flexibility (one may want to under- or over-filter the waveform for special functions), the antialias filter is independently controlled. Utilization of the exponential tuning feature of the 2050 allows a 1,000-to-1 tuning range with a step size so small (0.7%) it is inaudible.

The dynamic waveshaping filter can take on many forms, but here the simple state-variable type is used. Two channels of the 10-bit multiplexed DAC are used to control center frequency and Q factor of the filter. Exponential tuning of both parameters at the rate of 100 steps/octave retains better than 0.7% resolution over a 1,000-to-1 range. A 2-bit word and some analog switches select the filter's operating mode.

A VCA built with a 3080 gain control element uses the remaining 10-bit DAC channel to control amplitude in steps of 1/10 dB with a theoretical range of 100 dB. Note that any nonlinear distortion in the VCA results in pure harmonic distortion of the waveform, since only one tone is being handled.

Interfacing to the control computer is not explicitly shown because of wide variations in computer types, word lengths, and personal bias. When updating the frequency control words, however, it is important that all 15 bits change simultaneously. When using an 8-bit host, this requirement is

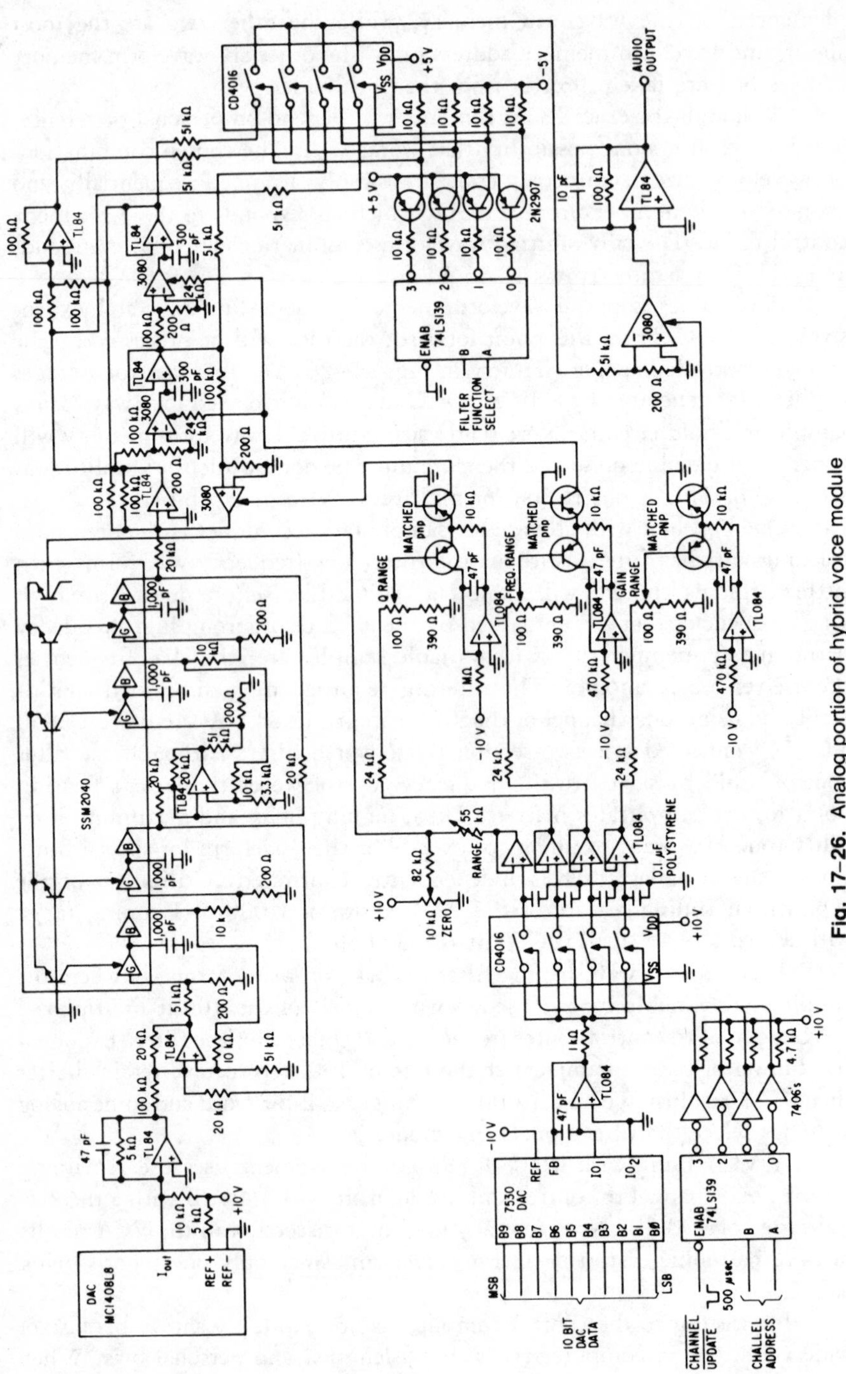

Fig. 17–26. Analog portion of hybrid voice module

taken care of with an additional buffer register much like the vector graphics oscilloscope interface described in Chapter 11. Writing into the waveform memory and multiplexed DAC memory should conform with the timing requirements of the RAM chips used.

18
Music Synthesis Software

With few exceptions, the entire discussion up to this point has concentrated on hardware-related items, both digital and analog. The key to a successful computer music system, particularly one utilizing direct synthesis techniques, however, is efficient and easy to use software. Actually in the final analysis, software is the real frontier in computer music regardless of the sound generation technique utilized. Little of the preceding hardware discussion can be considered "new" and almost certainly none of it is revolutionary. On the other hand, any given programmer with a suitable knowledge of music and synthesis techniques can create a music-oriented programming system significantly different from others that have been done and may possibly stage a software breakthrough. This is as it should be, since, after all, the general-purpose computer was conceived as a finite hardware device with infinite application possibilities through programming.

Computer music "systems," where a system is the combination of musical I/O hardware with software "glue," can be separated into two easily distinguishable groups. The first group covers systems designed for real-time performance directly from manual input devices such as keyboards and source-signal analysis. The second group covers "programmed" performance, either real-time or not, in which the sounds are carefully specified prior to the actual synthesis. While the former type of system has not been emphasized in this text, it is of interest to a great many people. In terms of software, however, such systems tend to be specialized for particular combinations of input devices and synthesis techniques. The second type of system tends to be much more general. Often, these develop along classic software system lines with the concepts of tasks, events, macros, supervisors, and languages being integral parts.

In this chapter, programming techniques for the programmed performance type of system will be discussed. In addition, the anatomy of a simplistic but expandable music software system will be described. It is immaterial whether the synthesis is performed in real time or not, since the "score" is definitely prepared outside of real time. In most cases, nonreal-time *delayed playback* direct synthesis will be assumed because it is more general

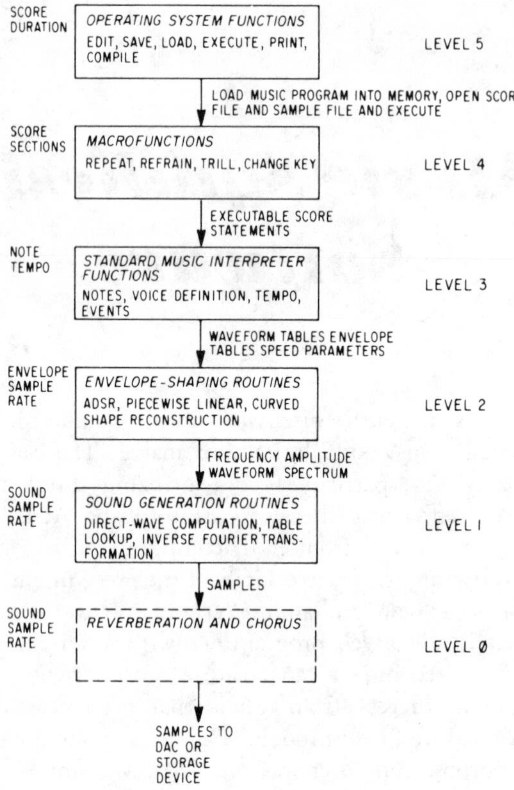

Fig. 18–1. Music software system hierarchy

and, in most respects, more difficult than real-time performance using external synthesis hardware.

Organization of Music Software Systems

Like most nontrivial software systems, a music synthesis software system is organized into a hierarchy of programs and functions. Figure 18–1 illustrates that at least five distinct levels can be identified ranging from the lowest level sample-by-sample computations to the highest level operating system functions. The levels are distinguished by the time scale at which they operate. The lower levels operate in the micro- and millisecond terms of individual waveform and envelope samples, while the higher levels operate on the scale of seconds associated with notes and phrases in the musical performance. Information flow is generally from the higher levels to the lower levels, although in some cases signaling in the opposite direction may be done.

Often, each level is served by a distinct program or set of subroutines and in fact the programming languages used may vary from level to level. Overall a music synthesis software system for programmed performance operates as an *interpretive* system that extracts information from the user-prepared score and then acts on the information. The higher levels do the information extraction and organization, while the lower levels do the actual execution.

The lowest level synthesis routines, which will be called "Level 1" routines, operate at the sample rate of the final sound. This means that a single "loop" through the synthesis routine generates only one sample of the final sound. Basically, the routine accepts sound *parameters* as input and generates sound samples as output. The output samples may be mixed with the output of other Level 1 routines or the same routine with different parameters. Details of the routine, of course, depend heavily on the synthesis method chosen. If waveform table lookup is the primary scheme utilized, then each loop involves the computation of a new lookup address based on a frequency parameter, actual table lookup based on a waveshape parameter, amplitude adjustment based on an amplitude parameter, and output based on a location parameter.

Usually, a Level 1 synthesis routine will generate a "block" of samples before returning to the next higher level. This saves most of the considerable overhead associated with call and return linkage and the passing of parameters. In the hierarchical system being outlined, the parameters of the sound being synthesized are assumed to be constant throughout the block. Often, a sample buffer is used to hold one or more blocks of samples. As samples are computed, they are algebraically *added* to corresponding samples in the buffer in a manner analogous to the audio bus of an analog voice modular system. If stereo or quad is being synthesized, there will be a distinct buffer for each channel of sound.

In some cases, there may be a "Level 0" routine that processes sound samples from the buffer before playing them through the DAC or writing them on a storage device. The usual function of such a routine is the addition of reverberation or a chorus effect to the sound. Parameters from the upper levels are often required to control the effects produced, particularly when they are used in a piece for dramatic contrast.

Level 2 routines operate at what can be called the "envelope sample rate." This is the rate at which the fundamental parameters needed by the Level 1 routines are updated and is equal to the audio sample rate divided by their block size. Rates of 50 s/s to 2,000 s/s are useful, which corresponds to update periods of 0.5 msec to 20 msec. Level 2 routines accept envelope parameters from the higher levels and supply sound parameters to the Level 1 routines. Envelope parameter descriptions vary widely, however, and a typical system may use different Level 2 routines simultaneously according to envelope type and description.

For example, amplitude envelope needs are often satisfied by the ADSR shape, which can be completely described by five parameters. It is the responsibility of a Level 2 routine to generate samples of the shape as needed, given the parameters, and then pass these samples as parameters to the Level 1 routines. A different Level 2 routine may produce arbitrary contour shapes using a piecewise linear or curvilinear approximation. With such approximations, the higher-level routine specifies segment endpoints, the amount of time spanned by the segment, and the segment shape (linear, concave, convex, etc.). Yet another might interpolate between tabulated samples of a shape that could be the result of a source-signal analysis, for example.

Level 3 routines comprise the bulk of the coding in the system. Their job is to accept music language statements, which are character strings, extract the information contained in them (or flag an error if the statement is incomprehensible), and supply parameters to Levels 1 and 2 routines. It is also responsible for setting up waveform and envelope shape tables, if used, in response to voicing statements in the score. It is hard to pin down the exact rate of execution for a Level 3 routine, but it is generally at the rate that notes are played. This is often called the "syllabic rate" from the corresponding level in the hierarchy of routines that comprise a typical speech synthesis system.

Level 4 programming is a superset of Level 3. In most music, there is a considerable amount of repetition that when added to the many conventions of standard music notation results in a conventional score much shorter than the corresponding computer score expressed as character strings. The concept of macroinstructions is useful in taking advantage of these properties of the score to reduce its size. Basically, a macroinstruction is a command to the macroexpander (the Level 4 routine under consideration) to convert a statement such as "repeat the following three-note sequence eight times" into eight repetitions of the three-note statement, which are then interpreted by the Level 3 routine just as if the user had actually written the sequence eight times. Most macroexpanders allow loops, conditional tests, counters, and procedure calls (subroutines), suggesting their use as a composition tool as well.

Even though they are not really part of the music software system, operating system functions on Level 5 have been included for completeness. These are the routines that allow the user to prepare and edit the score file, link and load the music system programs into memory, and control the reading of the score file and writing of the sample file in a delayed playback system. Depending on the installation, the operating system may range from a paper tape editor and loader to a full disk operating system. In a loosely structured music software system, the operating system is vital in its role of maintaining the data base.

Implementation of the Levels

Current thinking in computer science dictates that each of these levels be independently implemented as a separate program and linked together only for execution. In fact, each level should probably be broken down further into many subroutines. While this book is not the place to discuss modular and structured programming practices, it is clear that the major levels need not all be coded in the same programming language. In fact, the optimum balance between programming effort and music program speed requires that different languages be used on different levels.

There is a little question that Levels 0 and 1 should be implemented in assembly language for the machine being used. The reason, of course, is that they execute at the sound sample rate of 8 ks/s to 50 ks/s. Furthermore, for almost any personal computer, fixed-point (integer) arithmetic must be used for the sample calculations. Most programmers are unfamiliar with the fine points of fixed-point computation, having been spoiled by the floating-point capabilities of large mainframe computers or high-level languages. Since integer computation is vital to acceptable speed with microcomputers, it will be discussed in detail later.

In isolated instances, the lower-level routines have actually been implemented in the *microcode* of a microprogrammed minicomputer. This essentially means that new instructions are added to the computer's repertoire that facilitate sample computation. What is actually happening is that the internal machine registers and logical elements are being directly manipulated by the microcode at maximum speed without the overhead of reading instructions from main memory. Although two to three times faster, microprogramming is even more obscure and difficult than assembly programming. Also, only the larger minicomputers allow user microprogramming anyway.

Dedicated hardware such as was discussed in the previous chapter can be thought of as replacing Level 1 routines. If the dedicated hardware is intelligent, Level 2 may also be replaced. In computer-controlled analog systems, voltage-controlled oscillators, amplifiers, and filters perform the functions of Level 1 routines, while envelope generators do the Level 2 functions.

High-Level Languages

Level 3 routines are best implemented in a higher-level language, particularly in a delayed playback system. This level of the music system typically handles a relatively small volume of data but does a lot of character string scanning, data table maintenance, and decision making. Thus, only a small portion of the computational effort is spent in these routines, while a large portion of the programming effort is sunk into them. High-level languages tend to minimize the programming effort required while simultaneously making the programs easier to read and modify (if adequately commented). High-level languages for microcomputer systems almost invariably have features that make it easy to link to assembly level routines.

The natural question, of course, is: Which high-level language should be used in the upper levels of a music software system? Like microprocessor selection itself, language preference tends to be more a matter of personal experience (and taste) than scientific weighing of virtues and drawbacks. The following, therefore, amounts to nothing more than a summary of the author's biases, which, hopefully, are shared by a majority of readers.

The primary virtue of BASIC, of course, is its nearly universal implementation on microcomputer systems. Drawbacks are many but most serious are the lack of a true subroutine capability and a restricted variable-naming convention. Its formal mechanism for linking to assembly language leaves much to be desired, although tricks for enhancing it abound. These shortcomings make writing and implementation of large programs in BASIC more difficult than necessary. Nevertheless, BASIC is excellent for getting started, and after all, has been used in programming examples so far.

FORTRAN is the grandaddy of programming languages and is now available on some microcomputers. For musical purposes, it is very similar to BASIC but with subroutine and naming restrictions removed. It is, however, somewhat weaker in the handling of character string data than BASIC is. Since FORTRAN is compiled, it is faster than a BASIC program, which is usually interpreted. The best-known direct computer synthesis program, MUSIC V, is implemented in FORTRAN but is far too big and dependent on a big mainframe operating system to run on a microcomputer without extensive modification. FORTRAN would be a good choice for someone already familiar with it but should probably be bypassed by newcomers in favor of a more "modern" language.

COBOL, the most widely used big-computer language, is unsuitable for a music software system.

APL may be available on some microcomputers. While it is an excellent problem-solving language for those adept in its use, it is an extremely self-contained, "isolationist" language. This means that communication with the operating system, assembly language programs, and data files is poor or nonexistent. While not suitable for a music performance system, it may be useful in exploring computer *composition* techniques.

The remaining are called "block-structured" languages because of the way that statements are grouped together and the mechanism for variable storage allocation. These run the range in sophistication from integers-only subsets such as PL/M to overgrown monsters like ADA. Pascal, or its latest incarnation, Modula-2, is a fairly well-known language of this type that is extensively used in computer science education, largely due to the efforts of the University of Southern California at San Diego (UCSD), who first implemented it on a microcomputer. Many students are introduced to Pascal as their first formal language (if they had not encountered BASIC on their own earlier). A few years ago, Pascal promised to become the dominant language for large microcomputer software systems such as synthesis packages. This has not happened because of the lack of efficient optimizing compilers and largely unspecified methods of I/O and linkage with the operating system. The latter defect in turn begat a variety of incompatible solutions to the problem. Although Modula-2 has addressed this in the language specification, it is probably too late to help.

C is another structured language born in the commercial world and is probably the most used in large microcomputer software projects. It was developed at Bell Laboratories and is often seen in conjunction with UNIX, a very large time-sharing operating system (UNIX is in fact written in C). It is available as a stand-alone language for most microcomputer systems from the Z-80 and 6502 up to the 68000. In fact, a large and comprehensive delayed playback music synthesis system written in C (the CARL project at UCSD) is readily available and will be described in the next chapter. As mentioned in Chapter 5, C has structural features that allow for highly efficient object code generation—if the compiler takes advantage of them. In particular, the 68000 is a good match for the requirements of C because of its unsegmented memory addressing and numerous registers capable of holding 32-bit "double" values. The 8086 family (8088, 80186, 80286) is not as good because of the lack of those same features. In particular, their segmented addressing will either impose a 64K limit on the size of arrays, which could be a problem in musical applications, or will exact a severe space and time penalty if the compiler attempts to overcome it. A big advantage of C is that I/O and system call conventions are written into the language specification and thus differ little from one implementation to the next. A potential drawback of C is its often cryptic appearance, which makes adequate comments in programs essential.

One programming language property that is taking on increasing significance is *portability*. At the current rate of microprocessor evolution, it is quite likely that the computer being used will become obsolete in the course of music system development (this has happened three times to the author). Parts of the system implemented in a high-level language should be easily transportable to a new system if required. C promises to be very good in this respect. Although the low-level assembly language routines are not portable, they can usually be kept small, thus minimizing the effort needed to reimplement them on different hardware.

Low-Level Programming Techniques

Because they are executed so much, low-level sample computation routines completely dominate the speed characteristics of a direct computer synthesis system. Arithmetic operations in turn dominate the execution time of these low-level routines, particularly on a microcomputer. This is in stark contrast with most general-purpose assembly level programming in which arithmetic instructions are among the *least* used. Unless the reader has access to a mainframe or supermicrocomputer with floating-point hardware, it is a sure bet that these arithmetic operations will be of the fixed-point variety.

Even when floating-point hardware or subroutines are available, their speed is likely to be substantially less. The techniques of fixed-point computation are rapidly becoming an obscure art, however. In the next few pages these will be described to the depth necessary for use in digital signal-processing applications. Reasonable familiarity with the binary number system will be assumed. If the reader lacks such knowledge, introductory chapters of nearly any book on microprocessor programming can provide the background.

Adequately illustrating such a discussion requires an example microprocessor. Although Chapter 5 strongly suggested that the 68000 or other 16-bit machine should be used for direct synthesis applications, we will be using the 6502 microprocessor here for illustration. Such a choice can be rationalized in a couple of ways. First, programming just about any other choice would be easier, since the 6502 does not have hardware multiply or divide or even double byte add and subtract. Thus, understanding the given examples implemented on a 6502 will make similar implementation on a better machine seem simple in comparison. Another reason is that the 6502 is the basis of a great number of very inexpensive microcomputer systems. Later, the FFT subroutine presented in BASIC in Chapter 13 will be translated into 68000 assembly language to illustrate how integer arithmetic can be used in that type of algorithm on a processor that has better arithmetic capability.

The examples would not be very interesting unless actual synthesis and analysis experiments can be performed. A-to-D and D-to-A boards are available for most microcomputers, although they are seldom optimized for audio applications. Micro Technology Unlimited, however, has audio DAC and ADC systems at both the 8- and 16-bit levels that can be easily interfaced to most computers. The 8-bit units are designed for 8–10-ks/s sample rates and already have the necessary filters included. While these are definitely not hi-fi, they are indeed capable of illustrating all of the synthesis, modification, and analysis techniques described in previous chapters. Most experimentation will require a large memory buffer to hold a few seconds of sampled sound, although some real-time operations are possible. A 32K memory, for example, will hold 3–4 sec of sound at the sample rate for which these boards were designed. The 16-bit units, however, are truly hi-fi and include their own 32K sample buffer to simplify I/O programming as well as stereo and plug-in filter features. Of course, any of the circuits given in Chapters 7 and 12 can be used to build an audio DAC or ADC at considerable savings over commercial units.

Properties of Binary Arithmetic

Before plunging into programming examples, it is wise to review the characteristics of binary arithmetic that are important to signal processing. We will be dealing with two fundamentally different kinds of numbers, *signed* twos-complement numbers and *un*signed numbers. In an unsigned number, the weight of each bit is two raised to the bit number power. Thus, a single byte in the 6502 can represent any number from 0 through +255. Unsigned numbers are therefore always positive. In programming, they are normally used to represent addresses but in signal processing they are most useful as multiplying coefficients in digital filters, etc. Besides doubled dynamic range compared with signed numbers, the use of unsigned numbers simplifies the associated multiplications.

Signed twos-complement numbers are probably more familiar to most readers. The bit weights are the same as in unsigned numbers except that bit 7 (the leftmost) has a weight of −128. The number is negative only if this bit is a 1; thus, it is called the *sign bit*. The remaining bits are called *magnitude* bits, although it must be remembered that they have been complemented in the case of a negative number. A signed single-byte number can therefore represent quantities between −128 and +127. In signal processing, signed numbers are used to represent audio signal samples that invariably swing positive and negative.

A signed twos-complement number can be *negated*, that is, N converted to $-N$ or $-N$ converted to N, by complementing every bit in the number and then incrementing the result by one. This will not work for the number −128, however, because the increment operation overflows and the result becomes −128 again. Since negation will be required often in signal processing, mere existence of the largest negative number in a sample stream may cause an overflow that gives rise to a full-amplitude noise spike. Avoidance of such overflows usually requires an extra bit of precision in the numbers that may propagate when calculations are chained together. Thus, it is wise to prevent the occurrence of the largest negative number in synthesized samples and to search and correct ADC data by converting any −128s to −127 (which amounts to slight clipping rather than a full-scale noise spike) or the equivalent when other word lengths are used.

Fixed-point arithmetic is often equated with integer arithmetic because memory addresses are usually involved. In signal processing, fractions and mixed numbers are more common. There are at least two ways to think about such numbers. One involves the concept of a *scale factor*. The numbers being manipulated are considered to be the product of the actual quantity and a scale factor that the programmer keeps track of. The scale factor is chosen so that when it multiplies the numbers being handled, the results are pure integers, which are "compatible" with integer arithmetic. In the course of a chained calculation, the scale factors change so as to maintain the largest range of integers possible without overflowing the chosen word lengths.

The other method, which will be used here, involves the concept of a *binary* point. The function, meaning, and consequences of binary-point position are the same as they are with decimal points and decimal arithmetic. The microcomputer can be likened to an old mechanical calculator or a slide rule in which raw numbers are fed in and raw answers come out. It is the operator's responsibility to place the decimal point. Binary integers have the binary point to the right of the magnitude bits. Binary fractions have the binary point to the left of the magnitude bits. For unsigned numbers, this means to the left of *all* bits, while signed numbers have the point between the sign bit and the rest of the bits. Mixed numbers can have the binary point anywhere in between.

A good way to think of mixed binary numbers is to consider their *resolution*, which is the weight of the least significant bit, and their *range*, which is the largest number that can be represented. We will also be referring to their *integer part*, which is the string of bits to the left of the point, and their *fractional part*, which is the string to the right. Thus, a signed number with the binary points between bits 3 and 4 as illustrated in Fig. 18–2 has a resolution of 1/16 or 0.0625 and a range of 127/16 or 7.9375 (which can be called 8 for convenience). The integer part is bits 4-6 and the fractional part is bits 0-3. Integers, of course, have a resolution of unity and a range dependent on word size, while fractions have a range just short of unity and a resolution determined by word size.

The last property of binary numbers is word size or simply the number of bits allocated to the representation of the number. Arithmetic word sizes are usually chosen to be integer multiples of the computer's word size, or in the case of a sophisticated machine, a multiple of the smallest directly addressable data element, usually an 8-bit byte. When the word size of a number is greater than the word size of the machine, the number is said to be a *double-precision* or multiple-precision number. Thus, with the 6502 example machine, 16-bit numbers are double-precision quantities, 24 bits is triple-precision, etc.

Before the advent of microprocessors, visualization of multiple precision numbers on paper and in memory was a simple, unambiguous task. A double-precision number, for example, would be visualized as consisting of a high order, more significant part and a low order, less significant part. When written on paper, it is natural and even necessary to write the high order part to the left of the low order part. If one listed a portion of memory containing the number, it would be reasonable to expect it to look the same as it did on the notepad. However, many of the most popular microprocessors (6502 included) handle double-precision unsigned numbers (namely memory addresses) *low* byte first! Thus, the address bytes of instructions and indirect address pointers all appear on a memory dump *backward*. Furthermore, since address arithmetic is done one byte at a time, the programmer must be aware of this to get these operations done right.

The question, then, is: Should *all* numbers be stored and manipulated backward or just addresses? The author has tried it both ways and found neither to be completely satisfactory on the 6502. However, in signal-processing work, it is recommended that all numbers except addresses be

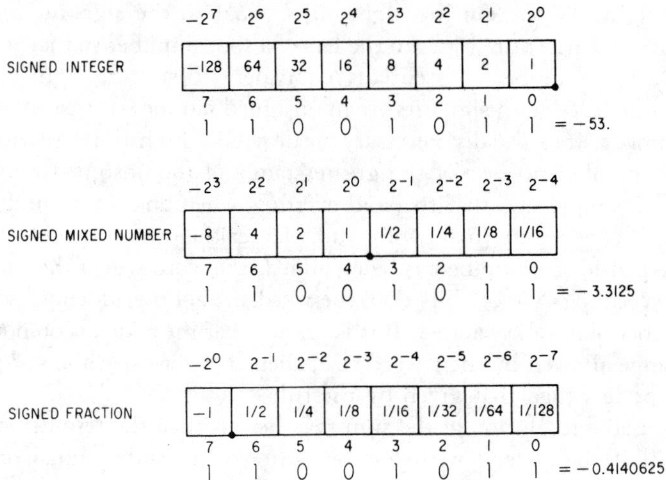

Fig. 18–2. Binary point placement

stored in natural order. One reason is that data arithmetic will predominate, which means that confusion will be only partial rather than total. The other reason is that 16- and 32-bit microprocessors, such as the 68000, directly handle the word sizes of interest—in natural order.

Addition and Subtraction

At this point, we are ready to discuss the effect of arithmetic operations on the various kinds of numbers. We will be discussing the four fundamental arithmetic operations (addition, subtraction, multiplication, and division) and their effect on the word size and binary point placement in the result. Rules governing mixed operands such as signed/unsigned and different word sizes will also be discussed.

Addition is the most fundamental operation and is usually considered the simplest. The operands of an addition are not distinguished from each other and are simply called *addends*. The following is a summary of the rules of binary addition of signed numbers:

1. The binary points of the addends must line up before addition unless scaling (multiplying or dividing by a power of 2) of one addend is specifically desired.
2. The range of the result can be up to twice as large as that of the widest range addend (one extra bit added to the integer part) and the resolution of the result is equal to that of the highest resolution addend (no change in the fractional part).

In heeding the first rule, it may be necessary to shift one of the addends with respect to the other. When shifting left, zeroes should be brought in from the right. When shifting right, bits equal to the sign bit must be brought in. Adding entire bytes to the left of a short number so that it can be added to a long number is essentially equivalent to shifting right so these bytes must be filled with sign bits. If an unsigned number is to be added to a signed number, it is usually necessary to provide a high order extension of the signed number because of the greater range of the unsigned number.

Rule 2 simply says that to avoid overflow when unknown numbers are added up, it is necessary to allow for sums larger than the addends. When a string of equal-length numbers is being added, the word size of the final sum will not exceed $\log_2 N$ more bits than the word sizes of the addends, where N is the number of numbers added. If it is known that the addends do not cover the full range allowed by their word size, then the word size allowed for the sum may be less than that given by the rule.

The usable resolution of the sum may be less than the resolution given by Rule 2. If the addend with less resolution is an audio signal or other "approximate" value, the usable resolution of the result cannot be any greater because of quantization noise.

In subtraction, there is a distinction between the operands. When done on paper, the top number is called the *minuend* and the number being subtracted is called the *subtrahend*. Twos-complement subtraction is generally accomplished by negating the subtrahend and adding the result to the minuend. This may be done either by a hardware subtract instruction or by actually complementing the subtrahend and adding. Since signed operands were assumed for addition anyway, the properties and rules for subtraction are the same as for addition.

Often, such as in digital filters, a quantity of numbers that partially cancel each other may be added up. A property of twos-complement arithmetic is that the *order* of addition/subtraction is immaterial. This is true even if intermediate sums overflow! This is a handy property to keep in mind because it may allow the word size of intermediate results to be the same as the addends.

Multiplication

The rules of binary multiplication are quite different from addition and subtraction. In particular, there is none governing location of the binary points of the operands. Those governing the range and resolution of the result are as follows:

1. The range of the result is the product of the ranges of the operands. This means that the number of magnitude bits in the integer part of the product is the *sum* of the number of magnitude bits in the integer parts of the operands.
2. The resolution of the result is the product of the resolutions of the

operands. This means that the number of fraction bits in the product is the sum of the number of fraction bits in the operands.

From the foregoing we can conclude that if the operands are of equal length, the result length is twice as great. Actually, it is one bit shorter when both operands are signed (provided that largest negative numbers are avoided). It is also easy to see that when both operands are fractions that the range of the result is unchanged, although the resolution is increased. Thus, fractional arithmetic is attractive because a chain of multiplications will not increase the range of numbers to be handled. Note that, if both operands are *signed* binary fractions, the binary point in the result will be *two* positions to the right of the sign bit of the result, that is, the sign bit will be duplicated. Thus, one would normally shift the double-length fractional product left one position before using it.

One may be tempted to conclude that the excess resolution that may result can always be discarded without any loss of significant data. This is not generally true if one of the factors is small. S/N *ratio* will be lost if the excess resolution is discarded in such a situation, but the absolute noise level relative to full scale will remain constant. Ideally, multiplication and other arithmetic operations are done with word lengths longer than the initial input samples or final output samples in order to eliminate "computational noise" from the results. Of course, this must be tempered by a possible increase in computation time, particularly when using machines like the 6502.

Division

Division is by far the most difficult fixed-point arithmetic operation to control. Fortunately, it is not needed very often in signal-processing work and in many of the remaining cases it can still be eliminated. Division operands must be carefully distinguished. The numerator is called the *dividend* and the denominator is called the *divisor*. Like multiplication, there is no restriction on the position of the operands' binary points, although there is definitely a practical restriction. Unlike multiplication, nothing concrete can be said in general about the range and resolution of a division result. This should be obvious, since division by very small numbers gives rise to a very large quotient, while for most operands there is no limit to how far the fractional part of the quotient can be carried.

Fixed-point binary division is customarily done with a dividend word length precisely double the divisor word length. The quotient is restricted to a word length equal to the divisor. With these restrictions, the rules of binary division are as follows:

1. The upper *half* of the dividend must be numerically *smaller* than the numerical value of the divisor to avoid overflow.

2. The range of the quotient is equal to the range of the dividend divided by the range of the divisor. This means that the number of bits in the integer part of the quotient is equal to the number of integer bits in the dividend *minus* the number of integer bits in the divisor.
3. The resolution of the quotient is equal to the resolution of the dividend divided by the resolution of the divisor. This means that the number of fraction bits in the quotient is equal to the number of fraction bits in the dividend *minus* the number of fraction bits in the divisor.

Examination of these rules reveals that one just can't win with division. For example, if both operands have the same word size and both are fractions, the one used for the dividend must be padded on the right by N zeroes, where N is the fraction size desired in the quotient. Thus, if the desired resolution is the same as the operands, the dividend must also be smaller than the divisor so that the range of the result is less than unity. The only way to cover all possible combinations (except a zero divisor) of two N-bit fractional operands without overflow or loss of resolution is to use a dividend $4N$ bits long and a divisor $2N$ bits long. The dividend used in the arithmetic operation would be the actual N dividend bits padded on the left by N zeroes (or sign bits if signed) and padded on the right by $2N$ zeroes. The divisor would similarly be padded by N zeroes on the right. The $2N$ quotient bits then allow N range bits ($N-1$ for signed operands) and N resolution bits. Fortunately, when division is needed in signal processing (usually for computing a scale factor), the values of the operands will be known well enough to avoid trouble.

Required Arithmetic Instructions

Regardless of whether hardware instructions are available or an arithmetic subroutine package is being used, there is a certain "complete set" of operations that is needed for straightforward signal-processing computation. Such a set is usually built around a particular word length. When hardware instructions are available, this is usually the machine's accumulator word length. Some of the operations produce or process double words, which then require a pair of registers to hold. In fact, classic single-accumulator computers usually had an accumulator extension or multiplier/quotient register, which was used to hold the low order half of double words.

For illustrating a fixed-point arithmetic package with the 6502, a word length of 8 bits will be used for simplicity, although 16 bits would be more practical in high-quality synthesis. Since the 6502 has very few registers, two bytes are set aside in memory for a double-word accumulator. The other operand if single byte or its address if double byte is passed to the subroutine in a register. Following is a list of the arithmetic operations and the operand word lengths that would be expected in such a package:

1. Double-word load accumulator
2. Double-word store accumulator
3. Double-word addition to accumulator
4. Double-word subtraction from accumulator
5. Double-word negation of accumulator
6. Double-word left shifting of accumulator
7. Double-word signed and unsigned right shifting of accumulator
8. Unsigned multiplication 8 × 8=16
9. Signed multiplication (uses unsigned multiplication as a subroutine) 8 × 8=15
10. Unsigned division 16/8=8
11. Signed division (uses unsigned division as a subroutine) 15/8=8

Double-word addition is necessary for forming sums of products that will in general be double-word values. Shifting operations are needed for scaling. Of course, single-word addition, subtraction, negation, and shifting are also necessary. It is often helpful to have a "load with sign extend" operation, which is used to translate a single-word signed value into a double-word one. It is surprising how many computers, both micro and mini, that claim to have complete hardware arithmetic capability fail to include all of these necessary operations.

A Fixed-Point Arithmetic Package for the 6502

Here we will briefly describe the 8-bit arithmetic package for the 6502 shown in Fig. 18–3. A pseudo-16-bit accumulator is assumed to exist in page zero memory at location ACCH for the high order half and ACCL for the low order half. All subroutines that require a double-byte second operand expect the address of the high-order half of the operand, which must be in page zero, to be in the X index register. Single-byte second operands are expected to be in the hardware accumulator.

Load and store are trivially simple. Although they can be easily done by in-line code in the calling program, using the subroutines will make a signal-processing program easier to read and later convert to a machine with hardware to replace this package.

Double-precision addition and subtraction are equally straightforward. Both process the low bytes first and then use the carry flag to transmit carry information to the high bytes. Note that the 6502 does not have add and subtract in which the carry flag is ignored. Therefore, it is frequently necessary to clear or set the carry before an addition or subtraction, respectively. Negation is performed by subtracting the pseudoaccumulator from zero, which turns out to be faster than complementing all of the bits and then incrementing.

```
0000                 ;        8-BIT ARITHMETIC PACKAGE FOR THE 6502
0000                 ;        ALL ROUTINES UTILIZE A 16 BIT PSEUDO ACCUMULATOR IN PAGE 0.
0000                 ;        ACCH IS THE HIGH BYTE AND ACCL IS THE LOW BYTE OF THE PSEUDO
0000                 ;        ACCUMULATOR.
0000                 ;        ROUTINES REQUIRING A DOUBLE BYTE SECOND OPERAND EXPECT X TO
0000                 ;        POINT TO THE HIGH BYTE OF THE OPERAND WHICH IS ASSUMED TO BE
0000                 ;        STORED ON PAGE ZERO.  ROUTINES REQUIRING A SINGLE BYTE SECOND
0000                 ;        OPERAND EXPECT IT TO BE IN THE HARDWARE ACCUMULATOR.
0000                 ;        ALL ROUTINES PRESERVE X, THEY MAY DESTROY A AND Y.
0000
0000                          *=     $B0          ; STORAGE AREA FOR ARITHMETIC PACKAGE
00B0            ACCH          *=*+   1            ; PSEUDO ACCUMULATOR HIGH BYTE
00B1            ACCL          *=*+   1            ; PSEUDO ACCUMULATOR LOW BYTE
00B2            TEMP1         *=*+   1            ; TEMPORARY STORAGE FOR UNSIGNED MPY/DIV
00B3            TEMP2         *=*+   1            ; TEMPORARY STORAGE FOR SIGNED MPY/DIV
00B4
00B4                          *=     $1000
1000                                              ; DOUBLE LOAD
1000 B500       DLD           LDA    0,X          ; MOVE HIGH BYTE FROM ADDRESS IN X
1002 85B0                     STA    ACCH         ; TO PSEUDO ACCUMULATOR
1004 B501                     LDA    1,X          ; MOVE LOW BYTE FROM ADDRESS IN X PLUS 1
1006 85B1                     STA    ACCL         ; TO PSEUDO ACCUMULATOR
1008 60                       RTS                 ; RETURN
1009
1009                                              ; DOUBLE STORE
1009 A5B0       DST           LDA    ACCH         ; MOVE HIGH BYTE FROM PSEUDO ACCUMULATOR
100B 9500                     STA    0,X          ; TO ADDRESS IN X
100D A5B1                     LDA    ACCL         ; MOVE LOW BYTE FROM PSEUDO ACCUMULATOR
100F 9501                     STA    1,X          ; TO ADDRESS IN X PLUS 1
1011 60                       RTS                 ; RETURN
1012
1012                                              ; DOUBLE ADD
1012 A5B1       DADD          LDA    ACCL         ; ADD LOW PART OF PSEUDO ACCUMULATOR
1014 18                       CLC                 ; TO LOW BYTE POINTED TO BY X+1
1015 7501                     ADC    1,X
1017 85B1                     STA    ACCL         ; AND PUT RESULT IN PSEUDO ACCUMULATOR
1019 A5B0                     LDA    ACCH         ; ADD HIGH PART OF PSEUDO ACCUMULATOR TO
101B 7500                     ADC    0,X          ; HIGH BYTE POINTED TO BY X
101D 85B0                     STA    ACCH         ; USING CARRY FROM LOW PARTS
101F 60                       RTS                 ; RETURN
1020
1020                                              ; DOUBLE SUBTRACT
1020 A5B1       DSUB          LDA    ACCL         ; SUBTRACT LOW BYTE POINTED TO BY X
1022 38                       SEC                 ; FROM LOW PART OF PSEUDO ACCUMULATOR
1023 F501                     SBC    1,X
1025 85B1                     STA    ACCL         ; AND PUT RESULT IN PSEUDO ACCUMULATOR
1027 A5B0                     LDA    ACCH         ; SUBTRACT HIGH BYTE POINTED TO BY X
1029 F500                     SBC    0,X          ; FROM HIGH PART OF PSEUDO ACCUMULATOR
102B 85B0                     STA    ACCH         ; USING BORROW FROM LOWER PARTS
102D 60                       RTS                 ; RETURN
102E
102E                                              ; DOUBLE NEGATE
102E 38         DNEG          SEC                 ; INITIALLY SET CARRY FOR SUBTRACTION
102F A900                     LDA    #0           ; NEGATE ACCH,ACCL BY SUBTRACTING
1031 E5B1                     SBC    ACCL         ; IT FROM ZERO.
1033 85B1                     STA    ACCL         ; LOW BYTE FIRST
1035 A900                     LDA    #0
1037 E5B0                     SBC    ACCH
1039 85B0                     STA    ACCH         ; THEN THE HIGH BYTE
103B 60                       RTS                 ; RETURN
103C
103C                                              ; DOUBLE SHIFT LEFT
103C 06B1       DSHL          ASL    ACCL         ; SHIFT LOW BYTE LEFT AND PUT OVERFLOW BIT
103E                                              ; IN CARRY FLAG
103E 26B0                     ROL    ACCH         ; SHIFT HIGH BYTE LEFT BRINGING IN OVERFLOW
1040                                              ; BIT
1040 60                       RTS                 ; RETURN
```

```
1041
1041                                   ; DOUBLE SHIFT RIGHT UNSIGNED
1041 46B0   DSHR    LSR   ACCH         ; SHIFT HIGH BYTE RIGHT AND PUT UNDERFLOW
1043                                   ; BIT IN CARRY FLAG
1043 66B1           ROR   ACCL         ; SHIFT LOW BYTE RIGHT BRINGING IN
1045                                   ; UNDERFLOW BIT
1045 60             RTS                ; RETURN
1046
1046                                   ; DOUBLE SHIFT RIGHT SIGNED
1046 A5B0   DSHRS   LDA   ACCH         ; FIRST COPY THE SIGN BIT INTO THE CARRY
1048 2A             ROL   A            ; FLAG
1049 66B0           ROR   ACCH         ; THEN SHIFT HIGH BYTE RIGHT BRINGING IN
104B 66B1           ROR   ACCL         ; COPY OF SIGN BIT AND CONTINUE AS ABOVE
104D 60             RTS                ; RETURN
104E
104E                                   ; UNSIGNED 8X8 MULTIPLY
104E                                   ; ENTER WITH MULTIPLICAND IN ACCUMULATOR
104E                                   ; ENTER WITH MULTIPLIER IN ACCL
104E                                   ; EXIT WITH DOUBLE LENGTH PRODUCT IN ACCH
104E                                   ; AND ACCL
104E 85B2   UMULT   STA   TEMP1        ; SAVE MULTIPLICAND
1050 A900   UMULT0  LDA   #0           ; ZERO UPPER PRODUCT
1052 85B0           STA   ACCH
1054 A009           LDY   #9           ; SET CYCLE COUNT
1056 18             CLC                ; INITIALLY CLEAR CARRY
1057 66B0   UMULT1  ROR   ACCH         ; SHIFT PSEUDO ACCUMULATOR RIGHT BRINGING
1059 66B1           ROR   ACCL         ; IN ANY OVERFLOW FROM PREVIOUS ADD AND
105B                                   ; SHIFTING OUT NEXT MULTIPLIER BIT
105B 88             DEY                ; DECREMENT CYCLE COUNT AND
105C F00C           BEQ   MULTRT       ; RETURN WHEN DONE
105E 90F7           BCC   UMULT1       ; SKIP ADDITION IF MULTIPLIER BIT WAS ZERO
1060 A5B0           LDA   ACCH         ; ADD SAVED MULTIPLICAND TO UPPER BYTE
1062 18             CLC                ; OF PSEUDO ACCUMULATOR
1063 65B2           ADC   TEMP1        ; BEING CAREFUL TO PRESERVE ANY POSSIBLE
1065 85B0           STA   ACCH         ; CARRY OUT
1067 4C5710         JMP   UMULT1       ; GO SHIFT PSEUDO ACCUMULATOR
106A 60     MULTRT  RTS
106B
106B                                   ; UNSIGNED 16/8 DIVIDE
106B                                   ; ENTER WITH 16 BIT DIVIDEND IN ACCH,ACCL
106B                                   ; ENTER WITH DIVISOR IN REGISTER A
106B                                   ; RETURN WITH QUOTIENT IN ACCL
106B                                   ; RETURN WITH REMAINDER IN ACCH
106B                                   ; DIVISOR MUST BE LARGER THAN ACCH TO
106B                                   ; AVOID OVERFLOW
106B 85B2   UDIV    STA   TEMP1        ; SAVE DIVISOR
106D A008           LDY   #8           ; SET CYCLE COUNT
106F 06B1           ASL   ACCL         ; SHIFT DIVIDEND LOW
1071 26B0   UDIV1   ROL   ACCH         ; SHIFT DIVIDEND HIGH
1073 B00B           BCS   UDIV2        ; JUMP IF A 1 SHIFTED OUT OF DIVIDEND
1075 A5B0           LDA   ACCH         ; SUBTRACT DIVISOR FROM ACCH
1077 38             SEC
1078 E5B2           SBC   TEMP1
107A 9010           BCC   UDIV4        ; JUMP TO SHIFT AND COUNT IF UNDERFLOW IS
107C                                   ; IMMENIENT, CARRY IS QUOTIENT BIT
107C 85B0           STA   ACCH         ; STORE DIFFERENCE IF NO UNDERFLOW, CARRY
107E                                   ; FLAG IS QUOTIENT BIT
107E B00C           BCS   UDIV4        ; GO TO SHIFT AND COUNT
1080 A5B0   UDIV2   LDA   ACCH         ; SUBTRACT DIVISOR FROM ACCH
1082 E5B2           SBC   TEMP1
1084 B005           BCS   UDIV3        ; SKIP IF UNDERFLOW IMMENIENT
1086 85B0           STA   ACCH         ; STORE DIFFERENCE IF NO UNDERFLOW
1088 38             SEC                ; QUOTIENT BIT IS A ONE
1089 B001           BCS   UDIV4        ; GO TO SHIFT AND COUNT
```

Fig. 18–3. Signal-processing math package for the 6502

```
108B 18      UDIV3   CLC             ; QUOTIENT BIT IS A ZERO
108C 26B1    UDIV4   ROL    ACCL     ; SHIFT DIVIDEND LOW PART
108E 88              DEY             ; COUNT ITERATIONS
108F D0E0            BNE    UDIV1    ; LOOP IF NOT DONE
1091 60              RTS             ; OTHERWISE RETURN
1092
1092                                 ; TWO QUADRANT MULTIPLY
1092                                 ; USAGE IS THE SAME AS WITH UMULT
1092                                 ; PSEUDO ACCUMULATOR CONTAINS THE SIGNED
1092                                 ; FACTOR AND THE MACHINE ACCUMULATOR
1092                                 ; CONTAINS THE UNSIGNED FACTOR
1092 85B2    MULT2Q  STA    TEMP1    ; SAVE UNSIGNED MULTIPLICAND
1094 A5B1            LDA    ACCL     ; SAVE SIGNED MULTIPLIER
1096 85B3            STA    TEMP2
1098 205010          JSR    UMULT0   ; DO AN UNSIGNED MULTIPLICATION
109B A5B3            LDA    TEMP2    ; TEST SIGN OF MULTIPLIER
109D 1007            BPL    MULT2R   ; GO RETURN IF POSITIVE
109F A5B0            LDA    ACCH     ; SUBTRACT MULTIPLICAND FROM HIGH PRODUCT
10A1 38              SEC
10A2 E5B2            SBC    TEMP1    ; IF MULTIPLIER IS NEGATIVE
10A4 85B0            STA    ACCH
10A6 60      MULT2R  RTS             ; RETURN
10A7
10A7                                 ; SIGNED MULTIPLY
10A7                                 ; USAGE IS THE SAME AS WITH UMULT
10A7 85B2    SMULT   STA    TEMP1    ; SAVE MULTIPLICAND
10A9 A5B1            LDA    ACCL     ; SAVE MULTIPLIER
10AB 85B3            STA    TEMP2
10AD 204E10          JSR    UMULT    ; DO AN UNSIGNED MULTIPLICATION
10B0 A5B2            LDA    TEMP1    ; TEST SIGN OF MULTIPLICAND
10B2 1007            BPL    SMULT1   ; JUMP AHEAD IF POSITIVE
10B4 A5B0            LDA    ACCH     ; SUBTRACT MULTIPLIER FROM HIGH PRODUCT
10B6 38              SEC             ; IF MULTIPLICAND IS NEGATIVE
10B7 E5B3            SBC    TEMP2
10B9 85B0            STA    ACCH
10BB A5B3    SMULT1  LDA    TEMP2    ; TEST SIGN OF MULTIPLIER
10BD 1007            BPL    SMULT2   ; GO RETURN IF POSITIVE
10BF A5B0            LDA    ACCH     ; SUBTRACT MULTIPLICAND FROM HIGH PRODUCT
10C1 38              SEC             ; IF MULTIPLIER IS NEGATIVE
10C2 E5B2            SBC    TEMP1
10C4 85B0            STA    ACCH
10C6 60      SMULT2  RTS             ; RETURN
10C7
10C7                                 ; TWO QUADRANT DIVIDE
10C7                                 ; USAGE IS THE SAME AS WITH UDIV
10C7                                 ; PSEUDO ACCUMULATOR CONTAINS THE SIGNED
10C7                                 ; DIVIDEND AND THE MACHINE ACCUMULATOR
10C7                                 ; CONTAINS THE UNSIGNED DIVISOR
10C7 85B2    DIV2Q   STA    TEMP1    ; SAVE DIVISOR
10C9 A5B0            LDA    ACCH     ; COMPUTE SIGN OF QUOTIENT
10CB 85B3            STA    TEMP2    ; SAVE THE SIGN UNTIL LATER
10CD A5B0            LDA    ACCH     ; TEST SIGN OF DIVIDEND
10CF 1003            BPL    DIV2Q1   ; SKIP IF POSITIVE
10D1 202E10          JSR    DNEG     ; TWOS COMPLEMENT DIVIDEND IF NEGATIVE
10D4 206B10  DIV2Q1  JSR    UDIV     ; DO THE DIVISON
10D7 A5B3            LDA    TEMP2    ; TEST DESIRED SIGN OF QUOTIENT
10D9 1008            BPL    DIV2Q2   ; GO RETURN IF SHOULD BE POSITIVE
10DB A5B1            LDA    ACCL     ; TWOS COMPLEMENT QUOTIENT IF SHOULD BE
10DD 49FF            EOR    #$FF     ; NEGATIVE
10DF 85B1            STA    ACCL
10E1 E6B1            INC    ACCL
10E3 60      DIV2Q2  RTS             ; RETURN
10E4
10E4                                 ; SIGNED DIVIDE
10E4                                 ; USAGE IS THE SAME AS WITH UDIV
10E4 85B2    SDIV    STA    TEMP1    ; SAVE DIVISOR
```

```
10E6 45B0              EOR   ACCH       ; COMPUTE SIGN OF QUOTIENT
10E8 85B3              STA   TEMP2      ; SAVE THE SIGN UNTIL LATER
10EA A5B0              LDA   ACCH       ; TEST SIGN OF DIVIDEND
10EC 1003              BPL   SDIV1      ; SKIP IF POSITIVE
10EE 202E10            JSR   DNEG       ; TWOS COMPLEMENT DIVIDEND IF NEGATIVE
10F1 A5B2      SDIV1   LDA   TEMP1      ; TEST SIGN OF DIVISOR
10F3 1005              BPL   SDIV2      ; JUMP IF POSITIVE
10F5 49FF              EOR   #$FF       ; TWOS COMPLEMENT DIVISOR IF NEGATIVE
10F7 18                CLC
10F8 6901              ADC   #1
10FA 206B10    SDIV2   JSR   UDIV       ; DO THE DIVISON
10FD A5B3              LDA   TEMP2      ; TEST DESIRED SIGN OF QUOTIENT
10FF 1008              BPL   SDIV3      ; GO RETURN IF SHOULD BE POSITIVE
1101 A5B1              LDA   ACCL       ; TWOS COMPLEMENT QUOTIENT IF SHOULD BE
1103 49FF              EOR   #$FF       ; NEGATIVE
1105 85B1              STA   ACCL
1107 E6B1              INC   ACCL
1109 60        SDIV3   RTS              ; RETURN
110A
  0 ERRORS IN PASS 2
```

Fig. 18–3. Signal-processing math package for the 6502 *(cont.)*.

The shift routines do one shift at a time, again using the carry flag to transfer bits from one byte to the other. Note that when shifting right the left byte is shifted first, whereas when shifting left the right byte is shifted first. A fair amount of fooling around is necessary to duplicate the sign bit when doing a signed shift right. A machine with decent arithmetic capability would explicitly provide a shift with sign-extend instruction. Note that the ability of the 6502 to directly modify memory greatly simplifies many operations on the pseudoaccumulator.

The basic multiplication subroutine handles two 8-bit unsigned numbers and produces a 16-bit unsigned product. While most computer users know that the proper way to multiply involves shifting and adding, the number of inefficient (or just plain incorrect) multiply subroutines that have been published (IC manufacturers are the worst offenders) indicates a general lack of understanding in this area. Minicomputer designers of the 1960s,

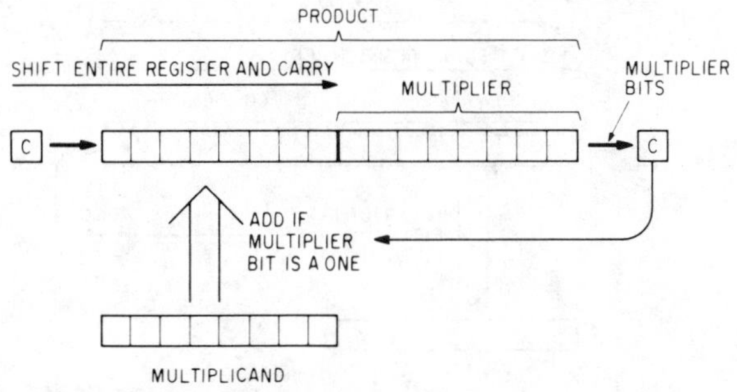

Fig. 18–4. Shift-and-add multiplication

however, did know how to multiply and as it turns out their hardware methods are highly efficient in software too.

Figure 18–4 illustrates the shift and add multiplication algorithm. Two "registers" are involved; the multiplicand register which is 8 bits long, and the 16-bit pseudoaccumulator. Prior to multiplication, the multiplicand is placed in the multiplicand register, the multiplier is placed in the low order half of the pseudoaccumulator, and the high order half is cleared. A shift and add cycle consists of shifting the entire pseudoaccumulator right one bit and testing the least significant bit shifted out. If this bit is a zero, the cycle is complete. If the bit is a one, the multiplicand register is *single-precision* added to the *upper half* of the pseudoaccumulator. This addition may overflow, so it is important to bring in the carry flag when the next shift cycle is done. A little thought will reveal that as the multiplication progresses the multiplier is "eaten away" at its right end and the product grows downward as the multiplier is shifted out. A total of 8½ cycles are needed to complete the operation. The half-cycle is a final shift of the pseudoaccumulator to bring in a possible overflow from the last addition and properly align the product.

The above algorithm is different from many that are published in that the product is shifted right and the multiplicand stands still rather than vice versa. Efficiency improvement is due to both product and multiplier shifting being handled simultaneously and the fact that only single-precision addition of the partial products is required. If the upper part of the pseudoaccumulator is not cleared prior to multiplication, its contents wind up being added to the product. Since this may be useful and actually saves a slight amount of time, the unsigned multiplication routine provides an alternate entry point that skips clearing the product. Note that binary multiplication, even with the "free add" included, cannot overflow.

Unsigned binary division, illustrated in Fig. 18–5, is precisely the reverse of multiplication. The algorithm can be described as a "shift and conditionally subtract" procedure, opposite that of multiplication. Again,

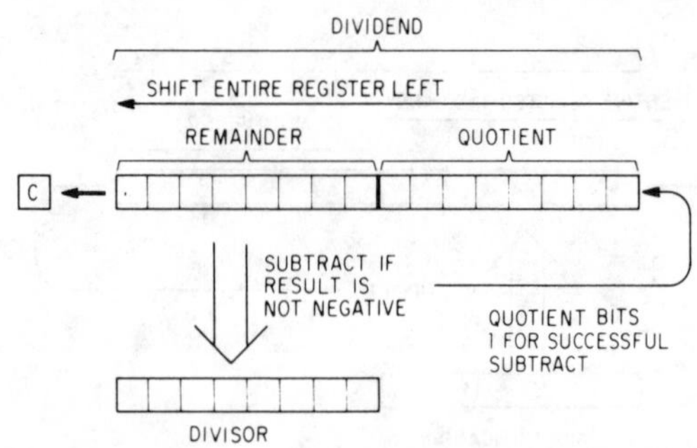

Fig. 18–5. Shift-and-subtract division

two registers are involved. The dividend is a double-length value, which is held in the pseudoaccumulator. The divisor is kept in the same register as the multiplicand was in multiplication and is not altered by the division routine.

A shift and subtract cycle begins by shifting the entire pseudoaccumulator left, being sure to bring in the carry flag on the right end. Next the divisor is *single-precision* subtracted from the high order half of the dividend and the result suspended. If the subtraction underflowed (that is, went negative, which is not allowed in unsigned arithmetic), the result is thrown away. If the subtraction did not underflow, the result replaces the high order portion of the dividend. Deciding whether an underflow occurred is a little tricky because a significant dividend bit may have been shifted out when the dividend was shifted left. The table below can be used to determine if an underflow occurred:

Carry from shift	*Carry from subtract*	*Underflow?*	*Quotient bit*
0	0	Yes	0
0	1	No	1
1	0	No	1
1	1	Yes	0

The quotient bit value from the table is saved in the carry flag and shifted into the pseudoaccumulator on the next cycle.

As the division progresses, the dividend is eaten away on the left by subtracting the divisor, while the quotient is shifted in bit by bit on the right. The final result finds the quotient in the right half and the remainder in the left half of the pseudoaccumulator. Eight-and-a-half shift/subtract cycles are required to complete the division. The last half cycle is necessary to bring in the last quotient bit without moving the remainder out of position. Note that a subsequent call to UMULTO, which would multiply the quotient by the divisor and add in the remainder, will recover the dividend exactly.

In signal processing both two-quadrant (unsigned × signed) and four quadrant (signed × signed) multiplication is needed. The obvious procedure is to take the absolute values of the operands, perform the operation, and then adjust the sign of the product according to the rules of algebra. The signed multiplication routine, however, uses a different approach that is more efficient and actually works with largest negative numbers. The idea is to go ahead and multiply the *raw* operands with the unsigned multiply routine and *correct* the result later.

The correction turns out to be quite simple. After unsigned multiplication, the multiplicand sign is tested. If it is negative, the multiplier is unsigned, single-precision subtracted from the upper half of the pseudoaccumulator. Then the multiplier sign is tested and the multiplicand is conditionally subtracted in the same manner. If one of the operands is unsigned, only the signed operand need be tested. The author does not know of a simple correction procedure for division so it is handled using the absolute-value method.

Example Programs

The best way to illustrate use of the arithmetic package and scaling techniques for fixed-point arithmetic is to actually study a couple of simple signal-processing programs. Two reasonably useful functions will be covered. The first is a generalized digital filter using the state-variable structure. The second is a Fourier series (SFT method) program designed to optimally fill 8-bit, 256-word waveform tables for low-budget direct synthesis.

Before tackling the digital filter programming, let's discuss exactly what the program should do and how it would be used. For full flexibility as a state-variable filter, one input sample is required, four output samples are produced, and two parameters are needed. The input and output samples are assumed to be 8-bit signed binary fractions. The dynamic range of frequency and Q parameters are maximized if they are unsigned values. Referring to Chapter 14, we recall that the useful range of the frequency and Q multipliers is 0 to 2. Therefore, the binary point will be between bits 6 and 7 in these 8-bit multipliers.

The digital filter will be programmed as a subroutine and the input sample will be passed to it in the accumulator. For ease of understanding, the four output samples will be stored in specific locations in memory and the two parameters will be taken from specific memory locations. Note that this, like all recursive digital filters, requires storage registers to hold values from sample to sample. Two 16-bit numbers will therefore be stored in dedicated memory locations as well. A truly general-purpose routine should have the *addresses* of input, output, parameter, and register storage passed to it to minimize data shuffling when using the same routine to simulate many different filters.

Figure 18–6 shows a signal flow diagram for the filter along with the sequence of calculations spelled out in detail. Note that all addition and subtraction operations are done using 16-bit arithmetic. In fact, except for the input sample itself, all addition and subtraction operands are 16 bits in length because they are the result of multiplications. Also note that while the result of a multiplication is allowed to have a range of 1.99, the result of all additions and subtractions must have a range of 0.99 or less.

It is apparent, then, that overflow can easily occur if the input signal is near maximum and the Q is high (Q factor low). This is simply a consequence of the fact that a digital filter can have a gain substantially greater than unity. One might be tempted to consider moving the binary point of the filter output to eliminate the possibility of overflow until the cumulative effect of cascading several such "scaled filters" in a general-purpose digital

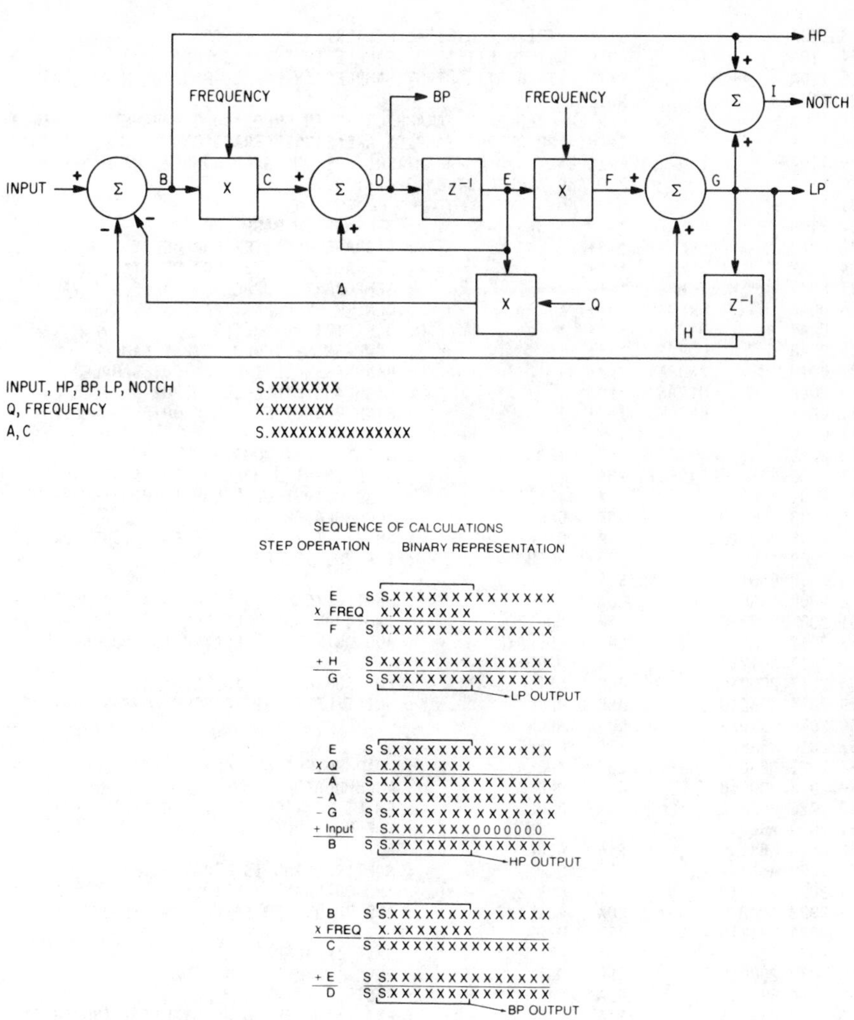

Fig. 18–6. Signal flow diagram of fixed-point arithmetic digital filter

synthesis system is considered. It can be a viable technique in dedicated filter applications such as a spectrum analyzer, however. Of course, with 8-bit samples and arithmetic, the programmer constantly walks a tightrope in keeping signal levels high to maximize S/N ratio, while keeping them low

```
110A             ;       STATE VARIABLE DIGITAL FILTER
110A             ;       ENTER WITH 8 BIT INPUT SAMPLE IN THE ACCUMULATOR
110A             ;       EXIT WITH 8 BIT OUTPUT SAMPLES IN LOPAS, BNDPAS, HIPAS, AND
110A             ;       NOTCH.
110A             ;       CENTER FREQUENCY PARAMETER IS IN FREQ AND Q PARAMETER IS IN Q.
110A             ;       INPUT AND OUTPUT SAMPLES ARE SIGNED FRACTIONS.
110A             ;       FREQUENCY AND Q PARAMETERS ARE UNSIGNED NUMBERS WITH A RANGE OF
110A             ;       2.0 AND A RESOLUTION OF 1/128.
110A
110A                     *=     $A0          ; STORAGE IN PAGE ZERO
00A0             DELAY1  *=*+   2            ; STORAGE REGISTER FOR DELAY 1
00A2             DELAY2  *=*+   2            ; STORAGE REGISTER FOR DELAY 2
00A4             TEMP    *=*+   2            ; TEMPORARY STORAGE FOR A 16 BIT VALUE
00A6             FREQ    *=*+   1            ; CENTER FREQUENCY PARAMETER
00A7             Q       *=*+   1            ; Q FACTOR PARAMETER
00A8             LOPAS   *=*+   1            ; LOWPASS FILTERED OUTPUT SAMPLE
00A9             BNDPAS  *=*+   1            ; BANDPASS FILTERED OUTPUT SAMPLE
00AA             HIPAS   *=*+   1            ; HIGHPASS FILTERED OUTPUT SAMPLE
00AB             BNDREJ  *=*+   1            ; BAND REJECT FILTERED OUTPUT SAMPLE
00AC
00AC                     *=     $2000        ; ORIGIN FOR PROGRAM
2000 48          SVDFLT  PHA                 ; SAVE INPUT SAMPLE ON THE STACK
2001 A2A0                LDX    #DELAY1      ; LOAD OUTPUT OF DELAY 1 INTO THE PSEUDO
2003 200010              JSR    DLD          ; ACCUMULATOR
2006 203C10              JSR    DSHL         ; SHIFT IT RIGHT 7 BIT POSITIONS FOR USE AS
2009 A5B0                LDA    ACCH         ; THE MULTIPLIER
200B 85B1                STA    ACCL
200D A5A6                LDA    FREQ         ; MULTIPLICAND IS FREQUENCY PARAMETER
200F 209210              JSR    MULT2Q       ; TWO QUADRANT MULTIPLY
2012 A2A2                LDX    #DELAY2      ; ADD OUTPUT OF DELAY 2 TO PRODUCT
2014 201210              JSR    DADD
2017 200910              JSR    DST          ; PUT SUM BACK INTO DELAY 2
201A 203C10              JSR    DSHL         ; SHIFT LEFT ONE TO FORM LOWPASS OUTPUT
201D A5B0                LDA    ACCH
201F 85A8                STA    LOPAS
2021 A2A0                LDX    #DELAY1      ; LOAD OUTPUT OF DELAY 1 INTO THE PSEUDO
2023 200010              JSR    DLD          ; ACCUMULATOR
2026 203C10              JSR    DSHL         ; SHIFT IT RIGHT 7 BIT POSITIONS FOR USE AS
2029 A5B0                LDA    ACCH         ; THE MULTIPLIER
202B 85B1                STA    ACCL
202D A5A7                LDA    Q            ; MULTIPLICAND IS Q PARAMETER
202F 209210              JSR    MULT2Q       ; TWO QUADRANT MULTIPLY
2032 A2A2                LDX    #DELAY2      ; ADD RESULT TO SAVED LOWPASS OUTPUT
2034 201210              JSR    DADD
2037 A2A4                LDX    #TEMP        ; SAVE IN TEMP1
2039 200910              JSR    DST
203C 68                  PLA                 ; RESTORE INPUT SAMPLE
203D 85B0                STA    ACCH         ; PUT INTO PSEUDO ACCUMULATOR AND SHIFT
203F A900                LDA    #0           ; RIGHT ONE
2041 85B1                STA    ACCL
2043 204610              JSR    DSHRS
2046 202010              JSR    DSUB         ; SUBTRACT SAVED SUM FROM INPUT SAMPLE TO
2049 200910              JSR    DST          ; SAVE RESULT FOR LATER USE IN NOTCH OUTPUT
204C 203C10              JSR    DSHL         ; FORM HIGHPASS OUTPUT
204F A5B0                LDA    ACCH
2051 85AA                STA    HIPAS
2053 85B1                STA    ACCL         ; IS ALSO MULTIPLIER
2055 A5A6                LDA    FREQ         ; MULTIPLY BY FREQ
2057 209210              JSR    MULT2Q
205A A2A0                LDX    #DELAY1      ; ADD OUTPUT OF DELAY 1 TO THE PRODUCT
205C 201210              JSR    DADD
205F 200910              JSR    DST          ; PUT SUM BACK INTO DELAY 1
2062 203C10              JSR    DSHL         ; SHIFT LEFT ONE BIT
2065 A5B0                LDA    ACCH
2067 85A9                STA    BNDPAS       ; HIGH BYTE IS BANDPASS OUTPUT
2069 A2A4                LDX    #TEMP        ; BAND REJECT OUTPUT IS DELAY2 PLUS TEMP1
```

```
206B 200010        JSR   DLD
206E A2A2          LDX   #DELAY2
2070 201210        JSR   DADD
2073 203C10        JSR   DSHL
2076 A5B0          LDA   ACCH
2078 85AB          STA   BNDREJ
207A 60            RTS               ; RETURN
207B
207B
  0 ERRORS IN PASS 2
```

Fig. 18–6. Signal flow diagram of fixed-point arithmetic digital filter *(cont.)*.

enough to avoid serious distortion caused by overflow. With 16-bit arithmetic, which is recommended for serious work, such problems are much less severe.

The second example program, which is shown in Fig. 18–7, is included to illustrate the use of division and as a useful program for experimentation. The idea is to take the spectral description of a harmonic waveform, compute samples for one cycle of it, and store them in a waveform table. With the 6502 example machine, the waveform table is assumed to be 256 samples long (one memory page), and to contain 8-bit signed samples.

Because of the limited resolution provided by 8 bits, it is advantageous to maximize the amplitude of the stored waveform. It is very difficult, however, to predict the magnitude of the largest peak of the waveform without actually computing an entire cycle, although it is easy to prove that the peak will not exceed the sum of the harmonic amplitudes. In most cases, it will be considerably less than this because of momentary phase cancellation, etc. Thus, it would be nice if the table-filling program would adjust the waveform amplitude automatically and optimally.

The program is actually just a collection of three subroutines. The point evaluator, FSEVAL, accepts a point number and a spectrum description and returns a 16-bit signed number representing the waveform at that point in time. The point number simply represents time to a resolution of 1/256 of a cycle. The scale factor determination routine, SCALE, calls FSEVAL 256 times in order to determine the absolute maximum sample value that will be encountered when the table is actually filled. The table-filling routine, FILL, also calls FSEVAL 256 times. The 16-bit values returned are divided by the maximum peak found by SCALE and stored in the waveform table as 8-bit values.

The spectrum description expected by these routines consists of pairs of 8-bit unsigned numbers, each of which corresponds to a harmonic in ascending order starting with zero (the dc component). The first member of the pair is the amplitude which is treated as an 8-bit unsigned fraction. The second member is the phase angle of the harmonic. Zero gives a cosine wave, 64 gives an inverted sine wave, 128 gives an inverted cosine, etc. A parameter called NHARM determines the highest harmonic number that will be con-

```
110A              ;  WAVEFORM TABLE FILL USING FOURIER SERIES
110A
110A                        *=      $80            ; STORAGE IN PAGE ZERO
0080             HRMACC     *=*+    2              ; HARMONIC ACCUMULATOR
0082             PNTNO      *=*+    1              ; POINT NUMBER WITHIN CYCLE OF WAVE
0083             NDXACC     *=*+    1              ; INDEXING ACCUMULATOR
0084             HRMCNT     *=*+    1              ; HARMONIC COUNTER
0085             MAX        *=*+    1              ; MAXIMUM WAVEFORM AMPLITUDE
0086             WAVETB     *=*+    2              ; ADDRESS OF WAVEFORM TABLE TO FILL
0088
0088             NHARM      *=*+    1              ; HIGHEST HARMONIC TO GENERATE (16 MAX)
0089             FSRAM      *=*+    32             ; ROOM FOR 16 HARMONIC AMPLITUDES AND
00A9                                               ; PHASES
00A9
00A9                        *=      $2000          ; PROGRAM ORIGIN
2000
2000              ;         WAVEFORM TABLE FILL ROUTINE
2000              ;         THIS SUBROUTINE FILLS THE WAVEFORM TABLE AT WAVETB WITH 256
2000              ;         SAMPLES OF THE WAVEFORM SPECIFIED BY THE SPECTRUM AT FSRAM.
2000              ;         MAX MUST HAVE BEEN PREVIOUSLY SET GREATER THAN TWICE THE
2000              ;         ABSOLUTE VALUE OF THE LARGEST SAMPLE THAT WILL BE ENCOUNTERED.
2000
2000 A900        FILL       LDA     #0             ; ZERO THE POINT NUMBER
2002 8582                   STA     PNTNO
2004 204020      FILL1      JSR     FSEVAL         ; EVALUATE A WAVEFORM POINT
2007 A580                   LDA     HRMACC         ; DIVIDE POINT BY MAXIMUM POINT FOR SCALING
2009 85B0                   STA     ACCH           ; FIRST TRANSFER POINT TO PSEUDO
200B A581                   LDA     HRMACC+1       ; ACCUMULATOR FOR USE AS THE DIVIDEND
200D 85B1                   STA     ACCL
200F A585                   LDA     MAX            ; LOAD MAX AS THE DIVISOR (UNSIGNED)
2011 20C710                 JSR     DIV2Q          ; DO A TWO QUADRANT DIVIDE
2014 A5B1                   LDA     ACCL           ; GET THE SIGNED QUOTIENT
2016 A482                   LDY     PNTNO          ; GET THE POINT NUMBER
2018 9186                   STA     (WAVETB),Y     ; STORE RESULT IN WAVEFORM TABLE
201A E682                   INC     PNTNO          ; INCREMENT THE POINT NUMBER
201C D0E6                   BNE     FILL1          ; GO FOR ANOTHER POINT IF NOT FINISHED
201E 60                     RTS                    ; RETURN WHEN FINISHED
201F
201F              ;         SCALE FACTOR DETERMINATION SUBROUTINE
201F              ;         THIS SUBROUTINE GOES THROUGH ONE CYCLE OF THE WAVEFORM DEFINED
201F              ;         BY THE SPECTRUM AT FSRAM AND FINDS THE POINT WITH THE MAXIMUM
201F              ;         MAGNITUDE.
201F              ;         THIS MAGNITUDE IS THEN DOUBLED AND INCREMENTED BY ONE AND
201F              ;         STORED AS AN UNSIGNED NUMBER.
201F
201F A900        SCALE      LDA     #0             ; ZERO THE POINT NUMBER
2021 8582                   STA     PNTNO
2023 8585                   STA     MAX            ; ZERO THE MAXIMUM MAGNITUDE
2025 204020      SCALE1     JSR     FSEVAL         ; EVALUATE A WAVEFORM POINT
2028 A580                   LDA     HRMACC         ; GET UPPER BYTE OF THE POINT
202A 1005                   BPL     SCALE2         ; SKIP IF POSITIVE
202C 49FF                   EOR     #$FF           ; NEGATE IF NEGATIVE
202E 18                     CLC
202F 6901                   ADC     #1
2031 C585        SCALE2     CMP     MAX            ; COMPARE WITH CURRENT MAXIMUM
2033 3002                   BMI     SCALE3         ; SKIP IF NOT GREATER
2035 8585                   STA     MAX            ; UPDATE MAXIMUM IF GREATER
2037 E682        SCALE3     INC     PNTNO          ; INCREMENT POINT NUMBER
2039 D0EA                   BNE     SCALE1         ; GO FOR NEXT POINT IF NOT DONE
203B 0685                   ASL     MAX            ; DOUBLE AND THEN INCREMENT MAXIMUM VALUE
203D E685                   INC     MAX            ; TO AVOID POSSIBLE DIVISON OVERFLOW
203F 60                     RTS                    ; AND RETURN
2040
2040              ;         FOURIER SERIES POINT EVALUATOR
2040              ;         THIS SUBROUTINE EVALUATES A POINT ON THE WAVEFORM SPECIFIED BY
2040              ;         THE SPECTRUM AT FSRAM.
2040              ;         NHARM SPECIFIES THE HIGHEST HARMONIC TO BE INCLUDED
```

```
2040            ;       PNTNO IS THE POINT NUMBER TO BE EVALUATED
2040            ;       THE COMPUTED POINT IS RETURNED IN HRMACC AS A 16 BIT TWOS
2040            ;       COMPLEMENT NUMBER
2040            ;       DESTROYS A AND Y, SAVES X
2040
2040 8A         FSEVAL  TXA                   ; SAVE INDEX X
2041 48                 PHA
2042 A900               LDA     #0            ; CLEAR HARMONIC ACCUMULATOR
2044 8580               STA     HRMACC
2046 8581               STA     HRMACC+1
2048 8584               STA     HRMCNT        ; ZERO HARMONIC COUNTER
204A 8583               STA     NDXACC        ; ZERO THE INDEXING ACCUMULATOR
204C A584       FSEV1   LDA     HRMCNT        ; GET CURRENT HARMONIC NUMBER AND DOUBLE IT
204E 0A                 ASL     A
204F AA                 TAX                   ; USE AS AN INDEX TO THE SPECTRUM TABLE
2050 B589               LDA     FSRAM,X       ; GET AMPLITUDE
2052 48                 PHA                   ; SAVE ON STACK TEMPORARILY
2053 B58A               LDA     FSRAM+1,X     ; GET PHASE
2055 6583               ADC     NDXACC        ; ADD IT TO THE INDEXING ACCUMULATOR
2057 AA                 TAX                   ; USE AS AN INDEX INTO THE COSINE TABLE
2058 BD8620             LDA     COSINE,X      ; GET COSINE
205B 85B1               STA     ACCL          ; SAVE AS MULTIPLICAND
205D 68                 PLA                   ; RESTORE AMPLITUDE
205E 209210             JSR     MULT2Q        ; MULTIPLY AMPLITUDE (UNSIGNED) BY COSINE
2061                                          ; (SIGNED)
2061 A204               LDX     #4            ; SHIFT PRODUCT RIGHT 4 FOR 12 BIT RESULT
2063 204610 FSEV2       JSR     DSHRS
2066 CA                 DEX
2067 D0FA               BNE     FSEV2
2069 A280               LDX     #HRMACC       ; ADD RESULT TO HARMONIC ACCUMULATOR
206B 201210             JSR     DADD
206E 200910             JSR     DST
2071 A584               LDA     HRMCNT        ; TEST IF CURRENT HARMONIC IS LAST ONE TO
2073 C588               CMP     NHARM         ; INCLUDE
2075 F00C               BEQ     FSEV3         ; GO RETURN IF SO
2077 E684               INC     HRMCNT        ; INCREMENT TO NEXT HARMONIC
2079 A582               LDA     PNTNO         ; ADD POINT NUMBER TO THE INDEXING
207B 18                 CLC                   ; ACCUMULATOR
207C 6583               ADC     NDXACC
207E 8583               STA     NDXACC
2080 4C4C20             JMP     FSEV1         ; LOOP FOR ANOTHER HARMONIC
2083 68         FSEV3   PLA                   ; RESTORE INDEX X
2084 AA                 TAX
2085 60                 RTS                   ; RETURN
2086
2086            ;       256 POINT COSINE TABLE, TWOS COMPLEMENT
2086
2086 7F   ..    COSINE  .BYTE   $7F,$7F,$7F,$7F,$7F,$7F,$7E,$7E
208E 7D   ..            .BYTE   $7D,$7D,$7C,$7B,$7A,$79,$78,$77
2096 76   ..            .BYTE   $76,$75,$73,$72,$71,$6F,$6D,$6C
209E 6A   ..            .BYTE   $6A,$68,$66,$65,$63,$61,$5E,$5C
20A6 5A   ..            .BYTE   $5A,$58,$56,$53,$51,$4E,$4C,$49
20AE 47   ..            .BYTE   $47,$44,$41,$3F,$3C,$39,$36,$33
20B6 31   ..            .BYTE   $31,$2E,$2B,$28,$25,$22,$1F,$1C
20BE 19   ..            .BYTE   $19,$16,$12,$0F,$0C,$09,$06,$03
20C6 00   ..            .BYTE   $00,$FD,$FA,$F7,$F4,$F1,$EE,$EA
20CE E7   ..            .BYTE   $E7,$E4,$E1,$DE,$DB,$D8,$D5,$D2
20D6 CF   ..            .BYTE   $CF,$CD,$CA,$C7,$C4,$C1,$BF,$BC
20DE B9   ..            .BYTE   $B9,$B7,$B4,$B2,$AF,$AD,$AA,$A8
20E6 A6   ..            .BYTE   $A6,$A4,$A2,$9F,$9D,$9B,$9A,$98
20EE 96   ..            .BYTE   $96,$94,$93,$91,$8F,$8E,$8D,$8B
20F6 8A   ..            .BYTE   $8A,$89,$88,$87,$86,$85,$84,$83
20FE 83   ..            .BYTE   $83,$82,$82,$81,$81,$81,$81,$81
2106 81   ..            .BYTE   $81,$81,$81,$81,$81,$81,$82,$82
```

Fig. 18–7. Waveform table filler

```
2106E 83  ..        .BYTE   $83,$83,$84,$85,$86,$87,$88,$89
2116 8A  ..        .BYTE   $8A,$8B,$8D,$8E,$8F,$91,$93,$94
211E 96  ..        .BYTE   $96,$98,$9A,$9B,$9D,$9F,$A2,$A4
2126 A6  ..        .BYTE   $A6,$A8,$AA,$AD,$AF,$B2,$B4,$B7
212E B9  ..        .BYTE   $B9,$BC,$BF,$C1,$C4,$C7,$CA,$CD
2136 CF  ..        .BYTE   $CF,$D2,$D5,$D8,$DB,$DE,$E1,$E4
213E E7  ..        .BYTE   $E7,$EA,$EE,$F1,$F4,$F7,$FA,$FD
2146 00  ..        .BYTE   $00,$03,$06,$09,$0C,$0F,$12,$16
214E 19  ..        .BYTE   $19,$1C,$1F,$22,$25,$28,$2B,$2E
2156 31  ..        .BYTE   $31,$33,$36,$39,$3C,$3F,$41,$44
215E 47  ..        .BYTE   $47,$49,$4C,$4E,$51,$53,$56,$58
2166 5A  ..        .BYTE   $5A,$5C,$5E,$61,$63,$65,$66,$68
216E 6A  ..        .BYTE   $6A,$6C,$6D,$6F,$71,$72,$73,$75
2176 76  ..        .BYTE   $76,$77,$78,$79,$7A,$7B,$7C,$7D
217E 7D  ..        .BYTE   $7D,$7E,$7E,$7F,$7F,$7F,$7F,$7F
2186
2186               .END
 0 ERRORS IN PASS 2
```

Fig. 18–7. Waveform table filler *(cont.)*.

sidered with smaller values giving faster computation. The scaling logic assumes that NHARM is never greater than 16, although this can be extended by modifying the scaling computation or restricting the amplitude sum to less than 16.

Looking closer at FSEVAL, it is seen that the product of a harmonic amplitude and a sine table entry is a full 16 bits. To avoid almost certain overflow when other harmonics are added in, the product is shifted right four times, which effectively moves the binary point between bits 11 and 10. This increases the range to 16 and reduces the resolution to 1/2,048. The increased range positively insures against overflow for up to 16 harmonics.

In scale, only the most significant byte of the 16-bit samples produced by FSEVAL is examined. Peak determination is by comparing the absolute value of the upper sample bytes with a current maximum, which is kept in MAX. This maximum is incremented by one before returning. Note that the binary point position of MAX is between bits 3 and 2.

The FILL routine normalizes the samples by simply dividing the 16-bit sample returned by FSEVAL by MAX. Since the binary points are in equivalent positions, the point position for the quotient will be between bits 6 and 7, making it a signed fraction ready for storage in the waveform table. Incrementing MAX by one in SCALE is required to avoid overflow in the division, which would occur when the peak point is divided by itself. Unfortunately, this action also introduces an error that reduces the scaled amplitude somewhat. Large values of MAX minimize this error, however. Thus, when a harmonic spectrum is prepared, the strongest harmonic should be given an amplitude of 0.996 (0.FF). A 16/32-bit arithmetic package would reduce the error to insignificance but would be about three times slower on the 6502. It is important to note that this error is only an amplitude error; it does not introduce excess noise beyond that due to the lower amplitude. Also note that only the highest peak is normalized. It is also possible to shift the baseline of the waveform to force positive and negative symmetry and thus insure use of all 256 quantization levels in the waveform table. Unfortunately, this may also introduce a significant dc component to the waveform, which may cause trouble, such as a "thump" when a fast amplitude envelope is applied.

Fast Fourier Transform for the 68000

For the last example, we will examine a translation of the complex FFT subroutine described in Chapter 13 from BASIC into 68000 assembly language. The main practical reason for being interested in an assembly language FFT is its much greater speed relative to one in a high-level language. For example, to transform 1024 complex data points (which could be 2048 real data points if a real transformation routine was also written), only 900 msec are required on a typical-speed 68000 compared to a minute or more for the BASIC program running on most systems. With smaller record sizes of 64 complex (128 real) points and a fast (12-MHz) 68000, one could approach *real-time* analysis of speech bandwidth (8 ks/s) data! For any practical use with real-world data, the accuracy of the routine will be equivalent to one using floating-point arithmetic.

Before describing the workings of the routine itself, let's examine the scaling properties of the FFT algorithm. First refer back to Fig. 13–15, in which the calculations involved in each "node" of the FFT were diagrammed. These calculations are all of the form:

$$(\text{NEWDATA}) = (\text{OLDDATA1}) + (\text{OLDDATA2}) \times \text{COS}(A) + (\text{OLDDATA3}) \times \text{SIN}(A)$$

where A is some angle, OLDDATA1, 2, and 3 are current values in the data array, and NEWDATA is a new value stored back into the data array. Doing a *range analysis* where the ranges of OLDDATA1, 2, and 3 are all the same, we find that the range of NEWDATA is at most 2.41 times larger than the OLDDATA ranges, which could occur when the angle A is 45°. In actual use inside an FFT, it turns out that the range of NEWDATA is only twice that of the OLDDATA values. The point is that, since all of the array data participates in calculations of this type for each column of nodes in the FFT butterfly diagram, it follows that the range for the array *doubles* as each column of nodes is evaluated. Since there are LOG_2N node columns in an N-point FFT calculation, the range of the final result array is simply N times the range of the original data array. In actuality, this theoretical result range will only be approached when the input signal contains a single-frequency component near full-scale amplitude and it has not been windowed.

There are numerous ways to handle this tendency for data values to double every iteration through the FFT algorithm. The first is to simply insure that the initial input data values are small enough so that after transformation they will still fit into the chosen data wordlength. This is perfectly feasible for a dedicated function single block size FFT routine (or hardware implementation of such a routine) but could get out of hand in a routine designed for a wide range of possible block sizes. Another possibility is to scan the data array after each iteration and divide all values by two. Unfortunately, this sacrifices small signal accuracy, when freedom from processing noise is needed most, in exchange for large signal-handling capability. Yet a third is to scale the calculations so that overflow is a distinct possibility and test for it during each iteration. If overflow does occur, divide the data array by two, recording the number of times this is done, and continue. This technique is called *conditional array scaling* and has the best tradeoff between accuracy and word size but suffers from additional complexity and an indefinite execution time as well as burdening successive processing steps with data having a variable scale factor.

Since the 68000 readily handles 32-bit data values, the brute-force technique mentioned first above will be used. The intial input data, intermediate results stored in the data arrays, and the output data will be 32-bit signed integers. The SIN and COS multipliers will be obtained from a table as 16-bit *unsigned* binary fractions. When multiplied by the 32-bit data values, a 48-bit product is obtained. The intermediate calculations within a node are performed using these 48-bit values, but the final node result that is stored back into the data array is just the most significant 32 bits. The sign of the COS multiplier is handled by conditionally adding or subtracting the product according to the angle. The SIN multiplier is always positive, since the angle is always between 0 and 180°. For maximum accuracy, SIN or COS multipliers of unity (1.0) are represented by a special value in the table, and multiplication is skipped when they are seen. Zero multipliers are also skipped, which gives a noticeable speed increase for the smaller record sizes, where zero and unity multipliers are proportionately abundant.

Figure 18–8 shows the assembled 68000 FFT subroutine listing. Arguments and instructions for its use are given in the first few lines and should be self-explanatory. When filling the data arrays with 32-bit values, it is desirable to shift the data left as far as allowable to maximize accuracy. For example, if the original data are signed 16-bit integers and the transform size is 512 complex points, the 16-bit data can be sign extended to 32 bits and then shifted left seven positions before being stored into the data arrays. This leaves 9-bit positions available for the nine doublings incurred by the nine FFT iterations needed for 512 points. However, if real data is being transformed and this routine is followed by a real transformation routine, only six shifts should be done because the real transformation also tends to double the array values. The subroutine is completely self-contained except for an external cosine table (not shown but instructions for its generation are included), which can be shared with other synthesis routines. Since all

```
001000                    ; FFT68 -- COMPLEX FAST FOURIER TRANSFORM SUBROUTINE FOR THE MC68000
001000
001000                    ; THIS SUBROUTINE PERFORMS THE DISCRETE FOURIER TRANSFORM ON COMPLEX DATA USING
001000                    ; THE "RADIX 2 TIME DECOMPOSITION WITH INPUT BIT REVERSAL" FFT ALGORITHM.
001000                    ; COMPUTATION IS DONE IN-PLACE (OUTPUT ARRAYS REPLACE INPUT ARRAYS).
001000                    ; AS WRITTEN AND USING THE SPECIFIED COSINE TABLE, UP TO 2048 COMPLEX DATA
001000                    ; POINTS (UP TO 4096 REAL DATA POINTS) CAN BE TRANSFORMED.
001000                    ; MEASURED EXECUTION TIMES AT 8MHZ, NO WAITS, 3% MEMORY REFRESH OVERHEAD:
001000                    ;
001000                    ;             # COMPLEX POINTS  TIME IN MILLISECONDS
001000                    ;                     32                 13
001000                    ;                     64                 32
001000                    ;                    128                 77
001000                    ;                    256                175
001000                    ;                    512                400
001000                    ;                   1024                900
001000                    ;                   2048               2000
001000
001000                    ; INPUT ARGUMENTS:
001000                    ;  A1 = ADDRESS OF INPUT ARRAY, REAL PARTS.
001000                    ;  A2 = ADDRESS OF INPUT ARRAY, IMAGINARY PARTS.
001000                    ;  A3 = ADDRESS OF COSINE TABLE (TABLE FORMAT DESCRIBED BELOW)
001000                    ;  D1 = LOG(2) OF NUMBER OF COMPLEX DATA POINTS, MAXIMUM VALUE IS 11
001000                    ;       EXAMPLE: D1=9=512 COMPLEX POINTS
001000
001000                    ; OUTPUT ARGUMENTS:
001000                    ;  NO CHECKING OF ARGUMENT VALIDITY IS PERFORMED.
001000                    ;  ALL REGISTERS ARE SAVED AND RESTORED.
001000                    ;  CONTENT OF TWO DATA ARRAYS IS TRANSFORMED.
001000                    ;  THE COSINE TABLE IS NOT ALTERED.
001000
001000                    ; DATA FORMAT:
001000                    ;  INPUT DATA SHOULD BE 32 BIT SIGNED INTEGERS.  TO INSURE THAT OVERFLOW CANNOT
001000                    ;    OCCUR, THE MAXIMUM INPUT MAGNITUDE SHOULD BE LESS THAN (2**31)/(2**K)
001000                    ;    WHERE K IS THE TRANSFORM SIZE ARGUMENT IN D1.
001000                    ;  OUTPUT DATA WILL ALSO BE 32 BIT SIGNED INTEGERS.  THE MAXIMUM MAGNITUDE OF
001000                    ;    OUTPUT VALUES WILL BE EQUAL TO OR LESS THAN THE MAGNITUDE OF THE INPUT
001000                    ;    DATA MULTIPLIED BY THE TRANSFORM SIZE.  THUS FOR 16 BIT INPUT DATA,
001000                    ;    A 2048 POINT TRANSFORM COULD PRODUCE VALUES AS LARGE 27 BITS.
001000                    ;  THE COSINE TABLE SHOULD HAVE 1025 ENTRIES, EACH A 16 BIT UNSIGNED INTEGER.
001000                    ;    THE TABLE SHOULD BE PREPARED USING THE FOLLOWING FORMULA:
001000                    ;    T=INT(65536*COS(3.141592653*I/2048)+.5)
001000                    ;    WHERE I IS THE TABLE ADDRESS (0 - 1024) AND T IS THE TABLE ENTRY.
001000                    ;    USING THIS FORMULA, THE FIRST 3 ENTRIES WILL BE 65536 WHICH WILL NOT FIT
001000                    ;    INTO 16 BITS.  THESE REPRESENT A BINARY FRACTION OF 1.0 AND SHOULD BE
001000                    ;    STORED INTO THE TABLE AS 32768 ($8000).  THE FFT ROUTINE CAN DETECT THIS
001000                    ;    VALUE AND SKIP MULTIPLICATION WHEN IT IS SEEN.
001000
001000 48E7FF8E FFT68    MOVEM.L D0-D7/A0/A4-A6,-(SP) SAVE ALL REGISTERS USED
001004 9EFC000C          SUB     #12,SP              RESERVE ROOM FOR 3 LONG WORDS ON THE STACK
001008 7E01              MOVEQ   #1,D7               COMPUTE NUMBER OF POINTS
00100A E367              ASL.W   D1,D7               D7 = 2^(D1) = N
00100C
00100C                    ; SCRAMBLE THE INPUT DATA ARRAYS
00100C
00100C 4283     SCR      CLR.L   D3                  D3=NORMAL BINARY COUNTER
00100E 4284              CLR.L   D4                  D4=BIT REVERSED BINARY COUNTER
001010 5241              ADDQ    #1,D1               D1=BIT# OF LSB OF BIT REVERSED COUNTER
001012 5843     SCR0     ADDQ    #4,D3               INCREMENT THE NORMAL COUNTER
001014 3A01              MOVE    D1,D5               D5=BIT# TO FLIP IN BIT REVERSED COUNTER
001016 0B44     SCR1     BCHG    D5,D4               FLIP CURRENT COUNTER BIT
001018 6704              BEQ.S   SCR2                DONE INCREMENT IF 0-TO-1 TRANSITION
00101A 51CDFFFA          DBRA    D5,SCR1             REPEAT FOR NEXT LOWER BIT IF 1-TO-0 TRANS.
00101E 0C450001 SCR2     CMP.W   #1,D5               TEST IF REVERSED COUNTER OVERFLOWED
```

Fig. 18–8. Assembled 68000 FFT subroutine listing

```
001022 6722                  BEQ.S   XFM                 JUMP OUT IF SO, DONE WITH SCRAMBLE
001024 B843                  CMP.W   D3,D4               COMPARE THE TWO COUNTERS
001026 6DEA                  BLT.S   SCRO                NO SWAP IF EQUAL OR NORMAL IS BIGGER
001028 2A313000              MOVE.L  0(A1,D3.W),D5       IF BIT REVERSED COUNTER IS BIGGER,
00102C 23B140003000          MOVE.L  0(A1,D4.W),0(A1,D3.W)  SWAP REAL ARRAY ENTRIES ADDRESSED BY
001032 23854000              MOVE.L  D5,0(A1,D4.W)          THE TWO COUNTERS
001036 2A323000              MOVE.L  0(A2,D3.W),D5
00103A 25B240003000          MOVE.L  0(A2,D4.W),0(A2,D3.W)  AND ALSO THE IMAGINARY ARRAY ENTRIES
001040 25854000              MOVE.L  D5,0(A2,D4.W)
001044 60CC                  BRA.S   SCRO                REPEAT UNTIL BIT REVERSED COUNTER OVERFLOWS
001046
001046              ; PERFORM THE FOURIER TRANSFORM PROPER
001046              ; NOTE: IN THIS SECTION, THE N3, N4, N7, N8 VARIABLES FROM THE BASIC PROGRAM
001046              ;       ARE ALL MULTIPLIED BY 4 TO SIMPLIFY INDEXING INTO THE DATA ARRAYS.
001046              ; A0 = N4,  A4 = N3,  A5 = N7  A6 = N8
001046              ;
001046
001046 E547          XFM      ASL.W   #2,D7               D7=4*N
001048 307C0004      ST3210   MOVE.W  #4,A0               N4=4
00104C               ST3211                               N6=N4+N4 COMPUTED WHEN NEEDED
00104C 387C0000      ST3212   MOVE    #0,A4               FOR N3=0 TO N4-4 STEP 4
001050               ST3212A
001050 200C          ST3213   MOVE.L  A4,D0               A=PI*N3/N4  (N3<N4, N4 IS POWER OF 2)
001052 C0FC1000               MULU    #4096,D0            ACTUALLY COMPUTE:   D0=4096*N3/N4
001056 3208                   MOVE    A0,D1               BECAUSE A IS REALLY A TABLE LOOKUP ADDRESS
001058 80C1                   DIVU    D1,D0
00105A 4285          ST3214   CLR.L   D5                  C=COS(A)
00105C 0C400800               CMP.W   #2048,D0            TEST SIZE OF A
001060 6F0A                   BLE.S   ST3214A             FOR A<=PI/2, GO DIRECTLY TO LOOKUP, SIGN IS +
001062 0A400FFF               EOR.W   #$0FFF,D0           FOR A>PI/2, COMPLEMENT LOOKUP ADDRESS FIRST,
001066 5240                   ADDQ.W  #1,D0
001068 08C5001F               BSET    #31,D5              SIGN IS -
00106C 3A330000      ST3214A  MOVE.W  0(A3,D0.W),D5       LOOKUP C, KEEP IN D5.W, SIGN IN BIT 31
001070 4286          ST3215   CLR.L   D6                  S=SIN(A)
001072 04400800               SUB.W   #2048,D0            SHIFT A TO RANGE OF -PI/2<=A<PI/2
001076 6A02                   BPL.S   ST3215A             ABSOLUTE VALUE OF NEW A
001078 4440                   NEG.W   D0
00107A 3C330000      ST3215A  MOVE.W  0(A3,D0.W),D6       LOOKUP S, KEEP IN D6.W, SIGN IN BIT 31
00107E 0886001F               BCLR    #31,D6              *** CHANGE TO BSET FOR INVERSE TRANSFORM ***
001082 2A4C          ST3216   MOVE.L  A4,A5               FOR N7=N3 TO 4*N-4 STEP N4*2
001084               ST3216A
001084 2C4D          ST3217   MOVE.L  A5,A6               N8=N7+N4
001086 DDC8                   ADDA.L  A0,A6
001088 2831E000      ST3218   MOVE.L  0(A1,A6),D4         T1=C*D1(N8)-S*D2(N8)   (D1,D2 ARE DATA ARRAYS)
00108C 2605                   MOVE.L  D5,D3               FIRST COMPUTE C*D1(N8)
00108E 4EB81118               JSR.S   TRGMPY              USING THE TRIGNOMETRIC MULTIPLY SUBROUTINE
001092 2E81                   MOVE.L  D1,(SP)             THEN SAVE 64 BIT RESULT ON THE STACK
001094 2F420004               MOVE.L  D2,4(SP)
001098 2832E000               MOVE.L  0(A2,A6),D4         NEXT COMPUTE S*D2(N8)
00109C 2606                   MOVE.L  D6,D3
00109E 4EB81118               JSR.S   TRGMPY
0010A2 202F0004               MOVE.L  4(SP),D0            NOW SUBTRACT D1:D2 FROM PREVIOUS RESULT LEFT
0010A6 9082                   SUB.L   D2,D0               ON THE STACK AND SAVE THE HIGH 32 BITS OF THE
0010A8 2017                   MOVE.L  (SP),D0             RESULT ON THE STACK AT (SP) AS T1
0010AA 9181                   SUBX.L  D1,D0
0010AC 2E80                   MOVE.L  D0,(SP)
0010AE 2832E000      ST3219   MOVE.L  0(A2,A6),D4         T2=C*D2(N8)-S*D1(N8)   (D1,D2 ARE DATA ARRAYS)
0010B2 2605                   MOVE.L  D5,D3               FIRST COMPUTE C*D2(N8)
0010B4 4EB81118               JSR.S   TRGMPY              USING THE TRIGNOMETRIC MULTIPLY SUBROUTINE
0010B8 2F410004               MOVE.L  D1,4(SP)            THEN SAVE 64 BIT RESULT ON THE STACK
0010BC 2F420008               MOVE.L  D2,8(SP)
0010C0 2831E000               MOVE.L  0(A1,A6),D4         NEXT COMPUTE S*D1(N8)
0010C4 2606                   MOVE.L  D6,D3
0010C6 4EB81118               JSR.S   TRGMPY
0010CA 282F0008               MOVE.L  8(SP),D4            NOW ADD D1:D2 TO PREVIOUS RESULT LEFT ON THE
0010CE D882                   ADD.L   D2,D4               STACK AND SAVE THE HIGH 32 BITS OF THE RESULT
0010D0 282F0004               MOVE.L  4(SP),D4            IN D4 AS T2
```

```
0010D4 D981                 ADDX.L  D1,D4
0010D6 2617                 MOVE.L  (SP),D3         RETRIEVE T1 FROM STACK, NOW D3=T1, D4=T2
0010D8 2031D000 ST3220      MOVE.L  0(A1,A5),D0     D1(N8)=D1(N7)-T1
0010DC 9083                 SUB.L   D3,D0
0010DE 2380E000             MOVE.L  D0,0(A1,A6)
0010E2 2032D000 ST3221      MOVE.L  0(A2,A5),D0     D2(N8)=D2(N7)-T2
0010E6 9084                 SUB.L   D4,D0
0010E8 2580E000             MOVE.L  D0,0(A2,A6)
0010EC D7B1D000 ST3222      ADD.L   D3,0(A1,A5)     D1(N7)=D1(N7)+T1
0010F0 D9B2D000 ST3223      ADD.L   D4,0(A2,A5)     D2(N7)=D2(N7)+T2
0010F4 DBC8     ST3224      ADD.L   A0,A5           NEXT N7     (FOR N7=N3 TO 4*N-4 STEP N4*2)
0010F6 DBC8                 ADD.L   A0,A5
0010F8 BBC7                 CMPA.L  D7,A5
0010FA 6D88                 BLT.S   ST3216A
0010FC D8FC0004 ST3225      ADD.W   #4,A4           NEXT N3     (FOR N3=0 TO N4-4 STEP 4)
001100 B9C8                 CMPA.L  A0,A4
001102 6D00FF4C             BLT     ST3212A
001106 D1C8     ST3226      ADD.L   A0,A0           N4=N4+N4
001108 B1C7     ST3227      CMPA.L  D7,A0           IF N4<4*N GOTO 3211
00110A 6D00FF40             BLT     ST3211
00110E DEFC000C             ADD     #12,SP          FREE UP SPACE RESERVED ON THE STACK
001112 4CDF71FF             MOVEM.L (SP)+,D0-D7/A0/A4-A6 RESTORE ALL REGISTERS USED
001116 4E75                 RTS                     RETURN TO CALLER
001118
001118          ; TRGMPY = SPECIAL TRIGONOMETRIC MULTIPLY SUBROUTINE
001118          ;          ENTER WITH SINE OR COSINE MAGNITUDE IN D3.W, SIGN IN D3(BIT31)
001118          ;          ENTER WITH 32 BIT SIGNED DATA VALUE IN D4.L
001118          ;          RETURN WITH 48 BIT SIGNED PRODUCT LEFT-JUSTIFIED IN D1 (HIGH) AND D2
001118          ;          USES D0-D2
001118
001118 4A43     TRGMPY      TST.W   D3              TEST FOR SPECIAL CASES OF SINE/COSINE
00111A 6606                 BNE.S   TRGMPYA
00111C 4281                 CLR.L   D1              RESULT=0 IF SINE/COSINE=0
00111E 4282                 CLR.L   D2
001120 4E75                 RTS
001122 0C438000 TRGMPYA     CMP.W   #$8000,D3
001126 6606                 BNE.S   TRGMPYB
001128 2204                 MOVE.L  D4,D1           RESULT=DATA IF SINE/COSINE MAGNITUDE=1.0
00112A 4282                 CLR.L   D2
00112C 6020                 BRA.S   TRGMPYC
00112E 2204     TRGMPYB     MOVE.L  D4,D1           PERFORM 16 (UNSIGNED) BY 32 (SIGNED) MULTIPLY
001130 4841                 SWAP    D1              MULTIPLIER IN D3.W, MULTIPLICAND IN D4.L
001132 C2C3                 MULU    D3,D1           RESULT IN D1 (HIGH) AND D2
001134 2404                 MOVE.L  D4,D2           HIGH PARTIAL PRODUCT IN D1
001136 C4C3                 MULU    D3,D2           LOW PARTIAL PRODUCT IN D2
001138 2002                 MOVE.L  D2,D0           ADD PARTIAL PRODUCTS AS FOLLOWS:
00113A 4240                 CLR.W   D0              D1    ¶XXXX¶XXXX¶             (X=4 BITS)
00113C 4840                 SWAP    D0              D2  +       ¶XXXX¶XXXX¶
00113E D280                 ADD.L   D0,D1               ----------------------
001140 4842                 SWAP    D2              D1:D2 ¶XXXX¶XXXX¶¶XXXX¶0000¶
001142 4242                 CLR.W   D2
001144 4A84                 TST.L   D4              SIGN CORRECTION FOR NEGATIVE DATA
001146 6A06                 BPL.S   TRGMPYC
001148 4841                 SWAP    D1              SUBTRACT MULTIPLIER FROM HIGH D2 IF
00114A 9243                 SUB.W   D3,D1           MULTIPLICAND WAS NEGATIVE
00114C 4841                 SWAP    D1
00114E 4A83     TRGMPYC     TST.L   D3              NEGATE RESULT IF SINE/COSINE WAS NEGATIVE
001150 6A04                 BPL.S   TRGMPYD
001152 4482                 NEG.L   D2
001154 4081                 NEGX.L  D1
001156 4E75     TRGMPYD     RTS                     RETURN
001158
001158                      END
 0 ERRORS IN PASS 2
```

Fig. 18–8. Assembled 68000 FFT subroutine listing (*cont.*)

temporary storage is in the machine registers (a big advantage of the 68000) and the stack, the routine could even be put into ROM if desired.

In general, the subroutine is a literal translation of the BASIC program of Fig. 13–17. However, the first portion, in which the data arrays are scrambled into bit-reversed order, has been redone. Although the algorithm used in the BASIC version is reasonably efficient for a high-level language implementation, using bit manipulation instructions is much faster in assembly language. Essentially, two counters are incremented from 0 to *N*-1, one normal and one bit-reversed, and the corresponding array elements are swapped whenever the bit-reversed counter is larger.

The second portion is reasonably straightforward except when multiplication by a sine or cosine is performed. What is actually needed is a 16-bit unsigned × 32-bit signed multiply to yield a 48-bit signed product, whereas the 68000 only provides 16 × 16-bit multiplies where both operands are either signed or unsigned. The desired result is achieved in the TRGMPY subroutine by treating the 32-bit signed multiplicand as an unsigned value, performing a 32 × 16-bit unsigned multiply using two of the 16 × 16-bit machine instructions, and then correcting the product by subtracting the unsigned multiplier from the most significant 16 bits of the 48-bit product if the multiplicand was negative. This routine also bypasses multiplication completely when the multiplier is zero or unity. If an inverse transform is required, the instruction in line 106 can be changed to a BSET instruction, which has the effect of negating the SIN multipliers.

For efficient transformation of real data, a complex-to-real transform routine can be coded using these same techniques and the BASIC version in Fig. 13–19 as a guide. Note that the complex-to-real transform uses cosine and sine angle increments half the size of the corresponding complex FFT. Thus, to actually transform 4096 real points using a 2048-point complex transform, either the cosine table will have to be made twice as large (and the given subroutine slightly modified to accommodate it), or the complex-to-real routine will have to interpolate in the given table. Of course, this problem does not arise for smaller transforms.

As coded, this subroutine gives results as accurate as 16-bit input data allow. For many analysis tasks, particularly those in which the final result is a plot or display, less accuracy is needed. This routine (and a companion complex-to-real routine) could in fact be rewritten for the 12-bit data and multipliers, which would probably increase the speed two to three times for transform sizes up to 256 points. Real-time analysis of speech bandwidth data then would be possible even on an 8-MHz 68000.

NOTRAN Music System

After coming this far, it is about time to see how the various synthesis and processing techniques can be put together to form a usable music software system. The system that will be described here is rather small and simple compared to mammoth systems like MUSIC V. Nevertheless, it should serve well as an example of how a system of manageable size (for one person) might be put together. A subset of the system to be described was actually implemented on a university minicomputer (about half as fast as an 8-MHz 68000) in 1970 and used to perform a Bach organ fugue[1] with considerable attention to detail. The version described here as well as logical extensions is within the capabilities of nearly any microcomputer given the necessary mass storage capacity and audio DAC.

The acronym for the system is NOTRAN, which is taken from the words, NOte TRANslation. Immediately it is apparent that the system is based on conventional music notation and the 12-tone scale with all of its trappings and as such it is seemingly bound to the performance of conventional sounding music. This is basically true but does not detract from its utility as a system organization example, and besides, far more people are experienced in conventional notation. Thus, the reader is allowed to concentrate on the system organization, which is the purpose of this section. In any case, the huge variety of techniques, options, and goals in music synthesis makes "assumptions to simplify the problem" absolutely necessary if any results at all are to be obtained. Extensions to cover other tuning and notation systems are certainly no more difficult than with other music software systems.

Another characteristic of the NOTRAN system as described here is that it is a programmed, delayed-playback, direct digital synthesis system. However, the three lowest levels of software could be replaced by dedicated synthesis hardware or an interface to an analog synthesizer to allow real-time operation. The basic syntax of the language itself is not optimized for minimum typing effort. Instead, it is designed for ease of understanding (by humans) and ease of interpretation (by computers). However, a macroprocessor can be used to define more advanced statements that may generate numerous basic NOTRAN statements.

Finally, NOTRAN statements are in strict *time order*. All sounds created by the NOTRAN system are discrete events having a starting time and a duration. The starting time is determined by the location of statements invoking the event, whereas the duration is determined both by the invocation statement and a corresponding "voice definition" statement. Once started, an event runs to completion independent of other events and statements.

In describing the NOTRAN system, the lowest-level routines and design considerations will be covered first. While this is in direct opposition

[1] The piece was "Toccata and Fugue in D Minor." The computer was an Adage Ambilog 200, which had a 30-bit word but for arithmetic behaved like a 15-bit machine. Twelve-bit samples were used and the sample rate was 32 ks/s, although four-to-one speedup of the audio tape was necessary to obtain that speed due to the low-density (556BPI) of the tape drives. Computation time for the 8-min piece was about 3.5 h.

to "top-down" philosophy, it offers a smooth transition from familiar concepts already covered to the unfamiliar ones being introduced. Where word sizes are given they were chosen for very high sound quality and can certainly be cut back for experimentation in 8-bit systems.

Level 1 Routines

The Level 1 or actual sound generation routines in a synthesis system in many ways determine the "character" of sounds generated by the system. The NOTRAN system utilizes two basic types of sounds, definitely pitched tones and percussive sounds. Accordingly, there are two Level 1 subroutines, one for each type of sound. Although only two subroutines are involved, each may be called several times with different arguments in order to generate simultaneous sounds. While actual listings of these two subroutines will not be given, it is expected that they will be written in assembly language. The actual code is quite straightforward and may in fact represent the majority of machine level coding required for the entire NOTRAN system.

As mentioned earlier, efficiency considerations dictate that Level 1 routines work with blocks of samples in order to minimize call/return overhead. All control parameters are assumed to be constant throughout the block. A good block size is about 1 msec of samples; thus, for example purposes we will assume a 30-ks/s sample rate and a 30-sample block size. The subroutine will therefore compute 30 samples before returning. For maximum flexibility, these 30 samples will be *added* to the contents of a 30-sample, 16-bit output buffer to effect mixing. The upper level routines will be using block counts for timing purposes so an exact 1-msec block size is convenient.

The tone generation subroutine will operate on the table lookup principle. A table size of 1,024 16-bit words is sufficient for very high quality but could be reduced to 256 8-bit words for lower-quality experimentation. In either case, the subroutine needs the following five arguments passed to it:

1. Address of the waveform table (16 or 32 bits)
2. Frequency parameters (16 to 32 bits)
3. Amplitude parameter (8 or 16 bits)
4. Address of sample buffer (16 or 32 bits)
5. Waveform table pointer (16 to 32 bits to match frequency parameter)

Note that the waveform table pointer will be changed by the computation, while the rest of the parameters are left alone.

The most efficient method of passing this information back and forth is to treat the five items as an *array* and simply pass the *address* of the array to the subroutine. Although the array size is fixed for this particular subroutine, other Level 1 subroutines may require a different array size and format. Thus, for ease of storage allocation by upper level routines and future expandability,

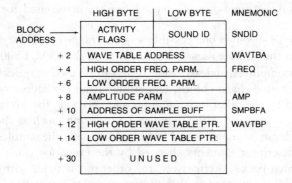

	HIGH BYTE	LOW BYTE	MNEMONIC
BLOCK ADDRESS →	ACTIVITY FLAGS	SOUND ID	SNDID
+ 2	WAVE TABLE ADDRESS		WAVTBA
+ 4	HIGH ORDER FREQ. PARM.		FREQ
+ 6	LOW ORDER FREQ. PARM.		
+ 8	AMPLITUDE PARM		AMP
+ 10	ADDRESS OF SAMPLE BUFF		SMPBFA
+ 12	HIGH ORDER WAVE TABLE PTR.		WAVTBP
+ 14	LOW ORDER WAVE TABLE PTR.		
+ 30	UNUSED		

Fig. 18–9. Sound control block for tone generator

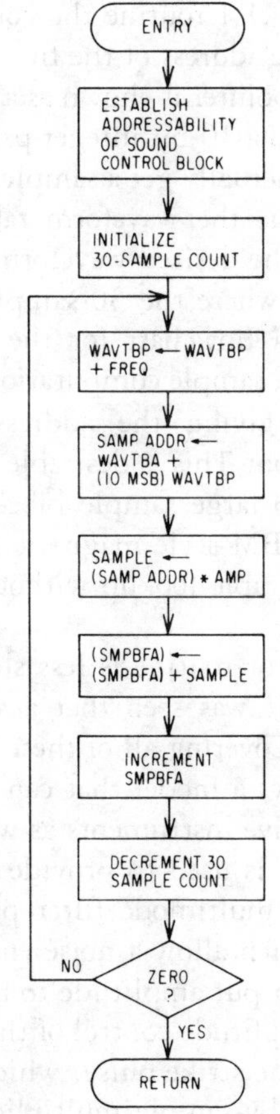

Fig. 18–10. Tone generator subroutine flowchart

a fixed argument array size of, say 32 bytes will be used for all Level 1 routines.

Figure 18–9 shows one possible way to arrange the five arguments into fields within the 32-byte *sound control block*. With the 6502, 68000, and most other microcomputers, indexed addressing can be used to quickly access the fields in the sound control block. One simply loads the address of the control block passed by the caller into a register and then uses fixed offsets to access the data. In a machine without indexed addressing, such as the 8080, the control block can be copied into a fixed memory area, the samples computed, and those descriptor elements changed by the execution (such as the table pointer) copied back. Alternatively, the order of the fields within the block can be carefully sequenced so that increment index instructions can be used to scan through them.

The initial byte of activity flags is used by the upper level routines to keep track of which control blocks are actually generating sound. The sound ID byte identifies which Level 1 routine the control block is formatted for. The wave table address is the address of the first entry of the waveform table being used. The wave table pointer is shown as a 32-bit value, which consists of a 22-bit fractional part and a 10-bit integer part. The integer part is added to the wave table address to actually get a sample. The frequency parameter is also shown as 32 bits and is the waveform table pointer increment. The amplitude parameter gives the desired waveform amplitude, while the sample buffer address indicates where the 30-sample buffer is located.

Figure 18–10 shows a flowchart for the tone generator subroutine. Essentially, it goes through a sample computation loop 30 times and returns. Note that the argument giving the address of the sample buffer is incremented during execution. This is desirable and minimizes the overhead associated with building up large sample blocks for mass storage devices, such as 3,000 samples for IBM-style magnetic tape. The other calculations perform standard waveform table lookup without interpolation as described in Chapter 13.

The percussion generator routine is less straightforward than the tone generator. In Chapter 15, it was seen that a wide variety of mechanisms produce percussive sounds. Covering all of these in a single subroutine is not practical. Figure 18–11 shows a model that can be used to approximate the majority of common percussive instruments as well as numerous others. The pulse-excited bandpass filter is used to provide a damped sine wave, while the white noise source and multimode filter provide filtered noise. Three gain controls are shown, which allow a noise envelope, the ratio of noise to damped wave, and overall output amplitude to be independently controlled. For maximum efficiency, amplitude control of the damped wave is controlled by varying the intensity of the strike pulse, which only has to be done once, rather than doing a sample-by-sample multiplication of the generator output.

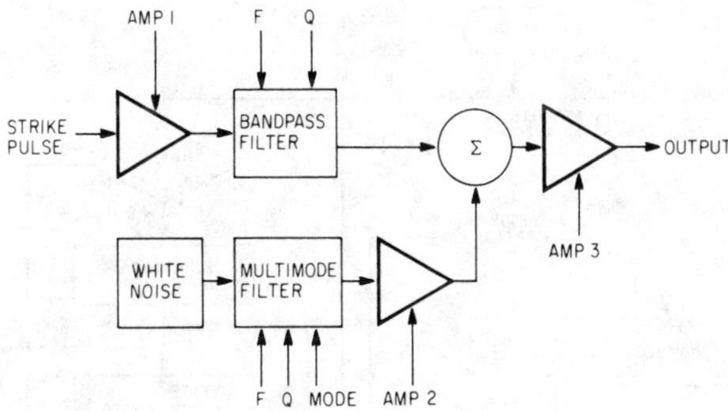

Fig. 18–11. Percussive sound model

	HIGH BYTE	LOW BYTE	MNEMONIC
BLOCK ADDRESS →	ACTIVITY FLAGS	SOUND ID	SNDID
+ 2	BANDPASS FILTER F		RESNF
+ 4	BANDPASS FILTER Q		RESNQ
+ 6	MULTIMODE FILTER F		MMFF
+ 8	MULTIMODE FILTER Q		MMFQ
+ 10	FILTER MODE		MMFM
+ 12	DAMPED SINE AMP		RESNAM
+ 14	FILTERED NOISE AMP		MMFAM
+ 16	OVERALL AMP		AMP
+ 18	ADDRESS OF SAMPLE BUFF		SMPBFA
+ 20	STORAGE FOR BANDPASS		RESND1
+ 22	FILTER		RESND2
+ 24	STORAGE FOR MULTIMODE		MMFD1
+ 26	FILTER		MMFD2
+ 28	NOISE REGISTER		NOISE
+ 30	UNUSED		

Fig. 18–12. Sound control block for percussion generator

The sound control block for percussive sounds is shown in Fig. 18–12. The data elements in the control block should be self-explanatory. Note that all but two bytes of the block are used and that many of them simply describe the percussive timbre, which is constant. In the tone generator control block, the actual waveform was stored elsewhere and a *pointer* to the information was given. This could also be done with the percussive generator and thus free up 10 bytes in its sound control block, although it was not.

Figure 18–13 is a flowchart of the major operations performed by the Level 1 percussion routine. Note that each half of the percussive sound model is checked for activity before computing the 30 samples. This saves considerable time when only half of the model is needed for simple percussive sounds.

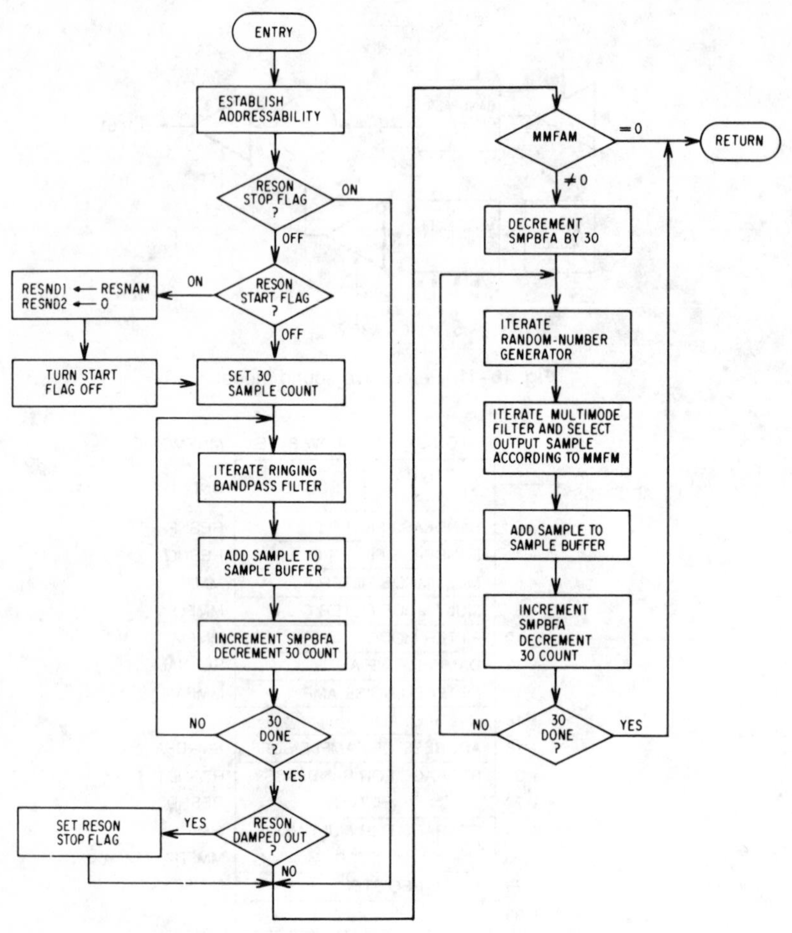

Fig. 18–13. Percussion generator subroutine flowchart

The envelope of the filtered noise is handled by higher level routines just as with the tone generator routine. The damped sine wave generator, however, supplies its own envelope because of the way it works. The activity flags are used to pass information about the damped wave generator to and from the calling routine. The *start flag* is set by the caller when the percussive sound is to be started. When the percussive routine sees the flag set, it initializes one of the bandpass filter registers (the digital state-variable type is assumed) to the damped wave amplitude and turns the start flag off. This operation is equivalent to striking the resonator, and thereafter the filter is iterated to produce the damped wave.

In theory, the wave amplitude will never reach zero so a mechanism is necessary to detect when a very small amplitude is reached so that the

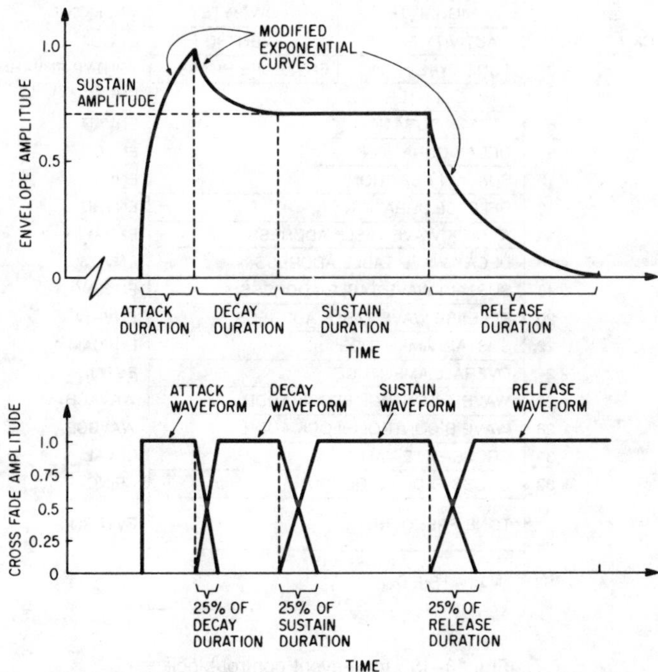

Fig. 18–14. Tone envelope details

percussive sound can be considered complete. Thus, at the end of every 30-sample block, the bandpass filter registers are examined (their absolute values are summed and compared with a constant representing perhaps 60 dB of decay), and if a low enough amplitude is seen, the *stop flag* is turned on.

Level 2 Generator Routines

Level 2 routines operate much like Level 1 routines except at a slower speed. They are primarily responsible for sequencing through envelopes in the synthesized sound. In this respect, they act much like waveform generators but at a 1-ks/s sample rate. Also, in order to crudely implement dynamic spectrum changes during a note, several waveform tables may be sequenced through in the course of the note. Cross-fading (time-variable interpolation) from one waveform table to the next is therefore handled in these routines as well. Also, there is a routine responsible for scanning the control blocks and insuring that all of the active ones contribute their samples to the sample buffer. Finally, there is a routine that controls the collection of 30 sample blocks into larger records and initiates writing of the records onto a mass storage device.

The most important Level 2 routine controls the execution of tone events. A tone event is basically a pitched note that uses the Level 1 tone

	HIGH BYTE	LOW BYTE	MNEMONIC
BLOCK ADDRESS	ACTIVITY FLAGS	EVENT ID	EVTID
+ 2	TONE TYPE	ENVELOPE PHASE #	TONTYP ENVPHN
+ 4	TIME COUNTER		ENVTC
+ 6	ATTACK DURATION		ENVAD
+ 8	DECAY DURATION		ENVDD
+ 10	SUSTAIN DURATION		ENVSD
+ 12	RELEASE DURATION		ENVRD
+ 14	ATTACK WAVE TABLE ADDRESS		ENVAW
+ 16	DECAY WAVE TABLE ADDRESS		ENVDW
+ 18	SUSTAIN WAVE TABLE ADDRESS		ENVSW
+ 20	RELEASE WAVE TABLE ADDRESS		ENVRW
+ 22	SUSTAIN AMPLITUDE		ENVSAM
+ 24	OVERALL AMPLITUDE		EVTAMP
+ 26	WAVE A CONTROL BLOCK ADDR.		WAVACB
+ 28	WAVE B CONTROL BLOCK ADDR.		WAVBCB
+ 30	CROSS-FADE VALUE		CFVAL
+ 32	CROSS-FADE INCREMENT		CFINC
+ 34 + 36	TONE FREQUENCY		EVTFRQ
+ 62	NOT USED		

Fig. 18–15. Tone-event control block

subroutine to generate sound. One important aspect of a tone event is its envelope, which is sketched in Fig. 18–14. This routine uses the standard ADSR envelope shape, which consists of four phases. To make life interesting, not only is the amplitude controlled by the envelope but the waveform is as well. Each envelope phase can correspond to a different waveform, which, although seemingly crude, is quite effective. A sudden switch from one wave table to the next might inject objectionable clicks, however, so a "cross-fading" technique is used.

From the foregoing it can be seen that this routine has several tasks to perform. It must sequence the envelope through its four phases according to several parameters, and it must generate an acceptable curve for each phase. During the cross-fading interval, two tones are being generated. Besides controlling the cross-fading itself, sound control blocks for the needed tones must be created, used, and deactivated. Although this routine is much more complex than the lower-level routines, it is executed far less frequently, which makes the extra time tolerable.

Figure 18–15 shows the *event control block* for tones. Since these blocks will tend to be large, an allocation of 64 bytes is assumed. The activity flags and event ID fields parallel those of sound control blocks. The tone type field indicates which type of tone generation subroutine is to be used if the system is ever expanded. The envelope phase number ranges from 1 to 4 to indicate which part of the envelope is being generated. The time counter is used to

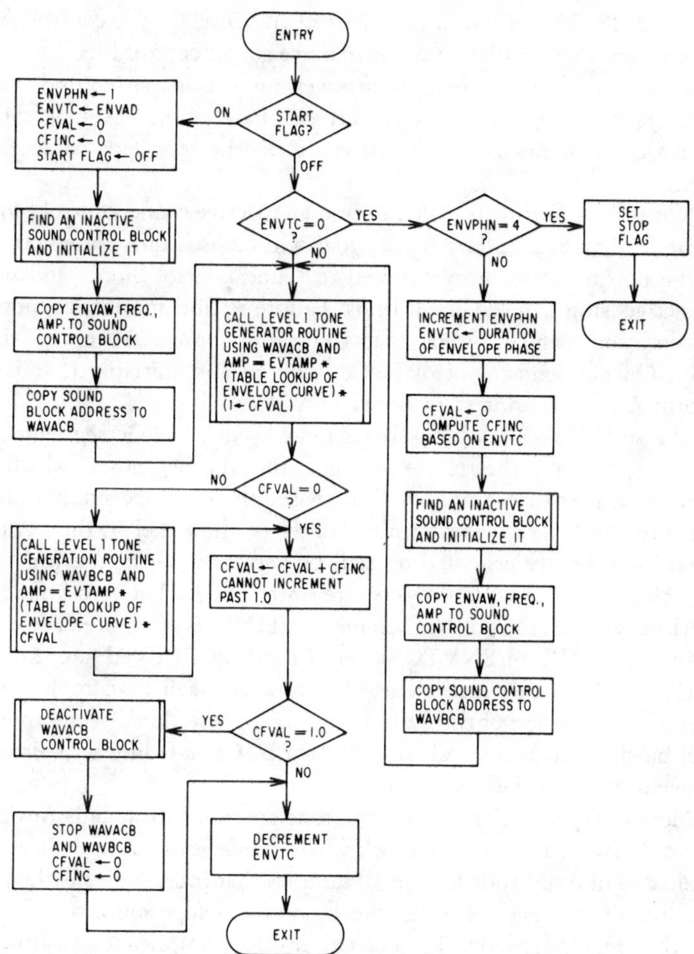

Fig. 18–16. Level 2 tone-control routine

count milliseconds during each phase. The next four parameters give the duration for each phase. Two additional parameters give the sustain amplitude relative to the peak amplitude of the attack (remember that the ADSR shape overshoots the sustain level during attack) and the overall amplitude of the entire event.

The remaining parameters are used to control waveform switching. Four parameters give waveform table addresses for each of the four envelope phases. Since sound control blocks must be created to generate sound, their addresses are stored in the event control block. The cross-fade value increases from 0 to 1.0 as the old waveform fades out and the new waveform fades in. The rate of fade is arbitrarily set to complete in one-quarter of the duration of the current envelope segment. The cross-fade increment is computed at the beginning of an envelope segment such that this is true.

Figure 18–16 is a rough flowchart of the Level 2 tone control routine. Start and stop flags similar to the percussive sound control block are used to control initiation and termination of the event. If this routine finds the start flag on, it initializes things for the attack phase of the envelope. Since no waveform cross-fade is used during the attack, the cross-fade parameters are zeroed.

Note that a routine is called to find an inactive sound control block and initialize it. This is a Level 2 utility that will be used quite often. It simply scans the portion of memory devoted to sound control blocks and uses the first inactive (stop flag on) one it finds. Failure to find an inactive block is an error condition, which means that too many sounds are going simultaneously. Once a sound control block is found and initialized, it is called waveform A and its address is stored in WAVACB.

The second decision block determines if an envelope segment has expired. If so, and it is the release segment, the stop flag is set, which means that the tone event is complete. Otherwise, the envelope phase number is incremented and the envelope time counter is initialized to the duration of the next phase. Since cross-fading will be necessary when entering the new phase, the cross-fade parameters are initialized. The cross-fade value (CFVAL) is set to zero and the increment (CFINC) is computed according to the formula CFINC=4/ENVTC, where CFINC and CFVAL are assumed to be fractions. With this increment, the cross-fade will be complete in one-quarter of the duration of the current envelope phase. Finally, another sound control block is set up and called waveform B. Cross-fading will always fade out waveform A and fade in waveform B.

Most of the time, entry into the tone control routine falls through the first two decisions and enters a block where the Level 1 routine for waveform A is called. The amplitude for the 30 samples that it computes is the product of the overall event amplitude, the current-envelope amplitude, and one minus the cross-fade value. The current-envelope amplitude is a function of the time counter (ENVTC) and the duration of the current-envelope phase.

In an analog-envelope generator, the attack, decay, and release curves are negative exponential functions, which never really reach their endpoints. In the digital domain, linear curves are easier to generate and also reach their endpoints but do not always "sound right," particularly with long duration envelopes. Here, a compromise is made in which the exponential curve is adjusted to reach the endpoint in three time constants. This may be accomplished as shown in Fig. 18–17 by computing a virtual endpoint 5.2% further away from the beginning point than the actual endpoint. For maximum efficiency in the envelope routine, the three-time constant exponential curve is stored in a table. Then a table lookup based on the envelope phase number, time counter, and envelope phase duration is performed according to the formulas given in the figure.

After waveform A samples are computed, a test is made to determine if cross-fading is in effect. If so, B waveform samples are also computed, which

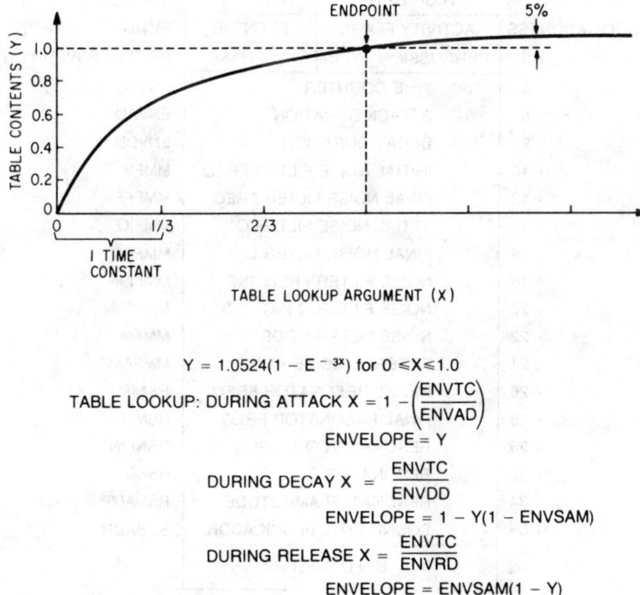

Fig. 18–17. Truncated exponential curve

are automatically added to the A samples in the sample buffer. The amplitude argument for B is the same as for A except that the cross-fade value is factored in differently so that wave B fades in. If cross-fading is not in effect, waveform B is bypassed.

After the 30 composite samples are computed, the cross-fade increment is added to the cross-fade value. If the sum reaches 1.0, which means that the A waveform is completely faded out, the A sound control block is deactivated and the B sound control block becomes a new A by swapping the control block addresses, WAVACB and WAVBCB, in the event control block. The cross-fade parameters are then zeroed to inhibit cross-fade processing until the next envelope phase is started. The final operation before a normal exit is decrementing the time counter.

Control of percussive events in most respects parallels that of tone events. The filtered noise envelope, for example, is controlled in a similar fashion but for simplicity is a simple attack–release shape. In order to broaden the range of sounds available from the simple model used, provisions are made for the noise filter and ringing resonator parameters to vary during the sound. Both the center frequency and *Q* factor for the noise filter may vary, while only the ringing frequency of the resonator is adjustable. A linear variation from a specified initial value to a specified final value is used. This variation scheme is well defined for the enveloped noise, which has a duration

	HIGH BYTE	LOW BYTE	MNEMONIC
BLOCK ADDRESS	ACTIVITY FLAGS	EVENT ID	EVTID
+ 2	PERCUSSION TYPE	ENV. PHASE #	PRCTYP ENVPHN
+ 4	TIME COUNTER		ENVTC
+ 6	ATTACK DURATION		ENVAD
+ 8	DECAY DURATION		ENVDD
+ 10	INITIAL NOISE FILTER FREQ.		MMFIF
+ 12	FINAL NOISE FILTER FREQ.		MMFFF
+ 14	INITIAL NOISE FILTER Q		MMFIQ
+ 16	FINAL NOISE FILTER Q		MMFFQ
+ 18	NOISE FILTER FREQ. INC.		MMFFIN
+ 20	NOISE FILTER Q INC.		MMFQIN
+ 22	NOISE FILTER MODE		MMFM
+ 24	FILTERED NOISE AMP.		MMFAMP
+ 26	INITIAL RESONATOR FREQ.		RSNIF
+ 28	FINAL RESONATOR FREQ.		RSNFF
+ 30	RESONATOR FREQ. INC.		RSNFIN
+ 32	RESONATOR Q		RSNQ
+ 34	RESONATOR AMPLITUDE		RSNAMP
+ 36	SOUND CNTL BLOCK ADDR.		SCBADR
+ 62	UNUSED		

Fig. 18–18. Percussion-event control block

that is the sum of attack and release times. The ringing bandpass filter does not have such a well-defined duration so for simplicity the "duration" is assumed to equal that of the enveloped noise. (If no enveloped noise is desired, its amplitude parameter may be set to zero but with an envelope defined to establish the "pseudoduration.")

The percussion event control block in Fig. 18–18 again contains a large number of parameters, most of which are manipulated similarly to those in the tone event control block. The main difference is control information for varying filter parameters during the event. For maximum efficiency, an "increment" (which can be negative) for each parameter is computed when the event is started, and the increment is added to the filter parameter every block of 30 samples.

Figure 18–19 is a flowchart of the percussion event control routine. Again, it is similar to the tone routine and in most respects is simpler. The major complication is that the "duration" of the filtered noise portion of the event may be different from that of the damped sine wave portion. No problem occurs if the damped wave is shorter, but, if it is longer, the event control block will have to be kept active beyond the end of the noise en-

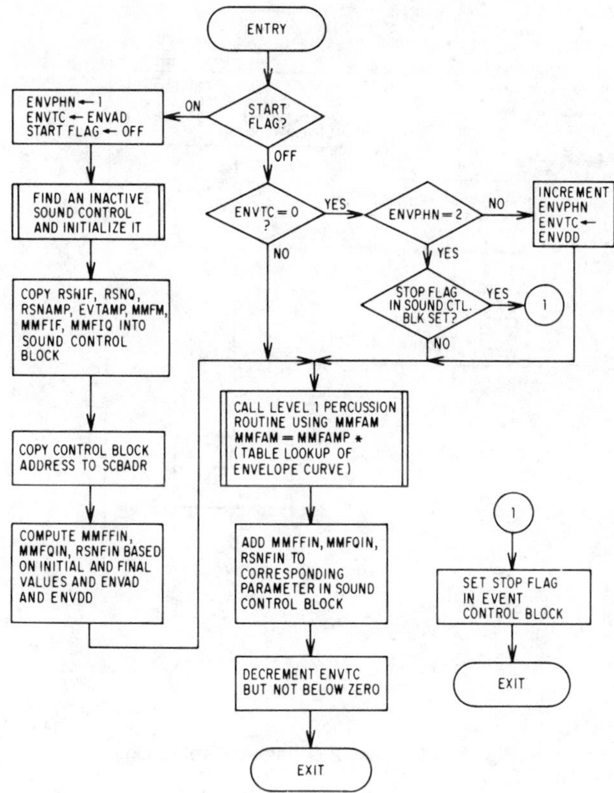

Fig. 18–19. Level 2 percussion-control routine

velope. This is accomplished by the bottom-most decision block, which does not allow the event control block stop flag to be set until the sound control block stop flag is set. This solution requires the envelope-sequencing logic to be smart enough to avoid overshooting the end of the envelope.

Level 2 Sequencing Routine

Up to this point, sound and envelope generator routines have been discussed. Although many sounds may be going simultaneously, there is only one copy of each generator subroutine in memory. The multiple sounds are the result of calling these routines with different event control blocks. The Level 2 sequencer routine is responsible for scanning the area of memory devoted to event control blocks and having each active one processed. This is the routine that is actually called by the Level 3 routines to be discussed.

Figure 18–20 is a flowchart for the sequencer routine. Entry is directly from the NOTRAN language interpreter and is with exactly one argument.

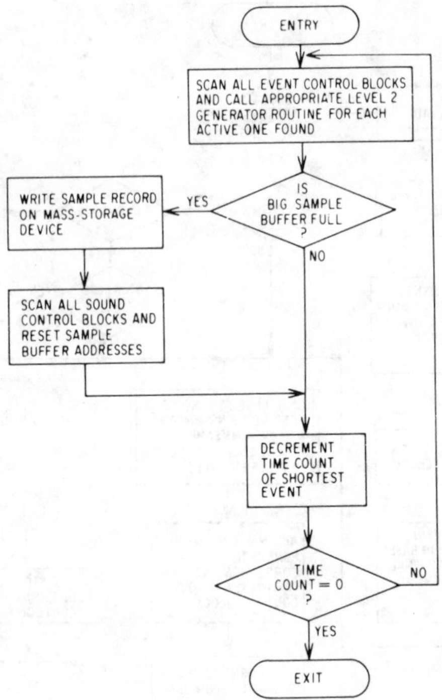

Fig. 18–20. Level 2 general-control routine

This argument specifies how many milliseconds of sound to generate before returning. Although no new events can be started *during* this interval, any number may terminate (as mentioned earlier, events are defined by their starting time and duration). New events can only be created by the NOTRAN interpreter when it is in control.

The first task is to scan the memory area devoted to event control blocks. Every active block found is further tested for the event type and the corresponding Level 2 generator routine is called. After a complete scan through all of the blocks, 30 samples have been added to the sample buffer and the buffer address pointers in all sound control blocks have been incremented by 30.

The next task is to determine if the large sample buffer is full. In the original implementation of NOTRAN, this buffer was 3,000 samples long, which would therefore hold 100 of the small sample blocks. If the large buffer is full, then a sample record would be written to the mass storage device. Following this, all of the sound control blocks would be scanned and their sample buffer addresses reset to the beginning of the large sample buffer. While this method of handling the sample buffer seems redundant (the buffer address field of all sound control blocks is the same), keeping the information separate and with the sounds facilitates implementation of stereo or quad at a later time.

The last task is to determine if the specified duration of sound generation has elapsed. The time argument that was passed to this routine is simply decremented and tested for zero. If the time has not elapsed, the routine is simply executed again for another 30 samples. When the time is elapsed, the Level 3 NOTRAN interpreter regains control so that more events can be started.

NOTRAN Language

Level 3 routines in the NOTRAN system are what actually look at NOTRAN statements. Like the lower-level routines, most of the work is simply the manipulation of tables of information. Before discussing what these routines do, a brief description of the NOTRAN language itself is in order. Note that up to this point the sound generation routines are completely independent (within the constraints imposed by the sound generation models) of the actual music language used. Thus, language freaks could completely restructure the language and still use the sound generation routines that have been discussed.

As briefly mentioned earlier, NOTRAN uses a *textual* representation of the musical score. In designing such a representation, one is immediately faced with a problem: how should the score, which is basically a two-dimensional structure, be represented as a one-dimensional character string? The two dimensions in this case are time in the horizontal direction and "voices" or "parts" in the vertical dimension. Thus, the music language designer must choose between a *vertical* representation where the score is coded chord-by-chord in strict time sequence and a *horizontal* representation in which all of the notes, from beginning to end, for the first voice are coded followed by notes for the next voice, etc.

The former is probably easier to read (it can be likened to a conductor's score, which shows all of the instrument parts at once), while the latter may be easier to transcribe from a printed score into language statements. Of course, when the music is actually played, it must be presented to the synthesis routines or synthesizer in vertical form so the individual parts of a horizontal score must be "merged" into an internal vertical form for performance. Such a merging routine can become quite complex and unless "checkpoints," such as measure boundaries, are included in the language, a single duration error in a voice may misalign that voice for the remainder of the piece. Thus, for simplicity, NOTRAN uses a vertical score representation.

Of course, printed music scores are primarily graphic in nature. This coupled with the improved graphic capabilities of modern microcomputers suggests an interactive graphic score editor rather than a text language and standard text editor program. This in fact is done frequently in commercial products (see Chapter 20), but the author is opposed to doing this in an experimental synthesis system from three standpoints. First, common graphics resolution in the 500 × 300 range and less is simply too low to provide satisfactory rendition of all the various music score marks and still show more than a few measures at once. Another is that the graphic score tells *what* to play but very little about *how* to play it. Special conventions, such as horizontal entry of one part at a time and a way to refer to voice definitions, are necessary to insure that notes are matched with the proper waveforms, envelopes, etc. While this problem can certainly be overcome in a system as simple as NOTRAN, one quickly becomes bogged down when adapting conventional score notation to a more comprehensive synthesis program. And finally, writing even a minimal score-editor program is a very large task for an individual to tackle, certainly much larger than the synthesis routines outlined so far. One can spend months or years to come up with a good score editor before getting into the sound-synthesis programming at all!

Returning to the NOTRAN language as currently defined, it is in many ways similar to a step-by-step procedural computer language like FORTRAN or BASIC. Music code in the language is broken up into individual *statements*.

Each statement uses one (or more) lines of text and almost always starts with a *keyword* such as TEMPO or VOICE. The keywords, besides being easy to read, make it easy for the interpreter to identify the type of statement. The boundaries between statements either denote the passage of time or simply separate blocks of information.

NOTRAN statement types can be divided into three different groups. First, there is the *specification* group, which is used to define the characteristics of something such as an "instrument." Specification statements are instantaneous and do not consume any time in the musical performance. Next, there are *control* statements, which influence what notes are to be played and how they are to be played but again they do not consume any time. Finally, there are *note* statements that actually cause sound to be generated. Usually, but not always, a duration is associated with each note. Later, we will discuss the importance of durations in sequencing and coordinating multiple, simultaneous sounds. NOTRAN statements are executed sequentially, one after another. The standard language has no provisions for loops or repeats, etc.; that function is left for a Level 4 macroprocessor.

VOICE Statement

The VOICE statement is a specification statement used to define all of the parameters associated with tone-type sounds. Thus, the envelope, amplitude, and waveform parameters associated with tones must be

```
Example:  VOICE2  AD=80; DD=50; RD=250; SA=45; VA=15;
                  AW=H1,50,50; H2,20,25; H4,30,60;
                  DW=H1,100; H2,80; H3,20; SW=H2,75; H3,50; H4;
                  RW=H1

          VOICEn where n is the voice ID number

          AD  Attack Duration in milliseconds

          DD  Decay Duration in milliseconds

          RD  Release Duration in milliseconds

          SA  Sustain Amplitude in percent of peak attack amplitude

          VA  Voice amplitude in percent of DAC full scale range

          AW  Attack Waveform

          DW  Decay Waveform

          SW  Sustain Waveform

          RW  Release Waveform

          Hn  Harmonic number
```

Fig. 18–21. Voice statement format. The example defines a voice ID of 2, and attack duration of 80 msec, decay duration of 50 msec, release duration of 250 msec, sustain amplitude 45% of attack amplitude, and total voice amplitude 15% of overflow level. The attack waveform consists of fundamental, second, and fourth harmonics with relative amplitudes of 50%, 20%, and 30% of the full waveform amplitude and phases of 180°, 90°, and 216°, respectively. The decay waveform has fundamental, second, and fourth harmonics with amplitudes of 50%, 40%, and 10% of the total and random phase angles. The sustain waveform has second, third, and fourth harmonics with amplitudes of 33.3%, 22.2%, and 44.4% of the total and random phases. The decay waveform contains only the fundamental harmonic, which is, of course, 100% of the waveform.

specified. The syntax of the VOICE statement could be as simple as a string of parameters (numbers) separated by commas (this, in fact, is how the original version of NOTRAN worked), but with possibly dozens of parameters, it becomes very difficult for the user to read the statement. Therefore, the convention of *keyword parameters* is adopted whereby each parameter is identified by a two-character mnemonic. This method also allows parameters to be scrambled or omitted if desired. The statement interpreter then supplies default parameters for the omitted ones. For example, if a simple AR envelope is desired, then only the attack and release parameters need to be specified and the interpreter will set the decay duration and sustain amplitude to zero and unity, respectively.

Parameters are separated by semicolons and optionally spaces. The semicolons act as a signal to the interpreter that more parameters, possibly on the next line, follow. Parameters probably should not be split across line boundaries (whether this is a requirement depends on the interpreter implementation), and besides, splitting makes the statement hard to read. Parameters that specify a duration are always in units of milliseconds. Parameters that specify an amplitude are in terms of percent. Depending on the parameter type, the values of related parameters may have to add up to 100% or less. With other parameter types, the percentage figures merely establish ratios and can add up to any value, although individual parameters must be less than 100%. With these conventions for numerical parameters, integers can normally be used; however, a decimal point and fractional part can be tacked on for additional precision.

Figure 18–21 shows an example voice statement and a list of the keyword parameters available. The number immediately following the VOICE keyword is the ID number for the voice. Note statements using the voice will specify the ID number. During the course of the music, a particular voice number may be redefined as often as desired. There is no restriction on the numbers that can be used.

The AD, DD, and RD parameters are used to specify the durations, in milliseconds, of three phases of the ADSR envelope. The duration of the sustain phase depends on the note being played. The first letter identifies the envelope phase and the D is a mnemonic for duration. If a parameter is omitted, zero (actually 1 msec) is assumed. SA refers to sustain amplitude and gives the sustain level relative to the peak overshoot of the attack. Note that the percent figure refers to voltage amplitude; thus, a specification of 50 would give a sustain level 6 dB below the attack peak. Omission of this parameter gives a default of 100%.

The voice amplitude (VA) parameter is very important. Its basic function is to specify the amplitude of the voice relative to that of other sounds. The importance is due to the requirement that the *sum* of all of the *voice amplitudes* of all *simultaneous sounds* must not exceed 100% if total freedom from overflow is desired. This means that if at some point in the musical score 15 simultaneous sounds have been built up, the VA parameters associated with each sound should not add up to more than 100%. Observing this rule will virtually guarantee (since the filtered noise used in percussion instruments is random, it cannot be absolutely guaranteed) that overflow will not occur when the sounds are summed in the sample buffer. In most cases, with a lot of simultaneous sounds, the amplitude sum could substantially exceed 100% without undue risk of overflow because of the low probability of envelope and waveform peaks all coinciding at the same time.

The remaining parameters define the four waveforms associated with the four envelope phases. These are organized into groups of parameters. A group starts with a keyword, such as AW for attack wave, followed by an equals sign, which signals that a group of parameters follows. Within the group may be several parameter subgroups, each of which corresponds to a harmonic. The subgroup starts with the keyletter H (harmonic) immediately followed by a number defining the harmonic number. Commas then separate the parameters in the subgroup. The first parameter after the harmonic number is amplitude (in percent) and the second is phase in units of $2\pi/100$ (thus, 50 specifies 180°, 25=90°, etc.). The last parameter in a subgroup is followed with a semicolon if any more subgroups or groups follow; otherwise, the end of the statement is assumed. If the phase parameter is omitted, a random-number generator determines the phase, and, if the amplitude parameter is omitted, a 100% amplitude is assumed. Omitted harmonics, of course, have zero amplitude. The amplitude percentages in a waveform specification simply indicate relative harmonic amplitudes; there is no restriction on their sum, since the waveform will be scaled after it is computed. DW, SW, and RW are similarly used to specify groups of parameters for the other three waveforms. If a waveform is not defined for an envelope phase, the waveform of the previous segment will be used, which saves space in the waveform table area of memory. The attack segment must have a waveform specified.

PRCUS Statement

The PRCUS statement, which is detailed in Fig. 18–22, defines the sound of a percussion instrument. The ID number and duration and amplitude parameters closely parallel those of the voice statement. Since a two-phase envelope is used, only the AD and RD parameters are needed.

The use of filtered noise in the percussion sound model creates some interesting problems in specifying the amplitude of the filtered noise. The worst problem is that the parameters specified for the filter will greatly influence the perceived as well as actual amplitude of the filtered noise. Although the interpreter could look at the filter bandwidth and adjust the amplitude parameter, the correction will be inaccurate if the bandwidth changes during the sound. For simplicity, the noise amplitude parameter should simply be passed through with any necessary correction supplied by the user. Another problem with filtered noise is the fact that its peak amplitude cannot be predicted with certainty even if uniformly distributed noise samples are used. Nevertheless, this will seldom cause a problem unless the noise filter bandwidth is quite small and the percussive voice amplitude is a sizable portion of the DAC's range. If a problem is encountered, it would be easy to incorporate a test in the percussion sound generation routine to clip excessively large filtered noise samples.

The noise filter mode parameter is different because it uses mnemonics for its value. While convenient for the user, mode numbers could be used just as well to simplify the interpreter program. Parameter transitions are specified by giving two numbers separated by commas, the first of which is the initial value of the parameter and the second is the final value. The

```
Example:  PRCUS4  AD=10; RD=70; NA=30; SA=70; VA=10;
                  NM=BP; NF=400,600; NQ=3; SF=100,90; SQ=15

          PRCUSn where n is the percussive voice ID number

          AD  Attack Duration for filtered noise in milliseconds

          RD  Release Duration for filtered noise in milliseconds

          NA  Filtered noise amplitude in percent

          SA  Damped sine wave amplitude in percent

          VA  Voice Amplitude in percent of DAC full scale range

          NM  Noise filter Mode

              BP  Bandpass

              LP  Low-Pass

              HP  High-Pass

              BR  Band-Reject

          NF  Noise filter Frequency in Hertz  initial,final

          NQ  Noise filter Q factor   initial,final

          SF  damped Sine wave Frequency in Hertz  initial,final

          SQ  damped Sine wave Q factor
```

Fig. 18–22. Percussion statement format. The example defines a percussive sound with an ID of 4, a filtered noise attack duration of 10 msec, filtered noise release duration of 70 msec, filtered noise amplitude of 30%, damped sine amplitude of 70%, and overall amplitude of 10% of the DAC range. The noise filter mode is bandpass, and its center frequency increases from 400 Hz to 600 Hz during the 80-msec combined duration of the envelope. The noise filter *Q* factor is constant at 3, giving a 3-dB bandwidth of 133 Hz at the beginning of the sound. The damped sine wave frequency decreases from 100 Hz at a rate that will make it 90 Hz when the filtered noise envelope expires. The damped sine wave *Q* of 15 will give a ring time to −60 dB of about 330 msec assuming a constant frequency.

parameters specifying *Q* are different from the others in that they are pure numbers rather than percents or durations.

Linear transition of the ringing filter frequency under the control of an unrelated process (the noise envelope) can lead to some interesting error situations if a decreasing frequency is specified. The problem occurs when the center frequency decreases all the way to zero before the ringing is damped enough to deactivate the sound. If this occurs, the frequency may go negative (and therefore seem to start increasing from zero) or it might get stuck. With the constant *Q* form of the ringing filter, sticking at zero frequency would probably prevent the sound control block from ever being deactivated, even though it is not producing an audible sound. Again, exceptional condition testing is probably necessary to eliminate the effects of this kind of error. The testing can be relatively infrequent, however.

Control Statements

The basic level of NOTRAN has very few control statements. Many more would undoubtedly be added if the language is extended via a macroprocessor. One of the basic control statements is the TEMPO statement. The TEMPO statement essentially specifies a correspondence between musical time in terms of quarter notes, etc., and real time. The statement format is simply the keyword TEMPO followed by a valid duration specification (see the section on note statements), an equals sign, and a number specifying the number of milliseconds assigned to that duration. An example statement is:

TEMPO *Q*=350

where *Q* refers to a quarter note and the 350 specifies that the quarter note has a duration of 350 msec. If the time signature (which does not need to be specified) is 4/4, then this corresponds to a metronome marking of 170 beats/min.

The only other control statements are START and STOP. These keywords require no parameters and are merely used to skip over code while the score is "debugged." Sound generation is started when a START statement is encountered and suspended when a STOP statement is seen. With sound generation suspended, statements are interpreted and thrown away at great speed, thus allowing rapid syntax checking or skipping of sections known to be correct.

Comment lines may be inserted simply by making the first character on the line an *. The interpreter then ignores the remainder of the line and goes to the next.

Note that there are no jump or repeat statements and no provisions for subroutines (refrains) in the basic language. A little thought will reveal that if these are implemented in the Level 3 interpreter that the entire NOTRAN score would have to be in memory at once. During actual sound synthesis much, if not most, of memory will be needed for waveform tables, control blocks, and sample buffers. Although the text could be kept on disk and randomly accessed in response to a jump or refrain statement, such a facility is beyond many microcomputer operating systems. In any case, these functions will be left to a higher-level macroprocessor that has all of memory available when run.

Note Statements

Note statements are the only ones that actually produce sound and take real time to execute. Whereas the other statements all began with a keyword, a note statement begins with either an ID number or simply one or more blanks. The statement ID number is not important to the interpreter but may be included to identify various portions of the score such as measure numbers to the user. The remainder of the note statement consists of one or more *event* (note) specifications. As before, a semicolon following a specification is a signal that more follow on the same or next line.

Quite a bit of information is needed in the specification such as the voice ID, pitch, duration, and articulation so the syntax is somewhat condensed to save space without unduly affecting readability. For a tone event, the specification starts with a number corresponding to the voice statement defining the "instrument" that will play the event. Immediately following the voice ID is a single letter pitch mnemonic, which is simply one of the letters A–G. If the basic pitch must be sharped or flatted, the letter is followed by a # or an @ sign, respectively. Following this is a single digit specifying the octave where C4 through B4 spans the octave starting at middle C. Note that the octave numbers "turn over" at C in accordance with usual musical practice.

After the voice and pitch have been specified, the duration is needed. In the original version of NOTRAN, standard fractions such as 1/4 were used for the duration. However, single-letter mnemonics will be used here for the common durations as listed below:

W	Whole note
H	Half note
Q	Quarter note
E	Eighth note
S	Sixteenth note
T	Thirty-second note

These stock durations may be modified by appending one or more dots (periods) or the digit 3. The dot extends the duration specified to its left by 50% and can be repeated if desired, that is, Q.. is 75% longer than a standard quarter note. The "3" modifier indicates a triplet, which has a duration two-thirds of that specified. This format is much faster to type than the old fractional form but may not be quite as flexible. For example, tied notes are not readily specified, although for most common cases dots can be used to simulate tied notes. A general solution to situations such as a half note tied to an eighth note is left to the reader's imagination. (In the original version, a simple 5/8 would have been used.)

The final variable to specify is articulation. Currently, only staccato is recognized and is indicated by the letter "S" following all other specifications. When normal (legato) notes are interpreted and given to the sound generation routines, the sustain duration is made equal to the note duration minus the attack and decay duration. Thus, the release phase of the note occurs beyond its musical stopping point. If the note duration is shorter than the attack plus decay time, the full attack, decay, and release phases are still executed. When staccato is specified, the sustain duration is made unconditionally zero.

Obviously, with so many options in statement construction, a great variety of note specifications is possible. Below is a list of some legal specifications and how they are interpreted:

97 3C4Q	Voice 3, middle C, quarter note duration (the 97 is a tag and is not processed)
4E@4E.	Voice 4, E-flat just above middle C, dotted eighth duration (equivalent to 3/16)
2F#3S3S	Voice 2, F-sharp just below middle C, part of a sixteenth note triplet in which three notes take the time normally required by two of them. Staccato articulation.
19B@5Q3..S	What a mess! The duration should evaluate to $1/4 \times 2/3 \times 3/2 \times 3/2 = 9/24$. Voice 19 and staccato articulation are specified.

In a long score, much of this information seems to be redundant. For example, a melody line might run for dozens of notes in the same octave, yet the octave number must be specified for each note. If it weren't for the fact that several notes with the same voice ID can be playing simultaneously, it would be easy to have the NOTRAN interpreter assume octave numbers. Of course, the melody could just as well be split between two octaves and such assumptions would probably lead to numerous errors. Again, a general solution to this and other redundancies is left to the reader.

Percussive note specifications are much simpler than tones because only the voice number really has to be specified. The form: Pn is used where the P signals a percussive voice and n refers to the ID of a percussive voice definition. For convenience in certain situations, a duration specification identical to that described above can be appended.

Sequencing and Overlap

Now that the events themselves are fully specified, all that remains is to define their sequencing, which relies on just two simple, but very powerful, concepts. The first is that every note statement represents a distinct *point* in time. These time points are in the same sequence as the note statements. All of the events within a single note statement *start* at the point in time corresponding to the statement. Once started, each event runs for its duration and stops when finished, *completely independent* of other events started by this or earlier statements.

The second key concept involves spacing of the time points. Simply put, the *shortest specified duration* in a note statement determines the amount of real time that elapses until the next note statement is executed. Thus, if a note statement specifies a quarter-note event, two eighth-note events, and a sixteenth-note event, time equal to a sixteenth-note duration will elapse

Fig. 18–23. Note-sequencing examples

before the next statement is executed. The fact that three other notes are still playing in no way affects interpretation of the next statement. Note that durations specified with Qs, Es, etc., are what count. Even though a staccato quarter note may sound for only a sixteenth-note duration, its time value is still a quarter, and if that is the shortest time value in the statement, it will control the delay before the next statement. Likewise, a percussive event with a specified duration (which need have no relation to its actual sound duration) can control the statement duration.

Often, it is necessary to go on to the next statement even sooner. The rest specification is provided for this purpose. A rest specification is simply the letter R followed by a duration specification. Its only effect is to be factored into the shortest duration evaluation and if indeed the rest is the shortest, it will control when the next statement is executed. This use of the rest is quite different from normal use in which a particular voice is instructed to be silent. In NOTRAN, no sound is created unless a note or percussion specification specifies it; thus, the usual rests are not needed.

However, if a period of silence is needed, a statement having a lone rest specification can be used.

Figure 18–23 shows some common musical situations and how they might be coded in NOTRAN. This sequencing method is quite general and should be able to handle any situation likely to be encountered in reasonably conventional scores.

Level 3 Routines

The primary function of Level 3 software is to decode the NOTRAN statements that were just described and extract their information content. Conversely, if a typing or specification error is found, the condition should be reported to the user. The routines for statement scanning and syntax checking, however, are in the realm of compilers and other language analysis programs and are therefore beyond the scope of this text. Basic NOTRAN as specified here is very simple in comparison with a typical programming language; thus, a statement interpreter should not be very difficult to write even by one experienced in general programming but inexperienced in compilers. In fact, a successful interpreter can be written with no knowledge of classic compiler theory at all, just common sense. The main danger, however, is a program that might misinterpret an erroneous statement rather than flag it as an error.

Once a statement is decoded, its information content is systematically stored in tables. In the case of a voice statement, for example, the various envelope parameters are stored in a table that describes the characteristics of that voice. The waveform parameters are then used to compute a waveform table (or tables) that is stored away, and a pointer to the table is stored along with the envelope parameters. The voice ID is also part of these data. Before allocating additional table space, a scan is performed to determine if the same voice ID had been defined previously. If so, the new information replaces the old; otherwise, more table space is allocated. Percussive voice definitions are handled in the same way except that the parameters are different and no waveform table is needed. TEMPO statements simply update a single tempo variable, which then influences all succeeding time calculations.

When an actual event is encountered in a note statement, several operations must be performed. First, the voice ID is extracted and used to locate the table of information created earlier when the corresponding voice statement was processed. Next, a new event control block (ECB) is created (by scanning the control block area until an inactive one is found), and pertinent information such as waveform table addresses and envelope parameters are copied over to it. The frequency parameter in the ECB is set by further scanning the specification for pitch information. Next, the duration and articulation specifications are analyzed and the information used in conjunction with the tempo variable to set the sustain duration. Finally, the duration is compared with the current "shortest duration," which is updated if longer. After all events in the statement are processed, the current shortest will be the actual shortest, which is then passed as an argument to the Level 2 ECB scanner routine.

Level 4 Routines

The preceding has described a functionally complete direct digital music synthesis system that is quite usable as is. However, even higher-level programming can be added to further ease its use and reduce the amount of typing effort needed to encode a score. In a nutshell, Level 4 programming accepts a string of "extended NOTRAN" statements as input and produces a longer string of "basic NOTRAN" statements as output. This output string is then run through the synthesis program (Levels 1–3) as a separate operation. The details of Level 4 programming will not be described, but perhaps a discussion of some ideas and possibilities will give a hint of what could be accomplished.

One easy-to-incorporate enhancement would be a key signature capability. A new control statement would be added whereby the user could specify the key in which the music was written. Note statements then could be coded without explicit sharps and flats except where necessary. The Level 4 processor would provide all of the accidentals in the output score. It might be necessary to provide a semipermanent override capability, however, to cover atonal and highly modulated scores. As mentioned before, other redundancies such as octave selection could also be removed with similar facilities.

A somewhat more complex enhancement would be a transposition facility. Orchestral scores, for example, are written for instruments that actually sound pitches different from what the score says (and the player thinks). A B-flat trumpet, for example, sounds B-flat when the player reads and fingers C. The trumpet part of the score, therefore, has been adjusted so that the correct pitches are played. With transposition capability, one could declare that voice 3, for example, was a B-flat voice and therefore directly use notes from a B-flat instrument score.

Sophisticated sequence control could also be added. Simple repeats and jumps are obvious but a subroutine capability can allow many weird and wonderful things to be done. Like a software subroutine, a musical subroutine can be written once and then called by name whenever it is needed. Power comes from the fact that a subroutine can in turn call another one and so on. Thus, very complex sequences can be built up from a relatively small number of statements. Much of the usefulness of software subroutines is due to the ability to pass *arguments* that then alter the action of the routine in a specific way for that particular call. Arguments such as key signature, pitch register, tempo, and voicing would allow great variety in the expression of a musical subroutine without rewriting it. Some really nice effects can be accomplished if a single voice line can be subroutined independent of other simultaneous voice lines.

Many other possibilities should come to mind. In fact, the appearance of the input language need not even bear a resemblance to NOTRAN. In this respect, "basic NOTRAN" would be used as a musical "machine language" with a high-level compiler generating code for it.

Level 0 Routines

Although seemingly out of sequence, Level 0 routines are discussed here because for most microcomputer direct synthesis installations they would comprise a separate program and separate pass of the data. As mentioned earlier, Level 0 routines operate on the individual sound samples produced by the Level 1 routines to introduce reverberation, choral effects, etc. The reader should not underestimate the utility of these simple techniques in enhancing and "de-mechanizing" the sound of even the most sophisticated synthesis methods.

The techniques described in Chapter 14, however, require large amounts of memory for simulated delay lines and therefore would probably not fit if implemented as part of the synthesis program. Thus, Level 0 functions would be written to read a sample stream from a mass storage device, process it, and write the altered stream on another device.

In some cases, the "acoustical environment" created by the Level 0 routines must change during the course of the score. If the ability to dynamically specify reverberation parameters is desired, the Level 0 program will also have to scan the score while processing the sample string. Virtually all of the score data will be ignored, but timing will have to be followed to determine where in the sample string to change reverberation parameters.

Sample Storage Devices

The mass-storage device used to hold computed sample data usually determines a delayed playback synthesis system's performance in two ways. First, its *average* data transfer rate limits the number of channels, sample size, and ultimately the sample rate that can be used. "Average" was emphasized because this figure is often much lower than the peak transfer rate often quoted in sales literature. With a disk, for example, nonproductive gaps between sectors, finite head movement time from one track to the next, and sector format restrictions, all subtract from theoretical average transfer rates. If the sample data are read using the computer's operating system as opposed to direct programming of the hardware, severe performance degradation can often occur due to operating system overhead. A 10-to-1 slowdown is not uncommon, thus making direct hardware programming a necessity in many cases.

The other performance determinant is, of course, mass-storage capacity. How storage capacity relates to continuous time capacity and other variables can be determined by applying these very simple formulas:

$$C = TNRB \qquad T = \frac{C}{NRB} \qquad R = \frac{C}{TNB} \qquad N = \frac{C}{TRB} \qquad B = \frac{C}{TNR}$$

where T is sound storage time in seconds, C is storage capacity in bytes, N is the number of sound channels (1 for mono, 2 for stereo, etc.), R is the sample rate in samples per second, and B is the number of bytes per sample (2 for 16-bit samples, 1.5 for 12-bit samples, etc.). Thus, with a 10M byte storage capacity, 16-bit samples, two channels, and 40-ks/s sample rate, the program length would be just over a minute. Conversely, one channel, 12-bit samples, and 25-ks/s would be over 4 min with only a slight effect on sound quality. One way to avoid the tyranny of these numbers is to use *two* mass storage devices with *removable* media. Then, assuming that the storage media can be swapped on one unit before the other is exhausted, one can obtain indefinite program lengths with a little manual intervention. Seldom are synthesis results archived on expensive computer media. Instead, when the project is complete, it is converted into analog form and recorded on conventional audiotape.

In the past, half-inch-wide digital magnetic tape was often used for sample storage, since disk space was simply too expensive to consider and the tape media was relatively cheap at around a dollar per megabyte. Such tape units are still used on large mainframe computers but are almost never seen on a microcomputer because of size (a moderate performance unit is as big as a large microwave oven and weighs 100 pounds) and expense ($2,000 and up). They are also clearly not random-access devices, which is necessary for applications other than strict sequential synthesis. Some of the newer "streaming" tape drives intended for backup of fixed disk data have potential for sample storage but tend to be as expensive as a disk of the same capacity and much less flexible.

Today, disks are almost universally used for sample storage. "Hard" disk drives with 5, 10, or even 20M byte capacity are so popular and reasonably priced now that they are built into many 16-bit microcomputers as standard equipment. Larger-capacity external units with 40, 80, and even 160M byte capacity are available, although the cost starts pushing past $2,000. These are all "fixed-media" disk drives, which means that the disk cannot be removed. Thus, sample data competes for storage space with the operating system and other programs and data stored on the disk. Removable media hard disk drives for microcomputers generally have capacities of only 5 or 10M byte, but, as mentioned earlier, two such drives could provide unlimited program length with some manual swapping. Even modern floppy disk drives can perform satisfactorily in many applications. Units are now available with up to 2.5M bytes on a 5-inch diskette, but the data transfer rate is limited to about 40K bytes per second.

Playback Program

After sound samples for the score are all computed and saved on a mass storage device, the last step is playing them back through the DAC for conventional recording. Because of the sustained high data rate involved and the requirement for an absolutely stable sample rate, this tends to be a highly specialized program that may not be easy to write. Most of the problems are due to the fact that samples are stored in blocks on the mass medium. With IBM-type tape, the time lapse between blocks is fairly constant and predictable. Disks are far more erratic. If the next sector is even barely missed, the playback program will have to wait a full revolution before reading it again. Even more time is wasted when a track seek is necessary. Also, rereading a block after an error is usually out of the question, so top-quality recording media are a must. The net effect of such an erratic input data flow is that as much memory as possible should be used as a data buffer.

Details of the playback program are heavily dependent on the system configuration. The ideal situation is an audio DAC that is interfaced to the system as a direct memory access (DMA) device and a mass storage system that is also a DMA device. The DAC could be configured so that it continuously scans, say, 16K words of memory in a circular fashion and generates an interrupt whenever wraparound occurs. The playback program then attempts to keep ahead of the DAC by reading records from the storage device. Of course, the records cannot be read too fast or the DAC may be "lapped." This, of course, assumes a system that can support simultaneous DMA, such as many of the larger bus-oriented 68000 and 8086 based computers.

A livable system can often be put together when only one of the two data streams is under DMA control. The easiest situation would be a DMA DAC coupled with a programmed transfer mass storage device. Execution time constraints on the playback program would remain lenient as long as sample entry into the buffer did not fall behind the DAC. Programmed transfer to the DAC with DMA sample reading is a less desirable situation. Assuming that the DAC is merely double-buffered (can hold one sample in a register while converting the previous one), the playback program must be free every sample period to get the next sample loaded before the previous one expires. While not difficult to do most of the time, the data must be kept flowing even while servicing exceptional conditions on the storage device such as an end of record interrupt or seeking to the next track. In either case, DMA activity must not lock the processor out for long periods of time.

The declining cost of memory is making another audio DAC interfacing option practical. The DAC itself could be equipped with a very large first-in–first-out data buffer and thereby greatly simplify both the writing and timing of a playback program. In fact, when using such a DAC, DMA data transfer is not necessary either from the storage device or to the DAC. In an all-programmed I/O system using a disk, for example, one could simply write a new programmed disk data transfer routine that stores bytes read from the disk data register directly into the DAC data register without ever going through the computer's own main memory at all. The DAC's buffer automatically bridges the unpredictable gaps in disk data flow provided the average transfer rate is great enough. Nowadays, it is perfectly feasible to have a 16K or 64K sample buffer built into the DAC, which is large enough to survive data flow interruptions up to a second or more depending on the sample rate.

The Author's Delayed-Playback Installation

To conclude this section, it seems appropriate to briefly describe the author's present delayed-playback synthesis setup as an example of what can be done with rather ordinary, currently available hardware. The computer is an MTU-130, an obscure 6502-based unit with 80K of standard memory, a 480 × 256 graphics display, two 8-inch floppy disk drives, and an excellent performance-oriented operating system. To the standard unit has been added an 8-MHz 68000 slave processor board with 256K of additional RAM. The audio D-to-A converter has gone through several revisions starting with 12 bits, mono, and a 256-sample buffer, followed by 12-bit stereo with A-to-D capability and a 1K buffer, and finally becoming 16 bits (with a 12-bit mode) and a 32K buffer. Although the disk drives use DMA data transfer into RAM, all three of the converter designs used programmed I/O; the current version in fact simply plugs into the computer's standard parallel printer port.

For digital audio recording and playback, the 8-inch floppy disks have a theoretical average transfer rate of about 40K bytes/sec and a capacity of 1.26M bytes. This is normally used to provide a single-channel 25-ks/s rate using 12-bit samples, which yields about 33 sec per disk. Block compounding is used, however, to obtain 16-bit dynamic range, and the two drives allow disk swapping for unlimited program length. Full 16-bit samples can also be transferred at 20 ks/s for 31 sec. For maximum usable disk storage capacity and transfer rate, a data format with 1K byte sectors is used. The 1K sectors are then divided into four 256-byte *sound blocks*, which is the basic unit of sound file storage. In 12-bit mode, each sound block holds 170 samples with the odd byte left over holding a gain value that is applied to the whole block. Direct programming of the disk hardware was necessary because the operating system runs at only 20K bytes/sec for disk data.

For music software, the NOTRAN system described in this chapter (less percussion) was coded into 6502 assembly language. The waveform tables used for tone synthesis are 256 points of 8 bits but with linear interpolation between points. Although the voice waveforms are only 8 bits before the amplitude envelope is applied, all later processing is carried to 16 bits of accuracy. This compromise greatly speeds up multiplication, which is a software subroutine on the 6502, and is nearly impossible to hear when several instruments are playing. The same Bach score transcribed 10 years earlier was run through the system and required about 5 hours of processing time for the 8 min piece; about a 40-to-1 ratio. In addition to NOTRAN, there is a playback program, a record program (A-to-D conversion into a sound file), a reverberation program, and several miscellaneous utilities.

For the immediate future, NOTRAN, of course, will be recoded into 68000 assembly language, which should provide about a 6-to-1 speedup along with greater precision (1K waveform tables with 16-bit samples). A pair of removable media 10M byte disk drives is also being added, which should allow stereo operation at 30–40 ks/s and several minutes per disk. Since the 68000 promises to be a popular microprocessor for music synthesis and can run high-level languages such as C reasonably efficiently, it should also be possible to run some of the other delayed-playback synthesis programs being developed at universities. The CARL system, which will be described in the next chapter, seems to have the most potential in this respect.

SECTION IV

Product Applications and the Future

At this point, it is time to describe some real-world applications of the theory studied in previous sections. In fact, there is probably no better way to get a feel for the *real* advantages and disadvantages of all of the synthesis and modification techniques described in those sections. This will also allow a chance to see how the market realities of cost, consumer acceptance, and ease of use enter into and usually dominate a product's technical design. The discussion will begin in Chapter 19 with serious applications in professional instrument design and university level research. Entertainment and novelty applications, which have been largely ignored so far, will be described in Chapter 20. And, finally, Chapter 21 takes a brief look at the potential future of computer-synthesized music.

19

Some Real Applications

In previous discussions, synthesis, modification, and analysis techniques were described as individual tools that could be used independently or combined in myriad ways to achieve a desired acoustical result. Indeed, in research applications of music and sound synthesis, one would probably prefer to have just the individual tools available without any externally imposed structure or limitations on how they may be used together. Whereas such a collection of tools really just constitutes an *environment* in which music creation can take place, a saleable product must be more organized for easy learning and less general for an acceptable cost. In fact, such a product is usually called a *synthesizer,* a term that has already been used frequently without really being defined.

Synthesizers in the Real World

In the context of this chapter, a synthesizer is essentially a self-contained machine designed to produce a wide variety of, hopefully, musical sounds in response to commands received from the outside. Any technology can be used to build a synthesizer (in the last century, pressure-actuated air columns were used), but, of course, analog and digital electronic techniques are of interest here. A true synthesizer already "knows" how to produce sound; an elaborate setup or programming procedure is not necessary to get at least simple sound out. Thus, a computer with a DAC alone is not a synthesizer, even though with programming it could produce any sound. However, a computer plus DAC bundled with a control interface and a ROM synthesis program could be sold as a synthesizer. Any practical synthesizer uses only a small subset of the many possible sound-generation techniques available. These may be chosen with generality, ease of control, or cost in mind according to the application ("market" in product planning terminology) the synthesizer will be designed for.

Live Performance Synthesizers

What, then, are the markets and applications for synthesizers? Many have been alluded to in previous chapters but were never focused upon.

Clearly, the mass market for synthesizers at this time is live performance in small bands by professional and semi-professional players. The term "mass market" implies two things. First, it refers to the needs of *average* potential customers, i.e., those with average skill, intelligence, and typically low interest in the technical aspects of their instruments. Second, because the mass market of average potential customers is so large (maybe 70–90% of the total market), it is where the competition is fiercest. There is a direct parallel apparent in the personal computer industry where mass market computers are promoted in terms of ease of use rather than flexibility or performance, and low cost rather than quality or reliability.

A mass market live performance synthesizer must be able to change patches ("sounds" and "programs" are common instruction manual terms) quickly and surely at any time. Quickly usually means instantaneously such as between musical phrases, and surely means a procedure so simple that embarrassing mistakes are unlikely. Typically, each combination of sound parameters is given a number and that combination can be called up by pressing one of 50 or so numbered keys or entering a two-digit number on a keypad. The parameters themselves are supplied by the manufacturer in printed, ROM, or digital cassette form or possibly determined by experiment during rehearsal. A live performance synthesizer must "sound good" in that it must not sound cheap or overtly electronic. Great flexibility and generality are usually secondary considerations as long as a reasonable range of sounds is possible. During sales demonstrations, realism in simulating conventional instruments is often promoted as an indication of the instrument's quality and flexibility. In actual use, where just the mood of a particular instrument's sound is preferable to a flawed duplication, such patches are infrequently used. Finally, a live performance synthesizer must be reasonably portable, at least by two people, and rugged and reliable enough so that it works upon arrival.

Studio Synthesizers

Of course, there are other markets for synthesizers, although much smaller than the mass market just described. One of these is *studio synthesizers,* which are used for creating music directly in recorded form rather than in a live performance situation. Although much studio work goes into creating record albums, the major use of studio synthesizers is in producing soundtracks for radio and TV ads and for the thousands of movies, TV programs, and documentaries released every year. Synthesized music has become so pervasive in this field that 50–75% of such "commercial music" is synthesized now. Although no attempt is made to simulate an orchestra, the sounds typically used are bland enough to avoid calling attention to themselves for all but the most critical listener. It is interesting to note that, although the studio synthesizer market is relatively small, its musical *product* is aimed at the very large mass market of TV and movie viewers and radio and album listeners.

While regular live performance synthesizers are certainly used in studio work, the requirements are different. For example, the ability to immediately change patches is less important because the tape can be edited later. Elaborate and complex programming and parameter setting schemes are admissable if they result in greater flexibility, since nobody hears the mistakes and evolution toward a desired sound. In fact, flexibility is the most important attribute because the synthesizer must adapt to a variety of very different musical situations; not just rock music on stage. Time is available to experiment in finding just the right sound, and, when it is found for a particular job, it need never be duplicated again. Sound quality is more important than in live performance where other instruments and the crowd (not to mention overloaded amplifier/speaker systems) tend to cover up subtle imperfections. Finally, a studio-oriented synthesizer need not be portable. In fact, many "studios" are built around a synthesizer in the owner's home and may consist of little more than the synthesizer and a multitrack tape machine.

Research Synthesizers

Another specialized application area is in academic research. Here, a synthesizer may be used in two ways. In psychoacoustic research (the study of human hearing perception), a synthesizer may be used to generate a very precise stimulus sound. The sounds needed, such as sine-wave bursts with controlled amplitude and frequency contours, are generally simple but must be very accurate and repeatable for reliable experimental results. Thus, a synthesizer for such research must be flexible (although the sounds needed may be simple, they are not necessarily musical and thus may not be in the repertoire of a "music" synthesizer) and accurate. The accuracy requirement often goes far beyond what is typically necessary for a synthesizer to "sound good." Distortion, frequency stability, and background noise must often be a factor of 10 better than accepted human perception limits to positively insure that experimental results are not affected. Frequently, specialized equipment is designed and built rather than buying a commercially available synthesizer either because something suitable doesn't exist or to save money. A computer with a high-quality DAC is probably the optimum choice for most of these needs, but then custom software must usually be written.

The other major research application is in studying synthesis techniques themselves. Here, extreme flexibility is the primary and oftentimes only requirement. Since the research object is new synthesis techniques, commercial synthesizers with fixed, built-in synthesis algorithms are unlikely to be of much interest. Instead, a programmable synthesizer in which the *structure* as well as the parameters can be changed is needed. Much current research is directed toward discovering simple synthesis techniques that give acceptable results in a limited number of cases rather than re-proving the generality of brute-force techniques such as direct harmonic synthesis. The FM, VOSIM, and nonlinear distortion techniques described earlier are the results of some of this research. Obviously, evaluation of new techniques involves psychoacoustic tests as well. Again, a direct computer synthesis system is probably the best low-cost solution to the immediate algorithm implementation and testing problem. However, the final goal of many such projects is the development of simpler and cheaper *hardware* using the new technique that performs audibly as well as earlier equipment using a more general technique. Thus, the academic research market is best served by D-to-A conversion equipment for general-purpose computers and specialized signal-processing computers rather than the typical packaged synthesizer.

Music Education

Music education is another fairly large market area with specialized requirements. Until recently, this market was served entirely by conventional instruments and almost by definition had no interest in electronic instruments. Now, however, the whole spectrum of personal computers and synthesizers is playing an increasing role in music education, particularly at the lower levels. It is becoming common for children to be first exposed to the mechanics of music (pitch, rhythm, melodies, notation, etc.) via some kind of simple music program on a home computer. Indeed, a big advantage of using such programs is that a child can produce a reasonably listenable final result as soon as the program is understood, long before any significant manual skills could be developed. This may in turn sustain interest through a child's critical interest-forming years.

In the intermediate stages involving ear training (learning to recognize intervals and chords) and music dictation training (learning to notate what is heard), drill programs on personal computers can be very helpful. More advanced instruction in compositional methods and analysis can also be more effectively done with interactive composition programs. It will probably be awhile before keyboard synthesizers make much headway in replacing the piano in performance training, although they could greatly reduce the boredom factor that causes many "piano students" to drop out after two or three years. Some of the very low-cost keyboard synthesizers becoming available may force their way into this realm on purely economic as well as pedantic grounds.

In most of the areas just mentioned, great synthesis power and flexibility are not required. In fact, a simple three- or four-voice square-wave synthesizer can be perfectly adequate in many cases. Modern personal computers usually have such capability built in as will be described in the next chapter. For more advanced needs, add-on products are available for the more popular computers that can have quite significant musical capabilities.

The Synthesizer Industry

The manufacture of synthesizers and related products is actually a 120 million dollar industry worldwide (estimated 1984 figures). Some 25 manufacturers are directly involved with making complete synthesizers, and many more make key parts such as keyboards and control panels. Since a synthesizer is almost entirely electronic, it is not surprising that a large segment of the industry actually resides in Japan while smaller portions are in Italy and Australia, to name a few. The United States, however, is the lion's share of the market at 65%.

The most striking feature of the synthesizer industry is that it is extremely competitive. Several large companies are involved (most of them are not exclusively synthesizer manufacturers or even muscial instrument manufacturers) as well as many smaller companies dedicated to synthesizer manufacture. No one manufacturer dominates the industry as is the case with, say, personal computers. Real innovation, such as the MIDI interface standard, frequently comes from the smaller companies, whereas the larger ones specialize in production efficiency, which lowers the cost of "mainstream" instruments.

Besides from each other, much of the competition in the synthesizer industry comes from conventional instruments. This war is largely fought in music stores; there is very little mail-order activity in synthesizers. Unfortunately, when dealing with average consumers, technical specifications and actual sonic performance may actually play a minor role in the buying decision. For example, many pianos and organs are bought as furniture! Considerations of styling, color, and perhaps the manufacturer's prestige may actually govern which unit will be bought. Even if the intention is to purchase and play a fine instrument, more often than not it will ultimately sit unused in a corner looking good. Even though a 50-pound portable synthesizer may cost the same, be easier to play, and could possibly sound like a full orchestra, it stands little chance of being purchased under these conditions.

Another striking feature of the synthesizer market is the incredibly fast pace of product innovation and obsolence. For example, the major synthesizer industry trade show is the twice-yearly NAMM show (National Association of Music Merchants). It is not unusual for an innovative product unveiled at one show to be answered by several similar but improved products at the next. What makes this even more amazing (at least to those whose background is in the computer industry) is that products shown are expected to be available, in production quantities, right then or at most 1–2 months later. The usual computer industry development lag of 1–2 years to announcement and 6 or more months of production delay after that has little chance in the synthesizer industry. In fact, the complete marketing life cycle (not useful life cycle) of a keyboard synthesizer is commonly 2 or perhaps 3 years at the most.

Hybrid Keyboard Synthesizers

In the mass market, the term "synthesizer" really means "keyboard synthesizer." As that name implies, the primary operator interface device is a piano-like keyboard, usually with 61 keys (five octaves), although 73 or even 88 for high-end and 49 for budget units are also seen. The keyboard is virtually always completely conventional. The keys are a standard size and shape and move a standard distance in response to a standard force. Many high-end units even attempt to simulate the inertia of piano keys by using weights, throw-bars, or other mechanisms. As in the computer market, any significant departure from such a "standard" keyboard meets vigorous customer resistance.

Besides the keyboard, the operator typically has two hand-operated variable controls available. These are frequently called "wheels" because of their smooth action and have a spring return to their center position. Usually, one of them is patched into all of the instrument's oscillators so that the whole instrument can be shifted flat or sharp and is called the pitch wheel or pitch bender. The other is available to be patched into any sound variable and is usually called the modulation wheel. Added to these hand-operated performance controls are one or two foot pedals that plug into jacks on the instrument. Usually, one is a simple on–off switch to control note sustain, while the other may be a variable control for volume or some other parameter.

The most visible distinction among keyboard synthesizers is in their control or *programming* panel. Every manufacturer and model is intentionally different, much like video games. Since most keyboard synthesizers are microprocessor-controlled internally, common digital devices such as push-button switches, thumbwheel switches, calculator keypads, light-emitting diodes (LEDs), and numeric displays are commonly used. It is not unusual for a front panel to be 8–10 inches high and as wide as the keyboard, with much of that area covered by dozens of individual buttons and lights and several different displays, button groups, and a keypad or two. Recent units have used alphanumeric and even low-resolution graphics liquid crystal and fluorescent displays and membrane buttons.

Readers with a computer background may question the wisdom of using all of this "stuff" when a small alphanumeric keyboard and CRT display would be much neater and more general. Part of the answer is historical, since current control panel practice is an evolution of simple early panels in which a CRT did not make sense. Also, CRTs are not always as rugged as might be desired for a portable live performance instrument. Studio-oriented keyboard synthesizers do exist that make use of a CRT display or in some cases a separate conventional CRT terminal. In the future, liquid crystal display panels may be able to approach CRT resolution at a competitive cost and thus negate these objections.

One very cost-effective method of implementing the sound generator in a keyboard synthesizer is to use *hybrid* circuitry. "Hybrid" here means a

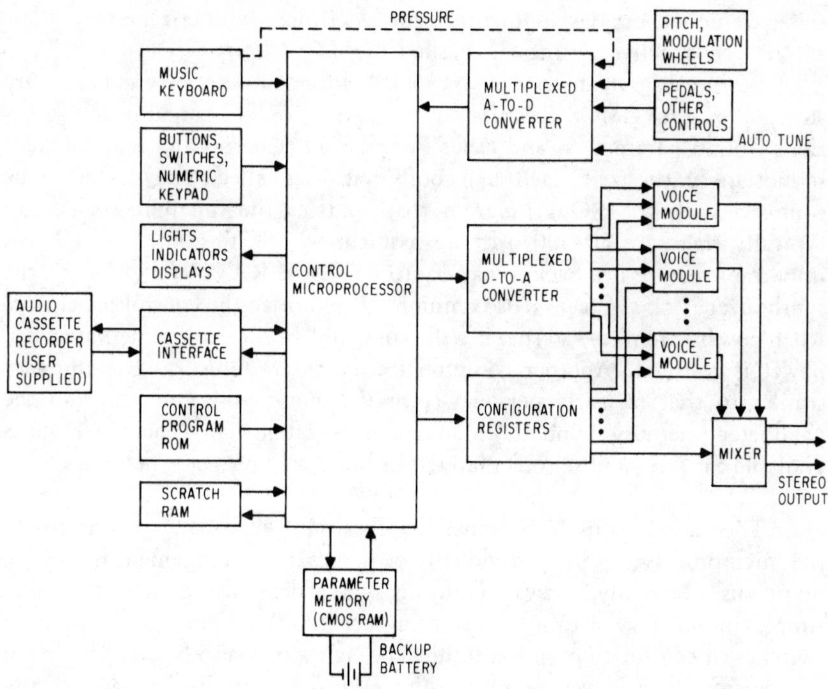

Fig. 19–1. Typical microprocessor-controlled hybrid keyboard synthesizer

combination of analog and digital circuitry, applying each where it is most advantageous. Control-type tasks are best handled by digital circuitry, particularly if it is microprocessor based. For example, implementing a multinote polyphonic keyboard would be extremely difficult with analog circuitry but is a straightforward exercise with digital circuitry as was demonstrated in Chapter 9. On the other hand, audio-signal-handling tasks such as filtering are much more economical to perform with analog circuitry. Thus, at this time, it is generally most cost-effective to use a hybrid approach to designing a moderate-performance, moderately priced keyboard synthesizer.

A Typical Hybrid Synthesizer

Figure 19–1 shows a generic block diagram of a microprocessor-controlled hybrid keyboard synthesizer. Central, of course, is the control microprocessor, which is typically one of the more powerful 8-bit units, although increasingly 16-bit architecture processors with 8-bit data buses or even true 16-bit units are being used. The microprocessor program always resides in permanent memory, either masked ROM or programmable ROM, and may be 8–32K or even more. EPROMs are frequently seen because sales volumes are often not high enough to justify ROM masking charges. Also, the extremely short development schedules of most synthesizers don't allow 10–20 weeks' delivery time for masked ROMs.

Besides a small amount of scratch RAM for computation and temporary storage, a larger CMOS RAM is normally used to hold patching configurations, sound parameters, and other information that specifies how different sounds are synthesized. Each such configuration is called a *program* (not to be confused with the ROM program that controls the microprocessor), and typically there are 50–100 or more requiring 2–4K to hold them all. An important feature is a backup battery to retain the RAM's content when the synthesizer is off. In fact, it is common to memorize the control panel state when power is removed so that it will "come up" in the exact same state when power is restored. Another common feature is an audio cassette interface similar to that on early personal computers for saving and restoring the parameter memory content. Manufacturers often have parameter tapes available for sale, and serious players can build a library of synthesizer voice tapes.

The various console buttons, switches, and keypads are connected to the microprocessor either individually or in a matrix arrangement if they are numerous. Generally, software performs switch debouncing and even makes simple momentary action pushbuttons act like alternate action latching switches in conjunction with a light. The lights may also be directly driven by register bits; however, multidigit seven-segment displays are usually multiplexed by software. For extensive alphanumeric panels, which may have 20–40 characters, "intelligent displays" may be used, which automatically refresh themselves. Then the synthesizer processor need only store bytes in a small RAM in the display.

The music keyboard is generally interfaced just like the one described in Chapter 9. Velocity sensing is performed by measuring the time differential between two contact closures. A more recent keyboard design has each key press two conductive rubber pads against patterns on a printed circuit board. One pad touches when the key is about one-third depressed, and the second touches at the three-quarter mark. The advantage of this approach is somewhat less contact bounce and significantly lower manufacturing cost in large volumes. One manufacturer even uses LEDs and photocells for zero bounce key position sensing. Because the keyboard must be scanned very rapidly and uniformly for accurate velocity sensing, it is sometimes given its own independent microprocessor rather than burdening the synthesizer's main processor with this task.

The actual sound-generating and control elements are on the right side of Fig. 19–1. Typically, each synthesizer voice is produced by a moderately small voice module that may either plug into an internal "synthesizer bus" or be part of a large synthesizer board. Such a module usually has two VCOs, two to four VCAs, and a VCF plus several analog switches for reconfiguring these elements in a number of useful, but not totally general, ways. The

Fig. 19–2. Rhodes "Chroma" keyboard synthesizer

needed control voltages are produced by a centralized, multiplexed D-to-A converter, usually 12 bits, and the analog configuration switches are controlled by external registers. Generally six to eight voice modules are included, although some synthesizers may be expandable. A final analog switch array selects the module outputs and mixes them into a stereo audio output.

A multiplexed A-to-D converter is also included to read the pitch and modulation wheels, variable footpedal, and other proportional operator controls. If the keyboard includes pressure sensing, this too is connected to the ADC. There may be either a single sensor under the entire keyboard or individual sensors under each key. Often a signal from the voice module output multiplexor is fed back to the ADC for diagnostic usage and *automatic tuning,* which will be described in the next section.

The Rhodes Chroma

Perhaps the best way to become familiar with the specifics of hybrid synthesizer technology is to briefly study a well-designed example unit. The Rhodes Chroma, pictured in Fig. 19–2, is one such synthesizer that sells in the $3,000–5,000 range. It is packaged into a wooden tabletop cabinet that weighs about 70 pounds and has a five-octave, 61-key keyboard, also made of wood. The control panel is mounted above the keyboard and is largely a printed plastic overlay sheet with an array of 50 membrane switches, several slide pots, several individual LEDs, a large two-digit display, and a smaller eight-digit display. One interesting feature is a solenoid "tapper" that literally thumps the control panel when any of the membrane switches is

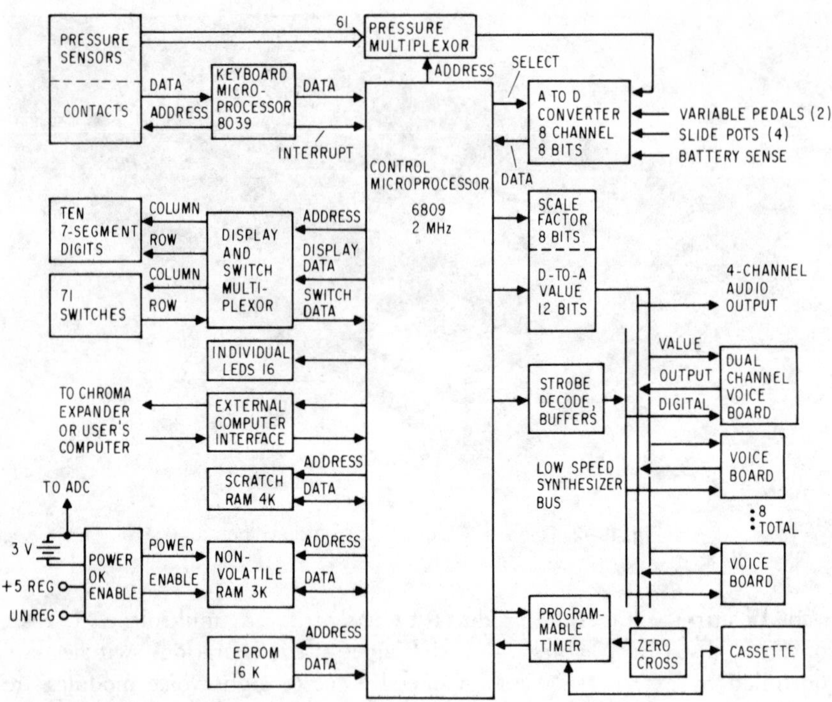

Fig. 19–3. Rhodes Chroma block diagram

activated. This gives a "tactile" feedback to the panel that is effective even in the 100-dB din of on-stage live performance. The customary "wheels" are two spring-return-to-center slide pots mounted alone immediately to the left of the keyboard.

Performance-wise, the Chroma has 16 oscillators that can be used for 16 independent, simple voices, although they are usually "paired" to make eight complex voices. The elements of each complex voice may be configured 16 different ways with each voice independently configurable. Included in these configurations are standard VCO-VCF-VCA, FM, and AM patches plus a digital "ring modulation" patch and a "sync" mode in which one oscillator "pulls" the frequency of the other. The oscillators as well as the filters and gain control elements are all analog with an automatic tuning feature to compensate for calibration errors and drift. Envelope generators, however, are "virtual" in that they are implemented in software and applied via the multiplexed DAC. Velocity sensing on the downstroke is standard, whereas individual key pressure is an optional feature.

Figure 19–3 is a specific block diagram of the Chroma, which is quite similar to the generic diagram described earlier. One difference is the use of a separate microprocessor, from a completely different family, to scan the keyboard contacts. The keyboard pressure sensors, however, are addressed by the main processor, which only looks at those associated with currently pressed keys. As is customary in pocket calculators, the matrix arrangement for the 10 seven-segment displays is also wired into the 71 membrane switches, thus saving some circuitry. The 16 individual LEDs, however, are driven directly by two 8-bit registers. An unusual feature is the external computer interface that is intended for connection to a Chroma *expander.* The 4K scratch RAM is used for holding expanded copies of currently active parameter lists and queues for data entering and leaving the external computer interface. The 3K CMOS RAM is sufficient to hold 100 complete patches, of which two can be in use at any one time. The program ROM at 16K is rather large, but, as is usually the case with software, the control program has grown to equal (actually slightly exceed) its capacity.

Since the A-to-D converter only needs to digitize eight variables that all come from the operator, an 8-channel 8-bit unit with a 100-μsec conversion time was sufficient. The 61 pressure sensors on the keyboard pass through a separate multiplexor into one of the ADC channels. The D-to-A converter actually consists of an 8-bit unit wired to supply the reference voltage to a 12-bit unit. Thus, the 8-bit DAC determines the *span* and thus the step size of the 12-bit main converter within a fairly narrow $\pm 6\%$ range. The variable scale factor is used by the automatic tuning routine that will be described later. The single-channel DAC output in conjunction with the outputs of a strobe decoder and buffer registers are routed as a bus to a synthesizer motherboard into which eight dual-channel voice boards are plugged. The strobes then can address a particular board and a particular parameter sample-and-hold on the board to give the effect of a multichannel DAC. The output of each voice can also be routed to another bus line that feeds into a zero-crossing detector used for automatic tuning. A special programmable timer circuit coordinates synthesizer operation by interrupting the control program at a constant rate, generating the cassette output signal and measuring the period for the cassette input and zero-crossing detector signals. All of these subsystems will be described in more detail in the following sections.

Dual-Channel Voice Board

Probably the most interesting subsystem is the dual-channel voice board, which is responsible for all sound generation in the Chroma. Eight boards are used and each plugs into a slot on the synthesizer bus. Figure 19–4 is a simplified schematic diagram of the board. Operation is completely controlled by 19 digital bits from three on-board registers and eight analog voltages from an eight-way demultiplexor and eight sample-and-holds on board. Thus, digital and analog demultiplexing is performed on each board from the common synthesizer bus rather than at a central location. In the drawing, a digital control signal is represented by a square-shaped terminal,

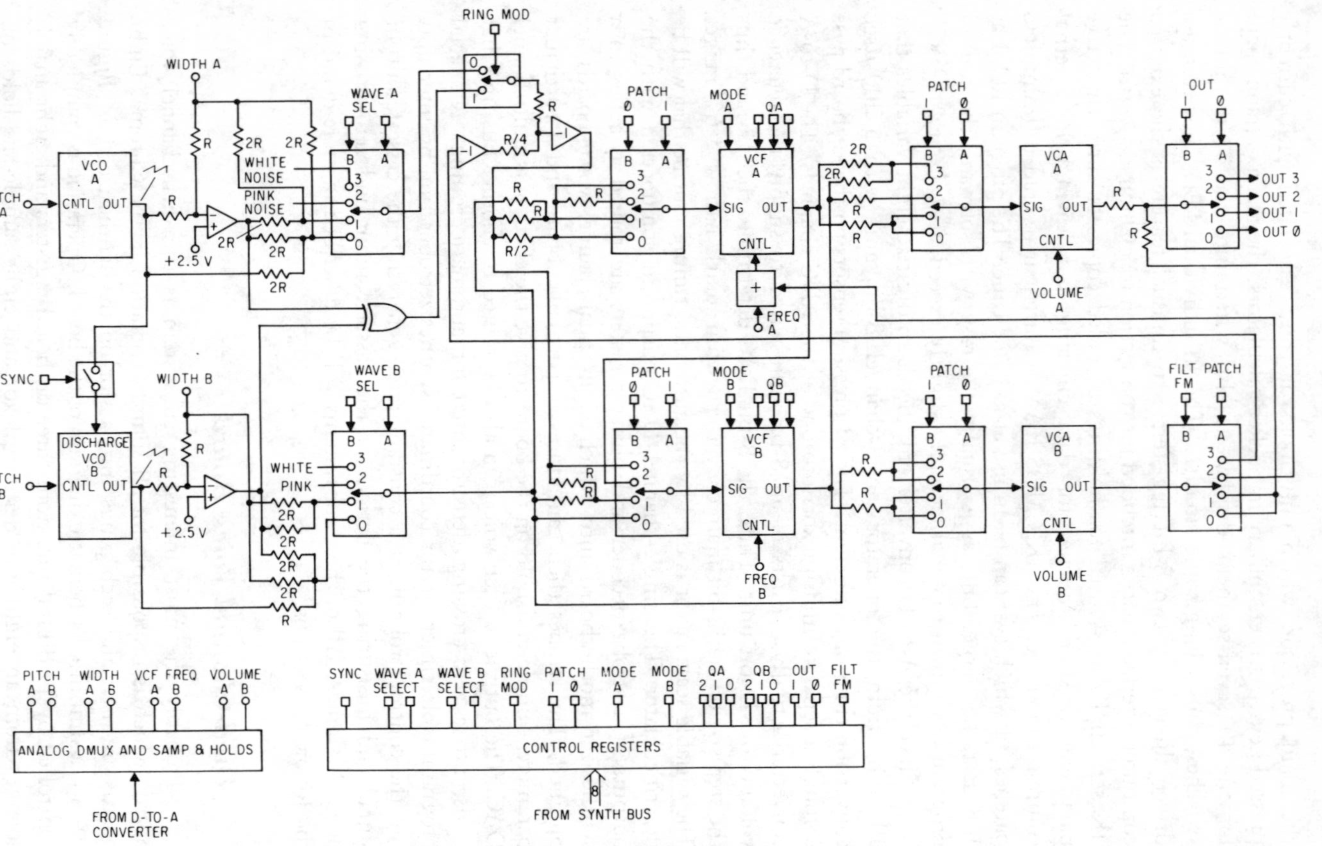

Fig. 19–4. Dual-channel voice board simplified schematic

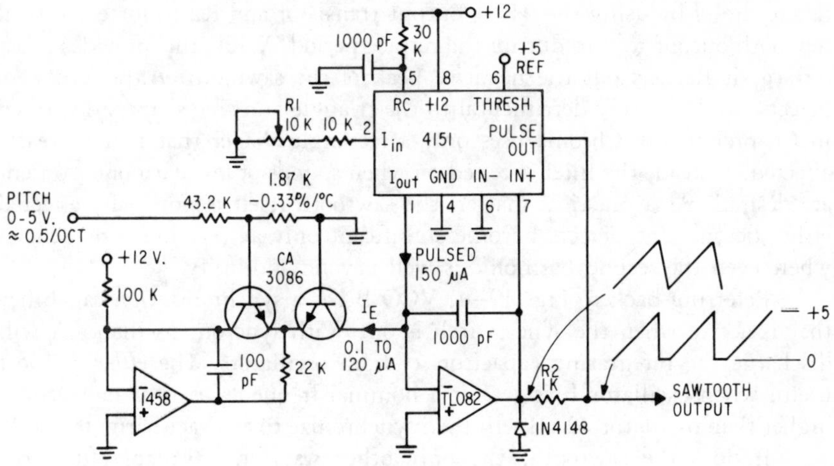

Fig. 19–5. VCO section of voice board

while an analog control signal uses a round terminal. Basically, the board is two VCO-VCF-VCA chains with a variety of programmable cross-connections between the two channels.

The two voltage-controlled oscillators, one of which is detailed in Fig. 19–5, are nearly identical and use the sawtooth-pulse type of circuit described in Chapter 6. The 0 to +5-V range pitch input voltage is scaled to approximately 0.5 V/octave in a conventional current output exponential converter. This current, which has a range of 100 nA to 120 μA, then feeds a conventional integrator, which uses a TL082 FET input op-amp and a 1,000-pF integrating capacitor.

The threshold comparator and discharge circuits, however, are part of a 4151 (Exar, Fairchild, Raytheon) "voltage-to-frequency converter" IC. This IC, which was designed for data acquisition rather than musical use, is a commonly available generic device. Its discharge circuit, rather than trying to short-circuit the integrating capacitor and discharge it as quickly as possible, consists of a switched current source. During the sawtooth retrace interval, which is fixed at 33 μsec by an internal one-shot (RC terminal), a positive current of 150 μA exits the I_{out} terminal, which counters the negative current from the exponential converter thus discharging the integrator. The combination of 33 μsec and 150 μA is set (via R1) to discharge the integrator from the 5-V threshold level back to exactly 0 V at low frequencies when I_E is small.

The point of all this is that the circuit is theoretically perfectly linear; there is no inherent "high-frequency droop" that can only be minimized in the usual short-circuit type of discharger. The price of this frequency accuracy improvement is a slow (33 μsec) sawtooth retrace time and a significant reduction in sawtooth amplitude at high frequencies. The slow retrace is taken care of by using the 4151's output transistor and R2 to force the final sawtooth output to zero during the retrace period. While this provides a fast retrace, it flattens out the negative peak of the sawtooth. Although these defects would be very detrimental to the triangle and sine shapers described in Chapter 6, the Chroma uses only a rectangle shaper that is not greatly affected. Instead, the filter is relied on when sounds of low harmonic content are desired. As a practical matter, the sawtooth itself is not really affected either because the defects become significant only at very high frequencies where even the second harmonic is well beyond audibility.

Referring back to Fig. 19–4, VCO B has a synchronization capability that is active when the sync switch is on. With sync on, oscillator A will discharge the integrating capacitors of both oscillators. The effect is most useful when oscillator B is set for a nominal frequency two or more times higher than oscillator A's. B will then synchronize to an exact harmonic of A.

Besides the sawtooth, the only other waveform available from the oscillator is a rectangle formed by comparing the sawtooth with a width control voltage. Since the sawtooth amplitude is 0–5 V and the width voltage covers the same range, duty cycles of 0–100% are possible. In fact, one way to mute an oscillator is to select the rectangle waveform and set either duty cycle extreme. In the Chroma, the rectangle width is commonly varied rapidly to create dynamic spectra and even a moderately effective chorus effect. One problem in doing this, however, is that the dc component can cause annoying thumps and low-frequency overload in audio systems when the width is varied rapidly. The problem is solved elegantly by using an inverting comparator in the rectangle shaper and then simply adding the width control voltage to the rectangle wave so as to cancel out its dc component!

The VCF section does use a specialized dual state-variable VCF chip, the Curtis 3350. In the Chroma only, the low-pass and high-pass configuration is used, which is selected by a single mode digital signal. Scaling of the frequency control input is the same as the oscillator scaling. "Q" or resonance is controlled directly by a local 3-bit D-to-A converter driven by the Q0-Q2 digital signals rather than by an analog voltage. Thus, Q is a static sound parameter that cannot be "logically connected" to an envelope. The Q control voltage developed by the 3-bit DAC is combined with the frequency control voltage to form a constant Q filter configuration. The Q varies in an exponential manner from under 1 for 000 to oscillation at 111. Some extra transistors added to the VCF chip insure oscillation at the highest Q setting but also gently limit the oscillation amplitude to about 3 V peak to prevent distortion.

The VCA section also uses a specialized VCA chip, the Curtis 3360. Exponential conversion of the volume control voltage is not performed; instead gain varies linearly from 0 to 1.0 as the control voltage varies from 0 to +5 V. Before entering the VCA chip, the gain control voltage is single-

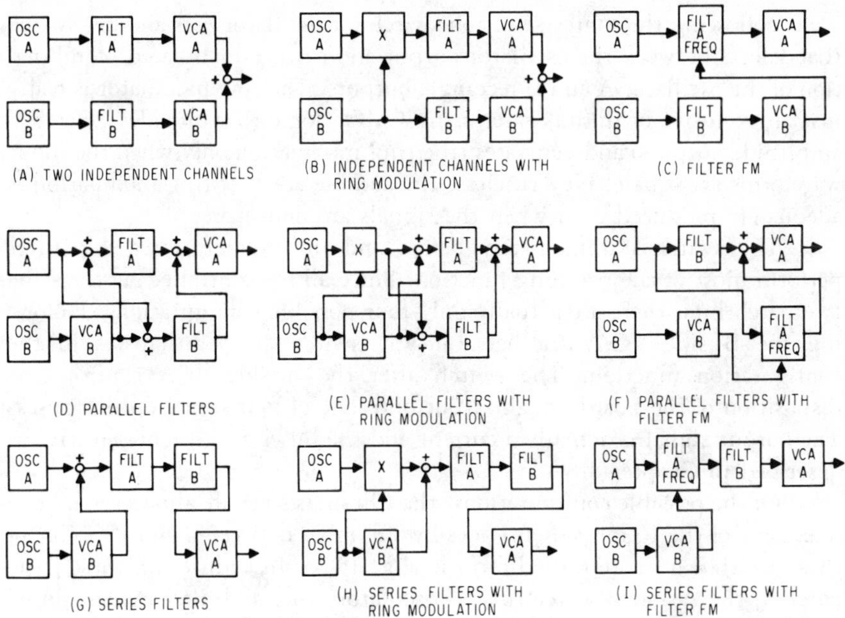

Fig. 19–6. Possible configurations of voice board. (A) Two independent channels. (B) Independent channels with ring modulation. (C) Filter FM. (D) Parallel filters. (E) Parallel filters with ring modulation. (F) Parallel filters with filter FM. (G) Series filters. (H) Series filters with ring modulation. (I) Series filters with filter FM.

pole RC low-pass-filtered with a time constant of about 1.3 msec. This prevents an unnatural "tic" sound when an instantaneous attack is applied to low-frequency sounds.

As can be seen, signal routing switches are scattered throughout the block diagram. Most of the switches are type 4052 dual 1-of-4 analog multiplexors. The first level of switching selects one of four possible sources for each oscillator output. These are rectangle, a mix of sawtooth and rectangle, white noise, and pink noise. It is interesting to note that an equal mix of a rectangle and a sawtooth waveform yields a result equivalent to mixing *two* sawtooth waves! The phasing between the two virtual sawtooth waveforms is determined by the rectangle width. Thus, varying the rectangle width will change the phasing as if the two waveforms were of slightly different frequency. In fact, periodic variation of the width sounds exactly like periodic beating between two oscillators and random variation gives a remarkably good chorus effect. Most Chroma patches make use of this surprising result to greatly increase the apparent richness of otherwise simple synthesized tones. The two noise sources are generated externally on the synthesizer bus motherboard and feed to all of the voice boards.

Following the source selection switch for oscillator A is another switch that selects between the oscillator output and a "ring-modulated" combination of the oscillator A and B rectangle outputs. The ring modulator is really just an exclusive-or digital gate (using CMOS logic that provides exact 5-V amplitude outputs) and generates true ring modulation only when the input waveforms are square. Nevertheless, the audible effect of ring modulation is adequately produced even when the signals are nonsquare.

The switches immediately before and immediately after the filters perform most of the patching function. Since all are controlled by the same two patch bits, there are actually only four possible configurations. Following the B side VCA, another four-way switch also participates in the configuration function. The switch after the A side VCA controls the disposition of the board's final output onto one of four signal output buses. The output signal is actually a current and the buses are current-sensitive as described in Chapter 8.

Of the possible configurations, the Chroma's software allows the user to select any of the 16 most useful ones by a number between 0 and 15. Nine of these are shown in simplified form in Fig. 19–6. In addition to these basic patches, the A and B waveforms, B oscillator sync, and filter modes can be selected to yield several dozen effective patches. By using the two filters in the parallel mode, a band-reject response is possible as well as dual-humped resonances. The series filter configuration allows a bandpass response as well as four-pole low-pass and high-pass shapes. It is interesting to note that frequency modulation of the oscillators is not provided for. Conversely, the filter center frequencies *can* be modulated. Since the oscillators cannot produce sine waves but the filters can (by using the Q7 setting), this makes sense. Also, many other strange effects are possible with lower *Q* settings.

Microprocessor Controller

The Chroma uses a Motorola 6809 ("B" version) 8-bit microprocessor operating at its highest rated clock speed of 2 MHz. The 6809 has been described by some as a "severely stripped 68000" and was indeed introduced a year or so before the 68000. It is in many ways more like the 6502, however. The bus control protocol, for example, is similar using a single "Phase 2" clock with a machine cycle that is the same length as a clock cycle. It has two 16-bit index registers and two 8-bit accumulators, which can be linked into a single 16-bit accumulator, as opposed to the 6502's 8-bit index registers and single accumulator. The addressing modes are similar but the 16-bit index registers make them more useful for large data arrays. There is also an 8×8 unsigned multiply (10 cycles) that is probably used frequently in the Chroma's control software. In all, the 6809 is about 50% more powerful than a 6502 of the same clock speed in this type of application.

The program is stored in eight 2716 EPROMs, each of which holds 2K bytes of program code. The fact that the current program version number is

14 is testament to why EPROMs are used. Of course, if such an instrument were being designed today, much larger EPROMs holding 8K or even all 16K bytes would probably be specified instead. The scratch RAM is eight type 2114 1K × 4-bit static RAM chips for a total of 4K bytes. Again, a new design would probably incorporate two type 6116 2K × 8-bit RAM chips instead.

For the nonvolatile RAM, six type 4334 RAM chips are used. These are functionally the same as 2114s but are CMOS to minimize battery drain during standby. Unfortunately, making a set of RAM chips nonvolatile is much more difficult than just connecting a battery to the RAM's power lead. During operation when the address and data lines are flipping about wildly, CMOS RAM still draws a substantial amount of power so a circuit to switch between battery and dc supply power is necessary. Also, while power is being applied or removed from the other circuitry, its action is indeterminate. Even a brief 100-nsec pulse on the write line during this time could alter stored data. In practice, fairly elaborate discrete transistor circuitry that responds predictably to changing power voltages is needed to prevent such transients.

D-to-A Converter

The D-to-A converter is actually on a separate I/O board along with drivers for the panel switches and lights. As shown in Fig. 19–7A, the D-to-A converter is really a two-stage device. The main converter is a 12-bit unit, but its reference voltage comes from a second 8-bit converter. When the reference converter's digital input is zero, the reference voltage for the 12-bit converter is about −4.33 V. When the digital input is all ones, the reference is about −4.95 V. Thus, the nominal 1.133-mV step size of the 12-bit DAC (reference centered at −4.64 V), can be varied + or −6.7%. Normally the oscillators are set for 0.43 V/octave, which is 384 DAC steps or 32 steps per semitone; a very convenient number. It is also small enough so that frequency stepping effects are completely inaudible.

The automatic tuning routines measure the actual oscillator and filter frequencies at selected low and high control voltages. From the result, an *offset* and a *slope* factor for each oscillator and filter can be determined. When an oscillator or filter sample-and-hold is selected by the software for updating, the slope factor is written into the reference DAC and the desired control value minus the offset is written into the main DAC. Except during this final output operation, all software routines can assume that each oscillator and filter has a precise tuning of 384 steps per octave and zero offset. Note that no software multiplication is required to implement the correction. In this particular application, even a single 16-bit DAC would not perform the correction as well. If a 16-bit DAC was used anyway, a 16 × 16-bit multiplication requiring three of the available 8 × 8 multiply instructions would be needed to perform the correction.

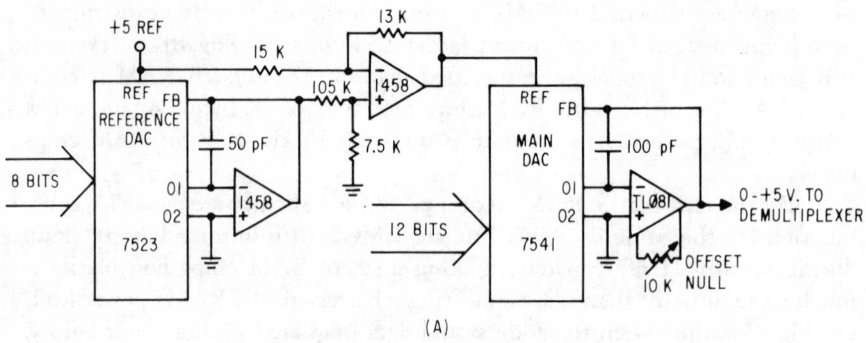

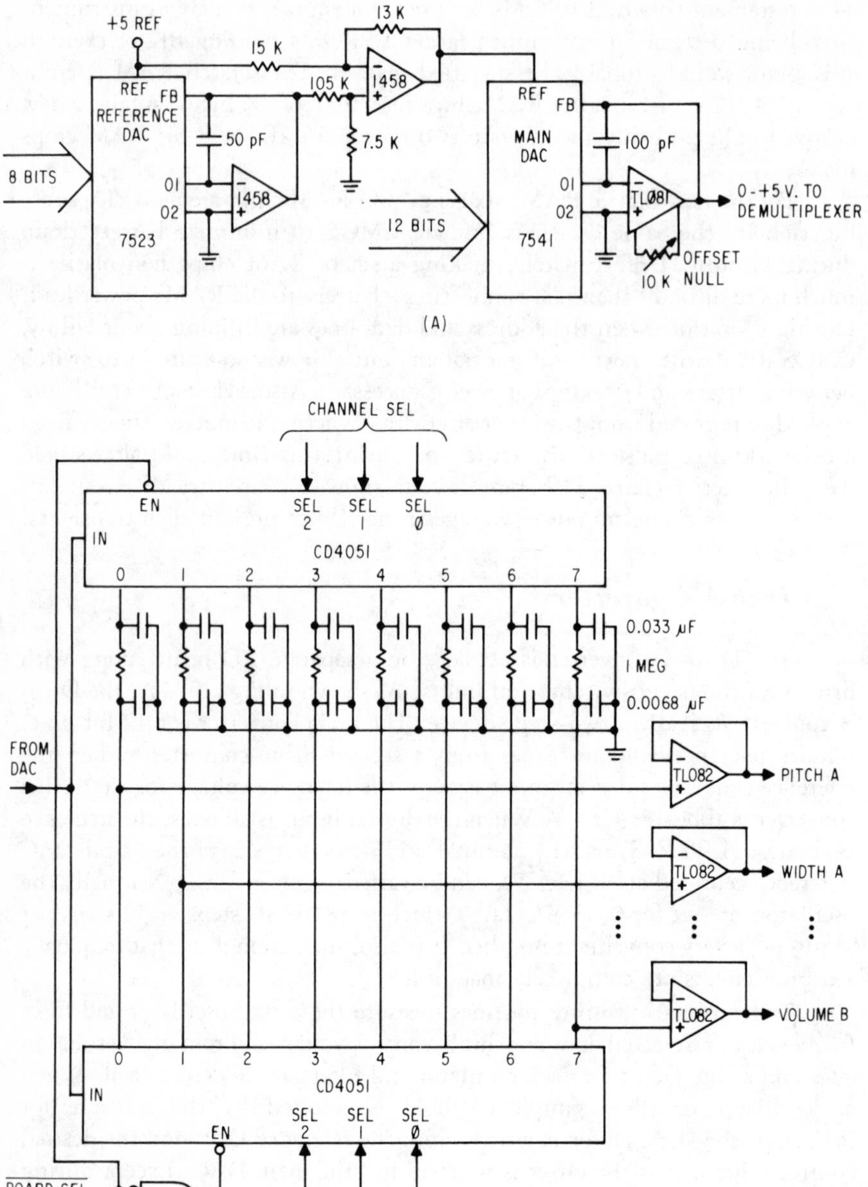

Fig. 19–7. Digital-to-analog converter system. (A) Variable-reference D-to-A converter. (B) Analog demultiplexor.

The analog demultiplexor in Fig. 19–7B has a unique feature that allows the computer some control over the transition times of analog control signals. For normal updating of the sample-and-holds, the top multiplexor only is enabled, which gives an immediate voltage change on the large (0.033 μF) hold capacitors. However, the actual control voltage is taken across the small (0.0068 μF) capacitors, which with the 1-MEG resistor gives a time constant of 6.8 msec. When the control computer desires an instantaneous voltage update, the bottom multiplexor is also enabled, which charges both capacitors to the new voltage. Of course, slower transition rates for envelopes are provided by writing successive values to the sample-and-holds in slow mode. Chroma software refreshes the sample-and-holds every 20 msec, which is 50 times per second. Because of the 1-MEG resistors, it was essential to use FET input op-amp buffers. The demultiplexor is actually on the voice boards, which greatly reduces the number of analog connections otherwise required.

External Computer Interface

When it was released, one of the Chroma's unique features was a high-speed parallel interface between its 6809 control computer and any kind of external digital device. Its primary purpose was to connect to a Chroma *expander,* which is identical to the Chroma except the keyboard is missing and the control program is slightly different. Increasing interest in personal computers by players, however, prompted full documentation of the interface hardware and command language so that an external computer could record keystrokes, play them back, and operate the control panel. The "Interface Manual" even shows an Apple II computer on the cover. The philosophy and command structure is similar to MIDI, which was discussed in Chapter 9, but, being parallel, the potential data rate is much higher.

The interface logic for data out consists of an 8-bit latch, a data out ready flip-flop, and an acknowledge input for a total of 10 lines. When the Chroma wishes to send a byte to an external computer or an expander, the byte is written into the data out register, which also sets the flip-flop. The external device responds by reading the data out lines and then sending a pulse on the acknowledge line, which resets the flip-flop. Having been reset, the flip-flop interrupts the Chroma's program, which then knows that it can send another byte.

The interface logic for data in uses a tri-state buffer for eight more data-in-lines and some gates to sense input data ready and generate input data taken signals. When an external device has a byte ready, it places it on the data in lines and raises the input data ready signal. This signal then interrupts the Chroma, which responds by reading the data through the tri-state buffer, which also pulses the input data taken signal. The remote device responds by dropping input data ready until it has another byte to send.

The interface thus allows completely *interlocked* data transfer simultaneously in both directions. Unlike MIDI, a data byte is not sent until the receiver indicates that it is ready to receive. The interface is in fact completely symmetrical; the expander has exactly the same interface logic as the Chroma and a "flipper" cable is used to mate them. The 20 lines of a 6522 parallel interface chip usually found in 6502-based personal computers can actually be connected directly to the Chroma interface and the handshaking and interrupt functions will operate properly.

Keyboard Scanner

A separate 8039 microprocessor is used to scan the Chroma's keyboard. It is unknown why this very different, slow, and difficult-to-program processor was used instead of a 6800 family member, but it is adequate. The 8039 is driven with an 8-MHz clock, which sounds fast but is divided on-chip by 15 to give a machine cycle of 1.9 μsec. A single 2716 EPROM holds the rather simple scanning program. The 61 keys are scanned once per millisecond using an algorithm similar to that described in Chapter 9. When a depression or release is recognized, the key ID number and a velocity value

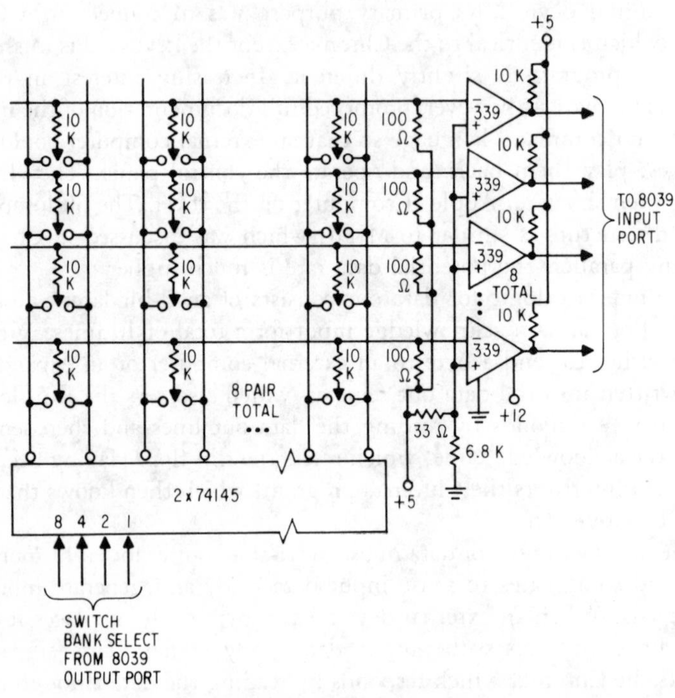

Fig. 19–8. Simplified schematic of keyswitch array

for that transition are written to latches that the main 6809 can read. The 6809 is also interrupted so that response to the keystroke is rapid.

Each keyboard key is equipped with a double-throw contact actuated by the rear edge of the weighted, wooden keys. The 61 keys, therefore, constitute 122 contacts, which are wired in a 16 × 8 *matrix* rather than to a bunch of digital multiplexor chips as in the Chapter 9 example. One potential problem with any kind of switch matrix is *sneak paths* that can occur when three or more switches are closed simultaneously. This is ususally dealt with by placing a diode in series with each switch but is handled differently in the Chroma.

Figure 19–8 shows a portion of the keyswitch matrix. The 8039 outputs a 4-bit "switch bank" number and reads back the state of eight switches in the bank. When a switch is closed, it draws a 0.5-mA current through its series 10K resistor and a 100-ohm sense resistor. The positive inputs of the comparators are all biased at 25 mV below +5V, whereas a closed key develops a 50-mV drop across the 100-ohm sense resistor. Besides limiting the current, the 10K series resistors prevent the formation of any significant sneak paths. The LM339 quad comparators are exceptionally cheap but are relatively slow at 1.2 μsec, requiring a wait state to be added when the 8039 reads a switch bank. Although this matrix arrangement is not as straightforward as using digital multiplexors, it does keep high-amplitude, high-speed digital signals out of the physically large keyboard contact area where they might generate unacceptable radio frequency interference.

Control Program and Panel Function

The most critical design aspect of a mass-market keyboard synthesizer is the control interface it presents to the user. In the Chroma, this is determined by the physical panel controls available and the logical structure of the control program. Unfortunately, a complete description of the user interface would require a chapter by itself so it will be very briefly summarized here.

Most panel operations revolve around the 50 numbered buttons, the two-digit and eight-digit displays, and a single "parameter value" slide pot. A few other buttons and lights are used to change operation modes and perform specific functions, such as setting a keyboard split or tuning. One important characteristic is that keyboard notes may be played at *any time* regardless of the panel mode. The only exception is during tuning or cassette dump/load operations.

There are two primary operating modes of the control panel. In the "program select mode," each of the 50 numbered keys is associated with a different "patch" or "sound." Simply pressing a button will instantly select the new patch for all subsequent notes, while silencing any that may already be sounding. Thus, during performance, different sounds may be selected rapidly and noiselessly. The large display always shows the currently selected patch number.

In the "parameter select mode," the patch number is frozen in the large display and each of the 50 keys selects a parameter instead. The left portion of the small display shows the currently selected *parameter number* and the right portion displays its *value*. The value displayed is what the parameter was last set to. The value may be changed temporarily by moving the parameter value slidepot. When movement is detected, the handle position is digitized and the result written into the display and internal parameter value. Different parameters have different numerical ranges. An on–off type of parameter for example has only two legal values: 0 and 1. Therefore, the lower half of the slidepot range will be converted to 0 and the upper half will be 1. Another parameter may have a range of 0–9, in which case the pot range is divided into 10 regions. A few parameters can range between −128 and +127 and the pot range is similarly divided. To aid in setting specific numerical values without constantly looking at the display, the panel tapper is activated whenever the slidepot handle moves into a new region. The whole operation is remarkably effective, even for parameters having 256 possible values. To permanently alter the displayed parameter value, another button must be pressed; otherwise it will revert to its previous value when another parameter is selected.

There are in fact 50 parameters for a sound. The first 25 are called *control* parameters and include such specifications as the voice board patch configuration, keyboard algorithm (ways of assigning keys to oscillators), output channel select, envelope parameters, and many others. There are actually two envelopes present and both are of the ADR (attack-decay-release) type. The second envelope can also be delayed with respect to the first (another parameter) allowing the creation of the ADSR shape as well as many others. Most envelope parameters can be modulated (altered) by other variables such as keystroke velocity, footpedal position, or even randomly. The other 25 parameters are called *audio* parameters and include items such as tuning offset, pitch control source, pitch control magnitude, waveshape, pulse width control source and magnitude, filter controls, and many others.

In nearly all cases, oscillators, filters, and amplifiers on a voice board are used together to make a single complex voice. Since there are 50 parameters for each half, the complex voice actually involves 100 distinct parameters that could all be different, although most of them are usually the same. These are referenced as the "A" and "B" groups. Depending on the panel mode, the user can examine/alter either A alone, B alone, or both simultaneously.

When "playing around" with a sound, the 100 parameters are actually copied from their slot in the nonvolatile CMOS memory into a temporary scratch area. The scratch sound can be altered in any way desired but will not be permanently changed until a specific sequence of buttons is pressed. This copying, in fact, occurs whenever a patch is selected in the program select mode and also includes "expanding" the compressed format used to conserve space in the CMOS memory into a format the control program can manipulate easily.

All-Digital Synthesizers

The previous section described what is essentially the epitome of analog synthesizer design. Of course, more basic waveshapes, filter modes, patching flexibility, and voice boards could be designed in to make a *bigger* instrument, but not really a *different* one. In the extremely competitive synthesizer world, as soon as one instrument design is complete and in production, work begins on a new design. Since instruments like the Chroma have taken analog sound generation technology about as far as it can go, real innovations must be in other areas. In the context of a hybrid instrument, most of the activity has been in more powerful control programs and more informative control panels. For example, many more software-generated envelopes and low-frequency modulator oscillators have been included in recent designs. Numeric readouts are being replaced by alphanumeric and even limited graphics displays to allow effective communication with the more complex control programs.

To come up with something truly new in a live performance synthesizer, it is becoming necessary to use digital synthesis techniques for the sound waveforms themselves as well as the envelope shapes. Of course, one immediate advantage of digital synthesis is its inherent accuracy. While automatic tuning is effective (provided it is performed about twice an hour and the room temperature is reasonably stable), it is not needed at all in a digital instrument. Also, factory adjustments, which must be touched up after a few years or when components are replaced, are not needed either. Finally, some synthesis algorithms, such as FM with reflected harmonic sidebands, are much more predictable when frequency uncertainties are zero.

The biggest advantage of digital, however, is that the whole spectrum of synthesis techniques is available. It should not be a surprise that the synthesis technique an instrument uses affects how the user "thinks about" sound. Whereas analog synthesis is virtually synonymous with subtractive (filter) synthesis, a digital system can be based on additive (harmonic), frequency modulation, nonlinear, direct waveshaping, or even VOSIM synthesis techniques. Besides these synthesis-from-scratch methods, modification techniques such as frequency shifting, dispersion, arbitrary filtering, envelope modification, and others are potentially available. Finally, an endless variety of parameter transferral, record-playback, and analysis-synthesis techniques are possible. No instrument uses all or even most of these possibilities, but they do provide a rich source of ideas for instrument designers.

On the negative side, it presently costs substantially more to develop and manufacture an all-digital synthesizer than a hybrid unit. If off-the-shelf components are used in the design, engineering effort and tooling costs may be affordable by a moderately small company, but then manufacturing costs will be quite high. For example, the cost of a single parallel multiplier chip can easily exceed the cost of 20 or more complete voltage-controlled oscillators. On the other hand, using custom chips can bring manufacturing costs down considerably, but then only the largest companies designing instruments for the broadest possible mass market can afford the development expense.

Nevertheless, at the time of this writing, "digital" is a hot buzzword not only in the synthesizer market but also the audiophile ("compact disks") and recording markets (digital multitrack recorders and all-digital studios). If a product is "digital," it is seen to be inherently better even if an objective evaluation may show it to be less flexible or more difficult to use than an equivalent older technology product. Thus, at this time, most new synthesizers being introduced are mostly, if not all, digital.

Synthesis from Sound Parameters

The development of digital synthesizers seems to be going in three rather distinct directions according to what designers perceive to be the greatest strength of digital technology. One of these is simply *synthesis from scratch* according to sound parameters in a live-performance keyboard instrument. The instrument's functional and design goals are similar to those of a hybrid synthesizer but with the advantages of digital technology, such as freedom from drift, present. Because of digital's inherent accuracy, digital instrument designers expect to be able to concentrate on providing more flexibility in parameter control and interaction and not have to worry very much about tuning correction, error accumulation, and the like. Beyond a certain sophistication point in the synthesizer's design, it becomes almost free (in production cost terms) to provide additional synthesis algorithms, more parameter modulations, and so forth. All that is really added is perhaps more memory to hold the additional programming and data. In fact, the flexibility limit in a live-performance keyboard instrument is often not set by the circuitry's capabilities but by an inability to design an effective human interface so that the user can learn the instrument in a finite time and effectively use all of the features. This problem is far more serious than what might be thought.

A good analogy might be word-processing programs for personal computers. Obviously, any small computer and a letter-quality printer is theoretically capable of producing any kind of text; it could even have typeset this entire book less figures (and for $3,000 one can purchase a laser printer that could typeset the text *and* draw all of the figures, except photographs, as clearly as you see them here). The rules of written English are fixed, and most

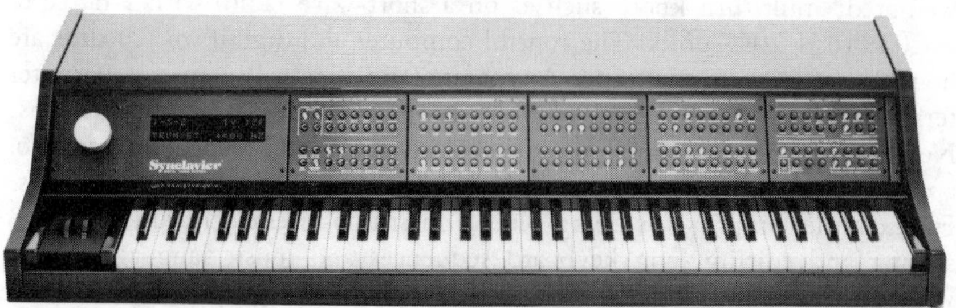

Fig. 19–9. Synclavier digital keyboard synthesizer

printers accept the same command set, yet there are a dozen or more different word-processing programs available for each computer type *and they all operate differently*. Reviews of such programs reveal that none of them does everything that might be desired, and different ones are weak in different areas. Most significant, though, is that those judged easiest to learn and use are also the most limited. Conversely, the few that are comprehensive are difficult to master and even these don't even begin to address the integration of figures into printed text. In essence, available digital hardware, both image synthesis and sound synthesis, presently far outstrips designers' ability to design effective and understandable user interfaces.

One way to tackle difficult control interface problems is to take a subset of the problem and solve it well instead. Thus, rather than trying to provide effective control interfaces for a variety of synthesis techniques, just one is selected and perhaps embellished a little to broaden its range of application. This approach shows up clearly in current keyboard digital synthesizers that typically offer just one primary synthesis technique.

One example is the Synclavier (Fig. 19–9) manufactured by New England Digital, which was also the first well-known all-digital keyboard synthesizer to become commercially available. The Synclavier is essentally an additive synthesis instrument with provisions for limited FM synthesis. Its internal hardware structure essentially consists of 8 (expandable to 32) waveform table scanners. Waveforms are computed from up to 24 harmonic specifications and placed into each table. A separate sine wave oscillator is associated with each table scanner as well and can frequency modulate the scanned out waveform. Thus, FM sidebands around each harmonic of the stored waveform are possible. Each table scanner has its own amplitude envelope and a single "note" can trigger up to four of these. Thus, a moderately complex spectral evolution can be produced. Such a hardware structure is relatively simple, being the same order of complexity as the Fourier series generator described in Chapter 17 for each set of eight table scanners.

The user interface for selecting and changing sound parameters is similar to the Chroma's except that the parameter value control is a large, weighted, multiturn knob (such as on a short-wave radio) with a range of −2048 to +2047 units. The control computer and digital voice boards are housed in a separate enclosure. A separate (and optional) graphics computer terminal is used for the more complex sound parameter setting operations. New software features are constantly being added to broaden the range of application and distinguish the Synclavier from other keyboard synthesizers. For example, emphasis is being placed on studio-oriented features, such as storing and editing long keyboard sequences and music language input, which ultimately will place it into the "toolbox" category to be described later.

Reconstruction of Digital Recordings

Another distinctly different development direction is instruments that effectively *play back digital recordings* of instrument sounds rather than trying to synthesize them from scratch. Of course, this idea is not new, having been tried centuries ago in pipe organs and more recently in the Mellotron (a multitrack tape loop with a different sound on each track), but digital technology and the very low cost of memory now makes its complete realization practical. The user of such an instrument doesn't think "oscillator A drives filter B in bandpass mode with envelope C modulating its center frequency, etc.," but rather "sound 27 is a muted trumpet, sound 63 is an orchestra string section, sound 119 is a bass recorder, etc." Thus, in the pure case, a user interface is very simple; just a bunch of stop-like numbered buttons, or a keypad. Conventional wisdom says that this kind of instrument should have a large market because most musically inclined people are unwilling to learn and deal with sound parameters.

In designing such an instrument, one quickly finds out that, while memory is cheap, it is not cheap enough to store the direct sound waveform of every note of every instrument in the repertoire. Actually, one can get by with direct digital recording of most unpitched percussive sounds such as drums because volume, which can be successfully adjusted as a *parameter* separate from the digital recording, is the only variable. Specialized *drum synthesizers* in fact do exactly that. Pitched percussive instruments like a piano are much more difficult because both pitch and volume are variables. The spectrum changes as a function of both frequency and of volume so external control of gain and memory scan speed are not usually satisfactory methods of controlling these two parameters. The situation is even worse for wind and directly fingered string instruments because playing technique becomes a third variable.

Thus, *data compression* of the digital recording becomes a crucial requirement, otherwise, tens or even hundreds of megabytes of memory are required. Unfortunately, manufacturers of emulation instruments are quite secretive about the specific techniques used, but it is possible to speculate a

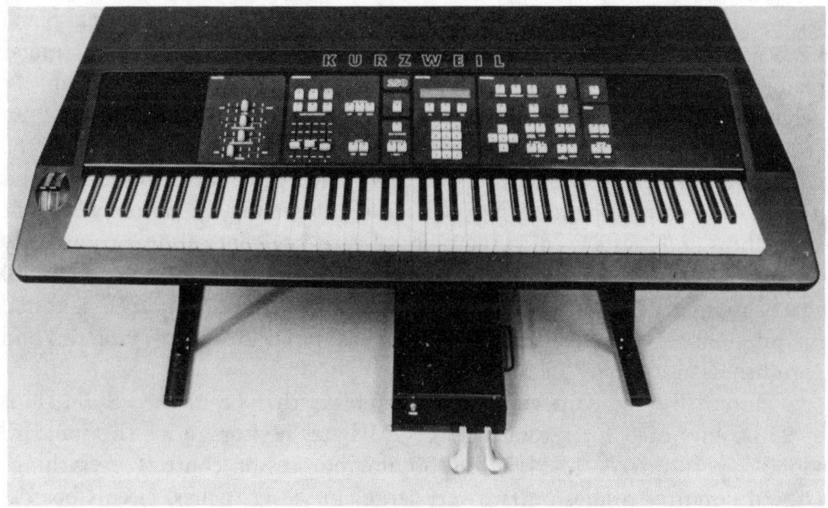

Fig. 19–10. Kurzweil-250 emulation synthesizer

little. One possibility is to encode the waveform samples more efficiently. For example, just the *differences* from one sample to the next might be stored. This is called *differential pulse-code modulation* and can easily compress well-behaved sample data by a factor of two. For pitched sounds, one might also arrange to store the differences from one *cycle* to the next as well. Logarithmic encoding of the samples is another way to achieve compression. Fully implemented along with provisions for skipping the encoding during particularly difficult sections like the initial attack, waveform coding can achieve compressions in the range of 3–10 with little or no degradation in the reproduced sound.

Another possibility is to store the time-varying *spectrum* of the instrument sounds using one of the techniques described in Chapter 16 rather than the waveform itself. Certain aspects of the sound not well represented by the time-varying harmonic spectrum, such as noise components, can be analyzed separately and added to the spectral description. The resulting data may be greatly compressed because the individual spectral envelopes can be approximated with line segments or higher-order curves and a variable frame rate can be used. Spectral variations at different pitches and volume levels may be handled by storing data for only a few well-chosen pitch and volume points over the instrument's range and then *interpolating* for a specific case. Of course, all of this processing "distorts" the recorded sounds substantially but can still provide a nearly perfect audible reconstruction.

One quite successful emulation instrument is the Kurzweil 250 (named after its inventor), which is pictured in Fig. 19–10. This is truly a top-flight machine with 88-key velocity-senstive wooden keyboard that has been fitted with weighted throw-bars in an attempt to duplicate the feel of a real piano keyboard. It has 12 standard orchestral sounds built in including grand piano, string *section*, trumpet, acoustic guitar, and Hammond organ; 14 percussion instruments including all kinds of drums and cymbals; an "endless glissando"; and a sine wave. Add-on ROM "voice modules" allow the repertoire to be expanded with instruments like a full chorus, both male and female. The control panel is devoted mostly to setting up various keyboard algorithms and splits even to the point of each key controlling a completely different sound. Splits can also overlap, which allows some keys to control two or more instruments playing in unison or at a constant interval. Limited modulations of the stored sounds such as pitch bending, vibrato, and "brightness" variations are also possible.

Internally, the Kurzweil 250 uses no fewer than 68 masked ROM chips of 256K bits each for a total of over 2M bytes of storage for the standard sound repertoire. A 10-MHz 68000 microprocessor controls everything. Digital circuitry resides on two very large (15 × 17 inches) circuit boards, while a surprisingly large amount of analog circuitry fills another board of similar size. Much of the analog circuitry is devoted to 12 completely independent voice channels where each channel includes a 12-bit CMOS type D-to-A converter, a sample-and-hold deglitcher, a programmable low-pass filter, and a programmable gain amplifier. The sample rate of each channel is also variable according to the instrument and note being played and ranges from 10 to 50 ks/s. A typical instrument's range is broken up into approximately 10 subranges with those at the extremes covering somewhat more than an octave, while those in the middle are about one-half octave wide. Different pitches within a range are produced by varying the sample rate. Sounds are stored as an attack portion, a sustain portion, and sometimes a decay portion. During exceptionally long sustains, the stored sustain portion, which averages about ¾ sec, is repeated. It appears that waveform coding is used for data compression, and the compression ratio is estimated to be in the 4-to-1 range for instruments like the string section.

To the author's ears, the accuracy of emulation is, for practical purposes, perfect. While the piano, violin, and other instruments actually recorded to prepare the voicing ROMs may not be the best in the world, they are probably better than what a potential buyer would otherwise have access to. If one knows exactly what to listen for and devises a suitable test score, some of the data compression artifacts can be detected. For example, with the piano sound, one can tell where the subrange boundaries are, while with the string section, repetition within long sustains can be detected.

The Kurzweil-250 seems to appeal mostly to people with a classical music background who might otherwise purchase a grand piano or large organ for their home. Aside from curiosity and challenging the company's slogan, "you can't tell the difference," the usual keyboard synthesizer customer has shown only moderate interest. To broaden its appeal to performing keyboard players, new features allowing greater flexibility in modulating the stored sounds and routines for computing and temporarily storing synthetic as well as sampled live sounds have been added as well as a MIDI interface.

"Toolbox" Synthesizers

The third developmental direction (and solution to the man–machine interface problem) is what will be called a "toolbox synthesizer." These provide a large collection of more or less disjointed software and hardware tools that can be used in sequence to build a composition. The control interface problem is greatly simplified because each tool performs a specific function and can be designed and implemented independently. It is the user's responsibility to determine how to use the functions together to produce a desired result. While they can be useful in live performance, a toolbox synthesizer is really a studio synthesizer. As such, the major design goal is maximum flexibility rather than efficiency in a performance environment.

Let's briefly look at what some of these tools might be and the sequence in which they might be used to produce, say, a low-budget film soundtrack. The composer would typically have a preliminary edit of the film and instructions from the director available. With these, a detailed list of the kind of music needed for each scene and its required duration is prepared. Next, musical ideas and score fragments are composed and notated using whatever method is familiar to the composer. Using the available score entry programs on the synthesizer, the score is then entered. Typical methods include direct music keyboard playing and the use of one or more music languages. After entry, score segments can typically be saved and inserted elsewhere, repeated, and modified in various ways such as transposition. For film work, it is also necessary to adjust the segment durations to match the scenes. This may be accomplished by deleting or adding phrases and small adjustments in tempo.

Once the score, which may be just the melody line, is in the system, the next step is orchestration. Up to now, some stock voice was probably used and the score was devoid of dynamic and voicing markings. One approach would be to search a library of already "designed" voices but, of course, it is more creative to construct new ones. Usually there are many different "voice editor" programs available using different synthesis techniques. For example, one program may allow the drawing of individual harmonic envelopes for use by an additive synthesis process. Another may allow interactive control over an FM synthesis setup or interactive drawing of nonlinear distortion curves or interactive design of digital filters. Yet another would begin by digitizing a natural sound and provide numerous ways of modifying or distorting it.

Once a library of voices is constructed, the score is edited again to include voice selection, dynamics, and additional musical lines. Depending

Fig. 19–11. Fairlight CMI "toolbox" synthesizer

on the synthesizer, the last step of combining musical lines may be done in real time on the synthesizer or in stages using a multitrack tape recorder. What is amazing (and gratifying) is that the entire process, which can result in a truly impressive soundtrack, may be accomplished by a single person in just a few weeks or months.

One example of what is effectively a toolbox synthesizer is the Fairlight CMI (Computer Musical Instrument), which was designed in Australia. This instrument is very popular in the studio and has in fact been used to produce countless film scores. The "terminal" part of the system, pictured in Fig. 19–11, consists of a movable 73-note music keyboard, an alphanumeric keyboard, and a graphics display screen. The display is rather mundane with a strictly black-and-white resolution of 256 × 512. Integrated into it, however, is an extremely effective light pen with resolution to the pixel for direct drawing of curves and pointing out displayed items. Except for the display, all of the computer and synthesizer circuitry is housed in a separate enclosure. Program and data storage is on 8-inch diskettes, and the two drives are mounted in this enclosure as well. Two 6800 microprocessors are used for the main control computer along with another in the music keyboard. Both processors have access to all system resources without mutual interference by taking advantage of the 6800's 6502-like two-phase clock. 64K bytes of read/write memory plus 16K for the graphics display is also present.

The synthesizer portion is also rather mundane but, as will be shown later, is very effective in practical situations. The logic for each of the eight voices is on a separate voice board. Each voice board has a 16K × 8 sample memory driving an 8-bit waveform DAC followed by an 8-bit multiplying amplitude DAC. In scanning the stored waveform, different pitches are produced by keeping the waveform pointer increment at unity and varying the sample rate. This is allowable, since the logic for each voice is independent of the other rather than being multiplexed. One interesting feature is that the table scanner treats the 16K memory as 128 *segments* of 128 samples each. Under direction from the control computer, the scanner may be instructed to cycle through a subset of the whole memory in integral numbers of segments.

Generally, the sound of an entire note is stored in the 16K sample memory including the attack, sustain, and decay. For pitched sounds, it is desirable for one cyle to fit into one segment. When a note of an arbitrary duration is played, the waveform scanner is instructed to scan sequentially through the attack portion, *loop* repeatedly through the segments representing the sustain portion, and finally scan sequentially through the remainder of the memory for the release. Although waveform resolution is only 8 bits, the dynamic range is considerably greater because of the separate gain control DAC. Also, since each voice is separately D-to-A converted and the quantization noise is purely harmonic due to the variable sample rate method of pitch control, the overall sound is of high quality after all.

The interactive graphics software supplied with the Fairlight is the key to its musical usefulness. This software consists of several independent programs that share common disk data bases. A proprietary, although conventional, disk-operating system loads requested programs into memory and maintains the files of voices and scores. Although the internal software organization is not at all unusual, the user interface and operator's manual is designed to hide the fact that multiple programs are being used and in fact even hide the concept of a computer program. Each program has a distinctive interactive graphics display format on the screen and is uniformly called a "page." The user's manual continually describes what can be "done" on each "page" as if each represented a portion of a massive control panel. The light pen is used extensively by all of the programs. About the only use of the alphanumeric keyboard is entering the names of *new* instruments and scores and in using the system's composition language.

Of the dozen or so pages available, a few will be briefly described here. Page 2, for example, is the disk file maintenance page, which allows all of the usual list/load/save/copy/delete DOS functions to be performed by pointing the light pen at a file name and a function name. Unfortunately, the floppy disks cannot carry out the functions as fast as the operator selects them, but certainly the approach is convenient.

Another page allows direct drawing of waveforms. A fine grid of 64 vertical lines is displayed for the light pen to "see" and the user can quite literally draw, as fast as desired, one cycle of a waveform to fill one segment of the waveform memory. Up to 128 different waveforms may be drawn to fill the memory, but typically only a few are drawn and the *waveshape interpolation* function used to compute intermediate shapes. Direct spectral entry is allowed on another page in a similar fashion. Here, 32 vertical grids are shown, each representing four waveform memory segments. With the light pen, up to 64 individual harmonic envelopes may be drawn with up to eight displayed at once. The envelope of interest is shown with a thicker line. The actual waveforms placed in memory are straight-line interpolations of the display values over the four segment intervals.

The "sound sampling" page is the most distinctive feature, however. An 8-bit A-to-D converter can sample from a microphone or high-level input directly into the waveform memory of a separate "master voice module." The sample rate may be varied over a wide range in order to fit the entire sound into the 16K memory or to match the sound's pitch period to the 128-sample segment size. Selectable low- and high-cut filters and an automatic trigger threshold with adjustable pretrigger delay are available. After a sound is captured, its overall amplitude envelope is displayed to allow level adjustment to make full use of the limited 8-bit dynamic range. As with the other pages, the light pen is used to select options and control operation.

Although these and other sound definition/capture programs are independent, they are linked together through disk files and retained contents of the waveform memory. Thus, the waveform drawing page may be used to view, and modify, a sampled sound waveform. The harmonic entry page may be used to view the spectrum of a drawn or sampled waveform. Another page is available for designating which segments of the waveform memory are to be the attack, looped sustain, and decay. It can even rearrange the segments or generate new segments that are combinations of other segments, all under light pen control. An important feature is that the keyboard is always active. As soon as a waveform is in memory, it can be played, at any pitch, at any step along the editing process.

A keyboard page is available for assigning different regions of the keyboard to different voices and assigning the eight available voices to stored sounds in various groupings. Another "patch page" is used to designate which synthesis parameters are controlled by the pedals, joystick, keyboard velocity sense, etc., all graphically with the light pen. A sequencer page is used to capture, edit, and merge keyboard sequences to build up to eight musical parts. A music language (MCL, Music Composition Language) and text editor are available to allow complex scores to be typed in and compiled into the internal sequence format. In all, the Fairlight CMI is a very flexible instrument that combines the best features of direct computer synthesis and performance-oriented keyboard synthesizers.

Direct Computer Synthesis Practice

Although keyboard and toolbox commercial digital synthesizers have essentially taken over the market for "working" instruments, there are still many unusual applications and research situations for which they are unsuited. Several of these, such as experiments in human perception, development of new synthesis techniques, and data compression algorithms, were mentioned earlier in this chapter. Add to these experimental *compositional* techniques and scores that simply do not lend themselves to "playing" on a keyboard and one realizes that there is still a great need for direct computer synthesis hardware and software. As would be expected, much of this kind of work is done in a university setting, but there are also a number of commercial studios and individual composers who make use of such equipment.

Whereas a toolbox synthesizer increases flexibility by "deintegrating" the usual keyboard synthesizer and making use of some standard computer graphics techniques, a direct computer synthesis system goes much further. First, there is the computer's operating system. Rather than being hidden behind a limited function "shell" program, the full array of file maintenance and other operating system commands are available. Although these commands must usually be typed in a rigid format, their great flexibility often allows otherwise repetitive tasks to be performed with just one command. Programs are even more individualized and disjointed. The data files that link them together can be defined by the user according to the application rather than having to conform to a rigid standardized format. In essence, there is total freedom—and the responsibility to use it productively.

The most significant feature of direct-synthesis systems is that writing new synthesis and manipulation programs is the norm. Full documentation of existing programs and data file formats are available to make the job straightforward. Contrast this with commercial toolbox synthesizers that make user programming difficult to impossible in order to protect proprietary rights. In most cases, direct-synthesis programs rely on conventional alphanumeric input rather than the nifty interactive graphics characteristic of the Fairlight and others. One reason is that only 10–20% of the effort in writing a typical interactive graphics program goes toward solving the problem; the rest is in the graphics interaction routines. Thus, in research situations, most programmers get by on the simplest user interface possible: typed commands. Another reason is that graphics programming is generally not "portable" among different computer types or even configurations. Thus, one group using Digital Equipment (DEC) computers would have a tough time sharing a well-done graphics program with another group using IBM equipment.

Real-Time Direct Synthesis

One constant research objective is to design and build hardware that can, in real time, perform the same synthesis and processing functions that a generalized delayed-playback software package can. Two approaches have

Fig. 19–12. Digital Music Systems DMX-1000 Signal Processing Computer

been taken to this problem. One is to choose a single but very general synthesis technique, such as waveform table scanning and then build a very large digital synthesizer using it. Sometimes the synthesizer structure can be very simple, with the difference being made up in volume. One such proposal has been to combine synthesizer boards each of which can produce 256 sine waves with individually controllable frequency and amplitude. The theory is that if enough of these are constructed (a good starting point would be the number of different perceivable frequencies that is in the low thousands range), then any sound could be produced. Although such machines are usually conceived as being one-of-a-kind and end up costing tens to hundreds of thousands of dollars to build, they are sometimes the basis of successful (and scaled down) commercial synthesizers.

Another approach is to split the difference between a general-purpose computer, which is inherently slow, and a fixed architecture but very fast machine like the one just described. The result is a "programmable signal

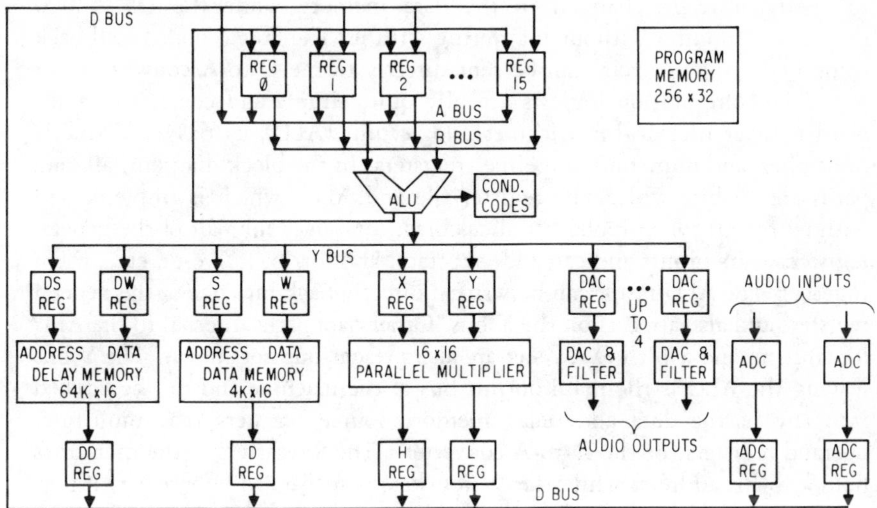

Fig. 19–13. Block Diagram of DMX-1000

processor" that is like a general-purpose computer but has an instruction set, register complement, and architecture optimized for repetitive sample calculation applications. It is the repetition (which makes pipelining possible) and specialization that allows such a machine to run synthesis calculations 5–50 times faster than a general-purpose computer of the same complexity and logic curcuit speed.

An example of this approach is the DMX-1000 Signal Processing Computer from Digital Music Systems, which is pictured in Fig. 19–12. This commercial, programmable, digital signal processor is actually an outgrowth from work done in the Electronic Music Studio at MIT. Packaged in a moderately small rack-mount enclosure, the DMX-1000 has a universal 8-bit parallel interface that can connect to almost any computer. Most users, however, drive it from a DEC PDP-11, primarily because most of the support software available is for that computer.

The DMX-1000 uses what is called a "Harvard architecture," in which the program memory is completely separate from the data memory. The simplified internal block diagram in Fig. 19–13 reveals that there are actually three memories: a 256 word × 32-bit program memory, a 4K × 16 data memory, and a 64K × 16-bit delay memory. The difference between the data and delay memories is that the latter is much slower (six machine cycles versus one) and is also optional. It is typically used to implement signal delays in reverberation simulation and digital filtering programs. The host computer can read and write any of the memories either continuously while the DMX-1000 is stopped or once each sample period while it is running. This allows programs to be loaded into the program memory and parameters to be dynamically changed in the data memory while the DMX-1000 program is running without interfering with it. The host can also read back computed results or they can be sent directly to the D-to-A converters.

The computation logic is actually quite simple and consists of a 16-word register file, 16-bit arithmetic logic unit (ALU), a 16 × 16 parallel multiplier, and numerous "pipeline" registers. In the block diagram, all data paths are 16 bits wide. The register file and ALU, which is implemented with four 2901 type bipolar bit-slice chips, can select any pair of the general registers as its inputs and can add, subtract, and, or, exclusive-or, etc., them together. The ALU result can be written directly back into one of the general registers and also appears on the Y bus. Other data paths internal to the ALU for shifting and a 17th Q register are also present but not shown. The Y bus leaving the ALU is the main output bus of the machine and can be latched into any of the data and delay memory source registers, the multiplier operand registers, or the D-to-A converters. The S registers of the memories hold a 16-bit address, while the W registers hold data to be written, if any, on the next machine cycle. The D bus is the main input bus onto which data read from either data memory, either half of the 32-bit product, or the A-to-D converters may be gated. The D bus then wraps around to the ALU general register inputs.

The DMX-1000 operates with a machine cycle time of 200 nsec, and all instructions require one machine cycle to execute. Every element of the system, except the delay memory, can perform its function in one machine cycle. Program memory is organized as a simple linear list of 256 sequential instructions with no branching except for one implied branch from the end of the program to the beginning. At the beginning of a sample period, four machine cycles are used to allow external access to the memories, trigger the ADCs, and other setup. Thereafter, instructions are executed sequentially at a 5-MHz rate until a halt instruction is encountered. At that point, the program may either loop immediately to the beginning or wait for the next sample pulse. Thus, one program loop is equal to one sample period. For a completely full program memory with 256 steps, the maximum sample rate is 19.3 ks/s. Program decision-making, which is necessary when computing line segment approximations, for example, is implemented by conditional execution according to the ALU condition codes. A failed conditional instruction simply performs as a one-cycle no-op.

Programming the DMX-1000 consists of establishing a bit pattern for each instruction in the sample loop. The 32 instruction bits are divided into a number of fields. For example, two 4-bit fields and another 3-bit field determine which general registers or other data sources are selected for the ALU inputs, while a 6-bit field determines the ALU operation. Additional fields determine which of the Y bus registers are loaded and which of the D bus registers are selected for the current machine cycle. Unlike most general-purpose computers, each element of the DMX-1000 can be performing simultaneously. Thus, the ALU can be adding two values, the multiplier can be working on two different values, and both data memories can be accessing all in the same machine cycle. Minimizing the size of programs, which directly minimizes execution time, involves careful study of the problem and careful programming to maximize concurrency. Thus, pipelining is actually the responsibility of the programmer, which can be much more effective than automatic pipelining. In this respect, DMX-1000 programming is even more difficult than traditional assembly language programming, but then there is much more room for creativity. A specialized assembler that runs on a PDP-11 is available to make the job somewhat easier. A complete music language compiler, called MUSIC-1000, is also available.

Using some of the stock coding supplied with the machine, it is possible to program up to 24 table-lookup oscillators, 8 FM oscillators, 10 second-order digital filters, and various combinations of these and other functions at a 19.3-ks/s sample rate. Although this is not a "large" amount of synthesizer functionality, the mix can be dynamically altered by rewriting the program memory, which can be done very quickly. The real power of this machine lies in its ability to "debug" instrument definitions and explore new synthesis techniques in real time for a limited number of voices using the exact same algorithms that a delayed-playback program would on a general-purpose computer. Even during a final delayed-playback run on the host computer using the whole "orchestra," the DMX-1000 can be used to greatly speed up repetitive synthesis calculations.

Delayed-Playback Direct Synthesis

For the most demanding applications, there is as yet no substitute for a software-based direct-synthesis program running on a general-purpose computer in the delayed-playback mode. Such programs for mainframe computers have been in existence since the early 1960s, when the original work was done at Bell Labs, and now form part of a large family tree. Currently used members include MUSIC V, which is written in FORTRAN for mainframes, MUSIC-360 which is in IBM 360 assembly language, MUSIC-11 in assembly language for the DEC PDP-11 line, and C-MUSIC which is written in the C programming language. Although the latter is typically run on PDP-11s and VAXs (a "supermini" computer also made by DEC), it is the only program in the series with the potential for running successfully on some of the more powerful microcomputer systems. All of these programs are similar in concept and usage with most differences due to the computers they run on and extra music language features. Development and maintenance of all of these programs is done at universities. Although some have stiff licensing fees, the market is just too small for any of them to become a profitable product.

To conclude this chapter, a brief look will be taken at the CARL (Computer Audio Research Laboratory) music system, which is a continuing development at the University of California at San Diego (UCSD). CARL is really a set of related programs that are normally configured to run under the UNIX operating system. This large time-sharing operating system runs most efficiently on VAX and PDP-11 computers but has also been successfully implemented on the more powerful 16-bit microcomputers using 68000, 16032, and 80286 microprocessors. Virtually all of the programs are written in the C language, which means that straightforward conversion to a different computer using UNIX is at least theoretically possible. The record and playback programs that operate the A/D/A conversion system, however, must be in assembly language so they would have to be rewritten for a different processor. All of the programs, including C language source code, may be licensed for a very nominal copying fee and by agreeing to some simple acknowledgment conditions.

One of the leading features of the UNIX operating system is an elegantly simple "tree-structured" directory system for disk data files. Since UNIX is a time-sharing operating system, each user has a separate branch of the directory. Likewise, each project being worked on can be a branch off the user branch and so forth. Directory links allow the same file to appear in different directories, thus avoiding multiple copies. Unfortunately, sound files are usually too big to be efficiently handled by the built-in UNIX file system. Also, substantial delays may sometimes be encountered during sequential access, which would be unacceptable during playback and recording operations. This problem is solved by defining a separate, simplified directory system for sound files, which is dedicated to a separate rigid disk drive. By using algorithms that favor physically sequential allocation of sound files and by using large block sizes, the *CSOUND* directory system meets the real-time acccess and high-speed data transfer required for digitized sound recording and playback.

At UCSD, for example, a 300M byte removable pack disk drive is used for sound file storage. Space is allocated in units of cylinders that are about 300K bytes each. For most operations, sound files are dynamic in size, but the A-to-D record program requires that the file length be specified in advance so that the written file is known to be physically sequential on the disk. Samples are stored in sound files as 16-bit, twos-complement integers called *shortsams* in CARL terminology. For stereo, shortsams are stored alternately in the file. In fact, the system handles up to four channels of sound data. Two sample rates are typically used; a 49,152 s/s ($= 3 \times 2^{14}$) rate for final results and one-third that rate for preliminary runs. At the higher rate, a 300 M byte disk pack holds about 43 minutes of monaural sound. Elsewhere in the system, particularly within CMUSIC and the other sample-processing programs, samples are manipulated as single-precision 32-bit *floatsams*. The use of floating-point arithmetic is virtually mandated when a high-level language such as C is used and does not greatly reduce computation speed on the large computers typically used to run UNIX.

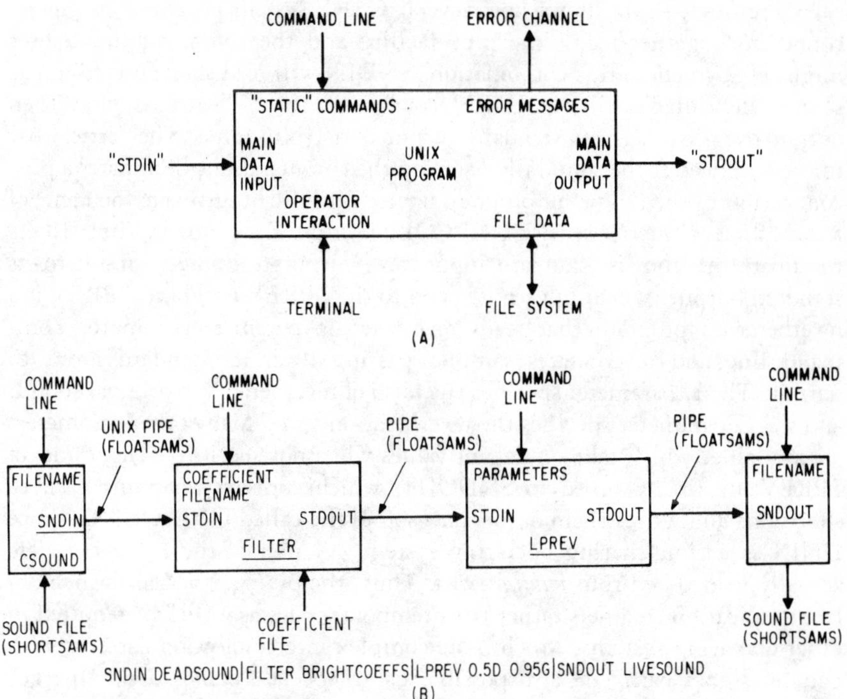

Fig. 19–14. Dataflow connections of UNIX programs. (A) Generalized UNIX program. (B) Four programs connected by UNIX pipes.

Another leading feature of UNIX is that otherwise separate programs can be "chained" together into networks with a simple command. This is used within CARL to combine sample generation and processing program modules almost like connecting them together with patchcords. Figure 19–14A is a "dataflow" diagram of a typical UNIX program. Programs are run by typing their names and perhaps some arguments on the UNIX *command line.* The program can read the arguments, which are usually file names and program options, from the command line input. Any error messages that may be generated are sent out over the errors channel, which can go to either the terminal or a file. Most programs also read and/or write data files using the standard UNIX file system. Such files may contain additional action specifications, data to be processed, or new data created by the program. For interactive programs, the terminal is used to receive additional operator commands and to display messages or results. Most important, however, are the STDIN and STDOUT data streams. These are simple sequential streams of bytes that are normally text characters but in the CARL system are sound samples. It is these two data streams that may be "connected" to other programs using the UNIX "pipe" facility.

Figure 19–14B shows how several CARL system programs might be connected together using the pipe facility and the command line a user might type to effect this combination. SNDIN will read shortsams from the sound file called DEADSOUND, convert them to floatsams, and then output them through its standard output to a UNIX pipe. The vertical bar immediately after the sound file name on the command line designates a pipe connection to the following program name. FILTER in turn gets the name of the coefficient file to use (BRIGHTCOEFFS) from the command line, filters the floatsams from its standard input, and outputs the filtered result to its standard output, which in turn is piped to the LPREV program. LPREV is a reverberation program that reads reverberation parameters from the command line and reverberates samples passing from its standard input to output. The D parameter specifies the ratio of reverberated to original sound, and the G parameter specifies the reverberation time. Many other parameters are available, which take on default values when not specified. The results of LPREV are finally piped to SNDOUT, which converts floatsams back to shortsams and writes them onto a new sound file called LIVESOUND. Since UNIX is a time-sharing operating system, all four of these programs are actually loaded and run *simultaneously.* Thus, the pipes are actual in-memory communication channels rather than temporary files as would be required in other operating systems. Much more complex interconnection patterns with parallel signal paths are also possible using special "branch" and "merge" programs.

C-MUSIC is the heart of the CARL system for synthesis applications. This program reads text from a score file and produces floatsams on its standard output for piping to other programs or writing into a sound file. The score file (or standard input if no file is specified) may have been prepared by the user with a text editor or may be the output from a macroexpander or high-level composition program. The brief discussion that follows should convey the flavor of C-MUSIC, which is also generally applicable to MUSIC-V, MUSIC-11, and other family members.

A C-MUSIC score consists of *statements,* each of which is terminated by a semicolon. Text enclosed in curly brackets ({}) may be placed anywhere as comments. Score statements are grouped into four overall *sections* as follows:

1. Options
2. Instrument definitions
3. Function (table) generation
4. Notelist

The options section contains statements that specify several global attributes applicable to the current "run" of C-MUSIC. These include the sample rate, number of sound output channels (one to four), the sizes of internal buffers, the random-number generator initial seed, and the default function length. The latter is the size of waveform and envelope shape tables used by the synthesis routines and is usually 1,024 entries. Options can also be specified on the command line, in which case they override those in the score.

At this point, it is probably better to describe the notelist, which is the actual score, first. The most fundamental notelist statement is the NOTE statement. It consists simply of the keyword NOTE followed by several parameter or "P-fields," each separated from the others by blanks. P1 is the keyword "NOTE" itself, while P2 is the "action time" and P3 is the name of the instrument that will play the note. The action time specifies when the note should start and is normally given in seconds. P4 is the duration of the note, also given in seconds, and is the last required parameter. Additional P-fields may be used if the instrument that will play the note requires them. By convention, P5 usually gives the amplitude and P6 the frequency of pitched notes. As many P-fields as desired may be used according to the complexity of the corresponding instrument definitions. Below are a few valid note statements in their simplest form:

```
NOTE 0.00 BLATT  .10   1.0   16
NOTE 0.15 BLEEP  .15  .707   220HZ
NOTE 0.20 BLIPP  .05  -3DB   4*261HZ  {Two octaves above
                                       {middle C
NOTE 0.50 BLOPP  .35  -5DB   1.5KHZ  5.7HZ  0.2SEC
NOTE 1.25 BLURP  .25   0DB   55HZ  V5  3*V7+2
```

The first note is played on an instrument called BLATT starting immediately at time zero and lasting for one-tenth of a second. Its amplitude is unity (the maximum amplitude allowable in C-MUSIC) and the frequency is 256 Hz. Actually, the frequency field gives the waveform table pointer *increment* value; thus, the wave frequency is actually P6*SR/FL, where P6 is the given P6 field value of 16, SR is the sample rate (default is 16,384 Hz), and FL is the wavetable or function length (default is 1024). The second note is similar but the "postop" hertz is used so that frequency can be specified in hertz rather than wavetable increments. Needless to say, this is usually done. The third note illustrates the decibel postop, which is useful in amplitude specification and the fact that arithmetic expressions can be used in specifying P-field values. In fact, nearly any kind of expression normally permitted in a programming language including functions such as SIN, COS, LN, EXP, SQRT, and even RAND can be used. In the fourth note, the "K" postop, which is a 1024 multiplier, is also included in the frequency specification to yield 1,536 Hz. Two additional parameters needed by the BLOPP instrument are also included. The SEC postop converts the given number, which is a waveform period here, into an increment. The last note makes use of *variables* in expressions for its P7 and P8 fields. V5 and V7 have

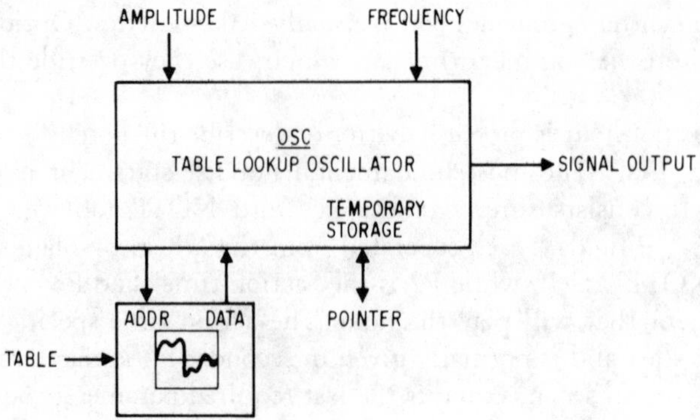

GENERAL FORM: OSC *OUTPUT AMPLITUDE FREQUENCY TABLE POINTER*

EXAMPLES:
1. OSC B1 P5 P6 F1 D
2. OSC B1 P5 P6 P7 D
3. OSC B2 B1 P6 F1 D
4. OSC B2 P5 B1 F1 D

Fig. 19–15. OSC Unit generator

presumably been defined previously in VAR statements, which influence all subsequent notes using them. Generally, in any source of significant size, variables, expressions, and macros (which have not been described) are used to make human reading and editing of the score much easier than these examples might imply.

The notelist can also contain VAR statements, which have already been mentioned, SEC statements, and MERGE statements. Besides V variables, the VAR statement can also specify P variables whose values are used as defaults when an instrument requries a P-field but the note statement does not specify one. The SEC statement defines the beginning of *sections* of the score in which local time always begins at zero. Thus, the timing of whole sections of the score may be made relative to other sections without having to change all of the note beginning times. Normally, note beginning times must be in sequence so that each is later than its predecessor. By using MERGE statements, one can cause C-MUSIC to sort note statements into time order before processing them. This allows, for example, horizontal score entry (one voice at a time; see Chapter 18) to be used instead of vertical entry and expressions involving variables (even the RAND function!) to be used in the starting time field. The TER statement is used at the end of the score and can specify an amount of trailing silence for notes and reverberation to decay.

The most interesting part of the score, and one that is responsible for C-MUSIC's flexibility, is the instrument definitions section. Instruments are defined by "patching" together *unit generators* in a manner analogous to voltage-controlled analog modules. Each unit generator is specified by a single statement within an instrument definition that gives the generator's name followed by several parameters, which specify where the inputs come from and where the output goes. Available unit generators include several kinds of oscillators, amplifiers, mixers, several different filters, delay lines, mathematical operators, nonlinear distorters (table lookup elements), noise generators, and the content of existing sound files. As many unit generators as desired may be combined in an instrument definition, and, since 32-bit floating-point arithmetic is used, error accumulation is generally not a concern.

Figure 19–15 shows a schematic representation of the OSC unit generator along with a prototype OSC statement. The statement begins with the keyword, OSC, followed by the name of an *I/O block* that will receive its output. I/O blocks are different from constants and parameters and are used to pass sample values among the unit generators in an instrument. The reason they are special is that signal samples are calculated in blocks to improve computation speed. I/O blocks are identified as B1, B2, . . . up to the limit of memory. The second and third fields specify the output amplitude and the increment for the table lookup pointer, respectively. Each may be parameters from note statements (P-type variables), V-type variables, constants, or other I/O blocks. The resulting amplitude value simply multiplies sample values read from the wavetable. The frequency of the oscillator is I*SR/FL, where I is the resulting increment value, SR is the prevailing sample rate, and FL is the length of the wavetable. The next field specifies which wavetable to use. Wavetables are created later in the function-generation section and are identified by number. Like the amplitude and increment fields, variables may be used to specify the function number to be used.

The last field effectively specifies the initial value of the waveform table pointer. If the letter D (for "dynamic" variable) is used, then the initial value is zero. Use of a P-type or a V-type variable allows the oscillator's initial phase to be controlled. Internally, a temporary storage location is allocated to hold the wavetable pointer when a note using the oscillator starts and is freed when the note ends. Every time a note starts, a new storage location is allocated so an instrument may play any number of notes simultaneously.

Also shown in Fig. 19–15 are some valid OSC statements. Example 1 is the simplest possible OSC statement. It outputs to I/O block number 1, uses function number 1 for its wavetable, and always starts its waveform at the beginning of the table. The amplitude of the note is specified by the fifth P-field in note statements that play it, and frequency is specified by the sixth P-field. Example 2 is similar except that the wavetable to be used may be specified in the note statements rather than being constant in the instrument definition. In example 3, the amplitude is the content of another I/O block from a previous statement that presumably has samples of an envelope shape. The same can be done for frequency as in Example 4 in which the content of B1 sets the instantaneous frequency.

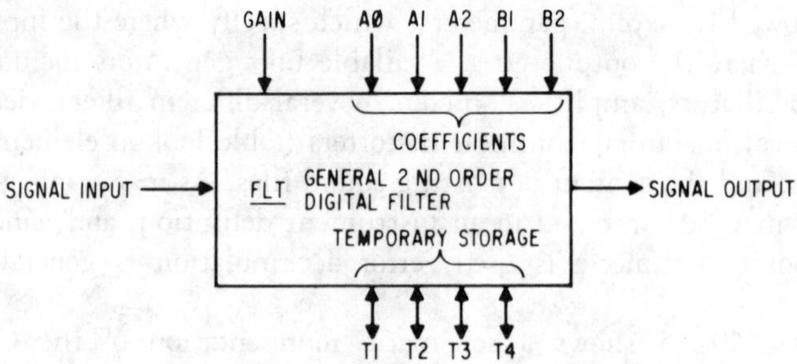

(A) FLT *OUTPUT INPUT GAIN AØ A1 A2 B1 B2 T1 T2 T3 T4*

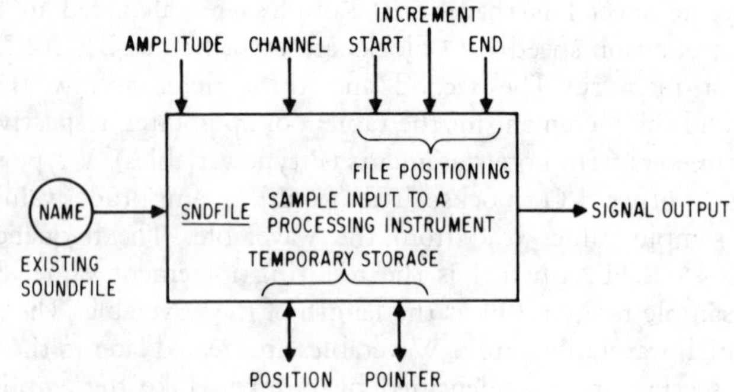

(B) SNDFILE *OUTPUT AMP INCREMENT NAME CHANNEL START END POSITION POINTER*

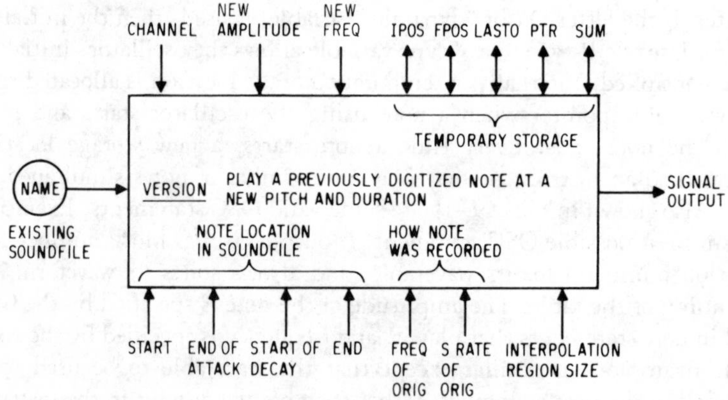

(C) VERSION *OUTPUT AMP NFREQ NAME CHANNEL START ENDATT BEGINDK END INTERPSIZ SRATEORIG FREQORIG T1 T2 T3 T4 T5*

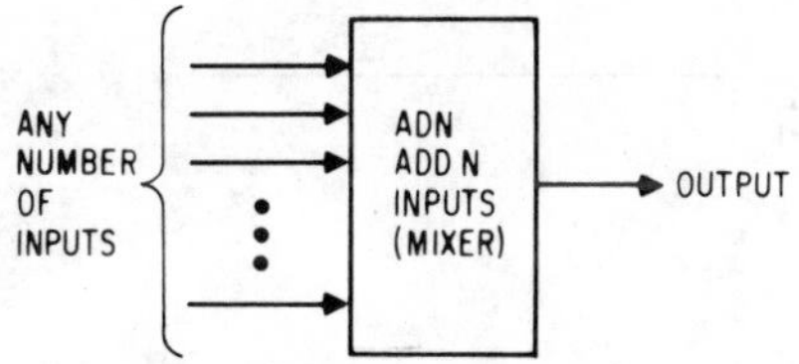

(D) ADN *OUTPUT INPUT1 INPUT2 •••*

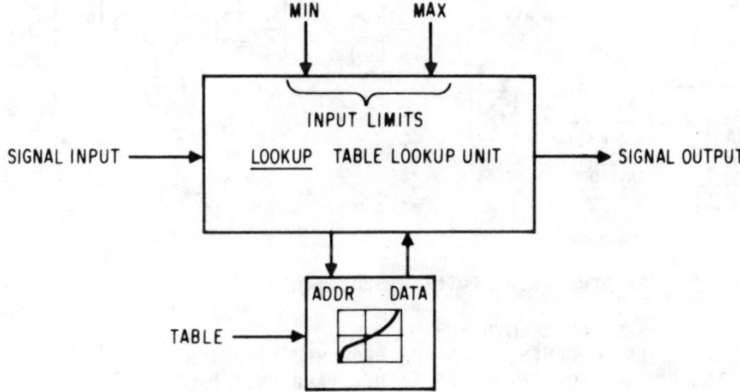

(E) LOOKUP *OUTPUT TABLE INPUT MIN MAX*

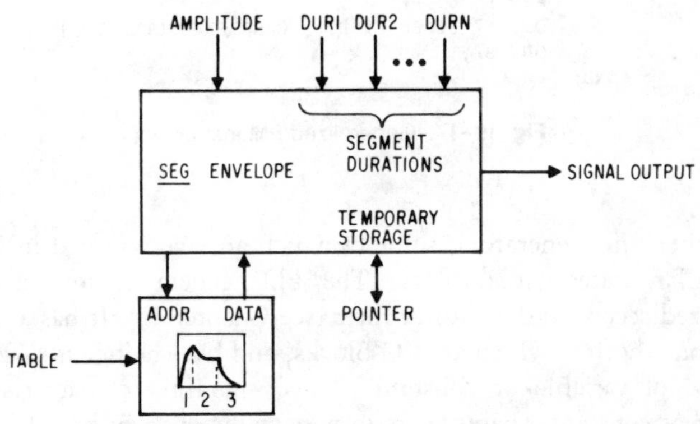

(F) SEG *OUTPUT AMP TABLE POINTER DUR1 DUR2 •••*

Fig. 19–16. Some additional unit generators. (A) FLT output input gain A0 A1 A2 B1 B2 T1 T2 T3 T4. (B) SNDFILE output amp increment name channel start end position pointer. (C) Version output amp NFREQ name channel start ENDATT BEGINDK END INTERPSIZ SRATEORIG FREQORIG T1 T2 T3 T4 T5. (D) ADN output input1 input2 .... (E) Lookup output table input min max. (F) SEG output amp table pointer DUR1 DUR2 ....

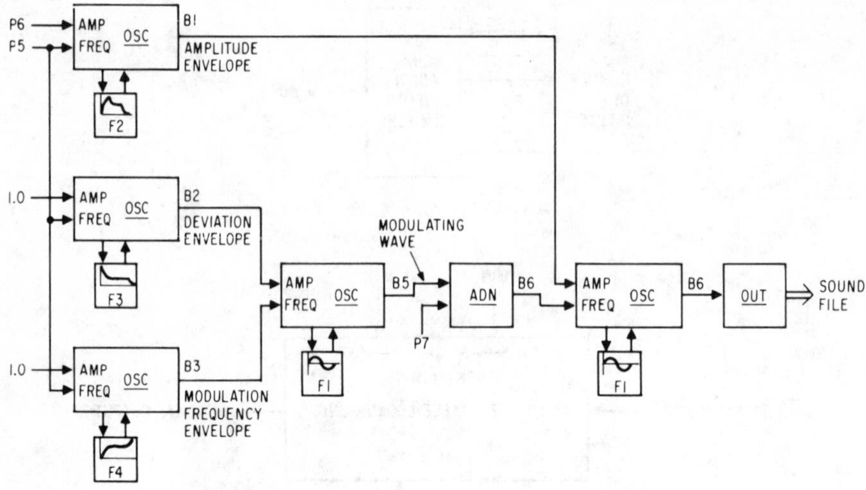


```
Instrument Definition Statements

SET FUNCLENGTH = 8K
INS 0 GENFM;  {P5=DUR, P6=AMP, P7=PITCH}
      OSC B1 P6 P5 F2 D;  {AMP ENVELOPE}
      OSC B2 1  P5 F3 D;  {DEV ENVELOPE}
      OSC B3 1  P5 F4 D;  {MOD FREQ ENVELOPE}
      OSC B5 B2 B3 F1 D;  {MODULATION OSCILLATOR}
      ADN B6 B5 P7;
      OSC B7 B1 B6 F1 D;  {CARRIER OSCILLATOR}
      OUT B7;
END;
```

Fig. 19–17. Generalized FM instrument

Other unit generators, some of which are diagrammed in Fig. 19–16, use similar statement formats. The FLT generator, for example, is a generalized second-order digital filter (see Chapter 14). It has a signal input and output, both of which are I/O blocks, and five coefficients, which can be any kind of variable or constant. Thus, the filter characteristics can be specified as constants, parameters in note statements, or by other signals via the I/O blocks. Also, since arithmetic expressions are allowed in any of the coefficient fields, the FLT statement may be set up for control in familiar terms such as center frequency and *Q* factor. FLT also requires four temporary values for the internal delays, which can be set to any specific initial value or allowed to default to zero. SNDFILE is not really a generator at all; it instead reads samples from an existing sound file. The various parameters include an amplitude factor, an increment for the read pointer (which should be 1.0 to read every sample), and starting and ending positions in the file. If more samples are read than exist between start and end positions, the pointer wraps around to the beginning as if the file was a huge waveform table. The

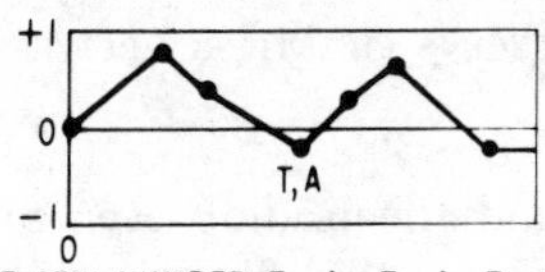

GEN DEFNTIME GEN1 NUMBER T_0, A_0 T_1, A_1 T_2, A_2 •••

GEN Ø GEN1 F1 0,0 0.2, 0.8 0.3, 0.42 0.5, −0.15 0.6, 0.2 0.7, 0.65 0.9, −0.25

(A) GEN1 = STRAIGHT-LINE SEGMENT GENERATOR (UNEQUALLY SPACED POINTS)

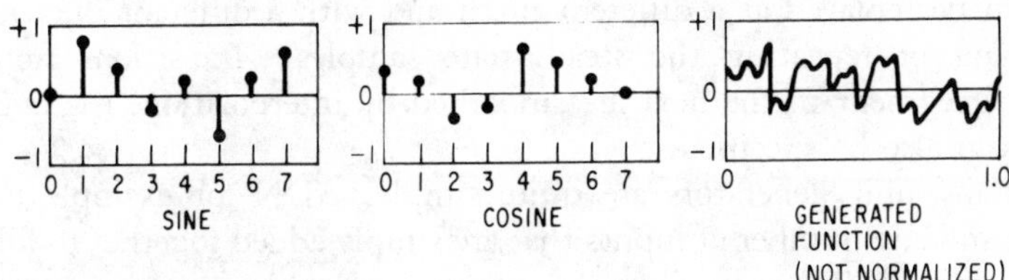

GEN DEFNTIME GEN2 NUMBER S_0 S_1 S_2 ••• C_0 C_1 C_2 •••

GEN Ø GEN1 F1 0 0.8 0.4 −0.2 0.2 −0.6 0.25 0.6 0.3 0.15 −0.4 −0.2 0.6 0.45 0.15 0

(B) GEN2 = FOURIER SERIES (SINE-COSINE FORM)

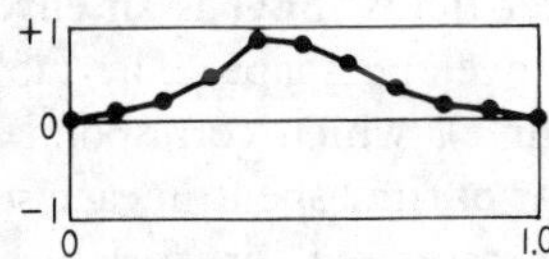

GEN DEFNTIME GEN3 NUMBER T_0 T_1 T_2 T_3 •••

GEN Ø GEN3 F2 0 0.08 0.21 0.5 0.9 0.85 0.63 0.36 0.15 0.10 0

(C) GEN3 = STRAIGHT-LINE SEGMENT GENERATOR (EQUALLY SPACED POINTS)

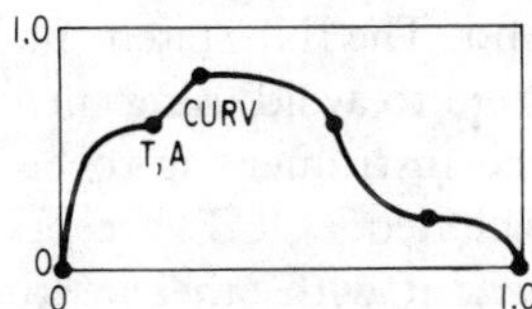

GEN DEFNTIME GEN 4 NUMBER T_0, A_0, $CURV_0$, T_1, A_1, $CURV_1$ ••• T_N, A_N

GEN Ø GEN4 F3 0, 0, −2 0.2, 0.6, 0 0.3, 0.8, 2 0.6, 0.6, −1 0.8, 0.2, 1 1.0, 0

(D) GEN4 = EXPONENTIAL LINE SEGMENT GENERATOR

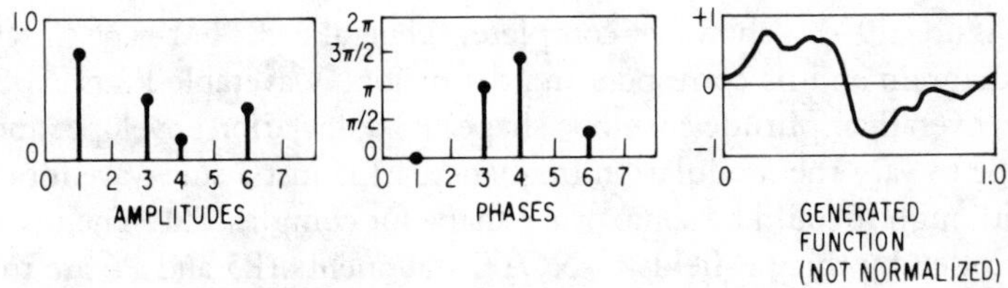

GEN DEFNTIME GEN5 NUMBER N_1, A_1, P_1 N_2, A_2, P_2 •••

GEN Ø GEN5 F2 1, 0.75, 0 3, 0.45, 3.14 4, 0.12, 4.2 6, 0.3, 1.4

(E) GEN5 = FOURIER SERIES (AMPLITUDE-PHASE FORM)

Fig. 19–18. Standard GEN functions. (A) GEN1 = Straight-line segment generator (unequally spaced points). (B) GEN2 = Fourier series (sine-cosine form). (C) GEN3 = Straight-line segment generator (equally spaced points). (D) GEN4 = Exponential line segment generator. (E) GEN5 = Fourier series (amplitude-phase form).

VERSION generator carries sound file reading even further. With VERSION, a particular note recorded in a sound file can be identified in terms of file positions for the beginning of the attack, beginning of steady-state, beginning of decay, and end of decay. Then, with additional parameters, the note can be replayed at a different pitch and with a different duration (by truncating or repeating the steady-state samples). Transitions from one envelope segment to the next are smoothed by interpolation, the degree of which can also be specified.

Many unit generators are quite simple. ADN for example has one output and any number of inputs that are simply added together to form the output. LOOKUP has an input, an output, and uses a wavetable to translate the input to the output. Two parameters also specify the expected range of inputs. Besides use as a nonlinear waveshaper, it can be used in a myriad of ways to tailor response curves in instruments more efficiently than using complex expressions in parameter fields. SEG is an envelope generator that uses a waveform table for the envelope shape. The table is divided into a number of segments (usually three), which correspond to envelope phases. Parameters determine the amount of time spent in each segment according to either constants in the SEG statement or variables from the NOTE statement. A very useful feature is that the duration of designated segments may be calculated automatically from the total note duration.

Complete instrument definitions require an INS statement at the beginning and an END statement at the end. The INS statement includes an "action time" field, which can be set nonzero to avoid using memory for the instrument definition until needed. If the instrument is to be heard, the OUT unit generator must also be included. OUT accepts the final instrument output as an I/O block and *sums* it with other instruments that may be playing into the C-MUSIC standard output sample stream, which will ultimately go to a sound file. For stereo or quad output, OUT requires two or four inputs. If an instrument is to sound in only one channel, the other inputs are set to zero.

Figure 19–17 shows a complete, generalized, FM-type instrument block diagram and its corresponding definition. Wavetable F2 is expected to have an overall amplitude envelope shape, F3 a deviation envelope, and F4 an envelope to vary the modulation frequency. F1 is just a sine wave for classical FM, although it could be some other shape for complex FM. The instrument is controlled by three P-fields in NOTE statements. P5 and P6 are the usual duration and amplitude parameters, while P7 sets the average ratio of modulation to carrier frequency. Below is the complete C-MUSIC instrument definition for this instrument, which is called GENFM. Note that, since FM synthesis can be adversely affected by table lookup truncation error, the size of F1 has been set to 8,192 samples.

The function generation score section specifies the content of wavetables. This section consists of a series of GEN statements, each of which will generate the contents of a numbered F table. The standard C-MUSIC function generator programs are identified by number; thus, GEN2 is a Fourier series waveform generator, while GEN3 is a line segment generator useful for defining envelope shapes. The reason for this is historical; user-written function generators can have any desired name. Figure 19–18 outlines the five standard GEN programs. The length of tables produced by the GEN programs can be specified with the SET FUNCLENGTH statement (in the options section) and defaults to 1024. Table lookups performed by the unit generators almost never use interpolation, since it is much slower and adequate memory is usually available for long tables.

20

Low-Cost Synthesis Techniques

While research and high-end applications of computer music synthesis enjoy the most glamour, more utilitarian applications are also important and can be interesting as well. A professional synthesizer, such as described in the previous chapter, would probably be considered "successful" if more than 5,000 were sold during its lifetime. At, say, $3,000 each, the gross income would be $15 million. A successful research system may have sales of only a few hundred units, but, even at its much higher price, there would be less total income. A popular musical toy, however, may very well sell in the millions of units. Even though the price might be only $30 or so, the income generated could be much greater than the two previous examples.

Designing sound-generation circuits for a high-volume toy or game is actually much more challenging than designing a professional or research synthesizer. In the latter case, the designer is interested mostly in a "clean" design that performs flawlessly. Manufacturing costs, while kept in mind during the design, are usually not of prime importance. In a high-volume product design, elimination of a single resistor with an installed cost of one cent can save $20,000 over a 2 million unit production run. That kind of savings is sufficient to justify having an engineer spend an entire *month* or more *full-time* studying whether that resistor can be removed. An excellent design in this context is one that is cheap to produce and performs adequately and safely.

Although fussing over individual components is often productive, the initial selection of synthesis technique is by far the most important decision to be made in a high-volume product design. In this chapter, some low-cost techniques will be examined and then their application to several low-cost products will be described.

Applications of Low-Cost Synthesis

Many types of products today use electronic sound generation in their operation. Mechanical sound generators, such as bells, buzzers, sirens, whistles, etc., are seldom heard anymore. Electronic generators are cheaper, offer a much wider variety of distinctive sounds, and can be smaller and louder with less power input than their mechanical counterparts. In consumer products, the use of sound generators is increasing dramatically. Cars beep when the key is left in, watches buzz on the hour, alarm clocks play reveille, and smoke alarms squeal when guests light up. The use of speech synthesis is also frequently heard in products such as microwave ovens, elevators, cars, and children's toys.

In video game design, proper selection and use of sound effects is almost as important as the screen graphics. In a well-designed game, every type of movement and event has a different sound associated with it. A trained listener can determine the state of the game and perhaps even keep score merely by listening. Often, a separate microprocessor is used exclusively to generate game sounds. Although uninformed charges that video game sounds are "carefully selected for maximum subliminal effect" are sometimes made, in reality they are chosen for generation ease. Most shots and explosions are simply bursts of filtered white noise, while the typical "laser zap" can be generated with a dozen instructions or so in the mircoprocessor program. However, more recent arcade game designs use multipart musical sequences and even speech synthesis to encourage players.

Moving into more musical applications, there are a large number of low-cost musical instruments on the market ranging from $30 toy keyboards to complete polyphonic synthesizers for a few hundred dollars. Many of these emphasize an ability to store keyboard sequences and play them back later, since this is easily implemented and requires little if any additional hardware. There are even $10 musical calculators that "play" the answer with a different pitch for each digit, $3 musical Christmas cards that play a tune when opened, and musical car horns for use late on Saturday nights. Several games make use of random note sequences to test the player's ability to remember them.

Except for the inexpensive synthesizers, most of these devices are monophonic and use a square or pulse waveform for the sound source. Where size is important, such as in the Christmas card, piezoelectric transducers are used. There are flat ceramic disks about 1 inch in diameter that give an extremely tinny sound due to a high self-resonant frequency and lack of a baffle. The toy organs and synthesizers usually have a standard dynamic speaker built in and occasionally an output jack for an external audio system.

Another large application area is in home and personal computers. Virtually every such computer made since the late 1970s has some means of sound generation built in. Sound is most commonly used in computer games, many of which are modeled after successful arcade versions. In business applications, audible feedback from keystrokes and discreet error beeps can dramatically improve operator accuracy. All computers with sound capability have music programs available for them. Even the simplest sound generators can, with proper programming, produce a complete range of note frequencies. In many cases, three or four simultaneous notes are possible and, in rare cases, timbre variations as well. For popular computers with minimal native sound generation capacity, there are usually a number of independently manufactured add-ons available. These typically consist of a plug-in synthesizer board and matching music software. The sophistication of these boards ranges from 3 square-wave voices to 16 fully programmable waveform generators. Frequently, the software includes a suitably simplified interactive graphics score editor and perhaps an instrument definition editor as well. A couple of products even include a music keyboard for live as well as programmed performance.

Techniques for Low-Cost Synthesis

The techniques used in low-cost sound-generating devices are not really different from those studied so far. Instead, the emphasis is shifted from considerations of flexibility and quality to those of cost and distinctiveness. In many product designs in which sound generation is just a small part, free choice of a synthesis technique might not be possible; available resources may have to be used instead. Thus, strange and ingenious circuit designs with limited general applicability sometimes evolve. Here, a few of the more straightforward low-cost synthesis techniques will be explored.

Interface Chip Timers

Many microprocessor-driven devices use one or more "peripheral interface chips" (PIC) in their design. A high-volume, relatively simple product may even use an all-in-one-chip microcomputer that also includes PIC functions. Most modern PICs include one or more programmable timers. These are normally used to simplify timing-related programming but can also sometimes be used as oscillators for sound generation.

Such timers are usually programmed in one of two ways. A *single-shot* timer for example typically has a 16-bit "counter register" that may be written into under program control. After writing, the register counts down at a fixed rate and generates an interrupt and perhaps an external pulse when it reaches zero. The timing reference is usually the microprocessor clock, which sometimes is passed through a programmable *prescaler* where it can be divided by a power of two before clocking the register. The counter register is normally readable as well so that the microprocessor program can determine how much time remains in the current interval. A *free-running* timer is similar except that it has an "interval register" that is separate from the counter register. When the counter reaches zero, it is automatically reloaded from the interval register and starts timing a new interval. Thus, variations in interrupt response time do not affect cumulative long-term accuracy such as keeping track of the time of day from 1-sec timing intervals.

Obviously, the free-running type is much more suitable as a programmable oscillator because a frequency control word can be written into the interval register once and the timer will then generate pulses at that frequency automatically without program intervention. Generally, the microsecond-wide pulses produced must be shaped before they can effectively operate a speaker. One possibility is to use the pulse to discharge a capacitor that is being constantly charged through a resistor or current source. This produces a sawtooth wave that is useful over a range of two to three octaves. Another possibility is to have the pulse trigger a single shot to produce a much wider pulse and thus a rectangular waveform. Sophisticated multichannel timer chips such as the Intel 8253 can be programmed so that one timer determines the frequency in free-running mode and triggers another timer in single-shot mode, thus producing a programmable duty cycle. The Motorola 6840 produces the same effect by splitting its 16-bit timer register into two 8-bit halves, one of which determines the waveform high time and the other determines the low time. Of course, the pulse output can also toggle a flip-flop for a square wave, a function built into some timer ICs.

One particular peripheral interface chip that has been used extensively for sound generation in low-cost personal computers is the 6522 "versatile interface adapter" (VIA). This remarkable IC has two full 8-bit I/O ports, two timers, and a multimode 8-bit shift register. In a typical computer, the ports are used to interface to a printer and control internal functions, while the timers and shift register are either not used or are connected to a small amplifier and internal speaker. Timer 1 is a standard 16-bit unit that can operate in free-running mode and produce a pulse or half-frequency square-wave output. The other timer is more interesting, however, because it can operate in conjunction with the shift register. Although its counter is also 16 bits, the interval register is only 8 bits, which limits frequency resolution somewhat. In one of its operating modes, the internal 8-bit shift register is *rotated* one position on each Timer 2 timeout. By writing different bit patterns into the shift register, different eight-segment waveforms can be produced on the shift register output pin for a number of different timbres (it is instructive to determine how many *audibly* different patterns there are). One can even set the shift register to shift at its maximum rate and then use different bit patterns to simulate a pulse-width modulated nine-level D-to-A converter for producing somewhat smoother waveforms. Also, since the two timers are independent, two simultaneous tones are readily produced. In all, the 6522 provides quite a lot of sound-generation function often for little or no added cost.

Timed Program Loops

Of course, the classic method of producing simple sounds by computer is the timed program loop. It is, in fact, so simple and fundamental (and interesting to novices) that it is frequently used as a programming example in elementary microprocessor technology courses. The basic idea is to provide an addressable flip-flop, either alone or as one of the bits of an output port, which an assembly language program can set to a one or a zero at will. The logic level voltage then is either connected to an on-board transistor switch driving a speaker or an external amplifier/speaker.

To produce a pulse of a constant frequency, the student is instructed to write a program to set the flip-flop to a one, immediately set it to a zero, and then enter a delay loop, which perhaps decrements a register until it becomes zero. After the delay, the program would jump to the beginning for another pulse. When the student has mastered this, techniques for making the delay variable, perhaps by reading the delay parameter from an input port, are then introduced. The utility of subroutines might be illustrated by altering the program for square or rectangular output using a single timing subroutine called with a different delay argument for the high and low portions of the waveform. Depending on the course, multitask programming might be introduced by having the student write a program to simulate two or three such oscillators, simultaneously producing different frequencies.

While this seems trivial compared with what has been covered earlier in this book, there are legitimate applications beyond being a teaching aid. In 1976–77, three-voice music programs using timed loops were state of the art in microcomputer music. Even today on many machines, such as the IBM PC and Apple II, it is the only viable way to produce sound without hardware add-ons. The musical Christmas cards and car horns mentioned earlier are really nothing more than minimal 4-bit single-chip microcomputers mask-programmed to play square-wave note sequences from stored scores using simple timed loops. Almost any computer program, even business programs, can benefit from the judicious use of sound, and usually a few dozen bytes of extra code are all that is needed.

Besides playing buzzy little melodies, single-bit timed-loop routines can produce a wide variety of sound effects as well. White noise is readily generated by programming one of the shift-register random-bit generators described in Chapter 15 and sending the bits to an output port. Some control over the noise spectrum can be secured by running the generator at different sample rates. Laser zaps and police siren effects can be produced by rapidly varying the delay parameter in a timed loop tone routine.

Figure 20–1 shows a simple but very effective "strange sound" generation program. The basic idea is to use two 16-bit simulated registers where the second (REG2) is successively added to the first (REG1). Each time REG1 overflows, the value of REG2 is incremented. After each inner loop, the lower half of REG1 is written to an output port. Each bit of this port will have a different sound sequence and more can be had by modifying the program to output the upper half of REG1 instead. The sounds produced by this routine are really wild and well worth the hour or so required to translate

```
0000                ; STRAGE SOUND EFFECT GENERATOR
0000
BFF0   =     PORT   =      $BFF0   ; OUTPUT PORT BITS TO AMPLIFIER
0000
0000                *=     0       ; SIMULATED REGISTERS IN PAGE 0
0000 0000    REG1   .WORD  0       ; 16-BIT OUTPUT REGISTER
0002 0100    REG2   .WORD  1       ; 16-BIT INCREMENT REGISTER
0004
0004                *=     $700    ; PROGRAM ORIGIN
0700                .ENTRY
0700 A500    SSOUND LDA    REG1    ; ADD REG2 TO REG1 WITH
0702 18             CLC            ; RESULT IN REG1
0703 6502           ADC    REG2    ; LOWER BYTE
0705 8500           STA    REG1
0707 8DF0BF         STA    PORT    ; MAKE LOWER BYTE AUDIBLE
070A A501           LDA    REG1+1  ; UPPER BYTE
070C 6503           ADC    REG2+1
070E 8501           STA    REG1+1
0710 90EE           BCC    SSOUND  ; REPEAT UNTIL REG1 OVERFLOWS
0712 E602           INC    REG2    ; INCREMENT REG2 WHEN REG1 OVERFLOWS
0714 D0EA           BNE    SSOUND  ; AND REPEAT INDEFINITELY
0716 E603           INC    REG2+1
0718 D0E6           BNE    SSOUND
071A E602           INC    REG2    ; DON´T LET REG2=0
071C 4C0007         JMP    SSOUND
```

Fig. 20–1. Sound effects generator

and enter the program into virtually any kind of computer. As written, the sequence of sounds repeats every 20 sec on a 1-MHz 6502-based computer. For practical use, as a sound-effects generator, desirable points in the sequence are determined, and the registers initialized to the corresponding values. The loop is then run the desired number of iterations and terminated.

One difficulty with timed loops is that the microprocessor is fully occupied while producing sound. Enough time for simple tasks, such as looking at a control panel, can be taken between notes, however, with little audible effect. A related problem is that the microprocessor must execute instructions at a known, stable rate. Computers that stop or interrupt the microprocessor to refresh memory, for example, would probably produce very rough sounding tones.

Simplified Direct Synthesis

For much more controlled sound effects and listenable music, many of the digital synthesis techniques described in Chapter 13 can be used, in simplified form, for low-cost sound generation. A common requirement, however, is a cheap D-to-A converter and a linear power amplifier (the single-bit timed-loop techniques could use a one-transistor switch). In large volumes, 8-bit D-to-A converter chips are well under $2, while half-watt audio amplifier ICs are under a dollar. For really low cost, one can get by with an 8-bit CMOS register, eight weighted 1% resistors, and a power Darlington transistor emitter-follower amplifier. In either case, a two-stage

```
0000                ; 4-VOICE WAVEFORM TABLE SCAN SYNTHESIS SUBROUTINE FOR 6502
0000                ; CALL WITH 4 FREQUENCY PARAMETERS IN FREQ1-FREQ4
0000                ; TONE FREQUENCY = (FREQ PARM)*.12715 HZ
0000                ; CALL ALSO WITH TEMPO AND DUR SET; DUR IS ZEROED ON RETURN
0000                ; CHORD DURATION = TEMPO*DUR*.00012 SECONDS
0000                ; SAMPLE PERIOD = 120US = 8.33KS/S     FOR 1MHZ PROCESSOR CLOCK
0000
BFF1 =        PORT    =       $BFF1       ; OUTPUT PORT BITS TO D-TO-A CONVERTER
0000
0000                  *=      0           ; STORAGE MUST BE IN PAGE 0 FOR SPEED
0000 0000     FREQ1   .WORD   0           ; FREQUENCY PARAMETER FOR VOICE 1
0002 0000     FREQ2   .WORD   0           ; FREQUENCY PARAMETER FOR VOICE 2
0004 0000     FREQ3   .WORD   0           ; FREQUENCY PARAMETER FOR VOICE 3
0006 0000     FREQ4   .WORD   0           ; FREQUENCY PARAMETER FOR VOICE 4
0008 00       TEMPO   .BYTE   0           ; CONTROLS TEMPO, NORMALLY STATIC
0009 00       DUR     .BYTE   0           ; CONTROLS CHORD DURATION
000A 0000     V1PT    .WORD   0           ; VOICE 1 WAVETABLE POINTER
000C 00       V1TAB   .BYTE   0           ; VOICE 1 WAVEFORM TABLE PAGE ADDRESS
000D 0000     V2PT    .WORD   0           ; VOICE 2
000F 00       V2TAB   .BYTE   0
0010 0000     V3PT    .WORD   0           ; VOICE 3
0012 00       V3TAB   .BYTE   0
0013 0000     V4PT    .WORD   0           ; VOICE 4
0015 00       V4TAB   .BYTE   0
0016
0016                  *=      $700
0700 A000     CHORD   LDY     #0          ; KEEP Y=0 FOR INDIRECT ADDRESSING
0702 A608     CHORD0  LDX     TEMPO       ; SET X TO TEMPO COUNT
0704 B10C     CHORD1  LDA     (V1TAB),Y   ; GET SAMPLE FROM VOICE 1 WAVETABLE
0706 8DF1BF           STA     PORT        ; OUTPUT TO THE DAC
0709 A50A             LDA     V1PT        ; ADD THE VOICE 1 FREQUENCY PARAMETER
070B 6500             ADC     FREQ1       ; TO THE VOICE 1 WAVETABLE POINTER
070D 850A             STA     V1PT        ; LOWER BYTE
070F A50B             LDA     V1PT+1
0711 6501             ADC     FREQ1+1
0713 850B             STA     V1PT+1      ; UPPER BYTE
0715 B10F             LDA     (V2TAB),Y   ; REPEAT FOR VOICE 2
0717 8DF1BF           STA     PORT        ; USE TIME-DIVISON MULTIPLEXING TO
071A A50D             LDA     V2PT        ; MIX THE 4 VOICES
071C 6502             ADC     FREQ2
071E 850D             STA     V2PT
0720 A50E             LDA     V2PT+1
0722 6503             ADC     FREQ2+1
0724 850E             STA     V2PT+1
0726 B112             LDA     (V3TAB),Y   ; REPEAT FOR VOICE 3
0728 8DF1BF           STA     PORT
072B A510             LDA     V3PT        ; CARRY NOT CLEARED PRIOR TO ADDING
072D 6504             ADC     FREQ3       ; FREQUENCY TO POINTER TO SAVE TIME
072F 8510             STA     V3PT        ; ALSO INTRODUCES SLIGHT RANDOM
0731 A511             LDA     V3PT+1      ; FREQUENCY ERROR WHICH LIVENS UP
0733 6505             ADC     FREQ3+1     ; THE SOUND
0735 8511             STA     V3PT+1
0737 B115             LDA     (V4TAB),Y   ; REPEAT FOR VOICE 4
0739 8DF1BF           STA     PORT        ; VOICE 4 IS SOMEWHAT LOUDER SINCE ITS
073C A513             LDA     V4PT        ; SAMPLE "DWELLS" IN THE DAC LONGER
073E 6506             ADC     FREQ4
0740 8513             STA     V4PT
0742 A514             LDA     V4PT+1
0744 6507             ADC     FREQ4+1
0746 8514             STA     V4PT+1
```

Fig. 20–2. Simplified four-voice waveform table scan for 6502

```
0748 CA                DEX               ; DECREMENT AND CHECK TEMPO COUNT
0749 D005              BNE     CHORD2    ; BRANCH TO TIME WASTE IF NOT RUN OUT
074B C609              DEC     DUR       ; DECREMENT AND CHECK DURATION COUNTER
074D D0B3              BNE     CHORD0    ; GO RELOAD TEMPO AND CONTINUE IF <> 0
074F 60                RTS               ; ELSE RETURN IF DURATION RAN OUT
0750 EA       CHORD2   NOP               ; EQUALIZE LOOP TIME BETWEEN RELOAD
0751 EA                NOP               ; TEMPO AND NOT RELAOD TEMPO
0752 4C0407            JMP     CHORD1
```

Fig. 20–2. Simplified four-voice waveform table scan for 6502 (*cont.*)

R-C filter or a judiciously selected woofer-type speaker can usually provide sufficient low-pass filtering. Once an audio DAC is present, whether it be in a game or a personal computer, the sounds producible are limited only by the imagination and skill of the programmer.

The most straightforward synthesis algorithm to use is waveform table scanning. Typically, the waveform table will be 256 entries with 8 bits per entry and no interpolation. For 6502 and similar microprocessors, the general scheme illustrated in Fig. 13–4 can be used to scan the waveform table. In fact, a complete routine capable of producing four simultaneous tones at a sample rate of 8.33 ks/s (for a 1-MHz 6502) requires only 85 bytes.

Such a routine is listed in Fig. 20–2. It is called with the 16-bit frequency parameters for the four voices (zero is used for silence) stored in FREQ1-FREQ4, a duration parameter stored in DUR, and a tempo parameter stored in TEMPO. The number of samples produced before returning is the product of TEMPO and DUR. Note that the four voice samples are mixed by presenting them successively to the D-to-A converter rather than adding them up. This avoids scaling and as written makes the fourth voice somewhat louder than the other three due to its increased dwell time. In effect, the low-pass filter performs the mixing function. With a smooth waveform stored in the table (to avoid aliasing of high harmonics), the routine is very effective in producing four-part organ music with just a hint of roughness due to the short table and programming shortcuts taken. In fact, including a Fourier series routine to compute the waveform table (perhaps from random harmonic amplitudes) requires just a couple of hundred additional bytes.

Other synthesis techniques have also been used in a similar context. Most 8-bit microprocessors are capable of producing one or two FM or nonlinear waveshaping voices. The VOSIM alogrithm has even been used to produce remarkably good synthesized speech, in real time, with nothing more than the audio DAC and some exceptionally clever programming. The increasing use of 16-bit internal architecture microprocessors with multiply instructions in even cost-sensitive products will extend further what can be done with two to three dollars worth of sound generation hardware.

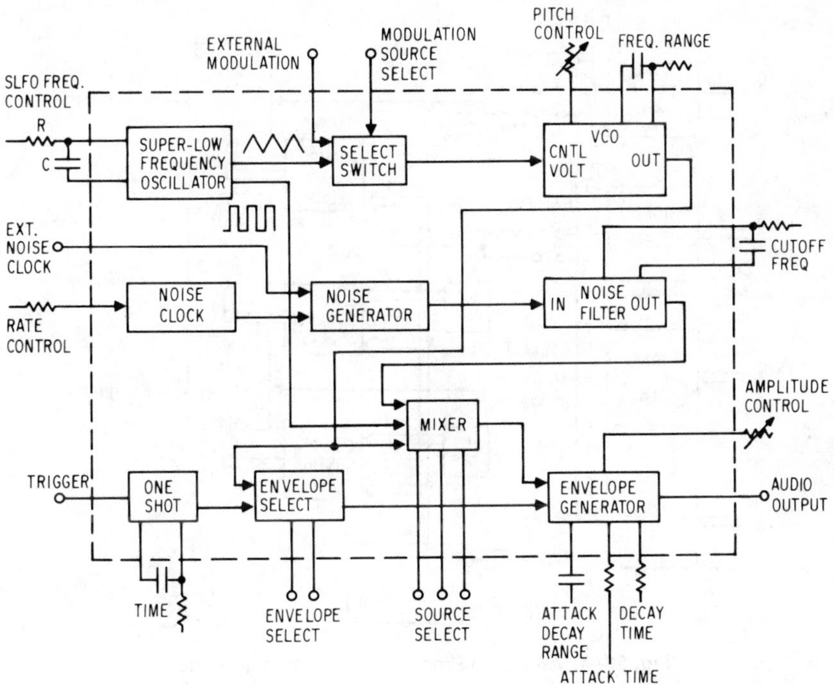

Fig. 20–3. SN76477 Complex sound generator block diagram

Sound Generator ICs

In many cases, specialized ICs are used for sound generation in games and personal computers. While this may not be the lowest cost alternative, such chips can greatly simplify programming by those unfamiliar with sound-generation principles and free up the processor for other tasks during sound generation. Actually, there are only a few sound chips on the open market to choose from. Many more are custom-designed units used only by one manufacturer, often in only one product.

One simple and inexpensive sound chip is the Texas Instruments SN76477. This is really a sound effects rather than a music generator and is "programmed" by connecting different value resistors and capacitors to several of its pins. However, the configuration of elements and, hence, the specific sound produced can be controlled by digital inputs that may either be a microprocessor output register or mechanical switches. In the block diagram in Fig. 20–3, it can be seen that the major sound sources are a voltage-controlled oscillator and a pseudo-random bit noise generator with a variable low-pass filter. The "super-low frequency" oscillator, which need not necessarily oscillate at a low frequency, can modulate the VCO frequency and

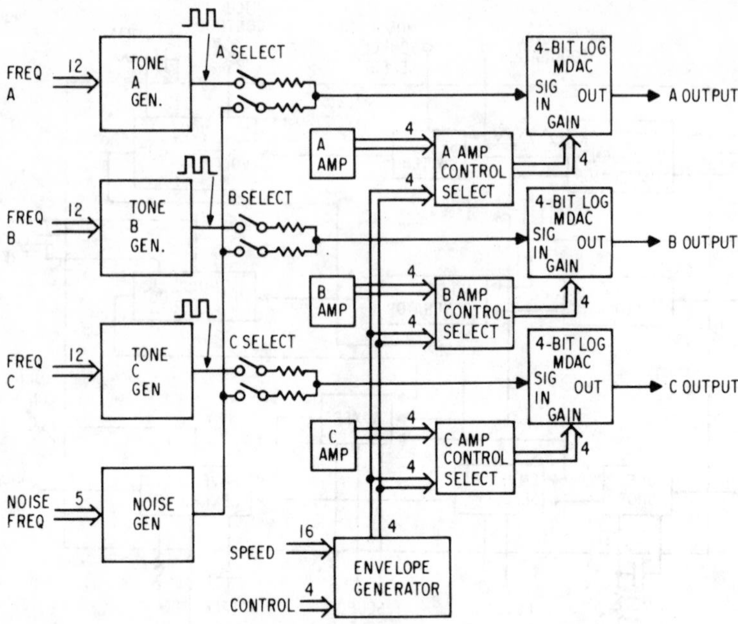

Fig. 20–4. AY-3-8910 Programmable sound generator

also trigger the envelope generator. By suitable selection of component values and setting of the configuration bits, quite a number of sound effects such as a chugging train, breathy whistle, "saucer lands," ray gun, gunshot, bird, clock, etc., are possible. In fact a popular toy consisting of the chip, several rotary switches, some pots, a few slide switches, a battery, and speaker was designed and sold as "The Sound Studio."

Another common sound chip is the General Instruments AY-3-8910. This by contrast is intended to be driven exclusively by a microprocessor and has been used in countless add-on music synthesizer boards for personal computers. Besides the sound generation circuit, its 40-pin package includes two 8-bit general-application I/O ports, although a 28-pin version (AY-3-8912) with one port and a 24-pin version (AY-3-8913) with none are also available. Figure 20–4 shows the internals of this chip, which are essentially three square-wave tone generators, a pseudorandom noise generator, three mixers, and a single envelope generator driving three multiplying DAC gain controls. Twelve-bit values control the frequency of the tone generators, while a 5-bit value controls the noise sample rate. A full 16 bits control the envelope generator *rate,* but the multiplying DACs themselves are very coarse with only 16 logarithmically distributed amplitude levels. The envelope generator can operate either in the normal single-shot mode or it can constantly recycle. Aside from the fixed square-wave timbre, it is possible to get some decent sounding music from one of these chips, considering the cost. Most add-on synthesizer boards use three, however, which allows for a pretty impressive kazoo choir.

In the area of custom sound chips, it is now relatively easy and practical to program a single-chip microcomputer to accept commands on one of its ports and respond by generating a sound, using software, on one or more of its other ports. The 6500/1, for example, is a 6502 CPU with 2K of masked ROM and 64 bytes of RAM plus a timer and four 8-bit I/O ports all in a 40-pin IC package. The Motorola 6801 is similar with a 6800 CPU but has 128 bytes of RAM and an 8 × 8 hardware multiply instruction. The Rockwell 6500/21 is unique in that it has *two* 6502 CPUs sharing the same ROM and RAM on a single chip, which would allow for very smooth sound generation where one CPU calculates the samples while the other updates waveform parameters. By adding an 8-bit DAC and filter to one of the ports on any of these units, quite a flexible and powerful sound and complex waveform generator can be had, often for under $10 in production quantities. One problem with all single-chip microcomputers is that RAM capacity is extremely limited. Thus, waveform tables, if used by the synthesis algorithm, must be fixed in the ROM.

As briefly mentioned in Chapter 17, one-chip digital signal processor ICs, which are programmed and applied much like the one-chip microcomputers, are also available. Advantages include on-chip converters and much greater processing power, which allows more complex synthesis algorithms to be used. However, their high cost, even in high volumes, rules out their use in the kinds of products being discussed here. Of course, if the product does indeed have a large volume potential (over 100K units) and the sound generator development budget is large enough ($100K and up), a completely custom sound chip can be designed. This in fact has been done for several home computers and musical instruments, some of which will be described in the next section.

Low-Cost Synthesis Products

There are, of course, dozens of products that use low-cost sound-generation and synthesis techniques in their operation. Most of them are uninteresting, but a few are unusual or clever enough to be described here. However, the marketing lifetime of these kinds of products is often extremely short, sometimes just a single "season." Therefore, it is entirely possible that few, if any, of these products will be actively marketed by the time you read this. Nevertheless, this section will illustrate which low-cost synthesis techniques and variations have been successful in real products.

"Toy" Keyboard Instruments

Toy electronic musical instruments seem almost by definition to be keyboard instruments. Actually, to a prospective buyer (a parent in most cases), an electronic horn or flute or ukulele somehow seems illogical.

One very inexpensive ($29) device marketed by Radio Shack is a two-octave electronic keyboard with built-in battery and speaker. It has a number of short single-note melodies already built into its memory that can be played automatically plus provision for user playing and storage (until power is switched off) of new note sequences. While the preprogrammed melodies have proper rhythm and accedentals (sharps and flats), note durations are lost when they are programmed by the user, and the keyboard has only white keys. Thus, the unit is strictly a toy, although the tone, which is a rectangular wave, is solid and robust. Only one IC, which is a reprogrammed calculator chip, and a few other components are present on the single printed circuit board, which also includes the keyboard contacts.

Casio is a company best known for calculators and digital watches. In the mid 1970s, in an attempt to inject some excitement into the calculator business, it began offering calculators with built-in digital clocks. The most popular models also had melody-playing alarms and a mode in which each keypress would play a different note and the "=" key would play out the entire answer through a piezoelectric speaker. This later evolved into a line of keyboard musical instruments that ranged from a $50 monophonic calculator/clock with a "real (miniaturized) music keyboard" and dynamic speaker to a $500 8-voice polyphonic wood-cased unit with full-sized four-octave keyboard, plus a number of models in between. Although there were no headlines in the popular press, these units stunned low-end synthesizer makers and experimenters (such as the author) with the capability that was being offered at prices less than one-quarter of prevailing levels.

Probably the most impressive member of the line, from a price–performance standpoint, is the Casiotone MT30. This $150 unit comes packaged in a 23-inch long plastic case with a three-octave, almost standard keyboard (key spacing is 85% of normal), 4-inch speaker, and output jack for an external speaker or amplifier. It is eight-note polyphonic and has a repertoire of 22 preprogrammed timbres. Although there is no provision for user creation of sounds, there are vibrato on/off and sustain on/off switches. The more expensive models differ by providing standard-sized keys, more keys, variable controls for effects like vibrato and sustain, and an "automatic arpeggio feature," in which a short keyboard sequence can be memorized and then repeated automatically while a melody is played over it.

Upon disassembling the unit, one finds a small (5 × 6 inch) circuit board with seven integrated circuits and about 75 discrete components mounted. One of the integrated circuits is an audio power amplifier, while another is a dual op-amp. Four more are CMOS hex inverters, which leaves just one 64-pin chip to do all of the work. Part of the keyboard switch matrix, which includes a series diode for each key, is mounted on this board, while the remainder is on another 3 × 11-inch board. The contacts are actually conductive rubber pads that bridge two parallel traces when a key is pressed. Both boards are single-sided.

Obviously, the key to the unit's operation lies in the 64-pin custom IC, which is also used in the other models. This all-digital IC both scans the keyboard and performs all of the synthesis calculations for up to eight simultaneous voices. Its final output is a 16-bit sampled digital signal, although only 10 bits are actually D-to-A converted in the MT30. The chip is driven by a 1.14-MHz tunable L-C oscillator and essentially simulates eight independent variable sample rate oscillators whose digital outputs are added together every two clock cycles to produce a composite digital waveform. The channel sample rates are quantitized in units of two clock cycles (1.75 μsec) and vary between 5 and 20 ks/s according to the note played. The DAC itself is external and in the MT-30 consists of CMOS buffers (4049) driving an R-2R resistor ladder network constructed with 1% and 5% resistors. The dual op-amp is used in the two-section (four-pole) Butterworth low-pass filter.

Most of the preprogrammed timbres are standard items such as piano, pipe organ, cello, accordion, glockenspiel, clarinet, plus a couple of electronic sounds such as "synthe-fuzz." The quality of emulation is certainly not up to professional standards but at least the sounds are distinctive. A more bothersome defect on the MT30 is severe distortion near the end of decay envelopes, which is probably due to having only 10-bit D-to-A conversion with 7–8-bit linearity likely. This is probably much less of a problem in the more expensive models. The synthesis technique used is straightforward wavetable scanning. Each note begins by scanning Table A during the attack and then gradually shifts to Table B for the sustain and decay. This can be thought of as a keypress actually triggering *two* fixed waveform notes at the same pitch but with different amplitude envelopes. The chip apparently has a small RAM that is capable of holding four pairs of wavetables at once. A front panel slide switch can instantly select one of them for playing. In "set mode," each white key represents a timbre and playing it copies a waveform from ROM into the particular wavetable RAM currently selected by the switch. Thus, any combination of four timbres can be placed on-line for playing. Waveforms are apparently stored in compressed form in the ROM, probably as a line-segment approximation, since the actual waveshapes seem to be quite simple.

Being so cheap, the Casio instruments have encouraged a bit of experimentation among musician/hobbyists. One simple modification is to add a wide range variable clock oscillator to the synthesizer chip. With a good sound system and the organ voice lowered two or three octaves with the variable clock, a pretty convincing "mighty Wurlitzer" sound can be produced. The latent automatic arpeggio feature can also be easily activated. All kinds of wild distortions are possible by gating off or scrambling the digital output words before they reach the DAC. Thus, a suitably modified Casio keyboard can become quite a special-effects device in a professional performance as well as an amazingly versatile toy.

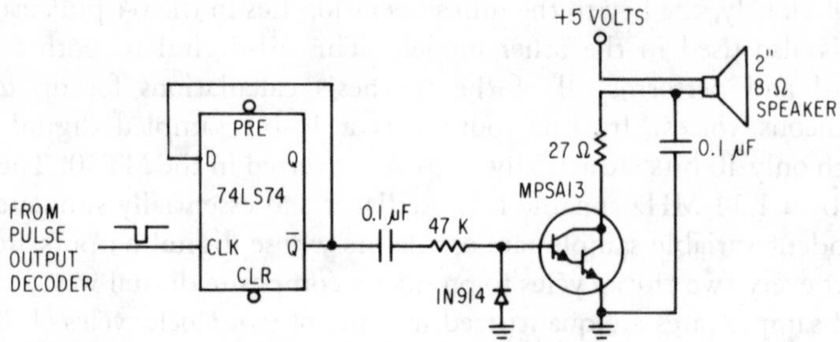

Fig. 20–5. Apple II sound port

Personal Computers

Nearly every personal computer on the market since the late 1970s has some kind of sound generator built in as standard equipment. Initially, these were nothing more than single output port bits that could be toggled by software such as were found in the Apple II and IBM PC computers. A few more addvanced machines, such as OSI, MTU, and Apple Macintosh, included an 8-bit DAC for sound generation. Commodore PET computers invariably used the shift register in their 6522 parallel I/O chip for sound. Other machines targeted more for home and game use often utilized specialized sound-generator chips having a few simple oscillators or even complete miniature synthesizers. For many of the popular computers with poor built-in sound capability, a number of add-on boards having surprisingly sophisticated synthesizers appeared. In the following section, a few of the more interesting sound-generation subsystems used in personal computers will be described.

The Apple II is a representative example of bit toggling sound. One feature of the Apple is a clever internal I/O port technique in which an 8-bit addressable latch (74LS259) functions as eight independently programmable latched output bits, and a 1-of-8 decoder functions as eight independently programmable pulse outputs, all in two 16-pin ICs. For sound, one of the pulse bits is used to toggle a flip-flop, which in turn drives a 2-inch speaker through a transistor buffer as shown in Fig. 20–5. Note that the coupling capacitor will eventually turn the driver transistor off when sound is not being generated, thus preventing dc current in the voice coil. To operate the generator, the program merely writes to address $ C030 whenever the waveform is to change polarity. Besides error beeps and buzzy one- and three-voice music programs (some with amazingly sophisticated graphic score entry front ends), "digital playback" of speech has been accomplished with the port. For this, speech is first differentiated (6 dB/octave high-pass filtered) and digitized with a 1-bit ADC at a sampling rate of 20 ks/s or more, which is about 2.5K bytes per second. For playback, the bit stream is

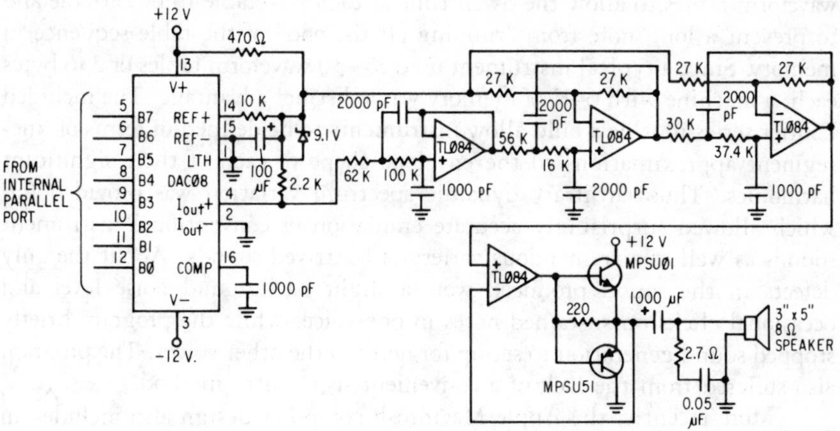

Fig. 20–6. Micro Technology Unlimited MTU-130 sound port

examined and the sound port toggled whenever the stream changes from 1 to 0 or vice-versa. For proper reproduction, the resulting waveform should be integrated (6 dB/octave low-pass filtered), but the sound is intelligible right out of the built-in speaker. The quality is comparable to that of severely distorted CB radio.

The Ohio Scientific C8P computer was probably the first to include a D-to-A converter for producing sound. Unfortunately, the designers chose an exponential rather than a linear DAC, which is very good for playback of digitized speech but difficult to program for multipart music synthesis. The machine also lacked an internal amplifier and speaker. The Micro Technology Unlimited MTU-130 computer, which was introduced in 1981, used an 8-bit DAC and had an unusually powerful built-in amplifier driving a 3 × 5 high-compliance speaker. Figure 20–6 shows the audio circuit used in the MTU-130 and subsequent models, which requires just two ICs for the DAC, six-pole filter, and power amplifier. The DAC was driven by an internal 8-bit parallel output port. Actually, the company manufactured several similar add-on DAC boards for other 6502-based computers such as the Apple II and PET well before the MTU-130 came out.

While there was nothing particularly innovative about the audio circuit, the 6502 music software available to drive it and the add-on boards was quite remarkable. The software was based on the routine listed in Fig. 20–2 but with an extension to allow, in effect, an independent envelope for each harmonic during the course of a note. This was accomplished by replacing the time wasting instructions at CHORD2 with code for periodically changing the memory page number of the waveform table at VxTAB, thus in effect dynamically switching through a *sequence* of waveform tables. The actual program used a separate 256-entry table with *pointers* to waveform tables to allow the dwell time at each wavetable to be variable and to prevent a long note from "running off the end" of the table sequence in memory. Since a typical instrument used 15–30 waveform tables of 256 bytes each, a machine with 64K of memory was a distinct advantage. The included Fourier series routine would allow instruments to be defined in terms of line-segment approximations to the envelope shape of each of their significant harmonics. Thus, arbitrary dynamic spectrum variation was provided for, which allowed surprisingly accurate emulation of conventional instrument sounds as well as a tremendous variety of contrived sounds. About the only defects in the sound produced were a slight background noise level and occasional clicks on sustained notes in one voice, while the program briefly stopped sound generation to set up for notes in the other voices. The program also suffered from the lack of a convenient score entry method.

More recently, the Apple Macintosh computer design also includes an 8-bit audio DAC. Besides having the much more powerful 68000 microprocessor available for computing sound samples, the DAC hardware repeatedly reads a 370-byte portion of memory automatically. A fixed frequency 22.26-kHz sample clock controls the delivery of data to the DAC rather than the execution time of a program loop. The presence of this clock and automatic data transfer circuit greatly simplifies sound-generation programming as well as solving the click between notes defect noted previously. In addition to the sample clock, an interrupt is available to signal when the 370-byte "sound buffer" has been completely scanned out by the DAC and is wrapping around to be scanned out again. Thus sound generation can operate on an interrupt basis and appear to be almost automatic. The interrupt service routine would compute 370 new samples as quickly as possible and return. Any time remaining from then until the next interrupt (which occurs 16.7 msec later) would be available for interpreting a music score, computing new waveform tables on the fly, updating the screen, and other uses. For example, with six voices and an algorithm similar to Fig. 20–2, a new sample would require about 30 microseconds to compute. To fill the 370 sample buffer then would require about 11.1 msec to which about 100 μsec of interrupt save and restore overhead should be added. This leaves about 5.5 msec available 60 times per second to perform other tasks. Although the capability for some truly impressive (for a personal computer) music generation is there, the author knows of no Macintosh music program that even begins to exploit it.

In 1980, Atari introduced their model 400 and 800 computers, which were unique at the time for using three custom integrated circuits along with a much faster than normal 1.79 MHz 6502 microprocessor. Two of these chips were dedicated to the Atari's video graphics display (Atari was best known at the time for arcade video games), while the third handled the alphanumeric keyboard, serial I/O bus, and sound. The sound-generator portion, which is block diagrammed in Fig. 20–7, probably represents the

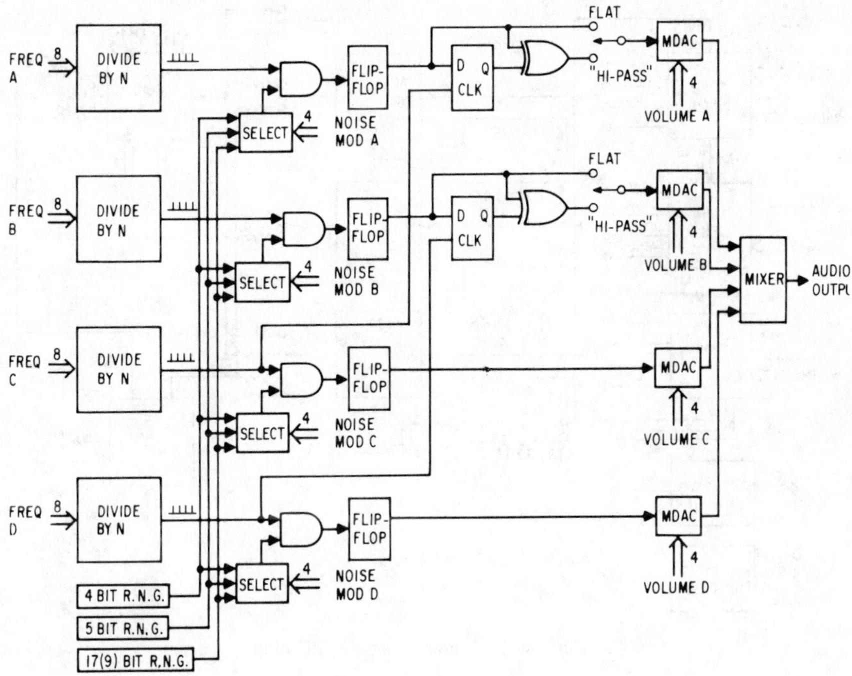

Fig. 20–7. Atari-800 sound-generator block diagram

ultimate that has been achieved with 1-bit D-to-A conversion. Since the Atari computers were primarily game machines, the ability to produce sound effects figured heavily in the sound-generator's design.

Basic pitched sounds are generated by four independent sound channels, each with an 8-bit divide-by-N counter, a noise modulator, and a 16-level volume control. To increase the range of accurate frequency generation from 8-bit dividers, a basis frequency of 16 or 64 kHz can be selected. Additionally, the channels can be combined pairwise to produce one 16-bit divider and two 8-bit ones or two 16-bit dividers. A useful feature is that a dc level can be selected rather than the frequency generator output, which then makes the volume control act like a 4-bit D-to-A converter.

For sound-effects use, the noise modulator serves to distort the pure square-wave tone in a number of different ways. Pulses from a channel's frequency divider are routed through an AND gate prior to toggling the output flip-flop. The other input to the gate can be a logic ONE (for pure tones), or various combinations of 4-bit, 5-bit, and 17-bit shift-register random-bit generators that are constantly clocked at 1.79 MHz. The effect is to delete some of the pulses that would otherwise reach the flip-flop and thus distort the sound. With the 17-bit generator, which can also be truncated to 9 bits, the resultant spectrum resembles bandpass-filtered noise with a center

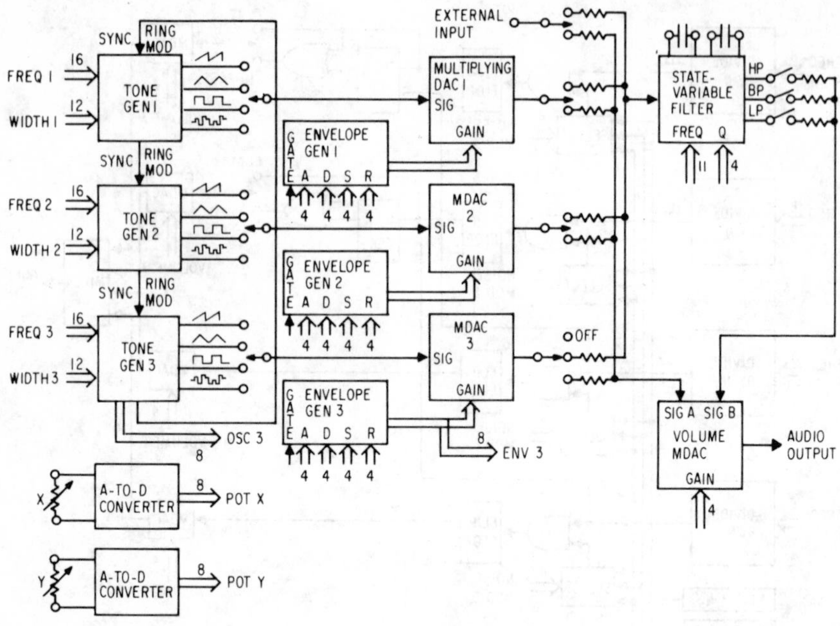

Fig. 20–8. Commodore-64 SID chip

frequency equal to the undistorted tone frequency. The shorter registers can generate a repeating beat pattern with the tone generator and thus produce a wide variety of droning-type sounds.

One final feature, which like the others is pure logical bit manipulation, is called "high-pass filtering." This amounts to a D-type flip-flop clocked by one of the frequency dividers and an exclusive-or gate as shown. If the flip-flop is clocked at a low frequency, the bottom input to the exclusive-or gate is relatively stable, and thus nearly all activity at the top input will pass to the output. As the clock frequency is increased, the two gate inputs differ, on the average, less and less, and thus the output consists of narrow pulses for those times when they do differ. The effect is most useful with noise signals, although an interesting chorus-like sound can be obtained if the flip-flop clock is very nearly equal to the tone frequency.

At the time of this writing, the Commodore-64 computer is by far the most popular in terms of number of units sold. It also has the greatest built-in musical capability of any microcomputer (with the possible exception of Macintosh's unrealized potential) and sells for only $200. Like the Atari machine, the secret lies in a custom chip, which, in this case, is dedicated to sound generation and A-to-D conversion of the game "paddle" pots. Unlike the Atari chip, however, the Commodore SID (sound interface device) chip is a hybrid having both digital circuits like counters and analog circuits like a programmable state-variable filter on the same chip.

Figure 20–8 is a functional block diagram of the SID integrated circuit. The unit basically consists of three tone generators, three envelope generators, a completely programmable multimode filter, and an overall volume control. A limited degree of patching among the elements and an external audio input is also possible. Standard sawtooth, triangle, and variable-width pulse waveforms are available from the tone generators as well as a noise waveform. The latter is produced by the voice's pulse output driving a shift register random number generator in which 8 of the bits are D-to-A converted to provide a truly random-looking waveform. A full 16 bits of frequency control and 12 bits of pulse width control make tuning errors and any stepping effect completely inaudible. The envelope generators operate automatically and have independently programmable attack, decay, and release durations (16 values for each from milliseconds to seconds on a quasi-exponential scale) and a programmable sustain level. High-pass, bandpass, and low-pass outputs from the filter can be selected, while 2,048 different cutoff frequencies and 16 different "*Q*" factors can be programmed. Quite obviously, SID is a miniature polyphonic analog synthesizer on a chip!

As shown in Fig. 20–9, no fewer than 29 8-bit registers control the SID chip. Twenty-five of these perform actual control functions and are *write-only.* Each of the three voices is controlled by a set of seven registers. Most of the bits and fields are self-explanatory, but a few are not. When set, the RING MOD bit causes the voice's triangle wave output to be a pseudo-ring modulation of its selected waveform and that of the next lower numbered voice. The modulation is actually an exclusive-or of the digital representations of the waveforms but sounds much like analog ring modulation. The SYNC bit causes this voice's waveform generator to reset when the next lower voice's waveform completes a cycle. The GATE bit triggers the envelope generator when it changes from a zero to a one and holds a sustain for as long as it is set. When it is reset, the release phase of the envelope starts.

Four more registers are used to control the filter and output amplifier. The mode bits are cumulative, thus setting HP and LP gives a band-reject response. The FILT1, 2, 3, and X bits select whether the corresponding source goes through the filter first or just passes directly to the output. The remaining four registers can be read to give the current position of two potentiometers, samples of the selected Voice 3 waveform, and samples of the Voice 3 envelope. The latter two functions, along with a software copy loop, allow Voice 3 to modulate other parameters such as the filter. The 3OFF filter control bit disconnects Voice 3 from the audio circuits when this mode is used.

The flexibility, ease of control, and relative precision of the SID chip, not to mention the couple of million Commodore-64 computers sold, have inspired some truly remarkable music software. Besides the usual score enter/edit/play type of programs, which are generally well done, there are also interactive sound-effect programs and even "live-performance" keyboard play

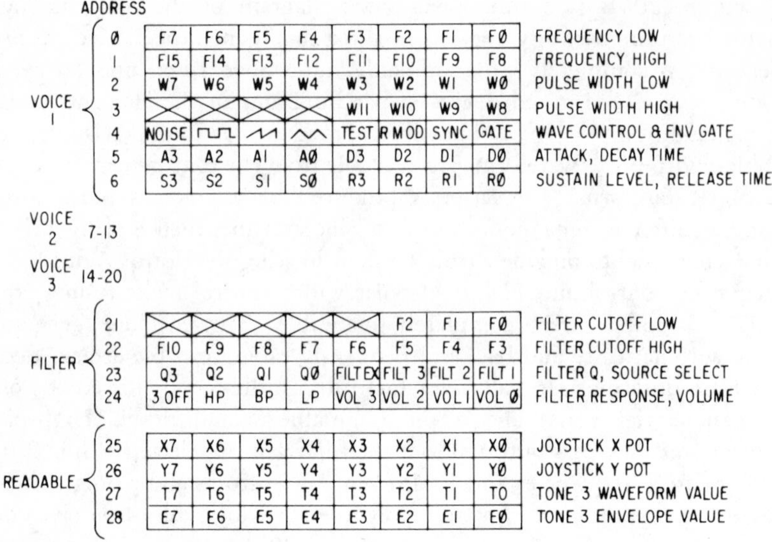

	ADDRESS									
VOICE 1	0	F7	F6	F5	F4	F3	F2	F1	F0	FREQUENCY LOW
	1	F15	F14	F13	F12	F11	F10	F9	F8	FREQUENCY HIGH
	2	W7	W6	W5	W4	W3	W2	W1	W0	PULSE WIDTH LOW
	3					W11	W10	W9	W8	PULSE WIDTH HIGH
	4	NOISE				TEST	R MOD	SYNC	GATE	WAVE CONTROL & ENV GATE
	5	A3	A2	A1	A0	D3	D2	D1	D0	ATTACK, DECAY TIME
	6	S3	S2	S1	S0	R3	R2	R1	R0	SUSTAIN LEVEL, RELEASE TIME
VOICE 2	7-13									
VOICE 3	14-20									
FILTER	21						F2	F1	F0	FILTER CUTOFF LOW
	22	F10	F9	F8	F7	F6	F5	F4	F3	FILTER CUTOFF HIGH
	23	Q3	Q2	Q1	Q0	FILTEX	FILT 3	FILT 2	FILT 1	FILTER Q, SOURCE SELECT
	24	3 OFF	HP	BP	LP	VOL 3	VOL 2	VOL 1	VOL 0	FILTER RESPONSE, VOLUME
READABLE	25	X7	X6	X5	X4	X3	X2	X1	X0	JOYSTICK X POT
	26	Y7	Y6	Y5	Y4	Y3	Y2	Y1	Y0	JOYSTICK Y POT
	27	T7	T6	T5	T4	T3	T2	T1	T0	TONE 3 WAVEFORM VALUE
	28	E7	E6	E5	E4	E3	E2	E1	E0	TONE 3 ENVELOPE VALUE

ATTACK-DECAY-RELEASE TIME CODES

CODE	ATTACK	DECAY/ RELEASE	CODE	ATTACK	DECAY/ RELEASE
0000	0.002	0.006	1000	0.100	0.300
0001	0.008	0.024	1001	0.250	0.750
0010	0.016	0.048	1010	0.500	1.5
0011	0.024	0.072	1011	0.800	2.4
0100	0.038	0.114	1100	1.0	3.0
0101	0.056	0.168	1101	3.0	9.0
0110	0.068	0.204	1110	5.0	15.0
0111	0.080	0.240	1111	8.0	24.0

Fig. 20–9. SID register layout

routines that display an analog synthesizer "console" complete with patch cords and control knobs operated by the game controls. The sound quality from the SID chip is generally quite good, although there are a few problems. One of these is a noticeable leakage from silent voices into the output, which creates a continuous background drone unless a zero frequency is selected as well.

Although the chip's exact internal structure is secret, it is probably based on the liberal use of multiplying D-to-A converters like the 7530 described in Chapter 7. The basic waveforms are undoubtedly produced by simple processing of the upper 8 bits of a 24-bit accumulator-divider driven by the computer's 1-MHz clock. The selected waveform is then converted into its analog equivalent by an 8-bit DAC. The digital envelope generator controls the amplitude of this analog signal with a multiplying DAC; probably 8 bits as well. The analog signals from each of the three voices are finally analog mixed, multiplied by the 4-bit volume DAC, and sent out. The filter most likely consists of two op-amp integrators (the integrating capacitors are connected externally) and three multiplying DACs; two to control the integrators' gain and thus cutoff frequency and one to control the *Q* feedback path. Athough the SID (official type number is 6581) was never made available on the open market, it could have formed the basis of an interesting keyboard synthesizer in which one chip would be used for each voice. Oscillators 1 and 2 would have produced the tone, while Oscillator 3 could have been used for modulation.

For popular computers without adequate built-in sound capability, there always seem to be a number of plug-in expansion boards available from independent companies to fill the need. S-100 computers were the first to enjoy this kind of support and even now have the highest-quality synthesizer expansions available, some well beyond the realm of "low-cost" items. The Radio Shack TRS-80 and Commodore PET computers also inspired a few music add-ons as well, but the Apple II has by far the greatest number of audio accessory boards available. Many of these are simple square-wave units based on the General Instruments AY-3-8913 chip described earlier, although at least one used a triple timer chip, while another was simply an 8-bit D-to-A converter with filter and amplifier. Perhaps the last word in Apple II synthesizers, however, is manufactured by Mountain Computer and is called, very simply, the MusicSystem.

The MusicSystem consists of two Apple II plug-in boards permanently connected together (Apple boards are very small at 2.75 × 5.5 inches) along with a quite sophisticated graphics score editor program. Functionally, the synthesizer implemented by these boards is quite simple. It amounts to 16-table lookup oscillators, each with an independent 16-bit frequency register, 8-bit amplitude register, and 8-bit waveform table page number. Waveform tables of 256 bytes are held in the computer's main memory and accessed by the boards using DMA (direct memory access). An interesting feature of the Apple II Plus, in fact, is its ability to perform DMA without any overhead associated with switching between the 6502 microprocessor and DMA devices. The synthesizer performs a DMA cycle every 2 μsec, which cuts the microprocessor speed exactly in half. With these DMA cycles going to the synthesizer voices in a round-robin fashion, each voice can get a new sample every 32 μsec, which is equivalent to a 31.25-ks/s rate. Multiplication of sample values read from memory by amplitude register contents is performed by a multiplying DAC, while mixing is performed by time-division multiplexing. They are, essentially, a hardware implementation of the table-lookup software routine described earlier. The synthesizer boards are constructed entirely from standard digital and analog integrated circuits and sell for around $400.

Using the 16 oscillators in a straightforward manner, one can obtain up to 16 static organ-like tones simultaneously. With software synthesis of *envelope* shapes and periodic updating of the amplitude register contents, any kind of envelope can also be added to the tones. For dynamic spectra sounds, the included software could combine from two to four oscillators, each with a different waveform table and delayed envelope shape, and thus effect interpolation among a series of waveforms. Actually, one could get the same effect for as many segments as desired with just two oscillators by alternately reassigning an oscillator's waveform table when its amplitude has cross-faded to zero.

The availability of such a high-quality, flexible synthesizer board set for the Apple II inspired at least two companies to offer a music keyboard and live-performance-oriented software to go with it. Alpha-Syntauri, for example, manufactured a four-octave velocity-sensitive keyboard that plugged into an interface board in another of the computer's expansion slots. Although the 6502 microprocessor only ran at half speed when the synthesizer was operating, there was plenty of power remaining to scan the keyboard and even update the display. Quite a lot of performance-oriented software similar to that built into stand-alone keyboard synthesizers was offered for the system. Additionally, an elaborate interactive graphics sound creation program, reminiscent of the Fairlight CMI, was also offered. Passport Designs offered a similar setup initially with their own digitally controlled analog synthesizer plug-in board. Later, however, they switched to the Mountain synthesizer for its greater number of voices and flexibility. Although both of these systems were quite popular with amateur and semiprofessional musicians, the sound quality produced by 8-bit truncating oscillators with 256-entry waveform tables was not quite up to professional standards.

21

The Future

Frequently, when giving talks at computer shows and technical society meetings, I am asked what the future holds in the field of electronic and computer music synthesis. The reply is often prefaced with the observation that short-range technology predictions, i.e., in the 2–10-year range, are usually overly optimistic, while longer-range predictions are often woefully short of the mark. In effect, the *evolution* of technology given a relatively stable base of underlying scientific knowledge is regulated primarily by economic factors, while *revolutionary* changes are driven by scientific breakthroughs that are inherently unpredictable.

For example, short-range predictions in 1940 about future technology in electric power generation were likely incorrect due to economic effects of the war. Meanwhile, nobody foresaw the development of nuclear power that occurred after the war, and most certainly none foresaw its present decline. In the early 1950s, it was said that only a handful of computers would ever be built because there would never be a general need for computation. Yet 20 years later, tens of thousands were in use by every medium- to large-sized company, university, and research laboratory in the country, and today, more than 30 years later, they number in the millions with no end in sight. Of course, many predictions are just plain wrong, regardless of the time scale. In 1973, shortly after the 8008 microprocessor was introduced, an industry spokesman claimed that microprocessors would never do much more than control traffic lights and certainly wouldn't have enough power to run programming languages like BASIC. Yet, less than a year later, the 8008 *was* running BASIC and even APL, a much more complex language.

There are at least four different approaches or mindsets one can take in making predictions and not all are the result of conscious, rational thought. First, one might take the "philosophical" approach in which the predictions made represent what the predictor thinks *should* happen to best serve society. The "wishful-thinking" approach is based on an unconscious hope that, by making a certain prediction, the chance of it actually happening is increased. This is seen most often in business and economic forecasting, particularly by the government in power. A group of people given significant time and resources are most likely to use a "scientific" approach in which a mathematical analysis of related past events and current trends is undertaken. While the resulting conclusions can then be objectively defended, such a thinktank approach is often not any more accurate than the first two highly biased approaches. The final method amounts to just an informal analysis of recent history and current trends along with some imagination that might have a chance at foreseeing major breakthroughs. This is within the power of an individual to do without a lot of effort and is what will be engaged in here.

The Music Technology Development Cycle

In this book, a large number of sound- and music-synthesis techniques have been described, explored, and in many cases, applied to practical use in equipment. Virtually all of these techniques were theorized long (20+ years) before their use in a practical commercial product. Harmonics, harmonic analysis, and harmonic synthesis, for example, were known about in the last century and even played around with (using special organ pipes) but only recently could be fully applied in a musical instrument. Experiments in drawing sound waves directly onto movie film were performed shortly after soundtracks were developed, but only recently has the technique proved practical on computer graphics screens. In essence, the kinds of musical applications discussed in this book are *technology driven.* It is technological advances, usually in other fields, that allow the application of most synthesis techniques to progress beyond the theoretical and experimental stage. Unfortunately, the electronic music field is generally not large or lucrative enough to drive technology itself.

Just a little study will reveal a remarkably consistent development sequence that applies to many fields besides music. First, there is the conception followed by theoretical study and eventually publication of a new technique in a scholarly paper. These are seldom seen, let alone understood by anyone besides other researchers in the same field. If the technique is of sufficient interest, it is then implemented on a one-time basis using institutional funds in an effort to learn more about its properties. In the past, this often meant building large, expensive, and specialized machines, but now it might amount to writing a program to simulate the process and then buying enough computer time to study its action. Generally, a couple of additional papers are published outlining the results of actual use followed by a period of dormancy during which nothing much happens. At this point, many ideas die, but eventually technology advances to the point where it becomes *possible* to incorporate the good ones into a "high-end" product of some sort. With further advances in technology, the new technique gradually becomes competitive with other existing techniques in "mid-range" products and begins to be used extensively. In the final stage, a truly good technique will become trivialized by common usage in "low-end" and toy products.

Thus, accurate prediction of the future of electronic musical instruments largely depends on an accurate knowledge of the "pool" of techniques available and accurate prediction of the course of electronic technology. Presumably, the former requirement has been met by reading this and related books listed in the bibliography, so we need only take a look at past and current trends in electronic technology.

Major Trends in Electronic Technology

Several major trends can be identified in electronic techhnology at this time. Probably most obvious is a shift to digital techniques and circuits when possible. While analog components such as op-amps, precision resistors, voltage-controlled oscillators, etc., are better than ever and are constantly improving, it is an evolutionary progression that merely gets a little closer to the limits imposed by the laws of physics. Actually, analog components have not really improved all that much and breakthroughs have been minor and rare. From the author's viewpoint, the greatest recent advance in analog circuit components was the introduction of "BIFET" op-amps in the mid-1970s. General-purpose versions of these offered 1/1,000 the bias current, 5 times the bandwidth, and 20 times the slew rate for a price that was only slightly higher than bipolar units. For synthesizer use, the other breakthrough was the integrated transconductance amplifier (3080 type) and more recently other integrated functions such as voltage-controlled oscillators and filters. Contrast these relatively minor improvements to those about to be described in the digital arena and the reason for the shift should be obvious. An additional factor to consider is an ongoing de-emphasis of linear circuit design techniques at colleges and universities as well as in the trade press. It is getting to the point in many companies that digital engineers are in abundance, but the one competent analog engineer there is a precious resource.

Memory Cost and Capacity

In the digital realm, the most dramatic advances are being made in memory devices. During the 1960s, core memory advanced from 1024 0.080-inch cores on a frame with a cycle time of 20 μsec to 64K and more 0.015-inch cores on a frame with a cycle time of 750 nsec. Costs likewise declined from a dollar or more *per bit* down to about 2 cents. Semiconductor memories got rolling in 1972 with the 1103 1K bit RAM chip, which was competitive with core in terms of speed and cost. 4K memory ICs were introduced in 1975, while 16Ks were available in 1977 but were not competitive until 1979. 64K RAM chips became competitive in 1982 and at the time of writing in early 1985, 256K RAMs are very nearly competitive at about $5 each in small quantities. In addition, 1M bit chips are working in a few labs, and at least one paper proposing a technique to realize a 4M bit RAM chip has been published.

Let's take a look at this data for a minute. First, the size of RAM chips has very consistently quadrupled about every 3 years and shows no signs of abating. Second, even though the chip capacity is rapidly increasing, the pricing of each new generation is roughly the same on a per-chip basis if not actually declining. Third, today's typical 256K RAM chips at 250-nsec cycle are only about twice as fast as the original 1103s at 570 nsec were. Spanning the 25 years from 1960 to the present, the density of memory in bits per square inch on a printed circuit board has increased from about 50 to about 500,000; a factor of 10,000 to 1. Speed has increased from 20 μsec to about 250 nsec, a factor of only 80. Cost, however, has declined from about $4.00 per bit to .002 cents per bit in 1985 dollars, a factor of 200,000 to 1!

In 1960, it would have cost over 60,000 1985 dollars or about the price of an average home for the memory to store a 1,024-entry waveform table for a music program. In 1985, that same table costs only 32 cents to store in read/write memory and even less in mass-produced masked ROM, which at a given time tends to be twice as dense and half as costly. In 3 years, the likelihood is that it will cost less than the price of a gumball to store such a table. Of all of the current technological trends, the declining cost of random-access memory will have by far the greatest influence on the future of music synthesis.

Small system disk storage has also progressed substantially from the original 8-inch 128K byte floppy disk drives introduced in 1972. Production floppies can now store 1.2M bytes on a 5-inch diskette or 800K bytes on a 3.5-inch diskette, and four times these densities have been demonstrated. Prices have also dropped from $2,000 (1985 dollars) for the original drives to just over $100 today. Small rigid disks have increased in capacity from 5M to 20M bytes and declined in cost from about $2,000 to under $300. For constant cost in the $3,000 range, small drives have increased from 10M to over 300M bytes. Now, optical read/write disk drives are poised for introduction with capacities from 500M to 2,000M bytes on a potentially very low-cost, removable, flexible disk.

Microprocessor Power

Microprocessor ICs are likewise improving in performance and price, although not nearly as dramatically as memories. In 1972, the standard 8008 cost $120 and could execute its rather weak instruction set at an average rate of one instruction every 30 μsec. In 1976, the 6502 cost $25 and executed a substantially stronger instruction set at the rate of one every 3 μsec for a power increase of perhaps 20 to 1 for one-fifth the cost. In 1984, the 68000, which is probably eight to ten times again as powerful as the 6502, could be purchased in the $25 range as well. Waiting in the wings (they were not generally available in early 1985) are 32-bit bus versions of the 68000 and other established 16-bit architectures that will be three to four times faster than their 16-bit predecessors given equal speed memory. Current prices are extremely high (around $500 for what samples are available) but will probably lower to the $2 range in about 3 years.

Now let's take a look at these figures. Since 1972, the power (speed) of microprocessors has increased about 600-fold while the cost has declined by a factor of 10 (remember inflation). More importantly, note that the rate of speed improvement is slowing down substantially, while the price point for high-end mature devices is stabilizing at the $25 level. The reason for the slowdown in speed improvement is that microprocessors are approaching the limit imposed by the speed of memory ICs and is not far from the physical limit of signal propagation along a bus system. Although the 600-fold speed increase doesn't sound like much compared to the 200,000-fold decrease in memory cost, consider this: The Concorde supersonic jet transport flies less than 600 times faster than a child can walk!

Although microprocessors themselves are now much faster than they once were, it often seems that the software that runs on them has not improved nearly as much, if at all, speedwise. In 1973 with the 8008, production programs were carefully handcrafted by a single person in assembly language. In 1985 with the 68000, production programs are more likely to be written rather hastily by a large group in a high-level language. Thus, a substantial portion of the available speed increase is being squandered by a decline in the quality of programming practice. This trend will likely continue as the cost of programming continues to increase in proportion to the cost of hardware. Of course, in specialized cases, such as a core sample computation loop, and with the proper motivation, this increased power is available for use. In fact, this potential for much better performing software given old-fashioned craftmanship and attention to detail means that opportunities still exist for creative individuals in the microcomputer software industry.

Custom Integrated Circuits

During the 1970s, all commercial (as opposed to military and aerospace) electronic systems were designed and constructed in basically the same way. Standard logic integrated circuits, memory ICs, and microprocessors were arranged on two-sided printed circuit boards, several of which would then be plugged into a backplane bus to make a system. Competitive edges were obtained by better design (fewer components required), using the latest high-density memories and high-speed processors, and selecting the optimum mix of features for the market being served. As standardization set in, the applicability and effectiveness of these competitive techniques declined until all of the competing systems were basically the same. At that point, only two system variables were left for competitive positioning: price and physical size. Since printed circuit technology is very much mature, a given number of components on a board will fall into a narrow range of physical sizes and costs. Other ways of reducing the cost and/ or size of the standardized system were needed.

Enter the custom integrated circuit. When one considers that a mid-range microprocessor, which might be the equivalent of a 12 × 12-inch board with 150 TTL IC packages mounted on it, is only 1/100 the size and at $5 perhaps 1/50 the cost, a powerful incentive to use custom ICs is seen. However, until fairly recently, development of even a moderately complex custom IC was a quarter million dollar proposition and not to be considered unless the production volume was to be in the hundreds of thousands. Nevertheless, some companies, notably Atari and Commodore who were mentioned in the previous chapter, did indeed incorporate custom ICs into their products, which gave them a tremendous competitive edge, both price- and performance-wise. Even in nonstandarized systems, another distinct advantage of using custom ICs is that a competitor, in order to duplicate the function, must either assemble the equivalent discrete logic at a substantial cost disadvantage, develop its own custom chip, or buy it from you at a healthy markup.

There are now available three degrees of chip customization. The highest level is called "full custom," in which the designer (actually a team) constructs the circuit from individual transistors in an optimum fashion that minimizes the chip area needed while meeting performance objectives. For example, an internal gate that drives only two other internal gates may use a different circuit topology or smaller transistors than one that drives five internal gates. Or the physical arrangement of the transistors might be altered in order to better fit an available space. This level has the best performance, highest development cost, and takes the longest (2–3 years) but is the densest and cheapest to manufacture. It is generally the approach IC manufacturers themselves use when developing new standard products.

The next lower level is called "standard cell" design. In effect, it is similar to choosing standard logic ICs and interconnecting them on a printed circuit board. In laying out a standard cell chip, the patterns of transistors and other components required for a particular standardized circuit function, such as a D-type flip-flop, are called up from a computer database, placed on the mask pattern, and interconnected with other such cells. The cells are fixed in drive capability, shape, and functional features just like discrete logic ICs are and thus require more space on the silicon chip. For large chips, even a modest increase in area can drive up manufacturing costs substantially because of reduced yields as well as fewer chips per wafer. However, standard cell chips are much less expensive to develop, perhaps one-quarter of the cost of full custom, because of greatly reduced design effort by less skilled designers (the cells can be treated as black boxes), and many fewer design iterations to get working chips. However, once a standard cell chip is designed, it is manufactured the same way as a full custom chip, which means that minimum-order quantities are quite large.

"Gate arrays" is the term used to identify the bottom level of IC customization. A gate array is a chip that already has a regular array of a few different cell types but without interconnections. Each cell in the chip's central area might be an array of three small transistors and five resistors that can be interconnected to form, say, a two-input NOR gate. By using components from adjacent cells, more complex functions such as flip-flops can also be formed. Around the chip's periphery might be other cells containing larger transistors for driving outputs or protection networks for receiving inputs. Design of a gate array then is purely a signal-routing problem, which may actually be more difficult than designing a standard cell chip. Additionally, gate arrays are less space-efficient than standard cells because typically only 60–70% of the available cells can be used due to routing space limitations. If a given design will not fit into a particular-sized gate array, then the next larger available array will have to be used instead.

The advantage of gate arrays, however, is that the customization process only affects the last one or two mask layers out of the dozen or so required to make a complete wafer. Thus, a gate array wafer can be passed through the first 10 masking steps and then *stocked* in large quantities. When a customer needs a run of a particular pattern, a few wafers are drawn from inventory, the last one or two masking steps performed, and then they are ready for testing, dicing, and packaging. The process is much like that used to produce masked read-only memories and can cost as little as $5,000–10,000 for having the masks made and the test sequence programmed. Most importantly, minimum-order quantities of chips may only be in the hundreds.

There is even a fourth level that is becoming significant and has exciting future potential. The same technology that is used for programmable read-only memories is now being used to establish the interconnection patterns in relatively simple gate array type chips called "programmable logic arrays" (PLA). These might typically have eight flip-flops, 32 16-input AND gates, eight four-input OR gates, and four or five miscellaneous gates around each flip-flop to control signal polarities, feedback, etc. Such chips can usually replace 5–10 standard logic ICs in the control sections of digital circuits. Since the user establishes the interconnection pattern with specialized programming equipment, the chips themselves can be mass produced, stocked, and sold in single-unit quantities if necessary.

Initially, all PLAs were programmed by blowing fuses on the chip and thus could only be programmed once. In 1984, however, *erasable* PLAs were introduced that could be erased by ultraviolet light as with erasable read-only memories. Even very small companies or individuals can use PLAs, since the only monetary investment is a programmer that can be built or purchased for $2,000–5,000. The major deterrents to widespread use of these arrays in 1985 are relatively high power consumption, speeds about half that of standard logic, and component costs higher than the logic they replace. The erasable versions, however, have the potential to solve the power problem and perhaps the component cost problem, since they are inherently denser.

Innovations in Packaging

As mentioned earlier, one way to compete in a market in which equipment specifications have become standardized is to make your product more compact. Since the late 1960s, the standard package for integrated circuits has been the dual-inline package or DIP. Common logic functions, like gates and flip-flops, use 14-, 16-, and 20-pin packages that take up roughly 1/2 square inch on a printed circuit board. Larger functions like microprocessors, read-only memories, and peripheral interface chips use 24-, 28-, 40-, and 64-pin packages that take from 1 to 3 square inches. As long as DIPs are used, everybody is limited to about the same circuit density. The main advantage of DIPs is that no specialized equipment is required to handle or insert them onto boards, although some relatively simple handling equipment is helpful in mass production. They are easy to work with when prototypes are built and there is a tremendous variety of sockets, wire-wrap panels, test clips, and other accessories available.

Recently, however, a number of high-density packaging alternatives have become available. The first ICs to be affected were large advanced microprocessors requiring 64 and more package pins. The "leadless chip carrier" (LCC) and "pin-grid array" (PGA) packages, for example, can contain a 68000 chip in under $1in^2$, while the 64-pin DIP equivalent requires $3in^2$. Even larger microprocessors, such as the 80186 and the 68020 are being offered *only* in such packages because DIPs with more than 64 pins are not available. Sockets are required for the LCC package but the PGA type can be soldered directly onto a board. A third new package type, called "surface mount" (SMT), has pins that lie parallel to the circuit board surface and are soldered on top rather than leads that pass through holes to be soldered on the bottom. Both large and small logic functions as well as transistors are available in SMT packages and are about one-third to one-quarter the area and much thinner than DIP equivalents. Sockets are generally not available for SMT components.

Using these new package styles can effect a dramatic increase in circuit functionality that can fit onto a standard-sized board. SMT 256K RAM chips, for example, can be packed about three times closer together, thus making possible 4M bytes of memory on a single 5 × 10-inch S-100 style board. With DIP packages, only 1M byte would be possible. In a system requiring 8M bytes of memory, the supplier of 1M byte boards is at a substantial competitive disadvantage even if his boards are cheaper per byte. With PGA and SMT components, one could package a 32-bit 68020 processor, 68881 floating-point processor, a hard/floppy disk controller, a CRT display generator, a couple of serial and parallel ports, and 2M bytes of memory all on *one* board measuring perhaps 8 × 8 × less than 1/2 inch thick.

The big disadvantage of these new packages, particularly the SMT types, is that specialized equipment *is* necessary to handle them. In addition, multilayer printed circuit boards and more expensive processing are necessary to run the increased number of signal lines that the increased component density requires. Since such boards are generally not repairable, a new board design may have to go through several iterations to perfect the layout before any systems at all can be shipped to customers. The net effect is that small companies may be unable to afford the new packaging technology. Also, since many advanced functions are only being offered in these packages, such companies may wind up being locked out of new devices as well.

Increasing Knowledge Base

In 1972, when microprocessors were introduced, knowledge about how computer systems were organized, how to program them, what their potential was, etc., was very rare indeed. Now, virtually anyone graduating from an engineering curriculum can program and electrical engineering graduates almost certainly know considerable detail about computer system organization and can design simple logic and interface circuits. Most of those specializing in digital technology can design a complete microprocessor-based system and program it in assembly language given written performance requirements. A good number will even know how to design chips and may have actually participated in a class project in which a custom chip was designed *and prototypes produced.*

Along with this greatly expanded knowledge of the mechanics of designing and building complex logic and microprocessor-based systems is increased knowledge of the algorithms that can be applied to make them perform useful tasks. The standard undergraduate linear systems courses (applied differential equations, etc.) are now supplemented (or perhaps even replaced) by courses in digital signal processing. Thus, many engineering students now are expected to know much of the material found in Chapters 13 and 14 of this book, although generally not in a musical context. Even music students may find that one of their required courses is a semester in electronic music production and another specifically in computer music with hands-on experience in both.

Besides formal training opportunities in these areas, a wealth of written and even social (clubs, etc.) information can now be found with virtually no effort at all. Computer-related magazines fill the racks at nearly every drugstore and computer-related books are one of the largest categories in many bookstores. New books, such as this one, distill technical information that was once accessible only in research papers scattered among dozens of scholarly journals.

The net result of this is that knowledge of many of the principles and techniques described in this book is becoming relatively common. Lack of know-how is becoming less of a barrier between a perceived musical need and action to meet it through digital and computer technology. The ready availability and relative cheapness of sophisticated logic components and powerful computers allows nearly anyone who wishes, to write software and build hardware to test some new idea the individual may have thought of. Translation of viable ideas into products is easier now than ever whether a new company is started for the purpose or an established one is approached. It is the expansion of knowledge that drives exponential growth of all technology and will surely continue to apply to musical technology as well.

So now it is time to get out the old silicon dioxide sphere and make some predictions for the next 10 years. One must, of course, assume that no major political or economic disruptions will occur in the meantime. Ten years from now it will be interesting to see how accurate these prognostications prove to be.

The Predictions

In analog components, look for continued gradual improvement in general-purpose op-amp performance and less of a price differential for premium-performance units. Someone will introduce a comprehensive line of digitally controlled analog functions including oscillators, amplifiers, and filters in which the digital side will interface directly with a microprocessor bus. Another company will introduce a large-scale mixed analog–digital chip that performs almost exactly like the dual voice board used in the Chroma synthesizer described in Chapter 19 but is programmed much like the SID chip described in Chapter 20. Finally, somebody will offer a hex or octal voltage follower op-amp in a 14- or 18-pin IC package.

In memory components, 1 Mbit RAM chips will be introduced in 1987 or 1988. While American manufacturers talk about putting these in some strange new package because the chip is too big to fit a standard DIP, Japanese manufacturers will introduce theirs in a standard 18-pin DIP that is pinned to be compatible with current 16-pin DIP-packaged 256K RAMs. Look also for 256K × 4-bit organization in a 22-pin DIP and a "pseudostatic" 64K × 16-bit device in a 40-pin SMT package. EPROMs with a 64K × 16-bit organization should also be introduced. Grave problems will be encountered while developing 4M bit RAMs so these are not likely to be available at all until 1993. The solution will be larger chip sizes made practical by virtually defect-free silicon crystals grown in space. Pricing of each generation will remain about the same at the chip level, which means that, by the early 1990s, read/write memory will be 1/16 of its 1985 cost. That 1K × 16-bit waveform table will then cost less than 2 cents to store in RAM or 1 cent to store in ROM.

No really new developments are expected in 8-bit microprocessors, although construction of current designs in CMOS and higher available clock rates will become the norm. Even so, 8-bit units will descend to the status of current 4-bit devices and continue to sell in large quantities. Current 16-bit microprocessors will become so cheap (less than $5) that they will be used in all low-end computers, while the 32-bitters being introduced in 1985 will be the norm for business-oriented personal computers. Somebody will finally figure out how to integrate a microprocessor and a dynamic RAM array on the same chip and thus offer one-chip microcomputers with enough RAM (like 8K) to be useful.

For consumer music products, look for portable synthesizers using digital playback of recorded sounds as their "synthesis" technique to become available for under $1,000 and with standard voice complements including all common acoustic instruments. Velocity- and pressure-sensitive keyboards will also be the norm on such instruments. Even cheap toy instruments (under $100) will have outstanding sonic capability (using real synthesis) but with cheap keyboards and cases. The typical home personal computer will have at least an eight-voice synthesizer as standard equipment, again using prerecorded sounds. A few sounds will be built in, while an infinite variety of others can be read from the standard optical disk drive on demand.

In professional live-performance synthesizers, design emphasis will shift from providing accurate emulation of acoustic instruments and an endless variety of contrived ones to improving the degree of interactive control the musician has over the sound. Keyboards will still be the dominant control device but will become divorced from the synthesizer and sold separately for the most part. Since even consumer keyboards will have independent pressure sensing, professional units must have additional control "dimensions," such as the key displacement mentioned in Chapter 9. These separate keyboards and other controllers will initially communicate with the synthesizers via MIDI. However, by 1990, look for a new music protocol to be developed as the weaknesses of MIDI become apparent. The new protocol will still be serial but will probably be based on some local area network protocol and matching interface chips developed earlier for business computer systems.

All-digital recording studios will also become common during this period. Studio synthesizers will more and more become just another "box" that is wired into the studio digital sound system. They will also be so good that a single individual, suitably armed with a digitized library of orchestral instrument sounds, will be able to "synthesize" a symphony orchestra with no qualifications and no audible compromises. One would hope that such a capability would not be used to produce yet another rehash of the classics. In any case, it will literally be possible to produce a piece of music that never exists in analog form until it reaches the speaker wires in the listener's home!

Appendix

Comparison of Popular Operational Amplifiers[1],[2]

Type	Bias current (nA)	Offset voltage (mV)	Unity-gain frequency (MHz)	Slew rate (V/μsec)	Output drive[3] (mA)	Process	Use[4]	Comments
741	80–500	2–6	1	0.5	20	Bipolar	GP	Most common op-amp in use
LM301	70–250	2–7.5	1	0.5	20	Bipolar	GP	External comp.
LM308	1.5–7	2–7.5	0.5	0.2	5	Bipolar	LP	Low power External comp.
LM318	150–500	4–10	15	70	20	Bipolar	HS	Low noise
NE531	400–1,500	2–6	1	35	20	Bipolar	HS	High speed without wide bandwidth
NE5534A	400–800	.5–2	10	13	30	Bipolar	GP,HS	Very low noise, designed for audio
LM324	45–250	2–7	1	0.5	20	Bipolar	GP	Quad unit
CA3130	0.005	8–15	4	10	5	BIMOS	GP	±7.5 V max. supply
CA3140	0.01–0.05	8–15	4.5	9	5	BIMOS	GP	Low negative-going output drive
LF356	0.03–0.2	3–10	5	12	15	BIFET	GP	General replacement
LF347	0.025–0.1	5–10	4	13	15	BIFET	GP	Quad unit
TL084	0.03–0.2	5–15	3	13	10	BIFET	GP	Quad unit

Notes:
[1]Where a range of values is given, the better figure is typical and the other figure is worst case. Single figures are typical.
[2]Specifications are for the "standard" grade; selected devices with better characteristics are available at a higher price.
[3]Output drive is for a voltage swing of at least two-thirds of the supply voltage.
[4]GP, general purpose; LP, low power; HS, high speed.

Bibliography

The following publications contain further detailed information on most of the topics presented in this book. The reader should be aware, however, that many of these references require considerable mathematical sophistication to comprehend. An asterisk appears in front of those that would be most valuable for further study.

Books

*Rabiner, L. R., and Schafer, R. W. *Digital Processing of Speech Signals.* Englewood Cliffs, New Jersey: Prentice-Hall, Inc., 1978.

Stearns, Samuel D. *Digital Signal Analysis.* Rochelle Park, New Jersey: Hayden Book Company, Inc., 1975.

*Oppenheim, Alan V. *Applications of Digital Signal Processing.* Englewood Cliffs, New Jersey: Prentice-Hall, Inc., 1978.

Gold, B., and Rader, Charles M. *Digital Processing of Signals.* New York: McGraw-Hill Book Company, 1969.

Hamming, R. W. *Digital Filters.* Englewood Cliffs, New Jersey: Prentice-Hall, Inc., 1977.

*Jung, Walter G. *IC Op-amp Cookbook.* Indianapolis: Howard W. Sams, 1974.

*Knuth, Donald E. *The Art of Computer Programming,* Vol. 2, *Semi-numerical Algorithms.* Reading, Massachusetts: Addison-Wesley Publishing Co., 1968.

Lam, Harry Y.-F. *Analog and Digital Filters.* Englewood Cliffs, New Jersey: Prentice-Hall, Inc., 1979.

Johnson, David E., and Hilburn, John L. *Rapid Practical Designs of Active Filters.* New York: John Wiley & Sons, Inc., 1975.

*Appleton, Jon H., and Perera, Ronald C. *The Development and Practice of Electronic Music.* Englewood Cliffs, New Jersey: Prentice-Hall, Inc., 1975.

*Mathews, Max V. *The Technology of Computer Music.* Cambridge, Massachusetts: MIT Press, 1969.

*Denes, Peter B., and Pinson, Elliot N. *The Speech Chain.* Bell Telephone Laboratories, 1963.

*Flanagan, J.L. *Speech Analysis Synthesis and Perception.* New York: Academic Press, Inc., 1965.

*Hutchins, Bernie. *Musical Engineer's Handbook.* New York: Electronotes, 1975.

Papers

Ashcraft, A., et al. "Noise in Real Time Digital Sound Generation." Proceedings 2nd Symposium on Small Computers in the Arts, 1982. IEEE Catalog Number 82CH1831-7.

Chamberlin, H. "Design and Simulation of a Real-Time Digital Sound Synthesizer." Master's Thesis, North Carolina State University, 1973.

Chowning, John M. "The Synthesis of Complex Audio Spectra by Means of Frequency Modulation." *Journal of the Audio Engineering Society,* Vol. 21, No. 7, Sept., 1973.

Le Brun, M. "Digital Waveshaping Synthesis." *Journal of the Audio Engineering Society,* Vol. 27, No. 4, 1979.

Schottstaedt, B. "The Simulation of Natural Instrument Tones using Frequency Modulation with a Complex Modulating Wave." *Computer Music Journal,* Vol. 1, No. 4, Nov., 1977.

Periodicals and Organizations

Computer Music Journal, The MIT Press, Journals Department, 28 Carleton Street, Cambridge, Massachusetts 02142.

ElectroNotes Newsletter, 1 Pheasant Lane, Ithaca, New York, 14850.

International Midi Association, 11857 Hartsook Street, North Hollywood, CA 91607. (Copy of current MIDI specification available for $1.50.)

Acronyms

ADC	analog-to-digital converter
ADSR	attack–decay–sustain–release envelope generator
AGC	automatic gain control
AR	attack–release envelope generator
BCD	binary coded decimal
BIFET	process name used by National Semiconductor Inc. to refer to the integration of bipolar and field-effect transistors on the same chip
BPF	bandpass filter
BPI	bytes per inch
CAS	column address strobe
CMOS	complementary metal-oxide field-effect transistor logic
CPU	central processing unit
CRT	cathode-ray tube
DAC	digital-to-analog converter
DIP	dual-inline package—most popular form of integrated circuit packaging

DMA	direct memory access
DOS	disk-operating system
FET	field-effect transistor
FFT	fast Fourier transform
FIFO	first-in-first-out buffer memory
IC	integrated circuit
IM	intermodulation
I/O	input/output
JFET	junction field-effect transistor
LPF	low-pass filter
LSB	least significant bit
MIPS	million instructions per second
MOSFET	metal-oxide field-effect transistor
MSB	most significant bit
NFET	N-channel field-effect transistor
OTA	operational transconductance amplifier
PLL	phase-locked loop
PROM	programmable read-only memory
RAM	read/write memory
RAS	row address strobe
rms	root-mean-square
RMW	read–modify–write
ROM	read-only memory
SAH	sample and hold
SFT	slow Fourier transform
S/N	signal-to-noise ratio
VCA	voltage-controlled amplifier
VCF	voltage-controlled filter
VCO	voltage-controlled oscillator
VFO	variable-frequency oscillator

Index